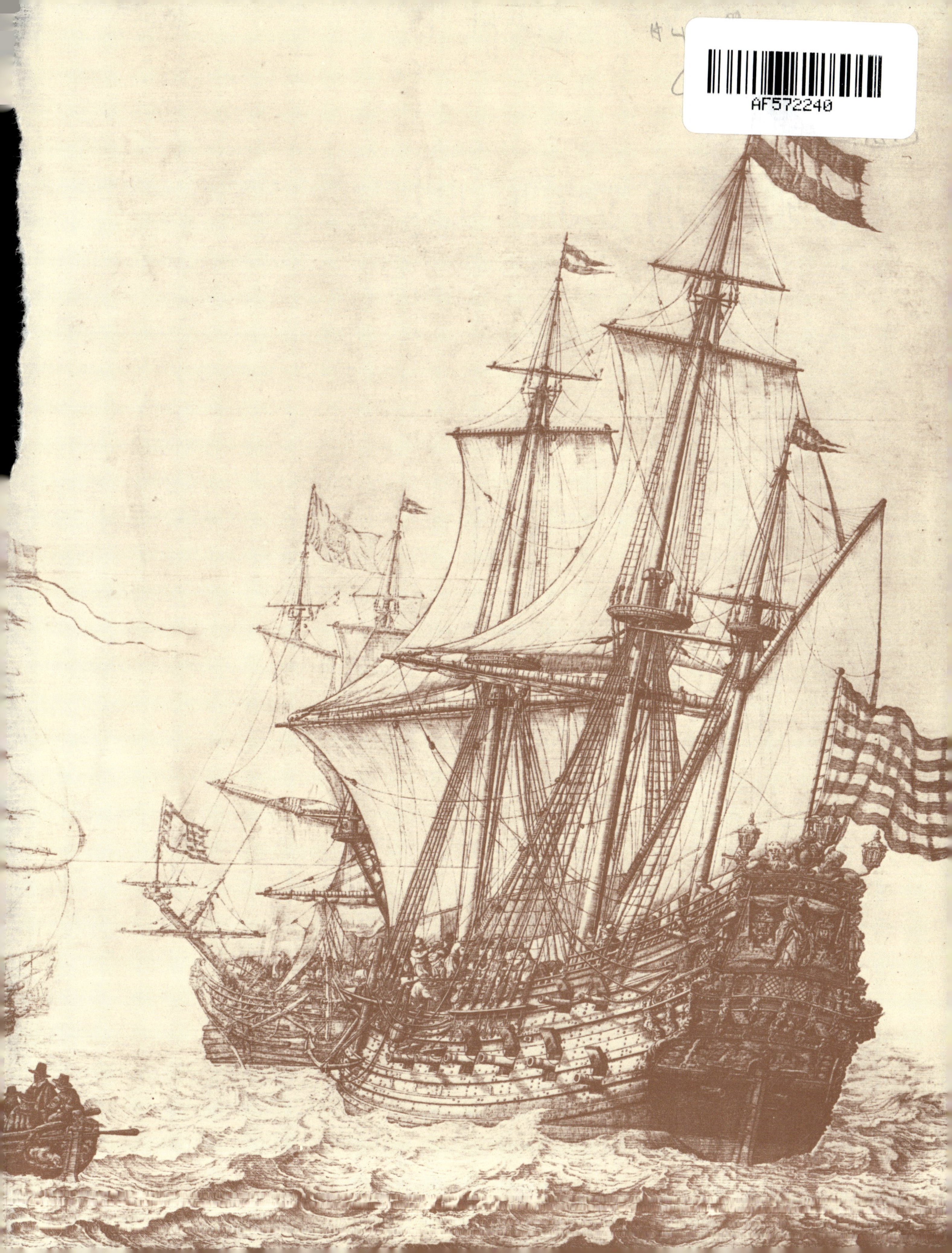

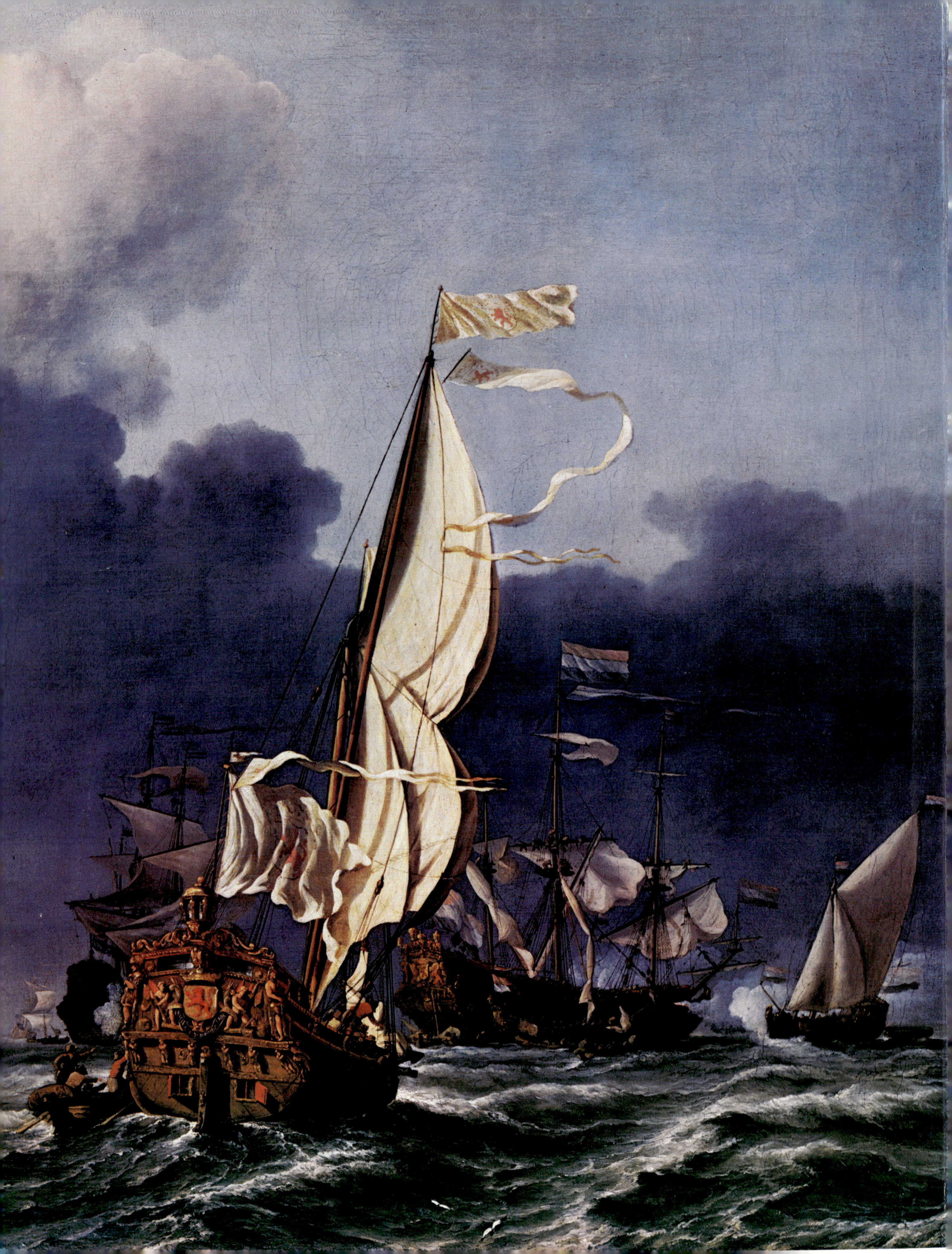

DICTIONARY OF SEA PAINTERS

E.H.H. Archibald

Antique Collectors' Club Ltd.

ISBN 0 902028 84 7

British Library CIP Data

Archibald, Edward H.H.
Dictionary of sea painters.
1. Painters — Biography
2. Marine painting
I. Title II. Antique Collectors' Club Ltd.
759.941 ND35

Published for the Antique Collectors' Club by the
Antique Collectors' Club Ltd.

Printed in England by Baron Publishing, Woodbridge, Suffolk

The vignettes used throughout the text are taken from issues of the *Naval Chronicle* of the first quarter of the 18th century.

Frontispiece: *A detail from a painting by Willem van de Velde, the Younger, of a Dutch States yacht. See Colour Plate IX.*

End papers: *A grisaille drawing by Willem van de Velde, the Elder, of the* Catarina *and other Dutch East Indiamen in 1649.*

DICTIONARY OF SEA PAINTERS

E.H.H. Archibald

Contents

Colour Plates

Abbreviations

A.S.M.A.	American Society of Marine Artists
B.I.	British Institution
F.S.	Free Society of Arts
F.S A.	Fellow of the Society of Antiquaries
N.A.	National Academician (America)
N.E.A.C.	New English Art Club
N.G.	National Gallery
N.P.G.	National Portrait Gallery
N.S.	National Society of Painters, Sculptors and Printmakers
N.W.S.	New Society of Painters in Watercolours
O.W.(C.).S.	Old Society of Painters in Watercolours
P.S.	Pastel Society
R.A.	Royal Academy
R.B.A.	Royal Society of British Artists
R.C.A.	Royal College of Art
R.D.S.	Royal Dublin Society
R.E.	Royal Society of Painter-Etchers and Engravers
R.G.S.	Royal Geographical Society
R.H.A.	Royal Hibernian Academy
R.I.	Royal Institute of Painters in Watercolours
R.I.A.	Royal Irish Academy
R.O.I.	Royal Institute of Oil Painters
R.P.	Royal Society of Portrait Painters
R.S.	Royal Society
R.S.A.	Royal Scottish Academy
R.S.M.A.	Royal Society of Marine Artists
R.S.W.	Royal Scottish Society of Painters in Watercolours
R.W.S.	Royal Society of Painters in Watercolours
S.Av.A.	Society of Aviation Artists
S.B.A.	Society of British Artists (Suffolk Street)

With the exception of the Royal Academies, nearly all the societies that now carry the prefix 'Royal' started without it.

Acknowledgements

I would first like to thank the Director of the National Maritime Museum, Mr. Basil Greenhill, and the Trustees for allowing me not only leave of absence from my post as Curator of Oil Paintings to write this *Dictionary,* but also the full use of the Museum's facilities and resources without which it could not have been done. I am also indebted to them for the loan of a great number of photographs of the Museum's paintings to illustrate the works of so many of the artists included. For the actual production of these photographs and transparencies thanks to Kenrick de Haan, Gillian Lewis and Caroline Hampton.

It has been a great comfort that the copy has been most professionally perused and checked by my colleagues, Pieter van der Merwe and Tim Wilson, and to have had the services of my Director's retired secretary, Mrs. Dorothy Beland, who has done such a wonderful job typing my drafts and letters which, as the illustrations show, received an excellent response from museums and art galleries round the world. Time restricted the number of museums that could be visited, but of those which I went to, it was a great pleasure to meet, and now to thank, their officers for their assistance.

In Australia and New Zealand I am particularly grateful to Miss Emma Devapriam, Miss Jennifer Fipps and Miss Annette Dickson of the National Gallery of Victoria at Melbourne, Miss Sylvia Carr of the National Library of Australia at Canberra, Miss Ann Mourot of the Library of New South Wales, Sydney, Mrs. Renee Free of the Art Gallery of New South Wales, Sydney, and Katherine Woodgate-Jones of the Auckland City Art Gallery, New Zealand.

In San Francisco a meeting with the Director of the National Maritime Museum, Mr. Karl Kortum, resulted in a flood of valuable material about recent American painters. In Washington friends such as John Stobart, the painter, and Malcolm Henderson, the art dealer, arranged introductions to Captain Roger Pineau, U.S.N., the Director of the Navy Memorial Museum in the naval dockyard, and Mr. James Cheevers of the U.S. Naval Academy Museum at Annapolis, which proved most fruitful. Every facility was offered to check through the great collections of the Mariner's Museum, Newport News, with assistance from John Sands.

In New York Mr. Cooney of the Frick Collection, and Dean Walker of the Metropolitan Museum, were most helpful. In Boston a friend and art dealer, Carl Crossman, was a tremendously kind host, and arranged meetings with Tom Parker of the Bostonian Society, Miss Schnieder of the Museum of Fine Arts, Paul Winfisky of the Peabody Museum of Salem, and Philip Chadwick Smith, late of that Museum, who made available his additions to the catalogue. Tom Hall of the New Bedford Whaling Museum, Robin Ashton, and Myra Rosenfeld at the Montreal Museum of Fine Arts also gave of their help and advice on my visits.

Although I did not meet her, Joyce McGrath of the National Library of Victoria, Melbourne, supplied a great deal of information on Australian artists, and Mark Myers, the painter, put me on to the track of numerous American artists.

In a final journey for the *Dictionary,* to Denmark and Sweden, my thanks are due to: Dr. Henningsen and Mrs. Paulson of the Maritime Museum at Kronborg Castle; Mr. Breda Morgenstiérne of the Royal Naval Museum, Copenhagen, who was, as always, the charming host; and Steen Aasberg and Erik Kristensen at Frederiksborg Castle and the Malmo Maritime Museum.

The *Dictionary* has been greatly enriched by Cliff and Wendy Meadway's beautiful interpretations of the historic flags, and excellent details of ship development and coastal craft.

Finally, it could not have been compiled at all, and certainly not in this form, without the enthusiasm and vision of my publisher.

Introduction

The evolvement of paintings of marine subjects occurred quite suddenly in the middle years of the sixteenth century, owing its emergence directly to the Reformation and the release of men's minds and spirits from the restrictions of choice imposed by the mediaeval church. This artistic flowering was initially confined to those parts of the new Protestant nations which already had a flourishing school of painters using sophisticated techniques — in effect the Netherlands.

As the burgeoning wealth of the Netherlanders in the seventeenth century was to be made mainly by sea trade, fishing and whaling, and as their lives were inextricably bound up with water and boats, it is not surprising that marine subjects were an important part of the output of the great Flemish and Dutch painting movements. By the third quarter of the seventeenth century not far short of a hundred painters had sustained themselves painting marine subjects, mainly in Antwerp, Amsterdam, Rotterdam, Haarlem, Hoorn, and even Utrecht. An amazing number of artists for a market to bear, considering the then, smaller, size of those towns and cities.

By the summer of 1672, however, the Dutch were fighting their third war with the English, now allied to the French, the Anglo-French fleet was blockading their coast and a French army was at Utrecht. Inevitably trade, and hence patronage, was at a low ebb. Curiously Charles II of England took advantage of this Dutch recession, and issued an invitation in June 1672, to Dutch artists and craftsmen to emigrate to England, where work and good patronage could be found.

In spite of the war, the Harwich to Hook of Holland sailing packet still sailed, and many Dutchmen took up the King's offer including, on the marine painting side, the Willem van de Veldes, Adriaen van Diest, J. van de Hagen and Jacob Knyff. The van de Veldes enjoyed the immediate patronage of the King and his brother, the Duke of York, and in 1673 sailed in a Government yacht to witness the three great sea battles of that year from the English side, just as they had so recently done from the Dutch.

The Dutch emigré painters were both the example and inspiration for the fine London-based school of English marine painters which was to emerge in the eighteenth century and, with the continuing decline in the Dutch school, London was to dominate marine painting throughout the eighteenth, nineteenth and into the twentieth centuries. In fact, the influence of the Dutch and English schools did seep back into the Roman Catholic countries, especially as so many Dutchmen had travelled to work and paint in France and Italy in the seventeenth century, and here the splendid marines of the Frenchman Joseph Vernet (1714-1789) come to mind.

The second great surge of sea painting was again to be in Northern Europe. Painters proliferated, encouraged not only by the patronage of an increasingly wealthy middle-class that liked to cover the walls of its houses with paintings, but also by the new and expanding public collections of paintings. In turn, the reaction to such stimuli, together with the generally high quality of professional nineteenth century painters, resulted in the formation of a number of excellent painting academies, and the expansion of existing ones. Foremost in the training of marine painters were the Royal Academy Schools in London, and those in Copenhagen, Stockholm and Düsseldorf.

An explosion in world trade following the navigation of world routes, spread the twin idea of painting and collecting marine paintings beyond Europe to America, and the number of professional sea painters in the nineteenth century must have increased by fourfold over that of the eighteenth century schools. Added to this, and since education became more widespread and the learning of painting fashionable, the number of amateurs, even good amateurs, became legion. Apart from the academy-trained professionals and the gifted amateurs, there were also the numerous professionals of the ship portrait, who flourished in every great port in the nineteenth century, and into the twentieth, offering owners and sailors, for a small sum and with varying degrees of skill, accurate portrayals of the vessels they loved.

In view of this enormous range of sea painters and sea paintings, and in order to assist students and collectors to identify and date pictures, I have included in the *Dictionary,* together with the artists and representative plates, illustrative material on the historic maritime flags, coastal craft, and ship development from the early seventeenth to the late nineteenth century, together with a brief synopsis of the importance of subject matter as an aid to dating paintings.

Finally, a note on the sequence of Plates. The basis on which the 695 black and white illustrations are arranged is, generally, date order. While this may appear a simple concept various problems arise.

a). Where an artist has been noted in the text as having influenced his contemporaries or those who followed him their works, as far as is possible and sensible, have been kept together. This is an obviously helpful arrangement for it facilitates comparison of unsigned works with a range of roughly similar painters shown in the book. It does however mean that such a grouping sometimes disrupts the strict date sequence as it applies to other artists outside the group.

b). Where a national or regional group of painters worked in broadly similar styles it seems sensible to group the works together for the reasons as given above, though it obviously presents the same problems in disrupting the strict chronological sequence.

c). In the 19th century, especially with ship portraits, more dated examples occur and hence a more strict adherence to chronological sequence has proved possible unless, of course, a) or b) above apply.

d). Several artists enjoyed long creative lives, for example Andreas Achenbach 1815-1910. Naturally examples of such artists' earlier and late works are included and these have to be kept together to facilitate comparison. This does however play havoc with chronology.

e). There remain those examples to which it is difficult to assign anything more than a rough chronological place.

No dictionary is ever complete or totally accurate and it is hoped that new information will be forthcoming which can, in due time, be incorporated in a second edition.

E.H.H. Archibald
July 1980

SEA PAINTINGS — Identification and Dating

Reference has been made in the introduction to the vast output of marine paintings in the last three centuries or so, and the collector can feel justifiably confused by this factor alone in identifying and dating works.

But further confusion arises when, added to the sheer quantity, one considers the various national styles of shipbuilding and the development over the years of shipbuilding techniques; as well as the subtle interweaving of economic, historic, political and climatic factors which affected ship development, styles of painting and flags.

Aids to identification and dating of sea paintings can be found in four main areas:—

1. Historic maritime flags
2. Ship profile development
3. Picture content and subject matter
4. Coastal craft

The following comments on each of these four areas do not set out to be comprehensive, but are based on factors most likely to be found in sea paintings and most likely to be helpful to the collector or researcher.

Historic Maritime Flags

Flags and Pendants of Command and Distinction, Ensigns and Jacks

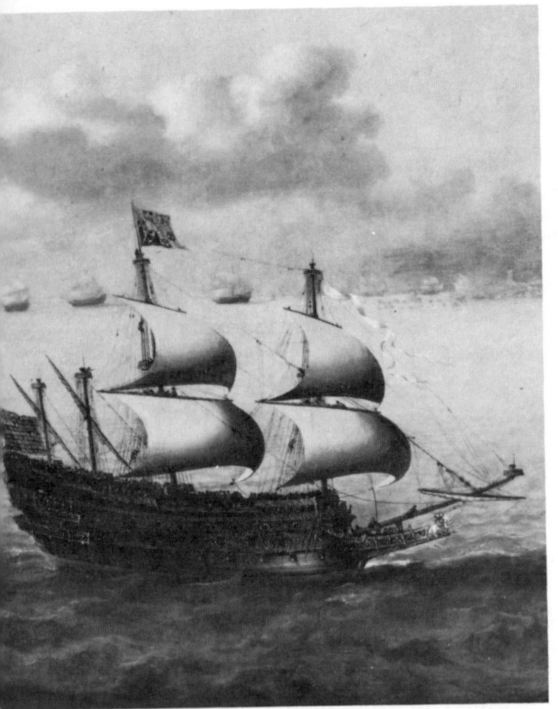

"The Prince Royal *in 1623" with Prince Charles and the Duke of Buckingham on board; detail of Plate 7, by H.C. Vroom. The ensign is striped blue, white and gold, with a cross of St. George in the first canton. The Royal Standard at the main is without the Prince's label (i.e. signifying mark), but the presence of Buckingham as Lord High Admiral entitled him to fly it as the King's representative.*

From the point of view of dating, the British have over the years provided the historian with a gratifying variety of flags which changed significantly from time to time. Up to the first Dutch war in 1652, English ships make only infrequent appearances, though the painter H.C. Vroom executed English commissions in the 1590s, particularly the cartoons for the Armada tapestries. Later, in 1613, he recorded, on the great picture at Haarlem, the arrival of the *Prince Royal* and other ships at Flushing (Colour Plate I), and again, in 1623, the English fleet arriving at Portsmouth. The St. George's flag was the one generally used in Elizabethan times, with the Royal Standard denoting the commander-in-chief. Ensigns were just emerging at the end of Elizabeth's reign; sometimes green and white, the Tudor colours; sometimes red and white, the Stuart colours; here again, the St. George's Cross begins to occupy the first canton, with the rest in multiple horizontal stripes; but in 1623 the fleet was wearing a multiple ensign of blue, white and gold stripes. The St. George's flags by this time had given way to Unions.

About 1625 the red ensign was adopted generally for the merchant and naval service, and remains today the senior ensign. Until 1707 it had the Cross of St. George in the first canton, until the Act of Union with Scotland added the saltire of St. Andrew to make a Union. This pertained until 1801 when, with the Act of Union with Ireland, the Irish saltire was added to the Union flag and to the ensign of all vessels. To this day only the Scottish Lights have a flag with the old type of Union.

The blue and white ensigns which appeared in Royal Naval ships from the middle of the seventeenth century existed to differentiate the three squadrons of the battle fleet, and identify the rank of the flag officer, but these date in the same way as the red. The white ensign, however, was without the large Cross of St. George which it has today, and which was introduced at the beginning of the eighteenth century to avoid confusion with the white Bourbon flags of France, with which country England was then at war.

England and Britain — Flags and Pendants

1. *Flag of the Lord Admiral, late 16th century and, with Stuart arms, into the early 17th century.*
2. *Royal Standard of the Tudors to 1603.*
3. *Royal Standard of the Stuarts 1603-1689, and of the Lord High Admiral from about 1618, also from 1702-1707.*
4. *Royal Standard of King William III 1689-1702, and of the Lord High Admiral.*
5. *Royal Standard of Queen Anne 1707-1714, and of the Lord High Admiral to 1709.*
6. *Royal Standard of King George I and the Hanoverians 1714-1801.*
7. *Royal Standard of King George III 1801-1816.*
8. *Royal Standard of King George III from 1816, after Hanover became a kingdom, until the death of King William IV in 1837.*
9. *Royal Standard of Queen Victoria, 1837, and of today. In the Scots arms the Scots lion takes precedence over the English leopards and so moves into the first canton. The two lower cantons are also reversed.*
10. *Admiralty Flag from about 1620 and Lord High Admiral's Flag since 1709.*
11. *Admiralty Flag of King James II 1685-1688.*
12. *Union Flag of the Stuarts and Hanoverians until 1801, also Flag of the Commander in Chief of the Fleet and of commanders on foreign stations until the early 18th century.*
13. *The Flag of Saint George, and of other Elizabethan and early Jacobean flag officers, then of flag officers of the white from about 1700 until 1864 and of all full admirals until today.*
14. *Flag of command of vice and rear admirals of the red from the Restoration of 1660 to 1864, and of admirals of the red from 1805 to 1864.*
15. *Flag of command of admirals, vice admirals and rear admirals of the white from the Restoration of 1660 to the French Wars of the 1690s.*
16. *Flag of command of admirals, vice admirals and rear admirals of the blue from the Restoration of 1660 until 1864.*
17. *Flag of the Generals at Sea in the Commonwealth c.1650 to 1658.*
18. *Other Commonwealth flag officers.*
19. *Commodores' broad pendant from 1674 to 1864, blue for second class commodores in the 19th century until 1864.*
20. *Commodores' broad pendant from 1864, with a red ball of difference for second class commodores.*

ENGLAND AND BRITAIN

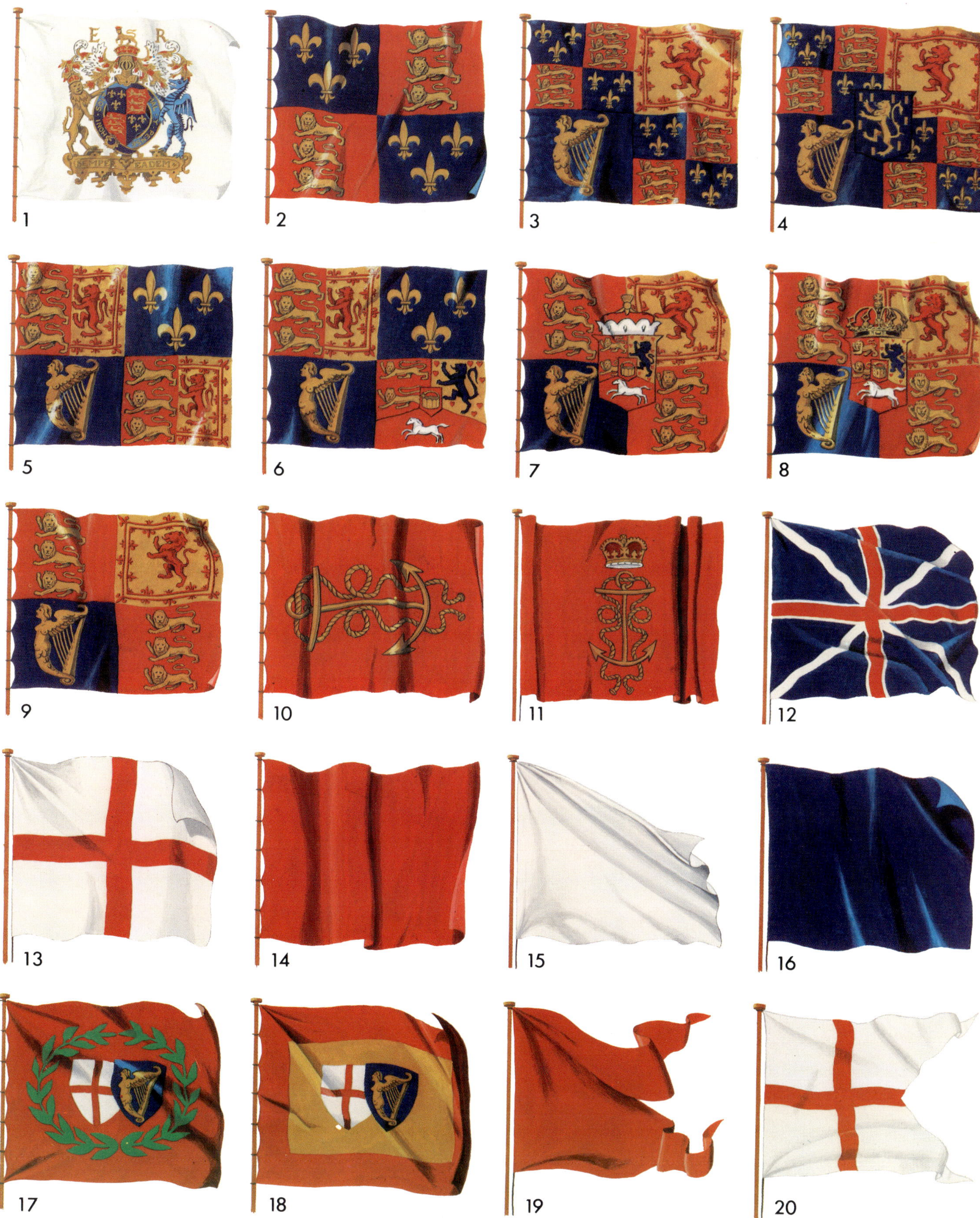

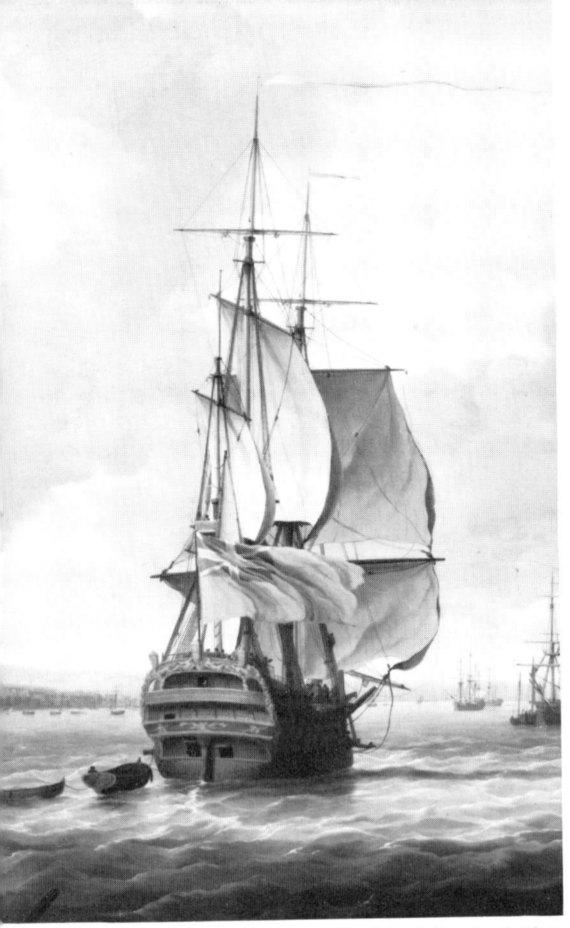

"A two-decker off Harwich," detail of Plate 212, by Charles Brooking. From 1707 the saltire of St. Andrew was put into the ensign. The ensign worn by this two-decker must be 40ft. in the fly (i.e. the full length to the outside edge), and is longer in proportion to its height than was the 17th century fashion.

A special mention must be made of the jacks and flags of the eleven years of the Commonwealth and Protectorate (1649-60) when the Union flag was dropped, and emblems for England and Ireland substituted. The jacks at the bows of the men-of-war had the St. George's Cross to the jackstaff and the harp for Ireland in the fly. Similar devices appeared in the command flags of the Generals-at-sea.

Two features distinguished the man-of-war from the merchantman from about 1650. One was the commissioning pendant, which was always worn at the mainmast-head, except when a flag officer was aboard, when it was struck and the admiral's flag worn instead. It might also be struck in the presence of a ship bearing a more senior captain, but this was only in the third quarter of the seventeenth century, before the introduction of broad pendants for commodores, dating from 1674. The other distinction for a man-of-war was, and is, the wearing of the King's jack, the union flag on the jackstaff; merchantmen wore the St. George's flag as a jack, except ships of the Honourable East India Company or the Levant Company. So long as ships had sprit-topmasts, the jacks were worn at sea, but when triangular headsails replaced the sprit-topsail in the 1720s, and the jib-boom was added to the bowsprit, it was no longer convenient to wear a jack at sea; though at anchor or in harbour it was and is always worn on the jackstaff.

The last big change in naval flags was the dropping of the three colours in the Fleet in 1864. Since then the merchant navy retains the senior ensign, the red. The white, the next senior, was adopted for all Royal Naval ships, and the blue, the junior, went to the Royal Naval Reserve and other Government services, those of the latter usually defaced with a departmental emblem.

The earliest yacht club, now called the Royal Cork, had and has a plain red ensign. The Yacht Club at Cowes had a plain red ensign and pendant from its formation in 1817 to the time the King joined in 1821, when a crown was introduced. In 1827 the Club's name was changed to the Royal Yacht Squadron, and in 1829, for reasons connected with customs and smuggling, it was ordered to adopt the white ensign to differentiate its ships from commercial craft. At the time members thought this implied down-grading in wearing a junior colour. The new pendant was a St. George's cross with a crown in the middle. Other yacht clubs adopted red or blue ensigns, either plain or defaced.

In the merchant service, the St. George's flag continued to be used as a jack in the seventeenth century until the adoption of the St. George's flag as a flag of command forced them to drop it; the white-bordered union was adopted in the middle of the nineteenth century. The Honourable East India Company was grand enough to have its own jack of multiple horizontal red and white stripes, and also its own ensign, the field similarly treated. These their ships were permitted to wear beyond St. Helena but, if the paintings and prints are anything to go by, seldom did. The red and white stripes on the flags of the ships of the Levant Company in the seventeenth century were broader and fewer. Though the pendant was forbidden them, the merchantmen wore wind vanes at their mast-heads, except the postal packets of the first forty years of the nineteenth century, which wore narrow red whip-pendants.

England and Britain — Flags and Pendants, Ensigns and Jacks

21. *Flag of vice admirals from 1864; rear admirals have a second ball in the third canton.*
22. *The red, white and blue pendants of private ships of the three squadrons of the battle fleet of the second half of the 17th century, and in general use after the Napoleonic Wars.*
23. *Pendant of ships on independent command, or common pendant, from 1660, and in general use from the early 18th century until after the Napoleonic Wars.*
24. *The St. George's flag worn by English ships in the 16th and early 17th century and as the merchant jack in the 17th century.*
25. *The green and white ensign, the Tudor colours worn in the 16th century.*
26. *The red and white ensign, the Stuart colours, worn by English ships in the early 17th century.*
27. *The ensign of the Royal Navy about 1620.*
28. *The jack of the Royal Navy from the early 17th century until 1801, except for the period of the Commonwealth and Protectorate, 1649-1660.*
29. *The senior ensign of the Royal Navy from 1625 to 1707, and of the merchant marine.*
30. *Ensign of the van squadron of the battle fleet 1660 to about 1700.*
31. *Ensign of the rear squadron of the battle fleet from 1660 to 1707.*
32. *Commonwealth jack 1650 to 1660.*
33. *Union flag and naval jack from 1801 to date.*
34. *White ensign from 1707 to 1801; red and blue ensigns also bore the Union.*
35. *Red ensign of the Royal Navy 1801 to 1864 and of the merchant marine from 1801. White and blue naval ensigns also bore this union.*

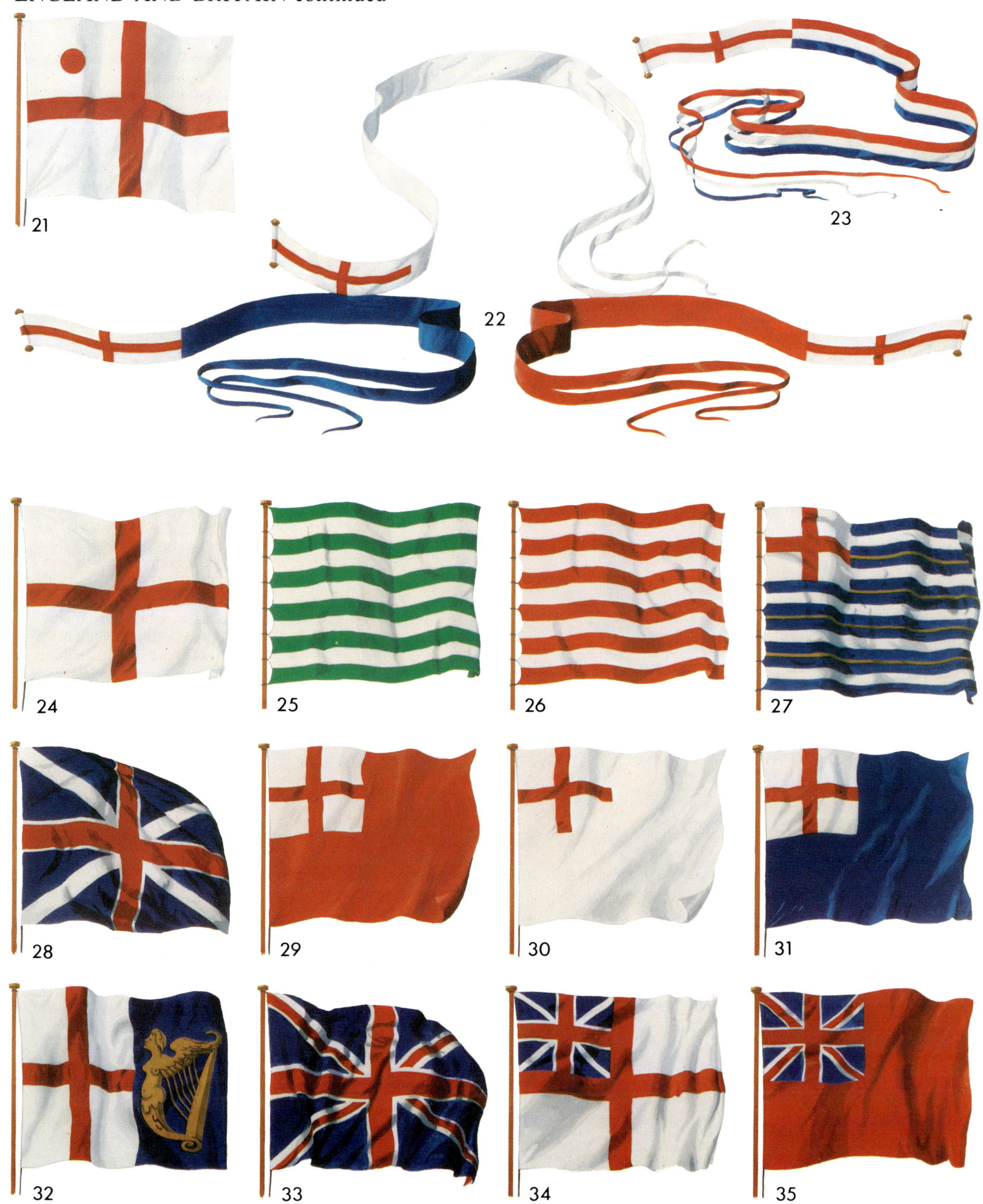
21
22
23
24
25
26
27
28
29
30
31
32
33
34
35

French ships figure increasingly commonly in the marine paintings of the eighteenth century and up to the end of the Napoleonic Wars. Until the Revolution and since the ordinance of 1661, all French naval flags, ensigns and pendants were plain white, except the King's galleys which wore sumptuous red ensigns covered with gold fleurs-de-lis with a blue shield with three fleurs-de-lis in the middle. Seventeenth century French merchant flags were blue with a white cross, but these gave way to white flags in the eighteenth century. After the 1789 Revolution the red, white and blue perpendicular stripes of the tricolour were at first placed in the first canton of the white flags, red to the staff. But in May 1794, the white field was dropped and the tricolour used alone, but now blue to the staff. This remained the

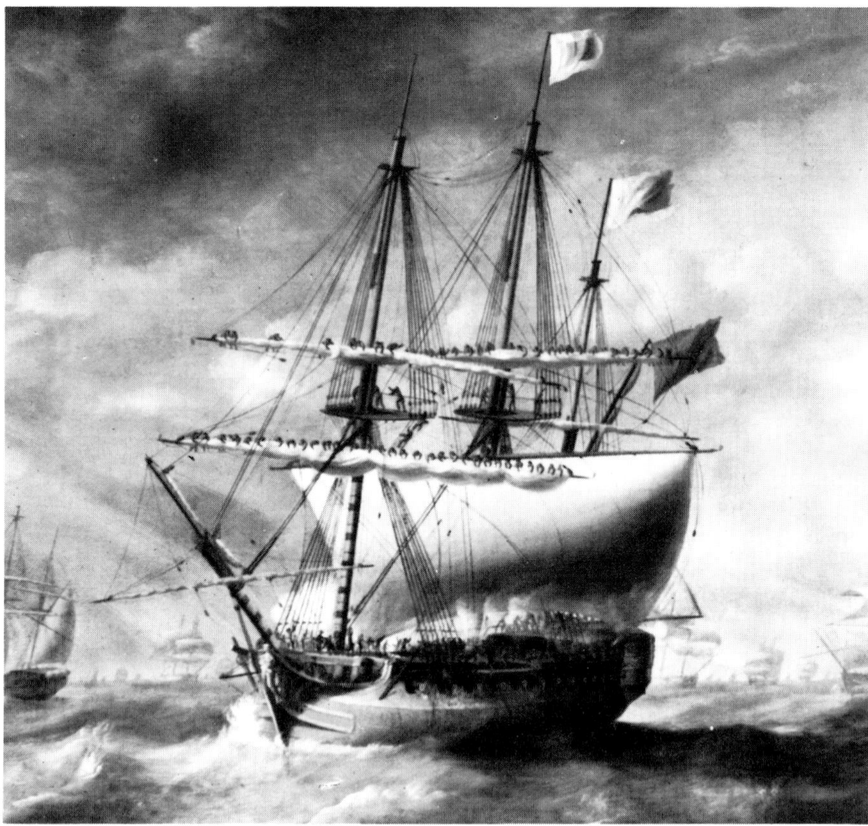

"The Ramillies *in 1782," detail of Plate 272, by Robert Dodd. An early example of an ensign worn at the peak, even though the mizzen sail is furled. Its boom (i.e. the mizzen boom), the reason for moving the ensign from its staff, can be seen sticking out over her stern.*

England and Britain — Ensigns and Jacks

36. *Ensign of the Honourable East India Company ships in the 17th century and to 1707.*
37. *Honourable East India Company jack.*
38. *Ensign of the Bombay Marine in the first half of the 19th century.*
39. *Ensign of Trinity House from 1801.*

France — Flags, Pendants and Ensigns

1. *Ensign of the Royal Galleys of France.*
2. *Royal Standard with the arms of France moderne.*
3. *The white flag of the Bourbons was the colour of all naval flags, ensigns and pendants, except the galley, in the royal service to the Revolution of 1789, and reverted after the fall of Napoleon.*
4. *Broad pendant of a French commodore.*
5. *First ensign of the Revolution, 1790 to May 1794.*
6. *Flag officer's flag of command 1790 to 1794.*
7. *Second ensign jack and flag of command of the Revolution and also of the Empire from May 1794 to 1814, then the Hundred Days in 1815, and from the overthrow of the Bourbons in 1830.*
8. *Standard of the Emperors Napoleon I and III, 1806 to 1815, 1848 to 1872.*
9. *Pendant of the Royal Galleys.*
10. *Bourbon pendant of the French Navy until 1789.*
11. *First naval pendant of the Revolution 1790 to 1794.*
12. *Second pendant of the Revolution, 1794, then 1815, then from 1830.*

ENGLAND AND BRITAIN continued

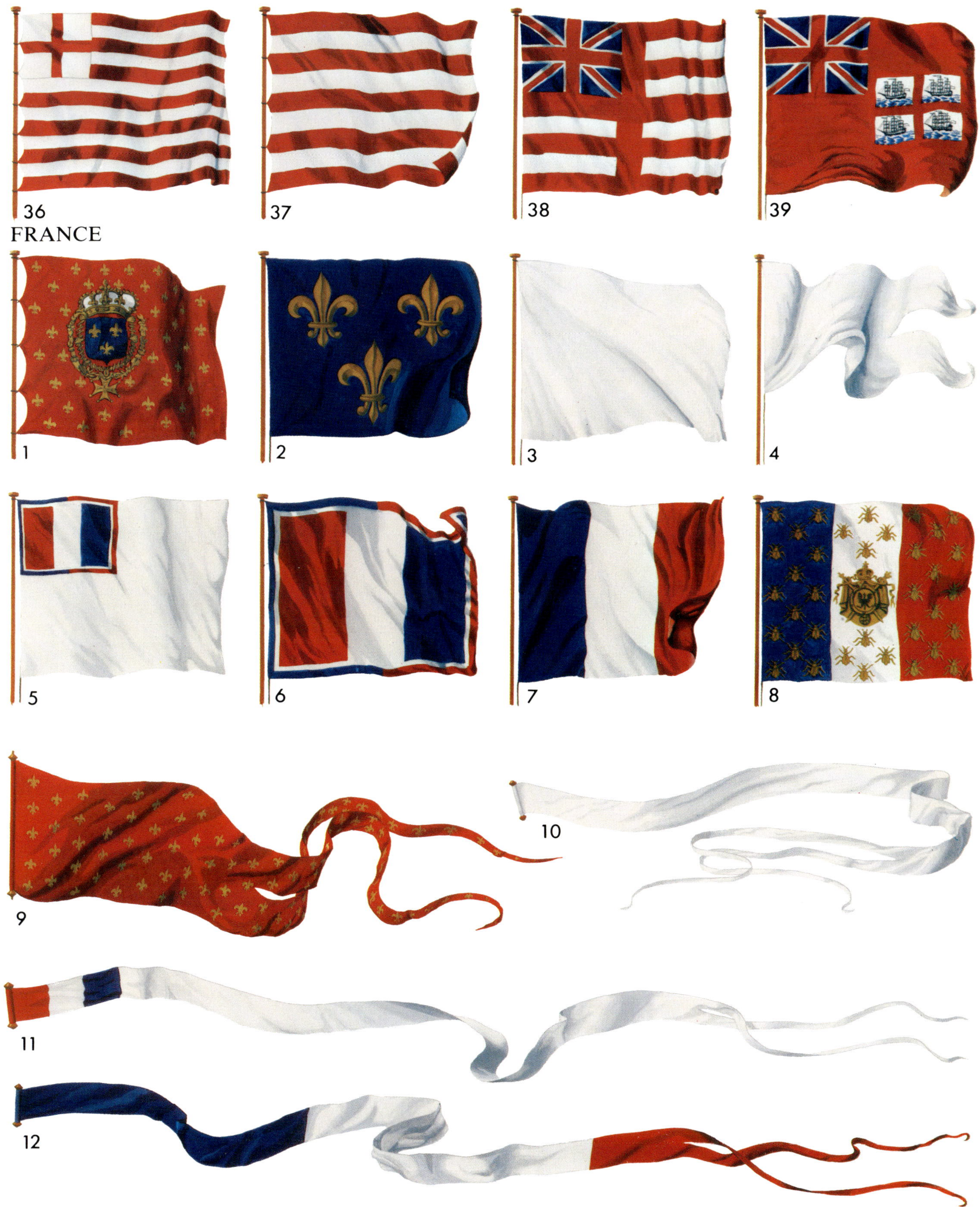

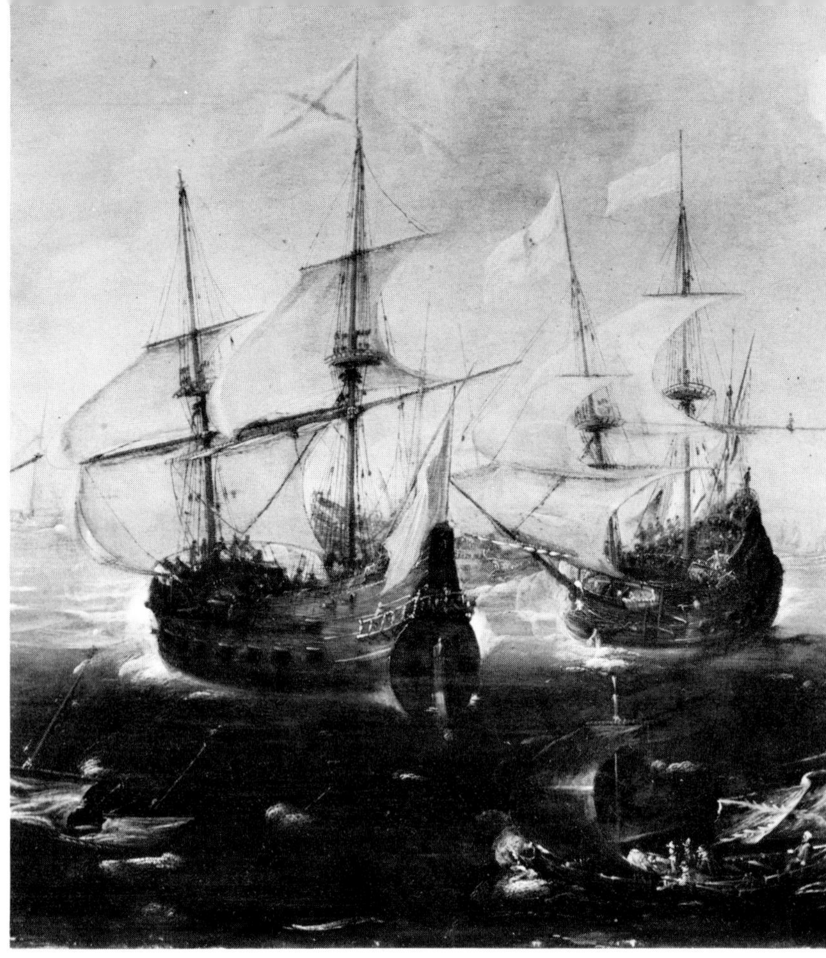

"Anglo-Spanish action of about 1600," detail from a work by Andries van Eertvelt. The central ship flies the Burgundian flag of the Spanish Netherlands, the red 'Ragged Cross'.

French flag until the Bourbon King, Louis XVIII, assumed the throne in 1814 and the white flag returned. The following year, for a hundred days, the tricolour was back. But after Waterloo, white flags were worn until the revolution of 1830, when King Louis Philippe restored the tricolour, which remains the French flag.

When the Bourbons took over the Spanish throne at the beginning of the eighteenth century, they took their white flags with them, on which, in order to avoid confusion with the French, the Spanish arms were placed, very large. In 1785 Spain reverted to red and gold in a horizontal tricolour, red, gold, red.

Since the Flemings and the Dutch were the first sea painters in the second quarter of the sixteenth century, the ships in those few early paintings that survive wear the flags of the Spanish Netherlands, notably the Burgundian flag, which featured the 'ragged cross', a red saltire on a white ground. Flags with multiple yellow and red horizontal stripes may appear, as do flags with the Spanish royal arms and, sometimes, flags with a religious figure on them.

The last quarter of the sixteenth century covers the Dutch struggle for independence from the Spanish, and the adoption of their own national flag, a blue, white and orange tricolour of horizontal stripes. The orange was changed to red in the 1620s, after which the flag only once, and briefly, changed, at the beginning of the Revolutionary Wars in the 1790s, when France overran the Netherlands and the Batavian Republic was formed; the tricolour was defaced with the figure of Liberty with a lion and foliage in the first canton. The flag reverted to the original tricolour and the only noteworthy point to be born in mind in this context is that for the first half of the seventeenth century Dutch ships of war in action are frequently shown wearing red ensigns, the 'Bloody Flag'. In addition, by 1650, men-of-war can be distinguished from merchantmen by the presence of a long tricolour pendant, usually at the mainmast head, but, where the ships formed part of the main fleet, also at the fore or mizzen, to denote the squadron to which they belonged. For the same purpose of identification, a flag called the 'Double Prince' was also used, which had multiple red, white and blue stripes. From the 1620s, men-of-war also wore a flag on the sprit-topmast, called a 'jack'.

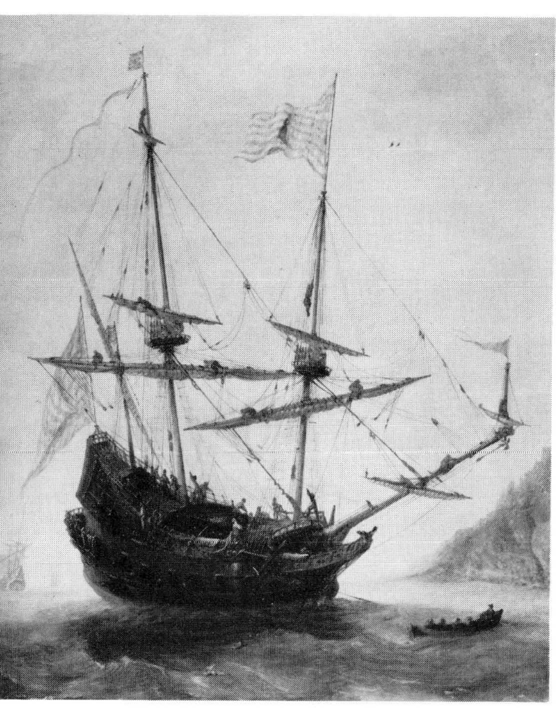

"A Spanish galleon of the early 17th century," detail of a picture by Andries van Eertvelt. The galleon wears a striped red and gold ensign, the traditional Spanish colours. The similar flag at the main is defaced by a religious figure, which was a common feature.

Among other national flags which may appear in paintings are the Swedish, a yellow cross on a blue field — swallow tailed for the men-of-war, plain for the merchant ships; this convention applies to the Danish flags, a white cross on a red field, as well as the Norwegian, a white bordered blue cross on a red field. When Norway and Sweden united in 1814, a union of their flags was designed. This was placed in the first canton of the ensign, until the union was dissolved in 1905. Danish naval flags and ensigns are a duller red to other Danish flags; Danish merchant vessels that carry mail also have swallow tailed ensigns defaced with a crown and bugle.

Ships of the Russian navy of the Czars wore white flags crossed by blue saltires, while merchantmen wore tricolour ensigns of horizontal bars of white, pale blue and red.

In the Mediterranean the ships of the Barbary pirates have blue flags with half moons, and blue and white striped flags. The Turks have similar half moons on red flags. The flags of ships and galleys of the Knights of Malta have a white Maltese cross on a red field. Other Mediterranean flags which may occur in paintings are the Genoese flag, like the St. George's flag a red cross on a white field; the flag of Tuscany, a red Maltese cross on a white field with red balls at the end of each arm; and the Venetian flag, a lion with a sword on a red field.

On the other side of the Atlantic, the War of American Independence produced the first version of the Stars and Stripes. Initially the union was kept in the first canton and, with thirteen red and white stripes, was called the Cambridge flag, after its place of origin. It seems, however, that the ships of the rebel navy in the late 1770s were wearing red, white and blue multi-striped flags with the union in the first canton, while merchant vessels had the stripes without the union flag in the first canton. The Stars and Stripes as we know it emerged after the War, initially with thirteen stars and thirteen stripes, but adding stars as new States joined the Union. Sometimes a ship portrait shows the stars in a circle. This was an early form of the flag, but may occur in paintings of as late as the second quarter of the nineteenth century.

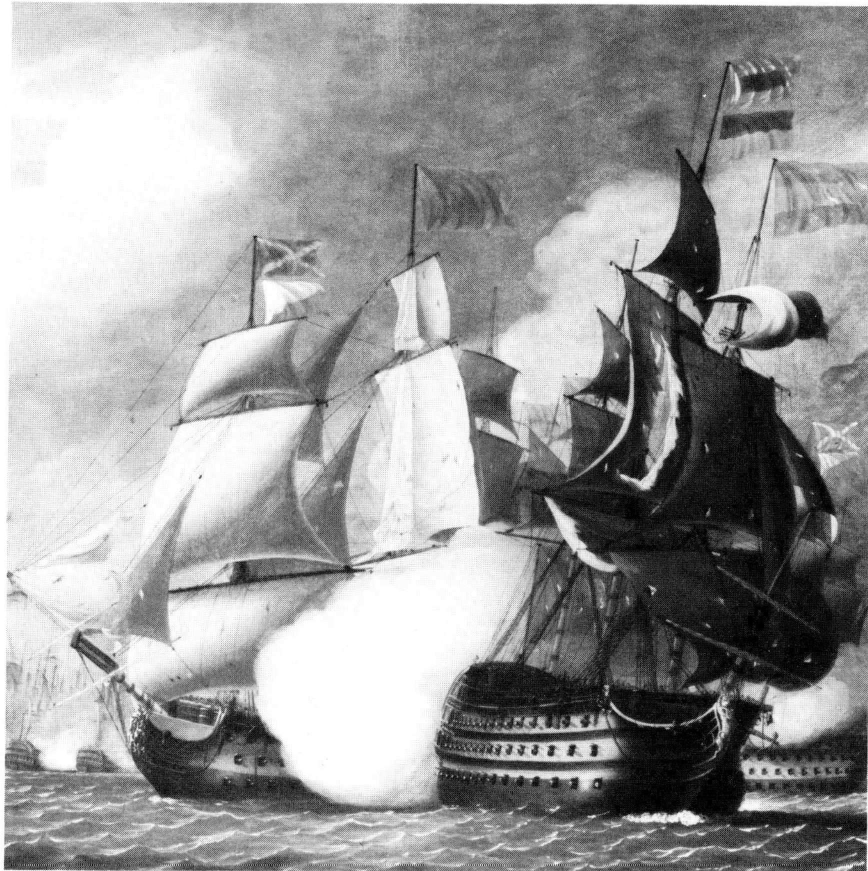

"The Salvadore del Mundo *at the battle of St. Vincent in 1797," detail of Plate 269, by Robert Cleveley. The Spanish vice-admiral's flag and the ensign by this time are composed by a bar of gold between two bars of red.*

SPAIN AND THE NETHERLANDS

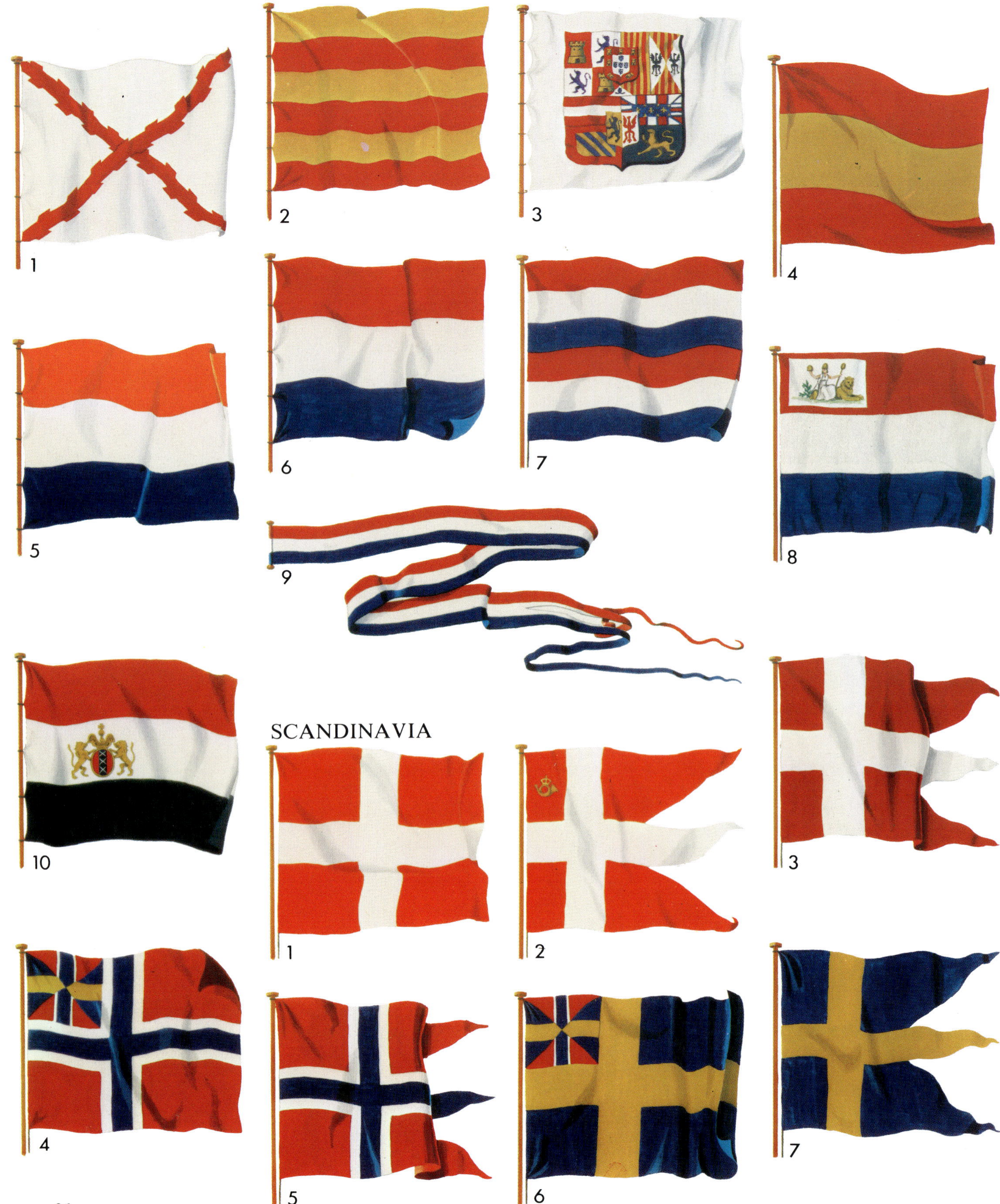

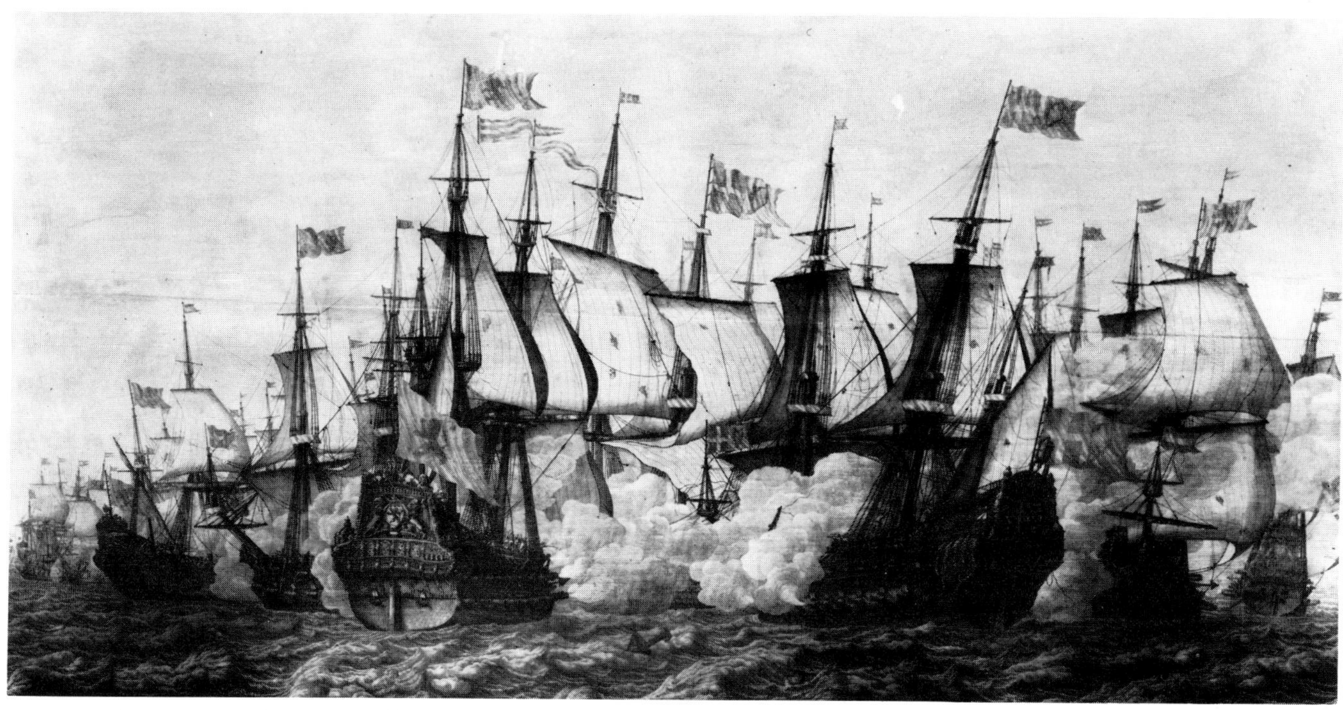

"Action of the First Dutch War in 1653," by Heerman Witmont (see Plate 95). Both the red ensign and the Union flag were dropped during the Commonwealth, and the cross of St. George and the Irish harp substituted. The Dutchmen are shown wearing flags bearing the lion of Holland.

Individual hoists worn on the mizzen-mast appeared for merchant ships in the second quarter of the nineteenth century. The Marryat Code, published between 1817 and 1878, was a hoist of four numbers beneath a distinguishing pendant with a ball in it. Thus a ship could communicate her name to another ship or to the shore by "making her number". This was not the only code for identifying ships at the time, but was the most widely used until the introduction of the International Commercial Code in 1857.

On the whole naval flags, and especially ensigns, were very large in the seventeenth and eighteenth centuries, over forty feet in the fly in a large ship, but in the nineteenth century they became progressively smaller, and it is often a sign that a picture of an old scene is by a modern hand if the flags are shown too small.

Spain and The Netherlands — Flags, Pendant, Ensigns and Jacks

1. *Flag of the Spanish Netherlands, or Burgundian flag, with the ragged cross, 16th century and first half of the 17th century. Could also be on a blue ground.*
2. *Spanish ensign and flag, 16th and 17th centuries.*
3. *Ensign of the Spanish Bourbon fleets, 1713 to 1785.*
4. *Spanish ensign, jack and flag of command from 1785.*
5. *First Dutch flag and ensign, from 1596 to about 1625.*
6. *Dutch ensign, jack and flag of command, naval and merchant, from about 1625.*
7. *Dutch 'Double Prince' flag of the Amsterdam Admiralty.*
8. *Dutch ensign and flags when The Netherlands were dominated by the French from 1794 to 1814 and called the Batavian Republic.*
9. *Dutch naval pendant from the 17th century.*
10. *Flag of Amsterdam from the 17th century.*

Scandinavia — Flags, Ensigns and Jacks

1. *Danish flag and merchant ensign.*
2. *Ensign of Danish merchant ships carrying mail.*
3. *Ensign, jack and flag of command of the Danish Royal Navy; a duller red than other Danish flags.*
4. *Flag and merchant ensign of Norway from 1814 to 1905.*
5. *Naval flag and ensign of Norway from 1905. Previously the union flag had been in the first canton.*
6. *Swedish flag and merchant ensign, 1814 to 1905.*
7. *Swedish naval ensign, jack and flag of command before 1814 and since 1905.*

OTHER EUROPEAN AND MEDITERRANEAN COUNTRIES AND CITIES

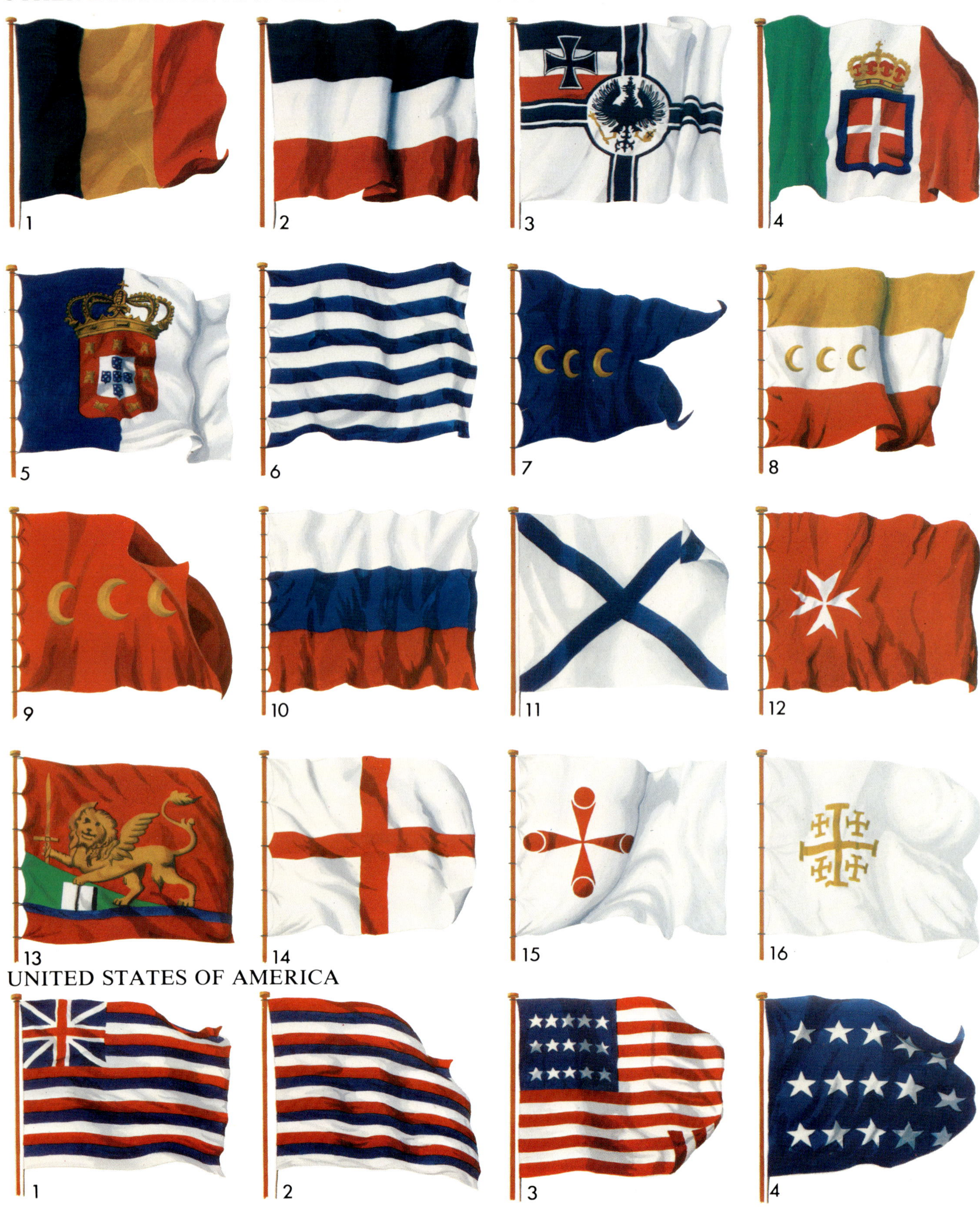

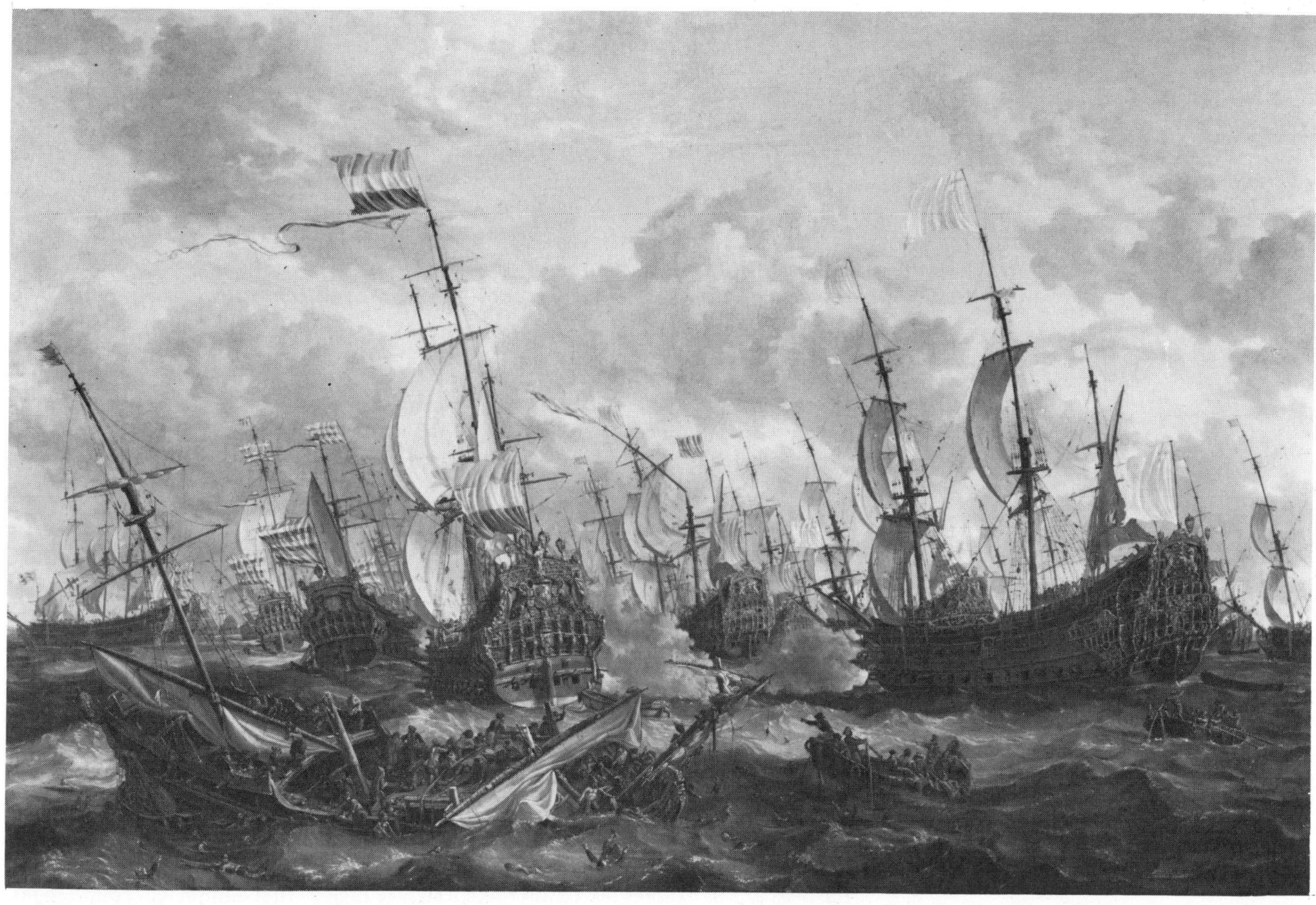

"The last day of the Four Days Fight between the English and the Dutch in 1666," by Abraham Storck (see Plate 160). The English Admiral of the White Squadron on the right hand side wears a white ensign and flag, though the admiral's flag should be plain, without the cross in the first canton. The Dutch ship in the middle is identified as that of their commander-in-chief since the Admiral's flag and the pendant are at the mainmast head, and most senior position, and indicate that his squadron was the central and main one. Beyond and slightly to the left is a Dutch squadron flying multi-striped flags and ensigns, in itself a distinction, but a further distinction is the placing of the pendants on the mizzen-masts, which indicates that the ships belonged to a rear squadron. The English commander-in-chief wears a red ensign and a union at the main, which is going by the board (i.e. shot away).

Other European and Mediterranean Flags, Ensigns and Jacks

1. *Belgian merchant and naval ensign and naval jack and flag of command from 1833.*
2. *German flag and merchant ensign from 1867 to the 1930s.*
3. *Ensign of the Imperial German Navy from 1871 to 1918.*
4. *Ensign of the Royal Italian Navy, from 1862 to 1945.*
5. *Ensign of the Portuguese Royal Navy, 19th and 20th centuries.*
6. *A flag of the Barbary pirates, 17th and 18th centuries.*
7. *A pendant of the Barbary pirates, 17th and 18th centuries.*
8. *A flag of the Barbary pirates of Salee, 17th century.*
9. *Turkish ensign and flag, 17th to 20th centuries.*
10. *Russian merchant ensign, 17th century to 1917.*
11. *Russian naval ensign, jack and admiral's flag, 18th century to 1917.*
12. *Flag of Malta.*
13. *Flag of Venice.*
14. *Flag of Genoa.*
15. *Flag of Tuscany.*
16. *The Jerusalem flag flown by pilgrim ships.*

United States of America — Flags and Ensigns

1. *Rebel American naval ensign, 1777.*
2. *Rebel American merchant ensign, 1777.*
3. *United States of America ensign, both naval and merchant, for 1795.*
4. *United States of America naval jack of 1795.*

Ship Profile Development

North European Ships

(Figure numbers refer to the drawings on pages 34 to 44, which give an illustrated view of ship development from 1600-1900.)

1600-1650

A general layout for large ships, which was to endure in modified forms for over two centuries, had been established by the last quarter of the sixteenth century. The Dutch and English ships were rather similar, with long, low beaks, open stern galleries and square tucks (Figures 1a and b) under their transoms. Spanish hulls had heavier poops and fo'c'sles, and a sort of covered balcony, like a penthouse, on their sterns (Figure 1d). In the early 1600s the English and Dutch men-of-war had light latticed spar-decks above their waists and quarter-decks, but this practice seems to have been abandoned by the middle of the century.

In rig the ships were normally three-masted, sometimes four, the aftermast in that case being called the bonaventura mizzen. They were not very heavily sparred, indicating that they were fairly tender, not to say crank (i.e. unstable when under sail), and on the whole only topsails are shown, though on the biggest ships a topgallant on the main may appear. The *Prince Royal* was exceptional in carrying a topgallant at the fore and a topsail on her bonaventura mizzen.

An important development in the second decade of the century was the development of the sprit topmast and sprit topsail (Figure 1c). Its appearance on the *Prince Royal* in 1610 was followed on other large ships, but in smaller ships not until the 1620s and 1630s.

1640-1700

By the start of the First Dutch War in 1652 profiles had altered considerably. The beaks were shorter and curved upwards (Figure 2d), and as the century progressed they were to get shorter and more curved (Figure 3a). The sterns had altered too, with closed stern galleries developing in the second quarter of the century and, in the case of the English, the round tuck (Figure 2b). The stern view of the *Sovereign of the Seas* of 1637 shows her to have had a square tuck as first completed; round tucks, the curving of the stern line up to the transom had, none the less, already been tried and by the middle of the century they became a general building feature, certainly in British naval yards. The Dutch continued with square tucks, as did the French (Figures 2a and c), whose enlarging navy begins to appear with increasing frequency in paintings of and after the Third Dutch War, 1672-3. In rig, the fourth or bonaventura mizzen-mast had by this time disappeared and huge topsails and main topgallants gave the ships a much loftier appearance.

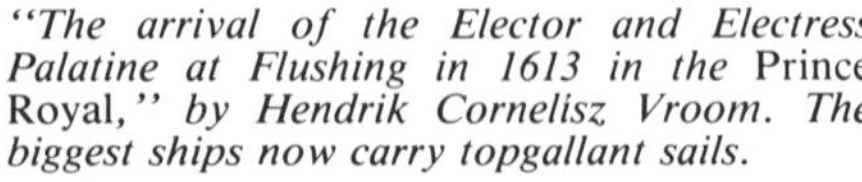

"The arrival of the Elector and Electress Palatine at Flushing in 1613 in the Prince Royal,*" by Hendrik Cornelisz Vroom. The biggest ships now carry topgallant sails.*

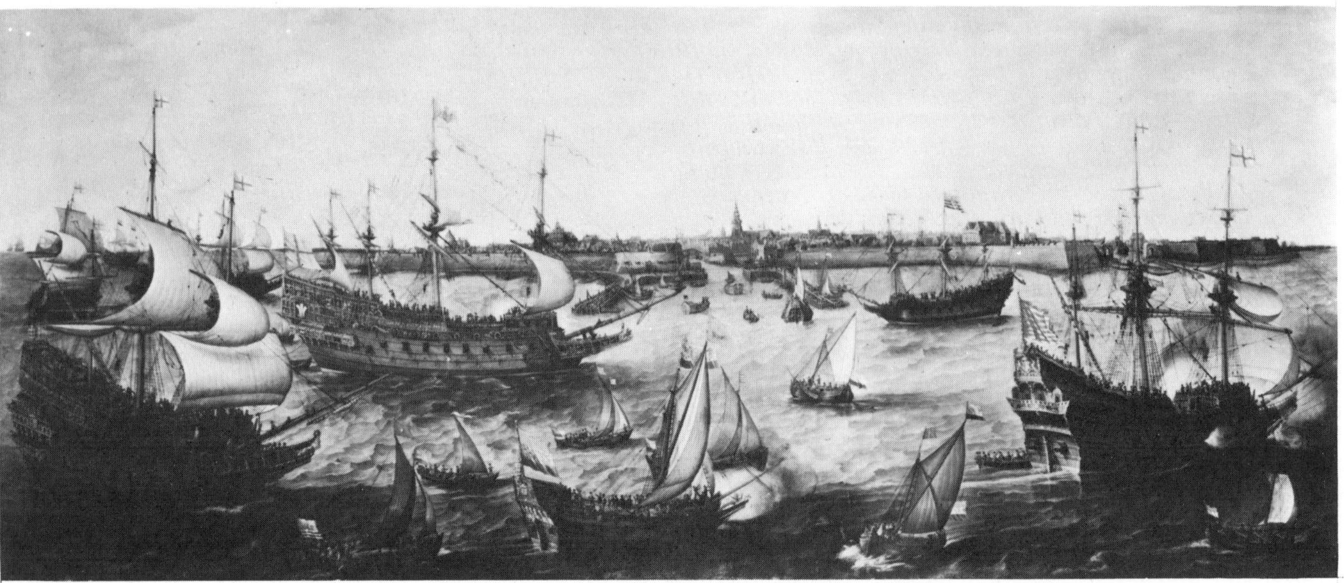

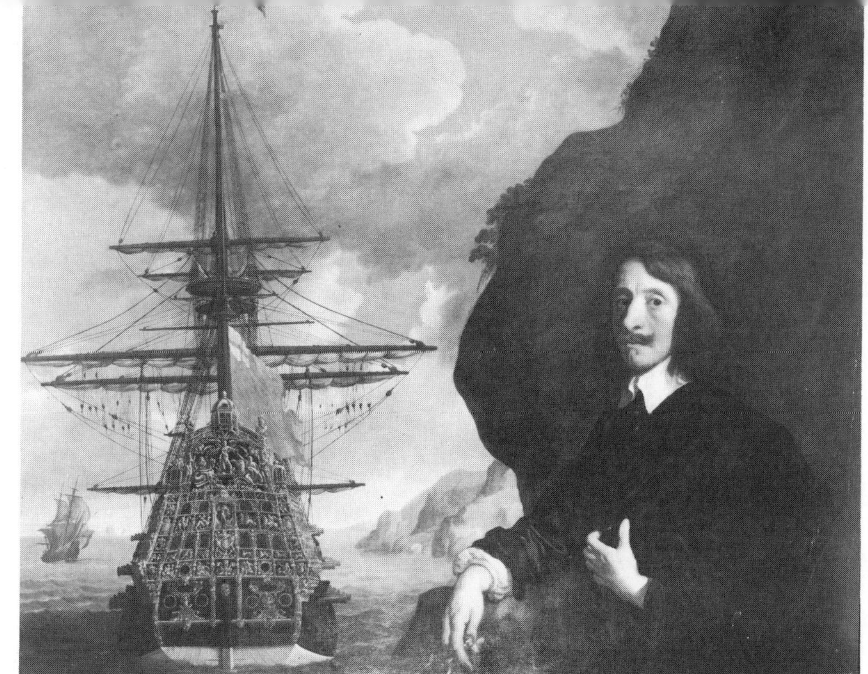

"Peter Pett and the Sovereign of the Seas,*" by Sir Peter Lely. She was launched in 1637 and this stern view (with her builder) shows the square tuck which was still the English fashion, but shortly to give way to the round tuck as in the* Royal Prince *below.*

Distinct diversions in style begin to appear between nations. In English ships after the Restoration in 1660, the area above the stern windows at upper-deck level (or from the middle-deck to the taffrails in three-deckers) was largely occupied by a large royal coat of arms (Figure 2b). In the 1670s and 1680s more stern windows appeared at quarter-deck level, and then in three-deckers at poop and even poop-royal level; consequently these coats of arms grew smaller and finally became badge size or disappeared altogether (Figure 3b).

English quarter galleries in the second half of the century were like lozenge-shaped badges; they were not part of the stern galleries as was the case with Dutch ships, in which the area between the single row of stern windows and the taffrail was usually given up to illustrating the vessel's name or origin (Figure 3c). However, as with the English coats of arms, this practice also died out as additional rows of windows appeared from the 1680s onwards. French stern design was different again, favouring open galleries; however, unlike the open galleries of the beginning of the century, these did not stick out from the hull of the ship, but tended to be contained within the line of the stern (Figure 2c).

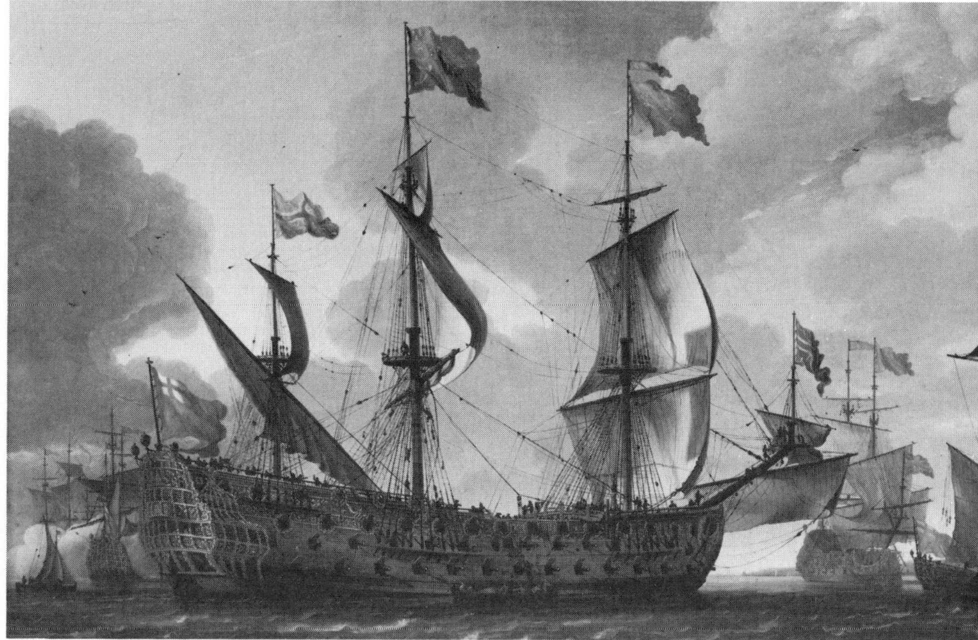

"The Royal Prince *in 1679," detail of a painting by Jan van Beecq. This illustrates the lofty appearance which the use of large topsails and main topgallants gave ships from the middle of the seventeenth century.*

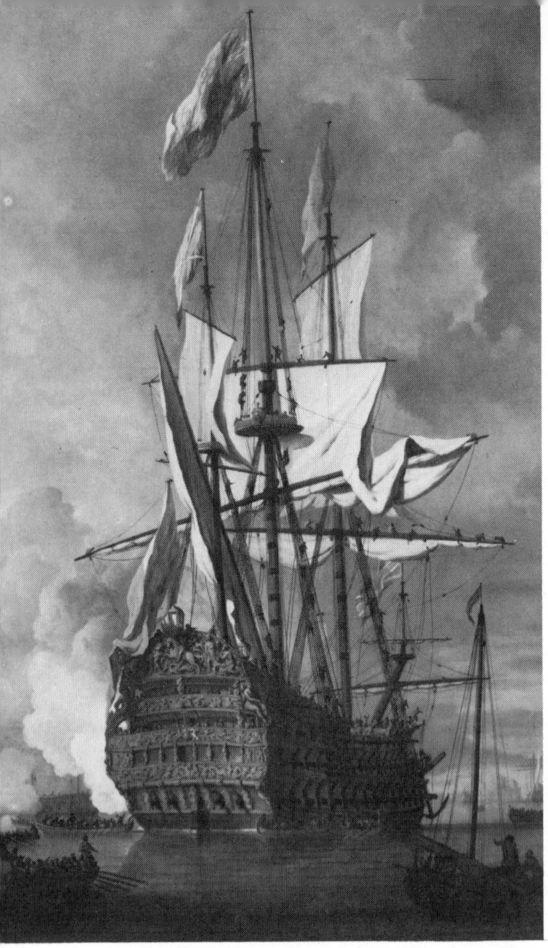

"The *Royal Sovereign* in 1704," by Willem van de Velde, the Younger, detail of Plate 156. The lavish carvings on this ship, which was built in 1701, were the immediate cause for ships' carved decorations to be confined to head and stern, with any further embellishments to be painted in.

1700-1780

Very early in the eighteenth century an important change took place in the appearance of ships of the Royal Navy. More recently in the same service a maxim given by petty officers to recruits went: "If it moves, salute it; if it doesn't, paint it." To an increasing degree in the Stuart navy you might substitute 'paint it' for 'carve it'. Not just the head and stern, but wreathed ports for the guns on the upper-decks, a carved entry port, catheads, the belfry and railings at the breaks of the poop, quarter-deck and fo'c'sle (Figures 3a and b). This lavishness continued inside the after cabins. In the case of the *Royal Sovereign* of 1701, the bill presented for her carved decorations was so large that their Lordships were moved to issue an order in 1703 confining such embellishments to the head and stern; the rest was to be painted (Figure 3d). This change of practice seems to have been followed by the builders of the East Indiamen and other large merchant ships. It not only changed the appearance of the ships but threw a large number of wood carvers out of work, many of whom sought work in churches and country houses, which explains the large amount of carving of that period still seen today around the country.

The beginning of the eighteenth century also saw the reappearance in English ships of the open stern gallery, now a recessed one (Figure 4b). At first this was often at upper-deck level in two-deckers and sometimes at quarter-deck level as well. By the second quarter of the century the lower gallery had, however, disappeared as being too near the water line; the upper one became standard for all ships up to near the end of the century (Figure 4c), and was revived in the early 1800s. In the second decade of the eighteenth century an important rig change took place. The sprit topmast and topsail gave way to a jib-boom and triangular head-sails (Figure 5a); this change, like most rig changes, started in the lower rates and worked up. Although sprit topmasts still figured in the rigging plans for first-rates until 1740, they do not seem to have been used as late as that in practice.

In the 1730s the stern galleries protruded over the stern and crossed the width of the ship, with a curved and carved taffrail arched above them (Figure 5c). The French had a similar system, but with the stern galleries curving round to join the quarter galleries. They also carried the ship's name on a label on the transom (Figure 4a), a practice the English did not adopt until 1772, and then without the label. Another change at this time was that the lower wales, that is, the extra planking which had been in two separate bands (Figure 3a), if not three, round the lower part of the ship's hull, merged into one (Figure 5a).

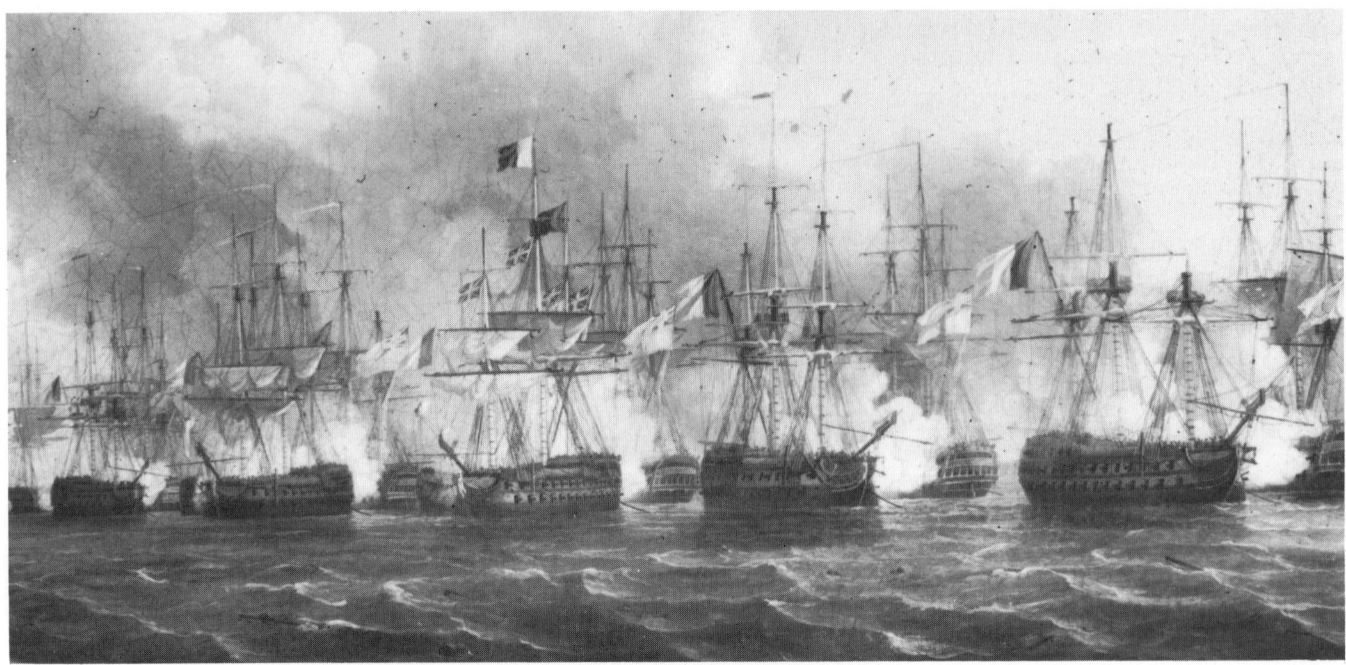

"The Battle of the Nile, August 1st, 1798," by Thomas Whitcombe. Nelson's flagship Vanguard *is left of centre in the picture. She still carries a lateen yard even at this late date, as indeed do the French ships in the picture.*

With the 1740s we are entering a period when little change of appearance took place for some time, so the raising of the main and fore chain-plates one deck in two-deckers in 1745 is important. Main and fore chain-plates are the fastenings to which the shrouds are brought down, and were traditionally at upper-deck level (Figure 3d). Commodore Anson, however, found that the *Centurion's* main and fore shrouds suffered storm damage off the Horn on his voyage round the world, and realised that raising them to quarter-deck level would ease this problem (Figure 5b). On his return, when he joined the Admiralty, it became official policy.

Another innovation of this period was the alteration of the lateen sail on the mizzen; this was cut vertically in two, the fore part being discarded, and the luff of the rear portion laced directly to the mizzen-mast (Figure 5c). This was logically and quickly followed in the lower rates by the cutting off of the mizzen yard at the mast, thus converting the lateen rig to a gaff (Figure 5d). This change was, however, not adopted by the larger ships and the East Indiamen until near the end of the century, the theory being that the lateen yard was a useful spar elsewhere if need for such arose. The *Vanguard,* Nelson's flagship at the Battle of the Nile in 1798, still had her lateen yard and is believed to have been the last vessel in the navy to be rigged in this way.

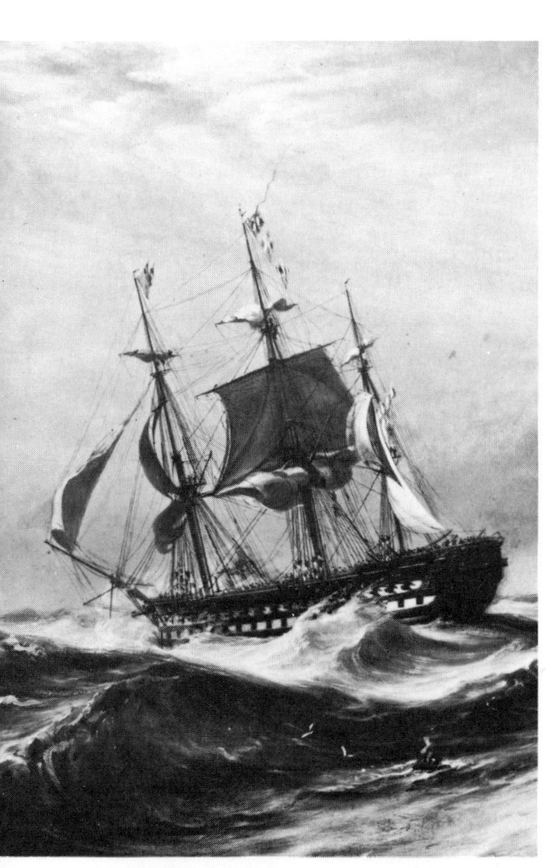

"Man overboard," by Oswald Walter Brierly, detail of Plate 496. In the early nineteenth century the navy adopted a black and white livery for its ships, as this painting from an incident in the Baltic in 1854 illustrates.

1780-1800

In 1779 the order went out for all naval ships to be copper-bottomed, the result being that bottoms and boot-toppings turned from white to weathered copper; ships also ceased to have their upper hulls 'payed', a type of varnishing, and were painted instead, which gave a dark lower hull and a buff upper (Figure 7a).

At the outbreak of the French Revolutionary Wars in 1793 the practice of putting the ship's name on her stern was discontinued for purposes of deception. The following year the dolphin striker was introduced to help the jib-boom support a flying jib-boom. This extra sail area forward needed to be balanced aft, so the gaff sail on the mizzen was enlarged, requiring it to be boomed out over the stern (Figure 7a). This had been a practice in cruising ships since the late 1770s; when ships were rigged in this way the ensign staff had to be struck and the ensign rehoisted at the head of the gaff-yard, a position known as the peak. Big ships, especially three-deckers, tended to hang on to their loose-footed gaffs until the end of the century, lashing their booms to the taffrail, but the boomed mizzen-sail soon came into general use. Its effect on the hoisting of ensigns in the Royal Navy remains to this day, ensigns still being worn on the ensign staff in harbour, but in some elevated position at sea. The practice also keeps the colours out of the field of fire, and makes them more easily seen.

1800 on

Up to the Battle of Trafalgar hulls were black and buff, though by 1805 painted in bands. About 1810 the navy adopted black and white, and this livery remained to the end of the wooden navy in the 1860s (Figure 7b). Black and white, or black alone, dominated the schemes of merchant ships, relieved sometimes by green hulls, a choice of colours which may have been something to do with the cost and durability of the paint.

From about the second quarter of the eighteenth century onwards, and with the appearance of iron built steamships later on, the design and development of ships was rapid and varied. Figures 8-11 show some of the most characteristic features typical of ship development from the early nineteenth century to its close.

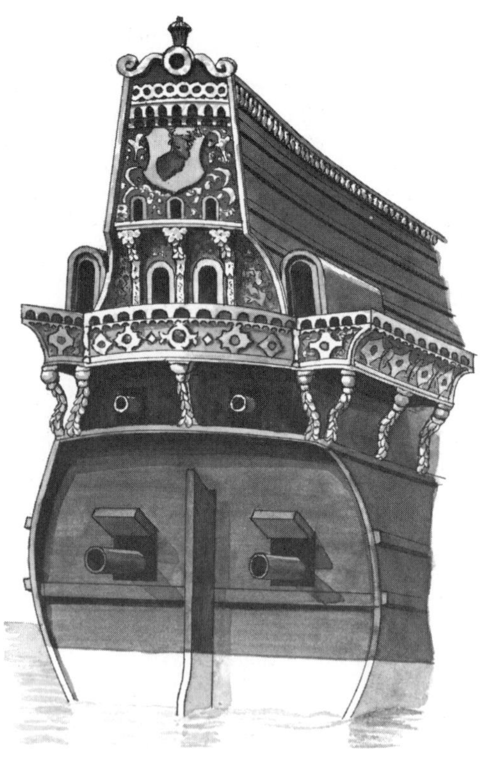

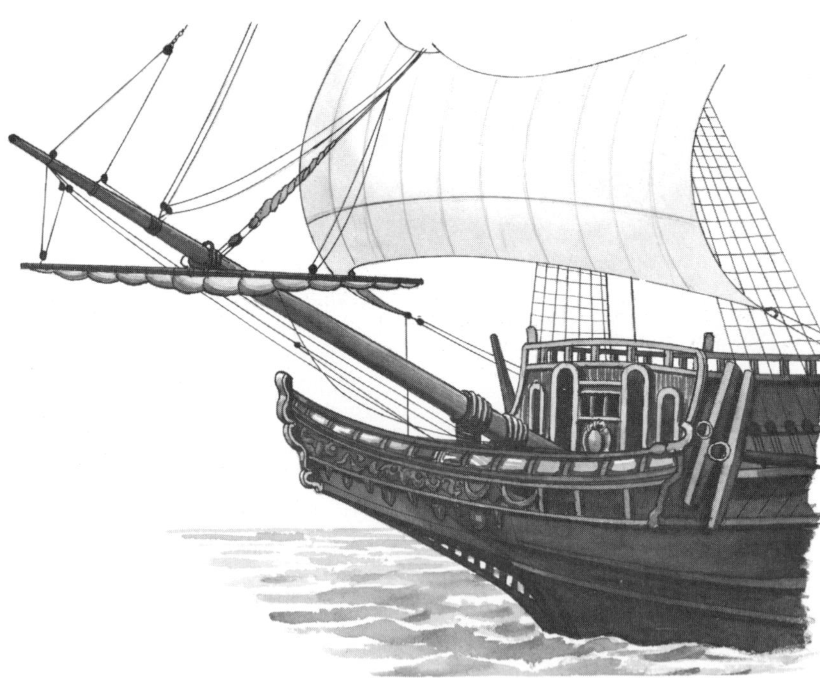

Ib. c.1600. The beak of a Dutch ship; the beaks of English ships were similar. Note the spritsail yard and sail, but the ship has not yet acquired the sprit topmast.

Ia. c.1600. The stern of a Dutch ship, characterised by a rather barrel-like lower hull with a square tuck below the transom and open stern galleries. There is a marked tumblehome to a very narrow poop. The white boot-topping is what shows of the painting of the underwater hull, with a mixture designed to discourage marine growth.

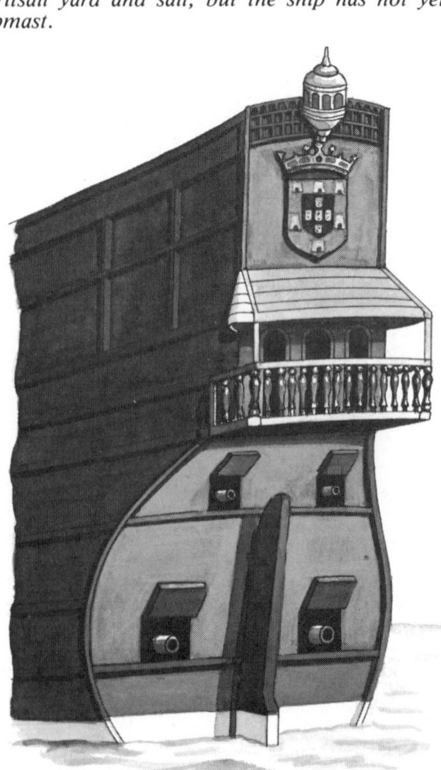

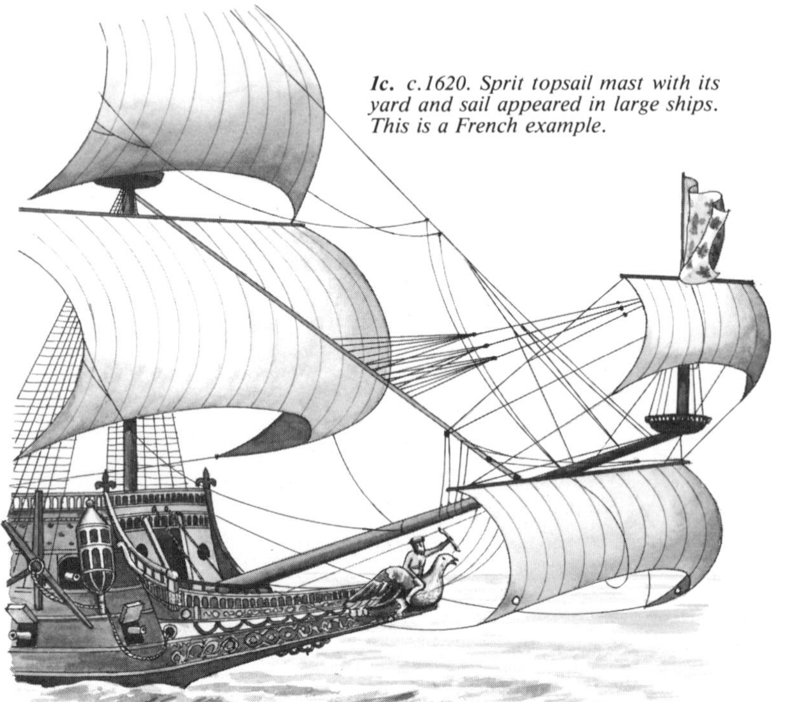

Ic. c.1620. Sprit topsail mast with its yard and sail appeared in large ships. This is a French example.

Id. c.1600. The stern of a Spanish ship. Note the appearance of a small gallery. By the 1630s the design of the stern had followed general European practice.

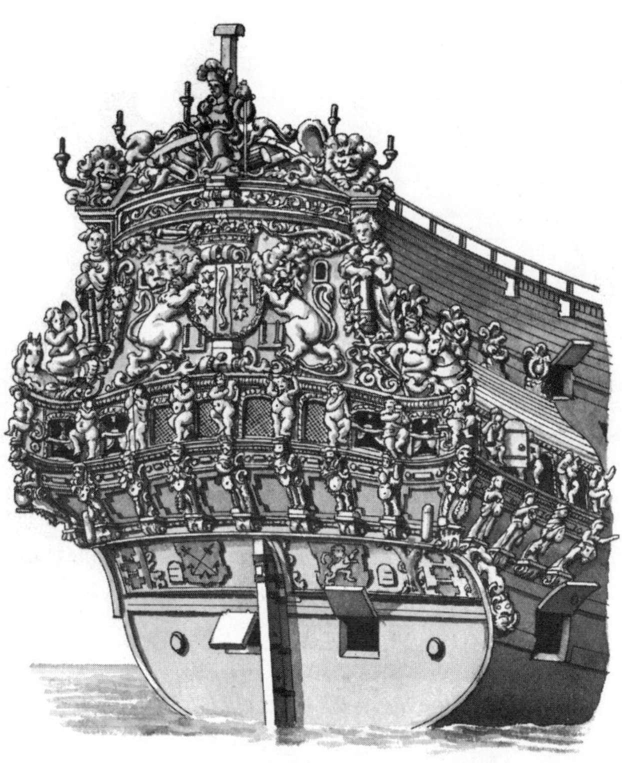

2a. The stern of the Dutch two-decker Gouda *of 1665. The stern galleries are now enclosed and richly carved. Above the stern windows and below the taffrail are the arms of Gouda and this area was used in Dutch ships to illustrate their names. Her poop is now much wider than in earlier ships.*

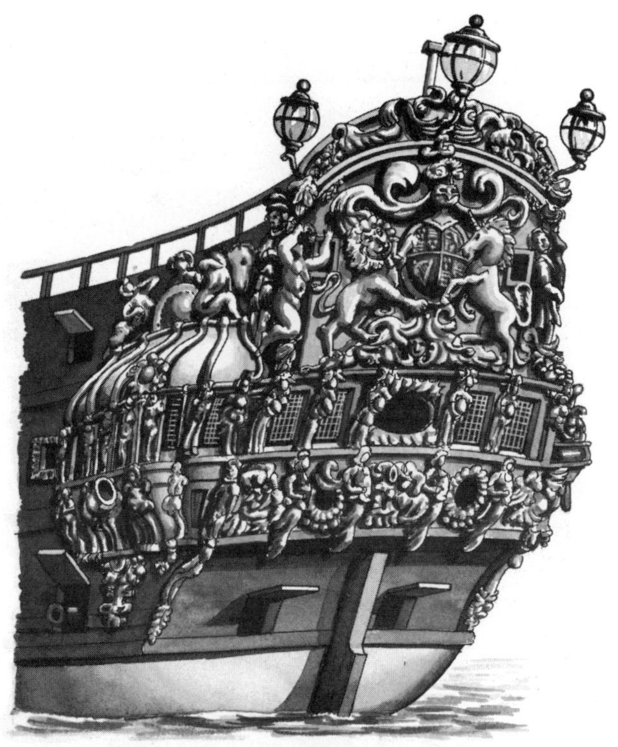

2b. An English stern of the third quarter of the 17th century. Note the adoption of the round tuck (the area from the waterline up to the transom), while the Dutch and French continued to build square tucks. Following the English practice the royal arms are always shown on the stern, the cipher only being changed on the death of a king. A further distinguishing feature between the English and Dutch was the quarter gallery. The English tended to have a greater vertical emphasis whereas on the Dutch ships this was more horizontal.

2c. A French stern of the third quarter of the 17th century, in this case the three-decker first-rate Reine *of 1667. Note the open stern galleries above the closed lower ones, and the wide square taffrail. The arms are those of Queen Marie Thérèse of France.*

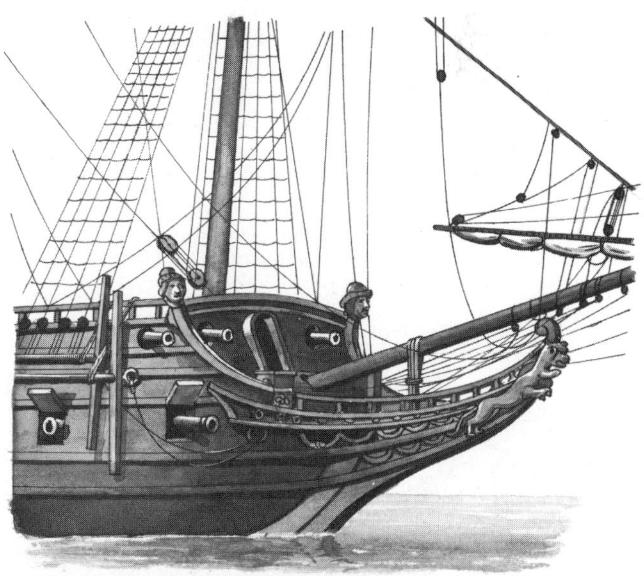

2d. North European beaks generally in the mid-17th century. The upward curve was to get shorter and steeper as the century progressed.

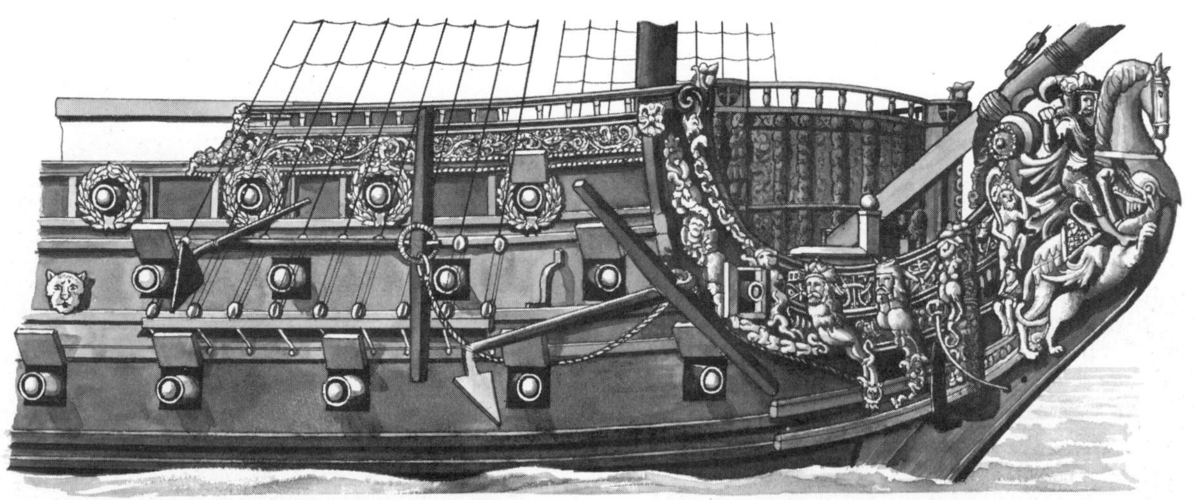

3a. The bows of an English first rate in the last quarter of the 17th century. Note the wreathed gunports on the upper deck, introduced in 1675 (previously they had been square); the wreathing continued until the general reduction in ornamentation. Only first and second rates had individual figureheads at this time, the first rate, as in the illustration, being highly ornate, the second rate being plainer. In 1706 the shroud plates in three-deckers were raised from middle-deck level, as here, to upper-deck level. These iron plates on the sides of the hull held the blocks to which the shrouds were brought down.

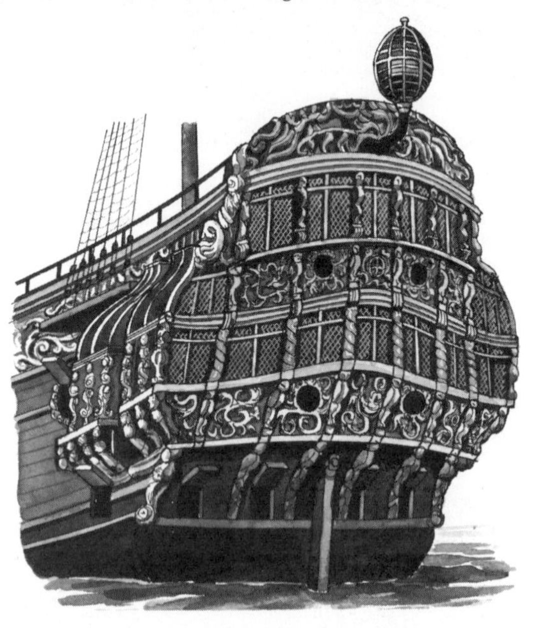

3b. An English stern about 1700. By this date there was a row of sternlights and the royal coat of arms was very much reduced in size or absent. Note also the continuing vertical design of the quarter galleries in contrast to the French and Dutch who continued to design theirs in a horizontal fashion.

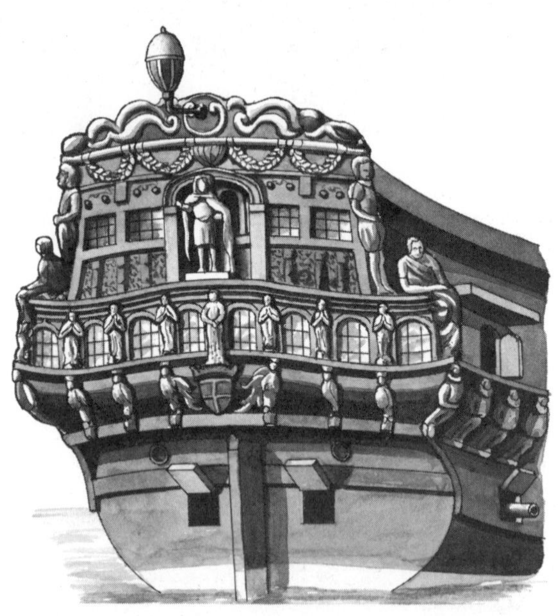

3c. A Dutch stern about 1700. The decoration has been drastically reduced as a result of general economies brought about by a series of wars. The central figurehead repeats the name of the ship. The quarter galleries have almost disappeared and now take the form of a gunport.

3d. From 1703 the carved decoration on ships of the Royal Navy was confined to the beak and stern galleries.

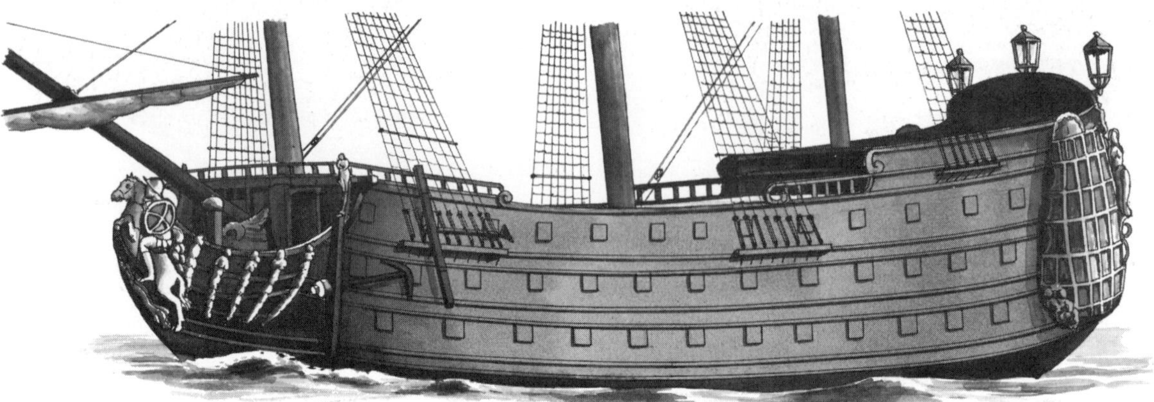

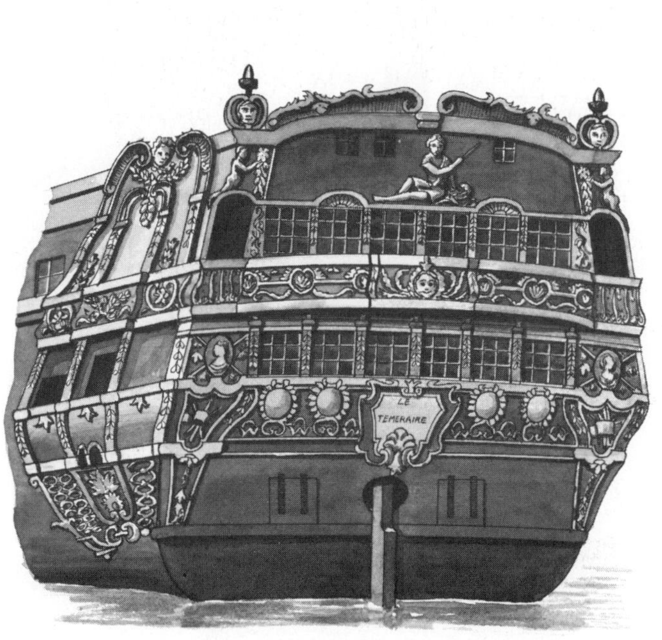

4a. *A French stern in the second quarter of the 18th century. Note the square quality has been retained with heavy galleries which go right round, a practice never followed in English ships. The addition of a name on a label or cartouche is also typical of French practice at this period.*

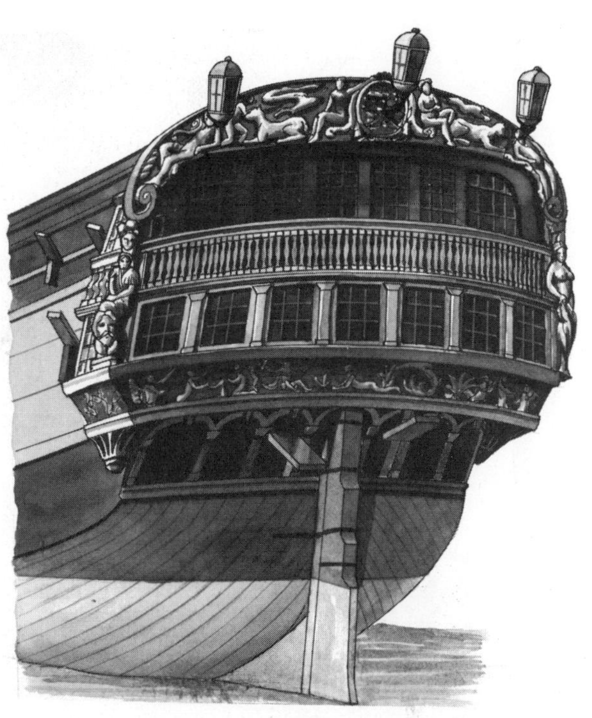

4b. *An English stern in the second quarter of the 18th century. The stern gallery has appeared but does not go right round as the equivalent French example. It was a design which continued for a considerable period.*

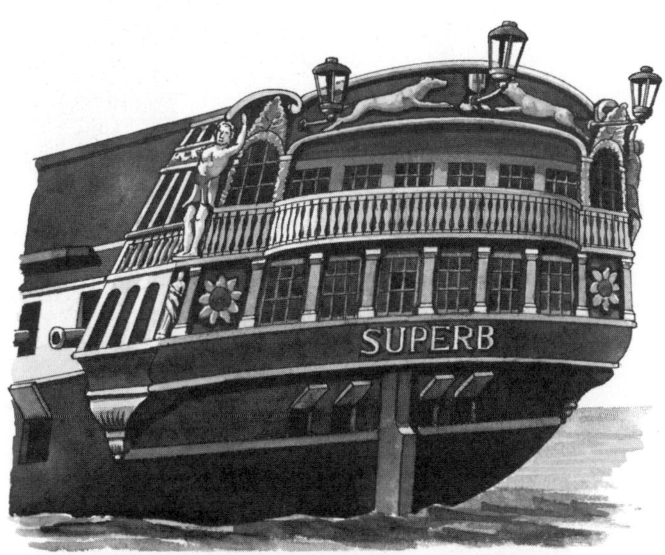

4c. *An English stern of about 1780. A slight change of fashion. Note that from 1779 ships of the Royal Navy were copper plated on their lower hulls so that their boot toppings no longer showed white or cream. The addition of the name appeared in 1772 and continued until the French Revolutionary Wars when anonymity was desirable.*

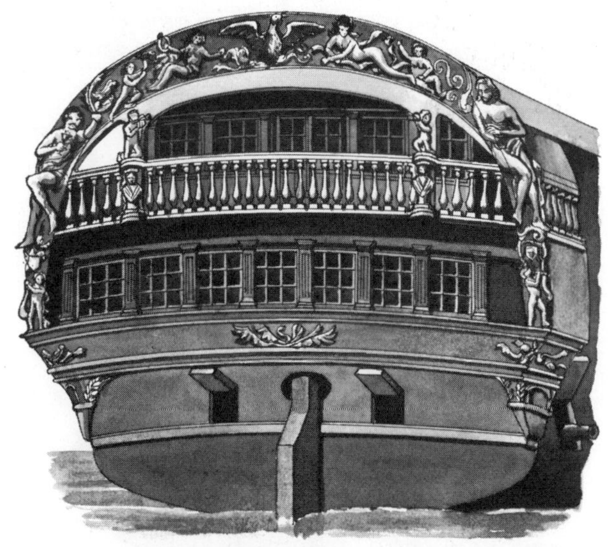

4d. *A Spanish stern in the second quarter of the 18th century. Similar to the French example but with a characteristic bow shape to the top which the French adopted later in the 18th century.*

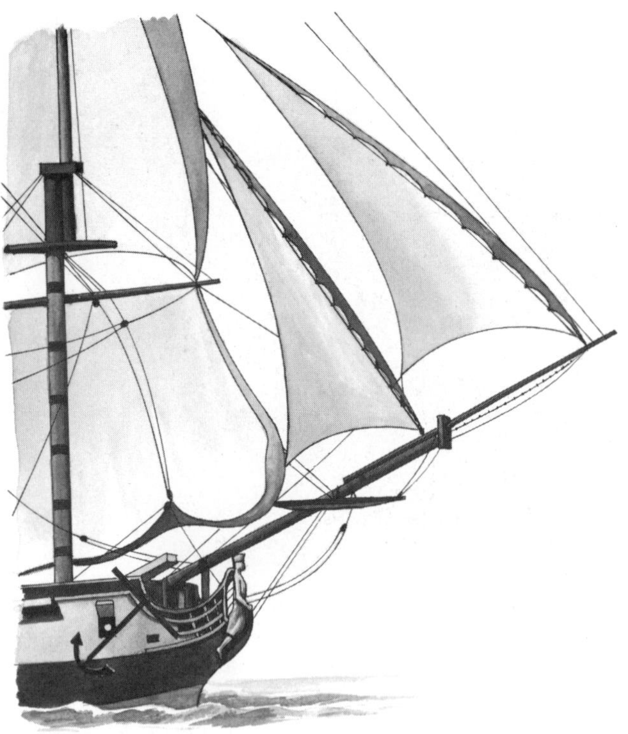

5a. In the 1720s the jib-boom and triangular head sails replaced the sprit-topmast in large ships as it had already done in small vessels. At this time too the wales, the two or three black painted bands of extra sheathing above the waterline, became one solid mass.

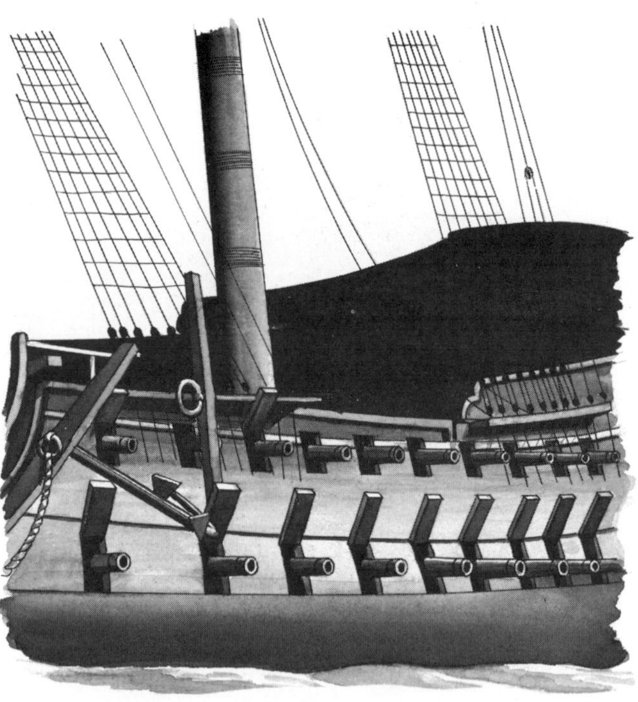

5b. As a result of Commodore Anson's experiences in the Centurion *off Cape Horn in 1739, the (main and fore) shroud plates in two-deckers were raised from upper-deck to quarter-deck level to reduce storm damage. This was in 1745; the change in three-deckers came in 1787. The delay in making the change in the larger boats was due to the fact that the shroud plates were further from the water and less damage was done.*

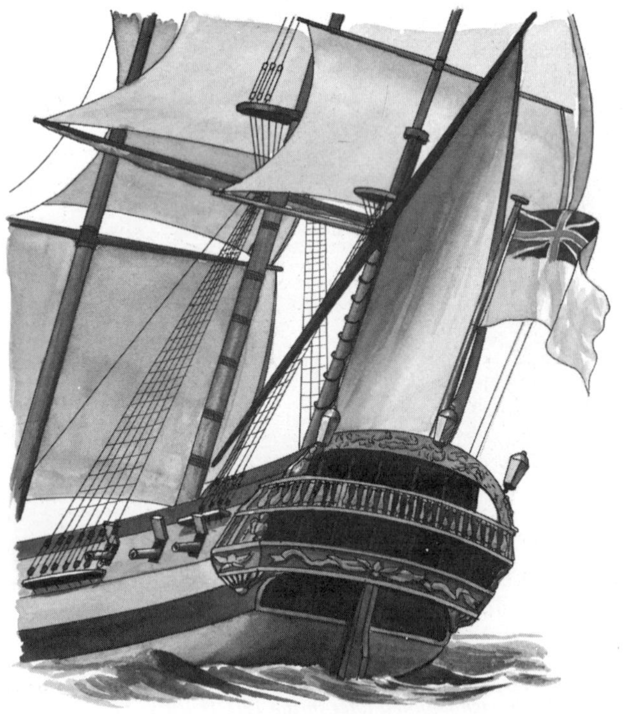

5c. In the 1740s the lateen mizzen-sail was modified by being cut off at the mast to which the luff of the sail was laced by ropes at intervals.

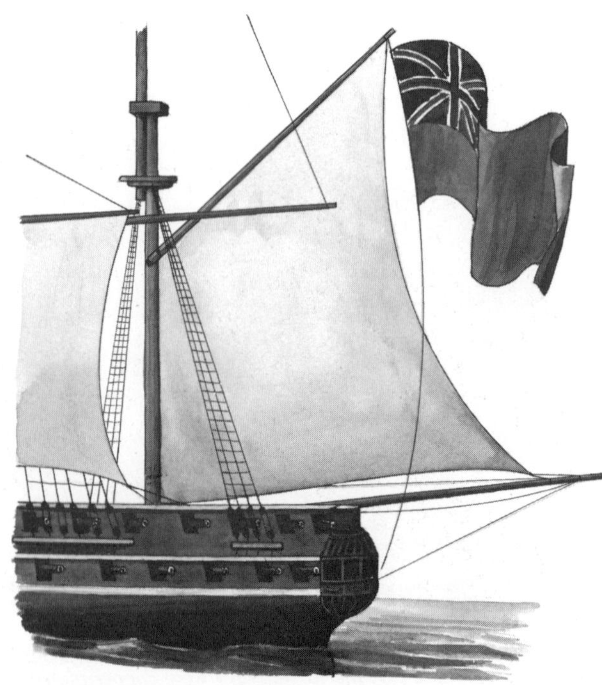

5d. In the 1770s the lateen yard was cut off at the mast to become a gaff yard in cruising ships and the size of the mizzen sail was enlarged by having its foot attached to a boom out over the stern. This meant the ensign staff had to be removed when at sea and the ensign worn at the peak. In harbour the boom was lashed so that the ensign staff could be re-stepped.

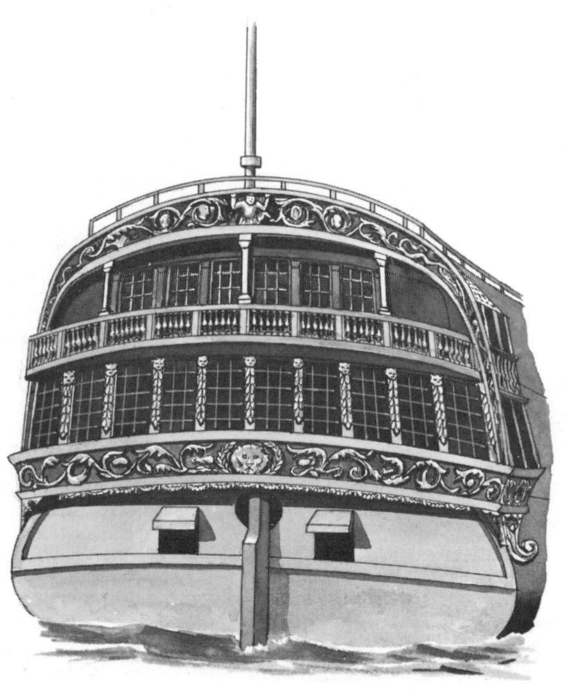

6a. The stern of a French two-decker of the period of the Revolutionary Wars, 1793-1815. Rather like the Spanish with a curved taffrail. The walking gallery, which is fairly prominent, goes across the width of the ship.

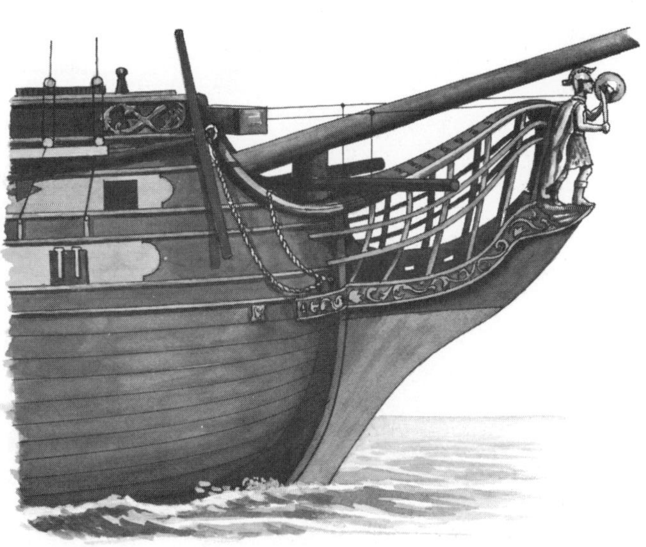

6b. The bow of a French two-decker of the period of the Revolutionary Wars. Note the large figurehead.

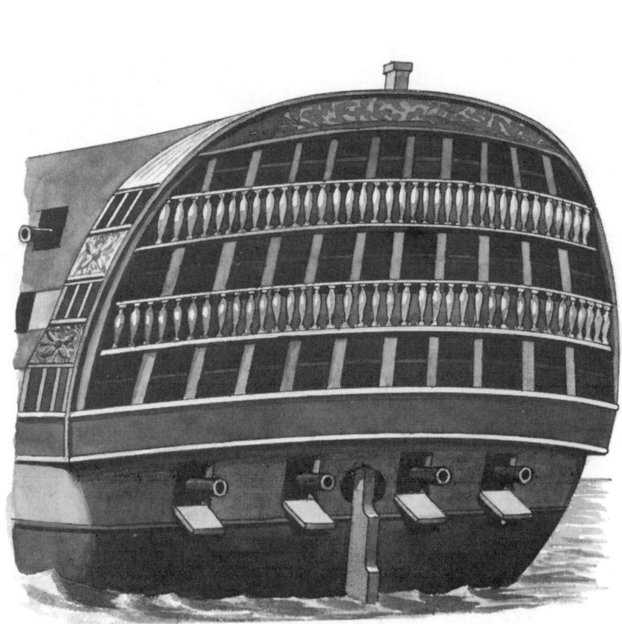

6c. The stern of a Spanish three-decker about 1800. The prominent feature is the bold curve of the outline.

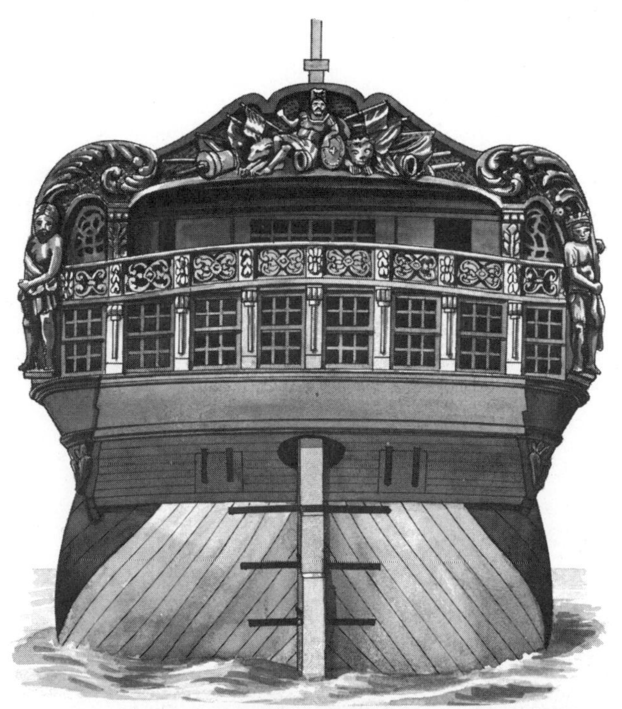

6d. The stern of a Dutch two-decker about 1800. By comparison with the English example (Figure 4c), it is heavier and more ornately treated.

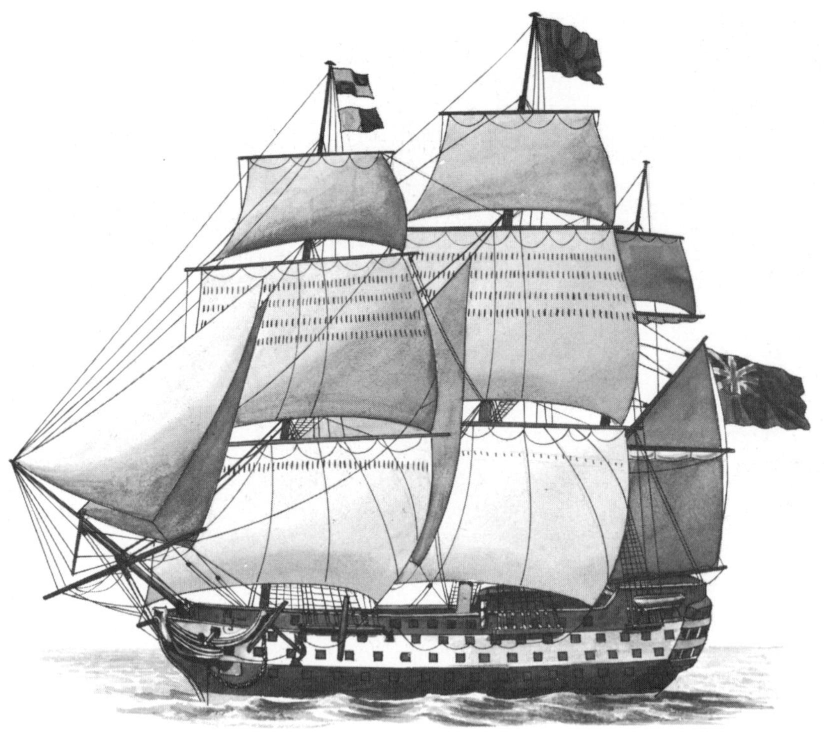

7a. *A first-rate of 1800. Since the early 1780s naval ships had been painted buff and black instead of being varnished, or 'payed'. In 1787 shroud plates in three-deckers were raised from upper-deck level to quarter-deck level, and in 1794 a spreader below the end of the bowsprit to support jib-booms, lengthened to carry flying jib-sails, was generally adopted and came to be known as a dolphin-striker. The lateen yard was retained in large ships until the 1790s and even after the mizzen gaff yard and boom had been fitted ships often appeared with the boom lashed by the ensign staff and carrying a loose footed mizzen-sail.*

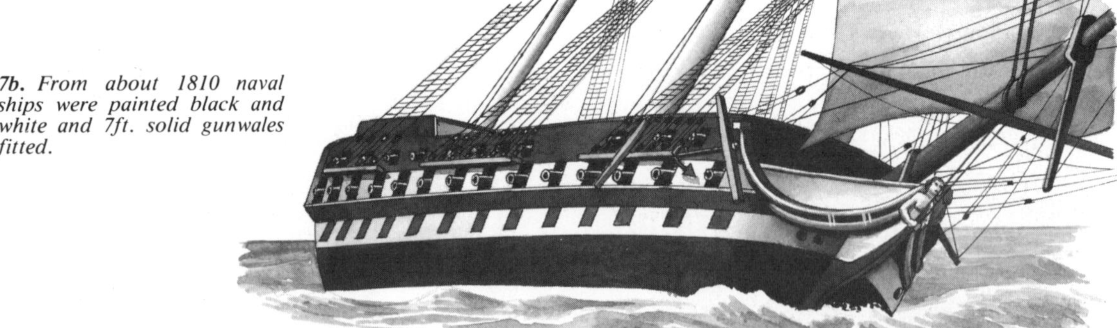

7b. *From about 1810 naval ships were painted black and white and 7ft. solid gunwales fitted.*

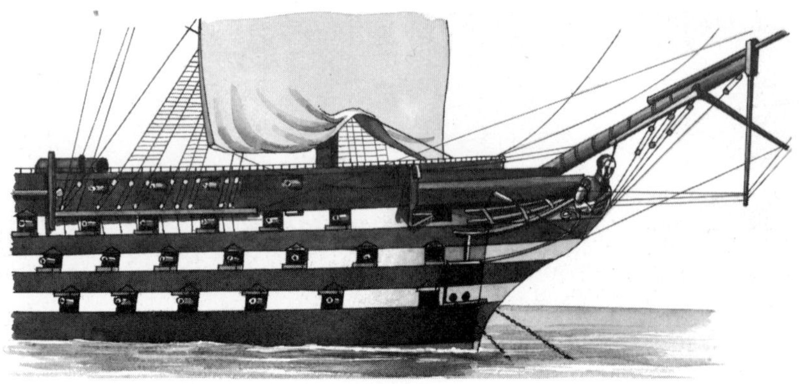

7c. *From about 1820 the filled-in bow appears with 7ft. solid gunwales above deck. Note retracted funnel. The steam assisted battle fleet was created in 1854. Cruising vessels, however, had had retracting funnels since the 1820s.*

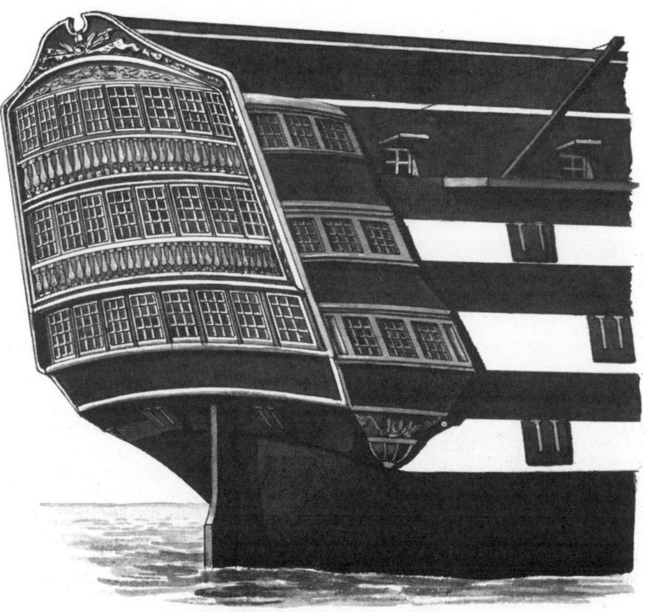

8a. The closed stern at the beginning of the 19th century. The vessel shown illustrates the Victory *after her refit. The practice at this time was to close the stern galleries though leaving the baluster effects intact. However, by about 1810 galleries, which were a popular feature, began to re-emerge.*

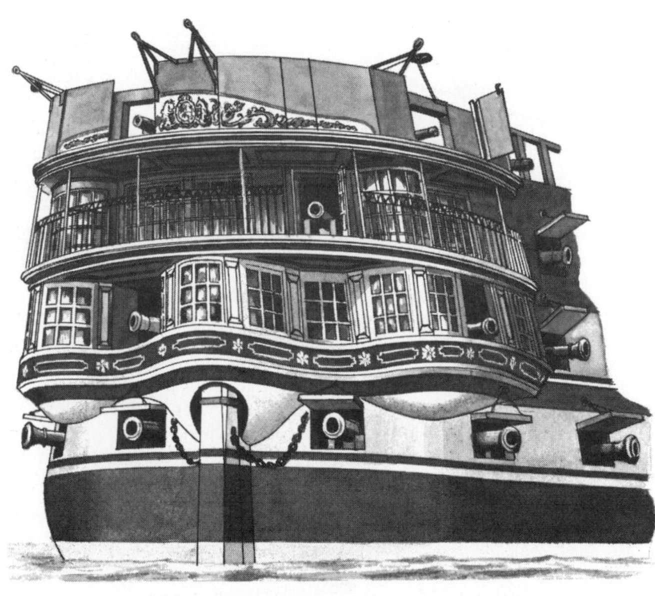

8b. One of the round sterns designed by Sir Robert Seppings during his period as Surveyor of the Navy, 1813-32. Note the iron sternwalks which started in the 1820s. This has a recessed gallery but the development was towards full sternwalks outside galleries, thus returning to the original concept (Figure 4b).

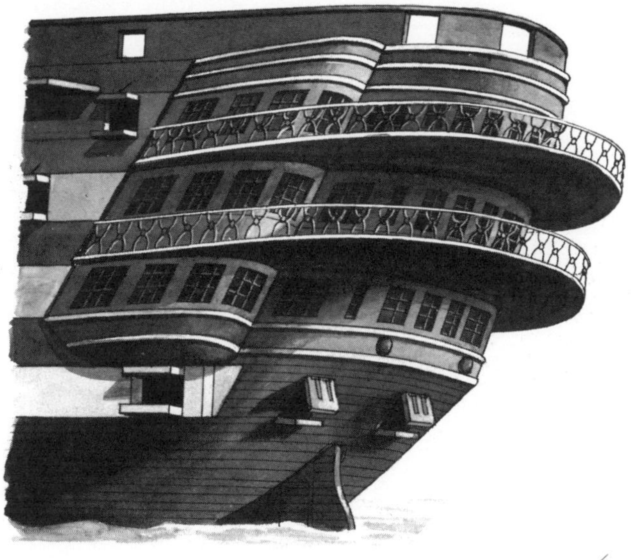

8c. In the 1830s and to the end of the era of the wooden line of battleships in the 1860s, naval design returned to more conventional stern galleries with the elliptical stern. This is the final stage in the development of the stern of the wooden liner.

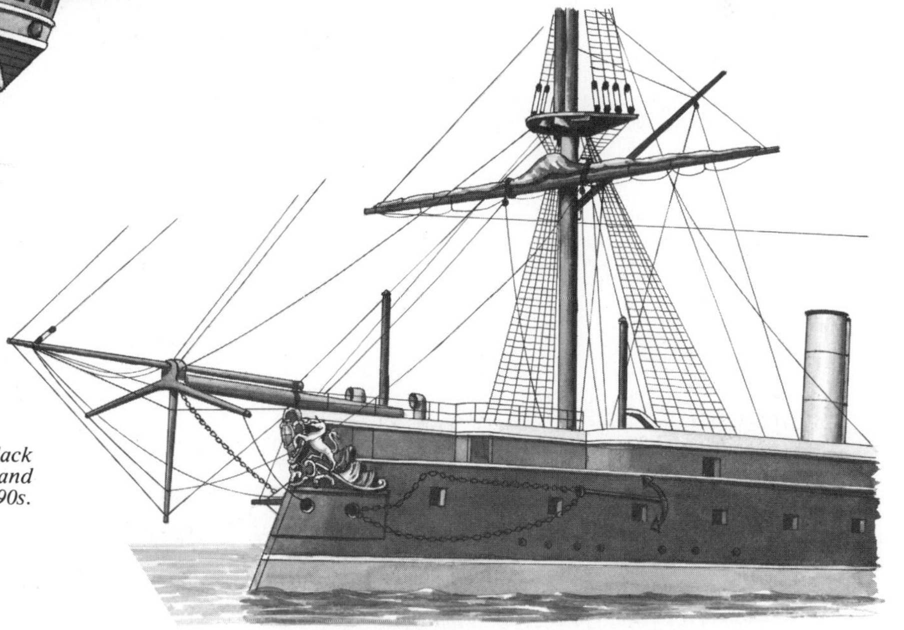

8d. The masted ironclads of the Black Battle Fleet first appeared in 1860 and served into the 1890s.

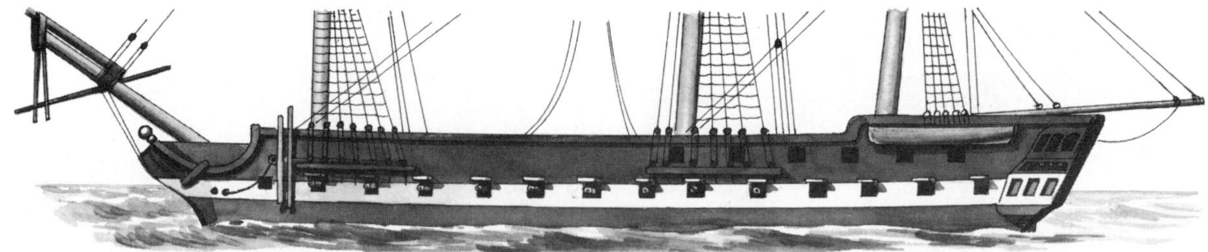

9a. An early 19th century East Indiaman. Note that the lower tier of gunports is on the upper-deck, in line with the lower stern galleries. This distinguishes them from naval two-deckers which have a tier on the deck below.

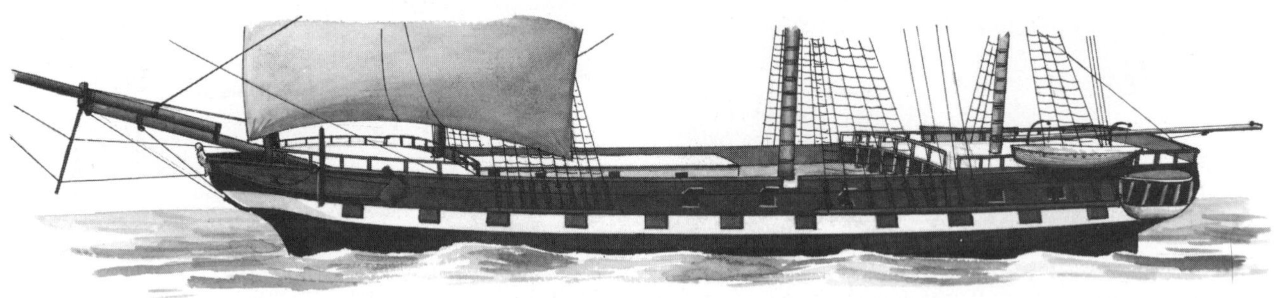

9b. Richard Green's improved East Indiamen from1837 are distinguished by having only one deck with stern galleries, the coach having been removed in favour of a lengthened quarter-deck. They were called Blackwall frigates, for while the old Indiamen were laid out like naval frigates with coaches, the new ones also looked like frigates. Such vessels worked throughout the century.

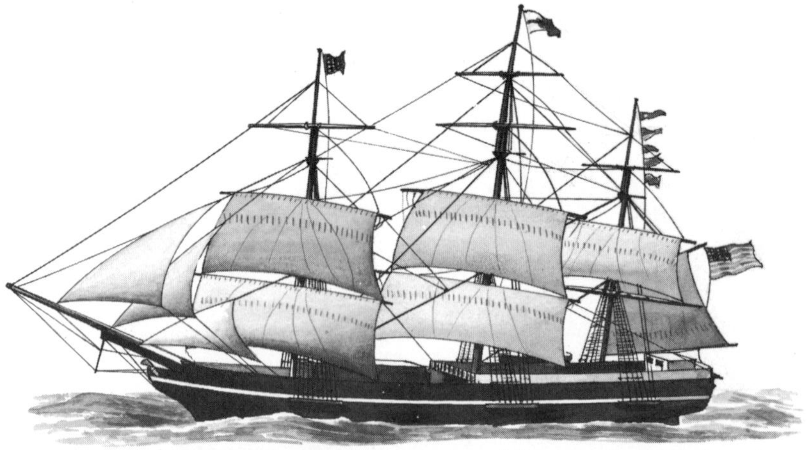

9c. An American North Atlantic passenger packet of the second and third quarters of the 19th century. Note the distinctive squared off stern typical of American vessels and the long quarter-deck to give maximum accommodation. Note also that the ship is underhatted (i.e. the masts do not rise to a great height) indicating the rough North Atlantic conditions.

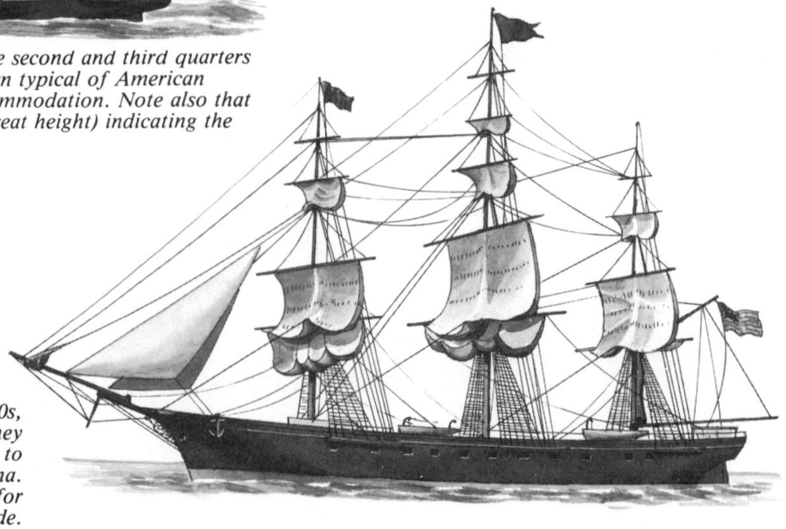

9d. The great American clipper-ships of the 1830s, on the other hand, had huge sail plans, as they were designed to work round the Horn to California with goldrush passengers, or to China. Some were bought by Liverpool shipowners for the Australian emigrant trade.

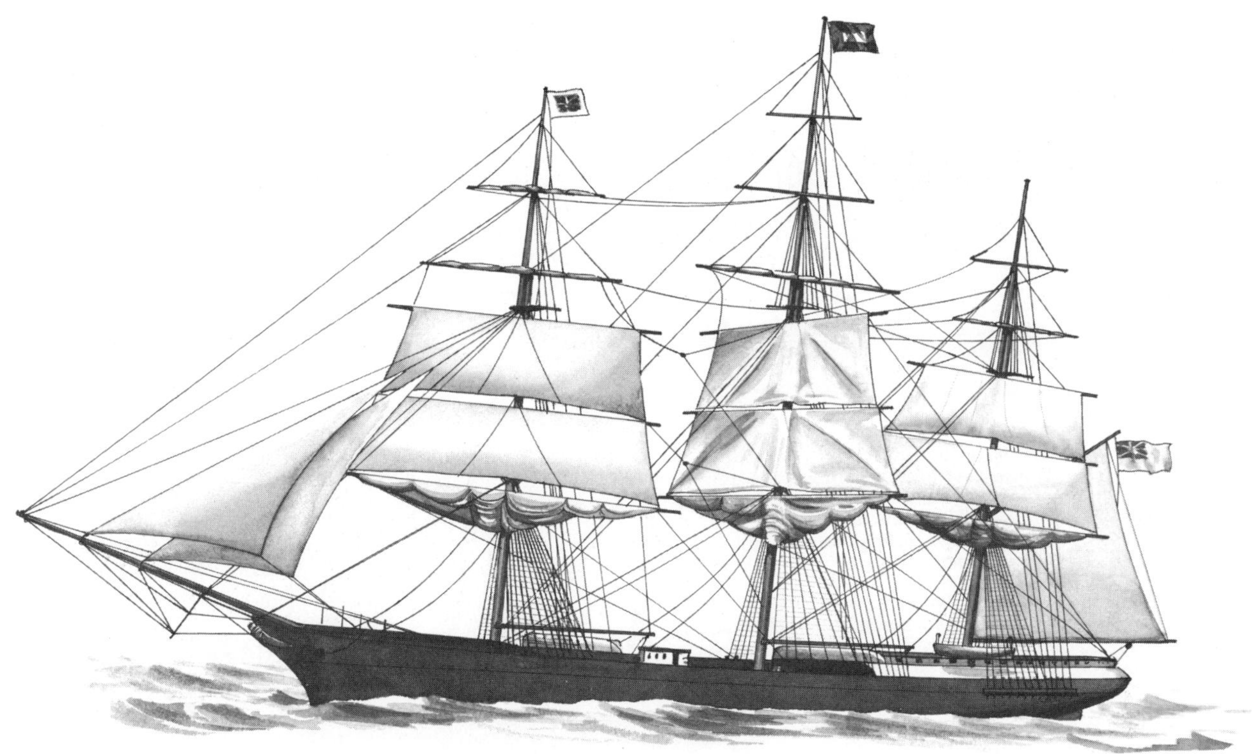

10a. *In the 1860s double topsails were introduced for easier handling, and by 1870 shrouds were generally secured inboard of the gunwales. In this ship the mizzen shrouds are still secured outboard because of her whale-backed poop, a feature that also indicates that she was built of iron. The double topsails were never used in the Royal Navy where shortage of manpower was not a problem.*

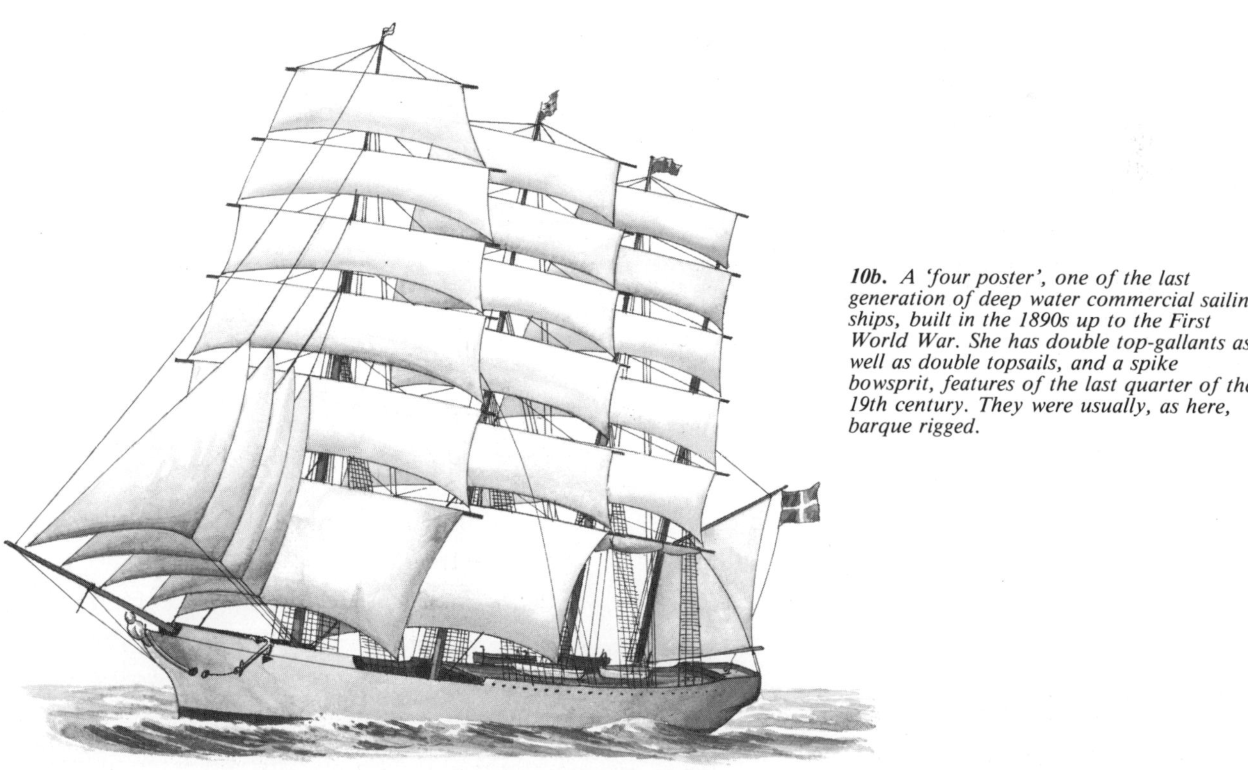

10b. *A 'four poster', one of the last generation of deep water commercial sailing ships, built in the 1890s up to the First World War. She has double top-gallants as well as double topsails, and a spike bowsprit, features of the last quarter of the 19th century. They were usually, as here, barque rigged.*

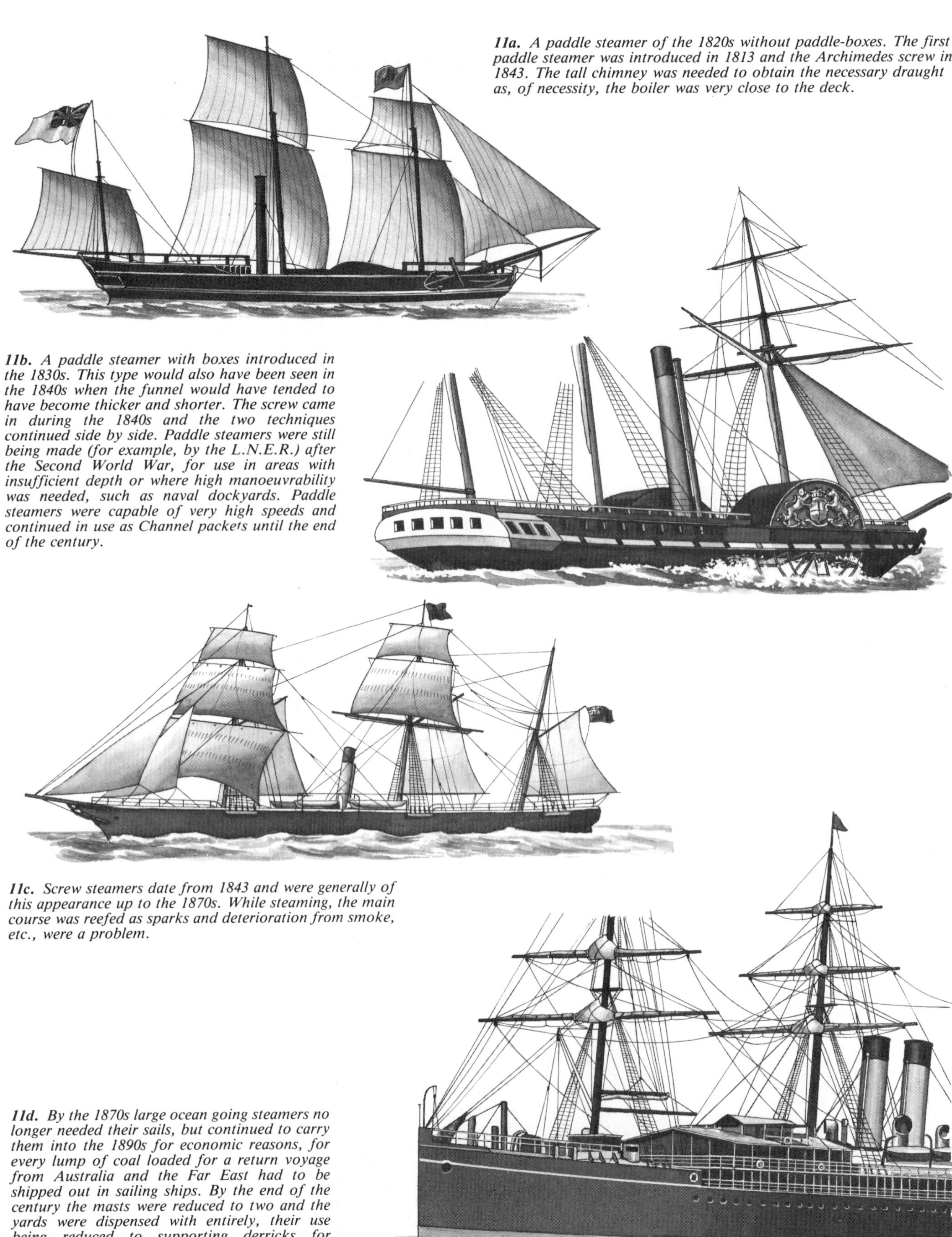

11a. A paddle steamer of the 1820s without paddle-boxes. The first paddle steamer was introduced in 1813 and the Archimedes screw in 1843. The tall chimney was needed to obtain the necessary draught as, of necessity, the boiler was very close to the deck.

11b. A paddle steamer with boxes introduced in the 1830s. This type would also have been seen in the 1840s when the funnel would have tended to have become thicker and shorter. The screw came in during the 1840s and the two techniques continued side by side. Paddle steamers were still being made (for example, by the L.N.E.R.) after the Second World War, for use in areas with insufficient depth or where high manoeuvrability was needed, such as naval dockyards. Paddle steamers were capable of very high speeds and continued in use as Channel packets until the end of the century.

11c. Screw steamers date from 1843 and were generally of this appearance up to the 1870s. While steaming, the main course was reefed as sparks and deterioration from smoke, etc., were a problem.

11d. By the 1870s large ocean going steamers no longer needed their sails, but continued to carry them into the 1890s for economic reasons, for every lump of coal loaded for a return voyage from Australia and the Far East had to be shipped out in sailing ships. By the end of the century the masts were reduced to two and the yards were dispensed with entirely, their use being reduced to supporting derricks for handling cargo and finally for wireless aerials (1910).

Picture Content and Subject Matter

In general the choice of subjects in marine paintings was controlled by the nationalities of the people who painted them, and by what was going on around them; for these reasons only types of vessel likely to appear in marine paintings over the years will be considered here.

There is a small group of Flemish-Italian paintings belonging to the mid-16th century which record historical events in the Mediterranean. The vessels depicted in them are high-castled carracks, galleasses and galleys. From that time on, the fighting galley remained basically the same until it disappeared in the second quarter of the 19th century. A feature of these 16th century galleys was the coloured awnings over their poops which almost brushed the water. These were progressively shortened in the seventeenth and eighteenth centuries.

When the Flemish and Dutch sea painters of the late sixteenth century were working, the ships they depicted were those of the Spanish Netherlands, their own small craft and (when the long struggle with Spain developed) the fights of the Sea Beggars, which were fought initially in these small craft. They also painted their English allies in action in the Armada campaign of 1588 and other battles that followed, until England made a separate peace with Spain.After this, though Vroom and Willaerts painted some important English subjects, the increasing hostility between Holland and England, arising from trade rivalries in the Mediterranean and Far East excludes most English subjects from Dutch paintings until the First Dutch War 1652-53, when, naturally enough, in view of the spectacle they provided, the battles were recorded. Also long excluded from Dutch painting were the Spanish, who are last found recorded at their defeat at the Battle of the Downs in 1639.

In a brief war in 1658 the Dutch beat the Swedes at the Battle of the Sound and pictures exist of this event. In 1665-67 there were the actions of the Second Anglo-Dutch War, followed by the Third of 1672-73, by which time the French navy was involved. An important development during and just after this war was the emigration of a number of leading Dutch marine painters to England, and many pictures of English interest were painted from this time; these cover the Third Dutch War and the Wars of the English and Spanish succession, 1689-1713, when the English and Dutch were allied against the French. The Mediterranean scenes may feature ships of all three nations if painted during a period of peace.

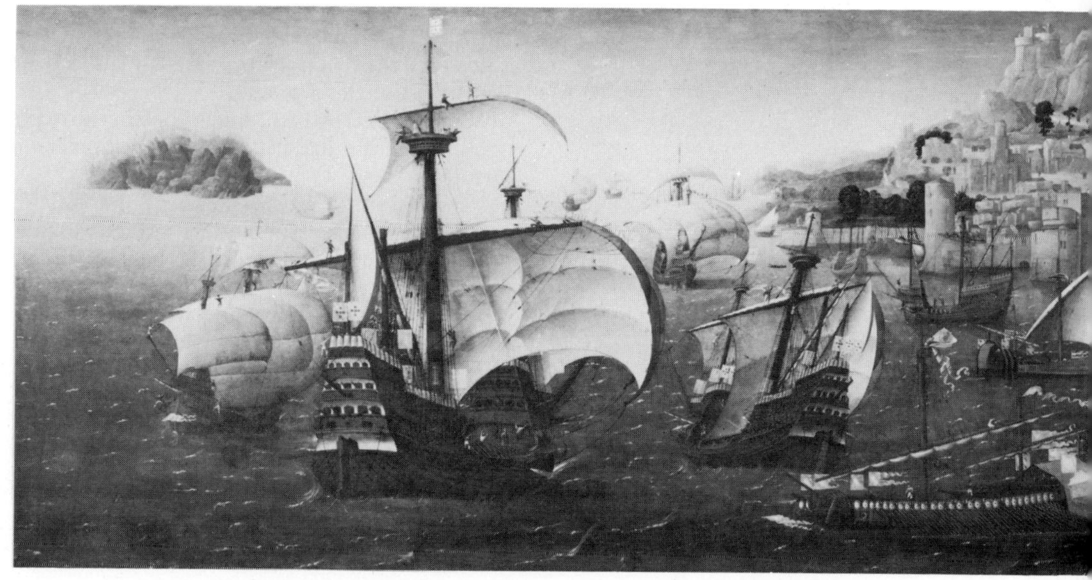

"The arrival of the Portuguese Infanta Beatriz at Villefranche, in the Santa Catarina de Monte Sinai, *to marry the Duke of Savoy, in 1522." This great carrack was built in 1511 in Cochin. Note the proportion of the beam to length, the huge fore- and after-castles and the two bonnets laced to her main sail, with their complicated sheeting.*

On the right are two fighting galleys of Savoy. Normally, and certainly in later times, a galley's only guns were mounted foreward in her rambata, firing over her ram. Here, in the nearest galley, a huge gun is mounted amidships. Another feature of the times is the great awning over the poop, which in the two galleys here nearly sweep the water. These became progressively shorter.

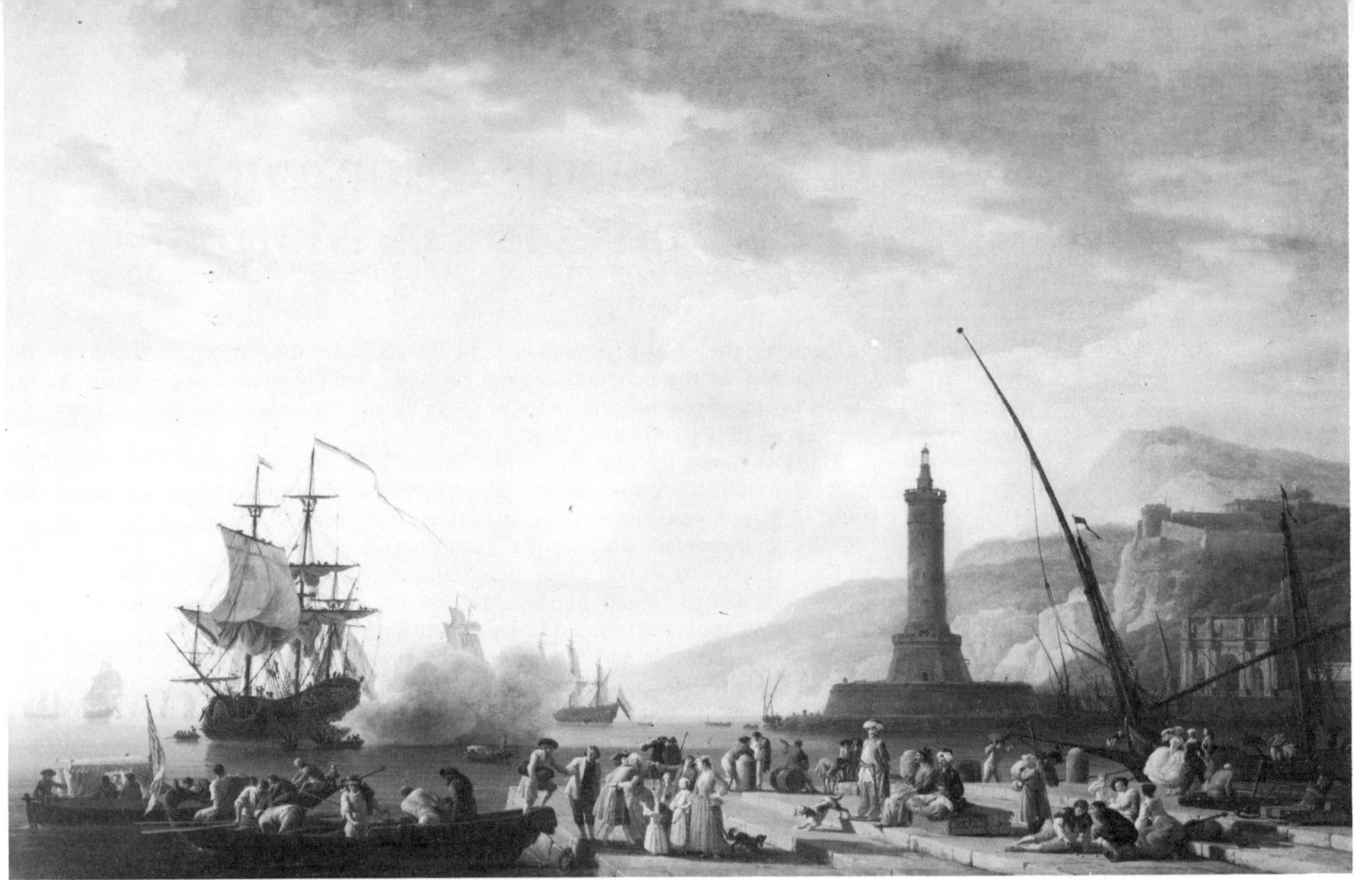

"Harbour scene at Naples, dated 1749," by Claude-Joseph Vernet (see Plate 232). One of the typically beautiful port scenes by this French painter.

In the eighteenth century the Dutch school of marine painters faded almost to oblivion and their heirs, the English painters, dominated the scene, especially in the field of history painting. In France, Vernet was painting his beautiful port scenes, but the recording of French sea battles seems to have been left to the crude primitives of Captain le Comte de Rossel.

Eighteenth century marine painting, therefore, is mainly concerned with English subjects; either general scenes or sea fights with the French, Spanish and occasionally the Dutch and Americans. With the long wars of the French Revolution (1793-1815) the list of combatants was augmented at various times by the Danes, Russians and Turks. It was from this period and shortly afterwards that there was a resurgence of the Dutch school, coupled with the emergence of good marine schools in Germany and Scandinavia, notably Denmark, and in every great port there blossomed the ship portraitist — a subject so diverse that its description is beyond the scope of this work.

Other aspects which, taken together or separately, may help in identification and dating are the pattern of the development of artistic style and, in port scenes, people's dress.

The pattern of the development of artistic style was largely dictated by one or two of the most successful masters who created an artistic fashion, which would in turn be adapted by their pupils, the best of whom would create another fashion and so identify a period. Each period will have in general its own palette, its own approach to drawing and subject, and will mirror the feeling of the times.

Dress can closely date a picture, especially if there are any who are fasionably dressed, and may also help to identify the place. Recourse to prints of the ports in the area may also aid in identifying the subject.

Coastal Craft

The identification of coastal craft can often be a valuable dating aid. To this end the wide range of vessels shown, both of type and in years, includes the majority of local craft which most frequently appear in sea paintings.

An English ketch-rigged royal yacht, c.1710. Most of the yachts were based at Gravesend or Greenwich, to take important people to, or collect them from, the Continent.

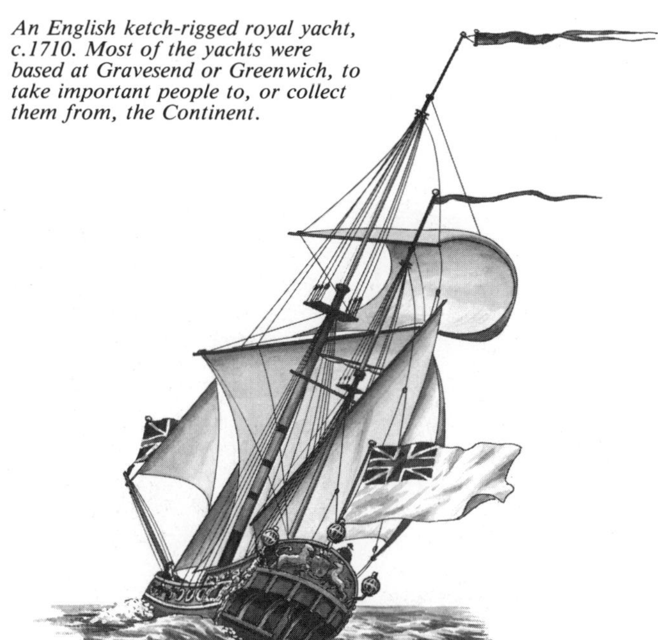

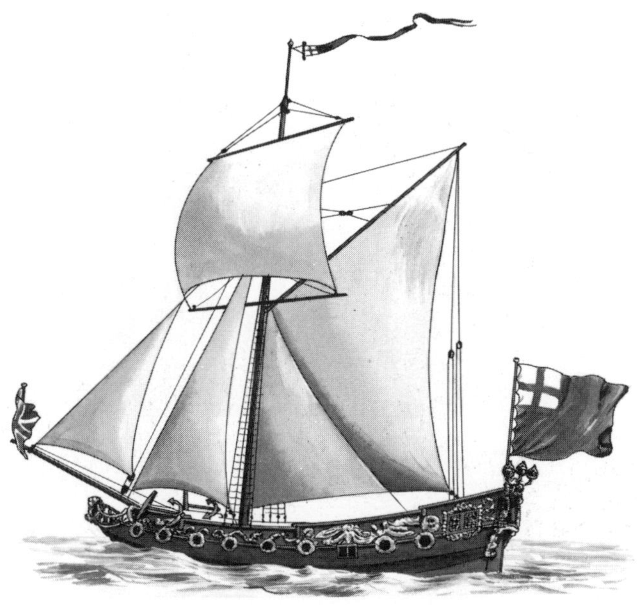

An English smack-rigged royal yacht from the late 17th to early 18th century. A number of these were later converted to ketch, as in the example on the left.

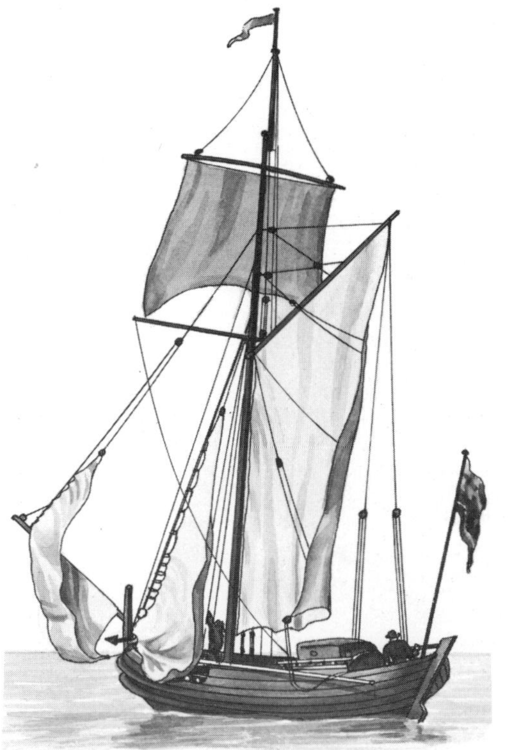

English hoy, 18th century.

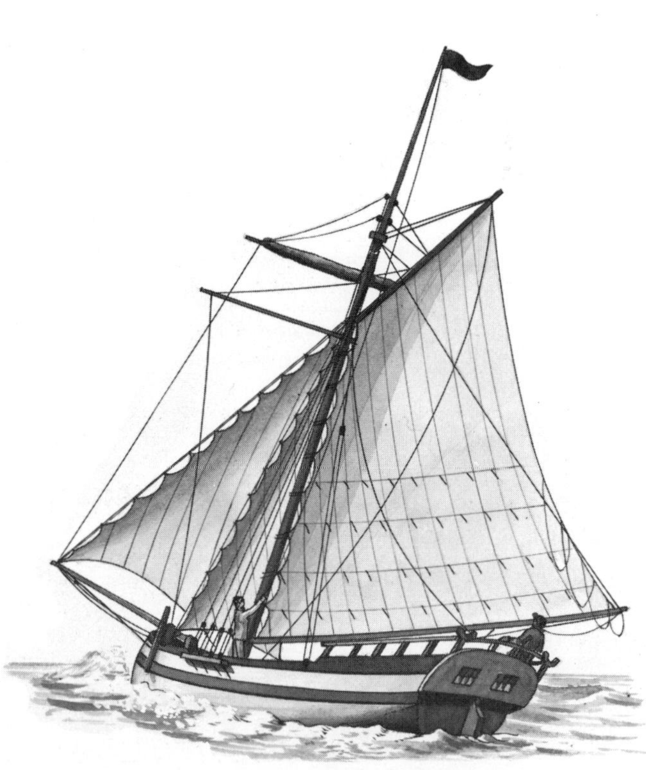

English cutter about 1790.

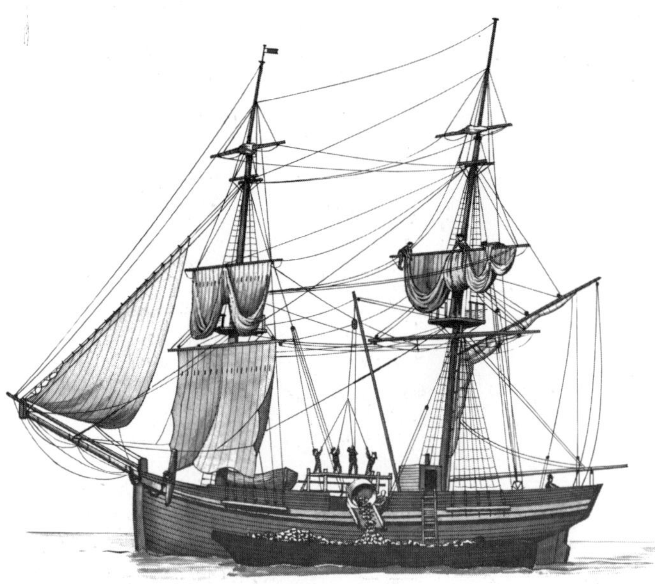

English collier brig, 18th and 19th centuries.

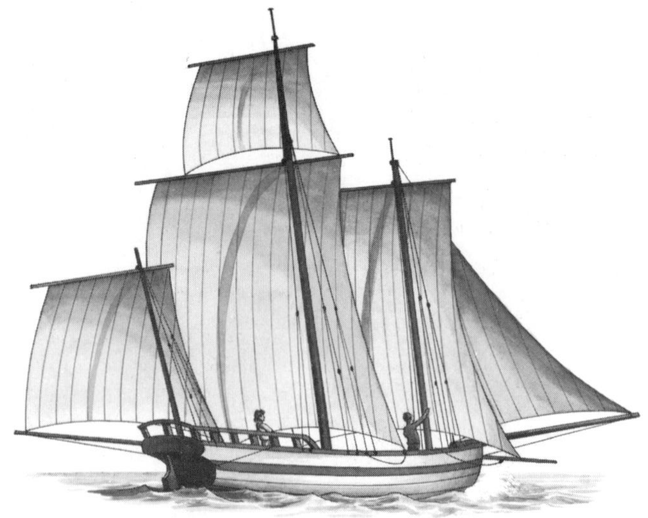

English lugger, early 19th century.

British frigate, about 1825.

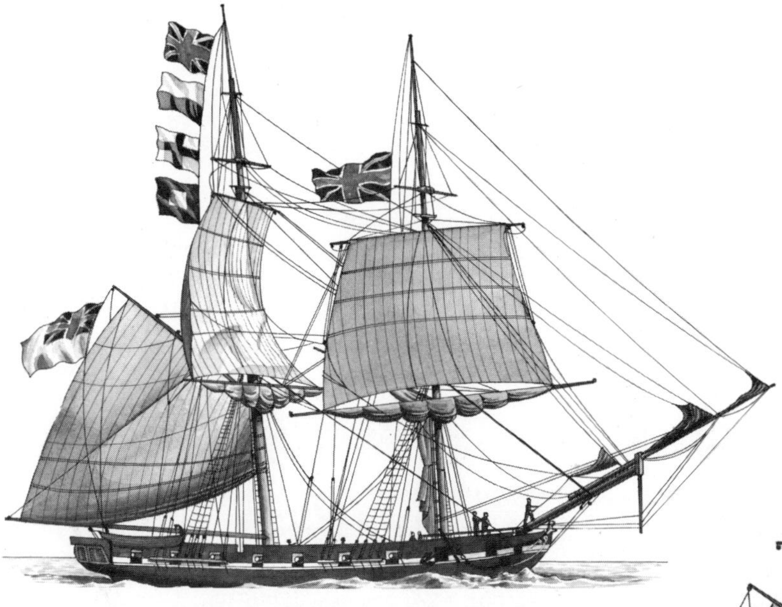

British brig-of-war, first half 19th century. The flag hoist 'shows her number', to identify her name, and the union at the fore is the signal that she is waiting for a pilot.

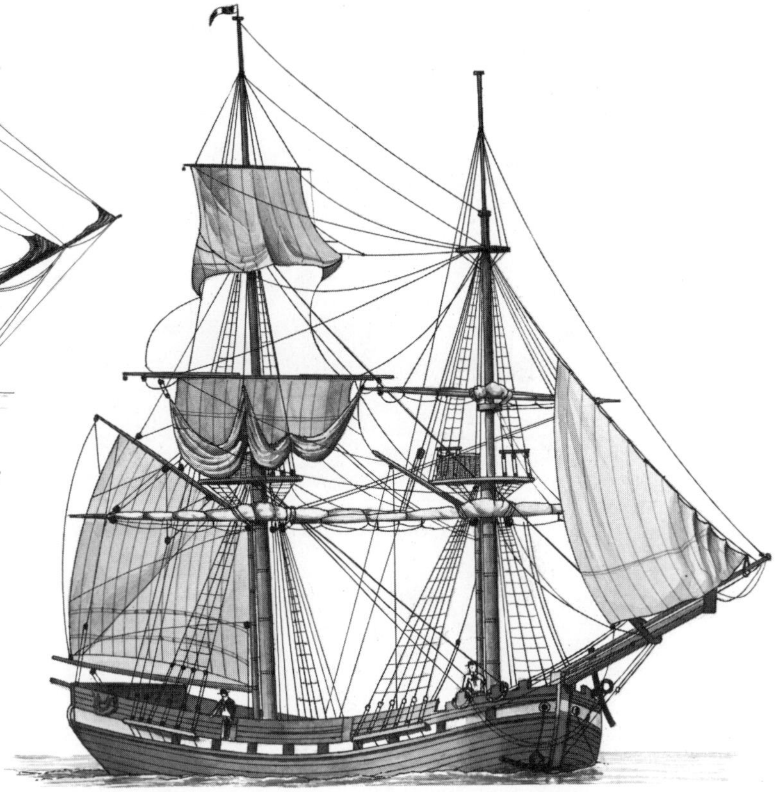

A merchant snow, first half 19th century. The distinguishing feature of the snow is that the mizzen sail is laced to a jigger mast which runs parallel and close up to the mizzen-mast. The jigger mast is smaller, easier to lace and stow. In the case of this vessel, she has another abaft the fore mast for a loose footed gaff.

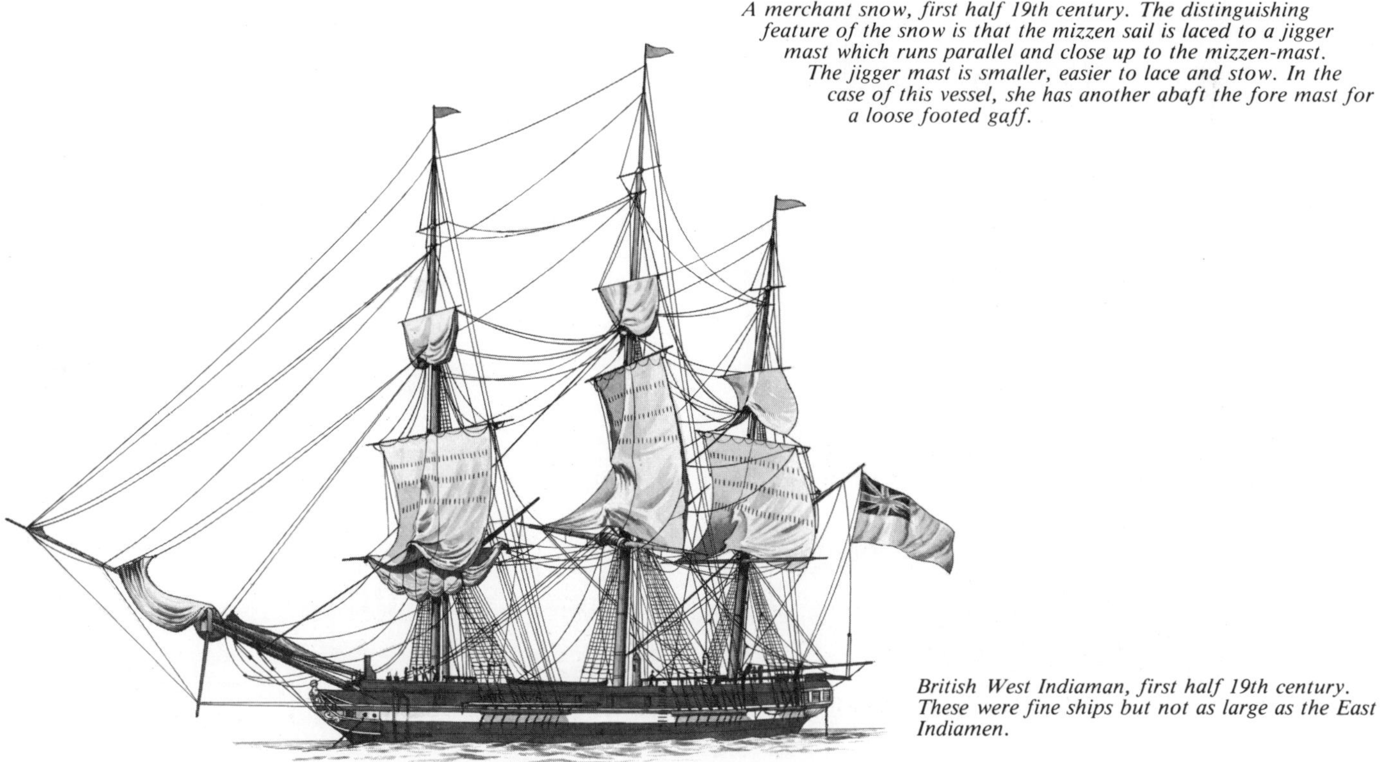

British West Indiaman, first half 19th century. These were fine ships but not as large as the East Indiamen.

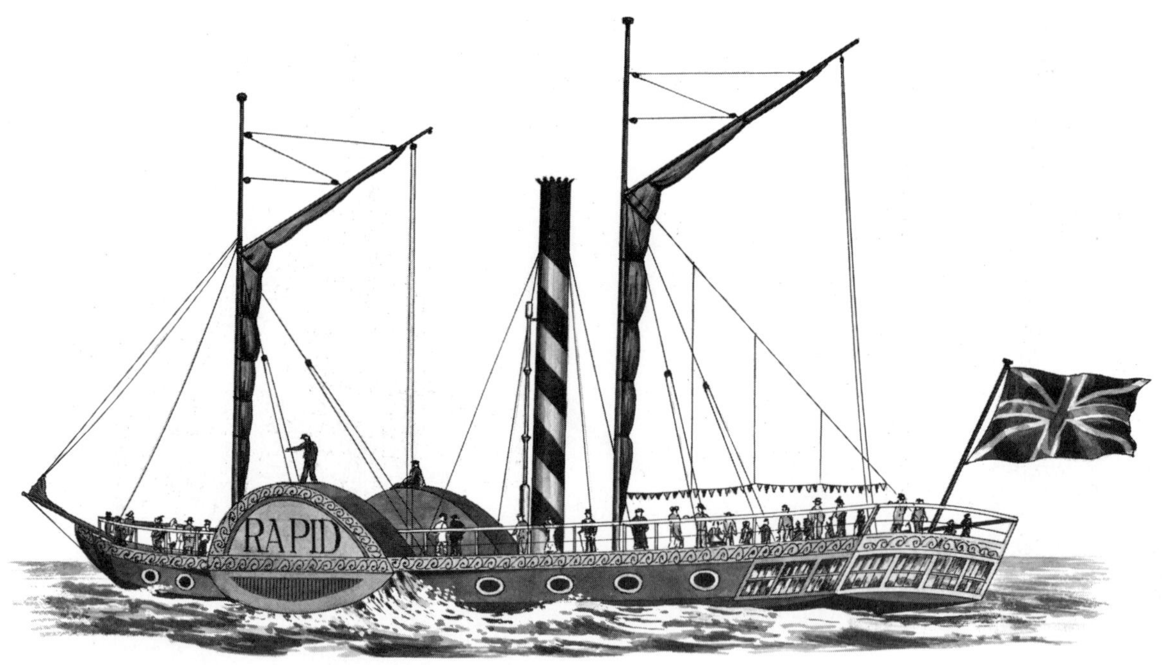

Gravesend steam packet, about 1835. With its tall chimney, this is the first generation of steam ships.

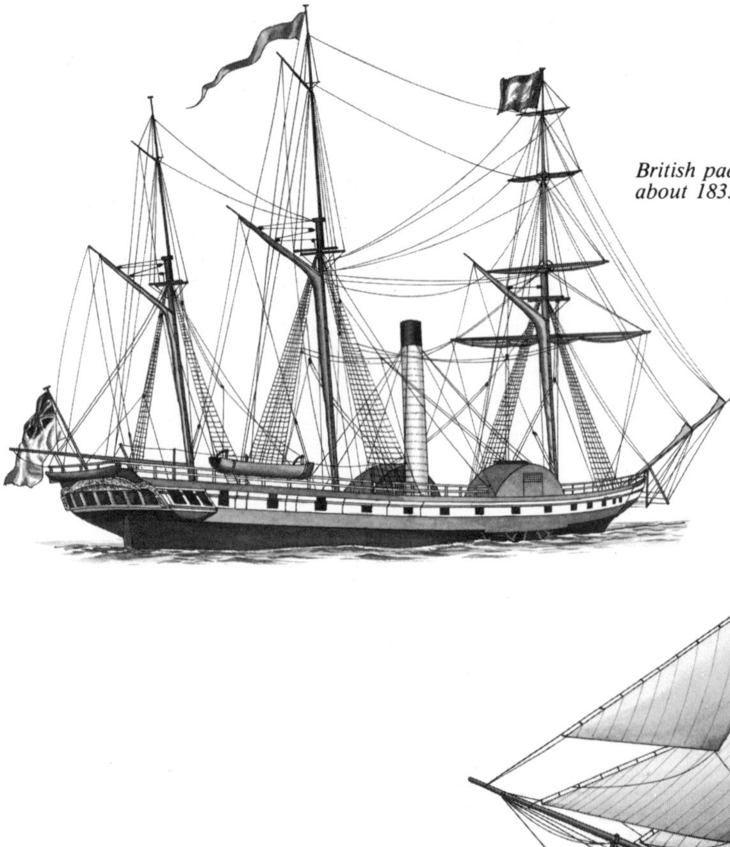

British paddle steamer mail packet, about 1835.

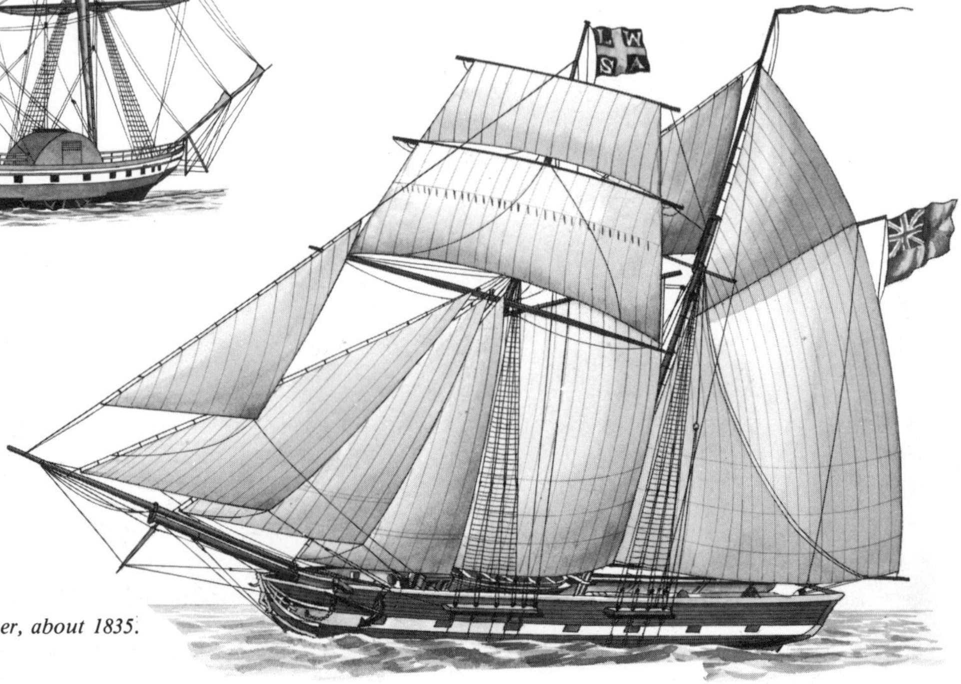

British topsail schooner, about 1835.

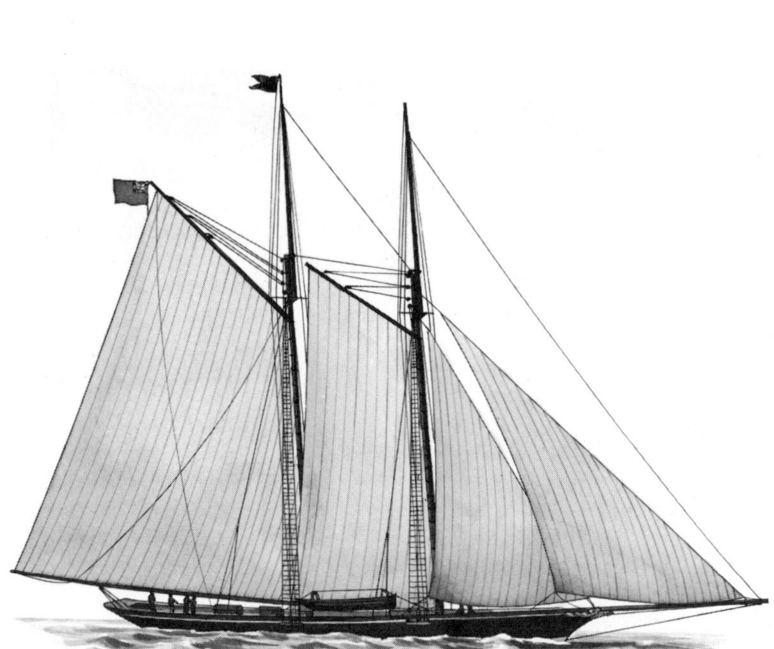

British schooner rigged yacht, which can be dated to the 1860s principally because of the pronounced curve to the bow. As the century progressed this gradually became straighter, until by the 1890s the yacht bow as we know it today became the norm.

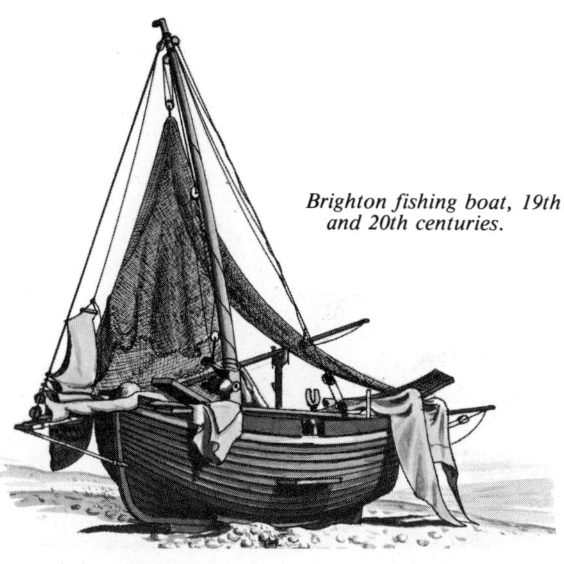

Brighton fishing boat, 19th and 20th centuries.

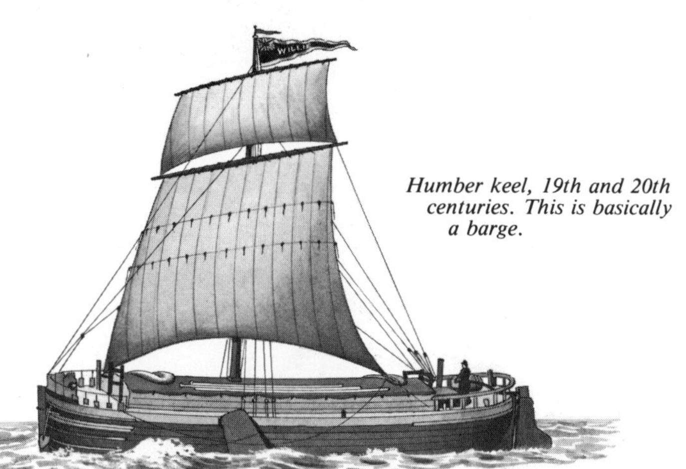

Humber keel, 19th and 20th centuries. This is basically a barge.

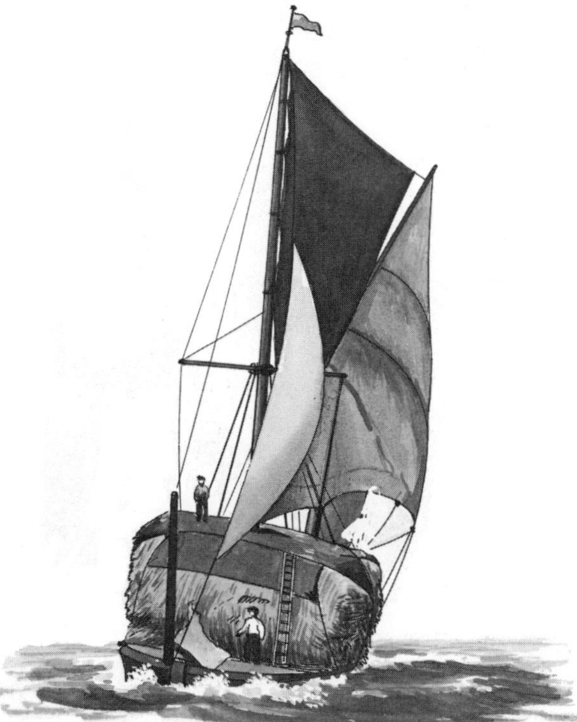

Thames hay barge, 19th and 20th centuries. These brought hay from the Essex farms for London's horses, and took the horse dung back to the farms.

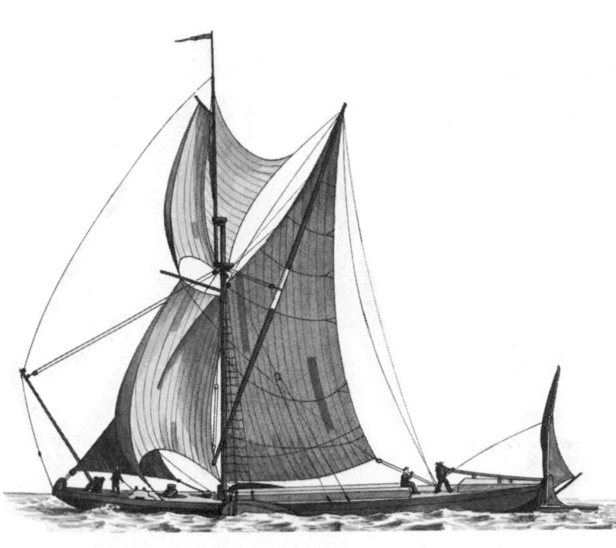

Swim-headed Thames barge, 19th and 20th centuries. This drawing shows the shape of bow still found on Thames lighters today.

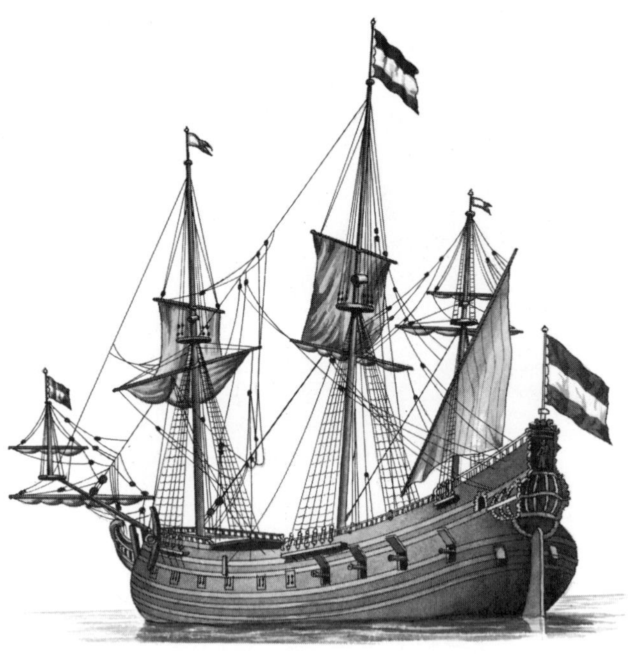

Dutch merchant flute, mid- to late 17th century. The shape of the stern gave these ships their name.

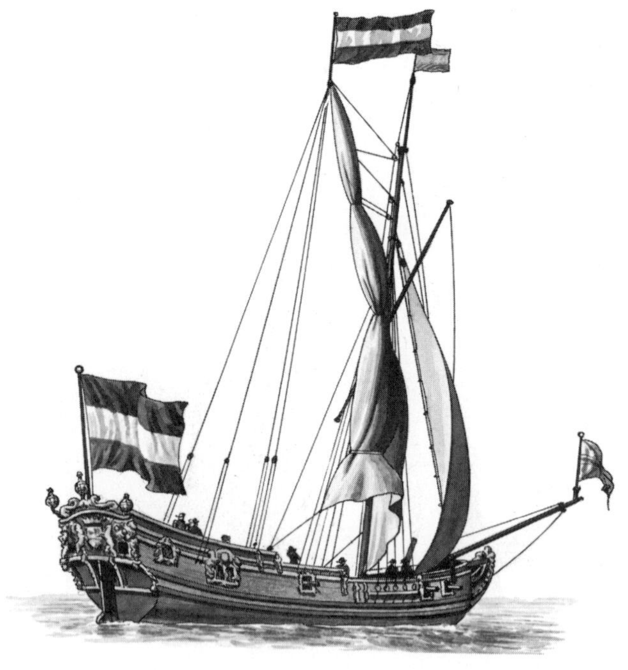

Dutch States yacht, third quarter 17th century.

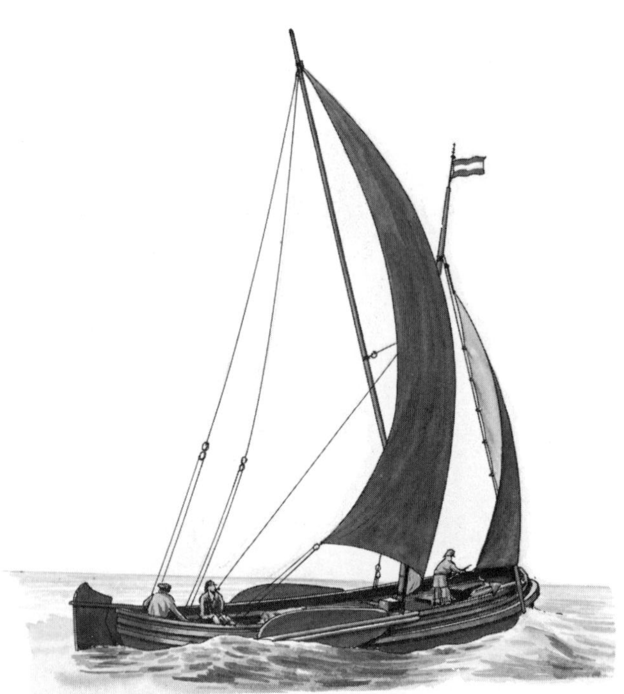

Dutch kaag, 17th and 18th centuries. These ships were sprit-rigged.

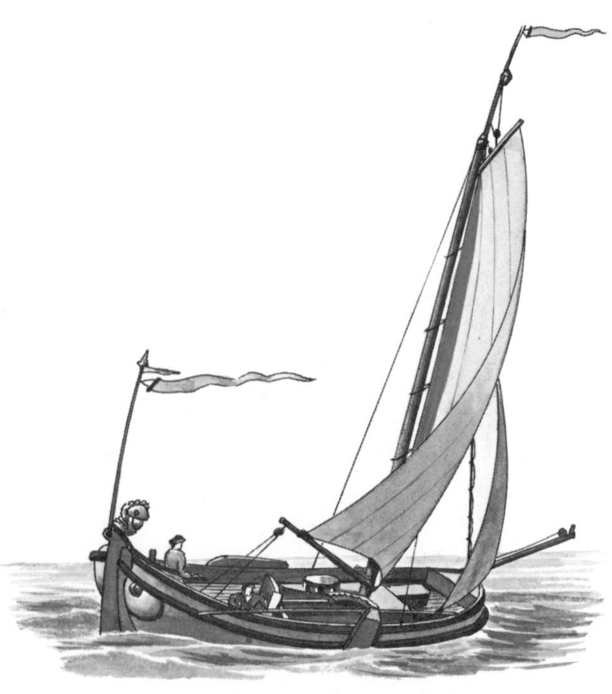

Dutch boeier-rigged yacht, 17th and 18th centuries.

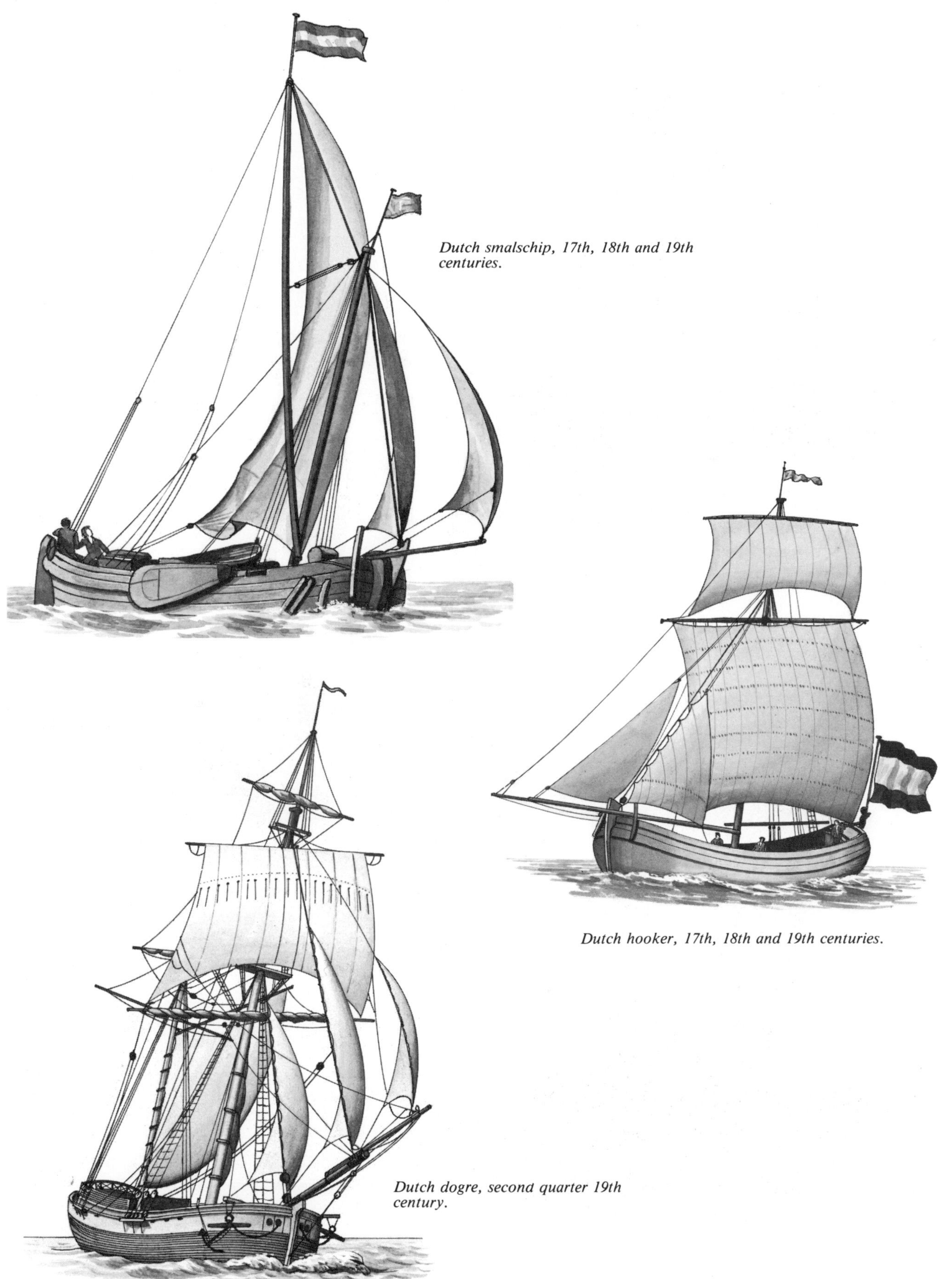

Dutch smalschip, 17th, 18th and 19th centuries.

Dutch hooker, 17th, 18th and 19th centuries.

Dutch dogre, second quarter 19th century.

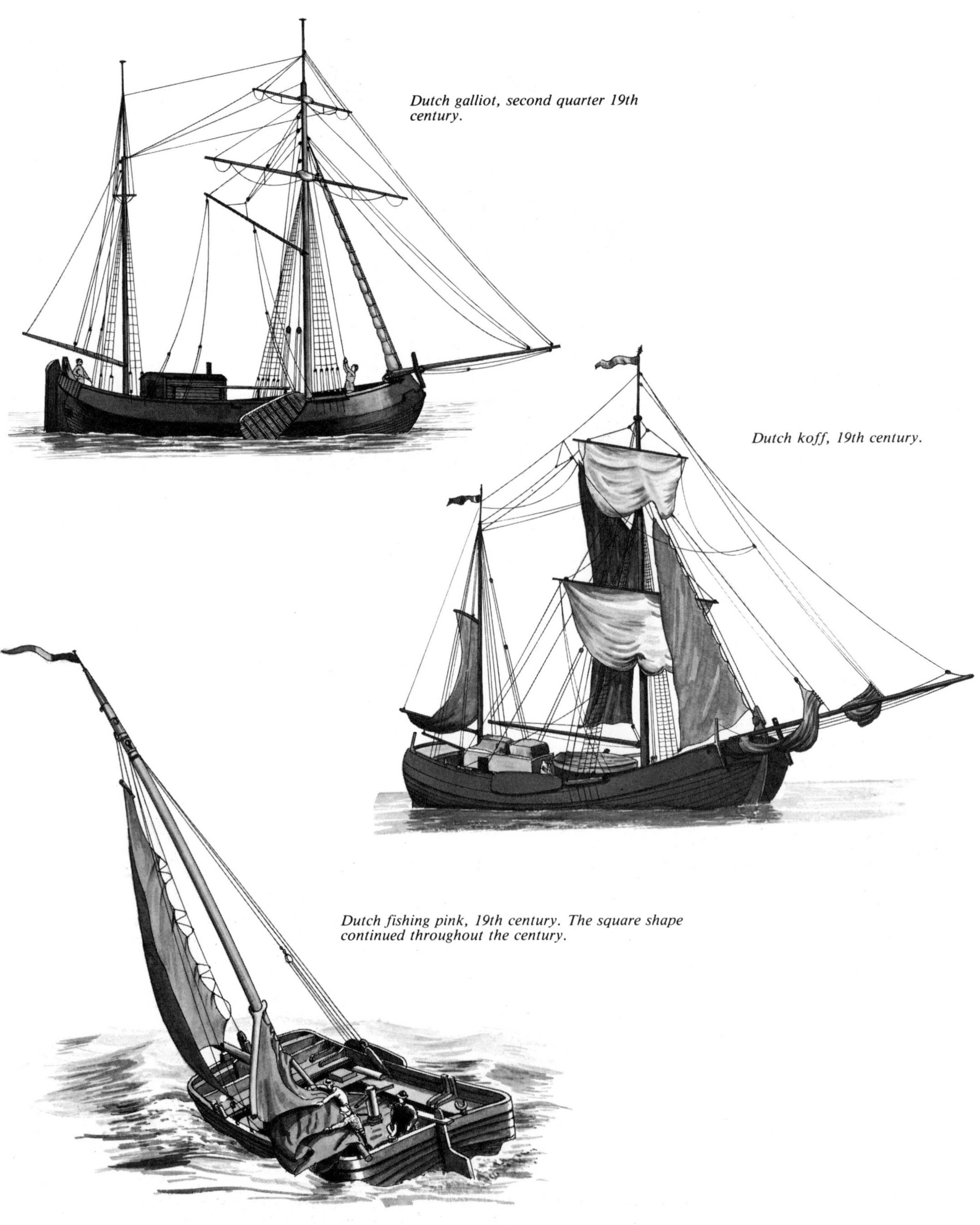

Dutch galliot, second quarter 19th century.

Dutch koff, 19th century.

Dutch fishing pink, 19th century. The square shape continued throughout the century.

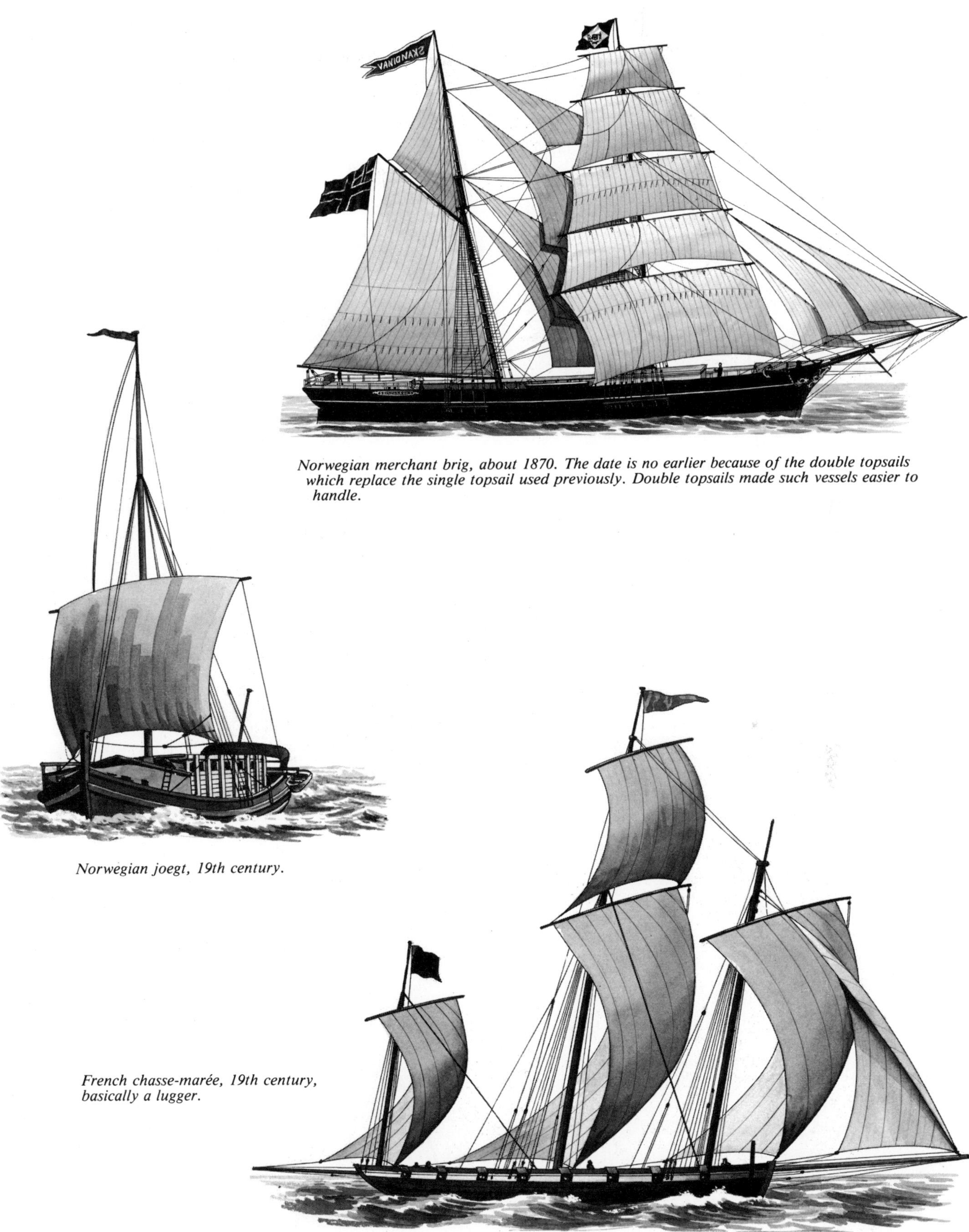

Norwegian merchant brig, about 1870. The date is no earlier because of the double topsails which replace the single topsail used previously. Double topsails made such vessels easier to handle.

Norwegian joegt, 19th century.

French chasse-marée, 19th century, basically a lugger.

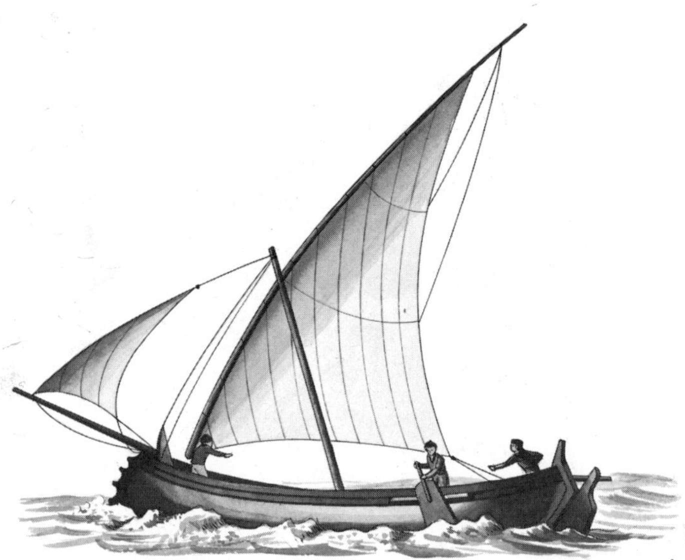

Portuguese bean cod, 18th and 19th centuries.

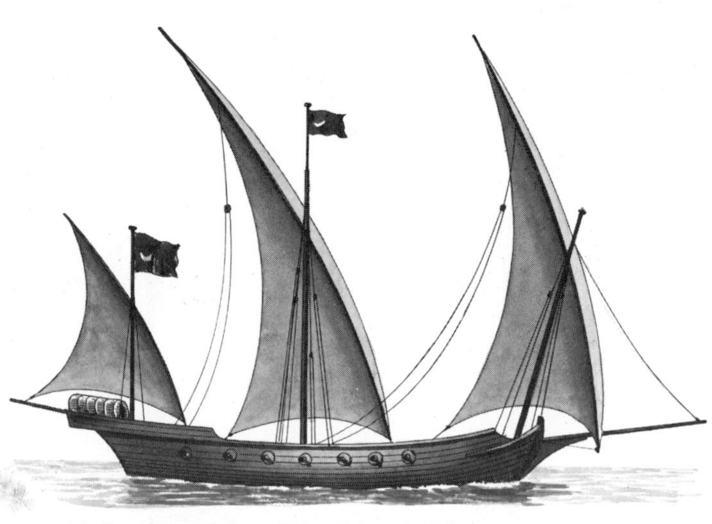

Mediterranean xebec, 17th, 18th and 19th centuries. It is lateen rigged as was favoured in that sea.

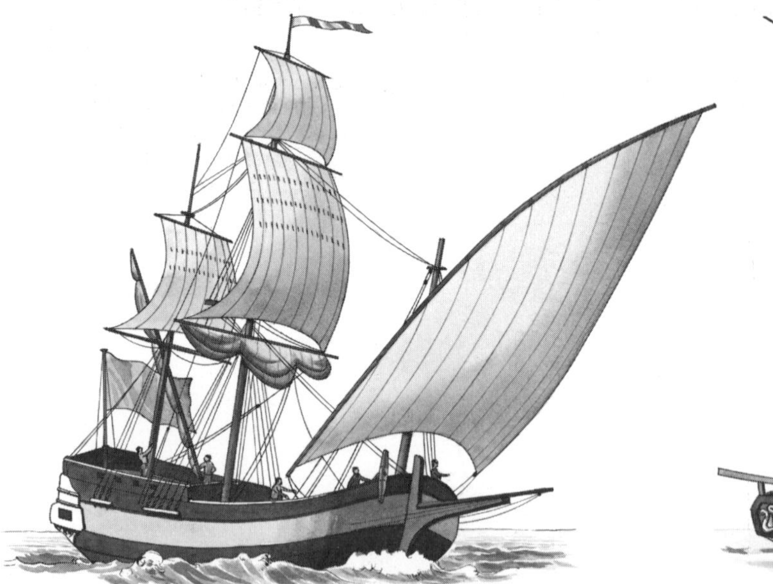

Mediterranean polacca, 18th and 19th centuries. The ratlines, by which sailors went up to the mast, were not necessarily standard in such vessels, and ladders are often found instead.

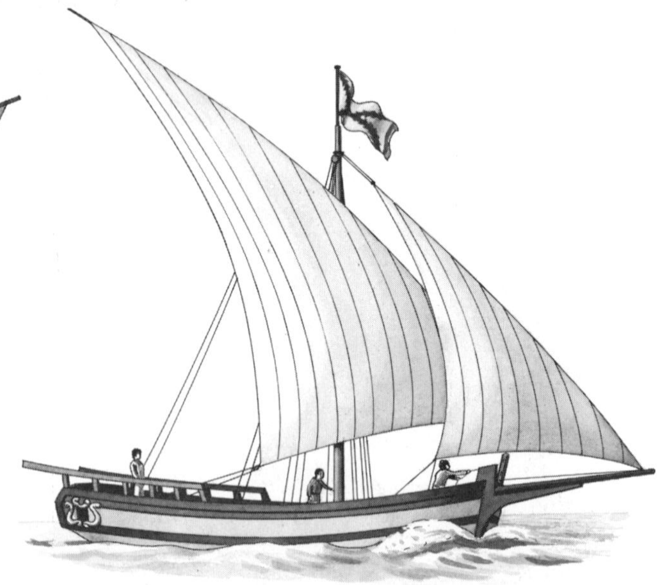

Mediterranean tartan, 18th and 19th centuries. A single-masted tartan, though they could also be two-masted.

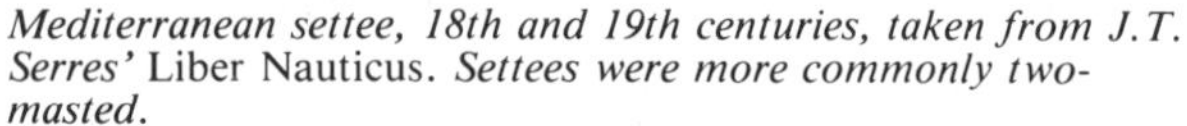

Mediterranean settee, 18th and 19th centuries, taken from J.T. Serres' Liber Nauticus. *Settees were more commonly two-masted.*

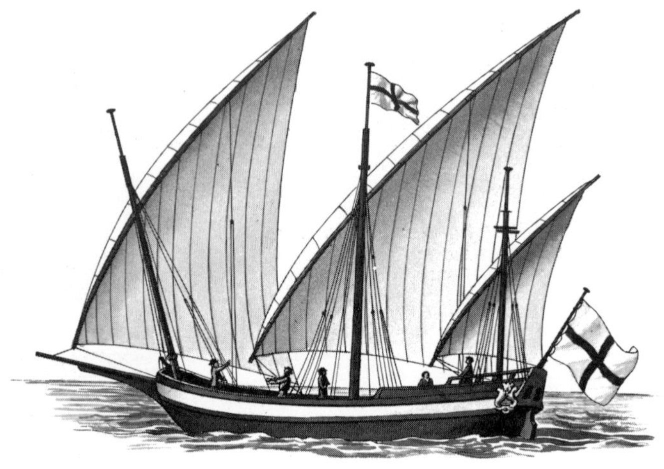

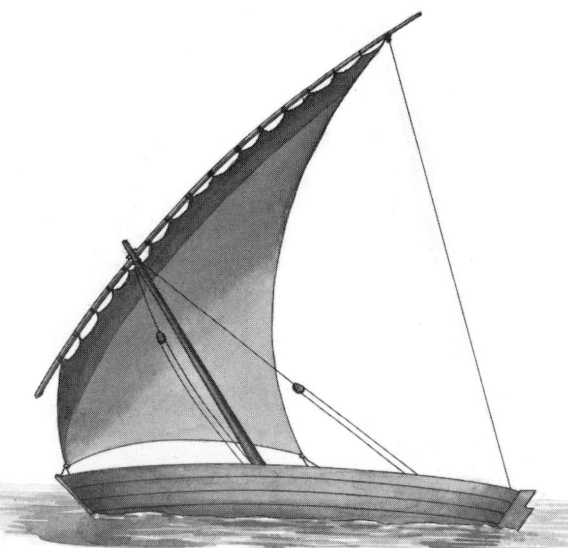

Indian dinghy, 18th, 19th and 20th centuries.

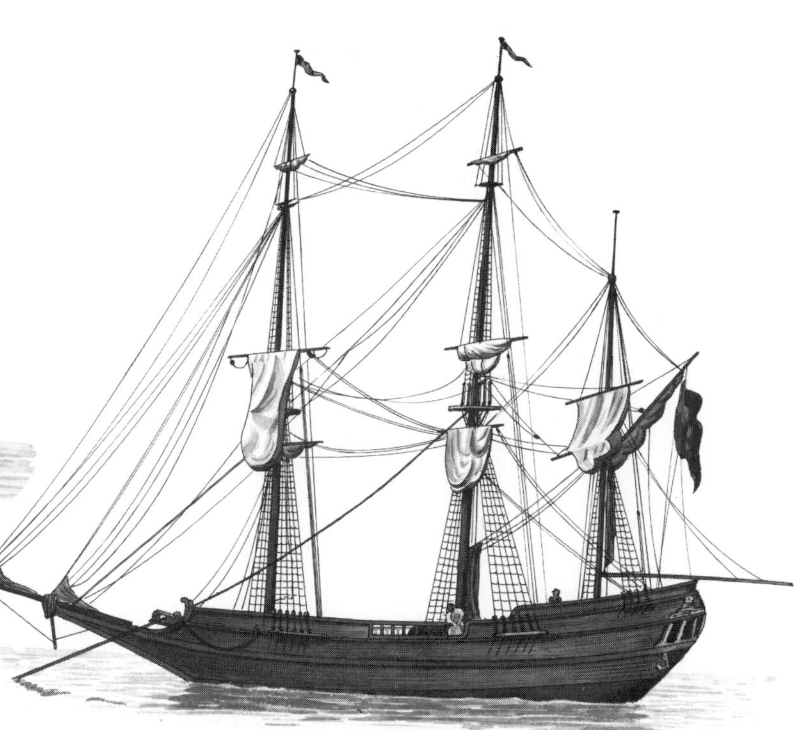

Indian grab, 18th and 19th centuries. The distinctive bow is characteristic of this vessel, which otherwise owes much to European developments.

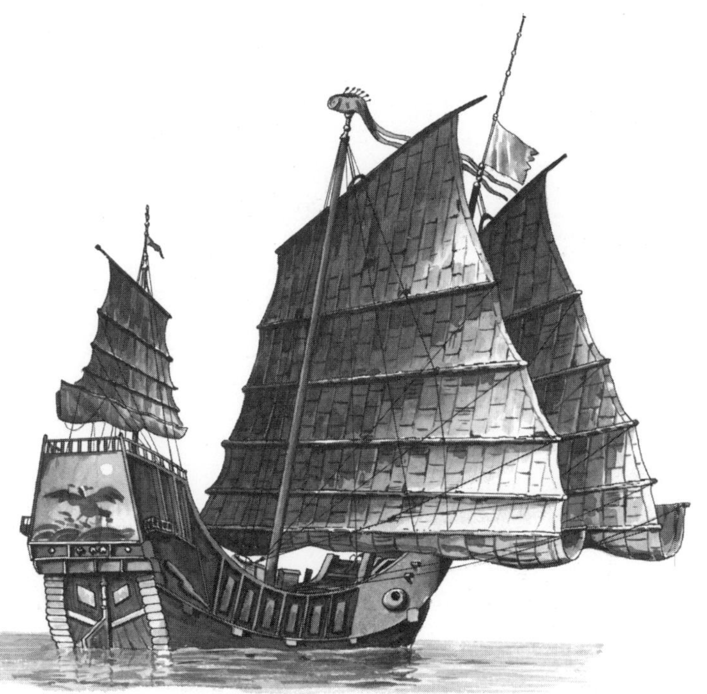

Chinese trading junk, 18th and 19th centuries. A very different ship from the Chinese war junk, right.

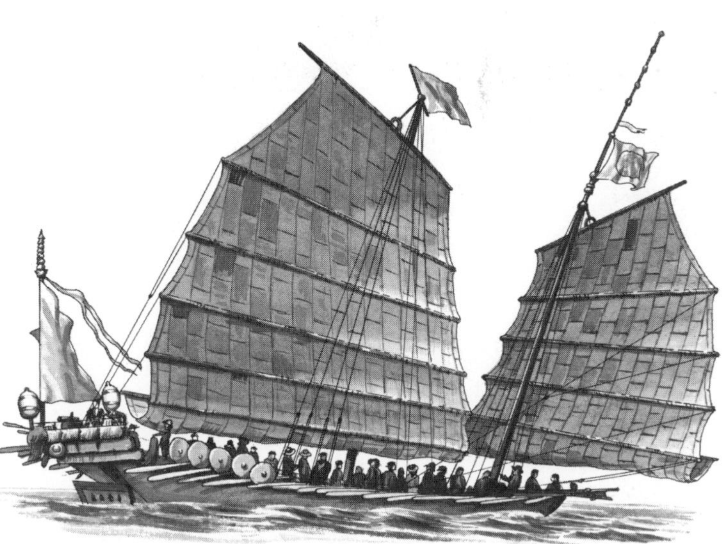

Chinese fighting junk, 18th and 19th centuries. The long low shape enabled them to be rowed.

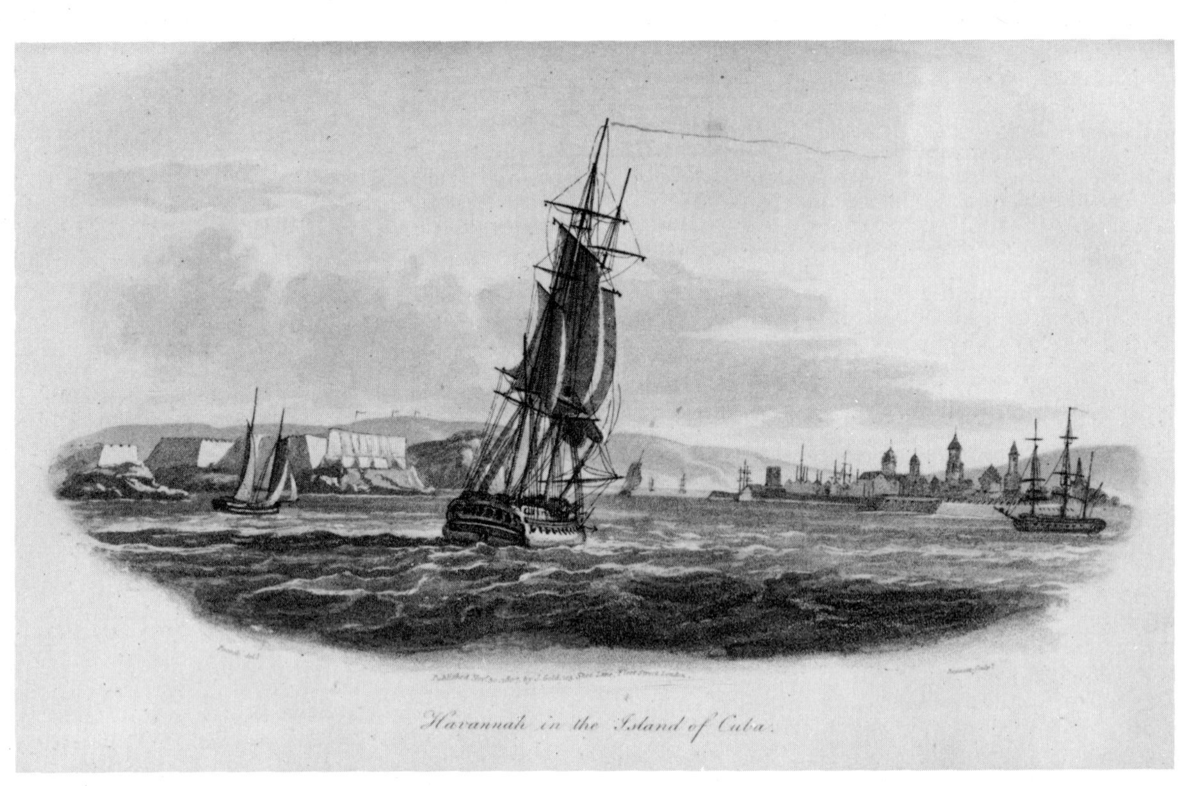
Havannah in the Island of Cuba.

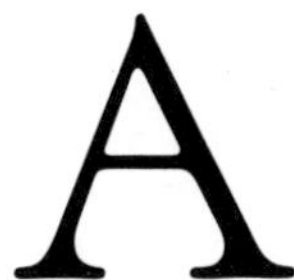

ACHENBACH, Andreas **1815-1910**
Born in Kassel, this artist was an important founder of the German 19th century Impressionist school. He studied in St. Petersburg in the late 1820s, where he was not considered a promising pupil. Moving to Düsseldorf, his style evolved from his own efforts and the study of nature. He travelled widely in the Baltic, and twenty years after settling in Düsseldorf, moved to Munich and then Frankfurt. He spent eight years in Capri from 1873. He died in Düsseldorf.

There appears to be a strong influence of the style of Eugène Isabey in the work of this fine painter, whose influence in the German school was considerable. Among his pupils was his brother Oswald, a landscape painter.

PLATES: 430, 431, 432.

EXAMPLES: Royal Museum of Art, Antwerp (1): Port of Ostend. Dahlem Museum, Berlin (3): View of Ostend; Scheveningen beach in the evening; Dutch port. Museum of Art, Bremen (1): The shore at Naples. Museum, Breslau (1): Norwegian coast scene. Wallraf-Richartz Museum, Cologne (1): Departure of a steamer. City Museum of Art, Düsseldorf (1): Storm. City Museum of Art, Frankfurt (1): Storm. City Art Gallery, Hanover (1): Port of Briel. Museum of Fine Art, Leipzig (2): Sailing of a steamer; Ostend. State Art Collections, Munich (4): two storm scenes; the North Sea; a marine.

ADAM, Edmond *see* **ADAM, Edouard**

ADAM, Edouard **d.c.1930**
A French ship portraitist working in Le Havre in the last half of the 19th century and up to 1930, when he ceased to be noted in the annual register. It seems likely, therefore, that he died 1929/30.

He was one of the best known of French ship portraitists whose son Edmond was also a ship portraitist. To avoid confusion, Edouard signed his pictures "E. Adam", while Edmond signed "Ed. Adam."

The National Maritime Museum, Greenwich, has a portrait of the barque *Victoria,* signed "Ed. Adam 1889", so this is presumably by Edmond. Another Edmond Adam, of a sailing vessel, is in the San Francisco Maritime Museum.

PLATES: 613, 614.

ADAMS, J.
A British ship portraitist working in Ryde, Isle of Wight, in the last quarter of the 19th century. The National Maritime Museum, Greenwich, has a painting by him of a sailing ship off the Needles, dated 1881.

AIVAZOFFSKI (AIVAZOUSKI) **1817-1900**
Ivan Constantinowitsch
Born at Theodosia in the Crimea, he was Russia's premier marine painter of the 19th century. He studied at the Academy of Fine Art in St. Petersburg, where he painted his first marines. When he was twenty-three he travelled in Europe and England, so it was presumably at this time that he was a pupil of Philippe Tanneur in Marseilles.

He returned to St. Petersburg in 1844 and became a member of the Academy. His total output was in excess of four thousand works, and in the year of his death he exhibited a painting in Paris called "The Ocean".

PLATE: 477.

EXAMPLES: Armenian State Picture Gallery (1): sunrise at Theodosia. Kronborg Castle, Helsingor (2): sea views of Constantinople. Russian State Museum, Leningrad (5): The Sun setting over the Crimea, 1862; The Wave, 1881; The Tenth Wave, 1850; The Sea by Moonlight, 1878; The Billow, 1889. State Tretyakov Gallery, Moscow (2): The Black Sea, 1881; The Rainbow, 1873. The Ivan Constantinowitsch Art Gallery, Theodosia, Crimea: a collection including the destruction of the Turkish Fleet in Cheseme Bay (1770), 1848; The Maria *caught in a Storm, 1892; A Shipwreck, 1878.*

ALBE, Gerhard
Swedish painter working in the second quarter of the 20th century. The National Maritime Museum in Stockholm has a painting of the four-masted barque *Abraham Rydeberg,* which received that name in 1929.

ALDRIDGE, Frederick James **1850-1933**
A marine painter from Worthing, Sussex, who exhibited in London from 1880 to 1901, including three paintings, two of the Channel, at the Royal Academy in 1896, 1897 and 1901. As well as being a painter, he was also an art dealer, and ran a picture gallery in Worthing under his name.

PLATE: 580.

ALLCOT, John O.B.E. **1888-1973**
Born in Derbyshire on November 13th, 1888, the son of a master mariner. The family moved to Liverpool, where in due course John was apprenticed to a firm of lithographers, though he cannot have been there long, since he went to sea at the age of sixteen for eight years. During this time his childhood interest in painting continued, and in 1912 he went ashore at Sydney, N.S.W., and set up as an artist. He never left the area, living at various times at Mosman, Bowral and Manley.

In the 1920s, at the instigation of a Mr. Douglas Johnston, and under the patronage of a Mr. Frederick Allen, he embarked on a series of paintings of incidents in Australian history, and for the rest of his life concentrated on such subjects and portraits of historic sailing ships. He eventually had a good practice, was elected a Fellow of the Royal Art Society in Sydney, and in 1970 was made an O.B.E. for services to the arts. He died in Sydney on July 13th, 1973.

In 1978 a leather bound, copiously illustrated, limited edition biography was published by the Copperfield Publishing Co. Pty. Ltd.; this was not so much a book as an act of homage — and £170 to the lucky five hundred.

PLATE: 677.

ALLEN, Thomas **d.1772/3**

He exhibited marines at the Free Society from 1767 to 1772, first from an address in Westminster then, in the final year,from Woolwich. It may be that he died in 1772/3.

ALLERTON, John Taylor **fl.1900**

A draper, stationer and photographer turned professional marine painter. Bridlington Library has several of his works.

ALLSTON, Washington A.R.A. **1779-1843**

Born in Charleston, South Carolina, he was first a classical scholar at Harvard, who travelled to England in 1801 and joined the Royal Academy Schools. He exhibited at the Royal Academy in 1802 and 1803, one of the pictures in 1802 being a coastal scene.

In 1804 he moved to Paris and then to Rome, where he settled until 1809, when he returned to America for a year's visit. On his return to Europe he began exhibiting again at the Royal Academy in 1814, and was elected an A.R.A. in 1818; his last picture exhibited there was in 1819, and he also exhibited at the British Institution between 1814 and 1818. None of these paintings were marines, but he did do coastal views. Later in life he returned to America and died in Cambridge, Massachusetts.

He was interested in the painting and literature of the Romantic Movement and was a friend of Washington Irving and Coleridge, who called him "the American Titian".

The Museum of Fine Arts at Boston has a painting called "The Rising of a Thunderstorm at Sea".

PLATE: 433.

ANDERSON, William **1757-1837**

Little is known of his early life except that he was born in Scotland and became a shipwright. He also learned to be a very finished painter, and about his thirtieth year he made his way south to London and set up as a marine painter. His style is firmly based on the Dutch 17th century school, and though he lived well into the 19th century he never made any concessions to the Romantic Movement.

Although he did some large canvases he is best known for his small, sometimes rather vapid calms, which sold well and still do. He first exhibited at the Royal Academy in 1787, and at the British Institution in 1810. Not all his exhibited paintings were marines: in 1822 his exhibit at the British Institution was a "Battle of Waterloo". At the Royal Academy in 1824 he exhibited a view of Berwick-on-Tweed and another of Tynemouth, which indicate the date that he journeyed to the north-east; here he became an influence on the Hull school of painters and particularly on the best of them, young John Ward, who copied at least one of his paintings of Greenwich Reach. Anderson's last exhibit at the Royal Academy, in 1834, was a major work, "Lord Howe's fleet at Spithead". He died in London on May 27th, 1837.

He was a friend of Julius Caesar Ibbotson, who is believed to have collaborated with him on some paintings. He had a son, William Guido Anderson, who joined the Royal Navy and was mortally wounded at the Battle of Copenhagen as midshipman in the *Bellona*. In 1799 he had exhibited a painting at the Royal Academy called "The *Wolverine* engaging two French luggers".

PLATES: 288, 289, 290, 291.

EXAMPLES: National Maritime Museum, Greenwich (9): Lord Howe's fleet at Spithead, 1790; The Capture of Martinique, 1794; Calder's Action, 1805 (a pair); The Return of King George IV to Greenwich, 1822; Troops embarking near Greenwich; The Thames at Limehouse Reach and Greenwich Reach (a pair); a 17th century subject of Dutch shipping with a flagship and a State yacht in the style of Bakhuizen. Ferens Art Gallery, Hull (1). Graves Art Gallery, Sheffield (1).

ANDREAE, Willem Lodewijk **1817-1873**

Born in The Hague, he was a reasonably good painter of river and harbour scenes, considering he was probably self-taught. Watercolours by him can be seen in the archives of The Hague and Leyden, where he died.

ANNEN, J.F.

A British primitive ship portraitist, working in the last quarter of the 19th century. The National Maritime Museum, Greenwich, has a painting by him of the brigantine *Aneroid* dated 1891.

ANTHONISSEN, Arnoldus **fl.1660s**

He was a pupil and presumably a relative of Hendrick van Anthonissen. He worked and lived in Middelburg, where in 1662 and 1663 he was the leader of the town council.

PLATE: 20.

ANTHONISSEN, Hendrick van **1606-aft.1656**

He was born in Antwerp. By marrying Judith Flessiers, a daughter of the painter Balthasar Flessiers, he became not only the pupil of Jan Porcellis, but also his brother-in-law, since Porcellis was married to Judith's sister, Jacquemintje. They lived in Leiderdrop in 1635, in Amsterdam in 1636, and in Rotterdam, 1645. He died in Amsterdam sometime after 1656.

His work is of the circle of Porcellis and de Vlieger in the Dutch realist school, but not of their quality.

PLATES: 52, 53, 54, 55.

EXAMPLES: Rijksmuseum, Amsterdam (2): Three Portuguese Galleons attacked by the Dutch in the Bay of Goa, 1639; Shipping on the Schelde. Scheepvaart Museum, Amsterdam (1): Battle of the Downs, 1639. Royal Museum of Fine Arts, Antwerp (1): a storm. Gemeentemuseum, Arnhem (1). Fitzwilliam Museum, Cambridge (1): View of Scheveningen. National Maritime Museum, Greenwich (1): Shipping in a Gale. Hermitage, Leningrad (3): rough seas. National Gallery, Oslo (1): Storm with lightning and a jetty. National Museum, Stockholm (1): Action between a Dutch ship and a ship of the Spanish Netherlands. National Gallery of Art, Washington (1): Ships in the Schelde estuary (this must be very early).

ANTHONISZ, Aert **1579-1620**
(formerly called Antum)

Born in Antwerp, this Protestant emigrant from Flanders was in Amsterdam by 1603, when he married there. Between 1604 and 1618 six children were born to the couple in that city, and the eldest boy, who called himself Hendrick van Anthonissen, also became a marine painter.

Although Anthonisz apparently spent most of his working life at Amsterdam he must have been associated with H.C. Vroom, not just because his work is so much like that master's (indeed, it has been the custom in some circles to ascribe to this artist Vroom-like pictures not thought good enough for Vroom) but because there are small signed copies by Anthonisz of two large Vrooms. Both are in the

Rijksmuseum in Amsterdam; one a jewel-like battle scene between the English and Spanish, the original of which is in a private collection in England, while the other of a ship off a port is a copy of an original Vroom in Bavaria. Indeed, his proven work indicates that he specialised in small, beautifully crafted paintings.

Aert Anthonisz died impoverished in Amsterdam and was buried there on September 5th, 1620.

PLATES: 8, 9, 10.

EXAMPLES: Rijksmuseum, Amsterdam (2): one signed and dated 1608, English and Spanish flagships in action; the other, The Eendracht *off Isselmonde, signed and dated 1617. Art Gallery, Emden (1). National Maritime Museum, Greenwich (2): both sea fights. Franz Hals Museum, Haarlem (1): Rough sea with shipping (attributed). Fine Art Museum, Prague (1): a storm, signed.*

ANTUM, Aert van *see* **ANTHONISZ, Aert**

ARNALD, George A.R.A. 1763-1841

Born in Berkshire, he was a pupil of William Pether, and was more a landscape and genre specialist than a marine painter, for of the vast output he exhibited at the Royal Academy between 1788 and the year of his death, only a few are of marine subjects. However, his most famous work is a marine, the *Orient* blowing up at the Battle of the Nile, 1798. This was exhibited at the British Institution in 1827 and presented by it to Greenwich Hospital. It is now in the National Maritime Museum, Greenwich.

He died in London on November 21st, 1841.

PLATE: 294.

ARNESEN, Vilhelm Karl Ferdinand b.1865

Born in Flensburg, Denmark, he was a marine painter who was a student at the Academy of Fine Arts at Copenhagen. He travelled widely in Europe and Asia.

EXAMPLES: Aalborg Museum (1): view of Copenhagen. State Museum for Fine Art, Copenhagen (2): A ship in an Atlantic storm; Copenhagen Roads. Also examples at the Royal Naval Museum, Copenhagen.

ARNESEN, Vilk

Scandinavian ship portraitist working in the latter part of the 19th century.

PLATE: 624.

ARNOLD, Edward c.1825-1866

An American ship portraitist of German origin, born in Heilbronn, Würtemberg. In the New Orleans directory for 1860 he is listed as a marine painter. Apart from ship portraits he also painted battle scenes. The Peabody Museum of Salem has a ship portrait dated 1858. He died in New Orleans on October 14th, 1866.

ARRIAGA, Esteban b.1922

Born in Tenerife, from the age of twelve to seventeen he studied at the Spanish School of Fine Arts and then entered the Naval Academy. He went to sea in 1946, and between 1948 and 1950 was an instructor aboard the four-masted topsail training schooner *Juan Sebastian Elcano,* where he spent his spare time painting.

As well as being a retired naval commander and artist he is also a qualified engineer. He has won the Premier Virgen del Carmen and other awards for his paintings.

The Museo Naval exhibits works by him, and he works in a studio in Malaga.

ASHTON, James 1860-1935

He was born in the Isle of Man. He taught art in York until he emigrated to Australia in 1884. There he taught at the Norwood School of Art in Adelaide from 1885 to 1895, and then, until 1926, at Alfred College in the same city where he later died. He was the founder and director of the Adelaide Academy of Arts.

His work, which is mainly seascapes, can be seen at the National Gallery of South Australia, Bendigo Art Gallery, and at Broken Hill.

ASHTON, James Daniel 1875-1942

Picture restorer, painter and ship modeller, resident in Hull.

ASKEW, John

The National Maritime Museum, Greenwich, has a painting of whalers in the ice. There is a painting, after Robert Dodd, of the Anglo-French action off the Channel Islands in 1794, signed and dated 1805.

ATKINS, George Henry 1811-1872

Baptised in Portsmouth, November 17th, 1811, he was the son of a shipwright. Having become a carver and gilder by trade he took up marine painting and published some of his works as lithographs. He also sold prints and built and repaired church organs in his workshop. From the late 1840s, he was organist of the Portsmouth Royal Naval Dockyard Chapel. In 1863 he built and owned St. George's Hall, where Dickens gave readings in 1866. He died in Portsmouth on July 23rd, 1872.

The National Maritime Museum, Greenwich, has lithographs of ship portraits after him, many by Dutton and Day. There is also one of his works in the City of Portsmouth Museum and Art Gallery.

ATKINS, Harry Joseph 1840-1916

He was born at Portsmouth on September 10th, 1840, and died at Hill Head, near Fareham, Hampshire, May 8th, 1916. He was the third son and fifth child of George Henry Atkins. As a youth he went to sea but a propensity to sea-sickness and the lack of prospects persuaded him to "swallow the anchor".

He turned schoolmaster, and, with the help of his father, bought Blenheim School in Fareham in 1864 of which he remained the owner and headmaster until he retired in 1892. He was an amateur marine painter in watercolours.

ATKINS, Samuel **fl.1787-1808**
He was a watercolourist who specialised in charming little shipping scenes. He first exhibited at the Royal Academy in 1787 and each successive year, except 1790, until 1796, from a variety of London addresses.

He then went on a voyage to the East Indies. By 1804 he had returned and exhibited a Chinese subject at the Royal Academy. He last exhibited in 1808 from an address in The Strand. It is tempting to think that he died at this time.

Examples of his work can be seen at the Ulster Museum, Belfast, the National Maritime Museum, Greenwich, the Leeds City Art Gallery, the British Museum, the Victoria and Albert Museum, the Mariners Museum, Newport News and the Ashmolean Museum, Oxford.

ATKINS, William Edward **c.1842-1910**
Born in Portsmouth, he was the youngest son of George Henry Atkins, and the only one to take up painting professionally. He specialised in watercolours of naval ships, and had a very large output. During the 1870s he was the Portsmouth naval correspondent and artist for the *Graphic*. He died there on March 8th, 1910.

The National Maritime Museum, Greenwich, and the City of Portsmouth Museum and Art Gallery both have collections of his watercolours.

AYLING, George S.M.A. **1887-1960**
He was born in London on August 27th, 1887, the son of a maker of oars and sculls who followed his father's trade for some years, then took up art, studying at the Putney School of Art.

Most of his work was done in docks and harbours, especially the Port of London. He exhibited at the Royal Academy, Royal Institute of Painters in Watercolours, Royal Society of British Artists, New English Art Club, and the Society of Marine Artists, of which he was a member.

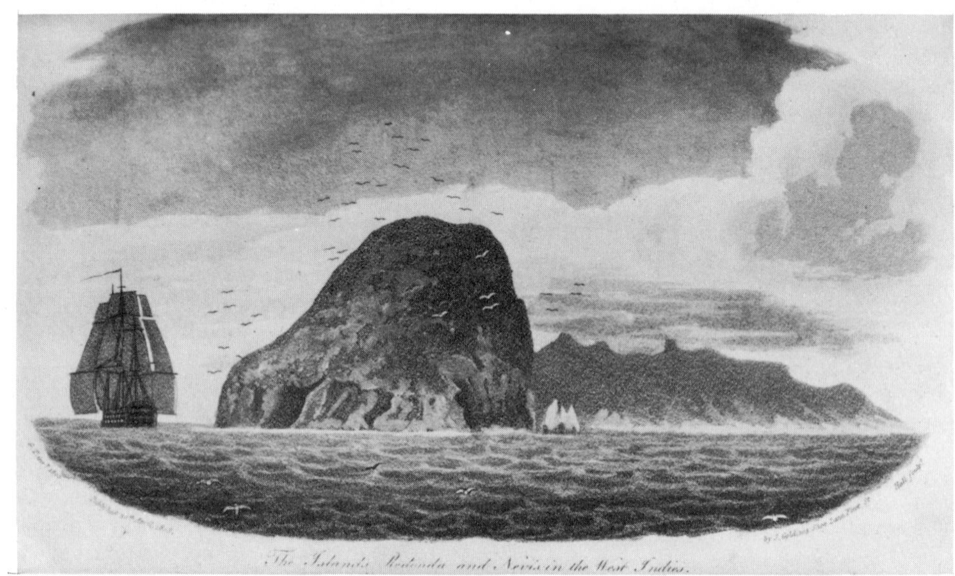

B

BAAGOE, Carl Emil **1829-1902**
Born in Copenhagen, he was mainly self-taught, though he did study for a time at the Academy of Arts at Copenhagen. He was an accomplished painter whose work has strong affinities with that of Christopher Eckersberg and, to some extent, Vilhelm Melbye.

The Maritime Museum at Kronborg Castle has ship portraits by him, and the Royal Naval Museum in Copenhagen also has examples of his work.

BACK, Robert **b.1922**
Born in Adelaide on October 4th, 1922. He is a marine painter who specialises in historical subjects. At sixteen he won the Royal Drawing Society's Gold Medal. At seventeen he won the Andrew Grant Scholarship to the Edinburgh College of Art, and at eighteen had a picture hung in the Royal Scottish Academy exhibition.

The war interrupted his career and he entered the Royal Navy. After the war he taught painting in schools and sailed. More recently he has turned to painting for a living, after a successful one-man exhibition at the Malcolm Henderson Gallery in London in 1974.

PLATE: 686.

BADGER, S.F.M. **fl.1893-1900**
An American ship portraitist working at the end of the 19th century. The Peabody Museum of Salem, has four works dated from 1893 to 1900.

BAGSHAWE, Joseph John Richard **1870-1909**
Born in London on July 1st, 1870, he was the fifth child and second son of W.H.G. Bagshawe, Q.C. (later judge) by his marriage to Harriet Teresa, a daughter of Clarkson Stanfield, R.A. (q.v.). He was educated at St. Augustine's, Ramsgate and Beaumont College, trained first at South Kensington, then with van Hove at Bruges and Hubert Vos in London. From 1896 to 1901 he lived periodically at Staithes, Yorkshire, being associated with the Staithes group of artists. In the latter year he married Mildred Turnbull, daughter of a Whitby shipowner, and made Whitby his permanent home, dying there on November 1st, 1909.

Most of Bagshawe's work was marine, concentrating on coast scenes, fishermen, their boats and occupations. Though largely a watercolourist he also worked in oils, creating rather sombre but lively compositions. He had a life-long experience of small boats and drew them with great skill; his delineation of the Yorkshire coble, accounted a difficult subject, was particularly good. He first exhibited at the Royal Academy in 1897, contemporary report praising his "Summer Sea" (R.A., 1904), "Towing the Spanish Prize", an Armada subject (R.A., 1905) and his "False Dawn". He was elected to the Royal Society of British Artists in 1904, exhibiting there from that year to his death. His best work was of the Yorkshire coast, then of the West of Ireland, but he also visited the sea ports of Normandy, Holland and Finland. He contributed a number of illustrated articles to journals like the *Field* and *Yachting Monthly*. There are examples of his work at the Pannett Art Gallery, Whitby.

BAKER, Captain R.E.
A merchant service officer who commanded ships in the New Zealand Shipping Company. In 1968 he exhibited a painting of the *Queen of the South,* paddle-steamer, in the Pool of London, at the Royal Society of Marine Artists annual exhibition. This was purchased for the National Maritime Museum, Greenwich, with the aid of the Society.

BAKHUIZEN, Ludolf **1631-1708**
Although he belongs to the Dutch school, he was German born and first worked as a calligrapher in his native town of Emden, where he was born on December 18th, 1631. However, while still a very young man, an interest in drawing and painting prompted him to emigrate to Amsterdam, where he at first followed his trade.

The early 1650s was the period when Willem van de Velde the Elder (q.v.) was perfecting his grisaille drawing technique in the same city; these drawings appear to have inspired young Bakhuizen, and he may well have taken tuition from van de Velde. Bakhuizen's grisailles are closely textured with tiny strokes of the reed pen in sepia ink.

He learnt to paint in oils in the studio of Albert van Everdingen, a landscape painter who did some marines, and more importantly in the studio of Hendrik Dubbels. Even in oils Bakhuizen, used to working in black and white, seems to have approached colour with caution. In his early works he was unique in the adoption of a black palette, relieved with grey-brown and flushes of pink on the landscape area of the pictures, which are generally wreck scenes. By the middle 1660s he had perfected a technique of luminous glazes with blue-grey seas, majestic skies and very dramatic light-and-shade compositions. This was his best period. Later his palette warmed and the dramatic effects became less sharp. At Greenwich there are two large monochrome views of a Dutch factory port in the East Indies, but they are not like the early black pictures and must have been a special commission later on.

Bakhuizen was a contemporary of the younger Willem van de Velde (q.v.), and he shared with him an accurate understanding of the ships he painted. He was deservedly successful in his lifetime and this must have influenced van de Velde to adopt some of his style, to the point where some van de Veldes of about 1670 have been mistaken for Bakhuizens.

He was curiously ambivalent about the spelling of his name, sometimes signing CK, and sometimes a Y instead of an I. This would be understandable if the various spellings fell into different periods, but they occur throughout his working life.

Bakhuizen must be placed in the first rank of marine painters; besides his oils he left drawings and engravings. He was also a convivial, generous man, who left money for a great wake to be held for him by his many friends after his death in Amsterdam on November 17th, 1708.

PLATES: 117, 118, 119, 120, 121.

EXAMPLES: Rijksmuseum, Amsterdam (17): 11 marines, 10 of them general shipping scenes or shipping from the shore, one of shipbuilding; two self portraits and a group in his studio; a group of his family diving on the Mussel Pier at Amsterdam; two portraits of his fourth wife Anna; one of his brother-in-law Jan de Hooghe; and one of his son Johannes holding a miniature of his father; view of Egmonde. Scheepvaaart Museum, Amsterdam (1): the Hollandia *off shore in a squall. Amsterdam Historische Museum (1): the* Mary *yacht with Dutch yachts and a Swedish one. Royal Museum of Fine Arts, Antwerp (1): Dutch man-of-war* Jacob. *Bode Museum, East Berlin (1): a wijdschip in a stiff breeze. Kunstmuseum, Berne (1): naval battle. Musée des Beaux-Arts, Bordeaux (1): marine. Museum of Fine Arts, Boston (1): shipping in a breeze off Amsterdam. Kunsthalle, Bremen (1): smalschip off a pier. Herzog Anton Ulrich-Museum, Brunswick (1): shipping off shore. Musée des Beaux-Arts d'Ixelles, Brussels (1): very large storm. National Gallery, Budapest (1): early shore scene. Wallraf-Richartz Museum, Cologne (2). State Fine Art Museum, Copenhagen (6): Battle of Texel, 1673: the* Royal Charles *being brought into Dutch waters, 1667; a calm; a storm; two scenes of coastal craft off shore. Gemäldegalerie, Darmstadt (1): Mediterranean port scene. Gemäldegalerie, Dresden (1): Battle of Texel, 1673, with* Tromp *and* Spragge *in action. National Gallery, Dublin (1): Returning Indiamen. National Gallery, Edinburgh (1): Stormy day with a fishing boat by a pier. The Pitti, Florence (1): storm. Gemäldegalerie, Frankfurt (1): Port of Amsterdam. Glasgow Art Gallery (5): including an early one of a ship being driven onto a high coast and a storm. National Maritime Museum, Greenwich (17): Boat action on the fourth day of the Four Days Fight, 1666; the* Royal Charles *being taken into Dutch waters, 1667; Battle of Barfleur, 1692; Battle of Vigo Bay, 1702; a pair of monochrome oils of a Dutch factory in the East Indies; an early one of ships being driven onto a rocky coast; ship repairing at Amsterdam; eight others and one grisaille of a yacht and shipping in harbour. Mauritshuis, The Hague (1): William III on horseback after arriving in Holland in 1692. Kunsthalle, Hamburg (2). Ferens Art Gallery, Hull (1): Small-craft in a rough sea. Gemäldegalerie, Leipzig (6). Hermitage Museum, Leningrad, several. National Gallery, London (6): the* Eendracht *and the Dutch fleet with a barge rowing to her in heavy weather; a small English vessel running down to a high coast; beach scene; estuary scene with a pier on the left; a Kaag and Indiamen off the Dutch coast; a Mediterranean port. Victoria and Albert Museum, London (1): shipping off a windmill. Dulwich Art Gallery, London (1): a shore scene in rough weather with fishing boats. Wallace Collection, London (2): storm; small craft. Victoria and Albert Museum, London (3): Ships off-shore in a rough sea and (at Apsley House) embarkation scene; Man of war at anchor in a rough sea. City Art Gallery, Manchester (2): Coast scene with small-craft; Man of war and small-craft. Alte Pinakothek, Munich (3): The English fleet off Scheveningen beach come to collect King Charles in 1660; an English royal yacht off a high coast; a Dutch merchantman and shipping off Amsterdam. Nantes Museum (1). Norwich Museum (1): squall. Louvre, Paris (2): an English royal yacht; fleet of Dutch Indiamen. National Museum, Posnan (1): Dutch flagship in a rough sea. Staatliche Gemäldegalerie, Schwerin (6): English royal yacht running into port and five general shipping. Staatsgalerie, Stuttgart (1): rough sea. Centraal Museum, Utrecht (1): shipping in heavy weather. Gallery of Academy of Fine Arts, Vienna (2): estuary scene with a pier, estuary scene with a yacht. Kunsthistorisches Museum, Vienna (1): Swedish Royal yacht at Amsterdam. Ypres Museum (1): storm. National Gallery of New Zealand, Wellington (1): Dutch yacht and a flagship off the coast.*

BAMFYLDE, Coplestone Warre **d.1791**

An English landscape artist who painted some quite well executed coastal views with shipping. Works exhibited at the Royal Academy between 1771 and 1783 included views of Exmouth and Southampton and a storm, which may or may not have been a marine. He also exhibited a view of Mount Edgecumbe from Mount Wise at the Society of Artists.

He is described in the Royal Academy catalogues as an honorary exhibitor, so was probably a gifted amateur.

BARD, James **1815-1897**

An American ship portraitist who worked in New York and who concentrated on steamships. He often worked in conjunction with his brother, John (1815-1856) (q.v.), who was presumably his twin. The Peabody Museum of Salem has three pictures by James and three by James and John, and the Mariners Museum at Newport News has one painting by James.

PLATE: 437.

BARD, John **1815-1856**

Presumably the twin brother of James (q.v.), he was also a ship portraitist, collaborating with his brother on some pictures (see previous entry).

The Peabody Museum of Salem has two of these watercolours.

BARKWORTH, Henry

A British ship portraitist working in the second quarter of the 19th century. The National Maritime Museum, Greenwich, has a portrait of the paddle steamer *Victoria,* built at Hull in 1837. This has a look of John Ward (q.v.), so it is possible that Barkworth was a Hull artist.

BARNSLEY, James MacDonald

A Canadian marine painter working in the second half of the 19th century. He was a pupil at the School of Fine Arts at Saint Louis and at the Académie Julian in Paris. He exhibited at the Paris Salon and the Artists Club at Denver, and was a member of the Art Association of Montreal. The Montreal Museum of Fine Arts has works by him, including two paintings of Dieppe harbour dated 1886.

PLATE: 587.

BARR, G.R.

A British ship portraitist working in the third quarter of the 19th century. The National Maritime Museum, Greenwich, has two pictures which are of good quality and were painted for the ships' London-based owner. These are the *Ellen Rodgers,* 1858, and the *Min,* 1862.

PLATE: 529.

BARTON, Mike J. **b.1933**

Born in South London he developed an early interest in ships and drawing. At fifteen he joined a commercial art studio as an apprentice, then went to the Regent Street Polytechnic and, after National Service, to the Ashmolean School of Art at Oxford.

His interest is in historic shipping which provides the subjects for his paintings. Though he works in various mediums, he prefers gouache. He has had commissions from shipping companies and publishers, and examples of his work can be seen at the Peabody Museum of Salem. He works as an illustrator for a publishing company and lives in Southend.

PLATE: 687.

BASTON, Thomas

Artist working in the first quarter of the 18th century. In the reign of George I, Thomas Bowles published an unimportant set of prints, "Twentytwo PRINTS of several of the CAPITAL SHIPS OF HIS Maj^ties ROYAL NAVY with Variety of other SEA PIECES after the Drawings of T. Baston."

The National Maritime Museum, Greenwich, has two drawings by him. This compiler knows of no oil paintings by him.

BATTEM, Gerrit **c.1636-1684**

Born in Rotterdam, a painter in the Dutch Realist style,he was a close contemporary of Willem van de Velde the Younger (q.v.) and Ludolf Bakhuizen (q.v.) and reflects their influence, though perhaps his closest affinity is to the slightly older artist, Abraham van Beyeren (q.v.).

He was orphaned as a small child and was tutored by the portrait painter Jan Daemen Cool. He spent some time in Utrecht, where he must have known the Willaerts brothers (qq.v.) though they do not appear to have made an impression on his style. As well as marines, he painted landscapes and still-life subjects.

He died in Rotterdam on October 28th, 1684.

PLATE: 83.

EXAMPLES: Musées Royaux des Beaux-Arts, Brussels (1): shipwreck in a storm. National Maritime Museum, Greenwich (2): a pair showing small craft in a fresh breeze, and a hooker off a jetty.

BAUR, Nicolaus **1767-1820**

He was born on September 12th, 1767, in Harlingen and died there on March 28th, 1820. He was the pupil of his father, Johannes Antonius, a portrait painter. He painted good quality landscapes and marines and was one of the principal Dutch 18th century marine painters.

EXAMPLES: Rijksmuseum, Amsterdam (6): the Rotterdam *on the Maas off Rotterdam; the* Amsterdam *in a gale on the Y at Amsterdam; four paintings of the bombardment of Algiers in 1816. Scheepvaart Museum, Amsterdam (1): view of Amsterdam. Gemeente Museum, Harlingen: two marines and river scenes.*

BEECHEY, Admiral Richard Brydges **1808-1895**

Born in London on May 17th, 1808, he was the youngest son, and second youngest child of eighteen born to Sir William Beechey, R.A.

He entered the Royal Naval College in 1821, and went to sea the following year. In 1825 he joined H.M.S. *Blossom* as a midshipman. She was commanded by his brother, Captain Frederick Beechey, and went on a three-year voyage of discovery in the Pacific. He was promoted to lieutenant on his return in 1828, to commander in 1846, captain in 1857, rear-admiral in 1875, vice-admiral in 1879, and admiral in 1885. He died in Southsea on March 8th, 1895.

He was a surveyor and in 1835 joined in a survey of Ireland. He went on half pay in 1856 and retired in 1864, further promotion being on seniority in retirement. He was therefore free to pursue his other profession, marine painting, and he must take the credit for being the best painter the navy ever produced. Whether or not he received any instruction from his famous father is not recorded but he must have studied under John Christian Schetky (q.v.) at the Royal Naval College at Portsmouth.

He first exhibited at the Royal Academy in 1832 and did so almost every year from 1858 to 1877. He also exhibited at the British Institution between 1833 and 1864, and at the Suffolk Street Galleries.

PLATES: 577, 578.

EXAMPLES: National Maritime Museum, Greenwich (5): "First Come First Served", which shows pilot cutters racing to a ship; Captain Markham's most northerly encampment; H.M.S. Erebus *and* Terror *in the ice; H.M.S.* Lord Warden *(on loan); H.M.S.* Scout *(on loan).*

BEECQ, Jan Karel Donatus van **1638-1722**

For an artist who is supposed to have been born in Amsterdam in 1638, it is surprising that his earliest known works date from the 1670s and are of English subjects. From his understanding of these it seems likely that he took advantage of Charles II's invitation to Dutch artists in 1672 and emigrated to England. His ships are beautifully crafted; the loving care with which he executed their decorations is reminiscent of the elder van de Velde (q.v.), and also has something of Abraham Storck's (q.v.) style.

There is a beautiful portrait at Greenwich of the first-rate *Royal Prince,* dated 1679. In 1681 he accepted an invitation from the Duc de Vendôme to go and work in Paris, and became a member of the Paris Académie in the same year. There are three paintings of French subjects by him dated 1684. Although he lived on to be over eighty, dying in Amsterdam on May 19th, 1722, there are no recorded 18th century works.

PLATE: 137.

EXAMPLES: Museum of Fine Arts, Copenhagen (4): a French three-decker at sea with a galley; calm with an English first-rate; an English flagship at anchor with a royal yacht and other shipping; a calm, with an English two-decker and other men-of-war. National Maritime Museum, Greenwich (2): shipping on the Bristol Avon; the Royal Prince *with a royal yacht and other men-of-war in a breeze. Los Angeles County Museum of Art (1): two English two-deckers off Greenwich. Malta Museum (1): an English ship. Musée de la Marine, Paris (2): junction of the French and English fleets in 1672; French attack on a Barbary port.*

BEELT, Abraham

Active in the middle and second half of the 17th century. Though little seems to be known about him, surviving paintings show him to have been a painter of quality and range. He seems to have had a taste for painting public occasions.

EXAMPLES: Rijksmuseum, Amsterdam (3): The Proclamation of the Peace of Münster in the Grote Market in Haarlem in 1648; The departure of Charles II for England from Scheveningen 1660; The Dutch herring fleet.

BEERSTRAATEN, Jan Abraham **1622-1666**
Born in Amsterdam on May 31st, 1622, he was a painter of sea battles and port scenes. His style derives from that of Claes Wou (q.v.), who was probably his master; though he may have been a pupil of Pieter van Soest (q.v.), whose work is also very similar and who, like Wou, was resident in Amsterdam. Beerstraaten was later a collaborator with Lingelbach (q.v.), who painted the figures in some of his pictures. As well as marines he painted landscapes, especially of winter scenes.

He usually signed "I. Beerstraaten", but a painting apparently by his hand and dated 1660, at Greenwich, is signed "Johan Beerstraaten." This would be too early for his son Johannes, born in 1653. Other children were Abraham born in 1644, Jacobus born in 1658, Magdalena born in 1660, and David born in 1661. He died in Amsterdam on July 1st, 1666.

PLATE: 74.

EXAMPLES (marines only): Rijksmuseum, Amsterdam (2): Battle of Scheveningen, 1653; Mediterranean port. Invalidenhuis, Arnhem (1): Action off Goa 1638. Museum of Art, Boston, Mass. (1): a Dutch State yacht and shipping in light airs. Bowes Museum (1): Mediterranean port. Museum of Fine Art, Copenhagen (1): rocky harbour. Gemäldegalerie, Dresden (3): ships wrecked on a rocky coast; shipping off the Dutch coast; ship off a high coast. Museum Merskoe, Gdansk (1): the Jupiter *off a port. National Maritime Museum, Greenwich (1): Battle of Scheveningen, 1653. Groningen Museum (1): ships of war; Gemäldegalerie, Leipzig (1). Kunsthalle, Mannheim (1): Battle of the First Dutch War (Scheveningen ?). Bavarian State Museums, Munich (4): Battle of the First Dutch War; a Dutch State yacht and a ship of Zeeland; a ship of Zeeland and fishing boats off-shore; a ship wrecked on a high coast with a castle. Boymans Museum, Rotterdam (1): mountainous coast with a port. Nationalmuseum, Stockholm (2): port of Venice; beach scene with an island castle and shipping. Albertina Museum, Vienna (1): Battle of Scheveningen, 1653. Waddesdon Manor, Bucks. (1): action of the Second Dutch War.*

BEERSTRAATEN, Johannes
Artist working in the third quarter of the 17th century. A painter of port scenes, especially of the fanciful Mediterranean type, and of winter landscapes. What his relationship to Jan Abraham (q.v.) was we do not know, except that pictures by him have been wrongly ascribed to Jan Abraham.

PLATE: 75.

EXAMPLES: National Maritime Museum, Greenwich (2): both fanciful Mediterranean port scenes, one signed Johan Beerstraaten. Louvre, Paris (1): view of Genoa. National Gallery, Prague (1): ships off a Mediterranean coast. Nationalmuseum, Stockholm (1): view of Venice.

BEEST, Albertus van **1820-1860**
Born in Rotterdam. He was already an established painter who had worked with the Dutch fleet, and accompanied Prince Henry of the Netherlands to the East, before he moved to America in 1845, dying in New York in 1860. He worked for some time with William Bradford (q.v.) mainly in watercolour.

PLATES: 457, 458, 459, 460.

EXAMPLES: Fodor Museum, Amsterdam (1): river view. Rijks Print Collection, Amsterdam (60 drawings). The Museum of Fine Arts in Boston, Mass. (1): Dordrecht harbour entrance with a merchant vessel. Teylers Museum, Haarlem (drawings). Rijks Print Collection, Leyden (a drawing). New Bedford Whaling Museum (3). Rijksmuseum "Kroller-Muller", Otterlo (34 drawings). Boymans Museum, Rotterdam (5 and drawings): shore scene on Zeeland coast, 1843; calm; rough sea; storm; view of the Gulf of Naples. Prins Hendrik Museum, Rotterdam (10 drawings).

BELL, R.
A British ship portraitist working in the second quarter of the 19th century, probably in Liverpool. The National Maritime Museum, Greenwich, has a painting by him of the Black Ball Line ship *Gladiator* off the Welsh coast, dated 1845. It is of good quality, very like the work of Joseph Heard (q.v.).

PLATE: 387.

BELLEVOIS, Jacob Andriaensz **1621-1675**
Born in Rotterdam, a painter in the Dutch realist style who specialised in scenes of ships being thrown onto rocky coasts, a fashionable theme of his time, although he also did some port scenes. His style owes a lot to Simon de Vlieger (q.v.) and something to Bonaventura Peeters (q.v.). He died on September 17th, 1675, in Rotterdam.

PLATES: 21, 22.

EXAMPLES: Rijksmusem, Amsterdam (1): storm. Herzog Anton Ulrich-Museum, Brunswick (1): ships wrecked on a rocky coast. National Maritime Museum, Greenwich (2): vessel in a storm off a rock with a castle, one the sketch for the other. Mauritshuis, The Hague (1): ships in an estuary. Kunsthalle, Hamburg (1): rough seas. Fuerstliche Lammling, Lichtenstein (1): storm. Museum of Mayence (1). Prado, Madrid (1): port scene.

BENNETTER, Hendrik Wilhelm **b.1874**
Born in Paris on April 24th, 1874, he was the son of Johan Jacob, and moved to Norway when five or six. His father taught him drawing as a child, and in 1894 he went to the Academy of Arts at Antwerp.

BENNETTER, Johan Jacob **1822-1904**
Born in Oslo, on September 30th, 1822, he was originally a sailor turned painter. In 1844 he studied at the school of drawing in Oslo, and in 1849 won a scholarship to work in The Hague, where he studied under Louis Meijer (q.v.). In 1852 he went to Paris and worked with Theodore Gudin, and exhibited at the Paris Salon from 1855 to 1870. In 1880 he returned to his native land, where he settled. He died on March 29th, 1904.

BENSON, John P. **1865-1947**
An American marine painter of good quality. The Peabody Museum of Salem, has a watercolour and two oils, one given by the artist.

PLATE: 649.

BENTABOLE, Louis **1827-1880**
He was a pupil of Eugène Isabey (q.v.), and exhibited at the Paris Salon from 1847. Born in Paris, he died there on November 30th, 1880.

PLATE: 499.

EXAMPLES: Musée des Beaux-Arts, La Rochelle (1): a view on the coast of Brittany. Musée Saint-Denis, Rheims (1): a beach scene. Musée des Beaux-Arts et de Céramique, Rouen (1): a beach scene.

BENTLEY, Charles **1806-1854**
Born in London, the son of a carpenter, he was apprenticed to the engraver Theodore Fielding. He was the friend of another of Fielding's pupils, William Callow (q.v.), who worked in Paris at the end of and after Bonington's life, when his influence was fresh. This connection could have been the reason for the strong flavour of Bonington in Bentley's work. Apart from his engravings, he seems to have worked only in watercolours. He died in London on September 4th, 1854.

His exhibits at the British Institution between 1843 and 1854 indicate that he visited, at least, Holland, France, Scotland and Ireland. He also exhibited at the Old and New Watercolour Societies.

Examples of his work may be found in the Ulster Museum, Belfast; Birmingham Art Gallery; Blackburn Art Gallery; Leeds City Art Gallery; British Museum; Victoria and Albert Museum; Newport Art Gallery and the Castle Museum, Norwich.

BERGEN, Claus **1885-1964**
Born in Stuttgart on April 4th, 1885, he was the son of Fritz Bergen, the illustrator and portrait painter. He attended the Munich Academy under Karl von Marr, and became a book illustrator under another illustrator called Karl Mays. He then studied in England and America. Around 1910 he was working in Munich and Düsseldorf.

In 1914 he became Marine Painter to Kaiser Wilhelm II and the German naval command, and made paintings of the High Seas Fleet, and of the Battle of Jutland in 1916. After the war he again visited America, and on his return continued to paint marines. A lot of his commissions were from public bodies and the paintings are of impressive size. He is thought to have died in Garmisch on October 4th, 1964.

PLATES: 647, 648.

EXAMPLES: the German Maritime Museum, Bremerhaven (1): The liner Columbus *at New York, 1924. The National Maritime Museum, Greenwich (4): a deck scene on a U-boat; Hipper's battle cruisers in action at the Battle of Jutland 1916; A Nazi wreath on the North Sea in Memory of Jutland; The "pocket battleship"* Admiral von Scheer *bombarding the Spanish coast during the civil war, 1937. The Navy Memorial Museum, Washington Navy Yard, (2): Going to England; a "pocket battleship".*

BERGER, Johann Christian **1803-1871**
Born in Linkoping, Sweden. An army officer, who resigned with the rank of captain and took up painting at the Stockholm Academy. He continued his studies in Paris and in London, where he exhibited at the British Institution in 1837 and 1839. He died in Uppsala.

PLATE: 406.

EXAMPLES: Lansmuseum, Linkoping (at least one). National Gallery, Oslo (1): a view of Golland. Nationalmuseum, Stockholm (1): View of Antwerp.

BEVERLEY, William Roxby **1811-1889**
Born in Richmond, Surrey, he came of a Yorkshire theatrical family whose real name was Roxby, the name of Beverley being added for professional reasons by his father. He was essentially a theatrical scene painter and the most important figure in that field in the 19th century after Clarkson Stanfield (q.v.). Notably, he combined innovatory painting techniques with remarkable mechanical ingenuity, and was the first theatrical painter capable of easel-painting who was content to let his reputation rest on his theatrical work, the theatre having become respectable.

He combined this with an interest in marine and some landscape painting, and exhibited at the Royal Academy from 1865 to 1880, all his contributions there being of coastal or fishing boat scenes. He died on May 17th, 1889 in Hampstead, London.

EXAMPLES: Ulster Museum, Belfast; Bridport Art Gallery; Fitzwilliam Museum, Cambridge; National Gallery of Scotland, Edinburgh; National Maritime Museum, Greenwich; Leeds City Art Gallery; Leicester City Art Gallery; British Museum, London; Newport Art Gallery; Portsmouth City Museum and Art Gallery.

BEYEREN, Abraham Hendricksz van **1620/1-1690**
Born in The Hague and died in Overschie, this artist is best known for his beautiful flower and still-life paintings, although he also painted marines, mainly of small craft in inland waters. An early example with a green sea indicates that he initially followed in the Flemish tradition but his later paintings have grey seas in the Dutch realist style. He was in the Guild of Delft in 1641.

PLATE: 82.

EXAMPLES: Stedelijk Museum, Alkmaar (1): fish on the shore with distant shipping. Rijksmuseum, Amsterdam (one marine). Landesmuseum, Bonn (1): estuary scene. Museum of Fine Arts, Budapest (at least one): small craft off a town. Glasgow Museum and Art Gallery (1). National Maritime Museum, Greenwich (1): fishing boats in an estuary. Gemäldegalerie, Leipzig (1). Hermitage Museum, Leningrad (5): most still-life subjects. City Art Gallery, Manchester (1): Fishing boats off a coast. Johnson Collection, Philadelphia (1): estuary scene. Boymans Museum, Rotterdam (one marine). Nationalmuseum, Stockholm (one marine). Castle Museum, York (1): Seascape with galliots.

BIERSTADT, Albert **1830-1902**
Born in Solingen near Düsseldorf, he became a pupil of the Düsseldorf Academy, then the centre of the German landscape and marine school. After travelling in Europe he went to America, where he visited and painted the Rocky Mountains and Colorado. Some of these works he sent for exhibition at the Royal Academy in London between 1869 and 1884. He died in New York in 1902.

The Museum of Fine Arts in Boston has a painting called "The Wreck of the *Ancon* in Loring Bay, Alaska."

PLATE: 551.

BILLE, Carle Ludvig **1815-1898**
Born in Copenhagen he was a sailor turned artist who won a scholarship to the Copenhagen Academy. He developed a style which must have influenced Vilhelm Melbye (q.v.), whose work is very close. This made him popular with Scandinavian and British collectors.

His son, Wilhelm Victor, was his pupil and also painted marines. The Frederiksborg Museum, Zealand, has a painting of the burning of the *Von der Tann* in 1850. Examples can also be seen at the Royal Naval Museum, Copenhagen.

PLATE: 452.

BINKS, Thomas **1799-1852**
Hull painter and decorator, a pupil of Thomas Meggitt of Hull. The Ferens Art Gallery has a whaling scene by him and one of three paddle steamers in Hull Roads. The National Maritime Museum, Greenwich, has a portrait of the sailing ship *East Indian*.

PLATE: 337.

BINKS, Thomas A. **fl.1840s**
Son of Thomas Binks, senior (q.v.), he may have died young, for his work has not been isolated from his father's. Described as a "Sign and Ship's Painter" in the directories from 1842-1848.

BIRCH, Thomas **1779-1851**
Born in London. In 1794, when he was fifteen, he emigrated to America with his father, an engraver and miniaturist. At first he was his father's pupil and assistant and helped with the engraving of views around Philadelphia. Later, when in his early twenties, he set up his own studio in Philadelphia as a portrait painter and was in due course elected to the Pennsylvania Academy of Fine Arts. He died there in 1851.

His choice of subject widened to marines and naval actions, as well as landscapes. Not being a sailor, and living far from the sea, the details of his compositions had to be researched. His sea fights covered the actions of the War of 1812.

PLATES: 329, 330, 331.

EXAMPLES: the Museum of Fine Arts, Boston; the Wadsworth Atheneum, Hartford, Conn.; the Fruitlands Museum, Harvard, Mass.; the Brooklyn Museum, New York; the Mariners Museum, Newport News, Virginia; the Pennsylvania Academy of Fine Arts; the Shelburne Museum, Vermont.

BIRCHALL, William M. **b.1884**
An American ship portraitist and illustrator, born in Iowa, who left America for England, and settled in Hastings.

PLATE: 651.

EXAMPLES: Folkestone Art Gallery (1): watercolour. National Maritime Museum, Greenwich (5): watercolours. Peabody Museum of Salem (7): watercolours.

BLAAUW, Pieter Aartsze **1744-1808**
Born in Hoorn on November 2nd, 1744, he was a Dutch carver of ship decoration, and sometime Master of the King's yacht. He was also a draughtsman and painter, mainly in watercolour. His works can be seen at the Scheepvaart Museum at Amsterdam, the Museum at Hoorn, and the Prins Hendrik Museum at Rotterdam. He died in Medemblik on December 2nd, 1808.

PLATE: 267.

BLACHE, Christian Vigilius **b.1838**
Born in Aarhus, Denmark, in 1838, he was a pupil of Carl Frederich Lorensen, and a student at the Academy of Fine Art in Copenhagen. He began exhibiting in 1863 and in the following year the Royal Museum for Art bought one of his paintings. He fought in the Schleswig-Holstein War of 1864. In 1872 he received a Danish Academy scholarship which enabled him to travel to Paris, Italy, Vienna, Dresden and Berlin.

The Maritime Museum at Kronborg Castle has a painting of shipping off Tre Kronner in 1860. The Royal Naval Museum, Copenhagen, also has works by him.

PLATES: 561, 562.

BLANDIN, Etienne **b.1903**
Born into a family of sailors, in St. Servan, near St. Malo, he intended to join them in going to sea. Unfortunately, while at the School of Navigation at St. Malo, he showed no aptitude for mathematics, a subject necessary for learning navigation, and after six months there he gave up his nautical aspirations. He turned to painting and found his metier first at the Art School at Reunes and then at the National School of Fine Arts in Paris, where he qualified.

His interest in the sea and ships prompted him to study them and in 1933 he had a successful marine exhibition in Brest and later in the Casino at St. Malo. Here his works were seen and admired by Admiral Darlan, at whose instigation he was appointed Official Painter to the Department of Marine, 1933.

He likes to paint the deep water sailing ships of the 19th and 20th centuries, and in 1951 he was made an honorary member of the Cape Horners Association. He has painted some eight hundred marines in oils, as well as drawings and works in gouache, which can be found in private collections throughout the world.

PLATE: 616.

BLANKERHOFF, Jan Heunisz **1628-1669**
Born in Alkmaar, he was in turn a pupil of Arend Teerling, then of Pieter Schayenborg, a still-life painter also of Alkmaar, Caesar van Everdingen, an Alkmaar portrait and history painter, and finally of Gerrit de Jong, an Alkmaar landscape painter.

After such a tuition it comes as no surprise to learn that he was elected to the Guild of Alkmaar in 1649. Such examples of his work as exist are in a grey palette and well executed, some very much in the manner of early works by Ludolf Bakhuizen (q.v.) and others, owing much to Jacob van Ruisdael and Abraham van Beyeren. The quality of his work suggests that had he not died young he would have developed into a major marine painter. He died in Amsterdam in 1669.

PLATES: 125, 126.

EXAMPLES: Stedelijk Museum, Alkmaar (1): Dutch ship wrecked on a rocky shore. Rijksmuseum, Amsterdam (1): Battle of the Zuider Zee 1573; this picture is on permanent loan to the Town Hall, Hoorn, for which it was originally commissioned. Nederlandsch Historich Scheepvaart Museum, Amsterdam (1): View of the Westerschelde, near Flushing. Bavarian Museum, Augsburg (2): rough sea scenes. Bristol Art Gallery (1): Dutch shipping in a breeze. Museum of Fine Arts, Copenhagen (1): A fishing pinck and a Dutch ship in a storm off a coast. Musée des Beaux Arts d'Ixelles, Brussels (1). Kunsthalle, Hamburg (1): Smalschip at anchor off shore. Kunsthalle, Karlsrühe (1): Ship wrecked on a rocky coast. Hermitage Museum, Leningrad (1).

BLAUVOET, Jacobus **1646-1701**
He was a pupil of Sorgh (q.v.) but sometimes painted more in the style of Verbeecq (q.v.). He was born in Rotterdam, where he also died on December 27th, 1701.

BLIJK, Frans Jacobus van der **1806-1876**
Born and died in Dordrecht. From the time he was fifteen until he was thirty he studied under Johannes Cornelis

Schotel (q.v.). He painted the coasts of Holland and France; between 1830 and 1840 he exhibited frequently in Germany, and also in The Hague between 1830 and 1875. The town archive at Dordrecht has drawings and there is a river view of Giessen in the Boymans Museum, Rotterdam.

BOEHME, Frederik Vilhelm
A painter who, while probably originally German, was working in Copenhagen in the early 18th century. The Museum of Fine Arts at Copenhagen has two romantic storm scenes of ships wrecked on rocky coasts; one in the style of Bonaventura Peeters (q.v.) and one dated 1704.

PLATES: 187, 188.

BOL, Cornelis **b.c.1580**
Born in Antwerp, he is thought to have been a pupil of one of the Sadeler brothers (qq.v.) and worked in Holland and England. Little is known of him, but a bible published in 1611 has a frontispiece by him. An indication of his life span is given by the signed painting in the Rijksmuseum, Amsterdam, of a Dutch ship engaging Spanish galleys, in which the ship cannot be earlier than about 1630.

BOND, William Joseph J.C. **1833-1926**
Born in Knotty Ash, near Liverpool, he was educated at Stonyhurst College, the Jesuit school, and afterwards intended to become a picture restorer, being apprenticed to a Thomas Griffiths in Liverpool. He began to sketch and, being encouraged, took to painting as a career. After his marriage in 1861 he moved for a time to Caernarvon but by 1865 had returned to Liverpool, where he died on March 1st, 1926.

He exhibited at the Liverpool Academy, of which he was made a member in 1859; also at the Royal Academy in 1871 and 1874, Suffolk Street between 1850 and 1870, the British Institution in 1858 and 1859, and the Liverpool Autumn Exhibition from 1871 to 1901.

At one time he was interested in the Pre-Raphaelites but later was influenced by the mature work of Turner (q.v.), to the point that some of his works have been offered as Turners. Of the fourteen paintings of his held by the Walker Art Gallery in Liverpool, ten are coastal scenes or marines.

BONE, Sir Muirhead, Kt. **1876-1953**
R.W.S., R.E., R.S.A.
Born on March 23rd, 1876, this great draughtsman and engraver was a pupil at the Glasgow School of Art at a time when the Glasgow School of Painting was in the ascendant. He was also an apprentice architect.

He set up as an art master in Ayre but lack of pupils forced him to move on and he went to London in 1901. In the First World War he became an official war artist and in 1917 a book of his lithographs was published, called *The Western Front*.

He was one of the instigators of the formation of the Imperial War Museum. In the Second World War he worked for the War Artists Commission and a number of his beautiful drawings are of naval subjects. He was also a trustee of the Tate Gallery and the National Gallery 1941-48 and was knighted in 1937. He died in Oxford on October 21st, 1953.

The Imperial War Museum has his official commissions of both World Wars and the Tate Gallery also has a few. A number of drawings of naval subjects in the Second World War are in the National Maritime Museum, Greenwich.

BONE, Stephen **1904-1958**
He was born in Chiswick, London on November 13th, 1904 and intended to be an artist from an early age. His education was at Bedales, the co-educational boarding school. After leaving school he travelled in Europe with his father, Muirhead Bone (q.v.), and must have been his pupil.

Stephen Bone was not essentially a marine painter, but is mentioned here because his work for the War Artists' Commission in the Second World War included many naval subjects, especially of the assault on the Normandy beaches in 1944. He also sailed with the aircraft carrier, H.M.S. *Pursuer*. His work for the Commission is divided between the Imperial War Museum and the National Maritime Museum, Greenwich. He died in London on September 15th, 1958.

BONFIELD, George Robert **1805-1898**
Born in Portsmouth, Hampshire, on February 4th, 1805, he emigrated with his family to America in 1816, and settled in Philadelphia. His father was a stonemason, and George was taught the trade, later working for a marble dealer, mainly on headstones. His work also took him to Bordentown to cut and decorate imported stone for the estate of Joseph Bonaparte, Napoleon's exiled brother. There he took to copying paintings in the house, encouraged to do so by Joseph Bonaparte.

In 1820 he exhibited a painting at the Pennsylvania Academy of Fine Arts, which prompted its president to arrange for Bonfield to take lessons there under Thomas Vest. He lived all the rest of his life in Philadelphia, painting high quality shipping scenes. He died there on July 27th, 1898.

His work may be found in the Museum of Fine Arts, Boston, the Mariners Museum, Newport News, the Philadelphia Maritime Museum and the Pennsylvania Academy of Fine Arts.

PLATE: 434.

BONINGTON, Richard Parkes **1802-1828**
Born in Arnold, near Nottingham on October 25th, 1802. His father, also Richard Bonington, had a varied career, as a drawing master, portrait painter, sailor, governor of Nottingham gaol. In 1817 or 1818 he went into the lace business at Calais.

With him went his family and Richard junior, already a skilled watercolourist in the English tradition, was able to meet the artists of the new French Romantic school, especially when the family moved on to Paris, where he met and was befriended by Eugène Delacroix. His first exhibits at the Paris Salon in 1824 were very well received. The following year he visited England and Scotland, and in 1826 exhibited two French coast scenes at the British Institution. The same year he travelled in Switzerland and Italy, returning to Paris via the Riviera.

In 1827 and 1828 he sent pictures, including French coast scenes, to the Royal Academy and the British Institution. He was then settled in Paris and had he lived, this, surely one of the most fresh, attractive and admired of English painters, would now be regarded as a French artist. Sadly a brain fever contracted in 1828 drove him to seek a cure in London, where he died on September 23rd, 1828, at the age of twenty-three.

EXAMPLES (marines only): Birmingham Art Gallery (2): French coast scenes. Ferens Art Gallery, Hull (1): coastal scene. The Hermitage Museum, Leningrad, has a large painting by him. Wallace Collection, London (5): sea piece off white cliffs; the Seine near Nantes, on the coast of Picardy; three watercolours. Victoria and Albert Museum, London (5 watercolours). Leicester Art Gallery (1): boat at a quay. Montreal Museum of Fine Arts (1): coastal view.

BORG, C.

Norwegian ship portraitist working in the first quarter of the 20th century. The Bergen Maritime Museum has one of the steamer *Nordpol,* with a Thames background, dated 1901.

BOS, Casper van den **1634-c.1656**

Born in Hoorn, this promising artist of grisaille pictures, died there shortly after 1656. What exists shows a delicate touch. In the Scheepvaart Museum in Amsterdam is one of a ship passing close inshore with a flute and a pinck, and at the Prins Hendrik Museum at Rotterdam is a view of shipping off Hoorn. Signed "C.J. van den Bos" (the C and J in monogram).

BOTTGER, Jacob Ahrend Heinrich **1781-1860**

A ship portraitist from Schleswig-Holstein (then Danish) who worked in Flensburg and Altona from 1833. Stiff and repetitive but quite well crafted. The Altonaer Museum has ten pen and wash drawings and the Maritime Museum at Kronborg Castle also has watercolour ship portraits.

PLATE: 429.

BOUDIN, Eugène Louis **1825-1908**

He was born in Honfleur, and died in Paris. This charming painter of the French Impressionist school, produced a vast number of mainly small paintings of shipping in the harbours of Northern France and the Low Countries, as well as beach scenes at fashionable watering places, with groups of elaborately dressed holiday-makers.

He was not a marine painter in the sense that a marine painter would depict shipping scenes in various sea conditions; he only painted what he saw, which seems to have been almost exclusively from dry land. He had a strong influence on marine painting which still lingers today. His biography, *La Vie et les Oeuvres d'Eugène Boudin,* was written by M.G. Caben.

His popularity has meant that his works can be seen in most major galleries of Europe and America, as well as many minor ones in France.

PLATE: 615.

BOUGH, Samuel R.S.A. **1822-1878**

Born in Carlisle January 8th, 1822, his father was butler to Sir Joseph Gilpin, the physician and, after marriage, a cobbler. His mother was also a servant in the house, and Samuel was the third child of five. He had some instruction in drawing from a friend of the family called John Dobson. At fifteen he was put in a solicitor's office to be a clerk, an arrangement which was not successful, and he was sent to London to learn engraving. He was soon back in Carlisle, where he set up a studio, selling some of his pictures in his father's shop.

He was strongly influenced by the work of John Constable, and had his first picture hung in the Royal Scottish Academy exhibition in 1844. The following year he left Carlisle to become scene-painter at the Theatre Royal, Manchester, and exhibited at the Manchester Royal Institution. In 1848 he moved to Glasgow as scene-painter at the Princess Theatre but, not thriving there, moved again to Hamilton, and then to Port Glasgow.

It was at this time, in the 1850s, that he was painting marines, and in 1855 he moved finally to Edinburgh, dying there on November 19th, 1878. He continued to exhibit at the Manchester Institute and the Royal Scottish Academy until 1877. He became R.S.A. in 1874. He also exhibited at the Royal Academy between 1856 and 1876.

PLATES: 517, 518.

EXAMPLES (marines only): Scottish National Gallery, Edinburgh (1): the Solway at Port Carlisle. City Art Gallery, Glasgow (3): Dutch vessels in the Thames; Dunkirk Harbour; seascape. National Maritime Museum, Greenwich (1): a view of a shipyard at Dumbarton.

BOURNE, G.W. **b.c.1860**

Born in Dover. The National Maritime Museum, Greenwich, has a painting of the crew of the sailing ship *Eblana* being rescued by the crew of the barque *Necapolis* on October 10th, 1878, during a violent storm. The painter was an apprentice on board the *Necapolis,* and Bourne also did a larger version which was exhibited in South Australia, where he settled.

BOUWMEESTER, Cornelisz **1670-1733**

Born and died in Rotterdam. The last of the masters of the art of making grisaille pictures, done in ink with a reed pen on a prepared panel or canvas, and called by the Dutch "penschilderen".

His work overlapped that of Adriaen and Roelot van Salm (qq.v.) but he brought a new dimension to the art by the use of sepia and black ink, which gives his grisailles an illusion of colour beyond what is actually there.

He usually signed with the initials "C.B.M.", but there is one at Greenwich signed "C/Boumeester". He was also a painter of tile pictures.

PLATES: 173, 174.

EXAMPLES: Fogg Museum, Boston, Mass. (1): a smalschip starboard quarter view (attributed). National Maritime Museum, Greenwich (6): The Jonge Prins te Paard *off Naples; several Dutch ships arriving at Naples; Dutch ships in a gale off a rocky coast; Dutch ships at anchor; an English fourth-rate close hauled; English ships in a gale. Historisch Museum, Rotterdam (1): shipping off Naples. Peabody Museum of Salem (1): Dutch men-of-war.*

BOYCE, William Thomas Nicholas **1867/8-1911**

Born in Blakeney, Norfolk, the son of a ship master who moved to South Shields while William was still a child, where he owned and commanded a number of collier brigs.

William was apprenticed as a joiner, but after a few years went into the drapery business, and worked for many years in a shop owned by a Mr. Thomas Crofton in the Market Place. From his youth he had been a keen amateur marine painter in watercolours, and by 1900 he had achieved sufficient success to quit the drapery business and work full time at his painting. He died on September 25th, 1911.

Of his thirteen children two, Herbert Walter and Norman Septimus, also were watercolourists. Examples of his work may be found in the Laing Art Gallery, Newcastle, and the South Shields and the Sunderland Art Galleries.

BOYCOTT-BROWN, Hugh R.S.M.A. b.1909

Born on April 27th, 1909, he was educated at Trent College, Derbyshire, and then at the Walford School of Art and Heatherly's, London. He also studied under Bernard Adams, R.O.I., and Sir Anersby Brown, R.A. He became the Art Master at the Royal Masonic Junior School at Bushey, Hertfordshire, in 1929, and remained there until 1969. He now lives and works at Saxmundham in Suffolk. He was in the Royal Air Force Volunteer Reserve during the Second World War (Coastal Command).

He likes to paint from nature on a rather small scale. He was elected to the Royal Society of Marine Artists in 1969. He exhibits at the Omell Gallery, Albemarle Street, London.

The National Maritime Museum, Greenwich, has one oil painting, and a watercolour on loan from the R.S.M.A., his diploma work.

PLATE: 689.

BRADFORD, William 1827-1892

Born in New Bedford, Massachusetts, he was a pupil of the Dutchman Albert van Beest (q.v.), with whom he shared a studio at Fairhaven, N.Y., and some of his works are joint efforts. After van Beests's death in 1860, Bradford made a series of expeditions into the polar regions and it is by his paintings of polar subjects that he is mainly remembered. These have an admirable clarity of style which indicates his debt to Robert Salmon and Fitz Hugh Lane (qq.v.).

He journeyed to Europe, and in 1875 he was received in England by Queen Victoria, who bought a painting "The Steamer *Panther* among the Icebergs and Field Ice in Melville Bay", which she ordered to be exhibited at the Royal Academy Exhibition of that year. In the 1880s he travelled widely in Western America, on which he afterwards gave lectures with slides from photographs that he had taken himself.

His paintings may be found in the Museum of Fine Arts, Boston, the New Bedford Whaling Museum, and the Mariners Museum, Newport News.

PLATE: 509.

BRAGER, Jean Baptiste Henri Durand *see* **DURAND-BRAGER, Jean Baptiste Henri**

BRAMWELL, Southby

The compiler has been unable to find out any details about this artist, but the National Maritime Museum, Greenwich, has an excellent painting signed by him of the "flat iron" collier *Croydon,* launched in 1951.

PLATE: 676.

BRANGWYN, Sir Frank William 1867-1956
R.A., R.W.S., P.R.B.A., R.E., H.R.S.A., H.V.P.S.M.A.

He was the son of a Welsh church architect, who ran a workshop for ecclesiastical furnishings in Bruges where Brangwyn was born on May 13th, 1867. Such early art training as he received he got from his father. He came to London with his family in 1875 and he practised drawing at the Victoria and Albert Museum from about 1880; from 1882-84 he worked in William Morris's workshop.

In 1885 he had his first painting hung at the Royal Academy; by 1889 he received enough commissions to enable him to travel widely, and he became involved in the Parisian art nouveau movement. Translated into paintings of galleons his art nouveau tendencies have tremendous impact, but he was also interested in scenes of sailors working ships, which are handled realistically.

He was much more than a marine painter. He is best known for his huge genre frescoes, one of which was in the Royal Mail liner *Empress of Britain,* and sank with her. He was also a designer of furniture and whole rooms, and an engraver.

He was elected A.R.A. in 1904, and R.A. in 1919. In 1952 he had the then unique honour, for a living artist, of a retrospective exhibition of his work in the Diploma Galleries of the Royal Academy. He was made a Freeman of Bruges in return for his gift of a large collection of his work, which is housed in a museum bearing his name. He died at Ditchling, Sussex, on June 11th, 1956.

PLATE: 603.

EXAMPLES (marines only): The City Art Gallery, Glasgow (1): A burial at sea. National Maritime Museum, Greenwich (1): Stowing the mainsail.

BRETT, John A.R.A. 1830-1902

Born in Bletchingley, Surrey, in 1830. He studied at the Royal Academy Schools, joining in 1853. He was strongly influenced by the Pre-Raphaelite movement, and was praised by Ruskin for his painting "The Stonebreaker". Later he concentrated on beautifully crafted shore scenes, especially in the West Country. He exhibited at the Royal Academy from 1856 to 1901 and was elected A.R.A. in 1880 — the same year that his "Britannia's Realm", a splendid sea view from Beachy Head, was bought for the Chantrey Bequest.

He was something of an eccentric and a keen amateur astronomer. About 1892 he built himself a remarkable house at Putney called Daisy Field. It was built round a strong central pillar on which was mounted his telescope and was one of the first houses in London to be centrally heated. The floors were of some composition like asphalt for ease of cleaning; there were no internal doors, and his seven children were discouraged from wearing clothes in the house. He died in Putney, London, on January 8th, 1902.

The Birmingham Art Gallery has four of his paintings, and the Tate Gallery has four. Only two of these are coastal views, and "Britannia's Realm" is on loan from the Tate Gallery to the National Maritime Museum, Greenwich.

BRETT, Oswald Longfield F.A.S.M.A. b.1921

Born in Sydney, New South Wales. At the age of twelve he was inspired by the work of the local marine painter John Allcot, and at fourteen he attempted to join Alan Villiers in the little sailing ship *Joseph Conrad,* but was prevented from doing so by his parents. Instead he studied fine art at the East Sydney Technical College, eventually becoming a pupil of John Allcot.

In the Second World War he joined the Cunard Line. When the *Queen Elizabeth* went to Sydney to pick up troops for service in the Middle East, Brett, having already had experience in the Australian coastal trade and deep water sailing ships, was therefore involved both in the *Queen Elizabeth* and the *Aquitania* in their trooping runs from New York to Great Britain, and it was in New York that he met the girl he was to marry after the war. He settled there and now lives and works in Levittown, N.Y.

His development as a painter was influenced and assisted by the American illustrator and marine painter Anton Otto Fischer. His subjects include both historical and contemporary scenes; notably a commission from the President of the Philippines for a painting of the barque *Kaiulani,* still afloat there, for presentation to President Johnson in 1964, and in 1971, thirty paintings about the Nantucket whaling industry for Douglas Fonda.

In 1976, to celebrate the bicentenary of the independence of the United States of America, an exhibition of his work was staged in his native Sydney.

In the National Maritime Museum, San Francisco, is a painting by him of the sailing ship *Balclutha.*

PLATE: 685.

BREUHAUS DE GROOT, Frans Arnold 1824-1872

He was born in Leyden in 1824 and studied under his father, Frans, and at the Academy at The Hague, from 1839 to 1847. From 1850 to 1861 he was in Amsterdam, and from then on in Brussels, where he died in 1872. He exhibited at Amsterdam and The Hague from 1843 to 1863. The Rijksmuseum, Amsterdam, has a painting of jetties on the English coast.

BRICHER, Alfred Thomson 1837-1908

Born in Portsmouth, New Hampshire, in 1837, an American painter of quality, whose work is close to his contemporary, James Hamilton. Denver Art Museum, Colorado, has a painting of schooners offshore.

BRIERLY, Sir Oswald Walter, Kt. 1817-1894
R.W.S., F.R.G.S.

Born in Chester on May 19th, 1817. His father was a doctor and amateur painter. After attending the Academy of Henry Sass, the genre and history painter, in Bloomsbury, he went to Plymouth to study naval architecture and rigging and his first exhibits accepted by the Royal Academy were of the *Pique* and *Gorgon* at Plymouth in 1839.

He must have been one of the most travelled of professional painters. In 1841, with a London stockbroker called Benjamin Boyd, he sailed for Sydney in the yacht *Wanderer,* where Boyd was to set up banking interests. Brierly settled for a time in Auckland, N.Z. In 1848 the royal naval surveyor, Captain Owen Stanley, offered to take him in H.M.S. *Rattlesnake* on a survey of the north and east coasts of Australia and he went on two voyages, keeping a valuable record with his drawings.

In 1850 Captain the Hon. Harry Keppel asked him to join him aboard H.M.S. *Meander,* which cruised in the Pacific and off the west coast of South America, before returning to England via the Straits of Magellan in July 1851. Eight lithographs by Brierly illustrated Keppel's book on this voyage. In 1854 Keppel was to accompany the Baltic fleet in the *St Jean d'Acre,* 101 guns, and again asked Brierly to come with him. Many of Brierly's watercolours of that first year of the Russian War were lithographed and published as *The English and French Fleets in the Baltic 1854.*

In 1855 he again accompanied Keppel, this time to the Black Sea for the final operations of the War. On his return the Queen asked him to sketch the fleet from the royal yacht during the great review on the fleet's return. This connection culminated in his becoming Marine Painter in Ordinary to the Queen on the death of Schetky (q.v.) in 1874 and he was knighted in 1885.

Continuing his travels, the Duke of Edinburgh, who had been appointed to command the frigate *Galatea,* asked him to accompany him on a voyage round the world, which lasted from February 1867 to June 1868 and some of his sketches illustrated a book about the voyage published in 1869. In 1868 he accompanied the Prince and Princess of Wales on a tour of the Nile and Black Sea.

He exhibited at the Royal Academy between 1839 and 1872, in which year he was elected to the Royal Society of Painters in Watercolours. He also exhibited at the Old and New Watercolour Societies, and in 1881 became Curator of the Painted Hall and Greenwich Hospital collections. He died in London on December 14th, 1894.

His oil paintings are rare, and his main contributions were the watercolours from which so many lithographs were made.

PLATE: 496, 497.

EXAMPLES: The Bristol Art Gallery (1): a marine. National Maritime Museum, Greenwich (1): "Man Overboard", which shows H.M.S. St Jean d'Acre *in the Baltic; also 20 watercolours and over 300 sketches and drawings; National Gallery of Victoria, Melbourne (1): Robert Blake blockading Prince Rupert's squadron in the Tagus in 1650. Art Gallery of New South Wales, Sydney (6 watercolours): Venice after the rain; a whaler off Cap Bonne-Esperance; a sketch of* Revel; *a whaler in the South Seas; Sydney 1842; defeat of the Armada. The Library of New South Wales, Sydney (3 watercolours): H.M.S.* Black Prince *in a storm; Going to Sea; the Wreck of the Spanish Armada 1588.*

BRIL, Paul 1554-1625

He was born in Antwerp in 1554 and died in Rome in 1625. He is believed to have been the son of Mattheus Bril, a pioneer of landscape painting, which would make him the younger brother of Mattheus Bril the younger, another landscape painter who also died in Rome in 1584.

Paul Bril was a pupil of Damien Oortelmans, a member of the Antwerp Guild. When he was twenty he went to Rome to join his brother, who was already an established artist there. During a successful career in Rome he took commissions from nine popes and apart from his landscape painting, for which he is chiefly known, was an engraver and a miniaturist, and painted some marine subjects. His importance to the history of marine painting stems mainly from his influence on Hendrick Cornelisz Vroom (q.v.), when that artist stayed in Rome.

Examples of his marine paintings are in the Galleria Palatina, Palazzo Pitti, Florence and the Alte Pinakothek, Munich.

BRISCOE, Arthur John Trevor **1873-1943**
R.I., R.E.

Born in Birkenhead on February 25th, 1873; he was educated at Shrewsbury School, studied art at the Slade School and at Julian's in Paris. He exhibited at the Royal Academy, the Royal Institute of Painters in Watercolours, and the English Art Club from 1896. He was a talented engraver and was elected an Associate of the Royal Society of Painters, Etchers and Engravers in 1930, and a full member in 1933; he was also a member of the Royal Institute of Painters in Watercolours in 1935.

He was a yachtsman and wrote a *Handbook on Sailing* under the name 'Clove Hitch'. He died on April 27th, 1943.

The National Maritime Museum, Greenwich, has a deck scene called "Clewing up the Main Sail", also a watercolour and a large collection of his etchings.

PLATE: 658.

BROOKING, Charles **1723-1759**

He was born in Deptford in 1723. No painter of the second generation of British marine artists contributed so much to the emergence of a national style as did Brooking, and no painter, then or after, did it better.

Not that his debt to the Dutch was not considerable, but the purity and clarity of his tones and glazes has more affinity to de Vlieger (q.v.) than to the later works of the van de Veldes (q.v.). There is a copy of a beach scene by de Vlieger at Greenwich, the original of which is in the Wallraf-Richartz Museum in Cologne. Brooking also was not averse to using van de Velde compositions or making actual copies, though always in his own style and palette. The copies he made of the "Royal visit to the Fleet 1672" show that he did them from the mezzotint and never saw the original, because he did not understand that the boat in the foreground was French and should have had white flags where he has put in red ones. Another interesting adaptation of a van de Velde are his versions of an English squadron in a gale at Greenwich, in which he has used the subject but brought the ships up to date. The best of these is in the Ferens Art Gallery in Hull but there is also a smaller version at Greenwich.

His favourite composition seems to have been the one he used for the great picture in the Foundling Hospital, the biggest Brooking in the world but far from the best. The small version at Greenwich and the stretched version in the Tate Gallery are exquisite.

Brooking accepted commissions for a number of naval actions of the War of Jenkins' Ear (1739), though in all cases these were skirmishes and he never undertook a fleet action. Almost all these are to be found at Greenwich but perhaps the most interesting is in private hands. This is a large panoramic view of La Rochelle and the Ile de Rhé, with between them the *Alexander* capturing the *Solebay* in 1746, showing the action in several phases, and very small in the composition.

Like so many other important artists, details of his life are irritatingly meagre. A Charles Brooking successfully tendered for some decorating work at Greenwich Hospital in 1729, and it is tempting to think that he was the artist's father. We know nothing of his training but there is a painting in America signed with the addition of "aged 17". He seems to have been similar to George Chambers (q.v.), in that both appear to have been largely self-taught and that their best work dates from the last ten years of their lives. The last five in Brooking's case were particularly good, after he had acquired the patronage of Taylor White, the Treasurer of the Foundling Hospital, who commissioned the great painting there.

It seems likely that the consumption that was killing him, plus a rather humble background, contributed to his lack of material success and kept him in the thrall of an unscrupulous dealer off Leicester Square. By comparison Samuel Scott (q.v.), a painter of lesser talent if more range, admired him greatly, and did far better, his prosperity being closely related to his social position and connections.

Two painters who owed a special debt to Brooking were Dominic Serres (q.v.), who may have been a pupil in his early years in London, and Francis Swaine (q.v.), who made copies of works by Brooking and who may also have been a pupil.

PLATES: 208, 209, 210, 211, 212, 213; COLOUR PLATE: XIV.

EXAMPLES: Glasgow Museum and Art Gallery (1): small vessel close hauled off a fort. National Maritime Museum, Greenwich (22): the Boscawen *engaging a fleet of French ships, 1745; the capture of the* Marquise d'Antin *and the* Louis Erasme *1745; and another of the same subject; capture of the* Glorioso *1747; a beach scene near Scheveningen (after Simon de Vlieger); a beach scene with men-of-war in the distance (after Willem van de Velde II); a hoy and other vessels becalmed; a cutter close hauled on the port tack; a galley and other vessels wrecked on a rocky coast; royal yachts in a gale; a two-decker and a frigate running into Harwich; a merchantman and a royal yacht off Dover; a two-decker in a light breeze; a snow at anchor; a vice-admiral of the red and a squadron at sea; an Indiaman lying-to in a breeze; Indiamen driven ashore in a storm; Indiamen after a storm; shipping becalmed in the Solent; an English squadron going to windward in a gale (based on a Willem van de Velde II); whalers in the ice. Ferens Art Gallery, Kingston-upon-Hull (1): an English squadron going to windward in a gale (based on a Willem van de Velde II). Tate Gallery, London (2): a vice-admiral of the red and a squadron at sea; coastal craft becalmed. Yale Centre for British Art, New Haven, Conn. (7): the coast near Scheveningen with fishing pinks on the shore (after Simon de Vlieger); fishing boats in a calm; a ship wrecked on a rocky coast; an English flagship under easy sail; English shipping in a breeze in the Channel; a ship on fire at night close to shore; a smack under sail in a light breeze in a river.*

BROOME, William

Painter who flourished in the last quarter of the 19th century. On January 5th, 1881, the sailing ship *Indian Chief* was wrecked on the Goodwin Sands, near the lightship. In terrible conditions, some of her crew were rescued by the Ramsgate lifeboat towed out to her by the tug *Aide*.

William Broome, who is thought to have been a native of Ramsgate, painted this epic. The picture was an immediate success, oleographs being made of it for sale in the same year. Encouraged by this, Broome did more paintings with variations on this subject, and indeed is thought to have painted little else, though the compiler does know of two storm scenes with fishing boats.

Ramsgate Public Library has a pair of the *Indian Chief* subject dated 1891.

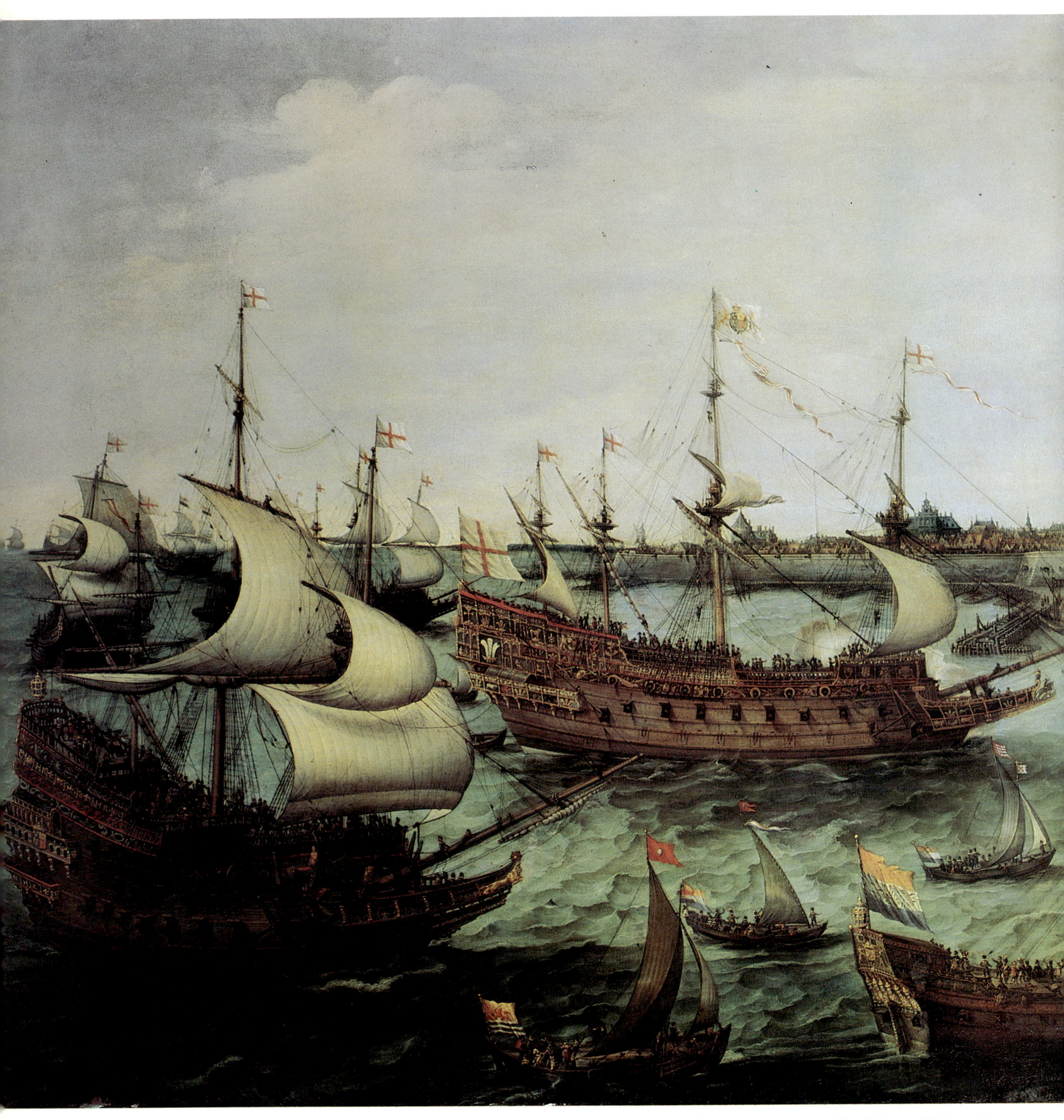

Colour Plate I. Hendrik Cornelisz Vroom, 1566-1640. ''The arrival of the Elector and Electress Palatine at Flushing in 1613 on the *Prince Royal*.'' Frans Hals Museum, Haarlem.

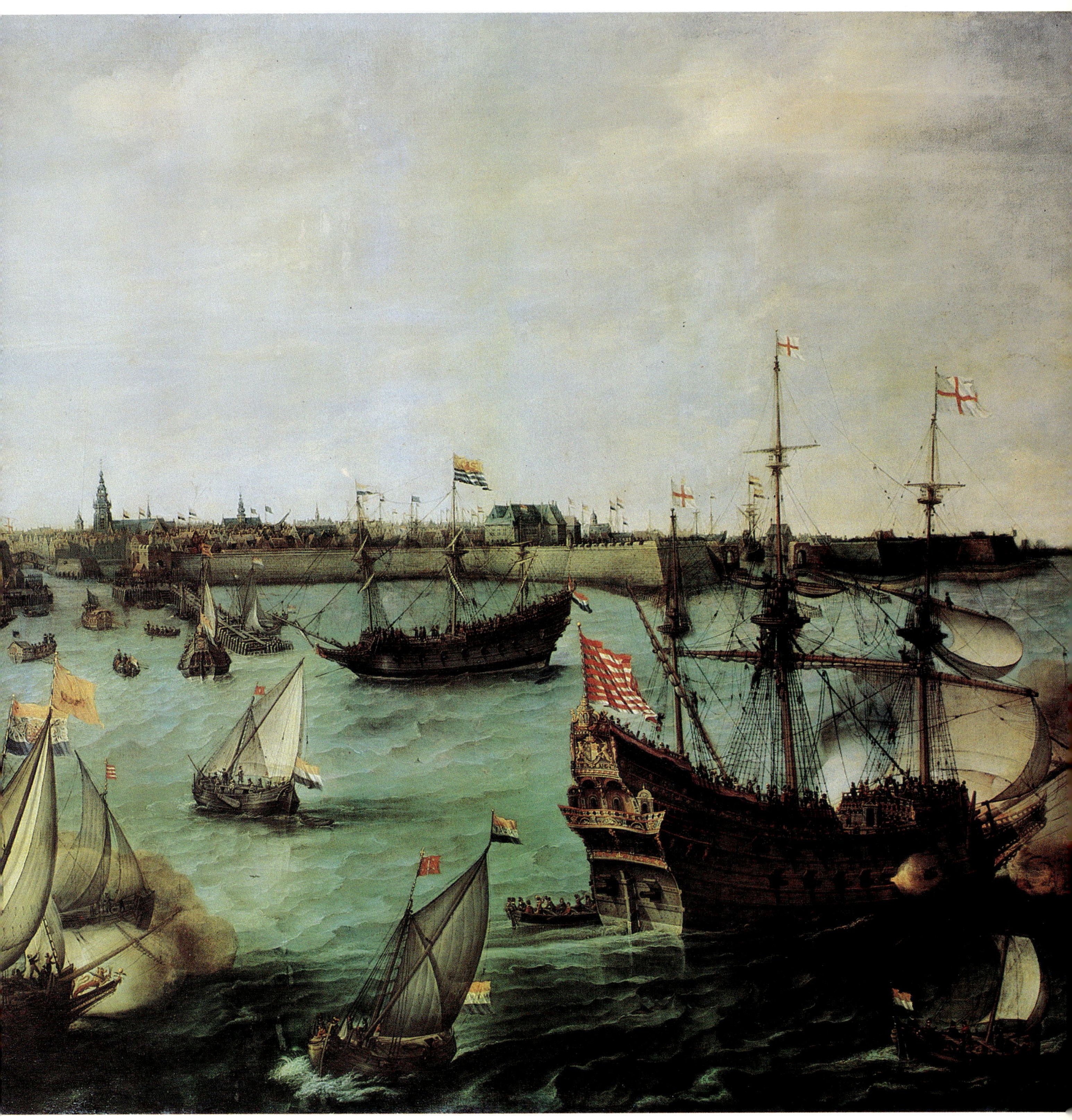

BROWN, Charles Porter **1855-1920**
An American painter who worked in Salem. As a young man he voyaged to Zanzibar, and his painting of the ship in which he sailed, the *Taria Topan,* is in the Peabody Museum, Salem, along with two other paintings by him.

BROWN, Harrison B. **1831-1915**
An American painter. The Peabody Museum, Salem, has a picture of H.M.S. *Monarch,* the turret ironclad, which, as a brand new ship, took the body of the American philanthropist, George Peabody, to America. Peabody was responsible for rehousing thousands of London's poor.

PLATE: 516.

BROWN, Samuel John Milton **1873-1965**
P.R.Camb.A.
Born at Wavertree, Liverpool, on April 13th, 1873. A pupil at the Liverpool School of Art 1888-1900. Adopted a style not unlike Somerscales (q.v.) and de Martino (q.v.). Exhibited at the Royal Institute of Painters in Watercolours and the Royal Cambrian Academy, of which he became President in 1937. He was also President of the Liverpool Academy of Arts, the Liverpool Sketching Club and the Flintshire Art Society. He was still living in 1954.

BRUEGHEL, Pieter **c.1528-1569**
Born at Brueghel, near Breda, about 1528, he took his name from his birthplace.

Though essentially a genre painter, he was moved, probably from seeing some Genoese school port scenes, to paint several marine scenes in which the shipping is given much more prominence than the port. The most notable of these is shipping off Naples, now in the Galleria Doria Pamphili in Rome. A lost picture of the Battle of Messina, painted during his visit to Italy, about 1552-54, has been engraved. In the Kunsthistorisches Museum in Vienna is a beautiful storm scene, said to have been painted at the end of his life, and his "Fall of Icarus" at the Musée des Beaux-Arts in Brussels has a good representation of a carrack on the left.

He was the pupil of a follower of Jerome Bosch, and Pieter Cock (q.v.), who took him to Antwerp, where he was elected a Free Master of the Painters Guild in 1551. His interest in maritime scenes is reflected in a series of engravings of types of ship. These and his paintings represent the first Flemish school works in maritime subjects.

He died in Brussels on September 5th, 1569.

BRUGADA, Antonio **c.1800-1863**
He was born and died in Madrid. He studied at the Royal Academy at San Fernando between 1818 and 1821, and then worked under Gudin in Paris. In 1841 he was made court painter in Madrid, where he specialised in marines, with a style reminiscent of the Dutch school. In the Museo Naval in Madrid there is a painting by him of Columbus arriving in America.

BRYANT, Charles David Jones **1883-1937**
Born in Sydney, as a young man he went to England and studied under the seascape painter Julius Olsson at St. Ives in Cornwall. He served as an official artist for the Australian Government in the First World War, and in all spent thirteen years away from Australia.

He visited New Guinea in 1923, also as an artist for the Government. After a visit to Sydney by the United States Pacific Fleet, he was commissioned to paint the fleet lying in Sydney Harbour, the painting being presented to the American President.

He was a member of the Society of British Artists and the Royal Institute of Oil Painters. He was one of the founders of the Manby Art Gallery. His work may be seen in the State Galleries in Adelaide, Melbourne and Sydney, and the Imperial War Museum, London.

BULL, Knud Geelmuyde **1811-1889**
Born in Bergen, Norway, died in Sydney, Australia. The Tasmanian Museum and Art Gallery has a painting of some quality by him of shipping off Hobart.

BUNN, George **fl.1897-1898**
The compiler has been unable to find any detailed references to this late 19th century Impressionist painter. But he suspects he was one of the Glasgow school. This is supported by the fact that a George Bunn briefly exhibited at the Glasgow Institute of Fine Arts, the Royal Scottish Academy, and the Royal Hibernian Academy at the end of the century.

BUONAMICO, Agostino (called Tassi) **1605-1644**
Born in Perugia, he went as a youth to Rome, where he was one of Paul Bril's pupils (q.v.). He was apparently of a wild nature and, because of some crime, served in the Tuscan galleys. This did not apparently put him off painting them, and they appear in his coastal and harbour scenes. Claude Gellée (q.v.) was one of his pupils. He is best known for his work in decorating palaces in Rome, such as the Quirinal and the Lancellotti. He died in Rome.

BURBURE, Louis de **b.1837**
Born in Brussels, he was a Belgian painter of marines; the Rijksmuseum, Amsterdam, has a view of warships saluting off Briel in celebration of the tercentenary of its capture from the Spanish.

BURGESS, Arthur James Wetherall **1879-1957**
R.I., R.O.I., V.P.S.M.A.
Born in Bombala, New South Wales, on January 6th, 1879. He studied art in Sydney and, after he came to England in 1901, at St. Ives in Cornwall. He exhibited at the Royal Academy from 1904, and at the Royal Institute of Oil Painters, the Royal Institute of Painters in Watercolours and the Paris Salon.

He worked as an illustrator for the *Graphic, Illustrated London News* and the *Sphere,* and for the Australian Government in the First World War. He was a founder member of the Society of Marine Artists and its Vice-President. He died in London on April 16th, 1957.

PLATE: 637.

EXAMPLES: The National Maritime Museum, Greenwich (4): The Grand Lady and the Usherettes (which shows the liner Rangitata *with tugs in the Port of London during the Second World War); High Water at the Bar; The Brotherhood of Seamen (showing the* Glengyle *picking up survivors); a standard merchantman of the First World War. Library of New South Wales, Sydney (1): Last of the old* Nelson *1900.*

BURRELL, James

Quite a good quality marine artist working in the third quarter of the 19th century, in a similar style to Jock Wilson. Exhibited one painting at the Royal Academy in 1863 from an address in Covent Garden, London (not a marine).

PLATE: 568.

BURWOOD, G.V.

A British ship portraitist working in the last quarter of the 19th century. The National Maritime Museum, Greenwich, has a painting by him of a Lowestoft trawler dated 1892.

BUTLAND, G.W. **fl.1831-1843**

It is rather significant that this artist exhibited at both the Royal Academy and the British Institution between the above dates, which may mean that he was born about 1810 and died in 1843/4.

In style his paintings resemble rather coarse E.W. Cooke's, and one of them at the National Maritime Museum, Greenwich, bore a false Cooke signature, which was accepted for some years. From 1831 to 1836 he exhibited from London addresses, then from Greenhithe in Kent, and from 1841 from Fulham.

PLATE: 469.

EXAMPLES: The National Maritime Museum, Greenwich (5): portrait of the East Indiaman the Earl of Hardwick; *the East Indiaman* Owen Glendower; *the Russian fleet at Malta in 1827; a paddle steamer off the Tyne; a tilt boat.*

BUTLER, Gaspar

A Neapolitan painter of the first half of the 18th century. The National Maritime Museum, Greenwich, has a painting of Admiral Sir George Byng's fleet at Naples in 1718.

BUTTERSWORTH, James Edward **1817-1894**

Probably born in London in December 1817, he was the son and pupil of the painter Thomas Buttersworth (q.v.), following his father in his profession and in a fairly similar style. Brought up in a time of peace, he concerned himself with general shipping and yachting scenes, rather than battle pieces.

Between 1845 and 1847 he emigrated with his family to America. He settled in West Hoboken near New York, and also may have had a studio in Brooklyn. In 1850 he first exhibited at the American Art Union, and throughout the 1850s he painted for Nathaniel Currier, who engraved and published his works.

He died in West Hoboken, New Jersey, on March 2nd, 1894.

EXAMPLES: United States Naval Academy Museum, Annapolis (1). Bath Marine Museum, Maine (1). The Bostonian Society, Boston, Mass (1). The Washington County Museum of Fine Arts, Hagerstown (2). Montclair Art Museum (1). Mystic Seaport Inc. (11). Newark Museum, N.J. (1). The Yale Centre for British Art, New Haven, Conn. (1). The Mariners Museum, Newport News, Virginia (12). The Museum of the City of New York (3). The Atwater Kent Museum, Philadelphia (2). Portland Museum of Art, Maine (1). Rhode Island Museum of Art, Providence (1). Virginia Museum of Fine Arts, Richmond (1). The Peabody Museum of Salem (6). Staten Island Institute of Arts (1). The Butler Institute of American Art, Youngstown, Ohio (1).

BUTTERSWORTH, Thomas **1768-1842**

Born in the Isle of Wight, May 5th, 1768. A seaman painter, who enlisted aboard His Majesty's Receiving Ship *Enterprise,* moored off the Tower, on August 17th, 1795. On the 19th he joined the *Caroline,* a new frigate fitting out for sea at Deptford, and was rated an able seaman at age twenty-seven. The following November he was appointed a master-at-arms, and in 1800 a midshipman. That same year he was invalided at Minorca and sent home. Nothing more is known of his naval service, but the National Maritime Museum, Greenwich, has a number of large watercolours of the Battle of St. Vincent (1797) and of the subsequent inshore blockading squadron off Cadiz, done in such a way as to make this compiler believe he was there. There are also Mediterranean subjects dated 1800, 1799 and 1797, which must have been done out there.

Although he was already painting, his being invalided out of the Navy must have been the spur for him to become a professional artist. He only exhibited one painting at the Royal Academy, in 1813, of the *Ville de Paris* off the Tagus (when he was living in Kennington, London) and one painting, the Battle of Trafalgar, at the British Institution in 1825 (when he was living at Trafalgar Street, Walworth).

He was never a very good painter but the best examples of his work are reasonably well crafted and of course he well understood the ships he painted. He was also a prolific painter, which is why the dealers have made him so expensive, for they know that plenty more will come on the market.

Until recently it was supposed that he died about 1827, but a painting by him of Queen Victoria's visit to Edinburgh in 1842, and other evidence, seems to establish that he died in London in November, 1842.

PLATES: 300, 301, 302, 303.

EXAMPLES: The United States Naval Academy Museum, Annapolis (2): a pair of paintings of the action between the Serapis *and* Bonhomme Richard, *1779. National Maritime Museum, Greenwich (17): The inshore blockading squadron off Cadiz 1797; The Battle of Trafalgar 1805 (a pair); The* Seahorse *capturing the* Bader Zaffer *1808; The attack on the* Aurora *by pirates 1812; Capture of the* Gypsy, *1812; The* Shannon *capturing the* Chesapeake, *1813; The Capture of the* President; *The loss of the East Indiaman* Kent *by fire, 1825; the* Glasgow *steamship picking up survivors; The* Iris; *The* Ville de Paris; *The* Warrior; *A smuggler chased by a brig; A lugger chased by a Revenue cutter; A cutter going to the help of a ship aground; plus 27 watercolours, mostly of actions and mostly large. City Art Gallery, Plymouth (1): shipping off Plymouth. The Peabody Museum of Salem (1): shipping in the Solent; plus two watercolours, one being of the inshore blockading squadron off Cadiz in 1797. Mariners Museum, Newport News (2): British fleet leaving Lisbon; East Indiaman* London. *Library of New South Wales, Sydney (1): action between an English brig and a French brig. Maritime Museum, Venice (1): two American frigates and two cutters offshore.*

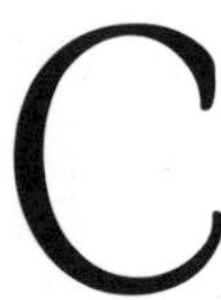

CABEL (KABEL), Adriaan van der **c.1631-1705**
Born at Rysewijck, near The Hague. He was a pupil of Jan van Goyen (q.v.). About 1656 he moved to Rome, where he stayed until 1668, adopting an Italian palette meanwhile. He then moved to Lyon, where he settled, dying there on January 16th, 1705. Though he painted marines, he was a general painter of landscapes, still-lifes, portraits and religious subjects. He also engraved.

PLATE: 87.

CALLANDER, Adam **fl.1780-1811**
This artist exhibited at the Royal Academy between 1780 and 1811, and at the British Institution from its first exhibition in 1806 to 1811. This indicates that he may have died in 1811/12, and that he may have been born about 1760. He exhibited from a London address in the Paddington area, and from 1783 from off Cavendish Square.

The National Maritime Museum, Greenwich, has a view of shipping off Madras, and another of St. Helena.

PLATE: 252.

CALLCOTT, Sir Augustus Wall R.A. **1779-1844**
Born on February 20th, 1779, in Kensington, London, where he also died. This artist was much admired in his lifetime, hence the knighthood in 1837, and was rated with Turner. He has now long ceased to be a household word. As a youth he trained as a musician and was for six years a chorister in Westminster Abbey; he then turned to painting and studied under Hoppner at the Royal Academy Schools to become a portrait painter. His first painting, hung at the Royal Academy in 1799, is a portrait and its success persuaded him to be a painter, but not of portraits. Thereafter nearly all his works were landscapes and coastal views, with a few genre pictures. He was elected an Associate in 1806 and a full Academician in 1809, exhibiting until the year of his death.

By contrast, when he began to exhibit at the British Institution, which he did from its first exhibition in 1806 until 1838, nearly all his exhibits are of genre subjects. In 1844, at the end of his life, he was appointed Conservator of the Royal Pictures.

EXAMPLES (marines only): National Maritime Museum, Greenwich (1): two men in a fishing boat. Tate Gallery, London (1): a coast scene. City Art Gallery, Manchester (2): view on the Thames; river scene with shipping; also a watercolour of the Pool of London. Nottingham (1): a river with shipping.

CALLCOTT, William James **fl.1844-1896**
These are the years between which he exhibited views and marines at the Royal Academy. He also exhibited at the British Institution in 1851 and 1852, also at Suffolk Street and the New Watercolour Society. He was an unsuccessful candidate for the New Watercolour Society in 1856, 1868 and 1874. There is an affinity with James Webb (q.v.) in his treatment and choice of subjects, but not of his quality.

CALLOW, H.
A British ship portraitist working in the third quarter of the 19th century. The National Maritime Museum, Greenwich, has a painting by him of the ship *Maidstone* in the China Seas, dated 1869.

PLATE: 569.

CALLOW, John A.O.W.C.S. **1822-1878**
Born on July 19th, 1822, in Greenwich, he was the younger brother and pupil of William (q.v.), and joined him in Paris in 1833. He returned and lived with his brother in Charlotte Street in 1844, dying in London on April 15th, 1878.

His exhibition work was curiously brief. He first exhibited at the Royal Academy in 1844, and then in 1854 to 1856, and at the British Institution from 1851 to 1855. He painted mainly in watercolours and taught drawing at Addiscombe Military Academy and the Royal Military Academy at Woolwich. He was an Associate of the Old Watercolour Society, and also exhibited at the Suffolk Street Galleries and the New Watercolour Society.

The Mariners Museum, Newport News, has a painting by him called "Calm Day, Portsmouth", the Northampton Art Gallery has a large oil painting by him of shipping in a breeze off Calais, and the City of York Art Gallery has "Fresh Breeze".

CALLOW, William **1812-1908**
Born in Greenwich on July 28th, 1812. At the age of sixteen or seventeen he went to Paris and studied under the animal painter Newton Fielding. Though only 19 he became teacher to the children of King Louis Philippe in 1831 as a result of his exhibits in the Paris Salon that year. He retained the post for seven years.

He travelled in Italy and Switzerland and returned to England with his brother and pupil, John (q.v.), in 1841. He was elected a member of the Old Watercolour Society in that year and later, from 1865 to 1870, was its secretary. In 1855 he moved to Great Missenden in Buckinghamshire, where he died on February 20th, 1908. He first exhibited at the Royal Academy in 1850 and thereafter most years to 1876. He exhibited at the British Institution from 1848 to 1867, missing only one year, 1855. He also exhibited at the New Watercolour Society and the Suffolk Street Galleries.

There is a biography of him by H.M. Cundall (1908), and one in preparation by Mrs. Jan Reynolds.

EXAMPLES: Birmingham Art Gallery (1). Bristol Art Gallery (2 watercolours). National Gallery, Dublin (3 watercolours). National Maritime Museum, Greenwich (2 watercolours). Tate Gallery (2): Richmond Castle; Grand Canal, Venice; also an album of 26 drawings done on the Continent. Victoria and Albert Museum (2 watercolours). Wallace Collection (1): Entering Harbour; also 12 watercolours. Reading Art Gallery (1): port scene.

CALVERT, Frederick **fl.1815-1844**

He was a native of Cork, who first exhibited at the Dublin Society of Artists and the Hibernian Society in 1815. He moved to London and in 1827, from an address in Pall Mall, exhibited a view of Dover Castle and one of Broughton Castle. He also exhibited at Suffolk Street.

In 1830 he published *Picturesque Views of Staffordshire and Shropshire,* and he also worked for the *Archaeological Journal.* The Victoria and Albert Museum and the British Museum hold watercolours by him, there is a view of Greenwich in oils at the National Maritime Museum, Greenwich, and the Walker Art Gallery, Liverpool, has an oil painting of shipping on the Mersey.

PLATE: 384.

CAMMILLIERI, Nicholas

Working in the second quarter of the 19th century, he was a Maltese ship portraitist who was clearly strongly influenced by the work of the Roux family (q.v.).

EXAMPLES: National Maritime Museum, Greenwich (5 ship portraits). Danish Maritime Museum, Kronborg Castle (3). Mariners Museum, Newport News, Virginia (4): Capture of the cutter Swift *by the xebec* Esperance, *1809; a United States naval squadron in the Mediterranean in 1839; U.S.S.* Constitution; *the brig* L'Aigle.

CAPELLE, Jan van de **1624-1679**

He was born in Amsterdam and died there on December 22nd, 1679. Although Capelle has for long been by far the most expensive of the Dutch marine painters, and so perhaps the most admired, he was a wealthy businessman who himself painted for pleasure. He is said to have been self-taught, but this seems unlikely, and it is highly probable that his friendship with de Vlieger (a man a quarter of a century older than him) involved a measure of tuition. He was fortunate that he grew up at a time when the Dutch school was at its apogee, a position to which he added considerable reinforcement. Unlike his great contemporary and fellow pupil of de Vlieger, Willem van de Velde the younger (q.v.), he was not a committed ship enthusiast, rather he perfected a style which produced the most wonderfully mystical, atmospheric calms, often in compositions crowded with small craft.

He was a major art collector in his time, and left a vast fortune to his seven children.

PLATES: 107, 108, 109.

EXAMPLES: Rijksmuseum, Amsterdam (3): two calms and a winter scene. Cannon Hall, Barnsley (1): River scene with ships becalmed. Barber Institute, Birmingham (1): Boats in a ruffled sea. Beziers (1). Musées Royaux des Beaux-Arts, Brussels (1): calm. Arts Institute, Chicago (1): calm. Wallraf Richartz-Museum, Cologne (1): calm. Glasgow Museum and Art Gallery (1): calm. National Maritime Museum, Greenwich (1 attributed). Musée de Lille (1). Kenwood House, London (1): calm. National Gallery, London (8): view of Owerschie and calms. City Art Gallery, Manchester (2): shipping in a calm; shipping off-shore in a calm. Frick Collection, New York (1). Metropolitan Museum, New York (1). Art Gallery, Rochester, New Zealand (1): calm. Boymans Museum, Rotterdam (1): calm. Nationalmuseum, Stockholm (1): shipping and a jetty. Toledo Museum of Art, Ohio (3). Kunsthistorisches Museum, Vienna (1): beach scene.

CARLEBUR, François, Junior **1821-1893**

Born and died in Dordrecht. He was self-taught, and originally an early photographer. He travelled and worked for a time in England and Scotland and exhibited at The Hague between 1853 and 1884.

EXAMPLES: Scheepvaart Museum, Amsterdam (1 marine sketch). Dordrecht Museum (1): view of Aberdeen. Mr. Simon van Gijn Museum, Dordrecht (1): merchantmen at sea. Dordrecht Archives (watercolours).

CARLEVARIS, Luca **1665-1731**
(called Casanobio, and also Luca de la Zenobio)

Born in Udine and died in Venice. The name Luca de la Zenobio refers to the name of his patrons. He was mainly a painter of Venetian and coastal scenes of high quality. In them the figures, animals and buildings have as much importance as the ships.

EXAMPLES: Gemäldegalerie, Darmstadt (1): Venetian scene. Gemäldegalerie, Dresden (1): reception of Austrian Ambassador at Venice.

CARMICHAEL, John Wilson **1800-1868**

Born in Newcastle-upon-Tyne, January 8th, 1800; he was christened John, not James, as some authorities have asserted. He was the son of a ship's carpenter and was apprenticed to a shipbuilder, and may have gone to sea. Hardly surprisingly, ships became his prime interest.

He may have been a pupil of the landscape artist, Thomas Miles Richardson, senior, who was a friend and had a studio adjoining Carmichael's in Blackett Street, Newcastle, where he had set up in 1823. It has been suggested that they collaborated in some of their works. Although Carmichael was never to become a great painter, he was certainly superior to his local contemporaries, such as the ship portraitist John Scott (q.v.), and so had a considerable success.

He exhibited at the Royal Academy from 1835 to 1859, and at the British Institution from 1846 to 1862. His exhibits there for the year 1847 give a London address, so he had moved from Newcastle that year or late in 1846. In 1854 the *Illustrated London News* employed him as their artist in the field in the Baltic theatre of what is commonly called the Crimean War. He therefore accompanied the Baltic fleet for the summer and again in 1855. He also travelled and painted in Europe.

The death of his son in 1862 affected him deeply and he never exhibited again, retiring to Scarborough, where he gave up painting in 1865, dying there on May 2nd, 1868. As an artist he belongs to the circle of Clarkson Stanfield (q.v.) and Edward William Cooke (q.v.) and at his best is the equal of Stanfield.

PLATES: 463, 464.

EXAMPLES (marines only): Shipley Art Gallery, Gateshead (6): haybarges and craft beating to Windward; shipping off a coast; a calm off Naples; Mediterranean craft off a coast; two merchantmen off a rocky coast; a frigate in a breeze; National Maritime Museum, Greenwich (4): The Bombardment of Swaeborg, 1855; two survey ships in the Antarctic and at anchor off a South Seas Island (a pair); a whaler in the Straits of Magellan. Ferens Art Gallery, Hull (1). Temple Newsam House, Leeds (1): a brig running into a harbour. Liverpool Museum (1). Laing Art Gallery, Newcastle (14): coastal scene with shipping and a windmill; off Staithes on the Yorkshire coast; off Leith; the entrance to Portsmouth Harbour; a rocky coast; a Dutch smack in a breeze; a dismasted ship scudding in a gale; Sunderland old pier and lighthouse in a gale; the Ann *of Hull at Newcastle; a Dutch boat becalmed off North Shields; Dutch vessels in a breeze; off Redcar; a river mouth; a ship close hauled in a stiff breeze. Nottingham Museum and Art Gallery (2): A frigate and a two-decker in the Mediterranean; fishing boats off North Yarmouth. Harris Museum, Preston (1): seascape. Peabody Museum of Salem (1): Opening of Sunderland Docks. South Shields Museum (6): Troops embarking on a P. & O. liner for India, 1853; Opening of Tyne Docks, 1859; The entrance to the Tyne; also another; The barque* Darius *off the Tyne; The brig* Elsewick *in two positions off the Tyne. Sunderland Art Gallery (7): A Keel close hauled; Two-deckers becalmed; A Dutch vessel with a frigate; a calm off Whitby; A brig off Calshot Castle; Sunderland Harbour in 1830; Sunderland Harbour 1864. City of York Art Gallery (5): Robin Hood's Bay; Whale Fishing; Action between* La Nymphe *and the* Cleopatra *1793; Queen Victoria's Arrival at Edinburgh in 1842; ships beating off a lee shore.*

CARTER, Henry Barlow **1803-1868**

Born in Scarborough. As a youth he joined the Royal Navy and was painting while still in the service. He exhibited at the Royal Academy between 1827 and 1830 while at Plymouth. He left the service, moved to Hull and married, becoming a master at the art school there. Later he moved back to his native Scarborough, then, after a brief sojourn in Bath, to Torquay where he died.

He was an exact contemporary of his fellow Yorkshire marine painter George Chambers and was strongly influenced by John Varley and the early watercolourists.

Examples of his work can be found at the Ferens Art Gallery, Hull; the British Museum and Victoria and Albert Museum; the Maidstone Art Gallery; City Art Gallery, Plymouth; City Art Gallery, Wakefield; Whitby Museum and Art Gallery; City Art Gallery, York and the Scarborough Art Gallery which has by far the largest collection.

CARTER, Peter **b.1920**

Born in London. Apprenticed as an engineer, and served in the Army during the Second World War. Moved to Devon from London in 1962 to study marine painting. Elected a member of the Royal Society of Marine Artists in 1969.

EXAMPLES: National Maritime Museum, Greenwich (1 watercolour — on loan): the Brixham trawler Leon Jeannine, *with another alongside.*

CARVILLE, J.E.

An American ship portraitist working in Port Arthur, Texas, in the first quarter of the 20th century. The Maritime Museum at Bergen has a portrait of the steamer *Caloric,* built in 1914.

PLATE: 635.

CASANOBIO *see* **CARLEVARIS, Luca**

CASANOVA, Francesco Giuseppe **1727-1802**

Born of Italian parents in London, he was the younger brother of the celebrated adventurer and libertine, Giovanni Casanova. His parents sent him as a youth to Venice, where he became the pupil of Guardi, and afterwards to Florence where he was taught to paint battle pieces by Simonini. He visited Paris in 1751 and in the following year settled in Dresden, where he remained for six years before returning to Paris, where he was admitted to the Académie Royale in 1763. In 1783 he went to Vienna, where Catherine the Great of Russia employed him to paint a series commemorating the victories of Potemkin over the Turks.

One of his pupils was Philippe de Lotherbourg (q.v.). He died at Bruhl near Vienna on July 8th, 1802. His battle pieces and landscapes are represented in a number of European galleries but not, apparently any of his marines.

CASSINELLI, H.

A French ship portraitist working in Le Havre in the middle of the 19th century. The Peabody Museum, Salem, has two watercolours.

PLATE: 415.

CASTRO, Lorenzo A.

Flourished in the third quarter of the 17th century. Probably the L.A. Castro who was master of the Lucas Guild at Antwerp in 1664-65, and was presumably a descendant of a Spaniard who had settled in the Spanish Netherlands.

Most of his pictures are of Mediterranean port scenes and he was clearly fond of galleys, which he portrays with a jewel-like elegance. His palette is reminiscent of the work of the Willaerts family (q.v.), but without their stylised treatment of water.

From the number of his works in England, compared to other places, it seems likely that he worked in England for a time, especially since the portrait of the *Sovereign of the Seas* at Great Parham, copied from the Payne engraving, must have been an English commission.

PLATE: 127.

EXAMPLES: Dulwich College Picture Gallery, London (5 plus one attributed): three Mediterranean port scenes; a Dutch flagship in the Zuider Zee; an action between the Dutch and Barbary corsairs; if the one of shipping at Amsterdam is by Castro, then it is a copy of an Abraham Storck. Museum Gdansk (on loan from National Museum at Posnan) (1): Mediterranean harbour scene. National Maritime Museum, Greenwich (3): Battle of Actium signed '1672 Lorenzo A. Castro, F.C.'; Anglo-Barbary action with a sinking galley in the foreground; Mediterranean port scene. Museum, Ipswich (1): shipping off a jetty. Gallery of Academy of Fine Arts, Vienna (1 attributed): Mediterranean port scene.

CASTRO, Sebastian D.

Flourished in the second and third quarters of the 17th century. He was an Antwerp painter with a style so close to Andries van Eertvelt (q.v.) that his paintings have been held in collections as by that master, and are usually sold as Eertvelt's unless clearly signed. The inference is that he was at least a pupil of Eertvelt and perhaps a collaborator.

There is a good example in the Mariners Museum at Newport News, Virginia, which appears to be signed 'D. Caster' but this may be due to a former restoration. There are unsigned examples at the National Maritime Museum, Greenwich.

PLATES: 27, 28.

CEDERGREN, Per Vilhelm **1823-1896**

He was born and died in Stockholm. He was a pupil at the Academy there in 1844 and 1845, and he also studied abroad. From 1872 he had the post of official artist to the Ministry of Marine. The example of his work at the National Maritime Museum, Stockholm, though admittedly early, suggests a fairly modest talent.

PLATE: 353.

CHALON, John James R.A. **1778-1854**

This artist was more a landscape and genre artist but is included for his admirable painting of the *Bellerophon* at Plymouth in 1815, with Napoleon aboard; he also did some marines.

Born on March 27th, 1778, in Geneva, he was of a French protestant family who had fled France. In 1796 he joined the Royal Academy Schools of Art and he first exhibited at the Royal Academy in 1801, was elected an Associate in 1827 and a full Academician in 1841. He also exhibited at the British Institution from 1808 to 1843, and at the Old Watercolour Society. Personally he was almost invariably linked with his brother, A.E. Chalon, R.A.; both were founders and leading lights of the Sketching Society, 1808-1851. He died in London on November 4th, 1854.

COLOUR PLATE: XIX.

CHAMBERLAIN, Trevor **b.1933**
R.O.I., R.S.M.A., N.S.

Born in Hertford, he is a self-taught painter who was an architectural assistant until 1964, when he made painting his profession. He paints landscapes and urban scenes, as well as marines, and has held one-man shows at the Ash Barn Gallery, Petersfield, 1971 and 1975, the Munnings Gallery, Hertford, 1977, and the Clarges Gallery, London, 1977. He has also exhibited at joint exhibitions in Welwyn Garden City, Bromley, Petersfield and Hertford between 1967 and 1978.

He is a member of the Royal Institute of Oil Painters, the Royal Society of Marine Artists (elected 1970), the National Society of Painters, Sculptors and Printmakers, and the Wapping Group of Artists. In 1976 he won the Lord Mayor of London's Art Award.

PLATE: 688.

CHAMBERS, George, Senior **1803-1840**

Born in Whitby; his father was a sailor and his mother let lodgings. He went to a local school which charged a penny per week. As his mother could not afford twopence for George and his elder brother, John, only one brother would attend each week, taking it by turns. Even then he had to leave and go to work at the age of eight. At the age of ten he shipped aboard an uncle's Humber keel called the *Experiment*. He was so small a child that he slept in one of his uncle's seaboots. At twelve his father got his firm to take him as an apprentice in the brig *Equity,* under Captain Storr.

It was not a hopeful start for a painter, but apparently the urge to draw and paint was strong in him even at this time. Captain Storr seemed sympathetic to the idea of releasing him from his indenture to be a painter but procrastinated. One day when the *Equity* was in London docks he was invited aboard the *Sovereign* alongside and during a drinking bout Captain Braithwaite extracted a promise from him that he would arrange to let Chambers go. Fortunately Chambers had a letter from his mother saying that she could find him a place in a painter's shop, and this was taken as the necessary parental consent. Messrs. Chapman, the brig's owners, cancelled his indentures and Chambers was free in London to follow his chosen profession.

In fact, he immediately returned to Whitby and took a job in a house and ship painter's business run by a widow called Irvin. His skill at lettering and decoration of the hulls of visiting ships was such, that some of the captains brought him sketches of their ships among icebergs and got Chambers to make finished pictures on millboard. As commissions from shipmasters increased, he took lessons from a Whitby drawing master called Bird, the only instruction he ever had.

About 1820, after his mother's death, and "sick and tired" of Whitby he took ship to London, where he boarded with a married sister. He urgently needed a patron, and one happily appeared in Christopher Crawford, a Whitby man and ex-collier who kept the Waterman's Arms at Wapping, the chief haunt of the colliers' crews, having a room put aside for owners, another for captains and another for the sailors. Chambers' first work was of Whitby Beach. One of the sailors having told Crawford of Chambers' talents as a painter, the latter sought him out and commissioned a view of Whitby (including vessels that he had served in) to hang in the owners' room, known as the House of Lords.

This was so well received that more commissions came his way, beginning with one from Mr. Chapman, to whose firm he had previously been apprenticed. These early commissions were managed by Crawford, with the declared intention of keeping Chambers out of the clutches of the dealers. Although Chambers' beginnings are entirely concerned with merchantmen, it is by his naval commissions that he is most remembered. This came about after Captain the Hon. Thomas Capel, R.N., saw two of his pictures in the window of Mr. Smart, the picture framer in Greek Street, and recognised their nautical expertise as well as their quality. He purchased them and recommended Chambers to his aristocratic naval friends, such as Lord Mark Kerr, who introduced him to Mr. Carpenter, the Bond Street picture dealer. Chambers soon moved into apartments in Alfred Street, off Bedford Square. Mr. Carpenter showed him some Boningtons he had and said to Chambers that if he could do as well he would hang one up beside them; in a short time he did so.

Chambers could be said really to have arrived when King William IV purchased a picture of the opening of the new London Bridge, which pinpoints the date of his success as 1831. There followed important commissions culminating in the great painting of the "Bombardment of Algiers" for the Greenwich Hospital Gallery in 1836.

Chambers visited Holland twice during his life, but sadly the career of the most promising marine painter of his generation was to be brought to an end by tuberculosis. In August 1840 he took the *Dart* packet to Madeira in a last bid to regain his health, but he would not stay and came back with her to die a few weeks later in Brighton on October 28th, 1840.

Besides the quality and nautical expertise that made the work of George Chambers so admirable, there is the important matter of his use of perspective. It is doubtful that he ever heard of isometric perspective, as used by the van de Veldes (qq.v.) and their 18th century followers. He used viewer's perspective, which gave his pictures an immediacy and impact that was impossible using isometric perspective.

He exhibited at the British Institution from 1827 to 1840. He also exhibited at the Royal Academy, but only three pictures, in 1828, 1829 and 1839, and at the Old Watercolour Society. In 1836 he was elected a member of the Royal Society of Painters in Watercolours. In 1841 his friend, John Watkins, published his *Life and Career of George Chambers* — a most informative account despite its partisan tone and the rather dubious character of the author.

PLATES: 421, 422, 423, 424, 425; COLOUR PLATE: XXI.

EXAMPLES: Birmingham Art Gallery (1): Tilbury Fort. Ferens Art Gallery, Hull (1): shipping off Greenwich. National Maritime Museum, Greenwich (11): Battle of La Hogue 1692 (after Benjamin West); Capture of Porto Bello 1739 (after Samuel Scott); Battle of Camperdown 1797; Battle of Trafalgar 1805 (after Clarkson Stanfield); Bombardment of Algiers 1816 and the oil sketch for it; the Britannia *entering Portsmouth; a Dutch fishing vessel and other shipping; a fresh breeze off Cowes, a brig leaving Dover; Greenwich Hospital. Tate Gallery, London (1): Dutch East Indiaman weighing anchor. Laing Art Gallery, Newcastle-on-Tyne (1): Greenwich Hospital (study for the picture at Greenwich). Rotherham Art Gallery (1). Seattle Gallery of Art (1): Dutch barges going to market. Graves Art Gallery, Sheffield (1). Wisbech Museum, Cambridgeshire (2): pair of Houses of Parliament and the Port of London. York Art Gallery (1).*

CHAMBERS, George, Junior **b.1830**

Born in London, he was a son of George senior (q.v.), and exhibited at the Royal Academy between 1850 and 1861, and at the British Institution from 1848 to 1862. There is at Greenwich a watercolour by him of Cannon Street Station, so he was alive at least until 1867. The donor of this and another watercolour claimed that Chambers had given them to his father in settlement of a debt and that his aunt had been governess to the Chambers' children in Venezuela, where Chambers worked as an engineer. He further claimed that Chambers went to work for Val de Travers in Trinidad about 1900, and was killed in a riot. No substantiation of this statement has been forthcoming.

Chambers painted pleasing oil sketches of the Thames, etc, with a rather fluid medium.

PLATE: 520.

EXAMPLES: National Maritime Museum, Greenwich (2): the Bellot Memorial at Greenwich Hospital; the Isabel *lying off Deptford.*

CHAMBERS, Thomas **b.1815-aft.1866**

English born, he emigrated to America about 1832, working first in New York, then in Boston and Albany. He painted portraits, marines, landscapes and sea battles. He had a stylised, dramatic manner.

CHAMBERS, William **b.1815**

Born on January 23rd, 1815, he was a younger brother of George Chambers senior (q.v.) and one of seven. He took up painting ship portraits, more in the style of Huggins (q.v.) than his brother. George Chambers mentions him as being a painter in a letter of 1837. None of his work is in public collections.

The compiler has a painting by him, signed "W. Chambers" of the *Dart* packet, based either on the drawing George Chambers made of her on that last voyage to Madeira, or from the stipple of it in John Watkins' biography.

CHAPMAN, Carlton Theodore **1860-1926**

Born in New London, Ohio. He was a pupil at the National Academy and Art Students' League in New York, and afterwards at the Académie Julian in Paris. He was a member of the American Society of Artists and exhibited in New York, Philadelphia and at the International Exhibition at Chicago in 1893. He died in New York.

The Brooklyn Museum has a painting called "A Calm in Gloucester Harbour", and the Navy Memorial Museum in Washington a painting "Navy Yard".

CHAPMAN, Conrad Wise

Born in Rome, an American who was painting views of Charleston Harbour around the time of the American Civil War.

CHAPPELL, Reuben **1870-1940**

A ship portraitist who worked first in Goole, where he had been born, and then from 1904 at Par in Cornwall, a move he made for his health. He died there in 1940.

He painted ship portraits mainly of coastal craft. In 1924 he suffered a stroke which affected his sight and curtailed his output.

The Maritime Museum, Greenwich, has two portraits in oils and eight in watercolours, and there is at least one ship portrait by him in the Maritime Museum at Kronborg Castle.

PLATE: 609.

CHAPURAT, Aristide

A French ship portraitist working at Cette in the middle of the 19th century. The Peabody Museum of Salem has a watercolour dated 1849.

CHIDGEY, Captain Thomas **1855-1926**

A native of Watchet in Somerset, Captain Chidgey spent his working life working in West Country coastal craft. When he retired from the sea in 1919 he indulged a latent talent for painting, and spent his last years painting portraits of the sailing coastal craft that had been his life.

The National Maritime Museum, Greenwich, has a painting of a trading schooner by him.

CHUNG, ?W.E.

Chinese ship portraitist of the middle of the 19th century, working in Hong Kong. The Peabody Museum of Salem has one painting by him.

CHURCH, Frederick Edwin **1826-1900**
Born in Hartford, Connecticut, died in New York. In 1844 he became a pupil of Thomas Coles, who gave him his grounding in execution and style. This was Church's springboard to a much more imaginative and heroic approach to painting, which was inspired to a large extent by the works of Turner.

He liked to project his art towards a large public, with gallery sized paintings.

Like a number of his generation of American painters he was an avid traveller, both in the Americas and in Europe. There are good examples at the Wadsworth Atheneum, Hartford, Connecticut.

PLATE: 508.

CLAESSEN, Cornelisz **fl.c.1620**
It seems little is known of this artist, other than what can be deduced from his signed work, which is so like the style of Hendrik Cornelisz Vroom (q.v.) that it can be assumed that he was a contemporary and probably a pupil of his, living and working in Antwerp, and also an associate of Anthonisz (q.v.) and Eertvelt (q.v.)

At the National Maritime Museum, Greenwich, there is a panel of Dutch ships running before the wind, signed "Cornelis Claessen, fe.".

CLARK, C.
A British ship portraitist working in the second quarter of the 19th century. The Peabody Museum, Salem, has an oil by him of fairly high quality, dated 1833.

CLARK, C. Myron **1876-1925**
An American painter of sailing ship scenes. The Peabody Museum of Salem, has five oils, three of the U.S.S. *Constitution*.

CLARK, William **1803-1883**
Born in Greenock, Strathclyde, on June 26th, 1803. He was the son of a seaman, and grew up to become a house painter. His interest in ships and his desire to paint pictures resulted in his becoming a ship portraitist of good quality. He worked all his life in Greenock, dying there on November 11th, 1883.

The National Maritime Museum, Greenwich, has seven ship portraits and Liverpool Museum at least one. The National Library of Australia, Canberra (Rex Nan Kivell Collection) has a ship portrait, and the Peabody Museum of Salem has a view of Greenock dated 1830.

PLATE: 426.

CLAUDE (le) Lorraine *see* **GELLÉE, Claude**

CLAUSEN, C.
A Danish ship portraitist working at Elsinor in the second quarter of the 19th century. The Peabody Museum of Salem has four watercolours by him, all of American ships.

CLAYS, Paul-Jean **1819-1900**
Born in Bruges on November 27th, 1819, he ran away to sea from his boarding school in Boulogne. While working in the French coastal trade he discovered a talent for drawing, so left the sea for Paris where he became a pupil of Baron Gudin (q.v.) and Horace Vernet. After training he returned first to Bruges, before settling in Brussels. In 1867 he was made Chevalier of the Legion of Honour. He died in Brussels on February 10th, 1900.

Like so many marine painters of his generation his style strongly recalls the masters of the 17th century, and his subjects were also often of that period.

PLATE: 558.

EXAMPLES: Musées des Beaux Arts, Antwerp (3): view near Dordrecht in stormy weather; the Port of Dordrecht; the River Escaut on a still day. Stedlijk Museum voor Schone Kunsten, Bruges: three marines. Musée Royaux des Beaux Arts de Belgique, Brussels (4): the coast at Ostend; the Port of Antwerp; the River Escaut on a calm day; a wreck on the coast of Shetland. Hamburger Kunsthalle: two marines. Leicester Museums and Art Gallery (2): a ship saluting; a calm day on the Kel near Dordrecht. The National Gallery, London (3): the beach at Ault; a marine; a calm. Musées des Beaux Arts, Liège (1): a marine. Musée des Beaux Arts de la Ville de Mons (1): the return of the fishing fleet. Bayrische Staatsgemaldesammlungen, Munich (1): a seascape. Metropolitan Museum, New York (1): the celebration of the liberation of Escaut in 1863. Graves Art Gallery, Sheffield (3): Dutch fishing boats; a calm; a storm.

CLAYTON, Captain Matthew Thomas **1831-aft.1919**
Born in Selsey, Sussex. In 1863 he was captain of the *City of Brisbane* paddle liner. He intended to settle in Sydney, but went to Auckland, New Zealand, in 1864 as marine surveyor to the New Zealand Insurance Company, a post he held until 1902. He died in New Zealand sometime after 1919. He painted marines and historical scenes and was a self-taught artist.

EXAMPLES: The Auckland City Art Gallery (6): The Resolution*; Captain James Cook and* Adventure *off Cape Palliser in 1773; The ship* True Briton *off Cape Horn passing ice; The* Tangariro *; an unidentified vessel in heavy seas; The landing of Lieutenant Governor William Hobson from H.M.S.* Herald *at Waitangi on February 5th, 1840, for the signing of the Treaty.*

CLEVELEY, John, the Elder **c.1712-1777**
Born in Southwark, London; his father was a joiner and young Cleveley was apprenticed to another, Thomas Miller, in 1726, and later worked in the Royal Dockyard at Deptford, where he settled, dying there on May 21st, 1777. Where then, and from whom did he learn his considerable skills as a painter? One explanation could be that following the scandal of the cost of the carved decorations on the *Royal Sovereign* of 1701, the Admiralty decreed in 1704 that only the head and stern galleries of ships could have carved decorations, while the rest of the decorations must be in paint. Thus many woodcarvers were paid off in the Royal dockyards, and decorative painters taken on to paint the trophies of arms, classical figures, chariots, etc. which adorned the sides of most ships from head to stern at the level of the upper-deck gunwales and above. John Cleveley could have learnt to paint from one or some of these dockyard painters, and by his own genius refined his work to easel painting.

Surviving examples date from the late 1740s, so it does not seem that he took up painting seriously until he was in his thirties. From about 1747 until the middle 1750s he painted a series of launches of ships at Deptford, of high quality and closely observed, so closely that the experienced eye can roughly date them from the size of the tree growing beside the Master Shipwright's house. He also painted ship portraits, a few battle pieces and royal occasions, such as the review at Spithead in 1773, which he attended, and visited and painted in East Anglia. Apparently he did not feel he could give up his dockyard appointment, for in the year after his death in 1778, he is referred to in an administration order as "carpenter, belonging to His Majesty's ship *Victory* in the pay of His Mjs Navy." He did not, however, go to sea in her, since she did not commission until after his death, but he must have been attached to her in some way.

A weakness of Cleveley's output was a tendency to repeat a successful composition, with the result that a number of almost identical paintings of East Indiamen merely have different names on their sterns.

He had three sons: James became a ship's carpenter and was the *Resolution's* carpenter on Cook's third voyage. He never was an artist in the formal sense, but apparently did bring back from that voyage some competent drawings, from which his brother John made finished drawings which were then engraved.

The said John and his twin brother Robert (qq.v.), were born in 1747 and were presumably younger than James.

PLATES: 203, 204, 205, 206; COLOUR PLATE: XIII.

EXAMPLES: Glasgow City Art Gallery (1): a Thames scene. National Maritime Museum, Greenwich (16): Forest's *action off Cape Francois, 1757; the royal yacht* Royal Caroline; *the East Indiaman* Princess Royal; *the loss of the* Luxborough *galley in 1727 and the escape of some of the crew (a set of six pictures); the* Buckingham *on the stocks 1752; the* Royal George *off Deptford; the* St. Albans *floating out at Deptford; a ship on the stocks at Deptford; a sixth rate on the stocks; a sixth rate launched on the Orwell, near Ipswich; a brigantine. Yale Centre for British Art, New Haven, Conn. (1): a launch at Deptford with an East Indiaman lying off.*

CLEVELEY, John, the Younger **1747-1786**

Born at Deptford on Christmas Day, 1747, he was one of a pair of twins born to John Cleveley (q.v.); the other was Robert (q.v.). He followed his father into the Royal Dockyard at Deptford, where he trained as a shipwright. At the same time he shared his father's interest in painting, and became his pupil, and also took lessons from Paul Sandby (q.v.) at Woolwich.

The fact that his father was an established artist evidently helped the artistic side of his career, for, having exhibited two drawings at the Society of Artists Exhibition as early as 1767 and three drawings at the Royal Academy Exhibition in 1770, he was chosen as draughtsman to a Royal Society expedition to Iceland in 1772. On his return he exhibited two Icelandic views at the Royal Academy in 1773.

The entry in Graves's dictionary of Academy exhibitors is misleading, as the work of father and son has been combined. Thus, in the 1774 Royal Academy exhibition there are two paintings listed; one of George III's review of the fleet at Spithead on June 22nd, 1773, and one of the *Racehorse* and *Carcass* in the ice at Spitsbergen. The latter is of the Royal Society sponsored expedition under Captain Phipps to try and sail to the North Pole, which sailed on June 3rd, 1773, with John Junior aboard. The review therefore must have been covered by John the Elder.

In 1777, 1778 and 1779 John Junior exhibited views of Balem Castle at the mouth of the Tagus, so it looks as if he went on a voyage there and to Lisbon in 1776-77. He died on June 25th, 1786, probably in Pimlico, London.

His style is close to his father's, but in signed works he used a J as the initial, whereas his father used an I.

Birmingham City Art Gallery has a painting and the National Maritime Museum, Greenwich, has a small oil "The floating out of the *Alexander* at Deptford in 1778", and several watercolours, including three of the *Racehorse* and *Carcass* on Captain Phipps's expedition in 1773.

CLEVELEY, Robert **1747-1809**

Twin brother of John Junior (q.v.), he also went into the Royal Dockyard at Deptford, a place in which his father had influence, and became a caulker. Not surprisingly he did not care for it, and was apparently a fastidious lad, for he is said to have been the butt of his workmates for working in gloves.

In 1770 he volunteered into the Royal Navy as a clerk, and served as Captain William Locker's clerk in the *Thames* until 1773, when Captain George Vandeput took over command, and Robert followed him to the *Asia,* and so went to the North American and West Indies stations until discharged on her return in 1777.

His ambition was to be a painter, and as his brother John was the pupil of his father and Paul Sandby (q.v.), then it is fair to assume that Robert was too. Whereas his brother John went in for voyages of discovery, Robert took up battles, since this was a profitable line, during the American War of Independence. The profit lay in getting commissions for paintings that were to be engraved, and these engravings of British victories were best sellers with the public. This was also an area where important patronage could be sought and Robert, who had first exhibited at the Royal Academy in 1780, showed two paintings in 1790, on the subject of the Duke of Clarence's public engagements; he was appointed Draughtsman to His Royal Highness the following year. This connection must have been instrumental to his appointment as Marine Painter to the Prince Regent.

His work is not very like that of his father and brother, being more atmospheric and in tune with the later trends of the 18th century. He died in Dover on September 28th, 1809.

PLATES: 269, 270.

EXAMPLES: National Maritime Museum, Greenwich (4): a small view of the fleet at Spithead saluting King George III at his review in 1793; a pair of the Battle of St. Vincent 1797; a view of Deptford; also numerous drawings. The Laing Art Gallery, Newcastle (1).

CLIFFORD, Henry

He was assistant chief engineer of the cable laying aboard H.M.S. *Agamemnon* when she laid the first trans-Atlantic cable in 1857-58, and chief engineer aboard the *Great Eastern* when she laid the next trans-Atlantic cable in 1865-66. From 1864 to 1894 he was chief engineer to the Telegraph Construction and Maintenance Company.

The National Maritime Museum, Greenwich, has four competent paintings by him of the *Great Eastern* during her cable laying operations.

CLINT, Alfred **1807-1883**
Born and died in London. He was the son and pupil of George Clint, A.R.A. He first exhibited at the British Institution in 1828, and at the Royal Academy the following year. Most of his exhibits were coastal scenes and of high quality. He last exhibited at the British Institution in 1852, and at the Royal Academy in 1871.

He also exhibited with the Society of British Artists and was its secretary from 1858, and its president from 1870.

PLATE: 461.

COBB, Charles David P.R.S.M.A., R.O.I. **b.1921**
Born in Bromley, Kent, on May 13th, 1921. He attended the naval school, Pangbourne College, then went to Cambridge University on an engineering course. In 1940 he began war service in the Royal Navy and from 1943 to 1945 commanded motor torpedo boats. In 1946 he set up as a self-taught painter, living in a yacht at Newlyn. He was elected to the Society of Marine Artists in 1948 and is its president, elected in 1979. He signs his work "David Cobb". At the time of writing he is engaged in painting a set of some forty or fifty works of the naval side of the Second World War for the Royal Naval Museum, Portsmouth.

PLATES: 674, 675.

EXAMPLES: National Maritime Museum, Greenwich (6): The Cutty Sark *and the R.M.S.* Britannia *(his diploma picture on loan from the R.S.M.A.); The yacht* Golden Vanity; *The yacht* Mercury; Grenville *Class frigates; The Royal Barge off Portsmouth; "High Winds and Heavy Seas."*

COCK, Pieter **1502-1550**
Born at Aelst on August 14th, 1502, he was a pupil of Baraent van Orley, one of the first of the Flemish school painters of historical subjects. Cock travelled in Italy in the 1520s and then settled in Antwerp, where years later he was to know Pieter Brueghel (q.v.), who married his daughter Maria and was his pupil. Although not strictly a marine painter, he did a few port scenes, which are among the earliest of the Flemish school. He died in Brussels in 1550.

COLE, Thomas **1801-1848**
Like the Morans (qq.v.) Cole was a native of Bolton, Lancashire, and like them he emigrated to America, in Cole's case with his family shortly after the Napoleonic Wars. He exhibited an early interest in drawing and painting, and without any financial backing left a turbulent home to seek his fortune as an artist, first in Philadelphia and then in New York. Not surprisingly he suffered great privations before his talents were recognised and he became the leader of the Hudson River School.

He can hardly be classed as a marine painter but did river and coastal views. In the 1830s he travelled to Italy, France and England, where he exhibited at the Royal Academy and the British Institution in 1830 and 1831, none of the pictures being marines. He died in New York.

PLATE: 445.

COLLINS, H.
A British ship portraitist of rather superior quality, working in Liverpool in the first quarter of the 19th century.

PLATE: 332.

COLLS, Ebenezer **fl.1850s**
In the years 1852, 1853 and 1854 he exhibited at the British Institution from an address in Camden Town. The National Maritime Museum, Greenwich, has a pair of pictures supposed to show the loss of the *Droites de L'Homme* in 1797. One is a copy of the aquatint after W.J. Huggins of the early stage of the action with the *Indefatigable* raking her, but for the ultimate wreck scene he has copied a painting by J.C. Schetky (q.v.) of the *Endymion* rescuing an embayed French two-decker on the Spanish coast about 1803.

PLATE: 427.

COMMONS, Donald Gregor Grant **1855-1942**
Born in Onehungo, New Zealand, on February 1st 1855, he was the son of a marine engineer who owned a fleet of sailing vessels. Like his father, he too trained as an engineer at Auckland University. After he moved to Sydney in 1878 he joined the New South Wales Department of Public Works as an engineering draughtsman, and remained with them until his retirement in 1924.

After that he devoted himself entirely to painting, which before had been his hobby. In 1936 he gave a one-man exhibition. He died in Condobolin, New South Wales, in 1942.

In 1879 he exhibited a painting called "The Coast of Ben Buckler" at the First Australian Art Exhibition at the Crystal Palace, Sydney. This picture, which was subsequently exhibited in London and Paris, was afterwards bought by the National Art Gallery of New South Wales.

CONDY, Nicholas, the Elder **1799-1857**
Disappointingly little is known about this Plymouth born artist, who, with his son, are the most admired marine painters to come from that city. He favoured small canvases and liked to paint shore scenes with figures, and craft in the background. Most of his subjects are local to Plymouth, but one illustrated here indicates that he visited Ireland. He died on January 8th, 1857.

PLATE: 380.

EXAMPLES: The City Art Gallery, Plymouth (marines only) (4): H.M.S. Thetis *off Mount Wise; Plymouth's inner harbour; arrival of fishing boats at Teignmouth, Mount Edgcumbe and the Hamoaze; a watercolour of the Cattwater at Plymouth during a storm.*

CONDY, Nicholas Matthew, the Younger **1818-1851**
There has long been some confusion in separating out the works of the Condys. There is no firm guide line on their subjects, but Nicholas senior (q.v.) preferred shore scenes, while Nicholas preferred scenes of ships and yachts at sea. He was born in Plymouth and was intended for the army, which he entered but did not stay in long, joining his father to paint for the rest of his short life.

PLATES: 381, 382, 383.

EXAMPLES: The National Maritime Museum, Greenwich (5): the capture of the Gabriel *slaver in 1841; the Post Office packet* Sheldrake *off Falmouth; ships off Devonport; a three-decker; a frigate clawing off a rocky coast. The City Museum and Art Gallery, Plymouth (marines only) (3): the Royal William Victualling Yard in 1840; H.M.S.* Britannia; *Lord Yarborough's yacht* Falcon; *also a watercolour called "Sailing".*

CONSTANTINOWITSCH, Ivan *see*
AIVAZOFFSKI, Ivan Constantinowitsch

COOK, J.
Flourished in the second quarter of the 18th century. This artist was one of the followers of the van de Veldes (qq.v.) and one whose work has often been confused with that of Peter Monomy (q.v.), although it is much inferior. His paintings often depict the royal yachts of the period and there are several versions of a painting showing an English man-of-war in the harbour at Alexandria.

The National Maritime Museum, Greenwich, has one of these signed "J. Cook fecit", one of a two-decker saluting off-shore and one of a ketch-rigged royal yacht.

PLATE: 197.

COOKE, Edward William R.A. **1811-1880**
Born in London on March 27th, 1811, he was the artistically precocious son of George Cooke, the engraver, and was doing engravings of flowers for publication before he was ten. He is said to have studied architecture for a time under A.G. Pugin, but he developed a natural interest in ships, probably enhanced by his association with Clarkson Stanfield (q.v.) for whom he made sketches in 1826, and whom he greatly admired.

He published his famous *Shipping and Craft* in 1829, when only eighteen. He did not start to exhibit paintings until 1835, when they hung at the Royal Academy and the British Institution; he continued to exhibit at both places nearly every year until the British Institution closed in 1867, and he last exhibited at the Royal Academy in 1879.

Just as Clarkson Stanfield was regarded as the doyen of marine painters until his death in 1867, so subsequently did the mantle fall on his friend Cooke. Some of his most successful paintings derived from sketches made on the beaches of Holland, where he went first in 1837, and again in 1838, 1841, 1843, 1852 and 1860. His other favourite venue was Venice, which he first visited in 1850, and where he met Ruskin who was writing his *Stones of Venice.* He also travelled in Spain, North Africa, France, Denmark and Sweden. He was elected an A.R.A. in 1851, and an R.A. in 1864.

PLATES: 466, 467, 468.

EXAMPLES: Auckland City Art Gallery (drawings): one of pinks on Scheveningen beach. Shipley Art Gallery, Gateshead (1). National Maritime Museum, Greenwich (7): the review of the fleet by the Shah of Persia with H.M.S. Devastation *in the foreground, 1873; the battery at Portsmouth; beaching a pink in heavy weather on Scheveningen beach; Mediterranean beach scene; Fishing boats becalmed; Dutch yachts in a breeze; Dutch barges; also a large collection of drawings and watercolours. Tate Gallery, London (5): Dutch boats in a calm; The Boat House; Venetian canal; A mill near Oxford; A boat near Venice. National Gallery of New South Wales (2): Shrimpers on the Normandy coast; Venetian view.*

COOPSE, Pieter
Flourished in the second and third quarters of the 17th century. He was a pupil of Ludolf Bakhuizen (q.v.), from whom he learnt the use of dramatic lighting effects. He worked in Amsterdam, and is better known as an engraver.

There is a fine pair showing Dutch flutes in a breeze at the Alte Pinakothek, Munich.

PLATE: 13.

COPNALL, Frank T. **b.1870**
Born on April 27th, 1870. He was really a portrait painter, and was a member of the Liverpool Academy and the London Portrait Society, also President of the Liverpool Art Club and the Liverpool Sketching Club. He exhibited at the Royal Academy and the Royal Society of Portrait Painters.

The National Maritime Museum, Greenwich, has a rather good painting by him of the *Lusitania* leaving Liverpool in November 1907.

PLATE: 636.

CORBY, J.W.
A British ship portraitist working in the third quarter of the 19th century. The National Maritime Museum, Greenwich, has a painting by him of the sailing ship *St. Lawrence,* launched in 1852.

PLATE: 608.

CORNE, Michele-Felice **1762-1832**
Born in Elba, the French Revolutionary War apparently forced him into exile, and the American merchant, Elias Haskett Derby, took him to Salem in the *Mount Vernon.* He worked first as a portrait painter, but the shipping interests of the thriving port of Salem engendered in him a latent love of the sea, so that he was soon doing ship portraits as well. He also painted actions, especially during the War of 1812.

In 1805 he decorated the interior of the new building of the Salem East India Marine Society. About 1810 he moved to Boston, where he continued his decorating and painting. He died at Newport, Rhode Island.

There is an affinity to the Roux family (q.v.) and the Mediterranean ship portraitists in his work as might be expected.

The United States Naval Academy at Annapolis has examples, and there is a large collection of his work in oils, gouache and watercolour at the Peabody Museum of Salem.

PLATES: 326, 327.

CORSINI, Raffael
A ship portraitist in Smyrna in the third quarter of the 19th century. His quality is quite good if rather mannered in the style of Cammillieri (q.v.) and the Roux family (q.v.). He worked in watercolour.

The Mariners Museum, Newport News, has a portrait of the barque *Fruiter,* and two views of Smyrna, and the Peabody Museum of Salem has fifteen ship portraits.

PLATE: 629.

CORTE, Juan del **1597-1660**
Born and died in Madrid. Not really a marine painter, he is included here because his battle pieces included sea fights, though it must be said that in these the genre ingredient is more important than the marine. He was a pupil of Velasquez and became court painter to Philip III and Philip IV.

PLATE: 3.

EXAMPLES: Museo Naval, Madrid (1): galley action.

COTMAN, Miles Edmund **1810-1858**
Born in Norwich on February 5th, 1810, he was the eldest son and pupil of John Sell Cotman, who overshadows his life and work. He took over his father's art school in Norwich when the latter went to King's College as drawing master in 1834. Then two years later he joined him as his assistant, taking over the post on his father's death in 1842. Miles died in Norwich on January 23rd, 1858.

His work is like his father's, but inferior. Unlike his father, he was sufficiently committed to maritime subjects to find a place here. He exhibited at the British Institution between 1840 and 1856, at the Royal Academy between 1840 and 1851, and at Suffolk Street. The Castle Museum, Norwich, has "Dutch boats on the Medway".

PLATES: 471, 472.

COULTER, William Alexander **1849-1936**
Born in Glengariff, Co. Antrim, on March 7th, 1849. Said to have studied in Copenhagen under Vilhelm Melbye (q.v.), and in Paris under François Musin (q.v.) and also in Brussels. If so, he also found time to sail in deep water sailing ships before settling in California in 1868.

From 1896 to 1906 he worked as an illustrator on the San Francisco *Call*. He became a full-time marine painter of West Coast shipping scenes, especially of the sailing days. In 1935 he held a one-man exhibition in San Francisco of one hundred pictures which he had painted since his 80th birthday. He died in Sausalito, California, the following year on March 13th, in his eighty-eighth year.

Examples of his work are held by the National Maritime Museum of San Francisco.

COWEN, Percy Elton **1888-1923**
The Peabody Museum of Salem, has a well crafted, very realistic oil of a dock with a whaler by this American artist.

PLATE: 633.

COX, David **1783-1859**
Born in Birmingham on April 29th, 1783, and died there on June 18th, 1859.

An eminent watercolourist who painted some marines. However, only one of his works exhibited at the Royal Academy or British Institution, "Sandbanks near the Ford, Calais", can be described as a marine.

COZZENS, Frederick Schiller **1856-1928**
Born in New York and died in Livingston, Staten Island, March 8th, 1928. He was a student at the Rensselaer Polytechnic Institute. As a painter he worked in watercolour, and was best known for his yachting scenes, being himself a keen yachtsman. The Peabody Museum of Salem has five examples of his work.

CRASKELL, ?Thomas **fl.1748**
There is a large oil painting of Knowles' action off Havana 1748, signed T. Craskell, and a drawing by him of the burning of the Spanish ship *Africa,* also by Knowles in 1748, at the National Maritime Museum, Greenwich, which also holds an engraving after one of his pictures of the herring fishery off Shetland.

The quality of the oil painting is good, somewhere between Monamy (q.v.) and Scott (q.v.), so it is fair to assume that he was a promising artist who died too young to paint many pictures, or to exhibit at the Society of Artists in the early 1760s.

PLATE: 228.

CREPIN, Louis Philippe **1772-1851**
Born and died in Paris. He was a pupil of Joseph Vernet (q.v.), of Baron Regnault, the historical painter, and also of the genre painter, Hubert Robert. He specialised in historical subjects.

PLATES: 320, 321.

EXAMPLES: The United States Naval Academy, Annapolis (1): action between the Hyder Ally *and the* General Monck *1782. The Musée de la Marine, Paris (3): Nelson's attack on the Invasion Flotilla off Boulogne 1801; the action between the* Amelia *and the* Arethuse *off the Les Islands, West Africa, 1813; Louis XVI's visit to Cherbourg in 1786.*

CROOS, Jacob van **b.c.1637**
Flourished in the third quarter of the 17th century. Born in The Hague, he may have been the son of Antoine van Croos. He was in Amsterdam in 1659. Better known for his landscapes than marine paintings, there is a painting at Greenwich of a Dutch ship and galleys off a fortified town signed "J. van Croos". It was painted in the second half of the 17th century and is not of very high quality.

PLATE: 132.

CROOS, Pieter van der **c.1610-1677**
From such pictures as exist it is clear that this painter was strongly influenced by Bonaventura Peeters, the Elder (q.v.), both in his use of highlights and in his palette.

He was in the Lucas Guild in The Hague in 1647, the Alkemaar Guild in 1651, and at Amsterdam in 1661. A picture at the National Maritime Museum, Greenwich, called "Shipping off a jetty", is signed "P. Croos". He probably died at Tobago.

CROSS, Roy R.S.M.A., S.Av.A. b.1924

Born in London on April 23rd, 1924. His first interest was aeroplanes and he became a member of the Society of Aviation Artists in 1952. He was largely self-taught but did for a time study at the Camberwell School of Arts and Crafts and the St. Martin's School of Fine Arts. By the end of the Second World War he was a leading journalist and illustrator of aircraft subjects. In the 1960s his interest widened to the subject of historic sail, and he was much influenced by the work of Montague Dawson (q.v.).

His commitment to marine paintings of this type grew as his aircraft interests waned, and since he held his first one-man show in the Malcolm Henderson Gallery in the West End in 1973 he has been painting marines as a full-time profession. His output is entirely absorbed by the American market, which is very appreciative of well-researched and beautifully crafted paintings of historical maritime subjects.

He was elected a member of the Royal Society of Marine Artists in 1977.

PLATE: 692.

CULL, Alma Claude Burlton 1880-1931

We know little about this artist, but as a portrayer both in oils and watercolours of the ships and work of the Royal Navy in the first quarter of this century, he ranks second only to W.L. Wyllie. Towards the end of his life he lived in a house on the front at Lee on Solent, Hampshire, and after his death on January 27th, 1931 his widow lived on there, and put most of his oil paintings in storage in Portsmouth. These were unfortunately destroyed by enemy bombs during the Second World War.

He exhibited between the years 1906 and 1927, mainly at the Alpine Club Gallery, but also at the Walker Art Gallery, the London Salon, the Royal Academy and the Royal Institute of Painters in Watercolours.

After his widow's death, in 1954 the National Maritime Museum purchased from her estate the remaining two oils — one of the eve of the Coronation Review of 1911 and the other of the first Battle-cruiser Squadron about 1914, as well as seventy watercolours. From another source the Museum holds an oil of King Edward VII class battleships at sea.

PLATES: 639, 640.

CUNDALL, Charles Ernest 1890-1971
R.A., R.W.S., R.P., R.S.M.A., N.S., N.E.A.C.

Born in Stretford, Lancashire, on September 6th, 1890, he studied at the Manchester School of Art, then won a scholarship to the Royal College of Art. His studies were interrupted by the First World War, when he served with the Royal Fusiliers and was severely wounded in 1917. On recovery he resumed his studies at the R.C.A., and later went to the Slade. He exhibited at the Royal Academy in 1918, was elected A.R.A. in 1937, and R.A. in 1944. He died in London on November 4th, 1971.

Cundall is mainly remembered as a painter of crowd scenes and royal occasions but during the Second World War he worked for the War Artists' Commission with the Royal Air Force and the Royal Navy. After the war he accompanied the Royal family on their visit to South Africa aboard the battleship *Vanguard;* he himself was aboard one of the escorts.

Five of his marine works for the War Artists' Commission are at the National Maritime Museum, Greenwich, but some are at the Imperial War Museum.

PLATE: 671.

CUYP, Albert 1620-1691

Born in Dordrecht on October 20th, 1620, he died there on November 15th, 1691. This painter was the master of a wide range of subjects, including some marines, though mostly of river scenes. He was one of a family of painters and the pupil of his father, Jacob Gerritz Cuyp, who died in 1651. He made a good marriage and had independent means, which has prompted some regard for him as an amateur.

His output was large and much admired, especially among English collectors. He is widely represented in public galleries, and those which have examples of his river and seascapes are the museums at Dordrecht, La Fere, Montpelier, Rouen, Paris (the Louvre), and the National Gallery, Washington.

PLATE: 103.

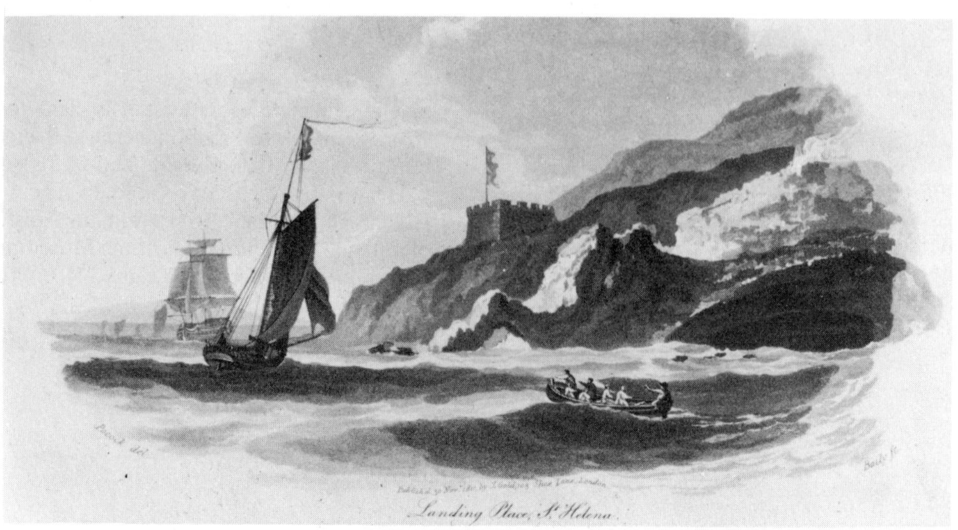

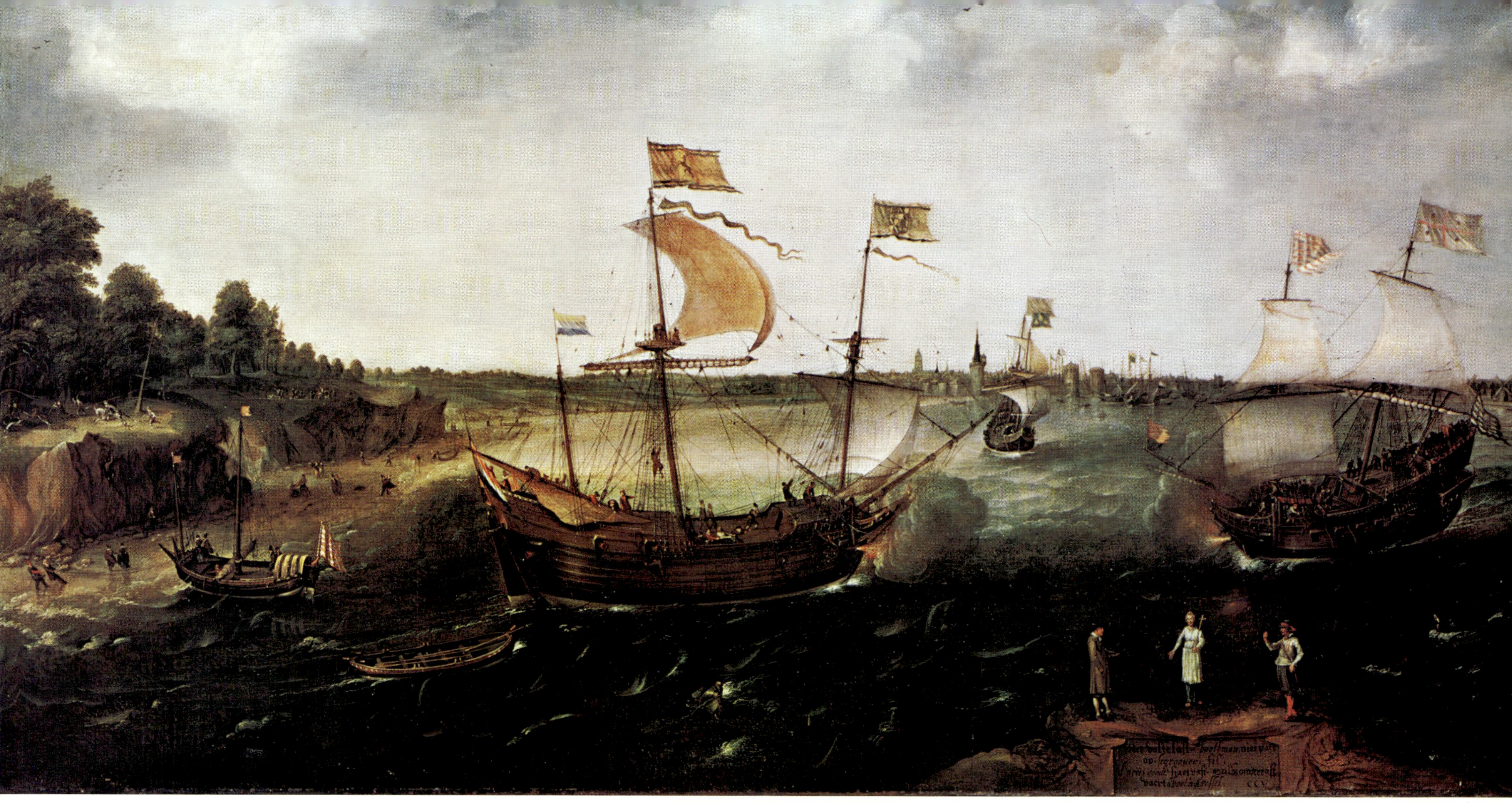

Colour Plate II. Cornelis Claesz van Wieringen, c.1580-1633. "An English privateer off La Rochelle, about 1627."
National Maritime Museum, Greenwich.

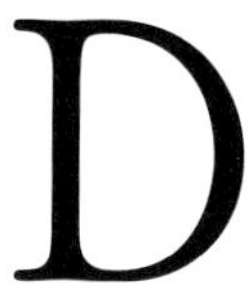

DAHL, Johan Christian Clausen **1788-1857**
Born in Bergen on February 24th, 1788, his parents were keen for him to take religious orders, but he wanted to be a painter, and joined the Academy at Copenhagen in 1811. In 1818 he went to Dresden, which, apart from visits to his native land to paint, and to Paris, was to be his permanent base, and where he was appointed Professor at the Academy of Art. He died there on October 4th, 1857. The National Gallery of Norway in Oslo has a number of paintings by him, but only the wreck scene illustrated is a marine.

PLATE: 346.

DAHL, Niels Carl Flindt **1812-1865**
Born at Faaborg in Denmark, he was a pupil at the Copenhagen Academy under Christoffer Eckersberg. In 1840 he voyaged to Lisbon and there is a view of the harbour there in the State Museum for Art in Copenhagen, purchased in 1843. The previous year he had been appointed Professor of Perspective at the Academy and in 1852 was awarded a travel scholarship by the Academy, with which he spent three years in the Mediterranean.

In 1864 he did a painting of the Battle of Heligoland which took place in that year. He died the following year in Copenhagen.

The Frederiksborg Museum, Zeeland, has a painting of Danish transports in Svenborgsund in 1848 and a Battle of Heligoland 1864. There are also examples in the Royal Naval Museum, Copenhagen.

DANBY, Francis **1793-1861**
Born in Wexford on November 16th, 1793, he was not really a marine painter, but the best known of that painting family. The paintings he exhibited at the Royal Academy between 1821 and his death include a few that might be construed as marines, as did those at the British Institution between 1820 and 1852. Examples in public galleries do not seem to include marines. He died on February 9th, 1861, in Exmouth.

DANBY, James Francis **1816-1875**
Born in Bristol, he was the eldest son and pupil of Francis Danby (q.v.). He specialised in sunsets and sunrises. He exhibited at the Royal Academy from 1842 to 1847, and every year from 1849 to 1874. He also exhibited at the British Institution every year from 1847 until it closed in 1867, as well as Suffolk Street. He died of apoplexy in London on October 22nd, 1875. The Birmingham Art Gallery has two of his paintings.

DANBY, Thomas R.W.S., R.H.A. **c.1818-1866**
Born in Bristol he was the younger son and pupil of Francis Danby and brother to James Francis (qq.v.), with whom he was taught and travelled in Europe. He was influenced by the work of Claude Gellée (q.v.) and exhibited at the Royal Academy between 1843 and 1882, but hardly showed any marines. He also showed work at the British Institution from 1841 (a wreck scene) to 1867 (posthumously), again mostly landscapes. He died on March 25th, 1866.

DANIELL, Thomas R.A. **1749-1840**
Born at Kingston-upon-Thames. His father, the landlord of "The Swan" at Chertsey in Surrey, apprenticed his son to a London coach builder in 1763. In 1772 he had his first painting hung in the Royal Academy. In fact, he was not a marine painter but is included here because, as the master and guardian of his nephew William Daniell (q.v.), he took him as his assistant on his famous voyage to China and India in 1786, where they remained travelling and recording the Indian scene until 1794. He was also a pioneer of aquatinting, a medium his nephew was to bring to such perfection.

Thomas never got over his Indian obsession, and although he continued to exhibit at the Royal Academy until 1828, and at the British Institution between 1806 and 1830, nearly all his paintings are of Indian and Far Eastern subjects.

DANIELL, William R.A. **1769-1837**
He was born at Kingston-upon-Thames. His father was a bricklayer who inherited his father's public house, "The Swan" at Chertsey. When he died in 1779, young William was taken to London by his artist uncle Thomas Daniell (q.v.), whose pupil he became.

In December 1784 Thomas obtained permission from the Hon. East India Company to "proceed to Bengal to follow his profession as an engraver" in an Indiaman, and to take his nephew as his assistant. They therefore sailed in the *Atlas* in April 1785. In fact, they arrived first at Whampoa in China in August, where they remained for some months before taking passage in a country ship for Calcutta. They travelled and sketched in India until 1794, when they sailed for home.

Thomas Daniell was a pioneer of aquatinting and his nephew studied hard to achieve the perfection that he did in this medium. The outcome was a series of beautiful large plates of their travels, and an illustrated book called *A Picturesque Voyage to India by the way of China,* 1810. Further travels round his native coasts produced another beautifully illustrated work, *A Voyage Round Great Britain,* 1814 to 1825. He also produced splendid plates of the Port of London.

In 1799 he joined the Royal Academy Schools of Art, although he had exhibited at the Royal Academy exhibitions since 1795. In 1807 he was elected an A.R.A. and in 1821 a full R.A. He also exhibited at the British Institution from

1807. In the 1825 exhibition he had three battle pieces; a pair of Trafalgar and one of the Nile and the former won him a prize of £100. He exhibited a Battle of Navarino in 1828.

The National Maritime Museum, Greenwich, has a view of the East India fleet at Angere Point, in the Sunda Strait in April 1794, also a bird's-eye-view of the East India Dock at Blackwall. At the Peabody Museum of Salem there are drawings of junks and Western craft and views of Wampoa.

PLATE: 293.

DANNENBERG, C.F.

An early 19th century ship portraitist who was probably based in Scandinavia. The Peabody Museum of Salem has two watercolours by him.

DAWSON, Henry **1811-1878**

Born in Hull on April 3rd, 1811. The following year his family moved to Nottingham. His working life started in a lace factory but he taught himself to paint and in 1835 started to paint for a living; in 1838 he took lessons from J.B. Pyne. In 1844 he moved to Liverpool, and in 1849 to London, and died in Chiswick on December 13th, 1878.

He had started to exhibit Derbyshire scenes at the Royal Academy and British Institution in 1841 but was soon showing coastal views and port scenes, especially the Port of London. He continued to exhibit at the British Institution until it closed in 1867, and at the Royal Academy until 1874. The hanging committee tended to sky his exhibits.

The Birmingham Art Gallery has a view of St. Paul's from the Thames, and one other; the Leicester Art Gallery has an example, and the Walker Art Gallery, Liverpool, has "The Harbour, Evening".

PLATE: 533.

DAWSON, Henry T. **fl.1860-1873**

A son of Henry Dawson (q.v.), he was more committed to marine painting. He exhibited at the British Institution from 1860 to 1867, and at the Royal Academy between 1866 and 1873.90

PLATE: 534.

DAWSON, Montague F.R.S.A., R.S.M.A. **1895-1973**

Born in Chiswick, London, he was the son of Henry Thomas Dawson, an engineer and keen yachtsman, who also painted marines, and the grandson of Henry Dawson (q.v.), the landscape painter. Early in his life Montague Dawson and his family moved to Smugglers House on Southampton Water, so he had every opportunity to indulge an inherited interest in ships. Although he never went to art school, he inherited flair for painting and in about 1910 he joined a commercial art studio in Bedford Row, London, where he worked on posters and illustration.

At the outbreak of the First World War he joined the Royal Navy and it was as a naval officer in Falmouth that he met Napier Hemy (q.v.), who had a powerful influence on his work. During this time too, he supplied illustrations for publication in the *Sphere*. These were normally in monochrome. In the Second World War he again worked for the *Sphere,* supplying them with pictures of historical events of the war.

After the First World War he set up as a painter and illustrator, concentrating on historical subjects and portraits of deep-water sailing ships, usually in a stiff breeze and a high sea. It was in the 1920s that he became contracted to Messrs. Frost and Reed, the art dealers, who from that time handled his whole output and reproduction rights. With them he became king of the "clipper-ship school".

From the early 1930s he lived at Milford-on-Sea in Hampshire, and he exhibited occasionally at the Royal Academy between 1917 and 1936. He also exhibited regularly at the Society of Marine Artists' exhibitions between 1946 and 1964 and was an elected member. He was also a Fellow of the Royal Society of Arts. He died in Midhurst, Sussex, on May 21st, 1973.

PLATES: 659, 660, 661.

EXAMPLES: National Maritime Museum, Greenwich (6): H.M.S. Inflexible *at the Battle of the Falkland Islands 1914 (on loan); H.M.S.* Inflexible *at the Dardanelles 1915 (on loan); H.M.S.* Implacable *at the Dardanelles 1915 (monochrome); H.M.S.* Repulse *in action with German light cruisers 1917 (on loan); R.M.S.* Mauretania; *The rescue of the* Macbeth *1941 (monochrome). Mariners Museum, Newport News (16): 13 of Second World War subjects; two of early sail subjects; a portrait of the Blackwall frigate* Macquarie.

DAWSON, Nelson **1859-1941**

Born in Lincolnshire, he was a marine painter in watercolours, and soft ground etcher, who settled in Chelsea and belonged to the circle of Whistler and Brangwyn. He married a flower painter, but their livelihood seems to have mainly depended on a workshop which turned out architectural fittings and wrought ironwork which they designed. He was a member of the Royal Society of Painter Etchers, and an Associate of the Royal Watercolour Society.

DE LACY, Charles John **c.1860-1936**

Born in Sunderland, he was the son of Robert De Lacy, an artist and professor of music. He was originally trained as an engineer and had experience in the Army and Navy. He trained as an artist at Lambeth, North Kensington and the National Gallery. He first exhibited at the Royal Academy in 1889, and also at the Royal Society of British Artists. In an entry in the 1929 *Who's Who in Art,* under recreation, he put "busman's holiday (painting something new)". His enthusiasm outran his talent, which was limited. He was keen on his service connections and was an honorary member of the Royal Marine Mess at Deal. He probably died in Cheam.

In his early years he worked as an illustrator for the *Illustrated London News, Graphic* and *Sporting and Dramatic* magazines as an illustrator.

PLATE: 610.

EXAMPLES: National Maritime Museum, Greenwich (2): Troops leaving in the Kinfauns Castle *for the Boer War in 1900; H.M.S.* Vindictive *alongside the Mole at Zeebrugge 1918.*

DENTON, Kenneth R.S.M.A. **b.1932**

Born in Chatham, Kent, Denton did his art training at the local art college, where he later lectured in the interior design department. In 1967 he resigned his teaching appointment to become a full-time landscape and marine artist. He has held a number of exhibitions and is a member of the Royal Society of Marine Artists.

PLATE: 693.

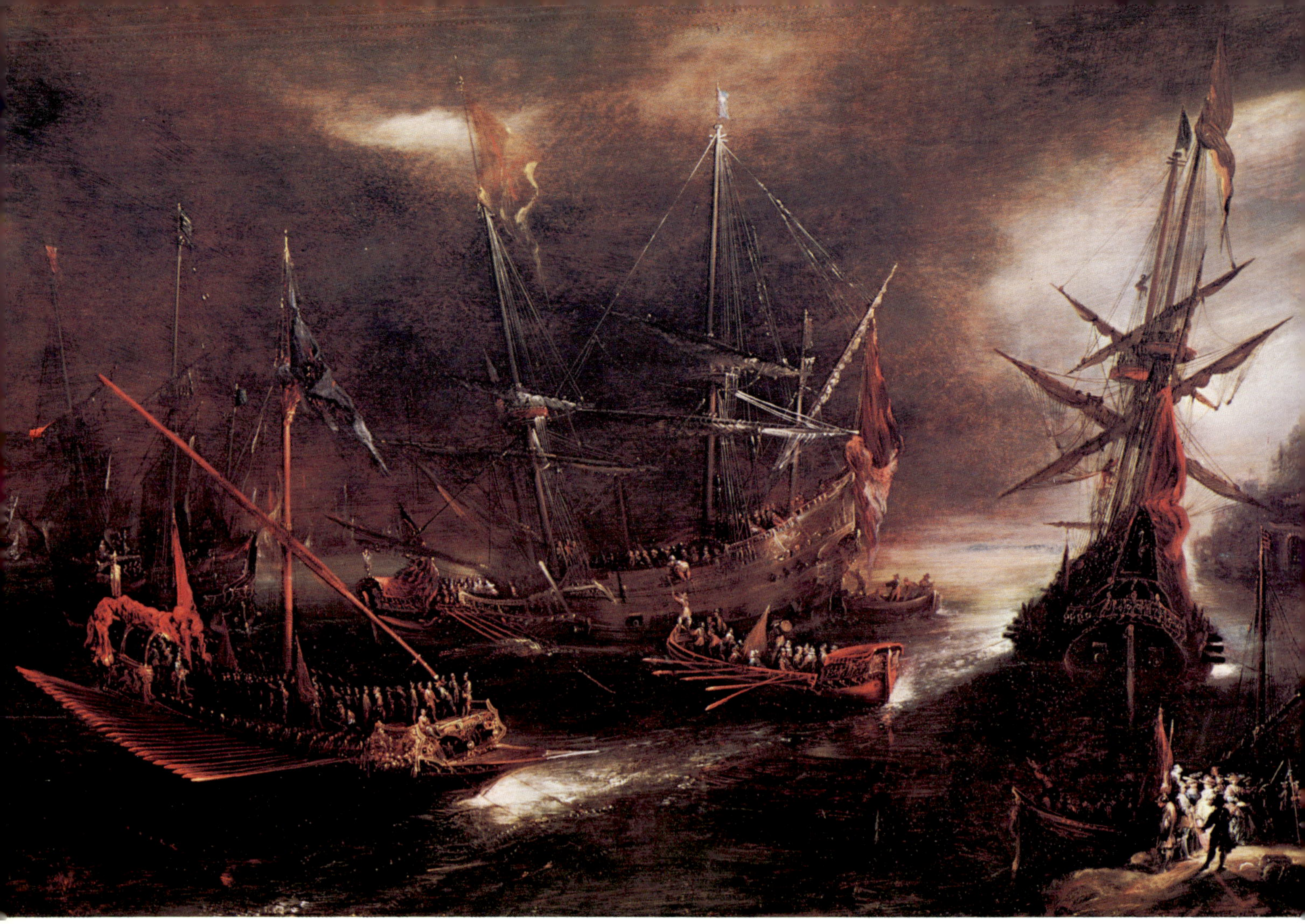

Colour Plate IV. Adam Willaerts, 1577-1664. "Dutch attacking a Spanish fortress." National Maritime Museum, Greenwich.

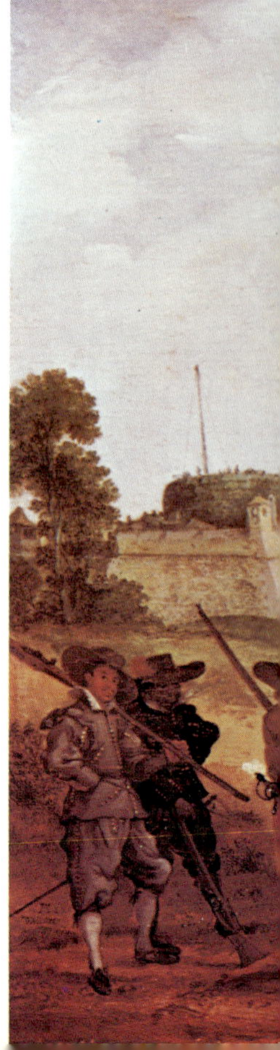

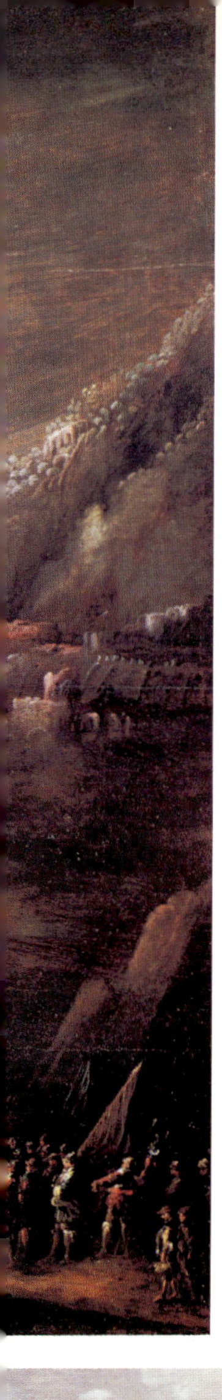

Colour Plate III. Andries van Eertvelt, 1590-1652. "The embarkation of Spanish troops." National Maritime Museum, Greenwich.

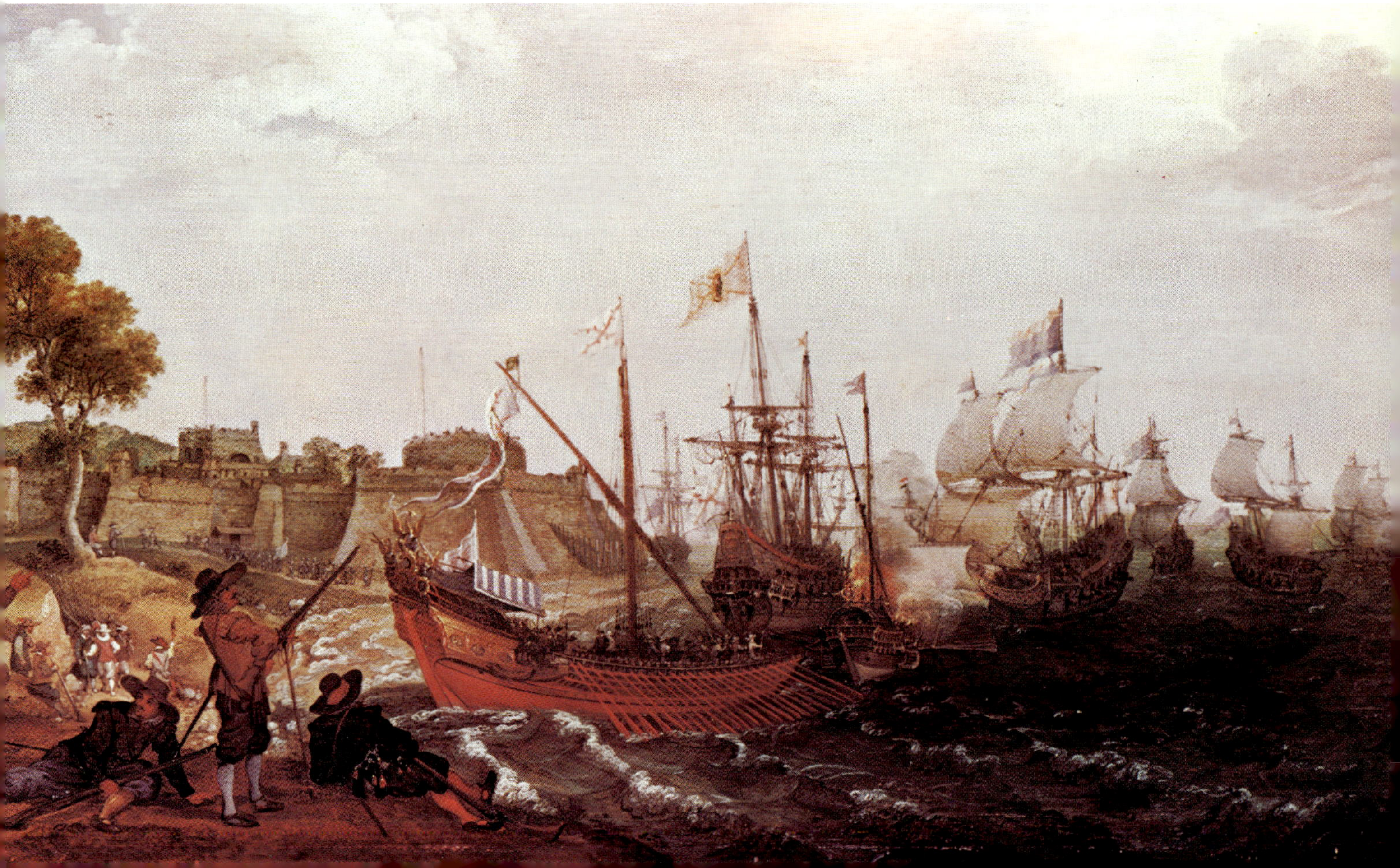

D'ESPOSITO, G.
A Maltese ship portraitist working in the middle of the 19th century. The Peabody Museum of Salem has three watercolours.

DESPREY, Louis Jean **1749-1804**
Born in Auxerre, France, he was not really a marine artist but a painter of historical subjects which included naval battles. He died in Stockholm.

EXAMPLES: National Maritime Museum, Stockholm (2): Battle of Heligoland, 1788; Battle of Svensksund, 1790.

DEVENTER, Willem Antonie van **1824-1893**
He was born in The Hague on June 30th, 1824. He attended The Hague Academy from 1843 to 1846 and then was a pupil of the landscape painter, Hendrick van de Sande Bakhuyzen. Except for the years 1856 to 1862 when he was in Amsterdam, he worked and died in his native city. The Rijksmuseum, Amsterdam, has two coast scenes, and his work can be found in the Fine Art Museum at The Hague, at the Boymans Museum and the Prins Hendrik Museum in Rotterdam.

PLATE: 554.

DIEMER, Michael Zeno **1867-1939**
Born on February 8th, 1867. He lived in Munich and was a painter of historical subjects, including naval ones.

There is a naval painting called "The Battle of St. Iago" at the Historical Museum at Lucerne.

DIEST, Adriaen van **1655-1704**
Born in The Hague, a son and pupil of Willem van Diest, he emigrated to England in 1672/3 at about the same time, and presumably for the same reasons as the van de Veldes (qq.v.). The war with France was going badly and patronage had fallen off. In June 1672 Charles II had invited Dutch craftsmen and artists to emigrate to England, in spite of the fact that the two countries were at war. This offer was especially attractive to artists who found in England a growing and flourishing market for paintings, especially portraits and marines; this could not be satisfied by a native school, which at that time could hardly be said to exist so far as marine painters were concerned.

It seems highly likely that he went straight into the van de Velde studio and that Willem the Younger was his master, for his copies of that master's work are the truest and his style the closest to it of all Willem's followers. He was also a landscape and animal painter and an engraver. Amongst his patrons was the Earl of Bath. He signed his work "A.V. Diest" or "A. Diest" and sometimes "A.D." on the back of the canvas.

PLATE: 164.

EXAMPLES: Bavarian Museum, Augsburg (1): Italian port scene. National Maritime Museum, Greenwich (3): two of the Battle of La Hogue, 1692, and one unidentified Anglo-French action.

DIEST, Jeronimus van **c.1631-1673**
Born and died in The Hague. He was the eldest child and pupil of Willem van Diest (q.v.). His style is very close to his father's so that they probably worked in the same studio.

PLATES: 112, 113, 114.

EXAMPLES: Rijksmuseum, Amsterdam (2): The captured Royal Charles *being taken to Holland, 1667; river scene. Scheepvaart Museum (1): Dutch herring fleet at sea. Gemäldegalerie, Kassel (1): river scene. Gemäldegalerie, Leipzig (1).*

DIEST, Willem Hermansz van **before 1610-aft.1663**
Born in The Hague, he was an early painter in the Dutch realist style, he was apparently influenced by van Beyeren and van Goyen, and later Zeeman and de Vlieger. He was the father and master of two marine painters, Adriaen and Jeronimus (qq.v.). He was a founder member of the Guild of St. Luke in The Hague in 1656.

PLATES: 56, 57.

EXAMPLES: The Rijksmuseum, Amsterdam (1): the beach at Scheveningen. Bridport Museum (1): harbour scene. National Maritime Museum, Greenwich (2): Battle of Leghorn 1653; ships' boats going ashore from a Dutch ship. Walker Art Gallery, Liverpool (1); Battle of Scheveningen. Bavarian State Art Collections, Munich (1): ships in a storm. National Museum, Stockholm (1): calm. Centraal Museum, Utrecht (2): Battle of the Sound 1658; shipping scene. Kunsthistorisches Museum, Vienna (1).

DIETZ, H.R.
Late 19th century ship portraitist; the Peabody Museum of Salem has an oil.

DIRCKS, Johann Peter **1813-c.1888**
A German primitive ship portraitist working at Oevelgonne, near Altona. The Altonaer Museum has two pen and wash drawings.

DIXON, Charles **1872-1934**
Born in Goring-on-Thames on December 8th, 1872, he was the son of the genre and history painter Alfred Dixon and he himself developed a taste for historical subjects, though always of naval interest. He was an illustrator and worked for the *Illustrated London News,* the *Sphere* and the *Graphic.* In a book called *Britannia's Bulwarks* he provided watercolours for all the colour plates. Watercolour was his favourite medium and he liked to do large ones very quickly.

He was a friend of Sir Thomas Lipton and went out with all five *Shamrocks* to record the America's Cup Races off Sandy Hook.

He exhibited at the Royal Academy from 1889, with pictures hanging most years. He also exhibited at the New Watercolour Society.

In 1900 he was elected a member of the Royal Institute of Painters in Watercolours. He died in Itchenor, Sussex on September 12th, 1934.

PLATES: 641, 642.

EXAMPLES: National Maritime Museum, Greenwich (2): Queen Victoria's Diamond Jubilee Review at Spithead 1897; H.M.S. Cardiff *leading the surrendered German High Seas Fleet into Rosyth 1918; also five watercolours. Marine Museum, Toronto (1 watercolour): Above Greenwich. Merseyside County Museums (1). The Library of New South Wales, Sydney (2): The* Cutty Sark *and the* Thermopylae, *H.M.A.S.* Australia.

DIXON, William **1774-c.1827**

Very little is known about this artist, but he is presumably the fifteen year old who joined the Academy Schools in December 1789. He exhibited at the Royal Academy in 1796 a large view of Perry's shipyard at Blackwall, which is now in the National Maritime Museum, Greenwich, and thereafter portraits and marines from time to time until 1824. His early addresses were in Rotherhithe and Limehouse. He also exhibited two pictures in the British Institution in 1808 and 1827; neither were marines.

DOBRILOVICH, G.M.

A ship portraitist working in Antwerp in the middle of the 19th century. The Peabody Museum of Salem has a watercolour by him.

DODD, Louis

In the last few years a number of beautifully crafted little paintings by this artist, of 18th century marine subjects and in the 18th century manner have been turning up in the salerooms. The painter is believed to be alive and well and living in Folkestone.

PLATE: 695.

DODD, Ralph **c.1756-1817**

The younger brother of the better known Robert (q.v.), he first exhibited at the Free Society in 1779 and again in 1780. In that year both brothers exhibited at the Society of Artists. In Graves' dictionary of contributors to the Royal Academy all the Dodd pictures are given to Ralph, which must be wrong. However, as Ralph became an engineer he can almost certainly be identified as the other "R. Dodd, Architect" who exhibited engineering drawings from 1799 to 1817. His painting is very like his brother's.

EXAMPLES: National Maritime Museum, Greenwich (2): The capture of the Amazone *by the* Santa Margarita 1783 (pair).

DODD, Robert **1748-1815**

He was one of the principal recorders of the naval side of the War of American Independence and of the French Revolutionary Wars. He not only painted the actions but engraved and published over a hundred of them as well, mostly in aquatint.

He first exhibited at the Society of Artists in 1780, the same year as his younger brother, Ralph Dodd (q.v.). Both painted battle pieces in a very similar manner and in Graves's dictionary of contributors to the Royal Academy exhibitions, all the works by Dodd, starting in 1782, are lumped together as by Ralph Dodd. This must be a mistake.

Robert Dodd's major work was the very large painting (76 by 134 inches) of the end of Lord Howe's victory on June 1st, 1794, showing the rescue of the crew of the sinking *Vengeur du Peuple.* This he painted in 1795, to hang in the dining room of his local inn, the "Half Way House" in the Commerical Road, and painted it *in situ* as it was too big to be taken in. It is now at Greenwich.

Although he could occasionally turn out a nicely finished work, his pictures on the whole are rather dull. He last exhibited at the Royal Academy in 1809 and died in London in February 1815.

PLATES: 271, 272, 273, 274.

EXAMPLES: The United States Naval Academy Museum, Annapolis (2): The action between the Serapis *and the* Bonhomme Richard, *1779; The Battle of the Nile, 1798. National Maritime Museum, Greenwich (19): the* Quebec *on fire after the action with the* Surveillante *1779; the* Artois *capturing two Dutch privateers 1781; action between the* Magicienne *and the* Sybille *1783 (a pair); the end of the Battle of the First of June 1794; Nelson forcing a passage through the Sound 1801; the Battle of Copenhagen 1801; the* Shannon *capturing the* Chesapeake *1813; the shortening sail at the approach of the fatal hurricane, 1782 (one of a set of five pictures of the loss of the* Ramillies); *the East Indiaman* Royal Charlotte; *The first rate* Victory *in 1792; the Pool of London; a frigate action about 1800 (a pair); a commodore coming to anchor.*

DODGE, J.T.

A ship portraitist working in Buenos Aires in the third quarter of the 19th century. The Peabody Museum of Salem has a watercolour by him.

DOMMELHUIZEN *see* **DOMMERSHUIZEN**

DOMMERSHUIZEN, Cornelis Christiaan **1842-1928**

Born in Utrecht on November 11th, 1842, and died at The Hague on May 23rd, 1928. On his birth certificate his name is spelt Dommelhuizen, and apparently he signed with both spellings. He was a traveller, working in America, Belgium, France and England. He exhibited in Amsterdam in 1866 and 1877, at The Hague in 1879, and in Rotterdam in the same year.

EXAMPLES: Scheepvart Museum, Amsterdam (2): the Nicot *(a pair). The Old Archive, The Hague (1): Scheveningen beach. Art Museum, Middelburg (1): view of the Town Hall. Centraal Museum, Utrecht (1): a seascape.*

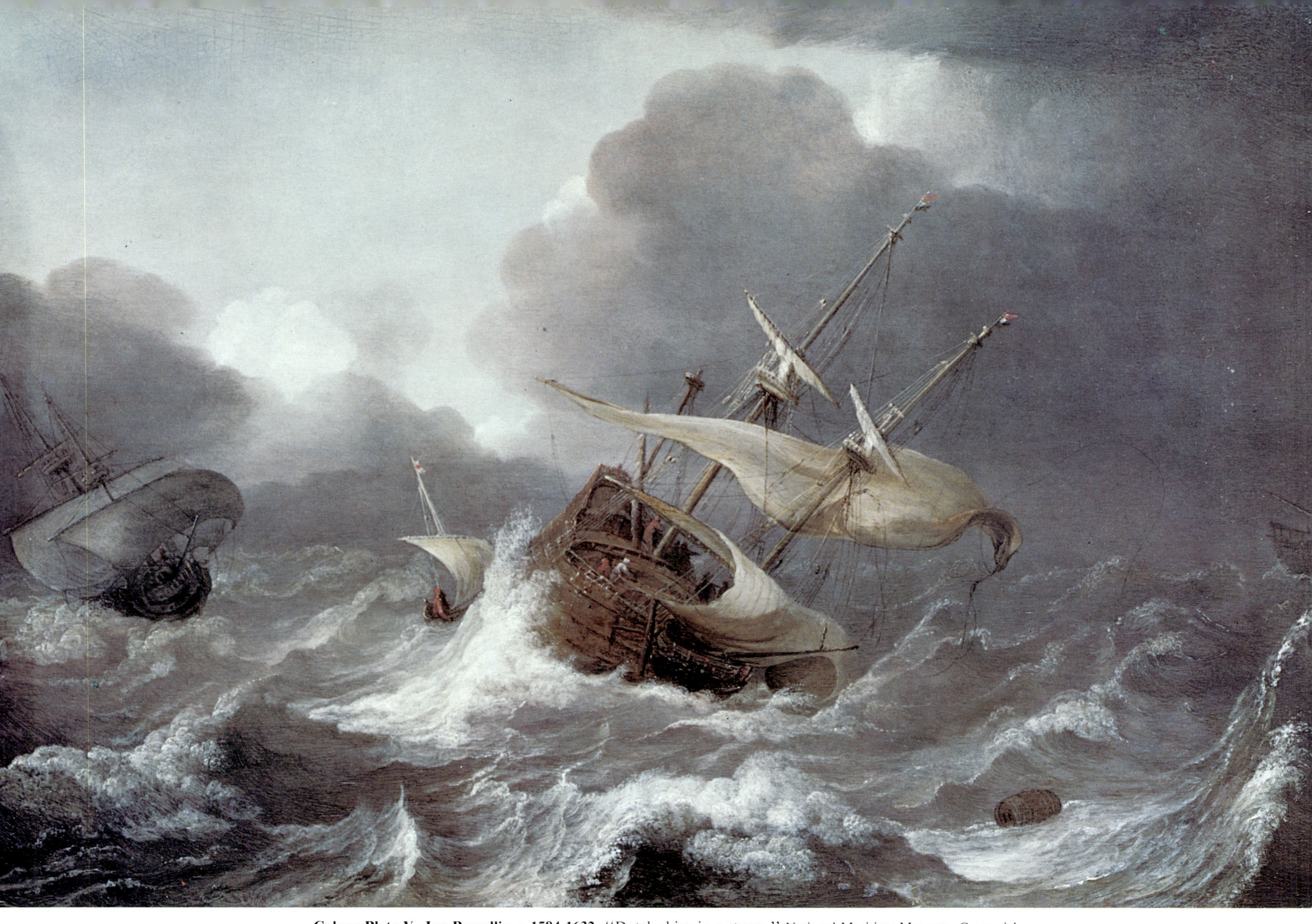

Colour Plate V. Jan Porcellis, c.1584-1632. ''Dutch ships in a storm.'' National Maritime Museum, Greenwich.

DOUGHTY, Thomas **1793-1856**
Born in Philadelphia and died in New York. He was a business man until he was thirty, when he decided to become a full-time artist and went to Paris to study. He also visited London and was probably living there in 1845. He exhibited at the British Institution in 1838, 1845 and 1846, and also at the Royal Academy in 1845.

The strange thing about these exhibits is that they are nearly all of American subjects, though presumably he had not been there for years. He was one of the few American artists of the period to become well-known in Europe.

PLATE: 462.

DOWINAR, B.M.
A British ship portraitist working in Leith in the third quarter of the 19th century. The National Maritime Museum, Greenwich, has a painting by him of the barque *Nile,* dated 1857.

PLATE: 522.

DREIBHOLZ, Christiaan Lodewijk Willem **1799-1874**
Born and died in Utrecht. He was a pupil of Johannes Christiaan Schotel (q.v.), and worked at Scheveningen from 1842 to 1866; he then moved back to his native Utrecht. He travelled in France and England, and in 1833 was elected to the Academy of Amsterdam.

PLATE: 373.

EXAMPLES: Rijksmuseum, Amsterdam (2): view of Dordrecht; storm. Bavarian State Collections, Munich (1): marine.

DREW, Clement **1806-1889**
Born in Kingston, Massachussetts. He worked in Boston and later Gloucester, Mass., painting ship portraits, seascapes and coastal views. He was also a lithographer and publisher of lithographs, an art dealer, figurehead carver and photographer.

The Mariners Museum, Newport News, has a portrait of the paddle steamer *Bangor,* and the Peabody Museum of Salem has twenty-four oil paintings by him, and twenty more attributed to him.

PLATE: 435.

DRUMMOND, Samuel A.R.A. **1765-1844**
His father joined Prince Charles Edward, the Young Pretender, in the 1745 rebellion, and was forced to flee the country for some years. Samuel was born in London on Christmas Day, 1765. He joined the navy when he was fourteen and served for seven years. He is said to have been present at three engagements, which could well be true since he was serving at the height of the American War of Independence.

He took up art as a pastellist and later turned to oils. Apparently he was self-taught, which seems remarkable given his quality. He was not a marine artist in the strict sense of the term, rather a portraitist and genre painter who had a taste for nautical subjects; his best known work, of which there are several versions, is of Nelson being carried below after being mortally wounded at the Battle of Trafalgar. He also did a few marines, mostly of naval battles, and there is a large Battle of Trafalgar at Greenwich.

He exhibited copiously at the Royal Academy from 1791 until the year of his death, and at the British Institution from 1806. He died in London in August, 1844.

PLATE: 299.

DUBBELS, Hendrick-Jacobsz **c.1620-1676**
Born in Amsterdam and died there on June 9th, 1676. A painter in the Dutch realist style and clearly influenced by his master, Simon de Vlieger (q.v.), and by Jan van de Cappelle (q.v.); his work can be of very high quality. His most illustrious pupil was Ludolf Bakhuisen (q.v.), and he appears to have lived and worked all his life in Amsterdam.

PLATES: 115, 116; COLOUR PLATE: VII.

EXAMPLES: Rijksmuseum, Amsterdam (4): Wassenaer van Obdam's fleet leaving the estuary of Texel, 1665; view of Batavia; two calms. Provensealmuseum, Bonn (1): rough sea. Fine Art Museum, Budapest (1): shore scene. State Museum for Fine Art, Copenhagen (2): large Dutch ship near the shore; shore scene with small craft. Gemäldegalerie, Dresden (1): small craft. Fine Art Museum, Düsseldorf (1): calm. Pitti Palace, Florence (1): marine. National Maritime Museum, Greenwich (2): calm; a smalschip passing under the bows of a Dutch flagship. Staatliche Kunstsammlungen, Kassel (1): calm. Museum of Fine Art, Leipzig (1): shore scene. National Gallery, London (1): calm. Prado, Madrid (1): marine. Boymans Museum, Rotterdam (1): a Dutch harbour after sundown. Schwerin Museum (1): a kaag in a breeze. Nationalmuseum, Stockholm (1): ships driving onto a rocky coast in a storm.

DUBREUIL, Chéri **fl.1860-1870**
A petty officer and helmsman in the French navy about the middle of the 19th century, he painted naval actions and arctic scenes, some of which have been reproduced.

EXAMPLES: Musée des Beaux Arts, Bordeaux (2): the bombardment of San Juan d'Ulloa, Vera Cruz, Mexico in 1838 and the bombardment of Tangier in 1844, painted in 1860 and 1862 respectively. The Musée de la Marine and the Bibliotheque Nationale have some reproductions.

DUNCAN, Edward R.W.S. **1803-1882**
Born in London on October 20th, 1803, he died there on April 11th, 1882. Ducan trained as an aquatint engraver under the Havells and his concentration on marine subjects, both as a painter and an engraver, was the result of his association with William John Huggins (q.v.), whose daughter, Bertha, he married. He collaborated with his father-in-law on some of his paintings and engraved many others.

He was mainly a watercolour painter, and most of his exhibited work was in the exhibitions of the Old and New Watercolour Societies; he was also an infrequent exhibitor at the Royal Academy between 1846 and 1873, at the British Institution between 1833 and 1857, and also at Suffolk Street.

At the National Maritime Museum, Greenwich, is a large painting of East Indiamen in the China Sea, signed by Huggins and Duncan, who appears to have painted the water; the Museum also holds a large collection of drawings and watercolours. Examples may also be found in the Birmingham Art Gallery, the Graves Art Gallery in Sheffield, the Victoria and Albert Museum, and the Walker Art Gallery, Liverpool.

PLATE: 401.

DUNN, Lawson **fl.1760**

The National Maritime Museum, Greenwich, has a competently painted picture of the action between the *Pitt* and the *St. Louis* in the Bay of Bengal in 1758. As the *Pitt* was commanded by Commodore Wilson, a Yorkshireman, the two possibilities (in the absence of any other evidence), are that Lawson Dunn was either working in Yorkshire, or in India.

DURAND-BRAGER, Jean Baptiste Henri **1814-1879**

Born in Dol and died in Paris. A traveller and a painter of naval history, who learnt his trade in the studio of Eugène Isabey (q.v.), he was a "reporter" in that he went on expeditions as the official artist; he also accepted commissions for battle pieces of heroic size from the French government, the Czar of Russia and the Emperor of Austria.

PLATE: 502.

EXAMPLES: Musée des Beaux-Arts, Bordeaux (1): action between the Niemen *and the* Amethyst *and* Arethusa, *1809. Musée de Laval (1): low tide. Musée des Beaux-Arts, Nantes (1): view of Eupatoria. Musée National de Versailles (1): bombardment of Sevastopol.*

DUTTON, Thomas Goldsworth **c.1819-1891**

He was not only the finest 19th century lithographer of shipping scenes and ship portraits but happily the most prolific. In 1844 he described himself as a "Lithographic artist, marine draughtsman and draughtsman on wood, 146 Fleet Str". The originals for the lithographs appear always to have been watercolours. He exhibited at Suffolk Street between 1858 and 1879.

For all his industry, he left only £60.16s.6d., and all to his faithful servant of twenty-one years, Mary Sextone, when he died aged 71 on March 12th, 1891, in Clapham.

At the National Maritime Museum, Greenwich, is a near complete collection of his published lithographs, and a few of his original watercolours. The Peabody Museum of Salem has a watercolour of H.M.S. *Monarch*.

PLATES: 478, 479.

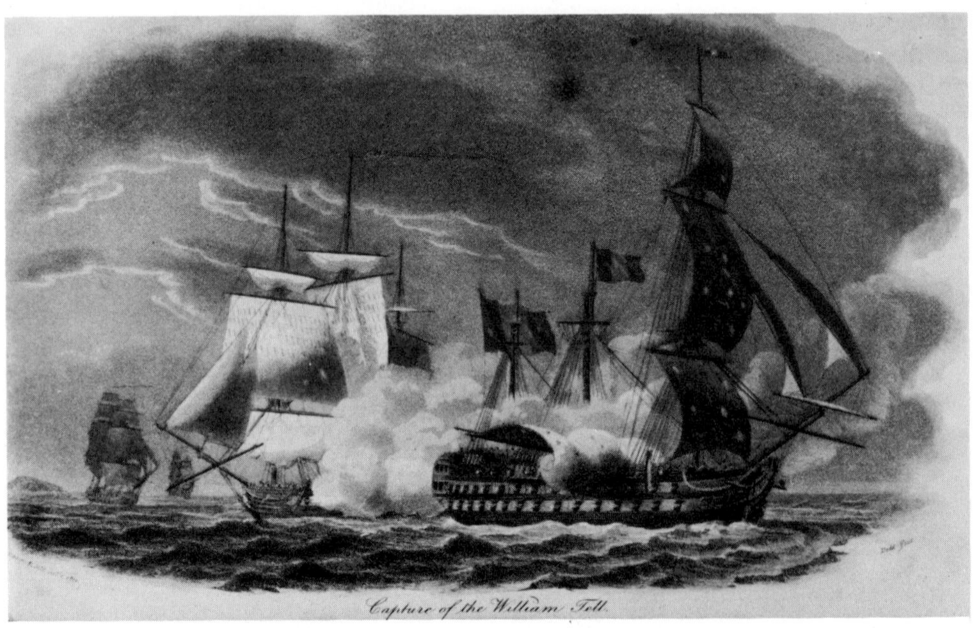

E

EAKINS, Thomas **1844-1916**
Born in Philadelphia. Portraitist, marine painter and teacher, who was at one time a lecturer at the Academy of Arts in Philadelphia. He was an admirable painter, though from his situation his subjects were rather confined to small boat scenes and rowing. He studied at the Academies of Philadelphia and Paris.

Examples of his marines may be found at the Museum of Fine Arts, Boston, the Metropolitan Museum of Art, New York, the Philadelphia Museum of Art, and the National Gallery, Washington.

EATON, William **1836-1896**
An American ship portraitist. The Peabody Museum of Salem has three of his oils.

ECKERSBERG, Christoffer Wilhelm **1783-1853**
Born in Sundeved, Schleswig-Holstein, on January 2nd, 1783, and died in Copenhagen on July 22nd, 1853. He was a pupil of Soren Abildgaard and Louis David. He later travelled to Rome and Paris before settling in Copenhagen where he practised painting over a wide range of subjects. In the field of marine painting he stands out as the best of the emerging school of Danish painters. In 1818 he was appointed a lecturer at the Copenhagen Academy of Fine Arts.

PLATES: 343, 344, 345.

EXAMPLES: Statens Museum for Kunst, Copenhagen (17 marines): the 84-gun man of war Dronning Marie; *ships in the Sound north of Kronborg Castle; the Russian ship of the line* Asow *off Elsinore; ships in the Roads of Copenhagen; the corvette* Galathea *in a gale in the North Sea; a frigate reefing sails in a freshening wind; a corvette off the cliffs of Moen; a frigate and some other ships cruising; two Russian ships of the line saluting; a corvette lying to form a conference with a brig in the West Indies; a Russian fleet at anchor off Elsinore; the corvette* Galathea *lying to assist the brig* St Jean *at dawn after a stormy night; the starboard battery and deck of the corvette* Najaden; *King Christian VIII on his steamship* Aegir; *a privateer outsailing a pursuing frigate; a calm with a boat pulling out to an American man of war; a corvette on the stocks. Other examples in Denmark are in the Royal Naval Museum, Copenhagen, and the Danish Maritime Museum in Kronborg Castle.*

EDGAR, W.
An Australian ship portraitist who sailed to San Francisco on the barque *Jane L. Stanford* in 1918 and settled there. The National Maritime Museum of San Francisco has three examples of his work, and the National Maritime Museum, Greenwich, a painting by him of the four-masted barque *Glencairn.*

PLATE: 634.

EERTVELT (ERTVELT), Andries van **1590-1652**
Born and died in Antwerp. If it is true that he was a pupil of H.C. Vroom's (q.v.) then he was the most distinguished of them to carry on the Flemish mannerist style. In any case the similarity of their interests must have involved them professionally. This is underlined by an early painting of Eertvelt's in the National Maritime Museum, which is a smaller version of the great Vroom in the Rijksmuseum, Amsterdam, showing the return of Houteman from the East in 1599. In this the ships are in the same positions but Eertvelt has painted the boats in the foreground to his own composition. Early Eertvelts of this type are colourful with glazes of a bright clarity and great precision of execution. They are never large and up to the 1960s were often wrongly attributed to the mythical "Aert van Antum", now known to be Aert Anthonisz (q.v.); this in turn suggests that Eertvelt may also have been one of his pupils.

Eertvelt was an artist whose palette and style changed over the years, his travels in Italy clearly influencing an artist who was an experimenter. Later works are more broadly painted and often much larger than earlier ones. The palette is less brightly varied and becomes more pastel in tone. He had a characteristic effect of making his rigging light against a dark background, though this device was copied by followers.

His best known pupils were Hendrick van Minderhout (q.v.), who was also his best pupil, Mathieu van Plattenberg (q.v.), who was his most successful pupil, Sebastian Castro, whose work is still usually mistaken for his master's, and Kasper van Eyck (q.v.).

Eertvelt was painted in Antwerp by Van Dyke in 1632; this portrait is now in Augsburg.

PLATES: 23, 24, 25, 26; COLOUR PLATE: III.

EXAMPLES: Museum of Bergues, near Dunkirk (1): Battle of Lepanto. Birmingham Art Gallery (1): galleys in action. Musée des Beaux-Arts, Ghent (1): ships in a storm with Barbary galleys wrecked on rocks (this painting is slightly larger, 70ins. x 138ins./175cm x 350cm, than the picture in Vienna and is probably the biggest Eertvelt in the world). Musée de Gratz (1): a Dutch river scene. National Maritime Museum, Greenwich (14): the return of Houtman's fleet to Amsterdam in 1599; the capture of San Salvador in 1624; Dutch ships running onto a rocky coast; loading timber in a northern port; Algerine ship off a Barbary port; Dutch ship running out of a harbour; Spanish galleon; Dutch ship at anchor off Genoa; daybreak after the bombardment of a port by Spanish ships; return of a Spanish expedition; action between English and Spanish ships; action between Spanish and Dutch ships; Spanish ships engaging Barbary galleys; embarkation of Spanish troops; Dutch yachts racing. The Hermitage, Leningrad (2): an action between Dutch and Spanish ships and a port scene. Musée de Maine (1 late marine). Alte Pinakothek, Munich (5): galleons and galleys in action; a Mediterranean port scene; fishing boats in a stiff breeze and galleys in action off a port (pair); Dutch vessels in a storm. Mariners Museum, Newport News (1): action between Spanish ships and Barbary pirates. Musée de la Marine, Paris (1): harbour scene. Musée de Valenciennes (1 marine). Kunsthistorisches Museum, Vienna (1): Spanish ships and galleys off a fort (a very large picture 73ins. x 125ins./184cm x 318cm).

ELLIOT, Thomas **fl.1790-1800**

This painter was working in Portsmouth in the last decade of the 18th century. His earliest known work, of which there are several versions, was of the Spanish Armament of 1790, showing the fleet mobilised at Spithead. There are also a number of versions of a pair of views showing the entrance to Portsmouth harbour, one of a three-decker leaving and one of ships at anchor from south of the harbour entrance; all these were painted in the late 1790s.

Although Elliot's style is modelled on that of Dominic Serres (q.v.), to whom his pictures have been mistakenly attributed, his talent was a much frailer one. It is presumed he died about 1800.

PLATE: 244.

ELLIOTT, Lieutenant William R.N. **fl.1784-1791**

The confusion as to which of the William Elliotts in the Royal Navy was the painter has never been satisfactorily resolved. The favourite has been the man who, having been previously in the merchant service, was master's mate of the *Roebuck* for four years, before passing for lieutenant on May 11th, 1782. He went on to be promoted to commander in 1790 and captain in 1810 and died in 1838.

If this identification is correct then it is odd that he should have ceased to exhibit in 1791 and that his latest known picture is of the *Victory* off Bastia in 1794. A painting of King George III reviewing the fleet at Spithead in 1789, signed Lieutenant W. Elliott, was exhibited at the Free Society in 1790; he exhibited there again in 1791. Previous to this he had exhibited at the Royal Academy every year from 1784 to 1789.

He went in for large canvases and painted battle pieces of reasonable quality.

PLATES: 253, 254.

EXAMPLES: The United States Naval Academy Museum, Annapolis (2): both of the action between the Serapis *and the* Bonhomme Richard, *1779. National Maritime Museum, Greenwich (2): Lord Howe's Relief of Gibraltar 1782; King George III in the* Southampton *reviewing the fleet at Spithead 1789.*

ELLIS, Edwin John **1841-1895**

Born in Nottingham. Like his master, Henry Dawson (q.v.), he started his working life in a Nottingham lace factory. He moved to London and set up as a landscape and coastal painter. He did not exhibit very much, showing only one work (not a marine) at the Royal Academy and one at Suffolk Street. He died on April 19th, 1895.

He was also a poet and book illustrator. Examples of his work are held by the Victoria and Albert Museum, Maidstone Museum, the City Art Gallery, Manchester, and the Castle Museum, Norwich.

ELLIS, Joseph F. **c.1783-1848**

In 1818 he moved from Ireland, where he was born, to London and specialised in making copies of Canalettos. He also painted marines rather in the manner of George Webster (q.v.), but in a harder style. He died on May 28th, 1848, at Richmond, Surrey.

He only exhibited twice at the Royal Academy, in 1819 and 1820, but had works at the British Institution from 1819 to 1822 and in 1829. He also exhibited at the Society of Artists.

PLATE: 365.

ELLIS, Vic R.S.M.A. **b.1921**

This contemporary artist, who lives at Leigh-on-Sea, sketches mainly around the Thames estuary and East Anglian coast and is a specialist on East Coast small craft. He was elected a member of the Royal Society of Marine Artists in 1969.

PLATE: 657.

ELZER, Hendrik Jacob **1808-c.1844**

Born and died in Amsterdam, he was a pupil of Hendrik Gerrit den Cate, the landscape and flower painter, and later became interested in marine painting from working in the studio of Johannes Christiaan Schotel (q.v.). In 1835 he became a member of the Royal Academy in Amsterdam.

EMERIC, F.J.

A French 18th century primitive. A single watercolour at the Peabody Museum of Salem, of a French 3-decker and dated 1782, is a forerunner of the style of the Roux family (qq.v.).

ERTVELT, Andries van *see* EERTVELT, Andries van

ESCHKE, Wilhelm Benjamin Hermann **1823-1900**

Born and died in Berlin. He was a pupil of the Berlin marine painter Wilhelm Krause and of Lepoittevin, in Paris. He afterwards settled in his native city, but travelled in Europe to paint. He exhibited three works at the Royal Academy Exhibitions in London: a Baltic coast scene in 1869, Freshwater Bay, Isle of Wight, in 1885 and Newlyn Harbour, Cornwall in 1889.

EXAMPLES: National Gallery of Victoria, Melbourne (1): Freshwater Bay, Isle of Wight. Art Gallery of New South Wales, Sydney (1): sunrise over the Isle of Wight.

EURICH, Richard Ernst R.A. **b.1903**

Born in Bradford on March 14th, 1903. He was a pupil at Bradford Grammar School, Bradford School of Arts and Crafts and the Slade School. During the Second World War he worked for the War Artists' Commission and his pictures, which are among the best, are divided between the Imperial War Museum, the National Maritime Museum and the Tate Gallery. Notable among the eleven canvases at Greenwich are the evacuation of Dunkirk 1940 and an ingenious view of the midget submarine attack on the *Scharnhorst* in 1943, as if seen in a fishtank.

PLATES: 669, 670.

EVERDINGEN, Allaert van **1621-1675**

Born in Alkmaar on June 18th, 1621, and died in Amsterdam on November 8th, 1675. A landscape painter who painted a few marines. He was first a pupil of Roeland Savery (q.v.) and after his death, of Pieter Molyn the Elder. Such marines as he painted usually had stormy subjects but his chief interest for the purposes of this work is that he was one of the masters of Ludolf Bakhuizen (q.v.).

PLATE: 16.

EXAMPLES (marines only): Avignon Museum (1). National Museum, Belgrade (1): rough sea in a canal. Gemäldegalerie, Frankfurt (1): storm. The Hermitage, Leningrad (1): entrance to a harbour. Bavarian State Collections, Munich (1): storm, with ship wrecked on a high coast. Johnson Collection, Philadelphia (1): small vessels beating to windward in a stiff breeze.

EVERETT, Herbert (John) **1876-1949**

He was the son of the rector of Dorchester where he was born on August 18th, 1876. The family travelled a good deal in Europe and he had his first lessons in painting from an Italian called Lantza Lugi in Munich.

Although he had been christened Herbert and was always known as such by his family, he did not like the name and called himself John instead. In October 1896 he moved to London to study at the Slade School of Art. This was at the time when Frederick Brown presided there, assisted by Henry Tonks, Walter Russell and Wilson Steer. William Orpen and Augustus John, Everett's particular friends, were also there as pupils, and all three lodged together in Everett's mother's house in Fitzroy Street.

In May 1898, after leaving the Slade, Everett shipped aboard the sailing ship *Iquique* as a "passenger" but borne on the books as a seaman, with a token payment of a shilling per month. In Capetown the captain bought a camera and plates which Everett used to take shipboard pictures. The *Iquique* sailed on to Sydney and home via the Horn, by which time Everett had been promoted to bo'sun. They docked at Gravesend on April 18th, 1899.

As well as taking photographs Everett had been sketching aboard ship, and he is unique in that a large part of his output consists of deck scenes on the ships he sailed in, or on other vessels. In 1901 he married a cousin and together they sailed to Hobart as passengers in the barque *Brierholm* in 1902. She hated it; he did very little work. Shortly after their return they sold the house in Fitzroy Street and moved to Dorset. For the time being this was the end of Everett's deep water sailing. He bought a 9-ton cutter called the *Walrus* and from that time until the First World War he painted mainly yachting and port scenes, many of them French.

The wartime security restrictions put an end to yachting and coastal sketching; so when his marriage broke up Everett returned to London and, after brief service in the army, worked on paintings about sea commerce for the Ministry of Information. He was particularly inspired by the "dazzle painted" method of camouflaging ships, invented by the painter Norman Wilkinson (q.v.).

After the war he used to paint the Surrey docks, then still frequented by big sailing ships, and the idea of sailing again in one of these resulted in a voyage to Texas in the barque *Birkdale,* from which he made many drawings and paintings. Despite the fact that it was getting harder and harder to find a berth on the fast disappearing sailing ships he made one more voyage, in 1928, in the Danish barque *Suzanne* (ex *Kylemore,* which is how his drawings are marked). She sailed to Martinique and again Everett used the experience to produced a mass of work, eighty-three oils and three hundred drawings.

Most years in the 1930s he would make a sea voyage, though now in steamers. He spent most of the war in Herefordshire so his work in this period is of landscape subjects. He never sold any of his work and lived on gradually diminishing private means. At the Slade he had been thought of as perhaps the most promising of a remarkable class, but while Orpen and John developed, Everett never achieved their success, nor sought it. His drawings, many in pastel, are very fine but much of his oil work is rather coarse in colouring. In 1923 he studied aquatinting in France and installed a large printing press in his studio in St. John's Wood. Some of his best work is in this medium.

He died in London in 1949 and left all his marines to the National Maritime Museum, Greenwich; the bequest amounts to 1,700 oil paintings and about twice as many drawings and engravings.

PLATES: 643, 644, 645.

EVERS, Carl G.

A contemporary painter of maritime subjects, both historical and contemporary, of a good quality. He was born in Germany though his father was English. He studied at the Slade School in London and in Sweden, before emigrating to the United States in 1947.

There is a gallery devoted to his paintings aboard the U.S.S. *Alabama,* the battleship docked as a memorial museum in Mobile, Alabama. The U.S. Naval Institute and the South Street Seaport Museum, New York, have examples of his work.

EYCK, Gaspar (Kaspar) van **1613-1673**

Born in Antwerp, he was one of the pupils of Andries van Eertvelt (q.v.), and carried on the Flemish mannerist tradition. Few of his pictures have survived and, coming from a well-to-do family, he perhaps did not feel any necessity to produce a large output. In his mid-forties his performance was further impaired by a mental breakdown, which recurred for the rest of his life, and is said to have been brought on by the death of his parents. He was a Master of the Guild of Antwerp in 1632 and afterwards lived for a time in Genoa before moving to Brussels, where his brother, Hendrick, looked after him, and where he also died.

PLATE: 31.

EXAMPLES: National Maritime Museum, Greenwich (1): Mediterranean coast scene. Maritime Museum, Haifa (1): coast scene. Staatliche Kunsthalle, Karlsruhe (1): harbour scene. Prado, Madrid (3): sea battle with galleys; two Mediterranean scenes of galleys and ships off castles.

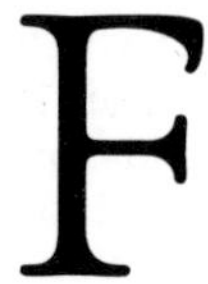

FANNEN, J. **fl.1893-1900**
The National Maritime Museum, Greenwich, has three ship portraits by this artist dated 1893, 1898 and 1901. One shows the barque *Camphill* passing through the Downs.

The Sunderland Art Gallery has a portrait of the barque *Regent* and it has been suggested that he was a Sunderland artist.

PLATE: 611.

FAXON, Richard **fl.1859-1875**
He was a native of Bordeaux and a pupil of the naval history painter Jean Durand-Brager (q.v.). He did not follow his master in this specialisation, though he did some historical subjects. He exhibited at the Paris Salon from 1859 to 1875.

PLATE: 503.

EXAMPLES: Brest (1): action between an English cutter and a Spanish schooner. Peabody Museum of Salem (1): American sailing ship Adriatic.

FEDELER, Carl **1837-1897**
He was the son and pupil of Carl Justin Harmen Fedeler (q.v.). An illustrator, he also painted on glass. Many of his paintings are in the Museum at Bremen, where he was born. He died in Bremerhaven.

FEDELER, Carl Justus Harmen **1799-1858**
Born and died in Bremen. He was an engraver and lithographer, as well as a painter. The City Art Gallery, Hanover, has a fishing boat scene by him, and the Peabody Museum of Salem a ship portrait in oils.

FEDI, Giuseppe
An early 19th century Neapolitan ship portraitist. The Peabody Museum of Salem has one signed watercolour and seven attributed to him.

FISCHER, Anton Otto **1882-1962**
Born in Munich on February 23rd, 1882, and died in Shandaken, New York, on March 26th, 1962. As a youth he went to Hamburg and to sea. In 1903 he was working in the British barque *Gwydyr Castle* when she put into New York, where he was paid off. Instead of getting another berth he stayed there crewing in yachts and instructing in seamanship in the school ship *St. Mary's.*

In 1904 he went to work for Arthur Frost, the painter and illustrator. In 1906 the Frost family moved to France and Fischer went back to crewing yachts, but by now he was determined to train to be an artist. At the end of the season he had saved seven hundred dollars, with which he went to Paris and enrolled in the Académie Julian and studied under Jean Paul Laurens. He returned to New York in 1908 and set up as a painter and illustrator. By 1912 he was established and successful, and best known for his illustrations of Jack London's stories. He became an American citizen in 1916. After the war he became one of America's most sought-after illustrators, and his drawings for the long-running series *Tug-Boat Annie* in the *Saturday Evening Post* are perhaps his best known works.

In the Second World War he did war posters and was commissioned in the U.S. Coastguard Service with the rank of lieutenant-commander. After the war he did a series of war pictures for *Life* magazine and wrote and illustrated a book called *Fo'c'sle Days,* 1947. Although he painted straight marines these often had strong genre overtones, and he seems to have preferred to include a human element.

Examples of his work are in the United States Naval Academy Museum, Annapolis, the Imperial War Museum, London, the Norwegian Maritime Museum in Oslo, and the Navy Memorial Museum, Navy Yard, Washington.

FISHER, Captain Roger Roland Sutton **b.1919**
C.B.E., D.S.C., R.N., F.R.S.A.
He was born on August 3rd, in Dover. He joined the Royal Navy in 1937, and rose to the rank of captain in the Supply and Secetariat branch. During his service he trained in the law and became a barrister. After his retirement, in 1973, he served as a Deputy Circuit Judge. At the same time he took up marine painting as a profession. He exhibits with the Royal Society of Marine Artists, the Armed Forces Art Society and the Wapping Group of Artists. The Board of Admiralty commissioned a number of paintings from him of the Silver Jubilee Review of the Fleet in 1977, one of which hangs in the Royal Yacht *Britannia.*

PLATE: 673.

FISHER, Rowland R.O.I., R.S.M.A. **1885-1969**
The son of a master mariner, he painted landscapes and marines in oils and was a member of the Royal Institute of Oil Painters, of the Royal Society of Marine Artists, and the St. Ives Society of Artists. He also exhibited at the Royal Academy. He lived for many years at Great Yarmouth in Norfolk, and was President of the Yarmouth and District Society of Artists. He died on May 14th, 1969.

FORREST, Captain Haughton **1825-1924**
Born at Boulogne on December 28th, 1825, he was the son of Captain T.A. Forrest of Forrest Lodge, near Windsor, a sometime military equerry to Queen Victoria. The compiler does not know what art training this painter had but the results show a precocious talent. Most of his early work seems to have been on commission, and one of his patrons was the Prince of Wales.

He served in the army for some years, then in the Post Office in London. About 1875 he left the country with the idea of settling in Southern Brazil. This proved unsuccessful and he moved on to Tasmania in 1876, where he settled in Hobart for the rest of his long life and devoted himself to painting. Some of his works were used for Tasmanian stamps in 1899. He died in Hobart.

PLATE: 487.

FOSTER, Deryck R.S.M.A. **b.1924**
Born in Hampshire, he studied art at Bournemouth and, after serving in the Second World War, continued his studies at the Central School of Art in London. A keen yachtsman, he has specialised in maritime subjects, especially yachting scenes and has exhibited at the Royal Society of Marine Artists since 1950. He was elected a member in 1964.

He lives in Yarmouth, Isle of Wight, where he has a studio and a gallery. His work can be seen at the Russell-Cotes Museum in Bournemouth, and at the National Maritime Museum, Greenwich, which has a yachting scene on loan from the R.S.M.A.

PLATE: 690.

FOWLES, Arthur Wellington **c.1815-aft.1878**
He was baptised at Ryde, Isle of Wight, on January 15th, 1815. He was the son of a Ryde greengrocer, who was clearly an admirer of the "Iron Duke", and appears to have lived and worked there all his life. His work is of fair quality and a lot of it concerns the local yachting scene. However, he also liked to commemorate occasions, especially Queen Victoria's connection with the island, and some of his paintings were used by the *Illustrated London News.* There is a picture by him of the loss of the *Royal George,* 1782, in Ryde Town Hall.

EXAMPLES: National Maritime Museum, Greenwich (5): a bird's eye view of Queen Victoria's arrival at Cherbourg in 1858; the pilot cutter Fox; *three small sketches of river scenes. Mariners Museum, Newport News, Virginia (1): a view of Ryde 1847. The Peabody Museum of Salem (4): the yacht* America; *the yacht* Corinne; *the yacht* Florinda; *an unidentified cutter and yacht.*

FRANCIA, Alexandre T. **c.1815-1884**
The date of his birth in Calais is thought to have been either 1815 or 1820. He was the pupil of his father, Louis Francia (q.v.) and exhibited at the Paris Salon between 1841 and 1866. He is presumably the "Count Alexendi T. Francia" who exhibited at the Royal Academy exhibitions of 1841, 1842 and 1867, and at the British Institution in 1842 and 1843. He died in Brussels.

EXAMPLES: Musée des Beaux-Arts, Calais (4).

FRANCIA, François Thomas Louis **1772-1839**
Born and died in Calais. In his early twenties he came to London, possibly to escape from the French Revolution, and exhibited his first picture at the Royal Academy Exhibition of 1795. He remained in England, becoming the secretary of the Society of Associated Artists in Watercolours and, in 1811, painter to the Duchess of York. Between 1795 and 1822 he exhibited eighty works at the Royal Academy exhibitions, and his style was noticeably affected by that of Turner (q.v.). He returned to Calais in 1817, and exhibited at the Salons du Louvre from 1835 until his death. It was in Calais in 1817 that Francia took on his most famous pupil, Richard Parkes Bonington (q.v.), whose work has a strong affinity to his master's.

EXAMPLES: Cecil Higgins Museum, Bedford (1): a fishing boat off Boulogne. Musée des Beaux-Arts, Calais (5). National Gallery, Dublin (1): view of Calais. Victoria and Albert Museum, London (watercolours). Manchester City Art Gallery (watercolours). Castle Museum, Norwich (2): both of the salvaging of a vessel off Yarmouth.

FRANCIS, W.
An American ship portraitist, working in Seattle in the 19th century. The Peabody Museum of Salem, has a gouache drawing by him.

FRASER, John R.B.A. **1858-1927**
He came from a nautical family. His brother, William, went to sea and in 1890, at the age of eighteen, was washed overboard and lost while outward-bound for Australia. His other brother, Rodney, also went to sea and rose to become a master; he too was later drowned.

In 1885 John Fraser sailed to North America without telling his family. He seems to have stayed there for three years and for the next twenty years travelled widely all over the world. It is not known where he studied, but his style from the beginning closely identifies with those of Thomas Somerscales and Edouardo de Martino (qq.v.), and changed surprisingly little during his whole working life.

There is an extant copy by him of Somerscales's famous "Off Valparaiso," but his affinity to de Martino in particular resulted in an intriguing development. De Martino was marine painter to several crowned heads, including Queen Victoria, Edward VII and George V. The result was that he had more commissions than he could handle. He therefore hit on the idea of getting Fraser to paint some of his commissions for him. He would then finish and sign them. In the case of one picture, for example, a portrait of one of Sir Thomas Lipton's *Shamrocks,* he only added a flag before signing it. At the time of de Martino's death in 1912, Fraser was working on a commission for the King of the man-of-war *Juno* of 1757. It was never delivered because de Martino was not there to sign it and is now at Greenwich. Fraser was subsequently in touch with de Martino's solicitors about six pictures which had been delivered but not paid for, and for which Fraser was seeking to get the money paid to him instead of to the de Martino estate.

Fraser first exhibited at the Royal Academy in 1880, and in every year from from 1885 to 1905, then in most years until 1919.

In later life he kept a print shop in the Grosvenor Road, Westminster, and sold reproductions; it was outside this shop that he dropped dead on April 25th, 1927. Between 1954 and 1956 his widow, who was by then living in one room in Wood Green, disposed of the residue of his studio to the National Maritime Museum, Greenwich. The collection comprises some sixty sketchbooks, sixty oil paintings and over one hundred watercolours.

PLATES: 595, 596.

FREITAG, C.
An American ship portraitist working in New York in the middle of the 19th century. The Peabody Museum of Salem has an oil by him.

FRENCH, Howard B.
An American painter working in California in the first half of this century. The Peabody Museum of Salem has an oil dated 1933.

FULLER, Edmund G. R.B.A. **fl.1888-1916**
A painter of good quality coastal scenes, marines, landscapes and figures, who initially exhibited from an address in London, but who, in 1891/2, joined the artists' colony in St. Ives in Cornwall. He was a member of the Royal Society of British Artists.

PLATE: 594.

FUNNO, Michele
A Neapolitan ship portraitist — a primitive — working in the second and third quarters of the 19th century. The Peabody Museum of Salem has three watercolours and a gouache by him.

FYRE, S.H.
A Glasgow ship portraitist working in the third quarter of the 19th century. The Peabody Museum of Salem has an oil by him of fairly good quality.

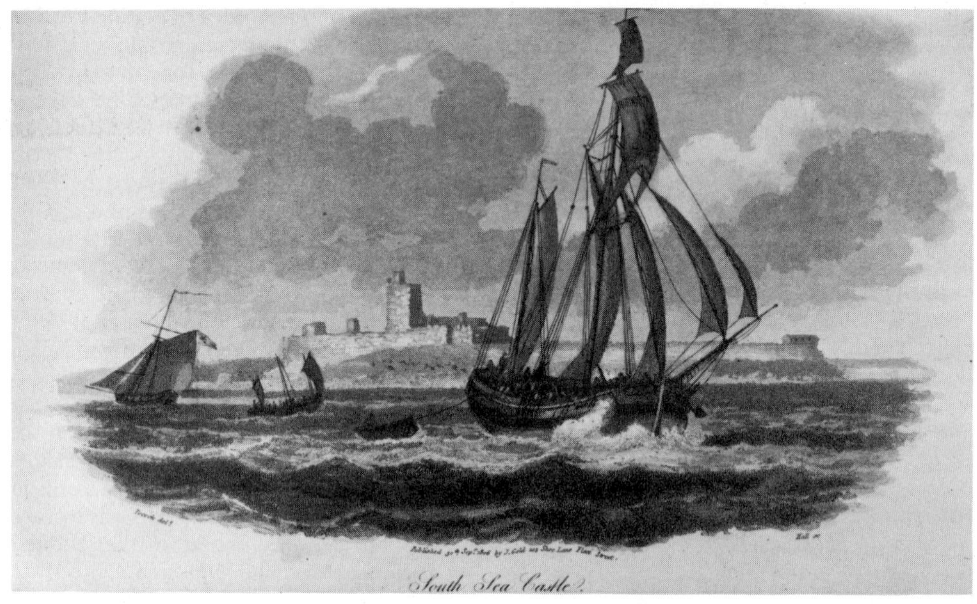

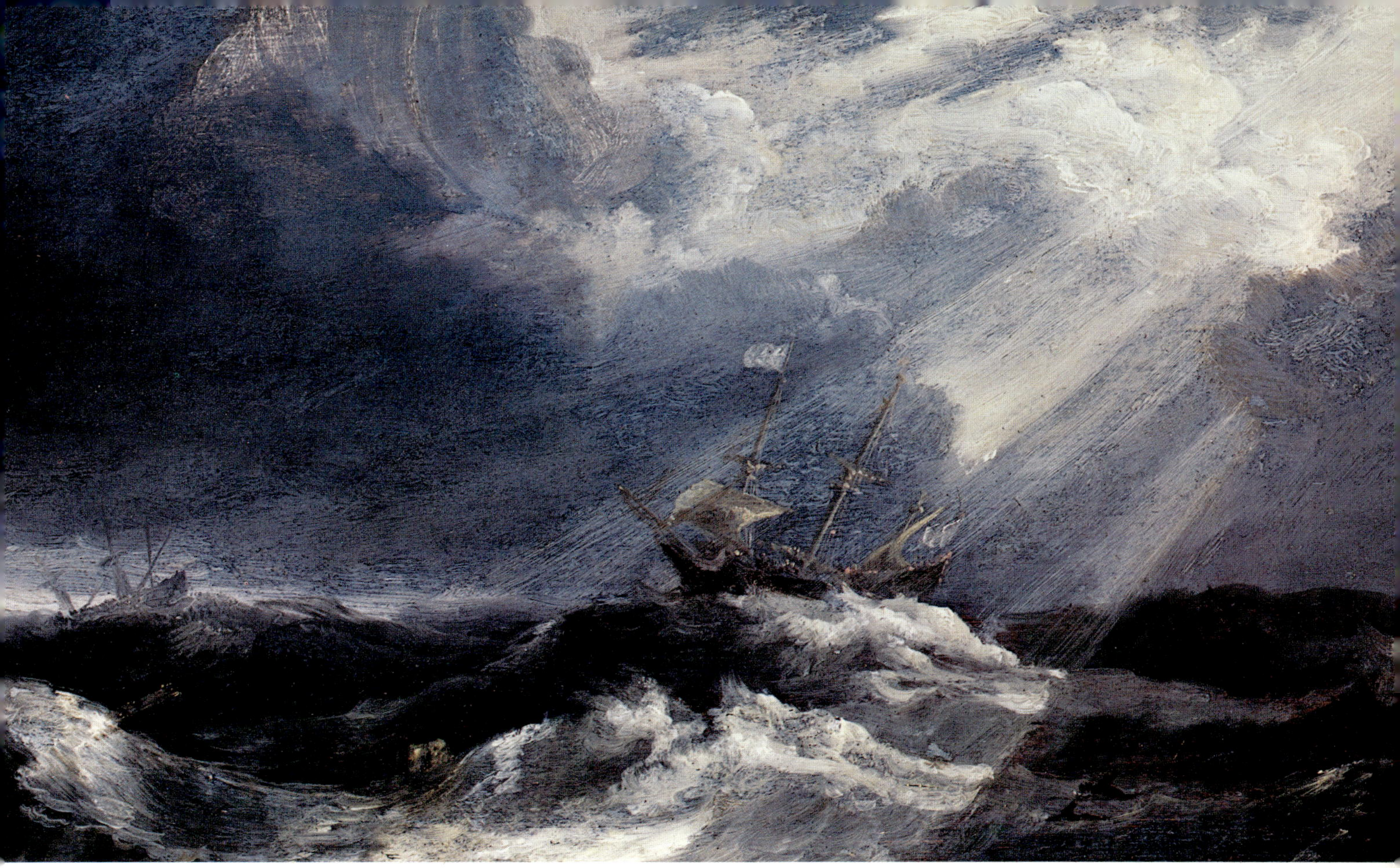

Colour Plate VI. Bonaventura Peeters, the Elder, 1614-1652. "A stormy day at sea." National Maritime Museum, Greenwich.

Colour Plate VII. Hendrick-Jacobsz Dubbels, c.1620-1676. "A smalschip passing under the bows of a Dutch flagship." National Maritime Museum, Greenwich.

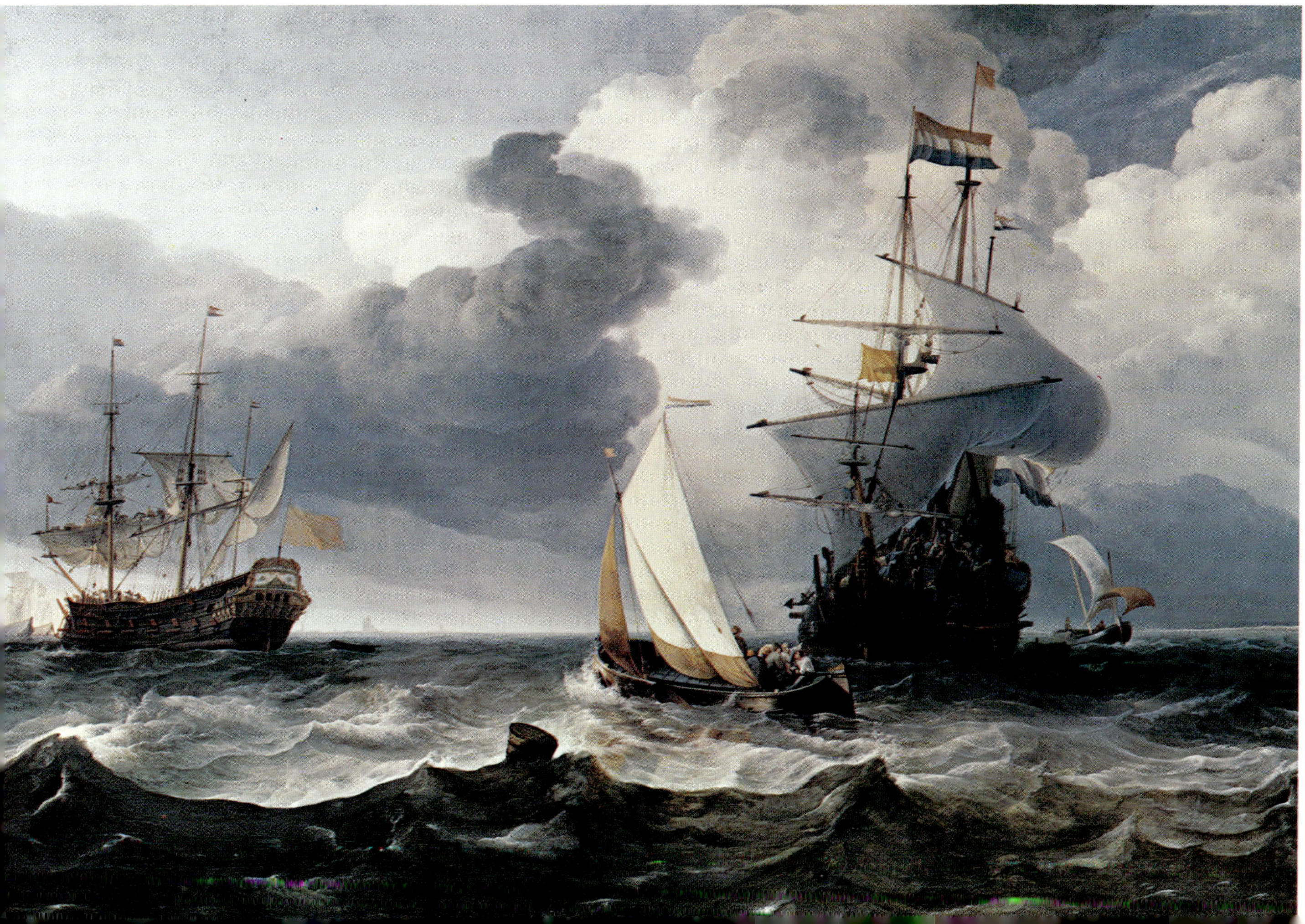

G

GALE, G.M.
A ship portraitist working in the third quarter of the 19th century, either British or American but more likely the latter. The Peabody Museum of Salem has an oil.

GALE, J.
The National Maritime Museum, Greenwich, has a pair of small paintings by him, dated about 1880; a Danish brig driven ashore, and a Danish steam frigate.

GALEA, Luigi Maria **1847-1917**
Born and died in Malta. A painter and restorer who studied in Malta and at Naples and Rome. He returned to work in Malta, where he had a similar practice to Gianni (q.v.), doing portraits of Royal Naval ships and views of Malta, especially Grand Harbour. Like Gianni, much of his output is to be found in England. From 1882 to 1885 he served as war artist for the Egyptian campaigns, and was present at Tel-el-Kebir. On the recommendation of Admiral Sir Charles Drury, who had been Commander-in-Chief, Mediterranean, 1907 to 1908, he was awarded a Royal Academy diploma.

The National Maritime Museum, Greenwich, has seven portraits of Royal Naval ships.

GALLARD-LEPINAY, Paul Charles Emmanuel **1842-1885**
Born in Aulnay near Brest on May 23rd, 1842, and died in Paris in March, 1885. A French marine painter who exhibited at the Paris Salon from 1864.

EXAMPLES: Rijksmuseum, Amsterdam (1): a ship off Venice. Musée de Cherbourg (1): visit of Grevy, Say and Gambetta to the French squadron at Cherbourg in 1880.

GAMAIN, Louis Honoré Fredéric **1803-1871**
Born in Crotoy on April 22nd, 1803; died in Le Havre on March 1st, 1871. He was a pupil of Baron Gudin (q.v.), and exhibited at the Paris Salon between 1833 and 1843. He seems to have been essentially a ship portraitist. The National Museum of History and Technology, Washington, has a painting of the Collins Line steamer *Atlantic* arriving at Liverpool on her maiden voyage on May 9th, 1850.

GARDNER, Derek George Montague **b.1914**
V.R.D., R.S.M.A.
Born on February 13th, 1914. A self-taught artist who specialises in historical maritime subjects but also paints from nature. He was a member of the Royal Naval Volunteer Reserve from 1934 to 1947, retiring with the rank of Commander. He was mentioned in dispatches in 1942 while in H.M.S. *Broke.* In civilian life he was a Chartered Civil Engineer until he retired in 1963. He was elected a member of the Royal Society of Marine Artists in 1966 and has had one-man shows at the Polak Gallery in London in 1972, 1975 and 1979.

PLATE: 682.

EXAMPLES: National Maritime Museum, Greenwich (2): the Garthpool; *a view of Erith Reach towards Dagenham. Bermuda Maritime Museum (1).*

GARLING, Frederick **1806-1873**
Born in London, he emigrated to Sydney as a child in 1814, and grew up to be a ship portraitist in watercolours. In 1826 he went as the artist on Captain James Stirling's expedition to Western Australia. He died in Sydney.

Examples of his work may be seen at the National Gallery of South Australia in Adelaide, the National Library at Canberra, the National Gallery of Western Australia at Perth, and the Dixon and Mitchell Libraries at Sydney.

GARNAIN, Louis
Ship portraitist working in the middle of the 19th century, apparently French and possibly from Honfleur. The Peabody Museum of Salem has a wash drawing by him, dated 1861.

GARNERAY, Ambroise Louis **1783-1857**
Born and died in Paris. A son of the painter Jean François Garneray, at thirteen he persuaded his father to let him go to sea in a man-of-war commanded by a cousin. In 1795 he was in the Indian Ocean serving in *La Confiance,* a privateer commanded by Robert Surcouf. Years later he did paintings of her taking the East Indiaman *Kent* in 1800, so perhaps he was still aboard her then. By 1805 he was back in the navy, when he was shipwrecked in the *Atalante* near the Cape of Good Hope. He was transferred to the frigate *Belle Poule,* but she was captured in 1806. He was consigned to the hulk *Prothée* in Portsmouth Harbour, and was to remain a prisoner until the end of the war in 1814.

He later described his life in the hulks in a book called *Captivité de L.G.* Conditions were grim and many of the prisoners turned their hands to a trade to make money to buy luxuries. The best known product of the prisoners were the bone models of ships, but Garneray, who had received some instruction in painting before he went to sea, determined to take it up again. He began with portraits, but later, in 1812, when he had learnt English and become an interpreter and a privileged prisoner, living ashore in a parole area, he executed a series of views of Portsmouth Harbour from the north, with the lines of prison hulks in the foreground. One of these is in the National Library of Australia (Rex Nan Kivell Collection), Canberra. In 1813 he nearly escaped and was only recaptured in the Channel in a boat by the *Vengeance*. He thus spent his last few months of captivity stripped of his privileges and in great privation.

Back in France he became a professional marine painter, exhibiting at the Paris Salon from 1817. In 1833 he became the director of the Museum of Fine Arts at Rouen, and in 1852 was created a Chevalier of the Légion d'Honneur.

PLATE: 324.

EXAMPLES: Musée d'Arras (1): the bombardment of Mogadore 1844. Musée Calvet, Avignon (1): naval action. Musée Municipal, Cambrai (1): beach scene. Musée Municipal, Douai (1): view of Escaut. National Maritime Museum, Greenwich (3): all views of the prison hulks in Portsmouth Harbour. Musée des Beaux-Arts, La Rochelle, (2): the taking of the East Indiaman Kent *by the privateer* Confiance *in the Bay of Bengal, 1800; a view of Amsterdam. Musée des Beaux-Arts, Le Havre (1): ships at anchor. Musée des Beaux-Arts, Nantes (2): Battle of Gravelines, 1588; Battle of Navarino, 1827. Musée Municipal, Narbonne (1): Battle of Navarino, 1827. Musée Cheret, Nice (1): the Dardanelles. Musée de la Marine, Paris (3): actions. City Museum and Art Gallery, Portsmouth (2): a pair of views of the prison hulks at Portsmouth. Musée des Beaux-Arts, Rochefort (1): the French frigate* La Virginie *in action 1795. Musée de Saint Malo (1): the taking of the East Indiaman* Kent *by the privateer* Confiance *in the Bay of Bengal, 1800.*

GARTHWAITE, W. **fl.1850**

It is strange and unfortunate that we know nothing about this talented mid-19th century artist.

The Shipley Art Gallery, Gateshead, has a fine painting of herring fishing boats, 1852, and Merseyside Museums have one called "Shipping off the Welsh Coast," 1852; the National Maritime Museum, Greenwich, has one of the ship *Hotspur* leaving Tynemouth, 1851.

GASQUY, Marius

A French marine painter working in Marseilles in the first half of the 19th century, probably mainly as a ship portraitist. The example in the Peabody Museum of Salem is of quite good quality and reminiscent of the work of the Roux family (q.v.).

GAVARRONE, Domenico

A Genoese ship portraitist working in the second and third quarters of the 19th century; a primitive. The Mariners Museum, Newport News, has a portrait of the American ship *Audubon,* and the Peabody Museum of Salem has five watercolours by him.

GEAR, Joseph W. **1769-1853**

Born in Gosport in 1769. He had a London address when he exhibited two paintings at the Royal Academy in 1815, of the review of the fleet at Spithead by the Duke of Clarence. At this time he was marine painter to the Duke of Sussex.

The date of his move to America is not known; however, the Peabody Museum of Salem has a collection of thirty-seven drawings and watercolours, mainly of British vessels, which includes a watercolour of the figurehead of the U.S.S. *Washington,* and these are thought to have been done about 1820. The Museum also has nine watercolours attributed to him. He died in Cambridge, Mass., in 1853.

GEEL, Jan (Joost) van **1631-1698**

Born in Rotterdam, he was a merchant as well as a painter of marines and genre subjects and travelled in France, Germany and England. The Museum of Fine Arts at Lyon has a marine by him. He died in Rotterdam in 1698.

GELLÉE, Claude **1600-1682**
(called Claude (le) Lorraine)

He was born in Champagne in the Vosges but as a very young man he went with some friends to Rome, where he became a servant to the landscape and marine painter Agostino Buonamico (q.v.). This job turned out to be the springboard of one of the world's greatest landscape painters, who also did some marines; for his master, finding him interested, gave him a grounding in painting. Although his paintings usually have some title from a story in the Bible, the ostensible subject and the figures are quite secondary and the interest is heavily weighted on the side of landscape and shipping. He was one of the most widely admired and influential of painters in both the 18th and early 19th centuries. As a young man he travelled widely in Europe, but returned to Rome, where he settled and where he died in 1682.

PLATES: 1, 2.

EXAMPLES: Amberg Museum, Bavaria (1): seaport. Cincinnati Art Museum (1): coastal view. Wallraf-Richartz Museum, Cologne (1): A classical harbour scene with mourning Heliardae. Uffizi Gallery, Florence (1): seaport. Gotha Gallery (1): marine view. Grenoble Museum (1): seaport. Hermitage Museum, Leningrad (3): seaports. Dulwich Art Gallery, London (2): embarkation of St. Pauline; seaport. National Gallery, London (3): embarkation of St. Ursula; embarkation of the Queen of Sheba. Metropolitan Museum, New York (1): The Trojan women setting fire to their fleet. Prado Museum, Madrid (1): embarkation of St. Pauline. Bavarian State Collection, Munich (1): seaport. Capodimonte Palace, Naples (1): marine view. Louvre, Paris (7): disembarkation of Cleopatra; four port scenes; two marines. Nationalmuseum, Stockholm (1): seaport. Centraal Museum, Utrecht (1): coastal view.

GIANNI, G. (?Giacomo, ?Gennaro)

Artist working in the second half of the 19th century. Although he apparently spent his working life in Malta, he is not thought to have been Maltese, but a native of southern Italy. The similarity of his style to that of the de Simones (qq.v.) of Naples suggests an origin there, and perhaps he was one of their pupils.

His principal patrons were British naval officers, who commissioned portraits of their ships, views of the fleet in the Grand Harbour, Valletta, and so on.

He painted mainly in oils and the National Maritime Museum, Greenwich, has two views of Grand Harbour, dated 1876, a portrait of H.M.S. *Agincourt,* 1882, and two pictures showing H.M.S. *Alexandra* and units of the Mediterranean fleet in the Grand Harbour, dated 1888.

PLATES: 588, 589.

GIFFORD, Charles B.

An American painter of modest talent, working in the middle of the 19th century. The Peabody Museum of Salem has an oil by him, and he is also represented in the New Bedford Whaling Museum.

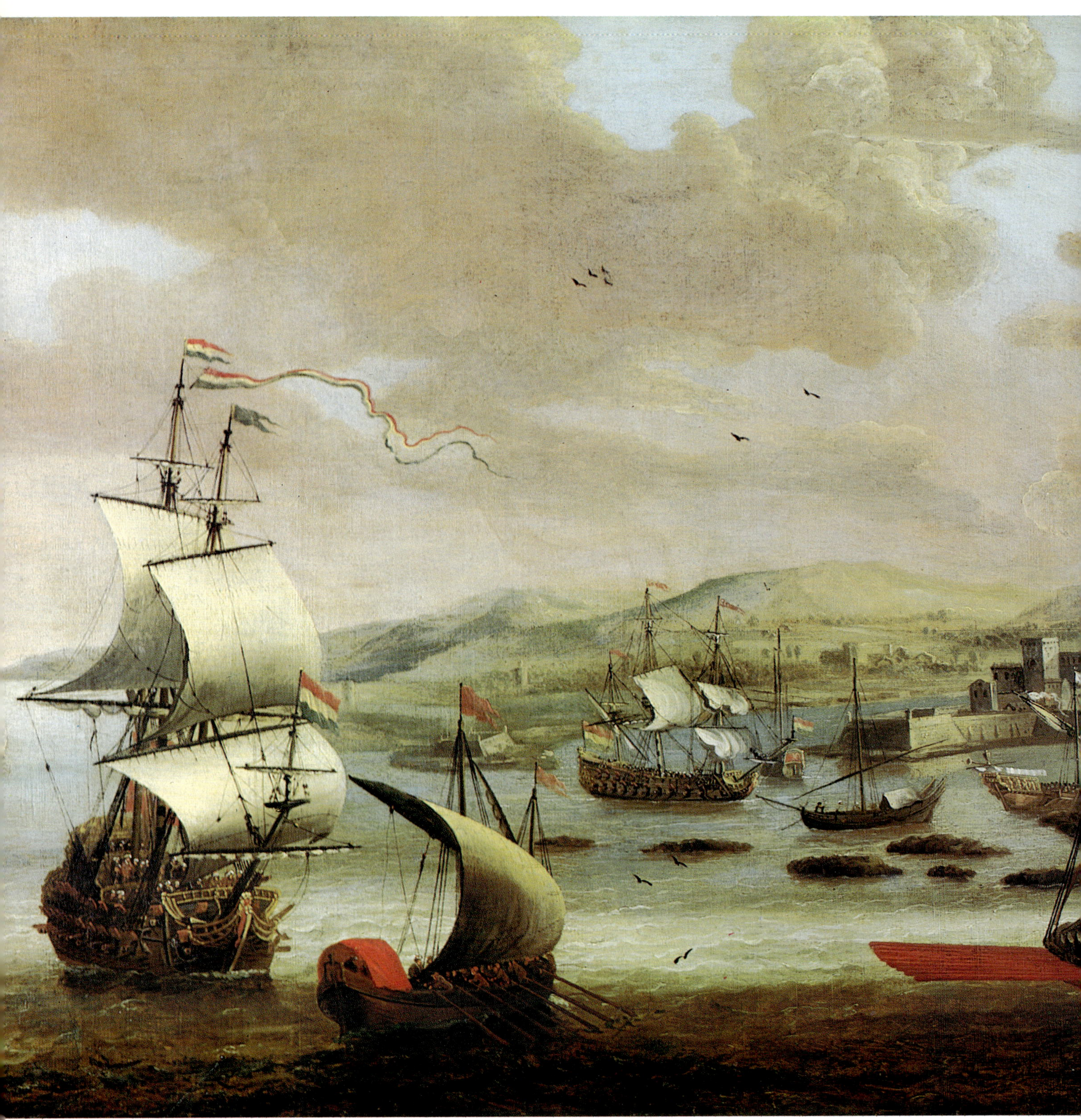

Colour Plate VIII. Jacob Knyff, 1638-1681. "Ships at Constantinople." Private collection.

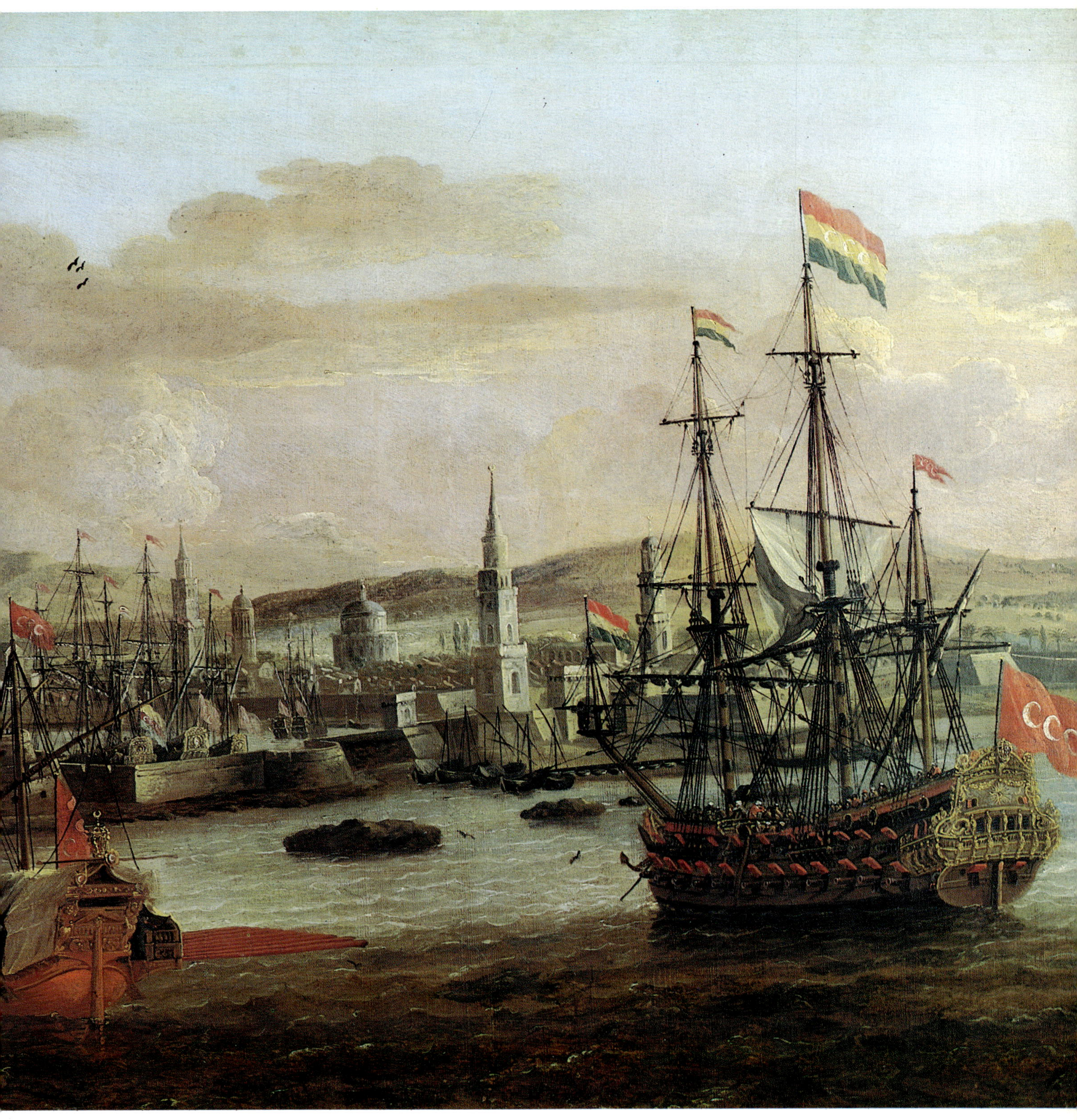

GILBERT, Pierre Julien **1783-1860**
Born in Brest he was a pupil there first of Nicholas Ozanne (q.v.) and then of Louis Crépin (q.v.) in Paris or Brest. He later became professor of drawing at the school of the Marine Royale. In 1830 he went as the official artist with the expedition to capture Algiers. He died in Brest in 1860.

PLATE: 322.

EXAMPLES: Musée de Cherbourg (2): marines. Musée des Beaux-Arts Nancy (1): landing of the army at Algiers, 1830. Musée de Saint Brieuc (1): the entrance to Toulon roadstead. Musée National de Versailles (10): all naval actions. Most, or all, of these have been transferred to the Musée de la Marine, Paris.

GILKERSON, William **b.1936**
He was born in Milwaukee, Wisconsin, on July 25th,1936, and first went to sea as a mess boy in a Norwegian freighter. He has followed the sea ever since, though now in his own boat. As an artist he works in oils and watercolours and also specialises in scrimshaw work. The subjects of his paintings are mainly sailing vessels and shipboard scenes.

He had a one man show at the National Maritime Museum, San Francisco, in 1973, and again there, with John Stobart, in 1975. Other one man shows were at the International Marine Archives, Nantucket, 1976, and aboard the historic ship *Wanderbird* at Sausalito, 1977. He has written and illustrated two books: *Gilkerson on War,* 1964, and *The Scrimshander,* 1975, and is working on a third to be called *An Adventurous Voyage.*

Examples of his work can be found in the United States Naval Institute Museum, International Archives, Nantucket, Mystic Seaport Museum, Peabody Museum of Salem, Kendal Whaling Museum and the National Maritime Museum, San Francisco.

PLATE: 653.

GLOVER, Sybil Mullen R.I., R.W.A., R.S.M.A.
A 20th century watercolour painter of marines and landscapes who was a pupil at the St. Martin's School of Art. To some extent she has specialised in scenes of the tidal estuaries of East Anglia but now lives at Stoke, Plymouth, and paints West Coast scenes.

She is a member of the Royal Society of Marine Artists, elected in 1964, and has also exhibited at the Royal Academy, the Royal Institute of Oil Painters, the Royal Scottish Academy, the New English Art Club and the Paris Salon, where she has won gold and silver medals.

Examples of her work can be found in the Brighton Art Gallery, the National Maritime Museum, Greenwich, Plymouth Museum and Art Gallery and the Walsall Art Gallery.

PLATE: 694.

GODERIS, Hans **fl.1625**
He was a pupil and close follower of Jan Porcellis, and like him his palette was of closely toned greys and browns, with the colour provided by the clothes of the figures. He worked in Haarlem, at least between 1622 and 1628.

The National Maritime Museum, Greenwich, has two examples; one is of fishing boats in a rough sea, which is in a painted oval; the other is a river scene signed H. Goderis, 1625 (the H and G in monogram). At the Santa Barbara Museum of Fine Art, California, there is also a scene of vessels beating into a harbour, signed H.G.

PLATE: 43.

GOEDHART, Jan Catharinus Adriaan **b.1893**
Born at Tolwa Asahan, Sumatra, on June 26th, 1893. He worked in The Hague and in the 1950s was considered the doyen of Dutch marine painters. In 1958 he was commissioned by the Netherlands Association of Sea Painters to paint a picture of the Royal Yacht *Britannia,* with the Queen and Prince Philip aboard, arriving in Dutch waters for a state visit in March 1958. This picture was presented in 1960 to the Queen, who has lent it to the National Maritime Museum, Greenwich.

GORE, Charles **1729-1807**
Born in Horkstow, Lincolnshire, on December 5th, 1729, he died in Weimar on January 22nd, 1807. His family were well off so that he drew and painted in watercolours, not for a living, but as a recreation. Although he never exhibited, he was extremely industrious and skilled.

He greatly admired the Willem van de Veldes (qq.v.) and did numerous drawings of 17th century subjects in their manner, some based on their drawings. He was working in Southampton in the middle of the century but in 1773, in an effort to recoup his wife's health, they went to Italy by sea and travelled there, in Corsica and on the Riviera. During this tour he made valuable drawings of the ancient ruins they visited.

He returned in 1781 and became a member of the Dilettante Society. After visiting Florence again he settled for the rest of his life at the court of the Duke of Weimar.

Examples of his work can be found in the Gloucester City Art Gallery, National Maritime Museum, Greenwich, Leeds City Art Gallery, British Museum and the Ashmolean Museum, Oxford.

GOYEN, Jan van **1596-1666**
Born in Leyden on January 13th, 1596. This celebrated artist, who is known to all for his riverscapes, also painted some seascapes. His father, an amateur artist, put his son into the studio of Henri Klok, a decorator of glass; from there he moved to Hoorn and studied under a painter called Willem Gerritz.

He later received some instruction from Esaias van de Velde. He worked for a time at Haarlem but returned to Leyden, where he married and lived for some fifteen years until about 1631. He finally settled in The Hague, where he was elected to the Guild in 1640, and he died there in 1666.

Van Goyen developed the trend away from the colourful mannerist painters begun by Jan Porcellis (q.v.) and the Dutch realists, so that much of his work is almost monochrome, generally using muddy greens or greenish browns, or just browns. Many of his paintings have an austere delicacy which can degenerate into feebleness; his best work (and there is a great deal of it) can be of extraordinary beauty.

As his paintings are so numerous and admired, there is hardly any great museum holding Dutch old master paintings where he is not represented.

PLATES: 84, 85, 86.

GRANDIN, Eugène
A French ship portraitist working in Le Havre in the third quarter of the 19th century. The Peabody Museum of Salem has five watercolours by him dated between 1850 and 1874.

GRANT, Gordon Hope **1875-1962**
Born in San Francisco on June 7th, 1875, the son of a Scots banker with nautical connections, he was put aboard the sailing ship *City of Madras* at the age of thirteen, and sailed round the Horn to Glasgow and the Fife Academy at Kirkcaldy to fulfil his father's wish for him to have a Scottish education.

In 1893 he was about to join the Clyde Ship Building Company when his watercolours were noticed by the editor of a London magazine, which resulted in his moving to London and a three-year course at the Heatherley Art School. At the end of his course he returned to San Francisco and worked as an illustrator on the *Examiner* and then the *Chronicle*. In the late 1890s he moved to New York, and in 1899 went to South Africa to cover the Boer War for *Harper's Weekly*. In 1900 he joined the staff of *Puck*, and worked for them for ten years. When the United States entered the First World War Grant was employed by the Morale Branch of the General Staff in Washington to design posters.

After the war he became a full-time marine artist in oils, watercolours, lithographs and etchings. He concentrated on historic sail subjects, and exhibited widely in America and the Paris Salon. In 1925 he made a voyage to the Bering sea in the sailing ship *Star of Alaska*. He wrote and illustrated a number of books on the sea. *Sail Ho* about life on a windjammer, *Greasy Luck* about whaling, *The Story of the Ship, Ships under Sail, The Secret Voyage, Sketchbook*. He was one of the best known and successful practitioners of his art of his day. He died in New York on May 7th, 1962.

The United States Naval Academy Museum at Annapolis has a painting by him of the U.S.S. *Monongahela;* the Metropolitan Museum, New York, has examples and the Peabody Museum of Salem has one of the U.S.S. *Constitution*.

GRAVENBROECK, Orazio and Charles Laurent
There is confusion about these two artists, if indeed they were two artists. An Orazio is said to have been working in 1760 and certainly one known example would agree with that date.

An artist of the name Orazio Gravenbroeck — though surely another man — is supposed to have been working in Paris in the 1730s. At about the same time a Charles Laurent Gravenbroeck was working for the Court of Louis XV.

GREENWOOD, George Parker
A Liverpool artist working in the last quarter of the 19th century and the first quarter of the present one. He was not only a ship portraitist, but also a general marine painter of reasonably good quality.

The National Maritime Museum, Greenwich, has a portrait of the ship *Lyttleton* and another of the White Star liner *Adriatic* leaving Liverpool in 1887. The Liverpool Museums have two paintings of the White Star liner *Germanic* dated 1877, and a view of the Mersey dated 1904.

GREGERSEN, Julius **1860-1935**
A German painter working at Flensburg in Schleswig-Holstein. The Altonaer Museum, Hamburg, has two port scenes and a portrait of a schooner by him and the Maritime Museum at Bergen has one picture of the steamer *Hera*.

PLATE: 619.

GREGORY, Arthur Victor **1869-1957**
Born in Melbourne in 1869, he died there on July 10th, 1957. His father, George F. Gregory (q.v.), was a draughtsman with the Thames Iron Works who went to Australia during the Gold Rush and set up in Melbourne as a marine painter in 1854.

Arthur Victor and his brother, William, both became painters, Arthur Victor turning out straightforward, rather brightly coloured ship portraits.

The State Library of Victoria Historical Picture Collection has fifteen of his watercolours.

GREGORY, Charles Dickson **b.1850**
Born in London, he went to Australia as a baby, returning to London at the age of twenty-two to study at the Royal Academy Schools. He returned to Australia and was a founder member of the Victorian Academy of Arts.

His work, which includes paintings of birds, can be seen in the National Gallery of South Australia in Adelaide, the National Gallery of Victoria in Melbourne, and the National Gallery of New South Wales in Sydney.

GREGORY, George F. **1815-?1885**
Born in England. An Australian ship portraitist working in Melbourne; rather primitive. The Peabody Museum of Salem has three of his watercolours. (See also Arthur Victor Gregory.)

PLATE: 446.

GREGORY, William *see* **GREGORY, Arthur Victor**

GREVENBROECK, Orazio *see* **GRAVENBROECK**

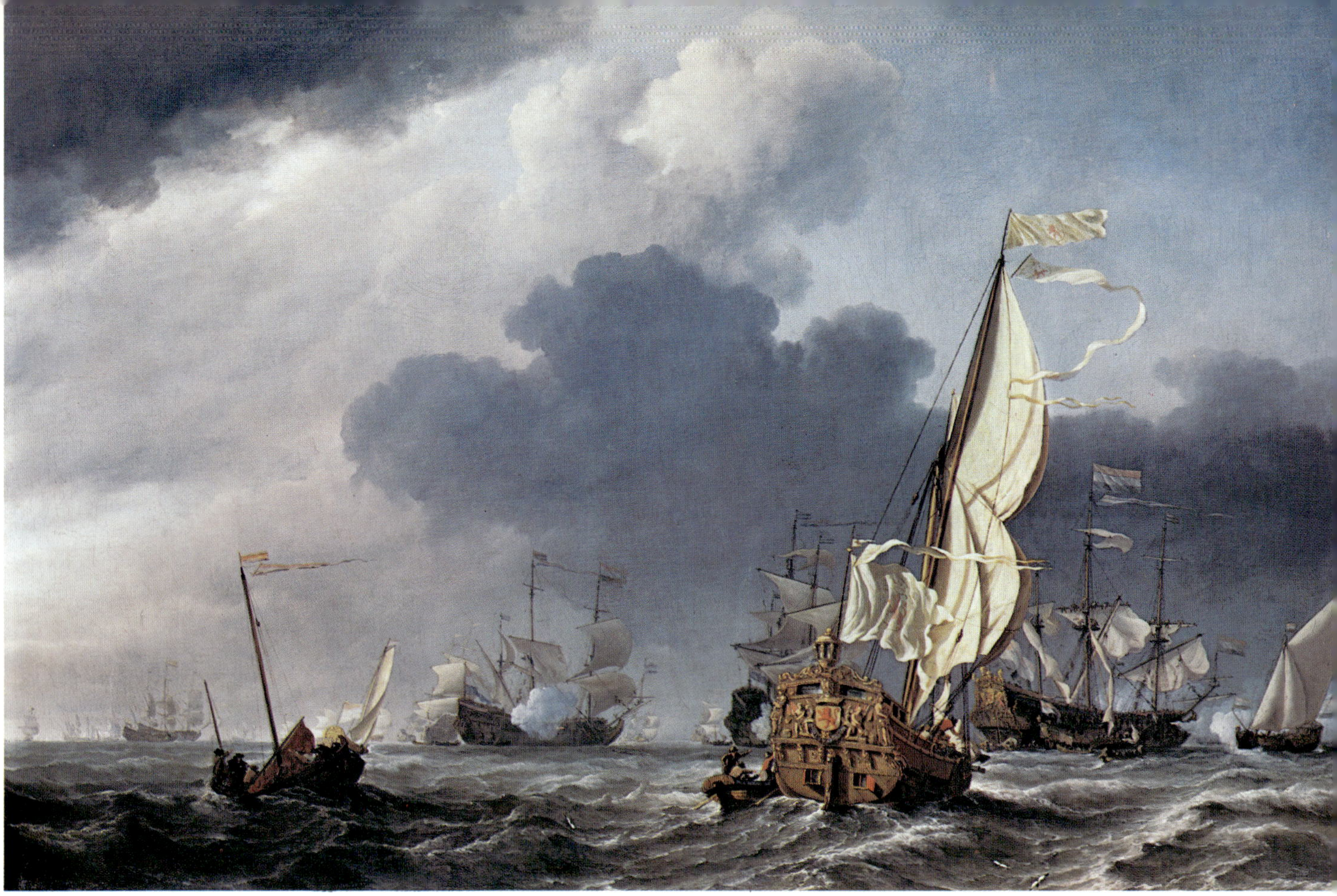

Colour Plate IX. Willem van de Velde, the Younger, 1633-1707. ''A Dutch States yacht running down on the fleet.'' National Maritime Museum, Greenwich.

Colour Plate X. Robert Woodcock, 1692-1728. ''An English third-rate getting under way.'' National Maritime Museum, Greenwich.

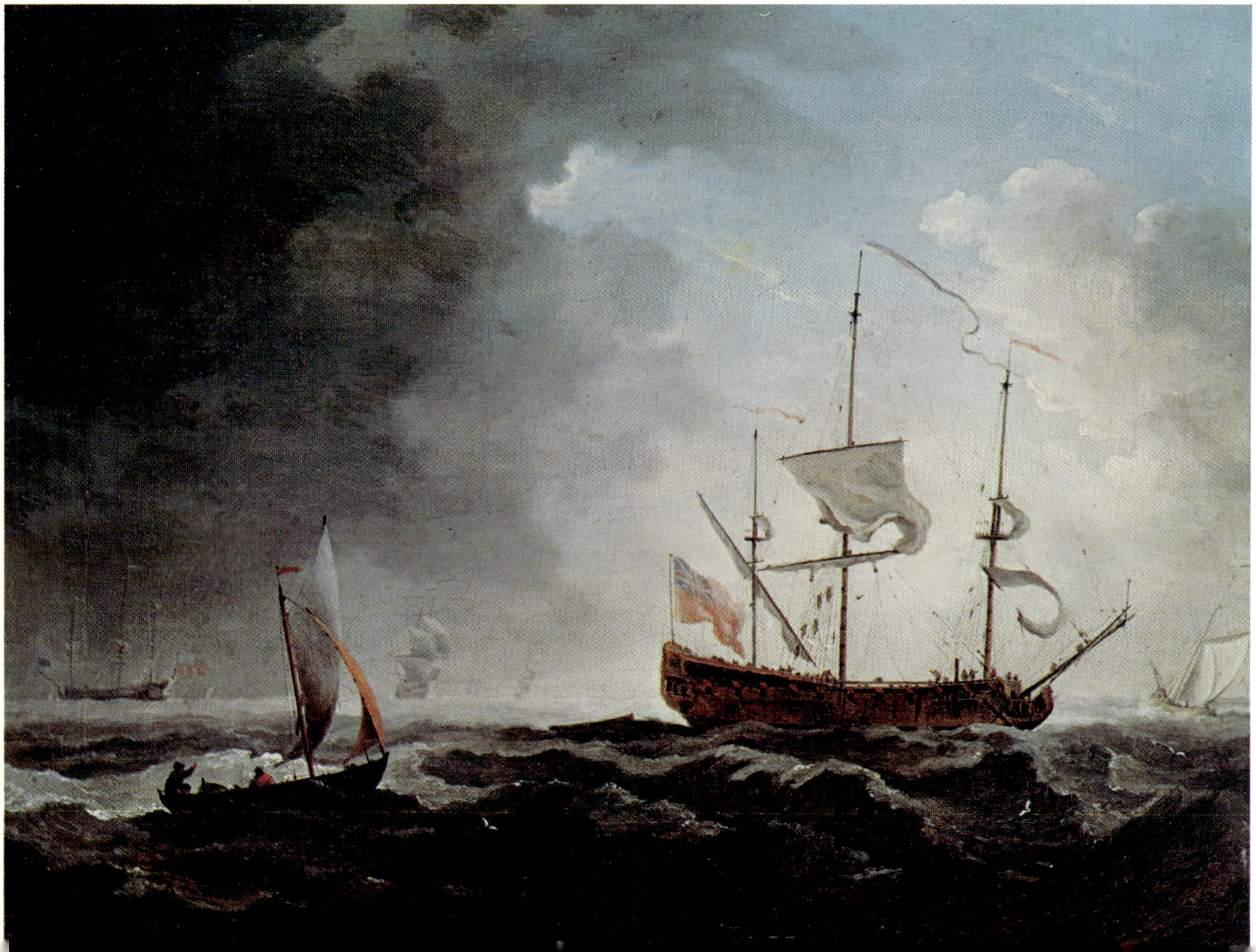

GRIBBLE, Bernard Finegan R.B.C., S.M.A. 1873-1962
Born on May 10th, 1873, he was the son of the architect of the Brompton Oratory and was educated at the College of St. Francis Saviour at Bruges. He then trained at the Royal College of Art, South Kensington, and under Albert Toft, the sculptor, and became a specialist in maritime history. In 1912 he was made marine painter to the Worshipful Company of Shipwrights; he exhibited at the Royal Academy, the Paris Salon and the Society of Marine Artists, of which he was a member. His early work is signed Bernard F. Gribble, later work without the F.

EXAMPLES: The United States Naval Academy Museum, Annapolis (2): The Return of the Mayflower; *U.S. destroyers off Queenstown 4/5/1917, U.S. destroyer rescuing a British seaplane. Russell-Cotes Museum, Bournemouth (1): Market Street, Poole. City Art Gallery, Bristol (1): "the Doomed Fleet". Federal Parliament House, Canberra (1): "Our Golden Argosies". National Maritime Museum, Greenwich (4): Lord Nelson being rowed out to* Victory *at Spithead 1805; the destroyer H.M.S.* Bedouin; *the first-rate* Royal Sovereign; *the destroyer* Wallace. *City Art Gallery, Plymouth (2): the surrender of the Pirate Captain; departure of the Pilgrim Fathers. Peabody Museum of Salem (1): watercolour of destroyers. Navy Memorial Museum, Washington Navy Yard (1): Surrender of the German High Seas Fleet, 1918.*

GRIFFIER, Jan, the Elder c.1651-1718
Born in Amsterdam, he was a pupil of the landscape painters Jacob van Looten and Roland Roghman. Though he initially specialised in flower painting, he turned to landscape and made a reputation with his views of the Rhine.

Once settled in London he painted successful views of the Thames and at the National Maritime Museum, Greenwich, there is a fine, large painting of shipping off Greenwich. He died in London in 1718.

GRIFFIN, William
A painter of the Hull school working in the second and third quarters of the 19th century, sometimes in collaboration with a T. Meggitt and son.

GRIMELUND, Johannes Martin b.1842
Born in Christiania (Oslo), a Norwegian landscape and marine painter who also worked in Paris, where he was made a Chevalier of the Legion of Honour in 1892. The National Gallery in Oslo has a painting by him of the port of Antwerp.

PLATE: 545.

GROENEWEGEN, Gerrit 1754-1826
Born in Rotterdam on October 16th, 1754, died in Rotterdam on August 7th, 1826. He was trained as a ship's carpenter but lost his right leg in an accident, and turned to making ships' draughts. He took lessons in drawing at this time from Nicholas Muys. He became a painter, mainly in watercolour, a designer of wallpapers, especially of seascapes, and also an etcher.

The Scheepvaart Museum, Amsterdam, has watercolours and etchings by him; the town record office in Delft has some drawings, as has the city record office in Rotterdam, and the Boymans van Beunigen Museum in the same city.

GRUIJTER, Jacob Willem 1856-1908
Born in Amsterdam in 1856; died in Egmond aan Zee in 1908. He exhibited at The Hague in 1884.

EXAMPLES: Scheepvaart Museum, Amsterdam (1): a regatta on the Y at Amsterdam.

GRUYTER, Jacob de
Artist working in the third quarter of the 17th century. A signed painting of a sea battle is so close in style to that of Hendrik van Minderhout (q.v.) as to suggest that he was most probably his pupil. This is made the more likely by the fact that both lived in Rotterdam.

PLATE: 35.

EXAMPLES: Rijksmuseum, Amsterdam (1): Dutch ships off a northern coast. National Maritime Museum, Greenwich (3): a Zeeland ship off Flushing; a Middelburg ship off Antwerp; a rock in a sea; one attributed, shipping off Rotterdam.

GRUYTER, Willem, Junior 1817-1880
Born in Amsterdam 1817; died in Amsterdam 1880. He was a pupil of Hermanus Koekkoek, and exhibited at Amsterdam and The Hague between 1843 and 1875.

EXAMPLES: The Rijksmuseum, Amsterdam, have a view of shipping in Bremerhaven Roads. Scheepvaart Museum, Amsterdam (1): a Dutch paddle steamer. There are drawings at the Fodor Museum, Amsterdam, and the Prins Hendrik Museum, Rotterdam.

GUDE, Hans Frederick 1825-1903
Born in Christiania (Oslo) in 1825; died in Berlin, 1903. He went in 1841 to Dusseldorf, then the centre of a flourishing painting school, where he studied under Johann Wilhelm Schermer and the marine painter Andreas Achenbach (q.v.). He specialised in marines and mountainous landscapes and on some of these works in collaboration with his fellow Norwegian, Adolph Tidemand.

He went back to Norway for three years in 1848 and then returned to Dusseldorf, where he succeeded Schermer as professor at the Academy until 1862. Then, after a year in Wales, he succeeded Schermer again, this time at the Academy at Karlsruhe. By this time he had become the doyen of Norwegian landscape and marine painters and was also very influential in the German school.

PLATE: 543.

EXAMPLES: National Gallery, Berlin (2): Norwegian coast scene; Viking ships. Museum of Art, Bremen (1): calm sea. State Museum for Art, Copenhagen (1): Norwegian port. Kunsthalle, Hamburg (1): marine. Gemaldegalerie, Hanover (1): Norwegian coast scene. Kunstalle, Leipzig (1): the Norwegian coast after a storm. National Gallery of Victoria, Melbourne (1): after the storm. National Gallery, Oslo (2): a timber vessel by a timber yard; fishing boats and coastal craft in an evening light. Nationalmuseum, Stockholm (3): marines. Gemäldegalerie, Stuttgart (1): calm sea.

GUDIN, Baron Jean Antoine Théodore **1802-1880**
(called Théodore Gudin)

Born in Paris on August 15th, 1802; died in Boulogne-sur-Seine, Paris, April 12th, 1880. He was a pupil at the Ecole des Beaux-Arts in Paris at a time when the romantic movement was the fashion. He developed a taste for historical naval subjects on a large scale and became France's leading painter of sea battles. They were the sort of paintings that required royal and state patronage and this he got, probably through his good social standing.

He also painted coastal views and it was this sort of subject, rather than his historical paintings, that he exhibited at the Royal Academy at irregular intervals between 1837 and 1873. He was a friend of Sir David Wilkie and perhaps this has a bearing on the fact that in later life he spent much of his time in Scotland.

Most of his historical pictures are in French and European public galleries, especially the Musée de la Marine in Paris. The only one in a British public collection is a storm, in the Wallace Collection in London.

PLATES: 407, 408, 409, 410.

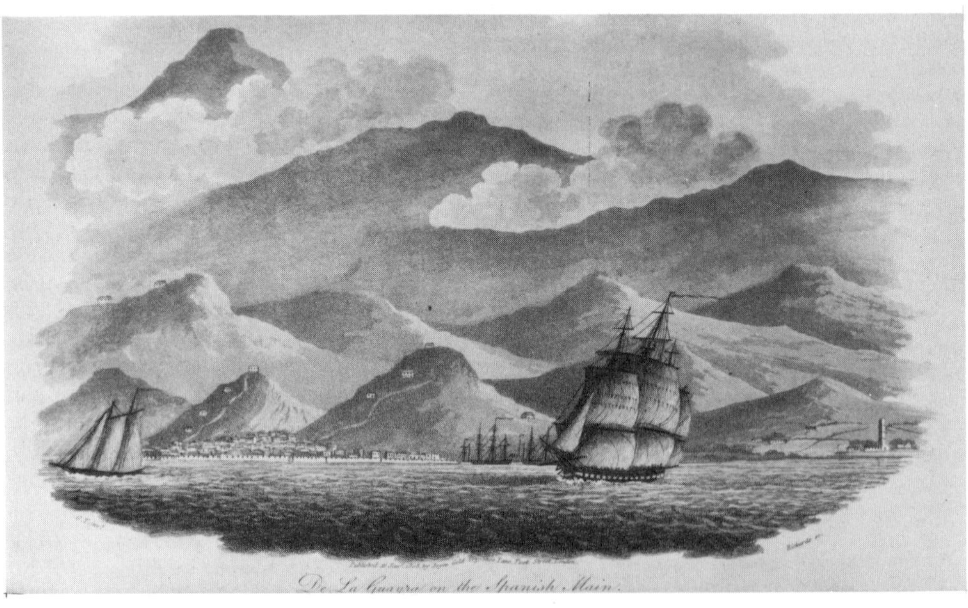

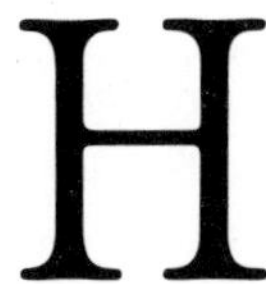

HACCOU, Johannes Cornelis **1798-1839**
A younger brother of Lodewijk (q.v.), he was born in Middelburg, on April 18th, 1798, and like his brother was a pupil of J.H. Koekkoek (q.v.). He travelled in Switzerland, France and Germany before settling in London where he exhibited just one picture at the Royal Academy, a marine, in 1836. He liked to paint 17th century subjects in the manner of Willem van de Velde the Younger (q.v.), and was a general painter as well as a marine painter. The Boymans van Beunigen Museum, Rotterdam, has three watercolour seascapes by him.

HACCOU, Lodewijk Gillis **b.1792**
He was born in Middelburg on November 27th, 1792, a brother of Johannes Cornelis (q.v.). A watercolourist, he was a pupil of J.H. Koekkoek. The Scheepvaart Museum, Amsterdam, has examples.

HACKERT, Jacob Philippe **1737-1807**
(called Hackert of Italy)
Born in Prenzlau, he was really a landscape painter who did some marines. His father, Philippe, was a portrait painter in Prenzlau and Jacob studied at the Berlin Academy. He then settled in Italy, living at various times in Rome, Naples and Florence, where he died. He was court painter to King Ferdinand IV of Naples and also did work for the Empress Catherine of Russia.

He worked in gouache and engraved, as well as painting in oils.

EXAMPLES: (marines only): Gemäldegalerie, Weimar (1).

HAECKEN, J. van
Said to have been called Joseph, he was working in England in the first quarter of the 18th century, painting rather indifferent pictures in a style derived from Willem van de Velde II (q.v.). Signed "J. v. Haecken". He is not the same man as J. van der Hagen (q.v.).

The National Maritime Museum, Greenwich, has a painting of English men-of-war in a calm.

PLATE: 182.

HAGEN, Johann van der **b.1675**
Born in The Hague in 1675; died before 1745. He is said to have come to London about the end of the 17th century but this artist, and his relation William, or Willem (q.v.), are to be approached with caution. In recent times two eminent scholars have added their labours to others in attempting a positive identification of these artists, and have largely failed.

What we do known is that certain extant paintings in the style of Willem van de Velde II are signed "J. v. Hagen" and that it was his daughter, Bernarda, who married Willem van de Velde II's son Cornelius.

Strickland's *Dictionary of Irish Artists* claims that he moved from London to Dublin at the end of his life. His death occurred before 1745 for he is mentioned as "the late" in a note of that date. His work is so modelled on van de Velde's that one wonders if he was not working in his studio.

The National Maritime Museum, Greenwich, has three paintings by him of English ships in storms.

PLATES: 183, 184.

HAGEN, Willem van der
There is a view of Waterford in Ireland dated 1736 by this artist owned by Waterford Town Council, also the strange allegorical signed painting of William III landing at Carrickfergus, now in the Ulster Museum in Belfast. These have brought up the question of which van der Hagen went to Ireland.

The answer may be both. For if Johann (q.v.) went to Dublin why not his family? There is no evidence to support the theory that Willem was Johann's son, except that he was apparently in Ireland in 1736. He was given to painting large panoramic port scenes; including Gibraltar, Portsmouth and Falmouth.

PLATES: 185, 186.

HAGG, Rear-Admiral Jacob **1839-1931**
Born on Kallhammarsvik Island of Gotland on July 21st, 1839; died in Stockholm April 15th, 1931. He entered the Swedish Royal Navy in about 1860, rose to flag rank in 1899, retiring in 1904. He was a signals specialist and reformed the Swedish navy's system. When Norway and Sweden separated in 1905 his advice on the form of the new Swedish flag was accepted. He was also a naval historian and in his retirement he joined the Society for Nautical Research in London, and contributed to its journal, the *Mariner's Mirror*.

His interest in drawing and painting began early and matured as his knowledge of ship archaeology increased.

Examples of his work can be found in the National Maritime Museum in Stockholm and the Maritime Museum in Goteborg.

HALL, Alfred S.
A British primitive ship portraitist working in the third quarter of the 19th century. The National Maritime Museum, Greenwich, has a painting by him of the trawler *Madden,* dated 1869.

HALSALL, William Formby **1841-1919**
A talented American ship portraitist. The Peabody Museum of Salem has six oils by him and a drawing of a pilot schooner.

PLATE: 585.

HAMILTON, James **1819-1878**

Born in Ireland; died in San Francisco. He was a self-taught artist based in Philadelphia, though he travelled widely. He was called "the American Turner" because of his admiration for that artist, and for the influence Turner had on his work.

As well as shipping scenes, he painted naval actions, and took commissions for book illustrations. He is represented at the Brooklyn Museum, New York: last days of Pompeii. At the Shelburne Museum, Vermont: fishermen at sea; and at Yale University Gallery: capture of the *Serapis* by Paul Jones.

PLATE: 482.

HAMMELEW, C.

A Danish ship portraitist working in Copenhagen in the first and second quarters of the 19th century. The Peabody Museum of Salem has a watercolour dated 1825.

HANSEN, J.

A German ship portraitist working in Altona in the second quarter of the 19th century and in the usual stiff and stylised manner. The Altonaer Museum, Hamburg, has four pen and wash drawings by him.

PLATE: 456.

HANSON, Albert J. **1866-1914**

Born in New South Wales. He studied at the Royal Art Society of New South Wales School. In 1889 he moved to New Zealand, where he ran an art school at Dunedin. He later returned to Sydney. His work can be found in the Auckland and Dunedin Art galleries, and in the Australian State galleries.

HANSTEEN, Nils Severin Lynge **1855-1912**

Born in Selbo, Norway, and died in Christiania, now Oslo. Having studied at the academies of Christiania, Karlsruhe and Munich, he settled in Copenhagen and from 1879 exhibited at Bremen, Vienna and Munich. He was awarded a bronze medal at the Paris Exhibition of 1889.

The National Gallery in Oslo has a painting of a steamer and a schooner in a gale, dated 1890.

HARDORFF, Hermann Rudolf **1816-1907**

Born and died in Hamburg. He was a pupil of his father, a portrait and history painter. His style is typical of the mid-19th century but skilful and well finished. He worked at Hamburg and Dresden.

HARDY, Thomas Bush R.B.A. **1842-1897**

Born in Sheffield on May 3rd, 1842 and died in London on December 15th, 1897. A prolific artist in watercolours whose views of the Thames and coastal shipping are spread across the country's art galleries. He was capable of delicate work on a small scale, especially in his early days, but his larger, later works tend to be rather coarse. He exhibited at the Royal Academy between 1872 and 1897, also at Suffolk Street and the New Watercolour Society. He was elected a member of the Royal Society of British Artists in 1884.

EXAMPLES: Haworth Art Gallery, Accrington; Cartwright Hall, Bradford; Bristol City Art Gallery; Dundee City Art Gallery; Eastbourne Art Gallery; National Maritime Museum, Greenwich; Gray Art Gallery, Hartlepool; Leeds City Art Gallery; Leicester Art Gallery; British Museum; Victoria and Albert Museum; City Art Gallery, Manchester; Newport Art Gallery; Sydney Art Gallery, New South Wales.

HARNACK, Fid R.S.M.A. **b.1897**

In 1930 he sailed in the three-masted barque *Alastor* from London to Bothnia and he is an enthusiast of square rigged sailing ships. He is also a keen yachtsman with two and a half ton gaff rigged sloop called *Ben Gunn.*

Harnack is an illustrator for yachting magazines and was elected to the Society of Marine Artists in 1949. His diploma picture, "Cruising", is on loan to the National Maritime Museum, Greenwich.

HARRIS, James **1810-1887**

Born in Exeter in 1810 and died in Reynoldston, Glamorganshire on June 19th, 1887. He was the elder son of John Harris, a carver and gilder and also a painter. About 1828 the family moved to Swansea. James went to London sometime in the middle 1830s, where he was introduced to George Chambers (q.v.) by Calvert Jones and is said to have worked in Chambers's studio for a time. As well as a painter he is said to have been a seaman who had rounded the Horn in copper ore ships.

On his father's death in 1836 he returned to Swansea to help his mother with the business of picture-framing and supplying artists' materials. In 1882 he retired and moved to Reynoldston, where Edward Duncan was a regular visitor. He exhibited at the Royal Academy in 1859 and 1862.

The National Maritime Museum, Greenwich, has a portrait of the *Roxburgh Castle,* Swansea Museum has twelve paintings and the Glyn Vivian Art Gallery, Swansea, has six.

HARRIS, Captain William

A primitive British ship portraitist working in the West Country in the third quarter of the 20th century. He had worked in coastal sailing vessels, and in 1971 presented two paintings of muffies to the National Maritime Museum, Greenwich.

HARWOOD, John

Little is known of this artist but he painted good quality marines in the style of Robert Salmon (q.v.). He exhibited at the Royal Academy from an address in Southwark, London, between 1818 and 1828 (the year that Salmon left for America). The Peabody Museum of Salem has a painting of whalers in the Arctic.

PLATES: 341, 342.

HASELTINE, William Stanley **1835-1900**

Born in Philadelphia. At the age of nineteen he went to Düsseldorf, which was then the centre of a flourishing school of landscape and marine painters. He died in Rome. The style he developed has a pleasing clarity and craftsmanship, not unlike that of his fellow American, Alfred Bricher (q.v.). Haseltine himself spent most of his life in Europe. The Mariners Museum, Newport News, has a painting by him called "Rocks at Nahant".

PLATE: 511.

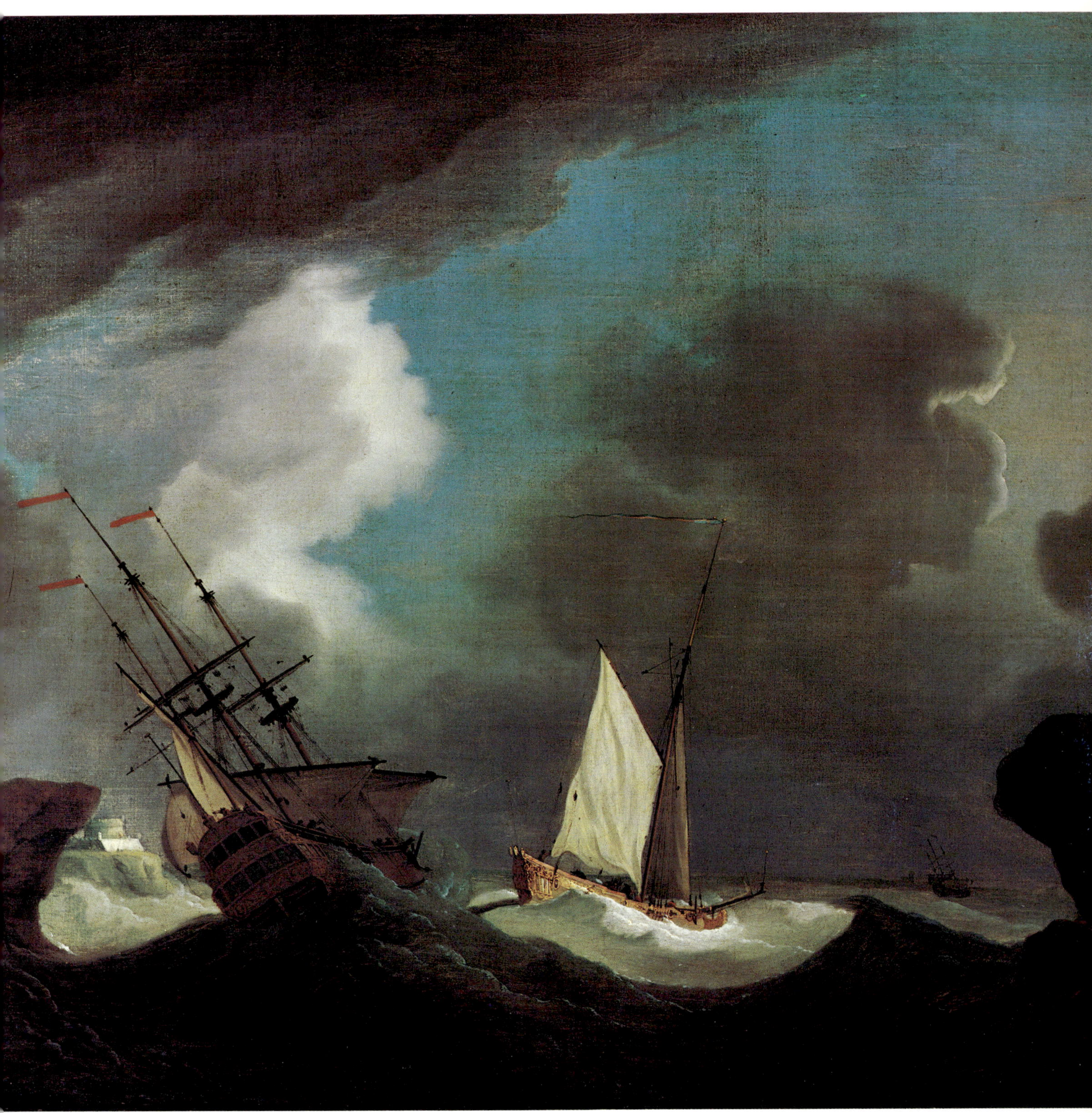

Colour Plate XI. Peter Monamy, 1681-1749. ''A royal yacht and an Indiaman off a rocky coast with a castle.'' National Maritime Museum, Greenwich.

HAYES, Edwin R.H.A., R.I. **1819-1904**

Born in Bristol on June 7th, 1819, he died in London on November 7th, 1904. He went to live in the Dublin area at an early age and is said to have been a pupil at the Royal Hibernian Academy, of which he was to become a member in 1870.

His first exhibit at the British Institution in 1854 was from an address in Dublin but in 1855 an address in Greenwich was given; it was in this year he also first exhibited at the Royal Academy. He continued to exhibit at the British Institution until 1867, and at the Royal Academy until the year of his death. He also exhibited at the Society of British Artists, the New Watercolour Society, the Grosvenor Gallery and the New Gallery.

PLATES: 526, 527, 528.

EXAMPLES: Bristol City Art Gallery (2): Falmouth Harbour; storm passing off Dordrecht. South African National Gallery, Capetown (1): Southend-on-Sea. Welsh National Gallery, Cardiff (1): a brigantine off Yarmouth. Shipley Art Gallery, Gateshead (1): off Boulogne. National Maritime Museum, Greenwich (1): the Wasp *captures the* Reindeer *1814. City Art Gallery, Leeds (1): sunset. City Art Gallery, Leicester (1): a trawler off Gorleston. Tate Gallery, London (1): sunset from Harlyn Bar, Cornwall. National Gallery of Victoria, Melbourne (1): fishing boats at Granton. Salford Art Gallery (1): view of Dover. Graves Art Gallery, Sheffield (1): marine.*

HAYES, G. **fl.c.1890**

The National Maritime Museum, Greenwich, has a painting of a swim-headed stumpy barge off Dover by this artist.

HEADE, Martin Johnson **1819-1904**

Born in Bucks County, Pennsylvania and died in Florida. Like so many of his generation of artists, he took full advantage of the new facilities for travel, both abroad and in his own country. He evolved a style very much like that of Fitz Hugh Lane (q.v.), though there does not seem to be any direct evidence that they knew each other.

He was also a painter of portraits and an ornithologist, with a special interest in humming birds, of which he made many studies hoping to illustrate a book on them but never finding a publisher to finance it.

PLATES: 450, 451.

EXAMPLES: Museum of Fine Arts, Boston; Shelburne Museum, Vermont; National Gallery, Washington.

HEARD, Joseph **1799-1859**

Born in Whitehaven on March 7th, 1799, he died in Liverpool on November 17th, 1859. With Samuel Walters (q.v.) he must stand as the top ranking Liverpool ship portraitist of the 19th century. He first practised in his native Whitehaven, and moved to Liverpool in 1834. Though he is often confused with his contemporary Liverpool artists, Walters and Macfarlane (qq.v.), he has a couple of idiosyncrasies, a little curved bow wave, and a steamer usually somewhere in the background. He also painted human portraits.

The National Maritime Museum, Greenwich, has seven ship portraits, the Merseyside County Museums four and the Peabody Museum of Salem, three.

PLATE: 386

HEEMSKERCK VAN BEEST, Jacob Edward **1828-1894**

Born in Kampen and died at The Hague. He was a pupil of a master of the Dutch modern school, Dirk van Lokhorst. He painted naval historical pictures as well as general shipping scenes, for which his training as a naval officer (1842-53) stood him in good stead.

From 1853-66 he worked at Utrecht, then from 1867-76 at The Hague. From 1879-85 he was at Dalfsen, near Zurolle.

He exhibited at Amsterdam and The Hague from 1856 to 1875.

EXAMPLES: Rijksmuseum, Amsterdam (4): the Dutch, English, French and American squadrons in Japanese waters, 1864; H.M.S. Medusa *facing a passage between Kyusku and Honshu, 1864; the Zuider Zee off Amsterdam; 17th century ships at sea. Scheepvaart Museum, Amsterdam (3): Prins Hendrik expedition, 1847; a man-of-war; pirate action. Stedelijk Museum, Amsterdam (1): view of Amsterdam. Gemeentemuseum, The Hague (2): Malaysian fisherman; a wreck scene. Stania State Museum, Oenkerk: seascape. Prins Hendrik Museum, Rotterdam (1): a frigate (crayon). Boymans Museum, Rotterdam (1): the Maas at Rotterdam.*

HELGASON, Edward **b.1895**

Born in Iceland, in his early teens he worked on a cod fishing boat out of Reykjavik. Then in 1913 he went to Norway and served on whalers for eight years. In 1925 he made his first salmon fishing voyage aboard an Alaska Packer ship, so that all his deep water experience was in sail. He later was the owner skipper of a West Coast tuna boat, and during the Second World War served in troopships and afterwards liners, until he retired from the sea in 1951, to take up full-time marine painting. In 1974 he had an exhibition of his paintings in the San Francisco Maritime Museum.

HEMY, Bernard Benedict **1855-1913**

If he was the younger brother of Charles and Thomas Hemy (qq.v.), the latter of whom was born aboard the ship *Madawaska* on the way to Australia, then Bernard must have been born in Australia, not Newcastle, as has been stated. Like his brothers he too returned to Tyneside and it seems likely he attended the Newcastle Art School. Unlike his brothers, however, he stayed in North Shields all his life painting on the north-east coast.

He never exhibited at the Royal Academy and there are no known examples of his work in public collections.

HEMY, Charles Napier R.A., R.W.S. **1841-1917**

Born in Newcastle-on-Tyne, May 24th, 1841 and died in Falmouth, 1917. Eldest of the three Hemy brothers, and the best known. In 1852 his family emigrated to Australia in the sailing ship *Madawaska*. He returned to England about 1855 and signed on for a time aboard a merchant brig.

He then decided to enter a monastery, spending three years at the Dominican House in Newcastle and at a monastery at Lyons in France. He was painting at this time, and finally decided to come out into the world and paint for a living. He studied at the Newcastle School of Art under the history painter William Bell Scott, then at Antwerp under another history and portrait painter, Baron Leys.

Hemy himself was not given to historical subjects, preferring coastal views and fishing scenes; with the latter, such as in "Pilchards", purchased for the Chantrey Bequest in 1897, the figure painting is the important part. He first exhibited at the Royal Academy in 1869, was elected an

A.R.A. in 1897 and an R.A. in 1910. He lived in London from 1870 to 1881, then at Falmouth, where he had a boat fitted out as a studio and used to follow the fishing boats and coastal craft to make sketches.

EXAMPLES: National Maritime Museum, Greenwich: "Pilchards" (on loan from the Tate Gallery). Walker Art Gallery, Liverpool: "A nautical argument". Laing Art Gallery, Newcastle: "Through Air and Water". National Gallery of New South Wales, Sydney: "Smugglers chased by a revenue cutter".

HEMY, Thomas Marie Madawaska **1852-1937**

He was born aboard the sailing ship *Madawaska* while his parents and elder brother, Charles Napier, were emigrating to Australia. Like his elder brother, he also returned to Tyneside about 1873 and studied at the Newcastle School of Art under William Cozens Way and at Antwerp under Charles Verlat, the history and portrait painter.

He exhibited at the Royal Academy from a North Shields address in 1874 and 1875; then there is a gap until he next exhibited from a London address from 1883. The Laing Art Gallery, Newcastle, has a watercolour called "A Bit of Old Greenwich", the Sunderland Art Gallery has a painting called "Old Sunderland", and the Library of New South Wales, Sydney, a painting of the ship *Orient*.

HERNBERG, Ernst

A Swedish ship portraitist working in the first quarter of the 19th century. The National Maritime Museum in Stockholm has a painting by him.

HEWITT, Jackson **b.1914**

Working in the Seattle area, he has been described as the doyen of American marine painters of the Northwest Coast. He served in deep water sailing ships in his youth and later in the Air Corps. His great interest is in naval archaeology which he has applied to painting finely crafted and carefully researched historical subjects. He uses a mixed media which resembles watercolour. Twelve of his paintings are on permanent display in a maritime gallery at the Oregon Historical Society in Portland. The Columbia River Maritime Museum in Astoria and the Washington State Historical Society in Tacoma also have works by him.

HEYNERTZ, D.G.

A Dutch primitive ship portraitist working in the second quarter of the 19th century. The Peabody Museum of Salem has a watercolour by him.

HILL, Samuel Prout **1820-1861**

Presumably of English origin, he emigrated to Hobart, Tasmania in 1842. He soon moved to Sydney where, in 1845, he became the secretary and librarian of the Mechanic's School of Arts until 1848, when he appears to have moved back to Hobart, living there until his death in 1861.

There he became a journalist and leader writer on the *Hobart Town Mercury*. He was also a poet and a painter of marines. The State Library of Victoria Historical Picture Collection has twenty watercolours by him.

HODGES, William R.A. **1744-1797**

London born, he was the son of a blacksmith in Drury Lane, and went to William Shipley's School and afterwards, in 1757 or '58, was apprenticed to the painter, Richard Wilson, for five years or more. Before photography it was the practice of major scientific expeditions to take artists with them to record what they found, and Hodges was offered such a post on James Cook's second voyage in 1772. The aim of this expedition was to establish or debunk once and for all, the presence of a great southern inhabited continent in what we know as Antarctica. The expedition returned in 1775, bringing with it a vast number of Hodges' drawings and small oils on panel. Some of these he used to paint on large canvases and he exhibited them at the Royal Academy in 1776.

They were of great artistic interest and originality of style, neither romantic nor academic, but sometimes bordering on the impressionist in his bold handling of the paint; perhaps it was this that the public was not quite ready for, since he did not get the patronage he needed. He did, however, win enough patronage from Warren Hastings to take him to India in 1780, where he stayed for four years and returned having made a good deal of money. He resumed exhibiting at the Royal Academy and was elected an R.A. in 1787.

None the less, success again eluded him. Nearly all his exhibits until 1789 are of scenes from his travels to the East, which might have been unfashionable, but Thomas Daniell (q.v.) painted Eastern scenes exclusively for years and he was successful. So it looks as if it was his style that was again the trouble. In 1794 he admitted defeat and retired to the West Country. Here he was involved in a banking venture which failed and he committed suicide.

A large number of engravings were made from the original paintings of his travels. Looking at the list of his exhibited works, it has to be admitted that he was no marine painter; he is included here because his work on Cook's voyage had to include some marine views, which are not only of great beauty as regards colour but have an obvious historical interest. Of these, there is a set of twenty-five paintings which have been the property of the Admiralty since being painted, all of which are on loan to the National Maritime Museum, Greenwich. A version of the *Resolution* and *Adventure* at Tahiti is in the Paul Mellon Collection.

PLATE: 236.

HOFFMAN, C.

A Dutch ship portraitist working in the second quarter of the 19th century; fairly primitive. The Peabody Museum of Salem has an oil.

HOFFMANN, Georges Johannes **1833-1873**

He was born and died in The Hague. He was a pupil of Louis Meijer (q.v.) and exhibited at Amsterdam and The Hague from 1857 to 1872.

PLATE: 379.

EXAMPLES: Rijksmuseum, Amsterdam (1): fishing vessel in a rough sea. Gemeentemuseum, The Hague, (1): rough sea.

HOGER, C.W.

A Danish ship portraitist working in the second quarter of the 19th century; rather primitive. The Peabody Museum of Salem has a watercolour.

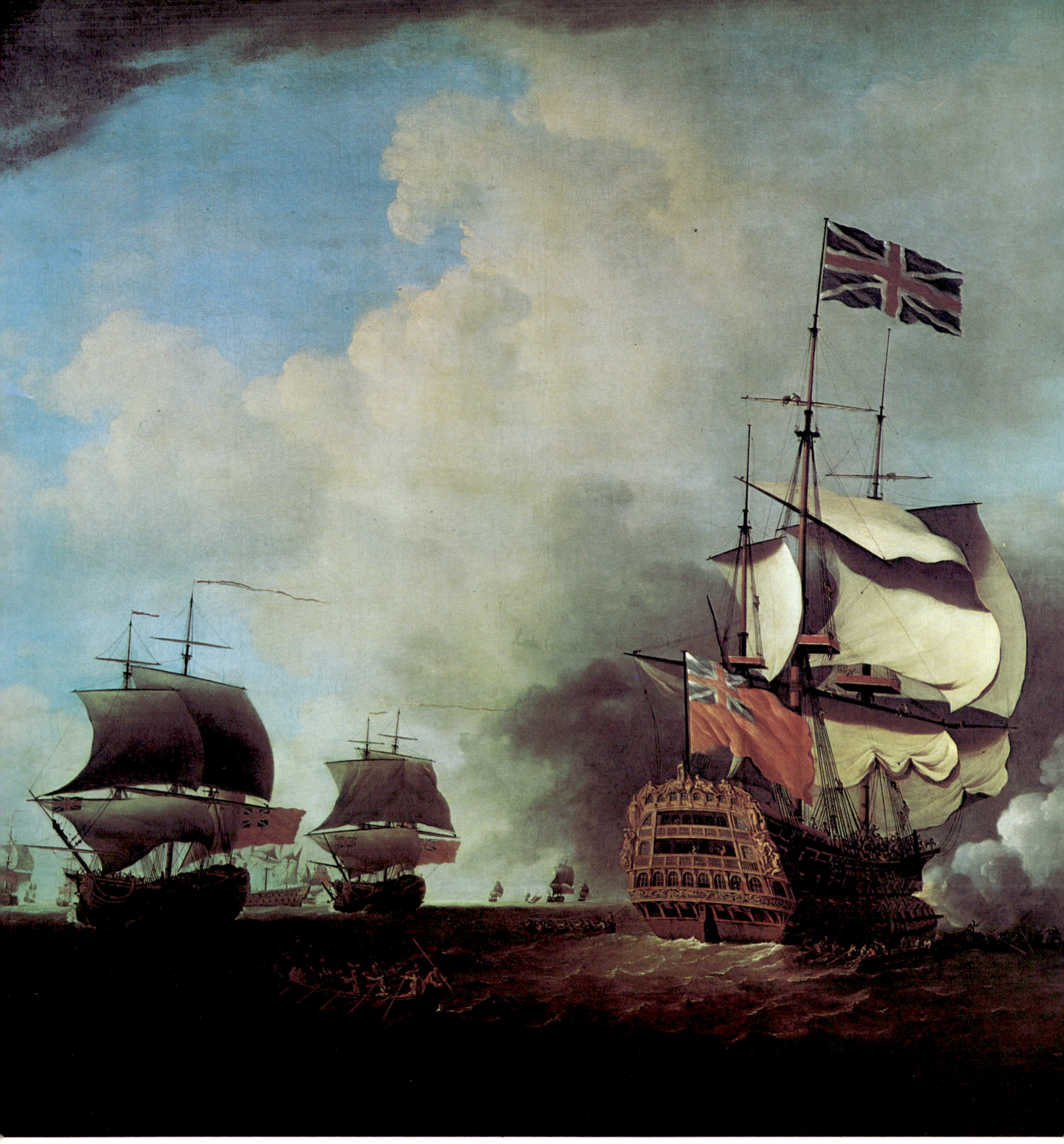

Colour Plate XII. Samuel Scott, 1701/2-1772. "The *Royal William* shortening sail." National Maritime Museum, Greenwich.

HOLM, Peter Christian **1823-1888**

A German ship portraitist working in Altona and Hamburg and with Lorenz and Heinrich Petersen (qq.v.).

The Altonaer Museum has seven paintings by him, nine signed by him and Lorenz Petersen, and four by him and Heinrich Petersen.

PLATES: 547, 548, 549, 550.

HOLMAN, Francis **d.1790**

In spite of his being one of the major marine painters of the 18th century, little is known about him. He first exhibited at the Free Society in 1767 from an address in Bell Dock, Wapping. Except for 1769, he continued to exhibit with the Free Society until 1772.

He then switched to the Royal Academy in 1774, where he exhibited marines every year until 1784 from addresses in Shadwell.

He was an industrious artist, whose views of shipyards, sea actions, ship portraits and general shipping scenes are still plentiful. However, it must be said that while he perfectly understood his subjects, he was a dull performer. His one famous pupil was Thomas Luny (q.v.), whose early work is like his master's, but who went on to greater things.

PLATES: 217, 218, 219, 220, 221.

EXAMPLES: National Maritime Museum, Greenwich (11): Barrington's Action at St. Lucia, 1778; the Moonlight Battle of St. Vincent, 1780; the launch of the Venerable *at Blackwall yard; a view of Blackwall Yard; a shipyard on the Thames; the brig sloop* Roebuck *with her American prizes, 1778; the East Indiaman* Duke of Portland; *the privateer* Fly; *a merchantman about 1760; a two-decker off Dover; shipping in the Downs. Peabody Museum of Salem (4): a set of the action between the American rebel ships* Hancock, Fox *and* Boston, *and the British* Rainbow *and* Flora, *1777. Library of New South Wales, Sydney (1): the* Adventure *and* Resolution.

HOLST, Johannes **1880-1965**

A German painter of fair quality working in Altenwerder, near Hamburg. The Altonaer Museum, Hamburg, has four paintings by him and the Deutsche Schiffahrtsmuseum, Bremerhaven, at least two other oils, one a portrait of the *Preussen*.

PLATE: 618.

HOMER, Winslow **1836-1910**

He was born in Boston and died in Prout's Neck, Maine. His earliest work was in lithography, which he took up at the age of nine. In 1865 he was a pupil at the National Academy of Design and in the following year travelled to France. He developed into one of America's greatest painters, whose work often has great impact. There are several biographies.

His work can be seen at the Museum of Fine Art, Boston, the Fogg Art Museum, Cambridge, Mass., the Museum of Fine Arts, Philadelphia, and the National Gallery, Washington.

PLATE: 515.

HOOD, John

This artist specialised in large pen and wash drawings of shipping scenes, mainly in the Thames near Limehouse where he lived, but also of naval engagements and general shipping pieces. Because of the clarity of detail this method makes possible, these drawings have an iconographic value rather like the Dutch grisailles had for the 17th century. Sometimes he used coloured washes.

He exhibited at the Free Society from 1762-71, missing only 1765, in which year he exhibited at the Society of Artists.

There are collections of his drawings at the British Museum and the National Maritime Museum, Greenwich.

HOOGERHEYDEN, Engel **1740-1809**

Born and died in Middelburg. He was a seaman turned artist who painted marines, sometimes in co-operation with Jacob Schwartzenbach (q.v.), the genre and portrait painter.

EXAMPLES: Rijksmuseum, Amsterdam (1): the Batavian Fleet off Veere; and with Schwartzenbach (2): the Dutch Fleet in Flushing Harbour; the Fleet leaving Flushing.

HOPPNER, Richard Belgrave **1786-1872**

Born on January 9th, 1786, he was the son of John Hoppner, R.A., the portrait painter. He was an honorary exhibitor at the Royal Academy in 1807, 1810 and 1811, all the exhibits being marines; and his "Bay of Cadiz" in 1810 and "View taken at Den Helder", suggest that he had travelled to these places. He also exhibited pictures at the British Institution between 1807 and 1827, all marines or connected with the sea. He died on August 6th, 1872.

HORNBROOK, Thomas Lyde **1780-1850**

He and the Condys (qq.v.), were leading Plymouth marine painters. Indeed, he became marine painter to H.R.H. the Duchess of Kent, and her daughter, the Princess Victoria. This probably occurred in 1833, when the Duchess and the Princess visited Plymouth and went on a cruise in the frigate *Forte* to inspect the Eddystone lighthouse.

Perhaps because he lived in a naval port his choice of subjects was mostly of scenes involving Royal Naval ships. Thus in 1836, when he first exhibited at the Royal Academy, all three pictures included named men-of-war. He exhibited only once more at the Royal Academy, in 1844. He also exhibited at Suffolk Street.

PLATES: 333, 334.

EXAMPLES: The United States Naval Academy Museum, Annapolis (1): Anglo-American action on Lake Borgne, 1814. The National Maritime Museum, Greenwich (3): the Anglo-American action on Lake Borgne, 1814; the Britannia *leaving Plymouth; a frigate in Barn Pool, Plymouth. Watling Art Gallery (2).*

HOSKINS, J.

A British ship portraitist working in the second half of the 19th century. The National Maritime Museum, Greenwich, has a painting by him of the steamer *Teuton,* launched in 1869.

PLATE: 575.

HOYER, Peter and Edward

Late 19th century marines signed by these two artists and of a very similar style and quality appear in the sale rooms from time to time. The National Maritime Museum, Greenwich, has one signed "P. Hoyer".

HUGE, Jurgan Frederick **1809-1878**

He emigrated from Germany at an early age and settled in Bridgeport, Connecticut, where he was a grocer and ship portraitist. He also painted harbour scenes there and in New York.

PLATE: 436.

EXAMPLES: Mariners Museum, Newport News (2): the Bridgeport ferry; the schooner Harriet Thomas.

HUGGINS, J.M. **fl.1840**

When he exhibited his one picture at the British Institution in 1842 he had an address in Leadenhall Street, London, but not at the same number as William Huggins (q.v.). However, his ship portraits are so similar in style to that artist's as to suggest a strong probability that he was his son and pupil.

PLATE: 402.

EXAMPLES: National Maritime Museum, Greenwich (2): the Matilda *and* Zephyr Castle; *the East Indiaman* Thomas Coutts.

HUGGINS, William John **1781-1845**

As a young man he served with the East India Company and we know that he was a steward and assistant to the purser aboard the *Perseverance,* which sailed for Bombay and China in December 1812, returning home in August 1814. This may have been his last voyage, for shortly afterwards he set up as a marine painter in Leadenhall Street, near the East India Company offices.

He specialised in ship portraiture, many of his pictures being engraved by his son-in-law, Edward Duncan (q.v.), who also worked on paintings with him and who was in fact the better artist. Though not generally admired by the critics, Huggins was popular with the public and especially with seafaring men. While the quality of his work is not much superior to the average run of 19th century ship portraitists the sheer volume of his output means that he made a valuable contribution to our knowledge of what the ships of his period looked like.

He first exhibited at the Royal Academy in 1817 and regularly after that until 1828, when for some reason there is a gap until 1835. In 1836 he was made marine painter to King William IV. He last exhibited at the Royal Academy in 1844, dying in London in 1845. He first exhibited at the British Institution in 1825 and then regularly from 1827-38; he last showed work there in 1844 and '45. His pair of paintings of the Battle of Trafalgar for the king were compared by him favourably to the one by Turner.

PLATES: 399, 400, 401; COLOUR PLATE: XX.

EXAMPLES: National Maritime Museum, Greenwich (26): the cutter Active *deceiving the Dutch with false signals to Duncan, 1797; the aftermath of the Battle of Trafalgar, 1805; the escape of the* Belvedere, *1812; King George IV aboard the Irish steam packet* Lightning, *1821; the capture of the slaver* Formidable *by H.M. schooner* Buzzard, *1834; a ketch in action with feluccas; an East India Company brig; East Indiamen in the China seas (on loan); 18 ship portraits, also 15 drawings and watercolours. Maritime Museum, Hull (1): the Northern Whale Fishery. Peabody Museum of Salem (1): the* Vansittart; *also two watercolours.*

HUGHES, J.

A fairly good quality ship portraitist working in the middle of the 19th century. His work looks British, but he could have been living in America. The Marine Museum, Bath, Maine, has a portrait of the American ship *Louisiana* dated 1873.

HULK, Abraham **1813-1897**

Born in London, he was the senior member, and the best known, of a family of Hulks who were painters. He went to Amsterdam as a pupil in the Academy there and of Jean Augustin Daiwaille, the portrait painter. In 1833-34 he visited North America and then returned to Holland. In 1870 he returned to London and lived there until his death in 1897.

He was a master of atmosphere in romantic calms but really a rather meretricious painter, considering how sought-after his work is.

He exhibited at Amsterdam, The Hague and Leeuwarden between 1843 and 1868, and at the Royal Academy in London in 1876 and 1890.

EXAMPLES: Gemeente-Archief, Dordrecht (1). Teylers Museum, Haarlem (1).

HULK, Hendrik **1842-1931**

Born in Amsterdam, he was a son of Abraham (q.v.) and his pupil. He worked in Haarlem, Enkhuizen and Nijkerk, before finally settling in Haarlem in 1876, dying there in 1931. He exhibited at Amsterdam in 1877 and The Hague in 1878. There are drawings of his in the Gemeente-Archief in Haarlem.

HUNT, E. Aubrey **1855-1922**

An American, born on February 17th, 1855, in Weymouth, Massachussetts, he came to England and settled there at an early age. He exhibited at the Royal Academy from 1881. He lived in London and Blackheath and in Hastings, where he died on November 22nd, 1922. He also exhibited at the Royal Society of British Artists and the Grosvenor Galleries.

The National Maritime Museum, Greenwich, has a painting of a Thames swim-headed barge; the Leeds Art Gallery has one of loading cattle, and Leicester Art Gallery has one of Venice.

PLATE: 586.

HUNTEN, F.

A ship portraitist, probably German, working in the third quarter of the 19th century. The National Maritime Museum, Greenwich, has a painting by him of the schooner *Mystery* off Heligoland in 1856.

I

IBBETSON, James B

An American ship portraitist working in the second quarter of the 19th century. The Peabody Museum of Salem has an oil.

INGLEFIELD, Admiral Sir Edward Augustus K.C.B., F.R.S. **1820-1894**

He was born in Cheltenham and died in London. This officer combined a successful naval career with an industrious artistic one. He was flag lieutenant to his father, Rear Admiral Samuel Hood Inglefield, on the South American station in 1845 and went in Lady Franklin's yacht *Fox* in search of Sir John Franklin, lost in the Arctic, in 1852. He published *A Summer Search for Sir John Franklin* in 1853, and was made a Fellow of the Royal Society and a post-captain that year.

He made two more Arctic voyages before going to the Black Sea during the Crimean War in 1855-56. He was second-in-command in the Mediterranean Fleet 1872-75, knighted 1877, and commander-in-chief on the North American station 1878-79.

On the art side, the strong influence of John Schetky (q.v.) makes one suppose that he was taught by him at the Naval Academy at Portsmouth. He worked mainly in watercolour, often on quite a large scale, though oil paintings by him also exist.

The National Library of Australia, Canberra, Rex Nan Kivell Collection, has the painting H.M.S. *Herald* off Macao.

The National Maritime Museum, Greenwich, has one of H.M.S. *Queen* after she had been cut down to a two-decker and given an engine. The Museum also holds a large collection of his watercolours, given by the family.

ISABEY, Louis Gabriel Eugène **1803-1886**

Born in Paris on July 22nd, 1803. Artistic success can often have more to do with social success than artistic genius. In the case of Eugène Isabey, the fact that he was the son and pupil of a famous father, the miniaturist Jean Baptiste Isabey, did much to ensure that his undoubted talents received early recognition. He was a leading member of what was called "the Men of 30", a group of romantic painters following the path of Bonington (q.v.).

In 1830 he was appointed official artist to the expedition which was to capture Algeria. He painted historical scenes and genre subjects, as well as marines and landscapes. Of these, the two latter are the best; they are fresh and brightly finished, his earlier work having a rather pale grey palette, which strengthened as he grew older.

He received many medals and honours, including being made a Chevalier of the Legion of Honour. He died in Paris on April 27th, 1886.

PLATES: 411, 412.

EXAMPLES: Wallace Collection, London (2): beach scenes. Montreal Museum of Fine Arts (1): the beach at Fécamp. Musée de Mulhouse (2): marines. Musée de Nantes (1): wreck of the Emily. *The Louvre, Paris (4): the embarkation of de Ruyter and Cornelis de Witt; the bridge; a marine; seaport. Musée de la Marine, Paris (2): the Battle of Texel, 1673; the visit of Queen Victoria to Tréport in 1843. Musée de Perigueux (1): seaport. Musée de Perpignon (1): marine. Musée de Poitiers (1): marine. Nationalmuseum, Stockholm (1): ships in an anchorage. Musée de Toulouse (1): view of Boulogne. City Art Gallery, York (2): boat in a storm; a Normandy fishing village.*

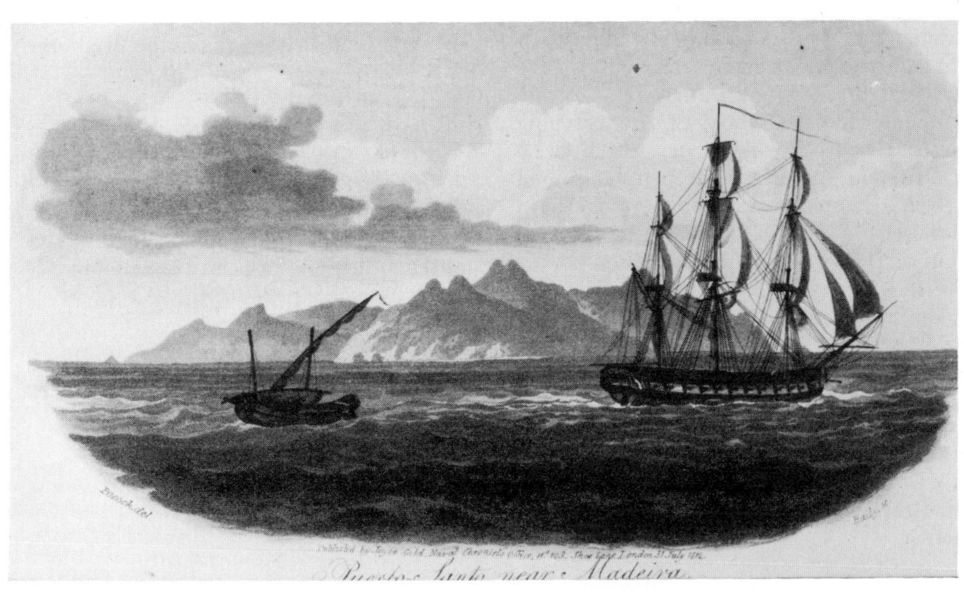

J

JACK, W.
A British ship portraitist working in the third quarter of the 19th century. The National Maritime Museum, Greenwich, has a painting by him of the paddle tug *Royal Alfred,* dated 1863.

JACOBSEN, Antonio Nicolo Gasparo 1850-1921
His studio was in West Hoboken, a suburb of New York, and he was the most successful of the late 19th and early 20th century American ship portraitists. Many of his works were commissions from European sea captains and owners and so found their way to Europe.

PLATE: 630.

EXAMPLES: Altonaer Museum (1). National Maritime Museum, Greenwich (1). Maritime Museum, Kronborg Castle (several). Mariners Museum, Newport News (275). Peabody Museum of Salem, 47 signed works and five attributed. He is also represented in the New Bedford Whaling Museum.

JAMES, David
Surprisingly little is known about this prolific painter of the sea. He first exhibited at the Royal Academy in 1886 from an address in Dalston, Cumberland, and from 1892-97 from an address in Maida Vale, London.

At his best he was a very skilful painter of the sea from the shore. The coastal views and the shipping were usually of secondary importance in the composition. His favourite locations were the West Country and the Isles of Scilly.

The National Maritime Museum has a fine, large example of breakers.

PLATE: 597.

JANES, Norman R.S.M.A. b.1892
Born in Egham, Surrey, he studied at the Regent Street Polytechnic before the First World War and then served in the infantry in France for the duration. He returned to civilian life in 1919 and studied at the Slade School of Fine Art and the Central School of Art and Design.

In 1928 he joined the Hornsey School of Art, teaching engraving, and later taught at the Slade. He became fascinated by the dwindling number of deep water sailing ships, which he drew and painted as and when they arrived in the Port of London. His interest in shipping and harbour scenes also took him to France where he painted the ports.

He served in the R.A.F. in the Second World War and since then has continued painting coastal scenes and harbours in Britain, France and Italy, particularly in Venice. He was elected a member of the Royal Society of Marine Artists in 1946 and has also exhibited at the Royal Academy since 1921, at the New English Art Club and at the Royal Society of Painters in Watercolours.

Examples of his work can be found in the National Maritime Museum, Greenwich, the British Museum and the Imperial War Museum.

PLATE: 655.

JANSEN, Harry J.
A ship portraitist working in Rotterdam in the first quarter of the 20th century. Two examples, one dated 1903 and the other dated 1913, are in the National Maritime Museum, Greenwich. There are also two oils in the Peabody Museum of Salem, one dated 1919, the other 1920.

PLATE: 623.

JANSEN, Hendrick Willebrord 1855-1908
Born in Nijnegen on December 12th, 1855, he studied at the Academy in Amsterdam under Auguste Allebe and de Wynveld. He then studied landscape at Arnhem and Doesburg and in 1888 went to Amsterdam where he concentrated on shipping scenes. He died in Ziest on November 4th, 1908.

EXAMPLES: Rijksmuseum, Amsterdam (1): Amsterdam on a rainy day. Mesdag Museum, The Hague (1): view of Amsterdam. Bavarian State Collections, Munich: the Port of Hoorn.

JENKINSON, J.
A good quality marine painter working in Liverpool in the first quarter of the 19th century. The Merseyside County Museums, Liverpool, have two ship portraits by him.

PLATE: 323.

JENNER, Isaac Walter 1836-1901
Born in Godalming, Surrey, on March 8th, 1836. Early in life he went to sea in oyster and crab smacks, then joined the Royal Navy, serving through the Russian war of 1854-56, and leaving it in 1865. He then took up marine painting, recalling episodes in his naval career and shipping scenes from memory.

In 1885 he emigrated to Australia, and founded the Queensland Art Society in Brisbane, where he died in 1901. Examples of his work can be seen in the Queensland Art Gallery in Brisbane, and the Brighton Art Gallery in Sussex.

JENSEN, Alfred 1859-1935
Born in Randers, Denmark, in 1859, he studied at Hamburg and at the Academy at Kassel, and spent some time at sea. He settled in Hamburg where he became Professor of the Arts and Crafts School. In 1901 he received a gold medal from an exhibition at Lyon. The Altonaer Museum, Hamburg, has a port scene by him.

JOHNSON, Marshall 1846-1921
An accomplished American marine painter, perhaps from Lovell in Maine. The Peabody Museum of Salem has three oils by him and some of his sketch books.

JOLI DE DIPI, Antonio **c.1700-1777**
Born in Modena, his profession was as a theatrical scene painter, but he was also a fine easel painter, not surprisingly, often on a grand scale. He was a pupil of Giovani Paolo Pannini. His work in theatres took him to Germany, England and Spain. The Prado Museum has two paintings of King Charles III embarking from Naples.

PLATES: 201, 202.

JONGKIND, Johan Barthold **1819-1891**
Born in Lattrop, Overyssel, on June 3rd, 1819. He was a pupil of Andreas Schelfhout and of the Academy at The Hague. He visited Paris in 1845 and afterwards worked in Holland, doing lithographs as well as paintings. He exhibited at Amsterdam in 1844 and worked on the north coast of France. He died in La Cote Saint André, near Grenoble on February 9th, 1891.

PLATE: 483.

EXAMPLES: Rijksmuseum, Amsterdam (2): marines; moonlit river scene; shipping at Rotterdam by moonlight. Stedelijk Museum, Amsterdam (2): Rotterdam harbour; seascape. Dordrecht Museum (1): view of Honfleur. Gemeentemuseum, The Hague (1): Normandy coast. The Louvre, Paris: a collection of watercolours. Boymans Museum, Rotterdam (1): view of Overichie.

JOY, John Cantiloe **1806-1866**
Born in Yarmouth, Isle of Wight, 1806, died in London, 1866. The younger of the two Joy brothers, who worked as a team all their lives and many of whose productions are joint efforts. John Cantiloe seems to have worked almost exclusively in watercolour, mainly doing views of men-of-war, often in an evening light and suffused with a characteristic purplish blue.

He and his brother were lucky to attract the patronage of Captain Thomas Manby, R.N., a wealthy collector with an estate in Norfolk. They were also employed by the government to paint scenes at Portsmouth in the 1830s. John exhibited at Suffolk Street in 1826 and 1827.

PLATES: 523, 524.

EXAMPLES: National Maritime Museum, Greenwich: 17 watercolours.

JOY, William **1803-1867**
Born in Yarmouth, Isle of Wight, in 1803; the elder of the two brothers Joy, he painted in oils as well as watercolours. He exhibited at the Royal Academy in 1824 and 1832, when he had an address in Great Yarmouth. The painting shown in the latter year was for his patron, Captain Manby, and illustrated that officer's invention for rescuing people from stranded ships. He also exhibited at the British Institution in 1823 and 1845, latterly from an address in Chichester, where he died in 1867.

PLATES: 523, 524, 525.

EXAMPLES: City Art Gallery, Birmingham (2). National Maritime Museum, Greenwich: a pair of the escape of the frigate Clyde *from the Nore Mutiny 1797; 8 watercolours and 5 more with his brother; Victoria and Albert Museum: 2 watercolours. Castle Museum, Norwich: 3 watercolours. Graves Art Gallery, Sheffield: 1 watercolour.*

JUGELET, Jean Marie Auguste **1805-1875**
Born in Finistère, Brittany, in 1805; died in Versailles in 1875. He was a pupil of Théodore Gudin and became a successful painter, exhibiting at the Paris Salon from 1831 to 1870. He received the Legion d'Honneur in 1847.

PLATE: 413.

EXAMPLES: Musée de Dieppe: the arrival of King Louis-Philippe at Dieppe. Musée Du Puy (1). Municipal Museum of Fine Art, Rochfort (2): the look-out on the Koat Ven; *action between the* Belle Poule *and the* Arethusa, *1778.*

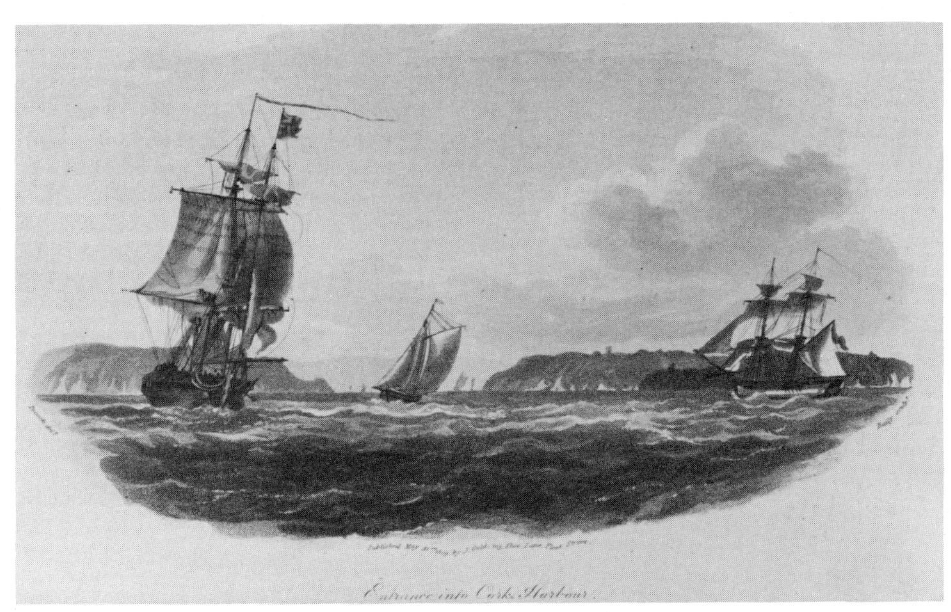

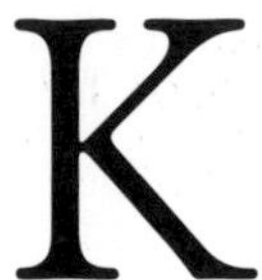

KABEL, Adriaan van der *see* **CABEL, Adriaan van der**

KANNEMANS, Christiaan Cornelis **1812-1884**
Born in Breda on July 13th, 1812, he was a pupil of Jan Hendrick Frederiks from the age of ten to twelve. He was later a house painter but developed as a marine artist, and eventually became a teacher at the Royal Military Academy at Breda. He died in Breda on January 3rd, 1884. He exhibited at The Hague 1843-75, and at Leeuwarden in 1855.

KENDRICK, Matthew R.H.A. **c.1797-1874**
Born in Dublin, he was a sailor turned painter who joined the Royal Dublin Society Schools in 1825. He exhibited at the Royal Hibernian Academy between 1827 and 1872, was elected an associate there in 1832 and an academician in 1850.

He moved to London in 1840 where he exhibited at the British Institution in 1842, 1844 and 1845, and at the Royal Academy in 1845. In 1848 he returned to Dublin and remained there until paralysis of the hands set in and he moved to London for treatment. He died in London on November 1st, 1874.

The National Maritime Museum, Greenwich, has one painting of a pilot cutter and a French smuggler, and the Peabody Museum of Salem has an example.

KENSETT, John Frederick **1818-1872**
Born in the County of Cheshire, in New Hampshire, in 1818. More a painter of coastal scenes and landscapes than a true marine painter, he was nevertheless an important influence on the American marine school of the second half of the 19th century.

His work is admirably crafted and clear. He started his artistic life in the studio of an engraver of bank notes and the discipline of that art form stood him in good stead.

In 1840 he worked his passage to England and remained there and in Rome for seven years. In 1845 he exhibited two pictures at the Royal Academy, one of which, "A peep at Windsor Castle", was acclaimed by the critics.

He returned to America in 1847 where he became a member of the National Academy in 1849. He died in New York in 1872. Examples of his work can be seen in the Museum of Fine Arts, Boston, and the National Gallery, Washington. He sometimes collaborated with Professor David Huntington of the University of Michigan.

PLATE: 481.

KENSINGTON, C.
A British ship portraitist working in the last quarter of the 19th century and the first quarter of the present one. The National Maritime Museum, Greenwich, has a painting of the barque *Westglen,* dated 1888.

PLATE: 593.

KENT, Leslie R.S.M.A. **b.1890**
Born in Finchley, London, on June 15th, 1890, he was educated at Bedales School and Leeds University, and studied painting under Frederick Milner at St. Ives in Cornwall. He was by profession a civil engineer from 1910 to 1945, and an artist in his spare time. After his retirement he took up oil painting professionally.

He has exhibited at the Royal Academy, Royal Scottish Academy, Paris Salon, Royal Society of British Artists, Royal Institute of Oil Painters, New English Art Club, Society of Marine Artists, etc. He has also held five one-man shows. He was elected a member of the Society of Marine Artists in 1938 and of the Royal Society of British Artists in 1940.

KERR, George Cochrane
He exhibited marines and coastal views at the Royal Academy between 1878 and 1897, also at Suffolk Street and the New Watercolour Society.

EXAMPLE: National Maritime Museum, Greenwich (1): the burning of H.M.S. Bombay *off Montevideo in 1864 (after R.B. Beechey).*

KIERS, George Laurens **1838-1916**
Born in Amsterdam in 1838, he died there in 1916. He was a pupil of the landscape painter Louis Meijer. He exhibited at The Hague and at Amsterdam from 1856 to 1878.

KLEIJNE, David **1754-1805**
Born in Bergen-op-Zoom in 1754, he died in Middelburg July 11th, 1805. A marine painter and draughtsman who became a master painter at Middelburg in 1777. Examples are held by the Scheepvaart Museum at Amsterdam, the Wallraf-Richartz Museum at Cologne, and the Prins Hendrik Museum at Rotterdam.

PLATE: 286.

KLOSS, Friedric Theodor **1802-1876**
Born in Brunswick on September 19th, 1802. He was a pupil of Martinus Schoumann in 1819. In 1828 he moved to Copenhagen, where he settled to paint marines, becoming a member of the Academy there, and master of drawing to the cadets of the Naval College. In 1844 he travelled in Italy. He died in Copenhagen on June 9th, 1876.

PLATE: 405

EXAMPLES: Statens Museum for Kunst, Copenhagen (9): the arrival of the frigate Havfruen *at Arhus; Danish men-of-war off Iceland; Danish men-of-war in the roads of Copenhagen; a French man-of-war cutting away her masts in a storm; Danish men-of-war in the roads of Warnemunde; the Danish frigate* Nymphen *in a storm; the harbour of Nyborg with the cutter* Neptun. *There are also examples at the Orlogsmuseet, Copenhagen.*

KNELL, John Henry **b.c.1818**

Possibly born in London c.1818, and presumably the younger brother of William Adolphus Knell (q.v.), since they shared the same address. He exhibited coastal views at the Royal Academy in 1833 and 1834.

KNELL, William Adolphus **c.1808-1875**

Thought to have been born in London in 1808, he was the best known and the best performer of this family of painters. He was strongly influenced by the romantic movement, and made a copy of de Loutherbourg's "Battle of the First of June 1794". His style varies a good deal and perhaps his most effective painting is his "Battle of Camperdown" at Greenwich, painted in 1848. There is a certain coarseness that pervades his work. He died in London on July 10th, 1875.

He exhibited at the Royal Academy between 1815 and 1866 and at the British Institution between 1827 and 1867.

PLATES: 438, 439.

EXAMPLES: National Maritime Museum, Greenwich (10): the Battle of Camperdown 1797 (on loan); Dance's action in the Strait of Malocca 1804; the Warrior *protecting a convoy 1807; the* Pearl *capturing the slaver* Vengador *and the* Opposicao *(a pair); H.M.S.* Marlborough *and H.M.S.* Minotaur; *the* Morley; *the* Mountstewart Elphinstone; *an East Indiaman in the Thames; a Brixham trawler.*

KNELL, William Callcott **c.1830-aft.1876**

Born possibly in London in about 1830, he died after 1876. It has been suggested that he was the brother of William Adolphus Knell (q.v.) but it is improbable that there would have been two brothers called William. It seems much more likely that he was William Adolphus's son, as they shared the same address when William Callcott first exhibited in 1848 at the Royal Academy. He continued to exhibit there until 1862 and at the British Institution between 1861 and 1865. Why he stopped exhibiting is a mystery, for paintings exist signed at least as late as 1876. He was probably his father's pupil, his work being similar, but inferior, to his father's later style.

KNIGHT, George **fl.1875**

Little is known of this artist. A contemporary painting by him of Cleopatra's needle being towed to England belongs to the National Maritime Museum, Greenwich, and the Museum also owns a small pair of paintings of fishing boats and a coaster being washed up on a beach, but these are not of high quality.

KNYFF, Jacob **1638-1681**

Born in Haarlem in December 1638. By June 1672 the war with France and England was going badly for the Dutch, especially on land. King Charles II made a proclamation inviting Dutch artists to come to England and work, even though the two countries were at war. Since patronage had almost dried up in Holland, a number of Dutch painters took advantage of the offer, and of the marine artists among them by far the best known were the two Willem van de Veldes and Jacob Knyff.

Since none of them spoke any English, so far as we know, they were rather isolated and must have had to rely on each other for company. It may be that Knyff worked in the van de Veldes' studio because there are copies by him of their works.

For several years, up to 1971, some art historians thought that Knyff was the most likely candidate to be the true hand of Isaac Sailmaker. Then a well documented Sailmaker turned up, and it was realised that this group of paintings could not be by Sailmaker after all. For a year they remained unidentified, until a painting signed by Knyff came on the market, and the group received its proper attribution. Jacob was the son of Wouter Knyff, and after working in Haarlem, later had a studio in Paris for a time. He died in London in 1681.

PLATES: 165, 166, 167; COLOUR PLATE: VIII.

EXAMPLES: National Maritime Museum, Greenwich (4): English ships attacking a Barbary port (copy of a Willem van de Velde I); a French flagship off Calais; a dock scene at an English port; the Royal Charles *with ships and galleys off a southern port — this last is a huge picture, probably meant to depict Katherine of Braganza being accompanied from Lisbon in 1662.*

KOBELL, Hendrick **1751-1779**

Born in Rotterdam in 1751, he was a pupil at the Amsterdam Academy in 1770 and 1771. Having already travelled to London in 1769 and exhibited a sea battle scene at the Free Society Exhibition in 1770, he visited Paris in 1772. He died in Rotterdam in 1779.

He seems to have worked mainly in watercolours and was also an engraver.

EXAMPLES: Rijksmuseum, Amsterdam (3): a shipwreck; the Dutch expedition of 1777; the roads at Batavia. Fodor Museum, Amsterdam (2): battle of the Third Dutch War 1672/3; a marine. Gemeente Archief, Amsterdam, Teylers Stichting Museum, Haarlem, Boymans Museum, Rotterdam: watercolours.

KOEKKOEK, Hermanus, Senior **1815-1882**

Born in Middelburg in 1815, he was the youngest of the four painter sons of Johannes Hermanus, who was also his master. He worked in Amsterdam from 1832 to 1858, then at Nieuwer-Amstel until he returned to Amsterdam in 1873. He became a member of the Royal Academy in Amsterdam in 1840 and of the Rotterdam Society in 1841. In 1876 he exhibited a painting at the Royal Academy, London, called "A Fresh Breeze on the French Coast".

His work is very similar to his father's, especially his calms, though somewhat more romantic as one would expect.

He exhibited at Amsterdam, Rotterdam and The Hague from 1836 to 1881, and died in Haarlem in 1882.

PLATES: 397, 398.

EXAMPLES: Stedelijk Museum, Amsterdam (7). Courtrai Museum (1). Paul Tetar Museum, Delft (1). City Art Gallery, Glasgow (1). Groningen Museum (1). Musée Du Havre (1). National Gallery, Melbourne (1). Boymans Museum, Rotterdam (2). Prins Hendrik Museum, Rotterdam (1). Graves Art Gallery, Sheffield (2).

KOEKKOEK, Hermanus, Junior **1836-1895**

Born in Amsterdam in 1836, he was a pupil of his father Hermanus Snr. (q.v.), and painted in the same style. He exhibited in Amsterdam in 1860, 1875 and 1881, in The Hague in 1859 and 1863, in Leeuwarden in 1855, and in Rotterdam in 1862. He does not seem to be represented in any public gallery. He died near London in 1895.

KOEKKOEK, Johannes **1811-1851**

Born in Middelburg in 1811; died in Breda in 1831. The third son of Johannes Hermanus, who was his master. Sadly he died before his twentieth birthday, so his output was limited. What there is shows great promise but there are apparently none of his works in public collections.

KOEKKOEK, Johannes Hermanus **1778-1851**

Born at Veere, Island of Walcheren in 1778; died in Amsterdam in 1851. The founding father of the Koekkoek family of painters, two of whom, Hermanus and Johannes (qq.v.), also became marine painters; Barend and Martinus Adrianus stuck to landscapes. Two of his grandsons by Hermanus also became marine painters, J.H.B. Koekkoek and Hermanus Koekkoek Junior. Johannes Hermanus was self-taught and in his early years worked at a wallpaper factory in Middelburg. From 1826 to 1833 he was in Durgerdam and then moved to Amsterdam, where he became a member of the Royal Academy. He was the most talented of the marine painters in his family. He exhibited at Haarlem in 1825 and at The Hague and Amsterdam from 1827 to 1833.

PLATES 393, 394, 395, 396.

EXAMPLES: Scheepvaart Museum, Amsterdam (3). Simon van Gijn Museum, Dordrecht (3). Boymans Museum, Rotterdam (1). Works also in: City Art Gallery, Bristol; Bavarian State Collections, Munich; museums in Hamburg and Mayence.

KOEKKOEK, Johannes Hermanus Barend **1840-1912**

Born in Amsterdam in 1840, he died in Hilversum in 1912. He exhibited landscapes, marines and coastal scenes at Amsterdam, Rotterdam, The Hague and Leeuwarden from 1862 to 1887. There are no works listed in public collections.

KOETS, Hermanus **1663-aft.1711**

Born in Middelburg in 1663. He was a pupil of the portrait and genre painter Zacharias Blijhoof, and painted portraits as well as marines. He also engraved and was a ship modeller. He died probably in Amsterdam soon after 1711.

KONG WEIN

A Chinese ship portraitist working in Calcutta in the last quarter of the 19th century. The National Maritime Museum, Greenwich, has a painting by him of the ship *Four Winds,* launched 1885, wrecked 1899.

KOOL (KOOLEN), Willem Gillsz **1608/9-1666**

Born in Haarlem, he died there in October, 1666. He was a member of the guild at Haarlem in 1638 and its doyen in 1656.

PLATE: 133.

EXAMPLES: Musée de Bordeaux (1): a fish market on the beach. Landesmuseum, Darmstadt (1): a beach scene. Frans Hals Museum, Haarlem: landing fish. Hermitage, Leningrad (3): beach scenes.

KOSTER, Everhardus **1817-1892**

Born in The Hague, he was a pupil at The Hague Academy under Johannes van Hove, and then at the City Institute, Frankfurt am Main. He returned to Holland in 1848 and worked in Amsterdam. In 1856 and 1857 he visited England and from the following year until 1878 was director of the Haarlem Pavilion. He died in Dordrecht in 1892.

He exhibited at The Hague and Amsterdam from 1837 to 1878 and at Leeuwarden from 1859 to 1863. His works are fairly widely spread in Holland and can be found in the galleries of Amsterdam, The Hague and Rotterdam, and in Utrecht Cathedral.

PLATE: 474.

KRAUSE, Wilhelm August Leopold Christian **1803-1864**

Born in Dersau. Neither of his masters, Kolbe and Wack, were marine painters. In his late teens he worked in Dresden, then moved to Berlin when he was twenty-one. What prompted him to paint seascapes before he had seen the sea, we will never know, but later he did see it when he went on a trip to Norway. He was made a member of the Berlin Academy of Fine Art in 1832. He died in Berlin in 1864.

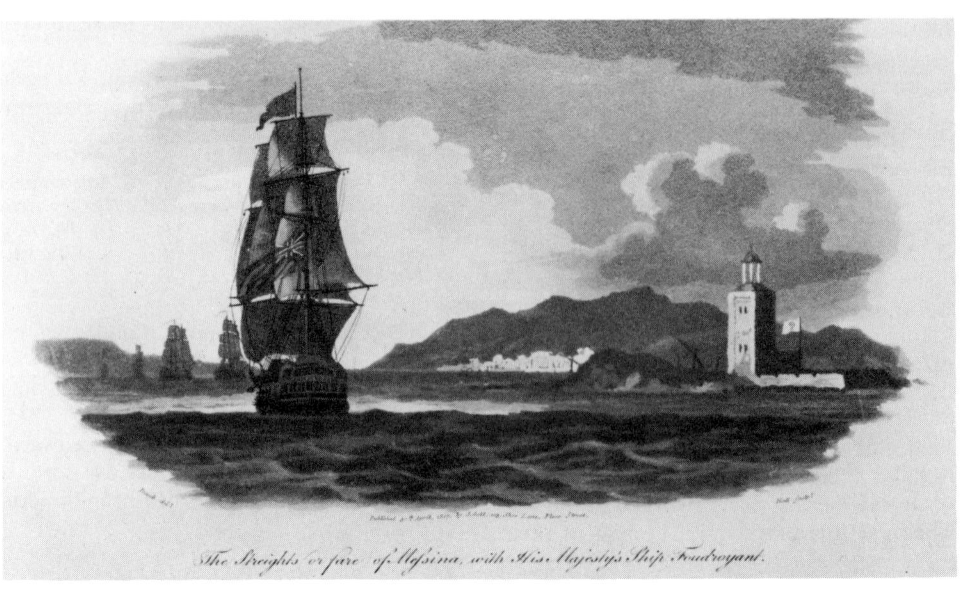

The Streights or fare of Messina, with His Majesty's Ship Foudroyant.

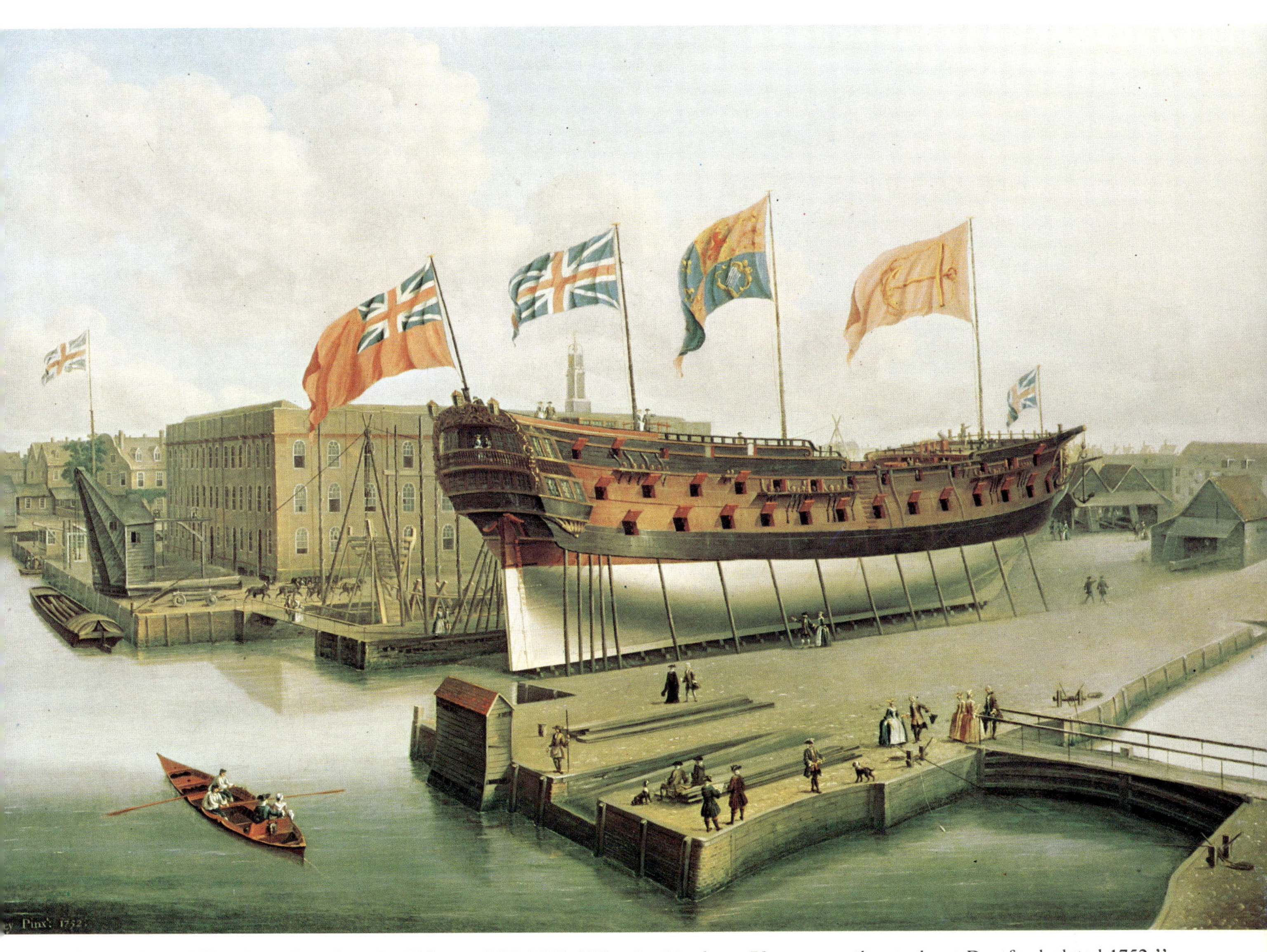

Colour Plate XIII. John Cleveley, the Elder, c.1712-1777. "The *Buckingham,* 70 guns, on the stocks at Deptford, dated 1752." National Maritime Museum, Greenwich.

L

LA CROIX, G.F. de

Painter working in the second and third quarters of the 18th century. It is strange that an artist who was probably Claude-Joseph Vernet's (q.v.) best pupil, and who has long been well known to collectors as "Lacroix de Marseille" is so poorly recorded. This was presumably his native city, though he died in Paris about 1780.

He emulated his master and did similar compositions though more prone to moonlight scenes.

EXAMPLES: Musée Calvert, Avignon (2): marine and a storm scene. Musée des Beaux-Arts, Dijon (3): moonlight scene; storm; sundown.

LAI SUNG

A Chinese ship portraitist working in Hong Kong in the middle of the 19th century. The Peabody Museum of Salem has six of his oils.

LANE, Fitz Hugh **1804-1865**

Born in Cape Ann, Massachusetts, in 1804, this painter is of the second generation of what is called the Hudson River school. He had a great success in his lifetime as being perhaps the first American marine painter of sophisticated quality, and he strongly influenced the next generation, especially Martin Johnson Heade (q.v.). There is a simplicity and straightforwardness about his style that sometimes suggests the influence of Robert Salmon (q.v.).

Examples of his work can be seen at the Museum of Fine Arts, Boston, The Bostonian Society, the Mariners Museum, Newport News, the Virginia Museum of Fine Arts, Richmond, the Peabody Museum of Salem and the Shelburne Museum, Vermont.

PLATES: 447, 448, 449.

LANGMAID, Lieut.-Com. Roland John Robb R.N. **c.1897-c.1960**

His commission as a lieutenant dates from 1919, which roughly fixes his year of birth. He appears to have fallen a victim to "Geddes's Axe" in the early 1920s, when the personnel of the Royal Navy was drastically reduced. In the Second World War he rejoined and served for most of the war in the shore based H.M.S. *Nile* in Egypt. It was here that he was appointed artist to the Mediterranean Fleet by Admiral Sir Andrew Cunningham. The upshot of this was a book about its operations called *The Med,* which he wrote and illustrated, published in 1948. He also wrote and illustrated a book in 1937 called *The King's Ships Through the Ages.*

The National Maritime Museum, Greenwich, has a collection of seventeen of his wartime paintings of events in the Mediterranean, and a portrait of Admiral Sir Andrew Cunningham later Viscount Cunningham of Hyndhope.

PLATE: 666.

LARSEN, Carl Frederick Emmanuel **1823-1859**

Born and died in Copenhagen. He was a pupil of Eckersberg and of the Copenhagen Academy. He travelled and painted widely in Europe.

PLATES: 354, 355.

EXAMPLES: Statens Museum for Kunst, Copenhagen (8): ships off the coast of Zealand; evening off Marseilles; Harbour at Nieuwe Diep, Holland; Danish ship of the line Valdemar *in the Sound; rocky coast near Marseilles; marine; a frigate at anchor; Copenhagen Roads. There are also examples in the Royal Naval Museum, Copenhagen.*

LARSSON, Simeon Markus **1825-1864**

Born in Ostergotland, Sweden, in 1825, he studied at the Stockholm Academy, then under Anton Melbye in Copenhagen, and with Andreas Achenbach in Düsseldorf. He worked in Paris in the mid-1850s, then in Russia and finally in London, where he died in 1864.

PLATES: 356, 357.

EXAMPLES: Maritime Museum, Krönborg Castle, Denmark (1): a steamer on fire. Lansmuseum, Linkoping, Sweden (1): a frigate and a brig in a storm. Nationalmuseum, Stockholm (2): storm; shipwreck.

LAWSON, J.L. **fl.1930s**

He was an Admiralty pilot for Gibraltar and Devonport between the wars. The National Maritime Museum, Greenwich, has a painting by him of the wreck of the *Herzogin Cecilie,* dated 1936.

LEATHAM, William J. **fl.1840s-1850s**

A painter who specialised in storm scenes and sea dramas. The only painting he exhibited at the British Institution was in 1847, of a drowning he had witnessed, called "A man overboard".

He first exhibited at the Royal Academy in 1840, and between then and 1855. The Brighton Art Gallery has three oils: Battle of the Nile 1798, Battle of Trafalgar 1805, Off Shoreham, and a watercolour of the Brighton Chain Pier; the National Maritime Museum, Greenwich, has three watercolours: the Bombardment of Acre 1840, frigates at sea, and a fishing boat with a Dutch ship at anchor.

LEAVITT, John Faunce **b.1905**

A talented American painter of historical sailing ships. The Peabody Museum of Salem has two oils and fifty-one watercolours and drawings.

PLATE: 652.

LEBRETON, Louis **d.1866**

A Parisian painter of marines, who exhibited at the Paris Salon from 1841 to 1849. A wash drawing of New York Harbour, of about 1860, was in the sale-rooms in 1971 and suggests that he journeyed to America.

The Peabody Museum of Salem has a painting of the *Astrolabe* and *Zelée* stranded on the Detract de Torres during the Dumont d'Urville expedition, for which Lebreton was the official artist; this is dated 1856.

PLATE: 500.

LEE, Joseph

An American landscape painter and ship portraitist who was working in the San Francisco Bay area in the second half of the 19th century. The National Maritime Museum of San Francisco has a portrait of the barquentine *Catherine Sudden,* built in 1878.

LEEMANS, T. **fl.c.1720**

Surviving paintings signed "T. Leemans" show him to have been a follower of Willem van de Velde II (q.v.), in the generation of Peter Monamy (q.v.). Known examples date to around 1720; though inferior to Monamy they have a finished, glossy quality. One distinctive feature is his tendency to exaggerate the sparring of his ships, particularly the length of the yards.

LEPOITTEVIN, Eugène Modeste Edmond **1806-1870**

Born in Paris 1806, his real name Poidevin; died at Auteuil, 1870. He was a pupil of Louis Hersent, the portrait and genre painter, who also taught him lithography. He was also a pupil of Xavier Le Prince, the landscape and genre painter.

He exhibited at the Paris Salon from 1830 and was awarded medals in the years 1831, 1836, 1848 and 1855.

It is perhaps as a lithographer that he is best remembered.

PLATE: 414.

EXAMPLES: (Marines only): Musée de Picardy, Amiens (1): shipwreck. Altonaer Museum, Hamburg (1): launch of a ship. Musée de Nantes (1). Musée National de Versailles (1): Battle of Encho, 1346.

LEPORT, John

The National Maritime Museum, Greenwich, has a crude portrait of the barque *General Picton* by him, dated July 1886. It is doubtful that he painted for a living.

LEVER, Richard Hagley **1876-1958**

Born in Adelaide in 1876, he first studied there under James Ashton, then went to England in 1902 and studied at St. Ives in Cornwall under Julius Olsson and A.M. Talmadge. He moved on to Paris and then to America where he became an instructor in seascape painting at the Art Students' League in New York. He remained to become a successful marine painter, and died there in 1958.

He was a member of the American National Academy of Design, the Society of American Painters and Engravers, Connecticut Academy of Fine Arts and the Royal British Artists. His work may be seen at the National Gallery of South Australia in Adelaide, the National Gallery of New South Wales in Sydney and the Metropolitan Museum in New York.

LEYDEN, Jan van

Painter working in the second and third quarters of the 17th century. This artist was mannerist in style and relates to Jan Beerstraaten (q.v.), Pieter van Soest (q.v.) and Claes Wou (q.v.), but he is not of the highest quality.

PLATE: 81.

EXAMPLES: Rijksmuseum, Amsterdam (1): Dutch in the Medway capturing Sheerness. *National Maritime Museum, Greenwich (1): the* Amelia *in action in the First Dutch War, 1652/3.0*

LIDDELL, J.D.

The Peabody Museum of Salem has a good quality painting of a paddle-tug with a brigantine in tow off Ramsgate pier, about 1870. No further information on the artist has come to light.

LINGELBACH, Johannes **1622-1674**

Born in Frankfurt in 1622; died in Amsterdam 1674. Lingelbach was not primarily a marine painter, perhaps being chiefly interested in genre painting with landscape. None the less he did paint marines, battle scenes and port scenes of admirable quality.

In 1637 he moved with his family from Frankfurt to Amsterdam, and then was in Paris from 1642 to 1644. He returned to Amsterdam for several years before going to Rome in 1650, where he stayed six years. During all this time he was being very well instructed, but by whom in particular it is not known. There was, however, a wealth of teaching talent available, and the report that he was a pupil of Wouverman in Haarlem seems credible. He remained in Amsterdam for the rest of his life, an important member of the Dutch School. He signed his work "J. Lingelbach".

PLATES: 76, 77, 78.

EXAMPLES: Marines only. Rijksmuseum, Amsterdam (6): three port scenes; two beach scenes showing the departure of Charles II for England in 1660; a distant view of the Battle of Leghorn, 1653. Prince Bishop's Palace, Bamberg (1): naval action. Herzog Anton Ulrich Museum, Brunswick (1): seafight between Christian and Turkish galleys. Statens Museum for Kunst, Copenhagen (2): Mediterranean port; galley action between Christians and Turks. Gemäldegalerie, Dresden (1): port scene. Gemäldegalerie, Düsseldorf (1): Mediterranean port scene. Gemäldegalerie, Frankfurt (1): Mediterranean port. Old Gallery, Graz, Austria (1): Mediterranean port. Landesgalerie, Hanover (1): Mediterranean port scene. Hermitage, Leningrad (1): view of Venice. Metropolitan Museum, New York (1): naval action. Louvre, Paris (1): Mediterranean port. Kunsthistorisches Museum, Vienna (1): port scene.

LISTER-LISTER, William **1859-1943**

Born in Sydney in 1859, died in 1943. He studied in England at the Bedford Art School, then spent two years in France before going on to Glasgow, where he joined the St. Mungo Art Club. He exhibited at the Royal Scottish Academy at the age of seventeen.

He returned to Sydney in 1888, where he became the President of the Royal Art Society of New South Wales from 1897 to 1941. He was known for his coastal views of New South Wales.

He is represented in the Australian State Art galleries, the National Gallery of New Zealand, Wellington, and the National Gallery of Wales in Cardiff.

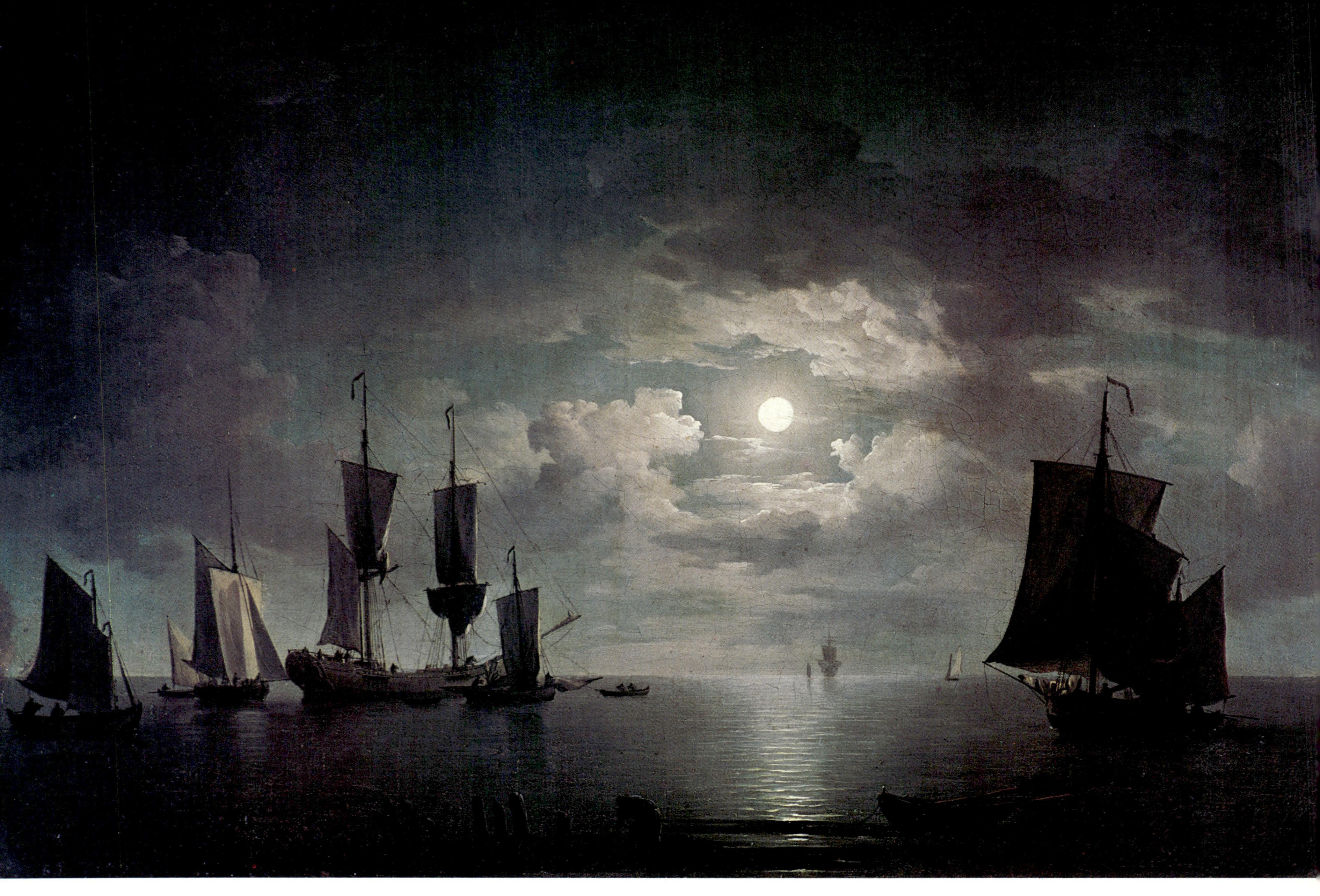

Colour Plate XIV. Charles Brooking, 1723-1759. ''An English merchant brig and coastal craft becalmed by moonlight.'' Private collection.

LIVESAY, John
He was appointed writing master at the Royal Naval Academy at Portsmouth in April 1799 and retired in 1832. He was also a competent watercolourist of maritime subjects; there are examples in the National Maritime Museum, Greenwich.

LOCHER, Carl **1851-1915**
Born in Flensburg, he was a Danish painter of coastal scenes, who exhibited in Berlin, Hamburg and Munich from 1878. The Statens Museum for Kunst at Copenhagen has three examples, two being beach scenes, the third depicting the funeral of King Frederik VII in 1863. There are also examples in the Royal Naval Museum, Copenhagen. He died in Skagen in 1915.

PLATE: 563.

LOEFF, Jacob Gerritsz
Painter working in the second and third quarters of the 17th century. His style is rather mannered with a grey or brown palette and not of the first quality. His identity has been lost until recently because, in the case of the Greenwich pictures listed, he mostly signed with initials.

PLATES: 58, 59.

EXAMPLES: Rijksmuseum, Amsterdam (2). National Maritime Museum, Greenwich (2, a pair): de Witte in action with Dunkirkers, 1641. Hermitage, Leningrad (1): small vessels off a port.

LOOS, John F.
A Belgian ship portraitist working in Antwerp in the third quarter of the 19th century. The Peabody Museum of Salem has four oils by him.

LORRAINE, Claude (le) *see* **GELLÉE**

LOUTHERBOURG, Philippe Jacques de R.A. **1740-1812**
Born in Strasbourg on October 31st, 1740; died in Chiswick, London, on March 11th, 1812. He studied first under his father, a miniaturist, then in Paris under Carl Vanloo, the genre and portrait painter, and last under the battle and marine painter, Francesco Casanova. He was already an established painter in France, painter to the King, a member of the French Royal Academy and of the Academy of Marseilles, when, in 1771, he came to London. The man instrumental in causing de Loutherbourg to settle in London was the actor David Garrick, who, after some trial work, engaged him in 1773 as scene director at Drury Lane Theatre with the enormous salary of £500 per year. He continued in this position for ten years, and in 1781 first exhibited his Eidophusikon or mechanical theatre, in which one of the most successful displays was of a painted and mechanical shipwreck.

In this, in his theatre work and his general art, de Loutherbourg was preoccupied with the recreation of dramatic naturalistic light effects. He was a leader of the Romantic movement and had a considerable influence on the direction marine painting was to take in the early 19th century. He particularly influenced the young J.M.W. Turner, who had a high regard for his work.

He started to exhibit at the Royal Academy in 1772, and continued to do so most years until his death, being elected a member in 1781. It must be admitted that very few of the paintings exhibited were marines and his influence on the marine painters rests mainly on a small number of heroic battle pieces which he painted at the turn of the century. Of these the finest are the huge "Battle of the Glorious First of June 1794" at the National Maritime Museum, Greenwich, the two smaller but very fine battle scenes: "Camperdown 1797" and "Nile 1798" at the Tate Gallery, and the Landing in Egypt 1801 painted for General Lord Abercrombie, which is still with his family.

The Bristol Art Gallery has his "Cutting out of the *Chevrette,* 1801". Less successful is his "Battle of Gravelines 1588", also at Greenwich. His remaining marines seem to be coast scenes, usually dramatic in form and weather. Other pictures are at the Victoria Art Gallery, Bath, "Smugglers Landing in a Storm"; National Gallery, Dublin, "A Mediterranean Tempest"; the Metropolitan Museum, New York, "The Fête of the Tunny Fishers at Marseilles"; Landesmuseum, Oldenburg, "Shipwreck on a Rocky Coast"; Ashmolean Museum, Oxford, "Beach Scene with Smugglers"; Art Gallery, Southampton, "Shipwreck with Banditti"; National Museum, Stockholm, "A Shipwreck"; Fine Art Academy, Vienna, "A Storm with Rocks and Figures"; City Art Gallery, York, a picture called "The Wreckers". There are other coastal views in de Loutherbourg's *Picturesque Scenery of Great Britain* (1801) and *Romantic and Picturesque Scenery of England and Wales* (1805).

PLATES: 257, 258, 259, 260, 261.

LOVEWELL, R.
An American painter. The Peabody Museum of Salem has a rather good oil by him, dated 1878.

PLATE: 583.

LOWRY, Lawrence Stephen R.A. **1888-1976**
Born in Manchester on November 1st, 1888, he was the son of an estate agent and had a small private income, which enabled him to remain at art school in Manchester and Salford until he was thirty-three. When he was twenty-two his family moved to Salford and it is his scenes of working class life there that have become famous. In 1939 his mother died and ten years later he left Salford for a house at Mottram-in-Loudendale, on the borders of Lancashire. He never painted the local scene but travelled back to Manchester to sketch. He also painted marines, of a sort; they are very formalised with plain seas, but he also did some harbour scenes with shipping.

The National Maritime Museum, Greenwich, has a painting of the Thames at Greenwich, dated 1959.

LUDDERS, Heinrich Paul **1826-1897**

A German ship portraitist and composer working in Finkenwerder in Prussia. Perhaps his music was better than his paintings, which are not of high quality. The Altonaer Museum has three of his works.

LUDEKING, David

There is mention of him selling a picture in Amsterdam in 1661; and there exists a painting of a battle of the First Dutch War signed "D. Ludeking". The style is very close to Beerstraaten (q.v.) and Wou (q.v).

LUNY, Thomas **1759-1837**

Born in London in 1759; died in Teignmouth on September 30th, 1837. When he first exhibited at the Society of Artists in 1777 his address is given as "At Mr. Holman's, Johnson Str. St. George's". This means that he was Francis Holman's pupil and assistant at that time, and he may well have continued with Holman until he moved to Ratcliff Way, Stepney, in 1781/2.

His early work is very close to Holman's, except that he used a slightly lighter, warmer palette. He ceased to exhibit at the Society of Artists after 1778 and only ever exhibited one picture at the Free Society, in 1783, concentrating instead on the Royal Academy Exhibitions every year from 1780 to 1793. He showed nothing after 1793 until 1802, when he exhibited a "Battle of the Nile", and then nothing until the year of his death, when he exhibited three pictures.

He had ceased to paint by 1837, but the decision to exhibit would have been connected with the simultaneous exhibition of one hundred and thirty of his pictures in Old Bond Street. The fact that the exhibits cease in 1793, the year of the outbreak of the long French Revolutionary Wars, indicates that he did indeed join up. Why he should have done such a thing we do not know, but he is supposed to have been a purser in the Royal Navy, and to have served under Captain George Tobin, R.N. That officer retired to Teignmouth after paying off in 1814, and was certainly a close friend of Luny's there.

Luny's own retirement from the Navy, due to rheumatoid arthritis, is usually given as 1810 but by his own account seems to have been earlier. He kept an inventory of the pictures he painted with the title, the purchaser's name and the price. The first entries are in February 1807 and include views of London Bridge and of Blackfriars Bridge; however, two views of Teignmouth are among the entries for June, so it seems he arrived there in the summer of 1807. He remained there to paint for the rest of his life.

His disability was severe, confining him to a wheelchair and affecting his hands, so that he had to hold the brush between both hands, or strapped to his wrist. Even so, his output was prodigious, over 2,200 pictures between February 1807 and the last crabbed entry in his journal in December 1835. In some months there are twenty-five or twenty-six entries, which means that, assuming he did not work on Sundays, he was turning out a picture every working day. Add to this his output from the late 1770s until 1793 and his total life's work must have been close to 3,000 pictures. It is no wonder that the sale rooms are full of them.

Towards the end of his life he is said to have employed a genre painter called G. Gomputz to assist him. Most of his paintings sold for less than £5, though a proportion went for around £10, and some occasionally for as much as £25. He left £14,000 when he died.

PLATES: 282, 283, 284, 285; COLOUR PLATE: XVII.

EXAMPLES: The City Art Gallery, Bristol (2): Plymouth Sound and Mount Edgecumbe; seascape. Exeter Art Gallery (4): a ship wrecked under St. Michael's Mount; a coast scene with shipping and figures; a three-decker in a breeze off Plymouth; a coast scene. National Maritime Museum, Greenwich (40): Battle of Quiberon Bay 1759; Battle of Lagos 1759; three paintings of the Moonlight Battle of St. Vincent 1780; Battle of The Dogger Bank 1781; three pictures of the Battle of the Saints 1782; the Mediator *engaging French and American vessels 1782; capture of Port Royal, Martinique, 1794; Battle of St. Vincent 1797; two paintings of the Battle of the Nile 1798; Battle of Copenhagen 1801; Battle of Trafalgar 1805; the* Victorious *raking the* Rivoli *1812; Pellew's action off Toulon 1813; Bombardment of Algiers 1816; Battle of Navarino; the* Castor *and other merchant ships; the wreck of the* Dutton; *the East Indiaman* Good Hope; *a set of five paintings of the East Indiaman* Hindostan; *two paintings of the burning of the East Indiaman* Kent; *the East Indiaman* Northumberland; *the wreck of the brig* Warren; *the East Indiaman* York; *Ferry at Teignmouth; a cutter passing astern of an anchored frigate; a beach with three women; a Brixham trawler running into Torbay; a cutter chasing a French lugger; a ship at anchor off a village; a yacht race off Exmouth. Peabody Museum of Salem, Mass (1): the ship* Simon Taylor. *Swansea Museum (1): the frigate* Daedalus *in action. The Mariners Museum, Newport News (3): the* Caesar *and* Isis *off Greenwich; Battle of Trafalgar 1805; merchantman off Dover. Library of New South Wales, Sydney (1):* Resolution *and* Adventure *in the ice.*

LUSCOMB, William Henry **1805-1866**

Born in Bailston, New York, in 1805. An American ship portraitist who worked in Salem, Mass. in the 1840s and 1850s. The Peabody Museum of Salem has one signed drawing and five oils attributed to him.

LUSCOMBE, Henry A. **1820-aft.1868**

Born in Plymouth in May, 1820. With Hornbrook (q.v.) dying in 1850, and the Condys (qq.v.) in 1851 and 1857, Luscombe was left to record the naval scene around Plymouth in the 1860s. He exhibited at the Royal Academy between 1845 and 1865. The National Maritime Museum, Greenwich, has a painting by him of a frigate. Plymouth Art Gallery has a painting of American, British and Russian warships in Plymouth Harbour.

PLATE: 567.

LUZZO, Giovanni

An Italian ship portraitist working in Venice in the middle of the 19th century in a highly stylised, primitive manner. The Mariners Museum, Newport News, has a watercolour ship portrait dated 1858, and the Peabody Museum of Salem has three of his watercolours.

LUZZO, Vincenzo

An Italian ship portraitist working in Venice and Trieste in the middle of the 19th century. There is a pen and wash drawing at the Altonaer Museum signed "V. Luzzo" and another almost identical drawing, unsigned but attributed to Giovanni or Vincenzo, so there must have been two members of the family doing ship portraits. The Mariners Museum, Newport News, has a portrait dated 1870 of the brigantine *Giles Loring*.

LYLE, D.

An American ship portraitist working in Philadelphia in the third quarter of the 19th century. The National Maritime Museum, Greenwich, has a painting by him of the Cunard paddle liner *Persia,* dated 1856.

PLATE: 510.

LYNN, John **fl.1828-1838**

He exhibited marines between these dates at the British Institution, working from an address off the Commercial Road, London. His work is of fair quality but rather in the 18th century manner than the 19th century romantic and realistic tradition.

The National Maritime Museum, Greenwich, has three ship portraits by him; two of East Indiamen, the *Vernon* and *Seringapatam,* and one of a Bermudan schooner yacht.

PLATE: 419.

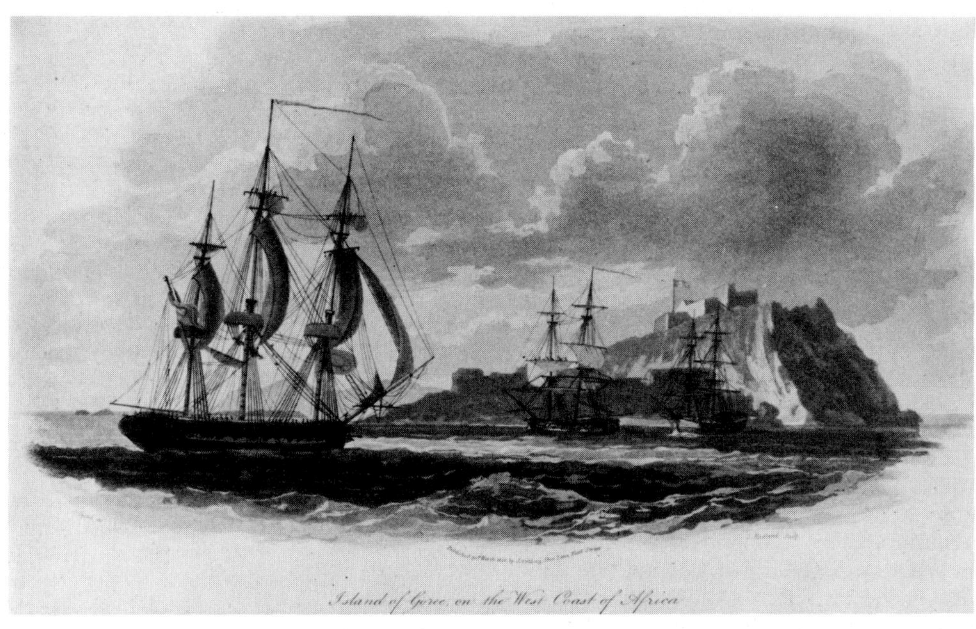

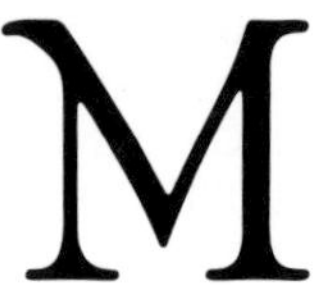

Mc is treated as if it were Mac; the next letter in the name determines the position of the entry.

MacALPINE, William
The frequency with which the paintings of this strange mid-19th century British artist turn up compels an entry here, even though no biographical details on him are known.

He was interested in coastal views and the aftermath of battles and storms; all are treated in a very romantic stylised manner and are influence, one might think, by Turner.

PLATE: 490.

MACFARLANE, D.
A British ship portraitist working in the second and third quarters of the 19th century. The background to his earlier works suggests he was based in Liverpool but his later paintings are of American subjects; one is of an American coastal brigantine off Boston Light, so it looks as if he emigrated to America, and possibly to Boston.

In his paintings one should find seagulls hovering over a bit of drift wood, which seems tohave been his trade mark.

The Bostonian Society has a painting by him of the *Titan* arriving dismasted at Liverpool; the National Maritime Museum, Greenwich, has three ship portraits by him, the Mariners Museum, Newport News, one, and the Peabody Museum of Salem two.

PLATES: 571, 572.

MACGREGOR, David Roy **b.1925**
M.A., F.R.Hist.S., A.R.I.B.A.
Born in Fulham, London, in 1925 and educated at Eton and Trinity College, Cambridge, where he took a degree in architecture. He studied painting under George F. Bradshaw and Julius Olsson (q.v.). As an undergraduate he had a one man show at the Hilton Gallery, Cambridge, and in 1974 another one in the Woodstock Gallery in London. He has also exhibited at the Royal Institute of Oil Painters, New English Art Club, Royal Society of Marine Artists, Royal Society of British Artists, and the Thames Valley Arts Club. He is best known as a leading expert on 19th century deep water sailing ships, and his publications include: *The Tea Clippers,* 1952, *The China Bird,* 1961, and *Fast Sailing Ships 1775-1875,* 1973, Daily Express Best Book of the Sea Award in 1973.

MACHEREN, Philip van
A Middelburg painter, who also worked in Rotterdam, in the third quarter of the 17th century. His works are rare, those known being signed "P.M.R." or "Ph van Macheren".

EXAMPLES: Town Hall, Flushing (1): view of Flushing. Town Hall, Veere (1): view of Veere.

McKELVEY, Frank R.H.A. **1895-1974**
Born Belvast 1895; died Holywood, Co. Down, June 1974. He studied art at the Belfast College of Art and was the doyen of Irish landscape and portrait painters in the third quarter of this century; he also did many coastal views.

Every year he went to the West of Ireland, Donegal in particular, to make sketches from which he might later do larger paintings. He received many commissions for portraits from official bodies and was elected to the Royal Hibernian Academy in 1930.

The National Maritime Museum, Greenwich, has a painting of an Aran Island curragh by him and examples of his work can be found in the National Gallery, Dublin, the Ulster Museum, Cork Public Museum, the Municipal Art Gallery, Limerick, and at Waterford.

MACLEOD ROBERTSON, Sheila **b.1927**
Born in Finchley, London on June 7th, 1927, she trained at the Watford and Central Schools of Art, and works in water-colours and oils. Her favourite subjects are the coasts of West Scotland and Cornwall. From 1947-53 she worked in a London display studio, and for several years afterwards as a freelance display artist.

She has exhibited at the Royal Institute of Oil Painters and the United Society of Artists. In 1969 she was elected a member of the Royal Society of Marine Artists and in 1970 to the St. Ives Society of Artists, Cornwall.

McPHERSON, Murdoch **1841-1915**
A Canadian watercolourist and copyist who apparently worked on his ship portraits in Salem, Mass. They are somewhat primitive. The Peabody Museum of Salem has fifty-five of them.

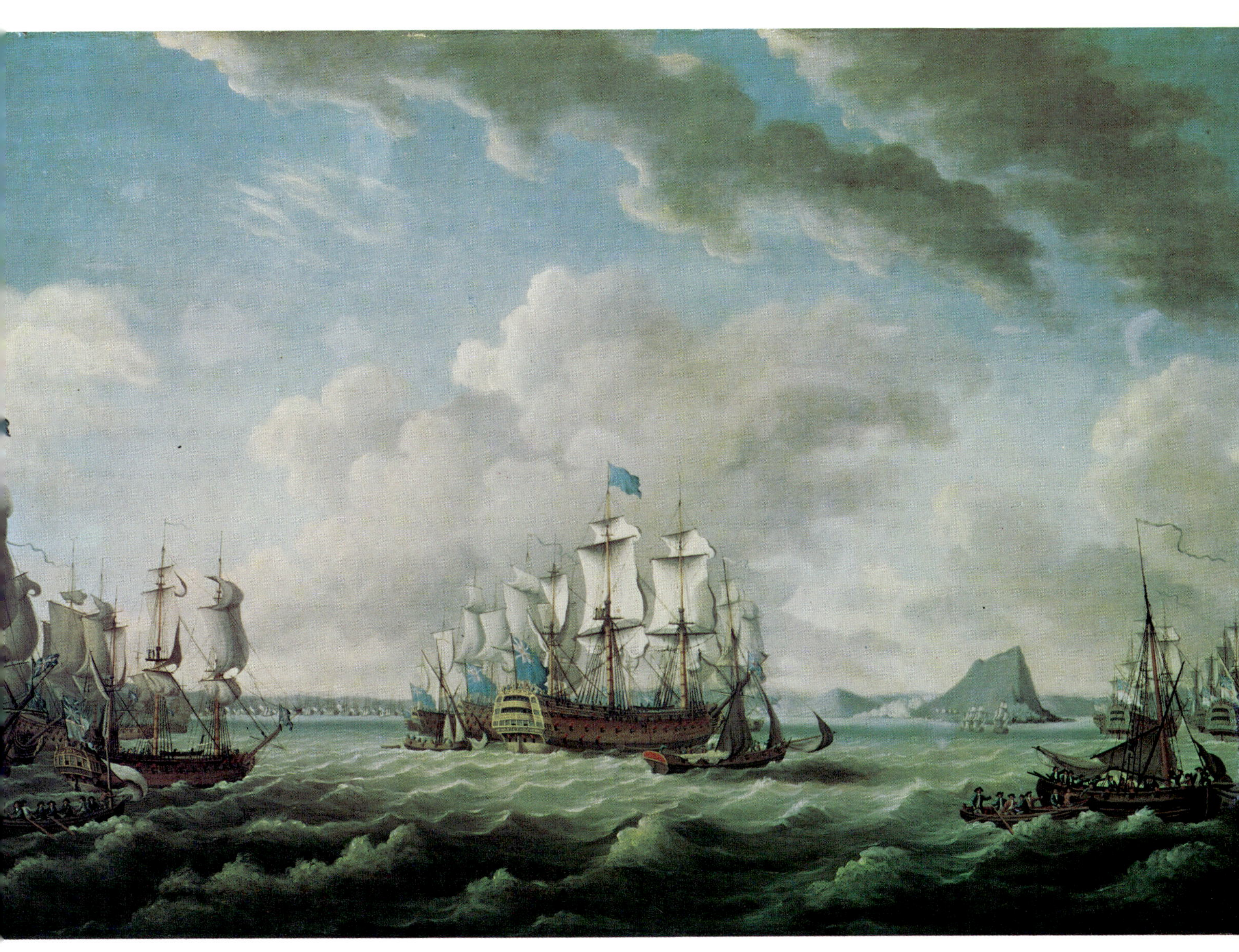

Colour Plate XV. Richard Paton, 1717-1791. ''Lord Howe's relief of Gibraltar in 1782.'' National Maritime Museum, Greenwich.

McTAGGART, William R.S.A., V.P.R.S.W. 1835-1910
Born Aros, Campbletown, October 23rd, 1835; died Broomieknowe, April 2nd, 1910. He was apprenticed to a Campbletown apothecary but was by then already painting portraits. In 1852 he went to Edinburgh and studied at the Trustees Academy for seven years. He first exhibited at the Royal Scottish Academy in 1855, was elected an associate in 1859 and an academician in 1870. He was Vice President of the Royal Scottish Society of Painters in Watercolours.

McTaggart was perhaps the most interesting Scottish painter of the 19th century. His early work was factual but beautifully crafted; then, like Turner (q.v.), he turned experimental painter in attempts to catch fleeting effects. Variations on the theme of emigration or embarkation were his favourite subject and as time went by the figures on the beach and the landscape almost melt into one. Since what he was trying to achieve was extremely difficult he obviously had his disasters, but his successes are splendid.

PLATE: 542.

EXAMPLES: Aberdeen Art Gallery. National Gallery of Scotland, Edinburgh. Glasgow Art Gallery. Kirkcaldy Art Gallery. Tate Gallery, London. National Gallery of Victoria, Melbourne: Lobster Fishers. Ashmolean Museum, Oxford. National Gallery of New South Wales, Sydney: Rainy Day at Canndale.

MADDERSTEG, Michiel 1659-1709
Born and died in Amsterdam. He was a pupil and emulator of Ludolf Bakhuizen (q.v.), and said to be his closest imitator. In 1698 he was court painter to the Elector of Brandenburg in Berlin. He signed himself "M.M.".

EXAMPLES: Museum of Aachen (1): seascape. Musée d'Aix la Chapelle (1): seascape. Gemäldegalerie, Hamburg (1): view of Amsterdam. Martin von Wagner Museum, Würzburg (1): ships in a gale.

MAHU, Cornelisz 1613-1689
Born and died in Antwerp, Essentially a still-life painter, he was also capable of painting marines of a high standard. He signed himself "C. Mahu" but there are apparently none of his works in public collections.

MAN, L.D. (or L. de) fl.1725
This artist was painting in England but was probably not British, as his style is Dutch though not in the Dutch tradition as manifested in England. It is carefully finished and rather static.

The National Maritime Museum, Greenwich, has three paintings of royal yachts.

PLATE: 189.

MANGLARD, Adrien 1695-1760
Born in Lyon on March 12th, 1695; died in Rome, July 31st, 1760. He became a member of the Académie Royale in Paris in 1736, though by then he was already settled in Rome, where he was to live, work and die. He was a member of the Academy of Saint Luke from 1735, and had a successful practice in marines, landscapes and historical subjects. In 1734 he took on his most famous pupil, Joseph Vernet (q.v.). Marine paintings by him may be found in museums in Avignon, Chârtres, Dijon, Epinal, Lyon, Montpellier, Nancy, Nântes, Paris (Louvre), Perigueux, Rome (Doria Pamphili), Rouen, and Vienna.

MARQUIS, James Richard R.H.A. c.1885
A Dublin painter of marines, who became a member of the Royal Hibernian Academy. He exhibited at the Royal Academy in 1862 and 1863, specialising in sunset scenes.

MARSH, William
An American ship portraitist working in the second quarter of the 19th century. The Peabody Museum of Salem has two oils dated 1843 and 1846, and a watercolour.

MARTIN, C.J. fl.1850s
The Peabody Museum of Salem has two high quality oils of native craft and shipping on the River Hoogli at Calcutta by this artist; one is inscribed "Painted by C.J. Martin for John W. Linzee, Calcutta, June 1852", and the other is dated 1853. No further information on Martin has come to light but he is said to have been American.

MARTINO, The Chevalier Edoardo de M.V.O. 1838-1912
Born in Meta, Kingdom of Naples in March 1838; died London May 21st, 1912. He was the son of a pilot in the Royal Neapolitan Navy and having trained at the Royal Naval College in Naples was commissioned in that service. When Italy was unified he found himself in the Italian Navy but, not relishing the changed atmosphere, he resigned in 1867 and went to Brazil.

It is not recorded where he got his grounding as an artist but it was probably at the Naval College. In Brazil he married and became attached to the court of the last Brazilian Emperor, Pedro II, who commissioned from him paintings of the war with Paraguay, 1868-69. In 1875 he moved to England, where his love of yachting and his social gifts brought him to the notice of the Prince and Princess of Wales, with whom he formed a close and lasting friendship. Edward is said never thereafter to have gone to sea without de Martino and it was when leaving for Victoria Station to see off Queen Alexandra the Queen Mother and the Empress of Russia, that de Martino collapsed and died.

His painting style brought a new realism, perhaps never before achieved, into British marine art. This was an instant success with the naval and yachting fraternity, and brought him into contact with Queen Victoria, who made him Marine Painter in Ordinary in 1894 as successor to Sir Oswald Brierly. This connection with the Court brought connections with other crowned heads and he accepted commissions from Kaiser Wilhelm II, Czar Nicholas II and from at least one of the Kings of Portugal; his daughter has said that he had over seventy orders and decorations. He was also official marine painter to the Royal Yacht Squadron.

He was an enthusiastic and knowledgeable student of ships. It was he who, one day at Osborne in 1899, told the Director of Naval Construction, Sir William White, that, if he kept piling modifications "to please the Queen" on the top of the new royal yacht, then fitting out at Portsmouth, the yacht would become unstable. He was right. When the dry dock was flooded, the *Victoria and Albert III* fell on her side; Sir William never spoke to de Martino again.

By the turn of the century he had more commissions than he could handle and chose a curious solution to his problem — though one with many good precedents. He got somebody else to paint some commissions, finishing and signing them himself. The artist in question was John Fraser (q.v.), and de Martino even applied his system to commissions from his Sovereign and such a close friend as Sir Thomas Lipton. Mrs. Fraser has recorded that a commission for one of Lipton's *Shamrocks* had only a flag added by de Martino before he signed it. After de Martino's death Fraser petitioned his executors to have the money owing for six pictures commissioned by King George V paid to himself rather than to de Martino's estate, as he claimed to have painted them.

In his later years de Martino signed himself Edwardo.

PLATE: 590.

EXAMPLES: National Maritime Museum, Greenwich (2): HMS Edinburgh *with anti-torpedo nets out in a mock exercise against torpedo boats; the Channel Squadron 1898.*

MASON, Frank Henry R.I., R.B.M. 1876-1965

Born in Seaton Carew, Co. Durham, October 1876, he was educated on the training ship *Conway* and went to sea, later becoming an engineer in the shipbuilding industry at Leeds and Hartlepool. He took up marine painting, mainly in watercolour and during the First World War served in the Royal Naval Volunteer Reserve as a lieutenant. He exhibited at the Royal Academy from 1900. He also illustrated books, designed posters for railway companies, and did a series of advertisements for "Senior Service" cigarettes.

Examples of his work can be found at Dundee Art Gallery, the National Maritime Museum, Greenwich, and the Gray Art Gallery, Hartlepool.

MATTHYS, Abraham 1581-1649

Born and died in Antwerp. He was a pupil of Tobias Haecht, the Antwerp landscape painter who was also Rubens' first master. In 1603, as a young man, he went to live in Rome and stayed there until 1619. He spent some time at sea in his father's whalers and such marines as he painted concentrate on whaling themes. Being a man of private means he was also a collector and, as regards marine painting, should perhaps really be described as a gifted amateur.

He also painted landscapes, still life and genre subjects. There is also a portrait by him of Bonaventura Peeters (q.v.) in the church at Hoboken, near Antwerp, where Peeters died.

EXAMPLES: National Maritime Museum, Greenwich (1); whaling scene.

MAXWELL, Donald 1877-1936

Born in London in 1877, he studied at the Royal College of Art and the Slade School. He was naval artist to the *Graphic* for 20 years and during the First World War was an official naval artist to the Admiralty. This took him to Palestine and Mesopotamia in 1918.

He accompanied the Prince of Wales on his tour of the East in 1921 and illustrated *The Prince of Wales's Eastern Book* which resulted from this. He illustrated a number of other travel and topographical books and lived at Rochester for many years, finally moving to Maidstone, where he died on July 25th 1936.

The National Maritime Museum, Greenwich, has two large canvases dating from the First World War, one called "Crisis" and the other "A Prize of War".

MAZZINGHI, Pietro

An Italian primitive ship portraitist who worked at Leghorn in the second quarter of the 19th century. The Peabody Museum of Salem has five watercolours by him.

MEADOWS, Arthur Joseph 1843-1907

A follower of Clarkson Stanfield (q.v.), whose style he copied. He exhibited at the Royal Academy between 1863 and 1872, at the British Institution between 1863 and 1867, and also at the Society of British Artists.

The National Maritime Museum, Greenwich, has one oil of fishing boats off a jetty.

PLATE: 576.

MEADOWS, James 1828-1888

Elder brother of Arthur Joseph Meadows (q.v.), he exhibited marines at both the Royal Academy and the British Institution between 1855 and 1863. He also exhibited at Suffolk Street Galleries.

MEARS, George

A British ship portraitist working in Newhaven, Sussex, in the last half of the 19th century. The National Maritime Museum, Greenwich, has nine paintings by him, the Mariners Museum, Newport News, one. The Peabody Museum of Salem has four of his works.

PLATE: 570.

Colour Plate XVI *(overleaf)*. **Nicholas Pocock, 1740-1821.** "A British sloop off a Mediterranean coast, 1787." Collection of Mrs. Thomas Geary.

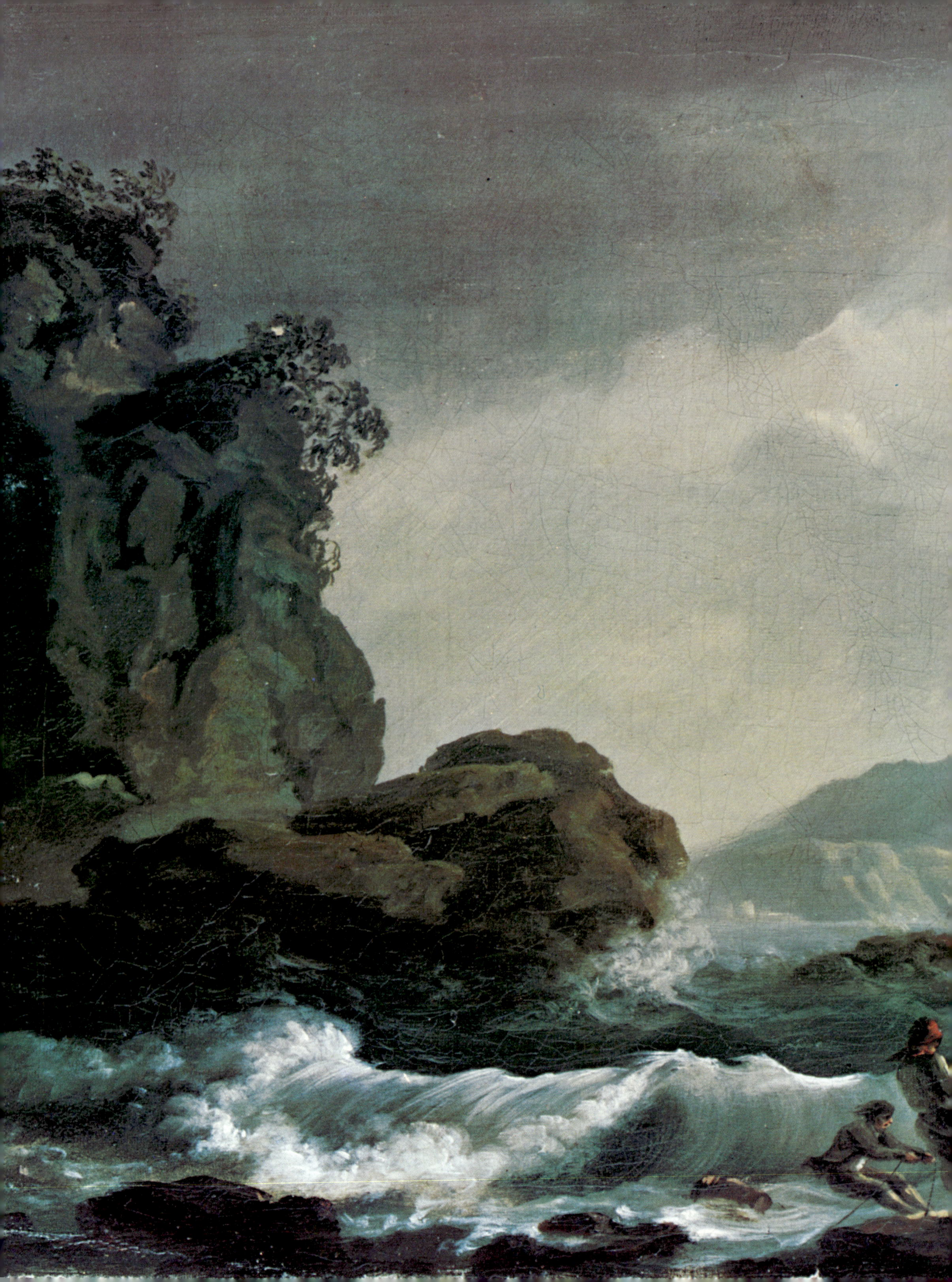

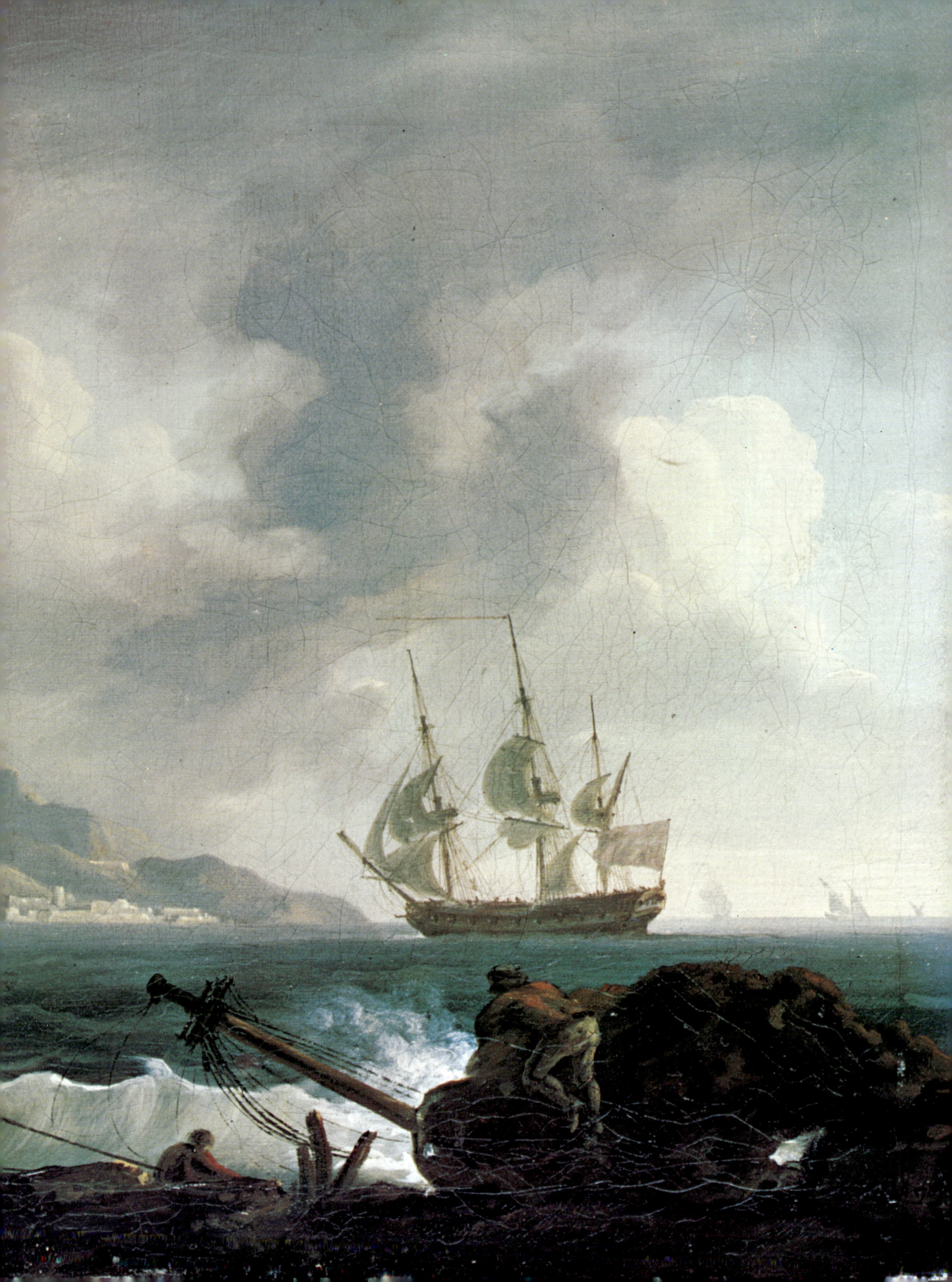

MEIJER, Johan Hendrik Louis **1809-1866**

Born in Amsterdam in 1809, he was a pupil of the Amsterdam Academy as well as of George Pieter Westenberg, the city and landscape painter, and of Jan Willem Pieneman, the genre painter. He afterwards collaborated with another genre painter, Joseph Jodocus Moerenhout.

From 1827 to 1830 he worked and studied in Paris, returning to Amsterdam and then moving to Deventer. In 1841 he was back in Paris, where he exhibited at the Salon in 1843 and 1844. He returned to Holland and settled in The Hague in 1847, where he practised lithography as well as painting. He died in Utrecht in 1866.

He exhibited at Amsterdam and The Hague from 1833 to 1863. Many of the next generation of Dutch marine painters were his pupils.

PLATES: 377, 378.

EXAMPLES: Rijksmuseum, Amsterdam (5): the capture of Palembang; coast scene; storm in the Straits of Dover; coastal craft; self portrait. Fodor Museum, Amsterdam (2): rough sea scenes. Stedelijk Museum, Amsterdam (1): rescue at sea on the Spanish coast. Nederlandsch Historisch Scheepvaart Museum, Amsterdam (2): a Dutch squadron off Genoa; man overboard. Musée de Dijon (1): action between the Abeille *and the* Alacrity *1811. Museum of Dordrecht (2): sailing craft; a sailing ship and a steam boat. Grenoble Museum (1): a ship off the Normandy coast. Gemeentemuseum, The Hague (1): Neapolitan fisherman. Musée Du Puy (1): fishermen off Normandy. Museum of Leeuwarden (1): marine. Museo Espanol de Arte Contemporaneo, Madrid (3): view of Oldenbourg; view of Ostend; marine. Musée National de Versailles (1): landing of Napoleon I at Frejus. Museum Boymans-van Beuningen, Rotterdam (2): rough sea scene; seascape. Centraal Museum der Germeente (2): seascape; beach scene.*

MELBYE, Daniel Hermann Anton **1818-1875**

Born in Copenhagen in 1818. Known as Anton, and the eldest of three painter brothers, he had early experience of ships through working in a shipbuilding yard. He then became a pupil of Denmark's leading marine painter, Eckersberg (q.v.). He exhibited at Charlottenborg, near Copenhagen, in 1840. Before moving to Paris in 1847 he numbered King Christian VIII among his patrons and in Paris he enjoyed the patronage of King Louis Philippe and the Emperor Napoleon III. In 1847 he was attached to the Danish Embassy at Constantinople and took commissions from the Porte. He died in Paris in 1875.

PLATES: 347, 348.

EXAMPLES: Musée de Baguères (1): fishing boats in the English Channel. Statens Museum for Kunst, Copenhagen (7): a Shetland fishing boat off the Orkneys in stormy weather; a Danish corvette in open sea after a gale; the Battle of Koge Bay, 1677; Eddystone lighthouse; a river landscape in France; and two seascapes. Orlogsmuseet, Copenhagen: several. Kunsthalle, Hamburg (4): Copenhagen Harbour; Battle of Heligoland 1864; the Needles, Isle of Wight; the open sea. Maritime Museum, Kronborg Castle (1). Hermitage, Leningrad (2). Nationalmuseum, Stockholm (1): Mediterranean scene.

MELBYE, Fritz Sigfried Georg **1826-1896**

Born in Helsingor in 1826, he was the youngest of the Melbye brothers and a pupil of his brother Anton (q.v.). He began exhibiting in Copenhagen in 1849. He travelled in the West Indies, where he met Camille Pissarro and went with him in 1852 to Venezuela. He set up as a marine painter in the Port of La Guaira and worked there for nine years. After this he moved to New York and then to China, where he died in Shanghai in 1896.

The Maritime Museum at Kronborg Castle has a painting by him of the *Charlotte Amalie* off the island of St. Thomas.

PLATE: 349.

MELBYE, Vilhelm **1824-1882**

Born Helsingor 1824; died Roskilde 1882. The second of the three Melbye brothers, he is also the best known. He studied at the Academy of Art at Copenhagen under his brother Anton. Near the end of his life, in 1880, he became head of the Academy.

As he worked for many years abroad, in London, Düsseldorf and Paris, his paintings achieved a wide international popularity. His romantic style is at its most successful when he depicts a drama at sea, like a shipwreck. Between 1853 and 1867 he exhibited eleven pictures at the Royal Academy Exhibitions. He seems to have called himself Wilhelm in later life, as he signed his work "W. Melbye".

PLATES: 453, 454.

EXAMPLES: Statens Museum for Kunst, Copenhagen (1): a Danish pilot boat in stormy weather. Orlogsmuseet, Copenhagen: several. Frederiksborg Museum, Zealand: the burning of the Von der Tann *in 1850. National Maritime Museum, Greenwich (1): a frigate clawing off a rocky coast. Lansmuseum, Linkoping, Sweden (1): a paddle-steamer passing a Norwegian lighthouse, 1863. National Gallery of New South Wales, Sydney (1): morning after the Gale with a ship on the Rocks.*

MELLISH, Thomas

Very little is known about this artist. He exhibited a pair of sea pieces at the Society of Artists in 1761, and a moonlight scene in 1763. In 1766 he exhibited a moonlight view with shipping and a view of Dover with shipping, from an address in Hoxton Square in London. The latest dated pictures known are 1778.

His quality varies, but at his best he has been mistaken for Samuel Scott (q.v.), and some years ago some of his paintings actually hung in an exhibition devoted to Samuel Scott. Indeed, one of them in a well-known private collection had for many years been attributed to Charles Brooking (q.v.).

PLATE: 207.

EXAMPLES: Shipley Art Gallery (1): coast scene with shipping and a castle. National Maritime Museum, Greenwich (1): a 50-gun ship off Woolwich viewed from Galleon's Point. Ferens Art Gallery, Hull (1): view of Charleston, South Carolina.

MEMLING, Hans **d.1494**

Born at Memlingen, near Mayance, or Memline, near Alkmaar, between 1425 and 1440; died 11th August, 1494, at Bruges.

An early Flemish painter of historical scenes and portraits; he was not really a marine painter but is included for the maritime interest of his famous "Caisse de Sainte Ursule" at the Saint Jean Hospital at Bruges, with its fine ship representations.

MESDAG, Hendrik Willem **1831-1915**

Born at Groningen in 1831; died at The Hague 1915. He was a pupil of the landscape painter Willem Roelof and of Alma-Tadema, the painter of classical genre situation scenes. He concentrated on fishing and harbour subjects and exhibited at the Paris Salon in the 1870s and 1880s. In The Hague he started his own museum, which contains the circular panorama of Scheveningen, called the Panorama Mesdag.

His work inclines towards the impressionist, and he was an influential figure in the development of this style. The French gave him the Légion d'Honneur.

PLATES: 555, 556.

EXAMPLES: Marines: Rijksmuseum, Amsterdam (9): five beach scenes with fishing boats; three of fishing boats at sea and one of a lighthouse in a storm. Stedelijk Museum, Amsterdam (2): a beach scene and a seascape with ships. Musées Royaux d'Art et d'Histoire, Brussels (1): after the storm. National Museum of Art, Budapest (1): vessels at Scheveningen. Dordrecht Museum (2): shrimpers; fishing boats in breakers. Groningen Museum (3): ship at anchor; North Sea; North Sea in the evening. Gemeentemuseum, The Hague (2). Mesdag Museum (13) plus the panorama. Middelburg Museum (2). Montreal Museum of Fine Arts (2): boats on the shore; moonlight coastal scene. Oenkerk Museum (1). Boymans Museum, Rotterdam (2): calm and a storm. Centraal Museum der Germeente, Utrecht (1): beach scene.

MEYER, Hendrik de **c.1600-aft.1690**

Meyer was not so much a sea painter as a painter of thickly populated river and beach scenes, in a style reminiscent of Albert Cuyp (q.v.). He lived in Rotterdam and signed works are known between 1641 and 1683.

PLATE: 105.

EXAMPLES: Rijksmuseum, Amsterdam: the embarkation of Charles II from Scheveningen in 1660; a view of Dordrecht. Statens Museum for Kunst, Copenhagen: another embarkation of Charles II from Scheveningen in 1660; the embarkation of troops on a Dutch river.

MILES, Thomas Rose

A London painter of landscapes, coastal scenes and marines. He liked to paint stormy scenes, and exhibited at the Royal Academy between 1877 and 1888. The National Gallery of New South Wales, Sydney, has a seascape off Hastings.

PLATE: 607.

MILLER, Charles Keith

A Scottish ship portraitist working in Glasgow in the last quarter of the 19th century.

MINDEN, Heinrich von **1784-1837**

A German ship portraitist who also taught navigation in Kiel. The Altonaer Museum, Hamburg, has two pen and wash drawings by him.

MINDERHOUT, Hendrik van **1632-1696**

Born Rotterdam 1632. While nothing seems to be known of this artist before he went to Bruges in 1632, it is difficult to believe he could have acquired his special skill and style without the tuition of Andries van Eertvelt (q.v.). It was Minderhout who, above all, carried on the mannerist tradition of the Flemish school, even though he preferred a Dutch palette of silvery greys, not only in his ships and seas but in the stern galleries of his ships, which are always stylised and idealised. This manner is established in his early paintings, such as the two very large canvases of Bruges harbour, one at Bruges and the other in the Britannia Royal Naval College at Dartmouth. Both pictures also show his talent for figure painting, human or animal.

Among his early works he was inspired to paint some battle scenes, both of actions between the Dutch and Spanish, and later scenes of the Anglo-Dutch wars. They are of great elegance and dramatic content, though more in the spirit of the occasion than in strict attention to historical accuracy. The best of them are in private hands but there is a Battle of Lowestoft at the National Maritime Museum, Greenwich.

He lived on at Bruges until 1672, then moved to Antwerp, where he lived and worked until his death on July 22nd, 1696. Two of his five sons, Anton and Willem, became painters and were his pupils. In his later works, a strong predeliction for Mediterranean port scenes, along with the adoption of a warmer and more colourful palette, suggest that he at least visited Italy. The port scenes, with their pack-horses, camels, and artificially tall ships, are among the most beautiful and romantic paintings to come out of the great 17th century Netherlands school.

There are particularly fine examples of these Mediterranean port scenes at the National Gallery at Oslo, at the Musée Royal des Beaux-Arts at Antwerp, which has a large, almost square picture, and there is a large view of Leghorn at the National Maritime Museum, Greenwich. As this is dated 1670, his travels probably took place before his move to Antwerp. The National Maritime Museum also has a battle of Lowestoft by him.

Although he seems to have been happiest working on large canvases there are smaller examples, of which two unusual river scenes, dated 1688, are in the Prado at Madrid.

Other public galleries where his work may be seen are the Calvet Museum, Avignon; the Municipal Museum, Douai, has a harbour scene, the Dunkirk Museum has a battle scene; at Dyrham Park, a National Trust house, there are two fine pictures of a Mediterranean port and a slave market, and the Museum of Fine Arts at Rouen has a Mediterranean port scene.

PLATES: 32, 33, 34.

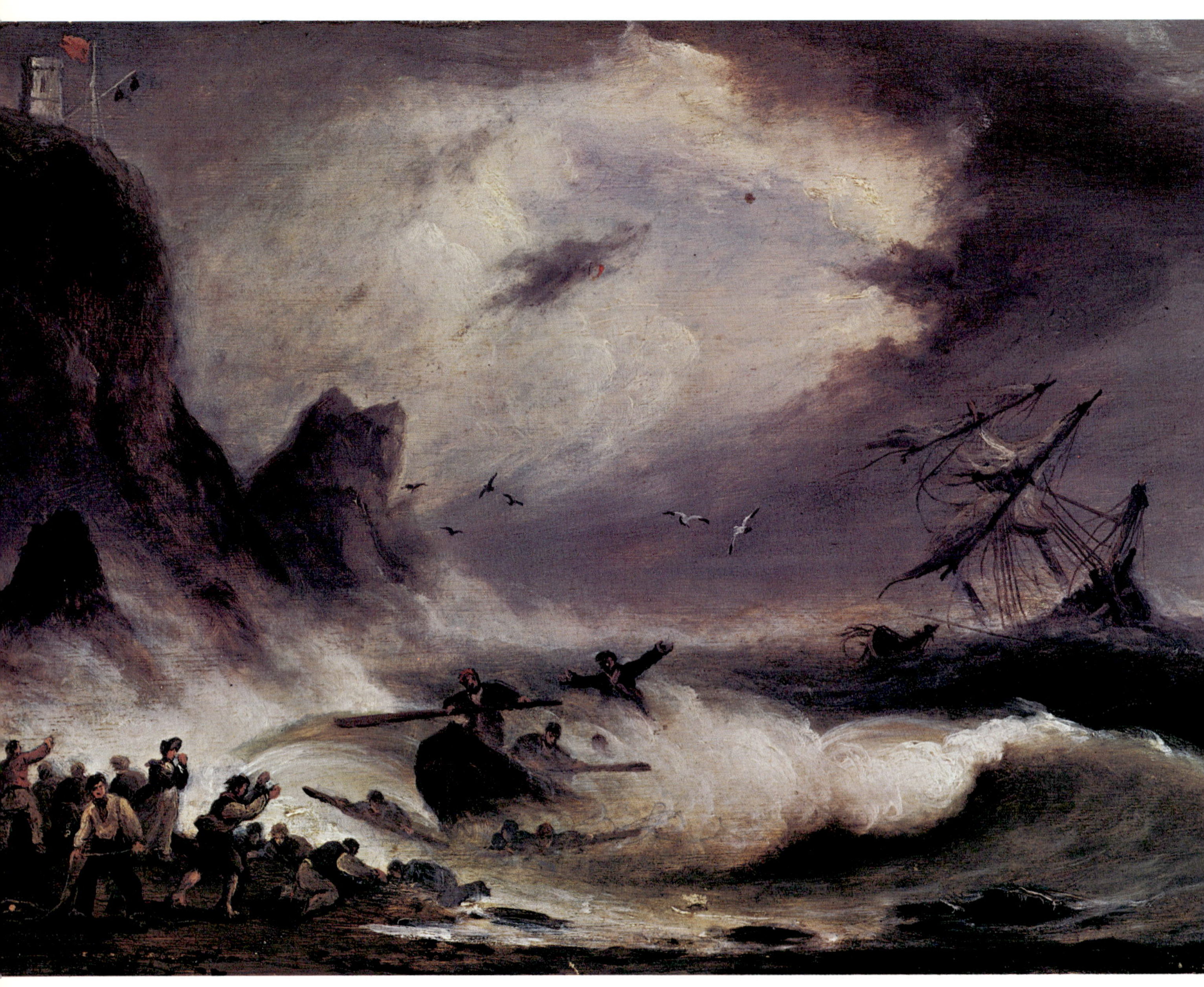

Colour Plate XVII. Thomas Luny, 1759-1837. "The loss of the brig *Warren,* dated 1828." National Maritime Museum, Greenwich.

MITCHELL, Thomas **1735-1790**

Like John Cleveley the Elder (q.v.), whom he must have known well, he combined the professions of marine painter and shipwright to the Admiralty throughout his career. In fact, Mitchell went far further in the latter service. In 1771 he was Builders' Assistant of His Majesty's Dockyard, Chatham, then filled the same position at Deptford; lastly he became Assistant Surveyor of the Navy. He did a supplement to the survey of harbours in 1774.

If he surpassed Cleveley in his naval career, he did not approach him as a painter. Although there was nothing amateur about his approach his style was dull and strongly influenced by Richard Paton (q.v.). He liked to undertake large battle pieces and exhibited at the Free Society between 1763 and 1780, and at the Royal Academy between 1774 and 1789.

PLATE: 255.

EXAMPLES: The United States Naval Academy Museum, Annapolis (1): the Serapis *engaging the* Bonhomme Richard *1779. National Maritime Museum, Greenwich (3): Battle of La Hogue 1692; action in the Hudson River 1776 (after Dominic Serres); Battle of the Saints 1782. Ferens Art Gallery, Hull (1): a man-of-war in a calm.*

MITCHELL, William Frederick **1845-1914**

Born at Calshot Castle, near Southampton, 1845; died Ryde, Isle of Wight, October 15th, 1914. He was a near deaf-mute and was known as Fred Mitchell. He had an arrangement with Griffins, a bookshop on the Hard, near the main gate of the Royal Naval Dockyard at Portsmouth, whereby they accepted orders on his behalf for portraits of ships of the Royal Navy, mainly from naval officers. A great many of these, which are all in watercolour, are preserved in the National Maritime Museum, Greenwich, which also has a small oil by him. There is an example in the Mariners Museum, Newport News.

MOHRMANN, John Henry **1857-1916**

A Belgian ship portraitist of good quality, working in Antwerp. His works can be found around the world.

PLATES: 621, 622.

EXAMPLES: Altonaer Museum, Hamburg (3). Peabody Museum of Salem (2). Also represented in the New Bedford Whaling Museum and the National Maritime Museum, Greenwich (2).

MOLLOY, Joseph **1798-1877**

Born and died in Belfast. He was a member of the Belfast Association of Artists and taught drawing at the Belfast Academical Institution. He painted a set of forty views of Belfast. The Ulster Museum, Belfast, has a view of Folkestone and one of Tilbury Fort.

PLATE: 385.

MONAMY, Peter **1681-1749**

Born London, 1681; died London, February 1749. Years of conjecture about the date of Monamy's birth seem to have been more or less settled by the finding of a record of his baptism. This took place at St. Olave's, Bermondsey, on 12th January, 1681. It is a pity his birth occured so early in the year, leaving a doubt as to whether he was actually born in 1680. However, the high rate of infant mortality and the importance attached to baptism in those days, made it normal for a child to be baptised within days of his birth. Monamy himself would have said he was born in 1680 since by the Julian calendar then in use, January was still in 1680. Whatever the chronological niceties, he was born in the Minories, a street between Aldgate and the Tower, to Peter and Dorothy Monamy. His father was a merchant and probably it was he who came from Jersey, as Vertue claimed his son did.

In the Painter Stainers' Company Binding Book is a record of his being apprenticed to a William Clarke for seven years in September 1696; in 1703 the same source records his being made a freeman of the company, which owns what is probably the biggest painting by Monamy in existence. In 1706 another baptism at St. Olave's, that of Margaret, described as the daughter of "Peter and Margaret Monamy, Painter", confirms that the earlier entries are indeed the right Monamy family. In 1708 he had a son Andrew, who would have been called after his uncle Andrew, the silversmith, who had originally persuaded Peter Monamy Snr. to come to London. There is a family tradition that before moving to Jersey the family lived in France and was called Bonamie. One of them, it is said, was in the King's service and after distinguishing himself in some way, the King said that in future his name should not be Bonamie but Mon-ami, hence Monamy.

Monamy's professional training was in house decoration and his elevation to marine painter seems to have derived from a natural talent and inclination, coupled with a love of ships and naval history. In this he was fortunate, arriving at a time when the van de Veldes (qq.v.) and other Dutch painters who had come to work in England had greatly heightened interest in shipping pictures and had created a growing market for them.

Monamy was probably largely self-taught, closely following the style of the younger Willem van de Velde (q.v.) and copying paintings by him. While he emerges with Samuel Scott (q.v.) as one of the two leading figures in the first generation of British marine painters, it cannot be said that his work ever approached the sublime and indeed it is very uneven in quality. What can be said, is that he worked industriously for at least forty years and has left us a rich heritage of paintings illustrating the nation's naval history in the first half of the 18th century. His work is an excellent record of ships of the period and provides a mass of pleasing general shipping scenes.

In 1726 he presented the Painter Stainers' Company with a fine calm scene, which was unfortunately lost in the blitz in the Second World War. Their present example was presented to them in the 19th century.

PLATES: 192, 193, 194, 195, 196; COLOUR PLATE: XI.

EXAMPLES: National Gallery, Dublin (1): sea piece. City Art Gallery, Glasgow (1): Battle of Barfleur 1692. National Maritime Museum, Greenwich (21): the Mary Rose *action 1669; the burning of the* Royal James *at Solebay 1672 (after W. van de Velde II); the destruction of the* Soleil Royal *1692; the capture of the* San Josef *1739; the capture of the* Princesa *1740; the loss of the* Victory *1744; the capture of Louisbourg 1745; the royal yacht* Isabella*; the royal yacht* Peregrine*; an East Indiaman (perhaps part of a larger picture, and said to have decorated Vauxhall Gardens); an English man-of-war becalmed near the shore; an English ship becalmed; a flagship becalmed with a yacht saluting; a fleet coming to anchor; an Indiaman and a royal yacht in a storm off a rocky coast; a first-rate; a ketch rigged royal yacht becalmed; a ship saluting a fort on the* *left; a ship saluting a fort; a man-of-war firing a gun at sundown; three first-rates, flagships, becalmed. Metropolitan Museum, New York: a large painting of the* Royal William *in a calm. National Gallery of New South Wales, Sydney (1); French ships in action with Barbary pirates.*

MONASTERI, Giuseppe
An Italian ship portraitist working in Palermo in the third quarter of the 19th century. The Peabody Museum of Salem has a watercolour by him dated 1881.

MONTAGUE, Alfred **fl.1835-1870**
This artist first exhibited at the Royal Academy in 1836 from an address in Frith Street, London. In 1846 he was at Clewer Green, near Windsor, in 1854 at Englefield Green, and finally at Blackheath Hill, Greenwich, his last exhibit being in the 1870 exhibition. He also exhibited at Suffolk Street. Only a small proportion of his exhibits were marines, but his stormy scenes are of good quality. The number of Dutch and French views exhibited in the 1840s and 1850s show that he travelled in those countries. The Salford Art Gallery has an example of his work and the City of York Art Gallery has a coastal view.

PLATE: 537.

MONTARDIER
A French ship portraitist working at Le Havre in the first half of the 19th century. He was among the earlier exponents of the simple 19th century ship portrait. The Peabody Museum of Salem has thirteen of his watercolours.

MOORE, Henry R.A., R.W.S. **1831-1895**
Born in York on March 7th, 1831; died in Margate on June 22nd, 1895. This interesting artist was preoccupied with experimenting with effects in his seas rather like McTaggart and, like him, the result was a very varied and uneven output. The best is of splendid quality but there are many failures. He was the son and pupil of the portrait painter William Moore at the York School of Art and afterwards attended the Royal Academy Schools.

He first exhibited at the Royal Academy in 1853 and in 1885 was elected an ARA, the same year as his exhibit "Catspaws off the Land" was bought for the Chantrey Bequest; in 1893 he was elected an RA. He also exhibited at the British Institution 1855-67, the Society of British Artists 1866-75, and at the Royal Institute of Oil Painters.

PLATE: 579; COLOUR PLATE: XXIII.

EXAMPLES: Auckland City Art Gallery (1): a fishing boat wrecked on a beach. Birmingham Museum and Art Gallery (5): the Newhaven packet; summer in Cornwall; "Driven by Stress of Weather"; "Abandoned"; "In the Moray Forth". Blackburn Museum and Art Gallery (1): a storm in the Mediterranean. National Maritime Museum, Greenwich (1): setting nets on the coast of North Wales. Tate Gallery (1): "Catspaws off the Land". City of York Art Gallery (2): Crossing the Bar; Calm before the Storm.

MOORE, John **1820-1902**
Called John Moore of Ipswich, he exhibited locally at the annual exhibition of the Ipswich Art Society between 1875 and 1901, but though locally admired, never became nationally known as he did not exhibit in London. He excelled at rough sea subjects, but in a manner that must have appeared a little old fashioned in the last quarter of the 19th century. There is an example in the Ipswich Museum.

PLATE: 532.

MOOY, Cornelisz Pietersz **1656-1693**
Born and died in Rotterdam. He was a draughtsman in the art of making grisaille pictures and, of all the artists in this field, his work is the closest to the elder Willem van de Velde's (q.v.). It is thus difficult to believe that he could have achieved such proficiency without having been his pupil. He also painted monochrome pictures in oils.

PLATE: 101.

EXAMPLES: Gemeentemuseum, Arnhem (1): seascape. Musée des Beaux-Arts, Caen (1): two men-of-war in a rough sea. National Maritime Museum, Greenwich (2): the Eendracht, Zeven Provincien *and other Dutch men-of-war; Dutch vessels off a fort. Staatliches Museum, Kassel (1): shipping off Rotterdam. Maritiem Museum "Prins Hendrik", Rotterdam (1): man-of-war in a storm off rocks.*

MOOY, Jan **1776-1847**
An early Dutch ship portraitist, he had a characteristic manner of painting ensigns, so that the fly falls over and appears perpendicular below the rest of the ensign. The Peabody Museum of Salem has three signed watercolours and one attributed; two are dated 1818 and 1822.

MORAN, Edward **1829-1901**
Born in Bolton, Lancashire, on August 19th, 1829, he emigrated as a young man to the United States of America and became a pupil of James Hamilton in Philadelphia. Later he returned to England and studied in the Royal Academy Schools, and later still in Paris. In 1877 he settled in New York, and had a successful practice in marines, landscapes and genre historical subjects. He died there on June 19th 1901.

The United States Naval Academy Museum, Annapolis, has "Sunset, New York Bay", the Denver Art Museum, Colorado, has an example and the Walker Art Centre, Minneapolis, has "A Squall in the Channel".

PLATE: 582.

MORAN, Thomas **1837-1926**
A younger brother and pupil of Edward Moran (q.v.), he also was born in Bolton, on January 12th, 1837. He too went to America, where he became a pillar of what is called the Hudson River school. He travelled in Europe and exhibited one painting, not a marine, at the Royal Academy in 1879. He ended his long life in Santa Barbara, California. The Walker Art Centre, Minneapolis, has a view of Venice at sunset.

MOREL, Casparus Johannes **1798-1861**
Born and died in Amsterdam. He exhibited at Amsterdam in 1828 and 1834, and at The Hague in 1830. The Scheepvaart Museum, Amsterdam, has a painting of the *Jacoba Cornelia Clasina* arriving in Batavia Roads, dated 1857.

PLATE: 552.

MORETY, André
Called Raboul of Villefranche, he was a French ship portraitist working in the first quarter of the 19th century. His work has that clarity which was characteristic of the Roux family (qq.v.) and the Marseilles group of ship portraitists. The Peabody Museum of Salem has two watercolours.

MORGAN, H.J.
A British ship portraitist working in the last quarter of the 19th century, probably an amateur.

The National Maritime Museum, Greenwich, has five small portraits of British warships by him.

MORSE, F.A.
Quite a good quality ship portraitist working in the last quarter of the 19th century, if the one oil painting in the Peabody Museum of Salem is anything to go by. Nothing else is known about this artist but he was probably an American.

MOSES, Henry **c.1782-1870**
Born in London, c.1782; died Cowley, Oxford, February 28th, 1870. He was chiefly an engraver and in the 1820s engraved and published several booklets of *Sketches of Shipping, Views of Portsmouth Harbour* (1824), *Visit of the Duke of Clarence to Portsmouth* (1827), and *Six Views of the* Columbine *and the Experimental Squadron* (1830).

There are two oil paintings by him at the National Maritime Museum, Greenwich, both of the Duchess of Clarence in the *Royal Sovereign* yacht, reviewing the Russian squadron at Spithead in 1827.

PLATE: 363.

MULIER, Pieter, the Elder **1615-1670**
Born at Haarlem in 1615, died and was buried at Haarlem on April 22nd, 1670.

Although he would have been only seventeen when Jan Porcellis (q.v.) died, the influence of Porcellis' work is so strong that one wonders if he was his pupil. He adopted the grey tonal palette of the Dutch realist school, and was mainly concerned with scenes of shipping in fresh breezes or storms. The latter are sometimes in the form of long rhythmic seas, which imitate the storms of Claesz Wou (q.v.) in composition, though not in palette. He was a member of the Guild of Haarlem.

PLATES: 46, 47, 48.

EXAMPLES: The Museum of Fine Arts, Boston (1): ships in a gale. Staatliche Kunstsammlungen, Dresden (1): a beach scene. Gateshead Museum (1). National Maritime Museum, Greenwich (5): two storm scenes; a fishing scene; a vessel off a rock; and a late one of a ship off a rocky coast. National Gallery, Prague (1): possibly a view of Trouke.

MULIER, Pieter, the Younger (called Tempesta) c.1636-1701
Born at Haarlem about 1636; died in Milan June 29th, 1701.

He is assumed to have been the son of Pieter the Elder (q.v.) and his pupil, though he painted hunting scenes in the style of Hans Snyders, as well as marines. In the latter subject he was even more given to storm scenes than his father, so much so that he came to be called "Tempesta".

In 1667 he was in Antwerp, where he met a Carmelite monk who persuaded him that he wanted to join the church. With this intention he went to Rome but once there, instead of taking orders, he started a successful painting practice, with a studio and pupils. His style of painting at this time was apparently strongly influenced by the work of the late Mathieu van Plattenberg (q.v.), who had worked for years in Florence and specialised in stormy scenes of ships being thrown onto rocky coasts. It is an interesting reflection of changes in public taste, that in the mid-17th century these scenes of violent nautical disasters, or storms in general, were fashionable and regarded as a greater test of the artist's skill than calms.

Sometime in the 1670s he moved to Venice, where he had a love affair which resulted in his murdering his wife; as a result of this he spent five years in prison. On his release he took the name of Muller, and lived and worked under the protection of the Duke of Bracciano.

His palette is distinctive, combining warm browns and an unusual use of mauves with the green seas of his Flemish background.

PLATES: 49, 50, 51.

EXAMPLES: Fine Art Museum, Breslau: 2 storms. Museum of Fine Arts, Budapest (2): not marines. Staatliche Kunsthalle, Karlsrühe (1). Staatliche Kunstsammlungen, Kassel (1). Lincoln Museum (1): a landscape. Maidstone Museum (1): wreck scene. National Maritime Museum, Greenwich (3): a xebec and other shipping in a gale in the Mediterranean; ships wrecked on a rocky Mediterranean coast; Jonah and the whale. Pinacoteca Ambrosiana, Milan (1). Palazzo Colonna, Rome: a set of frescoes. Staatsgalerie, Stuttgart (2).

MUNCASTER, Claude Grahame **1903-1974**
P.R.S.M.A., R.W.S., R.O.I., R.B.A.
Born in Sutton, Sussex on July 4th, 1903, he was the son of the landscape painter Oliver Hall. His decision in 1923 to change his name to an old family one of Muncaster was made partly to avoid confusion with his father as a painter.

In the 1920s he made several voyages as a deck hand. Having been ship's painter in the Finnish barque *Favell,* he went out to Australia in a steam tramp and, arriving in Hobson's Bay, Melbourne, found there the four-masted barque *Olivebank,* one of Erikson's grain ships. He shipped aboard her and so became a Cape Horner, later writing a book about his voyage called *Rolling Round the Horn* (1933).

As a result of his experiences one of his specialities was deck scenes in sailing vessels. The only other artist to do this from first-hand knowledge was John Everett. During the Second World War he became a lieutenant-commander, RNVR, and a camouflage adviser.

He first exhibited at the Royal Academy in 1920 under his original name, Grahame Hall. He also exhibited at the Society of Marine Artists and was elected its President following the death of Charles Pears (q.v.) in 1957.

The National Maritime Museum, Greenwich, has his diploma picture on loan from the Royal Society of Marine Artists, "Gale Brewing in the Pentland Firth". The Tate Gallery has a painting by him called "The Demolition of Hay's Wharf", and Worthing Museum has a number of his works.

MURDAY, J.

A painter of ship portraits and shipping scenes of quite good quality, whose works are signed and dated in the second and third quarters of the 19th century. So far no details of his life have come to light.

EXAMPLES: National Maritime Museum, Greenwich (3): the barque Bernard; *a ship getting under way with troops on board; a transport. Peabody Museum of Salem (1): the schooner* Ellen Gillman. *National Maritime Museum, San Francisco (1): a barque among icebergs off Cape Horn.*

MURELL, W.

A British primitive ship portraitist working in the last quarter of the 19th century. The National Maritime Museum, Greenwich, has a painting by him.

PLATE: 605.

MUSIN, Auguste Henri **b.1852**

Born in Ostend on April 23rd, 1852; he was the son and pupil of François Etienne Musin (q.v.). He settled in Brussels and, like his father, won many medals. There are examples of his work in public galleries in Ostend, Compiégne and Rheims.

PLATE: 559.

MUSIN, François Etienne **1826-1888**

Born Ostend, October 4th, 1826; died Brussels, October 24th 1888. There does not seem to be much information on this successful and prolific artist, who, apart from winning many medals, was a Chevalier of the Order of Leopold, of Charles III and of the Liberator of Venezuela.

The National Maritime Museum, Greenwich, has a large painting by him of HMS *Erebus* in the ice and his work can be found in public galleries in Brussels, Courtrai, Montreal, Nice, Ostend, Rheims, Sheffield and Ypres.

PLATES: 504, 505, 506.

MYERS, Mark Richard R.S.M.A. **b.1945**

Born in San Mateo, California, on November 19th, 1945, he studied for a BA in history at Pomona College, California, 1967. His interest in deep-water merchant sail has been the driving force in his choice of subjects for his paintings. Since there is little of this now, he was fortunate to get a berth in the brigantine *Grethe* and the barque *Wanderer,* under Captain Alan Villiers when they were making the film *Hawaii* in 1965. The following year he was for a few months in the schooner *Te Vega* on oceanographic research work. Then in 1968 he was appointed mate for the transatlantic voyage of the ketch *Nonsuch,* built for the Hudson Bay Company in Appledore and supposed to be something like the Company's first 17th century vessel of that name.

He paints well crafted and researched scenes of historic sailing ships, mostly of the last hundred years. He started to exhibit at, and is now a member of, the Royal Society of Marine Artists, having been elected in 1975. Examples of his work can be found in the National Maritime Museum, Greenwich, the South Street Seaport Museum, New York, the North Devon Maritime Museum and the San Francisco Maritime Museum.

PLATE: 691.

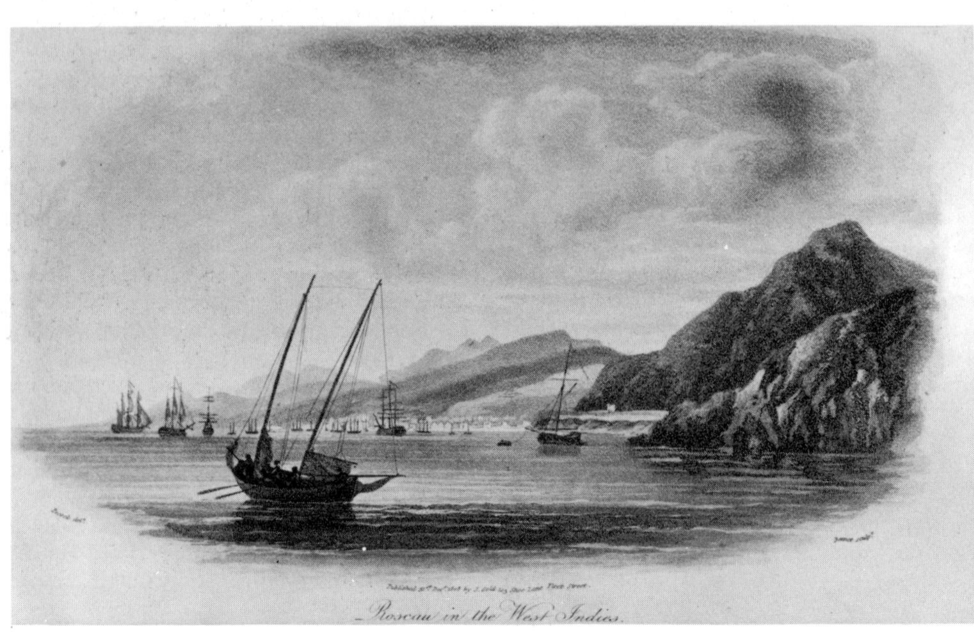

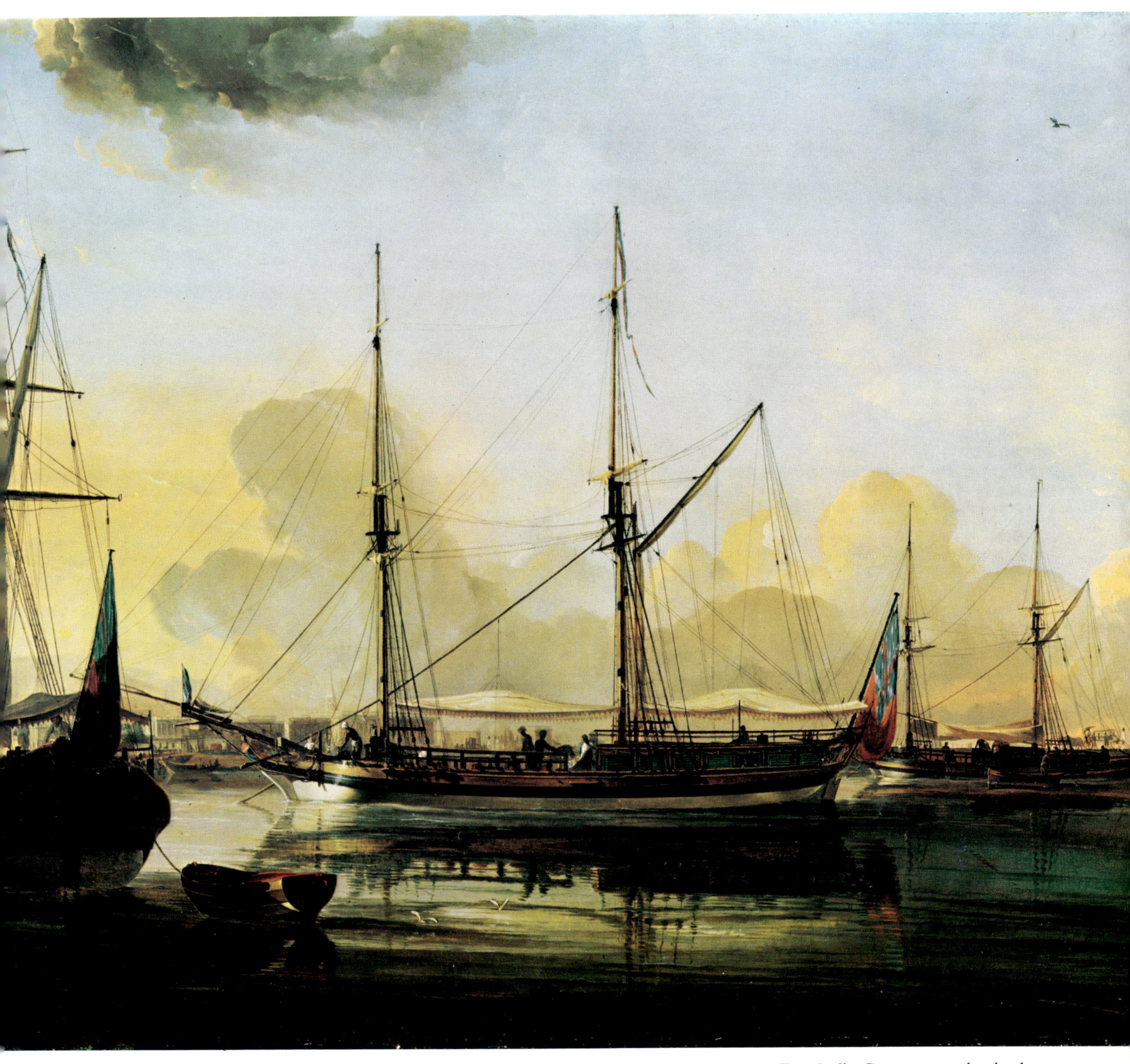

Colour Plate XVIII. Franz Balthazar Solvyns, 1760-1824. "The *Charlotte of Chittagong,* an East India Company yacht, in the Hooghly off Calcutta." National Maritime Museum, Greenwich.

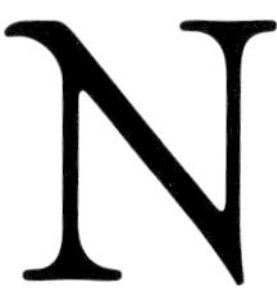

NAM CHEONG
A Chinese painter working in the middle of the 19th century. The Peabody Museum of Salem has an oil by him of Whampoa shipyard.

NAPIER, George Alexander **1827/8-1869**
Born Montrose, 1827/8, died Glasgow, 1869. A good quality ship portraitist working in Glasgow, about whom little is known. This was somewhat disconcerting for those people who paid large sums, five figures in one case, for a number of his paintings auctioned at the Gleneagles Hotel by Sotheby's in 1972.

NEUMANN, Johan Carl **1833-1891**
Born and died in Copenhagen. He was a pupil at the Copenhagen Academy and belonged to a highly talented generation of Danish marine painters. The Funen Art Museum at Odense has a painting by him of the Battle of Heligoland, 1864, and the State Museum for Art at Copenhagen has three paintings by him. The Frederiksborg Museum, Zealand, has paintings of the Danish fleet in the ice at Norborg in 1658 and the arrival of the Dutch fleet at Copenhagen in 1658. The Maritime Museum, Kronborg Castle, has a large painting of the Koch and Henderson fleet, and one of a Danish galleass leaving Helsingor. The Royal Naval Museum, Copenhagen, also has examples.

PLATE: 560.

NIBBS, Richard Henry **c.1816-1893**
Born and died in Brighton; he was educated at Worthing, where he later taught the violin and 'cello. For many years afterwards he played in the Theatre Royal orchestra in Brighton.

As a painter he is believed to have been self-taught, and in about 1840 a friend left him enough money to enable him to give up his music and concentrate on painting.

He first exhibited at the Royal Academy in 1841 and fairly frequently until 1888, mostly coastal views, but in 1849 a "Battle of Trafalgar" and a "Battle of the Nile". He also exhibited at the British Institution from 1841 to 1867, and at Suffolk Street.

In 1836 he published *Marine Sketches,* a set of ten plates of shipping scenes, then in 1850 his *Marine Sketchbook of Shipping Crafts,* and finally in 1876 *Shipping Coast Scenes and Antiquities of Sussex.*

PLATES: 492, 493, 494, 495.

EXAMPLES: The Royal Pavilion, Brighton (2): Queen Victoria landing on the Chain Pier at Brighton in 1843; HMS Vengeance *at Spithead and the yacht* America *1851. National Maritime Museum, Greenwich (6): "The First Shot of the War" showing the paddle sloop HMS* Fury *escaping from a Russian sailing squadron off Odessa; the* Essex *in the ice; the barque* Peeress; *a fishing smack running into Newhaven; a paddle tug towing a lifeboat to a wreck on the Goodwins in a gale; a hay barge off Sheerness.*

NICHOLLS, J.
It is one of the mysteries of marine painting that this artist, who painted the picture illustrated, signed and dated 1790, and which is built into the boardroom of the Admiralty as a companion to the van de Velde, should be a complete unknown. Only one other painting is known to be by him, that of the 1785 naval review, which belonged to the Seamen's Hospital Society at Greenwich. A man who could turn out two paintings of this quality must have painted more.

PLATE: 292.

NICKERSON, Vincent Douglas **1844-1910**
Born and died in Cleveland. He was the son of a sea captain and vessel agent, and married a Mary Le Frinier of the Cleveland shipbuilding firm. He took up marine painting in early middle age, and painted ship portraits from about 1882 until his death.

Examples of his work can be seen at the Great Lakes Historical Society Museum, Vermilion; the Mariners Museum, Newport News, Virginia, and the Milan Historical Museum, Ohio.

NIELSEN, Amaldus Clarin **1838-1900**
Born at Mandal in Norway on May 23rd, 1838, Nielsen studied art at Copenhagen, Düsseldorf and Karlsrühe, before settling in Christiania (Oslo) where he painted landscapes and coastal views, which were popular with the public. Examples of his work are in the Nasjonalgalleriet in Oslo.

PLATE: 544.

NIEMANN, Edmund John **1813-1876**
Born Islington, London, 1813; died Brixton, London, April 15th, 1876. He started work at thirteen as a clerk with Lloyds, but gave that up in 1839 to concentrate on painting. He exhibited at the Royal Academy between 1844 and 1872, and at the British Institution between 1845 and 1867, but only one or two of the exhibits were marines.

Examples may be seen at the British Museum, Victoria and Albert Museum, Rotherham Museum, and the Graves Museum, Sheffield. The National Gallery of New South Wales, Sydney has a view of Whitby by him.

PLATE: 498.

NOËL, Jules Achille **1815-1881**
Born in Quimper, Finisterre, on February 24th, 1815, he studied art in Brest, and then moved to Paris, exhibiting his first painting in the Salon in 1840. He continued to exhibit there until 1879 and was chiefly known for his coastal views in Normandy. He died in Alger, Algeria, on March 26th, 1881.

PLATE: 501; COLOUR PLATE: XXII.

EXAMPLES: Musée de Bernay: view of Brest. Musée de Briançon: Port of Brest. Musée de Chantilly: view of Treport. National

Maritime Museum, Greenwich: the Emperor Napoleon III receiving Queen Victoria aboard the Bretagne *at Cherbourg in August 1858 and fishing boats on the shore (watercolour). Musée de La Rochelle: the Port of Brest and cliffs at Quiberon. National Gallery of Victoria, Melbourne: a marine. Musée de Nancy: Brest Roads in a calm; a marine.*

NOOMS, Reinier (called Zeeman) c.1623-1667

Born and died in Amsterdam. As the name Zeeman suggests, his early life was spent at sea, from which he later turned to painting. His work is in the Dutch realist manner but he is not as austere in his palette as some of his contemporaries. A good craftsman with an obvious knowledge of shipping, his paintings are on the whole pleasant rather than stimulating.

In spite of this he had a successful, if rather short career, and for a time worked for the Brandenburg Court at Berlin. He is perhaps better known as an engraver than as a painter.

PLATES: 66, 67, 68, 69.

EXAMPLES: Musée d'Aix-la-Chapelle (1): rough sea. Rijksmuseum, Amsterdam (6): careening ships on the Y at Amsterdam; battle of Leghorn; view of Salee, Morocco; Tripoli; view of Tunis; view of Algiers. Scheepvaart Museum, Amsterdam (5): action of the First Dutch War; view of Amsterdam; two harbour scenes with ships being careened; shore scene with merchants and goods with two ships lying off. Cecil Higgins Museum, Bedford (1): coast scene with shipping and figures. Dahlem Museum, Berlin (1): beach scene. Fitzwilliam Museum, Cambridge (1): calm. Art Institute, Chicago (1): shore scene with small craft. Statens Museum for Kunst, Copenhagen (2): both with ships careening. Musée de Dieppe (1): port scene. Musée de Dijon (1). National Maritime Museum, Greenwich (7): battle of Leghorn; battle of the First Dutch War; view of Algiers; view of Tripoli; the Amelia; *shipbuilding at Santo Stefano; sea battle. Hamburger Kunsthalle: view of Amsterdam. Gemäldegalerie, Leipzig (1): shore scene. Hermitage, Leningrad (1): harbour scene. Musée de Mayence (1). Musée de Beaux Arts, Marseille (1). Louvre, Paris (2): view of the Louvre and a calm with fishing boats. Johnson Collection, Philadelphia (1): man-of-war and small craft in a calm. Musée de Rennes (1): naval battle. Boymans Museum, Rotterdam (3): shore scenes with shipping, one with the entrance to a walled town. Southend on Sea Museum (1): shipping off a coast. Nationalmuseum, Stockholm (2): shore scene with merchant shipping; calm with a ship being careened. Musée de Valenciennes (1).*

NOOTEBOOM, Jacobus Hendricus Johannes 1811-1878

Born in Groningen on October 9th, 1811, died in Amsterdam on June 1st, 1878. He was a pupil of the landscape painter Johannes Coucke at Ghent in 1830 and 1831. He afterwards travelled and studied in Belgium, Switzerland and Germany.

He exhibited at Amsterdam in 1834-74, The Hague 1835-43 and Leeuwarden in 1855. At the Castle of Chillon, near Geneva, there are paintings by him of a calm and a storm.

PLATE: 473.

NORMAN, Michael R.S.M.A. b.1933

He was born in Ipswich on August 20th, 1933 and did his art training at the Bournemouth College of Art. He still lives in the Ipswich area and specialises in coastal and river scenes in East Anglia. He has had one man shows in Ipswich, Colchester and Aldeburgh and was elected a member of the Royal Society of Marine Artists in 1977.

NORTON, Charles Wardlow 1848-1901

Born and died in Detroit. He was the son of a tugboat captain, and at the age of seventeen is listed in the Detroit city directory as a marine artist. In fact, he was painting rather primitive ship portraits. He was also a newspaper marine reporter, and later a vessel agent, and it was here that his real financial interests lay, so that when he died no mention was made in the local obituary of his earlier artistic career.

Examples of his work can be seen at the Dossin Great Lakes Museum, Detroit, the Mariners' Museum, Newport News, Virginia, the Milan Historical Museum, Ohio, and the Peabody Museum of Salem.

NORTON, William Edward 1843-1916

An American painter of modest talent. The Peabody Museum of Salem, has four signed oils and one attributed to him and the New Bedford Whaling Museum has one.

PLATE: 581.

NOWELL, William Calmody Com. R.N. c.1806-1883

A naval officer and amateur artist. In 1839 he was married in Malta to a daughter of the Marquis of Testaferrata. The quality of his painting is quite good.

The National Maritime Museum has two oils, units of the Mediterranean fleet about 1840, and the flagship of the Mediterranean fleet and other ships joining a French squadron at anchor in Turkish waters, also four watercolours of marine subjects.

NURSEY, Claude Lorraine 1820-1873

Born in Woodbridge, Suffolk, 1820; died January 2nd, 1873. As his names indicate he came of a painting family. He studied at the Central School of Design at Somerset House, London, and in 1840 was appointed to be master of the Leeds School of Design. In 1849 he went to teach at the Belfast School until about 1855, when he returned to East Anglia and to Norwich, where he was for some time secretary of the Norwich Fine Arts Association.

He was a landscape and marine painter; he exhibited one painting at the British Institution in 1844, and others in Suffolk Street, and at the Royal Hibernian Academy in 1854 and 1855.

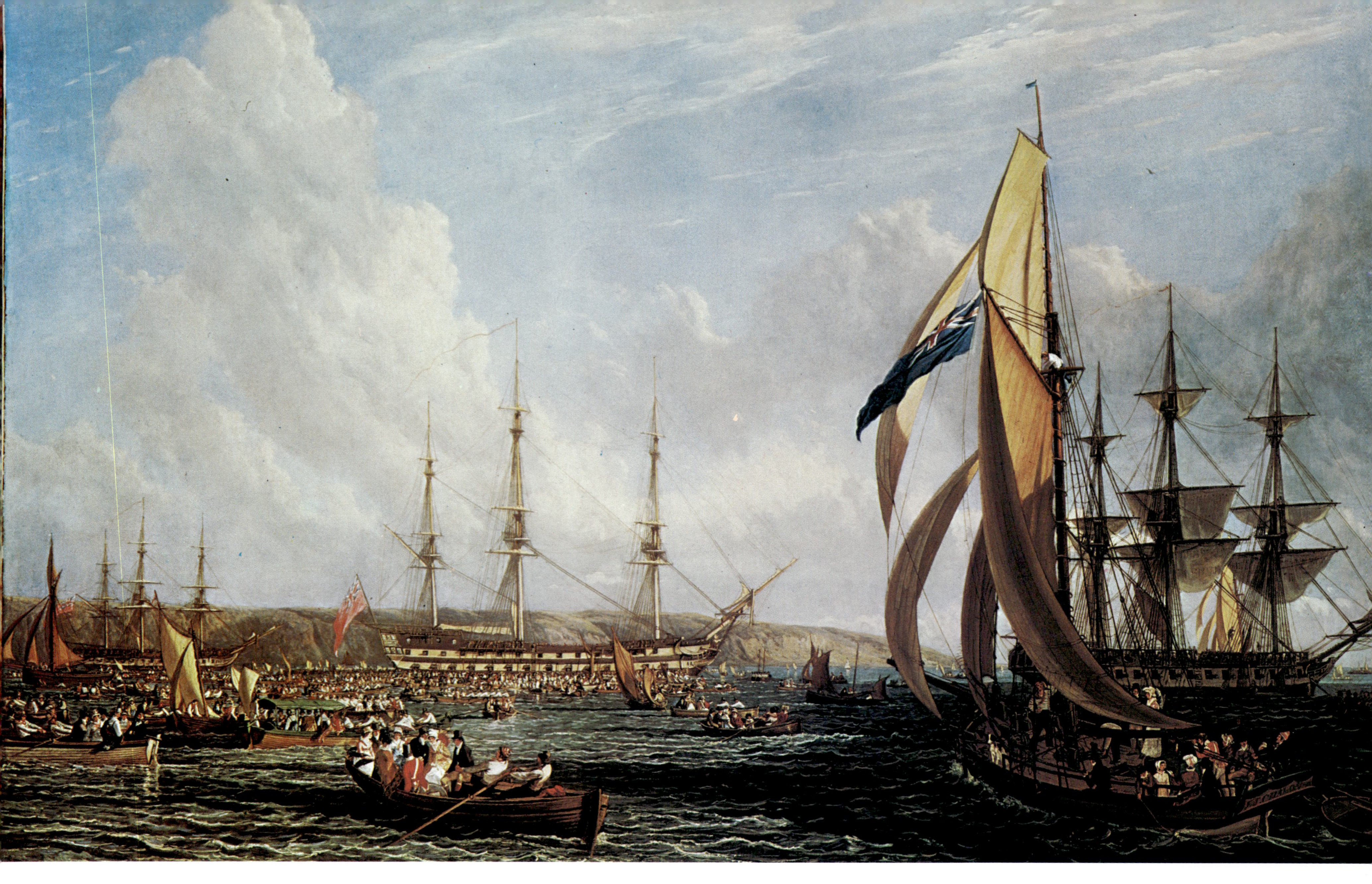

Colour Plate XIX. John James Chalon, 1778-1854. ''Napoleon aboard the *Bellerophon* at Plymouth in 1815.''
National Maritime Museum, Greenwich (Greenwich Hospital Collection).

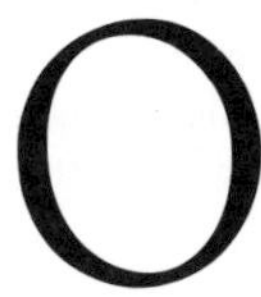

OLSEN, Carl Julius Emil **1818-1878**
Born and died in Copenhagen, he was a pupil at the Academy of Fine Art there and later worked with Anton Melbye (q.v.). The Maritime Museum, Kronborg Castle, has a painting of the *Weser* and *Adolfine* dated 1860.

OLSSON, Julius **1864-1942**
R.A., P.R.O.I., R.B.A., R.W.A., N.E.A.C.
Born in London on February 1st, 1864, the son of an English mother and a Swedish father. Without any formal training in art, he left commerce to paint and travel and exhibited his first painting at the Royal Academy in 1890. In 1896/7 he moved from London to St. Ives in Cornwall, where he became a pillar of the flourishing artists' colony there, and it is his seascapes painted on the Cornish coast that are his best known works. These are often moonlit scenes and it was one of them that the Chantrey Bequest bought in 1911.

In 1915 he returned to London and joined the Royal Naval Volunteer Reserve and became a lieutenant, though this compiler has been unable to find him in the Navy Lists. He remained in London after the war, becoming a Royal Academician in 1920 and later President of the Royal Institute of Oil Painters. After his house was bombed in the Second World War he moved to Dalkey on the outskirts of Dublin, where he died on September 8th, 1942.

Though his strong feeling for the sea comes across to us, his many artistic honours owe more perhaps to his presence and personality than to his rather messy Impressionist technique.

PLATE: 604.

EXAMPLES: National Maritime Museum, Greenwich (1): a moonlit seascape with a lighthouse on a headland. Tate Gallery, London (1): moonlit shore near St. Ives.

OPDENHOFF, George Willem (called Witzel) **1807-1873**
Born in Fulda, Prussia, in 1807, he was a pupil of the landscape painter Andreas Schelfhout and the marine painter Johannes Christiaan Schotel (q.v.). From 1835 to 1837 he worked in Breda and then travelled in France. After that he painted for a few years in Rotterdam, before settling near The Hague where he died in 1873.

He exhibited at The Hague from 1835 to 1861. The Gemeentemuseum there has a seascape by him.

PLATE: 374.

OS, Jan van **1744-1808**
Born at Middelharnis, Island of Oveflakkee, Holland, baptised February 23rd, 1744. He was a pupil of Aart Schouman. In 1773 he was elected to the Society of Painters at The Hague. As well as being a marine painter, he painted flowers and fruit. He died in The Hague on February 7th, 1808.

The Teylers Stichting Museum, Haarlem, has a river scene by him; other examples in Dutch museums seem to be flower pieces. The State Museum in Budapest has two port scenes, and there is a marine in the Museum of Valenciennes.

PLATE: 268.

OULESS, Philip John **1817-1885**
Born in Jersey on April 7th, 1817. He studied painting in Paris and then returned as a painter and a teacher to his native Jersey, where he died on June 22nd, 1885. His marines are mainly commissioned ship portraits but he also depicted occasions or events such as launches and wrecks. There are a number of his marines in the St. Helier Museum, Jersey; the National Maritime Museum, Greenwich, has a ship portrait by him.

His son, William, became an R.A. as a portrait painter, although at Greenwich there is a view of Greenwich Hospital by him.

PLATE: 521.

OVENDEN, F.W.
A London painter working in the second quarter of the 19th century in the style of George Chambers, Snr. (q.v.), though his work is coarser. He exhibited one picture, a coast scene, at the Royal Academy in 1836. He also exhibited at Suffolk Street.

PLATE: 428.

OWEN, Samuel **1768/9-1857**
He was mainly a watercolourist of coastal and fishing scenes but having first exhibited "A Sea View" at the Royal Academy in 1794, his next exhibit was of the action off Cape St. Vincent in 1797. This was followed in 1799 by three paintings of the *Director's* share of the Battle of Camperdown. His last exhibits, in 1802 and 1807, were general marine subjects. He died in Sunbury-on-Thames on December 8th, 1857.

Examples of his watercolours may be seen at the Birmingham Art Gallery, Fitzwilliam Museum, Cambridge, National Museum of Wales, Cardiff, National Maritime Museum, Greenwich, Leicester City Art Gallery, the British Museum and the Victoria and Albert Museum.

PLATE: 319.

OZANNE, Nicolas-Marie **1728-1811**
Born in Brest, 1728; died in Paris, 1811. He was a pupil of the genre and portrait painter Jules Roblin in 1743, and succeeded him as Professor of Drawing at the Pavillion at Brest. He was essentially a draughtsman rather than a painter, and as such achieved royal recognition as a recorder of events.

He covered Louis XV's visit to Le Havre in 1749, and in 1756 was in Toulon to record the departure of the Duc de Richelieu's expedition to take Minorca.

In 1762 he was made draughtsman to the Navy, and also commissioned to design and build pleasure vessels for the canal at Versailles. In 1769 he was instructing the son of the Dauphin in the building and working of ships. His younger brother Pierre (q.v.) was his pupil. The Musée de la Marine in Paris holds drawings by him.

OZANNE, Pierre **1737-1813**
Born and died in Brest. He was the pupil of his elder brother Nicolas-Marie (q.v.), and appears to have had similar tastes, for when his brother died in 1811 he succeeded him as draughtsman to the Navy, a post he held for two years only. There is a painting by him in the Museum at Cherbourg and he published a set of sixty engravings on types of vessels, called *Vaisseaux et Autres Bâtiments de Mer*.

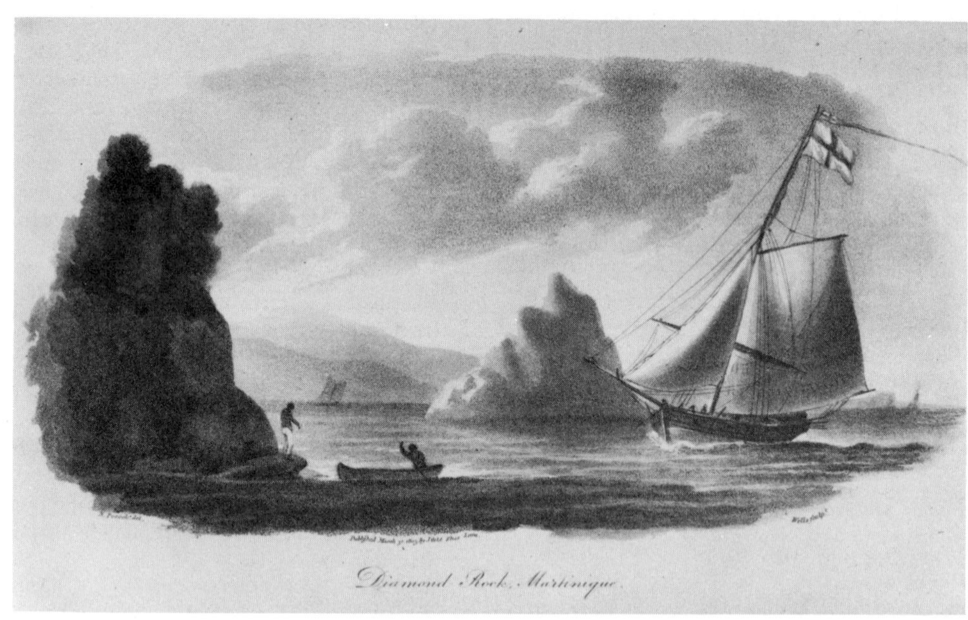

P

PADDAY, Charles M.

This artist exhibited marine subjects at the Royal Academy from 1890. The National Maritime Museum, Greenwich, has two monochrome yachting scenes in oil which were evidently done for illustrations at about the turn of the century.

PALLI, Felice

A ship portraitist working in Trieste in the second and third quarters of the 19th century. His work conforms to the style of the Marseilles school. The Peabody Museum of Salem has three watercolours by him, one dated 1834.

PANSING, Fred **b.1844**

Born in Bremen, the son of a manufacturer, he went to sea when he was sixteen. After five years, during which time he began to draw and paint, he emigrated to America and set up as a marine painter and ship portraitist. He was working into the first quarter of this century, and his pictures are of quite high quality.

PLATE: 617.

EXAMPLES: The Mariners Museum, Newport News (5); the Kaiser Wilhelm der Grosse; *the* Kaiser Wilhelm II; the Olympic; *a Hudson River paddle steamer; and another paddle steamer. Peabody Museum of Salem (3): oils.*

PARKE, Henry **c.1790-1845**

He was the pupil of, and later assistant to, Sir John Soane in his antiquarian pursuits; he was also an architect. His first exhibits at the Royal Academy, beginning in 1815, were all marines, including the example illustrated here, which was exhibited in 1817. After his travels in Italy, Greece and Egypt from 1820 to 1824, most of his exhibits were of ancient ruins, though there were some marines. He last exhibited in 1835. He died on May 5th, 1845.

Examples are held by the British Museum and Victoria and Albert Museum.

PLATE: 361.

PATON, Richard **1717-1791**

Born and died in London. Said to have been the youngest of an impoverished family, who sent him out as a child to beg in the streets. One day he accosted Commander (later Admiral) Sir Charles Knowles, on Tower Hill, and sufficiently impressed him to get an offer of a place in Knowles's ship, where he became assistant to the ship's painter.

From these unlikely beginnings, and presumably largely self-taught, he rose to be one of the principal painters of naval actions of the 18th century. In 1742, through some other patronage (not that of Knowles, who was in the West Indies), Paton was appointed Assistant Accountant in the Excise Office. Thus he was not dependent on his brush for a living and it does seem that he was a late starter as an artist. The first paintings to bring him to the public notice were of the Battle of Lagos 1759, and the capture of the *Foudroyant* in 1758; both of which were exhibited at the Society of Artists in 1762 and subsequently engraved. He continued to exhibit views and actions until 1770, when he resigned from the Society after a dispute over the placing of his picture of the Battle of Finisterre 1747. From 1776 to 1780 he exhibited at the Royal Academy.

Perhaps because he was self-taught and something of an experimenter, his work is uneven in quality and style; some of the best paintings show a strong influence of Samuel Scott (q.v.), others that of Charles Brooking (q.v.). He published engravings of his paintings, having them engraved by P.C. Canot.

PLATES: 214, 215, 216; COLOUR PLATE: XV.

EXAMPLES: United States Naval Academy Museum, Annapolis (1): the action between the Serapis *and the* Bonhomme Richard, *1779. National Maritime Museum, Greenwich (12): Battle of Barfleur 1692; Battle of Cape Pasaro 1718; capture of Port Louis, Cuba 1748; Battle of Quiberon Bay 1759; bombardment of Moro Castle, Havana 1762; the burning of the Turkish fleet in Cheseme Bay 1777; the moonlight Battle of St. Vincent 1780; Battle of the Dogger Bank 1781; two pictures of the Battle of the Saints 1782; Lord Howe's relief of Gibraltar 1782; Port Royal, Jamaica. The Hermitage, Leningrad (1). Shipley Art Gallery, Gateshead (1).*

PATTERSON, Charles Robert **1878-1958**

Born Southampton 1878. He was the son of the then head of the Whitehaven Ship Building Company of Southampton, and it is therefore a little surprising that he is said to have gone to sea at the age of thirteen.

In his twenties he left the sea and settled in America as a marine painter. He was also a naval historian and wrote on his own experiences and ship histories. An admirable technique, aided by a keen sense of authenticity make him one of the most admired of American marine painters. At the time of his death (in New York, October 1958) twenty-seven of his pictures formed a special exhibition at the Mariners Museum, Newport News. This museum has two paintings by this artist, the sailing ship *Emily F. Whitney* and the *McLaurin* at anchor, and a ship in a breeze. The Peabody Museum of Salem has a painting of a Blackballer and many sketches, and at the Navy Memorial Museum at the Washington Navy Yard there is a portrait of the U.S.S. *Mexico*.

PEARN, W.

A British primitive ship portraitist working in the third quarter of the 19th century. The National Maritime Museum, Greenwich, has three examples; one is dated 1870 and another 1880.

PEARS, Charles P.S.M.A., R.O.I. 1873-1958
Born in Pontefract, Yorkshire, on September 9th, 1873, he was educated at East Hardwick and Pomfret College and later became a professional illustrator who contributed to the *Illustrated London News, Graphic* and *Punch*. Among the books he illustrated were Masefield's *Salt Water Ballads,* Dana's *Two Years before the Mast* and the complete works of Charles Dickens.

During the First World War he held a commission in the Royal Marines and was also an official war artist to the Admiralty. In the Second World War he worked for the War Artists' Commission. These war paintings were of events and actions but not of things he saw himself. He was a keen yachtsman and an expert on ships, and brought a high degree of technical accuracy to his work. He had an unusual technique in the handling of water, evidently based on that of Canaletto. He was the first President of the Society of Marine Artists, later to have the prefix Royal. He published several books, including *From the Thames to the Seine, From the Thames to the Netherlands, South Coast Cruising* and *Going Foreign*. He died in Truro, Cornwall, in January 1958.

His First World War pictures are in the Imperial War Museum and his Second World War pictures are divided between the Imperial War Museum and the National Maritime Museum, Greenwich.

PLATES: 667, 668; COLOUR PLATE: XXVI.

PEETERS, Bonaventura, the Elder 1614-1652
Born Antwerp, July 1614; died Hoboken, near Antwerp, 25th July, 1652. The most talented of his family of painters, he was to produce some of the finest marines of the whole Flemish School, especially on a small scale. The best teaching studio in Antwerp when he was growing up was that of Andries van Eertvelt (q.v.), and as there are features in Peeters's work which reflect some of the latter's effects he was possibly a pupil of Eertvelt. He was an experimental painter whose style, like Eertvelt's, varied over the years. The early river scene at Brunswick is careful and Flemish, while the storm off Gibraltar at Greenwich is highly romantic. Later works in the Greenwich collection, like "Shipping off Hoorn", and the wonderful little "Stormy day at Sea", are more broadly treated and in the Dutch realist style. His popularity over the years is reflected in the large number of European galleries which hold works by him, more than for any other marine painter.

He became a master of the Guild of Antwerp in 1634, when he was twenty, and also had time to make sea voyages. His health was delicate, which prompted him to leave Antwerp for the better air of nearby Hoboken, where he lived with his sister Catharina and young brother Jan, both of whom he taught to paint marines. Of all the painters in the family Jan's work is closest to his eldest brother's later style.

His brother Gillis was not a marine painter but did co-operate with Peeters on a picture of the Siege of Calloo in 1639. It was Gillis's son, also named Bonaventura, who became a marine painter (q.v.).

PLATES: 70, 71; COLOUR PLATE: VI.

EXAMPLES: Musée d'Abbeville (1): storm. Rijksmuseum, Amsterdam (2): Dutch vessels off a jetty; a Polar bear hunt on a rocky coast. Musée Royal des Beaux-Arts, Antwerp (5): view of Antwerp; the quay at Antwerp; reception of St. Norbert at Antwerp in 1124; view of Middelburg; marine. Gemäldegalerie, Augsburg (2): storms. Holburne Museum, Bath (1): boats entering a harbour. Musée de Besançon (1): storm. Musée de Peinture de Bordeaux (1): storm. Herzog Anton Ulrich Museum, Brunswick (1): an unusual early river scene dated 1636. Bowdien College, Brunswick, Maine (1): galleys off Messina. Szépmüvészeli Múzeum, Budapest (4). Fitzwilliam Museum, Cambridge (4). Landesmuseum, Darmstadt (2): view of Dordrecht; storm with wrecks. Dayton Art Institute, Ohio (1): attributed. Stedelijk Museum, Delft (1): yachts off Antwerp. Musée de Douai (1). Gemäldegalerie, Dresden (2): one dated 1643 and the other 1652. Musée de Dunkerque (2). Staatliche Kunstakademie, Düsseldorf (1): by B. and Gillis Peeters. Narodowe Museum, Gdansk (1): English ship off a castle, probably meant for Elizabeth Castle, Jersey. National Maritime Museum, Greenwich (7). Kunsthalle, Hamburg (2): both signed and dated 1649. Landesgalerie, Hanover (1): storm. Wadsworth Athenaeum, Hartford, Conn. (1): attributed. Ferdinandeum, Innsbruck (1): English ship off a coast with a castle. Ipswich Museum (1). Staatliche Kunsthalle, Karlsruhe (1): shipping off Gibraltar. Staatliche Gemäldegalerie, Kassel (1). Musée de La Fère (3). Hermitage, Leningrad (1). Musée du Lille (1): ships wrecked on a rocky coast. City Art Gallery, Manchester (1): yacht in a choppy sea. Capodimonte Museum, Naples (2): both signed and dated 1636. Metropolitan Museum, New York (1): view of Antwerp. Nasjonalgalleriet, Oslo (1). Národni Galerie, Prague (1): signed and dated 1632. Staatengalerie, Schleissheim. Staatliches Museum, Schwerin. Brukenthal Museum, Sibiu, Rumania (1): ship in a harbour. Southend-on-Sea Museum (1): shipwreck. Nationalmuseum, Stockholm (1): early river scene. Museum of Strasbourg (1): storm. Centraal Museum der Gemeente, Utrecht (1). Musée de Valenciennes (1). Akademie der Bildenden Künste, Vienna (2). Museum of Weimar (1).

PEETERS, Bonaventura, the Younger 1648-1702
Born October 17th, 1648, died September 2nd, 1702. He was the son of Gillis Peeters, the elder Bonaventura Peeters' brother. His style is close though inferior to his illustrious uncle, so he was probably his pupil.

PEETERS, Catharina 1615-aft.1675
Born in Antwerp, 1615, she died there after 1675. A younger sister of Bonaventura Peeters, the Elder (q.v.) and elder sister of Jan (q.v.), she appears to have kept house for the former and brought up the latter at Hoboken, near Antwerp. She was also Bonaventura's pupil, and a naval battle scene by her is in the Kunsthistorisches Museum, Vienna.

PEETERS, Jan 1624-c.1679
Born Antwerp, April 1624; died Antwerp, c.1679. He was ten years younger than his brother Bonaventura, the Elder (q.v.) and nine years younger than his sister Catharina (q.v.). He was his brother's most apt pupil, adopting his later style so closely that their work of that period is sometimes difficult to tell apart. When he was twenty he moved to Antwerp and married a Catharine Buseliess. Although the children of this marriage became his pupils they were not apparently marine painters.

Like those of his elder brother, his paintings enjoyed a wide popularity and are to be found in a number of public galleries.

PLATE: 72.

EXAMPLES: Rijksmuseum, Amsterdam (1): Dutch in the Medway 1667 (attributed). Musée de Beaux-Arts, Antwerp. Musée des Beaux-Arts, Bordeaux (1). Szépmüveszeti Museum, Budapest (1): shipwreck scene. Gemäldegalerie, Darmstadt (1): whalers in a storm. Museum Narodowe, Gdansk (1): galley by a castle in a gale. National Maritime Museum, Greenwich (3): Dutch in the Medway 1667 (very similar to the attributed picture in the Rijksmuseum, Amsterdam); galleys in a storm off rocks; a grisaille of an English flute off Satalia. Gemäldegalerie, Kassel (1): dated 1667. Hermitage, Leningrad (1): ships driven onto a rocky coast; another attributed.

PELLEGRINI, Honoré **1793-1869**

A French ship portraitist working in Marseilles in the second and third quarters of the 19th century. Although his work is characteristic of the Marseilles school, it is stiffer than the typical output of the Roux family (qq.v.). The Peabody Museum of Salem has twenty-seven watercolours, dated between 1827 and 1866 and the Mariners Museum, Newport News, has five watercolours dated between 1829 and 1850.

PLATES: 313, 314.

PENNING, Nicolas Lodewijk **c.1764-1818**

He was born and died in The Hague, where he attended the Drawing Academy and where he won the gold medal for drawing in 1802. He was also a landscape painter.

PLATE: 325.

PETERSEN, Heinrich Andreas Sophus **1834-1916**

A German ship portraitist and son of Lorenz Petersen (q.v.), like him working in Altona and Hamburg. Like his father he also painted pictures jointly with Peter Holm (q.v.). The Altonaer Museum has four of these, and the Peabody Museum of Salem has three signed by Petersen only. The National Maritime Museum, Greenwich, has a portrait of the barque *Antagonist*.

PLATE: 550.

PETERSEN, Jacob **1774-1854**

A Danish ship portraitist working in Copenhagen whose style borders on the primitive. The Danish Maritime Museum in Kronborg Castle, Helsingor, has a very large collection of his work, nearly all watercolours, but some in gouache and in oils. The Royal Naval Museum in Copenhagen also has a few. The Peabody Museum of Salem has six signed watercolours by him, one gouache and watercolour, one certain oil and two attributed.

PLATE: 404.

PETERSEN, Lorenz **1803-1870**

A German ship portraitist working in Altona and Hamburg. Many of his pictures were joint efforts with Peter Holm (q.v.).

PLATES: 548, 549.

EXAMPLES: Altonaer Museum, Hamburg: 3 oils, 1 watercolour, and 9 signed by both Petersen and Holm. Peabody Museum of Salem (1).

PFEIFFER, J.H.

A German ship portraitist working in Altona in the second quarter of the 19th century, in a manner reminiscent of Jacob Petersen (q.v.). The Peabody Museum of Salem has a watercolour by him dated 1837.

PILLEMENT, Jean Baptiste **1728-1808**

Born and died in Lyon, this excellent artist studied in Paris and worked for a time in the Gobelins tapestry factory. He then went to Poland where he became a court painter and palace decorator to King Stanislaus Augustus. He later worked for the Duke of Liechtenstein, who commissioned ten paintings from him.

About 1755 he went to live in England, where he was a success, exhibiting at the Society of Artists and the Free Society between 1760 and 1780.

However, he was still very much the cosmopolitan, continuing to be the official painter to King Stanislaus and working for Queen Marie-Antoinette in Paris. It is therefore surprising that, when in his old age he retired to his native Lyon, he should have died poor.

He was an engraver as well as a painter, and did genre and landscape subjects of equal quality to his marines.

The latter are very reminiscent of the Dutch 17th century realist school, with a grey palette but bearing a strong influence of Claude-Joseph Vernet (q.v.).

PLATE: 234.

EXAMPLES: Marines only. Musée d'Abbeville (1). Musée des Beaux-Arts, Besançon (1): wreck scene.

PITTALUGA, Antonio

An Italian ship portraitist working in the second quarter of the 19th century. The Peabody Museum of Salem has three watercolours, one dated 1829.

PLATTENBERG, Mathieu van **c.1608-1660**
(also called PLATTEMONTAGNE)

Born in Antwerp about 1608, he was a pupil of Andries van Eertvelt (q.v.), and a painter of storms and ships wrecked on rocky coasts. As a young man he went to Florence, where in collaboration with another Netherlands painter, Jan Asselyn, he produced some portraits, landscapes and marines, all of which were successful. He moved on to Paris, where again he had success and he was made a member of the Académie Royale. It was in Paris that he started to call himself Plattemontagne. He died in Paris in 1660.

Of his storm-at-sea scenes, the Musée Royale des Beaux-Arts at Antwerp has one; the gallery in the Palace of the former Prince Bishops at Bamberg has two, and the National Maritime Museum, Greenwich, has three storms as well as one early scene in Dutch waters.

PLATES: 29, 30.

PLEIJSIER, Ary **1809-1879**

Born in Vlaardingen, 1809; died in Vreeland, 1879. He was a self-taught painter who worked in The Hague from 1842 to 1853; after that he could be found at Amsterdam and The Hague from 1843 to 1878, and at Leeuwarden in 1855 and 1859. Examples of his work can be found at the Paul Tetar van Elven Museum at Delft and the Boymans van Beunigen Museum, Rotterdam.

POCOCK, Nicholas **1740-1821**

Born in Bristol, 1740. He was the son of a well connected Bristol merchant, who had married a cousin of the Duke of Roxburgh. He went to sea, and in 1767 was in command of the *Lloyd,* a merchantman belonging to Richard Champion, the maker of Bristol porcelain. He was already an amateur painter, and each day, when he wrote up the *Lloyd's* log, he included a little wash drawing of her, showing the state of the weather or anything remarkable that had happened. Richard Champion's sister wrote in her journal that Pocock, "having a fine taste for drawing, he sometimes talked of giving up the sea."

What is thought to be his earliest surviving watercolour is one showing two views of the *Ruby* of Bristol and dated 1759. It is fairly primitive.

In 1780 he married and this additional stimulus to leave the sea and settle down seems to have been artistically decisive. In that year he sent a picture up to the Royal Academy and, though it arrived too late to be in the exhibition, he received an encouraging letter of advice from the President, Sir Joshua Reynolds. In 1782 he had two views around Bristol and two marines accepted, exhibiting thereafter in every year until 1812, and finally in 1815.

In 1789 he moved to London where, like Dominic Serres (q.v.) before him, his immense practical knowledge of ships and the sea and a "good address", immediately recommended him to naval clients to record their actions at sea, and so on. Indeed, Serres had only four years to live and Pocock was his obvious successor, though not without competition from such artists as Dodd (q.v.), Luny (q.v.) and Whitcombe (q.v.).

In 1794 he went briefly to sea with the fleet to witness the Battle of the Glorious First of June, and was thereafter busily employed recording the many actions of the long French Wars. This large output included a set of paintings to be engraved for Clarke and McArthur's biography of Lord Nelson.

In 1817, two years after he last exhibited at the Royal Academy he suffered a stroke, and the resulting paralysis appears to have prevented him from doing any further work. He died in Maidenhead on March 19th, 1821.

Two of his sons, Isaac and William Innes (q.v.) were also painters. The former, notable as a playwright, was a historical and portrait painter; the latter painted marines.

PLATES: 245, 246, 247, 248, 249, 250; COLOUR PLATE: XVI.

EXAMPLES: Ulster Museum, Belfast (3): Warren's action off Tory Island, 1798; beaching a boat in gale. City Art Gallery, Bristol (2): Southampton looking towards Netley Abbey; view of Bristol harbour. National Maritime Museum, Greenwich (23): Battle of Quiberon Bay 1759; repulse of French fleet in Frigate Bay, St. Kitts 1782; Battle of the Saints 1782; the Defence *at the Battle of the First of June 1794; the* Brunswick *after the battle 1794; the* Brunswick *breaking the line 1794; the* Brunswick *and* Vengeur *engaged at the Battle of the First of June 1794; the* Captain *capturing the* San Nicolas *and* San Josef *1797; capture of the* Resistance *and* Constance *1797; capture of Trinidad 1797; Battle of the Nile 1798; Cutting out of the* Hermione *1799; Battle of Copenhagen 1801; Battle of Trafalgar: Breaking the line; the end of the battle 1805; Duckworth's action off San Domingo 1806; H.M.S.* Triton; *Chatham Dockyard; London, Deptford Dockyard; Plymouth Dockyard; Woolwich Dockyard; East India fleet wearing 1807; Nelson's commands and flagships; in addition, approximately 200 watercolours, drawings, etc., and two illustrated log books of the Lloyd. Shipley Art Gallery, Gateshead (1): coastal scene.*

POCOCK, William Innes Lieut. R.N. 1783-1836

Born Bristol, June 1783, died Reading, March 13th, 1836. A son of Nicholas Pocock (q.v.), he followed his father's example and went to sea at the age of twelve. He seems to have been in merchantmen for some years, during which time he was involved in actions with the French. In 1805 he joined H.M. Frigate *Astrea* as a volunteer and fought the rest of the long Revolutionary Wars in the Royal Navy. In 1811 he became a lieutenant, but with the end of the wars in 1814 his employment at sea also ended.

His paintings are in his father's style and palette, so he may have been his pupil. During his service he kept sketchbooks of the places he visited and in 1815 he took advantage of the national interest in St. Helena to publish a set of five plates of the island with a lengthy description, while Napoleon was actually on his way there. The sketches for these were made when his ship, the *St. Albans,* put into St. Helena to repair storm damage about 1809. He did not like the place any more than Napoleon was destined to do.

The National Maritime Museum, Greenwich, has an oil of Louis XVIII in the yacht *Royal Sovereign* returning to France in 1814, and another, attributed, of the Battle of Copenhagen in 1801. The collection also holds sketch books and a large collection of watercolours.

PLATE: 251.

POMPE, Gerrit

Painter working in the second half of the 17th century. Said to be a pupil of Ludolf Bakhuizen (q.v.), his paintings are crisp and clear in style and well crafted, and he is like Bakhuizen in his lighting effects. Unlike so many marine painters, who tend to increase the dramatic impact of their ships by over-masting them, Pompe's ships are distinctly under-hatted, that is short in the masts and spars, a very distinctive feature which makes his work easily identifiable.

There are good examples at the National Maritime Museum, Greenwich, and at the Boymans van Beuningen Museum, Rotterdam. The one at Greenwich is signed "G. Pompe".

PLATE: 131.

PORCELLIS, Jan c.1584-1632

A product of the Spanish Netherlands, his family had Spanish origins. He married H.C. Vroom's daughter in 1605 and is believed to have been his pupil at Rotterdam. He has strong claims to be the innovator of the new Dutch realist palette; this moved away from the more colourful mannerist Flemish one and adopted a system of fairly low key, closely knit tonal values, based on the whole on the "pearl grey skies of Holland". This was to develop into an almost monochrome palette with some of the painters of the next generation, such as Simon de Vlieger and, in the extreme, with Jan van Goyen (qq.v.).

In his earlier works Porcellis' figures have a squat appearance reminiscent of Pieter Brueghel, though in later works they have a more 17th century look. He moved to Antwerp, where he became Master of the Guild in 1617, and then to Amsterdam and Haarlem, before finally settling at Soutermonde, near Leyden, where he died in 1632. His best known pupils were his son, Julius (q.v.), born in Rotterdam about 1609 and, much more important, Simon de Vlieger, born in the same city about 1600.

PLATES: 41, 42; COLOUR PLATE: V.

PORCELLIS, Julius **c.1609-1645**

Born at Rotterdam about 1609, died at Leyden in 1645. Son and pupil of Jan Porcellis (q.v.), Julius followed his father in the painting of close-toned pictures, but whereas his father favoured greys or browns, Julius affected bright creams or golds. His work is much inferior to his father's and can often be identified by his characteristic if somewhat unconvincing figure paintings. His paintings are not now common and have been confused with the father's because they both signed "I.P.".

PLATE: 44.

POWELL, Charles Martin **1775-1824**

Born in Chichester, he was a self-taught artist who was at some time a sailor. He adopted a Dutch style of painting, and though much of his output was small pot boilers for dealers, he was also capable of fine work. He exhibited at the Royal Academy between 1807 and 1821, and at the British Institution between 1813 and 1821. Subjects shown at the latter included historical subjects. He left a wife and eight children in poverty. Died May 31st, 1824.

PLATE: 362.

EXAMPLES: Shipley Art Gallery, Gateshead (1). National Maritime Museum, Greenwich (3): a two-decker running into Port Mahon; fishing boats in a breeze and shipping in a calm (pair).

PRESS, Captain Henry **1844-1920**

Born in England, February 26th, 1844, he died in Melbourne, July 26th, 1920. He emigrated first to Auckland, where he became a well known yachtsman. He sailed his yacht *Taniwha* to Melbourne to take part in a regatta and settled at Williamstown, near Melbourne. He later served for twenty-six years in the Victorian Pilot Service. He was a keen amateur marine painter.

The State Library of Victoria Historical Picture Collection has an oil painting by him called "Hobson's Bay and Williamstown Lighthouse, 1892".

PRESTON, W.

A British ship portraitist working in the fourth quarter of the 19th century. The Peabody Museum of Salem has one painting by him dated 1891.

PRINGLE, James Fulton **1788-1847**

An American marine painter and ship portraitist. The Mariners Museum, Newport News, has a portrait of a Blackballer dated 1841.

PROUT, Samuel F.S.A. **1783-1852**

Born Plymouth, September 17th, 1783; died Denmark Hill, London, February 10th, 1852. In 1796 the East Indiaman *Dutton,* full of troops and passengers, attempted to sail from Plymouth in a gale and was wrecked at the harbour entrance. This occasioned a heroic and successful rescue operation, organised by Captain Sir Edward Pellew and watched by a large crowd, which included the twelve year old Samuel Prout. This event made a strong impression on him, and he is said to have made many drawings of it. When he was eighteen a school friend, Benjamin Haydon, introduced him to the antiquarian John Britton, who employed him to make drawings of local architecture and then took him to London to study and improve.

Although he lived a normal span, he was dogged by ill-health from youth, and in 1805 he returned to Plymouth because London did not suit him. However, in 1808 he was back, and exhibiting at the Royal Academy, British Institution and especially the Old Watercolour Society.

Until 1818 these exhibits included a few marines and coastal views, but after his first Continental tour, he tended to specialise in scenes of romantic and heroic classical ruins. These are the subjects in which he was most influential and by which he is now best known.

There is a collection of drawings in pencil and watercolours at the National Maritime Museum, Greenwich, and there are also examples, though not necessarily marines, in nearly every major public collection in the country.

PLATE: 335.

PUGET, Pierre **1620-1694**

Born at Château Follet, near Marseilles in 1620. He was the son of a mason and was apprenticed to a ship-builder, for whom he executed some carved decorations for a ship. This was when he was sixteen; the following year he set out to work his way to Florence and Rome. He stayed in Florence about three years, during which time he helped with some ceiling paintings in the Pitti. He returned to Marseilles in 1643 and went back to designing and carving ship decoration, as well as painting portraits. Later he had commissions from the town, and from Aix and Toulon. About 1656 a serious illness obliged him to give up painting but for some reason allowed him to continue his sculptures. He died at Fougette, near Marseilles, in 1694.

None of the public galleries seems to have any of his marines but there is a fine drawing of a ship, showing the design of her decorations, in the Fitzwilliam Museum, Cambridge.

PURVIS, T.G.

A British ship portraitist working in Cardiff in the last quarter of the 19th century and the first quarter of the present one. He may have moved eventually to Greenwich.

The National Maritime Museum, Greenwich, has two examples, and the National Museum of Wales, Cardiff, has one.

PLATE: 606.

PYNE, James Baker **1800-1870**

Born in Bristol on December 5th, 1800; died in London on July 29th, 1870. His family intended him for the law and presumably did not encourage his predilection for painting, since he had to teach himself. He remained painting around Bristol until he was thirty-five, when he moved to London.

He had by then already been exhibiting at the British Institution since 1828 and he now started to exhibit at the Royal Academy from 1836. He also exhibited at the Society of British Artists, which elected him a member in 1842, and of which he was subsequently a vice-president.

He became an admirer and to some extent an imitator of Turner (q.v.) in his use of light effects. He was chiefly a coastal painter and only one of the examples in the Bristol Art Gallery could be described as a marine. The National Maritime Museum, Greenwich, has a view of St. Michael's Mount.

PLATE: 420.

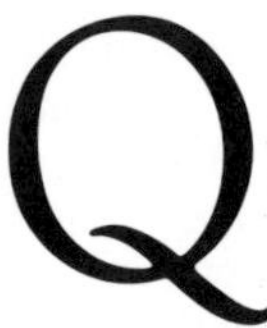

QUA SEES
A Chinese ship portraitist, working in Hong Kong in the third quarter of the 19th century. The Peabody Museum of Salem has an oil by him.

R

RAIGERSFELD, Rear Admiral Jeffrey Baron de **c.1770-1844**
He passed his examination for lieutenant in 1793, was promoted to commander in 1797, and made a post-captain in 1802; he became rear admiral in the retirement list in 1837. No details of his service are recorded.

He exhibited paintings at the Royal Academy as an honorary contributor in 1798, 1801, 1809 and 1811. One of the two paintings he exhibited in 1801 is now in the National Maritime Museum, Greenwich, and is of fair quality. It is entitled "View of Brest Harbour: the *Montagu,* one of the squadron of the Earl of St. Vincent, forcing the enemy's ships to shift their ground from Bertheaume Bay, August 16th 1800."

PLATE: 295.

RALEIGH, Charles Sidney **1830-1925**
This long-lived American ship portraitist worked in Monument, Masssachussetts. As well as ship portraits, he made his living by house, sign, carriage and ornamental painting. The Peabody Museum of Salem has three oil paintings by him, one dated 1877, another 1879. The New Bedford Whaling Museum has twenty-two works.

RAMSEY, G.
A British ship portraitist working in the last quarter of the 19th century. The National Maritime Museum, Greenwich, has a pair of oils, one of a Harwich sailing trawler and the other of a steam trawler.

RANDALL, Maurice.
The National Maritime Museum, Greenwich, has two large portraits of Union Castle Line ships, the *Arundel Castle* launched in 1921, and the *Caernarvon Castle* launched in 1926, which appear to have been painted in the 1920s.

READY, William James Durant **1823-1873**
Born in London, May 11th, 1823. A self-taught painter, mainly of south coast scenes, who did not exhibit until he was nearly forty, showing work at the British Institution in 1861, 1862 and 1863, and at the Royal Academy in 1867. According to Graves he signed himself, for some reason, W.F. Durant; according to others it was W.F.R. and W.R. In the example illustrated, the last two letters of the initials are J.R. He also exhibited a picture at Suffolk Street, and is said to have been a friend of the architectural painter David Roberts. At some point he went to America, where he lived for five years. He died in Brighton, November 29th, 1873.

PLATE: 519.

REDMORE, Henry **1820-1887**
Born and died in Hull. He lived and painted all his life in the north-east and had his studio in Regent Street, Hull. The quality of his work was good, with a pleasing palette tending to grey. He only exhibited once at the Royal Academy, in 1868, but may have put up pictures in other years. He and John Ward must rank as the two best painters of the Hull school, though not in the same tradition.

PLATES: 538, 539, 540.

EXAMPLES: The Ferens Art Gallery, Hull (4): Bamburgh Castle; boats off Whitby; fire at sea; shipwrecked.

REIMERS, Heinrich **1824-1900**
A ship portraitist working in Kiel in the second half of the 19th century. There are examples in the Maritime Museum, Bergen, the Altonaer Museum, Hamburg, and the National Maritime Museum, Stockholm.

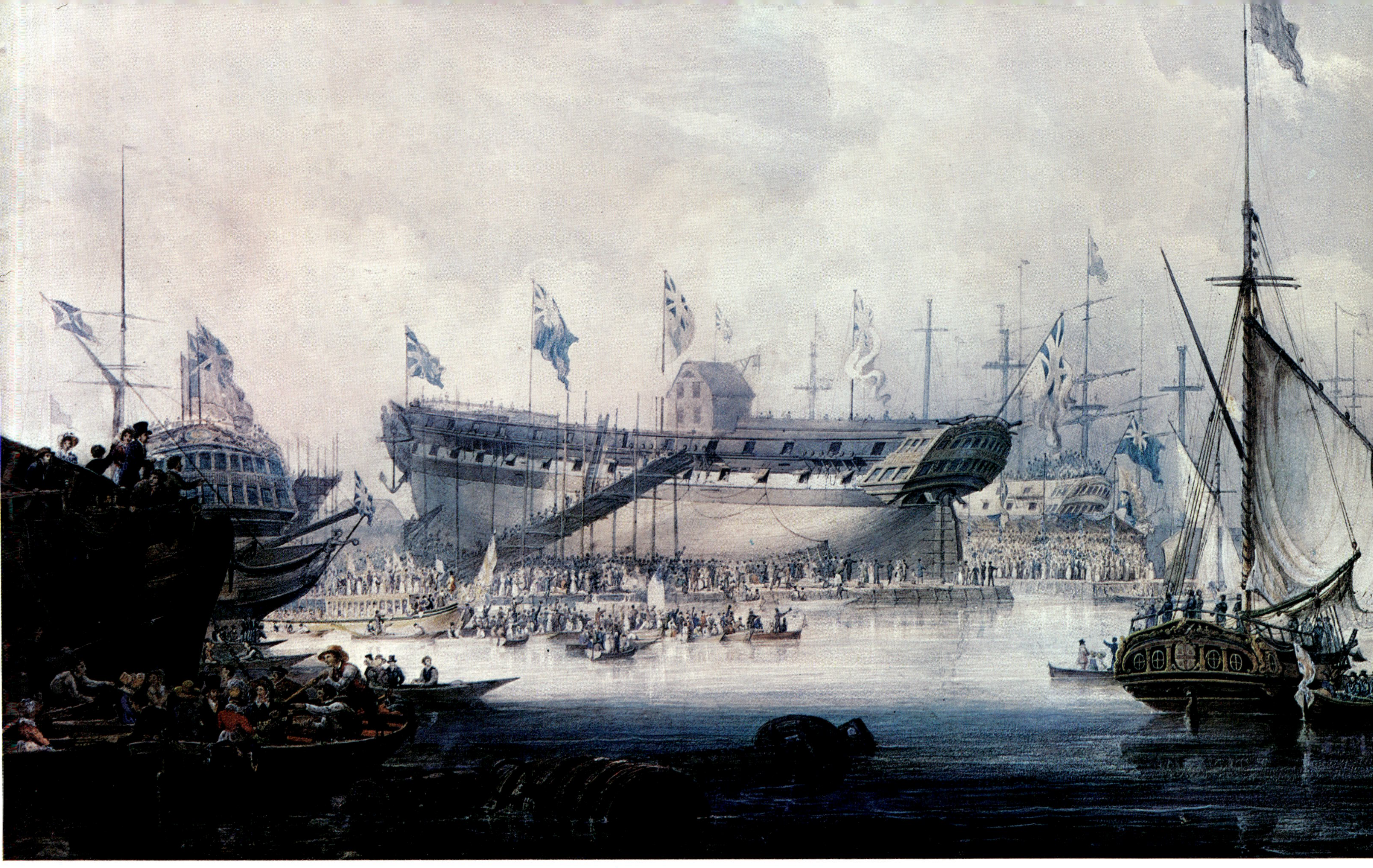

Colour Plate XX. William John Huggins, 1781-1845. "The launch of the East Indiaman *Edinburgh* at Blackwall yard in 1825." Watercolour. National Maritime Museum, Greenwich.

REINAGLE, George Philip **1802-1835**

He was a pupil of his father, Ramsay Richard Reinagle. In 1827 he accompanied Sir Edward Codrington's fleet during the campaign in the eastern Mediterranean over the issue of Greek independence, and was present at the Battle of Navarino. On his return he engraved two sets of lithographs, which were published by Colnaghi. One edition of seven plates deals with the events in the Bay of Patras leading up to the battle, and an edition of thirteen plates covers the battle itself.

In 1833 he accompanied Sir Charles Napier, when he commanded the naval force of Don Pedro which defeated the squadron of Don Miguel in the Portuguese Civil War. Two pairs of lithographs by Reinagle record this.

He first exhibited at the Royal Academy in 1822 but a promising career was cut short by his early death on December 6th, 1835.

PLATE: 403.

EXAMPLE: National Maritime Museum, Greenwich (1): the Battle of Navarino 1827.

RENAULT, Luigi P

An Italian ship portraitist working at Leghorn in the third quarter of the 19th century. The Altonaer Museum, Hamburg, has one oil; the Mariners Museum, Newport News, has two oils one dated 1858 and one 1873; the Peabody Museum of Salem has two oils both dated 1868, as well as a watercolour dated 1853 and a watercolour and gouache attributed to him.

PLATE: 628.

RENAULT, Michele

A ship portraitist working at Leghorn in the second quarter of the 19th century. The Altonaer Museum, Hamburg, has a watercolour.

RESMANN, Francesco

A ship portraitist working in Trieste in the early part of the 19th century. The Peabody Museum of Salem has a watercolour by him.

REUTERDAHL, Henry **1870-1925**

Born in Malmö, Sweden, on August 12th, 1870. Without much formal training he nevertheless grew up to be an illustrator, and at the age of twenty-one was sent by the magazine *Svea* on an assignment to Chicago to cover the World's Columbian Exhibition. It was on this visit to the States that he decided to make his home there.

He first worked as western artist for *Leslie's Weekly,* but his love of the sea and ships drove him east to New York. His particular interest was the navy, and he first caught the public eye with paintings of the Spanish-American War, reproduced in *Harper's Weekly* in 1897. In 1901 *Collier's Weekly* sent him to Europe to study the navies of the great powers, and in England he met Fred T. Jane, and became the American editor of *Jane's Fighting Ships.*

A number of his friends among American naval officers, particularly William Sims, were critical of some aspects of naval administration and warship design, and Reuterdahl wrote an article in *McClure's Magazine* in 1908, reflecting their views, which caused a Congressional investigation. He often sailed with the navy, and was a passenger and artist with the Great White Fleet, aboard the U.S.S. *Minnesota,* when it showed the flag round the world in 1907.

At the beginning of the First World War *Collier's* sent him to London as naval correspondent, and when America entered the war in 1917 he worked for the Navy Publicity Board, and was commissioned a lieutenant in the U.S.N.R.F., later being promoted lieutenant-commander. He designed recruiting posters, ships' camouflage, and painted some huge billboards in Times Square. After the war the Secretary of the Navy commissioned him to paint a series of large paintings showing the navy's work during the war. He never completed this task due to the advance of arterio-sclerosis, and he died in Washington, D.C., on December 20th, 1925.

As a painter he had a rather ebullient style, reminiscent of Frank Brangwyn, but though his paintings are strongly stylised, his knowledge and interest in the ships in his paintings ensured that individual vessels and classes are clearly identifiable.

Examples of his work may be seen at the United States Naval Academy Museum, Annapolis, and the Navy Memorial Museum, Washington Navy Yard.

PLATE: 626.

REYGERS, Johannes Hubertus **1767-1849**

Born in Gorinchem in 1767, Reygers was a self-taught artist, and later became the drawing master at the Academy in Middelburg. He was also a ship modeller. He died in Middelburg in 1849. There are watercolours by him in the Scheepvaart Museum, Amsterdam.

RICCI, Marco **1676-1729**

Born in Belluno, Italy in 1676. A landscape painter, who also painted storms at sea which appear to have been influenced by those of Pieter Mulier the Younger (Tempesta), whom he may have known. He came to England in 1710 but did not manage to attract success. He committed suicide in Venice in 1729.

PLATE: 104.

EXAMPLES: State Museum for Fine Art, Copenhagen (1): Christ on the Sea of Galilee. Kunsthistorisches Museum, Vienna (1): storm.

RICKETTS, Charles Robert **fl.c.1870**

He first exhibited at the Royal Academy from an address in Westminster in 1870, the work being "Discovery of the North West Passage." In 1871 he showed a wreck scene and other marines followed in 1873 and 1874. Apart from these and the fact that his son, Charles de Lourey Ricketts, was born in Geneva in 1866, we know no more about him. His style was close to that of Charles Seaforth.

RIEGEN, Nicolaas **1827-1889**

Born in Amsterdam, May 31st, 1827, he was a self-taught painter of seascapes and river scenes in a style characteristic of the early part of the century. He exhibited in Amsterdam and The Hague from 1853 to 1878, and at Leeuwarden in 1855. Died Amsterdam, November 27th, 1889.

The Rijksmuseum, Amsterdam, has a painting of a brig in a swell.

PLATE: 507.

RIETSCHOOF, Hendrik **1687-1746**

Born in Hoorn, 1687, he was the pupil and follower of his father, Jan Claesz (q.v.), with a similar if glossier style. The National Maritime Museum, Greenwich, has two paintings of Dutch shipping off a coast. Died in Koog by Zaandam in 1746.

PLATES: 141, 142.

RIETSCHOOF, Jan Claesz **c.1652-1719**

Born in Hoorn, about 1652, he was first a pupil of the Hoorn painter Abraham Liedts. He then must have moved to Amsterdam, as he became the pupil and closest imitator of Ludolf Bakhuizen. As his son Hendrik was born in Hoorn, he apparently returned to live and work in his native town after completing his studies, and he died there in 1719.

PLATES: 138, 139, 140.

EXAMPLES: Rijksmuseum, Amsterdam (2): ships in harbour in a calm; ships in harbour in gusty weather (a pair). National Maritime Museum, Greenwich (3): Dutch ships off the north of the Scheldt; Dutch man-of-war off a jetty; Dutch flute off a harbour. The Hermitage, Leningrad (1): a marine. National Museum, Stockholm (1): Dutch harbour scene with shipping and figures.

ROBERTO, Luigi

An Italian ship portraitist of a rather primitive style, working in Naples in the second half of the 19th century. The Peabody Museum of Salem has one signed watercolour dated 1883 and two watercolours and a gouache attributed to him.

ROBERTSON, William A.

An American painter and draughtsman, working in the second and third quarters of the present century. The Peabody Museum of Salem possesses a handsome oil of Admiral Byrd's *Bear* in the ice, dated 1960, and three watercolours.

ROBINS, H.

Paintings of marine subjects around Portsmouth and dating from the last quarter of the 19th century turn up from time to time, signed by this artist. One painting shows the dismasted *Eurydice* being towed into Portsmouth in 1878, after capsizing off the Isle of Wight.

ROBINS, Thomas Sewell **c.1809-1880**

On April 22nd 1829 Robins was admitted into the Royal Academy Schools where his professor for painting was Thomas Phillips, and lecturer for perspective, J.M.W. Turner.

In 1839 he was elected an associate of the New Watercolour Society, and exhibited 317 works there before he resigned in 1866. He was mainly a watercolour artist, though he did paint in oils. He is chiefly remembered for his yachting scenes; he also travelled abroad to the Mediterranean in about 1850, to Holland and to the Rhine in 1857, France in 1858 and Antwerp in 1860.

He exhibited six pictures at the Royal Academy between 1829 and 1874, and was a much more regular exhibitor at the British Institution between 1832 and 1863. He also exhibited at Suffolk Street. He died in Kensington, London, on August 9th, 1880.

Examples can be seen at the Haworth Museum, Accrington; Williamson Art Gallery, Birkenhead; Birmingham Art Gallery; Cartwright Hall, Bradford; Preston Manor, Brighton; National Maritime Museum, Greenwich; Victoria and Albert Museum, London; Newport Art Gallery; City of Portsmouth Museum and Art Gallery.

PLATE: 486.

ROBINSON, Gregory D.S.C. **1876-1967**

Born at St. Anthony, Cornwall, February 22nd, 1876. The son of an officer in the Royal Navy, he went to Christ's Hospital with a grant from a foundation for the sons of naval officers. While he was there one of his ship drawings was chosen by Queen Victoria, who gave him a gold pencil case. He afterwards did a three-year course at the Royal Academy schools.

The better to fit himself for life as a marine painter he made two long voyages, firstly in his father's ship H.M.S. *Wye,* to the West Coast of Africa and Ascension Island, and then round the world in the four-masted barque *Carradale.* In 1905 he married and settled down to raise a family at the Quay House at Hamble. During the First World War he was a lieutenant in the R.N.V.R. and won the D.S.C. for operations against German submarines.

As well as a painter he was a keen naval historian and a founder member of the Society for Nautical Research. In his later years he lived mostly in Woking so that he could be nearer to the Public Record Office, where he spent much of his time. He wrote and illustrated *Ships that have made History,* 1936, and *The Elizabethan Ship,* 1936, as well as many articles for the *Mariners Mirror.* His choice of subjects reflected his interests. He died on May 10th, 1967.

The National Maritime Museum, Greenwich, has drawings by him.

RODMELL, G. Hudson R.I., R.S.M.A. **b.1896**

Born in Hull in 1896, he went to the Hull School of Art with a scholarship. During the First World War, when he was rejected for military service on medical grounds, he worked in a lithographic printers and later as a draughtsman in the Royal Engineers. In 1919 he returned to the Hull School of Art for two years.

He was interested in designing shipping posters, in which his experience of printing stood him in good stead. He undertook work for many shipping firms. He has exhibited over many years at the Royal Academy, Royal Institute of Painters in Watercolours, Royal Society of British Artists, Society of Graphic Art, Salon de Marine, Paris. He was a founder member of the Society of Marine Artists, and the National Maritime Museum, Greenwich, has his diploma work for this body, "Gale Force 8", on loan.

ROPES, George **1788-1819**

An early American ship portraitist and painter of sea fights, who worked in Salem. He was deaf and dumb. While not untalented, his paintings are stylised, somewhat primitive and fairly close to his master, Michele Corne. The Peabody Museum of Salem has five oils, dated between 1805 and 1815, four oils attributed, one watercolour and gouache dated 1818, two watercolours dated 1811 and 1816, and two attributed, and two gouaches attributed.

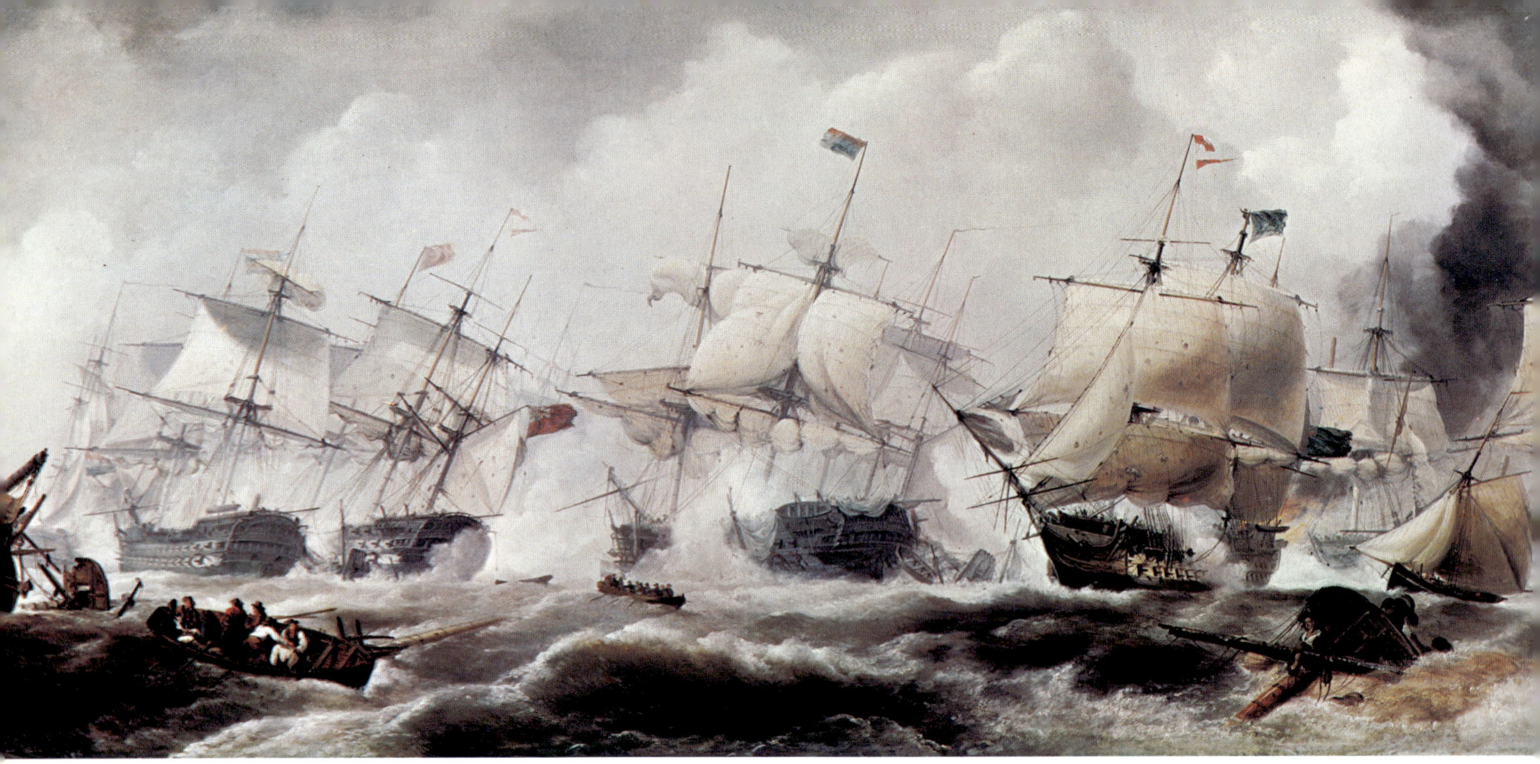

Colour Plate XXI. George Chambers, Senior, 1803-1840. "The Battle of Camperdown, 1797." Private collection (on loan to the National Maritime Museum, Greenwich).

Colour Plate XXII. Jules Achilles Noël, 1815-1881. "Napoleon III receiving Queen Victoria at Cherbourg, August 5th, 1858." National Maritime Museum, Greenwich.

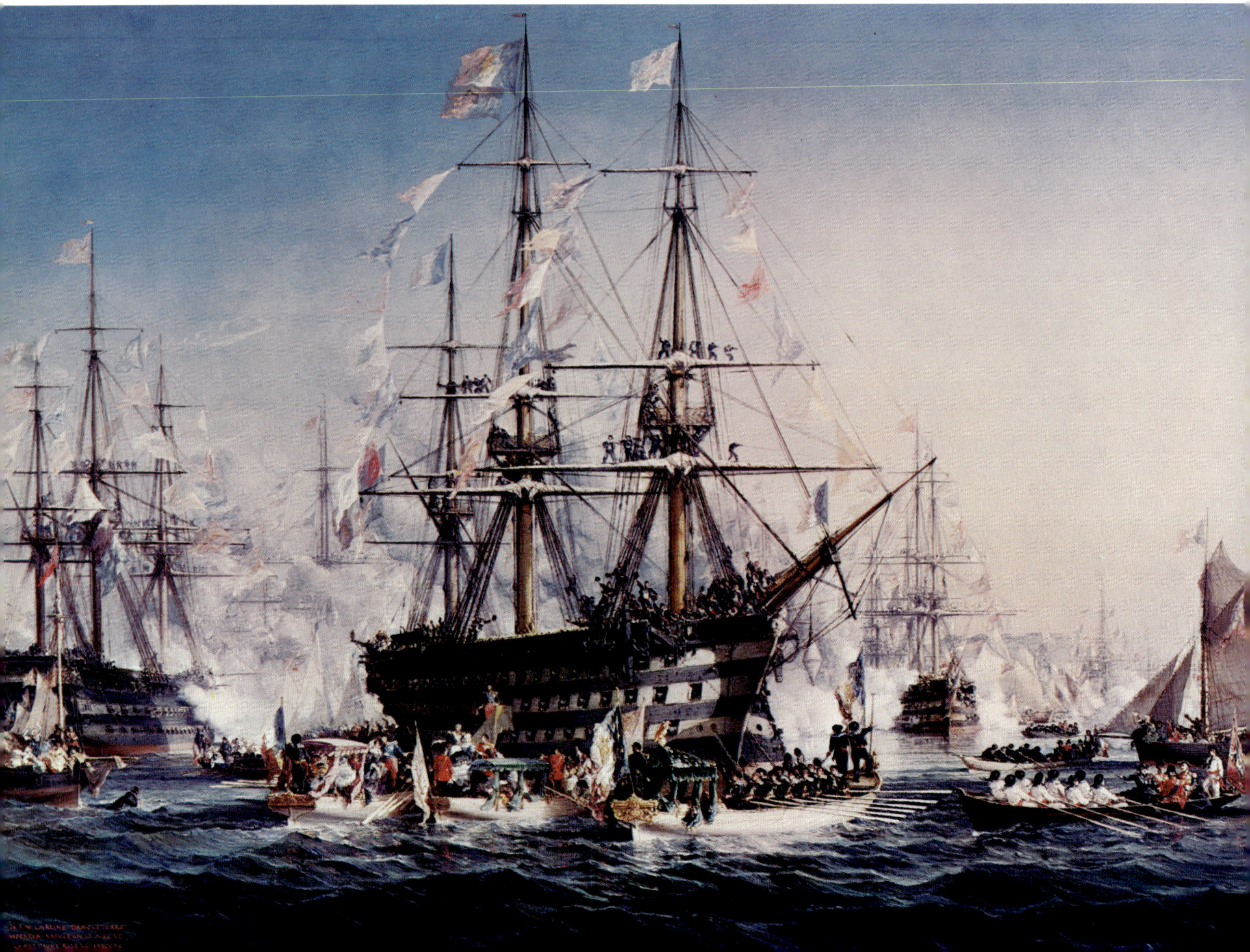

ROSNER, Charles **1894-aft.1975**

Born in Langendorf, Germany in 1894, Rosner was the son of a doctor, and as a child was taken on holiday to the port of Kolberg, a visit which triggered off in him a lifelong love of ships and the sea. He served in sailing ships, and had been five times round Cape Horn before he left the sea at the beginning of the First World War at Iquique in Peru, and worked in a copper mine for the rest of the war.

He then worked his way to the United States via Canada, where he married and settled in New York, an illegal immigrant. He took up full-time marine painting of historic sail subjects of a high standard, but never achieved the recognition he perhaps deserved. Sometime during his life in America he changed the spelling of his name from Rosner to Rossner. He died in New York sometime after February 1975.

There is a painting by him of the American barque *Adam W. Speiss,* dated 1933, in the Mariners Museum, Newport News.

PLATE: 654.

ROSSEL DE CERCY, Auguste Louis **1736-1804**
Capitaine le Marquis de

Born in Dompierre-sur-Mer, 1736. It is a severe reflection on the state of naval history painting in France in the late 18th century that the leading, and apparently only, practitioner should have been this naval officer and amateur artist.

The best that can be said of his efforts is that, being a seaman, he understood his subject, but after that his work can only be described as primitive. One of the problems in this subject area was that people only commissioned pictures of their victories and the public only bought prints of them if their country had won. As the French nearly always lost there were no commissions. By the same token, the painting of naval battles in England and the subsequent sale of engravings flourished exceedingly. It happened though, that during the American War of Independence the French navy did better than usual, especially out in India, where the Balli de Suffren fought Sir Edward Hughes to a draw in five separate actions. Consequently, the French Ministry of Marine was encouraged to commission some battle pieces in 1786. That their choice should have fallen on the gallant Marquis suggests that naval and social considerations were uppermost in the decision, plus the lack of a native alternative. They would have done better to have asked French-born Dominic Serres in London.

Rossel de Cercy died in Paris in 1804.

EXAMPLES: Musée de la Marine, Paris (10): capture of the frigate Minerva *by the* Concorde, *1778; capture of the frigate* Fox *by the* Junon, *1778; action between Rodney and de Guichen, 1780; action between the* Belle-Poule *and the* Arethusa, *1778; capture of the* Argo *by the* Nymphe; *the* Amphitrite, *action off Martinique, 1779; action between the* Scipion *and the* London, *1782; action between Suffren and Johnstone at Porto Praya, 1781; action between Suffren and Hughes off Negapatam, 1782; action between Suffren and Hughes off Gondelour, 1783.*

ROSSNER, Charles *see* **ROSNER, Charles**

ROUSSEL, C.

An American ship portraitist working in New Orleans in the first quarter of the 19th century. A portrait of the corsair *Alligator,* Captain Sam Griggs, exists; it is dated 1813 and is in a style very reminiscent of Joseph Ange Antoine Roux (q.v.). Thus it may be that Roussel was an immigrant to New Orleans from Marseilles.

PLATE: 328.

ROUX, Francois Geoffroi **1811-1882**

Born in Marseilles, he was the son and pupil of Joseph Ange Antoine Roux (q.v.), and worked on ship portraits in watercolour in the family workshop devoted to that purpose. His work is very similar to that of his father and brothers. He died in Marseilles in 1882.

The Musée de la Marine, Paris, has several watercolours; the Peabody Museum of Salem has five watercolours.

PLATE: 309.

ROUX, Frédéric **1805-1870**

Born in Marseilles in 1805, he was another son and pupil of Joseph Ange Antoine, who also worked with his father and brother, turning out high quality ship portraits in watercolour. He died in Marseilles in 1870.

The Musée de la Marine, Paris, has several watercolours; the Peabody Museum of Salem has fourteen watercolours, plus pencil drawings.

PLATE: 308.

ROUX, Joseph **1725-?1793**

Founding father of the Roux family of marine painters in Marseilles, and presumably the father and master of Joseph Ange Antoine. He died in Marseilles.

The Peabody Museum of Salem has two paintings: action between the *Serapis* and the *Bonhomme Richard,* 1779; action between a British East Indiaman and a French man-of-war.

PLATE: 256.

ROUX, Joseph Ange Antoine **1765-1835**

Born in Marseilles, he was the son of Joseph (q.v.) and the most successful of this family of marine painters; in turn he was the father and master of Mathieu Antoine, Frédéric and François Geoffroi (qq.v.) and his work was the inspiration for a generation of French and Italian ship portraitists, though his own productions outstripped them in scope and quality. He died in Marseilles in 1835.

He and his family were much patronised by American sea captains and owners, and many of their works, nearly all watercolours, are now in the U.S.A.

The Maritime Museum, Kronborg Castle has several portraits by him. The Mariners Museum, Newport News, has three watercolours, one a brig dated 1825. The Musée de la Marine, Paris, has several, including some actions; the Peabody Museum of Salem, thirty watercolours, two figures by the signal station at Montaudis, Philip de Saumarez's action with the French in Algeciras Bay in 1801, view of Montevideo, the rest ship portraits.

PLATE: 304, 305, 306.

ROUX, Louis **1817-1903**

A French ship portraitist working in Marseilles but not related to the family of Roux also engaged in ship portraiture.

The Mariners Museum, Newport News, has three watercolours and the Peabody Museum of Salem has five watercolours.

PLATES: 311, 312.

ROUX, Mathieu Antoine **1799-1872**

Born in Marseilles he was son and pupil of Joseph Ange Antoine (q.v.). His style is very close to that of his father's and he, too, concentrated on ship portraits in watercolours. He died in Marseilles in 1872.

The National Maritime Museum, Greenwich has five examples; the Peabody Museum of Salem has five watercolours, plus two attributed.

PLATE: 307.

ROUX, Ursula

A member of the French family working in Marseilles. The Peabody Museum of Salem has a watercolour of Marseilles harbour signed and dated 1827.

PLATE: 310.

RUISDAEL, Jacob Isaakszoon van **1628/9-1682**

Born in Haarleem in 1628/9. There is no positive evidence about who taught him but it seems highly likely that he and his cousin, Jacob Solomonsz, were taught by the latter's father, Solomonsz. Other Haarlem painters who are likely candidates were Cornelisz Hendriksz Vroom and Jan Wynaerts. Allardt van Everdingen in nearby Amsterdam has also been mentioned. After his early training he became a Mennonite and lived in their almshouse in Amsterdam in 1659, where he studied surgery.

However, he had shown a talent for painting at an early age and was persuaded by his friend, Nicholas Bercham, to take it up again, which he did with marvellous success. He was primarily a landscape painter but also did some marines, which are generally small vessels in very rough seas. He signed his work predominantly "J.V. Ruisdael", "J", or "J.V.R.", etc. He died in Haarlem in 1682.

PLATES: 123, 124.

EXAMPLES: Museum of Fine Arts, Boston (1): Dutch craft in a rough sea. Royal Museum of Fine Arts, Brussels (1): a rough day on Haarlemmermeer. National Gallery, London (1): Dutch vessels in a fresh breeze on Haarlemmermeer. Frick Collection, New York (1): the quay at Amsterdam. National Museum, Stockholm (1): storm clouds over the sea.

RUISDAEL, Solomon van **1600-1670**

Born in Naarden, he was the uncle, and possibly the master, of Jacob Ruisdael. This great landscape artist painted some river scenes and coastal marines. Examples of these may be found at the museums at Aix la Chapelle, Amiens, Amsterdam (Rijksmuseum), Antwerp, Berlin, Caen, Cologne, Detroit, Grenoble, Leningrad, London (National Gallery), Mayence, Munich, New York (Metropolitan), Rotterdam, Stockholm and Vienna. He died in Haarlem on November 1st, 1670.

PLATE: 122.

RUSSELL, Benjamin **1805-1885**

An American painter of primitive ship portraits. The Peabody Museum of Salem has three signed watercolours and two attributed.

RUSSELL, Edward J. **1835-1906**

An American ship portraitist and painter of historical naval actions of nice quality. The Peabody Museum of Salem has six watercolours, all signed but, curiously enough, all with dates in the early years of the 20th century, and one attributed.

PLATE: 512.

RUST, Johan Adolph **1828-1915**

Born in Amsterdam on April 13th, 1828, he was a pupil of the architectural painter Cornelis Springer and painted good quality seascapes and river scenes, rather in the manner of Schotel and Schoumann. He exhibited in Amsterdam and The Hague between 1853 and 1884, and at Leeuwarden in 1855. He died in Amsterdam on July 28th, 1915.

There are examples in the Rijksmuseum, the Stedelijk Museum and Scheepvaart Museum in Amsterdam; the Teylers-Stichting Museum, Haarlem and the Rijskmuseum, Kroller-Muller, Otterlo.

RYDER, Albert Pinkham **1847-1917**

Born in New Bedford, Massachusetts, on March 19th, 1847, he was a pupil at the National Academy in New York in 1872, became an Associate of it in 1902 and was elected an Academician in 1906. He was a general painter but the Metropolitan Museum in New York has, amongst others, "Workers of the Sea", and the Smithsonian Institute has "The Phantom Ship". The Museum of Fine Arts at Boston has a painting of a woman and a child adrift in a boat, called "Constance". He died in Elmhurst, N.Y., on March 28th, 1917.

RYLANDS, J.

A British ship portraitist working in Hull in the second quarter of the 19th century. A portrait exists of the merchant ship *Haidée,* dated 1849, painted in a rather primitive style.

S

SACHSE, Jochen
A living Hamburg painter of ship portraits, a number of which have appeared as colour reproductions.

SAILMAKER, Isaac **1633/4-1721**
Born in Scheveningen, this painter was almost an exact contemporary of the younger Willem van de Velde (q.v.). Vertue says he came very young to London and was a pupil of George Geldorp; also that he did a painting for Oliver Cromwell of the fleet off Mardyke when that town was taken.

When the van de Veldes and some other Dutch artists of superior talent came to work in England in the early 1670s he was eclipsed, but he outlived them all to go on painting into his extreme old age.

For a long time the lack of a signed painting by Sailmaker caused experts to doubt the traditional attribution of his works as not being good enough, and instead a hand that has now been identified as that of Jacob Knyff was preferred.

The identification of Jacob Knyff's work left a vacuum which fortunately was shortly afterwards filled when a well-documented Sailmaker painting of Rudyard's Eddystone lighthouse turned up and proved that the traditional identification had been the correct one all the time.

What is puzzling about the alleged span of his work is that existing identifiable works all appear to date from the last quarter of the 17th century and the first quarter of the 18th century.

Sailmaker died in London in 1721.

PLATES: 175, 176, 177, 178.

EXAMPLES: National Maritime Museum, Greenwich (9): Battle of Malaga 1704; painting of the English men-of-war, Assurance, Elizabeth, Tiger *and* Fairfax; *the first-rate* Britannia *of 1689; portrait of an East Indiaman; portrait of a smack rigged yacht; the East India Company Yard at Deptford; shipping in the Thames; shipping off a castle; Rudyard's Eddystone lighthouse (on loan).*

SALM, Adriaen van **c.1660-1720**
He was one of the last artists to specialise in the art of the grisaille or *penschilderen* picture. These were drawings in ink with a reed pen on gesso-prepared panels or canvases. As his earliest work appears to date from about 1690, he was probably born in the 1660s. Although he did some historical pictures of sea battles, he concentrated on depicting merchantmen, whaling and herring fishing scenes. He was fairly prolific in an art that was very painstaking and, though expert, his work comes nowhere near that of the elder Willem van de Velde, nor even that of his own contemporaries, Cornelisz Mooy or Cornelisz Bouwmeester. He was the father and master of Roelof van Salm (q.v.). He signed "A. Salm" or "V. Salm". He died in Delftshaven in 1720.

PLATES: 169, 170.

EXAMPLES: National Maritime Museum, Greenwich (17): Battle of Barfleur 1692; Forbin's attempt against Scotland 1708; five whaling scenes; four of the herring fleet; two of shipping off Rotterdam; one of shipping off Delftshaven; two harbour scenes; ships in a gale. Ferens Art Gallery, Hull (1): view of Leuvehaven, Rotterdam. Hermitage, Leningrad (8): Battle of Barfleur; Battle of Malaga; English ship rigged royal yacht; view of a city; whaling scene; herring fleet; shipbuilding; launch of a ship. Summer Palace, Leningrad (2): merchantmen off Petrograd. Victoria and Albert Museum, London (2): yachts in a breeze; naval engagements. Mariners Museum, Newport News (1): whaling scene. Prins Hendrik Museum, Rotterdam (3): flute off a rock in a gale; ship weighing anchor; merchant ship. Kendall Whaling Museum, Sharon, Mass., has at least one whaling scene.

SALM, Roelof van **1688-1765**
Born in Delftshaven, he was the pupil and second son of Adriaen van Salm (q.v.), and followed his father's style so closely that only the signature on the early works differentiates him from his father. In his later works the style of the ships date the pictures after the father's death. He signed his work "R.V. Salm". Roelof was the last significant Dutch artist to practise the art of making grisaille pictures. He died in Prinsland.

PLATES: 171, 172.

EXAMPLES: National Maritime Museum, Greenwich (5): three of the herring fleet; two of whalers. Prins Hendrik Museum, Rotterdam (1): sea battle. Peabody Museum of Salem (1): whalers.

SALMON, J.
It is strange that so good a painter should be so obscure. It was a J. Salmon who exhibited "On the Coast of Norfolk" at the British Institution in 1849 and, in 1853, "View near Tarnworth", both from an address in Camden Town, London. A J.F. Salmon exhibited a picture called "Near Ryde" at the Royal Academy in 1843 from an address in Prospect Place, which might be Finchley or Tottenham, both in London. The illustrated example is signed and dated "J. Salmon 1861".

PLATE: 531.

SALMON, Robert **1775-c.1845**
Born in Whitehaven in October/November 1775, he was the son of Francis Saloman, who was apparently a Whitehaven jeweller. We know little about his early life until he turns up in Liverpool in June 1806 at the age of thirty. Perhaps his twenties were spent in his father's shop, or perhaps he had been at sea, as his paintings show that he well understood how a sailing ship worked. He changed the spelling of his name from Saloman to Salmon.

He took to numbering his paintings, and against his No. 1, the Battle of Trafalgar, he noted "The first picture I painted". He must have meant the first picture he painted in Liverpool, for there are earlier dated examples. The painting of a dismasted brig under jury rig off Whitehaven, is dated 1802, and the style is already mature. So is the East Indiaman *Warley* off Blackwall dated 1804, which indicates he was in London at that time.

He remained in Liverpool until April 1811, when he moved

to Greenock. After that he moved back to Liverpool in October 1822, then to Greenock in 1826, to London in 1827, and in that year to Southampton, North Shields and Liverpool, whence he emigrated to America, arriving in Boston about New Year's Day, 1829. He remained in Boston until 1840, where he built up a successful practice, though it is curious to note from his inventory how many of the subjects are British scenes.

By 1840 his eyesight was failing, restricting his output, so he left Boston to return to Europe; we then lose sight of him, except that some small Italian views have surfaced, the latest dated 1845. His work was exhibited at a Boston exhibition of living artists in 1848; whether this is a true indication that he was still alive is uncertain but it was known there that he was already dead in 1851. Though he accepted many commissions for ship portraits, he had a greater range that that. His style is very individual. The ships themselves are painted with a precision and clarity of tone that is reminiscent of the Roux family, while his seas have a distinct formality, carefully crafted and disciplined in a quite individual style.

In Boston he was well regarded as a painter but thought to be an eccentric, solitary and irascible man. He had one pupil, a nephew called John Salmon, who came out to Boston to join him. Not surprisingly this did not work out, and the pupil left his uncle. His inventory lists 999 paintings up to 1840, but these do not include those painted after that date or before 1806.

PLATES: 338, 339, 340.

EXAMPLES: United States Naval Academy Museum, Annapolis, Maryland (2): North Shields, Co. Durham; Boston Harbour. Museum of Fine Arts, Boston (11): a British fleet off Algiers; the Ceres *privateer, a cutter and a lugger off North Shields; the ship* Duncan; *Plymouth Sound; Rainsford Island, Boston Harbour; rocks at Nahant; ship aground; south sea whaling; another whaling scene; storm at sea. The Boston Society (1): the wharves of Boston. Glasgow Museums and Art Galleries (2): launch of the* Christian; *a snow off Greenock. National Maritime Museum, Greenwich (5): the* Ariel *snow; a packet off Liverpool; a frigate coming to anchor in the Mersey; the ship* Anne; *the* Warley *East Indiaman. Walker Art Gallery, Liverpool (4): American ships in the Mersey; the ship* Arctic; *Liverpool Town Hall; view of the Mersey. New Britain Museum of American Art, Conn. (1): view of Algiers. Yale Centre for British Art, New Haven, Conn. (5): an Indiaman in the Mersey; the Low lighthouse, North Shields; the* Pomona *off Greenwich; ships in harbour; the* Favorite *off shore. Brooklyn Museum, New York (1): curious rocks on the coast of Scotland. Mariners Museum, Newport News, Virginia (8): the ship* Aristides *off Liverpool; Leith; North Shields; packet brig off Greenock; ship off Birkenhead; ship off Liverpool; shipping in the Mersey; view down the Clyde. Smith College Museum of Art, Northampton, Mass. (1): harbour scene. William A. Farnsworth Art Museum, Rockland, Maine (4): boat on shore; cutting blubber; packet* Bolton; *view of Burn Moore. Peabody Museum of Salem, Mass. (8): ship* Sea Mew; *British ship; Chelsea waterfront Mass.; French lugger in action with a British cutter; two views of the Mersey at Liverpool; packet* United States; *Scottish coast scene. Shelburne Museum, Vermont (2): ships in a storm; shipwreck on a rocky coast. Corcoran Gallery of Art, Washington (2): Boston Harbour; harbour scene. Wichita Art Museum, Kansas (1): harbour scene near Greenock. Worcester Museum of Art, Mass. (1): the ship* Huntress *of Wiscasset.*

SALTZMANN, Carl **1847-1923**

Born in Berlin, he was a pupil of Hermann Eschke, the Berlin marine painter, and studied at the Academy in Berlin, of which he later became the director. In 1878 he accompanied Prince Henry of Prussia on a voyage round the world, and ten years later made a similar voyage with Kaiser Wilhelm II.

He won medals in Berlin, Paris and Chicago. He died in Berlin in 1923.

PLATE: 620.

EXAMPLES: National Maritime Museum, Greenwich (1): the German High Seas Fleet on manoeuvres in 1908.

SANSOM, E.

A British ship portraitist working in the first quarter of the 20th century. The National Maritime Museum, Greenwich, has two paintings of the projected Chilean battleship *Libertad*. In fact, she and her sister ship never went to Chile, but were bought for the Royal Navy as the *Triumph* and *Swiftsure* in 1903.

SARGEANT, H.

A British marine painter working in Portsmouth in the middle of the 19th century. The National Maritime Museum, Greenwich, has a painting of the yacht *America* beating the Marquess of Anglesey's *Pearl* in 1851.

SARTORIUS, C.J. **c.1790-aft.1821**

Possibly born in London since, when he first exhibited at the Royal Academy, his address was the same as John F. Sartorius who painted sporting pictures; thus it is probable that the latter was his father. C.J. Sartorius only exhibited at four of the Royal Academy exhibitions, the last time being in 1821, and all the works shown were marine subjects. There is no known example in a public gallery. He died, possibly in London, after 1821.

SARTORIUS, Francis **1782-aft.1808**

Born in London, he was one of the family of painters better known for its sporting paintings, of whom his father, John N. Sartorius, was one of the most notable. Francis exhibited marines at the Royal Academy from 1799 until 1808, and he probably died shortly afterwards, since no later painting is known. Of his last five exhibits, three were of naval actions, which indicates that he was beginning to establish himself in that field.

PLATE: 298.

EXAMPLES: National Maritime Museum, Greenwich (7): the cutting out of the Curieux *1804; four frigates capturing Spanish treasure ships 1805; a pair of the action of the* Arrow *and* Acheron *against French frigates 1805; the* Curieux *capturing the* Dame Ernouf *1805; Hood's action off Rochefort 1806. The Castle Museum, Norwich (2): a pair of paintings of rescuing the crew of a wrecked vessel with the aid of Captain Manby's rocket and line.*

SATTLER, Herbert **1817-1904**

An American painter; the Peabody Museum of Salem possesses a rather exciting oil of a paddle steamer in a storm.

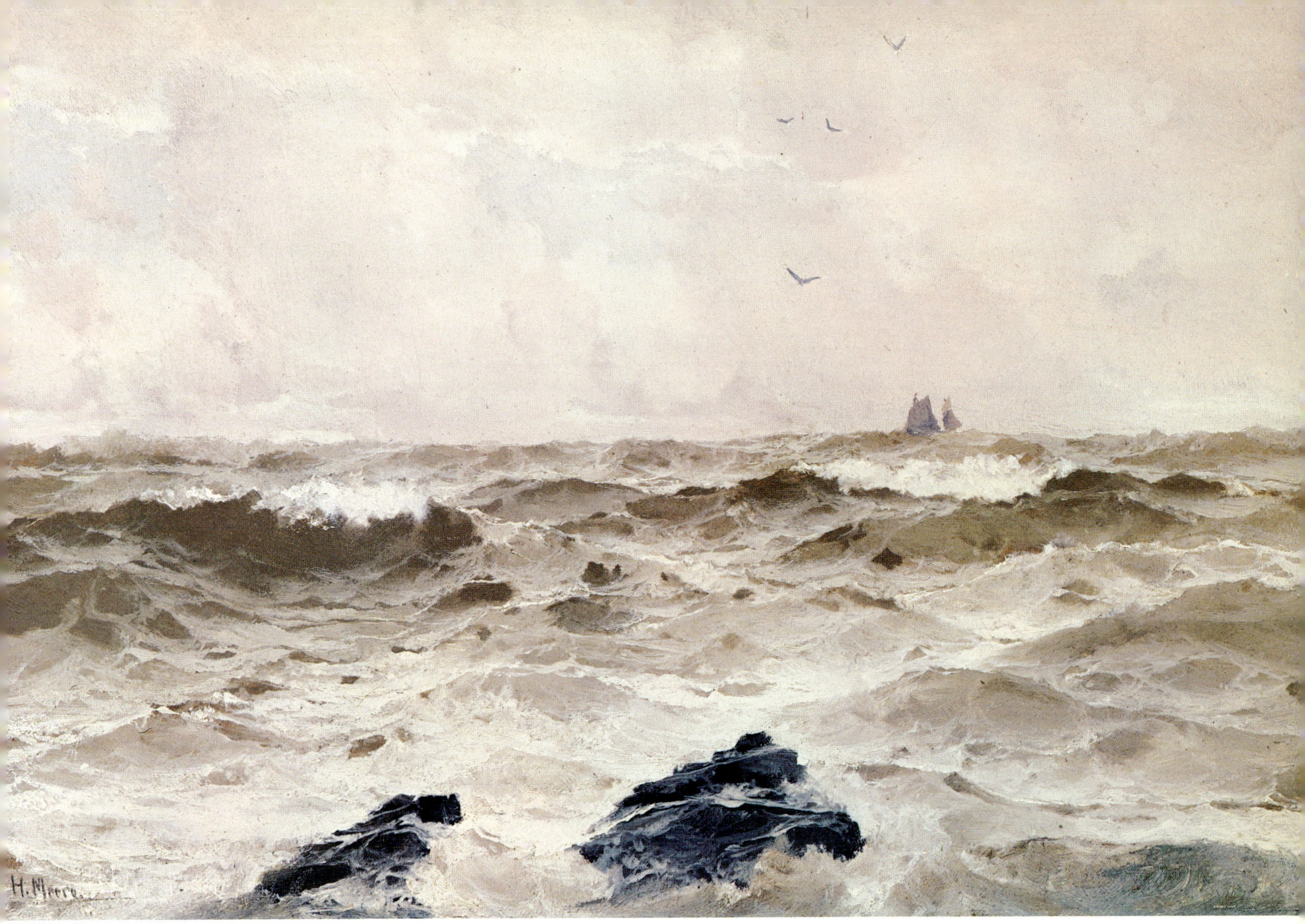

Colour Plate XXIII. Henry Moore, 1831-1895. ''Breakers off a rocky coast with a lugger.'' Private collection.

Colour Plate XXIV. William Lionel Wyllie, 1851-1931. '' 'Well done *Condor*', an incident at the bombardment of Alexandria in 1882.'' National Maritime Museum, Greenwich.

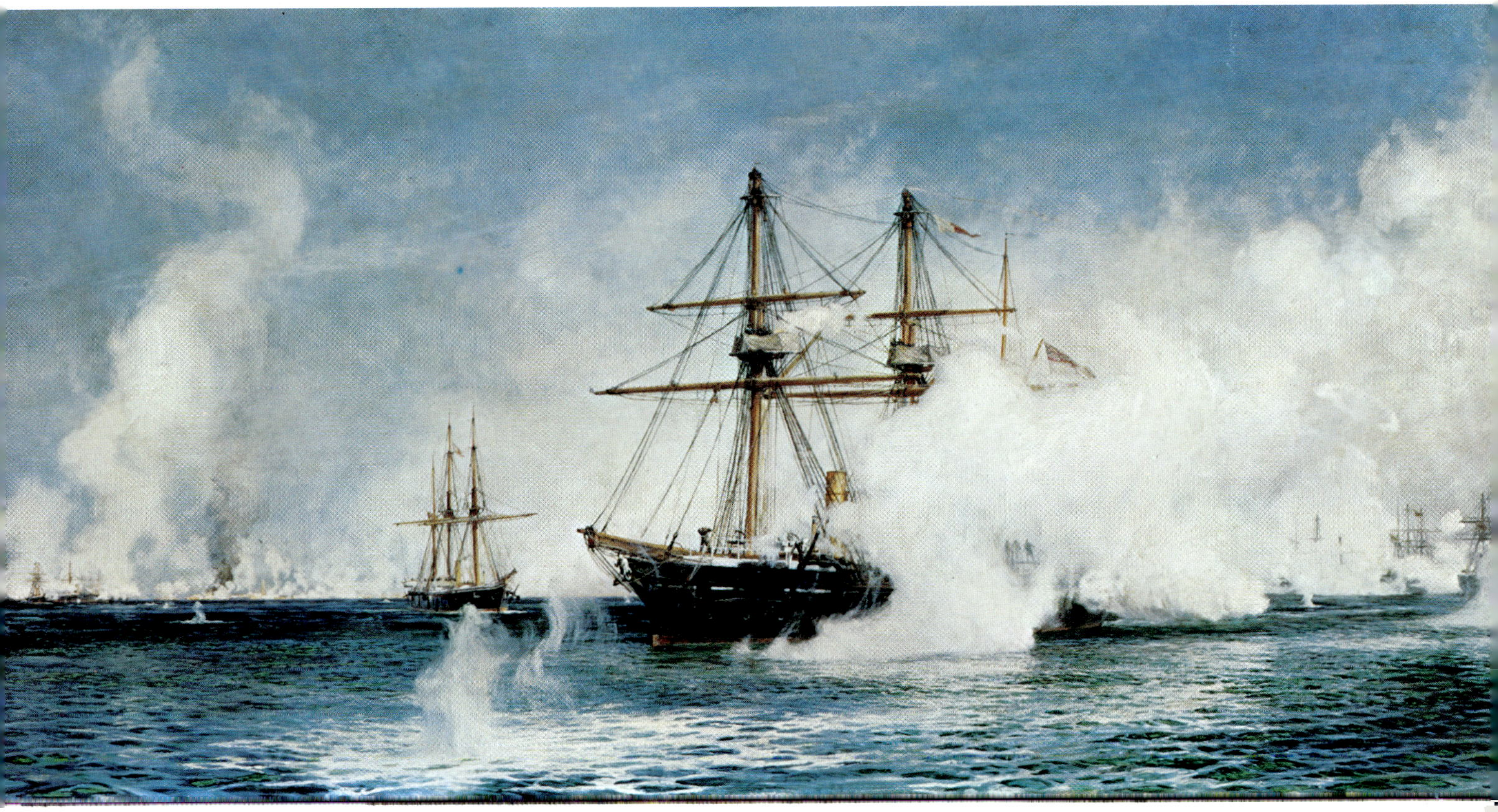

SAVERY, Pieter **d.c.1638**

An almost exact contemporary of Hendrick Cornelisz Vroom (q.v.) and, as a member of the Haarlem Guild in 1593, he must have known Vroom well. He therefore ranks as one of the founding fathers of the Netherlands marine painting school. He painted in the mannerist fashion of the Flemish School of his generation and his work is close both to that of Vroom and of Aert Anthonisz. His works are signed "Savery". He died in Haarlem c.1638.

There are apparently no examples of his marines in public collections.

SAVERY, Roeland Jacobsz **1576-1639**

He was born at Courtrai, the son and pupil of the painter Jacob Savery, and later a pupil of Hans Bol in Amsterdam. Though he painted marines, he was a general painter of landscapes, flowers and animals. In 1604 he went to Prague to work for the Emperor of Germany, Rudolf II, and after his deposition in 1611, for his brother, the Emperior Matthias, so that many of his works are still in Prague in the National Gallery.

He returned to Amsterdam in 1616, and later to Utrecht, where he joined the Guild in 1619. Though celebrated in his lifetime, he died in Utrecht, poor and insane. As can be seen from the marine illustrated his talent for them was only fair.

PLATE: 12.

SCHAEP, Henri Adolphe **1826-1870**

Little is recorded of this artist, who painted like the Schotels. There is a wreck scene of his in the Musée des Beaux-Arts in Antwerp.

SCHELLINKS, Willem **1627-1678**

A native of Amsterdam, he was a pupil of Karel du Jardin, the genre painter and portraitist, and also it is said of Johannes Lingelbach, the landscape painter. Indeed, Schellinks was not really a marine painter but a genre and landscape painter. However, he did paint several very good bird's-eye views of the Dutch attack on the Medway in 1667, in which the ships are well noted. It has been suggested that he was an agent of the Dutch Government during his visit to England during the Second Dutch War. He died in Amsterdam.

The views of the Medway at the Rijksmuseum and the Teachers Training College at Amsterdam, and the one in the National Maritime Museum, Greenwich, view the battle from above Sheerness, while the one in the Scheepvaart Museum, Amsterdam, and the one in the Musée d'Art et d'Histoire, Geneva, view it from high ground to the north of Rochester bridge, with soldiers in the foreground. Also at Greenwich is a large painting of the *Tiger* capturing the *Schakerloo* in 1675.

PLATES: 79, 80.

EXAMPLES: Hermitage, Leningrad (2): the beach at Scheveningen and another. Bavarian State Museums, Munich (1): Leghorn Harbour. The Louvre, Paris (3): Anglo-Dutch battle; view of Malta; Mediterranean port.

SCHETKY, John Christian **1778-1874**

Born in Edinburgh, August 11th, 1778. He was of Hungarian extraction and, from an early age, he displayed a keen interest in the sea and ships. He joined the frigate *Hind* in 1792, but for some reason his parents withdrew him after two years. His mother was an amateur artist and gave drawing lessons, so John was probably her pupil.

He took up teaching drawing, first at Oxford then, from 1808, at the Military College at Great Marlow, until in 1811 he found his niche at the Royal Naval Academy at Portsmouth; here his taste for things nautical, including his personal appearance, were given full rein. He remained there, a Professor of Drawing, for a quarter of a century, until the Admiralty's intention to close the Academy prompted him to make a change and he became Professor of Drawing at the East India College at Addiscombe. He finally retired in 1855.

He was a prolific painter with a keen eye for his subjects, which did much to mitigate a fairly modest artistic talent. However, as might be expected, the drawing is good and the paintings well crafted and finished. He tended to use a rather grey palette, with the characteristic use of a coppery brown. Here is another case that illustrates the importance of social as well as artistic talents in the pursuit of a successful career. Schetky's position at Portsmouth put him in a good position to be noticed and he took good advantage of this: he became in turn, Painter in Watercolours to H.R.H. The Duke of Clarence, then, in 1820, Marine Painter in Ordinary to King George IV.

He exhibited at the Royal Academy from 1805 to 1807; then there is a gap until 1821, which must have a connection with his appointment as marine painter to the King. Thereafter he exhibited every year or two until 1872; indeed, he became a more regular exhibitor in his later years, when he went to live in London. In 1825 he exhibited a major work of the Battle of Trafalgar at the British Institution, and it was really in such large battle pieces that he excelled. After his death, at the age of ninety-five in London on January 28, 1874, his widow wrote a biography of him called *Ninety Years of Work and Play.*

PLATES: 358, 359, 360.

EXAMPLES: National Maritime Museum, Greenwich (10): the cutting out of the Chevrette *1801; the loss of the* Magnificent *1804; H.M.S.* Columbine *and the Experimental Squadron; the cutter yacht* Gazelle; *a set of four paintings of the escape of H.M.S.* Pique; *two paintings of the salvage of treasure on the coast of Argentina by the crew of H.M.S.* Thetis. *The National Gallery of Scotland, Edinburgh (1). Castle Museum, Norwich (2): the frigate* Amelia *chasing the French frigate* Arethusa *1814; a frigate action by moonlight. Peabody Museum of Salem, Mass. (1): a Dutch shipping scene set in the 17th century.*

SCHIEDGES, Petrus Paulus **1813-1876**

Born in The Hague, attended the Technical College there and was a pupil of Louis Meijer. From 1871 until his death in The Hague he was the Keeper at the Gemeentemuseum there. As well as a painter he was a lithographer. He exhibited at Amsterdam, and at The Hague from 1827 to 1875. The Gemeentemuseum has a river scene; and the Prins Hendrik Museum, Rotterdam, has a landscape of morning by a river.

PLATE: 553.

SCHIERTZ, Franz Wilhelm **1813-1887**
Born in Leipzig, he was a pupil of Johan Christian Dahl at Dresden. He liked to paint coastal scenes in Norway and Sweden, and these are of good quality. He also painted views of seal hunting on the ice. The National Gallery in Oslo has fifteen of his drawings. He died in Balestrand, Norway.

SCHNARS-ALQUIST, Carl Wilhelm Hugo **1855-aft.1936**
Known as Hugo, he was born into a well established merchant family in Hamburg on October 10th, 1855. He worked in the family business and in banking before deciding to become a painter. Aided presumably by a long pocket, he studied in the U.S.A., England, Sweden, Denmark and Germany, where he was a mature student in the studio of Hans Frederik Gude (q.v.) in Karlsruhe or, if after 1886, in Berlin.

He was perhaps the most travelled of marine painters who was never a sailor. In the years 1890 to 1898 he made a world tour and subsequently eleven visits to the U.S.A., two to the West Indies, three to the Straits of Magellan, and also visited Africa, Australia, New Zealand and Tasmania. He was a member of the Institute for Nautical Studies in Berlin.

SCHOTEL, Johannes Christiaan **1787-1838**
A native of Dordrecht, he was a pupil and emulator of that other native of Dordrecht and reviver of the Dutch marine school, Martinus Schouman (q.v.), to whose work and quality he came very close. Before that he had been a soldier and then studied under the Dordrecht portrait painter Adriaan Meulemans.

PLATES: 370, 371.

EXAMPLES: Rijksmuseum, Amsterdam (2): a Dutch ship of the line and coastal craft in a rough sea; the beach at Rosenwerf. Scheepvaart Museum, Amsterdam (1): bombardment of Algiers, 1816; plus ten watercolour sketches of coastal scenes and shipping. Dordrecht Museum (1): rough sea scene. Boymans van Beuningen Museum, Rotterdam: 27 sketches. Prins Hendrik Museum, Rotterdam: a number of sketches of shipping. Shipley Art Gallery (1): a hoeker running before the wind.

SCHOTEL, Petrus Johannes **1808-1865**
Born in Dordrecht, he was the son and pupil of Johannes Christiaan, and his works are very similar to his father's. As well as being a painter, he was director of the School of Navigation at Medemblik. In 1856 he moved to Düsseldorf, and in 1865 he died in Dresden.

PLATE: 372.

EXAMPLES: Rijksmuseum, Amsterdam (2): a rough sea off Schouwen Island; The Willemssluis, Amsterdam. Stedelijk Museum, Amsterdam (2): a calm off Flushing; smalschips in a gale. Scheepvaart Museum, Amsterdam (3): two of Dutch squadrons commanded by Prins Hendrik; one of a Dutch squadron at Gibraltar. Gemäldegalerie, Haastretcht (1): harbour scene. Cheltenham Art Gallery (1): Dutch frigate taken aback. Museum Bisdom, Hanover (1): wreck scene. Boymans van Beuningen Museum, Rotterdam (1): view of the French coast.

SCHOULTZ, Johan Tietrich **c.1754-1807**
He was probably born in Sweden. In 1776 he enlisted in the Swedish naval artillery battalion, and ten years later was promoted to corporal. At the outbreak of the war with Russia, 1788-90, he was promoted to sergeant and later to sergeant major of the regiment. Considering that he was not discharged from his regiment until the year before his death, it is remarkable that he found time to paint at least ninety battle scenes, though we do not know how he learnt to do so. The results, which cover the Russian War, are stylised, capable, vigorous and, not surprisingly, historically accurate. His greatest patrons were his sovereigns Gustav III and Gustav IV, called Gustav Adolf, and Duke Karl. Fifteen paintings taken to Germany by Gustav IV, when he was deposed, were returned to Sweden in 1918, and form the National Maritime Museum's Schoultz collection. A further twenty-five battle pieces, which had originally belonged to Karl XIII, are in the National Museum of Art in Stockholm.

Schoultz was discharged from his post as sergeant major through ill-health in 1793, so probably did not continue in active service, and in 1806 he applied for a certificate of change of address to Bjarna in Finland, where he probably died.

SCHOUMAN, Martinus **1770-1838**
Born in Dordrecht in 1770, died in Breda in 1838. Dutch marine painting had sadly lapsed in the 18th century and Dordrecht was the home of its revival after 1800, Schouman being a leader of this movement. He was a pupil of his uncle Aart and of the landscape painter Michiel Versteeg, both Dordrecht painters. Apart from his seascapes of excellent dramatic quality, he was a painter of historical naval scenes and was the master of Johannes Schotel, who emulated his style and quality.

PLATE: 369.

EXAMPLES: Rijksmuseum, Amsterdam (4): Anglo-Dutch action off Boulogne, 1805; bombardment of Algiers, 1816; bombardment of Palembong, Sumatra, 1821; Dutch gunboat blowing up, 1831. Scheepvaart Museum, Amsterdam: sketches. Dordrecht Museum (1): yacht in a gale.

SCHRANZ (SCHREAUNCH), Anton **1769-1839**
Born in Ochsenhausen in 1769, nothing is known of him till he settled in Minorca where John (q.v.) was born in 1794. He seems to have spent most of the rest of his life there, for nearly all his known works are of views of Port Mahon, with ships of the Royal Navy. Late in life he apparently moved to Malta, where he died in 1839. His patrons included British naval officers, so that a number of his paintings are in private hands in England, though some of them have gone to America. There are apparently none in public collections.

SCHRANZ, John **1794-1882**
Born in Minorca, 1794; died Malta, 1882. Son and pupil of Anton (q.v.), his work is so close to that of his father that they are difficult to tell apart. All his known works are of Malta and all date from around the middle of the century, but what he did in early and later life is a mystery. His pictures are signed "Schranz".

EXAMPLES: National Maritime Museum, Greenwich (1): H.M.S. Howe *at Malta about 1842. Mariners Museum, Newport News (1): view of Port Mahon.*

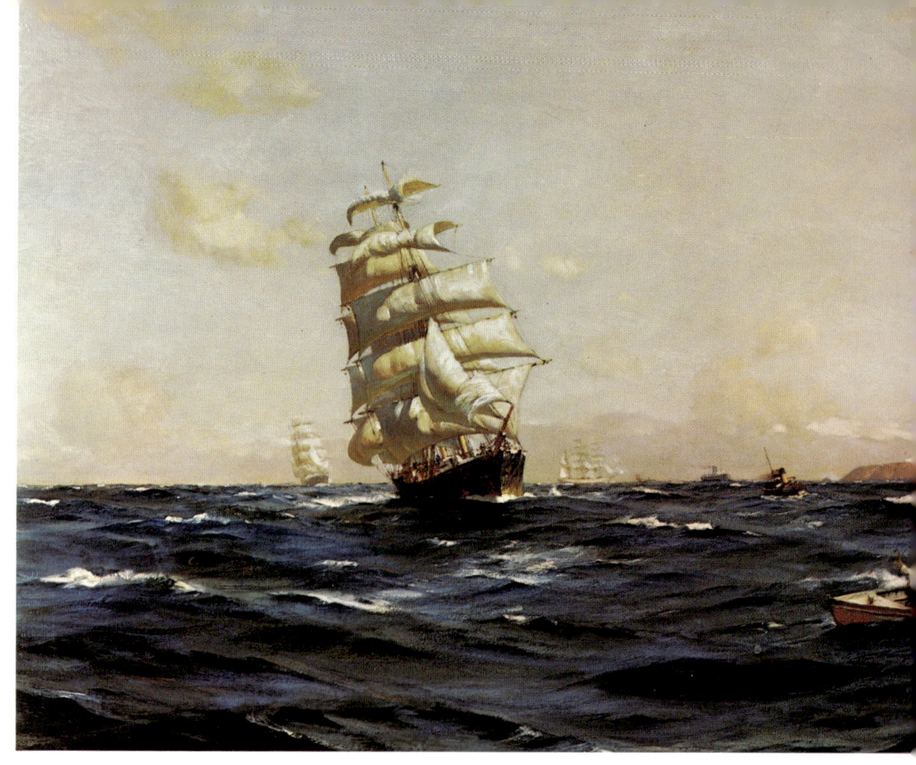

Colour Plate XXVI. Charles Pears, 1873-1958. " 'Line Ahead', the Home Fleet off the Needles, about 1930." Private collection (on loan to the National Maritime Museum, Greenwich).

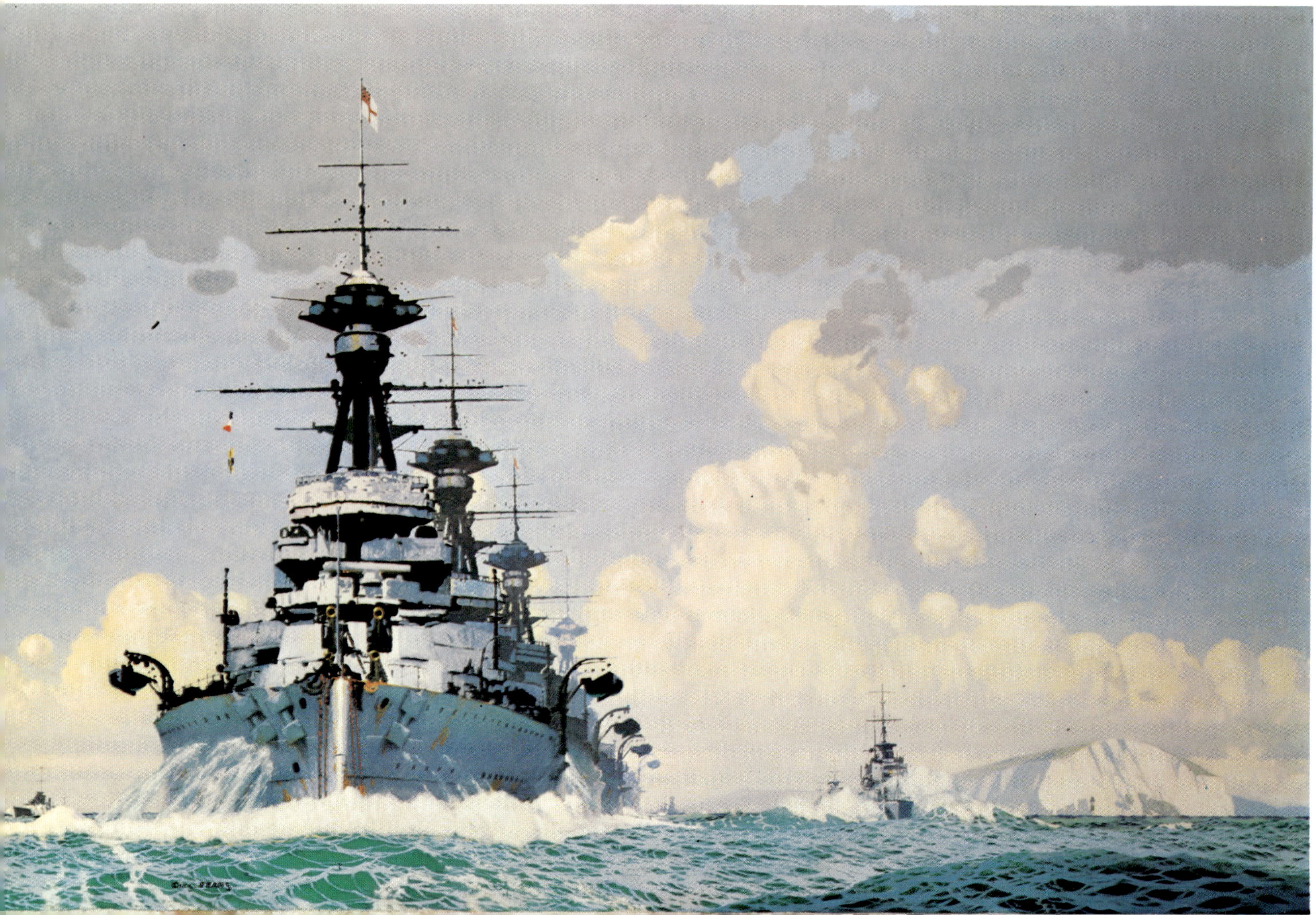

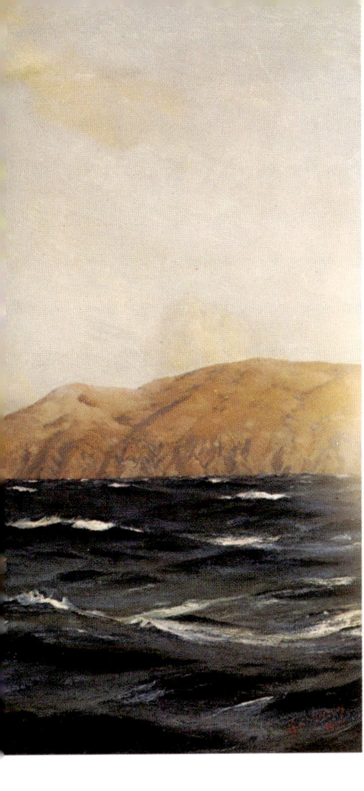

Colour Plate XXV. Thomas Jacques Somerscales, 1842-1927. "A merchant barque picking up a pilot in Valparaiso Bay, dated 1906." Private collection.

Colour Plate XXVII. Norman Wilkinson, 1878-1971. "H.M.S. *Malaya* about 1941." National Maritime Museum, Greenwich.

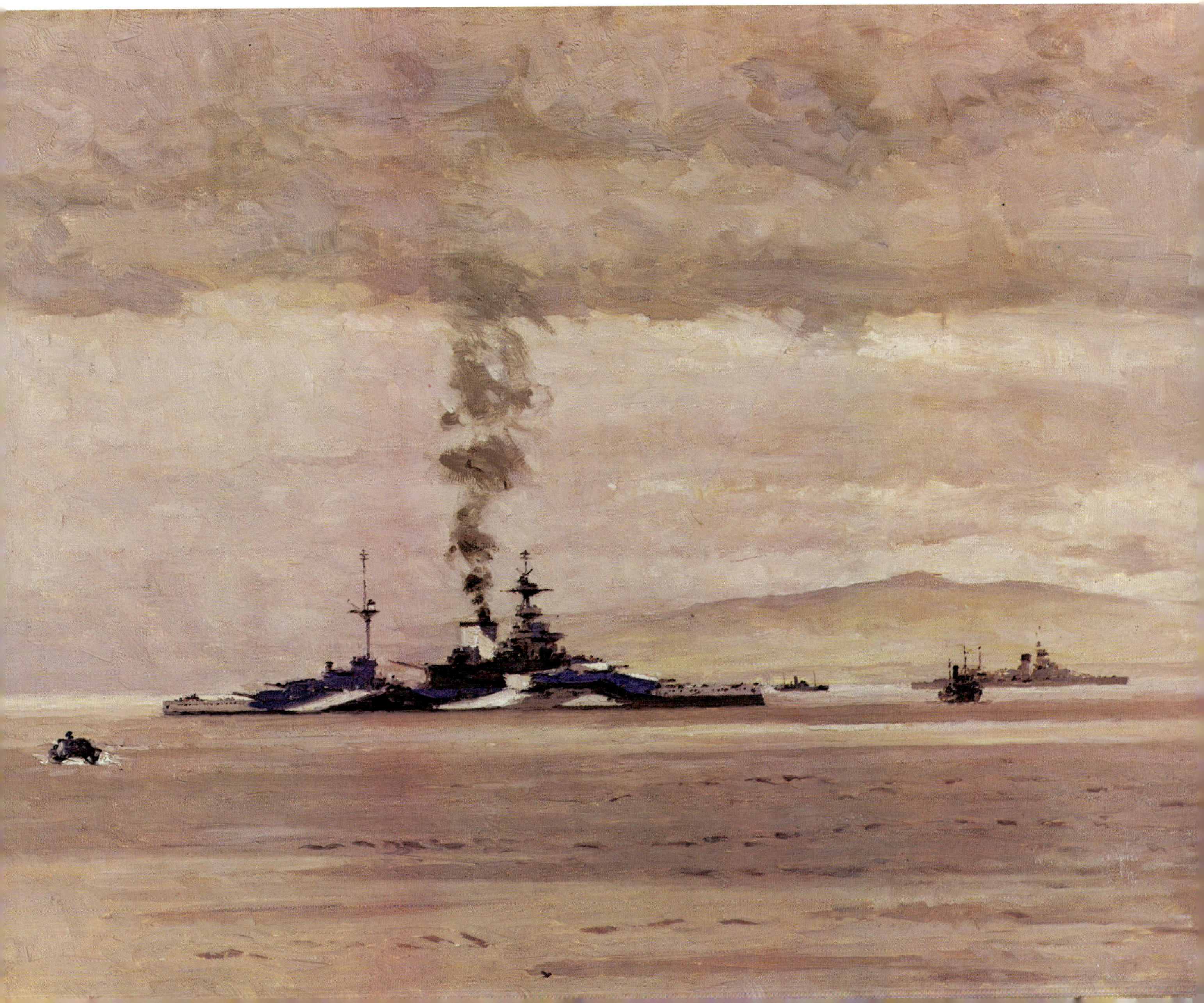

SCHREAUNCH *see* **SCHRANZ, Anton**

SCHUHMACHER, Thomas
An 18th century painter who has a scene of whalers in the ice at the Altonaer Museum in Hamburg.

PLATE: 227.

SCHULTZ, J.
A ship portraitist working in Riga in the second quarter of the 19th century. The Altonaer Museum, Hamburg, has three pen and wash drawings.

SCHUTZ, Johan Frederick **1817-1888**
Born 1817, he was a student, and later a lecturer, at the Middelburg Technical College. He exhibited at The Hague from 1843 until his death in Middelburg.

PLATE: 484.

EXAMPLES: Scheepvaart Museum, Amsterdam (1): the Dutch frigate Sambre, *dated 1864. Zeeland Museum, Middelburg (5): storm brewing; merchantman in a squall; a Dutch steam packet driven ashore in a storm, about 1850; a ship in distress; Flushing Roads.*

SCHUTZ, Willem Johannes **1854-1933**
Born in Middelburg, August 8th, 1854, he was a pupil of his father and exhibited between 1881 and 1884. The Frans Hals Museum at Haarlem has a watercolour dated 1897, and the Zeeland Museum, Middelburg, has two paintings: low water on the West Schelde and a rough sea scene. He died in Middelburg in 1933.

SCHWARTZENBACH, Jacob **1763-1805**
Born in Middelburg. The Rijksmuseum, Amsterdam, has two very late pictures, dated 1804, of the Dutch fleet at Flushing, both painted by him in collaboration with Engel Hoogerheyden, the Middelburg marine painter. He died in Veere in 1805.

PLATE: 297.

SCOTT, J.
A British ship portraitist working in the Newcastle-on-Tyne area in the second and third quarters of the 19th century. His style is close to that of W.J. Huggins (q.v.), and the quality good. Many of his portraits have a background of North Shields.

The National Maritime Museum, Greenwich, has six portraits in oils; the Mariners Museum, Newport News, has one, and the Peabody Museum of Salem has three.

PLATE: 465.

SCOTT, Samuel **1701/2-1772**
Born in London in 1701/2. Though twenty years junior to Peter Monamy (q.v.), Scott must rank with him as one of the two leaders in the first generation of English marine painters following on from the van de Veldes (qq.v.) and the other Dutch immigrant painters who came to London in the 1670s.

We know nothing of his training as an artist but it is significant, in view of his subsequent city views, that in 1732, when the East India Company commissioned a set of paintings of some of their ports of call and factories abroad, the architectural subjects were painted by George Lambert, while Scott was commissioned to paint in the shipping parts. This suggests that Scott's admiration for the Thames views produced by Canaletto during his stay in London in the 1740s, prompted him to acquire similar skills; for it is on views of London that Scott's reputation chiefly rests.

Scott was very much a townsman — no pastoral scenes for him; he was a friend of Hogarth, another townsman, with whom he shared a fellow feeling and an eye for the workaday world. This is beautifully expressed in his painting of Custom House Quay in the Victoria and Albert Museum; it is a picture that could not have been painted by the preceding generation who would have felt that they had to romanticise it.

On the purely marine side, Scott accepted commissions for the actions of the War of Jenkins' Ear and the Seven Years War, as well as for general shipping pieces; all were painted in his studio in Covent Garden. Materially, he was more successful than Peter Monamy and much more successful than poor Charles Brooking (q.v.), whose work he greatly admired, and justifiably. Since his work is comparable to that of Monamy's and inferior to Brooking's, his success stemmed partly from his superior social talents and connections. He is said to have been a warm-tempered and kindly man.

His love of the sea and ships did not extend to a desire to sail in them, for apart from one trip to Helvetsluys in one of the royal yachts in a squadron sent to collect George II, he never made another sea voyage. Indeed, one of the engravings commemorating a cruise down the Thames in a yacht with Hogarth and a party in 1732 shows him being pushed aboard.

Apart from his painting, which brought him a respectable income of £700 or £800 a year, he purchased the place of Deputy Clerk of Accounts to the Stamp Office; this brought in another £100 a year. Among his pupils were Sawrey Gilpin, who was with him from 1749 to 1758, and William Marlow from 1756 to 1761. About this time he retired to Bath to take the waters for gout, and he died there on October 12th, 1772.

PLATES: 198, 199, 200; COLOUR PLATE: XII.

EXAMPLES: National Maritime Museum, Greenwich (16): Wager's action off Cartagena 1708; capture of Porto Bello 1739; capture of Fort Chagre 1740; burning of Payata 1741; action between the Centurion *and the* Covadonga *1743; bombardment of Bastia 1745; action between the* Nottingham *and* Mars *1746; First Battle of Finisterre 1747; Battle of Havana 1748 (pair); fireship attack on the English fleet off Quebec 1759; fire raft attack on the English fleet off Quebec 1759; the* Royal William *shortening sail; a Danish timber bark getting under way; an English privateer engaging a French one; an English man-of-war saluting. Tate Gallery, London (5): First Battle of Finisterre 1747; Old London Bridge; Old Westminster Bridge; part of Old Westminster Bridge; Westminster from the Thames. Victoria and Albert Museum (1): Custom House Quay. Yale Centre for British Art, New Haven, Conn. (3): First Battle of Finisterre 1747; a small English ship coming into port; an English man-of-war close hauled in a breeze. Metropolitan Museum, New York (1): Westminster bridge under construction.*

SEAFORTH, Charles Henry **1801-aft.1853**
Born in 1801, probably in Naples, he studied at the Royal Academy Schools from 1823, exhibiting at the Royal Academy in 1822 and thereafter every year, except 1828, until 1845. Then there is a gap until 1852, when he sent pictures from Naples. This leads one to suppose that he went out there in 1845/6 and, since after 1853 he exhibited no more, may have died there in 1853/4.

He liked to paint on a fairly large scale and worked in a style which was his own interpretation of romanticism but, at the same time, foreshadowed realists like Somerscales and de Martino (qq.v.). In his choice of subject matter he had a predilection for the Royal Navy. He also exhibited at the British Institution from an address in Frith Street between 1825 and 1841, his first picture being a large and very fine Battle of Trafalgar, which recently passed through the sale rooms.

The National Maritime Museum, Greenwich, has two paintings, one of H.M. frigate *Forte* and one of a first-rate at Spithead.

PLATES: 440, 441.

SEAGO, Edward Brian R.B.A., R.W.S **1914-1974**
Born in Norwich on March 31st, 1914. When he was seven he suffered from a heart complaint which confined him to his room, where he occupied his time in drawing. On recovery he studied at the Royal Drawing Society, where he won a special prize at the age of fourteen. He later took lessons from Bernard Priestman. His early adult life was spent travelling with circuses and in 1933 he wrote and illustrated a book about them called *Sons of Sawdust*. He illustrated for the poet Masefield, served in the Royal Engineers in the Second World War and then passed the rest of his life in painting and writing. He died in London on January 19th, 1974.

He exhibited widely, including his famous annual one-man shows at Colnaghi's, where people were known to queue up outside from 6 in the morning so they could secure the picture of their choice. There were red stickers on most or all the exhibits at the end of the first day. This was the measure of his popularity.

He was a keen sailor and by no means exclusively a marine artist, his best known work being a portrait of Queen Elizabeth the Queen Mother and Princess Margaret, showing them in the Music Room at Buckingham Palace.

SEHLSTEDT, Elias **1808-1874**
Born in Harnosand, Sweden, in 1808; died in Sandhamn, near Stockholm, 1874. He was a gifted amateur painter and poet, and an example of his work can be seen at the Linkoping Museum.

SEMPLE, Joseph
A Belfast ship portraitist working in the third quarter of the 19th century. The National Maritime Museum, Greenwich, has two paintings by him of the barque *Grampus,* dated 1871, and the *William Yeo* in 1867. The Peabody Museum of Salem has one of the *Rinnie J. Carlton,* built in 1874.

SERRES, Dominic, the Elder **1722-1793**
Born near Auch in Gascony, in 1722, he came of a good family and was brought up in his father's country mansion at Beauperre. His uncle was an Archbishop of Rheims, and in Dominic's obituary in the *Gentleman's Magazine* he is called Comte Serres. He was sent to the famous English Benedictine school at Douai, which probably explains why he had no difficulties of communication when he came to England and accounts for his being a great anglophile.

His family intended him for the priesthood but to avoid this he ran away, first to Spain and, once there, to sea. His education would have enabled him to grasp the intricacies of navigation, and undoubtedly helped to bring him promotion and a command. He came to England after his ship had been captured, "during the war of 1752", according to Redgrave. Since, however, there was no war in 1752, it has been generally assumed that he came near the outset of the Seven Years War in 1756. None the less, there exists a painting, surely done in England and dated 1754. It is thus possible that he was captured late in the War of Jenkins' Ear in 1748/9.

He knew Charles Brooking (q.v.) and was strongly influenced by him when he began to make a living by his brush. His early works strained after the commercial market and are luminous calms with ships in romantic settings. However, once success came to him he adopted a more immediate approach to his subjects, painting them far more realistically.

Like Samuel Scott (q.v.) and unlike poor Brooking, his success probably had much to do with his social gifts, for he was not only educated but also a most likeable and charming man. This must have commended him to his gentlemen patrons, as did the fact that he was a practical seaman, to naval ones. Though a Frenchman, he became the most successful painter of the naval actions of the Seven Years War and the War of American Independence, from the British side. These paintings are most valuable historical documents and quite possibly more accurate than the written accounts. It must be admitted, however, that though well crafted, they are often artistically dull.

Serres was a founder member of the Royal Academy in 1768 and in the last year of his life was its librarian; he was also made marine painter to George III. He exhibited at the Royal Academy from 1769 to the year of his death, when seven of his pictures were shown there, and he also exhibited at the Free Society exhibitions and at the Incorporated Society of Artists, of which he became a member in 1765. He died in London on November 6, 1793.

PLATES: 237, 238, 239, 240, 241, 242, 243.

EXAMPLES: The United States Naval Academy Museum, Annapolis (1): forcing a passage on the Hudson River, 1776. National Gallery, Dublin (1): view of Torquay. National Maritime Museum, Greenwich (45): action between the Lion *and the* Elizabeth *and* Du Teillay *1745; capture of the* Duc de Chartres *1747; capture of Gheriah 1756; capture of Chandernagore 1757; the capture of the* Telemaque *by the* Experiment *1757; the* Monmouth *burning the* Rose *1758; three paintings of the attack on Goree 1758; capture of the* Comte de St. Florentine; *pair of paintings of the fireship and fire-raft attack on Saunders' fleet off Quebec 1759; two paintings of the Battle of Quiberon Bay 1759; Princess Charlotte arriving at Harwich 1761; capture of St. Lucia 1762; a set of eleven paintings of the taking of Havana in 1762 (on loan); Barrington's action off St. Lucia 1778; destruction of the American fleet in Penobscot Bay 1779; Battle of St. Vincent 1780; the capture of the* Esperance *by the*

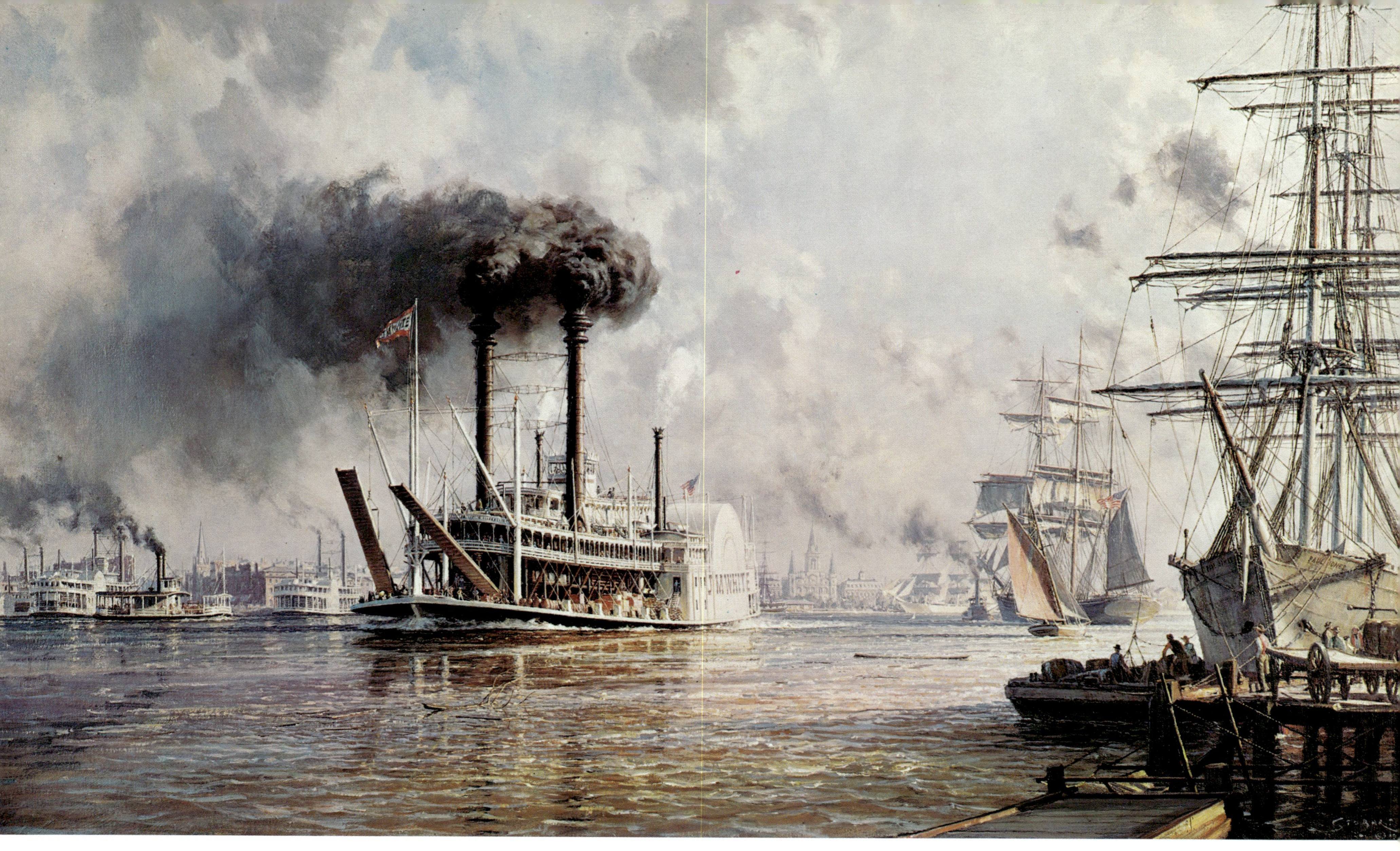

Colour Plate XXVIII. John Stobart, b.1929. "The *J.M. White* leaving New Orleans in 1878." Artist's collection.

Pearl *1780; the Battle of Negapatam 1782; the arrival of Their Sicilian Majesties at Naples 1785; the East Indiaman* Pitt; *the* Royal George; *the* St. George; *Drake's Island, Plymouth; shipping in the Hamoaze, Plymouth; a prize being brought into Plymouth; the Gun Wharf, Portsmouth; Dutch 17th century coastal craft on a fresh day (on loan); a Dutch ship saluting an English flagship in the Downs; a frigate; an English frigate chased by French frigates off the coast of India; the* Dorset *yacht close-hauled off Dover. Town Hall, Ipswich: a set of seven large paintings of the actions between Suffren and Hughes off the coast of India in 1782 and 1783, the eighth being that of Negapatam, at Greenwich.*

SERRES, Dominic, the Younger **?1761/2-?1804**
Born probably in London, he was the younger brother of John Thomas Serres (q.v.), and first exhibited at the Royal Academy in 1778, when he was listed as Master Serres. If he began exhibiting at the same age as his brother, sixteen, then he must have been born in the second half of 1761 or the first half of 1762.

He continued to exhibit until 1787, and then there is a gap until 1804, when he exhibited a view of the Bay of Naples; he showed nothing more. It is said that he developed health problems of a cerebro-spinal nature and that he went to live with his brother, who looked after him. If this is so, he was not living at John Thomas's address in 1804; and one wonders whether his view of the Bay of Naples was done from first hand knowledge from a visit there. From the evidence of his exhibited pictures, he did not follow his father and brother in choosing shipping subjects, though he painted some coastal views. The Victoria and Albert Museum has one watercolour.

SERRES, John Thomas **1759-1825**
Born in London, December 1759, he was the elder son and pupil of Dominic Serres, the Elder (q.v.) and was strongly influenced by the romanticism of Philip de Loutherbourg (q.v.) and the Romantic movement, though he never approached the quality of that master. Indeed, had it not been for his father's position and prestige it is doubtful if he would have gained the honours and position that he did.

On his father's death he succeeded him in his appointment as marine painter to King George III and to H.R.H. the Duke of Clarence. Then in 1800 he was appointed Marine Draughtsman to the Admiralty. Ever since George Anson's first lieutenant, Piercy Brett, in the *Centurion,* on the voyage round the world 1739-44, made drawings, subsequently engraved, of the coastlines they passed, the Admiralty had been conscious of the value of such views in identifying landfalls. Thus, Serres' task was to sail in naval ships round our coasts, down the western coasts of France and Spain and even into the Mediterranean, making drawings in the form of elevations. A selection of these were subsequently published in a book called *The Little Sea Torch* (1801).

Serres also taught drawing for a time at the Chelsea Naval School and in 1805 published a work called *Liber Nauticus;* this, which aimed to help students draw ships, contained plates after his own work and that of his father, illustrating different types of vessels. He did paint battle scenes but not many, and none on the grand scale of de Loutherbourg, which is a little surprising considering his admiration for that artist. In about 1817 he became one of the proprietors of the new Coburg Theatre and subsequently its scenic director.

Sadly this considerable professional success was more than counterbalanced by his disastrous marriage to a Miss Olivia Wilmot, an extravagant and immoral woman with notorious delusions of grandeur. She claimed to be the illegitimate daughter of H.R.H. the Duke of Cumberland, calling herself "Princess Olive of Cumberland" and passing on similar pretensions to her daughter. Her behaviour and debts ruined Serres, who lost all his favour at court and died in a debtors' prison in London on December 28th, 1825.

PLATES: 262, 263, 264, 265, 266.

EXAMPLES: National Maritime Museum, Greenwich (5): the Battle of Copenhagen 1801; the Barfleur; *the royal yacht* Royal Sovereign; *the Thames at Shillingford; third rates in a squall. Victoria and Albert Museum, London (1): the royal yacht* Dorset *passing Dublin lighthouse.*

SERRITELLI, Giovani
Illustrated is a good quality painting by this artist of H.M.S. *Caledonia* off Naples about 1868, wearing the flag of Vice-Admiral Lord Clarence Paget. Serritelli was presumably a Neapolitan, working in competition with the de Simones (qq.v.) but no other details are available.

PLATE: 564.

SETTLE, William Frederick **1821-1897**
Born in Hull, he was a nephew and pupil of John Ward (q.v.) the doyen of the Hull school of marine painters. He became the drawing master at the Hull Mechanic's Institute and moved to London in 1863. Though he never exhibited at the Royal Academy and had only one work shown at the British Institution exhibitions in 1867 (its last year), he somehow managed to reach the notice of Queen Victoria who was drawn to his delicately crafted little pictures and commissioned him to design nautical Christmas cards for her.

The National Maritime Museum, Greenwich, has a little painting of the H.M. frigate *Immortalité* with the royal yacht, *Victoria and Albert II,* H.M.S. *Warrior* and a cutter of the Royal Yacht Squadron, in the Solent about 1862, and the Ferens Art Gallery at Hull has two pictures.

PLATE: 535.

SHACKLETON, Keith P.R.S.M.A. **b.1923**
Born in Weybridge, Surrey, on January 16th, 1923. He is basically an ornithologist, who like many others has taught himself to record birds, especially in his case sea birds. He has developed a very successful technique for recording them in their element.

He was educated at Oundle and in the Second World War was in the R.A.F., where he worked on camouflage in Europe and the Far East, and was a war artist for the Department of Public Relations. His interest in birds extends to flying; he holds a pilot's licence and worked part-time for an aircraft sales firm after the war. He was a founder member of the Society of Aviation Artists, now the Guild of Aviation Artists, and was President of the Royal Society of Marine Artists, having been elected a member in 1962. He is also a founder member of the Society of Wildlife Artists and Chairman of the Artists' League of Great Britain.

He has published a number of books on wildlife subjects, *Tidelines, A Sailor's Guide to Ocean Birds, Wake, Wild Animals in Britain* and *Birds of the Atlantic Ocean.* His interests have taken him all over the world, including to both the North and South Polar regions. He has also exhibited at the Royal Academy and the Royal Society of British Artists.

The National Maritime Museum, Greenwich, holds a painting of shags.

PLATE: 683.

SHIMIDZU, H.

A Japanese ship portraitist working in Yokohama in the second quarter of the 20th century. The Peabody Museum of Salem has a watercolour by him of quite good quality, dated 1929.

SHOESMITH, Kenneth Denton **1896-1939**

Born in Halifax, he was brought up in Blackpool and in 1906 went as a cadet to the *Conway* training ship. She was then moored in the Mersey and Shoesmith spent most of his spare time drawing the passing ships. He was largely self-taught but did subscribe to a correspondence course called "Revival of Youthful Art League".

In 1909 he joined the Royal Mail Company as a junior officer, and continued in the merchant marine until the end of the First World War, by which time he found his duties as a chief officer allowed him too little time to paint. He became a professional painter living in London and specialising in poster designs, mainly for shipping firms, and especially for the Royal Mail. He had his first one-man show in Belfast in 1921, and exhibited at the Royal Academy and the Paris Salon.

In 1925 he was elected a member of the Royal Institute of Painters in Watercolour, and he was also a member of the British Society of Poster Designers. The highlight of his career was perhaps his being chosen in 1935 as one of the artists to paint murals in the great new Cunarder, *Queen Mary*. His work was strongly influenced by that of Frank Brangwyn. He died in Hampstead Garden Suburb, London, on April 6th, 1939.

In 1974 his widow, Mrs. Sarah Shoesmith, bequeathed such paintings, drawings and posters as he had kept to the Ulster Museum in Belfast.

SILAS, Ellis **1883-1971**

Born in London on July 13th, 1883, he was the son of the decorative artist and flower painter Louis Silas, and studied in his father's studio, designing fabrics and decor. He also studied under Walter Sickert.

He went to Australia and in the First World War was a war artist to the Australian Government, accompanying the A.N.Z.A.C.s to Gallipoli in 1915. As a result he published and illustrated a book called *Crusading at A.N.Z.A.C.* Between the wars he made a three-year painting expedition to Papua, about which he wrote a book called *A Primitive Arcadia.*

He was a member of the United and Ridley Art Societies and exhibited at the Royal Academy, the Royal Institute of Oil Painters and the Royal Institute of Painters in Watercolours. He was perhaps more a general painter than a marine artist, but his painting The Price of Glory, a large canvas of a battle of the First Dutch War, caused something of a stir when it was exhibited at the Royal Academy in 1934. It is now in the National Maritime Museum, along with a painting of H.M.S. *Wave* washed up on the beach at St. Ives, sketched on the spot in September 1952.

Silas died in London in May 1971.

SILLEMANS, Experiens **1611-1653**

Born and died in Amsterdam. An artist engaged in the drawing of *grisailles* in pen and ink on a gesso ground. They follow the style of Willem van de Velde the Elder (q.v.), who, though his exact contemporary, appears to have practised earlier and may have been his master. Even if he was he had nothing to fear from Sillemans. His father, Geoffrey Sillemans, was in the shipping business in Amsterdam and despite the evidence of his Dutch name is supposed to have been English.

A curious aspect of his work was his experiments with printing on to the gesso ground, then putting in a foreground by hand to give variety. This was apparently an attempt to put a cheap form of grisaille on to the market. There are examples of his work at the Rijksmuseum and the Scheepvaart Museum, Amsterdam, the Staatliche Museum, Berlin, and five at the National Maritime Museum, Greenwich.

PLATE: 102.

SILLEN, Herman Gustave af **1857-1908**

Born and died in Stockholm. He was Sweden's leading marine painter in his day and accepted commissions for large canvases of Swedish naval events. He studied in Paris and Berlin. His narrative style is close to that of Claus Bergen (q.v.).

Paintings by him can be seen in the Maritime Museum in Stockholm.

PLATE: 625.

SILO, Adam **1674-1766**

Born and died in Amsterdam. This talented man was a shipbuilder, in whose yard Peter the Great once worked when he helped build the *Peter and Paul*. The Czar became a patron.

Silo was a ship designer and draughtsman first, and a gifted amateur painter second. He studied under Abraham Storck (q.v.) whose style he emulated, and he was also an engraver.

PLATE: 181.

EXAMPLES: National Maritime Museum, Greenwich (1): Dutch whalers in the ice. Hermitage, Leningrad (5). Summer Palace, Leningrad (13): the herring fleet and others. New Bedford Whaling Museum (1).

SILVA, Francis Augustus **1835-1886**

The Peabody Museum of Salem has an atmospheric oil of schooners in a calm in Boston Bay at sunset.

PLATE: 513.

SIMONE, A. de
The best known of a family of Neapolitan ship portraitists working in the second half of the 19th century. He also painted some battle pieces, such as the Bombardment of Alexandria in 1882.

He worked in oils and watercolours, and the National Maritime Museum, Greenwich, has fourteen ship portraits in oils and a Bombardment of Alexandria, and eight portraits in watercolours. The Mariners Museum, Newport News, has a portrait of an American barque and the Maritime Museum at Kronborg Castle has one of a steam yacht in the Bay of Naples.

PLATES: 565, 566.

SIMONE, Tommaso de
One of the family of Neapolitan ship portraitists and marine painters working in the second half of the 19th century. The National Maritime Museum, Greenwich, has a painting by him of H.M.S. *Liffey* dated 1858.

SJORTSOM, S.P.
A Swedish ship portraitist working in Malmo in the second half of the 19th century. The Maritime Museum at Malmo has examples of his watercolours.

SLADE, Captain W.J.
A British primitive ship portraitist working in Bideford in the first quarter of the 20th century. The National Maritime Museum, Greenwich, has a painting by him of the schooner *M.A. James,* which was launched in 1900.

SLATER, John Falconer **1857-1937**
Born in Newcastle-on-Tyne on March 26th, 1857, this Northumberland artist emigrated to South Africa as a young man. However he soon returned to the Newcastle area, where he set up as a painter. He exhibited at the Royal Academy from 1889.

The National Maritime Museum, Greenwich, has a large painting by him of Whitley Bay, dated 1909.

SMIT, Aernout **1641-1710**
Born and died in Amsterdam. He was a pupil of Jan Blankerhoff, the second generation realist painter, and was a student at a time when the other great second generation painters in Amsterdam, such as the van de Veldes (qq.v.), Bakhuizen (q.v.), Cappelle (q.v.), and the Ruisdaels (qq.v.) at nearby Haarlem, were at the height of their powers and prestige.

Their influence, though not Cappelle's, are clearly seen in his work and in Smit's flowing seas there is almost a development from realism to naturalism. This is more apparent in his later work, his early work emulating Bakhuizen's (q.v.). He signed his work "A. Smit" or "A.S.".

PLATE: 135.

EXAMPLES: Provincial Museum, Bonn (1): rough seascape. The Palace, Compiègne (1): storm. Statens Museum for Kunst, Copenhagen (2): shipping off a coast (early); smalschips beating in a stiff breeze. Hessisches Landesmuseum, Darmstadt (1): a smalschip close hauled in a stiff breeze. Museum, Hamburg (1): storm. Kunsthalle, Karlsruhe (1): ships in a storm off a rocky coast. Museum, Mannheim (1). Nasjonalgalleriet, Oslo (1): an English flyboat running into a harbour and other shipping. Staatliches Museum, Schwerin (1): ships foundering off a rocky coast.

SMITH, D.W.
A ship portraitist of reasonable talent, either English or American, working in the third quarter of the 19th century. The Peabody Museum of Salem has an oil by him.

SMITH, Frank Vining **1879-1967**
Born in South Abington, Massachusetts, on August 25th, 1879. The name of his birthplace was changed to Whitman, so the school he attended is now Whitman High School. He studied at the School of the Museum of Fine Arts in Boston for two years, then at the Central Ontario School of Design.

He became a newspaper artist, mainly on the *Boston Journal* and *Boston Herald.* It was not until after the First World War, and his second marriage, that he began to make his mark as a marine painter of famous sailing ships of the 19th century. In 1924 he had his first one-man show at the Art Museum, Oberlin College, Ohio. In the following year he gave up his post on the *Boston Herald* to devote his time to the sea, painting marines in the winter and sailing in the summer. He was made a life member of the Cruising Club of America in 1956. His output was over a thousand paintings, some of which can be seen at the Mariners Museum, Newport News, Virginia, and one in the New Bedford Whaling Museum. He died in Hengham, near Boston, on July 30th, 1967.

PLATE: 650.

SMITH, Joseph B. **1798-1876**
Born and died in New York. He was the son of the minister of the John Street Methodist Church in New York, where he painted local scenes and ship portraits, notably the originals of the Currier and Ives engravings of the clipper ships *Adelaide, Great Republic, Ocean Express* and *Red Jacket.* He was assisted in his work by his son William.

The Peabody Museum of Salem has two oil paintings by him, one dated 1857.

SMITH, William Collingwood **1815-1887**
Born in Greenwich in 1815, he was the son of an amateur artist, and was encouraged to be a professional. He had some lessons from James D. Harding (q.v.), but was mainly self-taught.

He first exhibited at the Royal Academy in 1836, then at the British Institution in 1838 and thereafter at both up to 1855, when he ceased to exhibit at either, an indication that this was the time when he gave up oil painting for watercolours — a good proportion of which were marines. Thereafter he exhibited with the Old Watercolour Society, over a thousand items, turning away from marines to landscape subjects. He also exhibited at Suffolk Street, and had a very successful drawing and painting school. He died at Brixton Hill, March 15th, 1887.

Examples may be seen at the Towner Gallery, Eastbourne, National Maritime Museum, Greenwich, the British Museum and Stalybridge Art Gallery.

SMITH, Xanthus R. **1838-1929**
Born in Philadephia, 1838; died Weldon, North Carolina, December 2nd, 1929. He specialised in naval battle pieces. The United States Naval Academy, Annapolis, has a painting by him of the Battle of Mobile Bay 1864, and the Mariners Museum, Newport News, one of the sinking of the *Kearsage* by the *Alabama,* 1864.

PLATE: 514.

SMOUT, Lucas, the Younger **1671-1713**
Born and died in Antwerp. He was a pupil of the great Flemish mannerist painter Hendrick van Minderhout (q.v.), and this is very plain in the busy battle pieces in which Smout specialised. His painstaking compositions are beautifully crafted, highly finished and richly colourful. He signed his work "L. Smout".

The Musée Royal des Beaux-Arts, Antwerp, has a painting of a beach at Scheveningen; the Statens Museum for Kunst, Copenhagen, a sea fight off Kjoge Bay, Greenland, 1710.

SMYTH, Admiral William Henry **1788-1865**
K.F.M., D.C.L., V.P.R.S., P.R.A.S., F.R.G.S.
Born in Westminster, January 21st, 1788. He joined the East India Company in 1804 and transferred to the Royal Navy in 1805, serving in the East. After the war he surveyed most of the coasts of Sicily and Italy. On promotion to captain in 1828 he retired from active service and devoted himself to scientific writing.

He was a good amateur painter, and the National Maritime Museum, Greenwich, has a painting by him of the *Erebus* and *Terror* in the ice.

SOEST, Pieter Cornelisz van **1640-1667**
Although he was a burgomaster of Amsterdam in 1642 his best known marines date from the Second Dutch War, when he painted the Four Days Fight, 1666, and the Dutch attack on the Medway in 1667.

His work has a strong affinity to the battle pieces of Claesz Wou (q.v.), who may have been his master, and though his seas are grey his ships are rather colourful in the Flemish tradition. His battle pieces tend to be panoramic and are well crafted, if somewhat unsubtle in feeling.

PLATE: 73.

EXAMPLES: Musée d'Abbeville (1): sea battle. National Maritime Museum, Greenwich (4): all actions, two of the Four Days Fight, 1666, one of the Dutch in the Medway, 1667, one sea fight; Kunsthalle, Karlsruhe (1): shipping off a fort.

SOLDWEDEL, Kip
An American painter working today. Seaport 76, Rhode Island, sells a reproduction of one of his paintings, the rebel sloop *Providence* landing the party which captured Nassau in the Bahamas on March 3rd, 1776.

SOLVYNS, Franz Balthazar **1760-1824**
Born in Antwerp, July 6th, 1760, he was a pupil of Andreas de Quartenmont, the portrait and history painter, at Antwerp, and afterwards of François Vincent, the history painter, in Paris.

In 1789 he went to India, where he sketched and painted many aspects of Indian life. He made over three hundred etchings from his own originals including two series on local craft called *Pleasure Boats* and *Boats of Lading* which now make valuable references. Unfortunately for Solvyns they did not sell well, which caused him financial embarrassment, and may have been the reason for his taking a job in the Antwerp docks. He died in Antwerp, October 10th, 1824.

The National Maritime Museum, Greenwich, has a fine little panel of the East India Company's yacht *Charlotte of Chittagong* lying in the Hooghly River at Calcutta, and the Peabody Museum of Salem has a painting of East Indiamen at Calcutta.

COLOUR PLATE: XVIII.

SOMERSCALES, Thomas Jacques **1842-1927**
Born in Hull, October 30th, 1842, he was the son of a Hull shipmaster and was educated there and at the Normal College at Cheltenham. He is then said to have joined the Royal Navy as a schoolmaster about 1862, serving for seven years. While in the *Zealous,* flagship on the Pacific station, he picked up a fever at Tahiti. He transferred to the corvette *Clio,* but his health did not improve and he obtained the Admiral's permission to be invalided ashore at Valparaiso. This story comes from good sources and is probably true, but it would have been more conclusive if Somerscales' name could have been found among the appointments in the Navy Lists. According to them, the *Zealous* took up station in the Pacific early in 1867, when the *Clio* was already on station and Somerscales is not listed as being the instructor in either of them, though the post in the *Clio* is listed as vacant from the summer of 1867 to her return home late in 1868. This may be the period of Somerscales' stay on board her.

Ashore at Valparaiso he was offered a post as a drawing teacher at a school, but was sacked for his refusal to attend morning prayers. Two colleagues, named Peter Mackay and George Sutherland left with him, and together they started a new school. Somerscales soon took up painting in earnest and from 1874 gave instructions to pupils in Valparaiso and Santiago. He married George Sutherland's sister in 1874 and in 1892 they and their four sons returned to Hull.

In 1893 he exhibited his first picture at the Royal Academy, "A corvette shortening sail to pick up a shipwrecked crew". Its startling realism had a powerful effect on lovers of the sea.

His style had affinities with that of Edouard de Martino (q.v.) and John Fraser (q.v.), though it had evolved far away from their influence. In 1899 the Chantrey Bequest bought the famous "Off Valparaiso", which according to one of his daughters-in-law was painted over another picture. He kept his contacts in Chile and made a number of visits there. On one of them he took out with him a large canvas of "The First Naval Squadron of Chile", which had been commissioned to hang in the National Congress at Santiago. Another of his paintings, the action between the *Huascar* and the *Esmeralda* is in the Museum of Fine Arts in Santiago. The Auckland Art Gallery, New Zealand, has a picture called

"A Flying Squadron of the Old School", the National Maritime Museum, Greenwich, has two, "The sinking of the *Scharnhorst* at the Battle of the Falkland Islands, 1914", and "A Barque in a Gale". The Ferens Art Gallery has one and the Tate Gallery has "Off Valparaiso", a Chantrey Bequest picture.

Somerscales died in Hull on June 27th, 1927.

PLATE: 602; COLOUR PLATE: XXV.

SORENSEN, Carl Frederik **1818-1879**

Born in Besser, Island of Samsa, February 8th, 1818; died Copenhagen January 24th, 1879. A Danish marine painter of good quality, who, in 1846, was sent out to the Mediterranean in a Danish frigate to sketch the landfalls.

There is a collection of his work at the Royal Naval Museum, Copenhagen.

PLATES: 350, 351, 352.

EXAMPLES: Statens Museum for Kunst, Copenhagen (10): Shipwreck after a gale on the west coast of Jutland; Early summer morning: the roads of Elsinore; the skerries off the west coast of Sweden (two); ships off the coast of Iceland; a stretch of coast, Norway; a wreck on the west coast of Jutland at sunset; sailing ships south of Elsinore; low beach and sand dunes, Holland; sailing ships in misty weather. Frederiksborg Museum, Zealand (1): the Danish fleet blocking the Elbe 1849. The Maritime Museum, Kronborg Castle: a painting of the H.P. Priors fleet 1864. National Gallery, Oslo (1): view of Kronborg Castle. Nationalmuseum, Stockholm (3): Men-of-war before Elfaborg; marine; storm on the coast of Norway.

SORENSEN, F.I.

A ship portraitist, presumably of Scandinavian origin, but working in Cardiff about 1900.

The National Maritime Museum, Greenwich, has a painting by him of the tea clipper *Thermopylae*.

PLATE: 627.

SORGH, Hendrick Martensz Rokes **1611-1670**

Born and died in Rotterdam. He was essentially a genre painter who was said to be a pupil of Teniers the Younger (q.v.); since he was also strongly influenced by Brouwer who was in Antwerp when he was a young man, perhaps he was one of his pupils as well.

It seemed a point of honour for many Dutch 17th century painters to prove their versatility, and so Sorgh also painted some seascapes which, because he was an accomplished artist, are of good quality in the Dutch realist style. He was head of the Guild of Rotterdam in 1659 and signed his work "H. Sorgh" or "Sorg".

PLATES: 62, 63, 64.

EXAMPLES: Rijksmuseum, Amsterdam (1): storm on the Maas. Hermitage, Leningrad (1): vessels close-hauled in a breeze. City Art Gallery, Manchester (1): fishing boats in a choppy sea. Boymans van Beuningen Museum, Rotterdam (1): view of the Maas.

SORVIG family

In a place the size of 19th century Bergen, any painters who signed works with the same surname but various initials, were very likely related. The Bergen Maritime Museum has a collection. The earliest is a crude painting of a brigantine of about 1820 signed "F.M. Sorvig"; then there is one of a paddle steamer dated 1857 and signed "R. Sorvig". A painting of sailing merchantmen, dated 1861, is signed "F. Sorvig", another of timber boats, dated 1866, is signed "F.S." and a third, dated 1877, is signed "F.S. & T.S." Then there are two paintings signed "T. Sorvig", one of Bergen dated 1880, and one of timber boats, dated 1889. These Norwegian coastal craft were called *jaegts.*

There are also examples in the Maritime Museum, Kronborg Castle.

PLATE: 546.

SOULIES, Paul

A French ship portraitist working in Marseilles in the third quarter of the 19th century. The Mariners Museum, Newport News, has two watercolours by him, one dated 1858, and the Peabody Museum of Salem has one dated 1857.

PLATE: 557.

SPEER, John A. **b.1904**

Born in Auckland, he is a life-long lover of ships particularly naval, who took up watercolour painting seriously after serving through the Second World War with the Royal New Zealand Navy. He concentrates on ships and episodes of that navy.

PLATE: 656.

SPENCER, Richard B. and W.B.

Two British ship portraitists working in the second and third quarters of the 19th century, who may have been brothers. They also painted sea battles, copied from engravings after other artists but in their own style.

The National Maritime Museum, Greenwich, has thirteen ship portraits by them; the Mariners Museum, Newport News, has a Battle of Camperdown and a ship portrait signed "R.B. Spencer". The Peabody Museum of Salem has three ship portraits all signed by "R.B. Spencer".

PLATE: 489.

SPIN, Jacob **1806-1875**

Born and died in Amsterdam. A painter and draughtsman, mostly in watercolours. His work can be found in the Scheepvaart Museum, Amsterdam, the Prins Hendrik Museum, Rotterdam, and at Deventer and Dordrecht. The Peabody Museum of Salem has three watercolour ship portraits dated 1843, 1845 and 1855.

SPRAGUE, Howard Freeman **1871-1899**

Born in Huron, Ohio, he was a ship portraitist of the Great Lakes. In his late teens he moved to Superior, Duluth, Minnesota, where he took a job as an illustrator for the American Steel Barge Company. In 1899, after a trip to Puerto Rico as marine illustrator to a New York magazine, he died of tuberculosis in New York.

Examples of his work can be seen at the Dossin Great Lakes Museum, Detroit, the Great Lakes Historical Society Museum, Vermilion, the Fairport Marine Museum, Fairport Harbour, and the Mariners Museum, Newport News, Virginia.

PLATE: 632.

STAETS, Hendrik **fl.c.1635**

A painter of finely crafted marines in the Dutch realist manner, with a grey-brown palette. He was chiefly interested in the fashionable art of depicting storm-tossed ships off rocky coasts. His existence was rediscovered by Captain Eric Palmer about 1950 but no biographical details are known. His style stems from Jan Porcellis (q.v.) and has obvious affinities with those of Pieter Mulier I (q.v.), Simon de Vlieger (q.v.) and Jacob Bellevois (q.v.). He signed "H. Staets" and "H.S." in monogram.

PLATE: 45.

EXAMPLES: National Maritime Museum, Greenwich (3): two are of storms, one signed "H. Staets, 1655", and one of a Dutch Indiaman off a harbour.

STAINTON, George

A mid-19th century artist who painted atmospheric calms rather in the manner of Abraham Hulk (q.v.). Apparently he did not exhibit.

PLATE: 488.

STANFIELD, Clarkson **1793-1867**

Born in Sunderland, December 3rd, 1793, he was the fifth and youngest child of James Field Stanfield (1749-1824) by his first wife Mary Hoad of Cheltenham (died 1801). James Stanfield was an Irishman, sometime Catholic seminarist and an ex-seaman; he was well known in the north-east as an actor and author and at the time of his son's birth was trading as a spirit merchant in Sunderland.

Stanfield inherited his artistic talent from his mother and as a boy probably helped his father paint stage scenery; he also appeared occasionally as a child actor. In 1806 he was apprenticed to an heraldic coach painter but in 1808 went to sea in a Shields collier. In July 1812 in London he was pressed into the navy and served in H.M.S. *Namur,* the Sheerness guardship, under the alias "Roderick Bland". Here he reputedly painted scenery for amateur theatricals and so impressed the Sheerness Commissioner by his help in decorating the port admiral's ball-room that he was promised shore employment; the Commissioner's death however thwarted this chance and Stanfield remained afloat until December 1814, when he was invalided from the service. In March 1815 he obtained a berth as a seaman in the Indiaman *Warley* and sailed to China, returning in May the following year.

In September 1816, having missed his ship for a voyage to India, he was employed as a scene-painter at the East London Theatre (the "Royalty", Stepney), subsequently moving to the new Coburg (the "Old Vic") in 1818, and Astley's Amphitheatre, 1819-21. Touring with the last-named in Edinburgh in 1820-21, his father there introduced him to David Roberts (1796-1864), with whom he is associated as colleague, friend and rival. Both worked at the Coburg until December 1822 when they were engaged by Elliston, "the Great Lessee" of the Theatre Royal, Drury Lane. Here over the next twelve years, Stanfield established his dominance as the most brilliant theatrical painter of the age, with work which both raised scenic standards and had considerable effect on the development of popular taste in landscape art. He was particularly famous for his great "moving dioramas" in Christmas pantomimes; in these, vast land and seascape travelogues some twenty feet high and several hundred feet long unrolled across the stage with complex effects of painting, light and mechanics. He painted similar exhibitions for showing outside the theatre; panoramas of *The Destruction of Algiers,* 1816, and *The Battle of Navarino,* 1827, which he painted with Roberts and others, were toured in England and Europe (1824-29).

Stanfield's rise as an easel artist was contemporary with and encouraged by his scenic fame; though he worked very fast, the fact that he was so prolific in both areas simultaneously caused some astonishment. He first exhibited at the R.A. in 1820 and between 1830 and his death only failed to contribute there in 1839, due to a tour. Some of his early successes were at the B.I. (from 1820) and in 1823 he was an original member of the S.B.A. becoming its President for 1829, the last year in which he exhibited there. Though both a landscape and marine artist, Stanfield most successfully combined the two in coastal views. His best works tend to be of modest size, though he painted large exhibition pieces from an early stage; "Market Boat on the Scheldt" (B.I. 1826; Victoria and Albert Museum) is a good example, "Wreckers off Fort Rouge, Calais", a famous bad one, which none the less won the B.I. £50 premium in 1828 (private collection). In 1830, his stormy sea piece, "St. Michael's Mount" (R.A. 1830; National Gallery of Victoria, Melbourne) attracted William IV's attention and earned its author two royal commissions, "Portsmouth Harbour" and "The Opening of New London Bridge" (B.I. 1832, R.A. 1832). After this Stanfield's prosperity was assured; he was elected A.R.A. in 1832 and R.A. in February 1835, only weeks after giving up the theatre work for which he no longer had need or time.

The occasional scenic work which he later did for friends, especially the actor Macready, only added to his fame; his marine act-drop of the Eddystone light for his close friend Charles Dickens' amateur production of Wilkie Collins' *The Lighthouse* in 1855, is one of the earliest surviving pieces of English scene-painting (Dickens House, London).

Stanfield worked in both oil and watercolour, with very varied results. Generally his oils show the virtues and vices of his scenic training; he had a ready ability for dramatic and complex compositions and his best work is in a style of picturesque realism, painted with bright colour, great clarity and glowing surface effects. He was fascinated by objects rather than ideas and his work avoids violent extremes either in choice of subject or in treatment; "The Abandoned" (R.A. 1856; untraced) — a deserted hulk rolling on a heavy sea — is perhaps his only major oil to convey any powerful imaginative overtone. While his work was straight-forward and unpretentious, the demand for it too often led him to produce dull, contrived potboilers and even his best figure drawing tends to be wooden. Like other scene-painters he had difficulty in handling oil paint atmospherically and his early work is often hard and cold, though the mellower, loose handling of his later oils was much admired.

Few artists can have shown a greater real knowledge of ships and sea conditions than Stanfield. Ruskin thought him Turner's nearest rival as a delineator of cloud forms and said that the nautical knowledge in any of his marine works would have lasted one of the Old Masters a lifetime. The exaggeration reflects the esteem in which Stanfield was held, especially by those who saw his realism as the desirable antithesis to the "mysticism and oracularity" of Turner's later oils. Stanfield himself owed much to Turner's earlier work, and after his death was the undisputed master of British marine painting.

In contrast to his oils, Stanfield's sketches and watercolours are often lively and informal. Early watercolours can be mistaken for Bonington (q.v.) (Stanfield being one of those who capitalised on "le Boningtonisme") but his later work, especially of subjects for engraving is much denser and more finished. He was in fact almost entirely self-taught by his association with artist-scene-painters, notably those of northern connection. He was a friend and admirer of John "Jock" Wilson (q.v.) and was advised by Wilson's master, Alexander Nasmyth (q.v.); at the Coburg Theatre he worked for a time under J.T. Serres (q.v.).

He did much work for engraving beginning in 1827 with contributions to the *London and its Vicinity* of George Cooke, whose son Edward (q.v.) he encouraged as a painter and who became his principal follower. His wide British and European travels furnished material for other works, notably his own *Coast Scenery* (1836) and *Sketches on the Moselle* . . . etc. (1838); the latter contains useful studies of river craft. He also illustrated *The Pirate* and *The Three Cutters* (1836) and *Poor Jack* (1840), sea stories by his friend Captain Marryat.

Stanfield's work was often imitated. He received several artistic honours and was appointed the first Curator of Pictures at Greenwich Hospital in 1844. He was a man of striking appearance (portraits in the National Maritime Museum and the National Portrait Gallery) and widely liked for his simplicity and modesty; in later years he became a devout Catholic. He was twice married, having two children by his first wife (died 1821) and ten by his second; of these the fourth, George Clarkson (q.v.), was his pupil and the eldest to survive him. One of his grandsons, J.R. Bagshawe (q.v.), was also a marine painter. Stanfield is often wrongly called "William" in confusion with his half brother William James (1804-27) also a scene-painter. He died in Hampstead on May 18th, 1867.

Apart from the works named above, Stanfield's most notable marine oils are "The Battle of Trafalgar" (R.A. 1836; United Service Club, London); "The Day after the Wreck" (R.A. 1844; Graves Art Gallery, Sheffield); "On the Dogger Bank" (R.A. 1846; Victoria and Albert Museum); "HMS *Victory* towed into Gibraltar after Trafalgar" (R.A. 1853; Somerleyton Collection).

There is a range of his sketches and watercolours in the British Museum and the Victoria and Albert Museum, which also has other oils. There is a fine small oil ("Orford", 1833) in the Wallace Collection and a good later one ("Shakespeare Cliff, Dover"; R.A. 1863) in the National Maritime Museum; both collections have a few watercolours. There are other works in the Tate Gallery and interesting examples in many provincial collections.

PLATES: 416, 417, 418.

STANFIELD, George Clarkson **1828-1878**

Born on May 1st, 1828 at Buckingham Street, Strand, the second son of Clarkson Stanfield (q.v.) and his second wife Rebecca Adcock. He was trained by and worked with his father and also attended the R.A. schools. He painted both in oil and watercolour exhibiting at the B.I. (1844-67) and at the R.A. (1844-76). Most of his subjects were lake and river landscapes in Italy, Switzerland, down the Rhine and in France but he also painted some coastal views in France and Britain. He was strongly under his father's influence, personally and professionally, and his work is of the same stamp, though distinctively more laboured. In 1854 he married his cousin Maria Blackburn (a daughter of his father's half sister) and had three surviving sons. Both he and his wife were improvident and after his father's death his circumstances and health deteriorated. He died on March 22nd, 1878, of "liver disease" in the house of his sister, Mrs. Bagshawe, at Hampstead; he was 49.

A few examples of his watercolours are to be found in the British Museum, one in the Victoria and Albert Museum and others at Bristol, York and Cartwright Hall, Bradford. There are oils at York and Bristol and some in German collections (e.g. Bonn, Rheinisches Landesmuseum, and Trier); Benezit mentions others in Montreal and Melbourne.

PLATE: 536.

STANNARD, Alfred **1806-1889**

Born in Norwich in 1806; he died there, January 18th, 1889. He was the younger brother of Joseph Stannard (q.v.)and also painted for a living but not to his brother's standard. He exhibited at Norwich, and at the British Institution between 1826 and 1860 showing eight pictures, of which only one appears to have had a nautical theme.

PLATE: 376.

STANNARD, Joseph **1797-1830**

Born in Norwich, September 13th, 1797; he died there, December 7th, 1830. This admirable artist of the Norwich School was also a keen yachtsman. He was a pupil of Robert Ladbrook, the landscape painter. He was a member of the Norwich Society of Artists, exhibiting there and at the British Institution between 1819 and 1828; he also exhibited at the Society of British Artists.

He would undoubtedly have become much better known than he is had he not died young.

PLATE: 375.

STOBART, John R.S.M.A. **b.1929**

Born in Leicester on December 29th, 1929. He studied first at the Derby College of Art, 1946-50, and then at the Royal Academy Schools 1950-56. He first exhibited at the Royal Academy in 1952, also at the Royal Society of British Artists and the Society of Marine Artists. Elected to the Society of Marine Artists in 1956.

He lived in Farnham in the 1960s, where he studied to specialise in paintings of historic deep water sail, at which he achieved a very finished expertise. As there is a good market for this type of painting in America, he finally came to an agreement with the Kennedy Gallery in New York to market his paintings, and has moved himself and his family to Potomac Falls, near Washington. He has specialised in carefully researched scenes of American forts in the 19th century, which have become very popular in the form of signed and remarqued colour plates.

The National Maritime Museum, Greenwich, has a painting by him of H.M.Y. *Britannia* at the opening of the St. Lawrence Seaway in 1959, and the Peabody Museum of Salem has a view of Freetown Harbour with two Elder Dempster ships.

PLATE: 680; COLOUR PLATE: XXVIII.

STOOP, Dirck **c.1610-c.1686**

A native of Utrecht, he was in the Guild of Painters of Utrecht in 1638. In 1662 he was in Lisbon when the Earl of Sandwich arrived in the *Royal Charles* to collect Princess Catherine of Braganza and take her to England to marry King Charles II. Stoop painted the *Royal Charles* lying off Lisbon and accompanied the Princess to England where he produced a set of seven engravings of the journey and marriage. He apparently went back to Utrecht in 1678 but he must have kept up his English connections since he executed a set of three large pictures of the evacuation of Tangier for the Earl of Dartmouth, and that event occurred in 1683. He died in Utrecht about 1686.

Two of the Tangier pictures are on loan to the National Maritime Museum, Greenwich, and the third to the National Army Museum, London.

PLATE: 106.

STOOP, Willem van der **fl.1638-1665**

An Utrecht painter who joined the painters' guild there in 1638 and is known to have been there in 1643. Since he painted the Battle of Lowestoft in 1665, he continued to live there or in the vicinity. The plate illustrated, which is signed "W v Stoop", shows him to have been rather a primitive artist in the manner of Soest (q.v.), Beerstraten (q.v.) and Wou (q.v.). There are other examples of his work, one signed, in the mansion of Skokloster near Stockholm.

PLATE: 19.

STOOTER, Cornelisz Leonardsz **1620-1655**

Born in Leiden, he was a pupil of Julius Porcellis (q.v.), but this is not very evident from his surviving work, which is of pleasing quality, with a fresh brown palette and a nice sense of drama in his lighting effects.

He was doyen of the Leiden Guild in 1648 and died there in 1655. He signed his work "STO".

PLATE: 65.

EXAMPLES: Gemäldegalerie, Dresden (1): fishing vessels in a choppy sea. National Maritime Museum, Greenwich (1): fishing vessels in a choppy sea. Stedelijk Museum, Leiden (1): seascape.

STORCK, Abraham **1644-1710**

Born and died in Amsterdam. Though his master is not known, it may have been his father, Jan Jansen Storck (c.1603-c.1667). Someone good must have taught him since he became one of the best of the second generation Dutch School; and as he was brought up in the city that housed the studios of the van de Veldes (qq.v.) and of Bakhuizen (q.v.), perhaps he worked in one of them.

His style, with its highly finished and luminous glazes, is particularly close to that of Bakhuizen. His favourite subject was the harbour of his native city, busy with craft and people. He also painted fanciful Mediterranean views and accurate battle scenes.

Like the van de Veldes and Bakhuizen he well understood the technicalities of the ships he depicted, whether Dutch or foreign. His output was large and popular and he appears to have employed assistants to turn out "Storcks", many of which he would have worked on, and some of which he signed. This practice explains why the quality of work attributed to him varies so much. His brother Jacobus (q.v.), may also have been working in his studio. This attention to studio work has not helped the master's reputation but when the pictures are autograph throughout they are very fine. Unlike the van de Veldes and Bakhuizen he eschewed very large canvases. He signed his work "A. Storck", "A. Storck fecit" or "A.S."

PLATES: 158, 159, 160, 161, 162, 163.

EXAMPLES: Rijksmuseum, Amsterdam (7): the Russian delegation visiting Amsterdam; Enkhuizen Roads; whaling scene; three of Dutch ships in a Mediterranean harbour; Onrust Island, near Batavia. Amsterdam Historical Museum: Peter the Great at Amsterdam. Scheepvaart Museum, Amsterdam (5): Mediterranean harbour; Battle off Etna 1676; view of the Y at Amsterdam; two of Peter the Great on the Y inspecting the Peter and Paul. *Ulster Museum, Belfast (1): harbour scene. Museum at Bremen (1): view of Rotterdam. Brighton Museum (1): Mediterranean harbour. Brooklyn Museum (1): view of Amsterdam. Fitzwilliam Museum, Cambridge (1): Battle of Lowestoft 1665. Musée de Cherbourg (1): marine. Statens Museum for Kunst, Copenhagen (2): Dutch yacht and a flute off-shore; Battle of Agousta 1676 (also called "off Etna"). Gemäldegalerie, Dresden (1): shipping off Amsterdam. National Gallery, Dublin (1): harbour. National Gallery, Edinburgh (1): review before Peter the Great. Musée Ariana, Geneva (1): port scene. National Maritime Museum, Greenwich (13): Four Days Fight 1666; Battle of Texel; Venetian Pilgrim ship in an Italian port; review of Dutch yachts by Peter the Great; Dutch ships entering a Mediterranean port; Dutch ship off a fort; Dutch shipping in an estuary; shipping off a windmill; fishing boats in a gale off the Dutch coast; four of shipping off Amsterdam. Frans Halsmuseum, Haarlem (1): view of Haarlem in Winter. Mauritshuis, The Hague (1): beach scene. Museum de Bilden Kunst, Leipzig (1): Mediterranean fort. Hermitage, Leningrad (1): yachts in a breeze. National Gallery, London (1): the Maas at Rotterdam. Dulwich Art*

Gallery (1): English yacht passing a Dutch flagship off Rotterdam. Victoria and Albert Museum, Apsley House (1): shipping on a river. Maidstone Museum (2): seaport with ruins; seaport with merchants. City Art Gallery, Manchester (2): shipping; coast scene with figures and shipping. Bavarian State Museum, Munich (3): shipping in a breeze off Amsterdam; beach scene; inland water scene. Musée de la Marine, Paris (1): Four Days Fight 1666. Boymans Museum, Rotterdam (2): Mediterranean port; harbour in Winter. Prins Hendrik Museum, Rotterdam (1): whaling fleet. Schleissheim Museum (2). Schwerin (1): view of Venice. Southend-on-Sea Museum (1): shipping off a town. Springfield Museum of Art, Mass. (1): shipping becalmed off Amsterdam. Hallwye Museum, Stockholm (2): capture of the Swiftsure *1666; kaag in a breeze. Truro Museum (1): Mediterranean port scene. Centraal Museum der Gemeente, Utrecht (1): harbour scene. Akademie der Bildenden Künste, Vienna (2): Mediterranean harbour; Dutch yacht becalmed. Gemäldegalerie, Weimar (2): Mediterranean harbour; smalschip close hauled.*

STORCK, Jacobus **1641-aft.1693**

Born in Amsterdam in 1641, he was supposed to have died there before 1688 but there is a picture dated 1693 at Copenhagen.

He was the second son of Jan Jansen Storck (c.1603-c.1667), who may also have been his master. He preferred subjects in the waterways of Amsterdam and inland waters, rather than the open sea. His style and palette are very like that of his younger brother, Abraham (q.v.), and though the latter could hardly have been his master the similarity suggests that they may have worked closely together, or shared a family studio. He signed his work "J. Storck" or "J. Storck, fecit."

There was another brother, the eldest, called Johannes, who was born in 1630, he was not a marine painter but did landscapes and died about 1670.

EXAMPLES: Rijksmuseum, Amsterdam (1): Nijenrode Castle from the River Vecht. Statens Museum for Kunst, Copenhagen (2): Mediterranean Harbour scene; river scene off a fortified town (dated 1693). Museum at Emden (1): river scene. Museum at Gotha (1): view of Amsterdam. Hermitage, Leningrad (1): calm. Wallace Collection, London (1): castle by a river. Fine Art Museum, Philadelphia (1): view of Rotterdam. Boymans Museum, Rotterdam (2): the old fort of Rotterdam; Rotterdam in Winter.

STOREY, Terence Lionel R.S.M.A. **b.1923**

He studied at Sunderland Art School and Derby College of Art. During the war he was an engineering apprentice with Rolls Royce and then served in the Royal Air Force. After the war he worked in display and graphics but in 1971 he gave this up to become a full-time artist.

He has exhibited at the National Society, the Royal Society of British Artists, the Royal Institute of Oil Painters, and the New English Art Club. He was elected a member of the Royal Society of Marine Artists in 1972 and his diploma work is on loan to the National Maritime Museum, Greenwich. In 1977 he was commissioned by the Port of London Authority to paint "Royal Progress" during the Silver Jubilee Festival, to hang in the World Trade Centre.

STRANOVER, Tobias **c.1684-aft.1724**

Baptised at Nagy-Szeben, July 10th, 1684. Mainly a painter of still life subjects, but one who could clearly paint marines. He worked in Holland, London, Hamburg, Dresden and Hermannstadt.

PLATE: 134.

STUART, Alexander Charles **1831-1898**

Born in Scotland June 2nd, 1831, died in Chester, Pennsylvania, August 3rd, 1898. He was educated in Glasgow and later at Rugby School. His father had a brewery, which he hoped his son would take over. But after studying medicine he joined the Royal Navy, and later the U.S. Navy during the Civil War, and is said to have served in the iron armoured ship *Monitor*.

He married and settled in Chester, Pennsylvania, then in Wilmington, where he is listed in the town directories from 1881 to 1883 as a marine painter. He died in Chester, August 3rd, 1898.

He is best known for his ship portraits, especially the ships of the firm of Harlan and Hollingsworth.

STUART, William

His two exhibits at the Royal Academy in 1848 were a pair, "A Calm" and "A Gale", but at the British Institution, where he exhibited from 1848 to 1858, his pictures were of battles and historical subjects, and tended to be on the large side. He exhibited from the Manor House, Stepney, and though he projects a spirited feeling into his pictures, he did not know a great deal about the ships he was depicting.

The Thomas Coram Foundation for Children, formerly the Foundling Hospital, has his Battle of Trafalgar; the picture of the arrival in England of King George I, illustrated here, was exhibited in 1854.

PLATE: 491.

STUART, William E.D.

There appears to have been a whole family of painters in the Manor House at Stepney in the middle of the 19th century. Apart from William (q.v.), there was this W.E.D. Stuart, who was described when he first exhibited at the Royal Academy as 'Jnr.', and so was probably a William too. His address in 1846 had changed to 22 Stepney Causeway but two years later, when he first exhibited at the British Institution, it was again given as the Manor House. His first exhibit was the Battle of Trafalgar, which is similar in scale and to some extent in style to William's naval scenes, but has a mystical quality about it. He only exhibited one more marine there, the rest of his paintings being mainly of fruit and flowers.

If William was W.E.D.'s father, then Miss G.E. Stuart of the Manor House was probably his sister. She was all fruit and flowers! Even Mrs. William had one picture, called "Winter", exhibited at the British Institution.

PLATE: 470.

STUBBS, William Pierce **1842-1909**

Born in Bucksport, Maine, he was an American professional ship portraitist showing fairly straightforward broadside views of his subjects. The Peabody Museum of Salem has eight signed portraits, one attributed, and a view of his birthplace.

PLATE: 584.

STUCKEY, P.J.

He is a contemporary artist, working in Bristol, who specialises in historic sail subjects.

The National Maritime Museum, Greenwich, has a picture on loan called "Out Punt", showing the barque *Favell* picking up a pilot.

SUNQUA
A Chinese ship portraitist working in the second and third quarters of the 19th century. The Peabody Museum of Salem has eight oils.

SWAGERS, Franz **1756-1836**
Born in Utrecht in August 1756; he was a member of the Utrecht Art School in 1804. He went to Paris about 1810 where he exhibited at the Salon. He died in Paris in July 1836.

None of his pictures located in public collections is a marine.

PLATE: 287.

SWAINE, Francis **c.1720-1782**
Born before 1720. In a list for 1735 of clerks and officers employed by the Treasurer and Commissioners of His Majesty's Navy, Francis Swaine is listed as a messenger; so the generally held estimate of his birth date, about 1740, cannot be right. We do not know how he came to be a marine painter but he was a close contemporary of Charles Brooking (q.v.), whose work he sometimes copied. He was also strongly influenced by Peter Monamy (q.v.), especially in his treatment of studio calms. This is why his work has been mistaken for both those artists' and John Cleveley's (q.v.) as well.

He exhibited at the Free Society exhibitions from their inception in 1761 until the end of his life and, indeed, had put aside seven pictures for exhibition in 1783 which were included posthumously. The same thing was true for the Society of Artists exhibitions, where his work appeared from 1762 to 1783. It is curious that he never exhibited at the Royal Academy. He died in London in 1782.

On the whole Swaine liked to paint general shipping subjects, and often on a small scale. He also took commissions for actions, though in nothing like the numbers of Serres (q.v.) and Paton (q.v.).

PLATES: 222, 223, 224, 225, 226.

EXAMPLES: City Art Gallery, Glasgow (1): shipping in a breeze. National Maritime Museum, Greenwich (17): action between the Monmouth *and the* Foudroyant *1758; battle of Quiberon Bay 1759; English men-of-war at sea with the* Dorset *yacht wearing the Irish ensign in Dublin Bay; English men-of-war in a storm; shipping by moonlight; a royal yacht becalmed off a castle; an East Indiaman in stays, about 1750; pair of panels — an English commodore off a jetty and an Indiaman at sea; an English squadron getting under way; colliers at anchor; English yacht and fishing boat becalmed off the shore; a ship on fire; a Dutch Rear-Admiral at anchor with boats alongside; 2 Dutch ships at anchor with boats alongside; a lugger close-hauled in a strong breeze. Victoria and Albert Museum, London (2): ships leaving Dover; marine. Sigmund Samuel Canadiana Museum, Toronto (1): General Wolfe's headquarters in Gaspe Bay at the mouth of the St. Lawrence before the assault on Quebec 1759.*

SWAINE, Monamy **b.c.1750**
He was probably born in the early 1750s since his first exhibited picture, not a marine, was at the Free Society in 1769, when he was described as "Mr. Swaine Junior". His first name honoured the memory of Peter Monamy (q.v.), though his father, Francis (q.v.), seems to have had closer connections with Brooking since he copied some of his works. So perhaps young Swaine was fortunate not to have been named Brooking Swaine. He continued to exhibit at the Free Society until 1774, only two of his pictures being marines. After this records on him and his work peter out, and it may be that he died about this time.

The National Maritime Museum, Greenwich, has four upright marines by him, which are not of high quality, but in which the influence of the father is obvious.

PLATE: 275.

SWIFT, John Warkup **1815-1869**
Born in Hull in 1815; died Newcastle-on-Tyne, May 7th, 1869. He first went to sea, then came ashore to be a theatrical scene painter. He also took to painting rather good quality marines. Examples can be seen in the Shipley Art Gallery, Gateshead, the Ferens Art Gallery, Hull, and the Laing Art Gallery, Newcastle-on-Tyne.

PLATE: 476.

SYER, James **fl.1870s**
A son of John Syer (q.v.), he was known as J. Syer Jnr. He exhibited two paintings at the Royal Academy in 1872, a Cornish coastal scene and a wreck scene, also a view of St. Michael's Mount in 1873.

SYER, John **1815-1885**
Born in Atherston 1815, died in Exeter 1885. Although his son was called James (q.v.), they are referred to as J. Syer "Senior" and "Junior". John's early masters are not known but from 1848, when in his thirties, he was instructed by a British miniature painter called Fisher. He was primarily a landscape and coastal marine painter, though the picture illustrated here shows he could be an accomplished painter of the sea and ships.

PLATE: 475.

T

TAICHEONG
A Chinese ship portraitist working in Hong Kong in the second half of the 19th century. The Peabody Museum of Salem has an oil by him.

TANNEUR, Philippe **1795-1878**
Born and died in Marseilles. He was a pupil of Horace Vernet, the history painter, and his first exhibited paintings at the Paris Salon were of sea fights. He also exhibited four works at the Royal Academy Exhibition of 1841: Dutch shipping, view of St. Petersburg, the coast at Dover and a view in Normandy. The museums of Calais and Compiègne have marines, that of Draguignan, a view of Toulon Roads at sunset; at La Rochelle, there are two, the frigate *Belle Poule* and a shipwreck; at Montpellier, a marine; at Nantes, a calm; at Narbonne, a view near Bordeaux.

TASSI *see* **BUONAMICO, Agostino**

TAYLOR, Charles, the Elder **fl.1836-1871**
A London artist who first exhibited at the Royal Academy in 1836. His early exhibits were genre historical subjects, but in 1848 he showed "A Brig on the Sands unloading her Cargo", and from then on until 1871, the last year in which he exhibited, the subjects of his paintings were all marine.

TAYLOR, Charles, the Younger **fl.1843-1866**
He exhibited at the Royal Institution first in 1843, and between then and 1866; also at the Royal Academy in 1846, 1847 and 1849, mostly marines but some landscapes. His marines are in watercolours and in a style close to that of T.G. Dutton, with whom he collaborated and who lithographed some of his work. Taylor was also a lithographer, and examples of these and his watercolours can be found in the National Maritime Museum, Greenwich.

PLATE: 574.

TAYLOR, Robert **b.1946**
Born on February 11th, 1946, in Bath, where he still works. He specialises in naval scenes, to which he brings a high degree of technical knowledge. A colour print of his painting of H.M.S. *Cavalier,* countersigned by Lord Mountbatten, raised £20,000 for the *Cavalier* Trust. He has exhibited at galleries at home and abroad, including the Royal Society of Marine Artists' annual exhibitions.

TEUPKEN, D.A. **1801-1845**
A Dutch ship portraitist of Amsterdam, with a rather compelling style. The Altonaer Museum in Hamburg has four pen and wash drawings and the Peabody Museum of Salem one. The Maritime Museum at Kronborg Castle also has examples.

PLATE: 455.

THOMAS, Lieut. Robert Strickland R.N. **1787-1853**
Born October 18th, 1787; died between March 20th and June 20th, 1853. He entered the Royal Navy as an able seaman aboard the *Princess Charlotte,* frigate, in 1805. He was promoted to midshipman in her and it may be that he got his grounding in art in her gunroom, for her captain, George Tobin, was an enthusiastic amateur painter who later retired to Teignmouth and painted with Thomas Luny (q.v.). Thomas was master's mate in the sloop *Brisk* from 1807 to 1813, then joined the frigate *Creole* and was made acting lieutenant. She took part in the blockade of Cherbourg in 1814 and then cruised on the coast of Africa, where he contracted a disease that left him deaf, making him unfit for service, though he was confirmed in the rank of lieutenant in 1815.

He took up painting as a profession to augment his half pay and concentrated mainly on Royal Naval subjects; his pictures are well crafted and reminiscent of the Condys (qq.v.).

He only exhibited three pictures at the Royal Academy, in 1839, 1841 and 1842.

EXAMPLES: National Maritime Museum, Greenwich (5): Queen Victoria visiting H.M.S. Queen *at Portsmouth in 1842; H.M.S.* Britannia *leaving Malta in 1835; H.M.S.* Britannia *entering Portsmouth Harbour in 1835; the loss of H.M.S.* Hero *in 1811; H.M.S.* Raleigh.

THORNELY, Charles
This artist first started exhibiting marines at the Royal Academy in 1859 from an address in Paddington, London, and also at the British Institution from 1861 until it closed in 1867. He continued to exhibit at the Royal Academy until 1898.

According to Denys Brook-Hart, he liked to confuse by signing a number of aliases, such as William Thornely, or variations of Thornberry.

THORP, William Eric R.S.M.A., P.S. **b.1901**
Born in London, he was educated at the City of London School, and studied art under Herbert Dicksee and Herbert Schroder. At seventeen he was elected to the Artists' Society, the youngest member ever, and in 1917 joined the Langham Art Club, where one of the members was the marine painter Arthur Burgess (q.v.).

In 1947 Eric Thorp was one of the founder members of the Wapping Group and its President for the first five years. He was elected to the now Royal Society of Marine Artists in 1958, and the Pastel Society in 1952. He has also exhibited at the Royal Academy.

Public galleries holding examples of his work include the Guildhall Art Gallery and the National Maritime Museum, Greenwich, where his R.S.M.A. diploma picture "Early Morning on the River Orwell" is on loan.

TINDALL, B.
A British ship portraitist working in the south of England in the third quarter of the 19th century. His work is of quite good quality, and one known example is in the Peabody Museum of Salem.

TINDALL, Charles E.S. **1863-1951**
Born in Aberdeenshire in 1863, he emigrated to Australia, where he studied under Julian Ashton and Frank Mahony in Sydney. He was a member of the Art Society of New South Wales, and of the Australian Watercolour Institute. He knew Charles Conder, from whom he received encouragement.

He died in Sydney in 1951. His work can be seen in the National Gallery of New South Wales in Sydney.

TOLEDO, Juan de (called El Capitan) **1611-1665**
He was born in Lorca in south-west Spain. As a youth he went to Naples and joined the army. He also studied painting there under Aniello Falcone, and later, in Rome, under Michelangelo Cerquozzi, who was, among other things, a painter of battles. On his return to Spain he set himself up as a painter in Granada, concentrating on battle pieces. Later he moved to Talavera, Madrid and Alcala de Henares, and died in Madrid on February 1st, 1665.

He had a successful practice, but hardly qualified as a marine painter, since his three pieces depicting sea fights between the Spanish and Barbary pirates at the Prado concentrate more on the genre than the marine aspect.

PLATE: 4.

TORREY, Charles **1859-1921**
An American ship portraitist and copyist of reasonable competence. The Peabody Museum of Salem has eight oils by him.

TRUEKEN, M.
A German ship portraitist working in Altona in the third quarter of the 19th century. The Peabody Museum of Salem has a watercolour by him dated 1865.

TRUELSEN, Mathias Jacob Theodore **1836-1900**
A German ship portraitist who was also a lithographer and photographer in Altona. He was the son of Nis Nissen Truelsen (q.v.). The Altonaer Museum in Hamburg has a pen and wash drawing by him and the Maritime Museum, Kronborg Castle, has ship portraits.

TRUELSEN, Nis Nissen **1792-1862**
A German sailor turned ship portraitist who worked in Altona. He was the father of Mathias Truelsen (q.v.).

The Altonaer Museum, Hamburg, has a pen and wash drawing, and he is represented in the Royal Naval Museum, Copenhagen.

TUDGAY family
Efforts to find out details of this family of talented ship portraitists, working probably in London in the second half of the 19th century, have so far proved abortive, and as time goes by hopes of finding more must dim.

There are pictures signed with the initials F., J., L. and possibly I. Also pictures signed J. & L. and J. & F. They never exhibited.

EXAMPLES: J. Tudgay: Auckland City Art Gallery (1): a ship off Dover. F. Tudgay: National Maritime Museum, Greenwich (3): ship portraits. Peabody Museum of Salem (2): ship portraits. J. and F. Tudgay: Peabody Museum of Salem (1): ship portrait. L. Tudgay: Peabody Museum of Salem (1): Battle of Heligoland, 1864.

TUKE, Henry Scott R.A., R.W.S. **1858-1929**
Born York, June 12th, 1858, he was a pupil of the Slade School from 1875 to 1880, then studied in Italy and Paris under the history painter, Jean-Paul Laurens, 1881-3.

He settled in Newlyn in Cornwall and with Stanhope Forbes was a pillar of the Newlyn School. He painted boating scenes in which the main interest is usually in the nude bathers, for which he is best known. He also painted marines, human portraits and genre subjects. He later lived near Falmouth, where he died on March 30th, 1929.

He first exhibited at the Royal Academy in 1879. In 1889 his painting "All hands to the Pumps", was bought for the Chantrey Bequest, and is now on loan from the Tate Gallery to the National Maritime Museum. A.R.A. 1900, R.A. 1914. Other pictures of his, though not marines, can be seen at public galleries in Leeds, Liverpool, Munich, Nottingham and Sydney, Australia.

TURNER, Charles E. **1883-1965**
Born September 14th, 1883. A reticent man, it is difficult to find out much about him. He was an illustrator of the same generation as Norman Wilkinson (q.v.), and worked for the *Illustrated London News* and the *Sphere*. In the Second World War he painted naval actions where the camera was not present and these appeared as double-page spreads. His work is well-crafted, highly finished and the naval details expertly observed. For many years he lived at Looe in Cornwall. He died on April 14th, 1965.

PLATE: 672.

EXAMPLES: National Maritime Museum, Greenwich (7): sinking of the Bismarck *1941 sinking of the* Scharnhorst *1943; H.M.S.* Montrose *entering Reykjavik; H.M.S.* Vanguard *in dry dock at Plymouth; H.M.S.* Vanguard *being towed out of Portsmouth Harbour to the breakers 1960; H.M.S.* Vernon II *consisting of the battleships* Malaya *and* Ramillies *moored together in Portsmouth Harbour in 1945; H.M.S.* Woolston.

TURNER, Joseph Mallord William R.A. **1775-1851**
Born Covent Garden, London, April 23rd, 1775. He was the son of a barber in Maiden Lane, Covent Garden. His interest in drawing was early and precocious, and his father, who was later his business assistant, hung up some of his earliest drawings for sale in the barber's shop above which they lived. At fourteen he joined the Royal Academy Schools, and in 1790 the first of his paintings was accepted by the Academy for hanging in the annual exhibition.

The early exhibited works of Turner do not suggest any particular interest in marine subjects; from the early years of the 19th century, however, marine subjects began to appear and the sea excited a growing interest from an experimental artist who was more and more obsessed with capturing fleeting effects. As a young man Turner greatly admired de Loutherbourg (q.v.) and was much influenced by the Romantic movement. He visited the de Loutherbourgs so frequently that it is said that Mrs. de Loutherbourg, fearful that he was learning all her husband's secrets, barred him from the house.

His early marines were certainly encouraging, some being among the finest ever painted, such as "Calais Pier", 1803, and the great picture of Dutch fishing boats, which the Duke of Bridgewater commissioned as a companion to his splendid van de Velde the Younger (q.v.) of a similar subject. His few attempts at naval historical subjects were not so happy. No doubt inspired by the blowing up of the French flagship there, he painted a Battle of the Nile in 1798. In 1806 he began a painting of the Battle of Trafalgar, a deck scene rather than a marine, and unsuccessful. His next endeavour was a golden opportunity, which in the event proved a disaster. King George IV wished to commission a Battle of Trafalgar as a pair to the great de Loutherbourg of the Glorious First of June, to hang as a pair in the ante-room of St. James's Palace. The Trafalgar was painted in 1824, and although the *Victory* itself is very impressive, the picture as a whole fails. The King, who was as good a judge of art as any of his subjects, did not like it, the admirals hated it and the waiting ambassadors are said to have sneered at it. In the end the King got out of his predicament by giving both pictures to the naval gallery in Greenwich Hospital.

Matthew Henry Barker recalls a scene in the reign of William IV, the Sailor King, when Barker visited the Painted Hall at Greenwich and had the following conversation with one of the pensioners about the picture: "I don't like the picture," said he; "the perspective is bad and the ship is too long and flat; besides, the colour is unnatural." "Why, as for the matter of the perspective, Sir," replied the veteran, "that's just what his present Majesty, God bless him! observed when he came to look at it; and for the colour, says the King, 'why the painter must have thought he'd been cooking, for he has shoved the *Victory* into the hottest of the fire and done her brown'." The commission was a bitter experience for Turner.

His art in any case was progressing beyond the realities of the sea and ships, and any consideration of his massive and magnificent output of work, in oil and watercolour, in which the sea is a theme for poetic interpretation is certainly beyond the scope of a historical dictionary such as this. There is, of course, a vast literature on him; his original *Life* by G.W. Thornburg is notoriously inaccurate but an important source for many points. Far more reliable is A.W. Finberg's monumental *Chronicle biography*. Ruskin's *Modern Painters* is entirely founded on a justification of Turner and among many critical and catalogue works may be noted the following: *Turner* (R.A./Tate Exhibition 1975); *Turner Watercolours* (British Museum); Luke Herman, Butlin and Joll, *The Paintings of J.M.W. Turner,* 1958.

Only with "The Fighting *Temeraire* going to her last berth", painted in 1839, did he really successfully combine art and a naval occasion. On the other hand, Clarkson Stanfield (q.v.), the doyen of mid-19th century marine painters, had this to say to a friend, C.R. Leslie, who was critical of Turner's shipping paintings: "There is no doubt you are right, and I side with the sailors as far as his actual knowledge of the construction and working of a ship, but he possessed a wonderful discrimination and power on the character of the craft he depicted, and there is no mistaking whether he meant a man-of-war, a merchantman or a collier."

Turner continued to exhibit at the Royal Academy until 1850, and at the British Institution between 1806 and 1846. He died in Chelsea on December 19th, 1851.

On his death he bequeathed the very considerable contents of his studio to the nation. Thus, the famous (even notorious) "Turner Bequest" was housed first in the National Gallery; then, when the Tate Gallery was formed to take care of British and modern art, it was transferred there, though not all of it or all at once. Of this collection something less than fifty of the oil paintings are marine subjects, but there are also many sketches and watercolours, of which the great majority are in the British Museum.

PLATE: 315, 316, 317, 318.

EXAMPLES: Cecil Higgins Gallery, Bedford (1): a first-rate taking on stores. National Gallery of Wales, Cardiff (6). Museum of Fine Arts, Boston (1): the Slave Ship. National Maritime Museum, Greenwich (1): Battle of Trafalgar. Wadsworth Atheneum, Hartford, Conn. (1): Tromp's shallop at the entrance to the Scheldt. William Rockhill Nelson Gallery of Art, Kansas City (1): the fish market on Hastings beach. Tate Gallery, London (45): Tromp after the Battle of Dogger Bank 1752; landing of William of Orange at Torbay 1688; Battle of Trafalgar 1805; two sketches for the Battle of Trafalgar at Greenwich; Calais Pier with the arrival of an English packet 1802/3; shipwreck with fishing boats trying to rescue the crew 1803; Spithead with two captured Danish ships entering Portsmouth Harbour 1807-9; Bligh Sand near Sheerness with fishing boats trawling 1809; entrance to the Meuse with Orange Merchant *going to pieces on the bar c.1819; the Fighting* Temeraire *being tugged to her last berth 1838;* Peace *buried at sea 1841; snow storm with a steamboat off a harbour mouth 1842; fishing boats bringing a disabled ship into Port Ruysdael 1844; whalers 1845; Hurrah for the whaler* Erebus *1846; whaler's blubber entangled in the ice 1846; fire at sea (unfinished) c.1834; two of yacht racing in the Solent 1827; regatta at Cowes; two of shipping at Cowes; a ship aground c.1831; the burning of ships 1845; snow storm at a wreck with fishing boats 1842; shipping at the mouth of the Thames c.1807; coast scene with fishermen and boats c.1808; steamer and lightship; seascape with a sailing boat and a ship; and fifteen general seascapes. Iveagh Bequest, Kenwood, London (1): fishermen on a lee shore. Victoria and Albert Museum, London: mainly watercolours. British Museum: many watercolours. City Art Gallery, Manchester (1): Pas de Calais. Yale Centre for British Art, New Haven, Conn. (1): stormy sea breaking on a shore 1840-5. Metropolitan Museum, New York (2): a whaler; Saltash. Frick Collection, New York (4): Antwerp; vessels moored by Cologne; Dieppe Harbour; a Dutch boeier close hauled in a strong breeze. National Gallery of Canada, Ottawa (1): Shoeburyness with a fisherman hailing. City Art Gallery, York (1): study for the wreck of a transport ship.*

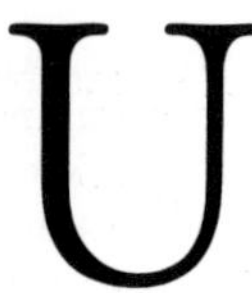

ULPTS, Captain Gerhards

A German merchant service officer, who was in the German Navy in the Second World War and served aboard the pocket battleship *Admiral Graf Spee,* though not on her last cruise.

In 1963 he painted a picture of her, which he and others who had served in her wished to present to the National Maritime Museum, Greenwich; this they did in person through the good offices of Sir Eugene Millington-Drake, who had been British ambassador to Uruguay at the time the *Graf Spee* was sunk in the River Plate in 1939.

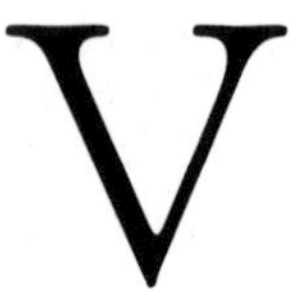

VALE, H. **fl.1700**

The paintings signed H. Vale are by the earliest known English marine painter, about whom little is known, except what can be deduced from his signed work. The National Maritime Museum, Greenwich, has a large painting of the relief of Barcelona by Admiral Sir John Leake in 1706 and a portrait of the *Royal Katherine* of a somewhat earlier date (on loan). A feature of both these paintings is a large decorative label in the top of the pictures, edged with shells and coral. The quality is good.

PLATES: 179, 180.

VALE, R. **fl.1700**

It is just possible that this Vale was a Richard Vale who died in Mitcham in 1716. The National Maritime Museum, Greenwich, has a painting signed R. Vale, of English men-of-war, one of which is wearing the royal standard of Queen Anne, after the Act of Union with Scotland of 1707. The quality is not up to that of the paintings signed H. Vale.

VELDE, Cornelis van de **c.1675-1729**

His marriage entry in the Knightbridge Chapel in 1699 Anglicises his name to Cornelius, but undoubtedly he would have been Cornelis to his Dutch family.

This marriage was to Bernada, daughter of J.C. van de Hagen who was a friend and follower of Cornelis' father, W. van de Velde the Younger (q.v.).

Cornelis was born in England after the family moved from Holland in 1672/3, and although he grew up to be an established marine painter, praised by J.C. Weyerman in his *De levens-beschrijvengen der Nederlandsche Konst Schilders,* 1729, as being "the best of all marine painters we could name", his identity managed to sink into obscurrity for many years.

Speculation as to which hand was his ended when a signed storm piece appeared on the London market in 1965, and was bought by the National Maritime Museum. This picture enabled identification of a number of others. Later a couple of signed calms came to light, which completed the identification. These are in a highly finished and detailed style, more like the work of his grandfather than of his father. The calms have a characteristic pinkness in the sky.

One feature which may have contributed to Cornelis' long obscurity is his crabbed little signature, which is difficult to read. His standing as an artist in his lifetime, however, may be judged to some extent from his being asked to report on the progress of the work of Sir James Thornhill in the Painted Hall at Greenwich in 1717.

The National Maritime Museum, Greenwich, has a painting of ships driving onto a rocky coast in a storm.

PLATES: 190, 191.

VELDE, Pieter van den **1634-aft.1687**

Born and died in Antwerp. Mainly a painter of battle scenes in the Flemish manner, though of middling quality.

PLATES: 110, 111.

EXAMPLES: Rijksmuseum, Amsterdam (2): the Battle of the Sound 1658; the Dutch in the Medway 1667. National Maritime Museum, Greenwich (2): shipping off a Mediterranean harbour; shipping off a rocky coast, both very small. Nationalmuseum, Stockholm (3): a port with a castle; a castle by the sea; a shipwreck.

VELDE, Willem van de, the Elder **1611-1693**

Born in Leiden, the son of a shipmaster, he went to sea as a boy. He married young and soon after the birth of his elder son, Willem the Younger (q.v.), in 1633, moved to Amsterdam; here his younger son, Adriaen, was born in 1636. Both boys were to grow up to be greater painters than their father, though only Willem inherited his father's love of the sea and ships. Adriaen, who was a pupil of his father, may have had too much of it as a child, for he turned his gaze firmly away from the sea and has left us rustic scenes of cows and people.

The elder van de Velde must be one of the earliest men, if not the earliest, to accompany a fleet into action as the official recording artist. Accompanying Marten Tromp's fleet in a galjoot in 1653 he was present at the Battle of Scheveningen and afterwards reported on it to the government. In 1658 he was with Wassenaer's fleet when it fought the Swedes at the Battle of the Sound. He afterwards regularly accompanied the Dutch fleet and at the outbreak of the Second Dutch War was present at the Battle of Lowestoft, but no picture was commissioned of this since the Dutch were badly beaten. The following year he was with the fleet during the Four Days Fight, June 1st-4th, 1666, after which the Council of State did order a picture. Up to this time van de Velde's finished works for sale had all been what we call grisaille drawings. These were pen and ink drawings on prepared gesso panels, or sometimes canvases. It is not clear whether van de Velde developed this art form himself or whether he learnt it from Heerman Witmont (q.v.), which seems the more likely. Unlike Witmont's work, which is generally done in sepia ink, van de Velde worked in black ink and he perfected his technique to a level never attained by anyone else; his grisailles, often four or five feet across, are one of the great glories of Dutch art.

It was a technique that enabled van de Velde to project in the finest detail his deep and expert knowledge of ships. They did, however, take weeks or months to complete and must have been a strain on the eyes. This combination of reasons led him to turn to oils, an art he probably learnt from his son in the late 1660s when they were working in the same studio.

He was with the fleet at the outbreak of the Third Dutch War and sketched the Battle of Solebay, May 28th, 1672. During that year the war went badly for the Dutch, with a French army at Utrecht, but in June King Charles II invited Dutch emigrants to England where, amongst other opportunities, there was a ready and increasing market for paintings. Even though the two countries were at war, the packet service between Briel and Harwich still ran and about 1672 or the beginning of 1673 the van de Veldes crossed by it to England. There is a painting at Greenwich signed in London in 1672 but as the Julian calendar still pertained, which made New Year's Day March 25th, it could have been painted in 1673 by the Gregorian calendar now in use.

The van de Veldes were immediately in receipt of royal patronage from the King and the Duke of York, to name but two, and the elder van de Velde was soon in an English yacht accompanying the English fleet to record the two Battles of Schooneveld in June, this time from the English viewpoint. In August, Charles II would not let him accompany the fleet when it sailed to fight the Battle of Texel for fear he might be killed.

From this time and for the last twenty years of his long life (he died in Greenwich on December 13th, 1693), the studio of van de Velde and his son Willem, dominated marine painting in England and their style and approach to their subjects were the models and inspiration for the first generation of English marine painters.

Also working in van de Velde's studio were other Dutch expatriots, J.C. van de Hagen, his grandson Cornelis (q.v.), almost certainly Adriaen van Diest (q.v.), and probably Jacob Knyff (q.v.). Van de Velde would have welcomed the company of his countrymen since he is not thought to have mastered the English tongue.

His grisailles are signed on the front, but oil paintings on canvas are usually signed on the back.

PLATES: 97, 98, 99, 100.

EXAMPLES: Grisaille pictures in public collections: Municipal Museum, Alkmaar: Battle of the Sound 1658. Rijksmuseum, Amsterdam (13): Battle of Dunkirk 1639; Battle of the Downs 1639; Battle of Scheveningen 1653; Battle of Leghorn 1653; two of the Battle of the Sound 1658; the action at Bergen 1665; the Council of War before the Four Days Fight 1666; the first day of the Four Days Fight 1666; two crowded scenes of Dutch yachts; a Dutch ship in a harbour after a battle; Dutch ships under sail. Scheepvaart Museum, Amsterdam (2): the Dutch ship Vergulde Zon; *Dutch ships before a light breeze. Kweekschool voor de Scheepvaart (1): action off Nieuwport 1653. Municipal Gallery, Cork (1): Dutch bezan yachts under sail. National Gallery of Scotland, Edinburgh (1): a Dutch ship and a Swedish flute near the shore. Palazzo Pitti, Florence (2): Battle of the Sound 1658; Dutch ships at sea. Poggio Imperiale, Florence (2): a pair of Dutch ships at sea. Frediksborg Museum, Zealand (1): Battle of the Sound 1658. National Maritime Museum, Greenwich (17): Battle of Scheveningen 1653; Battle of the Sound 1658; the Dutch fleet off Sheerness during the attack on the Medway 1667; the First Battle of Schooneveld 1673; a wijdschip and shipping off a harbour; a Dutch flagship off the shore; a Dutch flagship near the shore with a Swedish ship in the background; a Dutch ship lying to; the Dutch fleet near the shore; English ships in light airs; Dutch East Indiamen; Dutch merchantmen; Dutch yachts and a tavern by the shore; Dutch flagships close inshore; Dutch flagship near the shore; Dutch men-of-war and barges off a jetty; Dutch boeier yachts. Lakenhal, Leiden (1): Tromp's fleet off Katwijk. Musée des Beaux-Arts, Lille (1): Dutch flute and other ships near the shore. Hampton Court, London (1): the* Royal Prince *under sail (Royal Collection). Yale Centre for British Art, New Haven (1): shipping on the Mediterranean coast. Palazzo Chigi, Rome (1): the surrender of the* Royal Prince *1666. Prins Hendrik Museum, Rotterdam (5): Battle of the Sound 1658; the* Eendracht *at anchor; the* Mercurius *and other shipping; a galjoot under sail near the shore; two bezan yachts. Skokloster Castle, Sweden (1): Battle of Femeren 1644. Wellesley College Museum, Mass. (1): shipping off the Dutch coast.*

Oil paintings: Berkeley Castle, near Bristol (2): the Tiger *under sail in two positions; the* Tiger *with the King on board. National Maritime Museum, Greenwich (7): the Second Battle of Schooneveld 1673; the* Charles Galley; *the* Portsmouth *yacht; the* Royal Prince; *the* St. Andrew; *the* Woolwich; *English ships becalmed.*

VELDE, Willem van de, the Younger 1633-1707

Born in Leiden on December 18th, 1633, he was the elder son of Willem van de Velde the Elder (q.v.). He inherited his father's love of ships and the sea. He was a pupil of his father, who taught him to draw; he then went to Simon de Vlieger (q.v.), who taught him to paint. His earliest known painting is at Greenwich and is dated 1651, when he was seventeen or eighteen. It is of ships driving on to rocks in a storm, and is very much like his master's style but not yet nearly so good.

His early works are highly finished and carefully crafted. As he got older and more confident his style broadened and he achieved his effects with more economy of brushstrokes. His palette changed too, from predominantly grey in his Dutch period to warmer browns in his English period.

Drawing was the basis of the van de Veldes' art and both father and son poured out drawings all their lives. By these we know more about the appearance and decoration of Dutch, French and English ships of their time than we do about those of the 18th century.

In painting, the younger man was to excel his father; in drawing, though, he does not seem to have competed with him in attempting grisailles. Even so, many of the ship portraits are very similar but under magnification the drawings of the carved figures on the ships do not read in the older man's work, while in the younger man's drawings they do.

A feature of both men's drawings is that the ships are depicted in isometric perspective, thus enabling them to be used in paintings and grisailles at any distance in the composition. This is acceptable even though ships in the near foreground would not be seen in isometric perspective in reality; this means that there is a lack of immediacy about the van de Veldes' pictures which was to continue throughout the 18th century, since their followers also followed this practice. It was the 19th century painters like Turner and Chambers (qq.v.) who returned to viewer's perspective.

Young van de Velde joined his father's studio in Amsterdam and worked there for the next twenty years. Towards the end of this period he became influenced by the style of Ludolf Bakhuizen (q.v.), possibly because that artist was enjoying a considerable success, and so much so that the most notable of the Bakhuizen-type van de Veldes, the great Ellesmere picture, now in Toledo, Ohio, has been mistaken by both Dutch and English experts for a Bakhuizen; the handling of the paint in this is not however like Bakhuizen's.

Contemporary records in England relate that while father made the live drawings of the actions at sea, his son translated them into oil paintings, though it is true to say that father also made oils from his own drawings. Although the van de Veldes had received generous patronage both from King Charles and King James, they had no difficulty in welcoming Dutch William to the throne after the Glorious Revolution of 1688.

After his father's death in 1693, the mantle of being marine painter to the King and Queen fell onto Willem's shoulders and in 1694 the commanders of the fleet were ordered to provide food and accommodation for him and his servant as long as he stayed aboard any of Their Majesties' ships. In the following year he accompanied the Straights Fleet to the Mediterranean.

Like his father, he is not thought to have acquired much knowledge of the English language, which could account for the lack of any known English pupil, although between them the van de Veldes worked for a period of thirty-five years in England. Van de Velde the Younger died in Greenwich on April 6th, 1707.

Considering that both father and son lived to a good age and worked to the end of their lives, it is not surprising that their output was prodigious, and that much of it survives. At Greenwich alone there are 1,400 drawings, a mine of information on the naval scene in the second half of the 17th century.

He usually signed on the backs of canvases, but sometimes on the front; variously "W. van Velde J", "W.V. Velde der Jonge", "W.V. Velde", "W.V.V.", "W.V.V.J."

PLATES: 143, 144, 145, 146, 147, 148, 149, 150, 151, 152, 153, 154, 155, 156; COLOUR PLATE: IX.

EXAMPLES: Rijksmuseum, Amsterdam (16): capture of the Royal Prince *at the Four Days Fight 1666; English prizes after the Four Days Fight 1666; Battle of Solebay 1672; Battle of the Texel 1673; the* Gouden Leeuw *off Amsterdam after the Battle of the Texel 1673; the cannon shot; ship in a heavy sea, "the gust"; six calms; two of shipping in a breeze; fishing boats on a beach. Scheepvaart Museum, Amsterdam (1): English coastal scene. Musées Royaux des Beaux-Arts, Antwerp (1): calm. Gemäldegalerie, Berlin (1): ship saluting. Cannon Hall, Barnsley (1): calm. Musée de Besançon (1): harbour scene. Birkenhead Museum (1): St. Michael's Mount. Birmingham City Art Gallery (1): two-decker in a gale. Russell-Cotes Museum, Bournemouth (1): calm. City Art Gallery, Bristol (1): calm. Musées Royaux des Beaux-Arts, Brussels (1): shipping on the Zuider Zee. National Gallery, Budapest (1): men-of-war in a calm. Fitzwilliam Museum, Cambridge (1): storm. Canterbury Museum (1): seascape. Musée de Chantilly (1): calm. Wallraf-Richartz Museum, Cologne (1): storm. Statens Museum for Kunst, Copenhagen (3). Culzean Castle, Ayrshire (1): calm. Gemäldegalerie, Dresden (1): ships in a fresh breeze. National Gallery, Dublin (2): Dutch men-of-war at sea; English ships saluting. Musée de Dunkerque (1). National Gallery, Edinburgh (1): calm. Stadelsches Kunstinstitut, Frankfurt (2): calms. Gateshead Museum (3): seascapes with shipping. Glasgow Museum and Art Gallery (3): Dutch men-of-war at sea; Dutch States yacht running down on the fleet; evening gun. National Maritime Museum, Greenwich (36): action at Bergen 1665; Battle of Solebay 1672 (on loan from Ministry of Defence); burning of the* Royal James *at the Battle of Solebay 1672; five paintings of the Battle of Texel 1673; journey of Princess Mary and the Prince of Orange, "the Honeymoon Voyage", to Holland 1677; the* Kingfisher *and Barbary pirates 1681; Princess Mary arriving at Gravesend 1689; the* Resolution *in a gale; the* Royal Sovereign; *the* Royal Escape; *a ship lying to in a gale; two of English ships wrecked on a rocky coast; two of Dutch ships wrecked on a rocky coast; four storms; beach scene; arrival of the Dutch East India fleet; a Dutch States yacht running down to the fleet; shipping in a fresh breeze; a Dutch ship under way and two at anchor; Dutch vessels off a pier; an action between an English ship and Barbary pirates; an English squadron going to windward in a gale; English merchantmen in a Mediterranean harbour; moonlight; a vessel before a fresh breeze; a ship rigged yacht firing a salute; English royal yachts at sea. Musée de Grenoble (1): squadron at sea. Gemäldegalerie, Hamburg (1). Gemäldegalerie, Hanover (1): Battle of Solebay. Mauritshuis, The Hague (4): taking of the* Royal Prince; *three calms. Musée de Le Havre (3): ships dressed; rough sea; vessel on a beach. Staatliche Kunstsammlung, Kassel (3): calm; seascape; coastal scene. The Hermitage, Leningrad (2): calms. National Gallery, London (14): six of shipping in a breeze; six calms; two of shipping in a gale. Wallace Collection, London (8): Battle of Solebay 1672; Dutch men-of-war saluting in a calm; two calms with small vessels; embarkation of William of Orange from Hellevoetsluis in 1688; landing from ships of war; coast scene; shipping in a breeze. Musée de Lyon (2): Dutch squadron; calm. Bayerische Staatsgemäldesammlungen, Munich (3). Musée de Nantes (1): calm. Nottingham Museum (1): marine. Nuremburg (1): marine. Musée d'Orléans (1): naval battle. Louvre, Paris (3): a Dutch ship in a moderate breeze; a calm with a states yacht; calm with Dutch small craft. Petit Palais, Paris (1): calm. Netherlands Institute, Paris (3): beach scene; surrender of the* Royal Prince *1666; council of war in the Dutch fleet 1665. John G. Johnson Collection, Fine Art Museum, Philadelphia (1): calm. National Museum, Prague (1): rough sea scene. Reading Museum (1): ships at anchor. Boymans van Beuningen Museum, Rotterdam (3): dunes at Zandvoort; Texel Roads; calm. Musée de Rouen (1): sea battle. National Museum, Stockholm (4): shipping in a fresh breeze; three scenes with fishing vessels. National Gallery of New South Wales, Sydney (1): ship running in a storm. Toledo Museum of Art, Ohio (1): kaage close hauled. Akademie der Bildenkrint, Vienna (1): calm. Schlossmuseum, Weimar (2): estuary of the Maas; calm.*

VERBEECQ (Verbeeck), Cornelisz **c.1590-1635**

Born and died in Haarlem. Here is another artist whose early work suggests that he was almost certainly a pupil of Hendrik Cornelisz Vroom (q.v.); later works, however, show the strong influence of Jan Porcellis (q.v.), and though the style remains mannerist, the palette has adapted to the greys of the realist school.

There are three small paintings by him in the National Maritime Museum, Greenwich; a pair of early ones and a later storm with a whale. At the Heckscher Museum, Huntington, N.Y., there is a picture of the attack on Goletta in 1609.

PLATES: 14, 15.

VERBOECKHOVEN, Louis **1802-1889**

Born in Warneton, Belgium, 1802, he first worked and studied with his father and elder brother, neither of whom were marine artists, then travelled to complete his studies and turned to marine painting. He exhibited at the Paris Salon from 1842, and was a member of the Academy of Amsterdam. He won medals at Arras, Brussels, Cambrai and Lille. He died in Brussels in 1889.

EXAMPLES: Musée d'Aix (1): a shipping scene. Konintlijk Museum voor Schone Kunsten, Antwerp (1): a rough sea. Musée de Cambrai (2): marines. Musée de Cherbourg (1): low tide. Musée de La Fère (1): marine. Kunstmuseum, Leipzig (2): boats in a calm; boats in a rough sea. Musée d'Ypres (1): rough sea.

VERBRUGGEN, Jan **1712-1780**

Born in Enkhuizen, 1712. He was a marine and landscape painter, and an accomplished one to judge from his known works. He died in Woolwich in 1780.

PLATE: 235.

VERNET, Claude-Joseph **1714-1789**

Born in Avignon, August 14th, 1714. Called Joseph, he was brought up in Avignon and trained as an artist in a city that was one of the artistic centres of Europe. His talent was recognised at an early age, and the resulting patronage, especially that of the Marquise de Caumont and the Comte de Quinson, enabled him to travel to Rome in 1734, with letters of recommendation to Adrien Manglard. On the way he got his first sight of the sea at Marseilles. It was an experience that was to change his life; from then on he was to remain permanently fascinated by the sea, and will ever be remembered for the fanciful Mediterranean beach scenes and storms which are among the most charming marine paintings of the 18th century.

In Rome he had great success, and in 1743 was made a member of the Academy of St. Luke. In 1753 he returned to France and obtained the patronage of M. de Marigny, the brother of Madame de Pompadour. It was through this connection that he received his greatest commission, a set of the ports of France, painted over a period of years, and now housed in the Musée de la Marine in Paris.

These were his most definitive works, for Vernet was not primarily a ship painter and not at all a history painter. Much of the charm of his pictures is in the figure painting, with the ships usually part of the background. So popular were his works that they can be found in most state collections, with perhaps the largest collection in the Hermitage in Leningrad.

Vernet died in Paris on December 13th, 1789.

PLATES: 231, 232, 233.

VERNET, Jean Antoine **1716-1775**

Born Avignon 1716; died Naples 1775. He was a brother of Claude-Joseph Vernet (q.v.).

VERSCHUIR, Lieve Pietersz **1630-1686**

Born and died in Rotterdam. He is said to have been a pupil of Julius Porcellis (q.v.), and certainly he adopted a golden palette as well as a grey one, as did Porcellis. He is also supposed to have been a pupil of Simon de Vlieger (q.v.); this too seems likely. If he was also a pupil of Jan Beerstraaten (q.v.), as is also said, then no influence of that master is apparent in his work.

His father was a sculptor and from him he received a grounding in that art. A persistent theme of his paintings is the viewing of his subjects against a setting sun, a technique no doubt inspired by the paintings of Claude Gellée (q.v.), assuming that he had the opportunity of seeing them. He was an artist who strove after atmosphere in his paintings, such as Cappelle (q.v.) was achieving; however Verschuir's work falls far short in comparison.

PLATES: 128, 129, 130.

EXAMPLES: Rijksmuseum, Amsterdam (3) including Charles II arriving at Rotterdam on his way to his restoration to the throne in 1660. National Gallery, Budapest (1): Fire of London 1666. National Gallery, Dublin (1): port scene. National Maritime Museum, Greenwich (3): large action between Dutch ships and Barbary galleys; Four Days Fight 1666; Dutch States yacht. Alte Pinakothek, Munich (2): harbour scenes. Corsini Gallery, Rome (1). Boymans van Beuningen Museum, Rotterdam (2): Italian coast scenes. Museum of Strasbourg (1). Liechtenstein Gallery, Vienna (1).

VERVER, Abraham de **c.1590-1650**
(also called van Burghstrate)

His later work is amongst the greyest of the Dutch grey school, though his early work is, not unnaturally, in the Flemish tradition. In the Rijksmuseum, Amsterdam, there is a very large painting of his of the Battle of the Zuyder Zee in 1573, signed and dated 1621. Examples of his marines or coast scenes can also be seen in the National Maritime Museum, Greenwich, and the Municipal Museum at Mannheim. He died in Amsterdam in 1650.

VETTENWINKEL, Dirk **b.c.1787**

It is possible that his birth date was 1786, since we have the date of his baptism as January 14th, 1787. He was born and grew up in Amsterdam, where he became a shipwright and later a house and ship painter. He also painted ship portraits and was the father of the better known Hendrick Vettenwinkel Dzn.

VETTENWINKEL Dzn, Hendrick **1809-1878**

Born in Amsterdam, he grew up to join his father's house and ship painting business. Like his father he took up ship portraiture and was presumably his pupil. He also painted harbour scenes and genre subjects. The Rijksmuseum, Amsterdam, has a painting of the merchantman *Flew* sailing out of the Nieuwe Diep, and there are examples of his water-colours at the Scheepvaart Museum and the Fodor Museum, Amsterdam, as well as at the Teylers Stichting Museum, Haarlem.

VINCENT, George **1796-1836**
Born Norwich June 27th, 1796, he was a pupil of 'Old Crome' and exhibited at the Norwich Society from 1813. In 1819 he moved to London. He had already been exhibiting at the Royal Academy since 1814, and at the British Institution since 1815. None of the paintings exhibited were marines, and indeed, he does seem to have been mainly a landscape painter, but the painting illustrated shows him to have been capable of very finished marines. He died in London in 1836.

PLATE: 366.

VITRINGA, Wigerus **1657-1721**
Born Leeuwarden, 1657. In 1691 he joined the Guild of Alkmaar. He died in Wirdum, January 18th, 1721.

PLATE: 136.

EXAMPLES: The National Maritime Museum, Greenwich (1): a bear hunt in the Arctic. Fries Museum, Leeuwarden (1): a galjoot and Dutch shipping. There are also examples in public galleries at Bremen, Leningrad and Lille.

VLIEGER, Simon de **c.1600-1653**
Born in Rotterdam, this artist was the best pupil of Jan Porcellis (q.v.) and perhaps the one man who did more than anyone to perfect the Dutch realist manner. As the master of Willem van de Velde the Younger (q.v.) and Jan van de Capelle (q.v.), he was also the vehicle for ensuring its continuance and finest expression.

Although de Vlieger's palette was essentially grey, they are greys of lightness and delicacy, relieved with warm touches, which make his pictures among the greatest of the Dutch marine school. Like his master he does not seem to have interested himself much in pictures of historical scenes and battles; rather, he concentrated on the nautical scene around the Dutch coasts: ferry boats, fishing boats, landing the catch. He also painted more fanciful themes, such as rocky cliffs, either with calm seas, or the fashionable stormy shipwrecks.

As well as being a pupil of Jan Porcellis, he is also supposed to have been taught by Willem van de Velde the Elder (q.v.), a man some ten years his junior. If he was it can only have been for draughtsmanship, though it is thought that de Vlieger never did any grisaille drawings.

In the National Maritime Museum, Greenwich, there is a storm piece by Willem van de Velde the Younger, signed and dated 1651, when the artist was seventeen; it shows the young painter trying to emulate his master de Vlieger as exactly as he could in the same subject but with limited success; he was soon to move on into a style of his own. As well as being the master of the younger van de Velde and Capelle, de Vlieger also taught Hendrick Dubbels (q.v.), and probably Lieve Verschuir (q.v.).

In 1627 he married and later moved to Amsterdam, where he became a Freeman of the city in 1643. His fame ensured that his works became widespread and they are now found in most major collections.

Vlieger died in Weesp in 1653.

PLATES: 88, 89, 90, 91, 92, 93, 94.

EXAMPLES: Musée d'Aix (2): calm and storm. Rijksmuseum, Amsterdam (2): Dutch and Spanish action on the Slaak 1631; estuary scene; a third not a marine, plus three more pictures attributed to de Vlieger. Musée Royal de Beaux-Arts, Antwerp (1): calm. Fine Art Museum, Auxburg (1): coast scene. Bowes Museum, Barnard Castle (1): the Amelia *off a rocky coast. Dahlem Museum, Berlin (1): fishing boat. Gemäldegalerie, Bonn (1). Fogg Museum, Boston (1): shipwreck. Kunsthalle, Bremen (1): small vessels close hauled in a breeze. Herzog Anton Ulrich Museum, Brunswick (1): ships in distress in a heavy sea off rocks. Museum of Fine Arts, Budapest (examples). Fitzwilliam Museum, Cambridge (4). Statens Museum for Kunst, Copenhagen (3): the River Maas near Rotterdam; ships at sea; seascape. Gemäldegalerie, Darmstadt (1): calm by moonlight. Museum of Art, Detroit (1): calm on the banks of the Meuse. Staatliche Gemäldegalerie, Dresden (1): shipping in a storm off a rocky coast. National Gallery of Scotland, Edinburgh (1): Dutch flagship. Museum of Frankfurt (1): ship firing a gun. Museum of Gothenburg (1). National Maritime Museum, Greenwich (8): a squally day in a Dutch estuary; shipping off the English coast; the beach at Scheveningen with fisherfolk; Dutch ships at anchor off a rocky coast; two of Dutch shipping becalmed off a rocky coast; a ferry; a yacht; two attributed. Mauritshuis, The Hague (1): beach scene. Kunsthalle, Hamburg (1). Museum of Hanover (2). Gemäldegalerie, Kassel (1): shipping in a fresh breeze. Gemäldegalerie, Leipzig (1): rough sea. Hermitage, Leningrad (9): scene called "Arrival of William of Orange at Rotterdam"; port scene; seascapes with shipping and small craft. Summer Palace of Peter the Great, Leningrad (1): Dutch yacht and ships becalmed. National Gallery, London (2): shipping at a pier; estuary scene. City Art Gallery, Manchester (1): shipping in an estuary on a windy day. Academy of Middleburg (1): beach scene. Alte Pinakothek, Munich (3): fishing boats off a jetty; fishing boat at sea; fishing scene in a calm. Metropolitan Museum, New York (1): calm. Louvre, Paris (1). Johnson Collection, Philadelphia (1): calm. National Gallery, Prague (1): calm. Schwerin Museum (3): two calms and a rough sea scene. Nationalmuseum, Stockholm (1): coast scene with fishing vessels. Akademie der Bilden Kunst, Vienna (2): estuary scene and a calm. Kunsthistorisches Museum, Vienna (1): yacht becalmed. Museum of Volne (1): beach scene at Scheveningen. Van der Heycht Museum, Wappenthal (1): Dutch ship before the wind.*

VOGELAER, Pieter **1641-1720**
Born in Zierikzee in 1641, this artist made rather poor grisaille pictures and is also said to have been a sculptor and silversmith. He signed his work "P. Vogelaer". He died in Amsterdam in 1720.

PLATE: 168.

EXAMPLES: Rijksmuseum, Amsterdam (1): Dutch herring fleet. National Maritime Museum, Greenwich (2): Dutch three-decker Prins Hendrik; *Dutch East Indiamen in a storm. Prins Hendrik Museum, Rotterdam (1): a Mediterranean port scene with Dutch ships and galleys viewed from the battery.*

VRIES, J.C. **1804-aft.1850**
Born in Amsterdam, he was a pupil at the Amsterdam Academy from 1823 to 1825, and afterwards of Odenaere and Pallinck at Brussels. He worked in Amsterdam from 1836 to 1850, when he emigrated to America. He died near Boston, Mass., after 1850.

VRIES, Joachim de **b.c.1600**
Born in Sneek, he was a painter in the Dutch realist tradition, using a grey palette, and working at Delft in the second quarter of the 17th century. Such paintings as exist are similar to the work of Abraham Verver (q.v.).

EXAMPLES: National Maritime Museum, Greenwich (2): a Dutch whaling scene, signed "J.D.V.", and a Dutch ship before the wind, signed "JVries".

VRIES, Joghem de **fl.1750-1790**

He apparently lived and worked in Zaandam. The Rijksmuseum in Amsterdam has a very respectable whaling scene by him.

VROOM, Cornelis Hendriksz **1591-1661**

Born and died in Haarlem. Son and pupil of Hendrik Cornelisz Vroom (q.v.), his marines follow his father's work fairly closely but are distinct in their clarity of tone and in the use of a blue background sea, which is absent from his father's palette.

Examples of his marines still in existence are not numerous and tend to be battle pieces. He seems to have been more interested in landscapes, forest scenes in particular. In 1628 he travelled to England and visited the Court, where his father was well known. His best known picture, the destruction of Spinola's galleys in the Channel in 1602 is now in the Rijksmuseum.

PLATES: 60, 61.

EXAMPLES: Rijksmuseum, Amsterdam (1): Dutch ships ramming Spinola's galleys, October 3rd, 1602, signed and dated 1617. Gemäldegalerie, Staatliches Museum, Berlin (1): a landscape. Statens Museum for Kunst, Copenhagen (4): all landscapes. Glasgow Art Gallery (1): landscape. Frans Hals Museum, Haarlem (1): landscape. National Maritime Museum, Greenwich (1): ships of the Spanish Netherlands in action with Barbary galleys. Victoria and Albert Museum, Ham House, London (1): galleys in action.

VROOM, Hendrik Cornelisz **1566-1640**

Born and died in Haarlem. Although Pieter Brueghel (q.v.) had painted a few marines and Vroom was only three when he died, it is Vroom who is regarded as the father of marine painting. He pioneered the painting of naval scenes and battles in a manner never seen before. His approach to his work clearly shows a love and understanding of ships and a strong interest in naval history.

In the Rijksmuseum in Amsterdam is the large "Return to Amsterdam of Cornelis de Houtman from Sumatra in 1599". The large "Heemskerk's Defeat of the Spanish at Gibraltar in 1607", is at the National Maritime Museum, Greenwich. As well as Dutch commissions he also had English patrons. The Lord Admiral, the Earl of Nottingham, had him make cartoons for a set of tapestries on the Spanish Armada campaign of 1588. These tapestries were one of the State's great treasures until they were burnt with the Houses of Parliament in 1834. The cartoons have also disappeared, so that only an 18th century set of engravings by W.H. Pyne remains to show us what they looked like. Vroom did another painting of this campaign, the "Battle of Gravelines" which is in the Ferdinandeum Museum at Innsbruck and which is the finest picture of the event in existence.

Another important English commission was for two large paintings showing the English fleet arriving in the Solent led by the *Prince Royal,* bearing Prince Charles and the Duke of Buckingham on their return from Spain in October, 1623. Two similar pictures were painted: that for the King is in the Royal Collection, that for the Duke in the National Maritime Museum.

The finest of all his marine paintings also depicts a largely English event, the "Arrival of the Elector and the Electress Palatine at Flushing". The Elector had just married a daughter of James I, Princess Elizabeth, and they had sailed from Margate in May, 1613, in the *Prince Royal.* This picture is in the Frans Hals Museum, Haarlem, and nothing draws more attention to Vroom's care for the minutiae of naval detail than his depiction of that great ship in the Haarlem and the Greenwich pictures. In the Haarlem picture she is shown fully rigged for summer sailing, while in the Greenwich picture she is shown in winter rig with her sprit-topmast and other uppermost masts and yards sent down.

Although a Dutchman from Haarlem, Vroom was brought up to a Flemish palette, which he maintained all his life and although he out-lived Jan Porcellis (q.v.), his pupil and pioneer of the grey Dutch School, by eight years, his seas remained a deep green to the end. His early instruction in painting was from his stepfather, Cornelisz Hendricksen, a decorator of pottery.

As a young man Vroom lived first in Rotterdam and then travelled to Italy. In Rome he became acquainted with Paul Bril, the landscape painter and an important figure on the Roman artistic scene. He returned to Haarlem but was soon planning another journey abroad, this time to Seville. In order to keep himself while he was there he painted a number of religious subjects to take with him and sell. It was just as well he did, for the ship he took was wrecked near Lisbon and the local inhabitants, thinking they were English corsairs who had been raiding the coast, were going to kill the survivors. Fortunately Vroom had managed to rescue his paintings and showed them to the Portuguese. On seeing them they said, "These men are not Englishmen, they are Christians", and Vroom and his companions were saved. If examples of these paintings still exist they go unrecognised.

His travels must have fostered a natural inclination to the sea and ships and from this time he concentrated on marine subjects, becoming the doyen in his field and the inspiration of his followers. These were of the Flemish and the Dutch Schools, for he was made a member of the Painters' Guild at Antwerp in 1616, where hs most notable pupil was Andries van Eertvelt (q.v.). Later he returned to his native Haarlem, and there taught the first generation of Dutch School marine painters.

PLATES: 5, 6, 7; COLOUR PLATE I.

EXAMPLES: Stedelijk Museum, Alkmaar (1): view of Alkmaar. Galleria Palatina, Pitti Palace, Florence (1): marine. National Maritime Museum, Greenwich (5): Heemskerk's defeat of the Spanish at Gibraltar, 1607; the return of Prince Charles from Spain, 1623; trading in the East; a Dutch ship off a castle; a Dutch ship and fishing boats in a fresh breeze. Frans Hals Museum, Haarlem (5): the arrival of the Elector and the Electress Palatine at Flushing, 1613; Zeeland ship; a view of Haarlem; a view of the Y of Sparendam, with Haarlem in the background. West Freesch Museum (1): view of Hoorn. Museum Nacional de Arte Antigua, Lisbon (1): naval battle. Ashmolean Museum, Oxford (1): shipping off the Dutch coast.

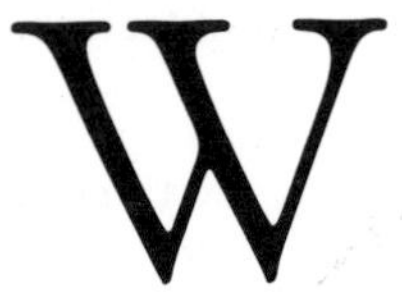

WAGNER, Corny
This painter was working in London in 1890, when he received a commission from Cory Brothers to paint a picture of *Atlas I,* the coaling pontoon. This picture is now in the National Maritime Museum, Greenwich.

WALDORP, Antonie **1803-1866**
Born at Huis ten Bosch, near The Hague, 1803. He attended The Hague Academy and was a pupil of Johannes Breckenheymer and, for a short time in 1833, of Wijnand Nuyen. He became a member of the Royal Academy at Amsterdam in 1836, exhibiting at The Hague and Amsterdam from 1830 to 1863, and at Leeuwarden in 1855. He died in Amsterdam in 1866.

Many Dutch art galleries have examples.

WALES, George Canning **1868-1940**
An American draughtsman and illustrator; he contributed to Howard Chappelle's *History of American Sailing Ships.*

The Peabody Museum of Salem has drawings by him.

WALES-SMITH, Captain Arthur Douglas R.N. 1888-1966
Born on January 20th, 1888. He retired from the Royal Navy before the Second World War but on its outbreak returned to work in the Naval Ordnance Department with the rank of Commander. After the war he hyphenated the "Wales" (which had been one of his Christian names) to the "Smith".

His painting of the Battle of Jutland at Greenwich is signed "D.W. Smith", but he later signed "Douglas Wales". Then when he emigrated to South Africa in 1948 he found a Wiles and a Wales already painting there so he added Smith to his signature. He died in South Africa on July 12th, 1966.

Wales-Smith specialised in naval scenes of the First and Second World Wars and portraits of well known naval officers, done from photographs. After his death his widow and son presented six portraits in oils and four in pastel, two paintings of Jutland 1916, and a painting of minesweeping trawlers, to the National Maritime Museum, Greenwich.

WALLIS, Alfred **1855-1942**
Born at Devonport on August 18th, 1855. At the age of nine he went to sea, and later was a fisherman on the Cornish coast. He was almost illiterate, but in 1925, in old age, he took up painting marines. His materials were as primitive as the results. He would paint on anything that came to hand, bits of cardboard, etc., for he had no money for proper materials.

He was patronised by Christopher Wood and Ben Nicholson. Wallis died in Madron workhouse, near Penzance, on August 29th, 1942.

His pictures were not saleable during his lifetime, but subsequently he has become a cult figure of modern art, and his works are expensive, ten of them being enshrined in the Tate Gallery. Auckland City Art Gallery has an oil painting by him of a four funnelled liner.

PLATE: 612.

WALTER, Joseph **1783-1856**
Born in Bristol in 1783, this artist must rank, after Nicholas Pocock (q.v.), as Bristol's best marine painter, and the best who never moved to London. Although on his death certificate he is described as a "Ship Portrait Painter", he was more than that. He drew well, and his clean, clear, if somewhat grey, palette is pleasing. As well as ship portraits he recorded such events as the floating out of the *Great Britain* in 1843, and the last of three paintings which were exhibited at the Royal Academy between 1836 and 1847, is of the Spanish Armament of 1790; that is to say, the Channel Fleet at Spithead that year, under Admiral Lord Howe.

He seems to have lived and worked all his life at an address in Trinity Street, Bristol; he died in Bristol on June 7th, 1856, after a long and painful illness.

PLATES: 442, 443, 444.

EXAMPLES: Bristol Art Gallery (10): the Great Western *on her fifth passage from Bristol to New York in 1838; the Mouth of the Avon; the ship* Severn; *Bristol Harbour 1837; the* Great Western *off Portishead; Bristol Harbour 1836; the old Floating Harbour at Sea Mills, Bristol; a ship before the wind; and another similar; National Maritime Museum, Greenwich (4): the West Indiaman* Britannia; *Bristol Harbour; shipping in the Bristol Channel (a version of the Mouth of the Avon at Bristol): a brig entering Bristol Avon. Peabody Museum of Salem (2): the steamer* Great Britain; *steamer* Great Western. *Library of New South Wales, Sydney (1): a frigate off shore.*

WALTERS, George Stanfield **1838-1924**
Born Liverpool 1838, he was the eldest son of Samuel Walters (q.v.) and was his pupil and assistant. His first picture to be accepted for exhibition at the Royal Academy was in 1860, and he exhibited there most years until his death in London on July 24th, 1924.

He did not inherit his father's obsession with ships and the sea, and many of his works were of general coastal views, and so on.

PLATE: 573.

WALTERS, Miles **1774-1849**
Born at Ilfracombe, Devon, 1774, he was apprenticed as a shipwright and went to sea. He is said to have left the sea and settled in London about 1805, but his son, Samuel (q.v.), who was to become the best known of the family, was born at sea as late as 1811. He then moved his family to Liverpool, where he established a framing, carving and gilding business. All this time he was turning out simple ship portraits, some of the later ones in collaboration with his son, Samuel. He died in Liverpool in 1849.

The Liverpool Museums have a well attributed painting of the *Antigua* packet by him. The Peabody Museum of Salem has a well attributed one of the American ship *Hercules,* also one of the American packet *Birmingham,* signed "Walters and Son, 1830".

PLATES: 388, 389, 390.

WALTERS, Samuel **1811-1882**

Born at sea November 1st, 1811, he was the son of Miles Walters (q.v.), who may have instructed him. By 1834 he had set up as a marine painter with a studio in his father's picture-framing premises.

In 1845 he moved his family to London but this was not a success and he returned to Liverpool, where he prospered by capitalising on the city's great shipping boom. Although he might be regarded as just another ship portraitist, he was rather more than that, having paintings accepted for hanging at the Royal Academy between 1842 and 1861; many of these were of general coastal subjects. Walters died in Bootle on March 5th, 1882.

PLATES: 389, 390, 391.

EXAMPLES: The Manx Museum, Isle of Man (2): ship portraits. National Maritime Museum, Greenwich (11): ship portraits. Merseyside Museums (1): ship portrait. Walker Art Gallery (8): Port of Liverpool; the Great Gale of January 1839; View of the Mersey; Returning to Ireland and 4 ship portraits. New Bedford Whaling Museum (1). Mariners Museum, Newport News (14): ship portraits. Peabody Museum of Salem (7): ship portraits, and one other signed by his father as well. National Museum of History and Technology, Washington (1): the Blackballer Isaac Webb.

WARD, John **1798-1849**

Born in Hull, December 28th, 1798, he was the son of a master mariner of Hull and was apprenticed as a house and ship painter, a trade he followed all his working life, even though he had also become a successful artist, who remains the best known and most admired of the Hull School of marine painters. He was influenced by William Anderson and copied some of his pictures.

He exhibited at the Royal Academy between 1840 and 1847, and at the British Institution between 1843 and 1847.

Ward also made engravings of many of his own works, which were published. Some of his most successful compositions are Arctic scenes, of which he had first hand knowledge from sailing with the whaling fleet.

The other well known painters of the Hull School, which flourished around him, were his fellow apprentices, Thomas Binks and William Griffin. It was always a school of rather local interest and this is reflected in the dearth of paintings by Ward in public galleries outside Hull. The Ferens Art Gallery and the Hull Maritime Museum have examples; and at the Peabody Museum of Salem there is a painting by him of the Hull steamers *Rob Roy, Queen of Scotland* and the *Helen McGregor*.

He died in Hull on September 28th, 1849.

PLATES: 367, 368.

WARD, William **1761-1801**

Born and died in Hull. A ship portraitist who was presumably a kinsman of John Ward. His main business was running his fleet of whalers and so as an artist he must be regarded as a gifted amateur. The Peabody Museum of Salem has seven drawings by him.

WAUGH, Frederick Judd N.A. **1861-1940**

Born Bordentown, New Jersey, September 13th, 1861, he studied at the Pennsylvania Academy of Fine Arts, and at the Julian Academy in Paris. He exhibited there in 1892, and in London from 1894 to 1905, after which he returned to America. Soon after his arrival there he painted a large canvas called "The Roaring Forties" which was bought by the Metropolitan Museum.

He settled first in Montclair, New Jersey, then in Gloucester and Kent in Connecticut. Finally he moved to Provincetown, Mass., in 1927, where he built an unusual studio of old ships' timbers on the outer shore of Cape Cod. Here he painted the coastal scenes for which he became celebrated. He died in Provincetown on September 12th, 1940.

His work may be found in a number of American museums, including the Art Institute of Chicago, the Metropolitan and Brooklyn Museums of New York, the Los Angeles Museum of History, the Museum of Fine Arts of Houston, the City Art Museum, St. Louis, the Toledo Museum of Art, the Pasadena Art Institute and the Mariners Museum, Newport News.

PLATE: 631.

WEATHERILL, George **1810-1890**

Born on September 18th, 1810, he was a son of a farmer at Staithes in Yorkshire. As a youth he became a solicitor's clerk at Whitby where he settled. He moved from the law to banking, and became head cashier at Simpson and Chapman's Bank, and all this time was a keen amateur watercolourist of marine subjects. About the age of fifty he suffered a nervous breakdown, after which he gave up the bank and turned professional artist. His chief patron was a Yorkshire county alderman called R.E. Pannett, who founded the art gallery at Whitby that bears his name, and which houses a large collection of Weatherill's work. Although he never moved from the Whitby area, he had a reputation for being a prodigious walker in it. He died on August 30th, 1890.

WEBB, Archibald **c.1800-c.1866**

He exhibited his first picture, of the Battle of Trafalgar, at the British Institution in 1825 and continued to show works there quite frequently until 1866. He only exhibited one marine at the Royal Academy, in 1841. As his address was the same as James Webb's (q.v.) when the latter first exhibited in 1852, it seems likely that he was James's father.

The National Maritime Museum, Greenwich, has a painting by him of a fishing lugger off the coast of Kent.

PLATE: 485.

WEBB, James **1825-1895**

Born Chelsea, London, 1825. This pleasing painter especially liked dramatic coastal scenes for his subjects, so that St. Michael's Mount, Ischia, Bamburgh Castle and San Sebastian were natural choices.

He first exhibited at the Royal Academy in 1853 and then most years until 1888; he also exhibited at the British Institution from 1852 to 1867, at Suffolk Street, at the New Watercolour Society and at the Grosvenor Galleries.

He died in London in 1895.

PLATES: 591, 592.

EXAMPLES: Marines only. Art Gallery of South Australia, Adelaide (1): Dordrecht Roads. Russell Cotes Museum, Bournemouth (1): Dutch fishing boats unloading. Bristol Art Gallery (3): Bamburgh Castle; Calshot Castle; sunset in Dutch waters. City Art Gallery, Glasgow (2): view of Constantinople; the harbour of Clovelly, Devon. National Maritime Museum, Greenwich (2): San Sebastian; a swim-headed barge. Liverpool Museums (1): Bamburgh Castle. Tate Gallery, London (1): Le Mont-Saint-Michel. National Gallery of Victoria, Melbourne (2): Rotterdam; scene in the Thames. Phoenix Museum of Art (1): Ischia. Reading Art Gallery (2): St. Antoine; Bilbao; view on the Thames. Laing Art Gallery, Sheffield (1): Mont-Saint-Michel.

WEBER, Theodore **1838-1907**

Born in Leipzig in 1838; he studied under Wilhelm Krause in Berlin from 1854 until 1856, when he settled in Paris and began exhibiting at the Salon. He died there in 1907.

EXAMPLES: Wallraf-Richartz Museum, Cologne (1): view of Flushing. Musée de Dijon (1): storm. Museum of Leipzig (1): after the storm. National Gallery, Melbourne (1): fishing boats leaving Boulogne. Museum of Mulhouse (2): roadstead of Boulogne; a rainy day at Treport. Nottingham Museum (1): fishing boat at sea. National Museum of Fine Art, Rio de Janeiro (1): storm. Art Gallery of New South Wales, Sydney (1): view of Ostend.

WEBSTER, George **fl.1797-1832**

Disappointingly little is known about this excellent artist, whose style is distinctive and whose pictures are full of the drama of the sea. His address when he first exhibited in 1797 was at Temple Bar, but by 1806 he had moved to the Angel, Islington, where he remained. His first picture to be hung at the Royal Academy was in 1826. He also exhibited at the British Institution between 1816 and 1832. In 1801 he showed a view of the Gold Coast "taken on the spot", and in 1821 a Dutch view and another of Mount Lebanon.

The National Maritime Museum, Greenwich, has a small painting of a two-decker leaving Portsmouth, and a larger canvas of an East Indiaman off Dover.

PLATE: 364.

WELLS, Thomas Winchester **b.1916**
A.I.C.H., F.A.S.M.A.

Born in Chicago, 1916. In 1936 he went on an Arctic expedition in the schooner *Effie M. Morrissey* and in the following year dory fishing in Gloucester schooners. In 1938/9 he served aboard the grain ship *Passat* to Australia and back to Europe via the Horn. He then took a Bachelor of Fine Arts degree at Yale before joining the U.S. naval reserve in 1942.

After the Second World War he held the appointment of Technical Illustrator in Naval Underwater Weapons Systems from 1950 to 1972, which arose from his wartime experience as the leader of a team of naval salvage divers.

In 1948 he won a Washington State Capitol mural design award for the Puget Sound Maritime History. Between 1972 and 1979 he has held eleven successful one man shows on the West Coast and has a commission to paint the ships of the Matson Navigation Company. He is a Fellow of the American Society of Marine Artists and lives in Seattle.

PLATE: 684.

WESSON, Edward R.I., R.B.A., R.S.M.A. **b.1910**

Born at Blackheath, London, April 29th, 1910. He was educated at Colfe Grammar School, taught himself to paint in watercolours and first practised his art by the nearby Thames and the Surrey Docks. During the Second World War he was commissioned in 1940 into the Honourable Artillery Company and fought in North Africa, Sicily and Italy, while continuing to paint in his spare time.

Since the war he has had nineteen one-man exhibitions in Britain and four in Belgium. In 1952 he was elected a member of the Royal Institute of Painters in Watercolours, in 1957 to the Society of Marine Artists (now Royal) and in 1963 to the Royal Society of British Artists. He writes on painting in *The Artist* and *Leisure Painter* magazines, and conducts painting courses. His Royal Society of Marine Artists diploma work is in the National Maritime Museum, Greenwich, and his works can also be found in the collections of the Guildhall Art Gallery in the City of London and the Maidstone Municipal Gallery.

WEST, Benjamin Franklin **1818-1854**

An American ship portraitist with a rather stiff, primitive style who lived and worked in Salem. The Peabody Museum of Salem has six signed oils and twenty-two attributed.

PLATE: 480.

WESTALL, William A.R.A. **1781-1850**

Born Hertford in 1781. He was not a marine painter by inclination, but it happened that at the age of eighteen and while a student at the Royal Academy Schools, he was chosen by the Admiralty as draughtsman to accompany Captain Matthew Flinders in H.M.S. *Investigator* on a voyage of discovery around Australia. The return voyage to England was made in the *Porpoise* and when this ship was wrecked on a coral reef Westall and most of the crew had to stay on the reef for eight weeks before Flinders could reach Port Jackson in an open boat and get help. Views painted by Westall as a result of this voyage were exhibited both at the Royal Academy and the British Institution. He died in London in 1850.

The National Maritime Museum, Greenwich, has "Wreck Reef" (on loan from the Admiralty), and the Tate Gallery has "The Deluge".

PLATE: 296.

WEYTS, Carolus Ludovicus **1828-1875**

A Belgian ship portraitist working in the third quarter of the 19th century. The Altonaer Museum, Hamburg, has five glass paintings. The Peabody Museum of Salem has an oil.

WEYTS, Petrus

A Belgian ship portraitist who was working in Antwerp in the first half of the 19th century, and who was probably the father and master of Carolus (q.v.), since their work is very similar. The Altonaer Museum, Hamburg, has a glass painting and the Peabody Museum of Salem has four signed oils and two attributed.

WHELDON, James H. **fl.1860-1880**

A painter of the Hull School; examples of his work can be seen at the Maritime Museum at Hull.

WHICHELO, C. John **1784-1865**
He was a pupil of John Varley and first exhibited at the Royal Academy in 1810, when he is described as Marine and Landscape Painter to H.R.H. the Prince Regent. He exhibited there rather infrequently until 1844, showing mostly landscapes. In 1826 he was elected an associate of the Old Watercolour Society. He died in London in 1865.

Birmingham Art Gallery has "Old Men-of-War, Portsmouth Harbour" and the National Maritime Museum, Greenwich, has a painting he exhibited at the Royal Academy in 1816 called "A packet and an American ship coming into Margate in a storm".

PLATE: 336.

WHIPPLE, Seth Area **1855-1901**
Born near New Baltimore 1855, he was a Great Lakes ship portraitist who worked in Detroit before he moved to Bay City, Michigan, where he supervised the draughting department of the Davidson Ship Yard in the 1890s. He died in Bay City in 1901.

Examples of his work may be seen at the Dossin Great Lakes Museum and the Henry Ford Museum, Dearborn, Michigan.

WHISTLER, James Abbott McNeill P.R.B.A. **1834-1903**
Born in Lowell, Mass., July 10th, 1834. Whistler was only marginally a marine painter, but did many Thames views. As a boy he lived in Russia and in England, his father at that time working in both countries as an engineer.

He went to the U.S. Military Academy at West Point but did not graduate, then worked as a cartographer in the U.S. Navy, where he learnt to etch. In 1855 he moved to Paris and in 1859 to London, where he settled and became one of the most lively figures of late Victorian society. He was President of the Royal Society of British Artists and is acknowledged as one of the greatest etchers who ever lived. He exhibited at the Royal Academy from 1859 to 1879, also at Suffolk Street and the Grosvenor Gallery. He died in London on July 17th, 1903.

Examples of his coastal or marine paintings can be seen at the Chicago Art Institute, Glasgow Art Gallery, Wadsworth Atheneum, Hartford, Tate Gallery, Frick Collection, New York, and the Freer Art Gallery, Washington.

WHITCOMBE, Thomas **c.1752-1824**
In spite of much searching in national and local archives, information on the origins and death of this eminent artist still eludes us. Nobody contributed more to recording the naval side of the French Revolutionary Wars than Thomas Whitcombe and his output was vast. Apart from the paintings for the fifty plates in *The Naval Achievements of Great Britain,* published after the wars, he made paintings for at least one hundred more wartime engravings, as well as producing peaceful subjects.

He only exhibited one painting at the British Institution, in 1820, but at the Royal Academy he exhibited most years between 1783 and 1824, working from London addresses. His first exhibited painting, the "Destruction of the Floating Batteries before Gibraltar 1782" is very different in style from his mature work, which at its best is crisp and fresh, and of the four great recorders of the period, Pocock, Luny, Whitcombe and Dodd, their rating for artistic quality should place them in that order.

PLATES: 276, 277, 278, 279, 280, 281.

EXAMPLES: National Library of Australia, Canberra (8): the Britannia at Sydney; the Britannia *off Dover; three of the East Indiaman* Calcutta; *a pair of the capture of the* Calcutta; *the East Indiaman* Cabalva *wrecked on Mauritius, all from the Rex Nan Kivell Collection. The National Maritime Museum, Greenwich (35): the* Pearl *captures the* Santa Monica *1779; the Battle of the Saints 1782 (a pair); destruction of the floating batteries at Gibraltar 1782; Battle of Camperdown 1797; Battle of the Nile 1798 (a pair and a third one); Duckworth's passage of the Dardanelles 1807; the* Seahorse *capturing the* Badere-i -Zaffer *1808; the* Implacable *and the* Centaur *1808; capture of St. Paul Ile de Bourbon 1809; action between the* Spartan *and French and Neapolitan ships in the Bay of Naples 1810 (a pair); the* Macedonian *captured by the* United States *1812; two pictures of the bombardment of Algiers 1816; the* Blenheim; *the East Indiaman* Britannia; *the East Indiaman* Caesar; *the merchantman* Ealing Grove *(originally in two positions on one canvas, now separated into two); East Indiaman* Essex; *the smack* Mary; *East Indiamen* Minerva; Scaleby Castle *and* Charles Grant; *the merchantman* Phoenix; *the East Indiaman* Providence; *the* Sylph *with the cutter* Mary Anne; *the frigate* Undaunted; *the East Indiaman* Warren Hastings; *St. Peter Port, Guernsey; the Thames at Redriff; a merchantman off Dover; ships in a gale; a Trinity House cutter. Tate Gallery, London (1): the Battle of Camperdown. Library of New South Wales, Sydney (1): the* Harriet *in Torbay.*

WHITEHEAD, Alan **b.1952**
Born in the Isle of Sheppey, 1952. This self-taught painter in watercolours, who started painting during six years' service in the Royal Navy, now paints full time. His subjects are mainly from the east coast of England and the west coast of Sweden. He has had two one-man shows in Gothenburg and has exhibited in England, the U.S.A. and Australia.

WIERINGEN, Cornelis Claesz van **c.1580-1633**
Born in Haarlem about 1580. We do not know the identity of his master but his work follows closely the style of Hendrik Cornelisz Vroom (q.v.); later in life he adopted the Dutch realist palette of Jan Porcellis (q.v.). He seems to have lived and worked in Haarlem which, with Antwerp and nearby Amsterdam, was one of the centres of marine painting by the beginning of the 17th century. He died on 29th December, 1633.

Wieringen's principal work was a commission from the City of Amsterdam for a huge painting of Heemskerk's victory at Gibraltar in 1607, which was to be a present for Prince Mauritz. This is now in the Scheepvaart Museum in Amsterdam; the Rijksmuseum in the same city has a painting of the Spanish Armada off the English coast.

The National Maritime Museum at Greenwich has a fine example entitled "An English privateer off La Rochelle" and there are two large pictures in the Frans Hals Museum, Haarlem; one shows the arrival at Flushing of the Elector and Electress Palatine from England in 1613, and the other depicts the breaking of the boom at Damietta in ancient Egypt, though the scene is brought up to date in the 17th century. The Ashmolean Museum, Oxford, has one painting of a storm on Haarlemmer Meer.

PLATE: 11; COLOUR PLATE II.

WIKSTROM, Titus **d.1920**

A Swedish ship portrait painter with a rather primitive style. The National Maritime Museum in Stockholm has a portrait of the steamer *Gothe* dated 1874.

WIKSTROM, Titus **fl.1950**

This artist is, or was, probably related to the earlier Swedish ship portraitist of the same name (q.v.).

To commemorate the state visit of Queen Elizabeth II to Sweden in June 1956, King Gustave VI Adolphus commissioned him to paint the arrival of the Royal Yacht *Britannia* at Stockholm, which he presented to Her Majesty, who subsequently lent it to the National Maritime Museum.

PLATE: 681.

WILCOX, Leslie R.I., R.S.M.A. **b.1904**

Born in Fulham, London, in 1904. He is a self-taught artist who has nevertheless strong claims to be the doyen of British marine painters. His main interest is in historical subjects, and he has written and illustrated two books, *Anson's Voyage,* 1966, and *Mr. Pepys's Navy,* 1969. He is a member of the Royal Institute of Painters in Watercolours and the Royal Society of Marine Artists. He also has exhibited at the Royal Institute of Oil Painters, the Royal Scottish Society of Painters in Watercolours, and the Royal Society of British Artists.

PLATES: 678, 679.

EXAMPLES: National Maritime Museum, Greenwich (4): the Queen arriving at Sydney in the R.M.S. Gothic, *1954; the* Cutty Sark *going into dry dock at Greenwich (called "The Last Voyage of the* Cutty Sark"*) 1954; the* Victoria and Albert III *being towed out of Portsmouth Harbour to the breakers, 1954; and the start of the Tall Ships Race from Torbay, 1962 (R.S.M.A. diploma picture, on loan).*

WILKINSON, Norman C.B.E., P.R.W.S., R.I. 1878-1971

Born in Cambridge, November 24th, 1878. From the age of eight to fourteen he was a chorister at St. Paul's Cathedral and then after two years at Berkhamsted School, he went to live with his mother at Southsea, where his passion for ships and the sea and to be an artist found release in the Solent. At the Portsmouth School of Art he obtained an Art Master's Certificate, and also studied under Louis Grier at St. Ives. He made some voyages in coastal colliers, and one deep water voyage before settling in London to become an illustrator.

His first drawing to be accepted by the *Illustrated London News* was in 1898, and in 1901 they sent him to New York to cover Sir Thomas Lipton's attempt to recover the America's Cup with his *Shamrock II.* He continued to work with the *I.L.N.* until 1915, when he got a commission as an assistant paymaster in the Royal Naval Reserve. He was present at the Dardanelles campaign and in 1917 in his new rank of lieutenant in the Royal Naval Volunteer Reserve, commanded a motor patrol boat. It was at this time that he put forward the idea of dazzle painting ships as a means of confusing the aim of German gunners and torpedomen, and this was generally adopted by both the naval and merchant fleets.

He was one of the best known poster designers for shipping and railway companies. His first poster was in 1903, and was remarkable for the fact that sea dominated the composition, the packet ship being quite small in the background. In 1924 he persuaded a number of Royal Academicians to execute posters for the London, Midland and Scottish Railway Company.

A keen yachtsman, he was made Honorary Marine Painter to the Royal Yacht Squadron in 1919. He was also interested in aeroplanes and was a painter of the air. Thus, when the Second World War broke out in 1939, he became inspector of camouflage with the rank of Air Commodore. He was present at the Normandy invasion in 1944, sketching from the destroyer *Jervis.* From these sketches he executed some of his War at Sea series. This was a set of fifty-three oil paintings of naval and a few Coastal Command Royal Air Force incidents of the war, very carefully researched. They were exhibited at the National Gallery in 1944 and presented to the nation. It was the intention of the artist that the pictures should be kept together at Greenwich, but the Director of the Imperial War Museum kept twelve of them back, and was only persuaded to part with them on the intervention of the Prime Minister.

He was President of the Royal Society of Painters in Watercolours and the acknowledged doyen of British marine painters.

Apart from the War at Sea pictures, the National Maritime Museum, Greenwich, has a large painting of the steam yacht *Liberty* in the First World War, one of his poster paintings with a packet ship in the background and some watercolours. The Imperial War Museum has nine paintings of First World War subjects, mostly of the Dardanelles campaign, but one of a convoy of dazzle painted ships. Of Second World War subjects, it has three oils and three watercolours. The Peabody Museum of Salem has a painting of the White Star liner *Oceanic* (1872) passing the *Olympic* (1910).

PLATES: 662, 663, 664, 665; COLOUR PLATE XXVII.

WILLAERTS, Abraham **1603-1669**

Born and died in Utrecht. The elder of the two sons of Adam Willaerts (q.v.), who took up their father's profession as marine painters and were his pupils. Abraham also studied portraiture under another Utrecht painter, Jan Bylaert, and later in Paris under Simon Vouet. After leaving Paris he went into the service of Prince Mauritz in Holland and went on an expedition to Angola, where he recorded the natives that he saw.

Apart from his reputation as a portrait and genre painter, his fame as a marine artist must compare with his father's. Because he copied his father in his mannered style and choice of subject as well as being his artistic contemporary for some thirty years, their works may appear difficult to tell apart to the unpractised eye. One none the less gets the impression that while Adam believed in his fairy tales Abraham did not, and of both men's works his are in fact the inferior.

PLATE: 40.

EXAMPLES: Bergen Museum (1): beach scene. Herzog Anton Ulrich Museum, Brunswick (2): shore scenes. Statens Museum for Kunst, Copenhagen (1): Dutch attack on a Spanish stronghold. This picture is of the same action, from a different viewpoint, as the picture at Greenwich by Adam Willaerts. Stadel Institute, Frankfurt (1). National Maritime Museum, Greenwich (3): a small upright of a Spanish three-decker at Naples dated 1669, the year of his death; Zeeland ship at anchor; Anglo-Dutch action. Hermitage, Leningrad (2): Dutch ships in a harbour with a castle; storm. Fürstliche Collection, Liechtenstein (1): storm.

WILLAERTS, Adam **1577-1664**

Born in Antwerp, this charming artist, the head of a family of charming artists, occupies a unique place in the Netherlands marine school. His work has little to do with either the Flemish mannerists of the style of Hendrik Cornelisz Vroom (q.v.) and his followers, nor with Jan Porcellis (q.v.) and the Dutch realists.

This could partly be explained by his leaving Antwerp in 1600, at the age of twenty-three, for the inland city of Utrecht, where he lived for the rest of his long life and where he painted marines from memory, undisturbed by the influence of other marine painters.

First of all he was a genre painter, strongly influenced by the Brueghels (q.v.) and using their colourful palette. His seas and ships are in the Flemish mannerist tradition and the only concession he ever made to the rising Dutch School was to change his seas from green to grey in his later pictures, a convention followed by his sons and pupils Abraham and Isaac. They adopted their father's style very closely but never emulated his quality. A third son, Cornelisz, was a history painter.

Perhaps the Willaerts were not so cut off from the main stream as their work suggests. There are at least three paintings by Adam of the voyage from Margate to Flushing of the Elector and Electress Palatine in 1613, in which it is clear he had a fair idea what the *Prince Royal* looked like. Three of these pictures, which deal with the embarkation from different viewpoints, are in the National Maritime Museum, Greenwich, in the Royal Collection, and in the Scheepvaart Museum, Amsterdam (one in each); a fourth showing the fleet approaching Flushing is in private hands. However, even when dealing with historical subjects Willaerts imparts the feeling of a fairy tale.

PLATES: 36, 37, 38, 39; COLOUR PLATE: IV.

EXAMPLES: Rijksmuseum, Amsterdam (5): including two large paintings of Heemskirk's victory over the Spanish at Gibraltar in 1607, widely spaced in date, one painted 1617 and one 1639. Scheepvaart Museum, Amsterdam (2): arrival at Flushing of the Elector and Electress Palatine from Margate in 1613; coast scene with Dutch ships and a Venetian galley. Bowes Museum, Barnard Castle (1): Christ preaching by the sea of Galilee. Landesmuseum, Bonn (1). Herzog Anton Ulrich-Museum, Brunswick (2): coast scenes with fisherfolk. Statens Museum for Kunst, Copenhagen (1): Dutch-Spanish action. Dordrecht Museum (2): huge view of Dordrecht; storm. Musée de Douai (1). Gemäldegalerie, Dresden (1): coast scene. Emden Museum (1). Enschede (1): beach scene. Fine Art Institute, Frankfurt (1): storm. National Maritime Museum, Greenwich (5): embarkation of the Elector and Electress Palatine from Margate in 1613; departure of English East Indiamen, 1622; Dutch attacking a Spanish fortress; Jonah and the whale; Dutch ships off a rocky coast. Frans Hals Museum, Haarlem (1): action between Spanish galleys and Dutch ships. Kunsthalle, Hamburg (1). Fine Art Museum, Leipzig (1): shore scene. Hermitage, Leningrad (5): views of a town and a storm. Fürstliche Sammlung, Liechtenstein (1). Royal Collection, London (1): embarkation of Elector Palatine. Prado, Madrid (1): ships embarking. City Art Gallery, Manchester (1): Egmond aan Zee. Musée Cantine, Marseilles (1): moonlight scene. Bavarian State Museum, Munich (2): coast scenes. Metropolitan Museum, New York (1): river scene. Germanisches Museum, Nuremburg (1): canal scene. Ashmolean Museum, Oxford (1): vessels and a fish market. National Gallery, Prague (1): fishing boats off a coast. Boymans van Beuningen Museum, Rotterdam (1): portrait group by the Maas at Den Briel. Nationalmuseum, Stockholm (1): coast with figures and ships. Stuttgart Museum (1). Centraal Museum der Gemeente, Utrecht (3): St. Paul at Malta; beach scene; Dutch ships off the English coast. Kunsthistorisches Museum, Vienna (1): shipping off a fort. Martin von Wagner Museum, Würzburg (1): seaport with a fishmarket.

WILLAERTS, Isaac **1620-1693**

Born and died in Utrecht. The younger brother of Abraham (q.v.) and the son and pupil of Adam (q.v.); he apparently did not travel like his brother and concentrated on painting marines in his native town. His work is similar to his father's, but weaker. As he lived on for nearly thirty years after his father's death the updated ships prevent confusion with the latter's work.

EXAMPLES: National Maritime Museum, Greenwich (1): a French galley and Dutch men-of-war off a fort. Boymans van Beuningen Museum, Rotterdam (1): river scene. Staatsgalerie, Stuttgart (1): shore scene with fisherfolk. Centraal Museum der Gemeente, Utrecht (1): shore scene with Amsterdam ship.

WILLIAMS, J.W.

Probably an American ship portraitist, but one strongly influenced by the Marseilles School; he was working in the first quarter of the 19th century. The Peabody Museum of Salem has a watercolour dated 1809.

WILLIAMSON, Samuel **1792-1842**

Born Liverpool, 1792; died Liverpool, June 7th, 1842. In 1810 he was elected an associate member of the Liverpool Academy, and a full member the following year. Also in 1811 he exhibited his only picture at the Royal Academy, but not a marine.

EXAMPLES: Walker Art Gallery, Liverpool (4): North Shore, Liverpool; New Brighton Shore; fishing boats in heavy seas; fishing boats entering harbour.

WILLIAMSON, W.H.

This artist, with a style similar to many mid-19th century marine painters, exhibited at the Royal Academy in 1853, 1855 and 1875, and at the British Institution between 1856 and 1865. He must have travelled as his subjects include views such as "Mouth of the River Scheldt" and "Fishing boats off Fort Rouge, Calais".

PLATE: 541.

WILLOUGHBY, Robert **1768-1843**

He was a pioneer of the Hull school of marine painting and ship portraiture. He had a house painting business, but seems to have devoted himself to easel painting in later life. The Hull Maritime Museum has nine of his paintings. The National Maritime Museum, Greenwich, has a portrait of an old merchant captain signed "R. Willoughby, pinx" which may also be by him. The Peabody Museum of Salem has a painting of the whaler *Molly* in the ice.

WILSON, H.S.

A British ship portraitist, probably working in Liverpool in the third quarter of the 19th century. The Peabody Museum of Salem has two watercolours.

WILSON, John H. ('Jock') R.S.A. **1774-1855**
Born Old Cumnock, Ayr, August 17th, 1774. He was apprenticed to an Edinburgh house decorator called John Norie and received some instruction in drawing from Alexander Nasmyth. He later taught drawing for two years in Montrose. In 1798 he moved to London as a house painter but after he had decorated the Surrey Theatre he worked there in the scene-room and subsequently became scene-painter to Philip Astley in his Royal Amphitheatre. He also worked for Astley in Ireland and on the Continent, and it was on his scene painting that a great deal of his reputation rested. Though none of it survives, it was very influential and admired by, among others, that other scene painter and budding marine artist, Clarkson Stanfield (q.v.).

As an easel artist Wilson was and is most notable for his marines. He was more in tune with the sea than any contemporary Scottish painter, with the possible exception of John Thomson, and his work was much admired for its dramatic effects of light and storm. He tended to use bright, even raw, colour and was also inclined to be somewhat careless in his execution. He first exhibited at the Royal Academy in 1807 and thereafter most years until his death. He also exhibited at the British Institution from 1813, and at the Society of Artists, of which he was a foundation member in 1823 and President in 1827. Late in life he moved to Folkestone where he died on April 29th, 1855.

Examples of his work may be seen at the National Gallery of Scotland, Edinburgh, Folkestone Art Gallery, Leicester Art Gallery, Laing Art Gallery, Newcastle, Salford Art Gallery and Wolverhampton Art Gallery.

WILSON, John James **1818-1875**
Born in London, 1818. Son and pupil of 'Jock' Wilson (q.v.). He first exhibited at the Royal Academy in 1835, and at the British Institution in 1834. Perhaps in reaction to his father, none of his exhibited pictures were marines until 1849 but thereafter, until he ceased to exhibit in 1873, few were anything else. He also exhibited a large number of paintings at Suffolk Street. He died in Folkestone on January 30th, 1875.

Examples of his work can be seen at the Folkestone Art Gallery, the National Maritime Museum, Greenwich, Graves Art Gallery, Sheffield, and the Wolverhampton Art Gallery.

PLATE: 530.

WISHART, T. **fl.1798**
A rather primitive painting of the *Mediator* in action December 12th, 1782, signed "T. Wishart 1798", and which is a copy from the engraving after Dominic Serres (q.v.), is in the National Maritime Museum, Greenwich.

WITHAM, J.
A British ship portraitist working in Liverpool in the second half of the 19th century. The National Maritime Museum, Greenwich, has a portrait of the *William McGilvery* dated 1877, and the Manx Museum has one of the *Ben-my-Chree,* built 1875.

WITMONT, Heerman **c.1605-aft.1683**
Born and died in Delft. If he was not the inventor of what we called grisaille drawings (which the Dutch with more accuracy called *penschilderen*) then he and Willem van de Velde the Elder (q.v.) devised it between them, for they were friends and near contemporaries.

These drawings, which could measure as much as six feet across, were usually on oak panels but sometimes on canvas, especially the larger examples. They were drawn with a reed pen and ink on to a prepared gesso ground. This technique enabled its practitioners to achieve a high level of detail in their work, but this advantage was offset by the very laborious process required to create the texturing of the picture using only a pen.

These grisailles were very popular in the middle of the 17th century when Willem van de Velde the Elder was producing his masterpieces, and they continued to be produced into the 18th century. Only a very small number of people used this unique art form, and if van de Velde was its finest exponent, then Witmont came a good second. He was also an engraver and a member of the Guild of Delft from 1644.

The only examples in public collections seem to be two at the National Maritime Museum, Greenwich; one shows the *Eendracht* off Kronborg Castle; the other is an action of the First Dutch War, probably the Battle of The Gabbard, June 2nd, 1653. Both are signed "H. Witmont".

PLATES: 95, 96.

WITTEL, Gaspar Adriaansz van **1647-1736**
(called Vanvitelli)
Born in Amersfoort, Holland, in 1647, he was a pupil of his fellow townsman and landscape painter, Matthias Withoos. He went to Rome about 1674 and Italianised his name to Vanvitelli. He remained in Italy for the rest of his life, painting landscapes with classical ruins, harbour scenes, and so on. He died in Rome on September 13th, 1736. He painted very few marines but at the National Maritime Museum at Greenwich there is a view of Naples harbour by him.

WOOD, Frank Watson **1862-1953**
Born in Berwick-on-Tweed, 1862. He studied at the Berwick School of Art, and in 1886 went to the Newcastle School of Art as Second Master. From 1889 to 1899 he was headmaster at the White School of Art, and in 1900 moved to Portsmouth. It was here that he started to paint the Navy, accepting many commissions from naval officers for portraits of their ships and of naval exercises.

In 1918 he was invited with William Wyllie and John Lavery aboard the Grand Fleet flagship, H.M.S. *Queen Elizabeth,* to cover the surrender of the German High Seas Fleet. In 1938 he accompanied King George VI and Queen Elizabeth on their Canadian tour as official artist. He painted some oils but worked mostly in watercolour. He died in Strathyre, Perthshire, in 1953.

The National Maritime Museum, Greenwich, holds a collection of his work.

PLATE: 646.

WOOD, Peter Macdonagh R.S.M.A. b.1914

Born in Twickenham, London, he was brought up at Westcliff-on-Sea, near Southend. Having attended Southend Art School, then the Slade (where he won the Diploma of Fine Art), he went to Hornsey, where he obtained the Board of Education Art Teachers' Diploma. His father had maritime interests and Peter Wood served aboard a Finnish barque and a Norwegian steamer. A yachtsman, he has done illustrations for yachting magazines. In the Second World War he served in the Royal Army Ordinance Corps and since then he has worked for film companies as a naval adviser. He was elected to the Society of Marine Artists in 1955 and his diploma work, a view of Surrey Docks, is on loan to the National Maritime Museum, Greenwich.

WOODCOCK, Robert 1692-1728

A clerk in the Admiralty with a keen interest in ships, he made drawings of them and at the age of thirty took up painting in oils. His admiration for the works of the van de Veldes (qq.v.) led him to make many copies of their works. At Greenwich there is a remarkable version of the younger van de Velde's great painting of the *Gouden Leeuw* going into action at the Battle of Texel 1673, in which the latter is made into an English flagship and Spragge's *Royal Prince* into a Dutch flagship. Woodcock died in London at the age of thirty-six and his style had not escaped from the influence of the van de Veldes, but the versions of a third-rate getting under way show a confidence and originality which distinguishes his later works. One of these, dated 1726, is in the National Maritime Museum, Greenwich, which also owns a small painting based on the younger van de Velde's painting of the *Royal Sovereign,* but depicting the *Royal William* instead.

In the Paul Mellon Collection at Yale University there is a painting of the launch of a 50-gun ship, dated 1727. He signed his work "R.U." or "R. Woodcock".

PLATE: 157; COLOUR PLATE: X.

WORKMAN, Harold 1897-1975
R.B.A., R.O.I., R.Cam.A., R.S.M.A.

Born in Oldham, Lancashire, he was a pupil at the Oldham and Manchester Schools of Art. He painted in oils and watercolours, marines, landscapes, architectural subjects and interiors.

He was elected to the Royal Society of British Artists in 1937 and the Royal Institute of Oil Painters in 1948, and is a member of the Royal Society of Marine Artists and the Manchester Academy of Fine Arts. He was President of the United Society of Artists and exhibited at the Royal Academy, New English Art Club, etc.

His diploma work for the R.S.M.A., a view of Brixham, is on loan to the National Maritime Museum, Greenwich.

WORSLEY, John R.S.M.A. b.1919

Born in Kenya on February 16th, 1919, he was educated at St. Wilfred's, Seaford, and Brighton College and then spent three years at the School of Art at Goldsmith's College, at Deptford. During the Second World War he served in the Royal Navy. He was in the merchant cruiser H.M.S. *Laurentic* when she was sunk in the Atlantic in 1940. In 1942, as a lieutenant R.N.V.R., he was appointed Official Naval War Artist on the staff of the C-in-C Mediterranean. Among other events, he was present at the Italian landings at Reggio. In November 1943 he was captured by the Germans and spent the rest of the war in a prisoner-of-war camp. While there he did a number of oil portraits of fellow officers and drawings of life in the camp.

After the war he worked in Canada and the U.S.A. depicting life in Esso oil fields. He is an illustrator, mainly of children's books, and the honorary secretary to the Royal Society of Marine Artists, to which he was elected in 1946. He also exhibits at the Royal Academy and the New English Art Club.

His work for the War Artists Commission is mainly divided between the Imperial War Museum and the National Maritime Museum, Greenwich. Some of his wartime drawings are of marine subjects.

WOU, Claes (Claesz) 1592-1665

Born in Amsterdam in 1592, he was a painter of storms and of sea battles, of which the former are the more successful. Like Hendrik Cornelisz Vroom (q.v.) he was a painter in the Flemish tradition and his seas are dark green. His storms with ships tossed in great sweeping seas have considerable drama and were probably the inspiration for the storms of Pieter Mulier the Elder (q.v.), though Mulier developed them with a grey palette.

Wou's battle pieces are different from those of H.C. Vroom in that they still belong to the Flemish mannerist school, while taking a rather distant panoramic view of the battles. The battle pieces of Pieter van Soest (q.v.) and of Jan Beerstraaten (q.v.), appear to have been strongly influenced by Wou, who may have been their master.

Wou died in Amsterdam on May 15th, 1665.

PLATES: 17, 18.

EXAMPLES: National Museum of Fine Art, Budapest (1): ships in a heavy sea. Museum of Gdansk (1): ships wrecked on a rocky coast. Museum of Graz (1): shipping in heavy weather. National Maritime Museum, Greenwich (3): battle of Scheveningen 1653; two of shipping in heavy weather. Nationalmuseum, Stockholm (1): ships in a heavy sea.

WRIGHT, Richard 1735-1775

Born in Liverpool, he was called "Wright of Liverpool", or "Wright of the Isle of Man", though the reason for the latter appellation is a mystery: he did do a pair of paintings of Captain Elliot's action off the Isle of Man in 1760.

He was apparently self-taught and first exhibited at the Society of Artists in 1762, and thereafter every year until 1773. He exhibited one picture at the Free Society, "A Seapiece with a Squall of Rain", which won the highest premium, 30 guineas. He is best known for his curious picture called "The Fishery", which is of good quality with dramatic lighting. There is a cart in the foreground, the picture having been commissioned by a syndicate who planned an unlikely scheme to transport live fish in tanks full of sea water to inland customers. The weight factor in having enough water to support enough fish over rough roads and up and down hills must surely have been prohibitive.

He was aboard the royal yacht *Fubbs* in the squadron that went to Kiel in 1761 to collect Princess Charlotte of Mecklenburg-Strelitz to marry King George III. On the voyage to Harwich three severe storms blew them towards Norway and the crossing took ten days. Wright did several paintings of the ordeal and one of these was his first exhibited picture at the Society of Arts.

PLATES: 229, 230.

EXAMPLES: National Maritime Museum, Greenwich (2): the morning after the Battle of Quiberon Bay 1759; the Royal Charlotte *and consorts in a storm in the North Sea 1761. Walker Art Gallery, Liverpool (1): the Fishery.*

WYLLIE, Charles William R.O.I. 1859-1923
Born in London, February 18th, 1859, he was the younger brother of William Lionel Wyllie (q.v.) and in youth displayed an even more precocious talent. He first had a picture hung in the Royal Academy in 1872 when he was only thirteen years old and in 1877 his "Digging for Bait" was bought for the Chantrey Bequest.

Although his subjects were mainly coastal and harbour scenes, he did not have his brother's tremendous interest in and knowledge of ships and shipping. His style is not unlike his brother's but with a more pleasing sense of colour.

During the First World War he served as a naval camouflage expert in the rank of lieutenant R.N.V.R. As well as at the Royal Academy he exhibited at Suffolk Street, the New Watercolour Society, the Grosvenor Gallery and the New Gallery, London. He was a member of the Royal Institute of Oil Painters.

PLATE: 601.

EXAMPLES: National Maritime Museum, Greenwich (2): a rowing regatta off the training ship Worcester; *"The Dying Giant" (the breaking up of a wooden two-decker, on loan). Tate Gallery, London (1): "Digging for Bait".*

WYLLIE, Lieut. Col. Harold 1880-1973
O.B.E., R.S.M.A.
Born in London on June 20th, 1880. He was the eldest son of William Lionel Wyllie (q.v.) and he inherited his father's love of ships; in his case, however, this interest was not so much with the contemporary scene as in the development of the sailing ship in naval history. This involved him in a lifetime of research into shipping archaeology, on which he became a world expert. Thus it was that when he and his father were appointed to the committee to restore the *Victory* to her Trafalgar state, Harold Wyllie was put in charge of re-rigging her. He was also concerned with the preservation of the training ships *Foudroyant* and *Implacable* (ex-*Dugnay-Trouin,* the last French survivor from the battle of Trafalgar).

He exhibited at the Royal Academy and was a member of the Royal Society of Marine Artists. He worked in a rather similar style to his father, but because most of his subjects were historical his work lacks the freshness and spontaneity of William Lionel's. One of his major works is a series of battle pieces which cover the upper part of the walls of the mess at H.M.S. *Dolphin*. Among his later works was a sketch of the Battle of Trafalgar for the large mural in the Trafalgar Square Post Office; the mural itself was painted by others.

In the Boer War he went out with the West Kent Regiment as a lieutenant, and in the First World War he joined the Royal Flying Corps; he flew in action and later commanded squadrons in France and England, one of them being the first night-fighter unit. In the Second World War he commanded the training ship *Implacable* in Portsmouth harbour.

For many years he lived in Perthshire, in a house which his wife had inherited called "Hillhead of Dunkeld", and he was still accepting commissions there into his nineties. He died in London on December 22nd, 1973.

Wyllie was also an etcher and ship modeller. The National Maritime Museum, Greenwich, has on loan his diploma picture for the Royal Society of Marine Artists. This depicts the famous trial off Lisbon in 1847, when the old ex-French liner H.M.S. *Canopus* beat all Sir William Symonds' new ships of the line.

PLATE: 638.

WYLLIE, William Lionel R.A., R.I. 1851-1931
Born London, July 6th, 1851. He was the son of the genre painter William Morrison Wyllie, and had a younger brother Charles (q.v.) who grew up to be an accomplished marine artist.

Their father, who had studied in Paris, was extremely francophile, and decided partly for health reasons that the family would spend part of the year in a summer home in France and the remainder in a winter one in London. The French home was at Wimereux on the coast just north of Boulogne. William Lionel was first a student at Heatherley's Art School and then joined the Royal Academy school in 1865.

He exhibited his first painting at the Royal Academy in 1868 and in 1883 his picture of the Thames at Greenwich, called "Toil, Glitter, Grime and Wealth on a Flowing Tide", was purchased for the Chantrey Bequest. The subject of this picture — tugs working barges — was something of an innovation, as painters had formerly concentrated on the more decorative types of vessels; however, Wyllie's obsessive love for the sea and anything that floated on it, embraced every type and size of vessel. It moved him to cover every aspect of the working river and set a fashion that other artists followed. In 1889 he was elected A.R.A., by which time he had a house by Rochester and was busy painting the lower Thames and Medway. He was also spending much of his time in his yacht *Ladybird* and as well as painting, he was working as an illustrator for the *Graphic*.

In 1889 he was the guest of the White Star Company aboard their new liner *Teutonic* when, as an armed merchant cruiser, she went to the naval review at Spithead in honour of the new Kaiser Wilhelm II; during the subsequent manoeuvres he was aboard a Royal Naval ship. The previous year he had stayed on H.M.S. *Black Prince* in Ireland and in 1901 he was aboard the flagship *Majestic* to record the passing of Queen Victoria's body from Osborne, Isle of Wight, to Portsmouth. His connections with the Royal Navy were strengthened in 1906 when he bought Tower House in Old Portsmouth, on the waterfront at the entrance to the harbour. He was elected a full Royal Academician in 1909.

As well as painting from life he also painted historical scenes and events of the First World War. His largest painting, and one of his last, is the semi-circular panorama of the Battle of Trafalgar in the Royal Naval Museum in Portsmouth, where it is viewed through a full-size mock-up of the stern windows of the frigate *Euryalus*.

The quality of this work is not very high and indeed Wyllie's oil painting declined in quality from about the First World War, though his watercolours, his favourite medium, continued to be excellent. He was also a skilful engraver.

His output was prodigious. When he died in 1931 the watercolours in his studio were purchased for the proposed National Maritime Museum at Greenwich; on counting these were found to number about five thousand. A set of engravings, about two hundred, were also in the studio and these were offered to the Museum in the 1950s by Colonel Harold Wyllie. Messrs. Colnaghi were asked to value them, which they did at so low an estimate that the offer was withdrawn and they were dispersed in America.

One of Wyllie's last tasks was his work as a member of the committee supervising the restoration of H.M.S. *Victory* to her Trafalgar state, in a dry dock in Portsmouth dockyard.

He exhibited at the Society of British Artists, the New Watercolour Society and the Grosvenor Gallery. He died in Hampstead on April 6th, 1931.

Wyllie's published works include *Tidal Thames (188-), Marine Painting and Watercolour* (1901), *Nature's Laws and the Making of Pictures* (1903), *J.M.W. Turner* (1905), *London to the Nore* (1905), *Sketch Book* (1908), *Trafalgar, 21st October 1805* (1905), *Sea Fights of the Great War* and *More Sea Fights of the Great War* (1919), *Lionel Percy Smythe, his Life and Work* (1924).

His widow wrote a biography of him called *We were One;* Admiral Sir Cyprian Bridge contributed an article on him to the 1907 *Art Annual,* and F. Dolman a book called *W.L. Wyllie and his work* (1899).

PLATES: 598, 599, 600; COLOUR PLATE: XXIV.

EXAMPLES: Oil paintings. National Maritime Museum, Greenwich (13): "Well Done Condor*" (H.M.S.* Condor *at the bombardment of Alexandria 1882); the French fleet arriving at Spithead 1905; the burning of the Semaphore Tower at Portsmouth 1914; the loss of the* Invincible *1916; "Storm and Sunshine, a battle with the Elements" (the* Leonidas *as a powder hulk at Upnor); another picture of the* Leonidas; *R.M.S.* Teutonic *leaving Liverpool in 1889; H.M.S.* Victory *at Portsmouth; H.M.S.* Victory *on her last voyage to the dry dock; the Pool of London; the 2nd Cruiser Squadron 1909; fishing boats returning to Portsmouth; fishing boats on a beach at low tide. Guildhall Art Gallery, London (1): "Commerce and Sea Power". Tate Gallery, London (2): Battle of the Nile 1798; "Toil, Glitter, Grime and Wealth on a Flowing Tide" (on loan to the National Maritime Museum). Walker Art Gallery, Liverpool (1): "The Passing of a Great Queen"; National Gallery of New South Wales, Sydney (2): Herring Fishery and night scene.*

WYNDHAM-TUSTING, Albert

A contemporary painter and ex-Petty Officer in the Royal Navy, who presented the National Maritime Museum, Greenwich, with his painting of a trawler in a gale at night in 1970.

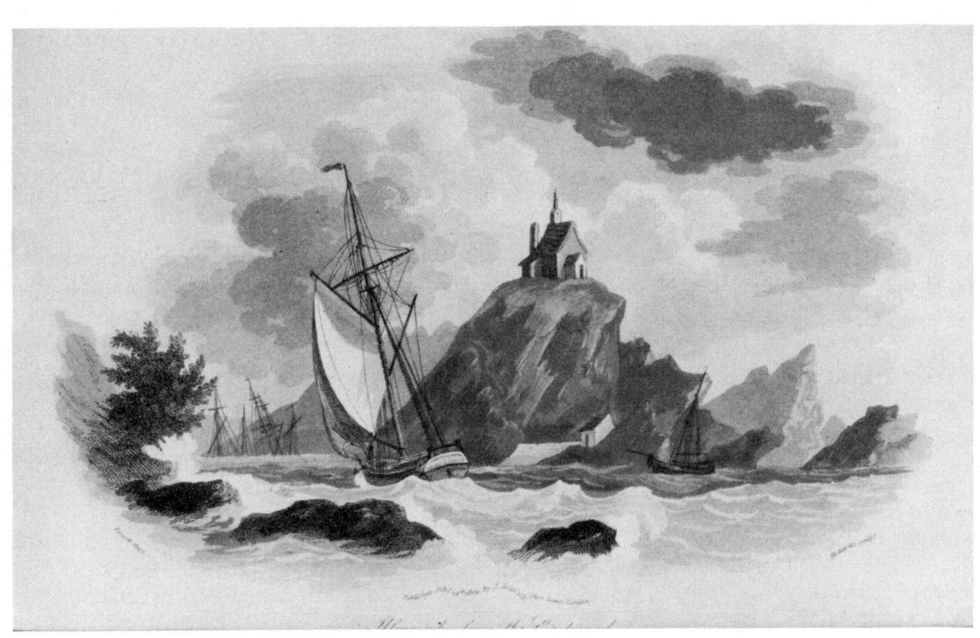

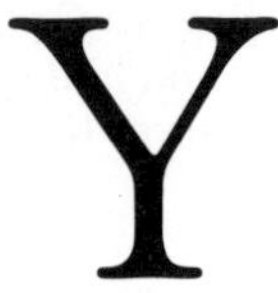

YATES, Lieutenant Thomas R.N. **c.1760-1796**

He passed for a lieutenant in the Royal Navy in 1782. At what date he gave up the sea to be a painter is not clear but he first exhibited at the Royal Academy in 1788 and continued to do so until 1794, specialising in actions and views of good quality. When the French Revolutionary War began he started to publish pictures of actions from his own drawings.

His paintings are rare because of his short working life. He shared a London house that had belonged to his great-uncle (Richard Yates, the comedian) with a Miss Jones and in August 1796 they were in dispute about who owned it, though it had clearly been left to her. After dinner on the afternoon of the 29th, his wife being out, Thomas took a stroll in the garden and Miss Jones locked him out. As he attempted to climb in through the kitchen window a Mr. Sellers, who had called in to protect Miss Jones, shot him. At the trial the jury returned a verdict of manslaughter; Sellers was fined one shilling and imprisoned for six months.

EXAMPLES: National Maritime Museum, Greenwich (1): the Scourge *capturing the* Sansculotte.

YORKE, William Howard **fl.1858-aft.1913**

A Liverpool ship portraitist working in competition with Samuel Walters (q.v.) and Joseph Heard (q.v.), but not as good as either of them.

Marion and Dorothy Brewington, in their catalogue of the paintings in the Peabody Museum of Salem, make the distinction that the three they hold signed "Wm York Lpool" are by a different hand, also working in Liverpool. It should be pointed out that these three are dated 1860, 1861 and 1864, while the earliest picture at Greenwich is dated 1866 and signed "W.H. Yorke". One explanation for a change of signature could be the presence of a ship portraitist signing himself "W.G. York Lpool". All but two of the ten signed ship portraits at Greenwich are signed "W.H. Yorke Lpool" but one dated 1874 is signed "W.H. York", and one dated 1871 is signed "W. Yorke Lpool".

The Peabody Museum of Salem also has five examples signed "W.H. Yorke Lpool".

It seems likely that Wm. York and W.H. Yorke was the same man. The latest example known to this compiler appeared in a sale at Sotheby's Belgravia in 1973, dated 1913.

PLATE: 392.

EXAMPLES: National Maritime Museum, Greenwich (11): ten signed and one firmly attributed. Liverpool Museums (1). Manx Museum, Isle of Man (1). Mystic Seaport, Conn. (1). Mariners Museum, Newport News (1). Peabody Museum of Salem (8). San Francisco Maritime Museum (1).

Z

ZEELANDER, Pieter de **fl.mid-17th century**

Believed to have been a Haarlem painter in the Dutch realist manner, strongly influenced by Jan Porcellis (q.v.) in his later grey period. He travelled to Rome, where he took the surname of Cafer or de Krafer.

EXAMPLES: Gemäldegalerie, Augsburg (1): rough sea. Museum of Bamberg (1). Städtisches Museum, Frankfurt am Main (1). National Maritime Museum, Greenwich (1): a flute and small vessels on a windy day. Alte Pinakothek, Munich (3): small pair of shipping off a rock and off a fort in windy weather, and fishing vessels in a gale.

ZEEMAN *see* **NOOMS, Reinier**

ZENOBIO, Luca de la *see* **CARLEVARIS, Luca**

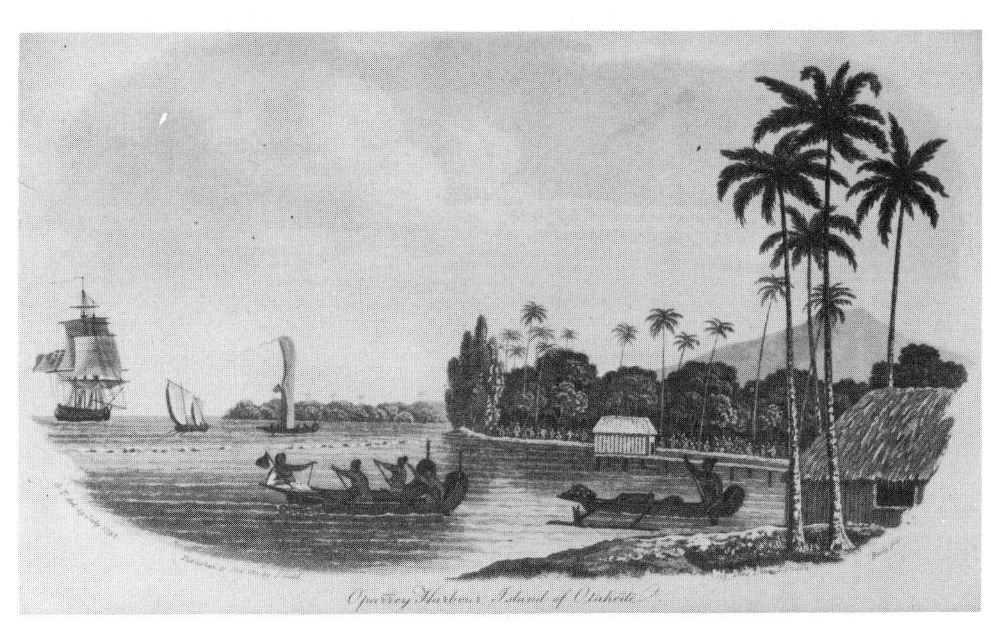

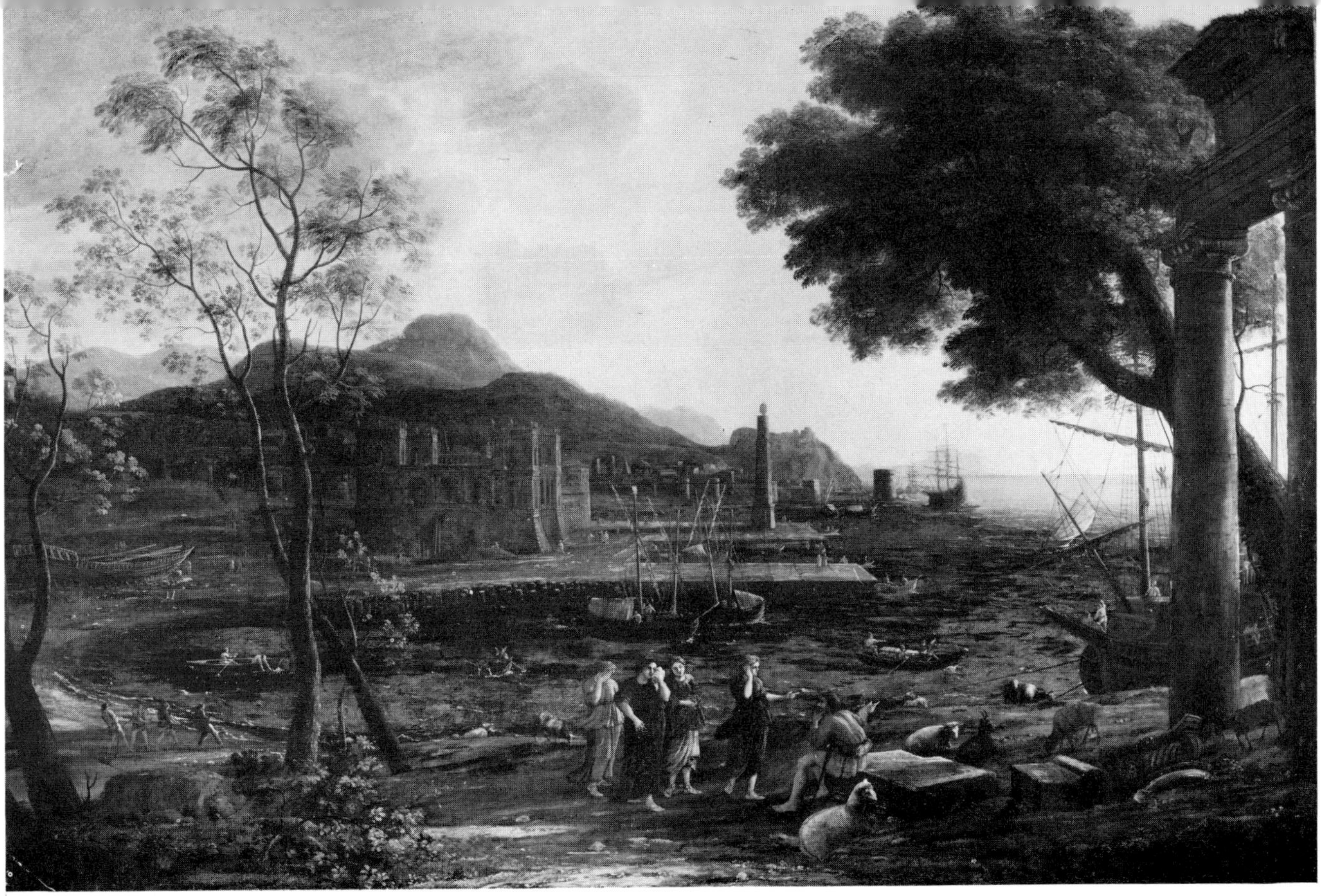

Plate 1. Claude Gellée, 1600-1682. "A classical harbour scene with mourning Heliardae." Wallraf-Richartz Museum, Cologne.

Plate 2. Claude Gellée, 1600-1682. "The Trojan women setting fire to their fleet." The Metropolitan Museum of Art (Fletcher Fund 1955), New York.

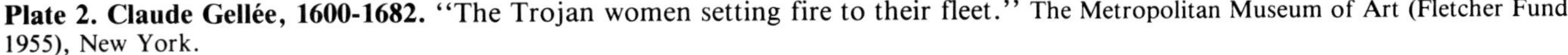

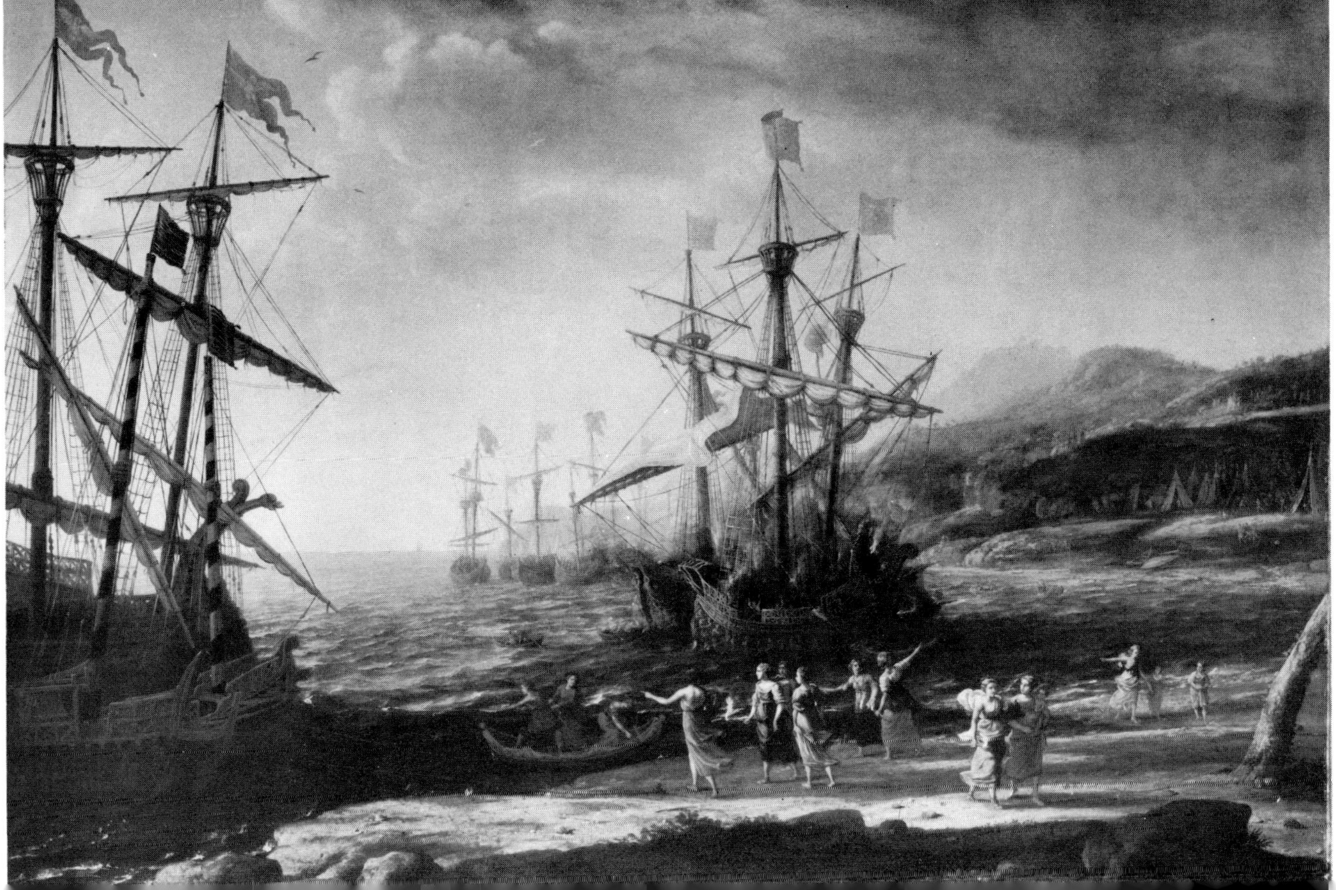

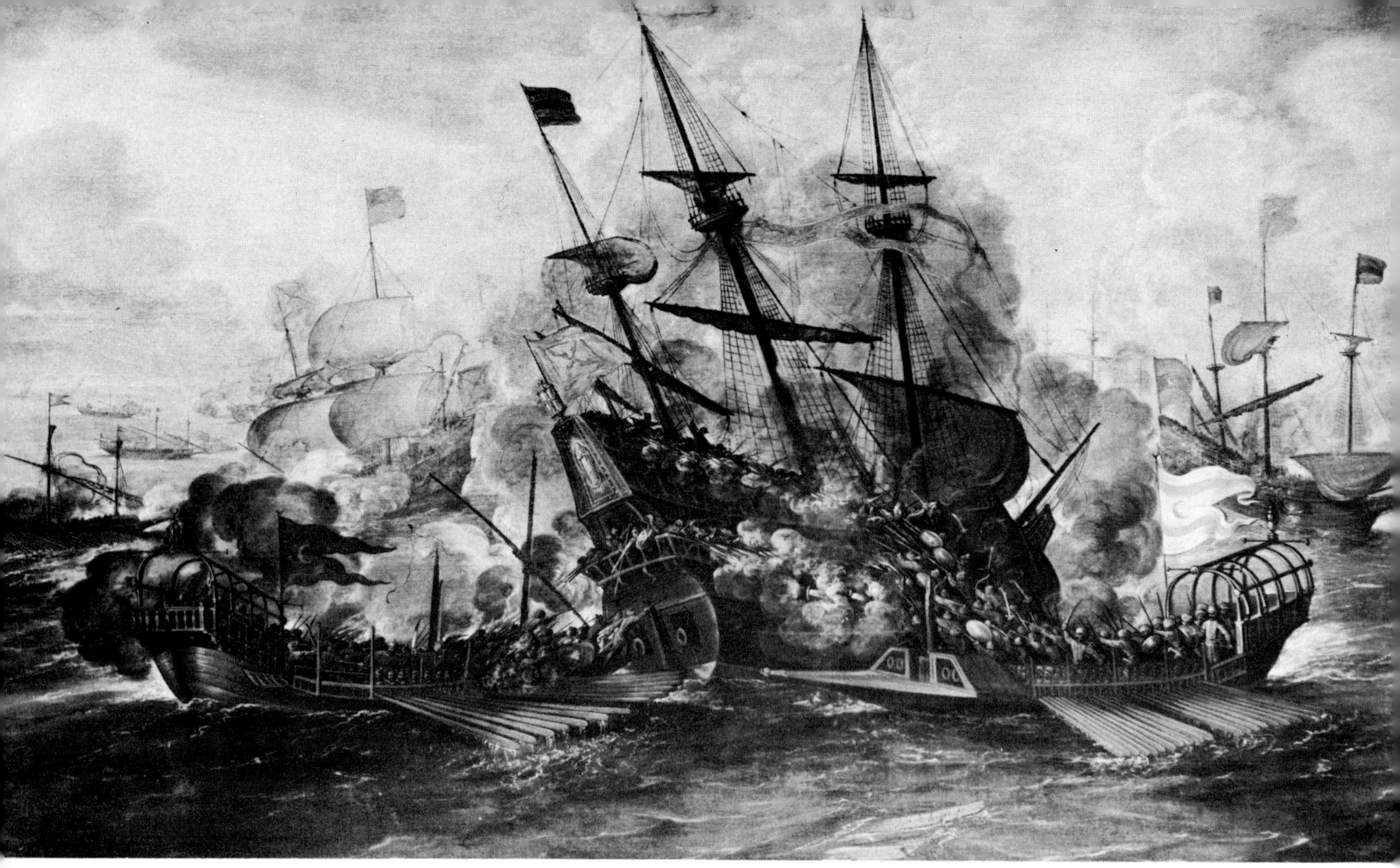

Plate 3. Juan del Corte, 1597-1660. "An action between Spanish ships and Turkish galleys." Museo Naval, Madrid.

Plate 4. Juan de Toledo, 1611-1665. "An action between a Spanish ship and two Barbary pirates." *The treatment of the people and their groupings suggests Spanish, or at least Mediterranean, overtones. Especially in the religious paintings of this period one finds the figures in the foreground relatively larger than the boats.* Prado Museum, Madrid.

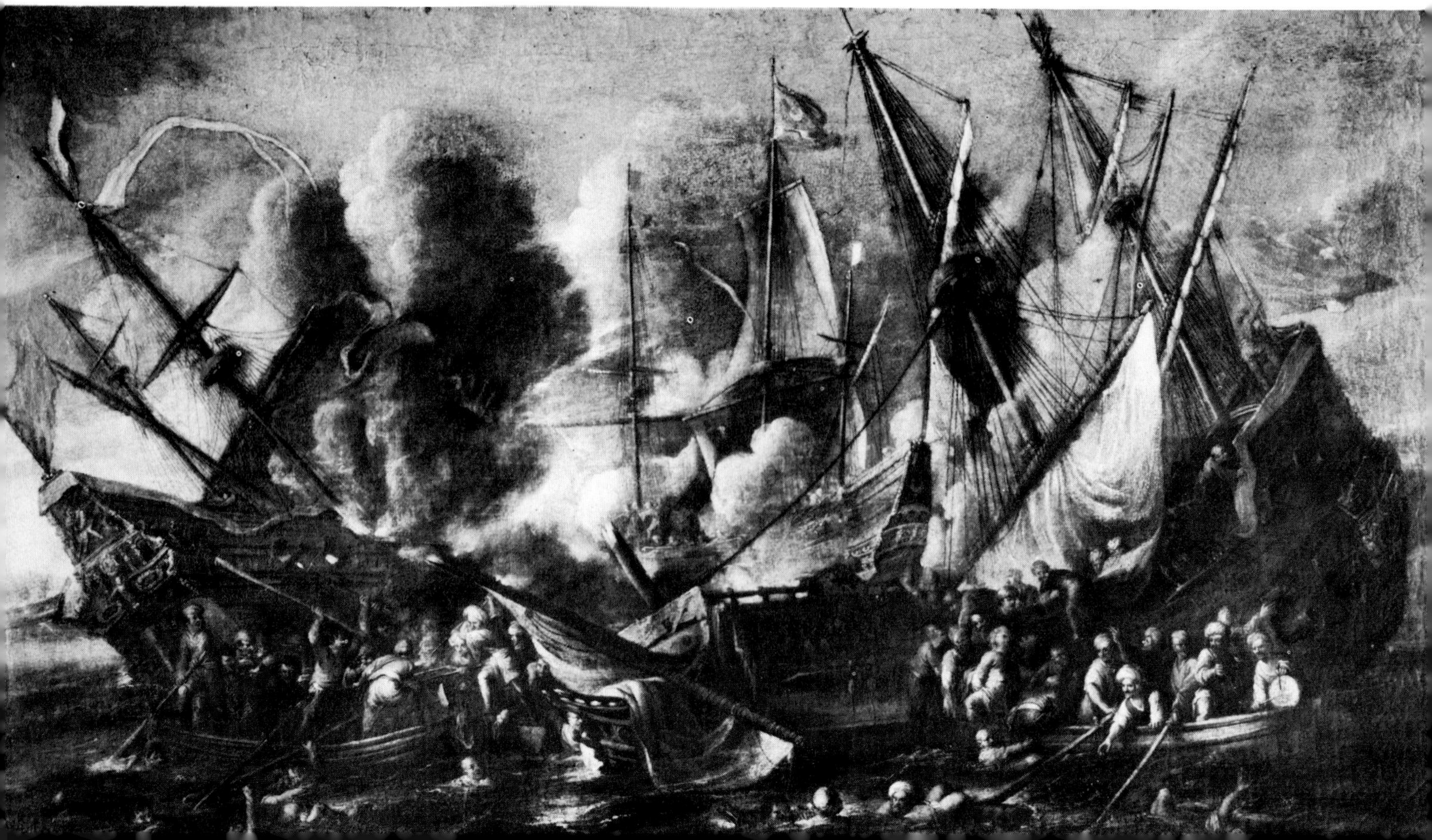

Plate 5. Hendrik Cornelisz Vroom, 1566-1640. ''The Battle of Gravelines in 1588.'' *Note the Spanish flagship, the* San Martin, *'a floating fort', bottom right, with its enormously high superstructures full of soldiers and armaments. Compare her to the English flagship, the* Ark Royal, *astern of her — no great ship, but a race-built galleon. The galleass beyond her had to raise her oars in order to fire her guns, so when the oars went up the opposition knew something was imminent.* Ferdinandeum Museum, Innsbruck.

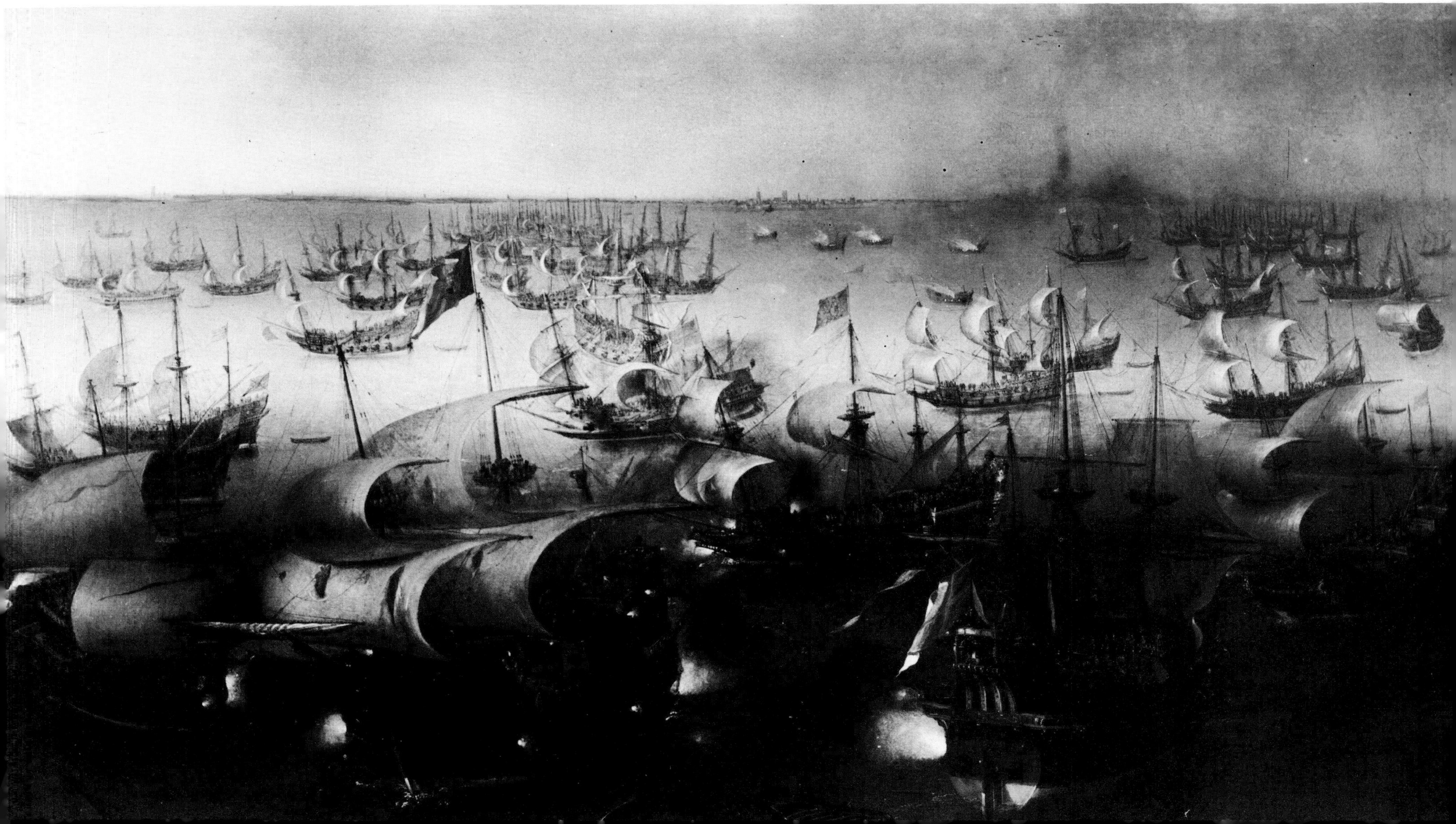

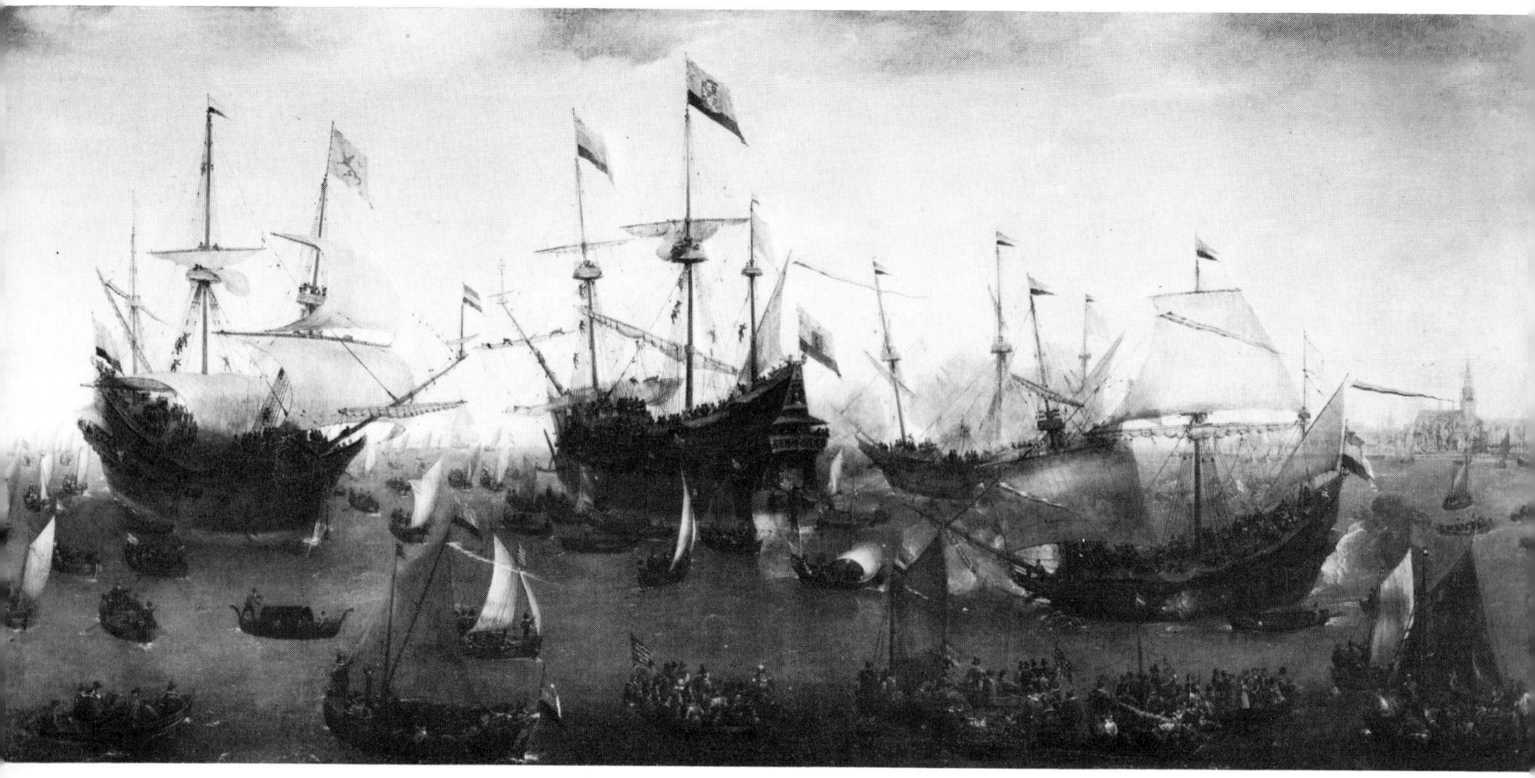

Plate 6. Hendrik Cornelisz Vroom, 1566-1640. "Return to Amsterdam of Cornelis de Houtman from the East Indies in 1599." *The four surviving ships of the Dutch fleet.* Rijksmuseum, Amsterdam.

Plate 7. Hendrik Cornelisz Vroom, 1566-1640. "The return of Prince Charles from Spain in 1623." *The English fleet is seen rounding the east end of the Isle of Wight and coming to Portsmouth Harbour, led by the* Prince Royal. *It was late in October and she is in winter rig with her topgallant masts on fore and main, and topmasts on mizzen and bonaventura mizzen sent down. (See Colour Plate I for her summer rig.)* National Maritime Museum, Greenwich.

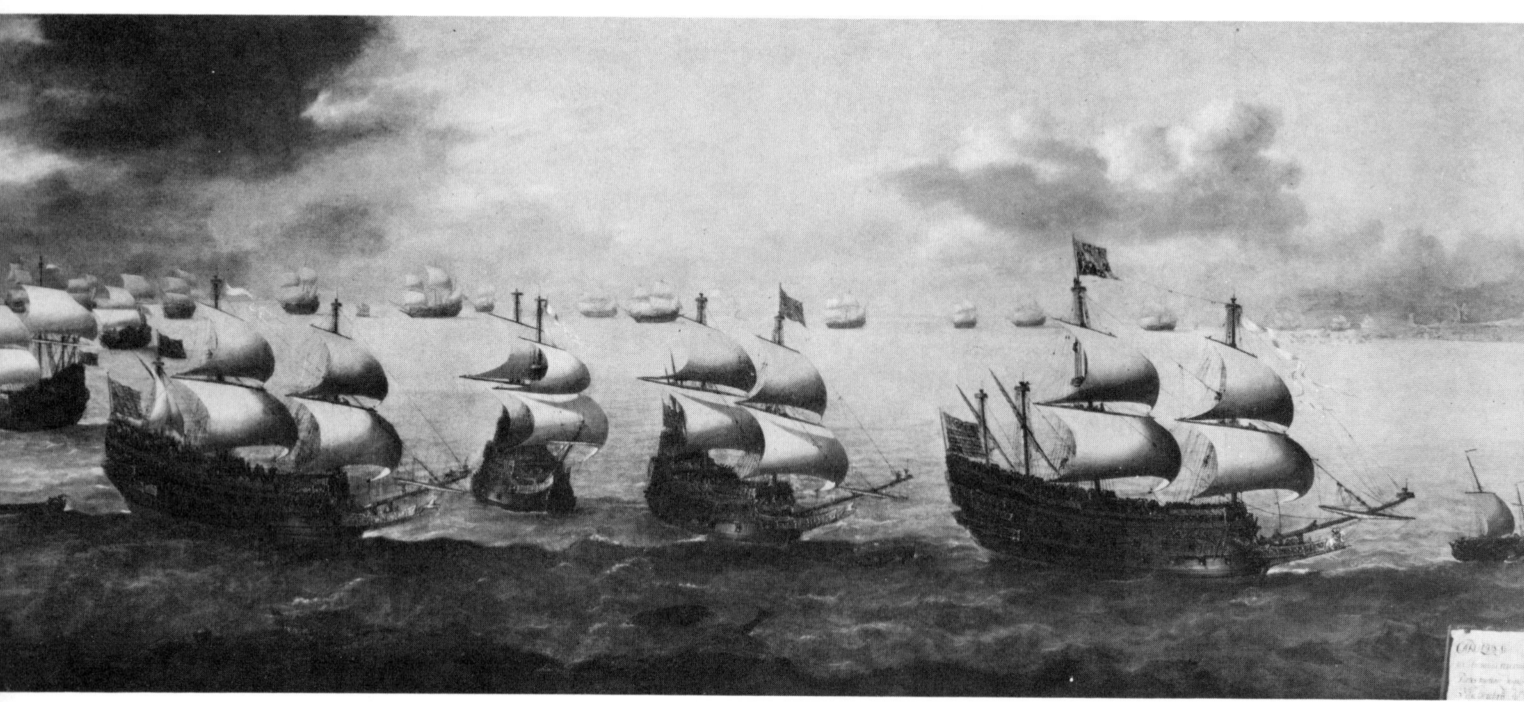

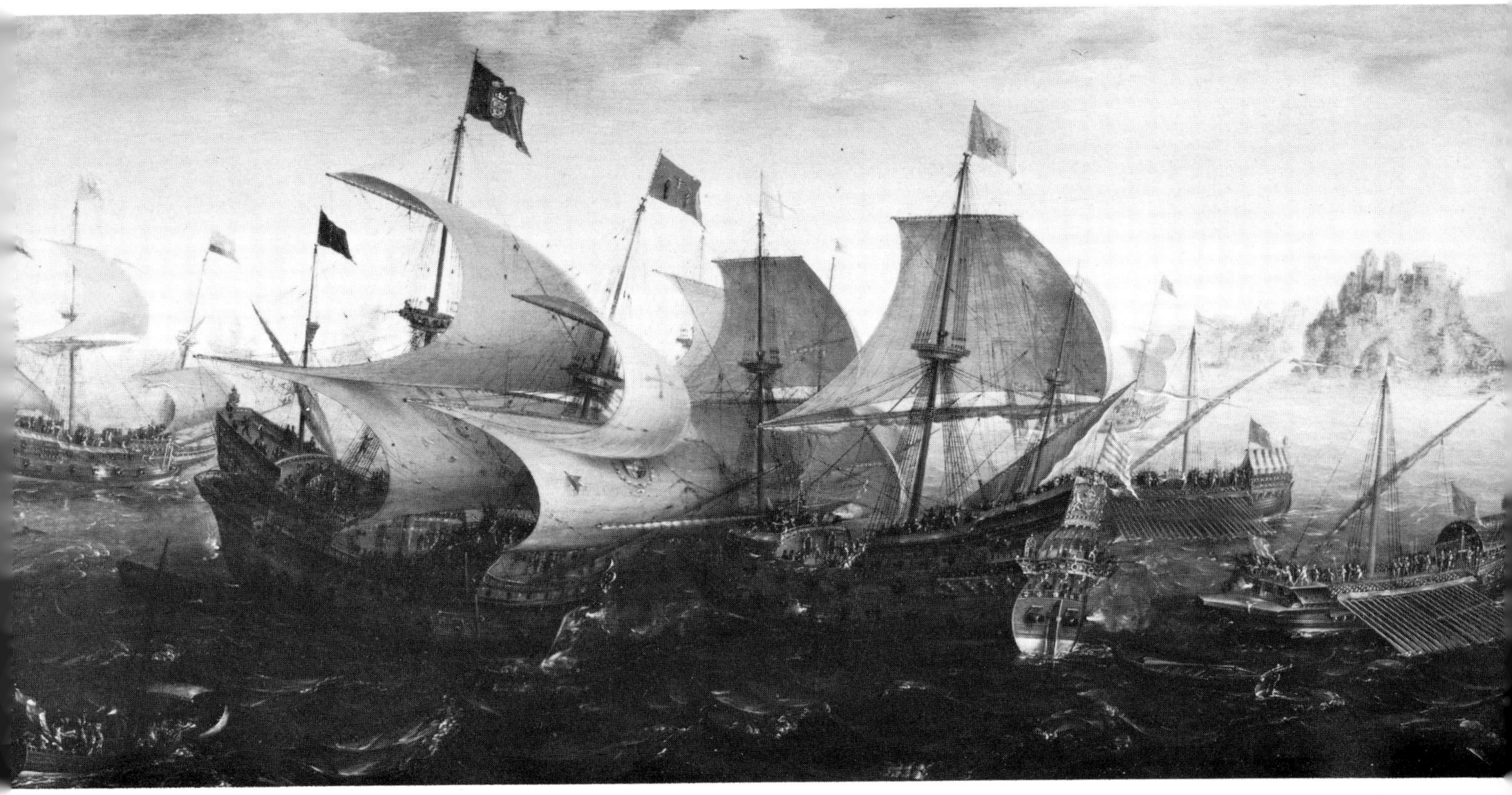

Plate 8. Aert Anthonisz, 1579-1620. "English and Spanish flagships in action." *From the presence of galleys one assumes this scene to be off the Spanish coast. In September 1602, Federigo Spinola brought nine Spanish galleys up through the Straits of Dover to cruise on the coast of Flanders. They were intercepted by a squadron commanded by Sir Richard Mansell, which destroyed all the ships but that of Spinola himself. Galleys like this had to be finely built, light and narrow, to get them any distance at all without exhausting the crew, but this in turn meant they were not as seaworthy as northern sailing ships.* Rijksmuseum, Amsterdam.

Plate 9. Aert Anthonisz, 1579-1620. "A sea fight between a Dutch ship and Spanish ships about 1600." *Both the large ships are galleons, rather than great ships, the latter being built very square with great fo'c'sles and poops, while the former had a lower fo'c'sle and a lighter poop and therefore a greater sheer.* Rheinisches Landesmuseum, Bonn.

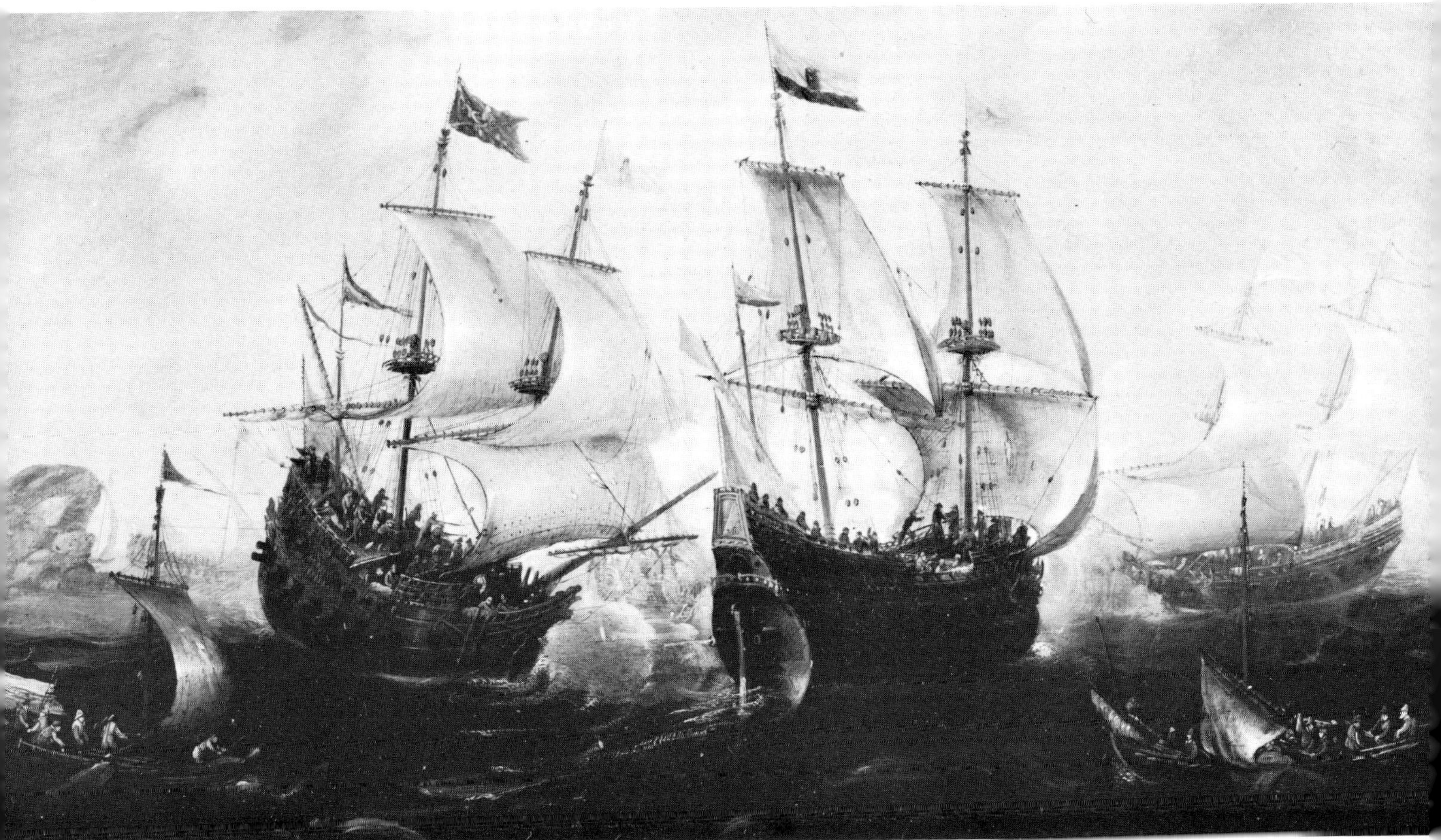

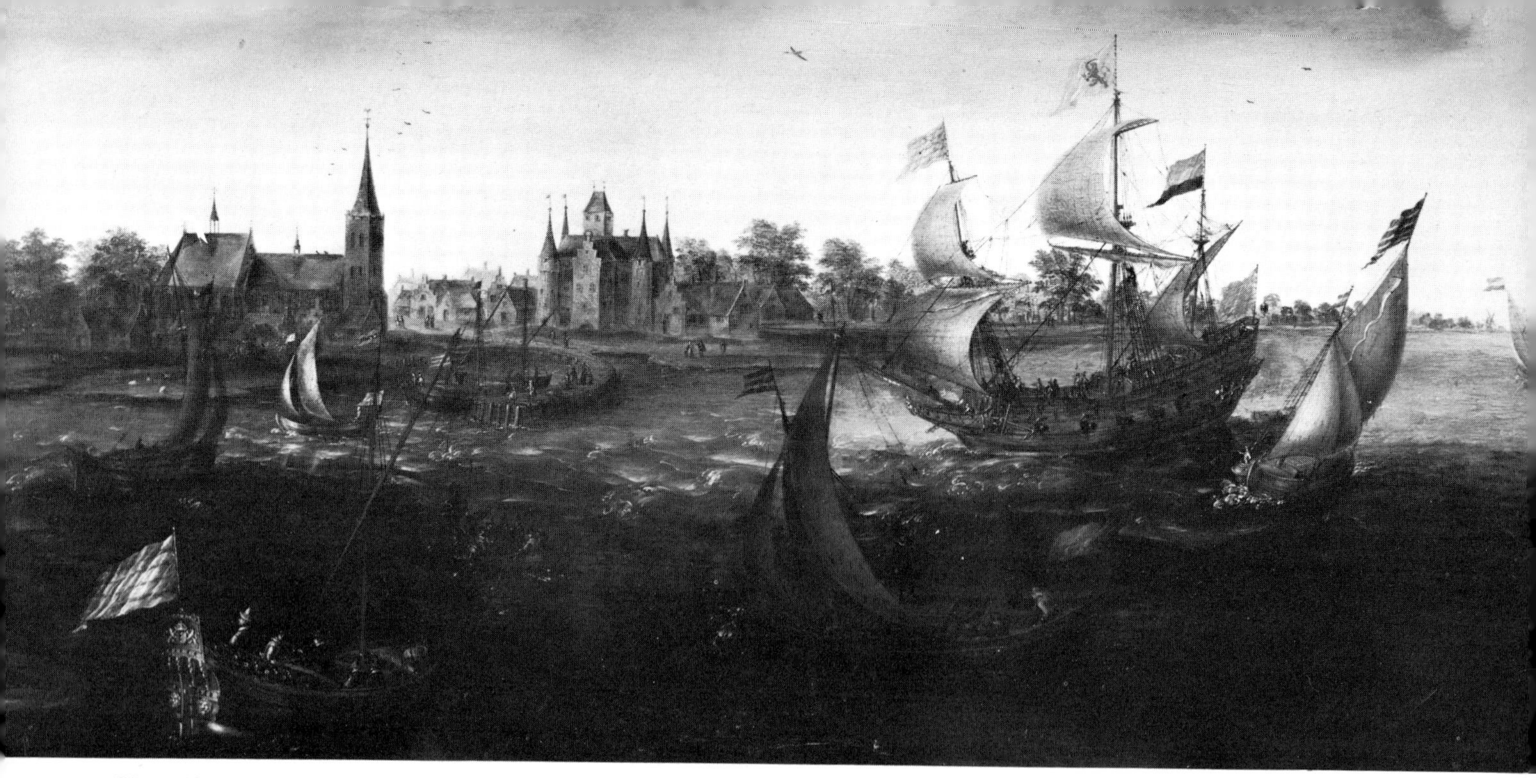

Plate 10. Aert Anthonisz, 1579-1620. "The *Eendracht* off Isselmonde in 1617," (after H.C. Vroom). *The absence of sprit-topmasts, which became general in the 1620s, supports the date, though as a generalisation artists tended not to change their styles over a period of twenty years or so. The striped flags on the foremasts probably indicate a port of origin, for instance green and white stripes would be Rotterdam.* Rijksmuseum, Amsterdam.

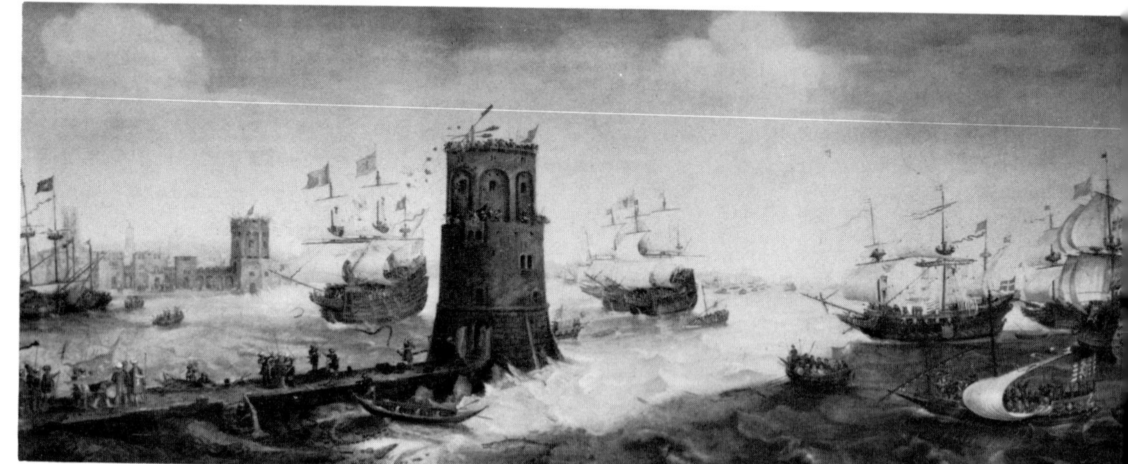

Plate 11. Cornelis Claesz van Wieringen, c.1580-1633. "The breaking of the boom at Damietta in 1259." *Damietta, a port in Lower Egypt, was captured from the Saracens on the seventh crusade led by Louis IX of France.* Frans Hals Museum, Haarlem.

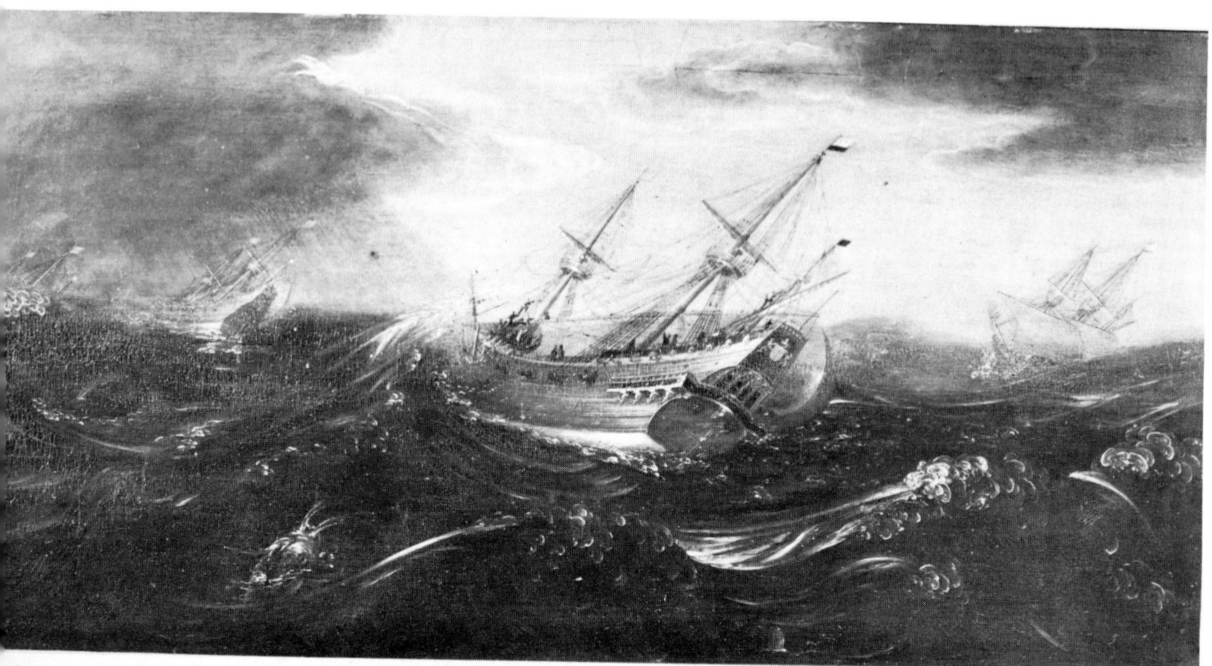

Plate 12. Roeland Jacobsz Savery, 1576-1639. "Dutch ships in a storm". Boymans-van Beuningen Museum, Rotterdam.

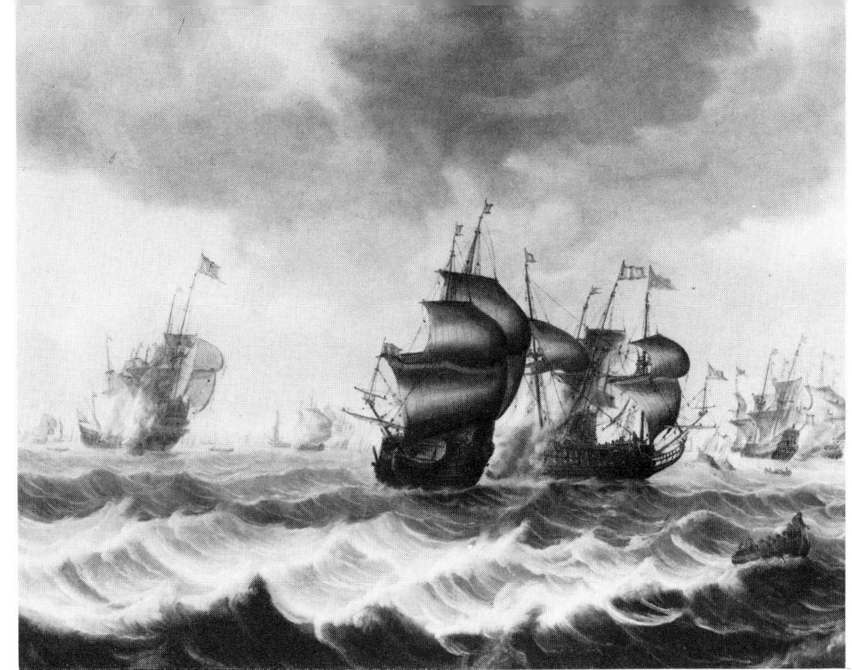

Plate 13. Pieter Coopse, fl. early to mid-17th century. "The Battle of the Downs in 1639." *A painting tending towards the grey Dutch palette, and very realistic when compared with the previous illustration.* Christie's.

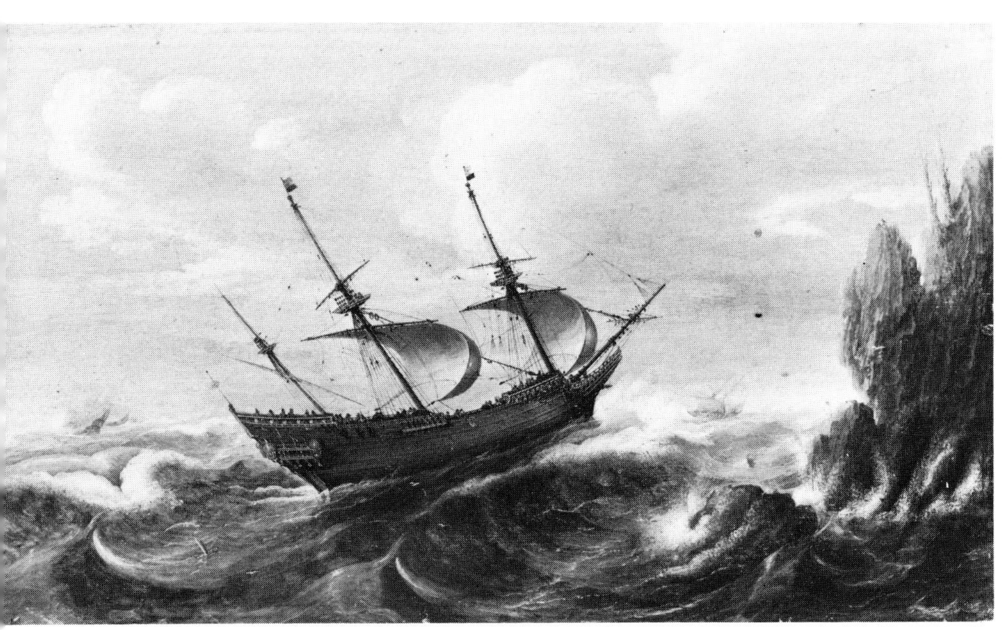

Plate 14. Cornelisz Verbeecq, c.1590-1635. "A Dutch ship driving onto rocks." *The sprit-topsail was used to help get the ship's head round when tacking, and was very difficult to handle in rough weather, as can be visualised from this painting.* Scheepvaart Museum, Amsterdam.

Plate 15. Cornelisz Verbeecq, c.1590-1635. "The Dutch East India fleet off St. Helena." Scheepvaart Museum, Amsterdam.

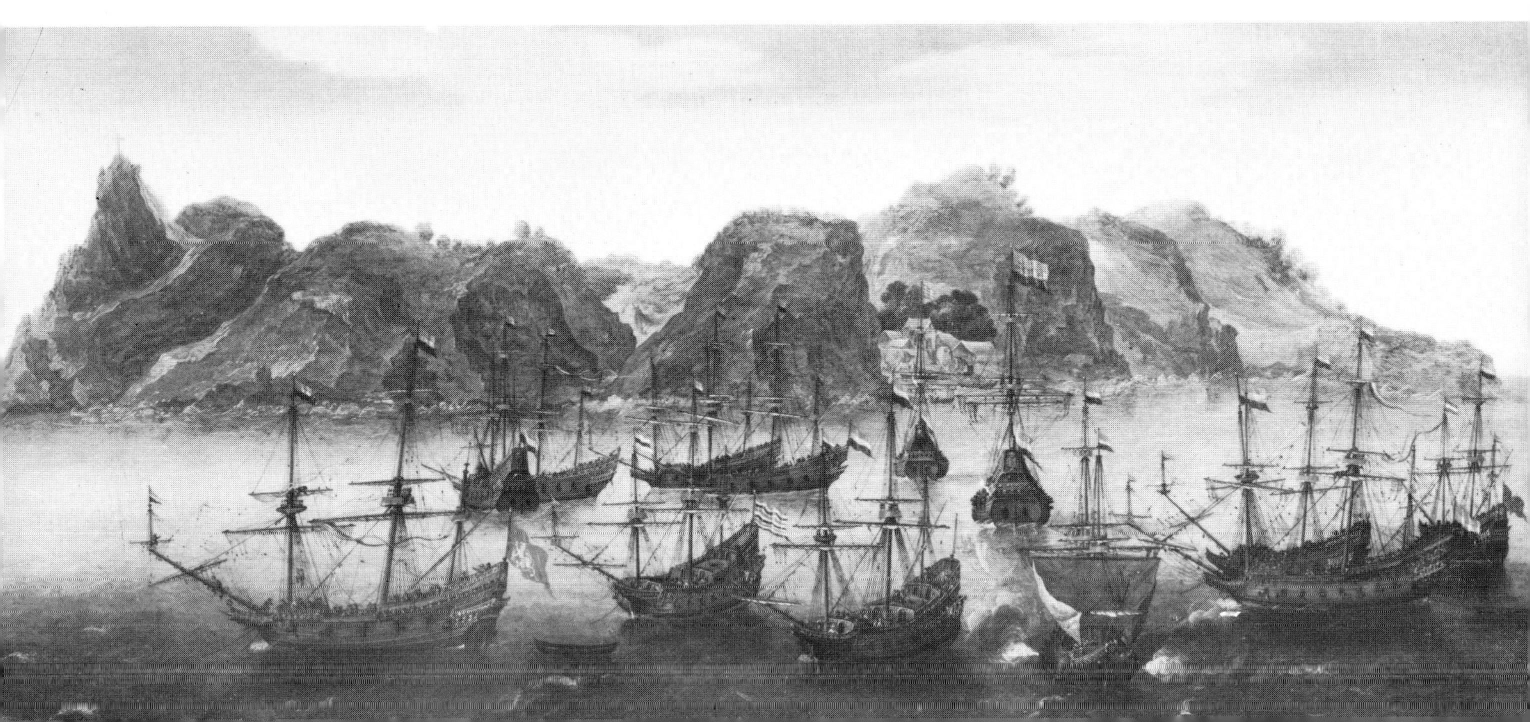

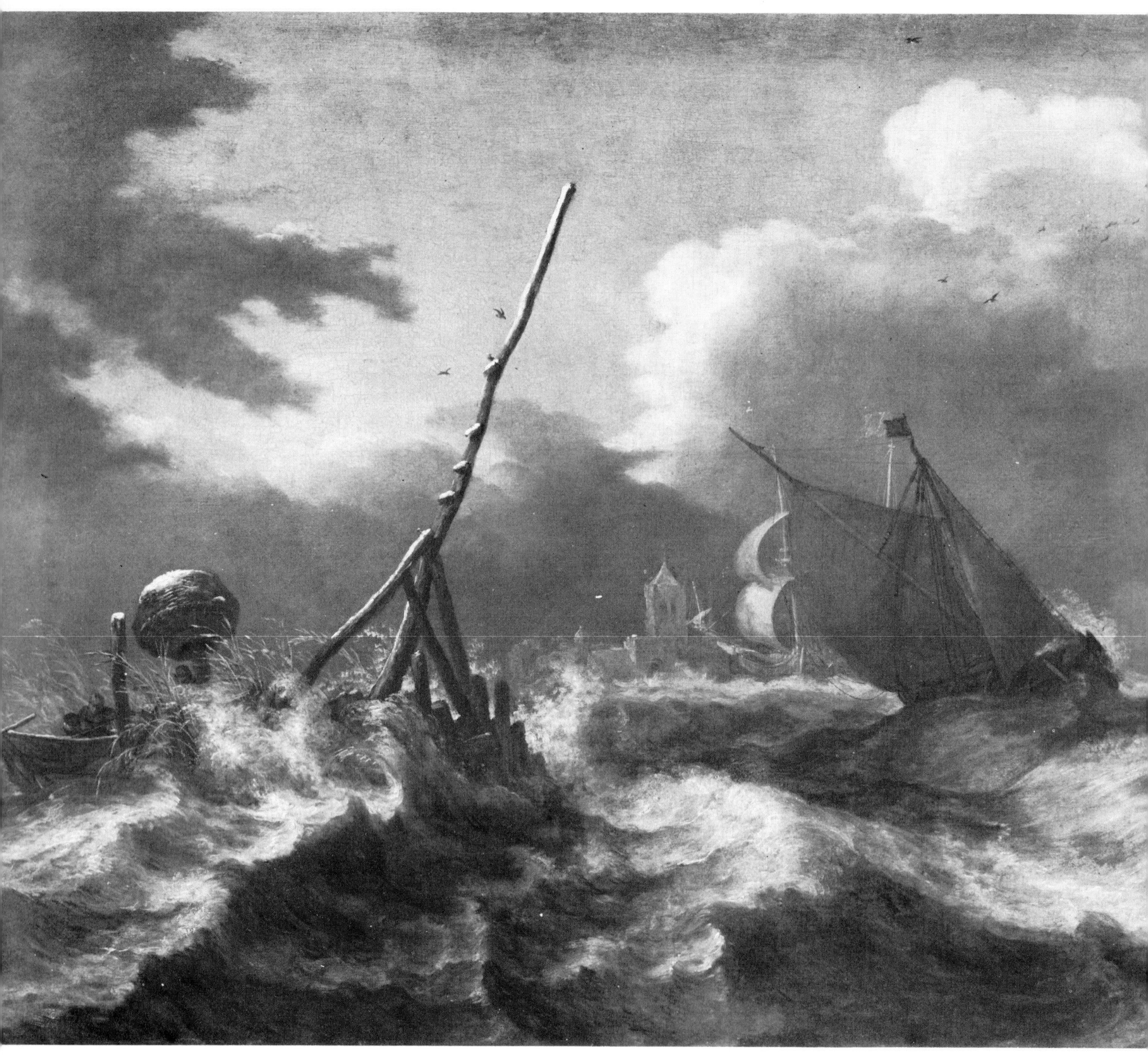

Plate 16. Allaert van Everdingen, 1621-1675. ''Storm in snowy weather.'' Musée Condé, Chantilly.

Plate 17. Claes Wou, 1592-1665. "The Battle of Scheveningen in 1653." National Maritime Museum, Greenwich.

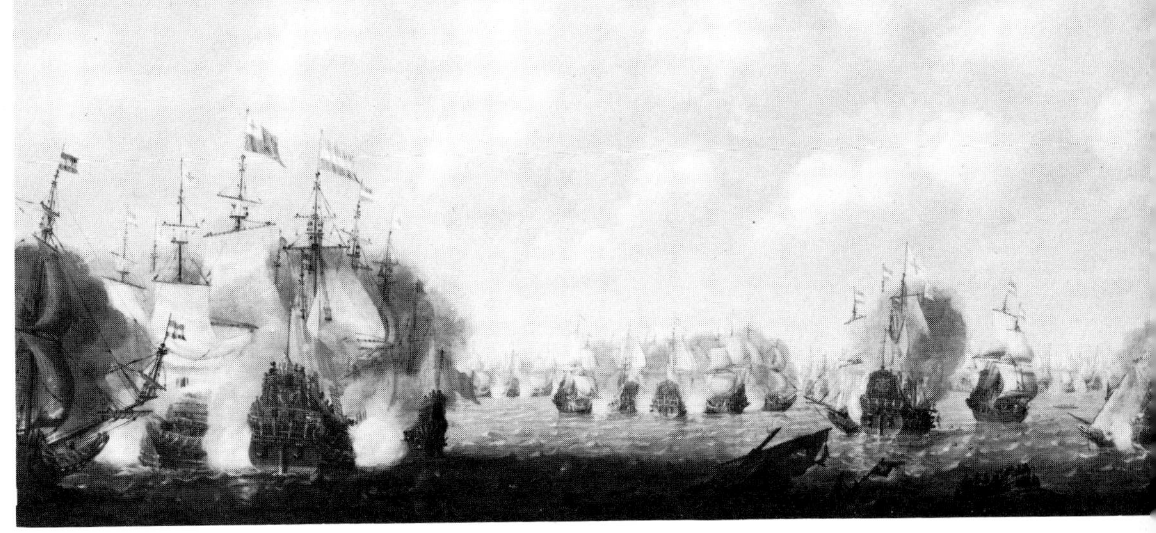

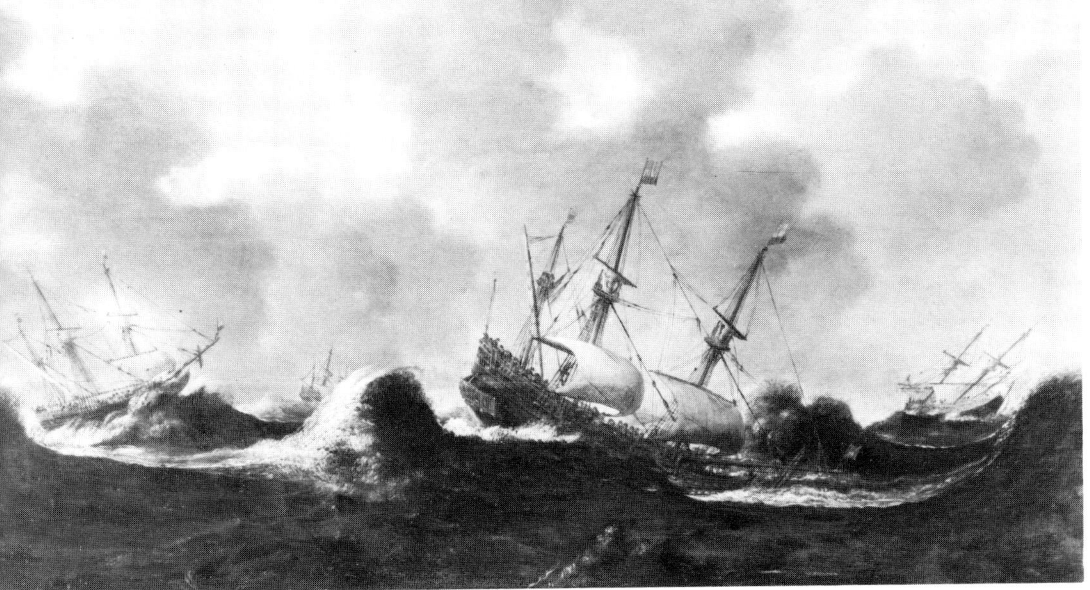

Plate 18. Claes Wou, 1592-1665. "Ships in a storm." *Wou enjoyed painting vessels in stormy seas, and this ship pile-driving is typical of his work.* Christie's.

Plate 19. Willem van der Stoop, fl.1638-1665. "The Battle of Lowestoft with the *Eendracht* blowing up in 1665." *As the Dutch were badly beaten in this encounter there were probably no Dutch commissions for pictures of the event; all the paintings were therefore painted from the English viewpoint — even if by Dutch painters. The* Eendracht *was the flagship of the Dutch commander-in-chief. The English commander-in-chief, the Duke of York, flew the Royal Standard of his brother King Charles II, as representing the King, rather than his own. This flagship was the* Royal Charles. Private collection (on loan to the National Maritime Museum, Greenwich).

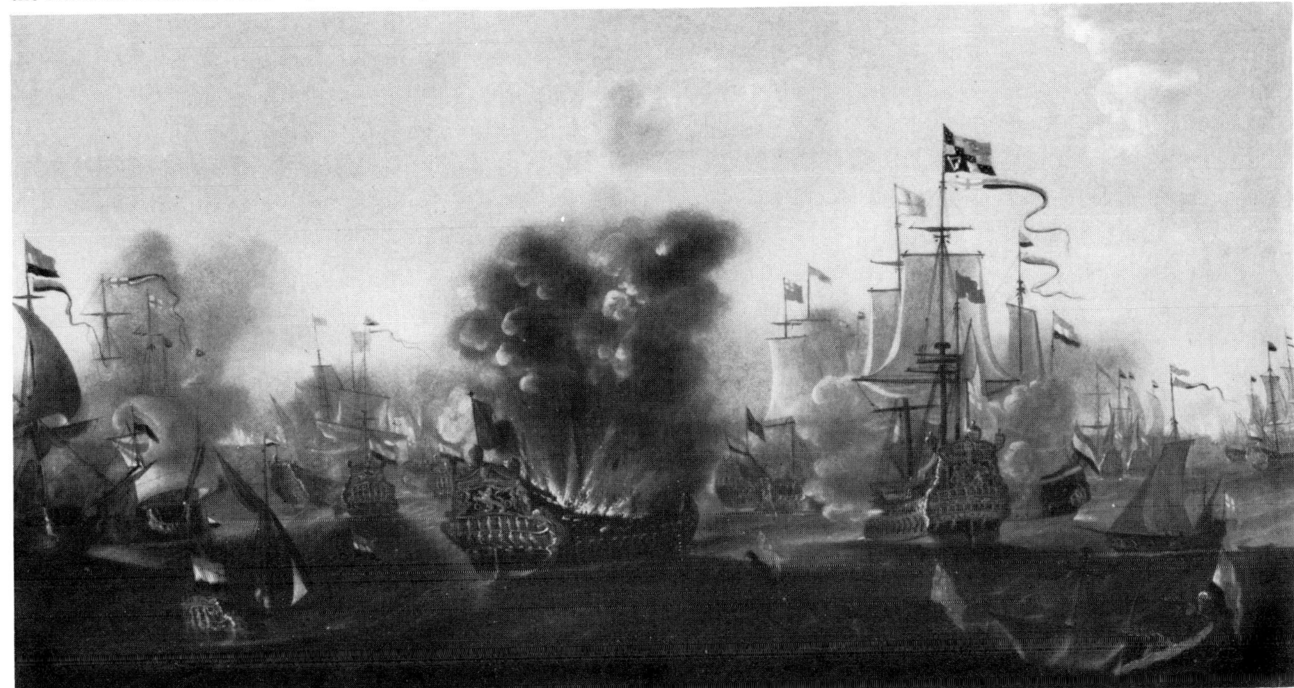

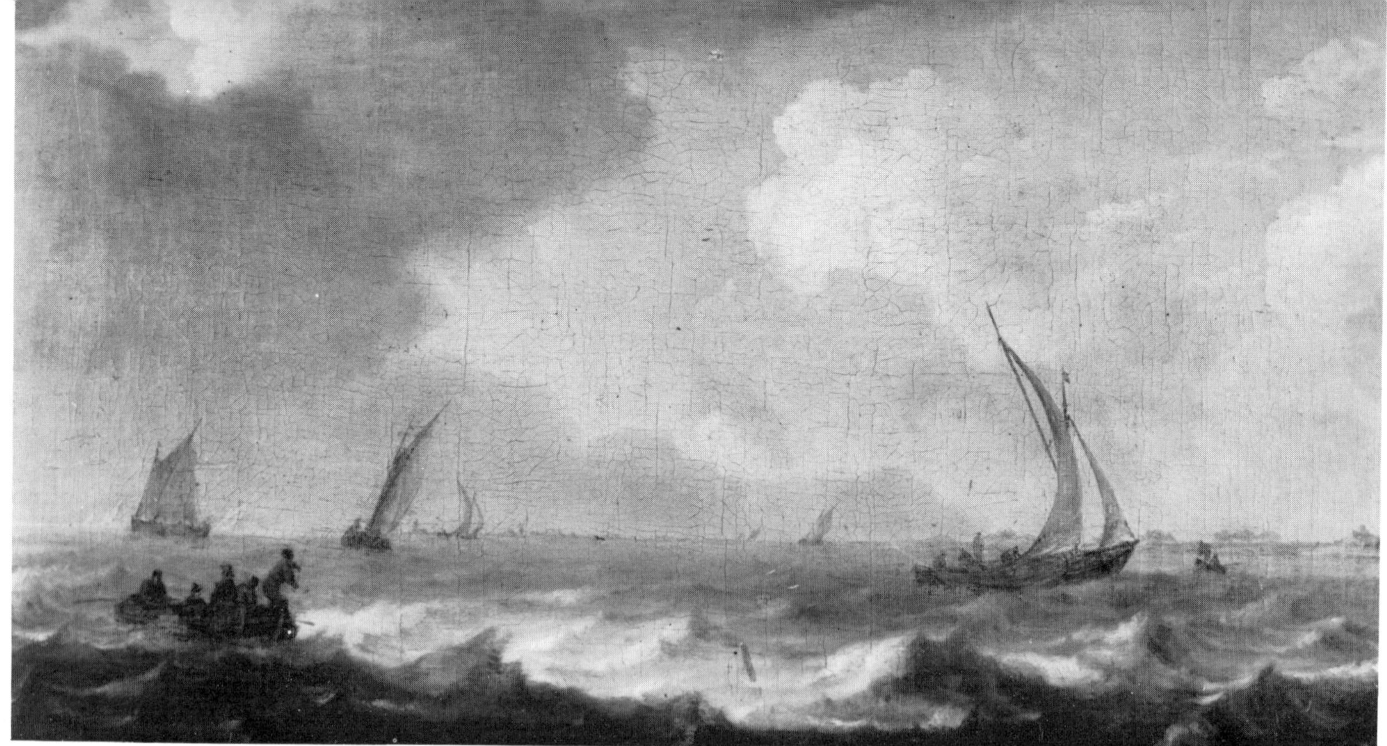

Plate 20. Arnoldus Anthonissen, fl.1660s. ''Dutch fishing boats in rough water.'' *A painting very much in the Dutch tradition, as opposed to the Flemish tradition which is characterised by a more colourful palette.* Stedelijk Museum, Leiden.

Plate 21. Jacob Andriaensz Bellevois, 1621-1675. ''A fishing boat off a rocky coast in a storm with a wreck.'' *A favourite theme with the Dutch was that of ships wrecked on rocky shores. Presumably because their coast was so undramatic they found such paintings exciting, and Bellevois was responsible for many similar scenes.* National Maritime Museum, Greenwich.

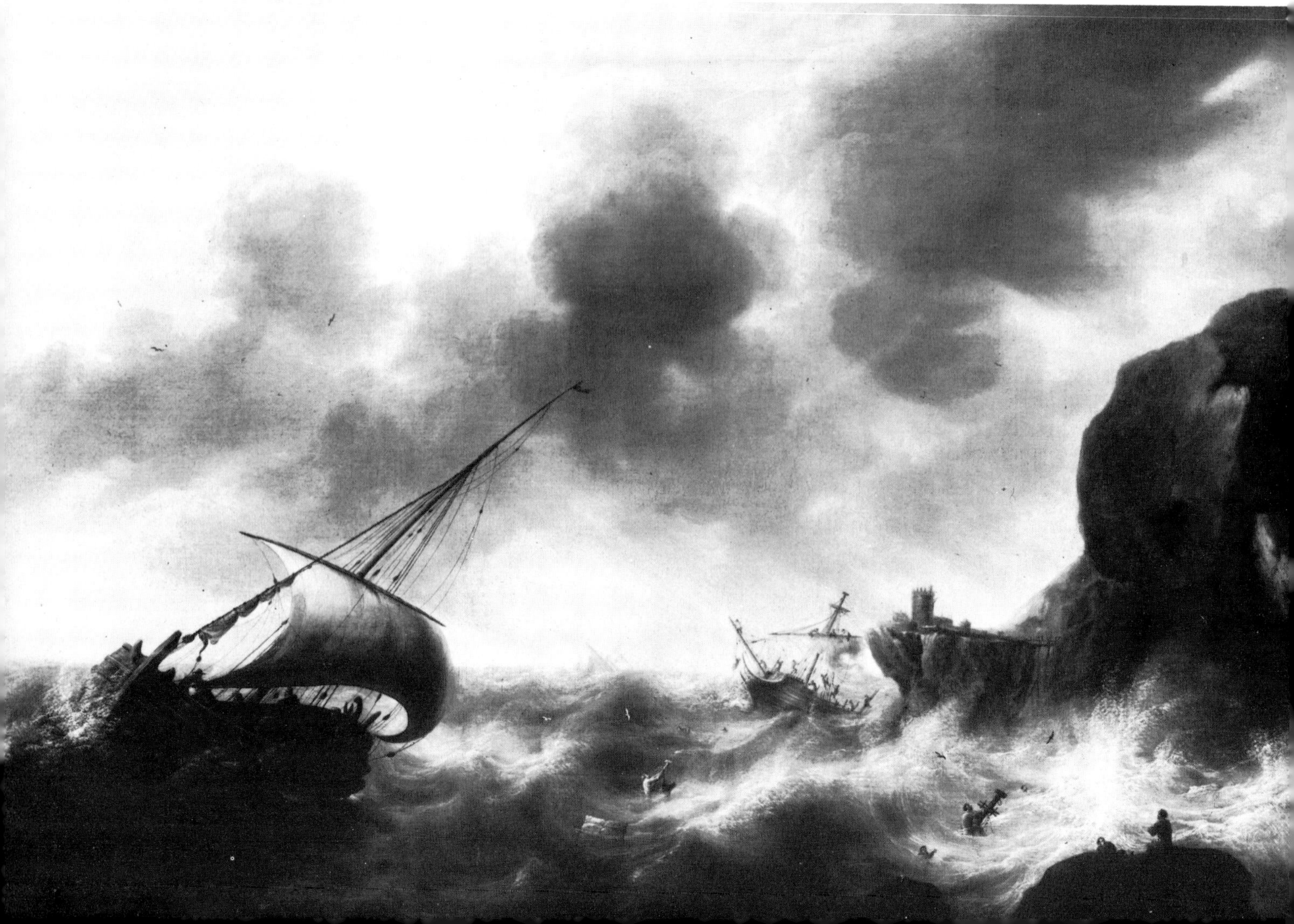

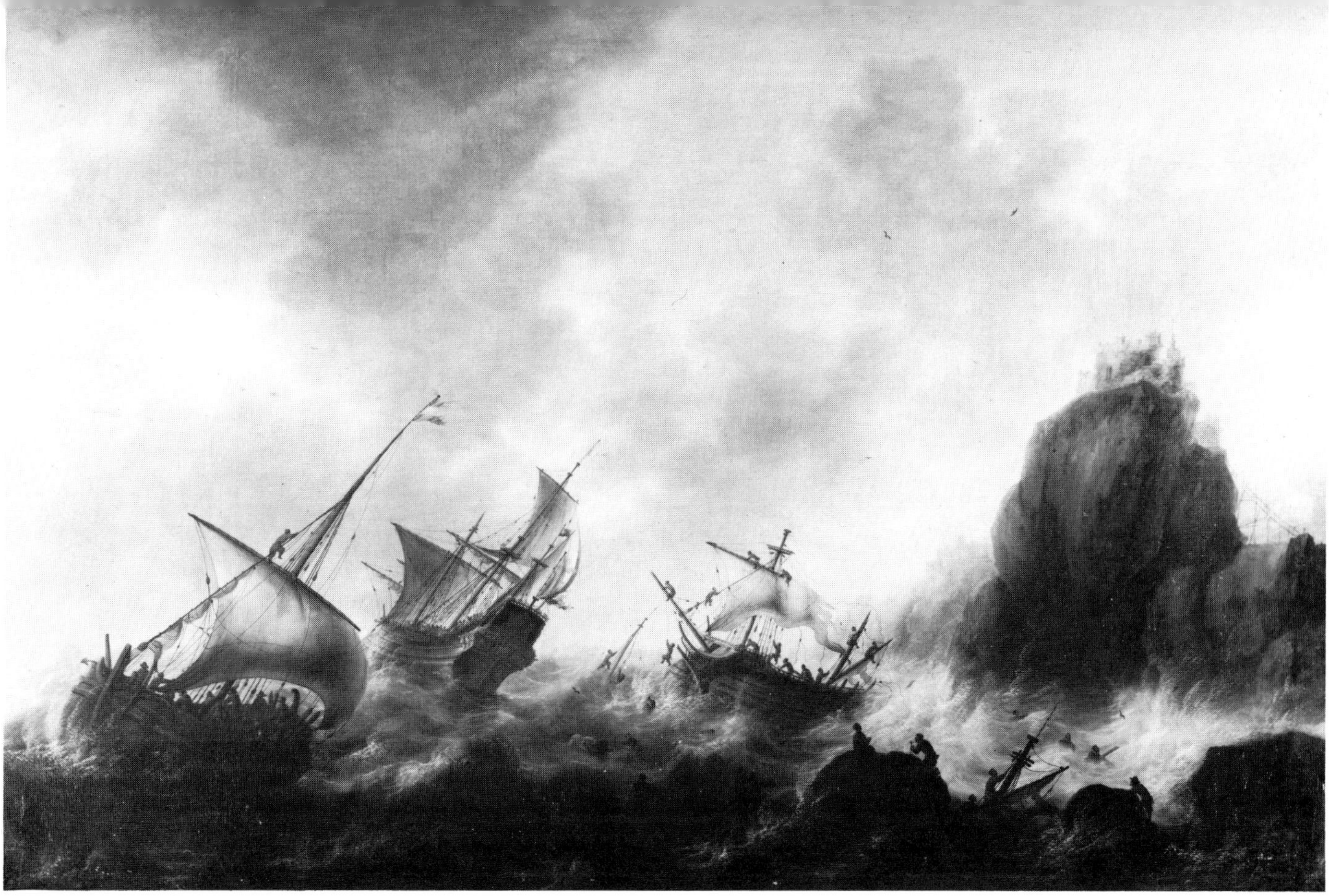

Plate 22. Jacob Andriaensz Bellevois, 1621-1675. "Ships wrecked on a rocky coast." Herzog Anton Ulrich-Museum, Brunswick.

Plate 23. Andries van Eertvelt, 1590-1652. "The return of Cornelis de Houtman from the East Indies with ships of the Dutch East India Company fleet to Amsterdam, 1599." *This is an early work based on the great painting by H.C Vroom, Plate 6.* National Maritime Museum, Greenwich.

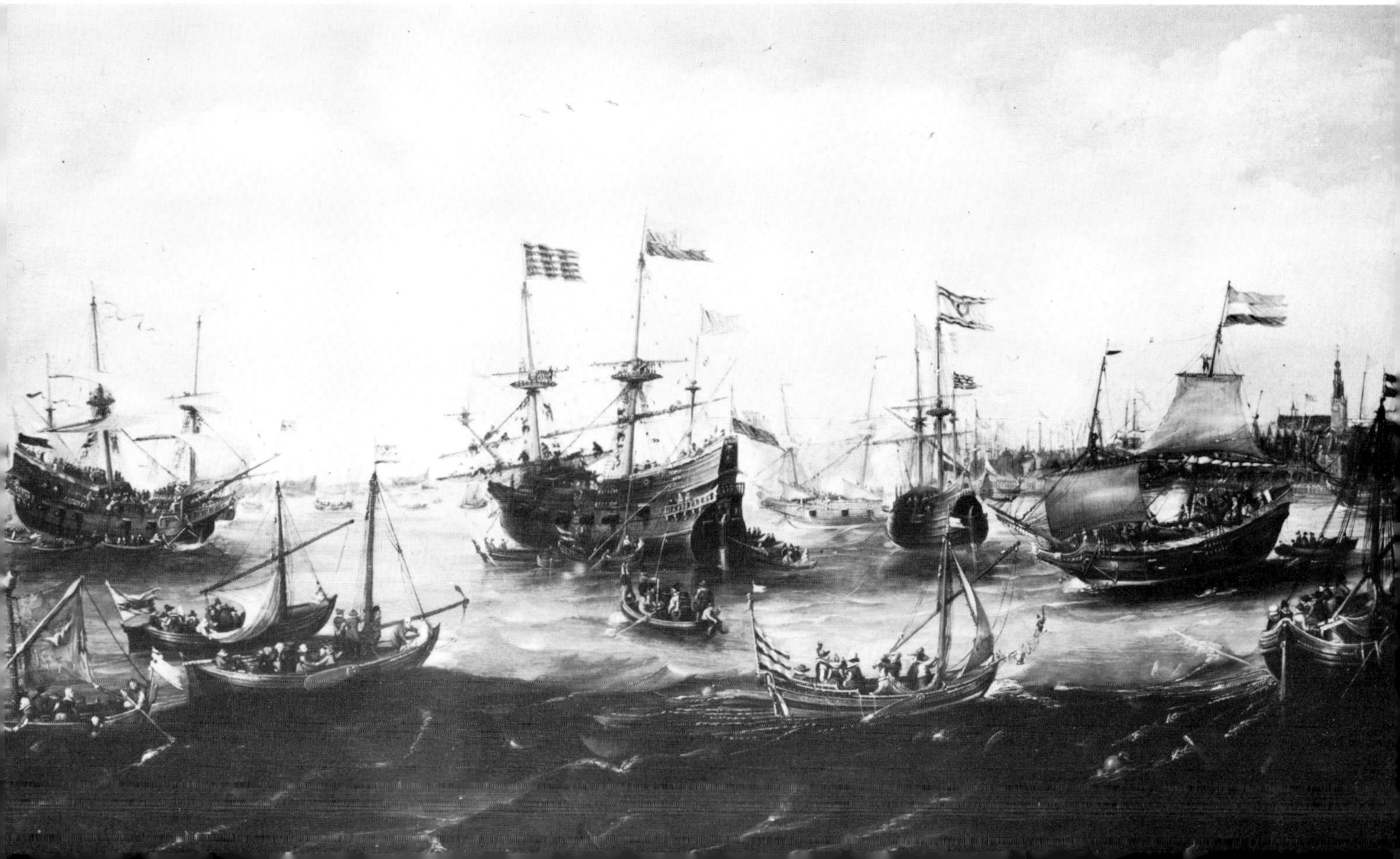

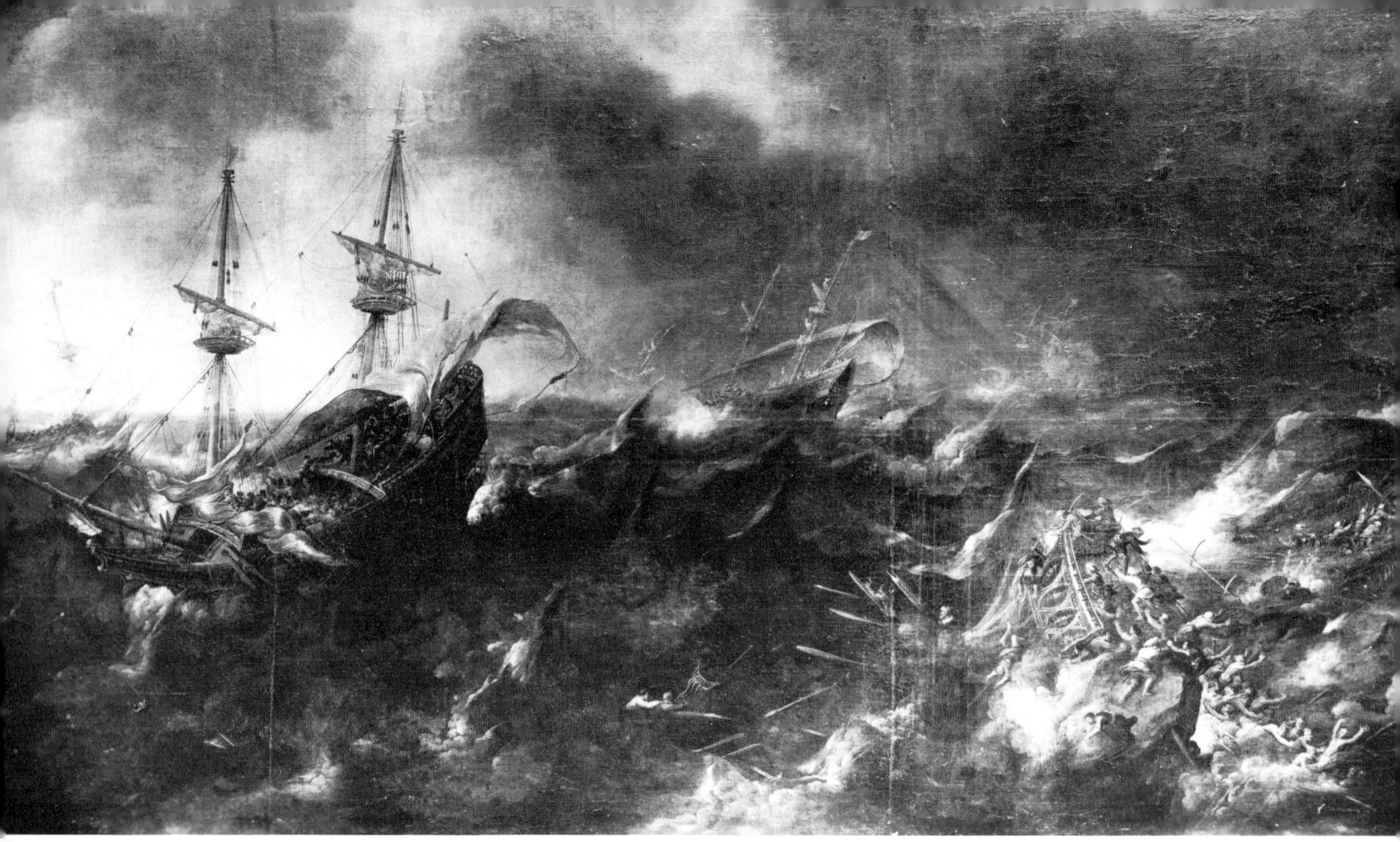

Plate 24. Andries van Eertvelt, 1590-1652. "Dutch ships in distress in a storm off a rocky coast, with Barbary galleys wrecked on it." *The reduced sail on the vessel on the left shows the 'tops' where the mainmast meets, or rather overlaps, the topmast. The 'tops' provided a platform from which the futtock shrouds could be spread to give maximum support. The mainsail has been dropped and the ship is lying-to under his lowered main.* Fine Art Museum, Ghent.

Plate 25. Andries van Eertvelt, 1590-1652. "Spanish ships and galleys off a fort." *Eertvelt perhaps did more than any marine artist to keep the Flemish tradition alive.* Kunsthistorisches Museum, Vienna.

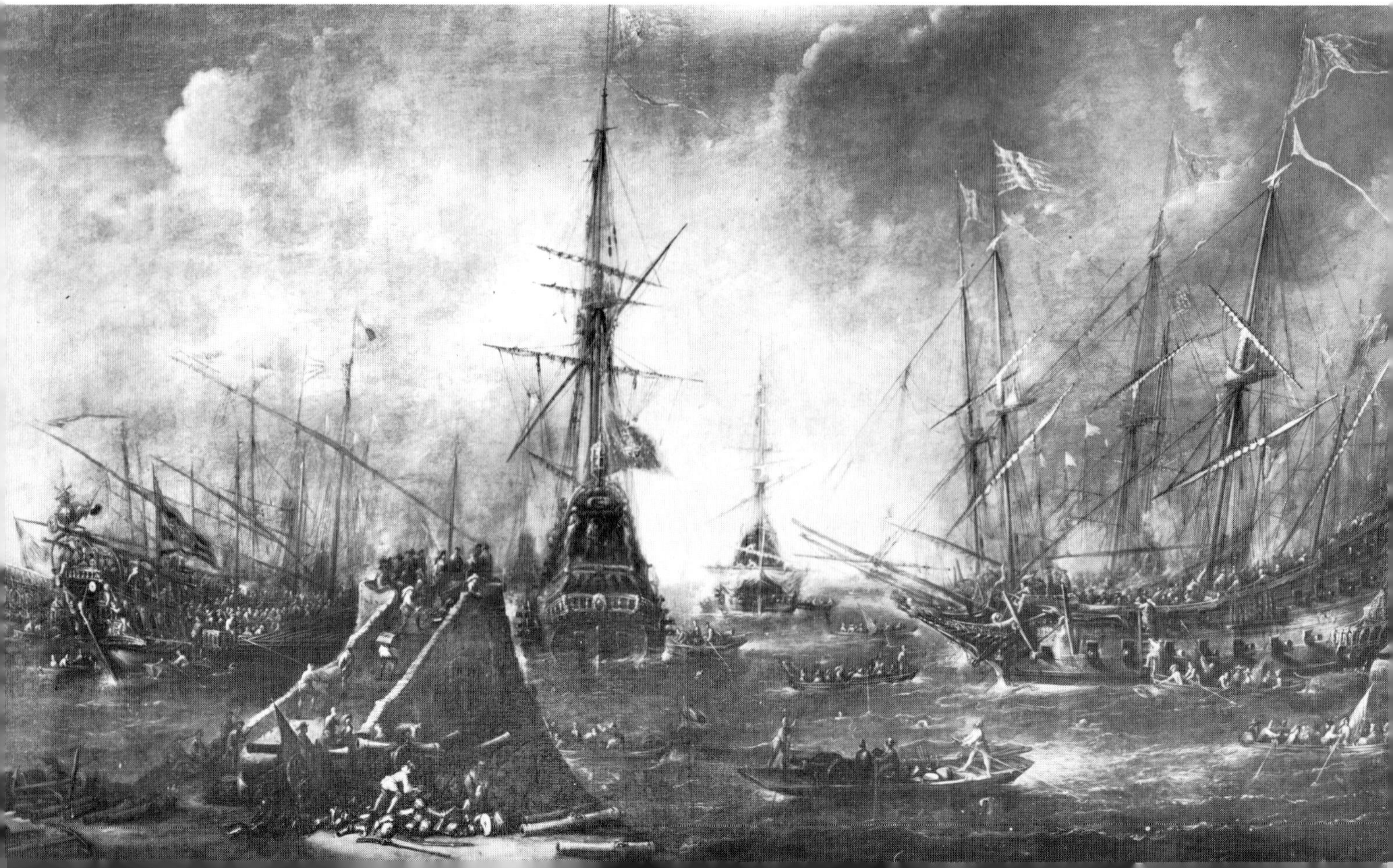

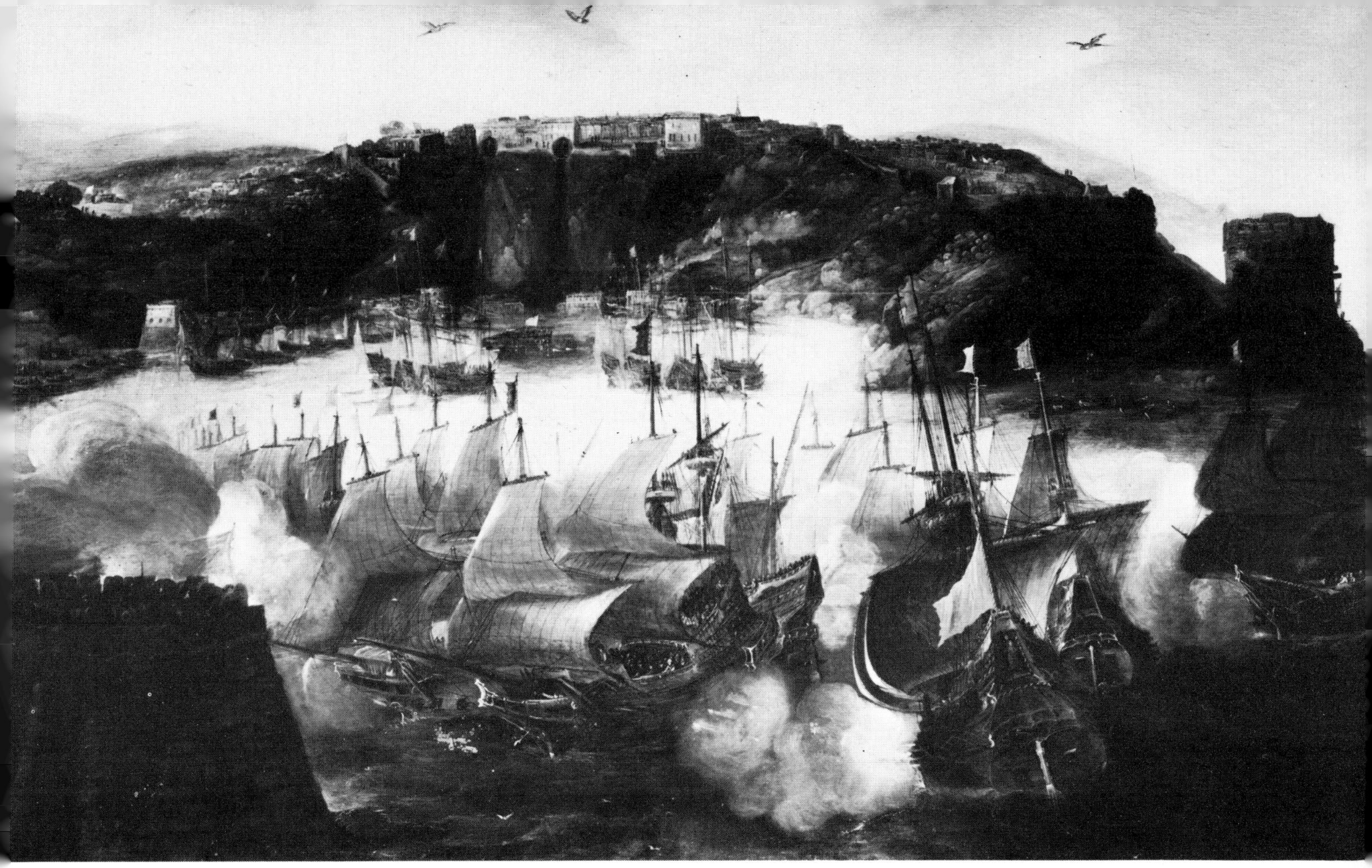

Plate 26. Andries van Eertvelt, 1590-1652. "The attack on San Salvador in 1624." *This city in Portuguese Brazil was captured on May 9th by a Dutch fleet commanded by Piet Hein. It is now called Bahia.* National Maritime Museum, Greenwich.

Plate 27. Sebastian D. Castro, fl. mid- to late 17th century. "An action between the Spanish and Barbary pirates." Mariners Museum, Newport News.

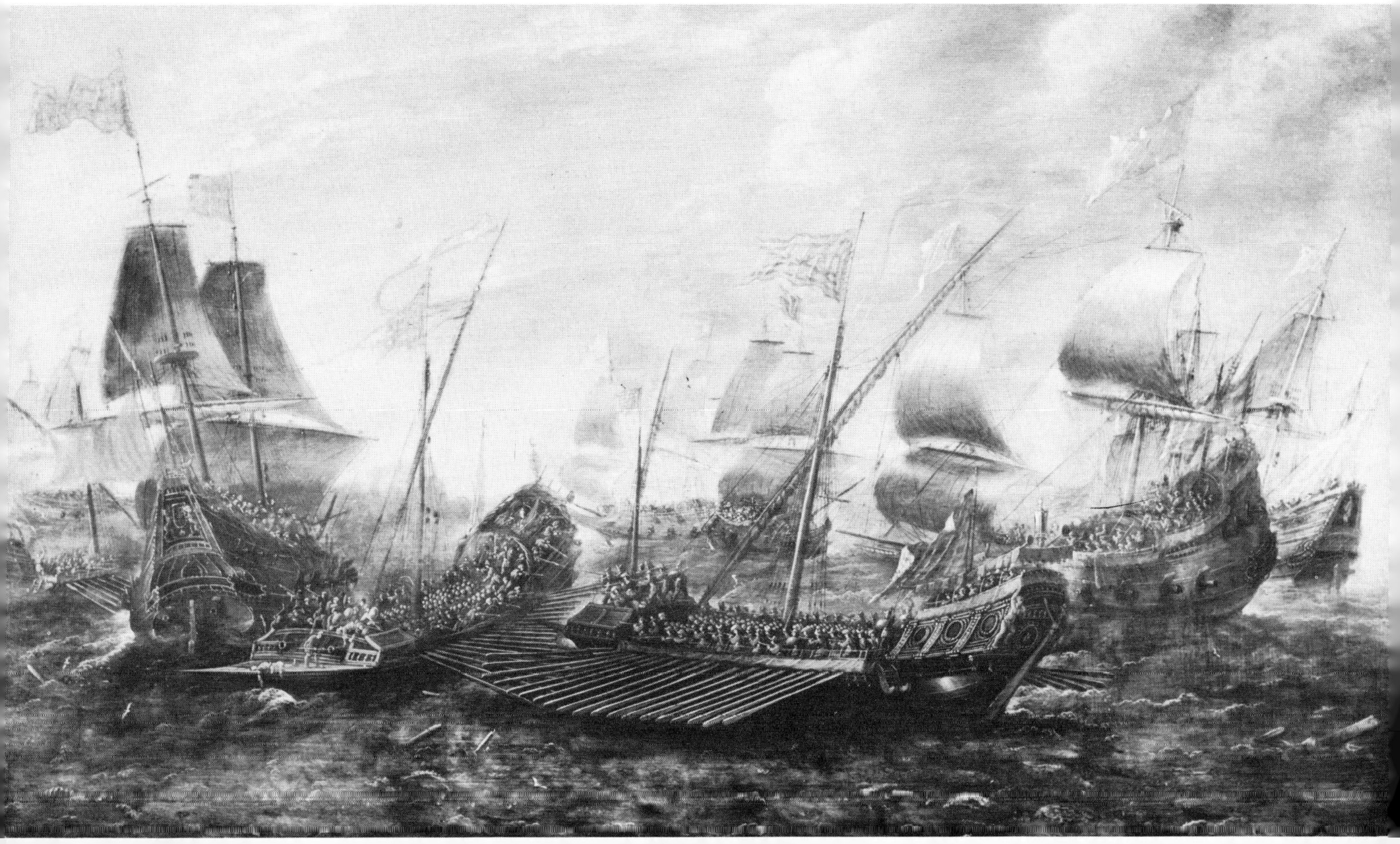

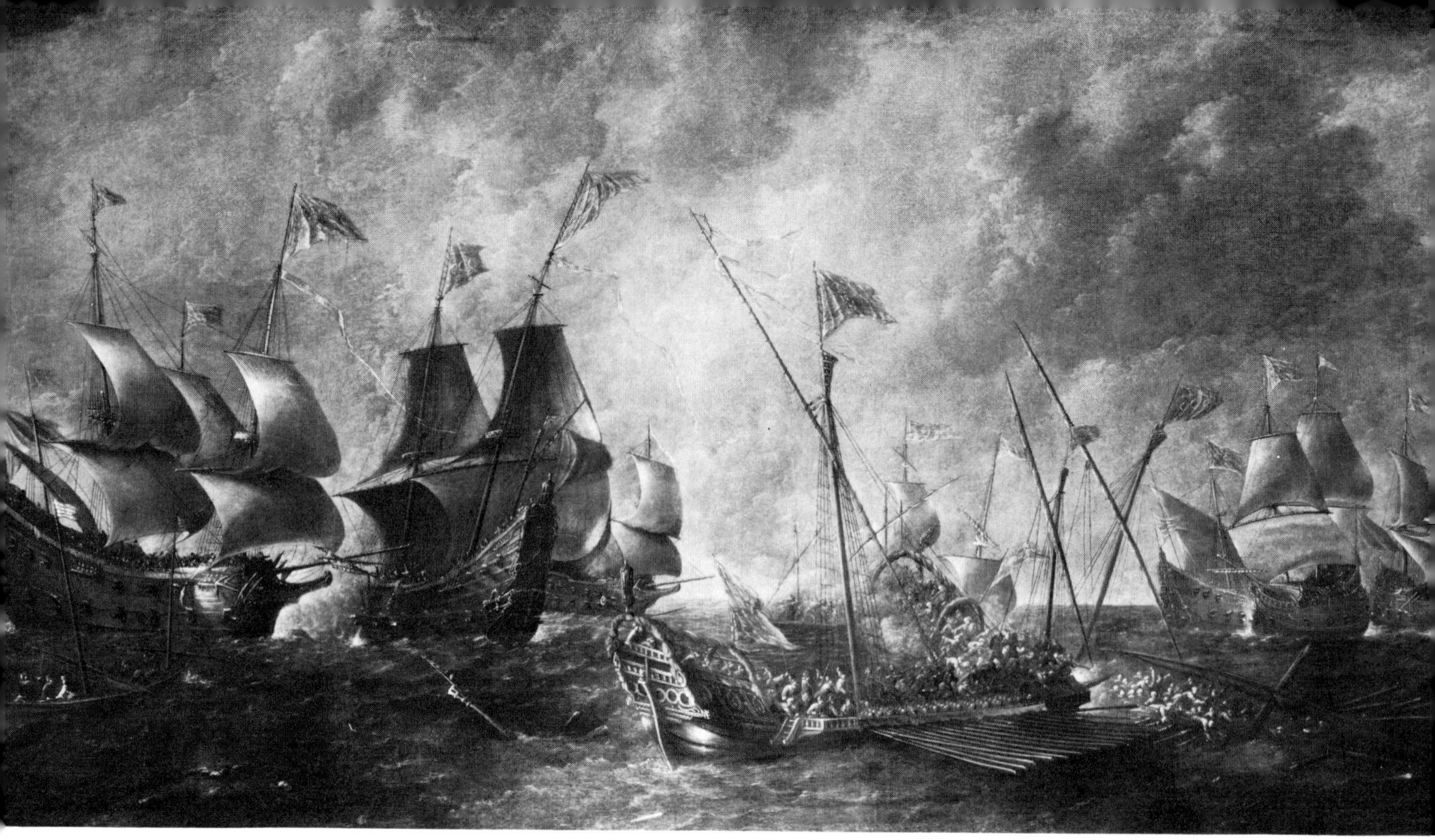

Plate 28. Sebastian D. Castro, fl. mid- to late 17th century. "An action between Spanish ships and Barbary pirates." *A painting which was attributed to Eertvelt until a signed Castro turned up. Castro used many of Eertvelt's painting techniques, not least of which is the similarity in the way the flags are treated.* National Maritime Museum, Greenwich.

Plate 29. Mathieu van Plattenberg, c.1608-1660. "Dutch shipping in an estuary." *An early picture by this artist, whose speciality was storm-at-sea scenes, as the next example illustrates.* National Maritime Museum, Greenwich.

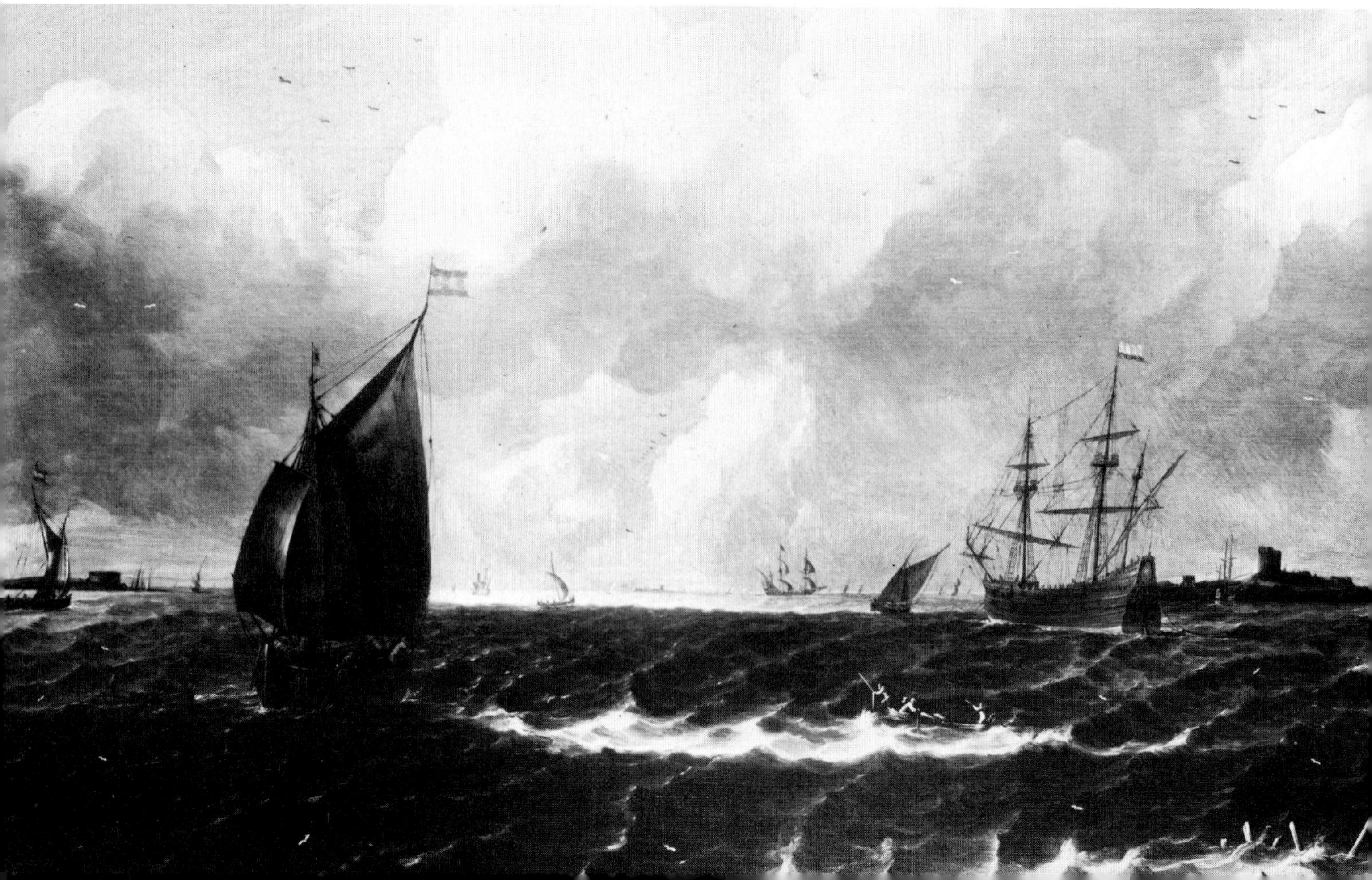

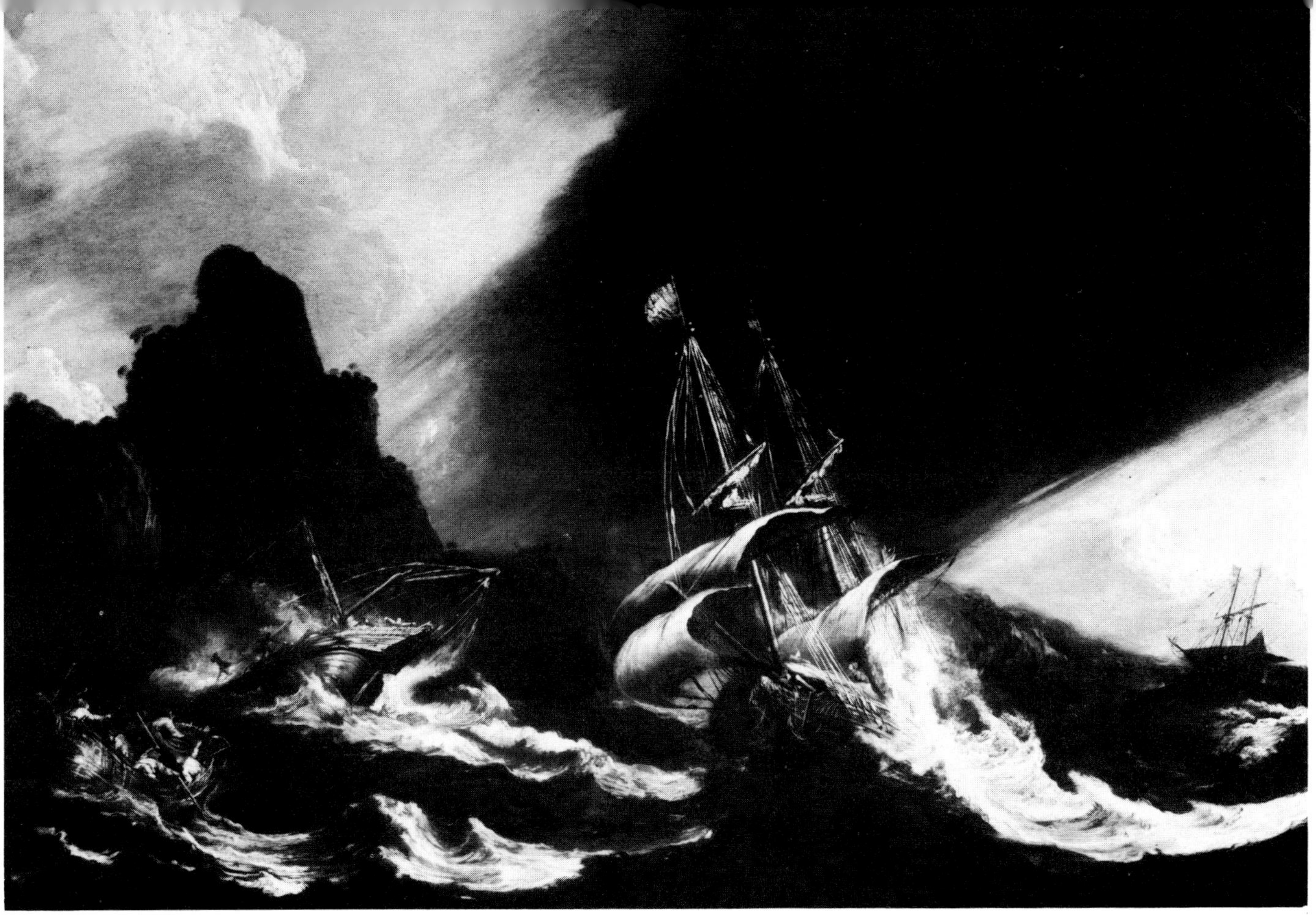

Plate 30. Mathieu van Plattenberg, c.1608-1660. "A galley and a Dutch ship wrecked on a rocky coast." *Painted after Plattenberg went to Italy, and a typical subject.* National Maritime Museum, Greenwich.

Plate 31. Gaspar van Eyck, 1613-1673. "A Mediterranean coast scene." *A fine quality and romantic painting by this obscure sea painter. The sea is worked in a very formalised manner.* National Maritime Museum, Greenwich.

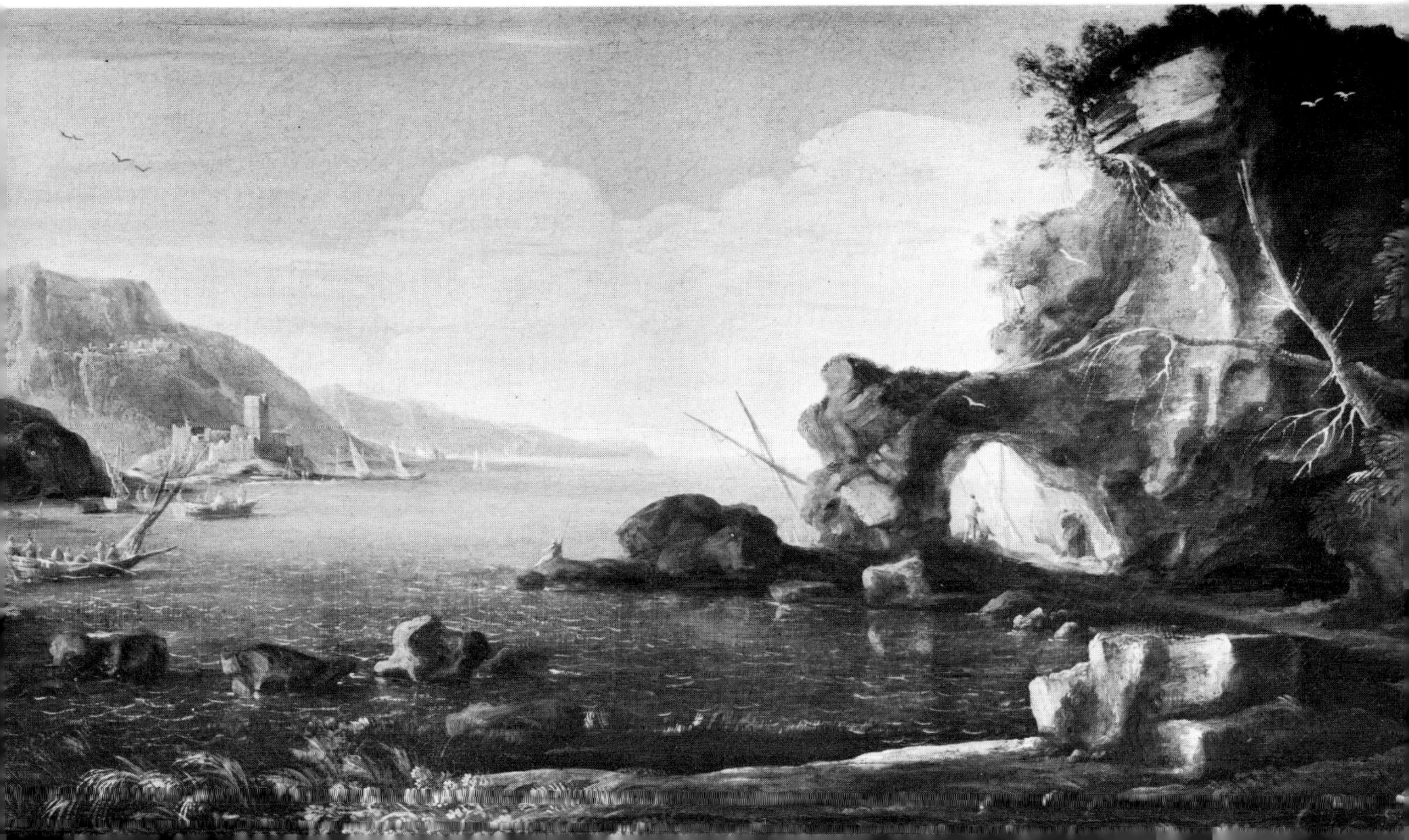

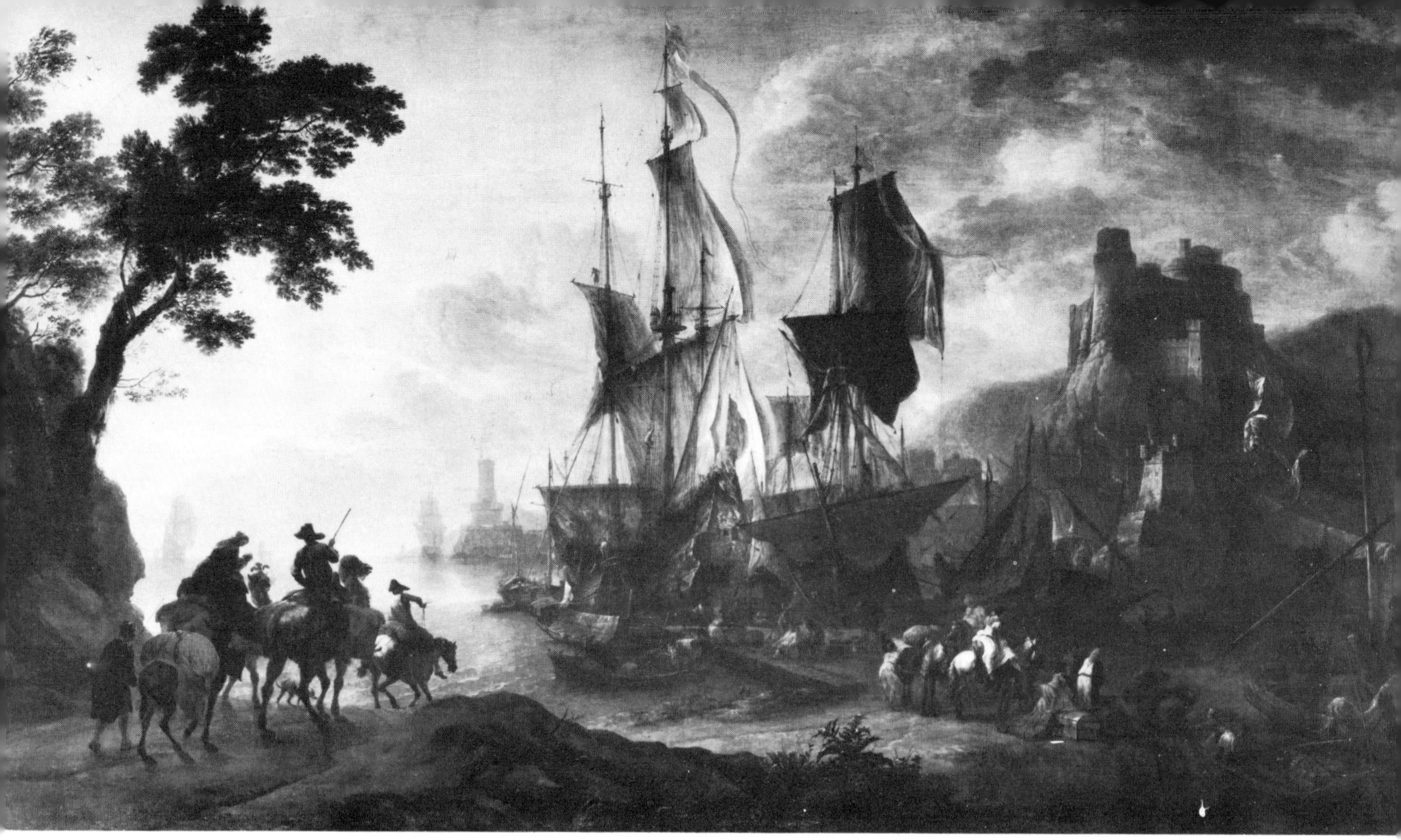

Plate 32. Hendrik van Minderhout, 1632-1696. ''A port in the Mediterranean.'' *One of Minderhout's romantic renderings of a Mediterranean port scene in which he displays his love of painting pack horses, camels and groups against the light. His ships are exaggerated with very tall masts, but he was less interested in the accuracy of the ships than in creating a romantic impression.* National Gallery, Oslo.

Plate 33. Hendrik van Minderhout, 1632-1696. ''The Battle of Lowestoft in 1665.'' *An excellent example of this artist's work, though not strictly accurate, since the English flagship on the left has been given a Dutch stern, with its square tuck and gallery.* National Maritime Museum, Greenwich.

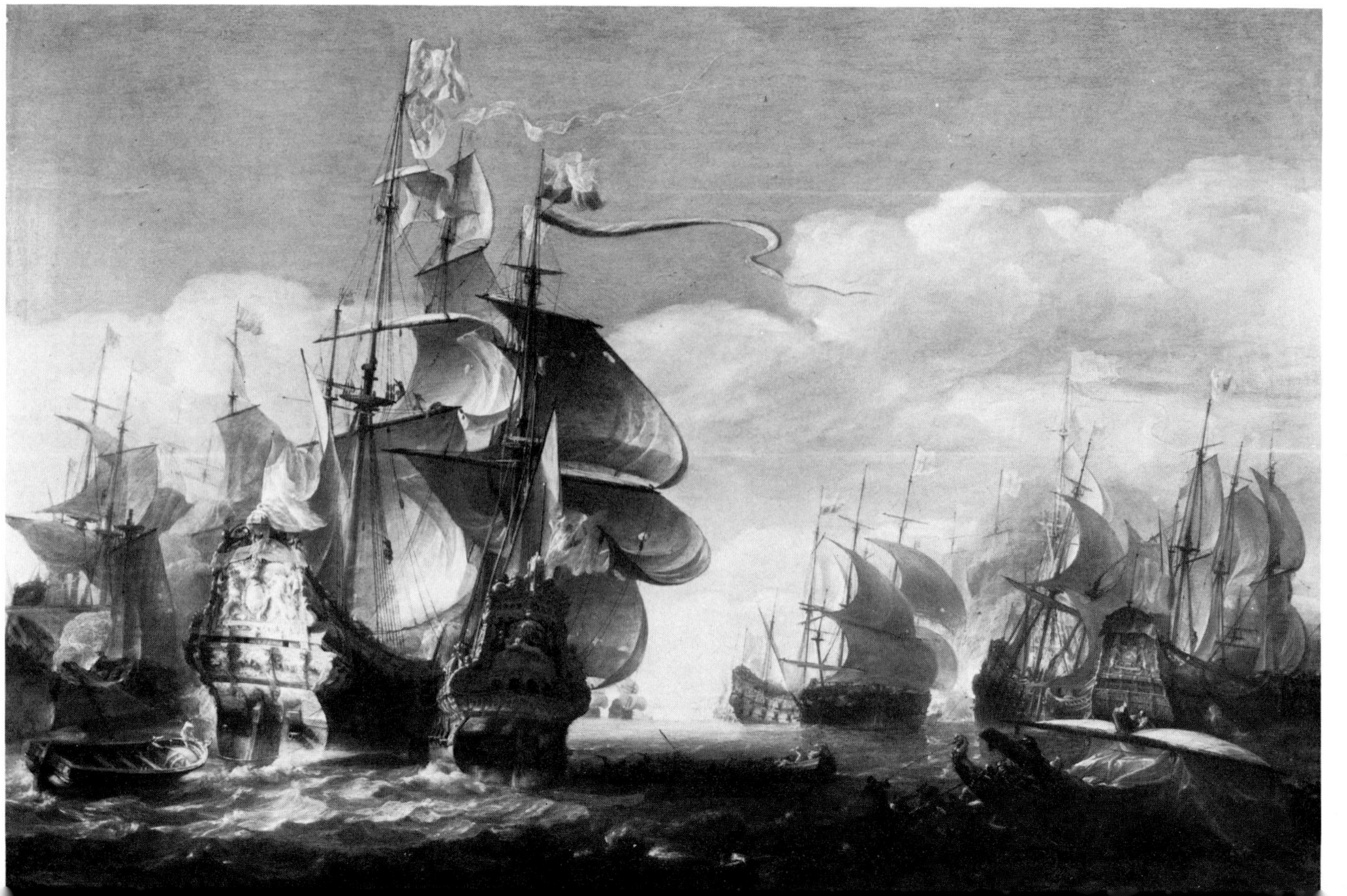

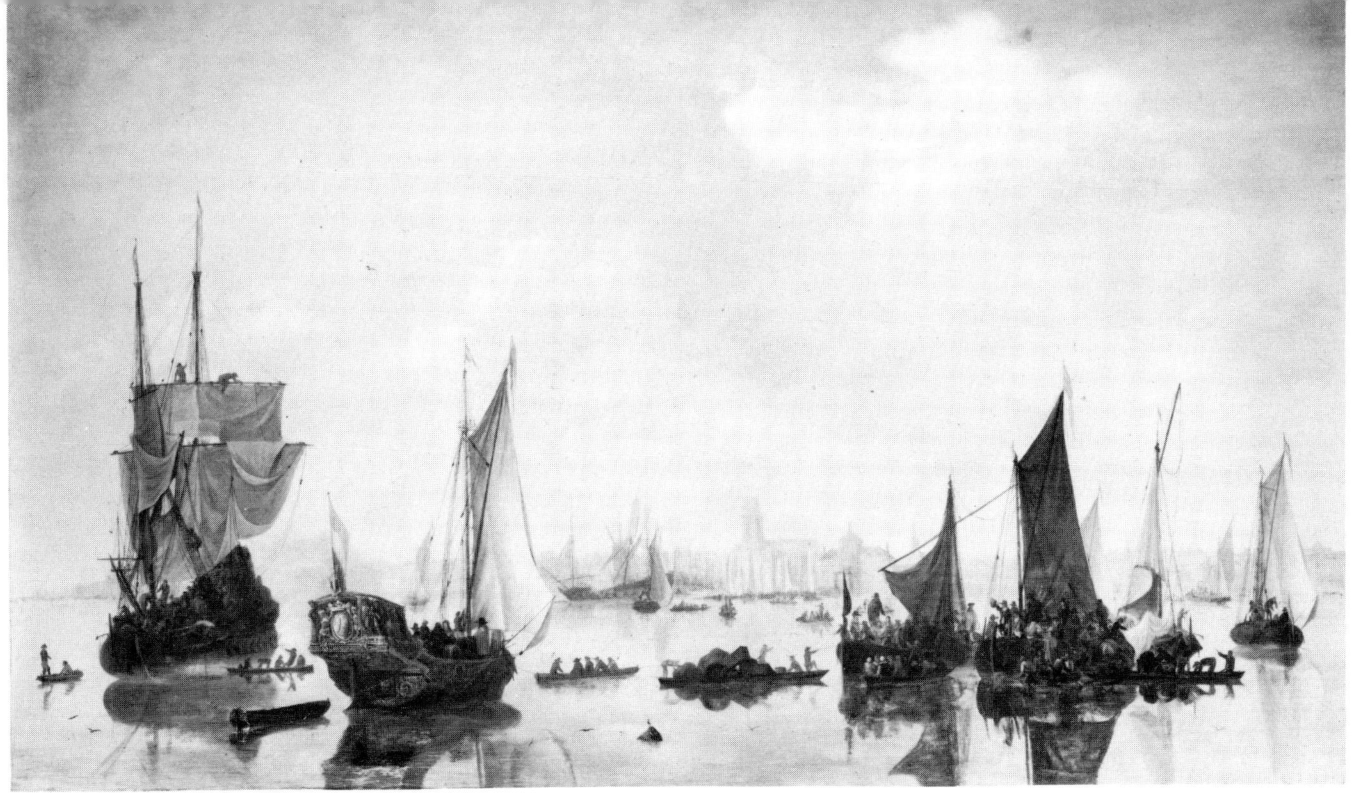

Plate 34. Hendrik van Minderhout, 1632-1696. ''A view of the River Maas before Rotterdam.'' *The attribution to Minderhout is the author's.* The Frick Collection, New York.

Plate 35. Jacob de Gruyter, fl. late 17th century. ''A Dutch and Spanish sea battle.'' *De Gruyter worked in the same studio as Hendrik van Minderhout and this painting, with all the same sort of exaggerations, is very like the Minderhout painting in Plate 33.* Private collection.

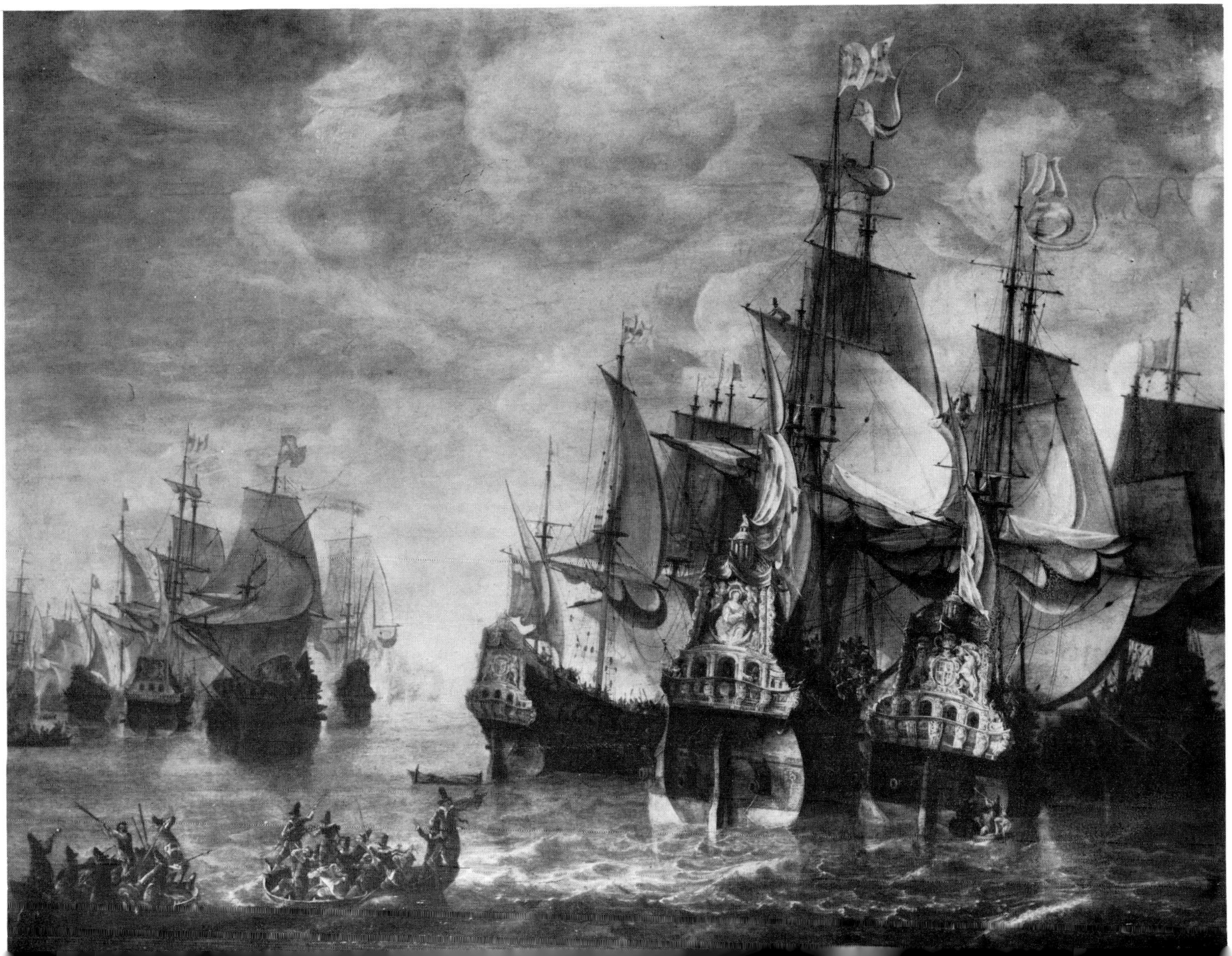

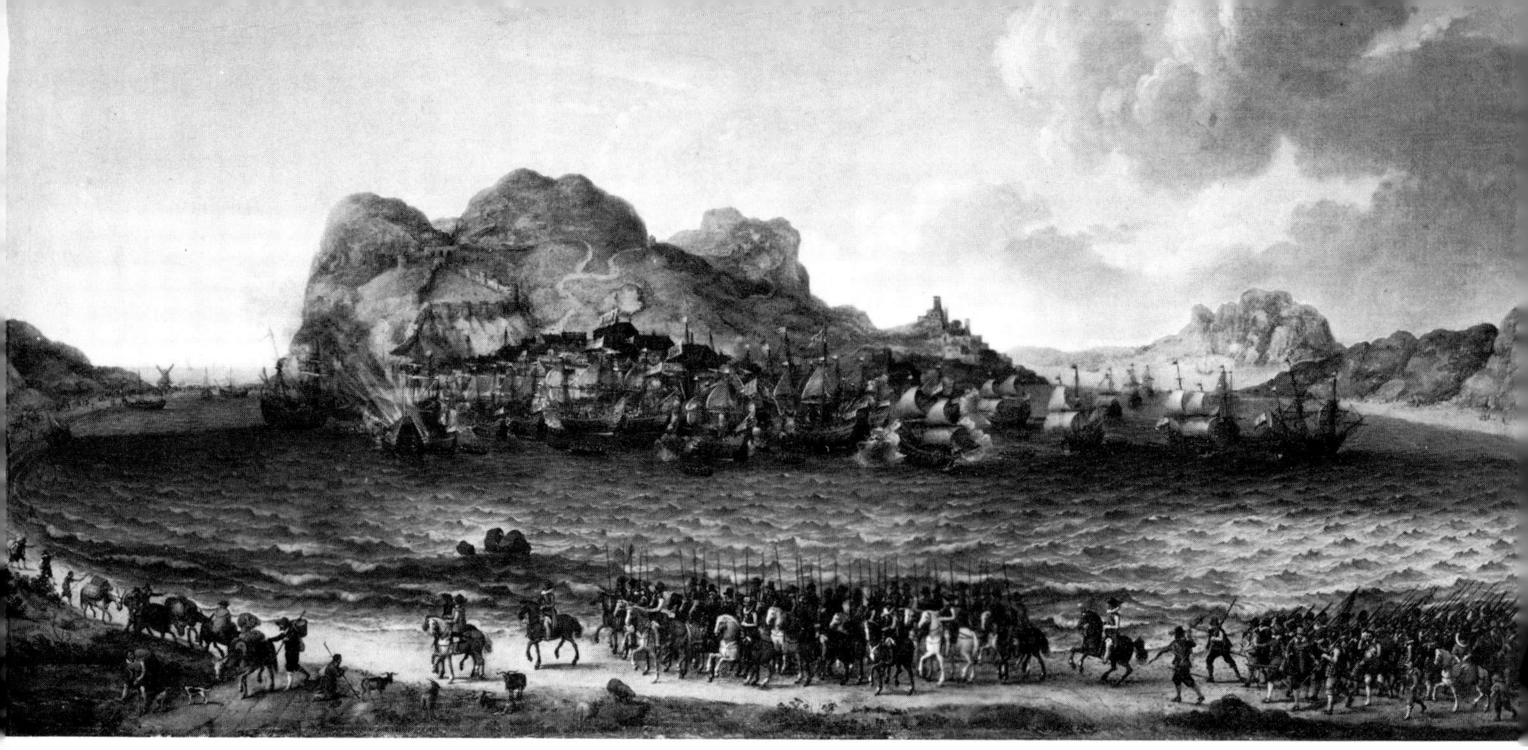

Plate 36. Adam Willaerts, 1577-1664. "The defeat of the Spanish at Gibraltar by the Dutch under Jacob van Heemskirk on April 25th, 1607." *A beautifully drawn Willaerts, showing his tremendous interest in large groups of people.* Rijksmuseum, Amsterdam.

Plate 37. Adam Willaerts, 1577-1664. "Jonah and the whale." *Willaerts painted in a very individual style and his master is not known. He was really more interested in figures, especially groups, than in ships, and his earlier works, like this one, use a green palette.* National Maritime Museum, Greenwich.

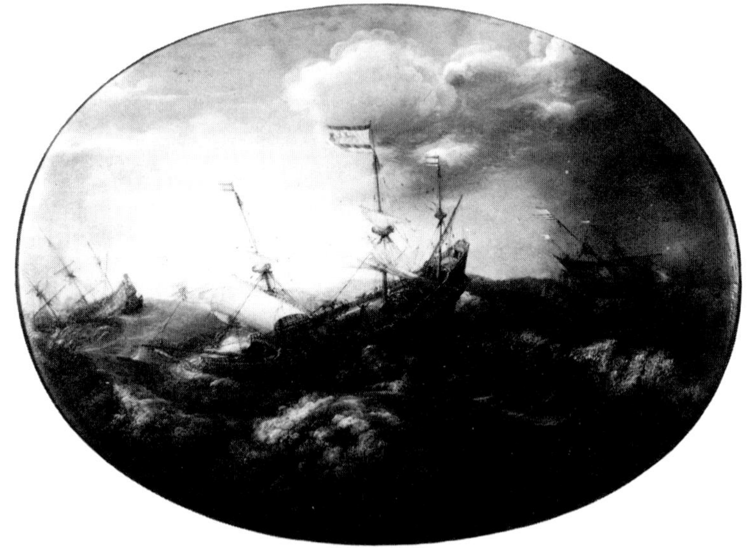

Plate 38. Adam Willaerts, 1577-1664. "Beach scene with shipping and a church." *A later Willaerts, using the grey palette.* Herzog Anton Ulrich-Museum, Brunswick.

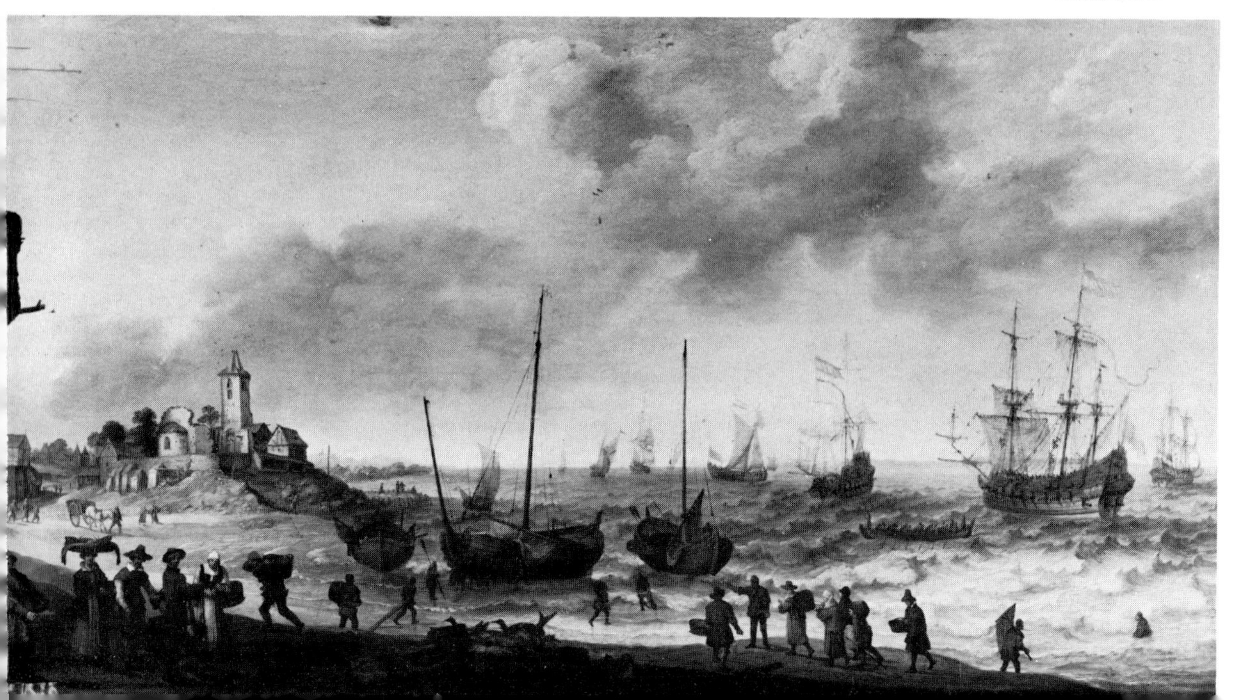

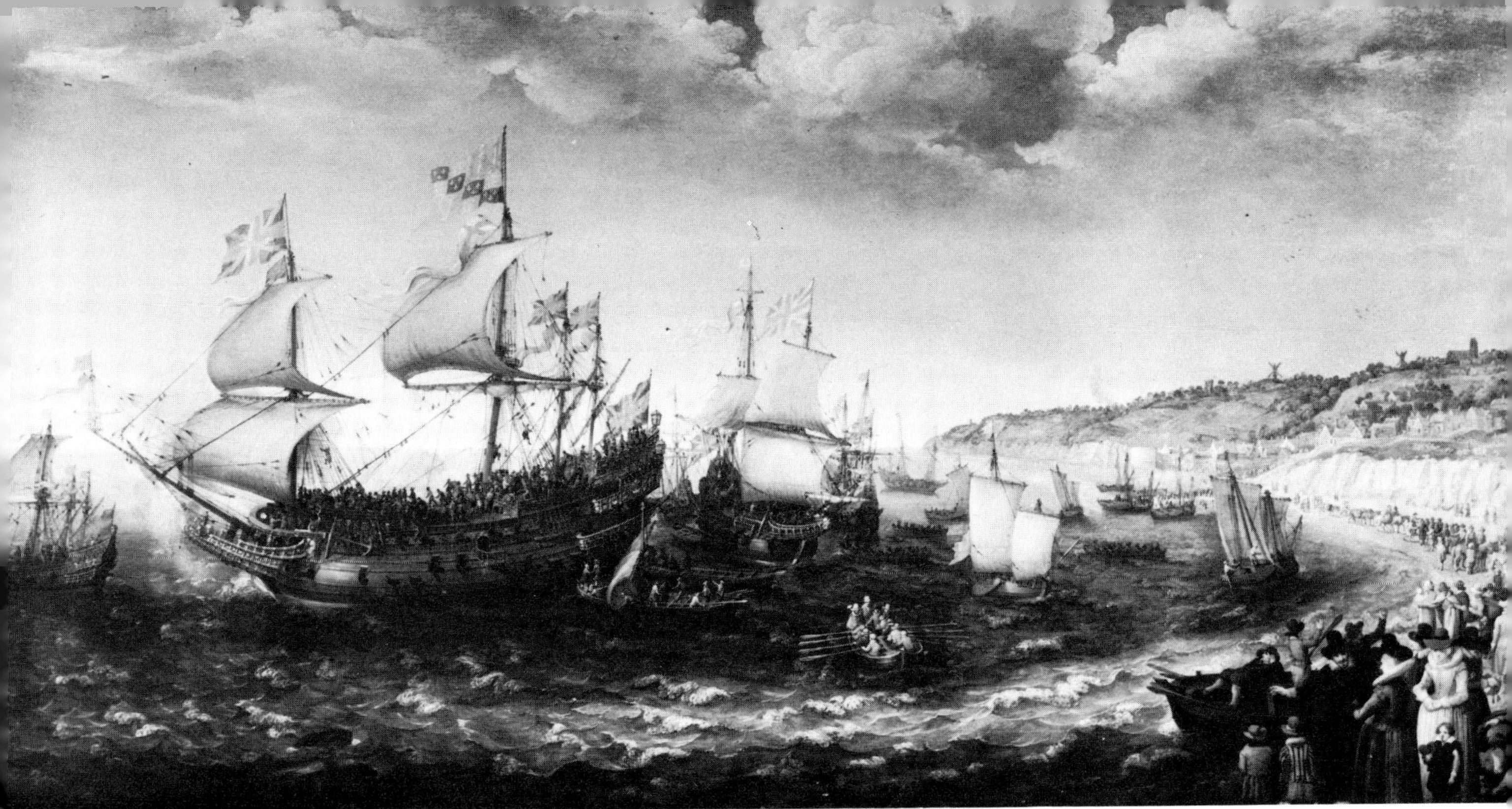

Plate 39. Adam Willaerts, 1577-1664. "The embarkation of the Elector and Electress Palatine from Margate in 1613." *Willaerts has the Lord Admiral's standard wrong. It is right in the Vroom painting (Colour Plate I). Buckingham had not arrived on the scene in 1613.* National Maritime Museum, Greenwich.

Plate 40. Abraham Willaerts, 1603-1669. "A Dutch attack on the Spanish, with men landing from boats, 1641." State Museum for Art, Copenhagen.

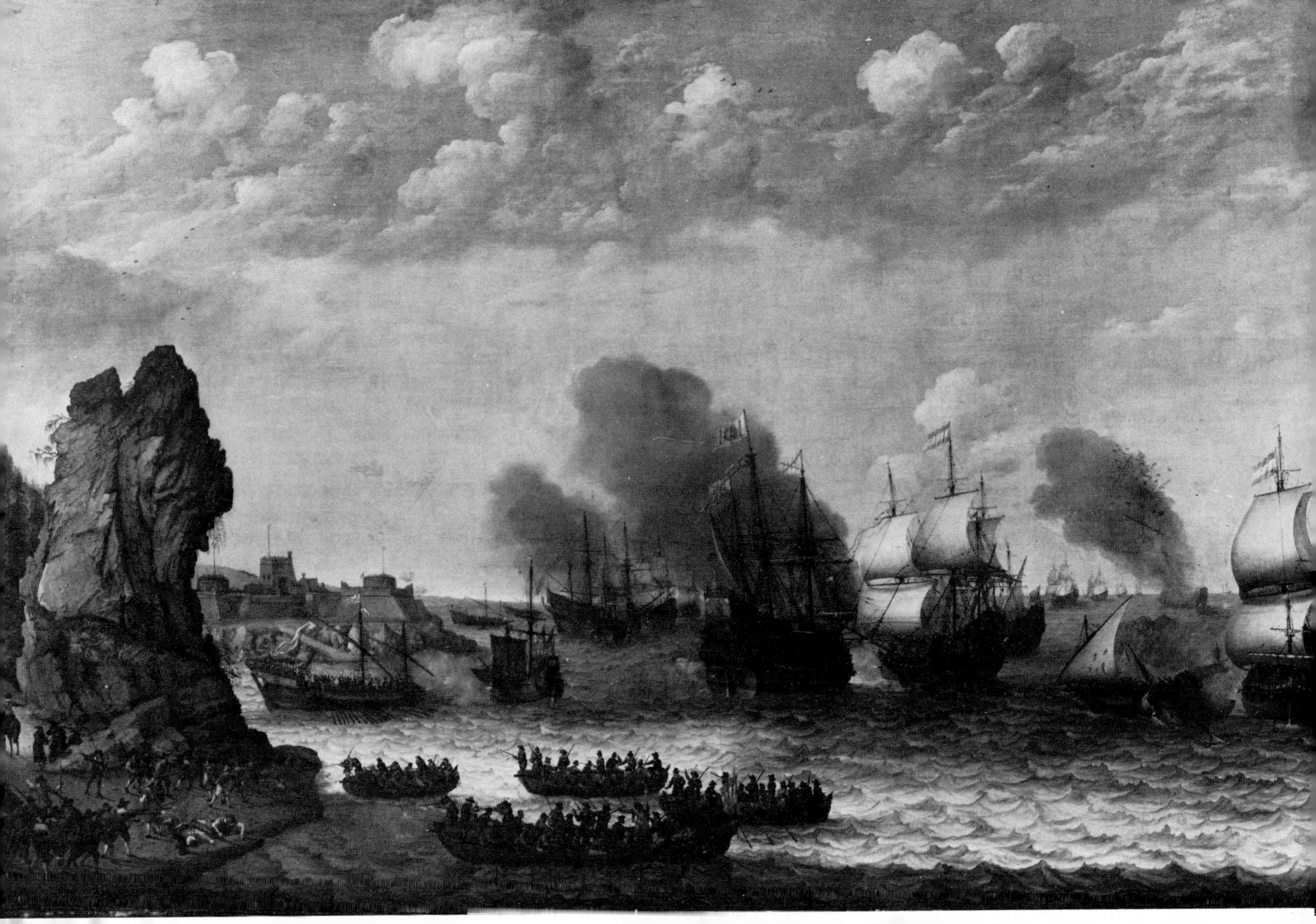

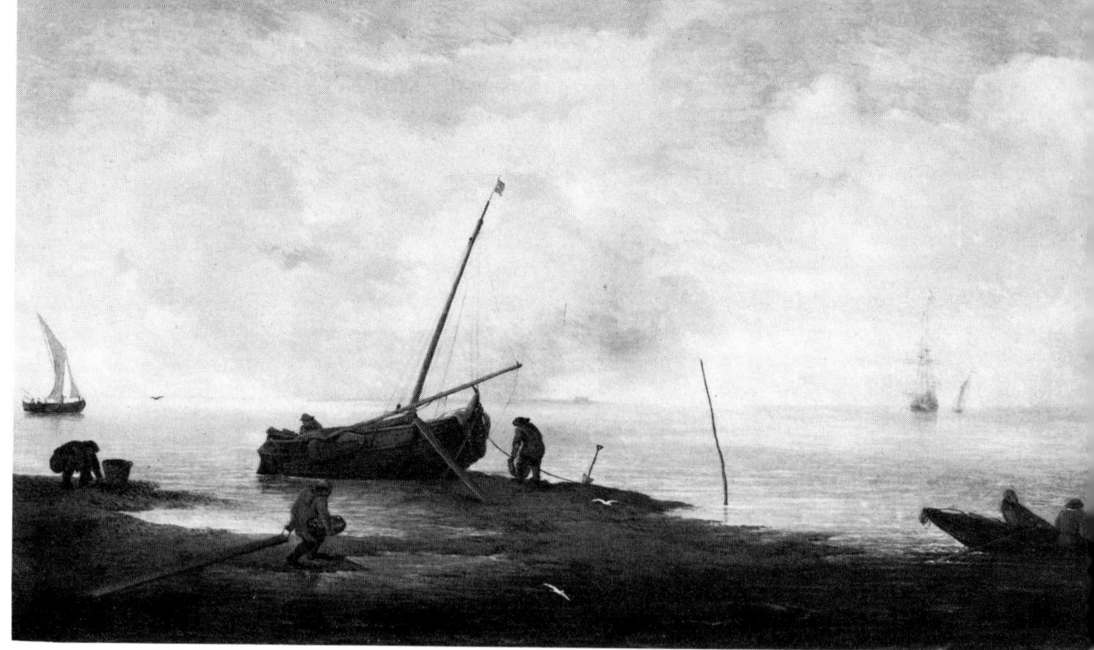

Plate 41. Jan Porcellis, c.1584-1632. "Mussel fishing." National Maritime Museum, Greenwich.

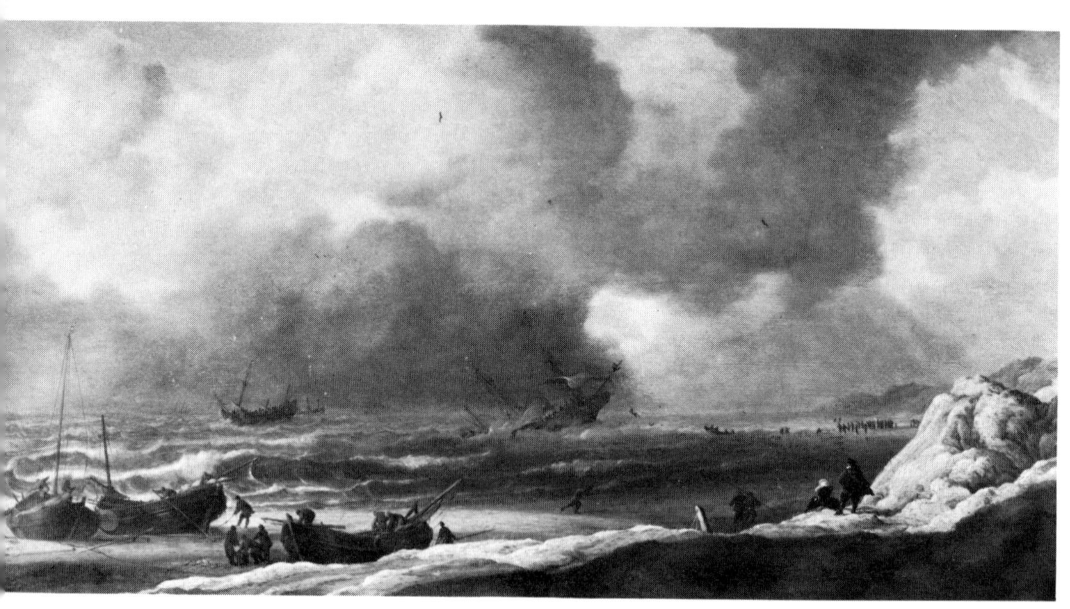

Plate 42. Jan Porcellis, c.1584-1632. "A ship foundering on the Dutch coast." *An excellent example of this artist's work, showing the Dutch realist palette of green/grey sky.* Maritshuis, The Hague.

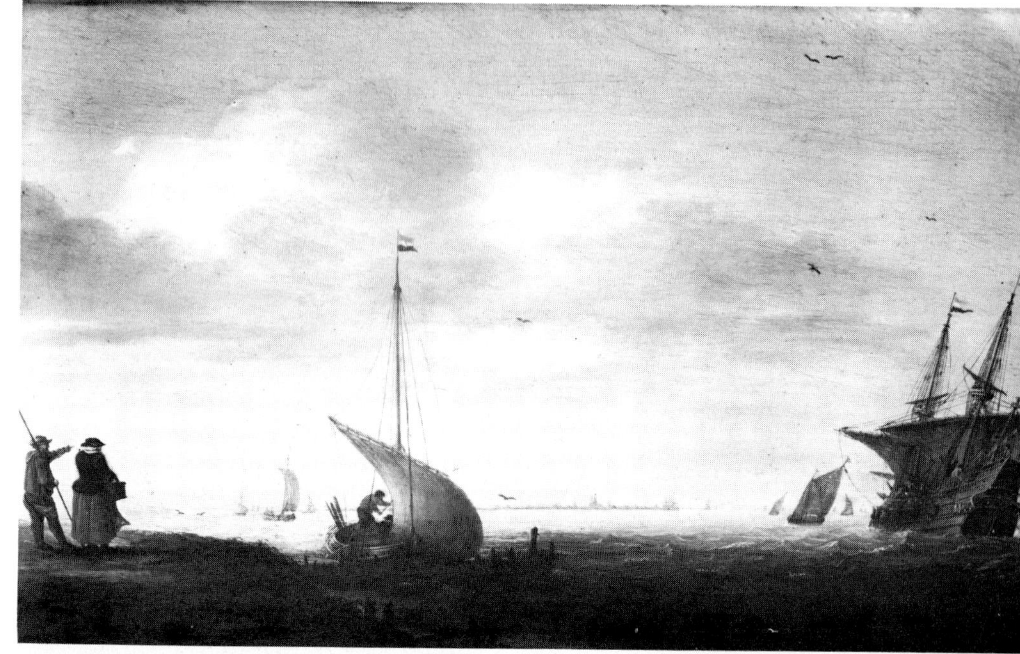

Plate 43. Hans Goderis, fl.1625. "Dutch shipping in inland waters." Boymans van Beuningen Museum, Rotterdam.

Plate 44. Julius Porcellis, c.1609-1645. "Dutch Mussel fishers." *Julius Porcellis' works can be distinguished from those of his father Jan, by the difference in treatment of the figures. Whereas Jan's are like Pieter Brueghel's brooding figures, Julius' are more up-to-date.* National Maritime Museum, Greenwich.

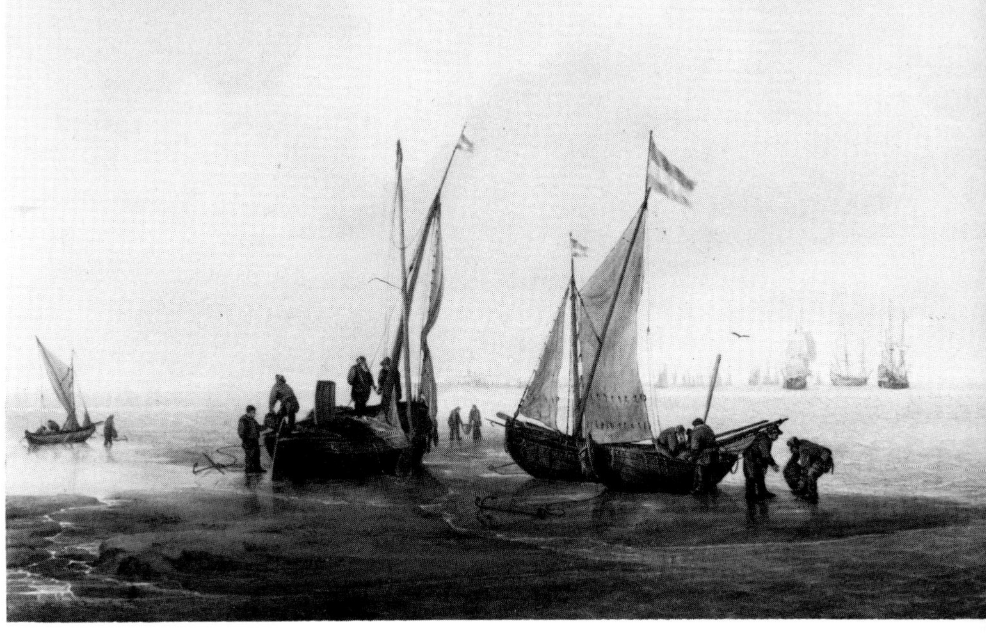

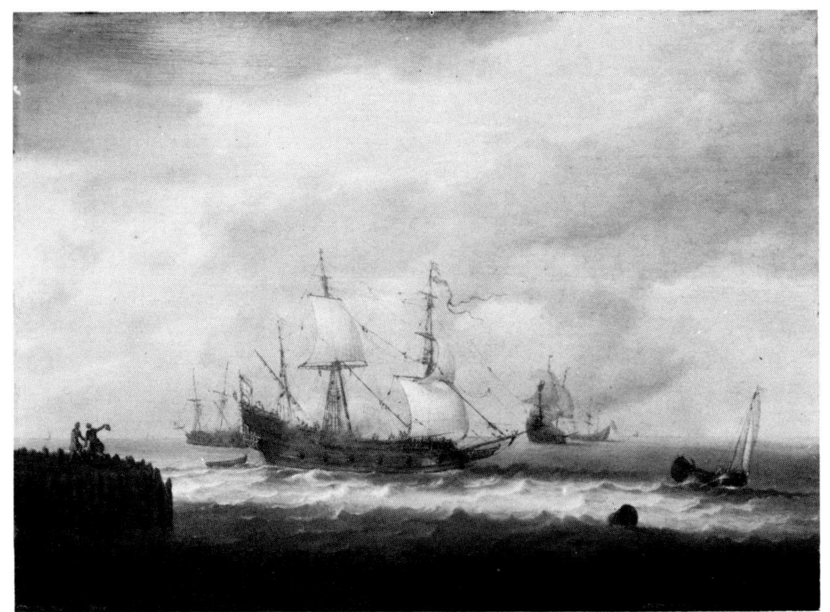

Plate 45. Hendrik Staets, fl.c.1635. "The departure of a Dutch East Indiaman." National Maritime Museum, Greenwich.

Plate 46. Pieter Mulier, the Elder, 1615-1670. "A Dutch ship in a stiff breeze off a rocky coast." National Maritime Museum, Greenwich.

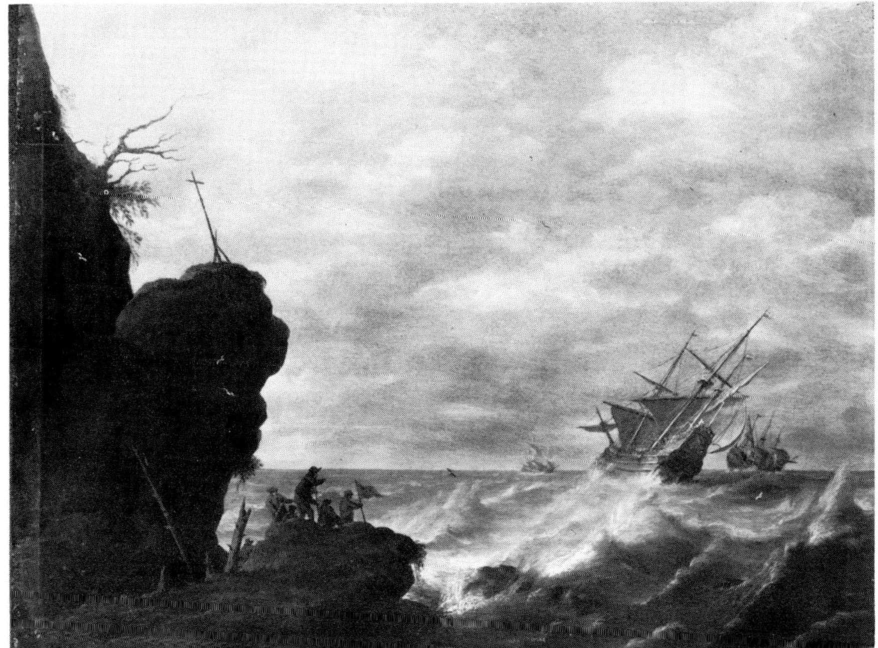

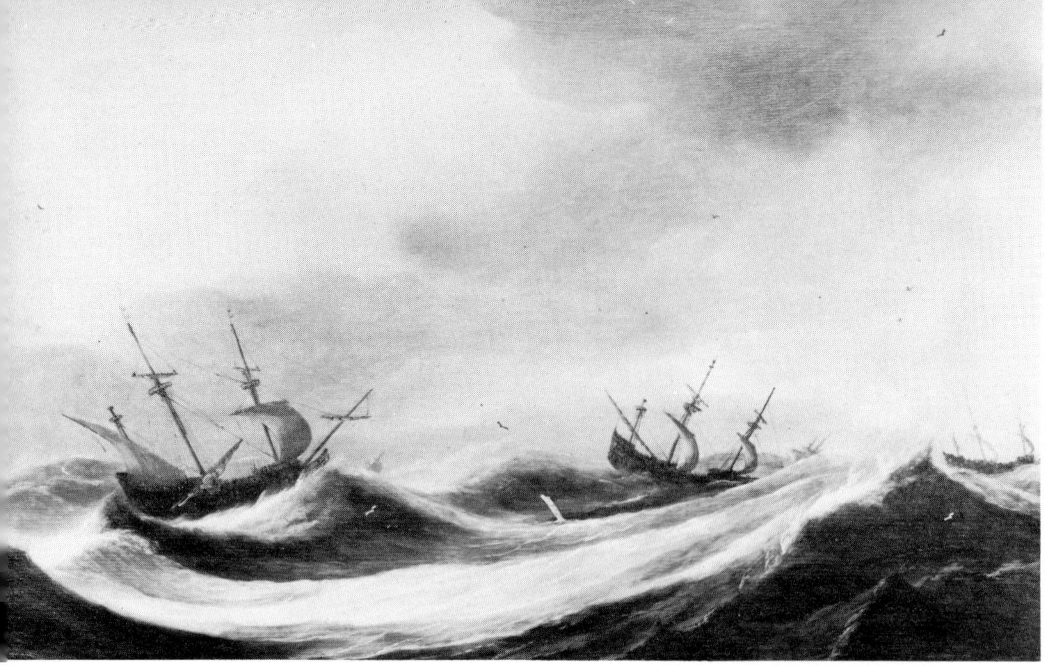

Plate 47. Pieter Mulier, the Elder, 1615-1670. "Dutch ships running before a storm." *A highly rhythmic work by Mulier Senior, who tended to a grey palette.* National Maritime Museum, Greenwich.

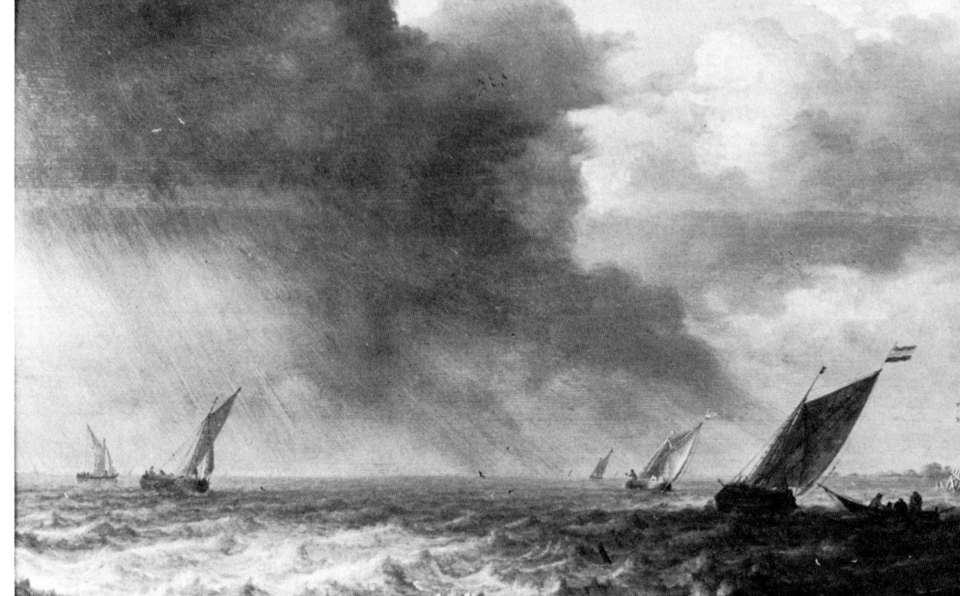

Plate 48. Pieter Mulier, the Elder, 1615-1670. "Dutch fishing boats in the Zuider Zee, squall approaching." Gemeentemuseum, Arnhem.

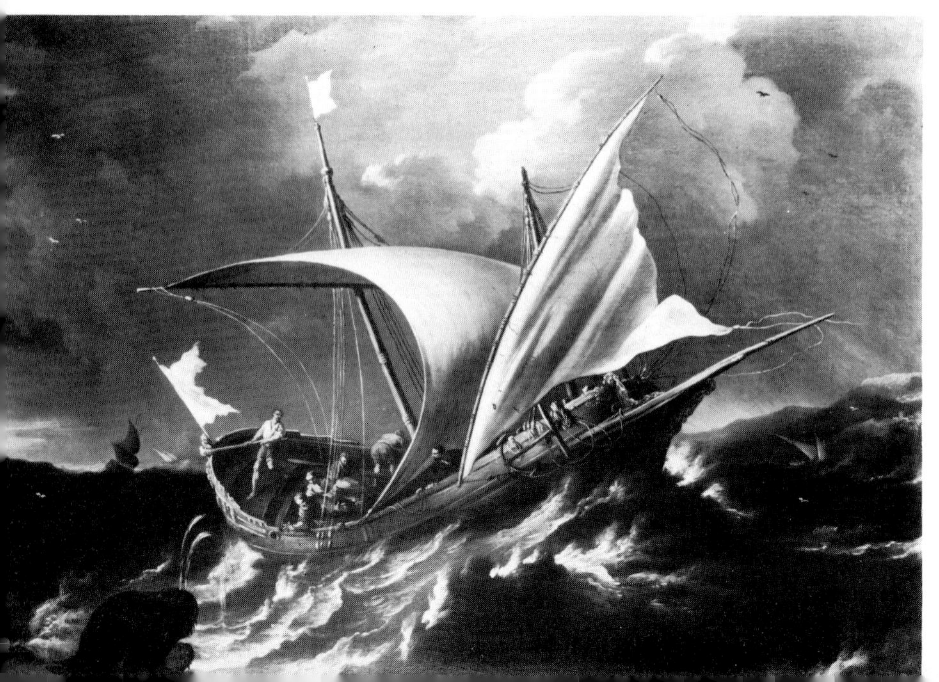

Plate 49. Pieter Mulier, the Younger, c.1636-1701. "Jonah and the whale." National Maritime Museum, Greenwich.

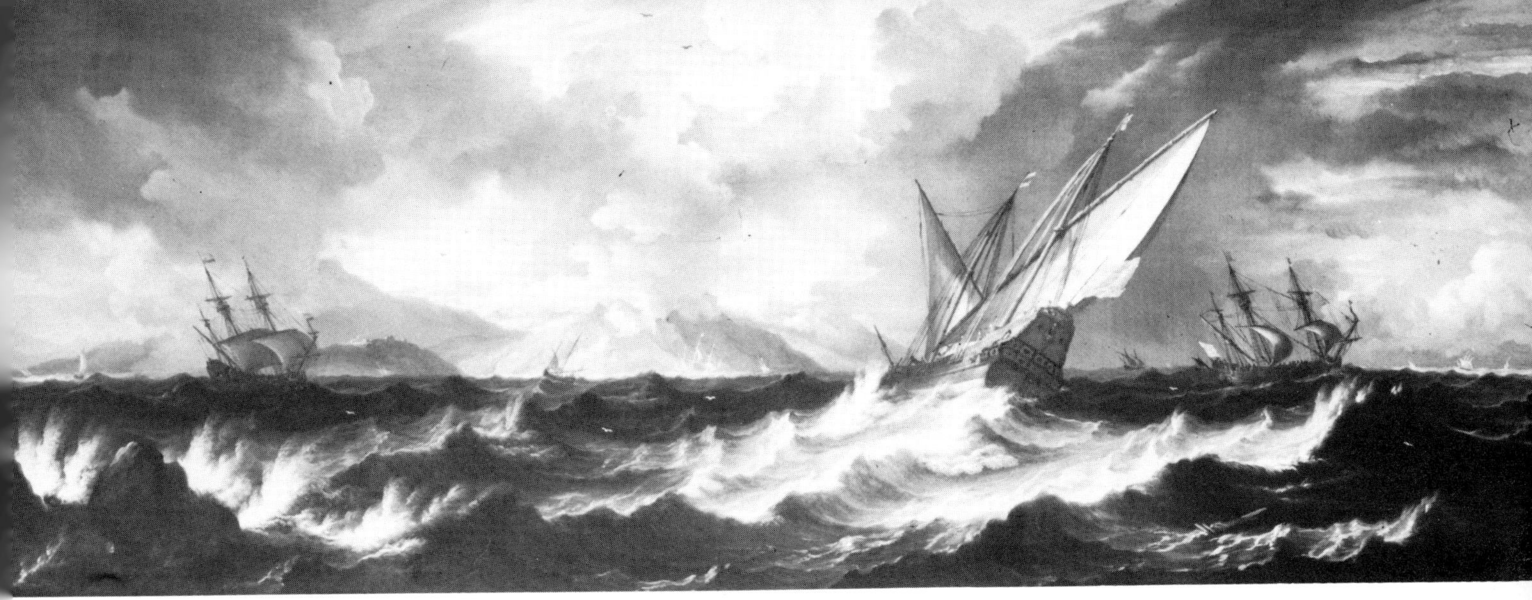

Plate 50. Pieter Mulier, the Younger, c.1636-1701. "A xebec and other shipping in a gale in the Mediterranean." National Maritime Museum, Greenwich.

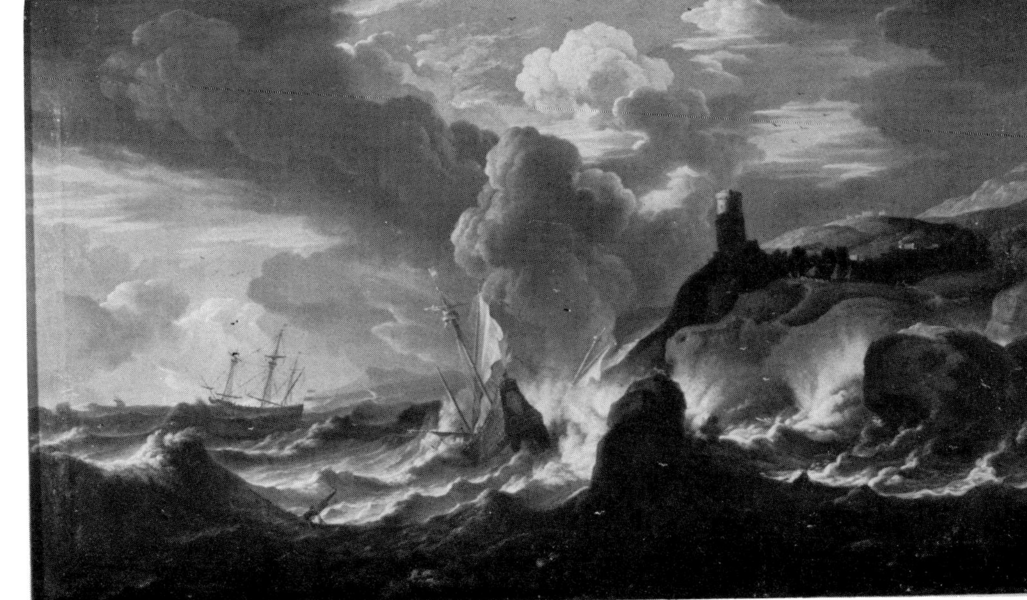

Plate 51. Pieter Mulier, the Younger, c.1636-1701. "Ships wrecked on a rocky Mediterranean coast." National Maritime Museum, Greenwich.

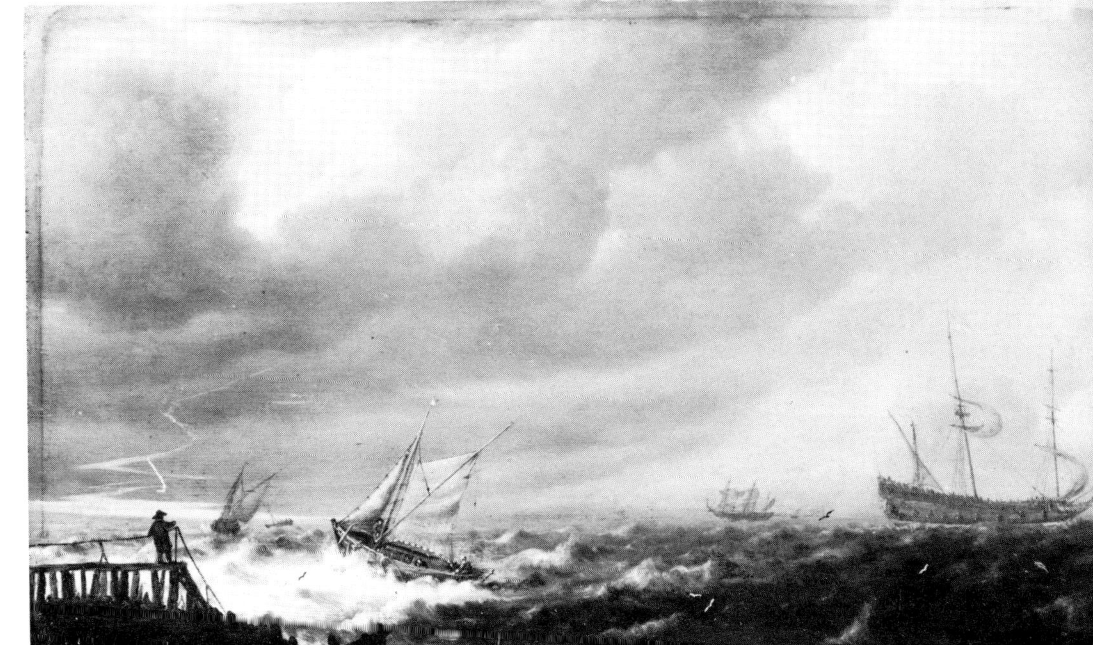

Plate 52. Hendrick van Anthonissen, 1606-aft.1656. "Storm with lightning and a jetty." National Gallery, Oslo.

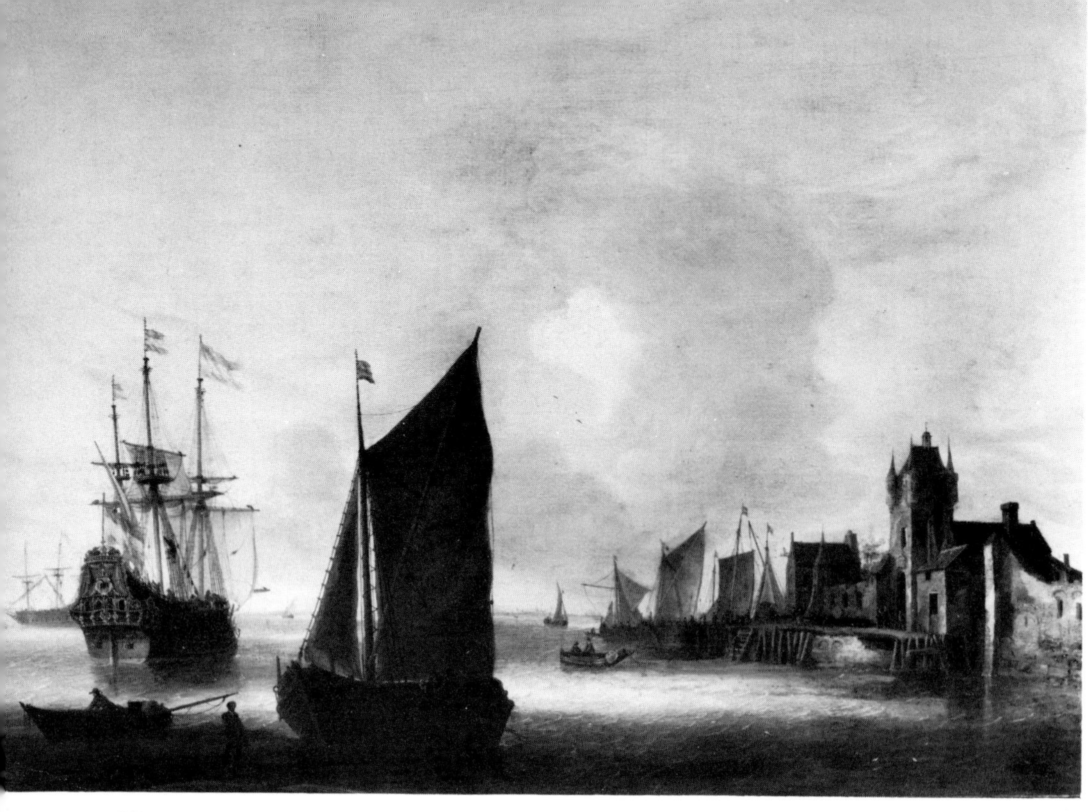

Plate 53. Hendrick van Anthonissen, 1606-aft.1656. "Shipping on the East Schelde near the Zuidhavenpoort, Zeirikzee." Rijksmuseum, Amsterdam.

Plate 54. Hendrick van Anthonissen, 1606-aft.1656. "Ships in the Schelde Estuary." *The small boat in the foreground is hooker rigged. It has two masts and a square sail on each.* National Gallery of Art, Washington.

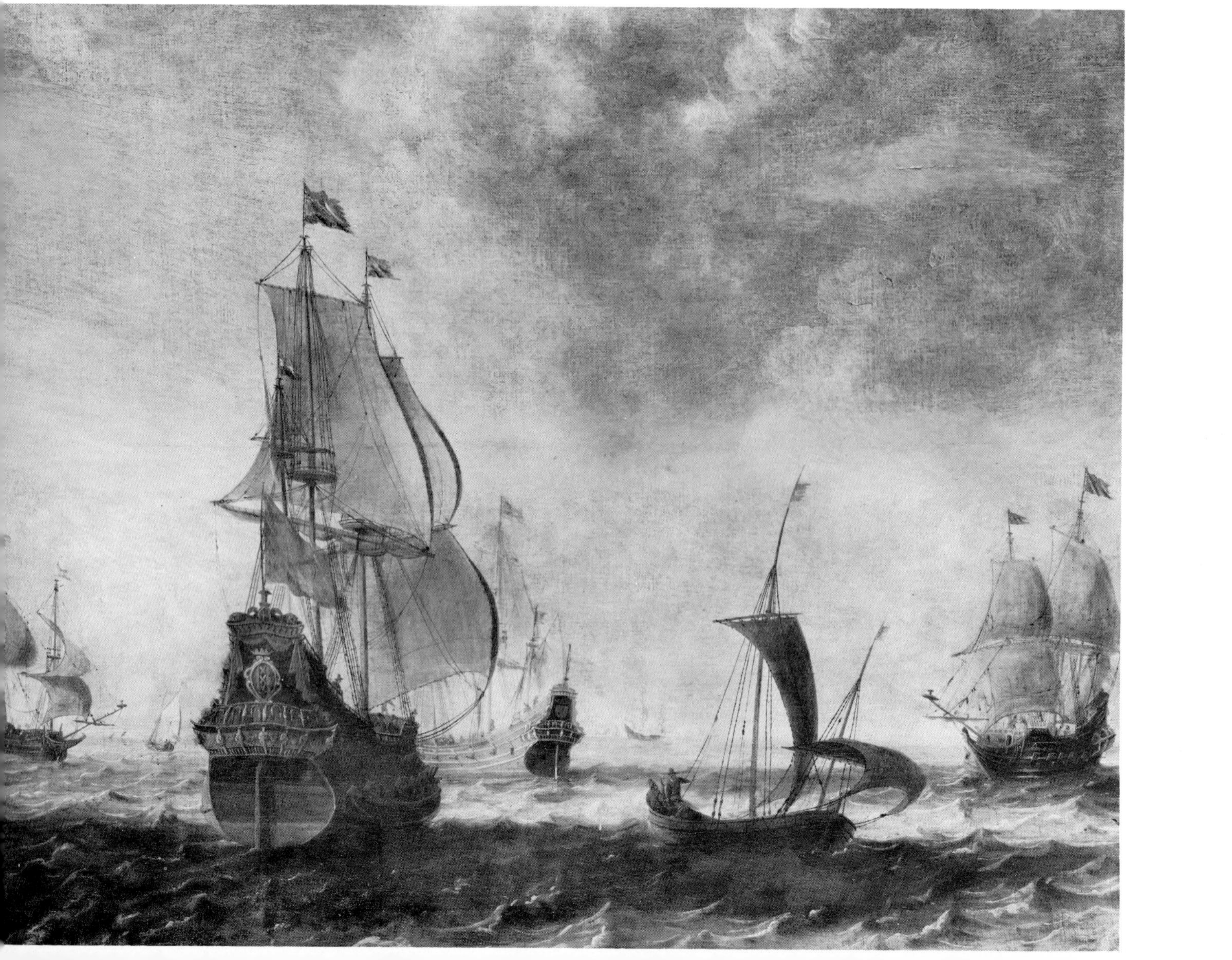

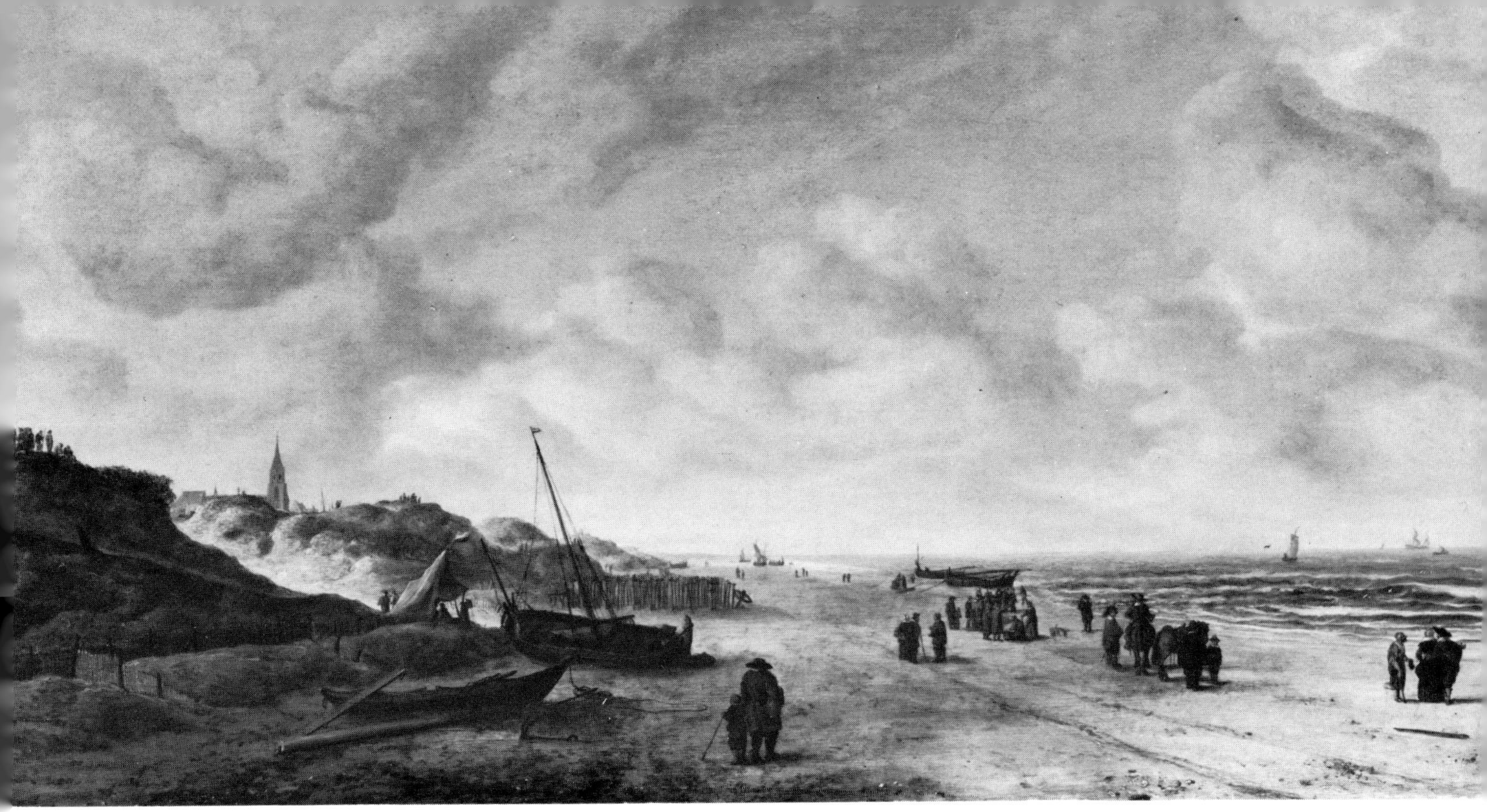

Plate 55. **Hendrick van Anthonissen, 1606-aft.1656.** "View of Scheveningen." Fitzwilliam Museum, Cambridge.

Plate 56. **Willem Hermansz van Diest, c.1610-aft.1663.** "The Battle of Leghorn in 1653." National Maritime Museum, Greenwich.

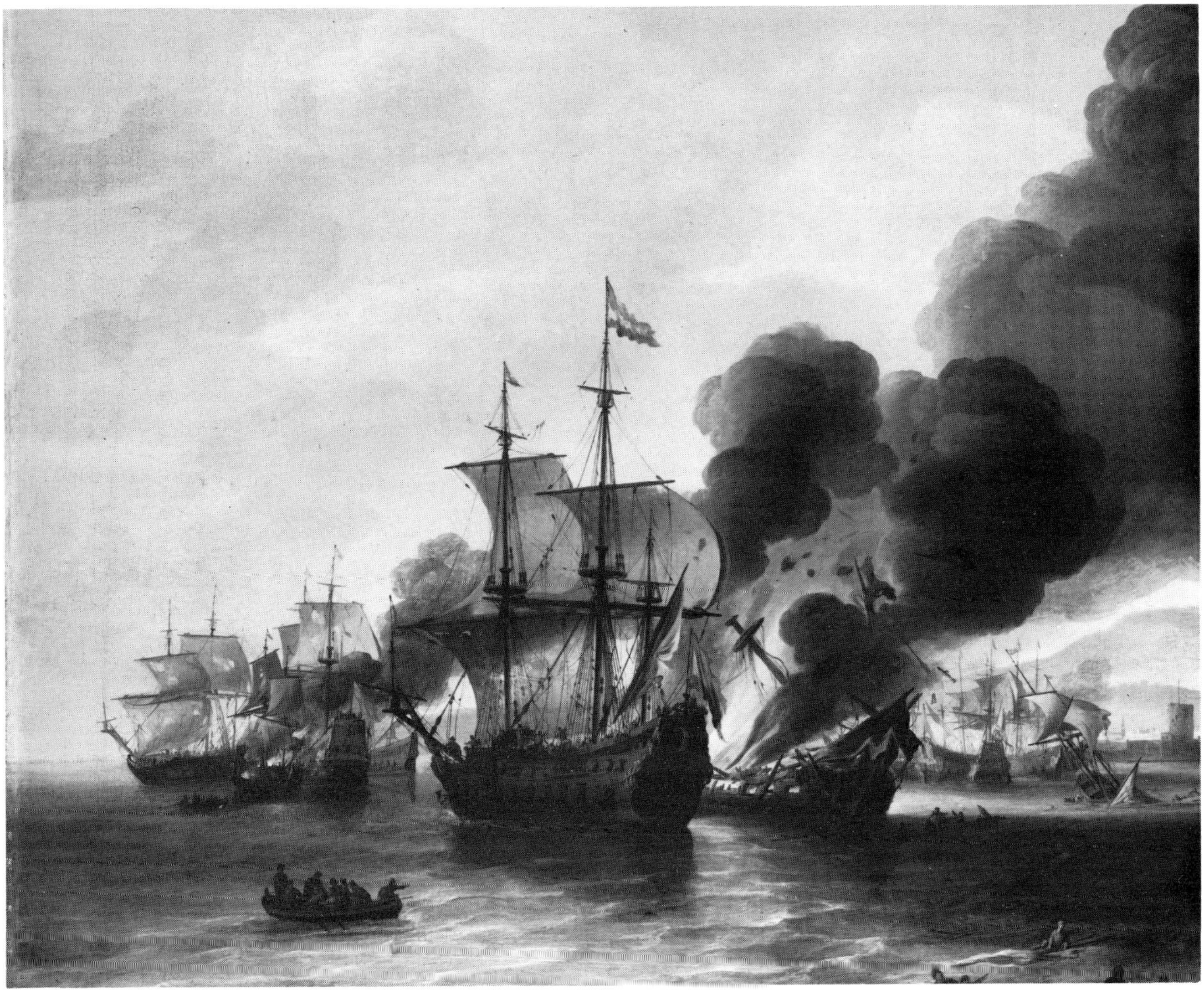

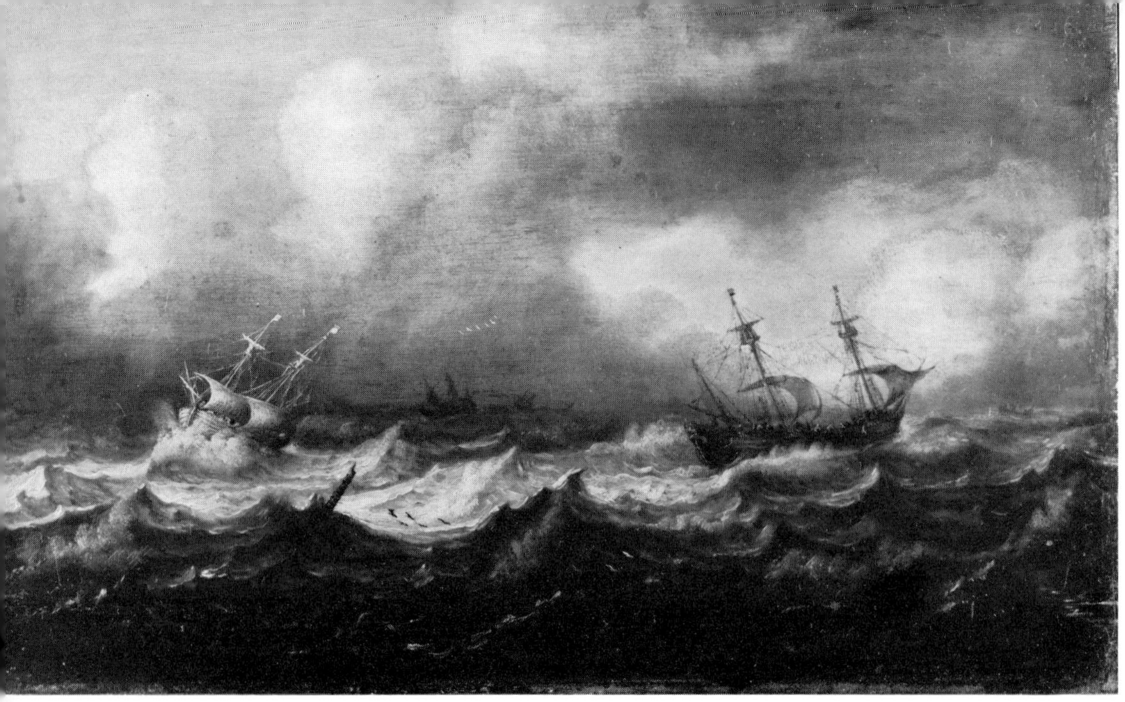

Plate 57. Willem Hermansz van Diest, c.1610-aft.1663. "Dutch ships in a storm." *This high quality work by a major Dutch sea painter has caught the feeling of confusion and panic.* Alte Pinakothek, Munich.

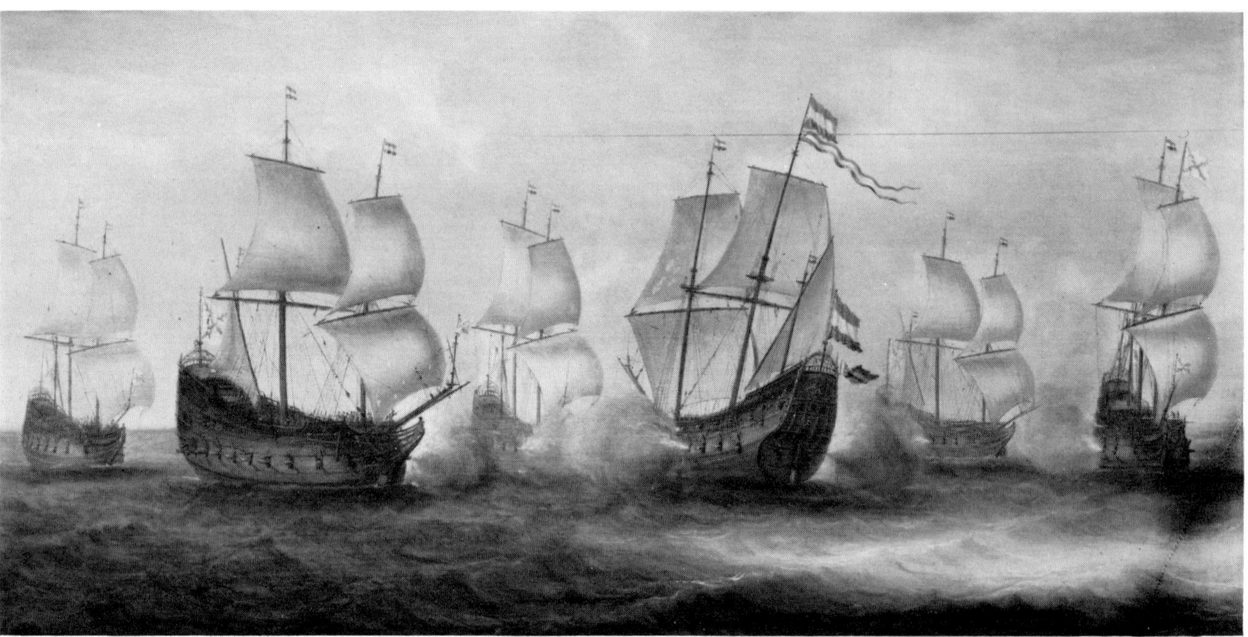

Plate 58. Jacob Gerritsz Loeff, fl. mid- to late 17th century. "De Witte in action with Dunkirkers." National Maritime Museum, Greenwich.

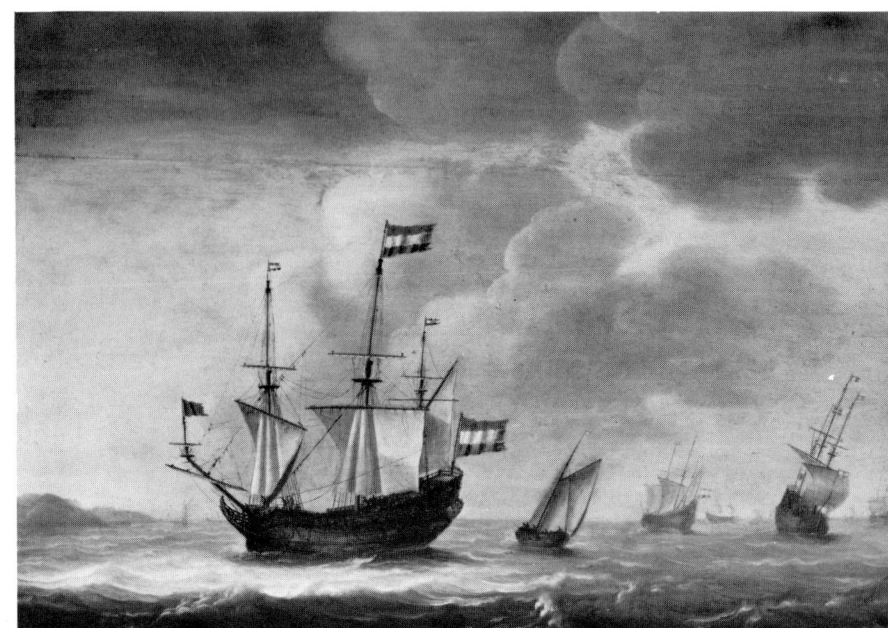

Plate 59. Jacob Gerritsz Loeff, fl. mid- to late 17th century. "Dutch shipping off a coast." Rijksmuseum, Amsterdam.

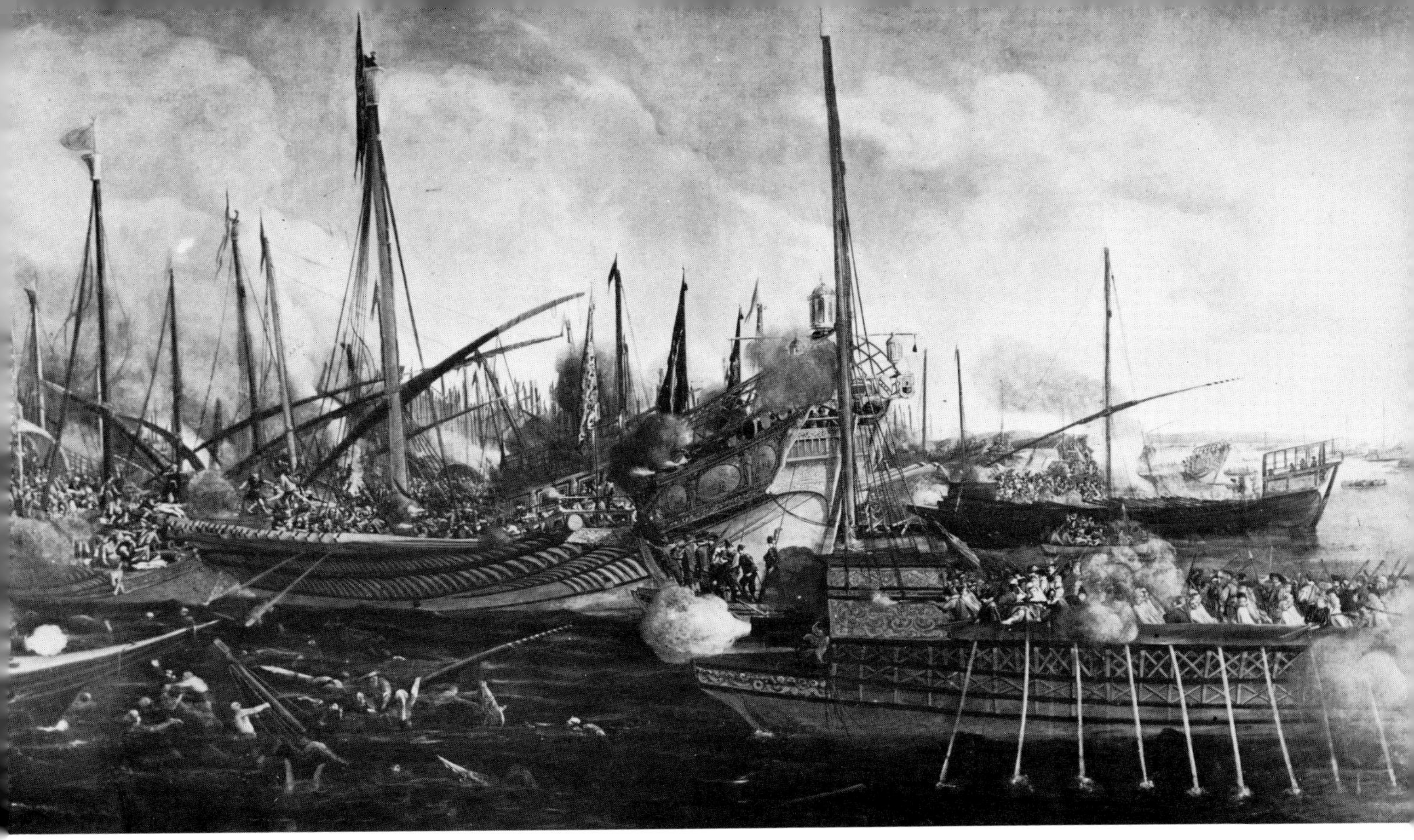

Plate 60. Cornelis Hendriksz Vroom, 1591-1661. "An action between Christian and Turkish galleys." *The typical clarity and clear delineation of this artist's work can be seen here. Another painter who liked to include figures in his works.* Victoria and Albert Museum, Ham House.

Plate 61. Cornelis Hendriksz Vroom, 1591-1661. "An action between a Spanish ship and Barbary galleys." *C.H. Vroom used a curious blue colour which occurs here on the right of the painting.* National Maritime Museum, Greenwich.

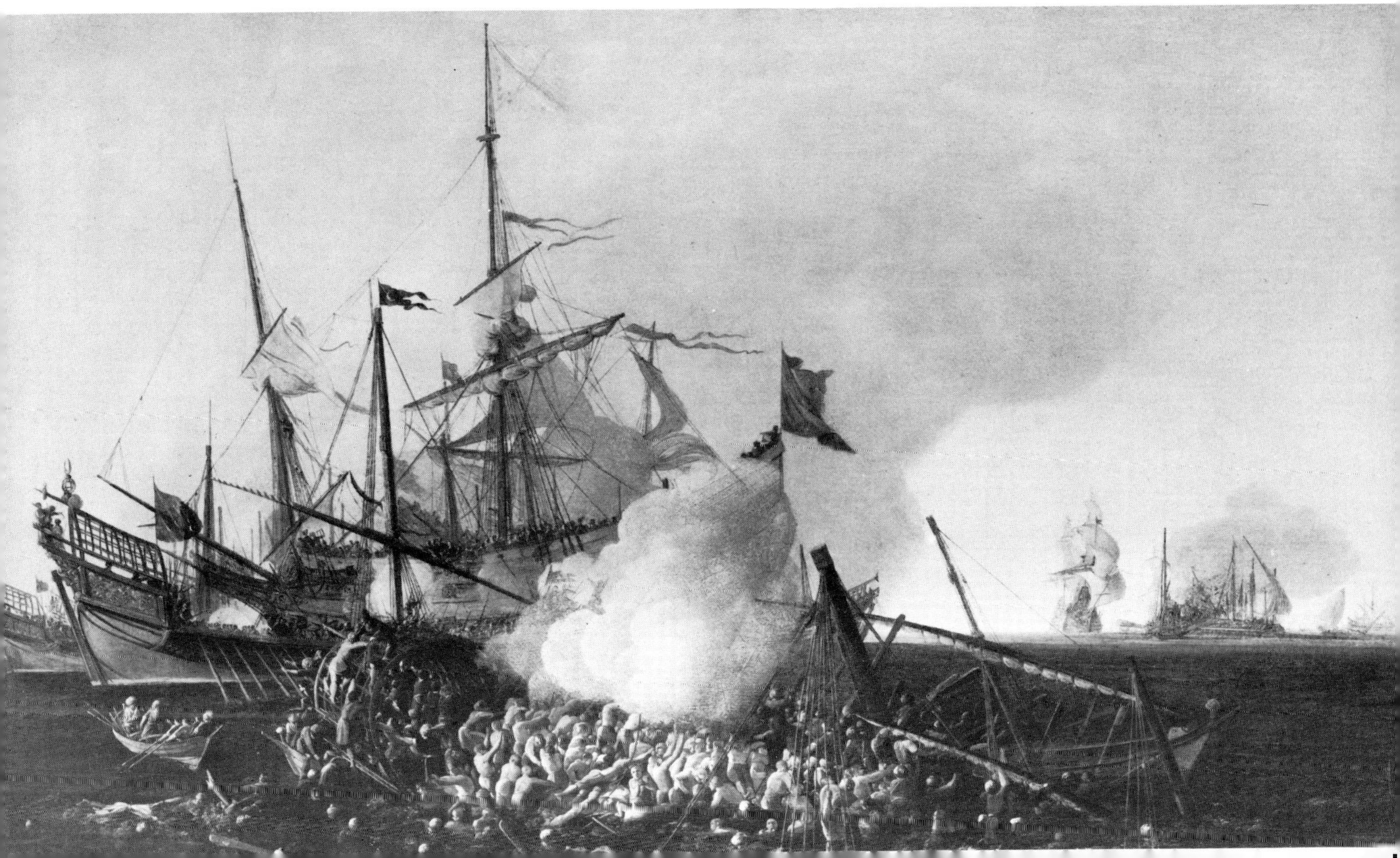

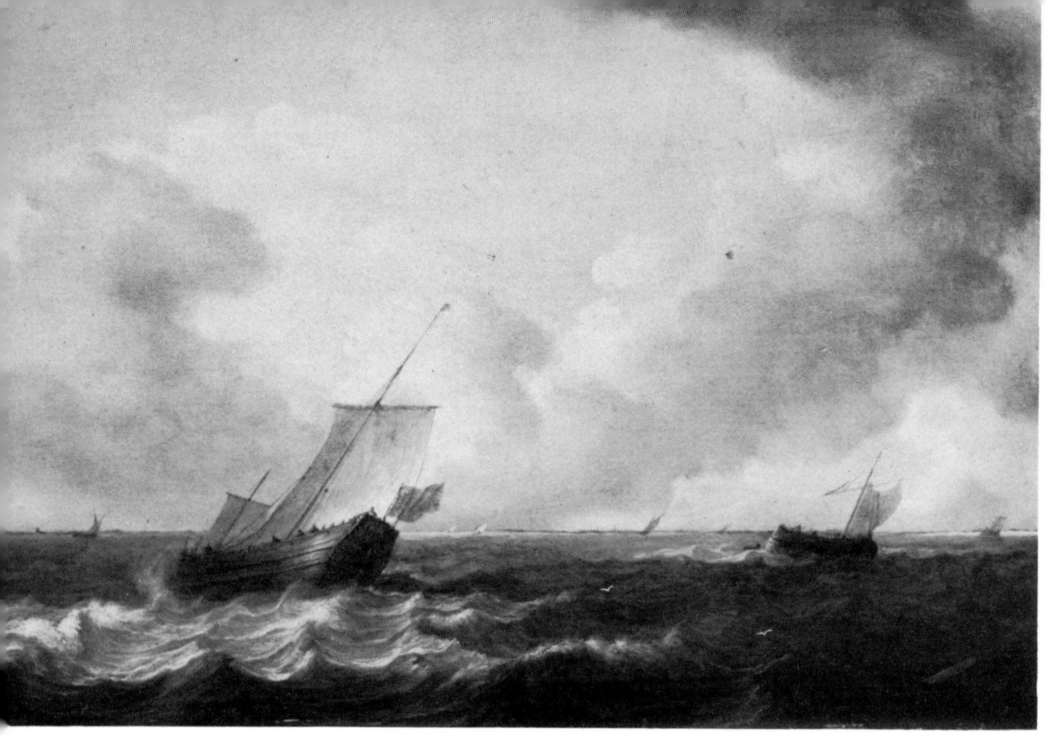

Plate 62. Hendrick Martensz Rokes Sorgh, 1611-1670. "An English snow off the Dutch coast." *The use of light and its effect on the sea is typical of this artist, whose work is very close to that of Simon de Vlieger (Plates 88-94).* National Maritime Museum, Greenwich.

Plate 63. Hendrick Martensz Rokes Sorgh, 1611-1670. "View of the River Maas." *Drawn with a grey Dutch palette and with a particularly linear quality. The wijdschip in the foreground is sprit-rigged and, like most Dutch small craft, has a lee-board, for sailing to windward.* Boymans-van Beuningen Museum, Rotterdam.

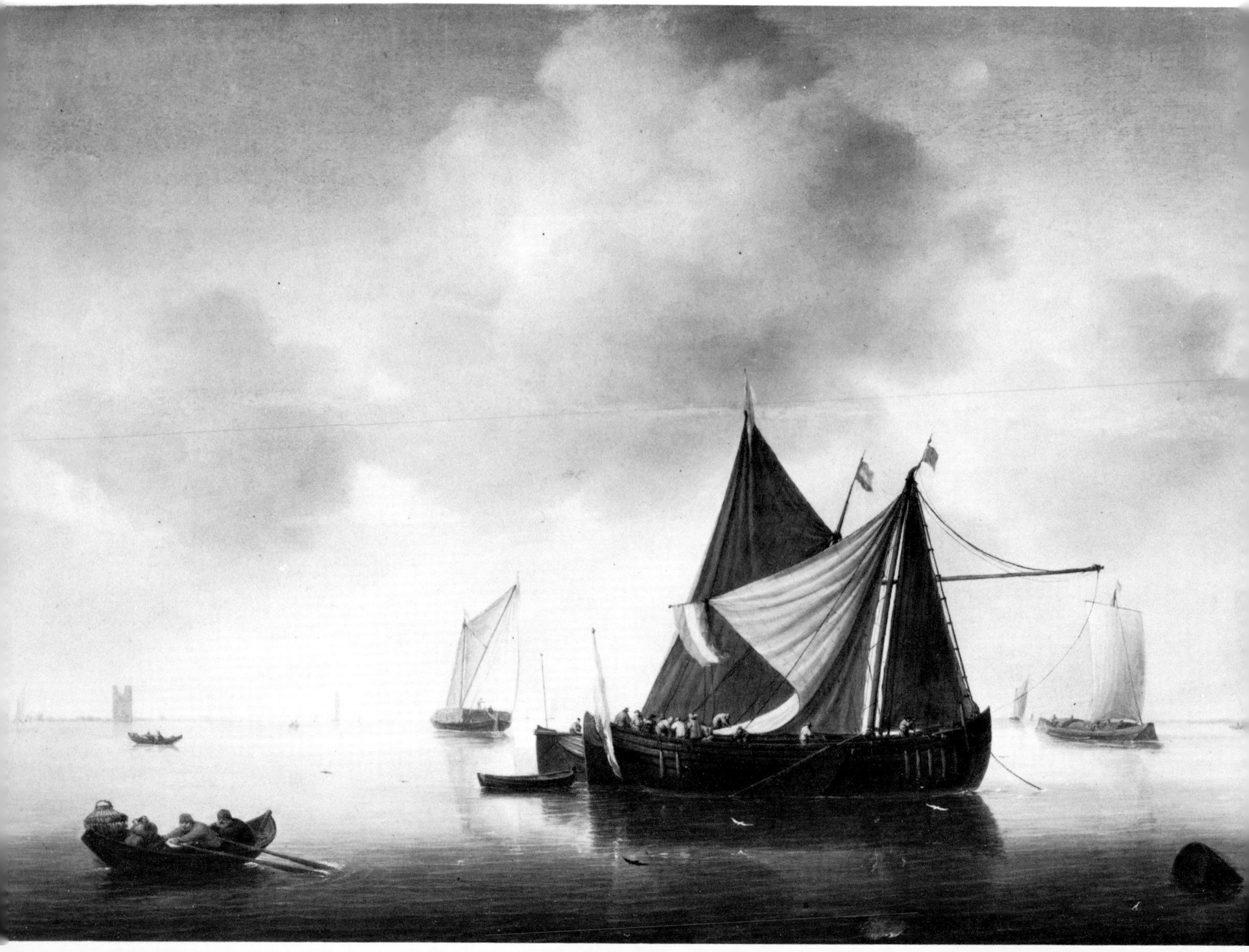

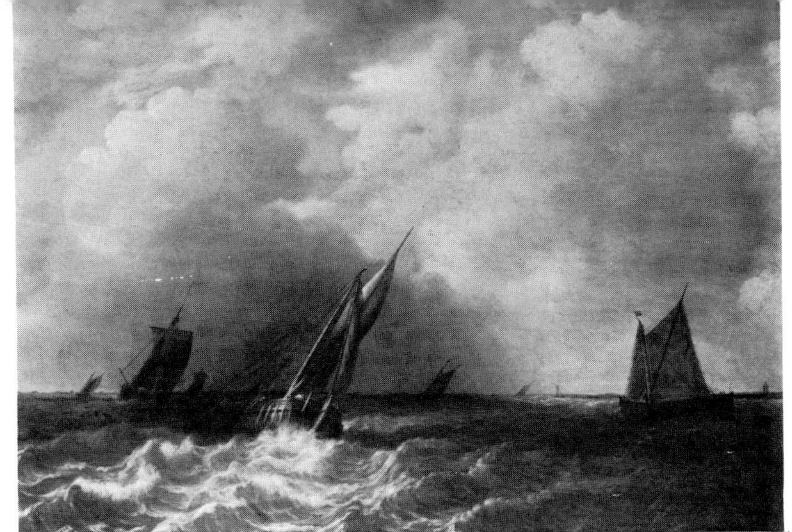

Plate 64. Hendrick Martensz Rokes Sorgh, 1611-1670. "Storm on the Maas, dated 1668." Rijksmuseum, Amsterdam.

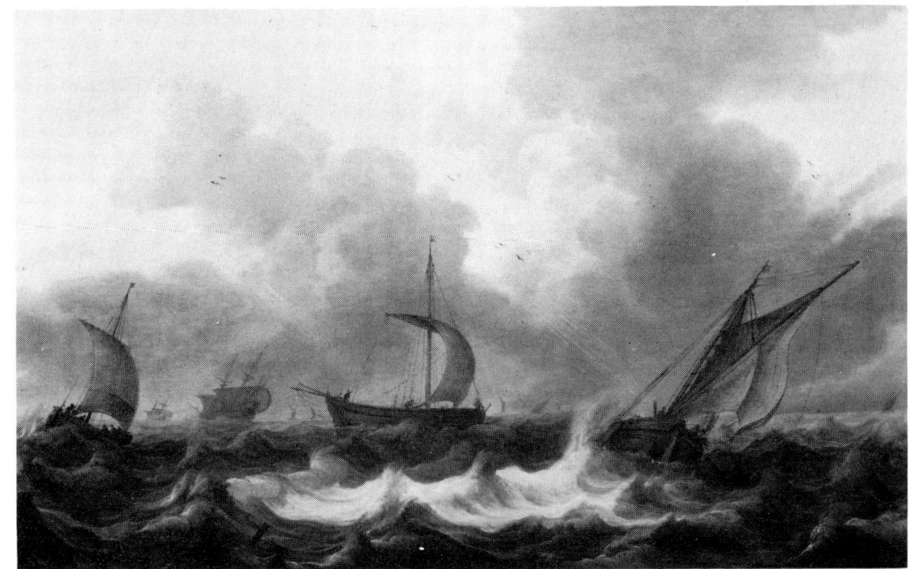

Plate 65. Cornelisz Leonardsz Stooter, 1620-1655. "Fishing vessels in a choppy sea." National Maritime Museum, Greenwich.

Plate 66. Reinier Nooms, c.1623-1667. "A Battle of the First Dutch War in 1652/3." National Maritime Museum, Greenwich.

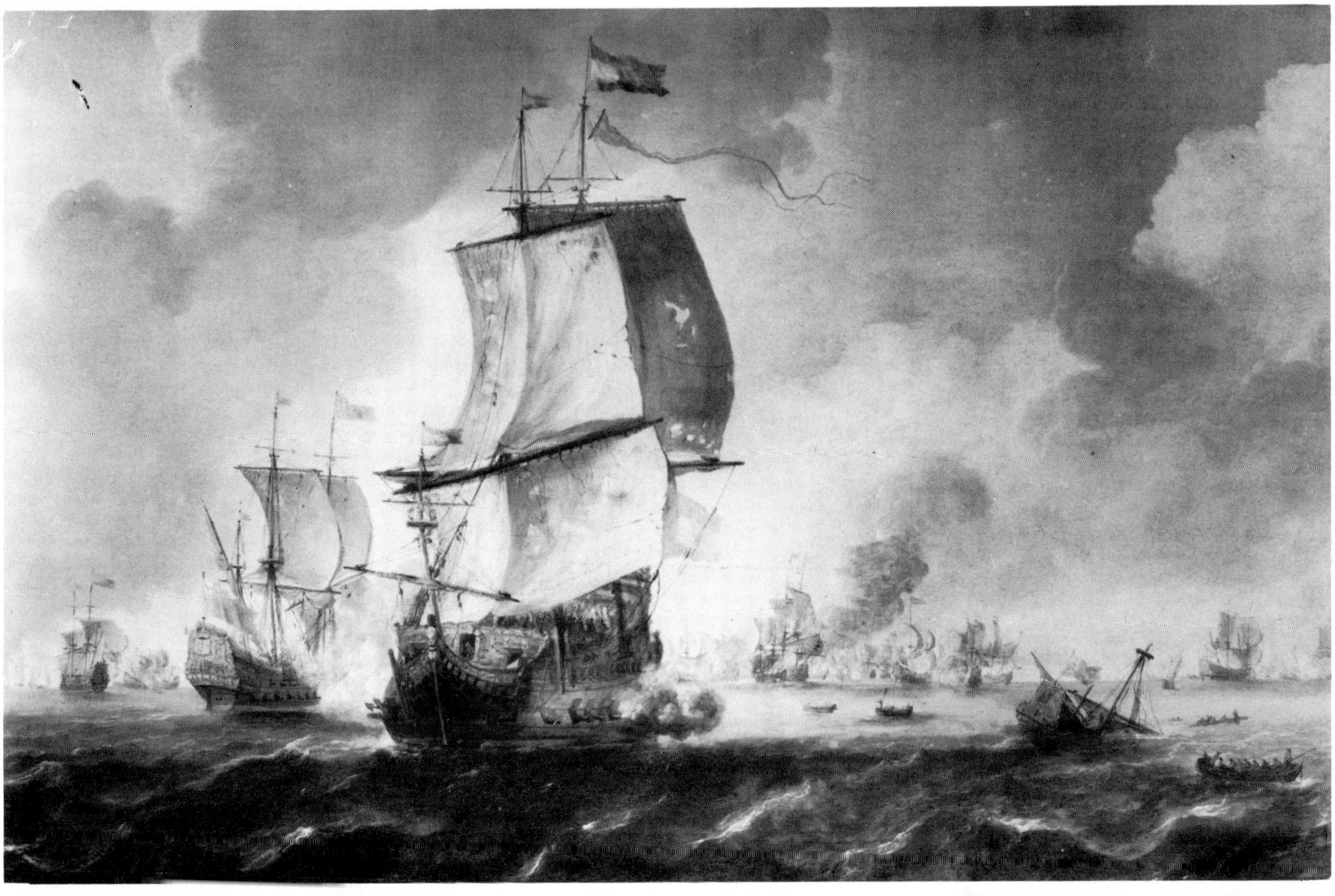

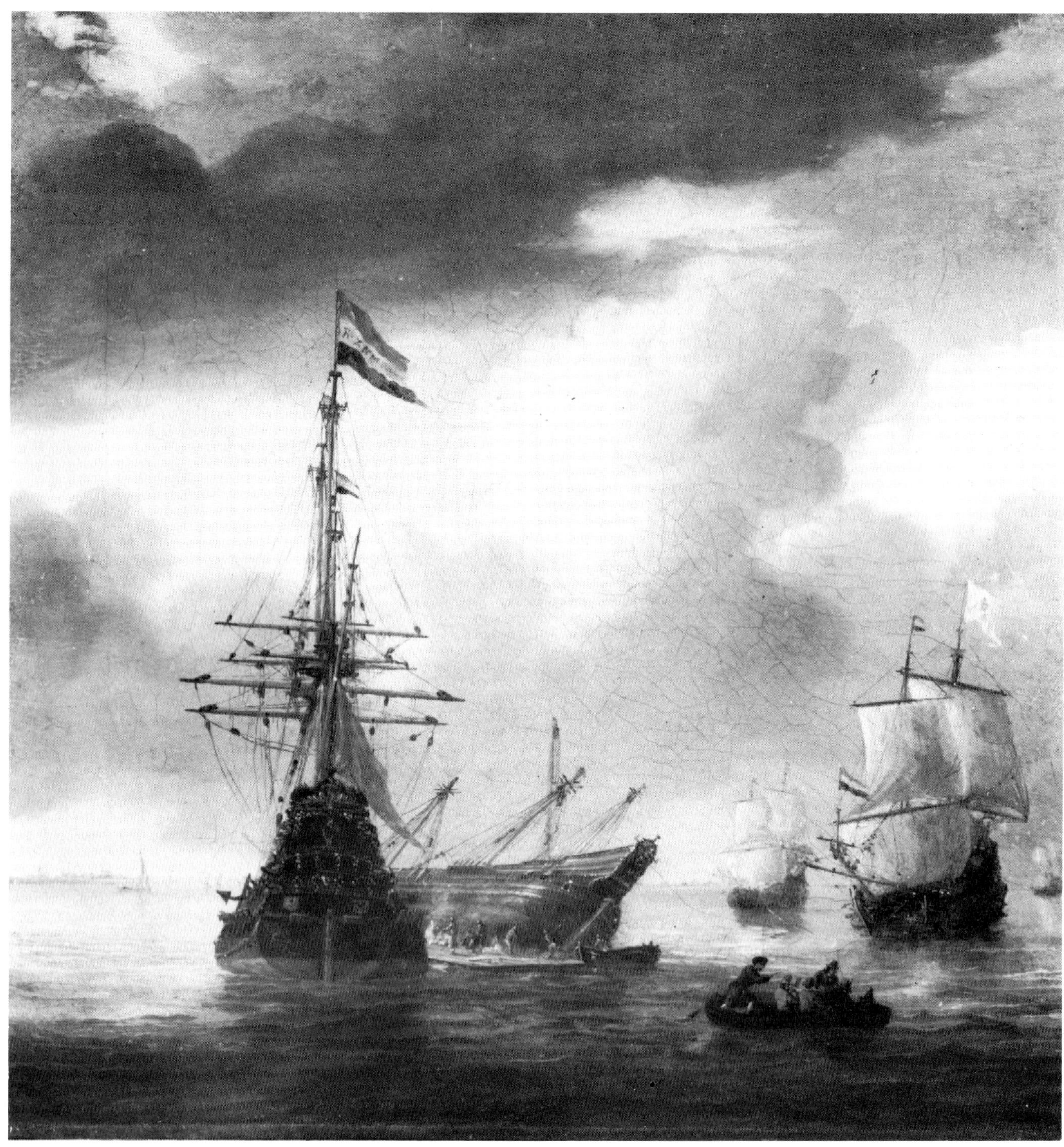

Plate 67. Reinier Nooms, c.1623-1667. "Dutch shipping with a merchant flute being careened." *Nooms painted quite a few pictures of careening.* Nationalmuseum, Stockholm.

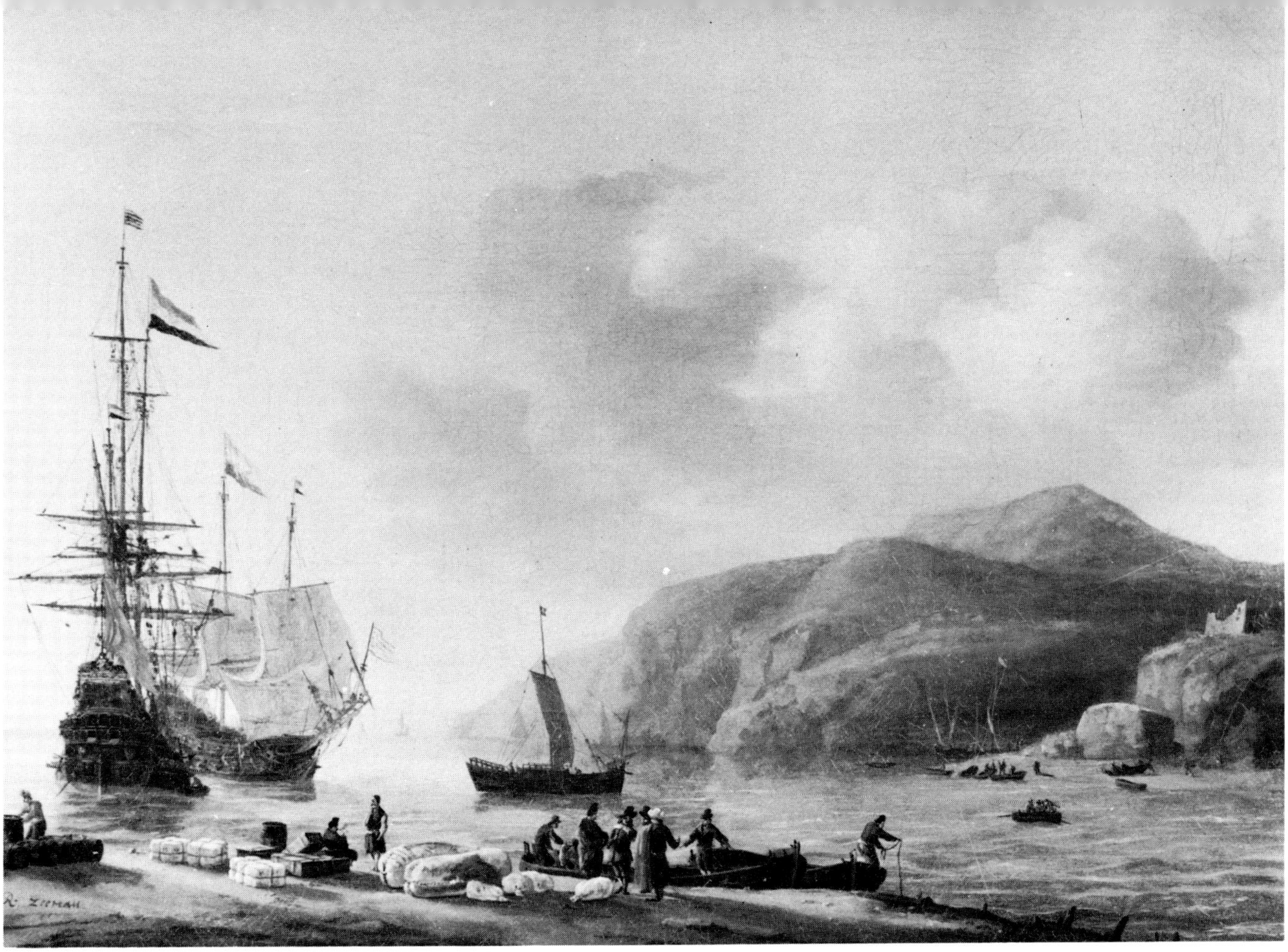

Plate 68. Reinier Nooms, c.1623-1667. "Shore scene with merchants and goods, with two ships lying off." Scheepvart Museum, Amsterdam.

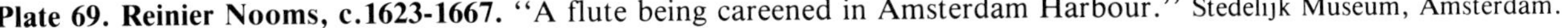

Plate 69. Reinier Nooms, c.1623-1667. "A flute being careened in Amsterdam Harbour." Stedelijk Museum, Amsterdam.

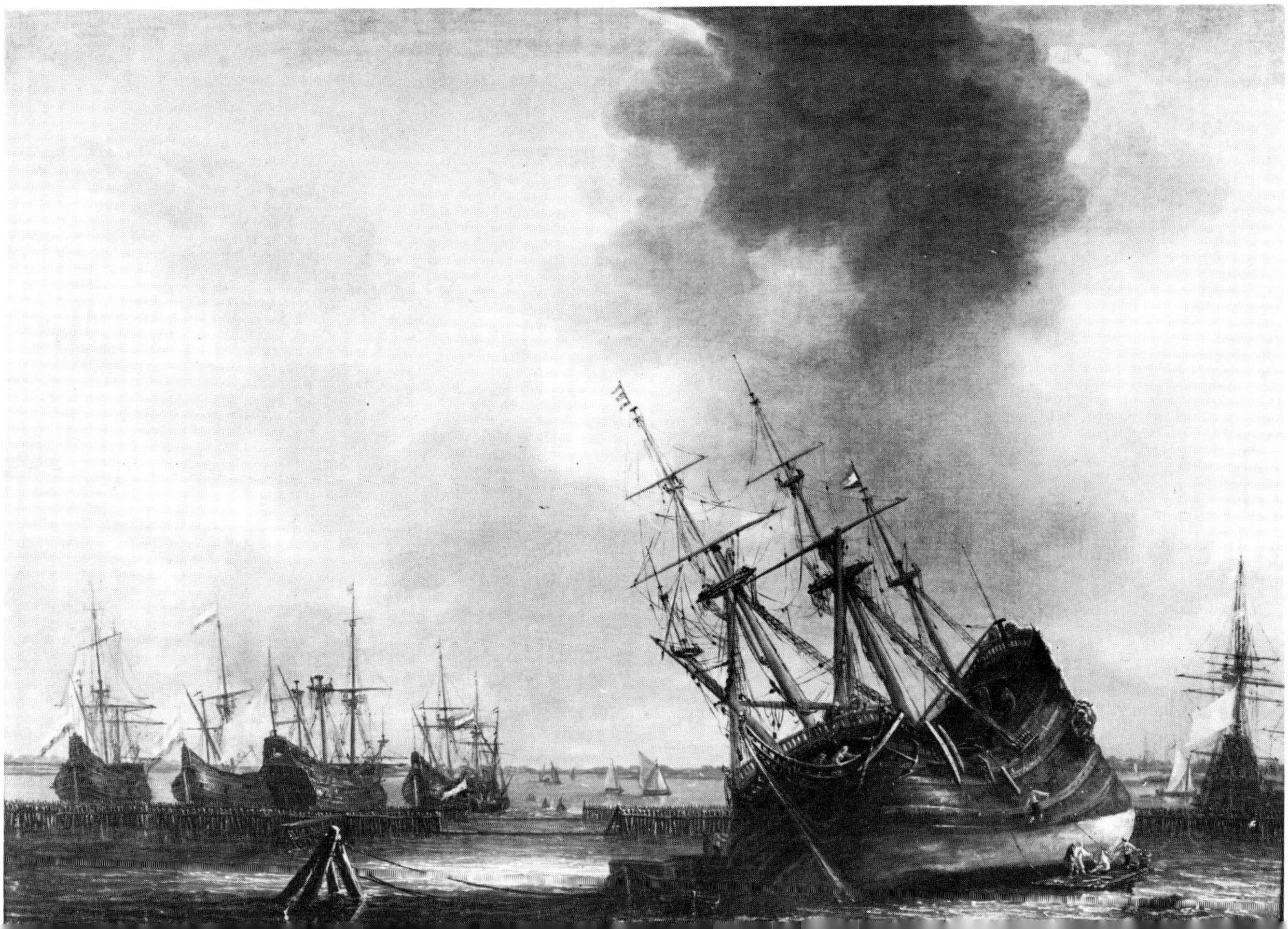

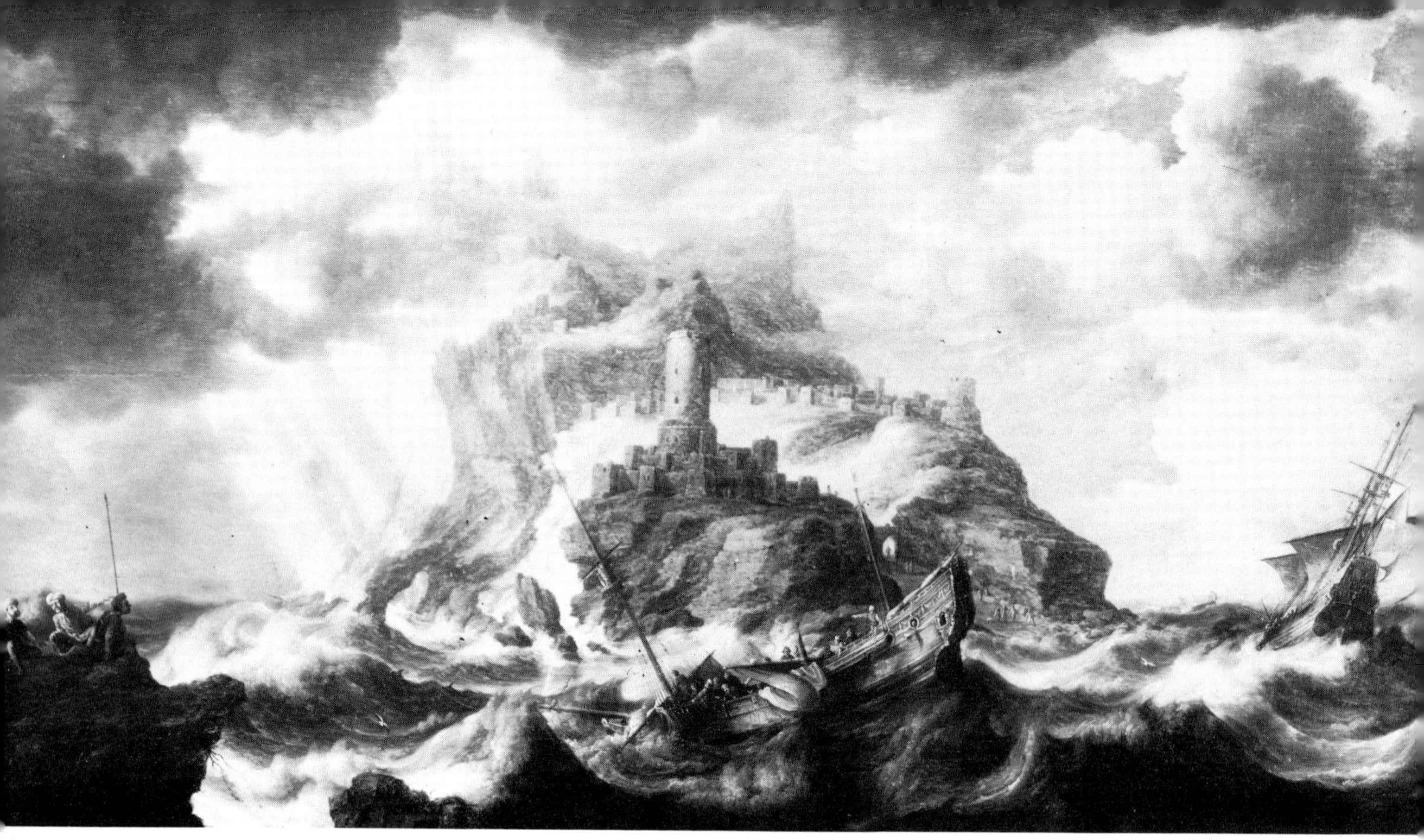

Plate 70. Bonaventura Peeters, the Elder, 1614-1652. "A dismasted ship in a heavy sea, with an island in the background." National Maritime Museum, Greenwich.

Plate 71. Bonaventura Peeters, the Elder, 1614-1652. "A galley and a Dutch ship driving onto a rocky coast in a storm." Kunsthistorisches Museum, Vienna.

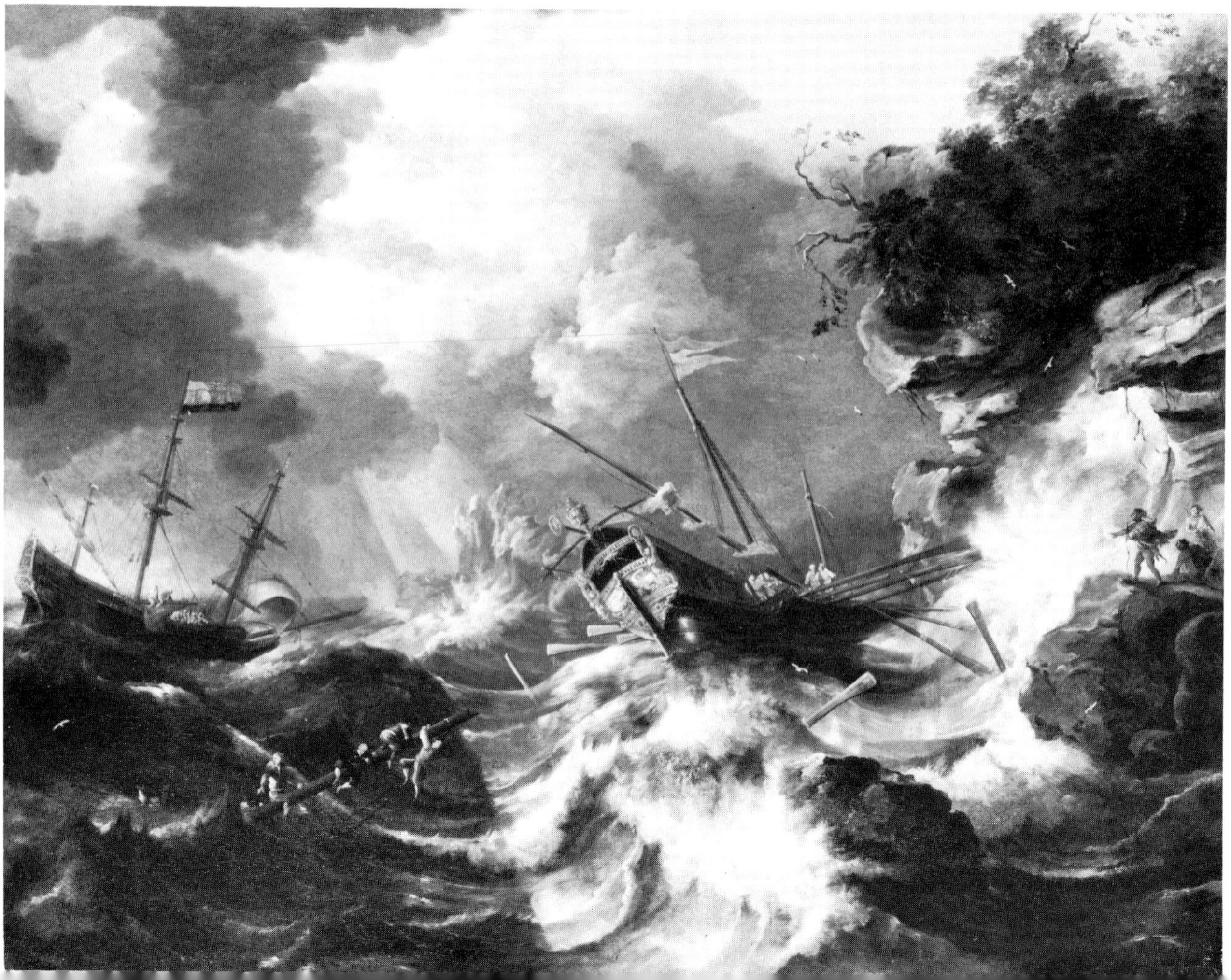

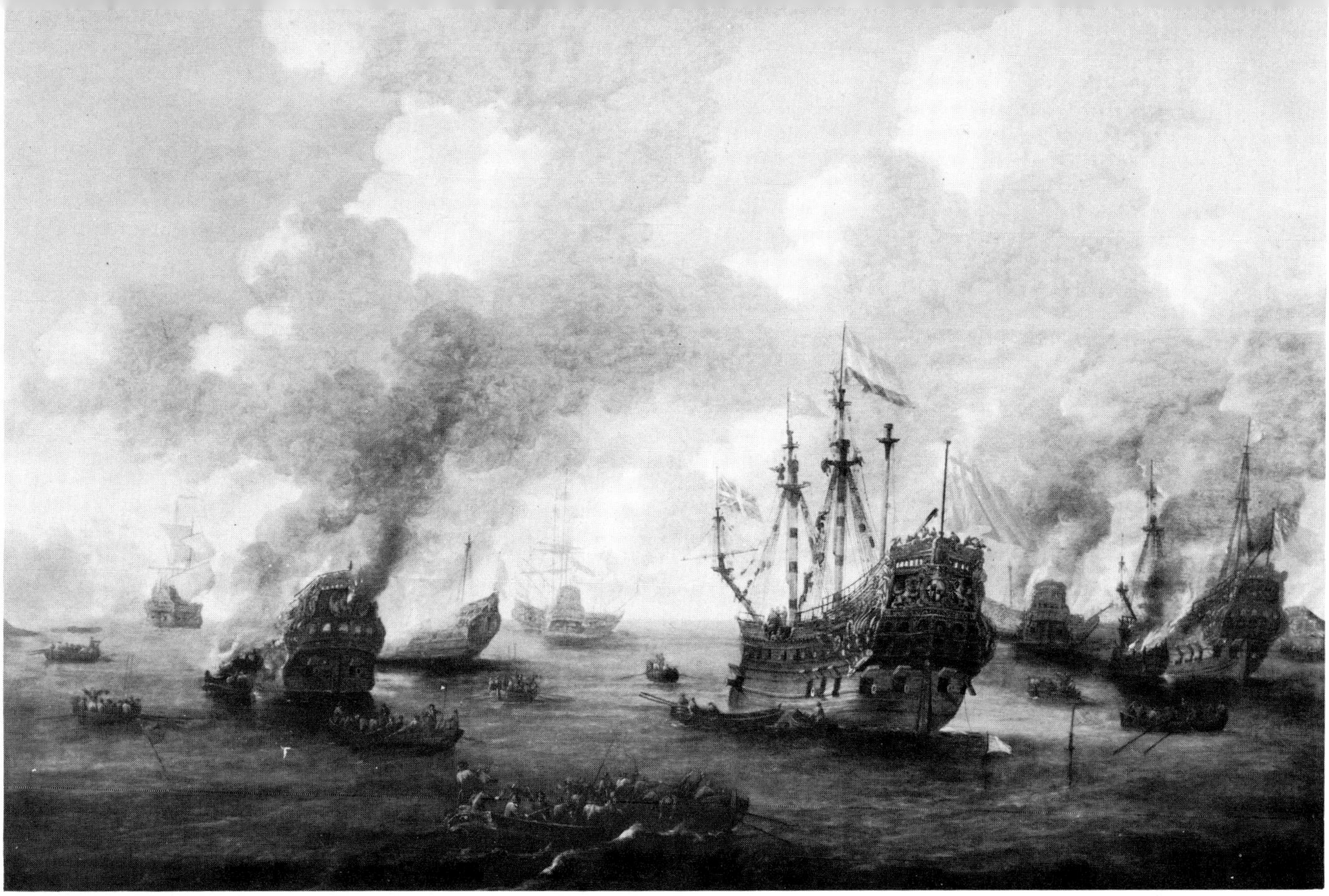

Plate 72. Jan Peeters, 1624-c.1679. "The Dutch attack on the Medway in 1667." *This shows the* Royal Charles *and ships of the English fleet being captured while lying in ordinary; that is to say, with spars sent down, most of their guns put ashore and the crew paid off. This was the practice for the winter months, or in time of peace.* National Maritime Museum, Greenwich.

Plate 73. Pieter Cornelisz van Soest, 1640-1667. "The Four Days Fight in 1666." National Maritime Museum, Greenwich.

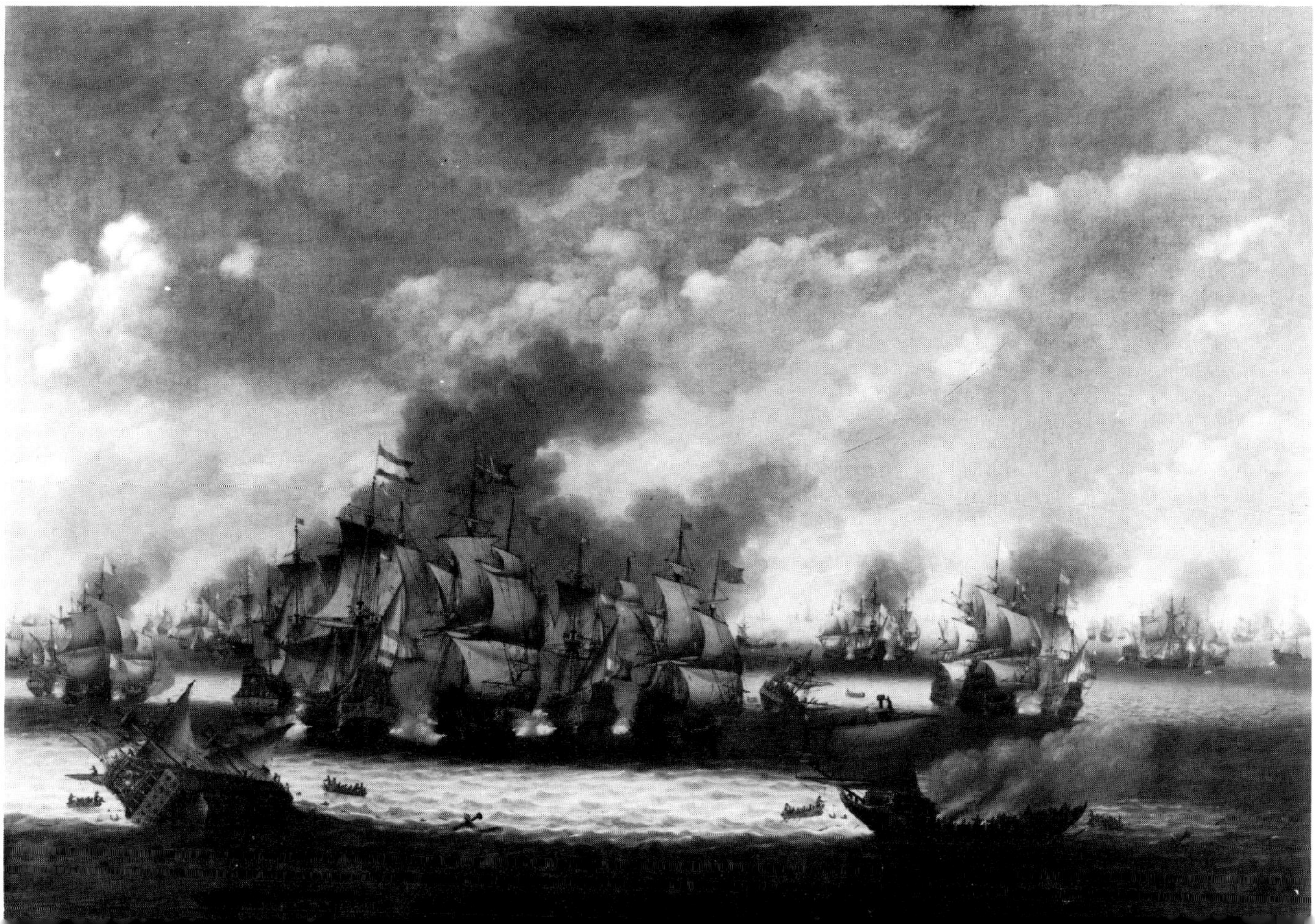

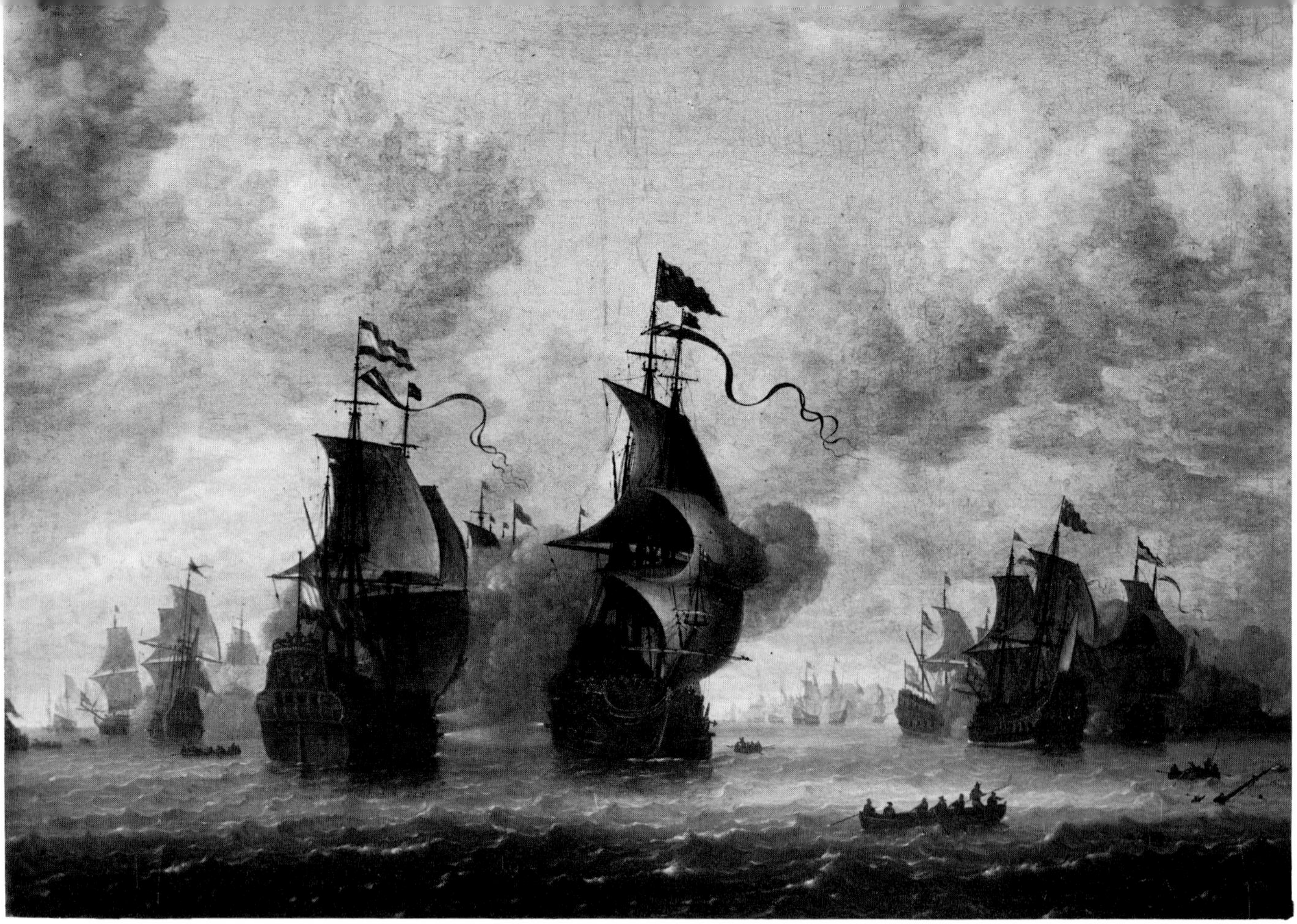

Plate 74. Jan Abraham Beerstraaten, 1622-1666. "A battle of the First Dutch War in 1652-3." Bavarian State Museums, Munich.

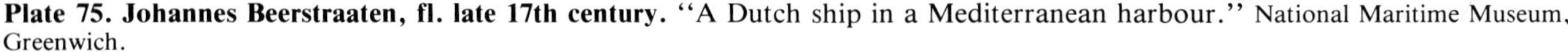

Plate 75. Johannes Beerstraaten, fl. late 17th century. "A Dutch ship in a Mediterranean harbour." National Maritime Museum, Greenwich.

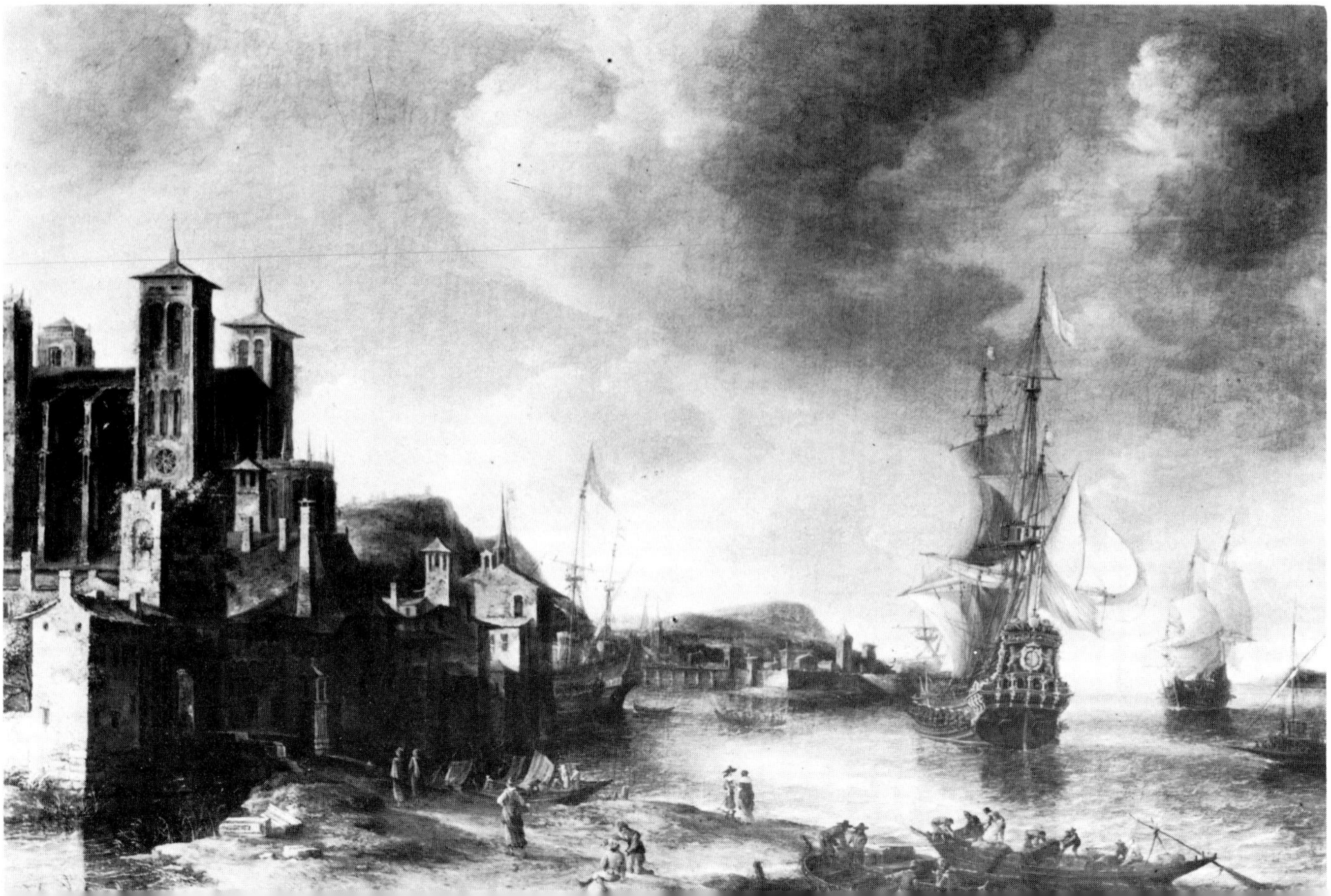

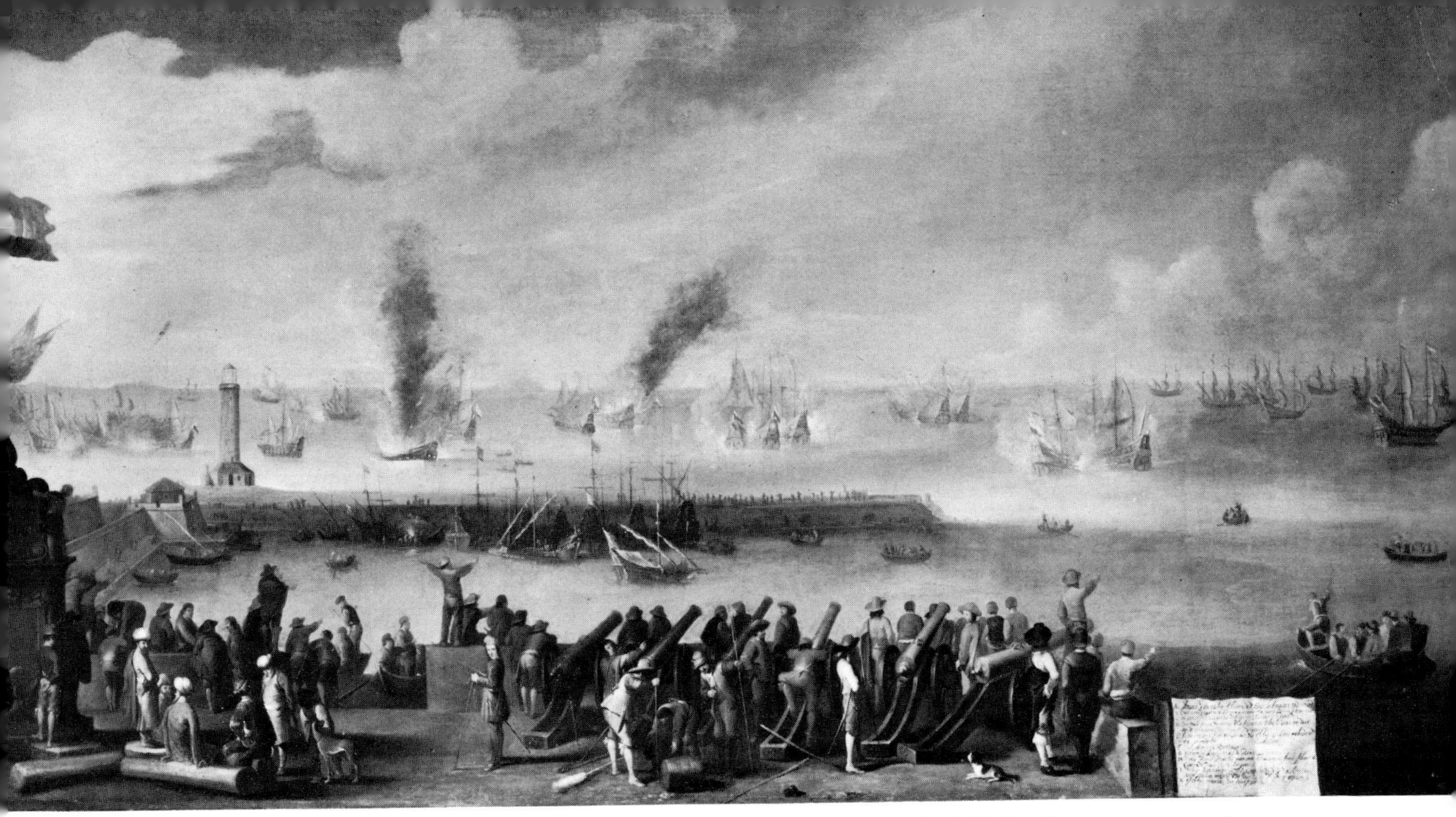

Plate 76. Johannes Lingelbach, 1622-1674. "A distant view of the Battle of Leghorn in 1653." Rijksmuseum, Amsterdam.

Plate 77. Johannes Lingelbach, 1622-1674. "Scheveningen beach; the departure of King Charles II for England in 1660." *More correctly a genre rather than a marine painter, Lingelbach has achieved a really fine quality here.* Rijksmuseum, Amsterdam.

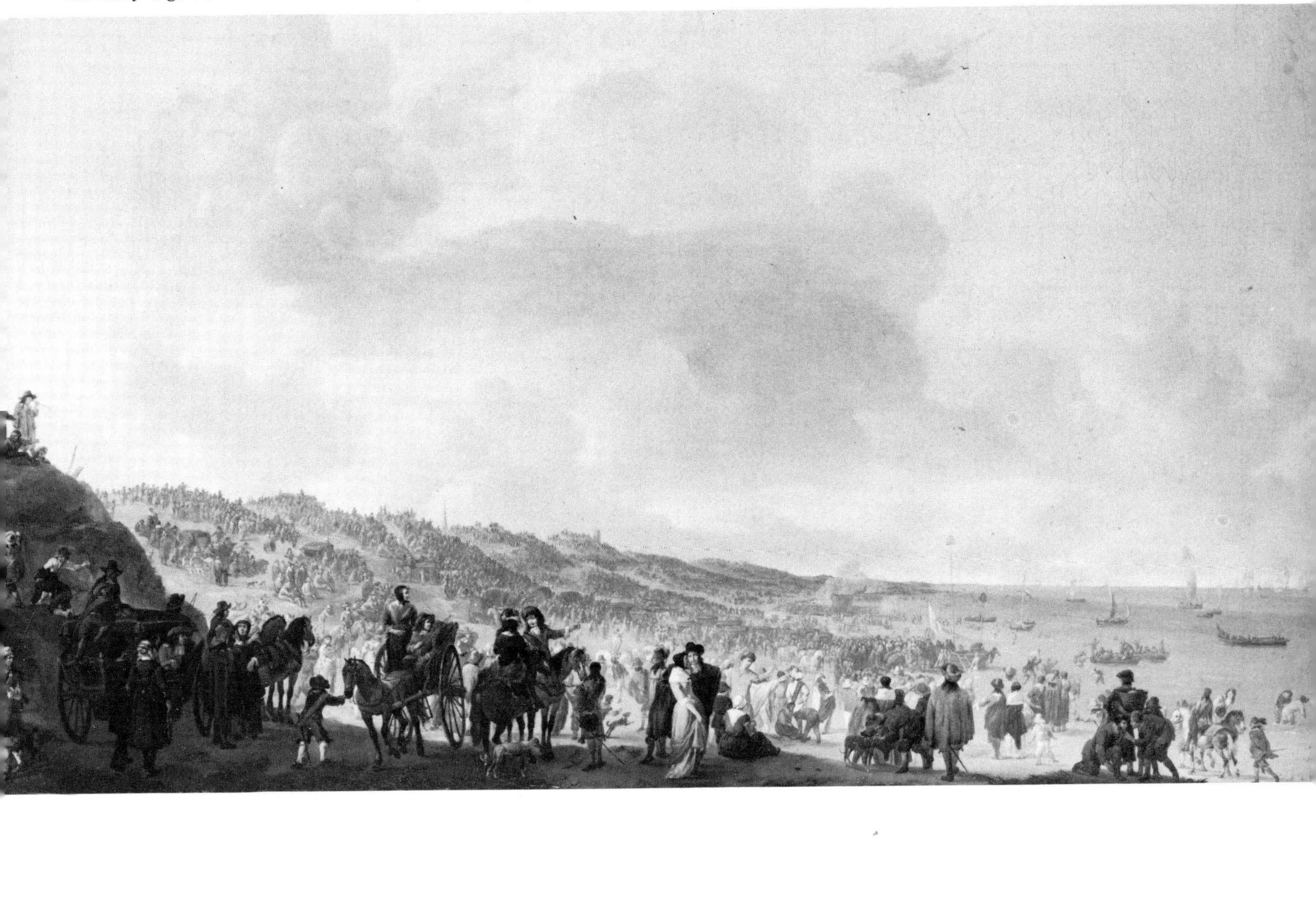

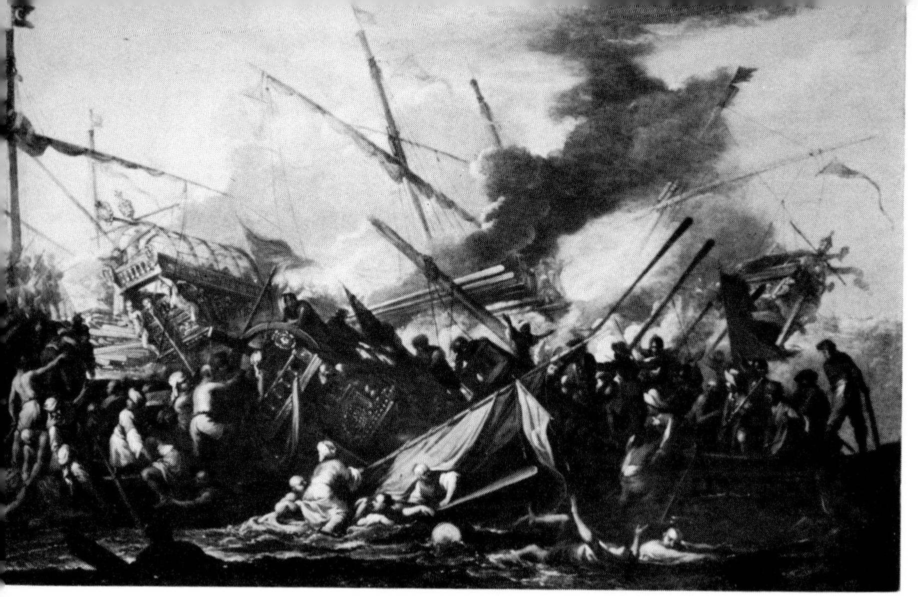

Plate 78. Johannes Lingelbach, 1622-1674. "An action between Turkish and Maltese galleys." Nationalmuseum, Stockholm.

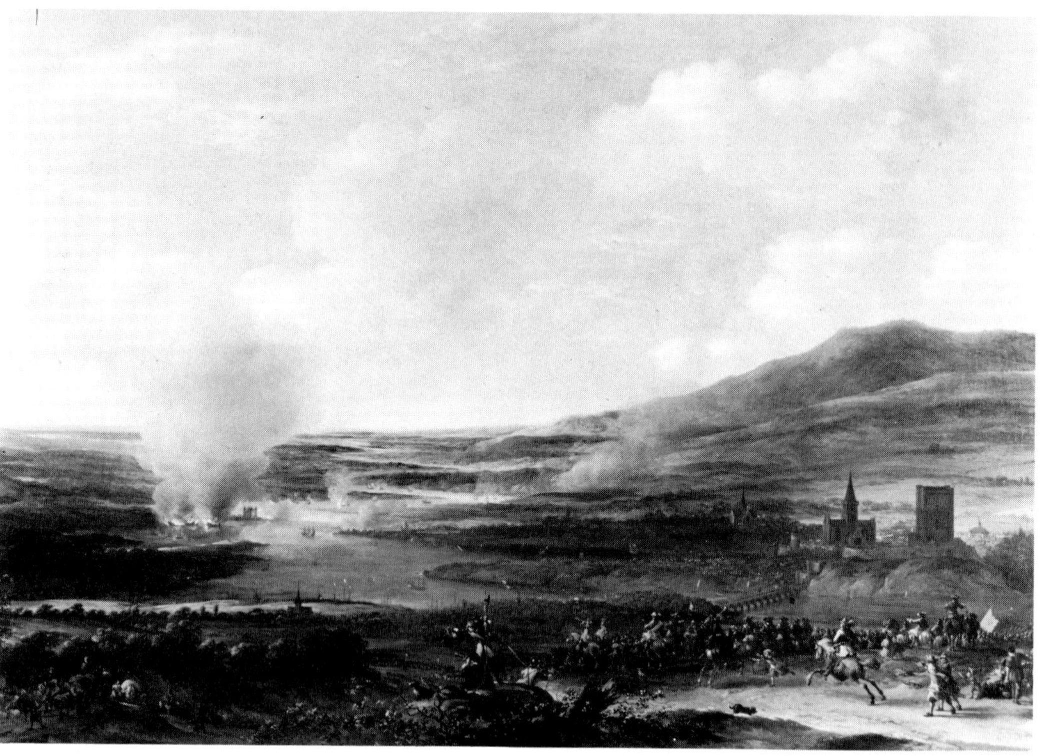

Plate 79. Willem Schellinks, 1627-1678. "The Dutch attack on the Medway in 1667." *A painter whose work bears a certain resemblance to Bakhuizen (Plates 117-121). The details of the ships are usually accurate.* Scheepvaart Museum, Amsterdam.

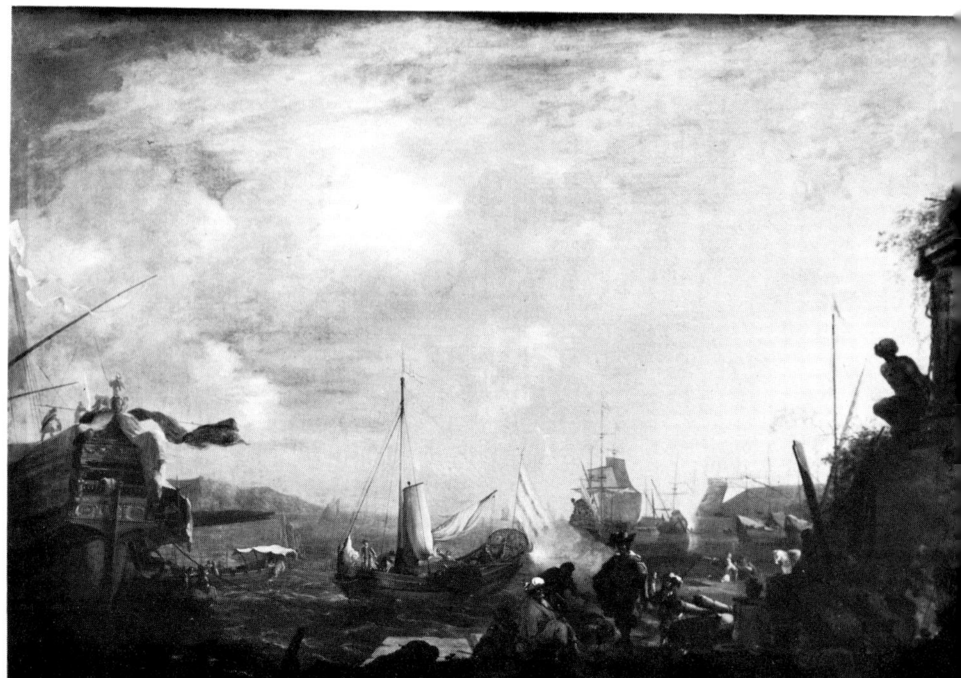

Plate 80. Willem Schellinks, 1627-1678. "Leghorn Harbour." Alte Pinakothek, Munich.

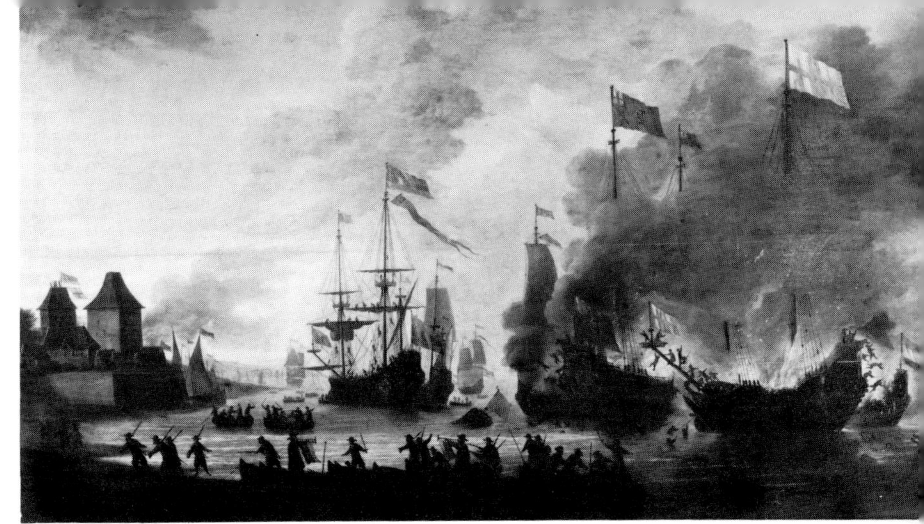

Plate 81. Jan van Leyden, fl. mid- to late 17th century. "The Dutch in the Medway in 1667." Rijksmuseum, Amsterdam.

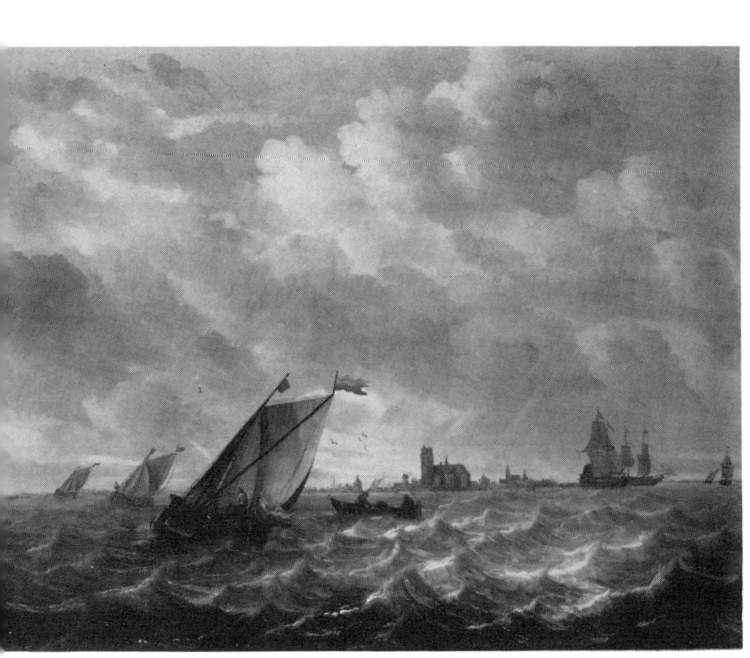

Plate 82. Abraham Hendricksz van Beyeren, c.1620-1690. "River view." Rijksmuseum, Amsterdam.

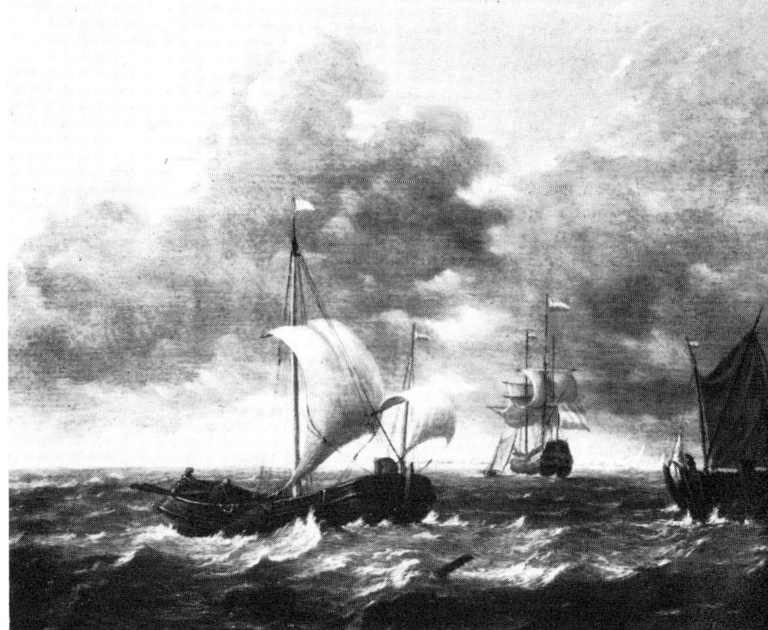

Plate 83. Gerrit Battem, c.1636-1684. "A Dutch hooker off a jetty." *A typical work of this little known Dutch artist.* National Maritime Museum, Greenwich.

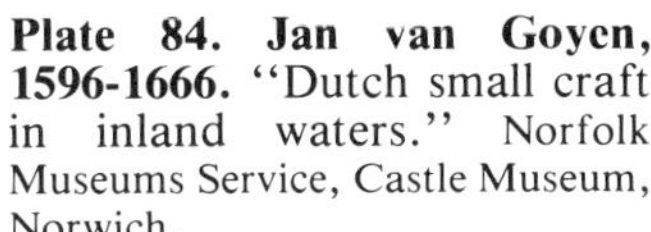

Plate 84. Jan van Goyen, 1596-1666. "Dutch small craft in inland waters." Norfolk Museums Service, Castle Museum, Norwich.

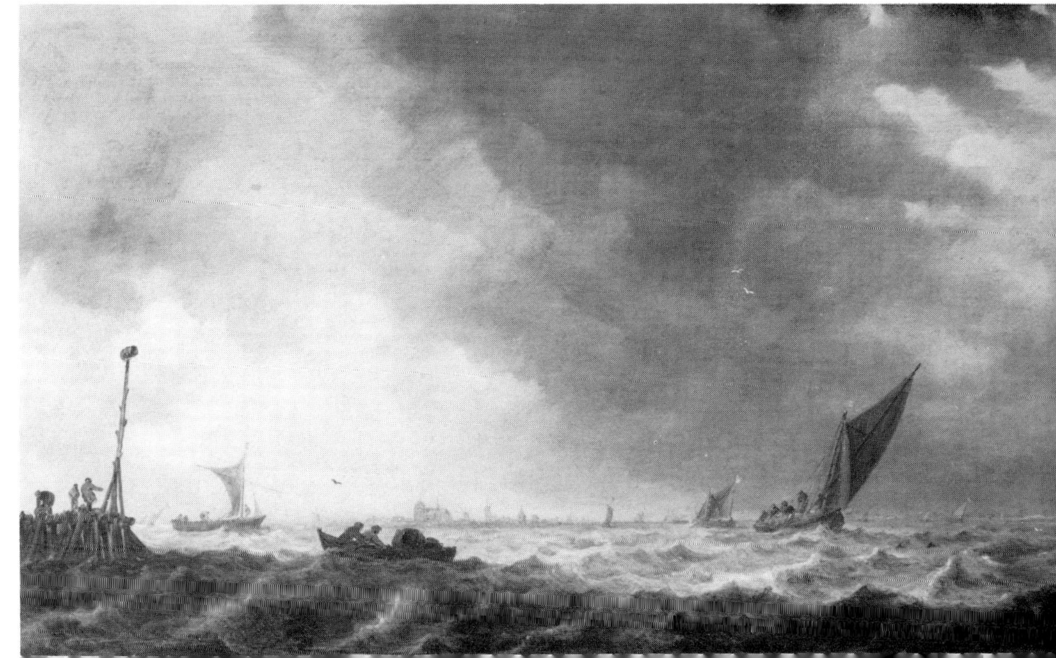

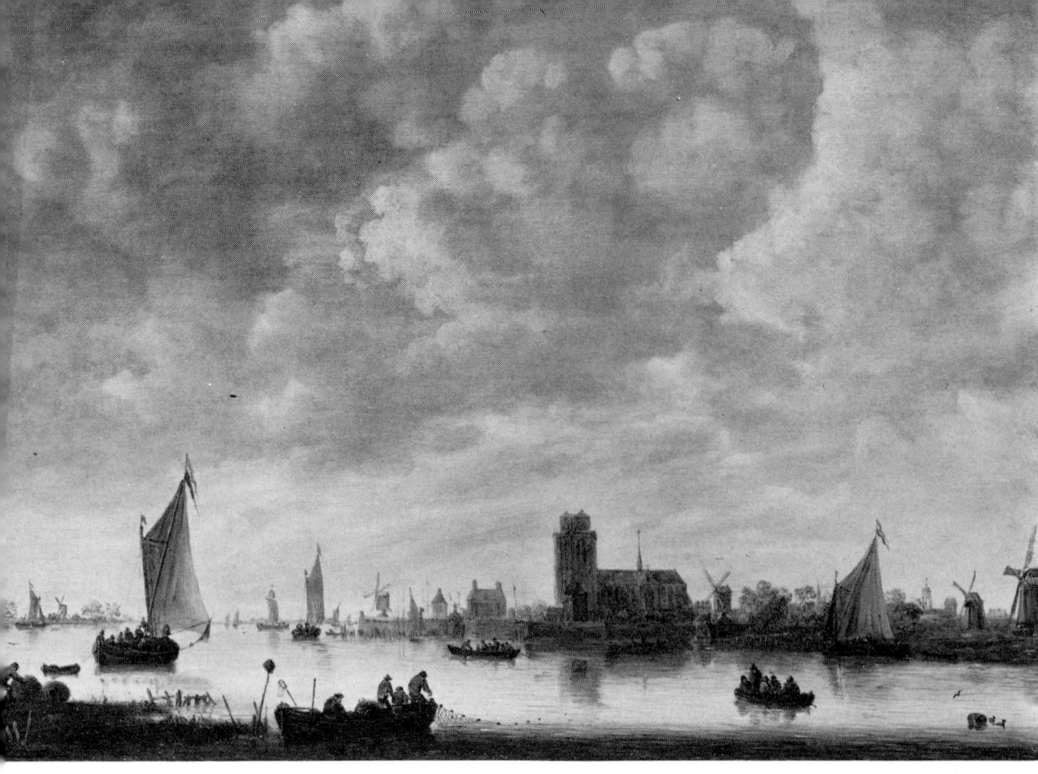

Plate 85. Jan van Goyen, 1596-1666. "Scene near Dordrecht." Rijksmuseum, Amsterdam.

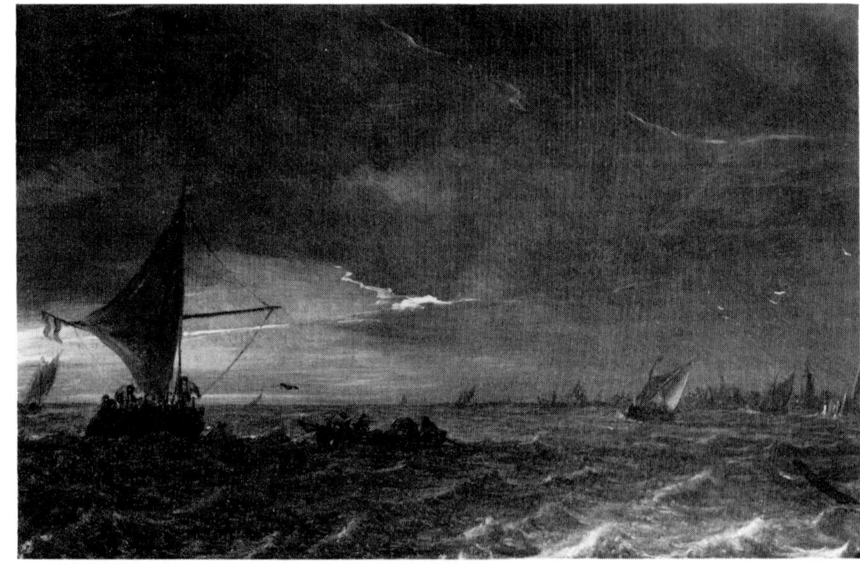

Plate 86. Jan van Goyen, 1596-1666. "Dutch fishing boats in an estuary." National Maritime Museum, Greenwich.

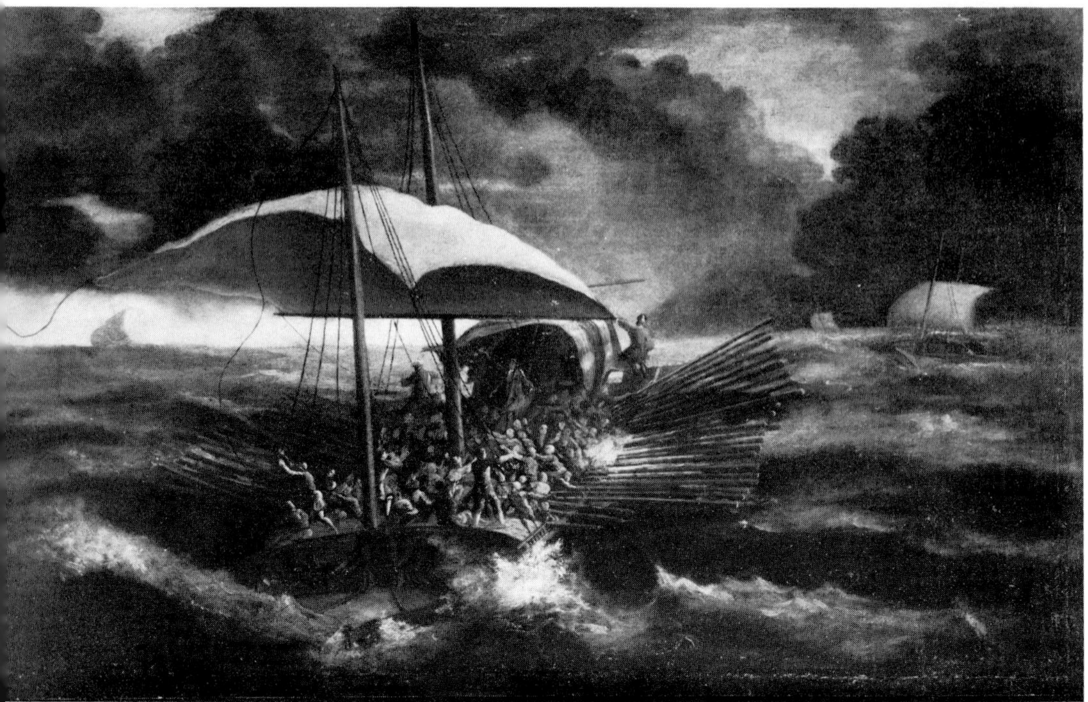

Plate 87. Adriaan van der Cabel, c.1631-1705. "A galley in distress." *A very dramatic painting by this Dutch artist.* Christie's.

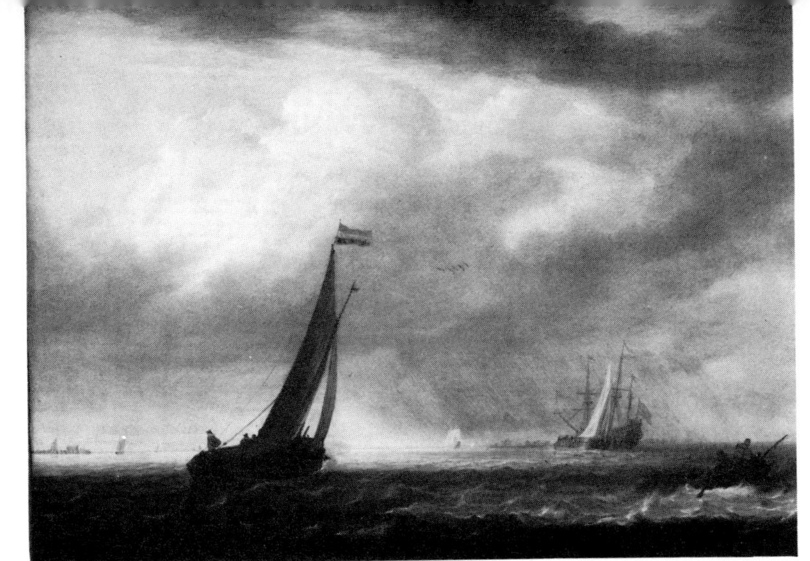

Plate 88. Simon de Vlieger, c.1600-1653. "A squally day in a Dutch estuary." National Maritime Museum, Greenwich.

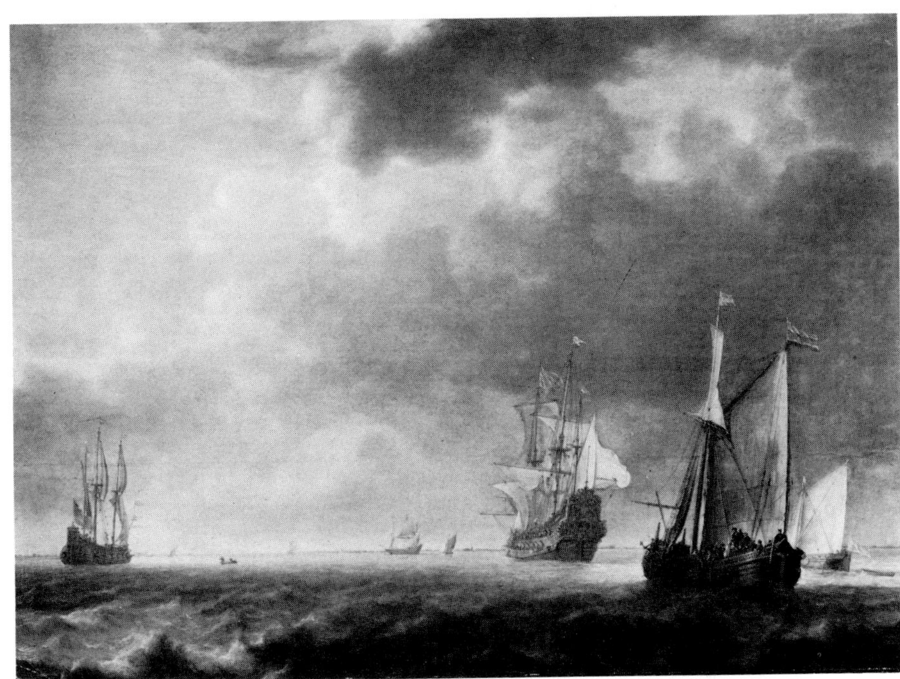

Plate 89. Simon de Vlieger, c.1600-1653. "Estuary scene." Rijksmuseum, Amsterdam.

Plate 90. Simon de Vlieger, c.1600-1653. "Action between the Spanish and the Dutch on the Slaak in September 1631." Rijksmuseum, Amsterdam.

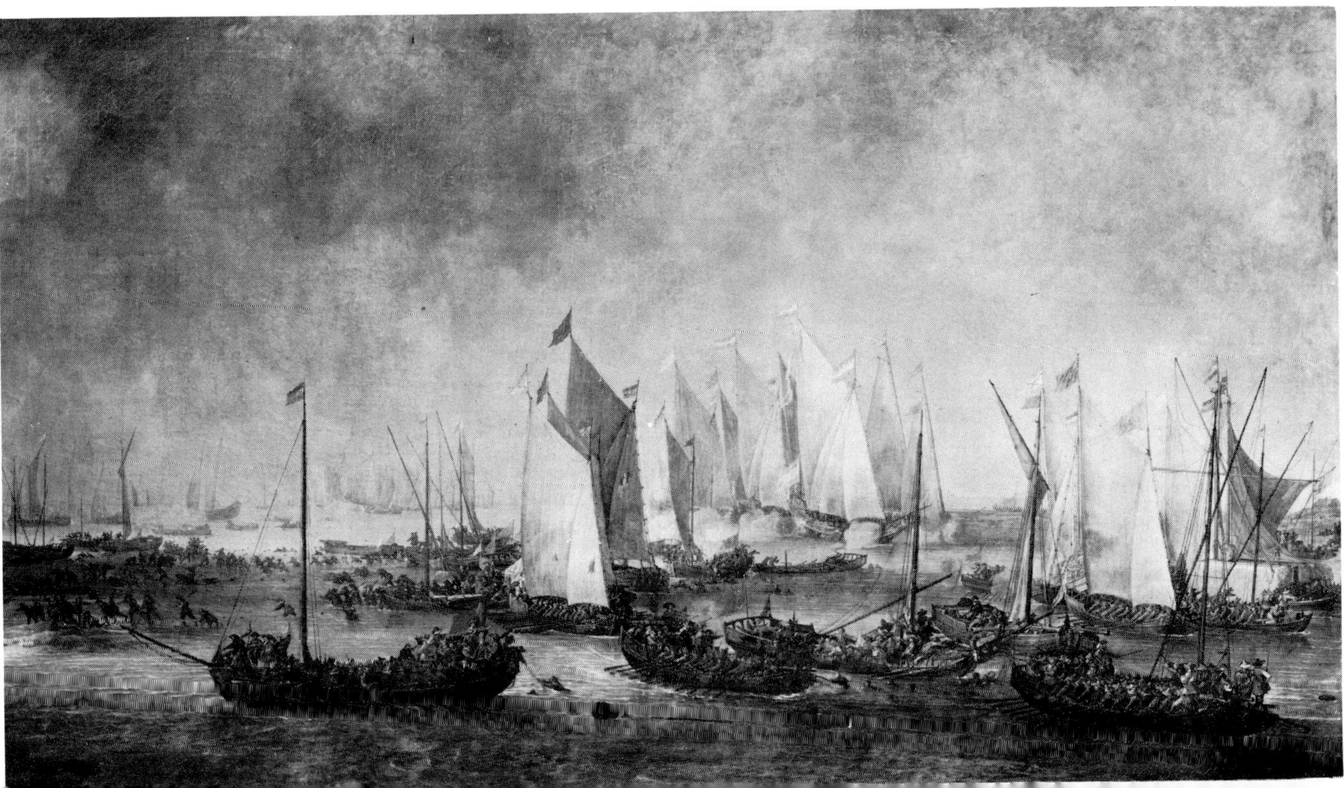

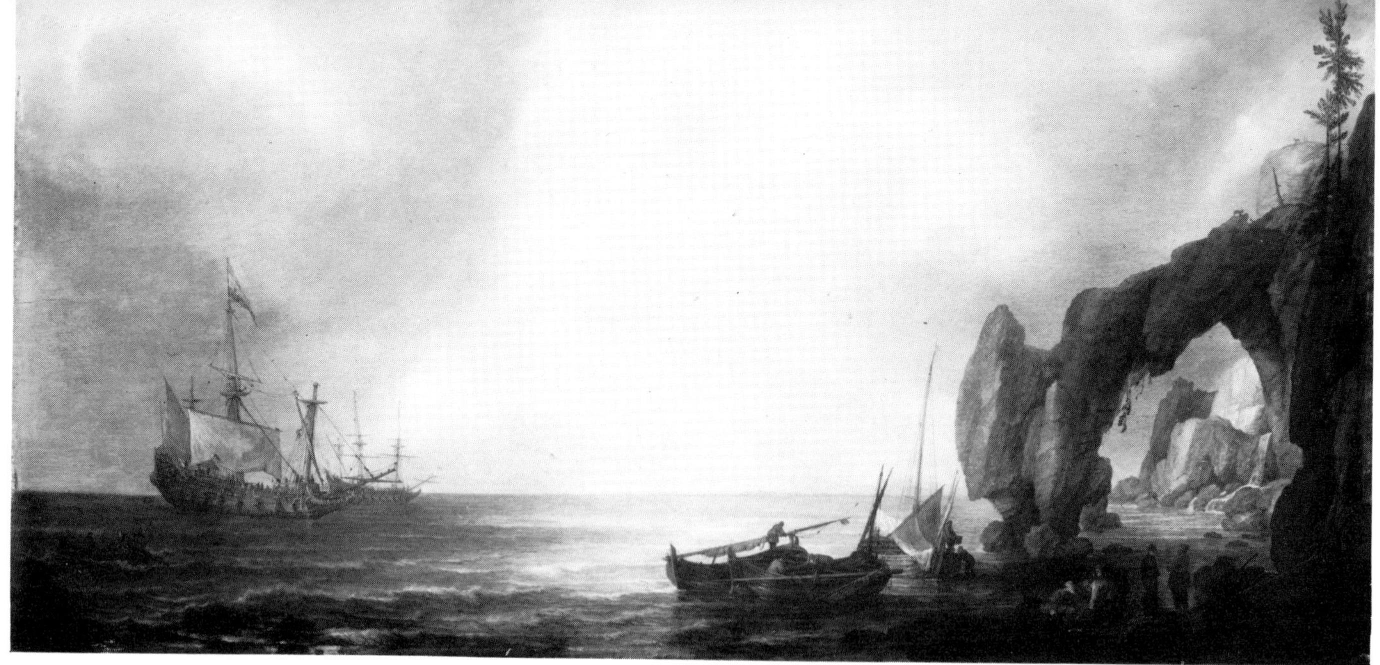

Plate 91. Simon de Vlieger, c.1600-1653. "Dutch ships at anchor off a rocky coast." *De Vlieger was more interested in painting coastal scenes than historical and battle scenes. His excellent use of light and the delicacy of his palette are both apparent in this painting.* National Maritime Museum, Greenwich.

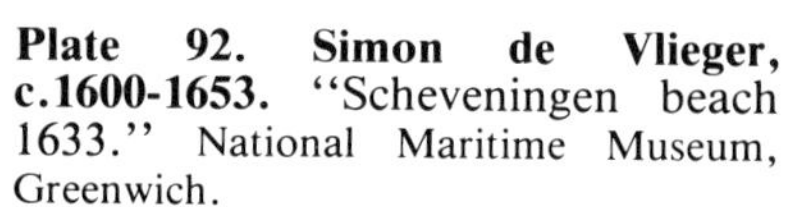

Plate 92. Simon de Vlieger, c.1600-1653. "Scheveningen beach 1633." National Maritime Museum, Greenwich.

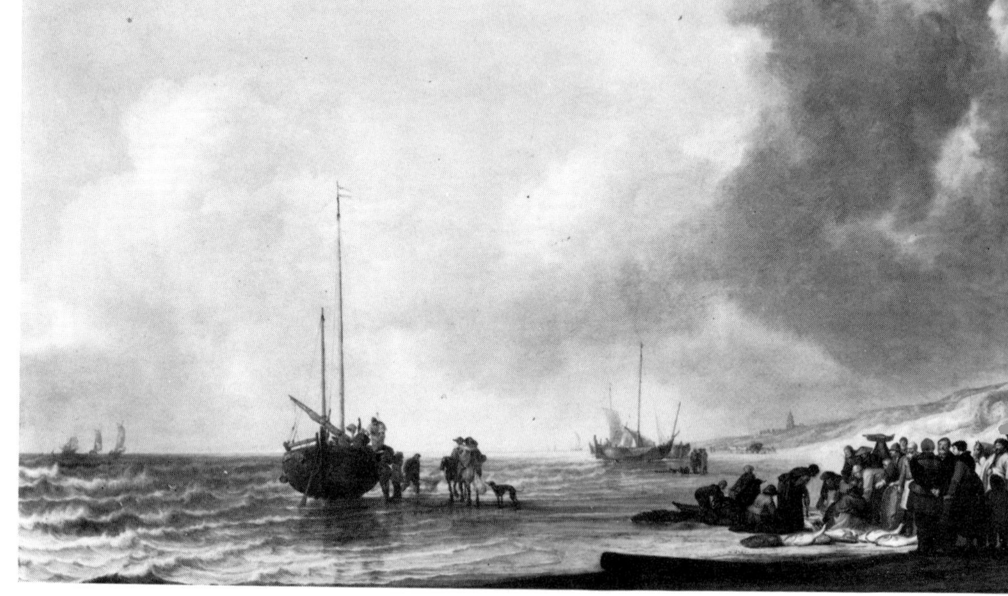

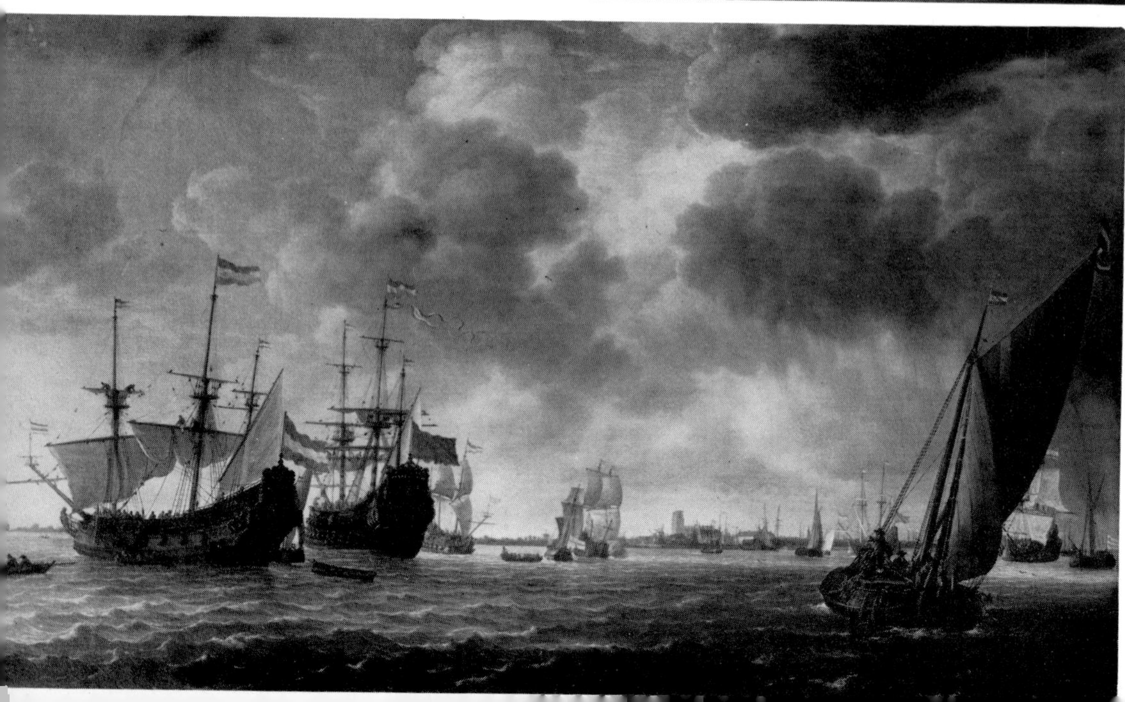

Plate 93. Simon de Vlieger, c.1600-1653. "The River Maas near Rotterdam." State Museum for Art, Copenhagen.

Plate 94. Simon de Vlieger, c.1600-1653. "The ferry boat." National Maritime Museum, Greenwich.

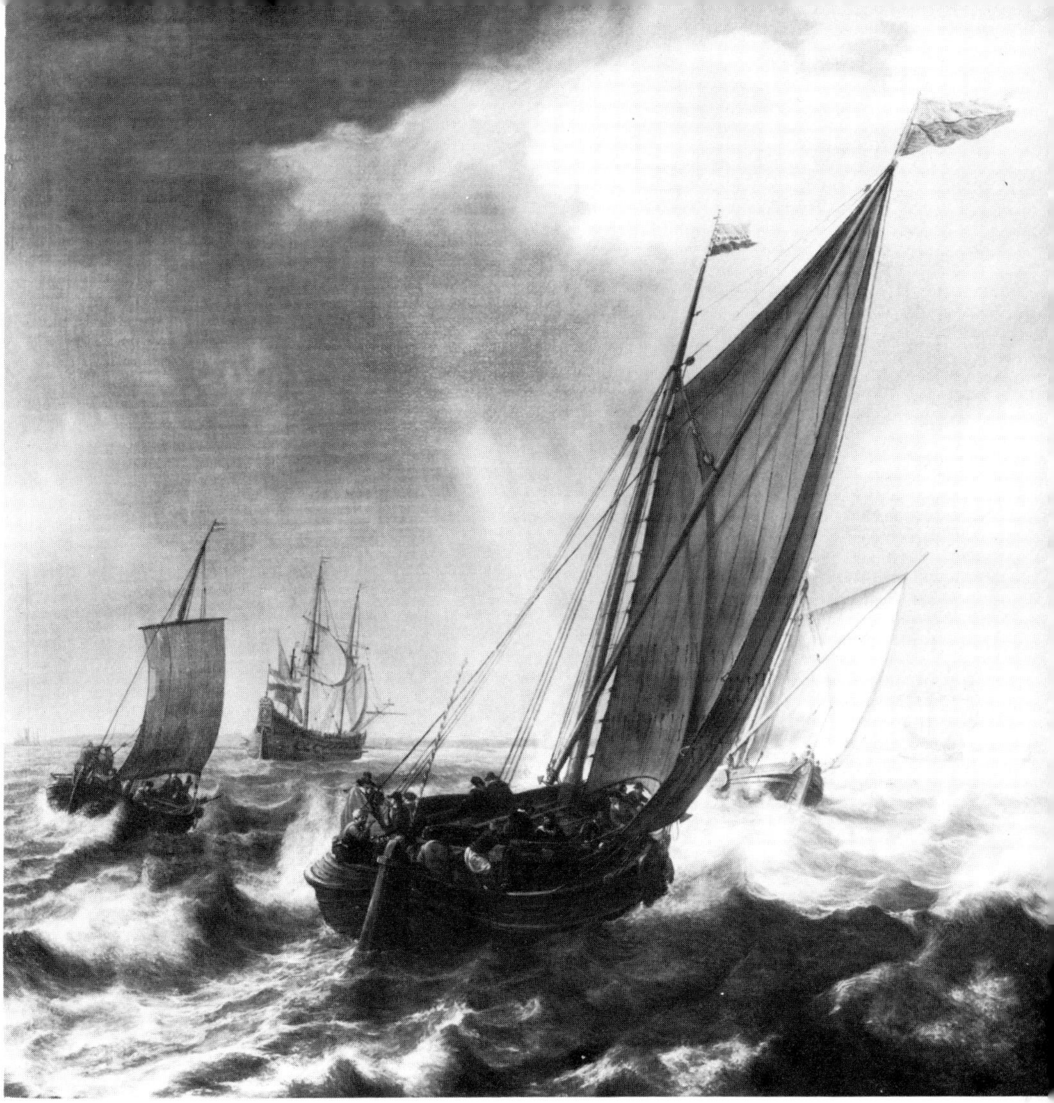

Plate 95. Heerman Witmont, c.1605-aft.1683. "The Battle of the Gabbard in 1653." *Both this and the next illustration are grisaille drawings by one of the earliest and finest exponents of this technique.* National Maritime Museum, Greenwich.

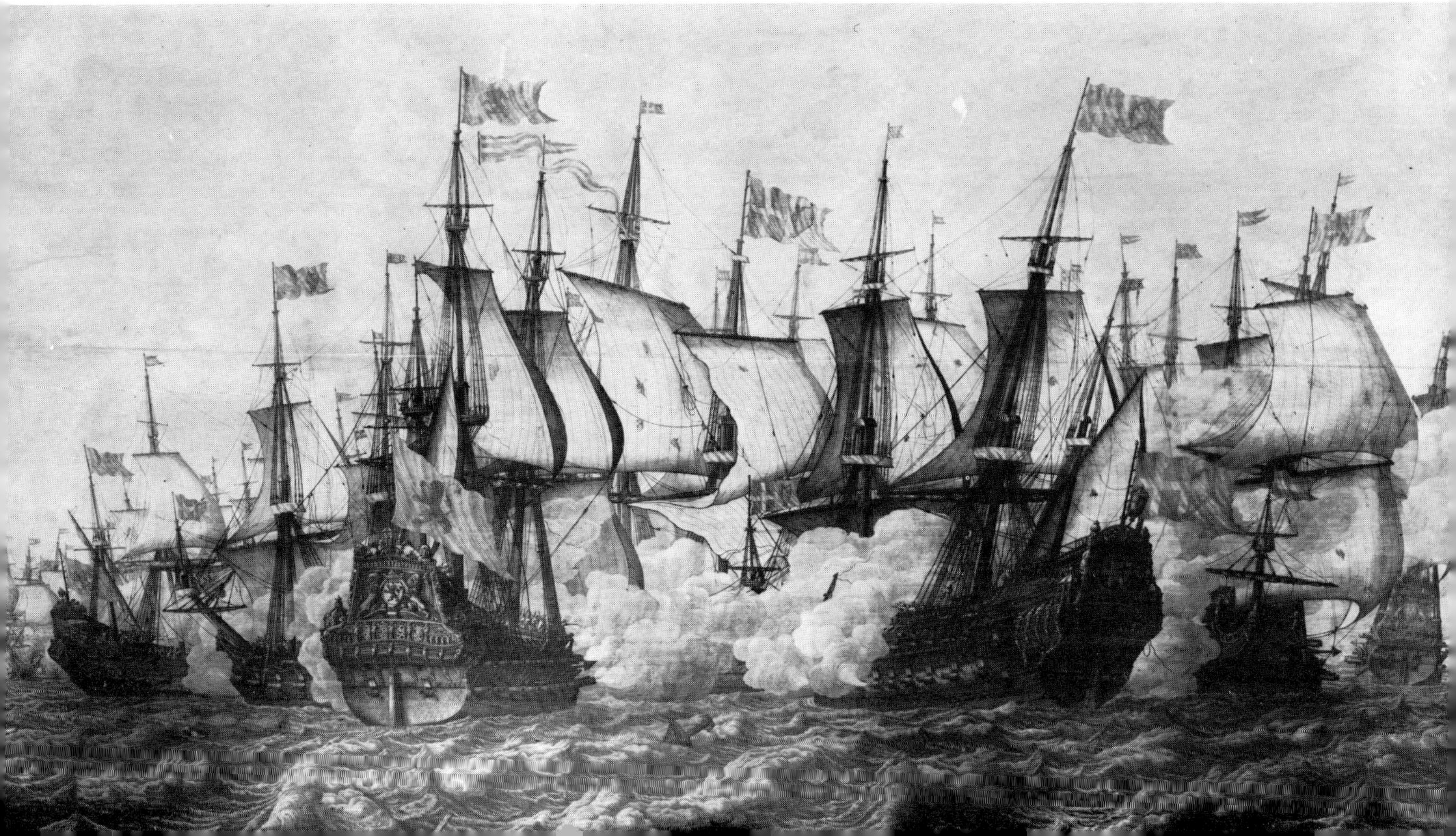

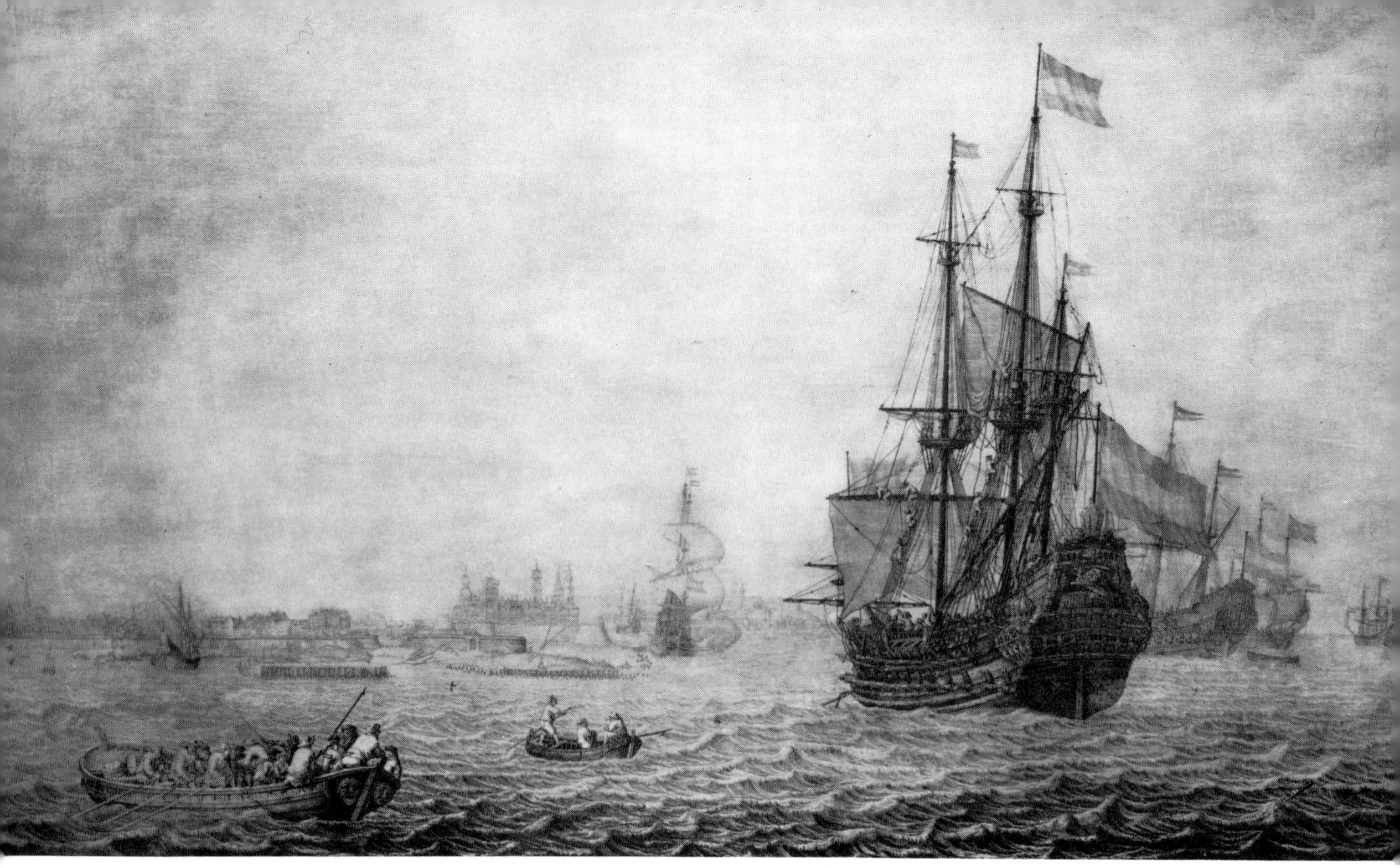

Plate 96. Heerman Witmont, c.1605-aft.1683. "The Dutch flagship *Eendracht* lying off Kronborg Castle in the Sound, dated 1654." *The principal flagship of the Dutch fleet at the Battle of Lowestoft in 1665, she blew up in action with the English flagship* Royal Charles. National Maritime Museum, Greenwich.

Plate 97. Willem van de Velde, the Elder, 1611-1693. "The Battle of the Sound between the Dutch and the Swedes in 1658." National Maritime Museum, Greenwich.

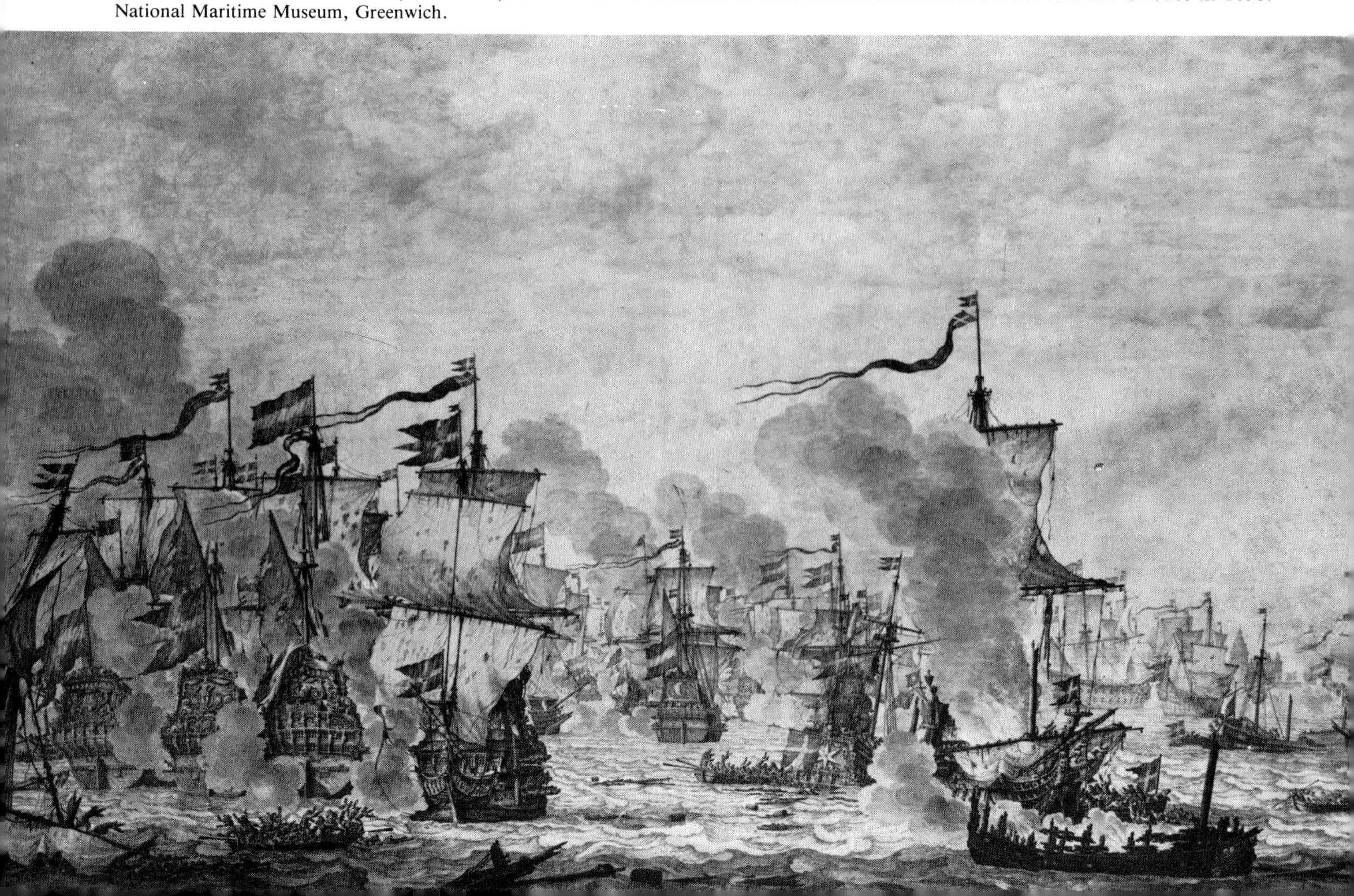

Plate 98. Willem van de Velde, the Elder, 1611-1693. "A Dutch flagship and a Swedish flagship close inshore." National Maritime Museum, Greenwich.

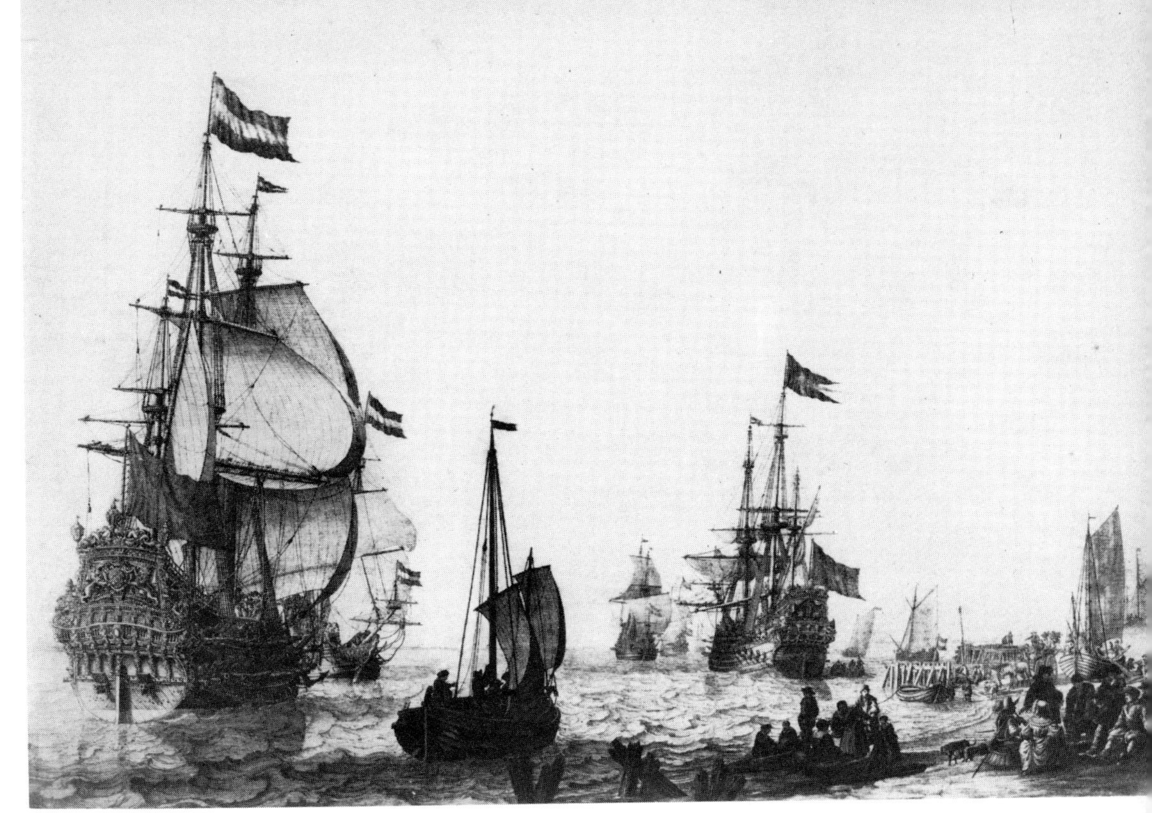

Plate 99. Willem van de Velde, the Elder, 1611-1693. "The Second Battle of Schooneveld, 4th June, 1673." *De Ruyter had returned to his anchorage after the action on 28th May, and this battle was the sequel to it, when he sailed out to give the allies battle again. When he broke off the action in the evening, no ships had been lost on either side. Prince Rupert commanded the Anglo-French fleet.* National Maritime Museum, Greenwich.

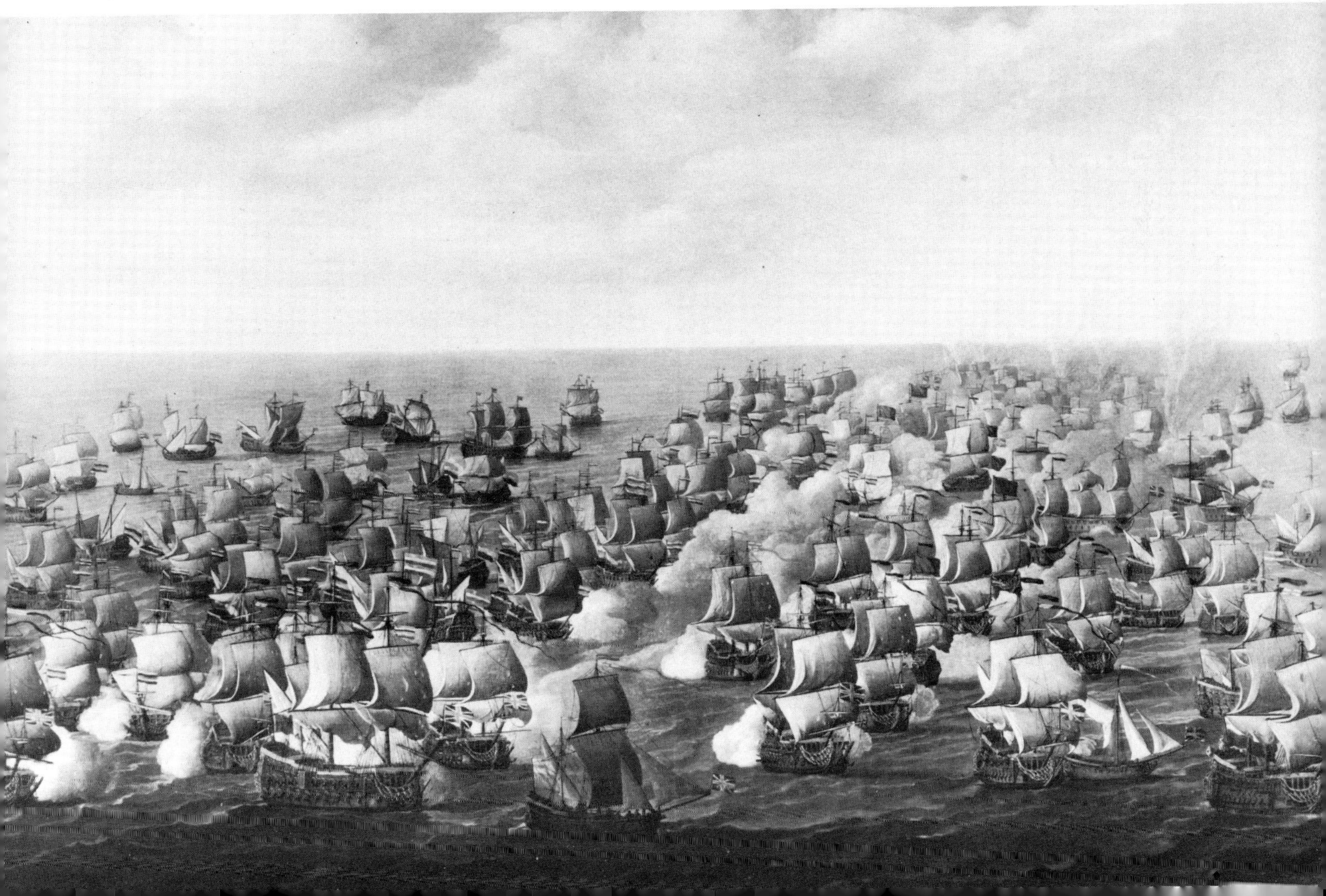

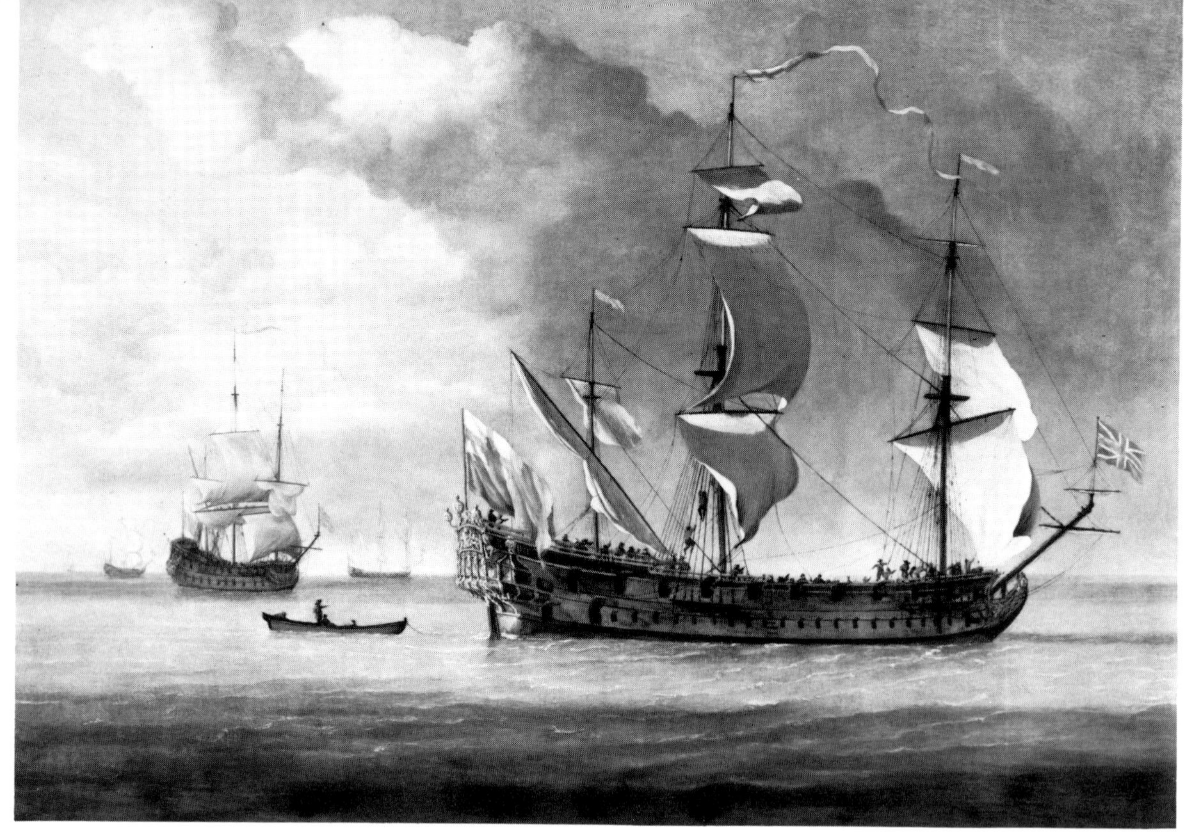

Plate 100. Willem van de Velde, the Elder, 1611-1693. "The *Charles Galley.*" *She and the* James Galley *were built to fight the Barbary galleys, so were given a tier of oar ports to give them freedom of movement independent of the wind.* National Maritime Museum, Greenwich (Greenwich Hospital Collection).

Plate 101. Cornelisz Pietersz Mooy, 1656-1693. "The *Eendracht, Zeven Provincien* and other Dutch men-of-war." National Maritime Museum, Greenwich.

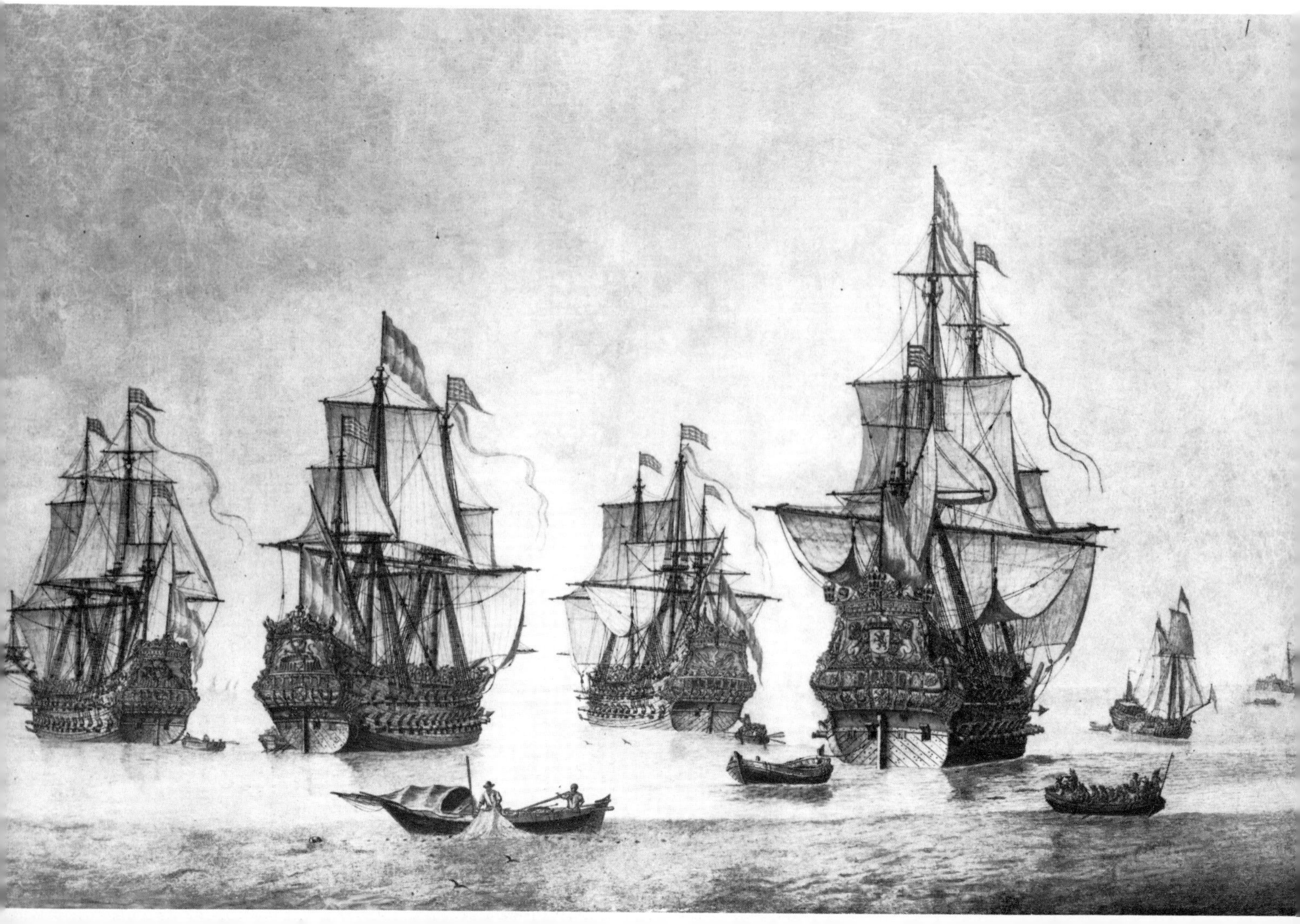

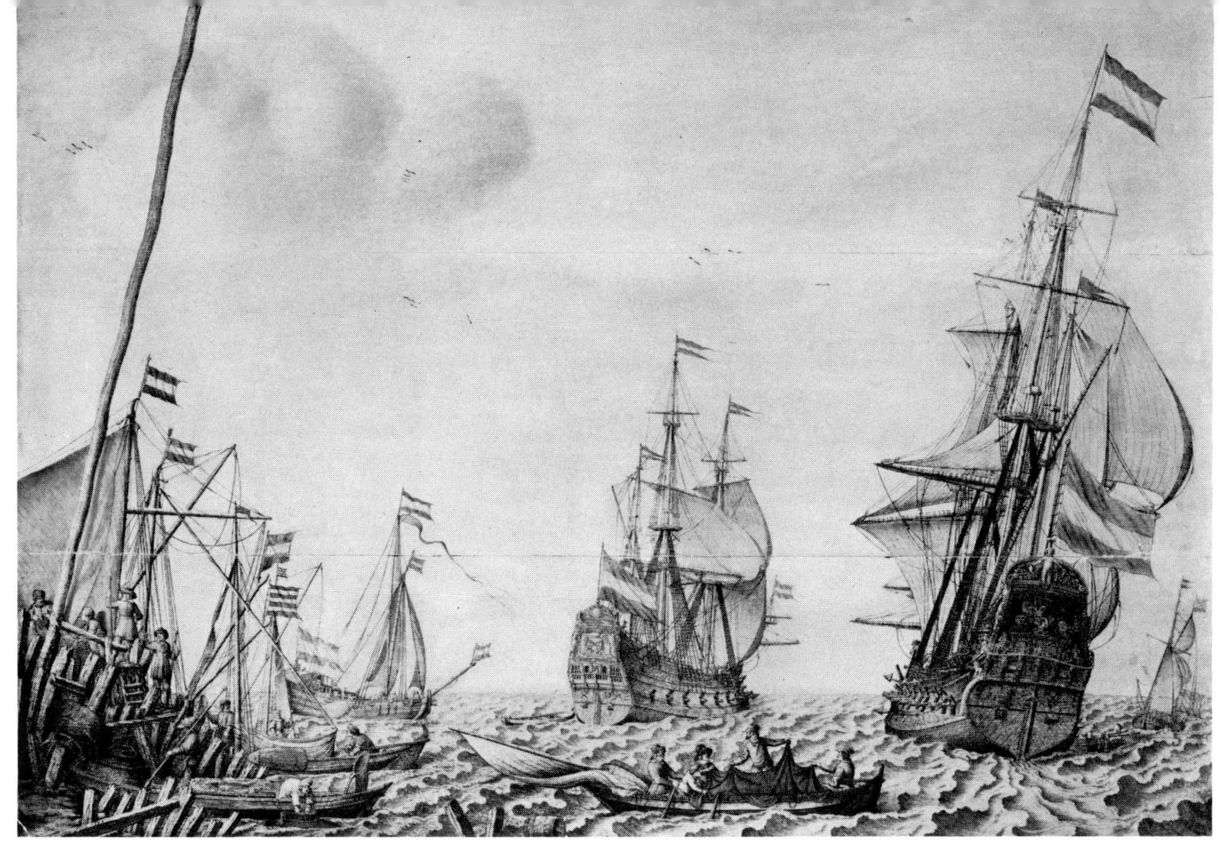

Plate 102. Experiens Sillemans, 1611-1653. "Dutch Indiamen off a jetty, dated 1641." Grisaille drawing. Rijksmuseum, Amsterdam.

Plate 103. Albert Cuyp, 1620-1691. "The Maas at Dordrecht." National Gallery of Art (Andrew Mellon Collection), Washington.

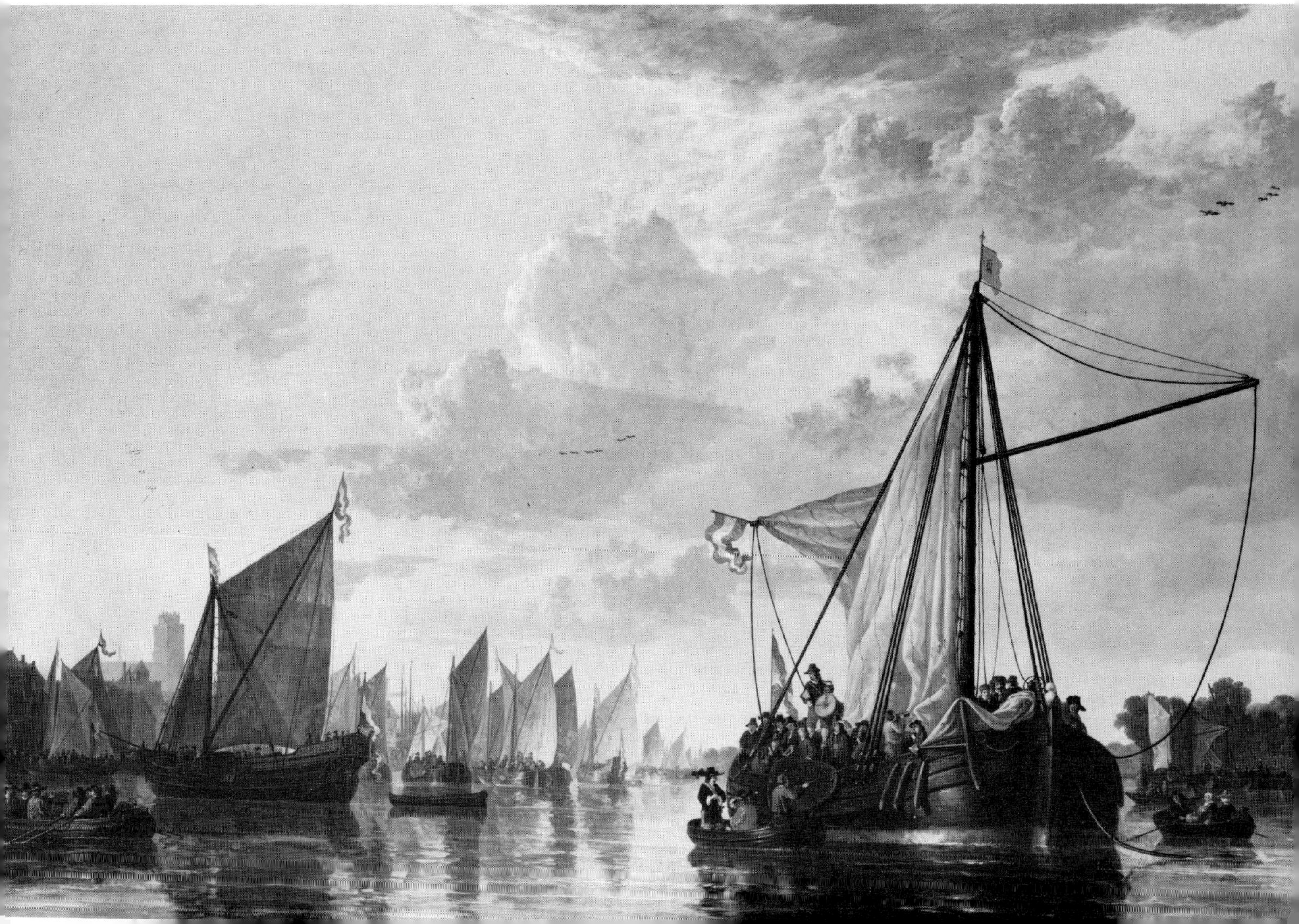

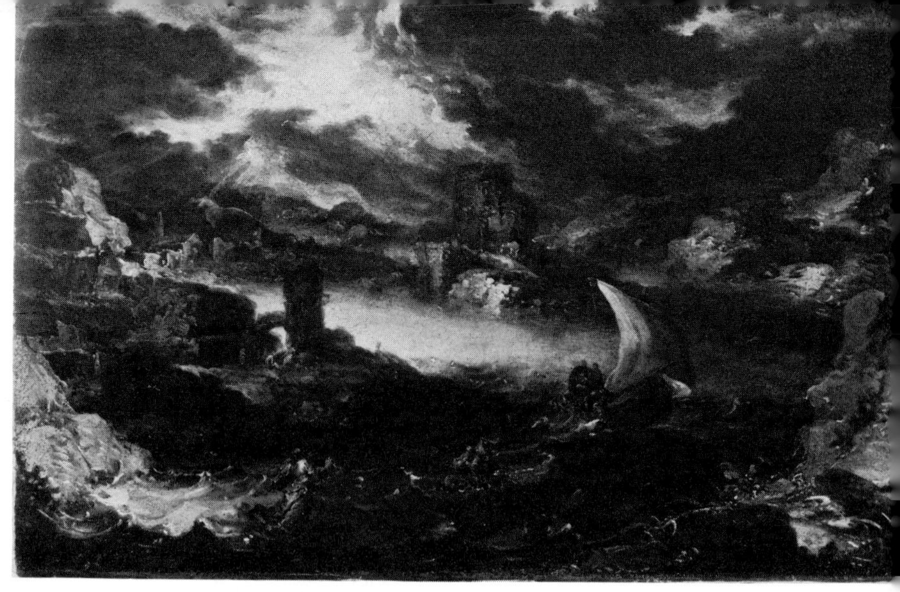

Plate 104. Marco Ricci, 1676-1729. "Christ on the sea of Galilee." *Very similar in style to Plattenburg (Plates 29, 30), this Italian artist painted a number of stormy, violent marine scenes, with slight delineation. His colours are black and heavy, sombre, dark greens.* State Museum for Fine Art, Copenhagen.

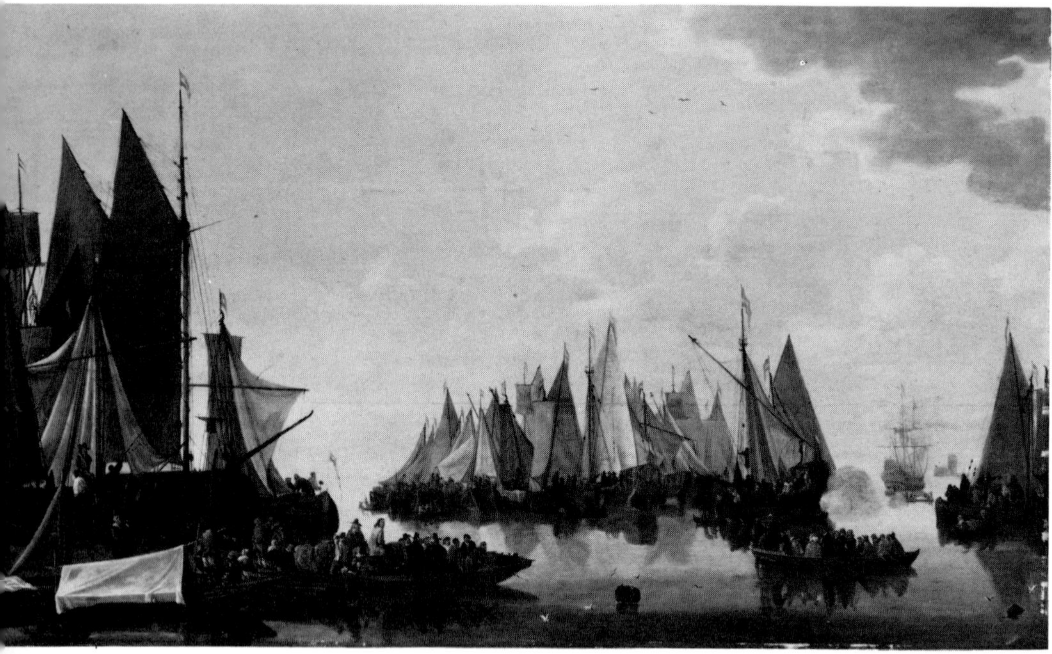

Plate 105. Hendrik de Meyer, c.1600-aft.1690. "The embarkation of troops on a Dutch river." State Museum for Fine Art, Copenhagen.

Plate 106. Dirck Stoop, c.1610-c.1686. "The *Royal Charles* off Lisbon in April 1662." *Lord Sandwich, who brought Charles II out of exile, was further employed to accompany Catherine of Braganza to England in the* Royal Charles. Private collection.

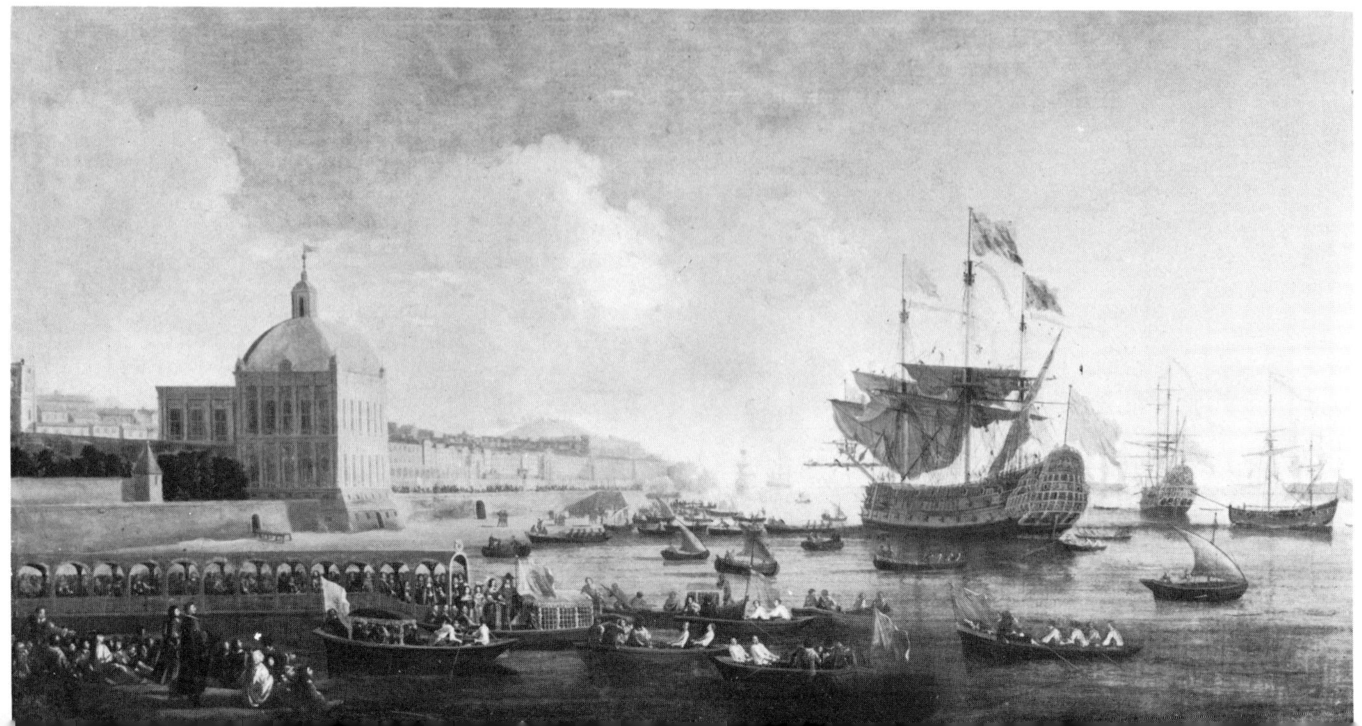

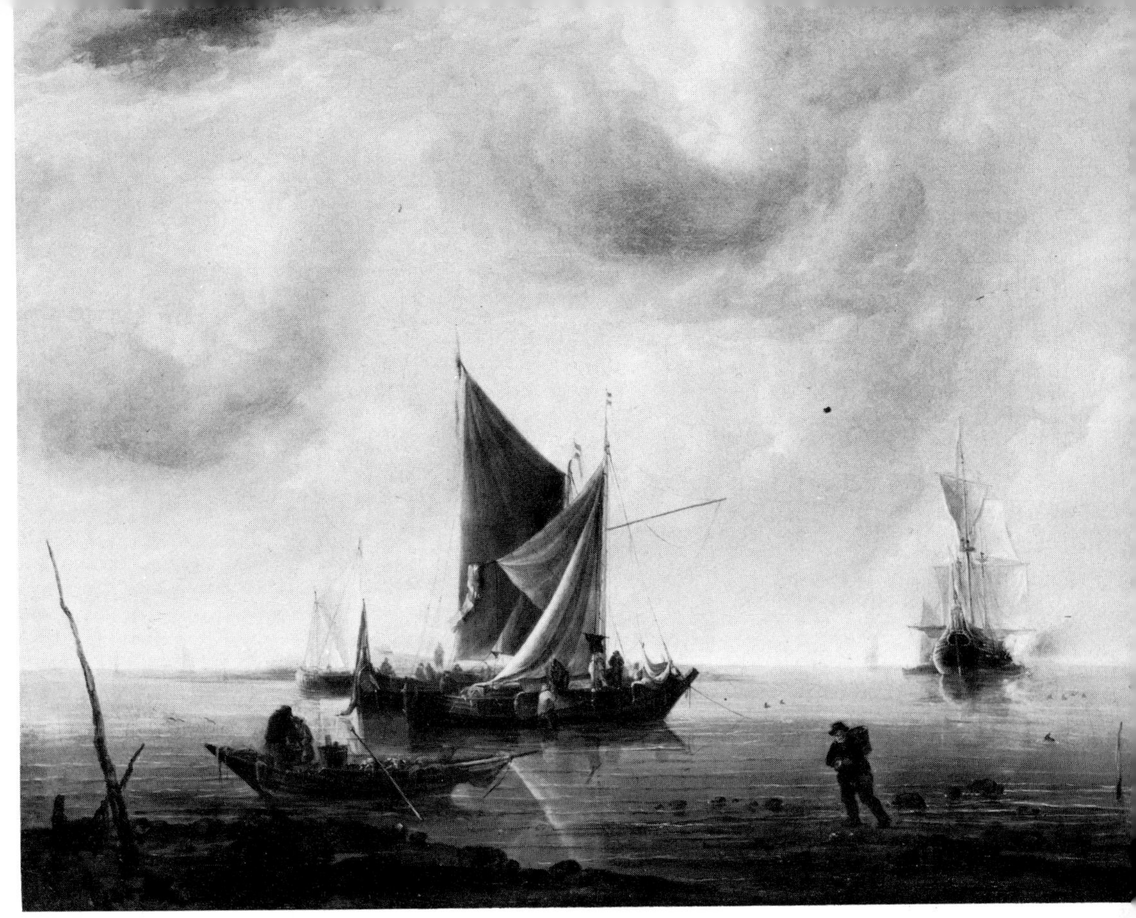

Plate 107. Jan van de Capelle, 1624-1679. ''A calm sea with fishing boats.'' *Capelle was one of the great masters.* Rijksmuseum, Amsterdam.

Plate 108. Jan van de Capelle, 1624-1679. ''A Dutch barge landing on a beach, with a states yacht beyona and other shipping in a calm.'' Private collection.

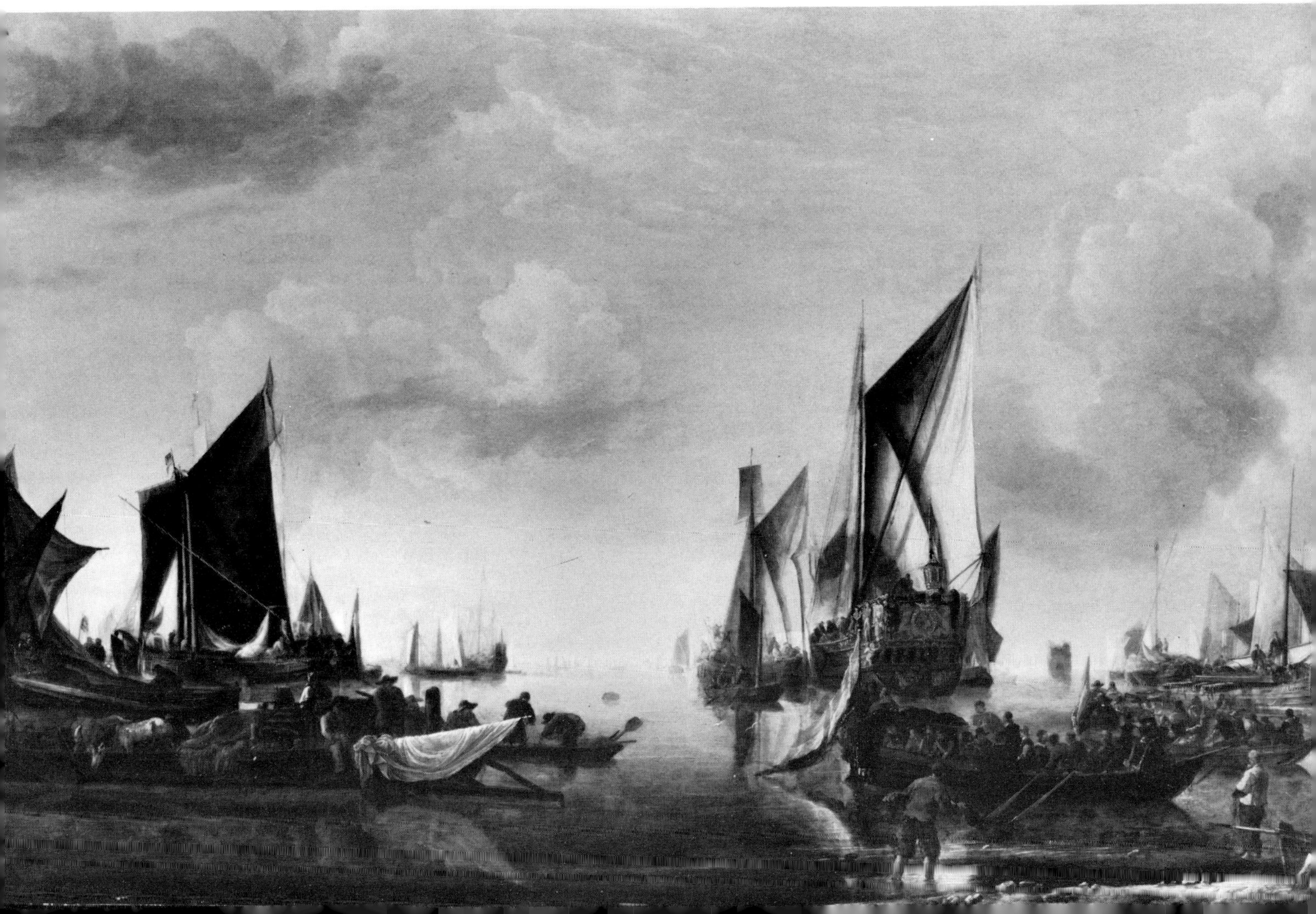

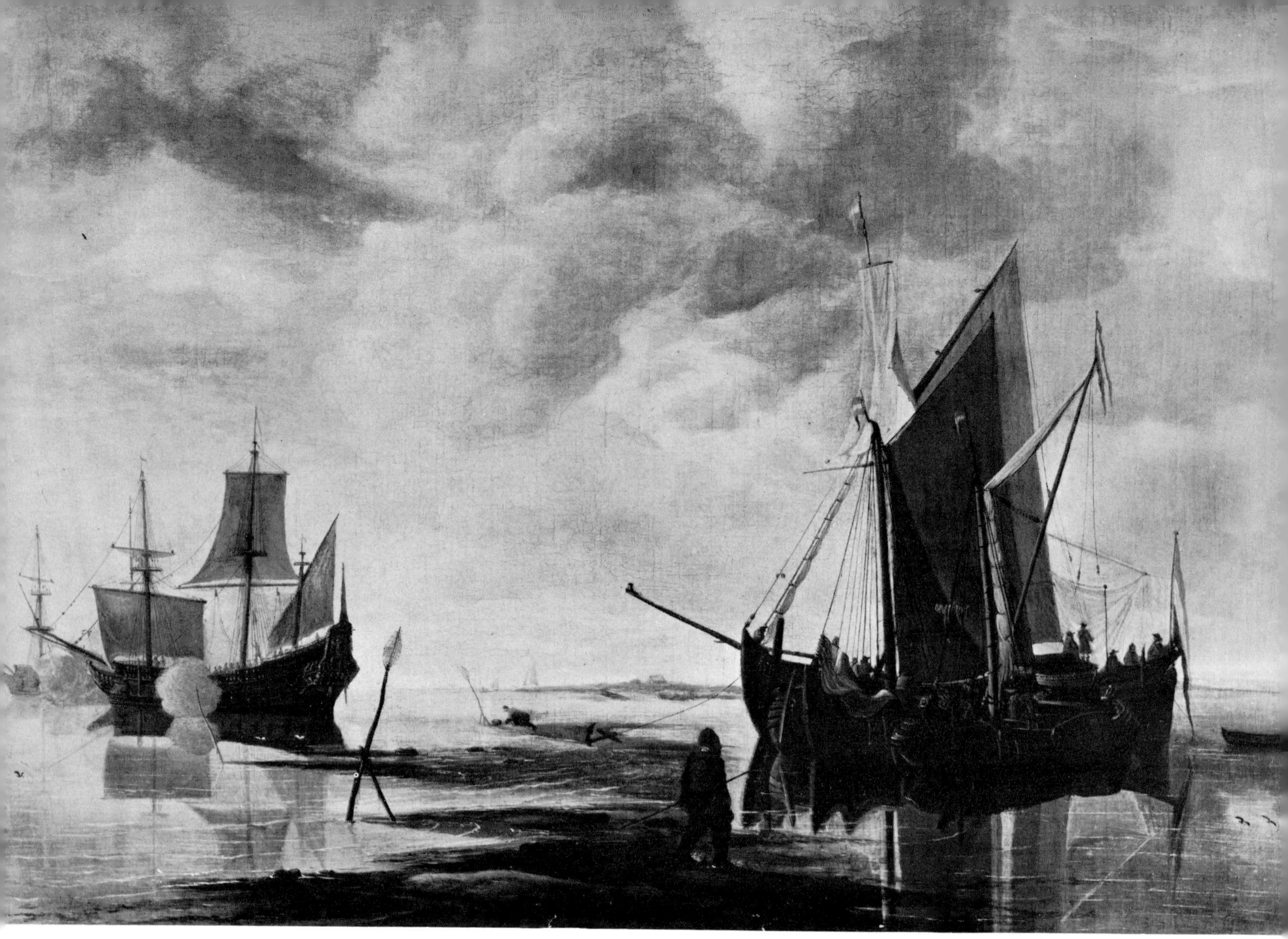

Plate 109. Jan van de Capelle, 1624-1679. "Dutch shipping becalmed at low tide off a beach." *Capelle's work can be confused with Cuyp's who painted similar scenes (Plate 103).* Kunsthistorisches Museum, Vienna.

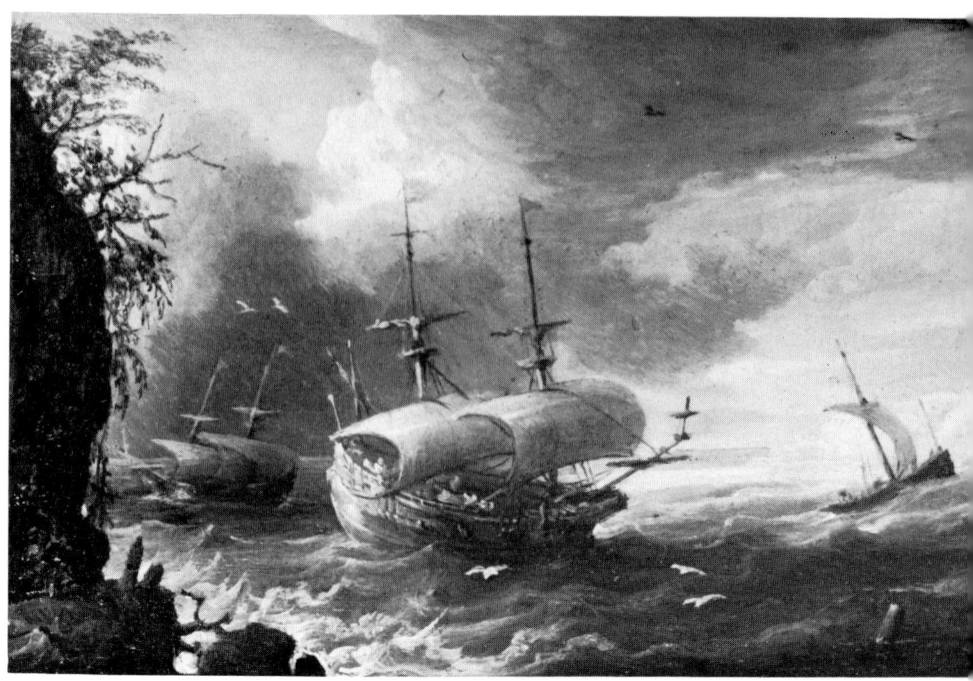

Plate 110. Pieter van den Velde, 1634-aft.1687. "Shipping off a rocky coast." *A tiny luminous sketch by this painter.* National Maritime Museum, Greenwich.

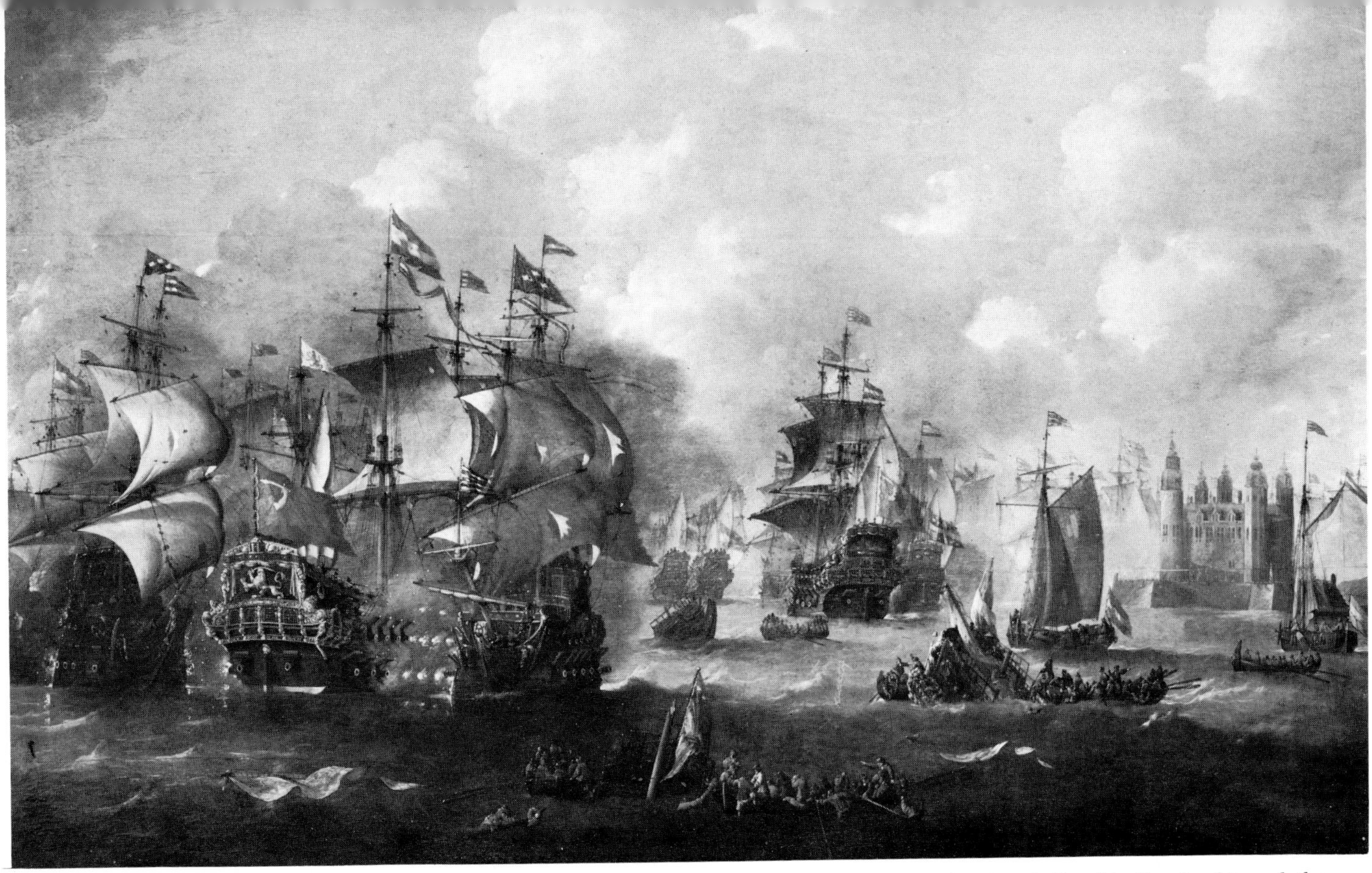

Plate 111. Pieter van den Velde, 1634-aft.1687. "The Battle of the Sound in 1658." *The Dutch flagship* Eendracht *and the Swedish flagship* Viktoria *are engaged to the left. Kronborg Castle is on the right.* Rijksmuseum, Amsterdam.

Plate 112. Jeronimus van Diest, 1631-1673. "The captured *Royal Charles* in Dutch waters in June 1667." *The British flag of the captured ship is towed behind, and the Dutch flag flown.* Rijksmuseum, Amsterdam.

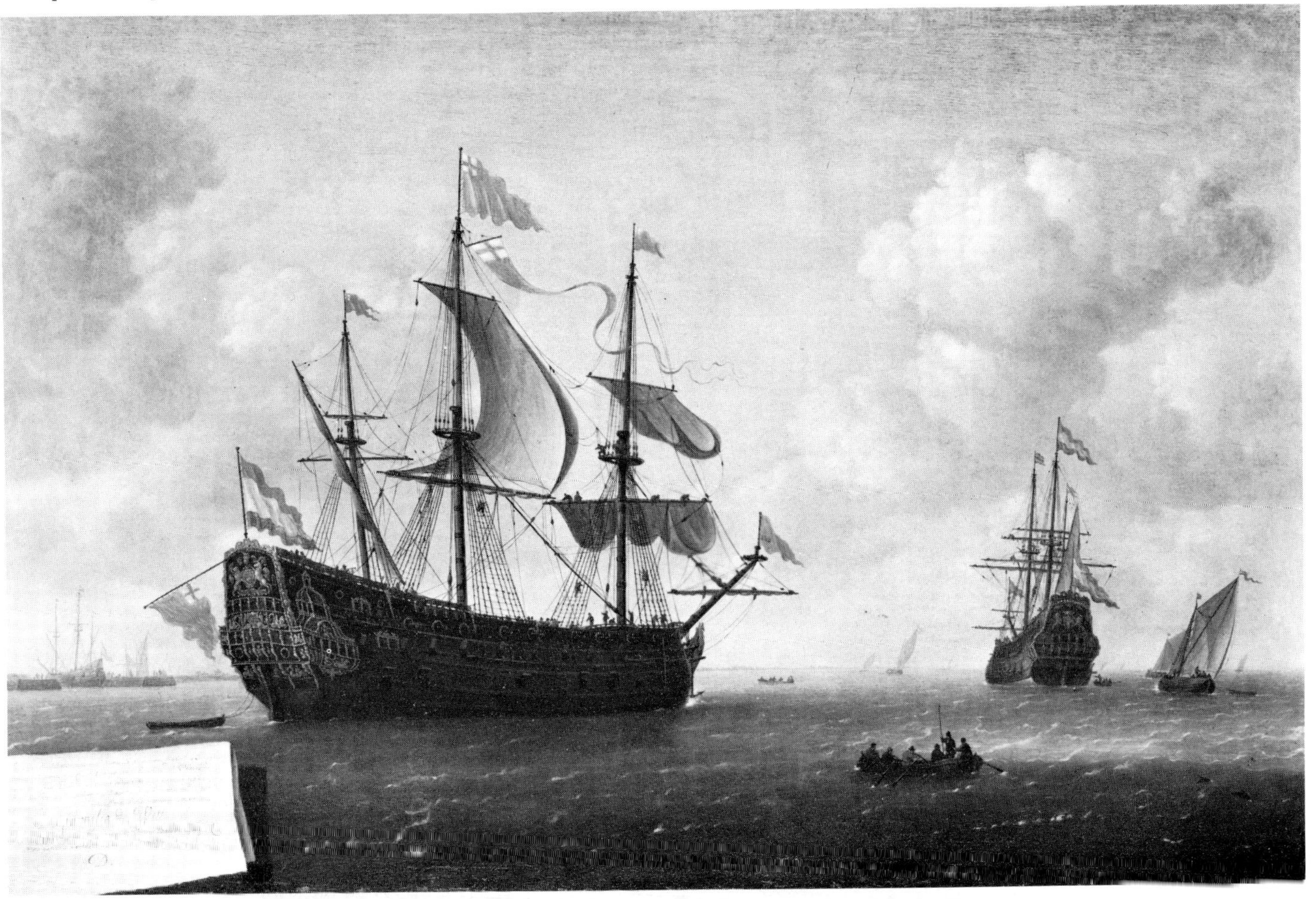

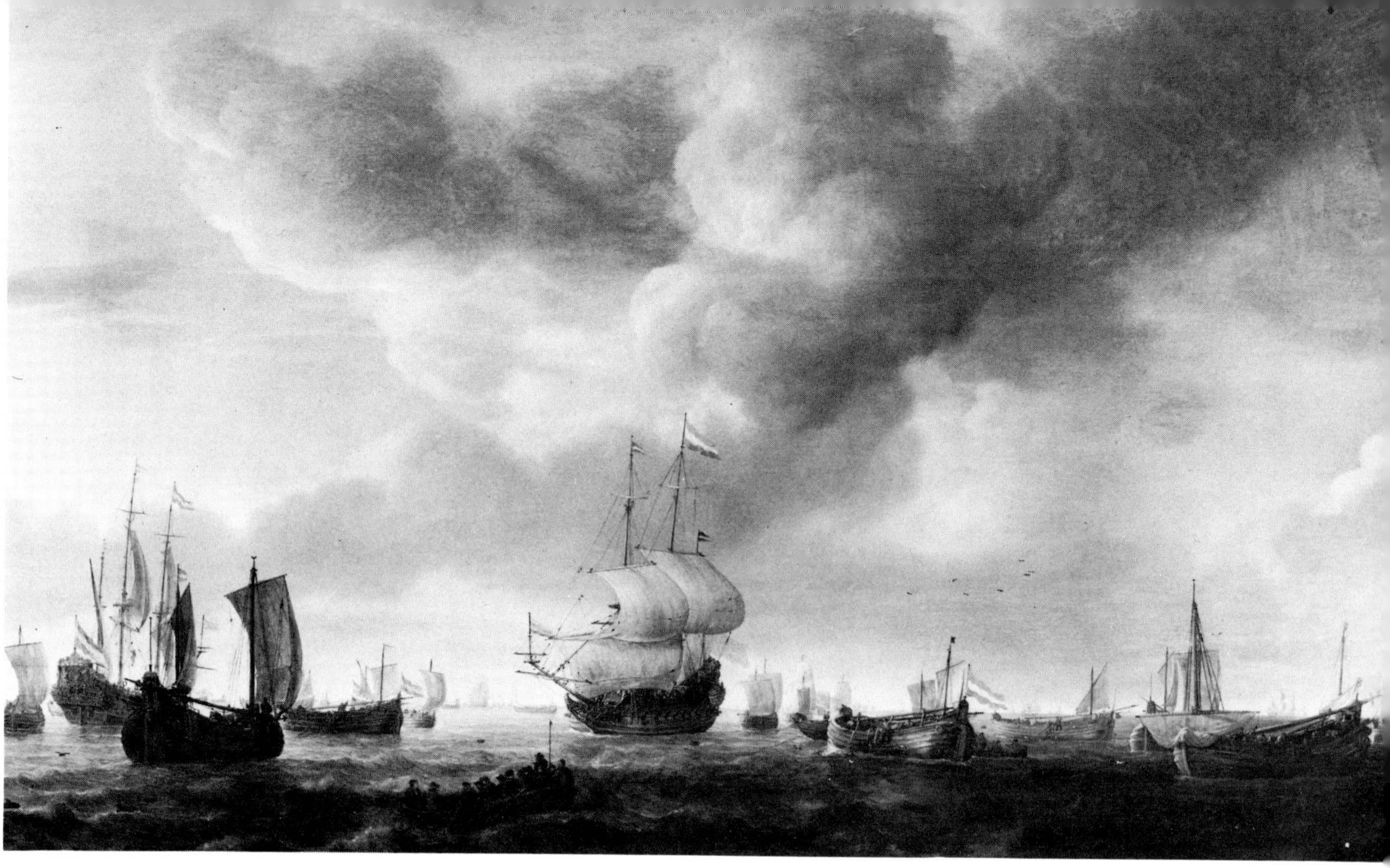

Plate 113. Jeronimus van Diest, 1631-1673. "The Dutch herring fleet with its escort." *A less well-known example of van Diest's work.* Scheepvaart Museum, Amsterdam.

Plate 114. Jeronimus van Diest, 1631-1673. "The *Eendracht.*" *The lion with cleaver insignia (the town's heraldic symbol) can be seen on the stern of the well-known Dutch flagship.* National Maritime Museum, Greenwich.

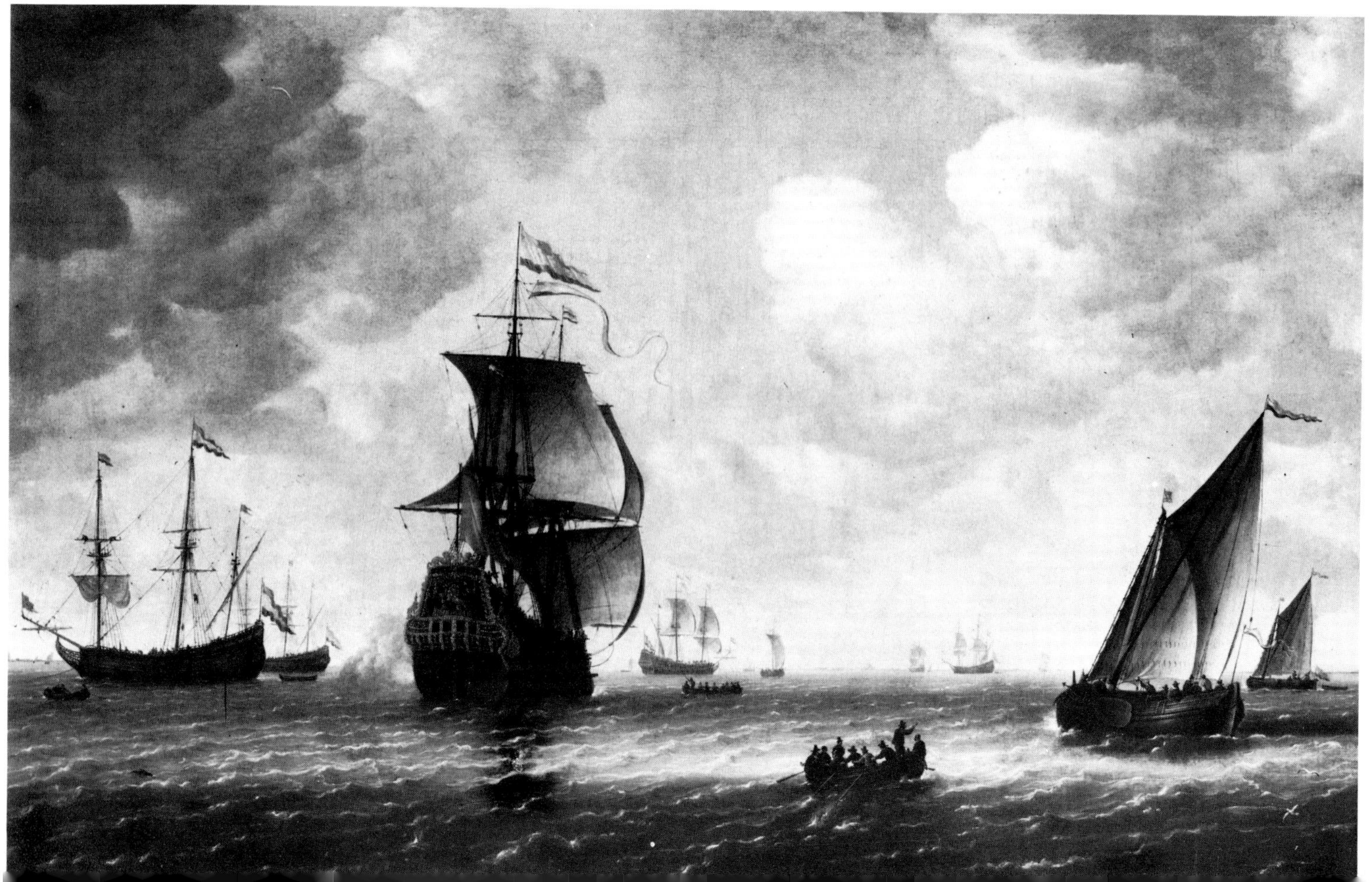

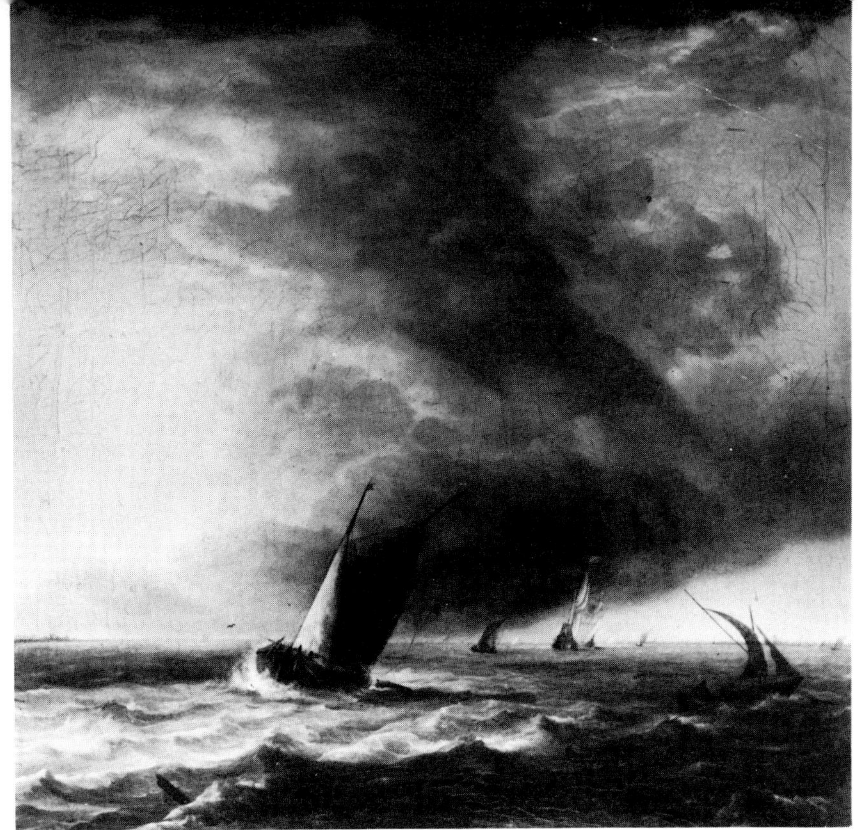

Plate 115. Hendrick-Jacobsz Dubbels, c.1620-1676. "A kaag in a breeze." *Dubbel's work can be confused with Bakhuizen's, who was Dubbels' most illustrious pupil.* Staatliches Museum, Schwerin.

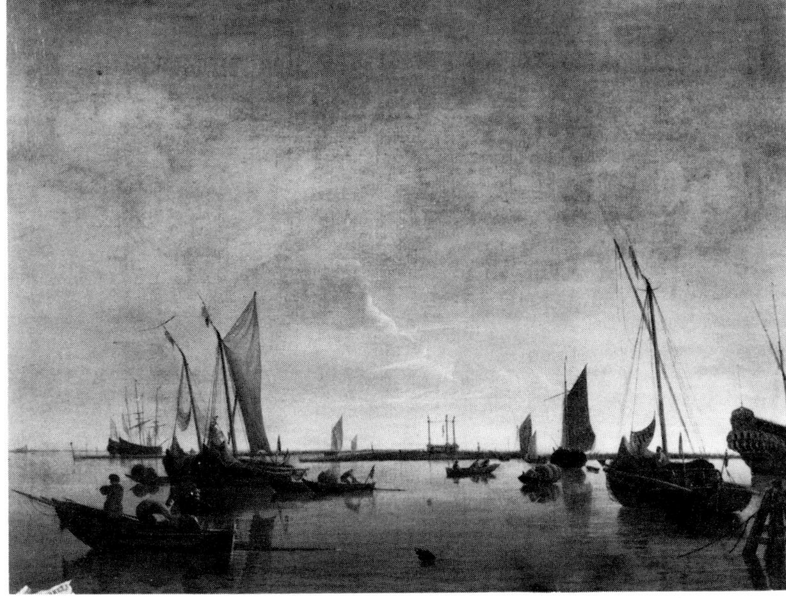

Plate 116. Hendrick-Jacobsz Dubbels, c.1620-1676. "A Dutch harbour after sundown." Boymans-van Beuningen Museum, Rotterdam.

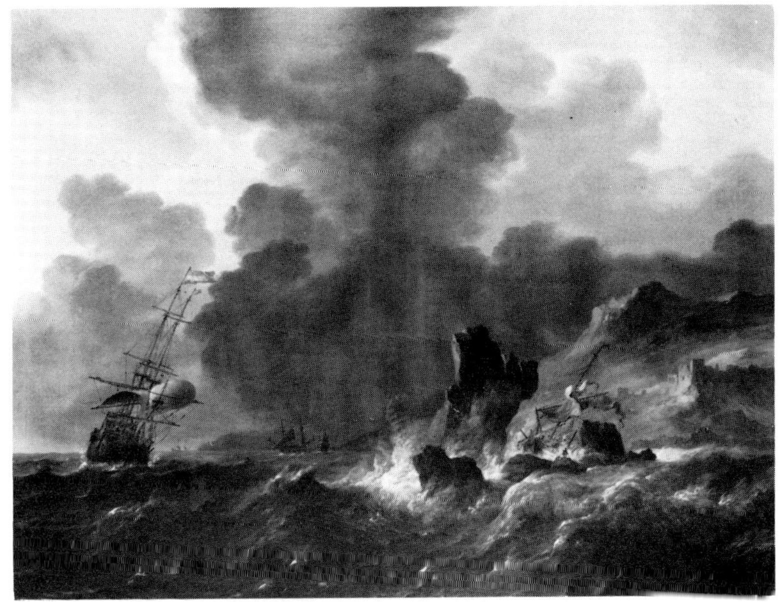

Plate 117. Ludolf Bakhuizen, 1631-1708. "A Dutch flagship off a rocky coast with a wreck." *A painting from the artist's early 'black' period.* National Maritime Museum, Greenwich.

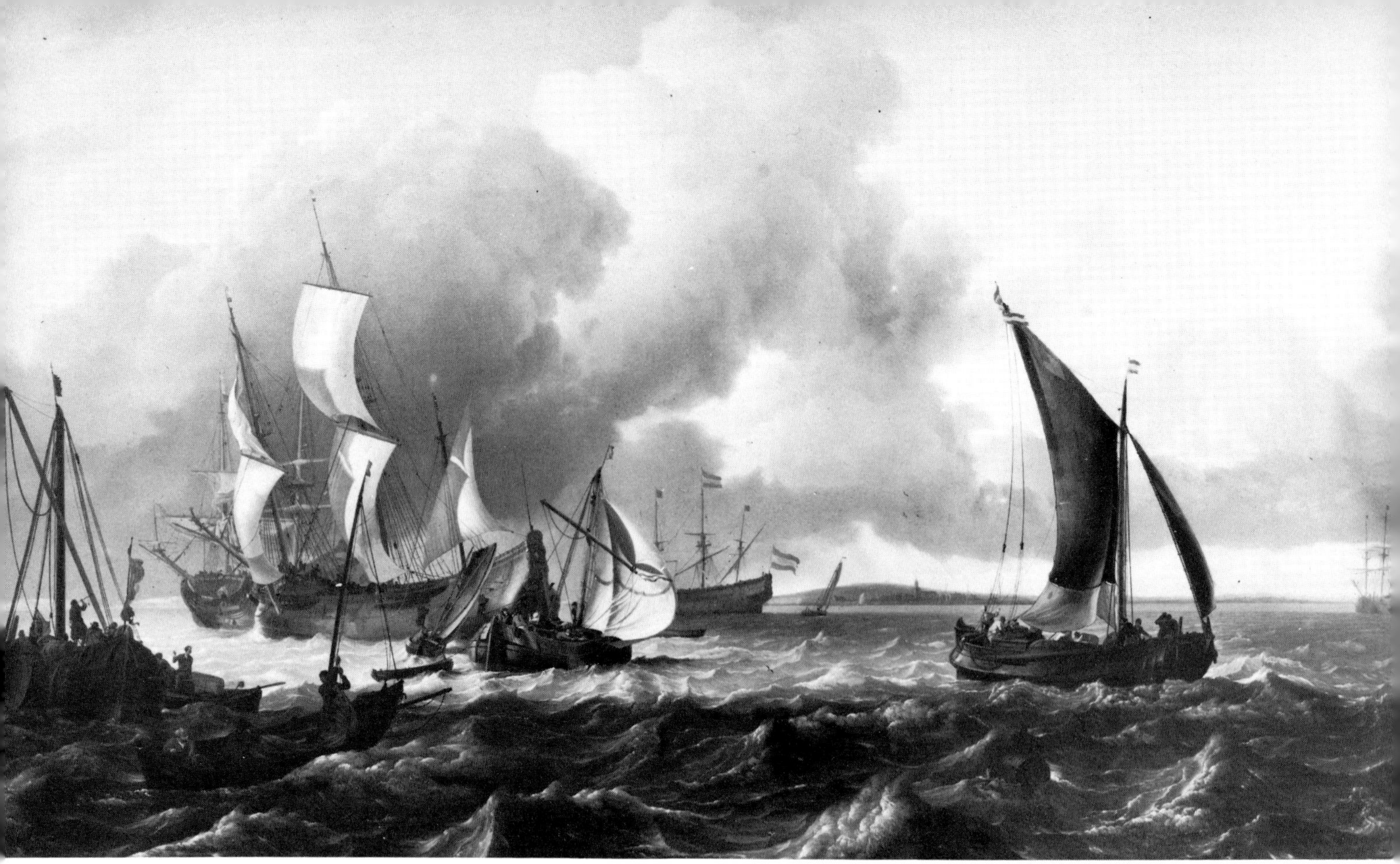

Plate 118. Ludolf Bakhuizen, 1631-1708. "Dutch shipping off the coast in a fresh breeze about 1665." *A painting from Bakhuizen's middle and best period. A highly realistic the luminous, icy blue sea.* National Maritime Museum, Greenwich.

Plate 119. Ludolf Bakhuizen, 1631-1708. "The *Royal Charles* being taken into Dutch waters after her capture in the Medway in 1667." National Maritime Museum, Greenwich.

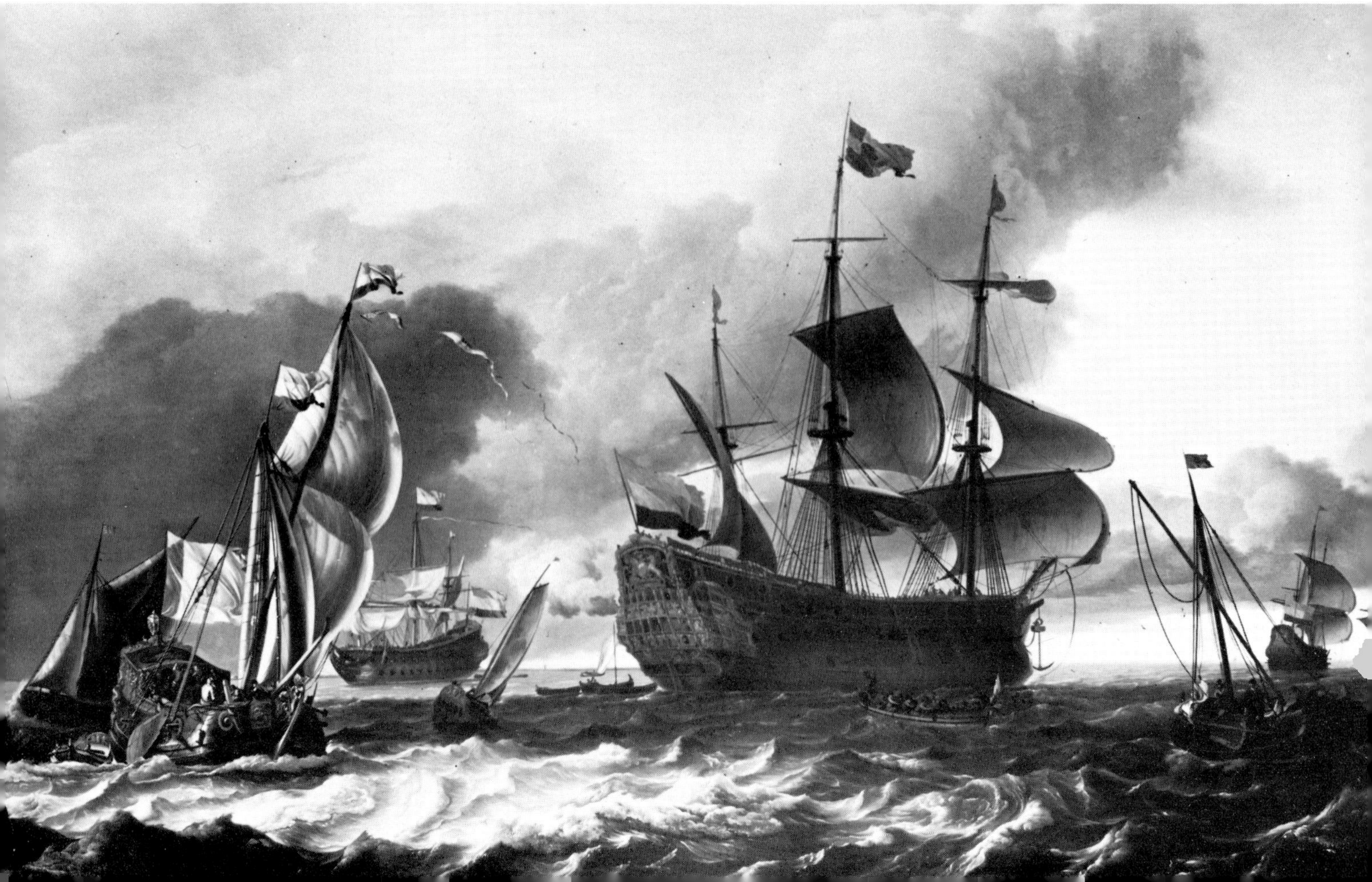

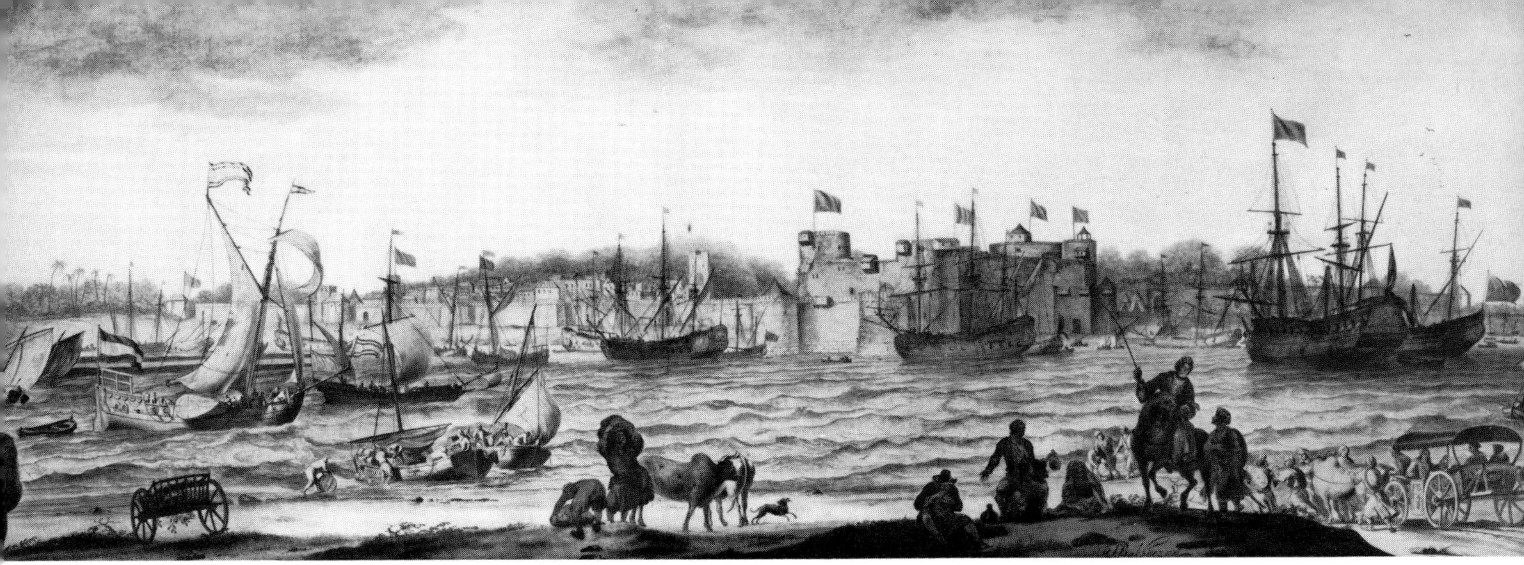

Plate 120. Ludolf Bakhuizen, 1631-1708. "Surat from the sea." *This is a monochrome painting.* National Maritime Museum, Greenwich.

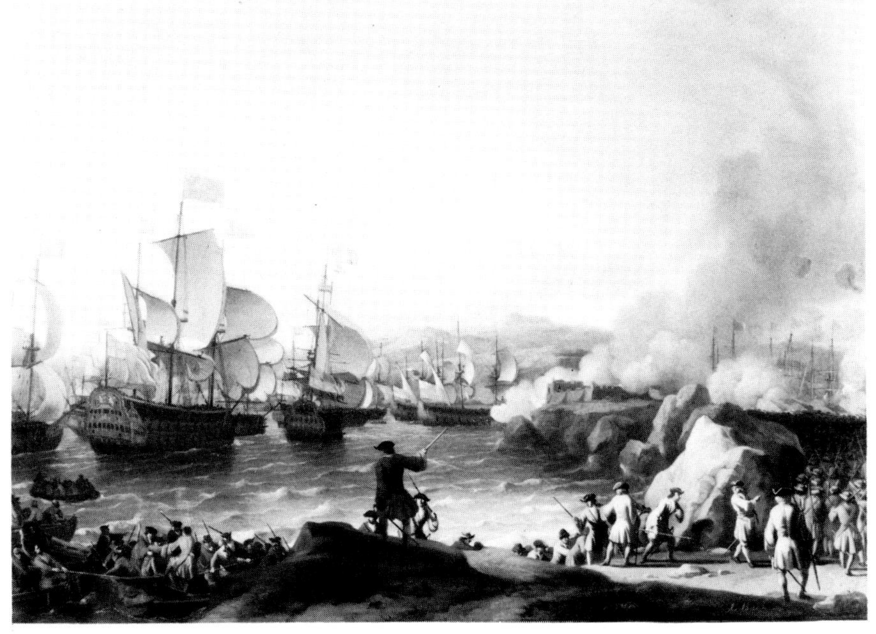

Plate 121. Ludolf Bakhuizen, 1631-1708. "The battle of Vigo Bay in 1702." *By this date the royal coat of arms on the stern has decreased in size to accommodate an increase in the number of stern ports. The hull design, however, has not yet altered appreciably.* National Maritime Museum, Greenwich.

Plate 122. Solomon van Ruisdael, 1600-1670. "Dutch fishermen in inland waters." *A painter with a style very similar to van Goyen (Plates 84, 85, 86).* State Art Collections, Kassel.

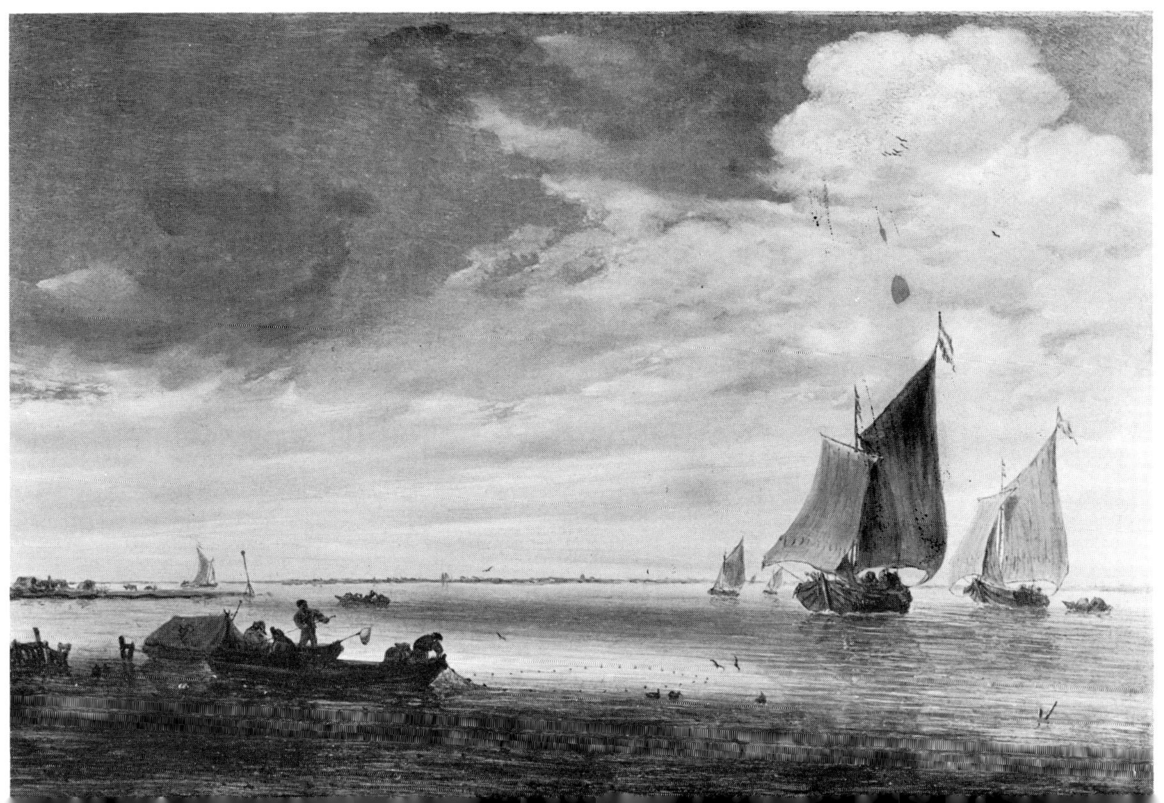

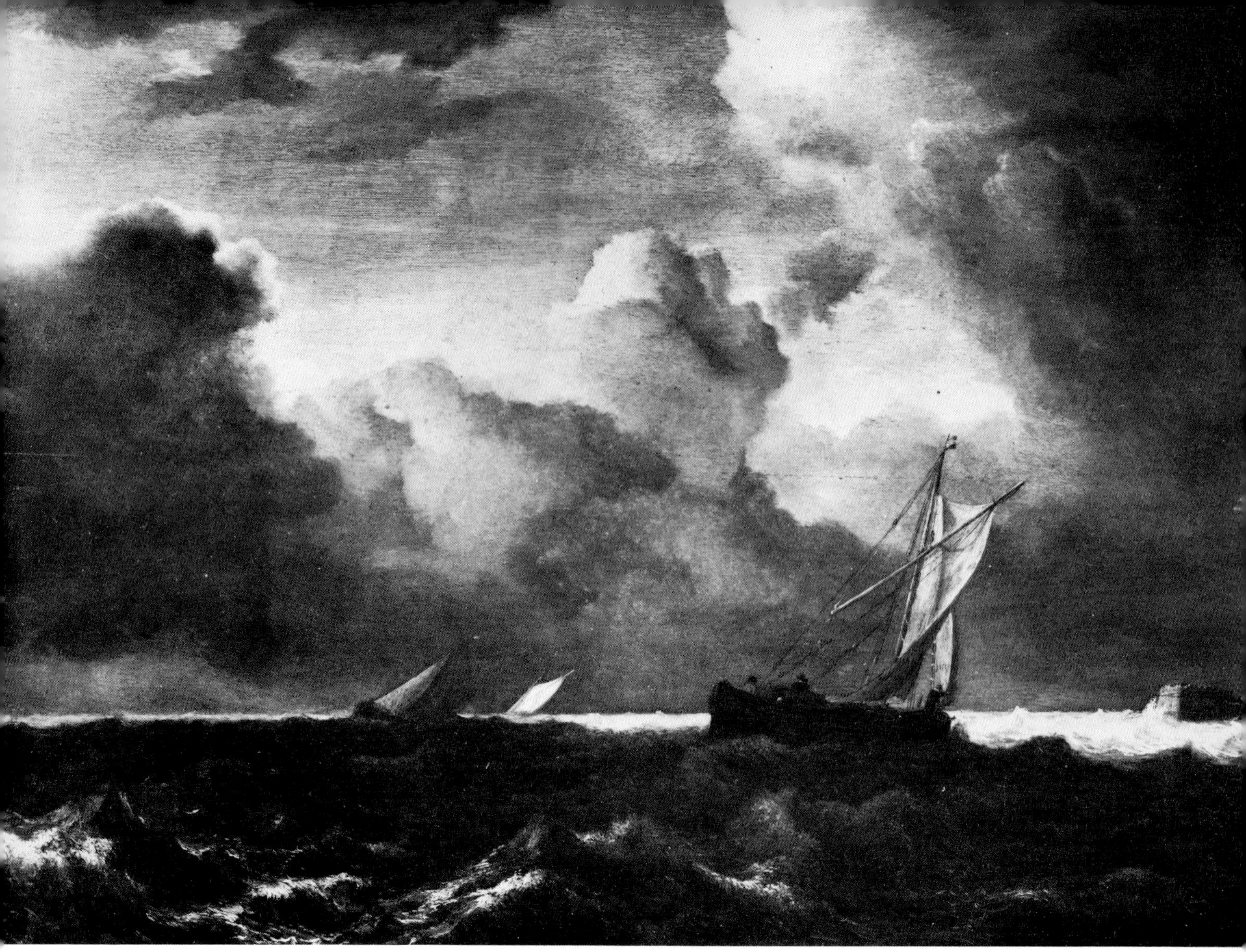

Plate 123. Jacob Isaakszoon van Ruisdael, 1628/9-1682. "Storm clouds over the sea." *The painter has achieved a marvellous sense of drama with the threatening clouds and light on the sea.* National Museum, Stockholm.

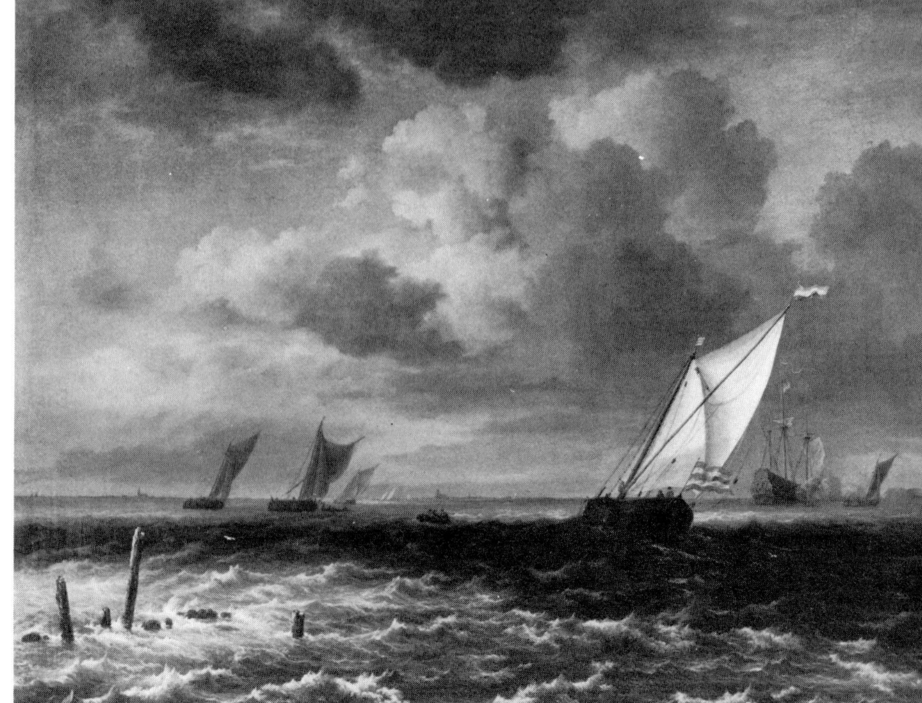

Plate 124. Jacob Isaakszoon van Ruisdael, 1628/9-1682. "A rough sea." *A less typical painting by this artist than the preceding plate.* Museum of Fine Arts (William F. Warden Fund), Boston.

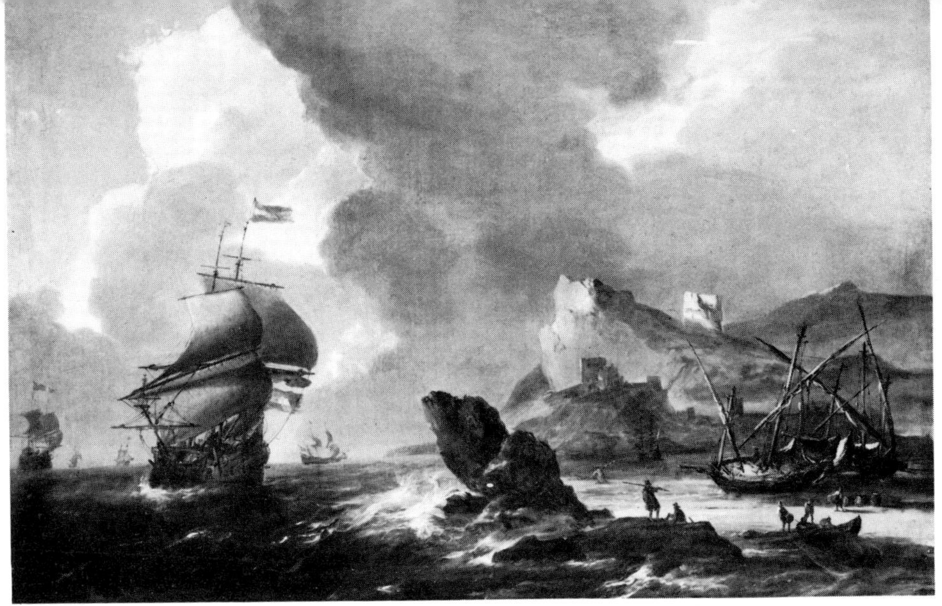

Plate 125. Jan Heunisz Blankerhoff, 1628-1669. "Shipping off a rocky coast." Christie's.

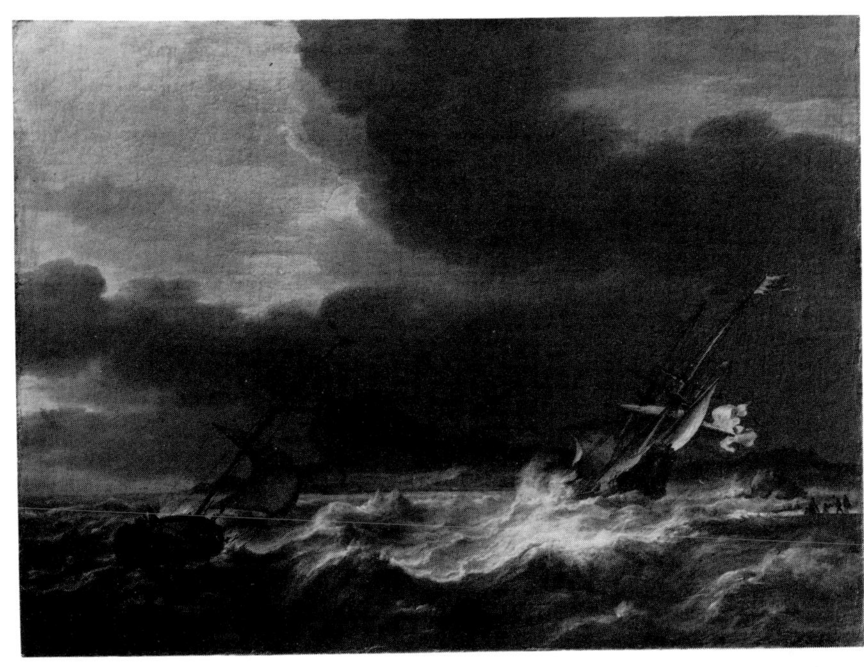

Plate 126. Jan Heunisz Blankerhoff, 1628-1669. "A fishing pink and a Dutch ship in a storm off a coast." Museum of Fine Arts, Copenhagen.

Plate 127. Lorenzo A. Castro, fl. late 17th century. "A Maltese galley and a Dutch man-of-war off a Mediterranean port." Dulwich College Picture Gallery.

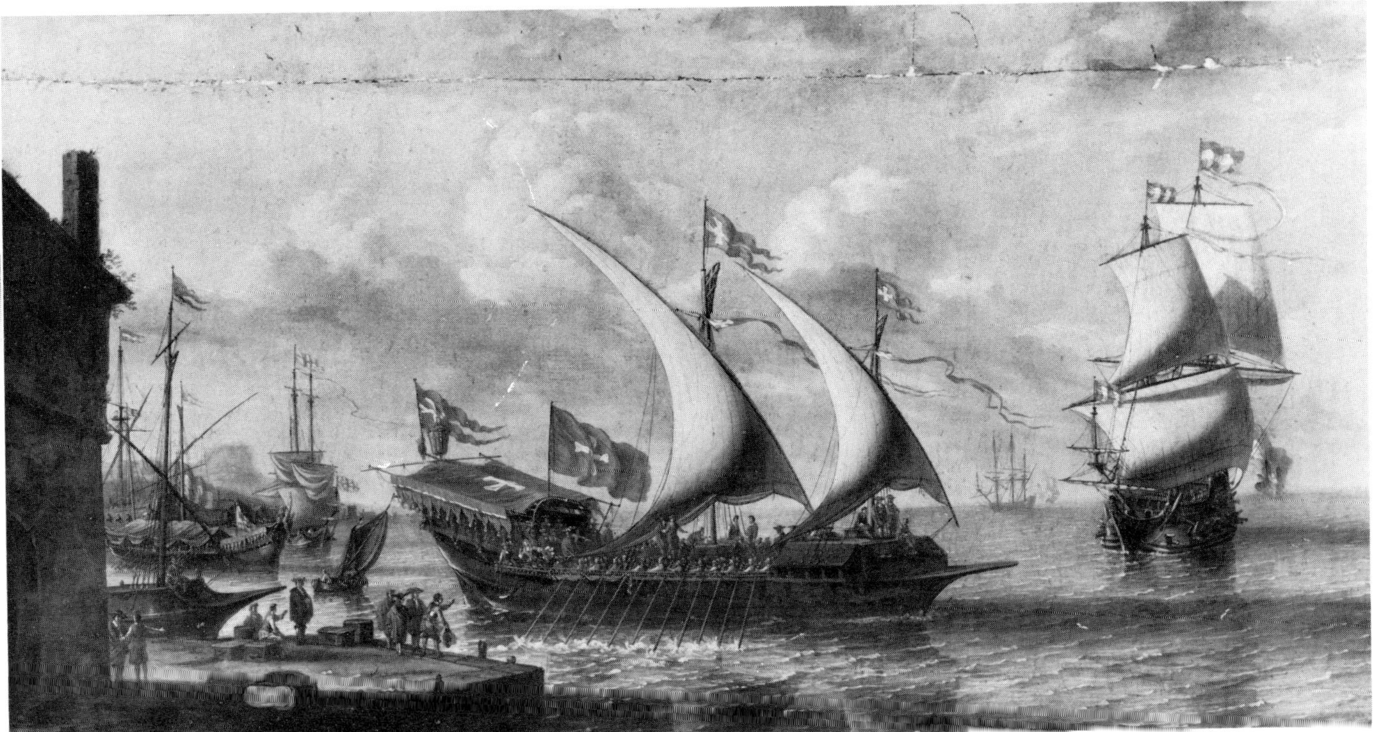

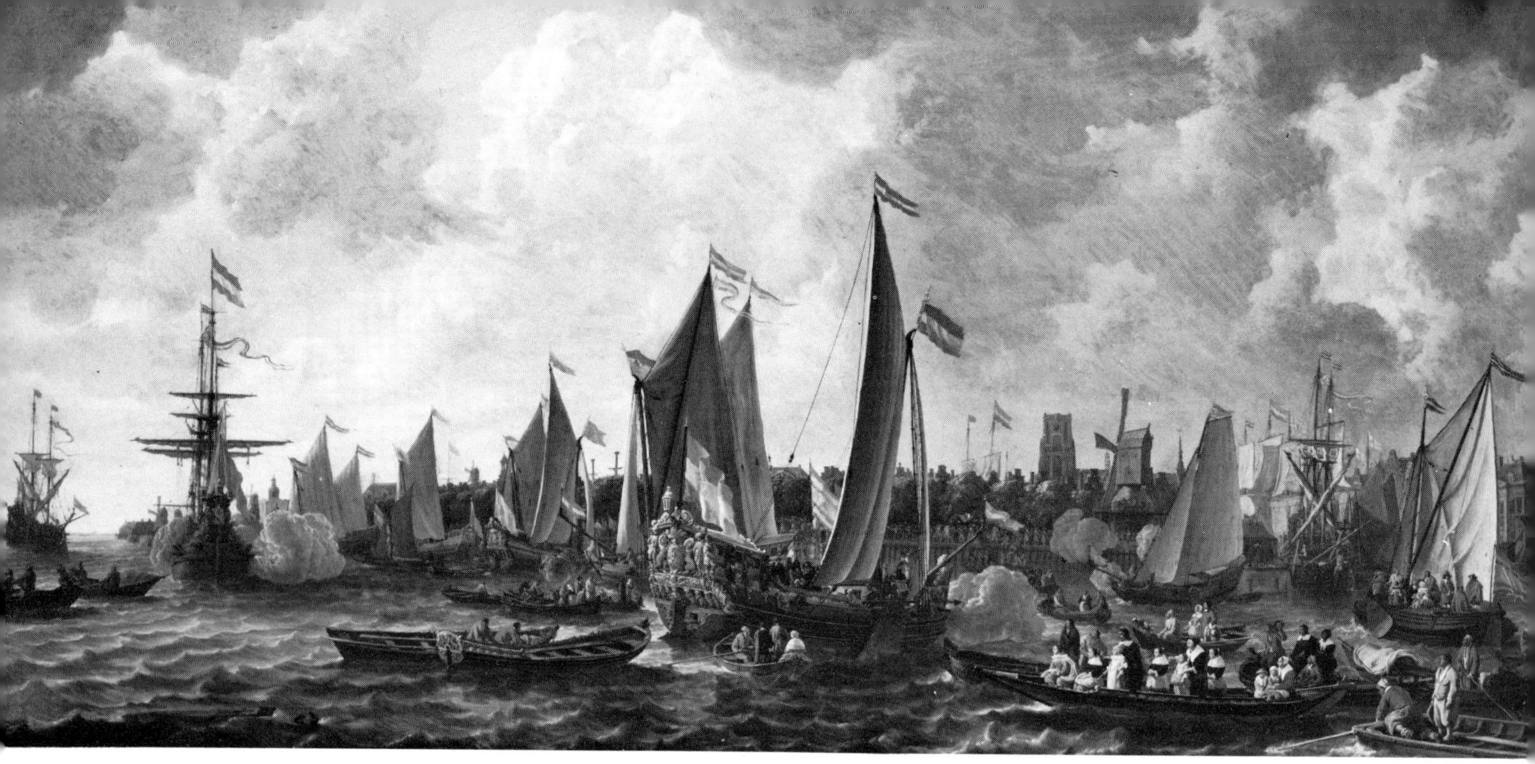

Plate 128. Lieve Pietersz Verschuir, 1630-1686. "The arrival of King Charles II at Rotterdam on his way to his restoration to the throne in May 1660." *Like Claude, one of Verschuir's characteristics was painting into the sun.* Rijksmuseum, Amsterdam.

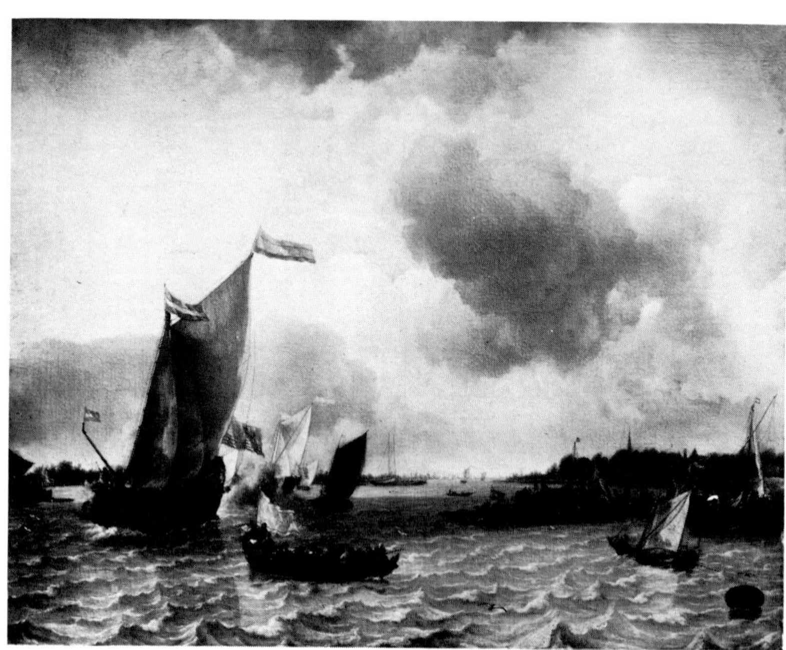

Plate 129. Lieve Pietersz Verschuir, 1630-1686. "A Dutch yacht and boats in inland waters." Alte Pinakothek, Munich.

Plate 130. Lieve Pietersz Verschuir, 1630-1686. "An action between a Dutch squadron and Barbary pirates about 1670." National Maritime Museum, Greenwich.

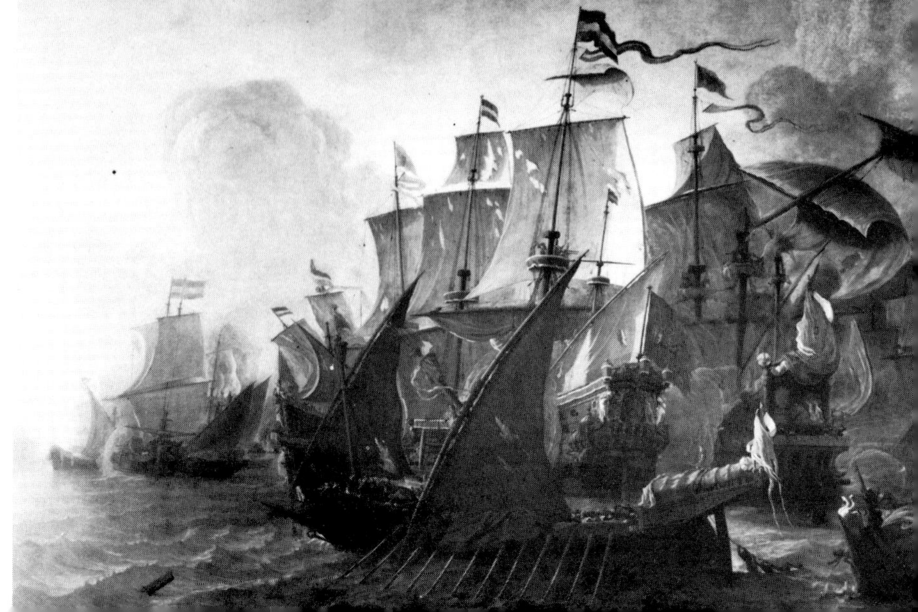

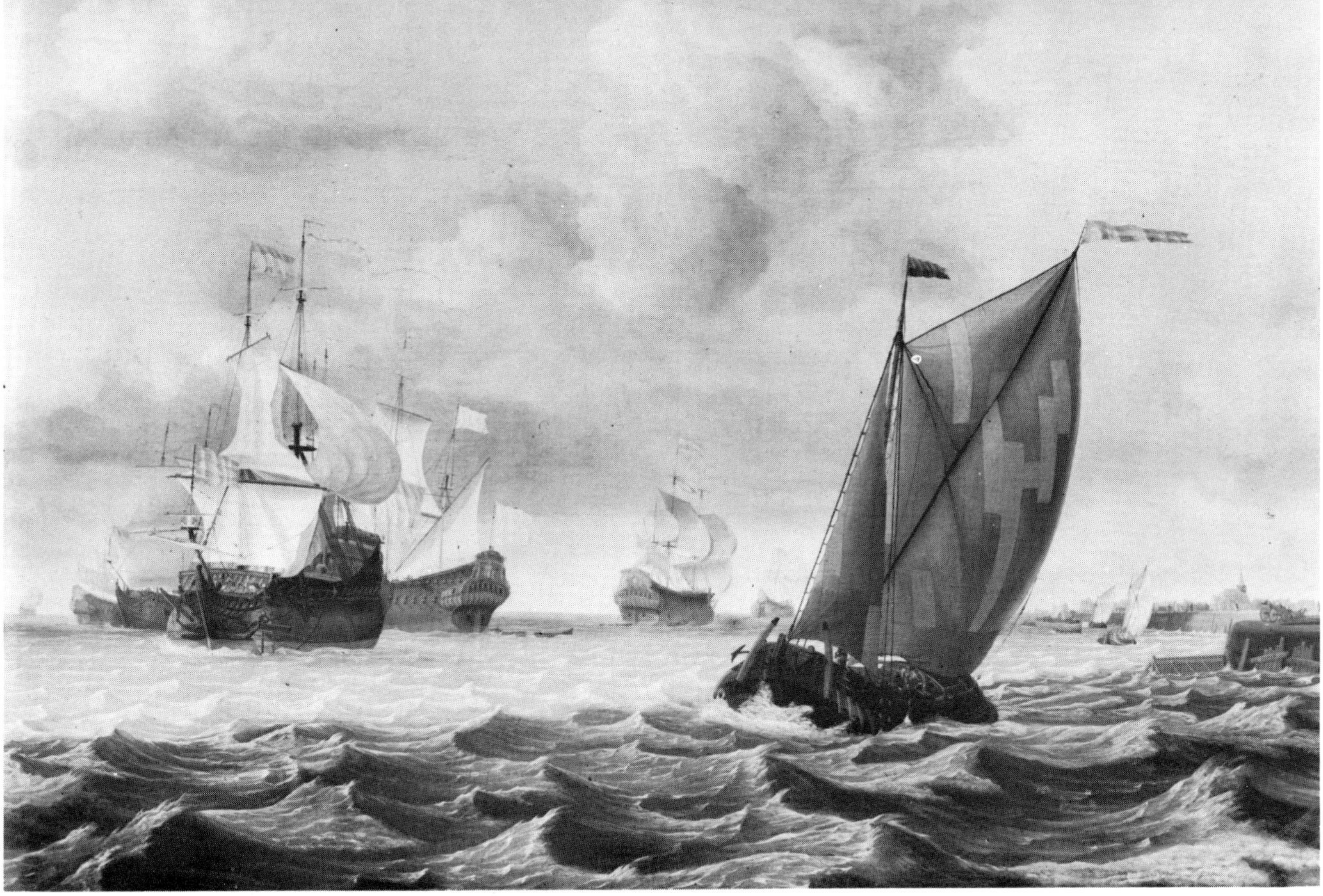

Plate 131. Gerrit Pompe, fl. mid- to late 17th century. "Shipping off a Dutch harbour." *Pompe was a fine quality marine artist, who painted carefully executed and well delineated seas, and identification is helped by the way he 'under hatted' his ships; that is to say, gave them rather short masts and low profiles. The size and lack of a naval pennant on the ship whose stern can be seen in the left middle distance suggests she is an Indiaman.* National Maritime Museum, Greenwich.

Plate 132. Jacob van Croos. b.c.1637. "A Dutch ship and galleys off a fortified town." *Imaginary Italianate scene. The sea particularly lacks realism.* National Maritime Museum, Greenwich.

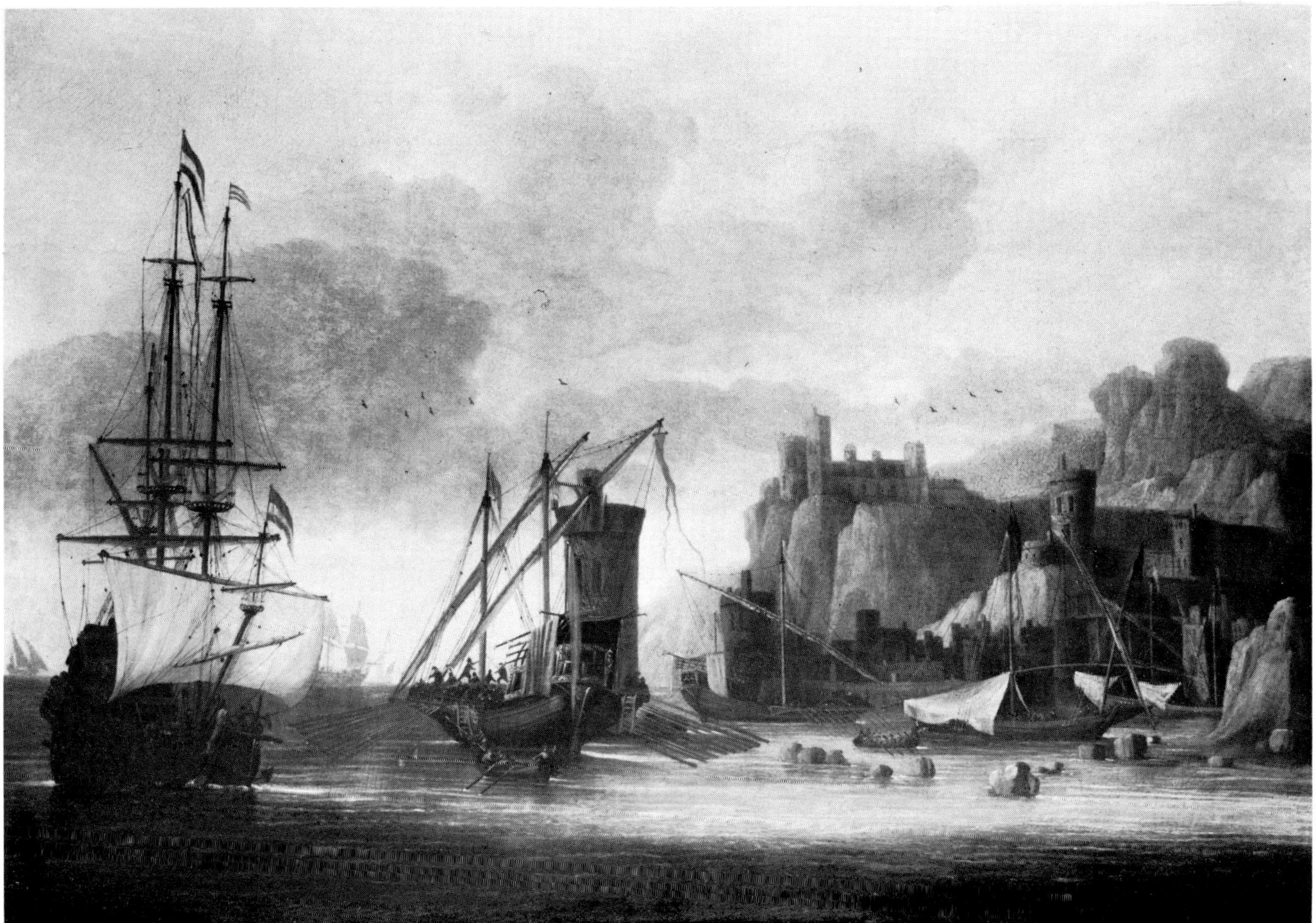

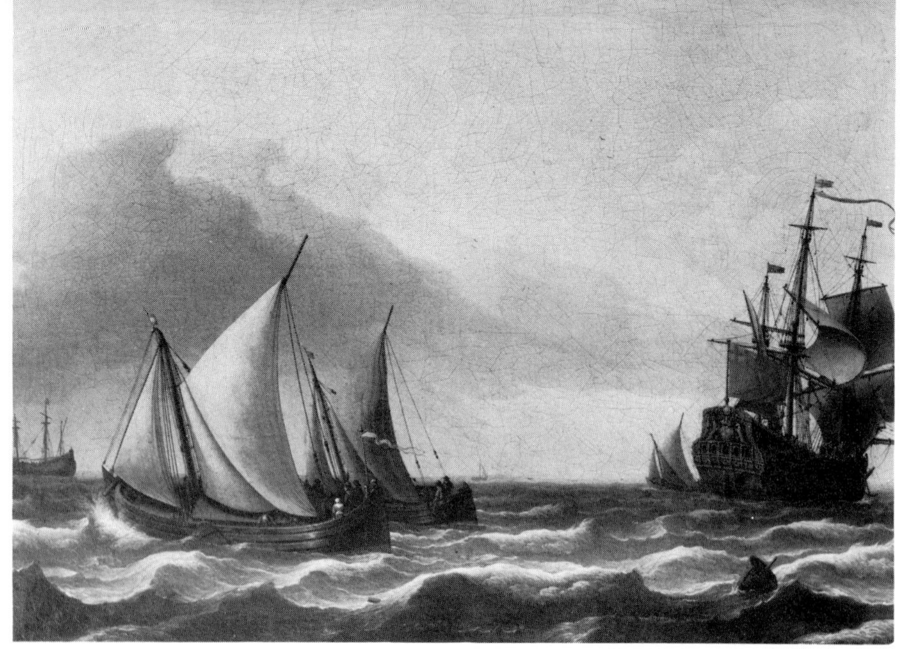

Plate 133. Willem Gillsz Kool, 1608/9-1666. "An English man-of-war and Dutch vessels in a breeze." Sotheby's.

Plate 134. Tobias Stranover, c.1684-aft.1724. "An English flag-ship off a port." Christie's.

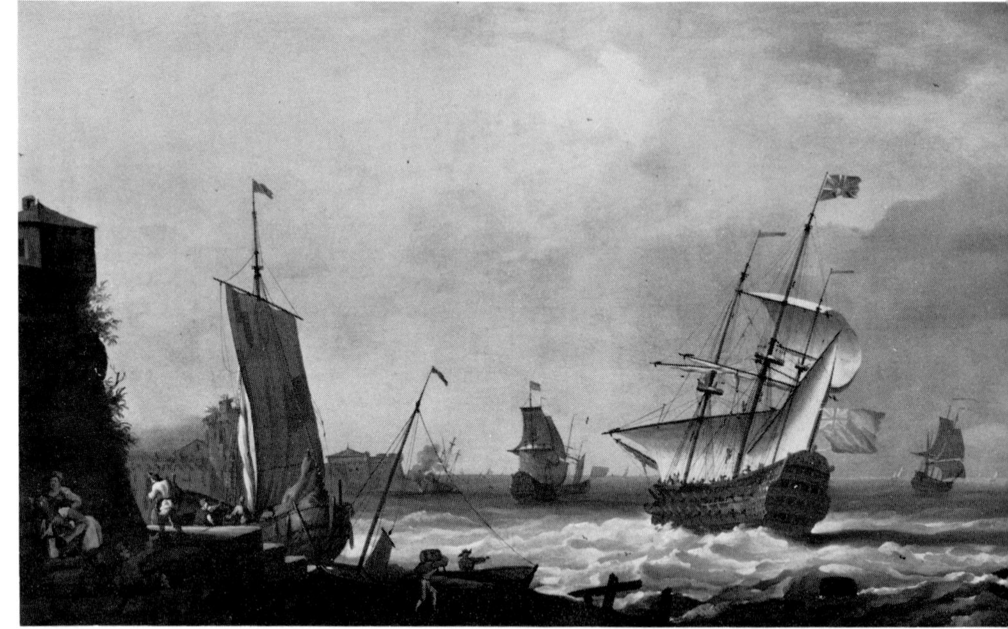

Plate 135. Aernout Smit, 1641-1710. "Dutch shipping in a stiff breeze off the coast." *The ship in the background is a flute (see Coastal Craft, page 52).* Hessisches Landesmuseum, Darmstadt.

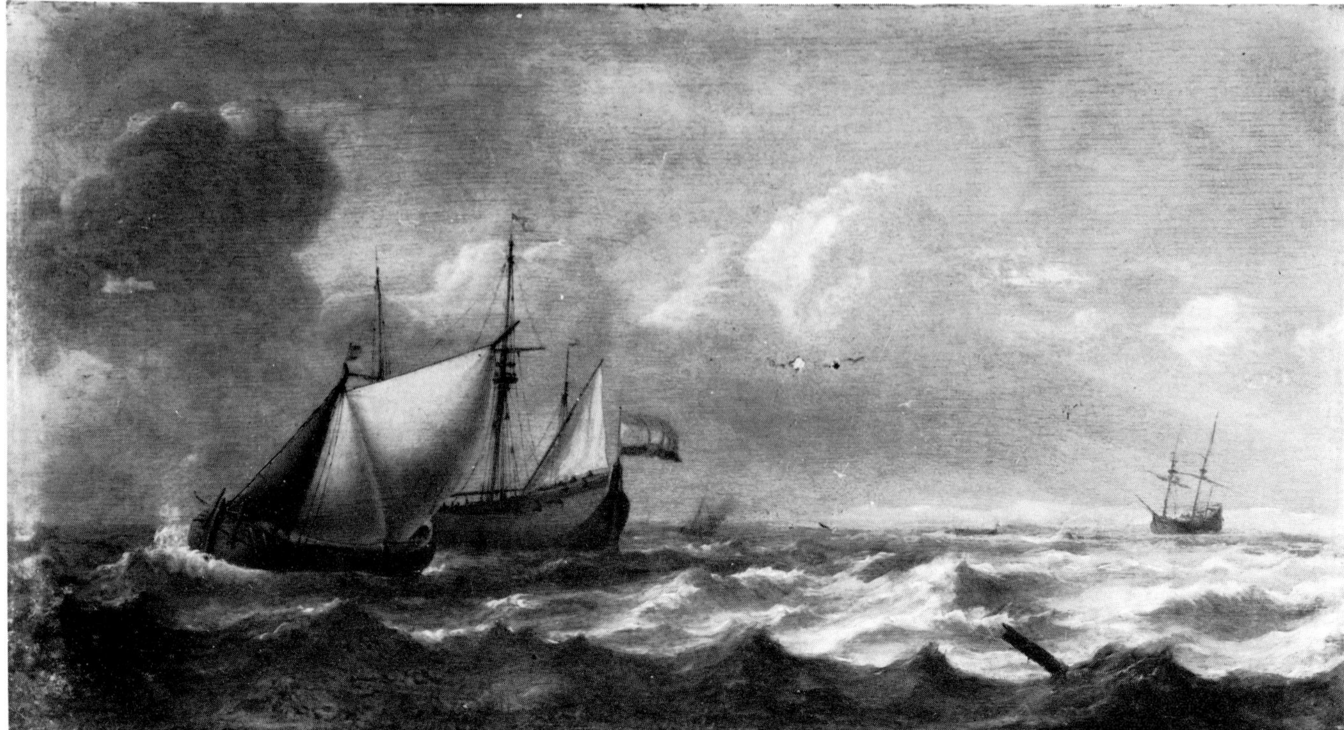

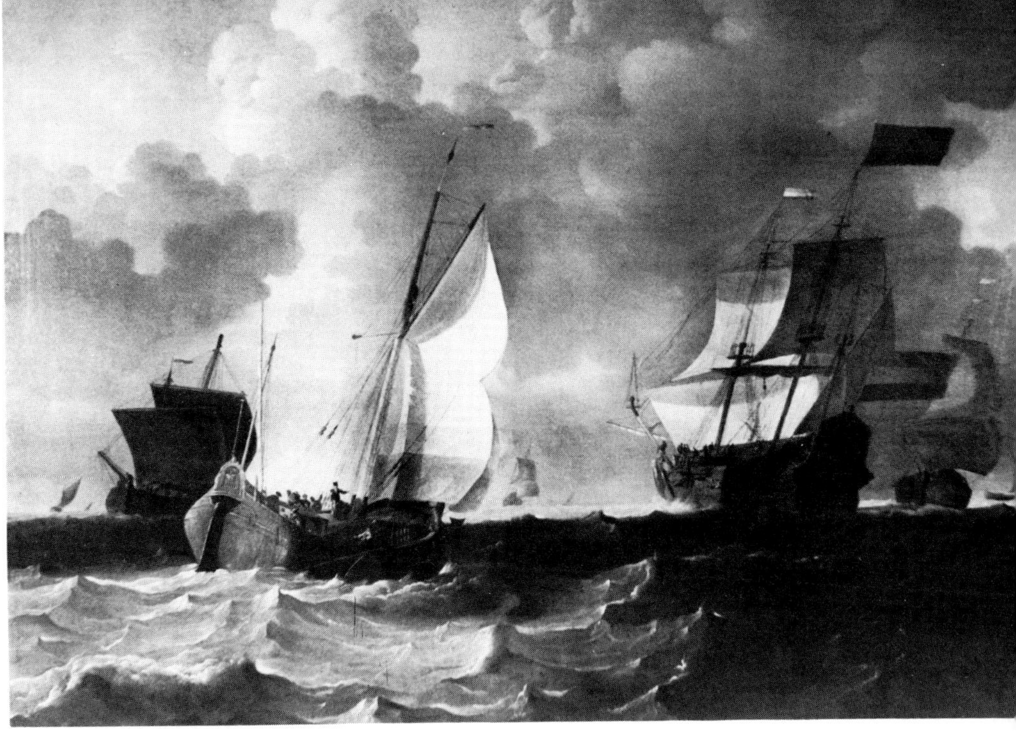

Plate 136. Wigerus Vitringa, 1657-1721. "A galjoot and Dutch shipping in a fresh breeze." Fries Museum, Leeuwarden.

Plate 137. Jan Karel Donatus van Beecq, 1638-1722. "Shipping on the Bristol Avon about 1680." *A glittering, colourful composition which shows the artist's skill in careful delineation of the ships and their decoration.* National Maritime Museum, Greenwich.

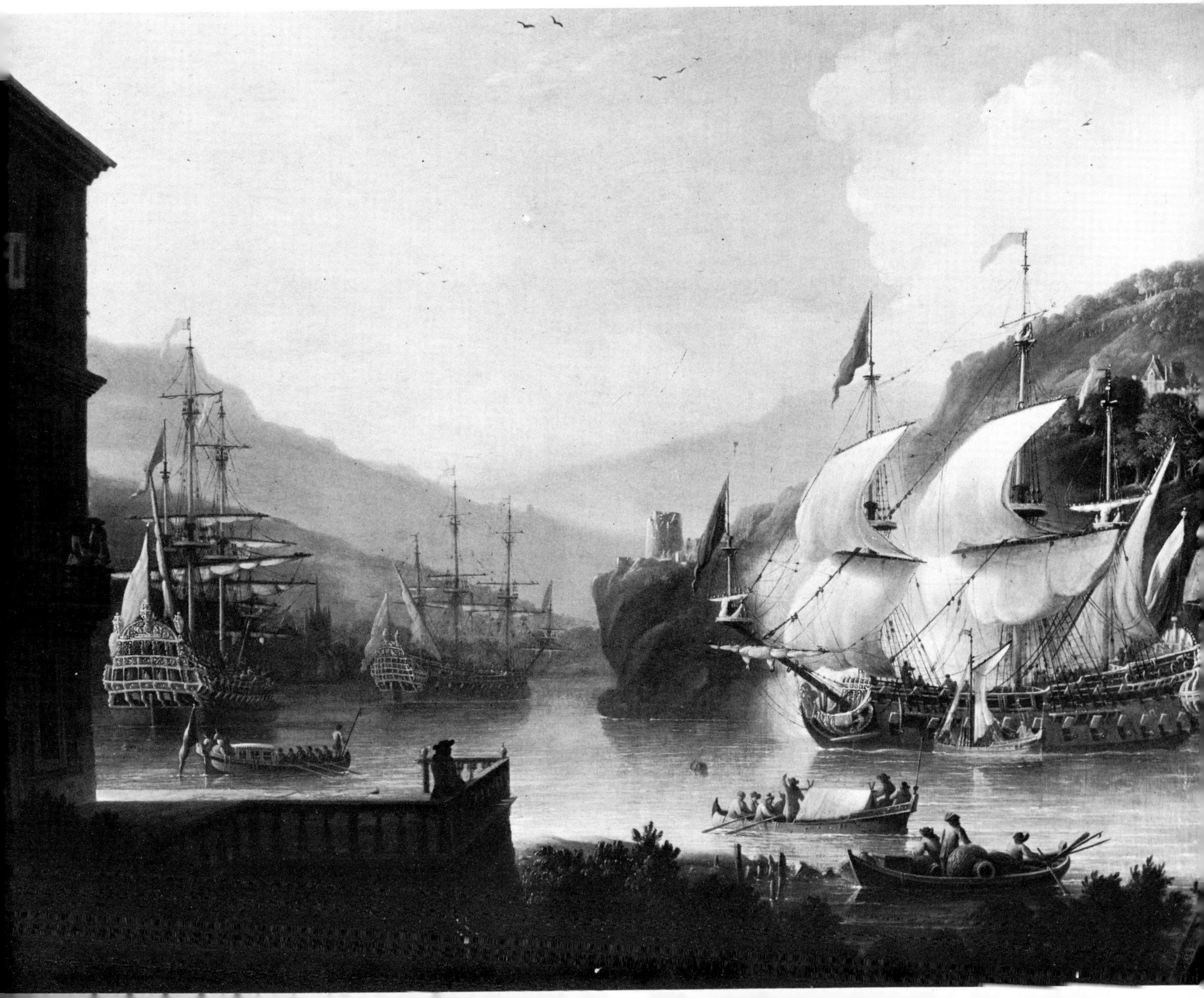

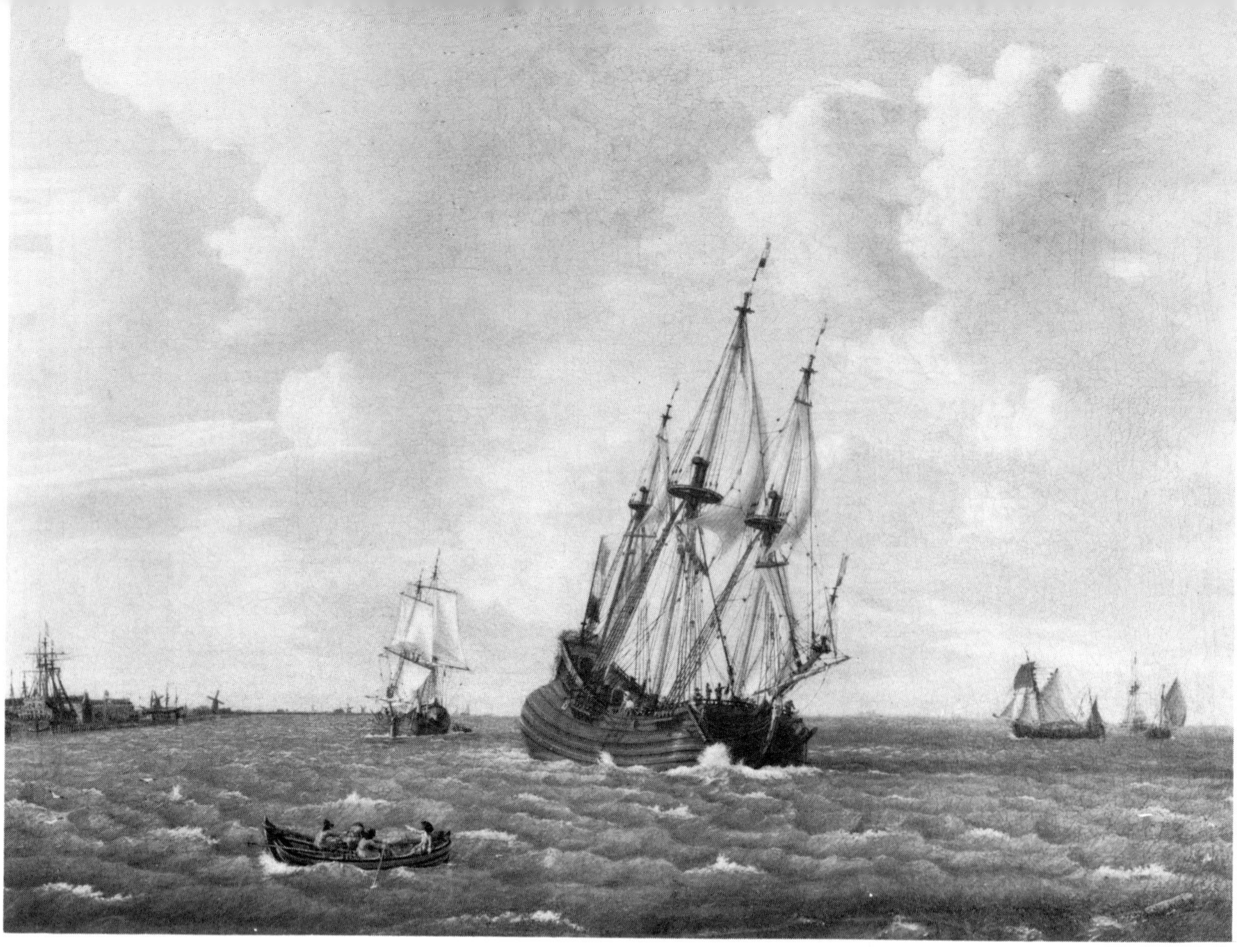

Plate 138. Jan Claesz Rietschoof, c.1652-1719. "A Dutch flute off a harbour about 1675." *The Dutch were subjected to a tax on the deck area and consequently ships were designed with sides curving sharply inwards — tumble home. If the topmasts appear to be unduly tilted it must be remembered that they were supported by heavy ropes which did not have the rigidity of modern materials.* National Maritime Museum, Greenwich.

Plate 139. Jan Claesz Reitschoof, c.1652-1719. "Dutch shipping, probably in the mouth of the Scheldt about 1680." National Maritime Museum, Greenwich.

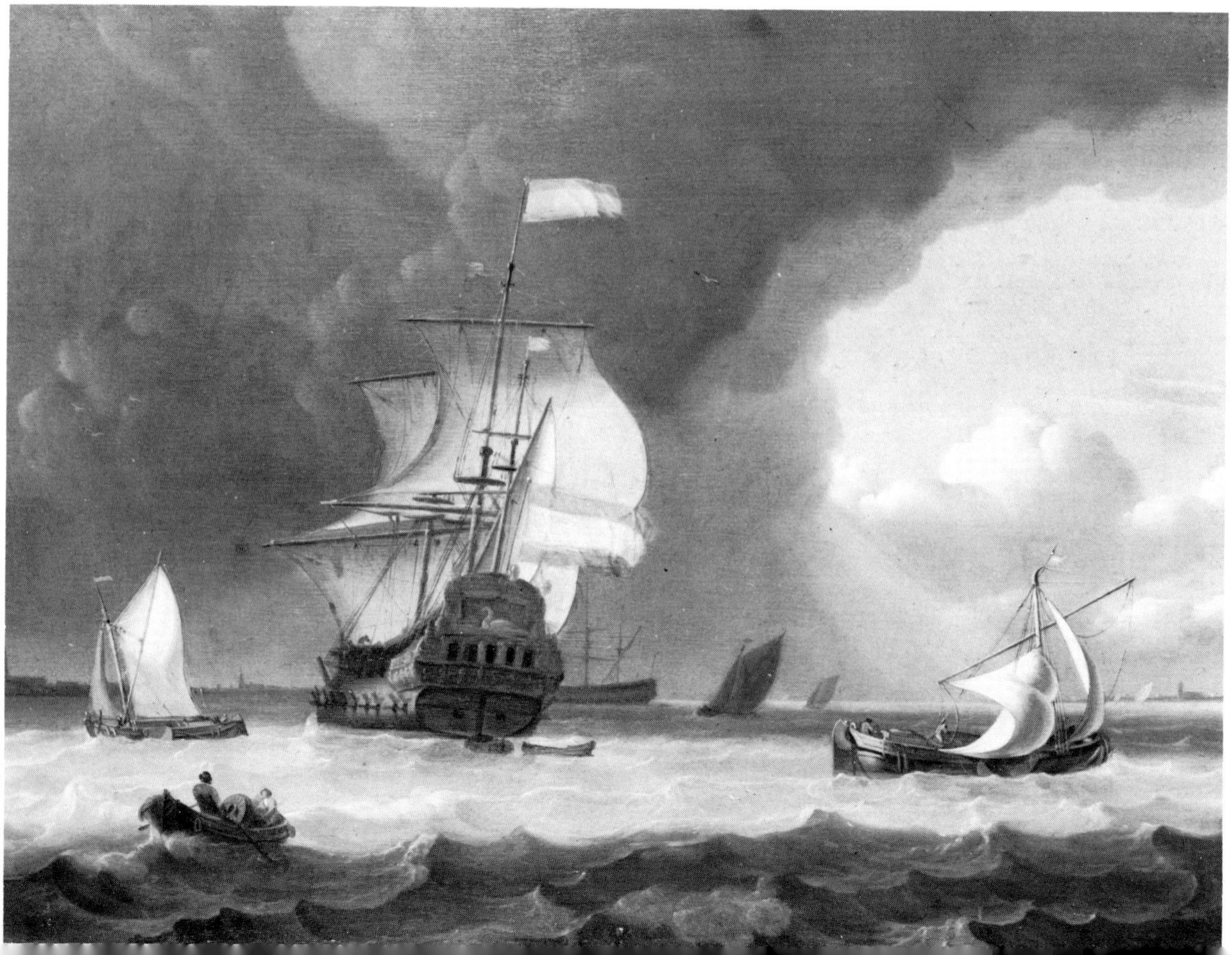

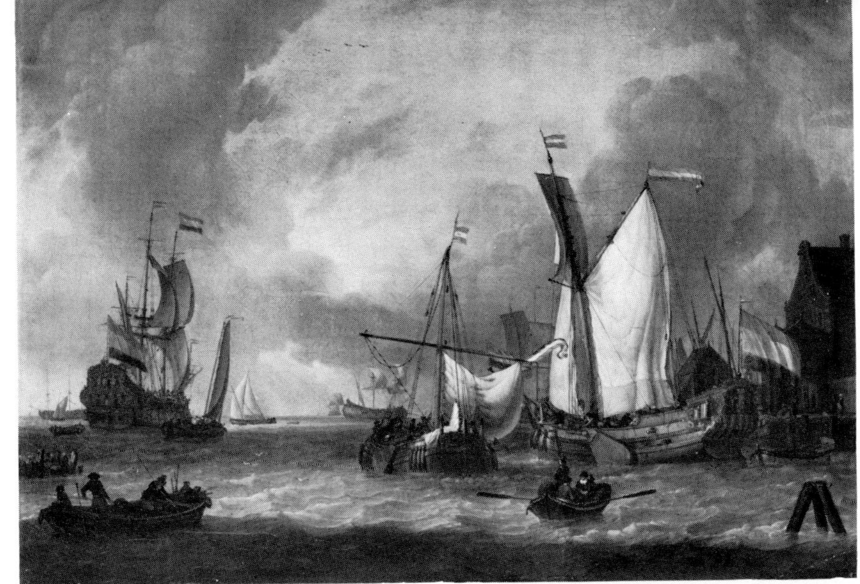

Plate 140. Jan Claesz Rietschoof, c.1652-1719. "Dutch shipping in harbour in gusty weather." Rijskmuseum, Amsterdam.

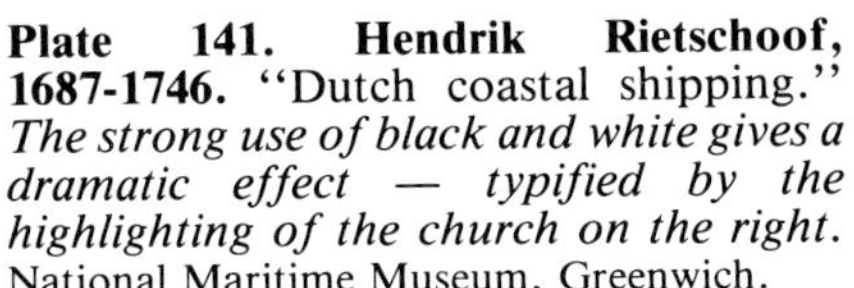

Plate 141. Hendrik Rietschoof, 1687-1746. "Dutch coastal shipping." *The strong use of black and white gives a dramatic effect — typified by the highlighting of the church on the right.* National Maritime Museum, Greenwich.

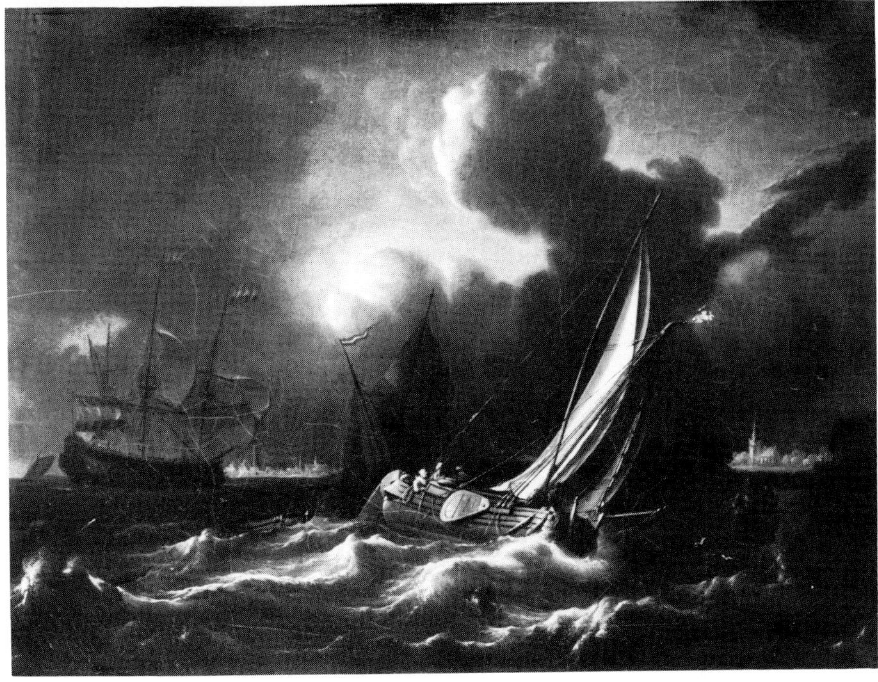

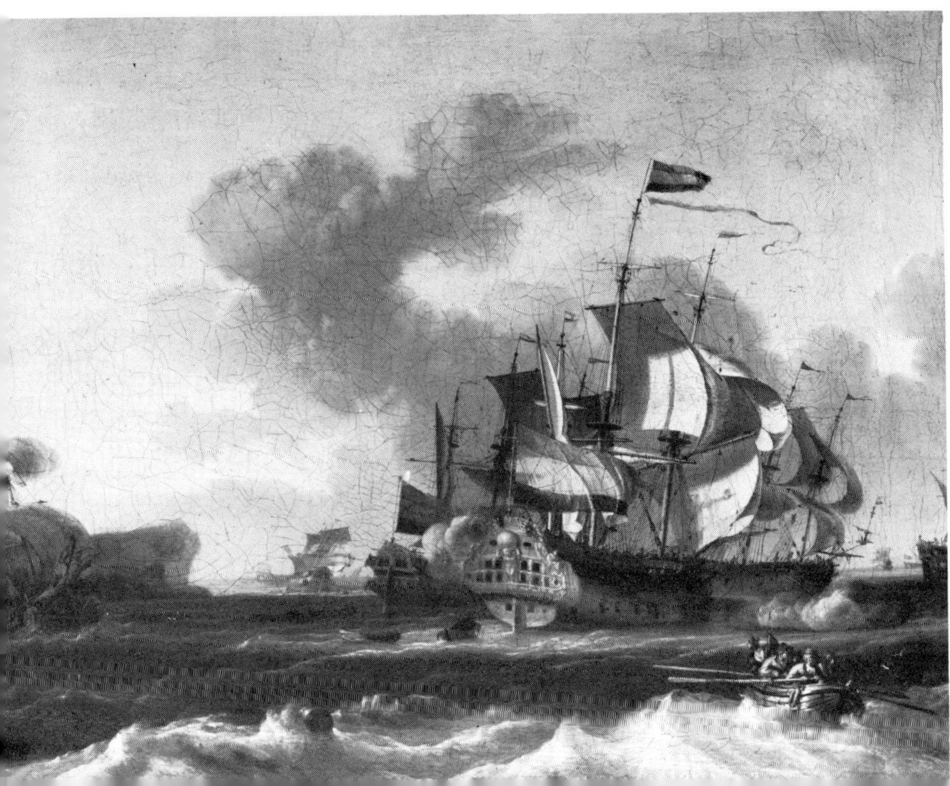

Plate 142. Hendrik Rietschoof, 1687-1746. "A Dutch flagship and shipping off a rocky coast about 1720." National Maritime Museum, Greenwich.

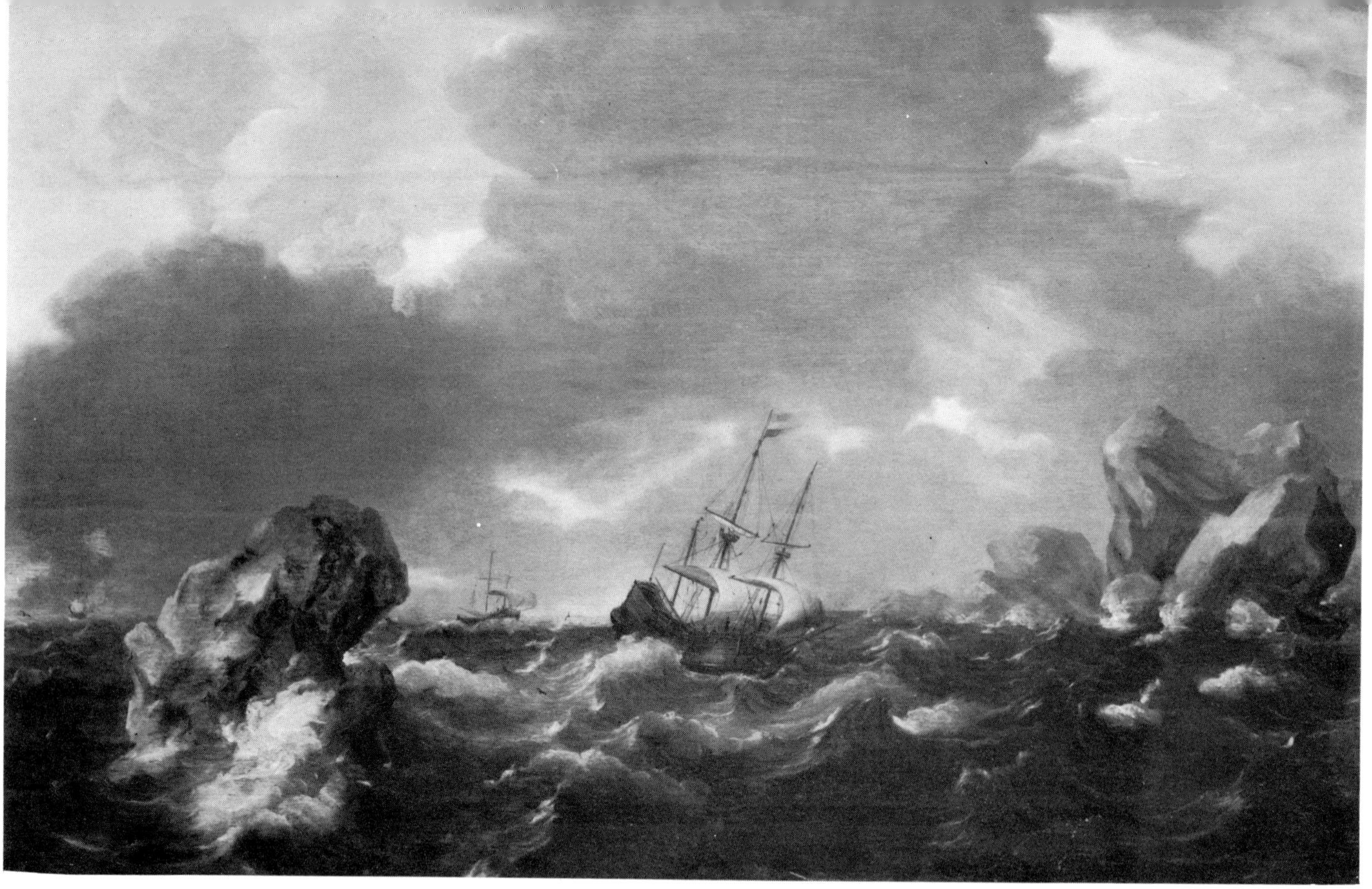

Plate 143. Willem van de Velde, the Younger, 1633-1707. "Dutch ships in a storm, driving onto a rocky coast, 1651." *The earliest known picture painted at the age of seventeen. Like a bad de Vlieger under whom he was then studying.* National Maritime Museum, Greenwich.

Plate 144. Willem van de Velde, the Younger, 1633-1707. "The return of a Dutch East India fleet about 1658." *A colourful early picture with jewel-like quality.* National Maritime Museum, Greenwich.

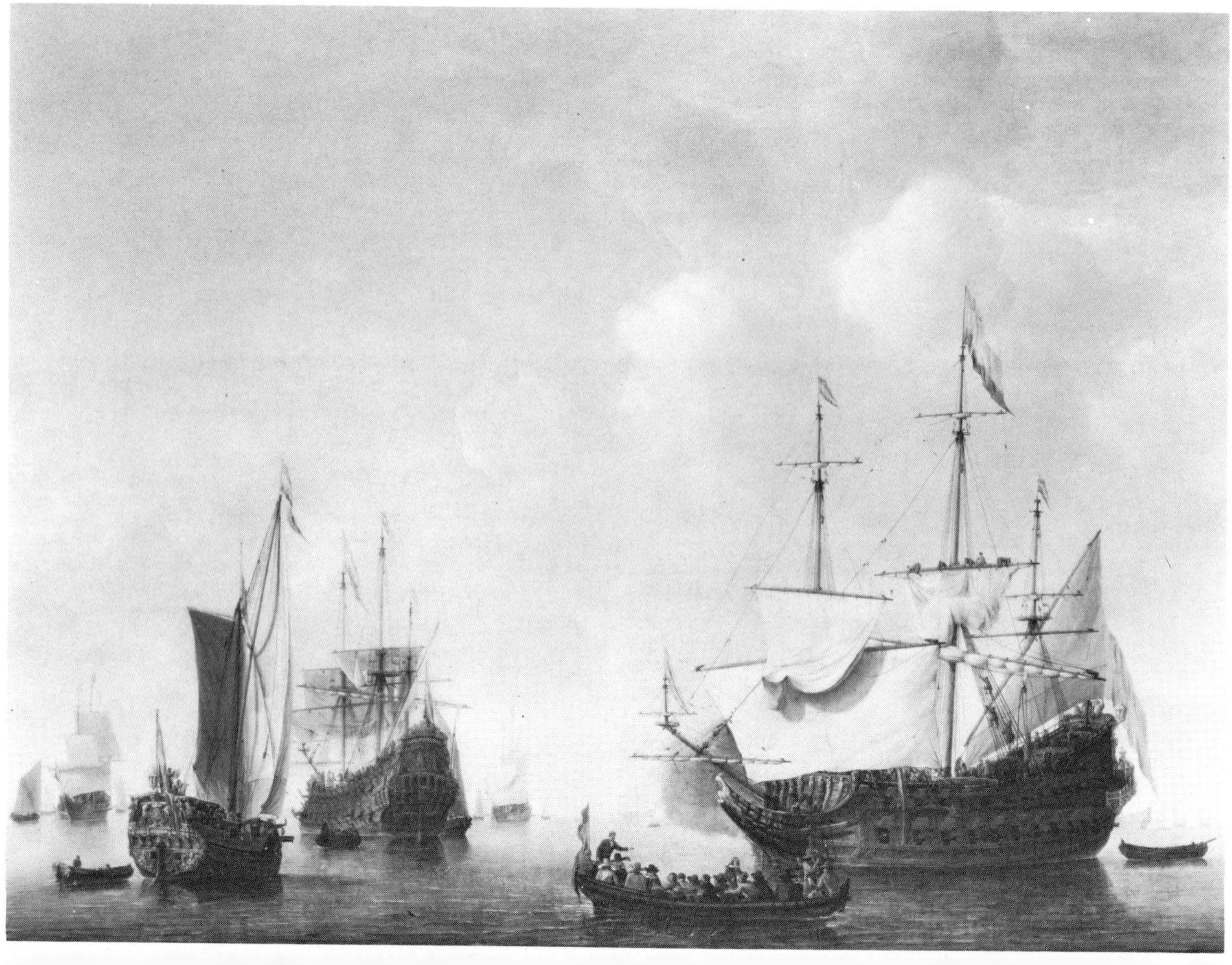

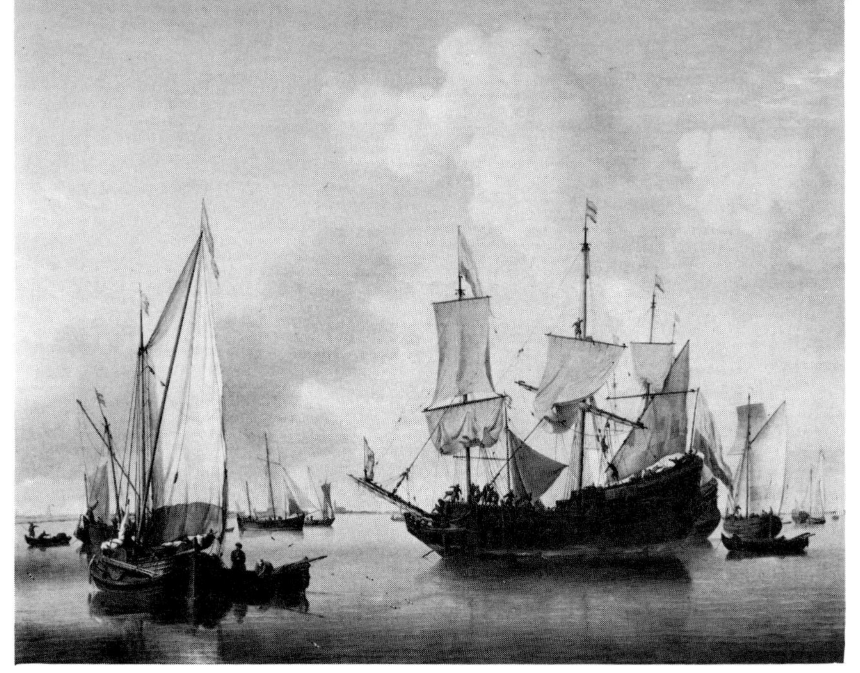

Plate 145. Willem van de Velde, the Younger, 1633-1707. "A Dutch merchantman come to anchor among coastal craft in a calm, c.1660." Rijksmuseum, Amsterdam.

Plate 146. Willem van de Velde, the Younger, 1633-1707. "Shipping in a fresh breeze, about 1660." *Typical painting of the middle Dutch period.* National Maritime Museum, Greenwich.

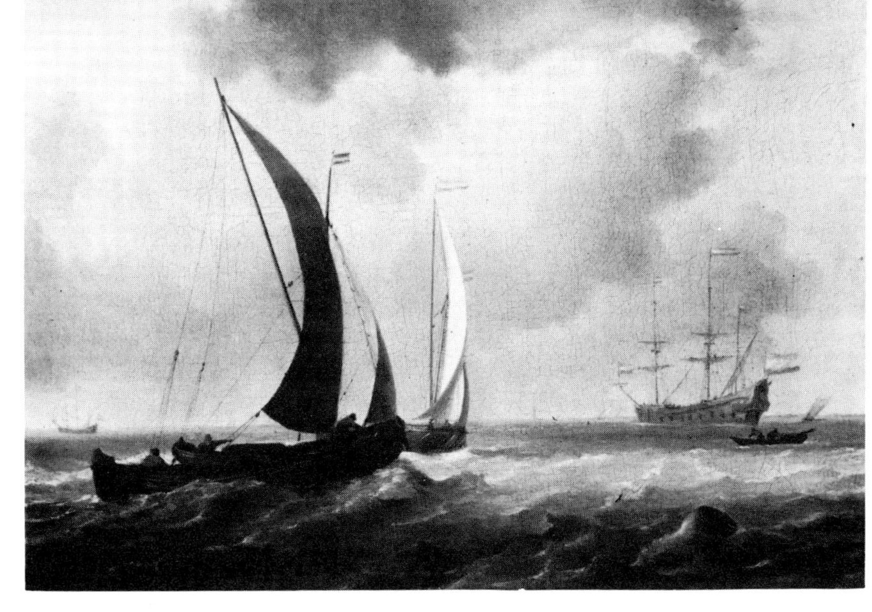

Plate 147. Willem van de Velde, the Younger, 1633-1707. "The action between the English and the Dutch East India fleet at Bergen, 1665." National Maritime Museum, Greenwich.

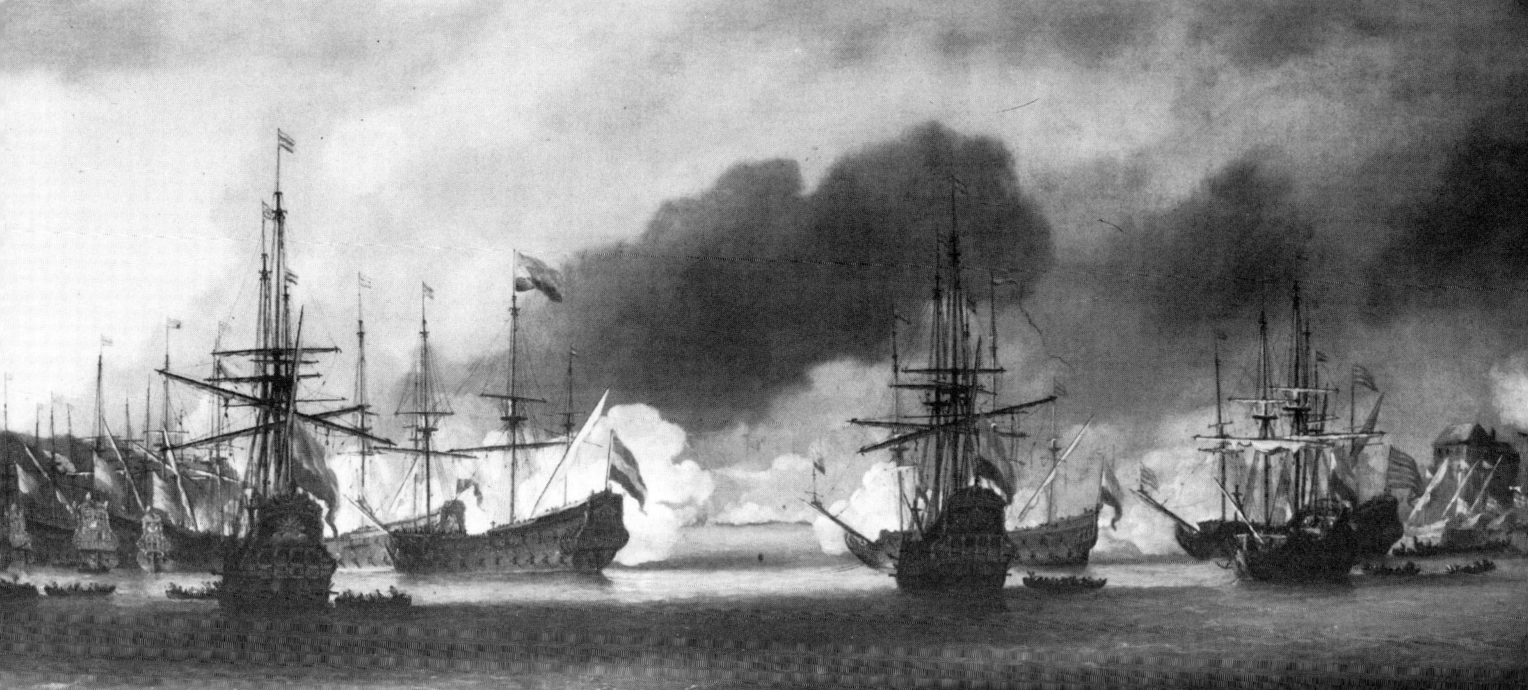

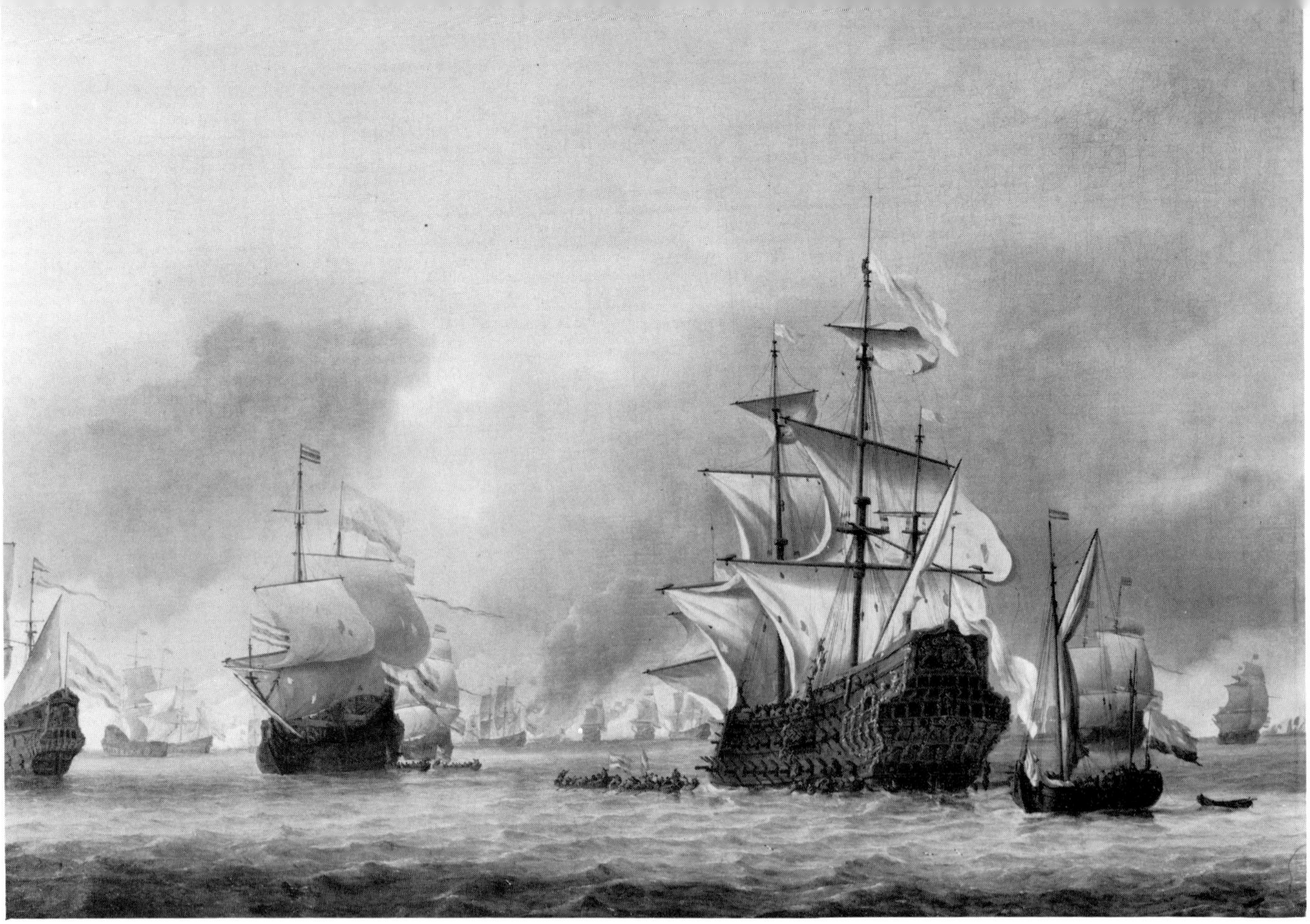

Plate 148. Willem van de Velde, the Younger, 1633-1707. "The capture of the *Royal Prince* during the Four Days Fight, 1666." *The painting recalls the incident on the third day of the Four Days Fight, June 3rd, 1666, when the* Royal Prince *grounded on the Galloper Sand.* Rijksmuseum, Amsterdam.

Plate 149. Willem van de Velde, the Younger, 1633-1707. "A kaag close-hauled in a fresh breeze, about 1671." *A big painting and one of the great van de Velde's, painted in the manner of Bakhuizen by using his dramatic lighting effects, but the paint handled in his own manner.* The Toledo Museum of Art, Ohio.

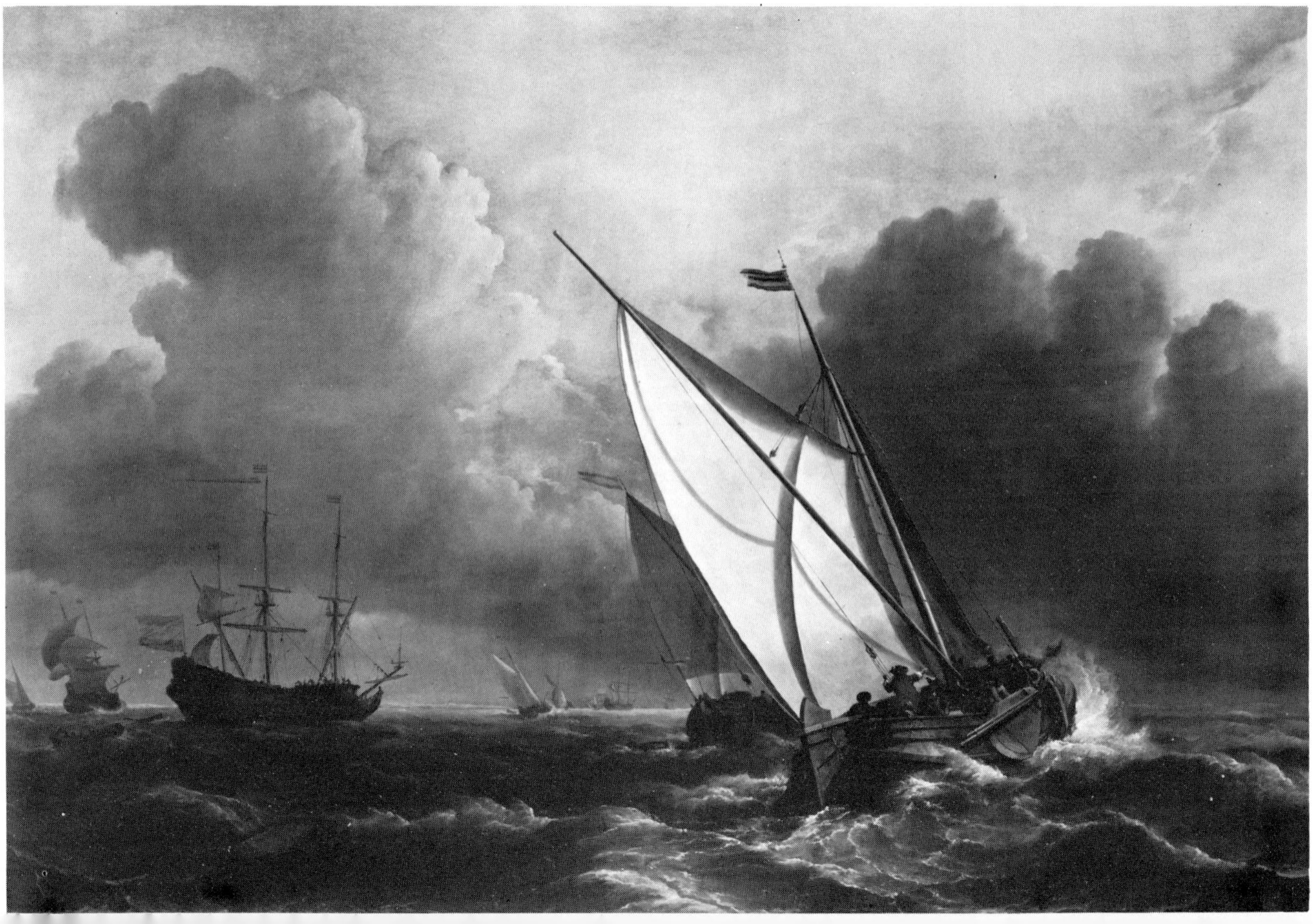

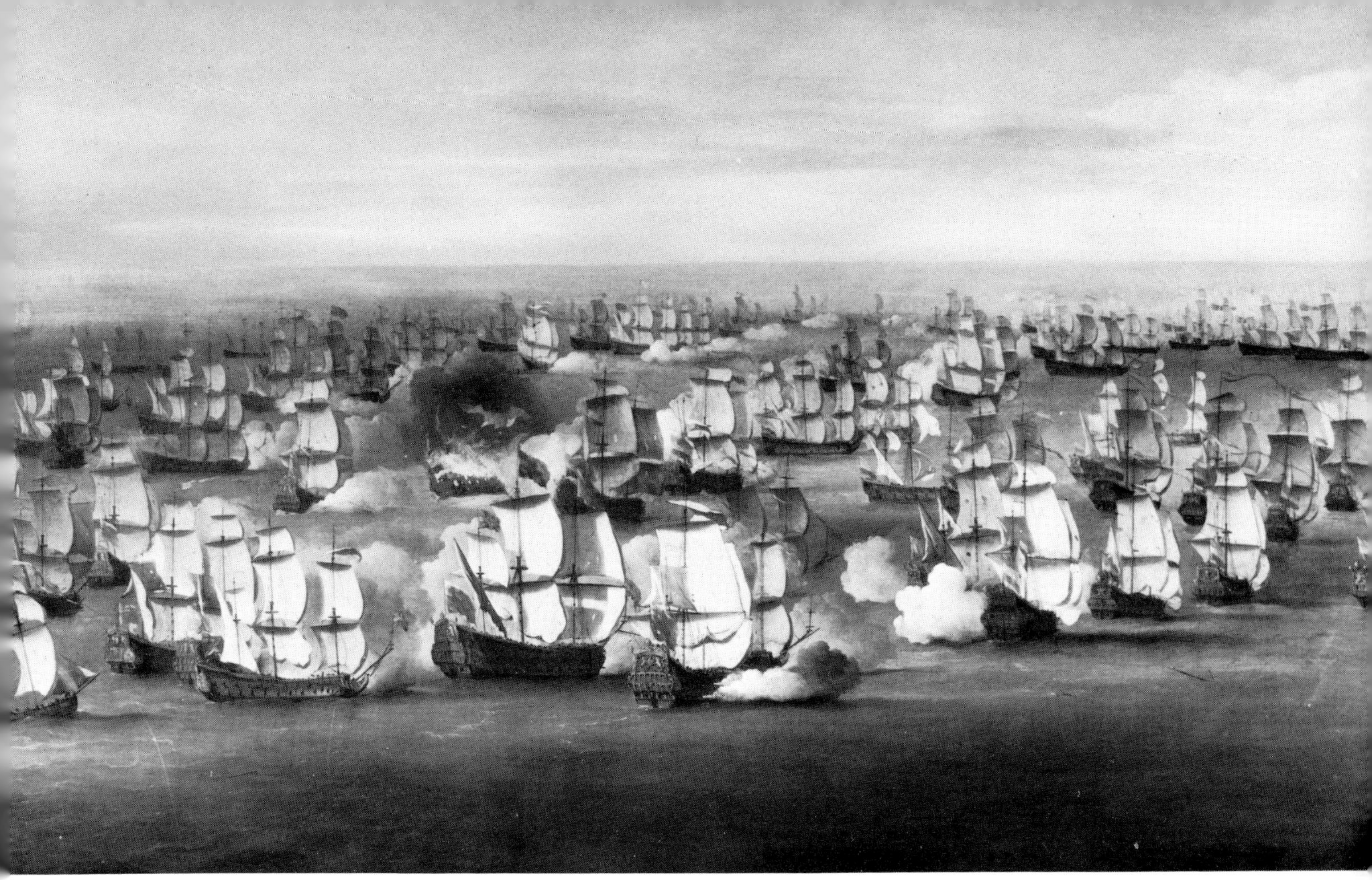

Plate 150. Willem van de Velde, the Younger, 1633-1707. "The Battle of Solebay in 1672." Ministry of Defence (on loan to the National Maritime Museum).

Plate 151. Willem van de Velde, the Younger, 1633-1707. "The *Gouden Leeuw* at the Battle of Texel in 1673." *Painted in England in 1687 on commission from Cornelis Tromp, whose flagship she was, this big painting is his finest battle piece.* National Maritime Museum, Greenwich.

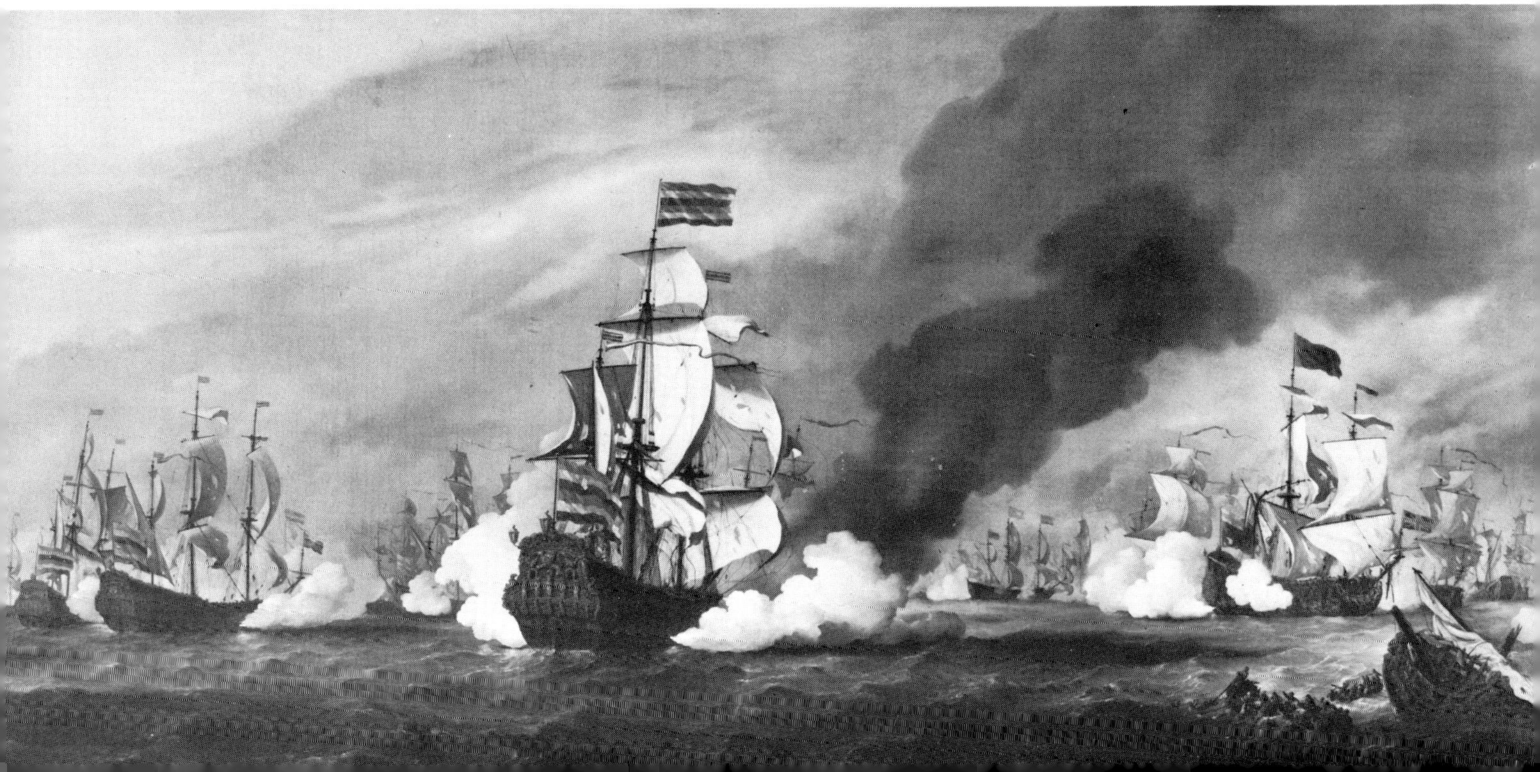

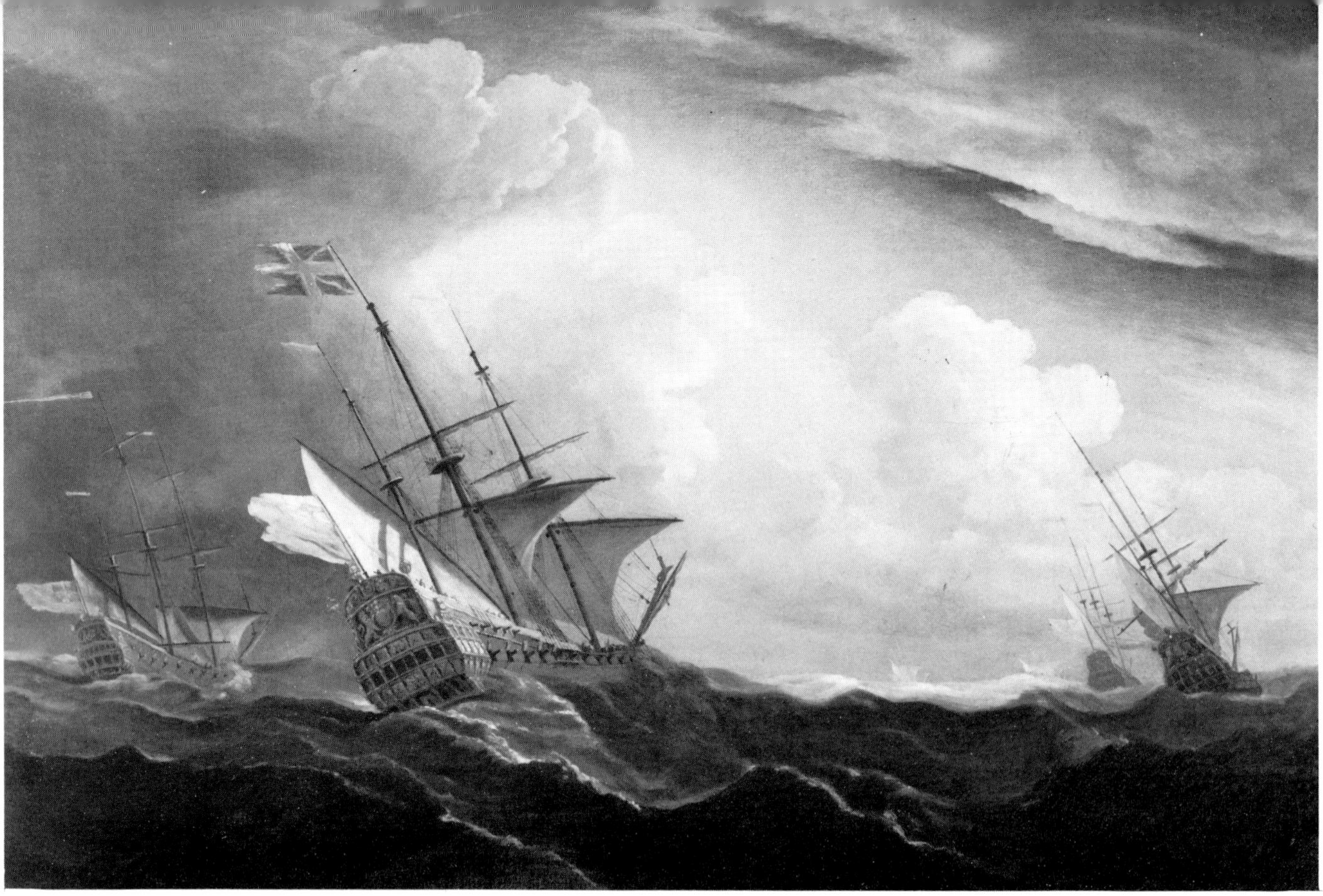

Plate 152. Willem van de Velde, the Younger, 1633-1707. "An English squadron going to windward in a gale." National Maritime Museum, Greenwich.

Plate 153. Willem van de Velde, the Younger, 1633-1707. "William of Orange and Princess Mary leaving for Holland in 1677." National Maritime Museum, Greenwich.

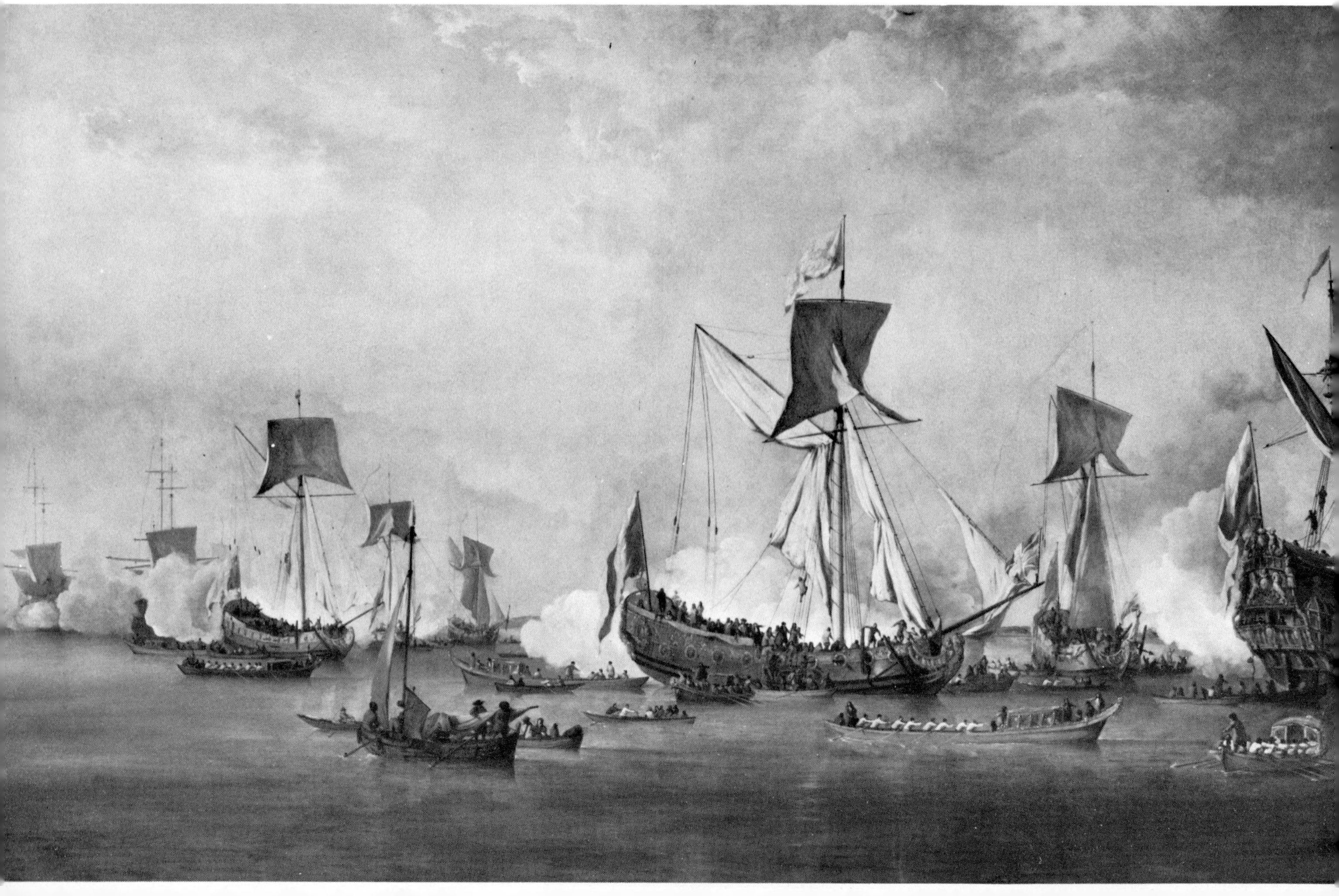

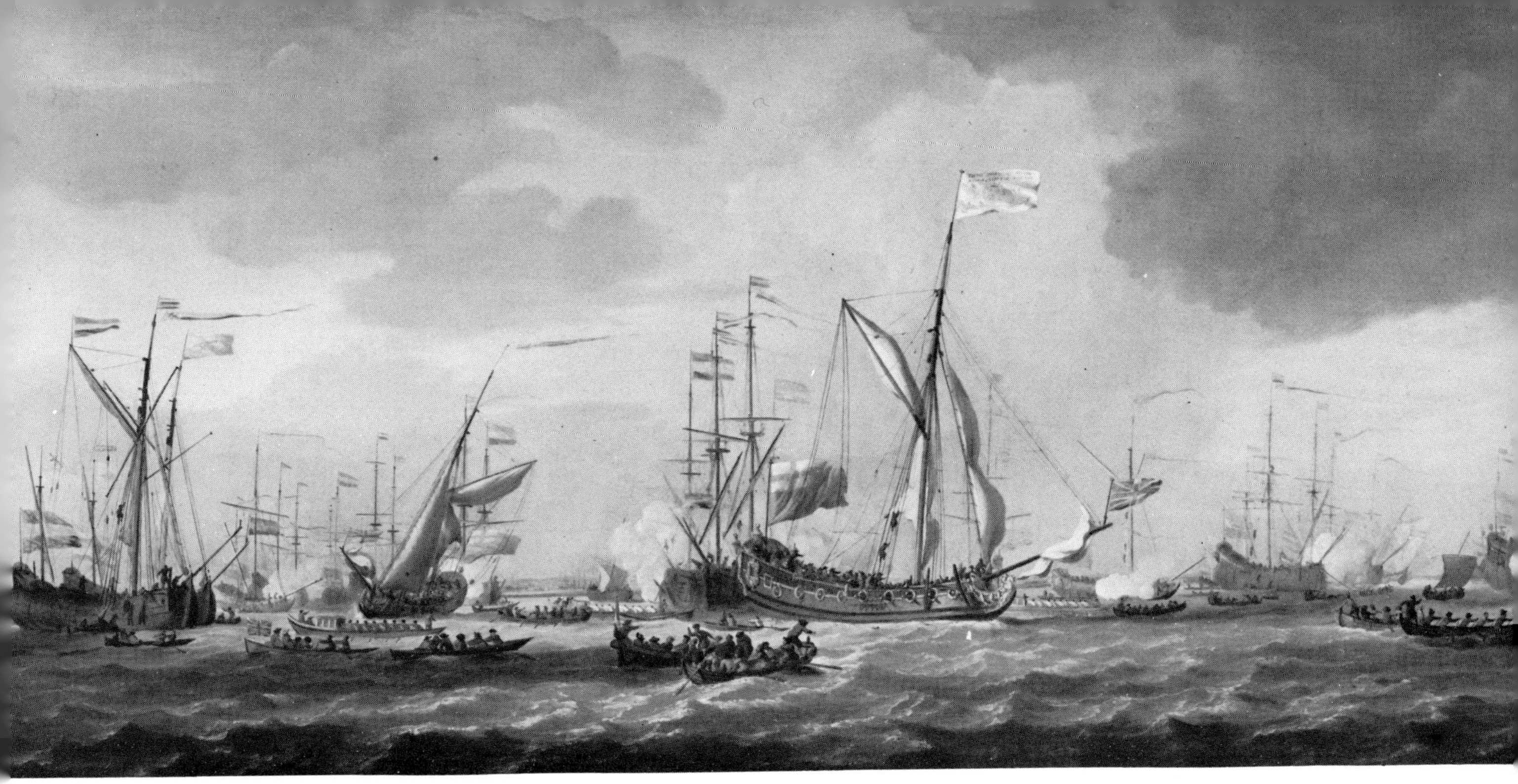

Plate 154. Willem van de Velde, the Younger, 1633-1707. "Princess Mary arriving at Gravesend in 1689." *In the centre is the* Mary, *a smack-rigged royal yacht, flying the Protestant standard.* National Maritime Museum, Greenwich.

Plate 155. Willem van de Velde, the Younger, 1633-1707. "English ships wrecked on rocks in a storm." *A black, highly dramatic picture.* National Maritime Museum, Greenwich.

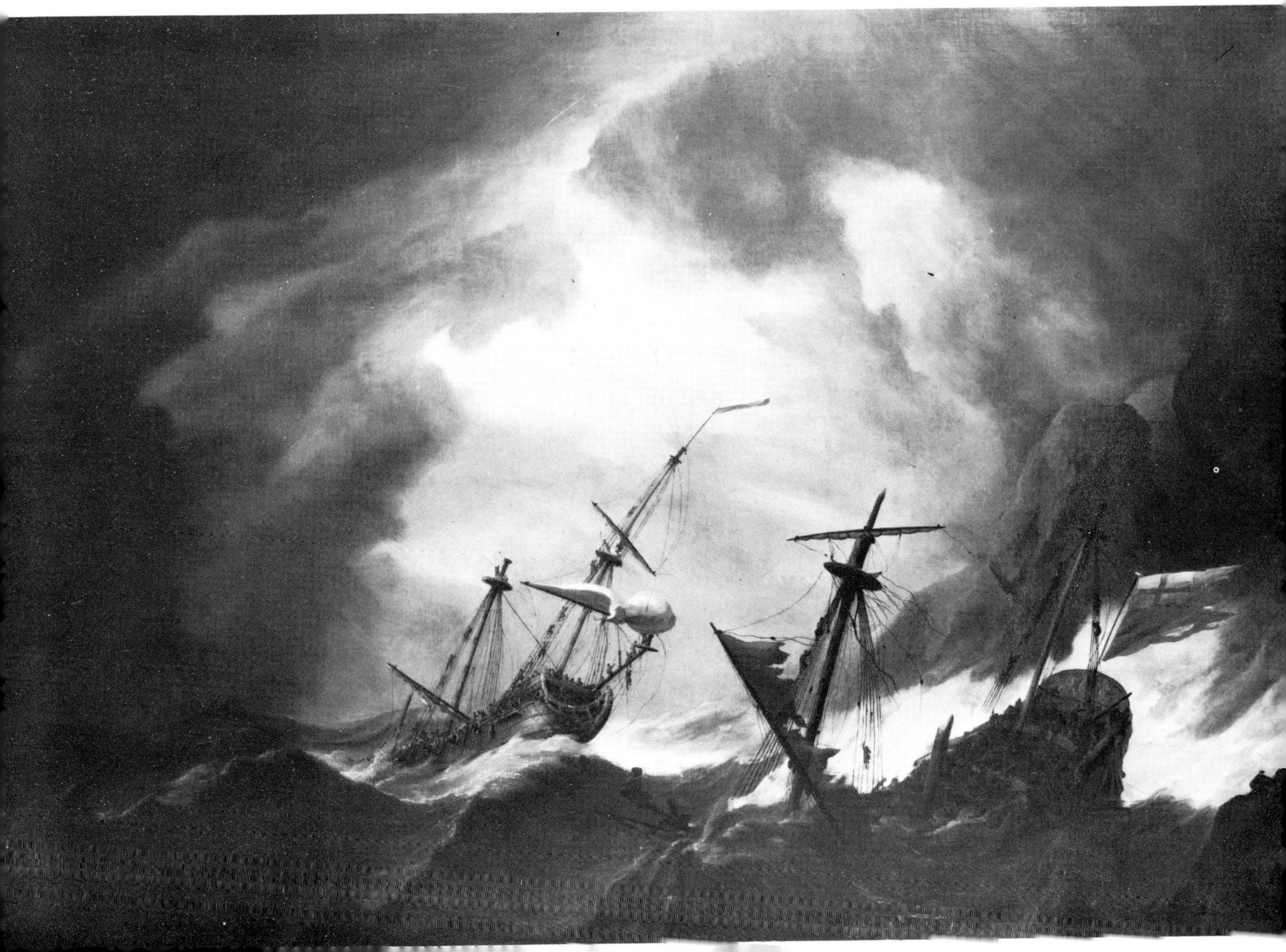

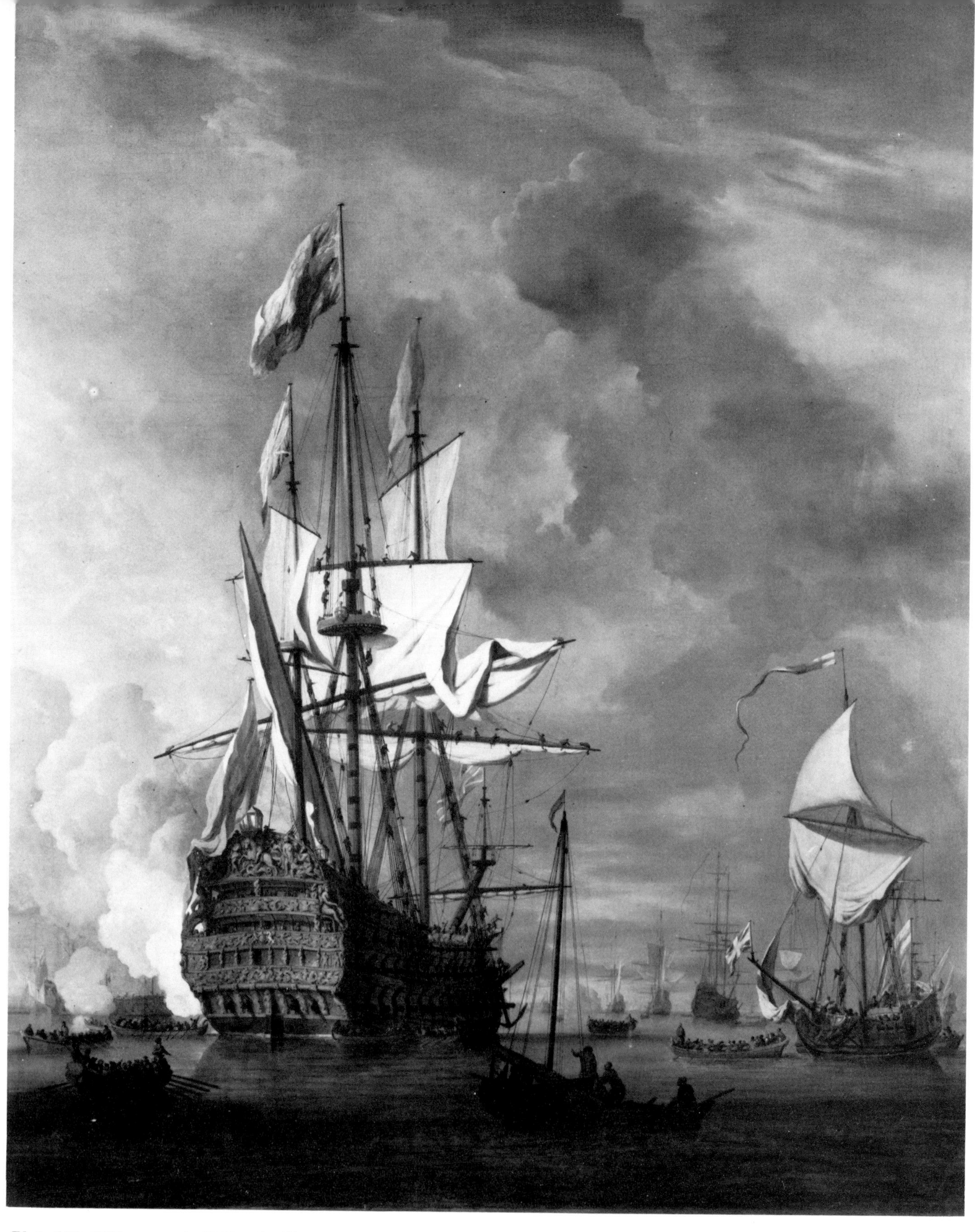

Plate 156. Willem van de Velde, the Younger, 1633-1707. "The *Royal Sovereign* in 1704." National Maritime Museum, Greenwich.

Plate 157. Robert Woodcock, 1692-1728. "The *Royal William* becalmed, about 1720." *This painting is based on the preceding work of the* Royal Sovereign *by the young van de Velde.* National Maritime Museum, Greenwich.

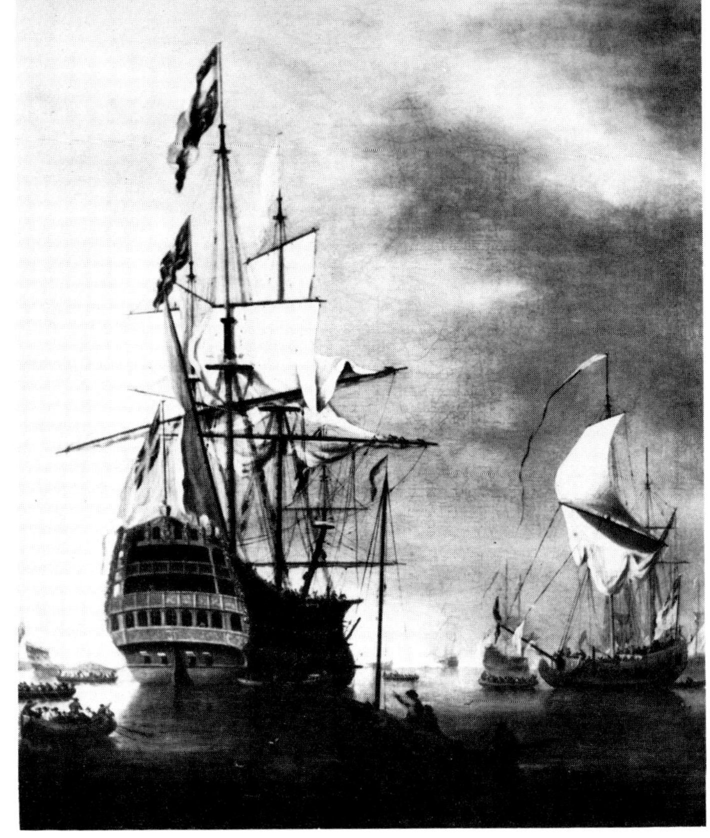

Plate 158. Abraham Storck, 1644-1710. "Shipping on the Y at Amsterdam." *The two yachts are privately owned, the one on the left by some very grand Dutchman. The ensign of the barge on the right bears the cypher of the Dutch West India Company. In the two boats in the foreground, as was the custom, the women do the rowing. Storck was a finished painter and an acute observer.* National Maritime Museum, Greenwich.

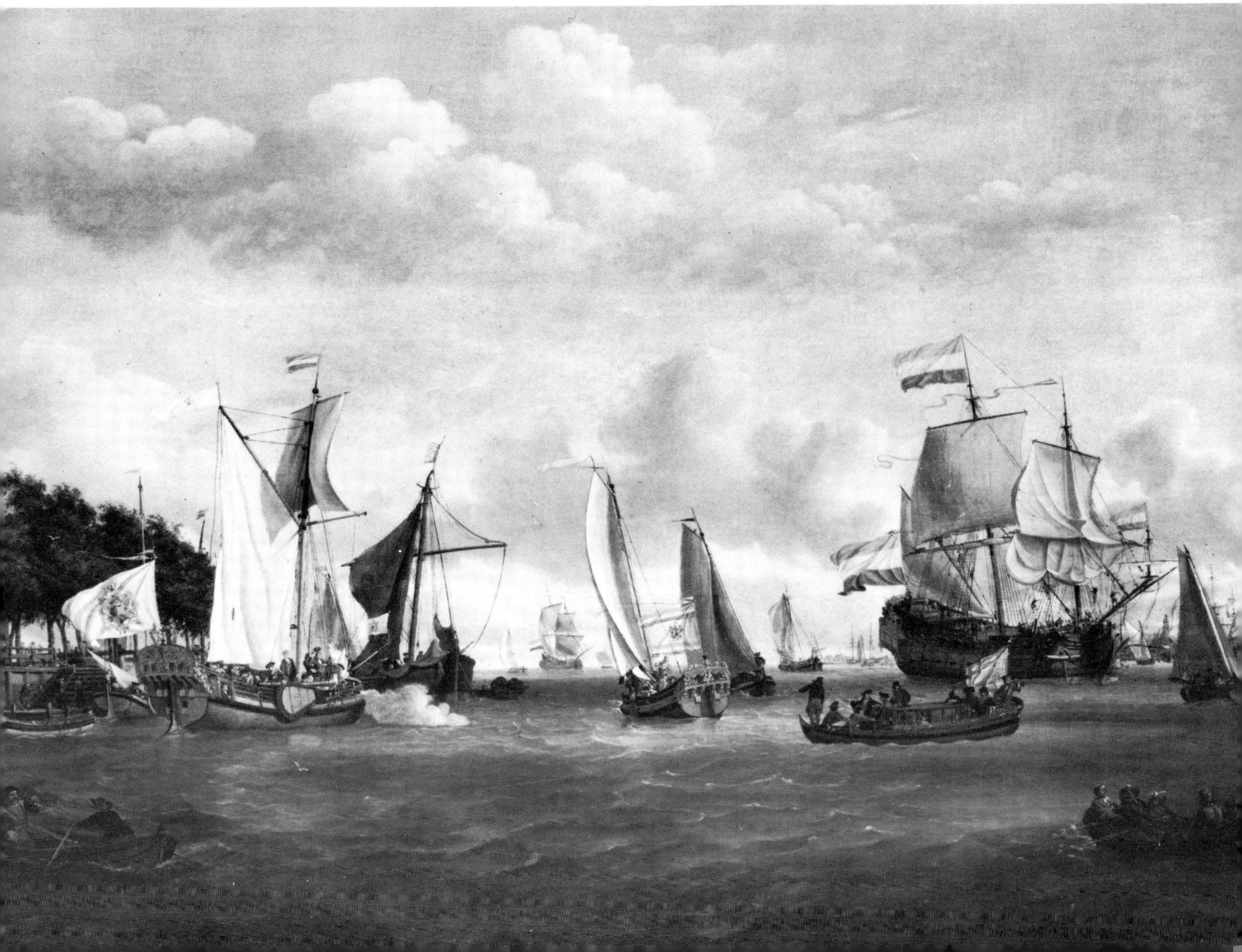

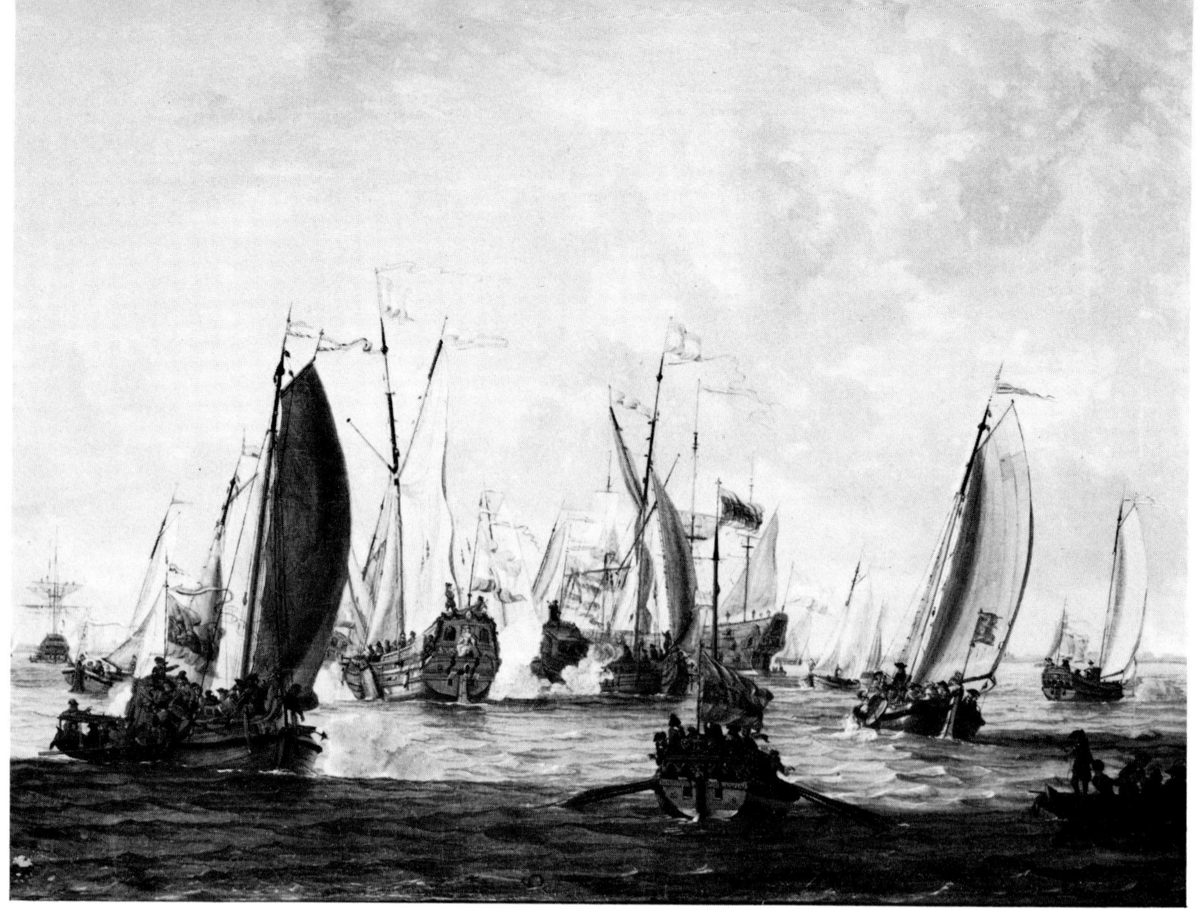

Plate 159. Abraham Storck, 1644-1710. "Czar Peter I going aboard in the Y off Amsterdam." Sotheby's.

Plate 160. Abraham Storck, 1644-1710. "The Four Days Fight in 1666." *The ship losing her main topmast is Prince Rupert of the Rhine's* Royal James *on the fourth day of the Four Days Fight, at 1.30 in the afternoon. The multi-striped ensigns of the Dutch ships on the left identified a squadron.* National Maritime Museum, Greenwich.

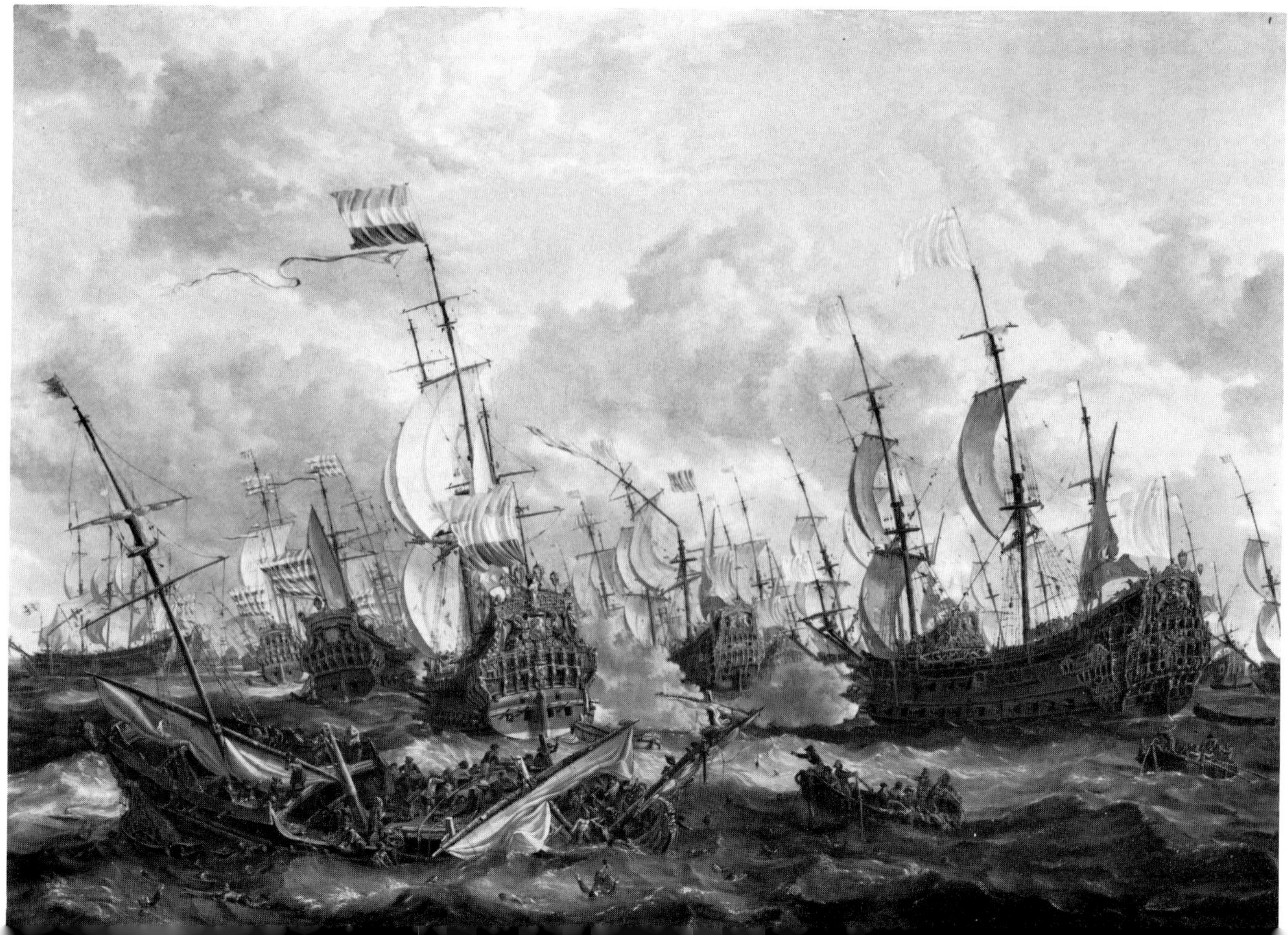

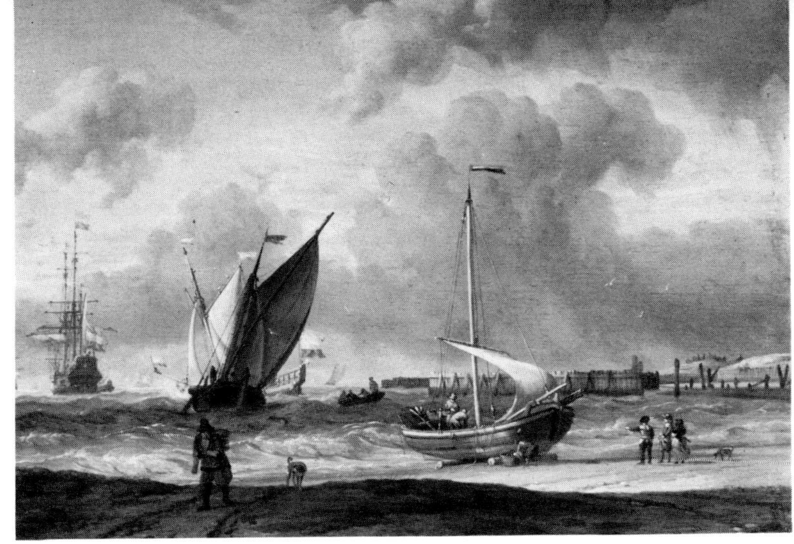

Plate 161. Abraham Storck, 1644-1710. "Fishing boats in a gale on the Dutch coast about 1670." *A tiny picture.* National Maritime Museum, Greenwich.

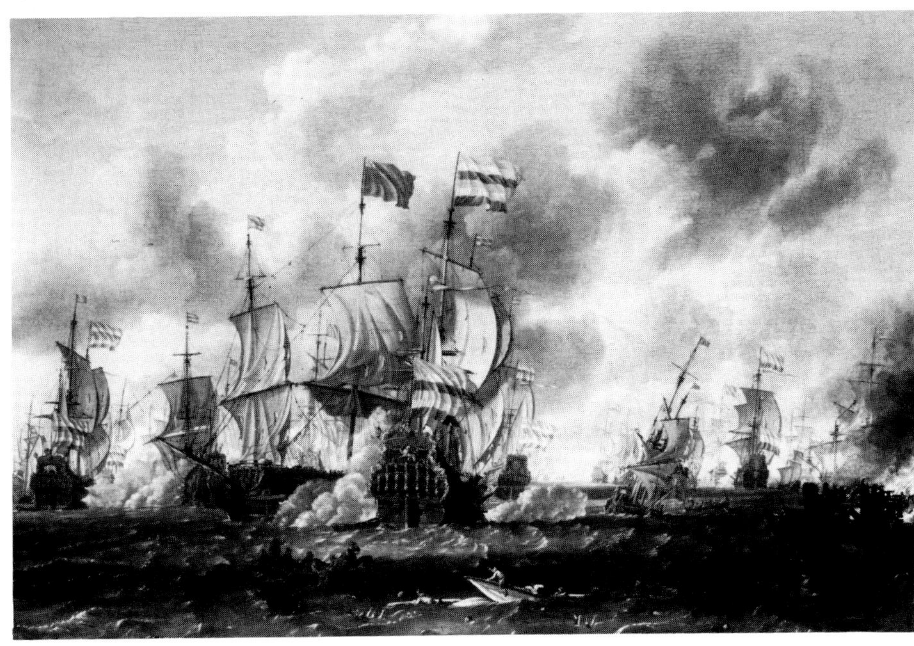

Plate 162. Abraham Storck, 1644-1710. "The Battle of Texel in 1673." *The 'double prince' ensign and flag on Cornelis Tromp's flagship is associated with the Admiralty of Amsterdam.* National Maritime Museum, Greenwich.

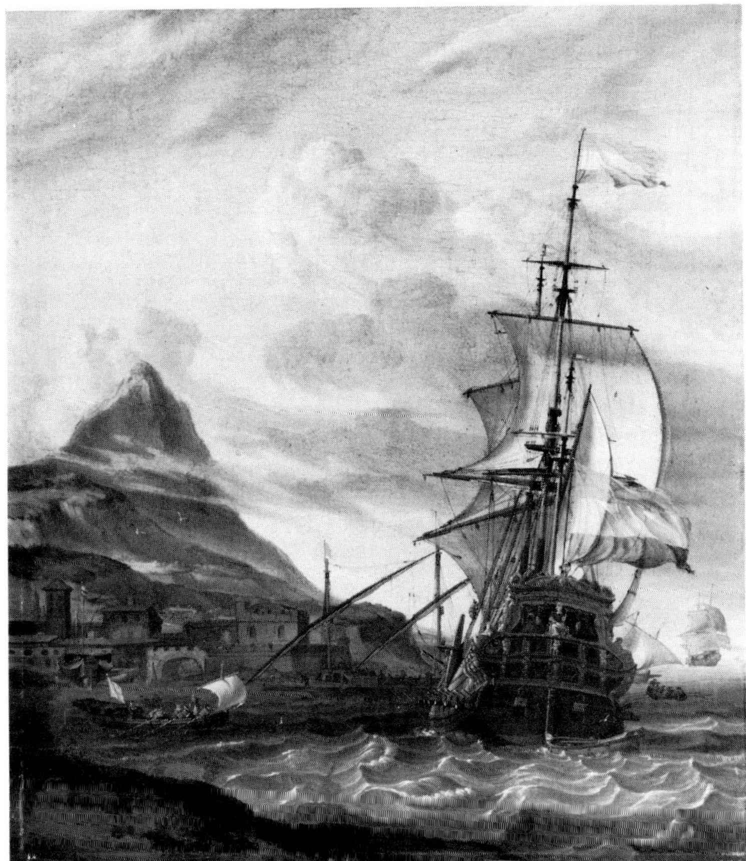

Plate 163. Abraham Storck, 1644-1710. "Dutch ships entering a Mediterranean port." National Maritime Museum, Greenwich.

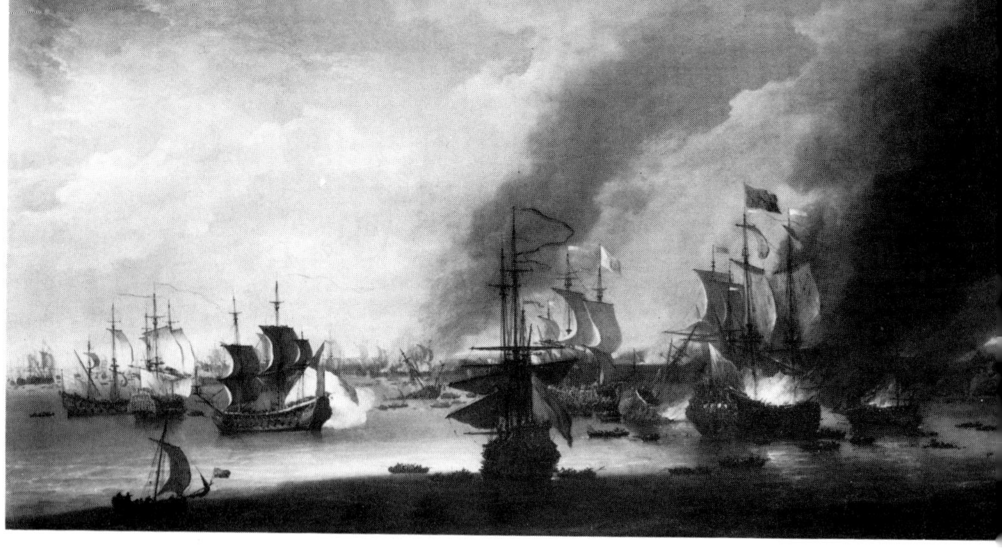

Plate 164. Adriaen van Diest, 1655-1704. "The destruction of the French fleet at La Hogue in 1692." *A good example of the work of the closest copier of the style and some of the paintings of van de Velde, the Younger. He sometimes signed 'AD' on the back of the canvas.* National Maritime Museum, Greenwich.

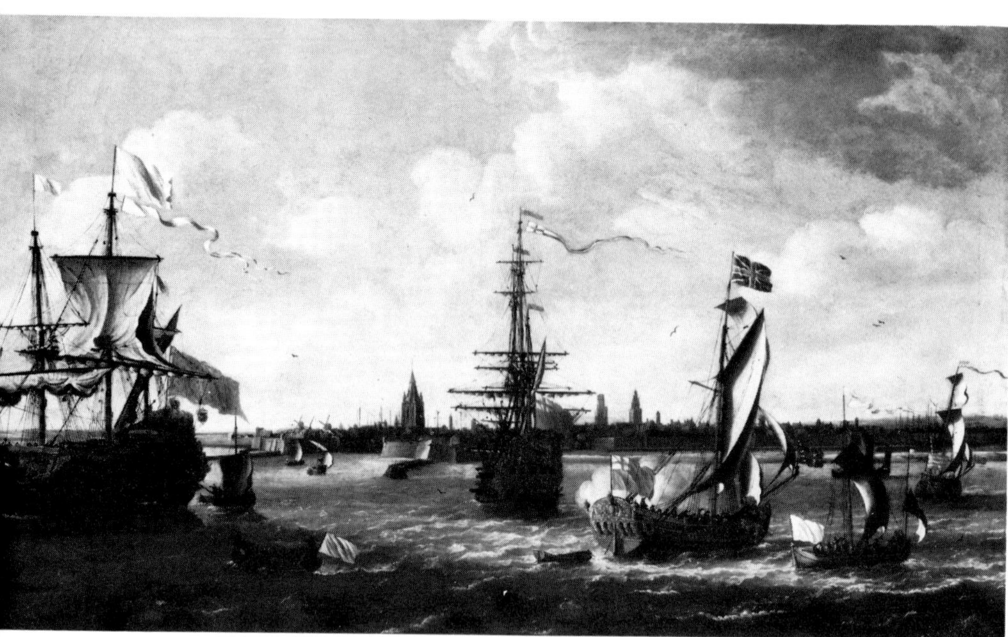

Plate 165. Jacob Knyff, 1638-1681. "French flagship off Calais." *The greyish green in the hulls and the manner of painting the sea are typical.* National Maritime Museum, Greenwich.

Plate 166. Jacob Knyff, 1638-1681. "An English first rate and galleys off a southern port." *A huge painting. It was normal for galleys to be covered in hot climates.* National Maritime Museum, Greenwich.

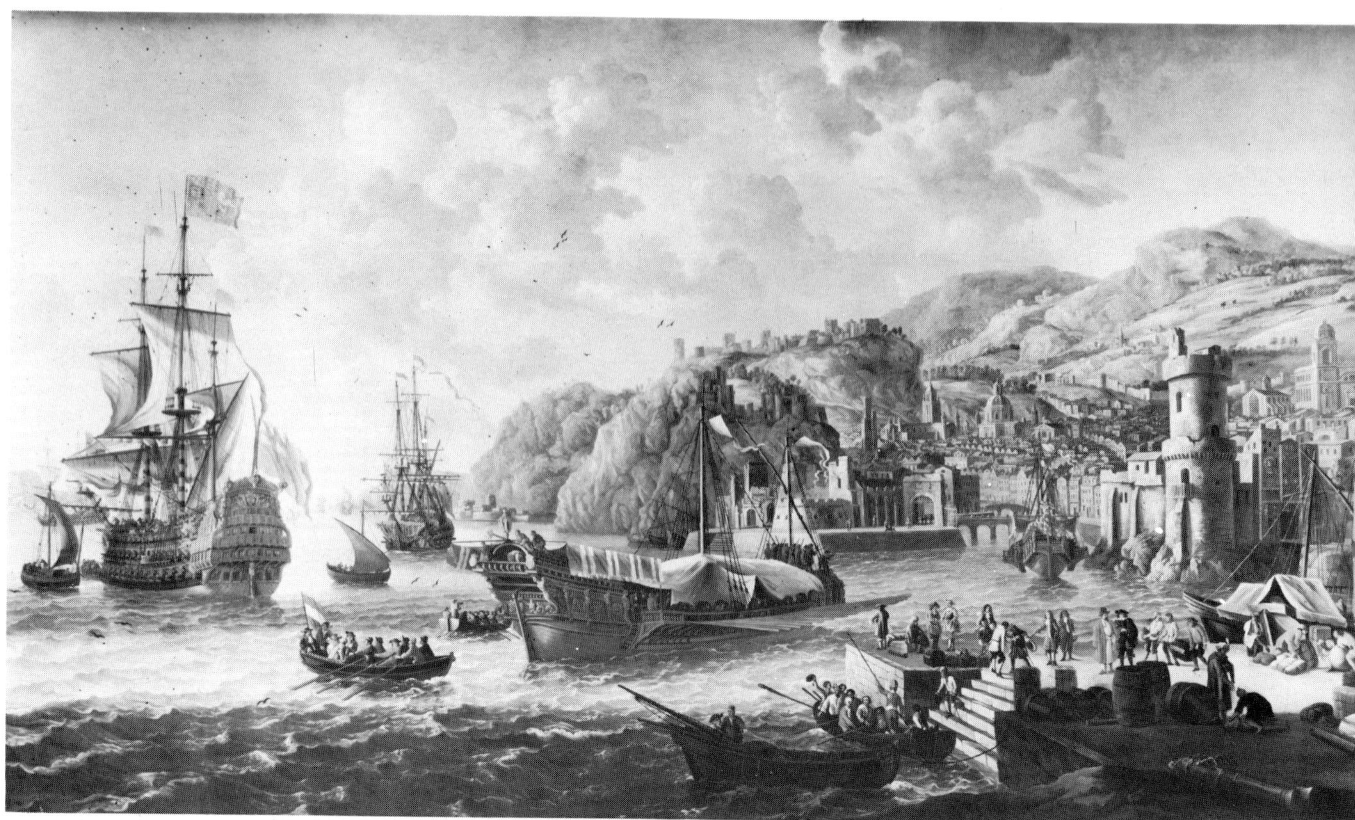

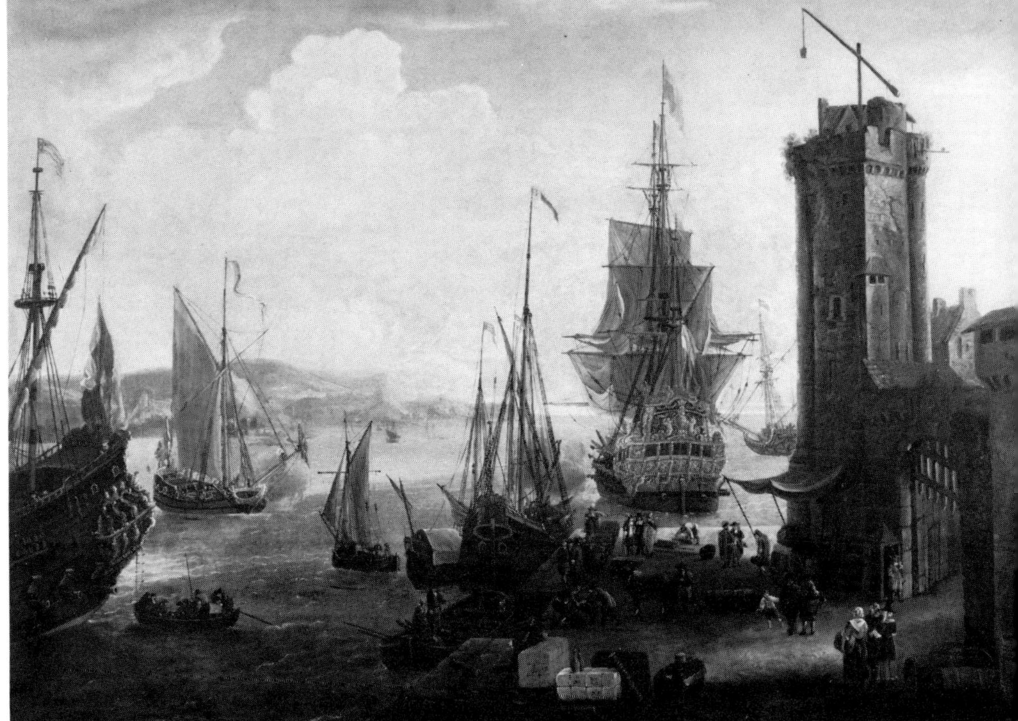

Plate 167. Jacob Knyff, 1638-1681. "A dock scene at an English port, about 1675." *It was the appearance of this signed picture in the sale rooms in 1972 that identified a whole group of Knyff paintings formerly attributed to Sailmaker.* National Maritime Museum, Greenwich.

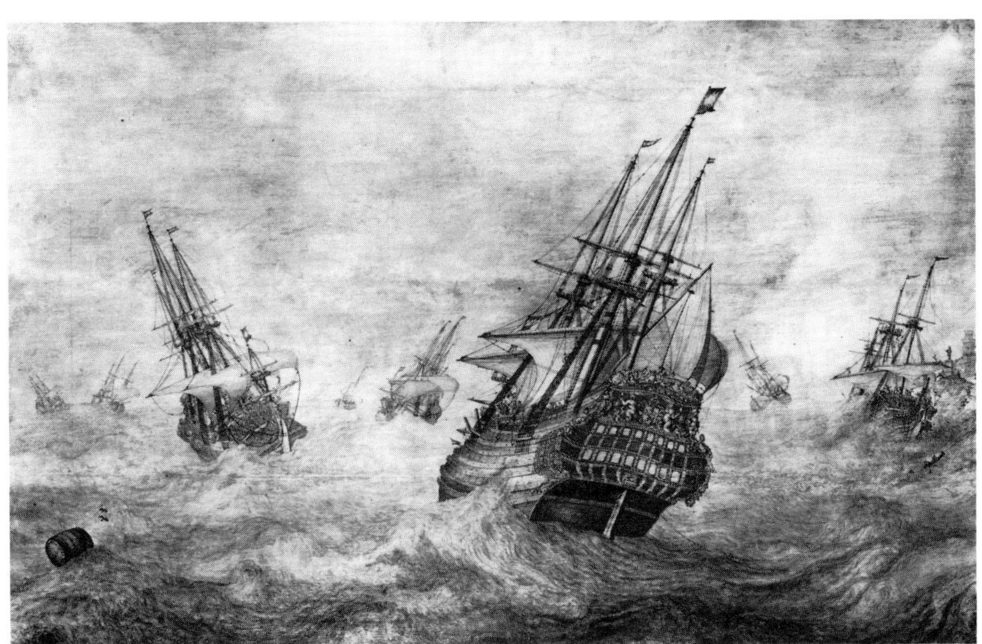

Plate 168. Pieter Vogelaer, 1641-1720. "Dutch East Indiamen in a storm, about 1680." *A late grisaille artist of modest talent, almost a primitive.* National Maritime Museum, Greenwich.

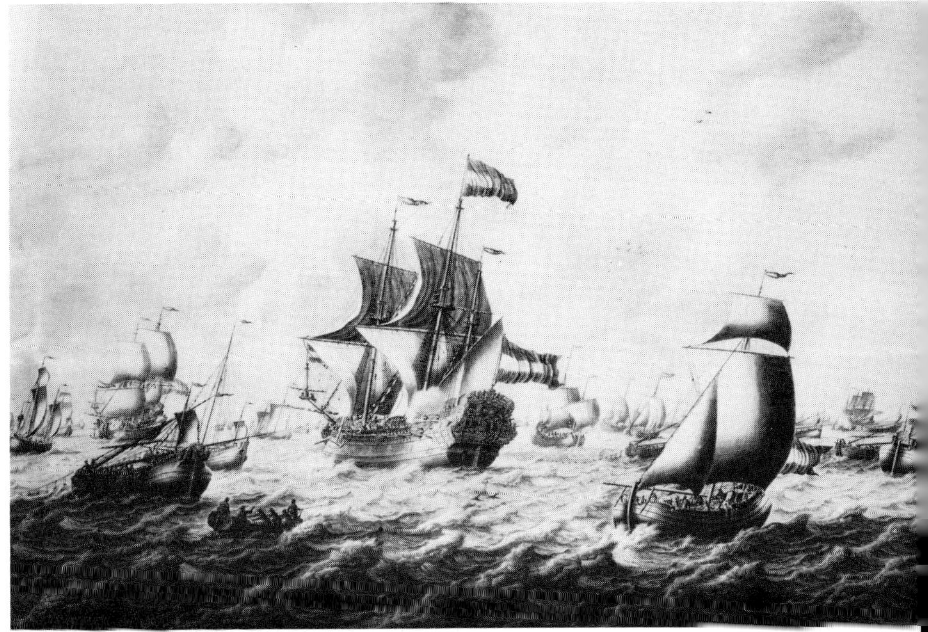

Plate 169. Adriaen van Salm, c.1660-1720. "Dutch herring busses with their guard ship, about 1700." *A typical subject of van Salm, well executed in grisaille. He was one of the last artists to use this medium, the last being Bouwmeester who was van Salm's superior in artistry.* National Maritime Museum, Greenwich.

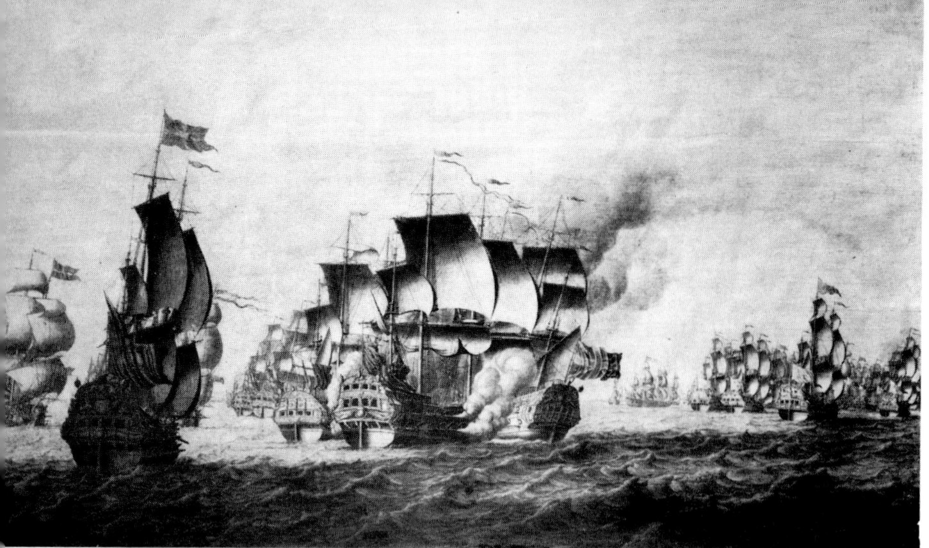

Plate 170. Adriaen van Salm, c.1660-1720. ''Forbin's attempt against Scotland in 1708.'' National Maritime Museum, Greenwich.

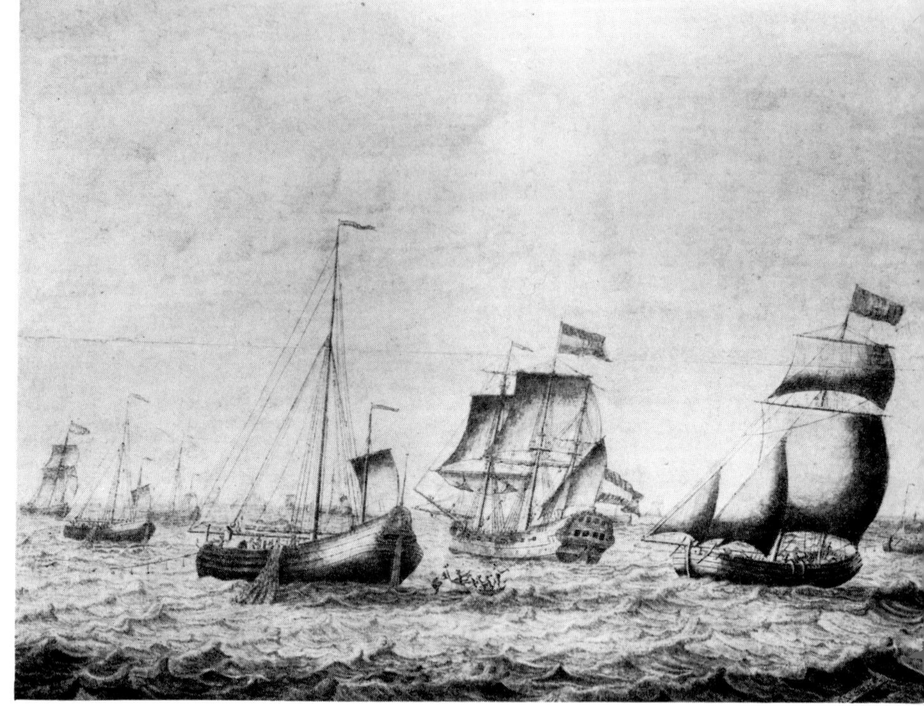

Plate 171. Roelof van Salm, 1688-1765. ''Dutch herring fishery about 1720.'' *The herring busses were drifters, the nets laid over their bows and a sail rigged aft to increase the stern drift.* National Maritime Museum, Greenwich.

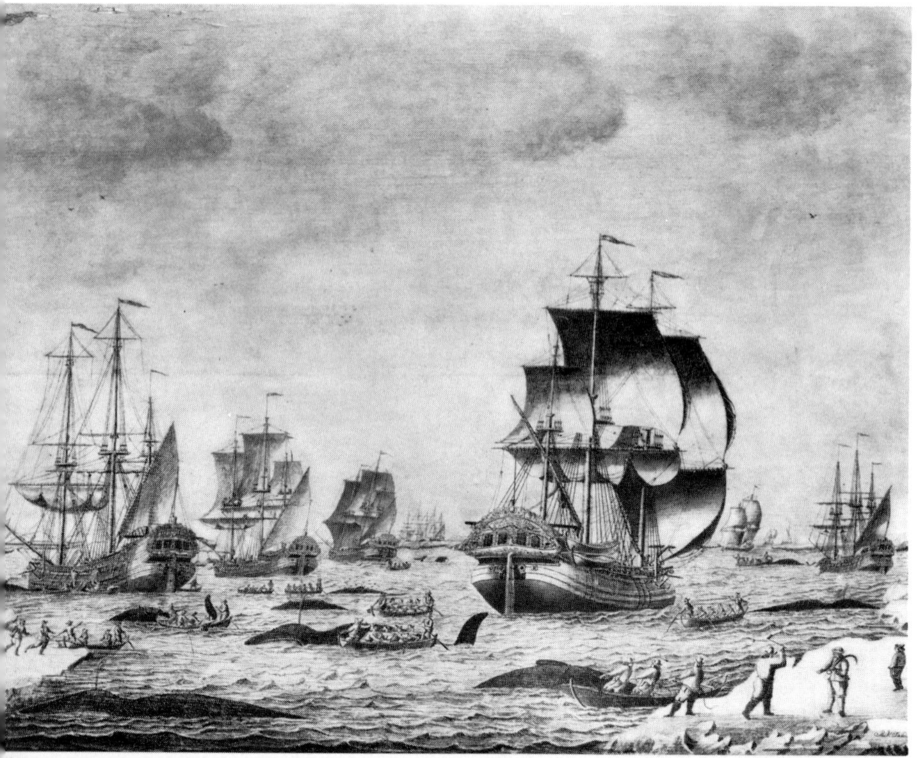

Plate 172. Roelof van Salm, 1688-1765. ''The Dutch whale fishery about 1720.'' National Maritime Museum, Greenwich.

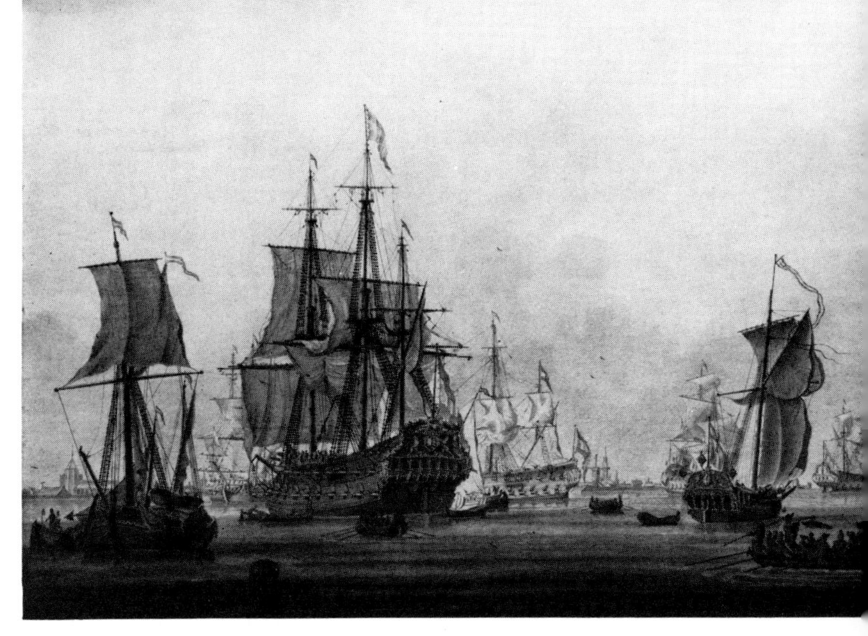

Plate 173. Cornelisz Bouwmeester, 1670-1733. "Dutch ships at anchor about 1700." National Maritime Museum, Greenwich.

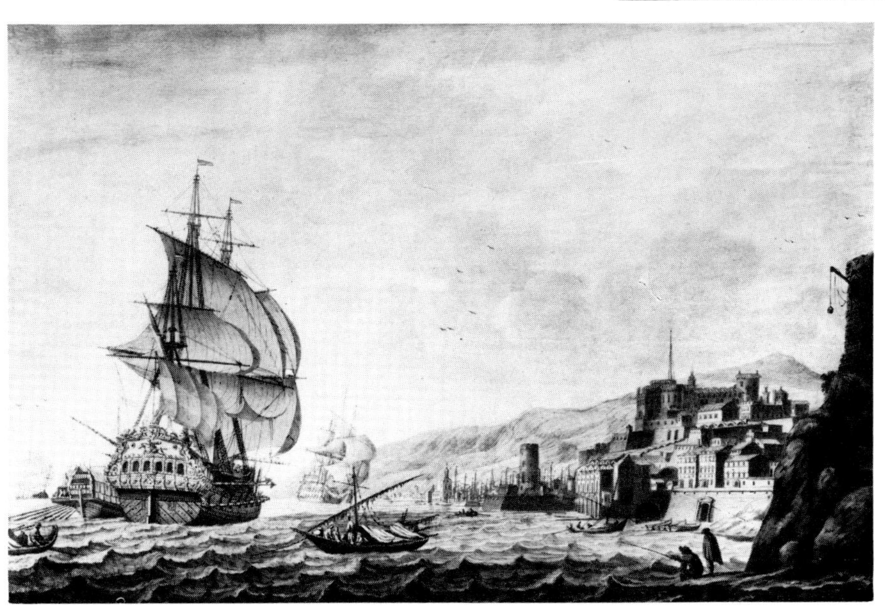

Plate 174. Cornelisz Bouwmeester, 1670-1733. "The Dutch ship *Jonge Prins te Paard* arriving at Naples, about 1720." *The last of the grisaille artists, Bouwmeester sometimes used sepia and black ink to give the effect of colour.* National Maritime Museum, Greenwich.

Plate 175. Isaac Sailmaker, 1633/4-1721. "East India Company yard in the Thames about 1670." National Maritime Museum, Greenwich.

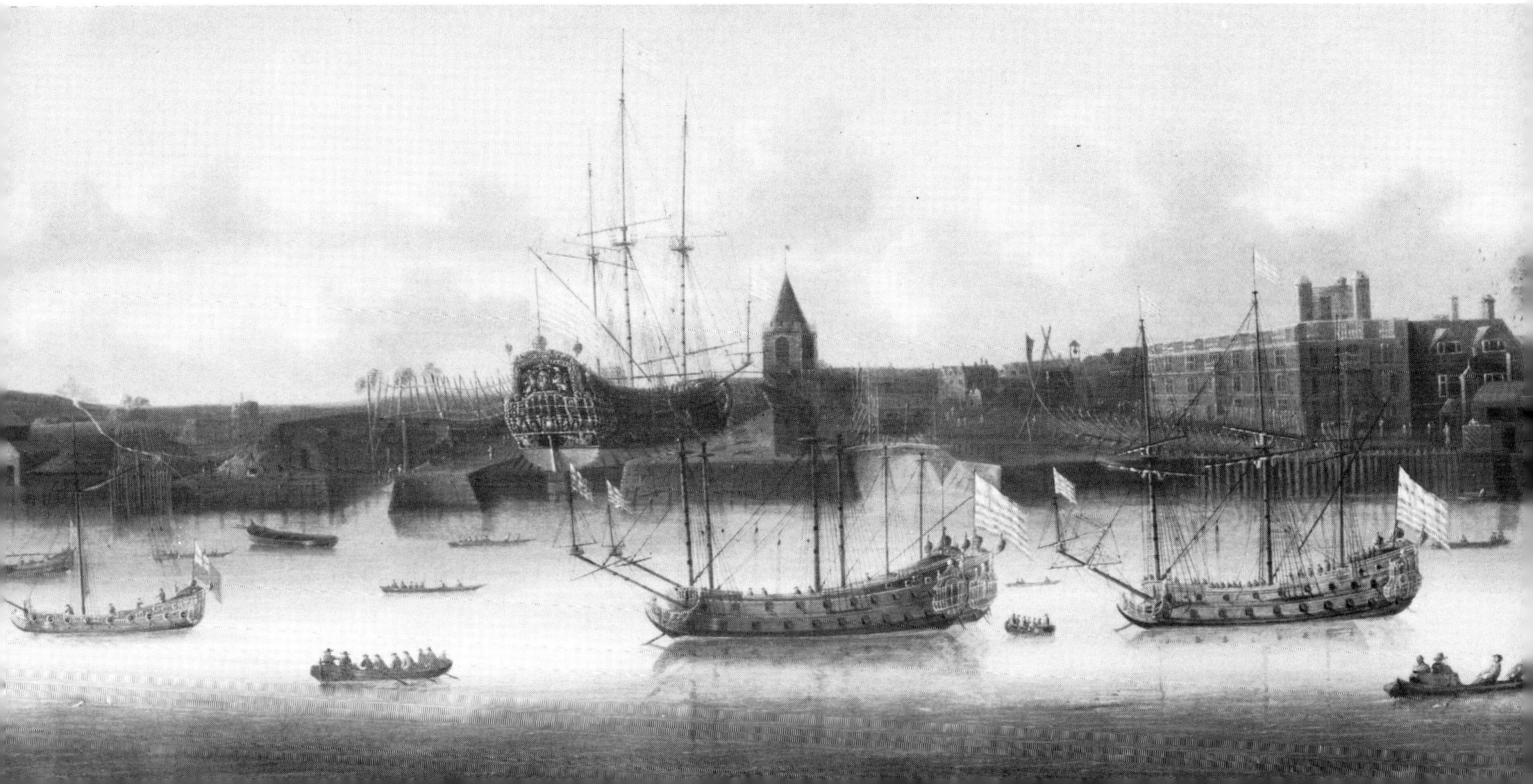

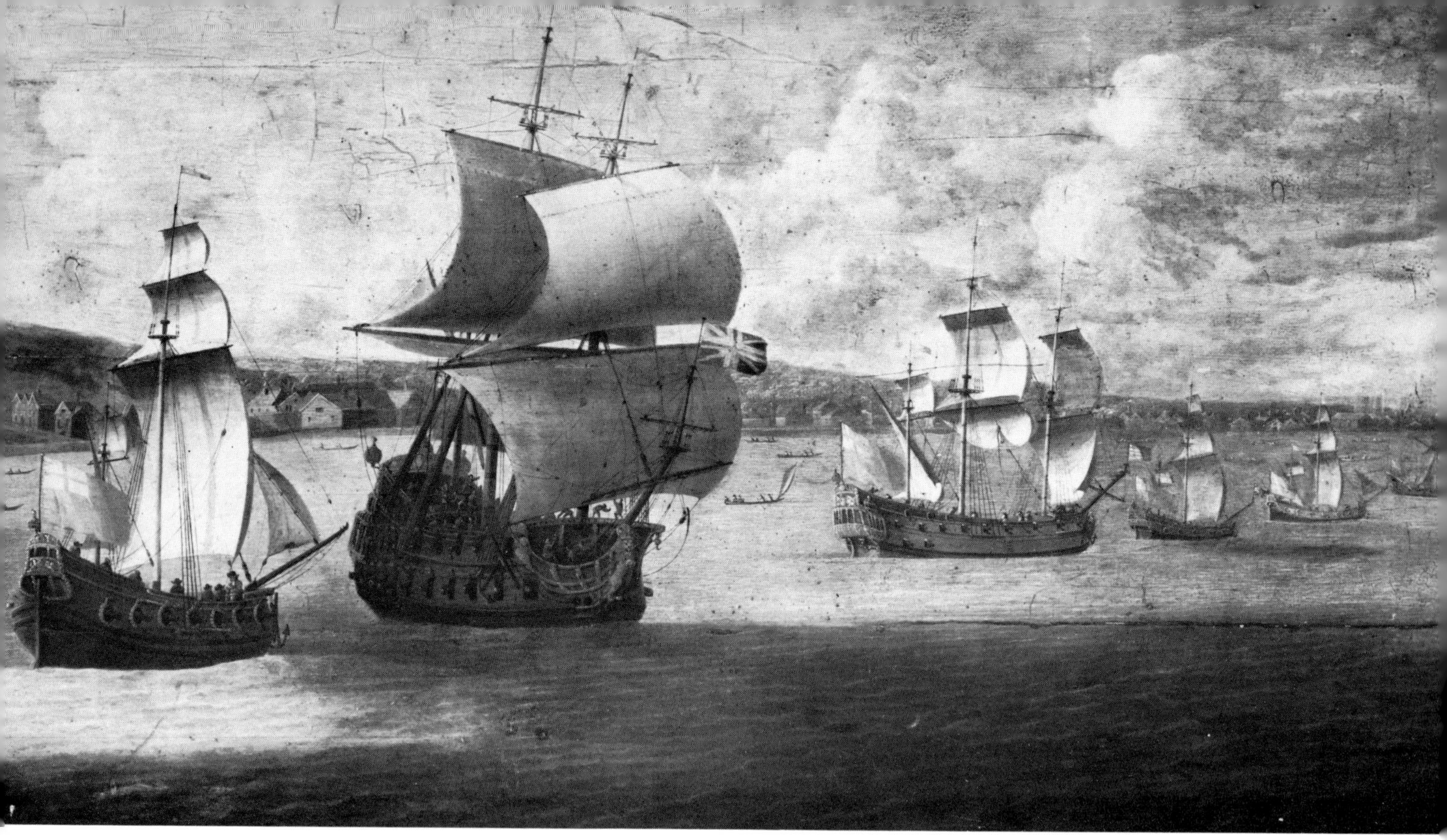

Plate 176. Isaac Sailmaker, 1633/4-1721. "Shipping in the Thames about 1670." National Maritime Museum, Greenwich.

Plate 177. Isaac Sailmaker, 1633/4-1721. "The first-rate *Britannia* of 1689." National Maritime Museum, Greenwich.

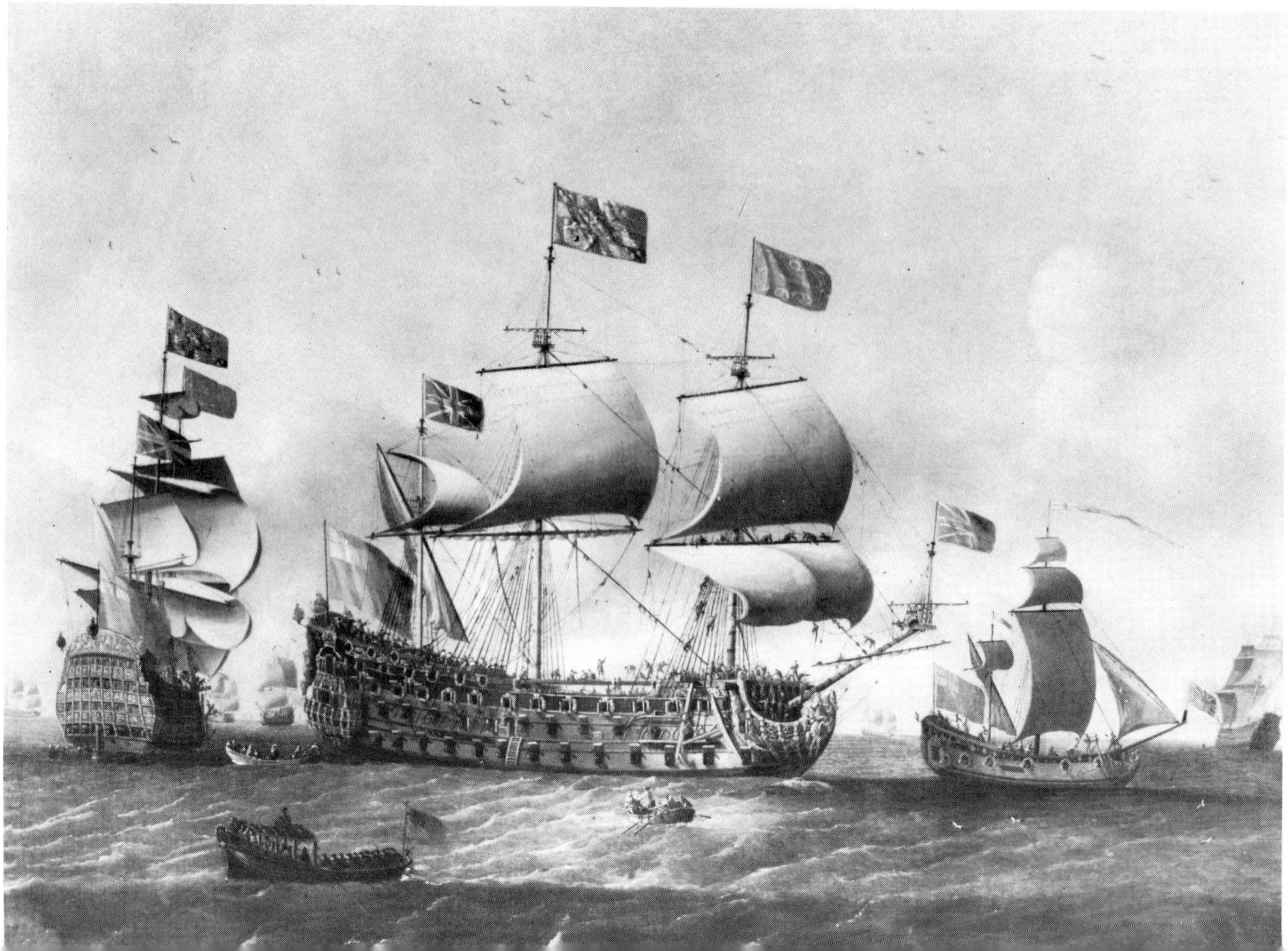

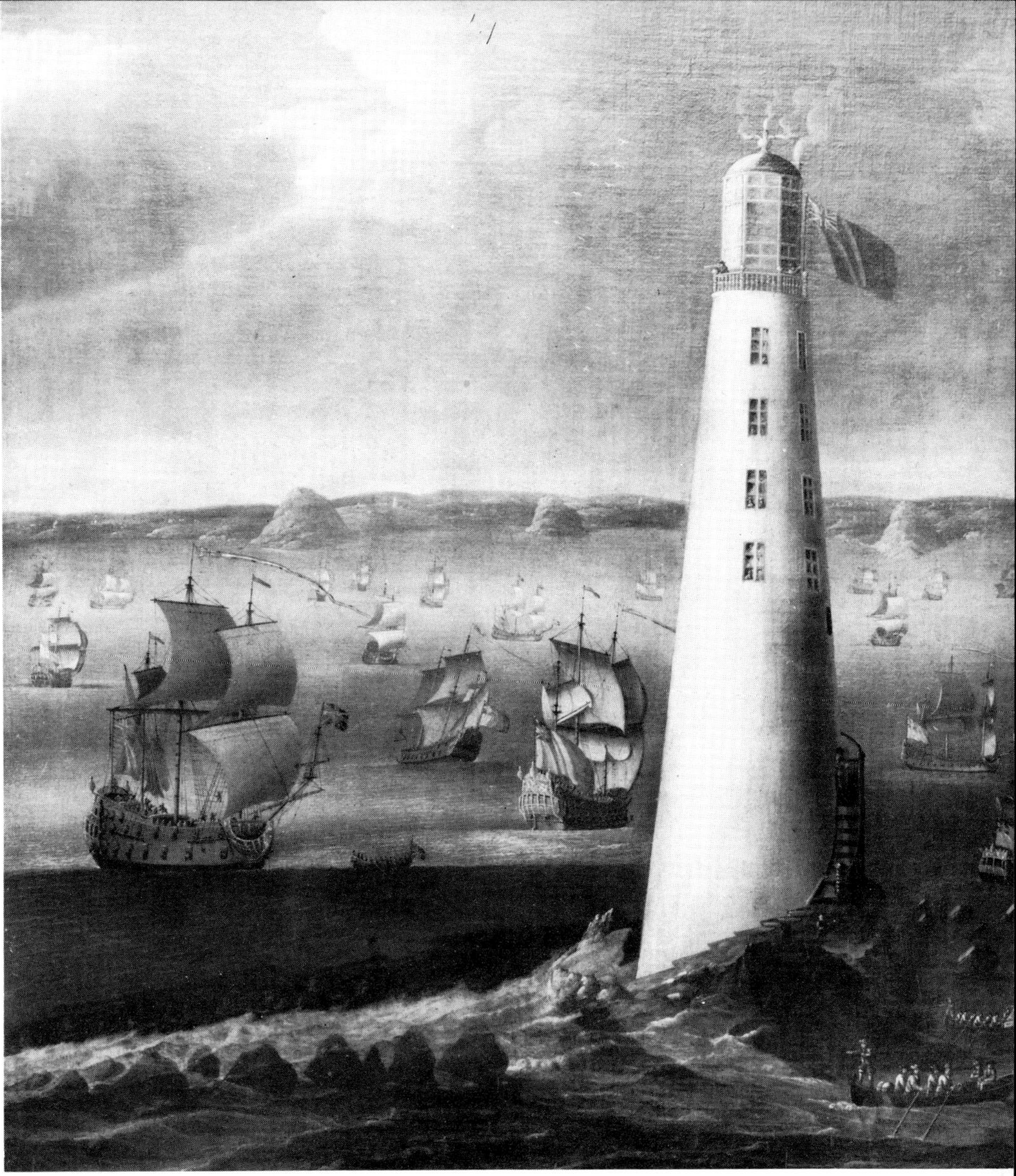

Plate 178. Isaac Sailmaker, 1633/4-1721. "Rudyard's Eddystone lighthouse, completed in 1709." *This well documented picture provided the key to the identification of this artist's work.* Private collection (on loan to the National Maritime Museum, Greenwich).

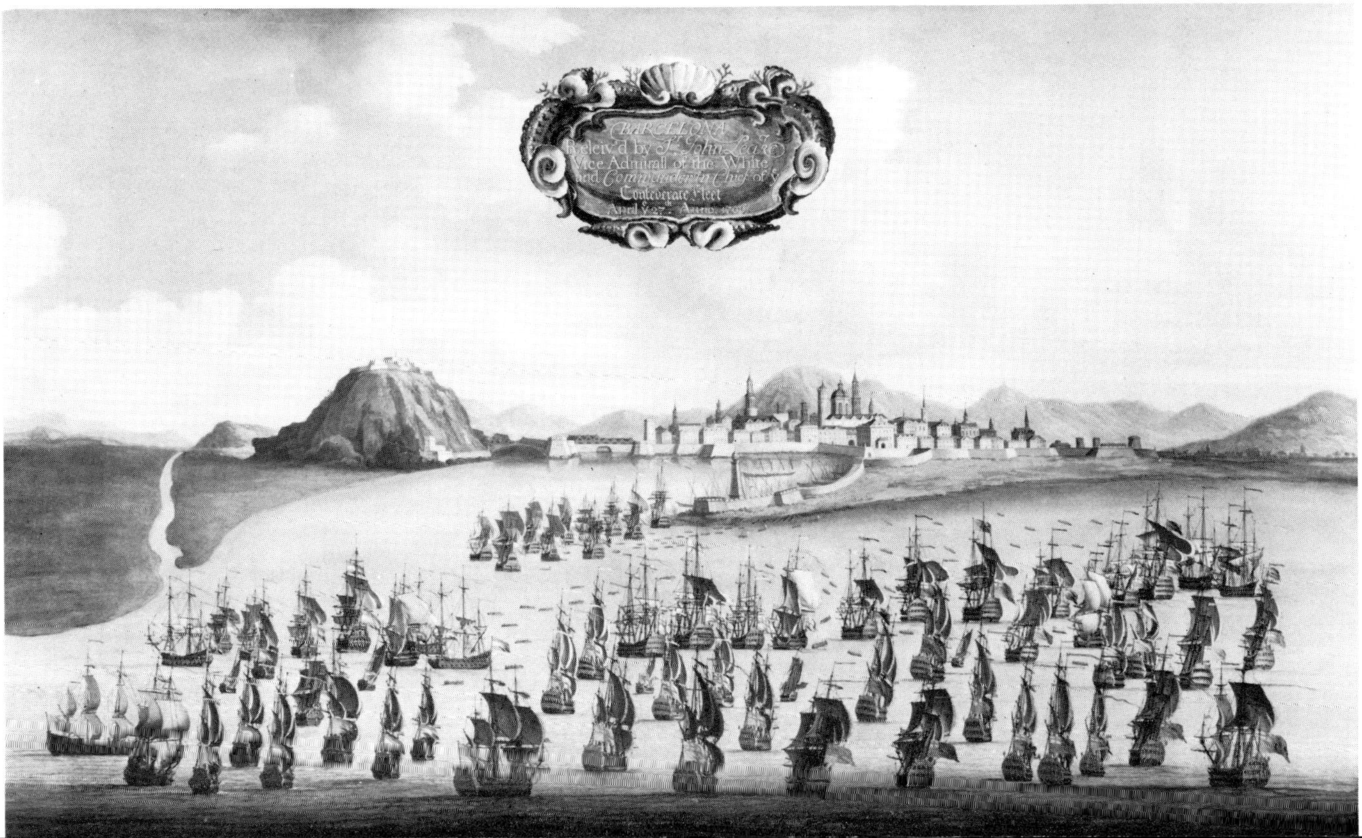

Plate 179. H. Vale, fl.1700. "The relief of Barcelona on August 29th, 1706, dated 1713." *The city was besieged by the French during the War of the Spanish Succession until Sir John Leake appeared with the Anglo-Dutch fleet. The French blockading squadron left and the siege was raised.* National Maritime Museum, Greenwich.

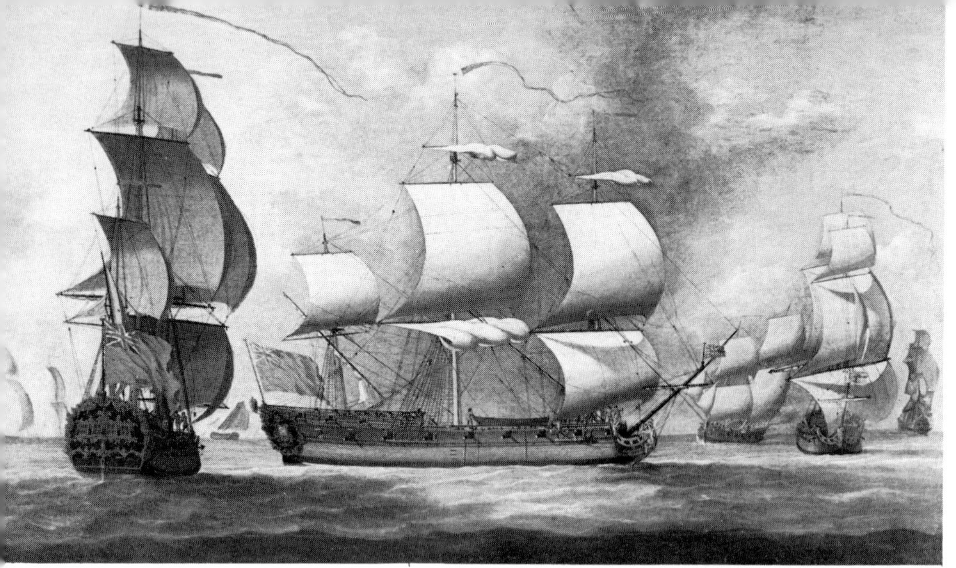

Plate 180. H. Vale, fl.1700. "An English sixth rate, dated 1714." *She is apparently a French prize because her stern galleries are in the French fashion.* Simon Carter Esq.

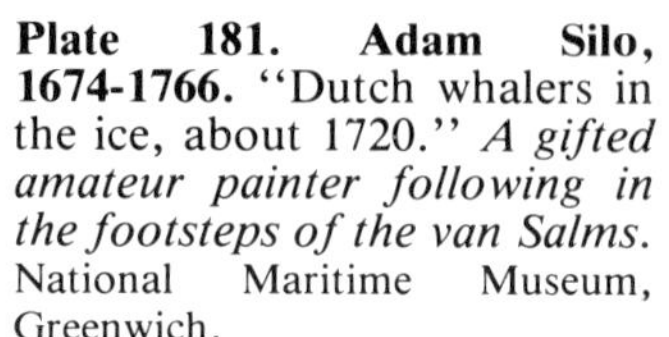

Plate 181. Adam Silo, 1674-1766. "Dutch whalers in the ice, about 1720." *A gifted amateur painter following in the footsteps of the van Salms.* National Maritime Museum, Greenwich.

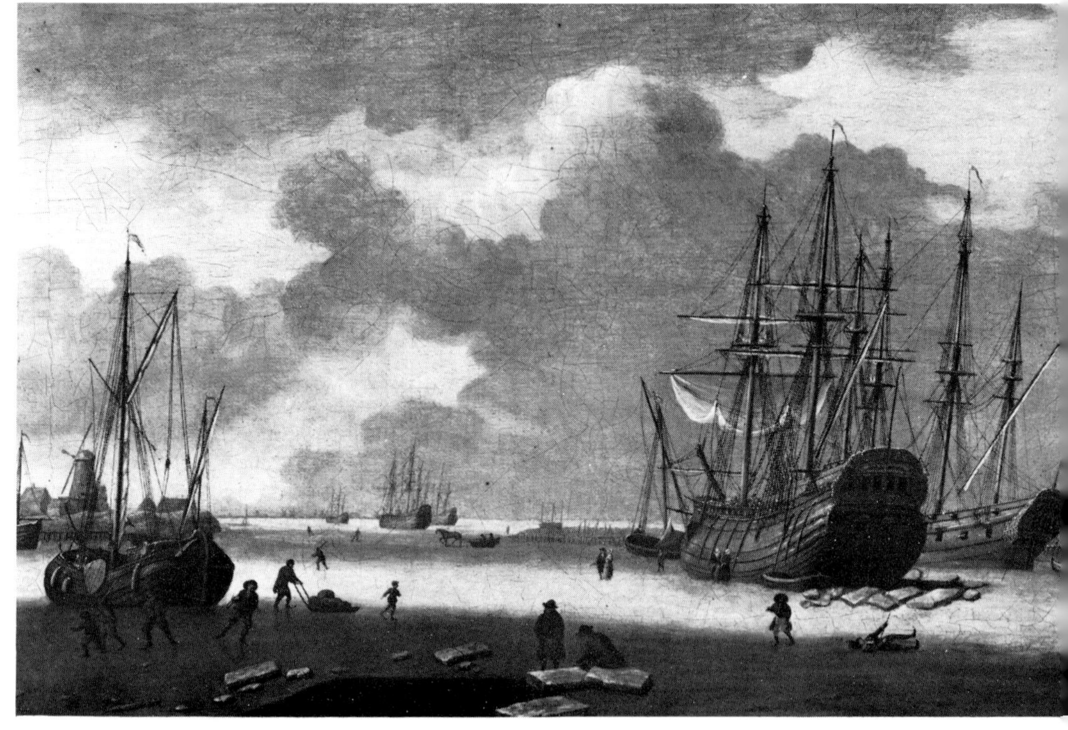

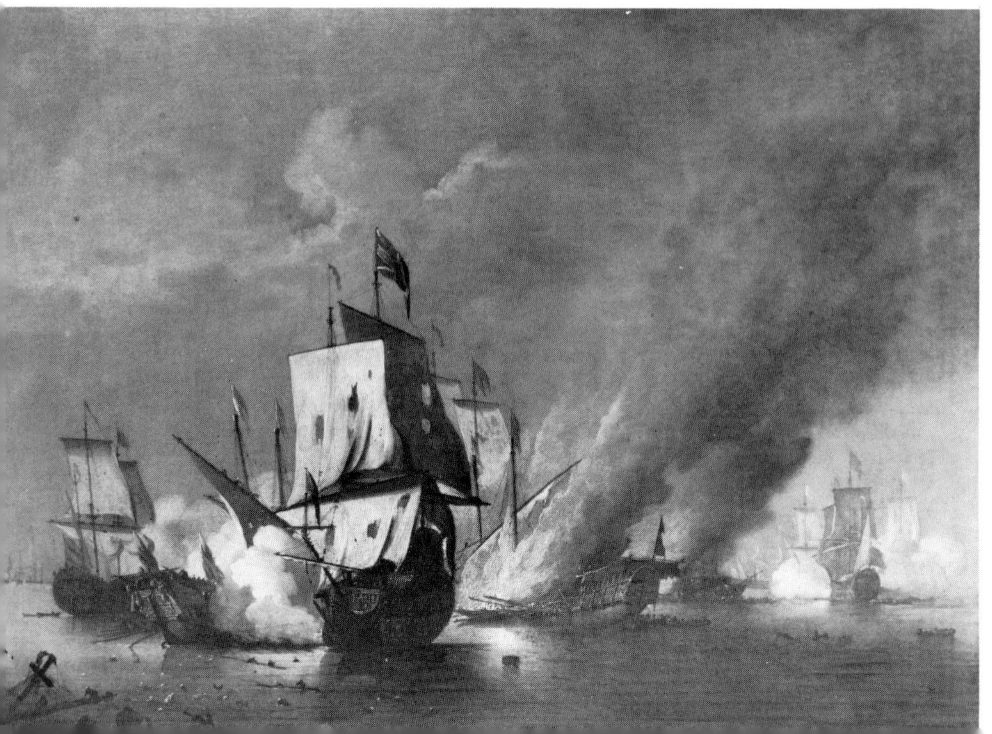

Plate 182. J. van Haecken, fl. early 18th century. "The flagship of the English Mediterranean squadron in action with galleys of the Barbary corsairs." *A minor artist painting in a style derived from the van de Veldes.* Sotheby's.

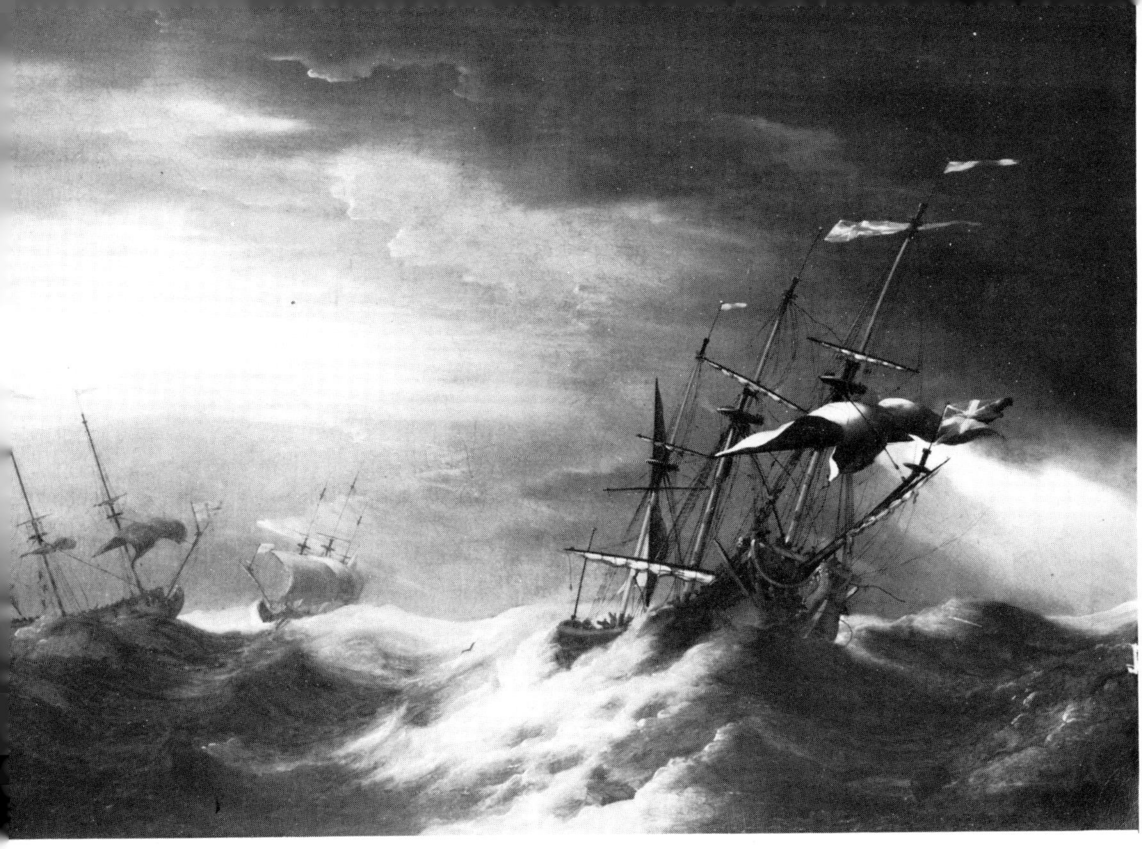

Plate 183. Johann van der Hagen, b.1675-c.1745. "English men-of-war in a storm, about 1690." National Maritime Museum, Greenwich.

Plate 184. Johann van der Hagen, b.1675-c.1745. "A ketch rigged royal yacht in a breeze, about 1720." *This artist probably worked in the van de Veldes' studio and copied their style. The painting of the stern shows a nice quality of reflected light and the rendering of the seas coming over the windward side and the peculiar, if not inaccurate, angle at which the bowsprit appears is typical of van der Hagen's work.* National Maritime Museum, Greenwich.

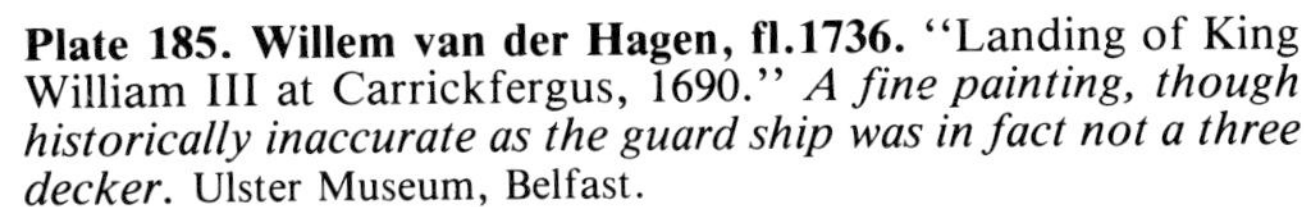

Plate 185. Willem van der Hagen, fl.1736. "Landing of King William III at Carrickfergus, 1690." *A fine painting, though historically inaccurate as the guard ship was in fact not a three decker.* Ulster Museum, Belfast.

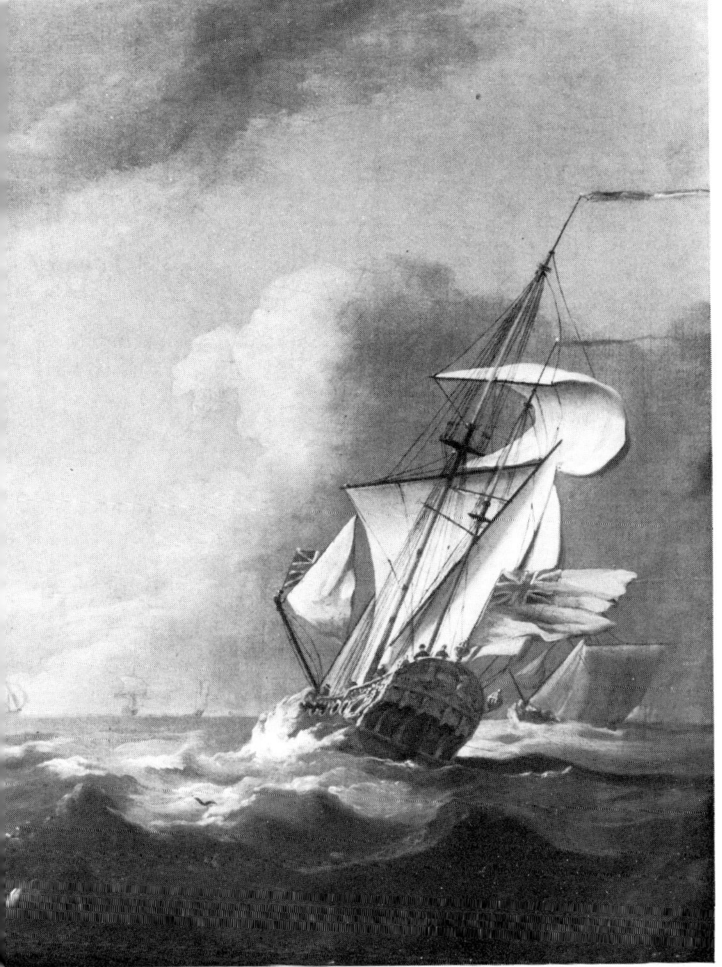

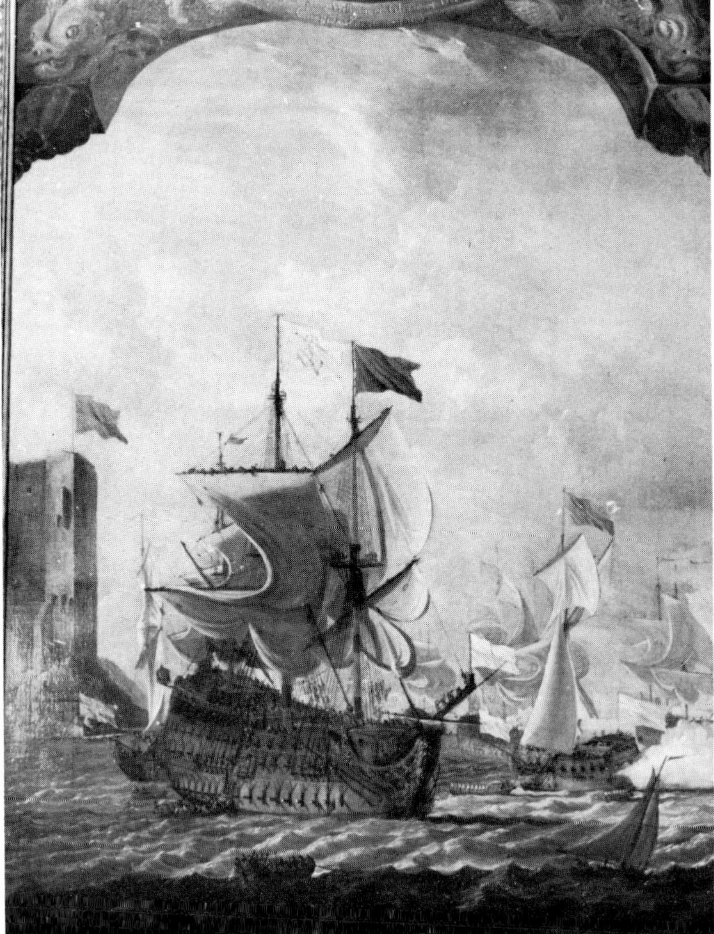

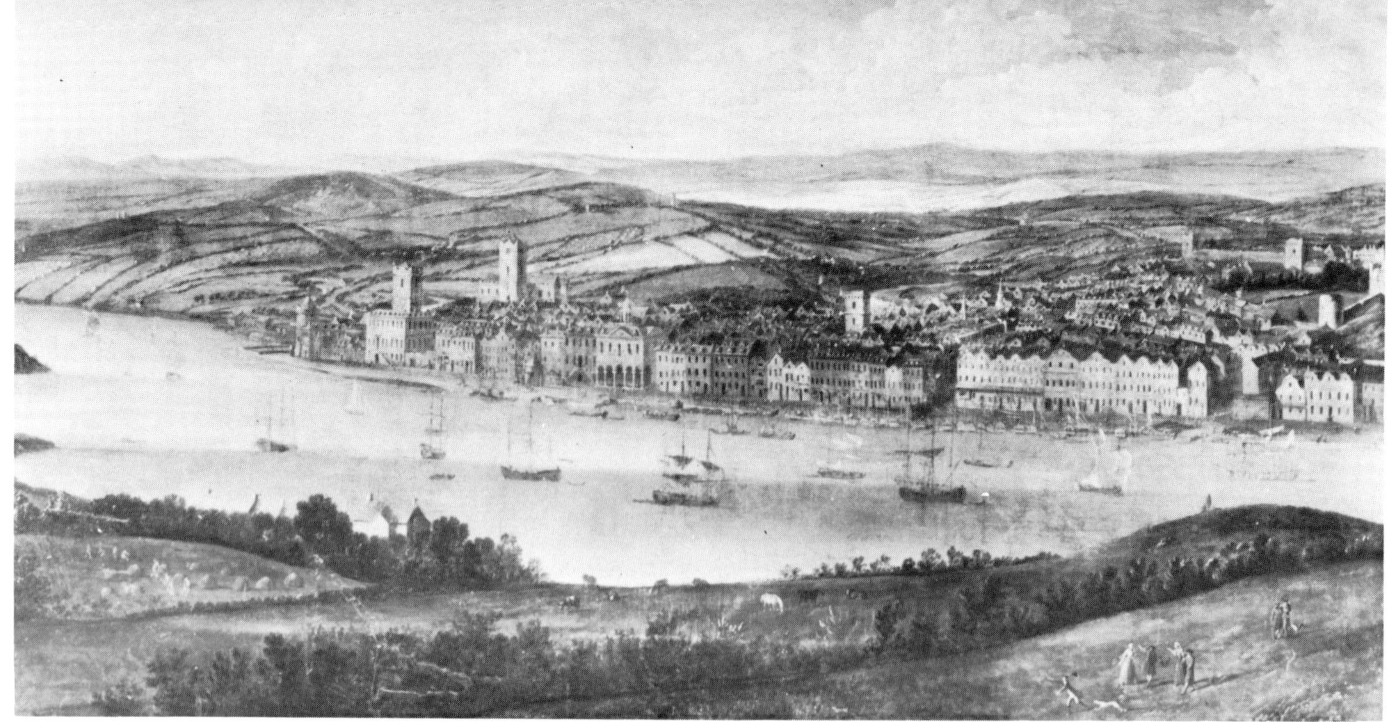

Plate 186. Willem van der Hagen, fl.1736. "View of Waterford, Ireland, dated 1736." Waterford Town Council.

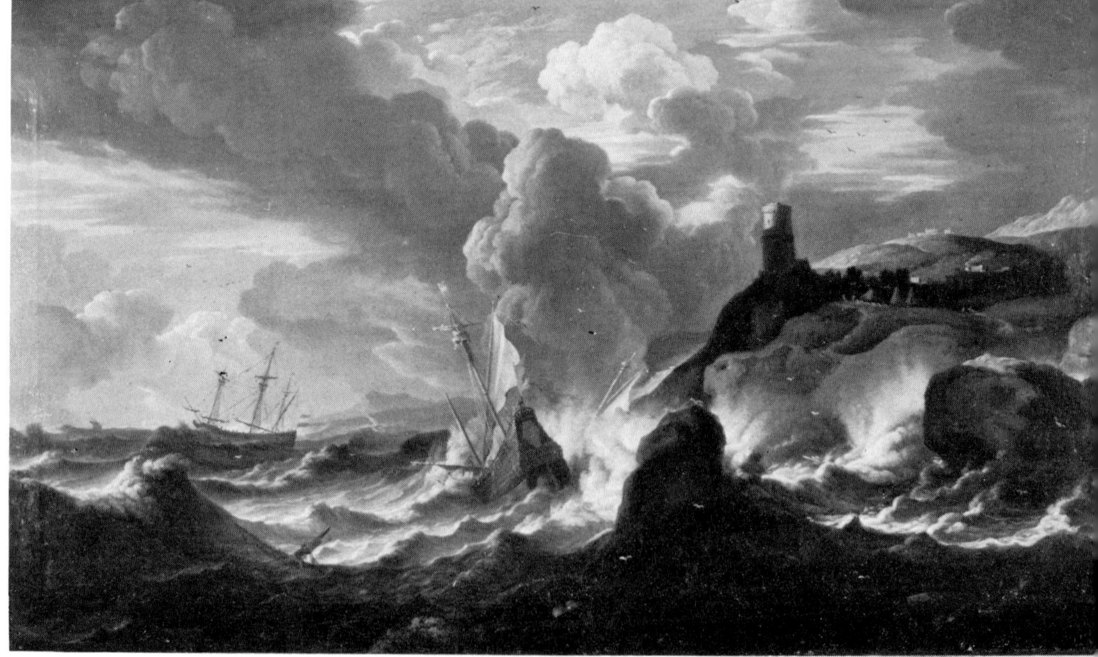

Plate 187. Frederik Vilhelm Boehme, fl. early 18th century. "A rocky coast with ships wrecked in a storm." *Very much in the style of Bonaventura Peeters (Plates 70 and 71).* Museum of Fine Arts, Copenhagen.

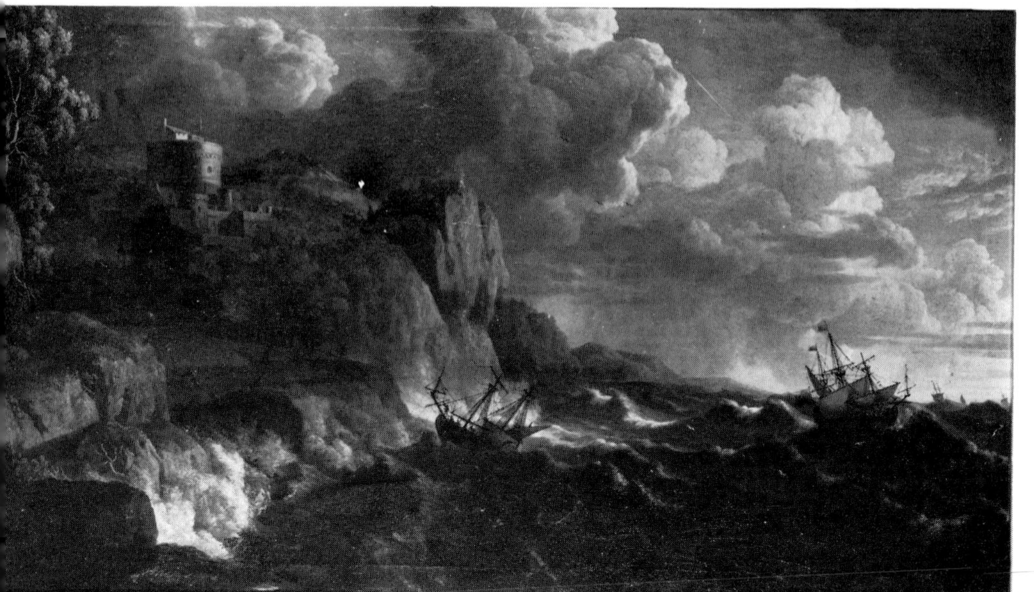

Plate 188. Frederik Vilhelm Boehme, fl. early 18th century. "Ships in distress off a high coast, dated 1704." Museum of Fine Arts, Copenhagen.

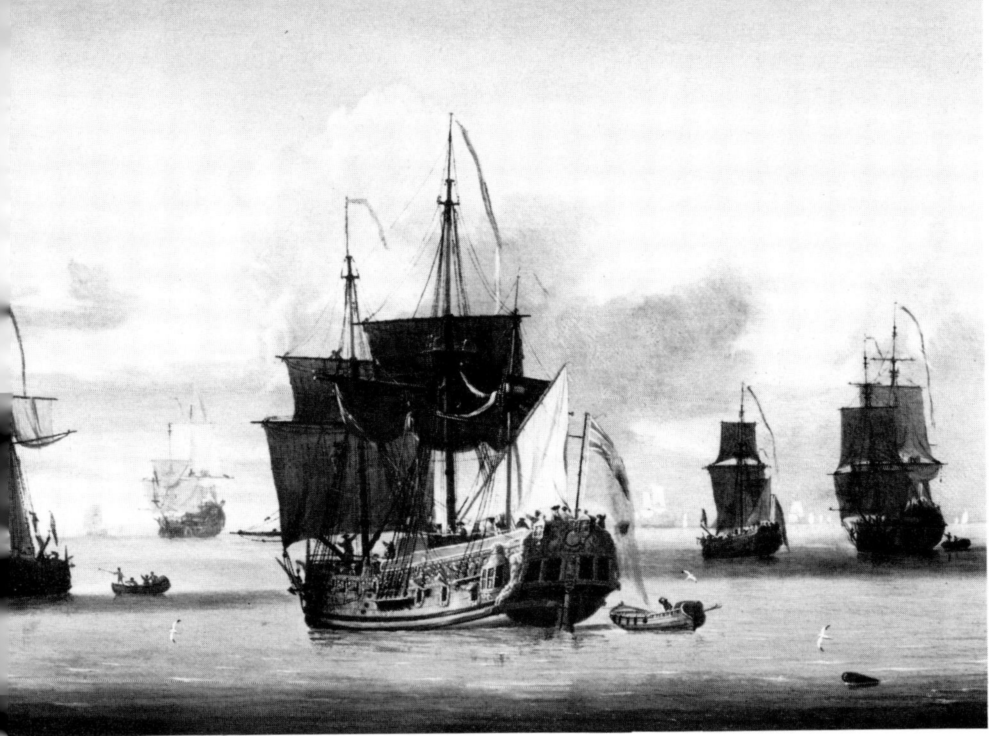

Plate 189. L.D. Man, fl.1725. "The royal yacht *Carolina,* about 1720." *This was the biggest of the royal yachts at the time and the only ship-rigged one.* National Maritime Museum, Greenwich.

Plate 190. Cornelis van de Velde, c.1675-1729. "East Indiamen driven on to a rocky coast in a storm, about 1720." National Maritime Museum, Greenwich.

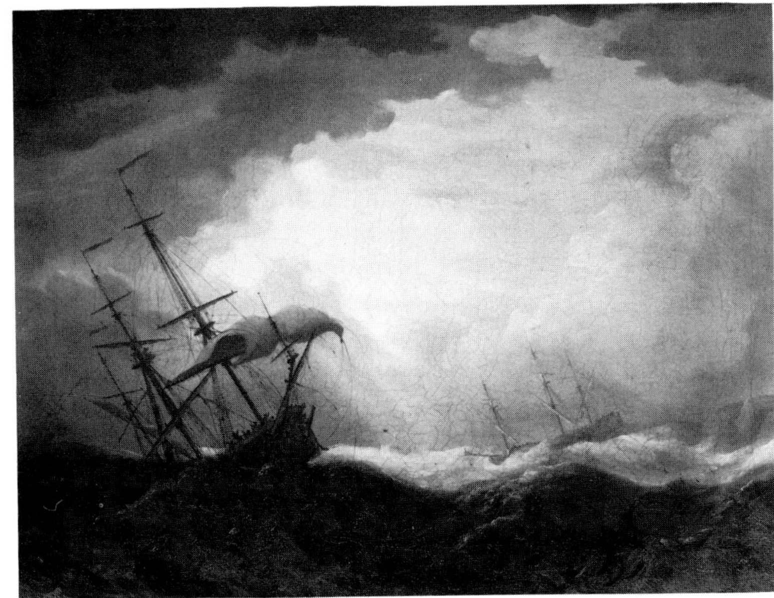

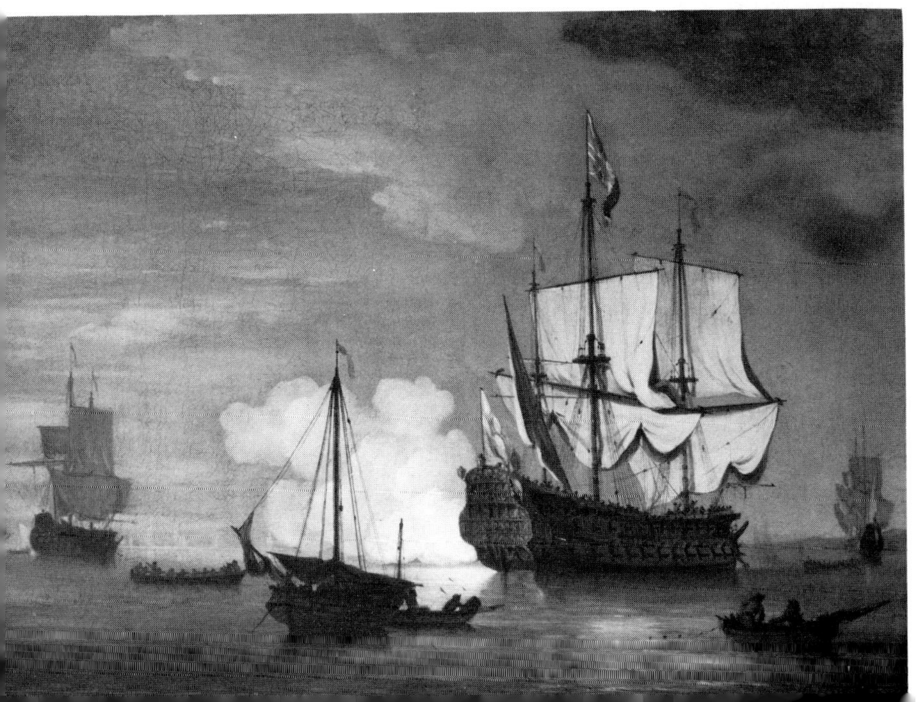

Plate 191. Cornelis van de Velde, c.1675-1729. "A two decker saluting, about 1700." *This is one of the typical calms characterised by its pink sky. His calms are more reminiscent of his grandfather van de Velde's work than his father's.* Private collection.

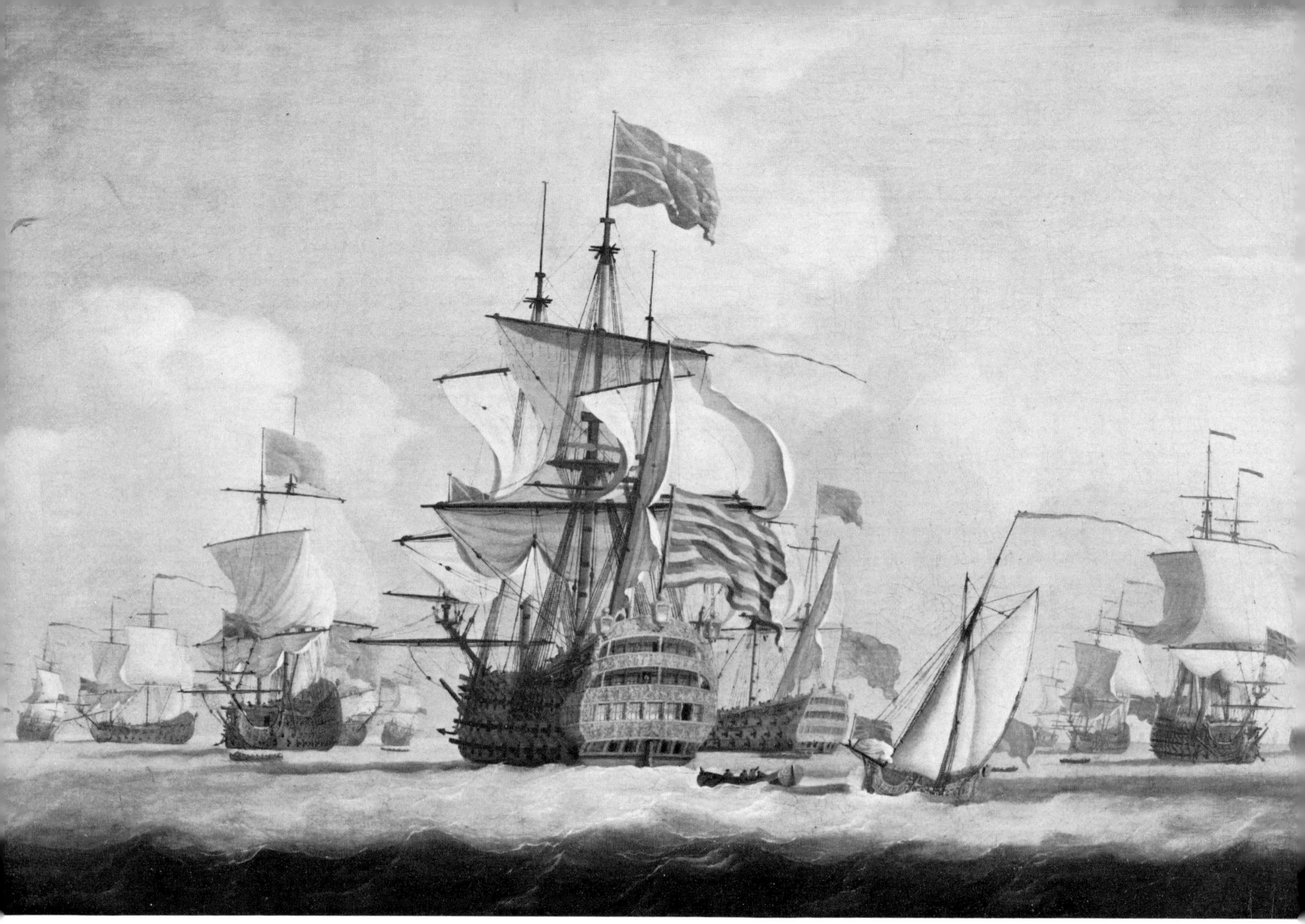

Plate 192. Peter Monamy, 1681-1749. "The English fleet coming to anchor, about 1715." *The major change in design of boats of this period is clearly demonstrated. The return of the stern gallery provides a progression that can be clearly seen on page 37 (Figure 4b).* National Maritime Museum, Greenwich.

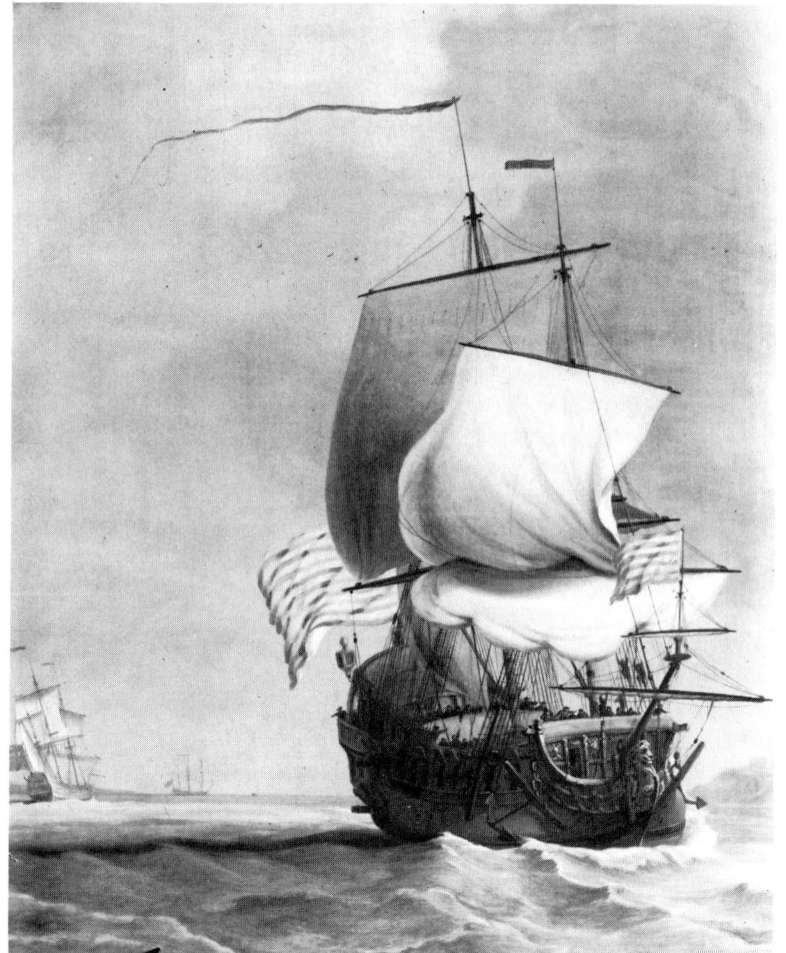

Plate 193. Peter Monamy, 1681-1749. "An East Indiaman in a breeze about 1720." *Monamy's profession was house painting and by tradition this work is supposed to have been part of the decorations for Vauxhall Gardens, which may account for the impression that it has been part of a larger picture.* National Maritime Museum, Greenwich.

Plate 194. Peter Monamy, 1681-1749. "An English flagship becalmed with a yacht saluting, about 1725." *A sensitively composed scene looking into the setting sun, which was not a device Monamy commonly employed.* National Maritime Museum, Greenwich.

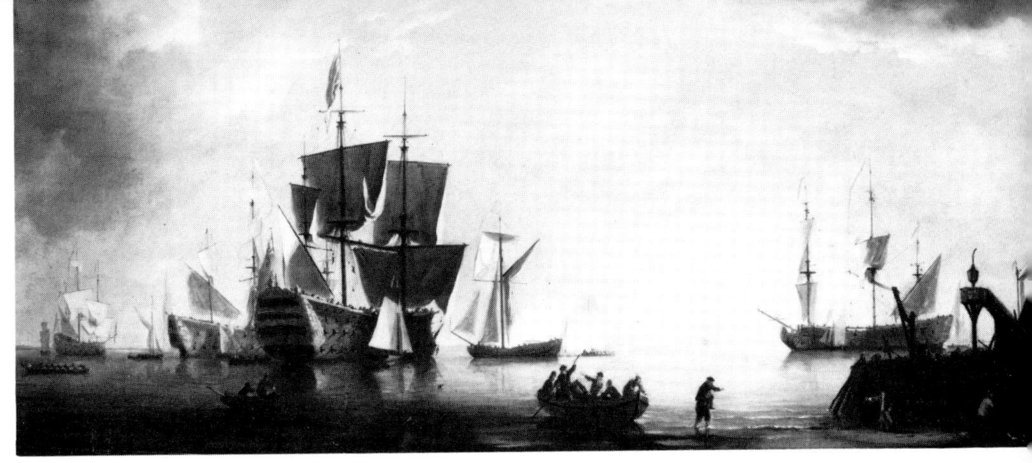

Plate 195. Peter Monamy, 1681-1749. "The capture of the *Princesa* in 1740." *A late example of Monamy's work.* National Maritime Museum, Greenwich.

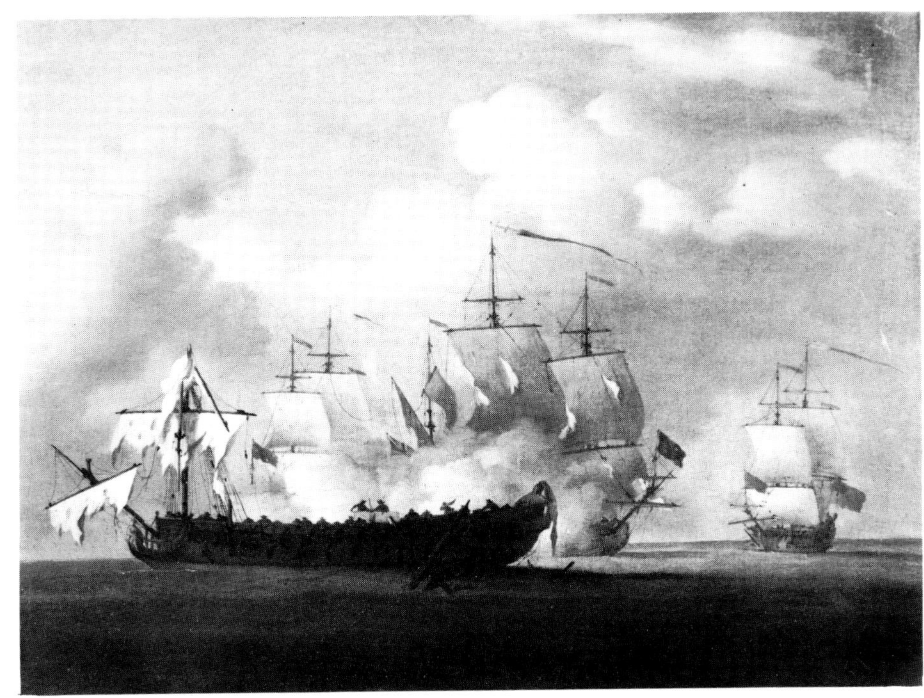

Plate 196. Peter Monamy, 1681-1749. "The capture of Louisbourg by Sir Peter Warren in 1745." *An example illustrating the wide variation of Monamy's style.* National Maritime Museum, Greenwich.

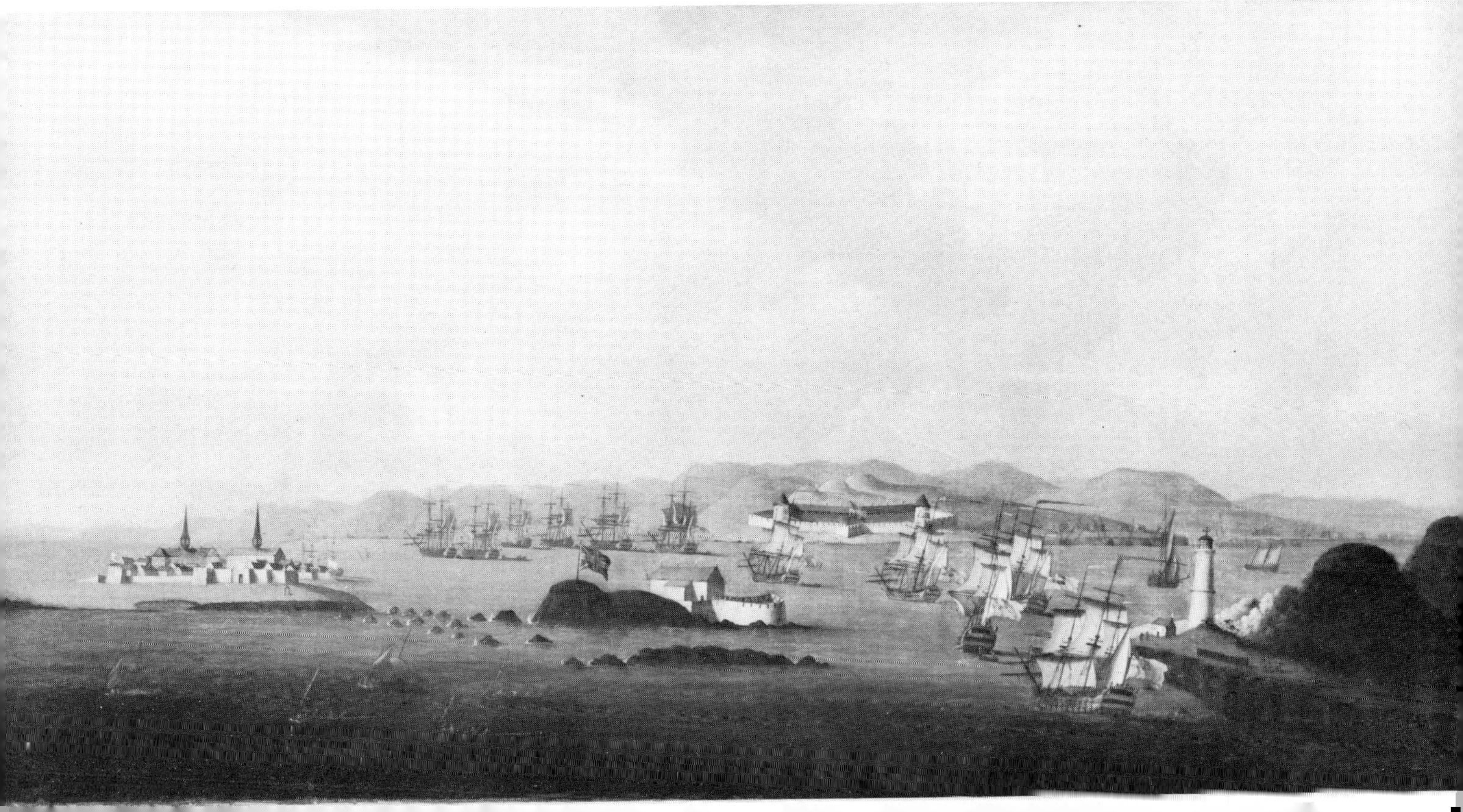

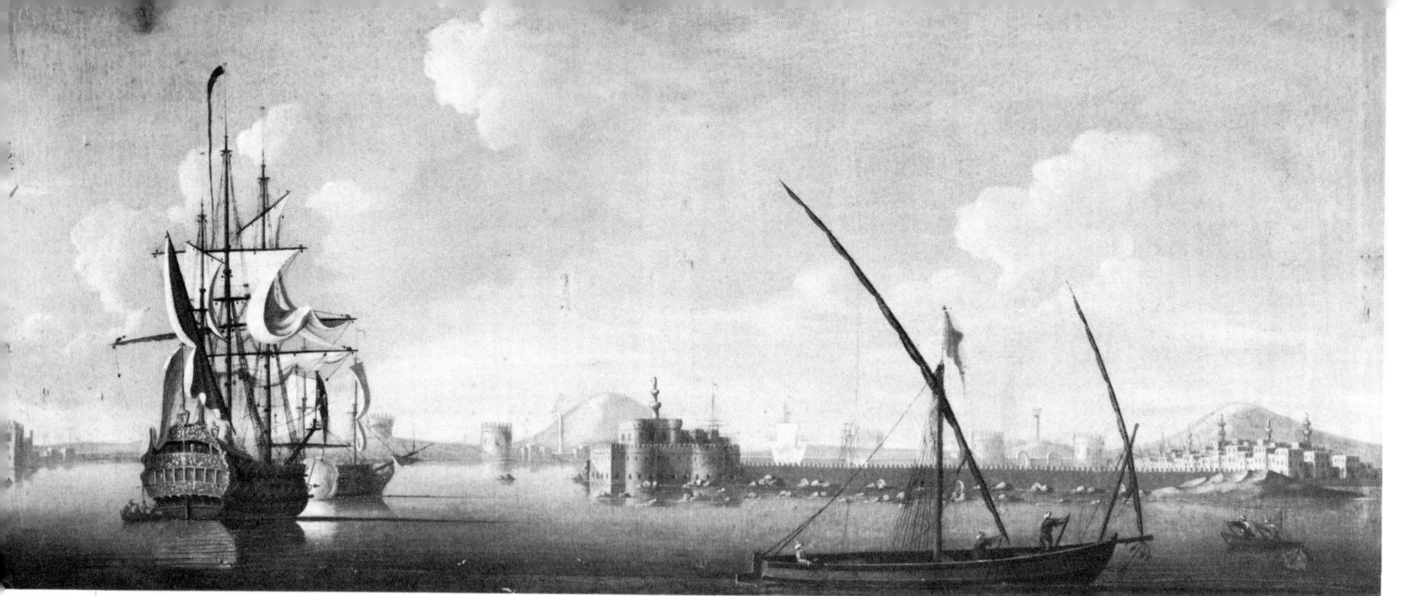

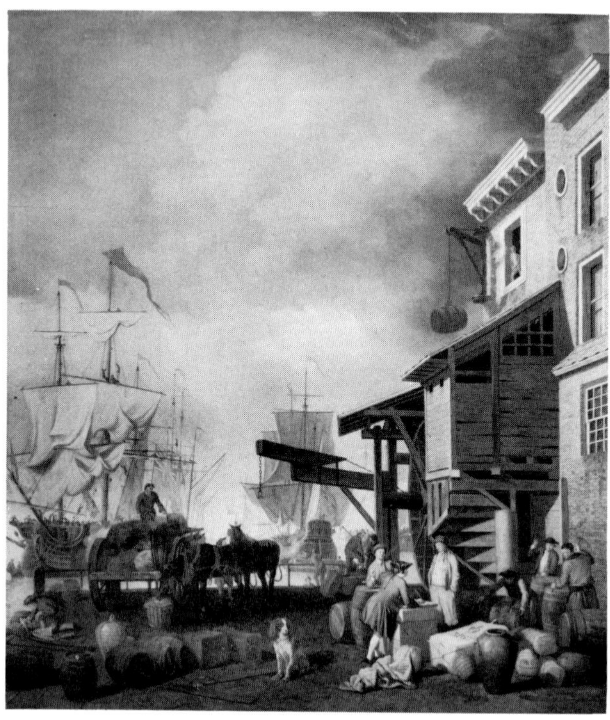

Plate 197. J. Cook, fl. early to mid-18th century. "An English man-of-war in the harbour at Alexandria, about 1720." *A typical example of the work of this artist who painted a number of pictures of Alexandria. Another follower of the van de Veldes.* National Maritime Museum, Greenwich.

Plate 198. Samuel Scott, 1701/2-1772. "Custom House Quay, London." *Scott's port scenes are considered by many to be among his finest works.* Victoria and Albert Museum.

Plate 199. Samuel Scott, 1701/2-1772. "The capture of Porto Bello in 1739." *By contrast a commissioned recording of a scene which perhaps lacks perspective in the relationship of the size of the castle and the ships.* National Maritime Museum, Greenwich.

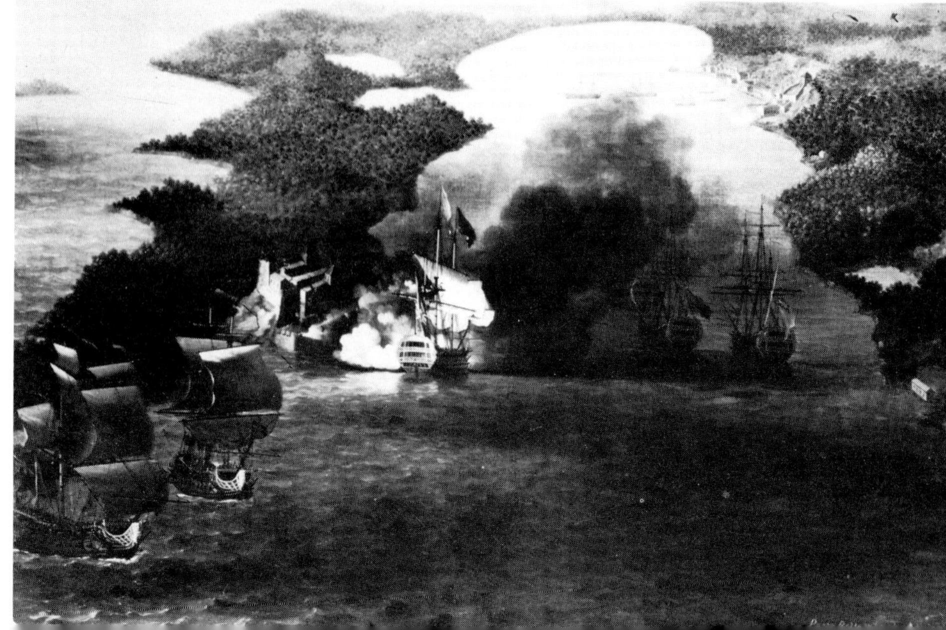

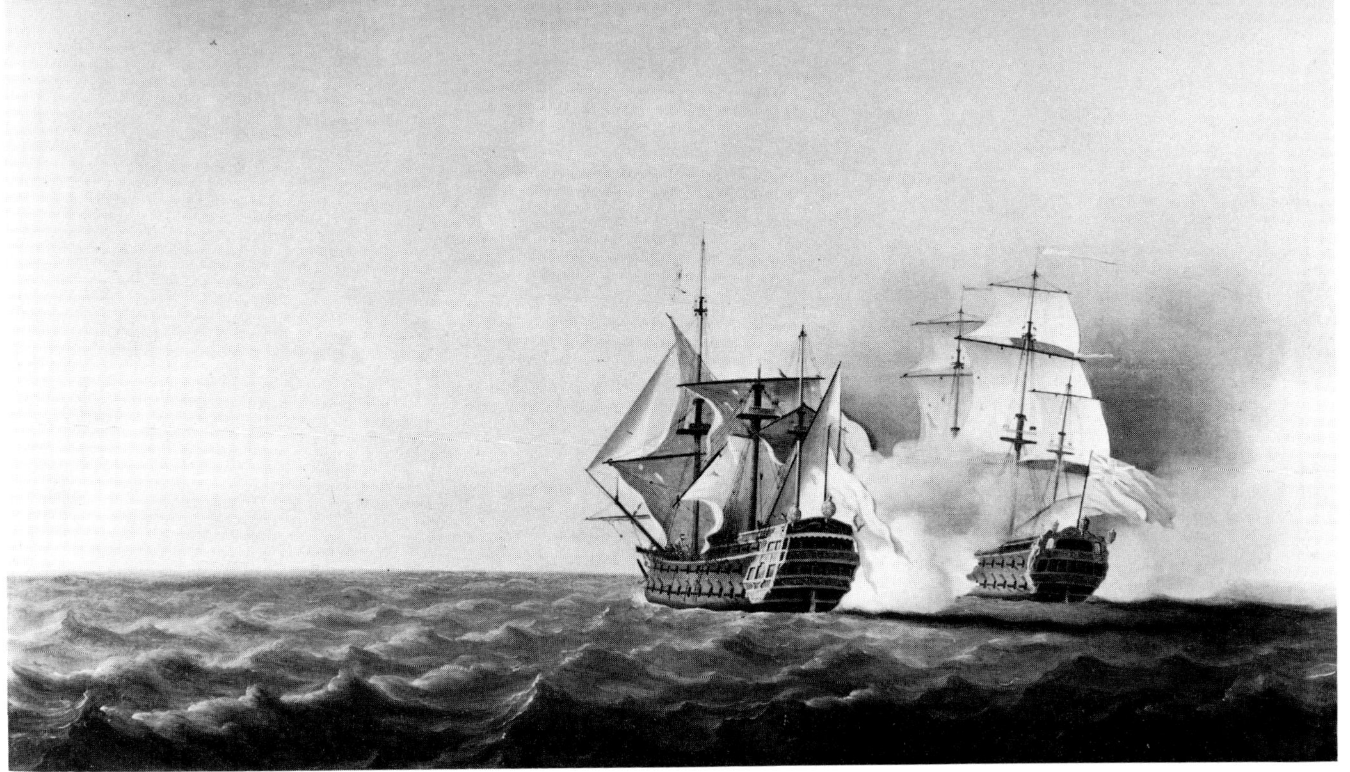

Plate 200. Samuel Scott, 1701/2-1772. "The action between the *Nottingham* and *Mars* in 1746." *Typically Scott shows more sea in this battle scene than would many of his contemporaries.* National Maritime Museum, Greenwich.

Plate 201. Antonio Joli de Dipi, c.1700-1777. "The Thames with a view of St. Paul's Cathedral and London Bridge." *At first glance a similarity to Canaletto might be suggested, but the very precise draughtsmanship and the tight disciplined work differentiates Joli de Dipi.* Colnaghi.

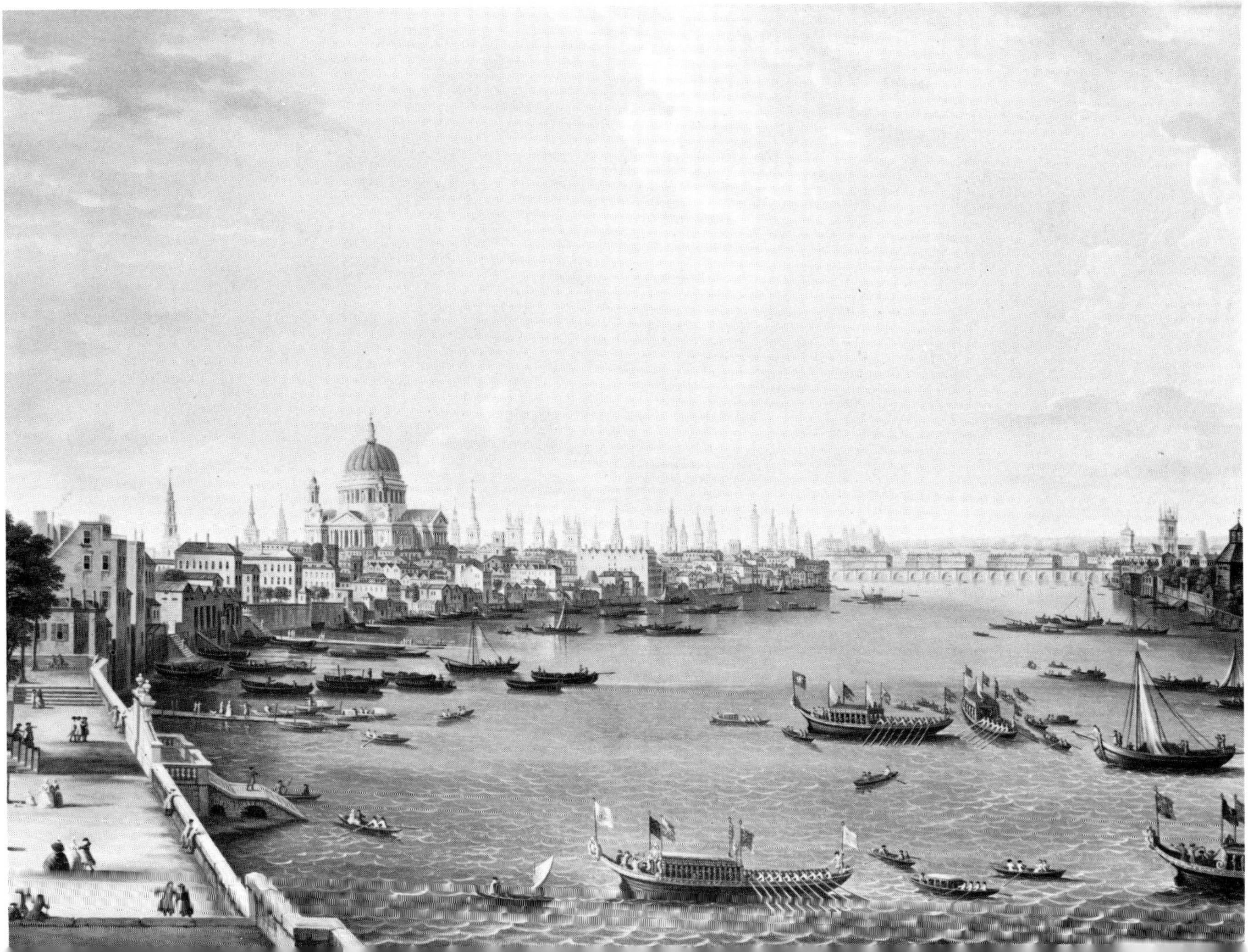

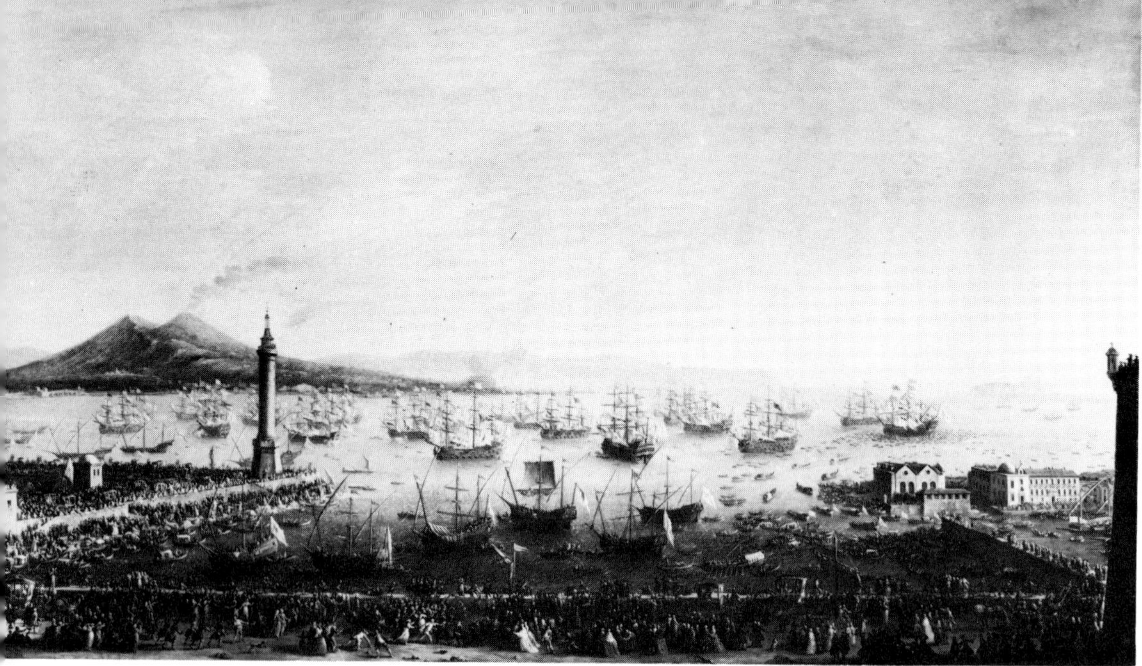

Plate 202. Antonio Joli de Dipi, c.1700-1777. "The embarkation of Charles III at Naples, dated 1759." *Perhaps Joli de Dipi's experience as a theatrical scene painter gave him a penchant for these grand scenes which are typical of his work.* Prado Museum, Madrid.

Plate 203. John Cleveley, the Elder, c.1712-1777. "The *Royal George* off Deptford, dated 1757." *There are a number of versions of this launch scene, but all with different ships on the right. This one is the biggest and grandest, with the new* Royal George *at anchor. This ship had been launched downstream at Woolwich the year before and never came up to Deptford, but Cleveley would have had drawings of her.* National Maritime Museum, Greenwich.

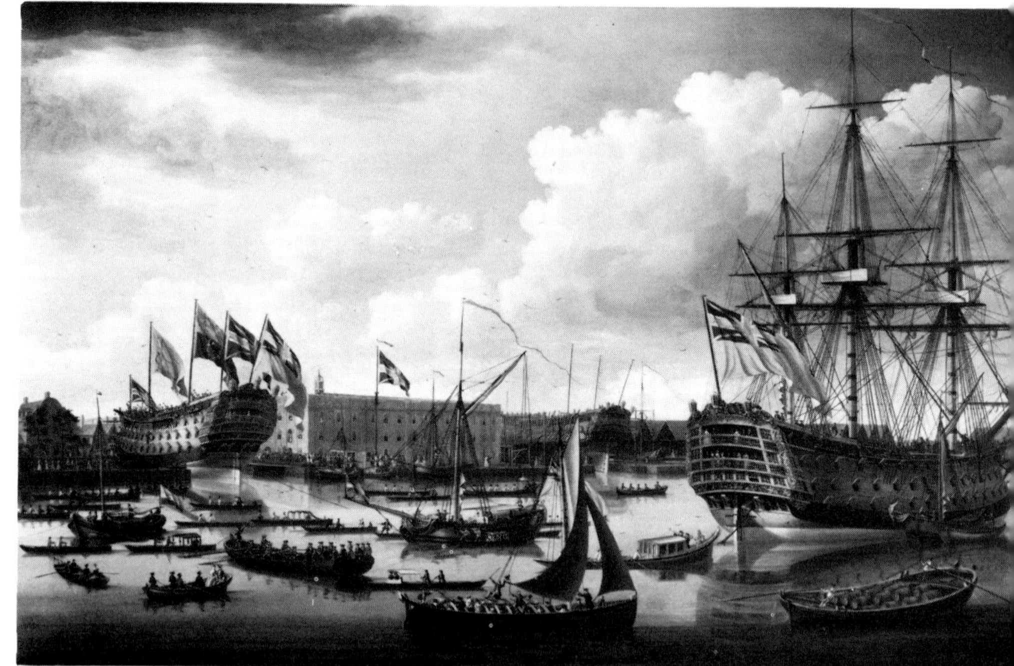

Plate 204. John Cleveley, the Elder, c.1712-1777. "The loss of the *Luxborough* galley in 1727." National Maritime Museum (Greenwich Hospital Collection).

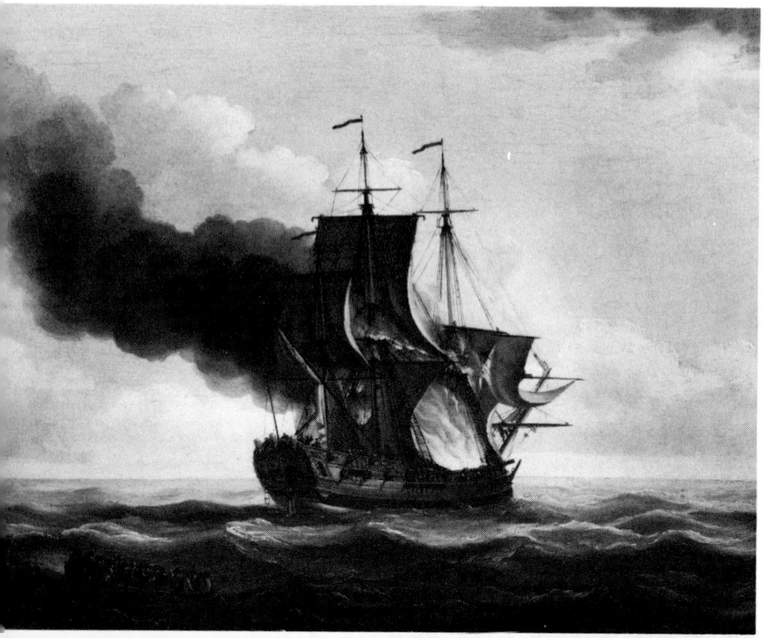

Plate 205. John Cleveley, the Elder, c.1712-1777. "A naval brigantine sloop 1752." National Maritime Museum, Greenwich.

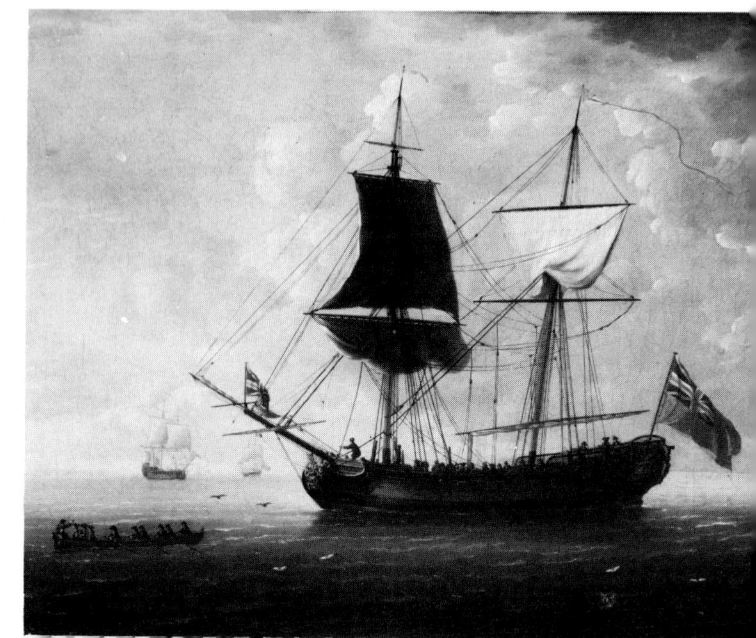

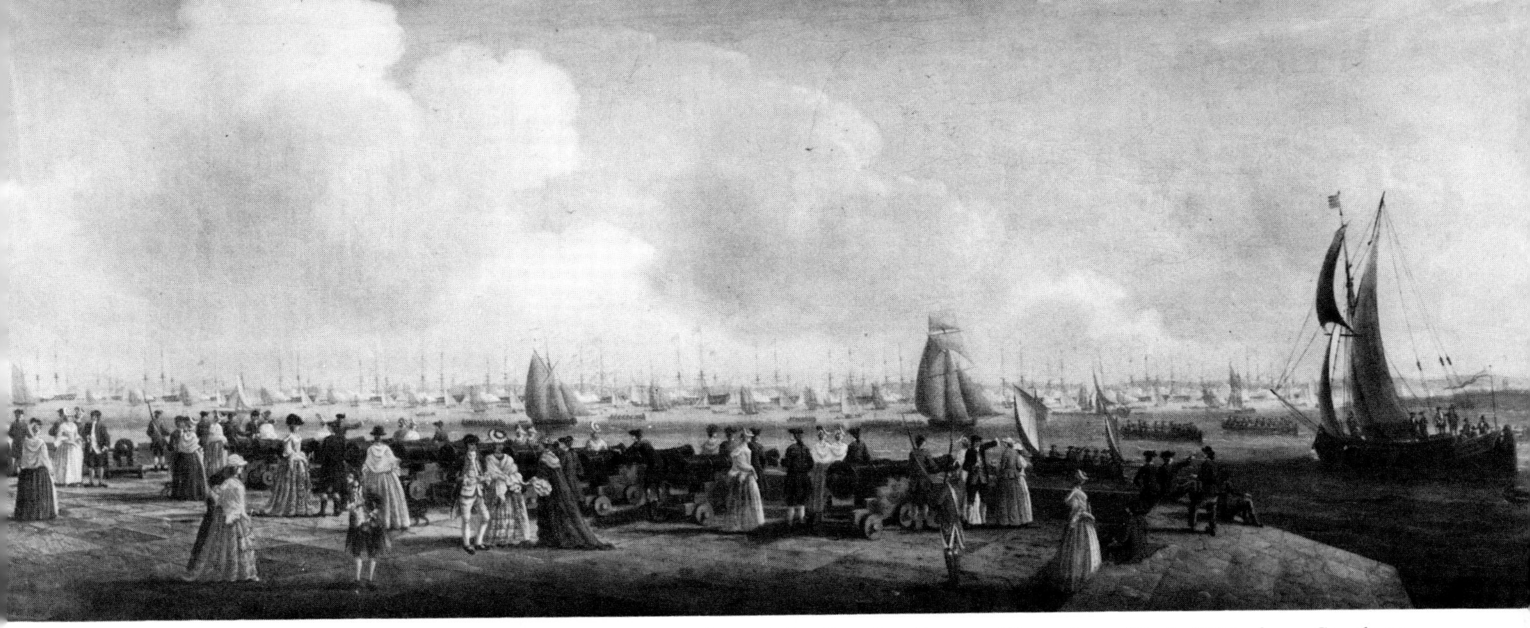

Plate 206. John Cleveley, the Elder, c.1712-1777. "The review of the fleet by George III on June 22nd, 1773, from Southsea Castle." Sotheby's.

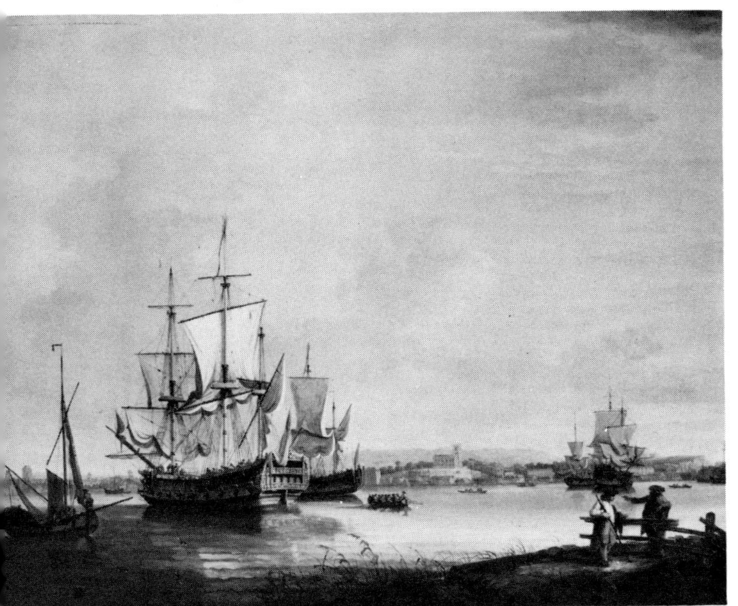

Plate 207. Thomas Mellish, fl. mid-18th century. "A 50-gun ship off Woolwich, 1748." *A painter who has been mistaken for Scott and even Brooking.* National Maritime Museum, Greenwich.

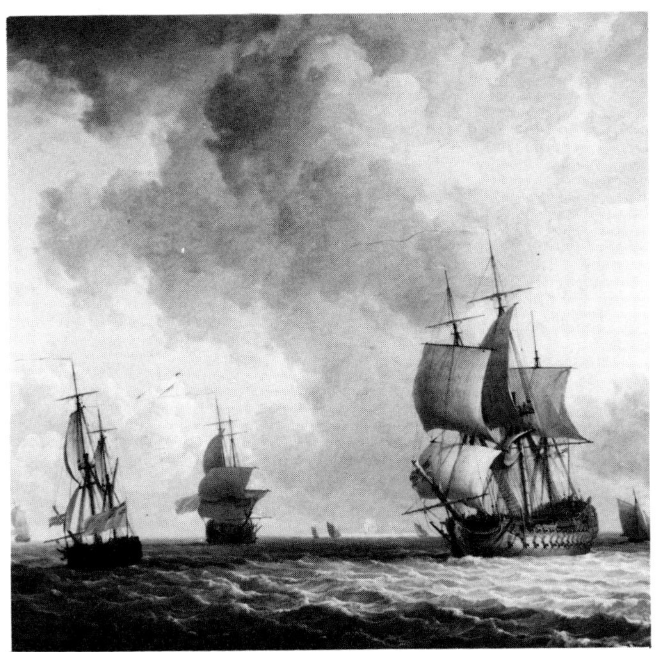

Plate 208. Charles Brooking, 1723-1759. "A two-decker in a light breeze." National Maritime Museum, Greenwich.

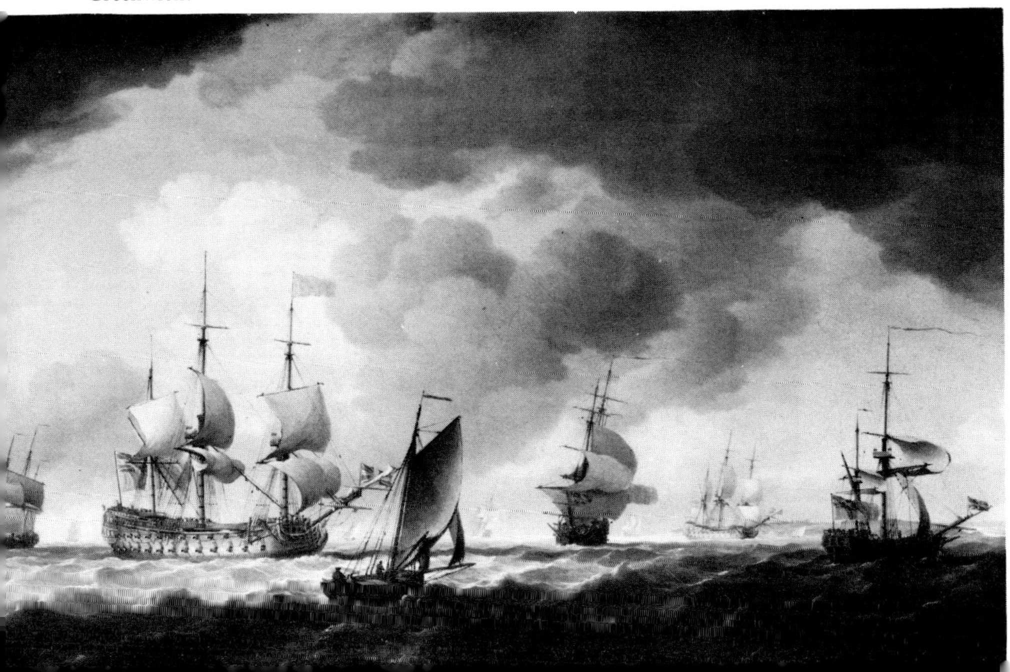

Plate 209. Charles Brooking, 1723-1759. "A vice admiral of the red and a squadron at sea." *A smaller version of the huge, less successful work in the Foundling Hospital.* National Maritime Museum, Greenwich.

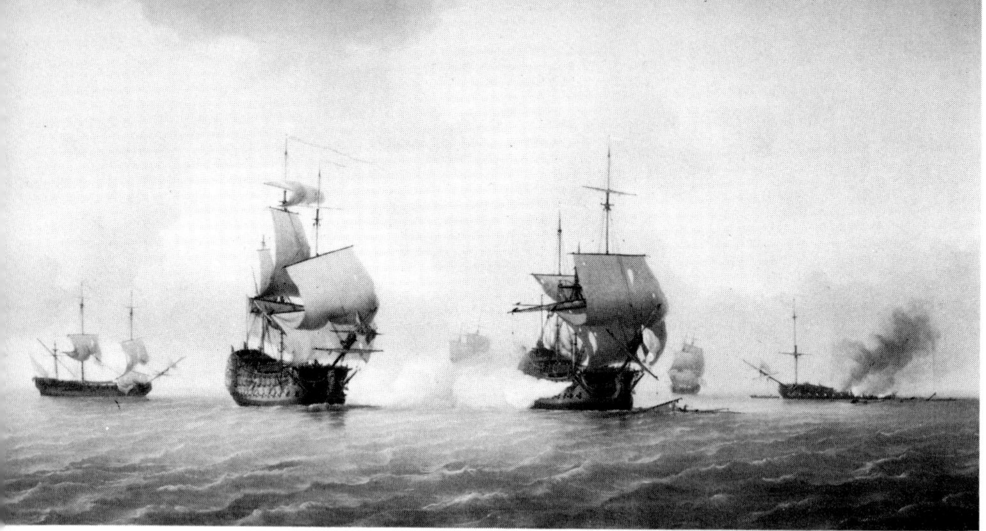

Plate 210. Charles Brooking, 1723-1759. "The capture of the *Glorioso* in 1747." National Maritime Museum, Greenwich.

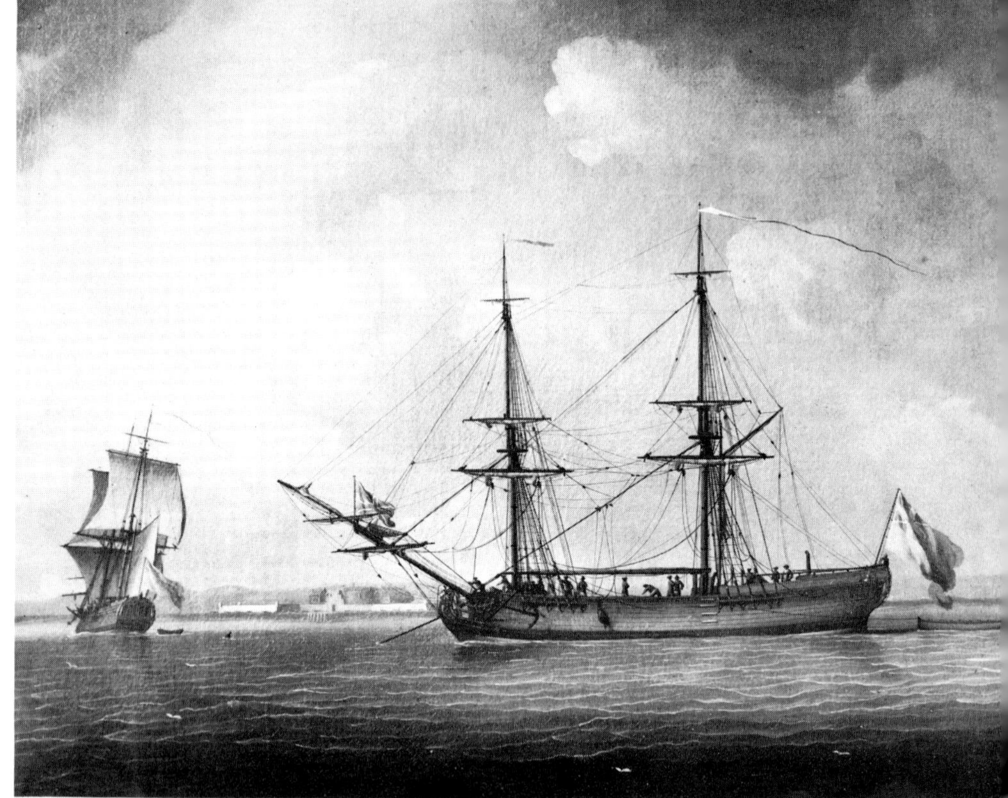

Plate 211. Charles Brooking, 1723-1759. "A snow at anchor." National Maritime Museum, Greenwich.

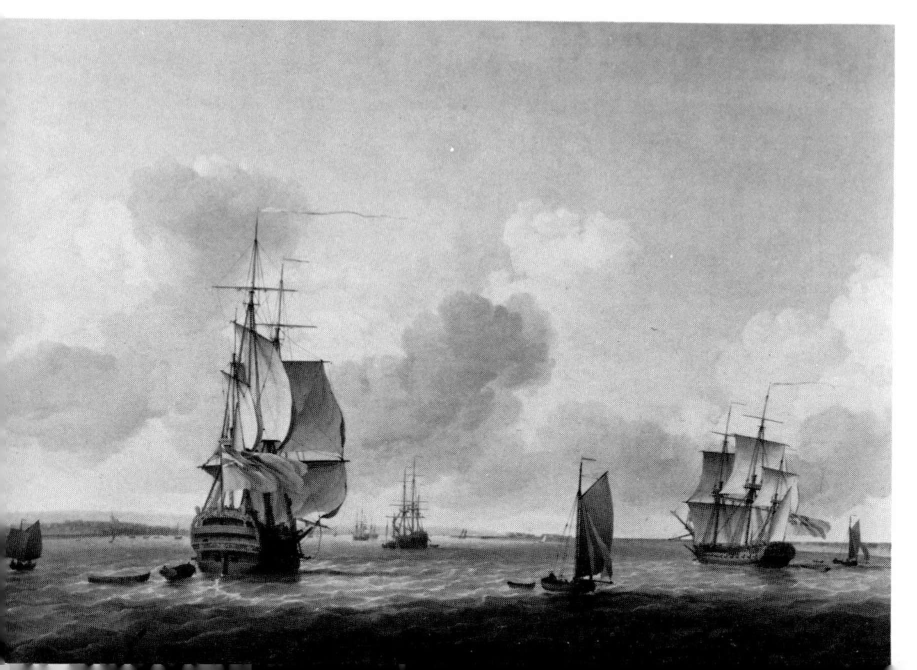

Plate 212. Charles Brooking, 1723-1759. "A two-decker and a frigate running into Harwich." *As the frigate must be the* Southampton *of 1757, this is a very late picture.* National Maritime Museum, Greenwich.

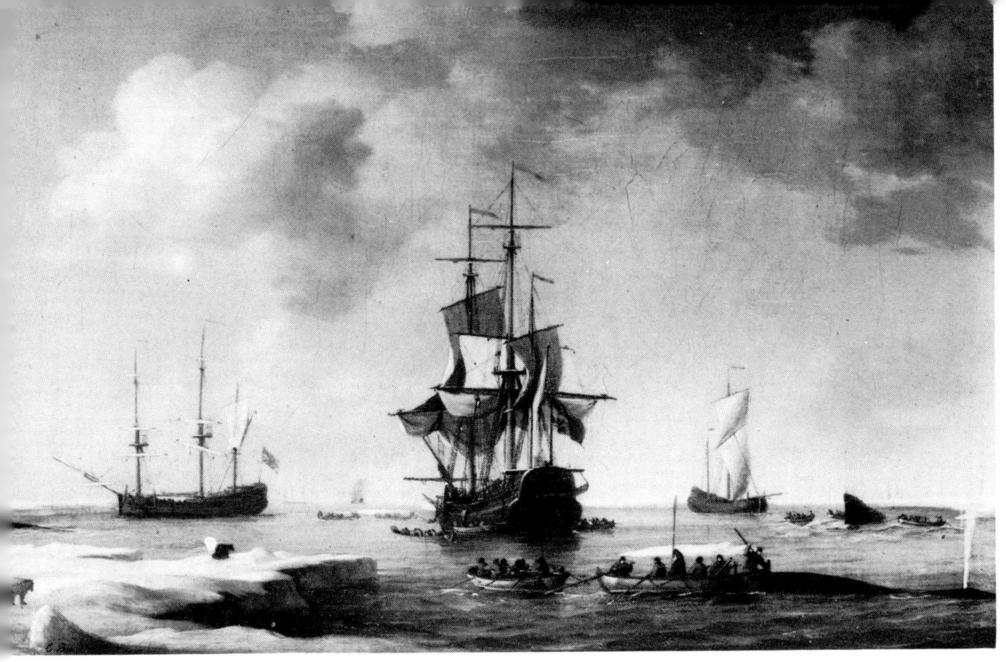

Plate 213. Charles Brooking, 1723-1759. "Whalers in the ice." *When fishing the union was hoisted on the ensign staff.* National Maritime Museum, Greenwich.

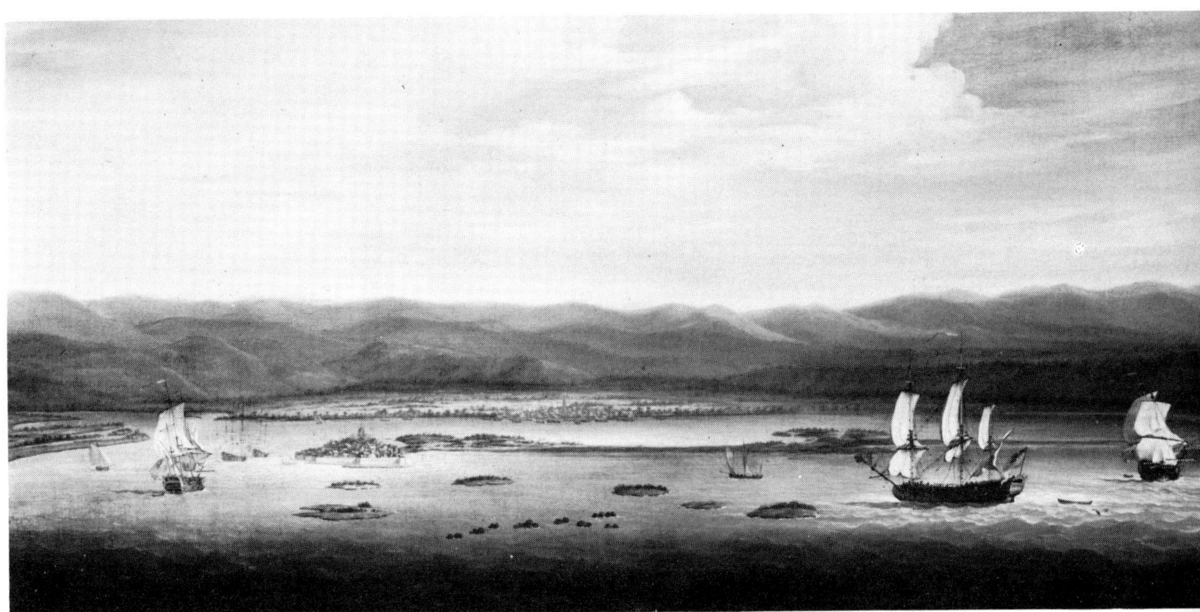

Plate 214. Richard Paton, 1717-1791. "Port Royal, Jamaica, about 1750." *A comparison of this with the next plate demonstrates the unevenness of this artist's work, due to his habitual experimentation.* National Maritime Museum, Greenwich.

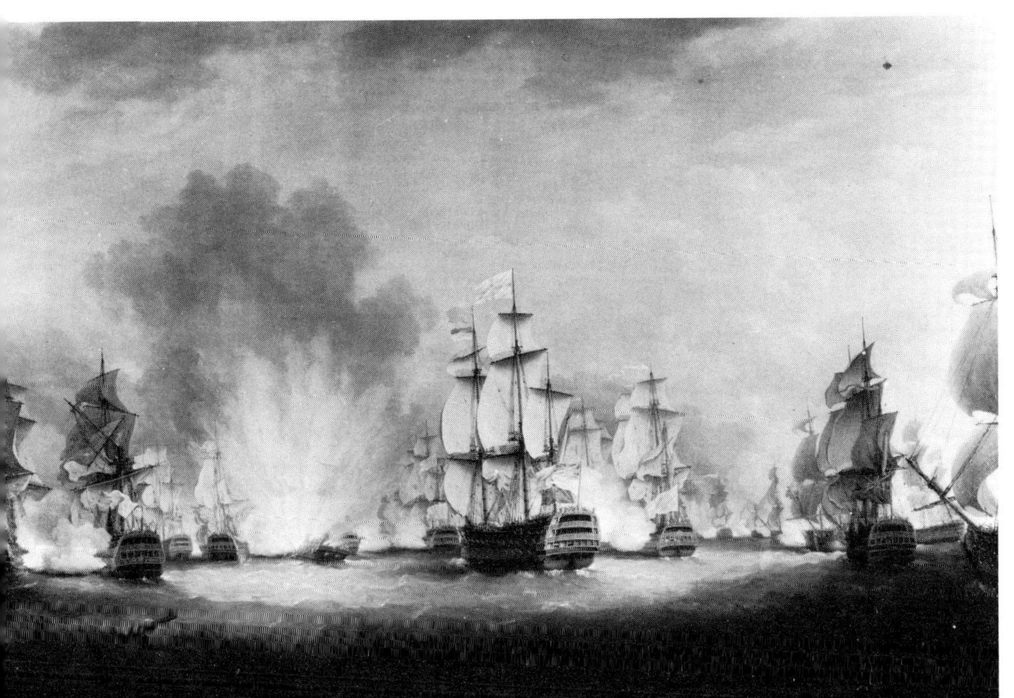

Plate 215. Richard Paton, 1717-1791. "The moonlight Battle of St. Vincent, January 16th, 1780." *Admiral Sir George Rodney intercepted a Spanish convoy and in a general chase the* San Domingo *blew up and six others were captured.* National Maritime Museum, Greenwich.

Plate 216. Richard Paton, 1717-1791. "Battle of the Dogger Bank in 1781." National Maritime Museum, Greenwich.

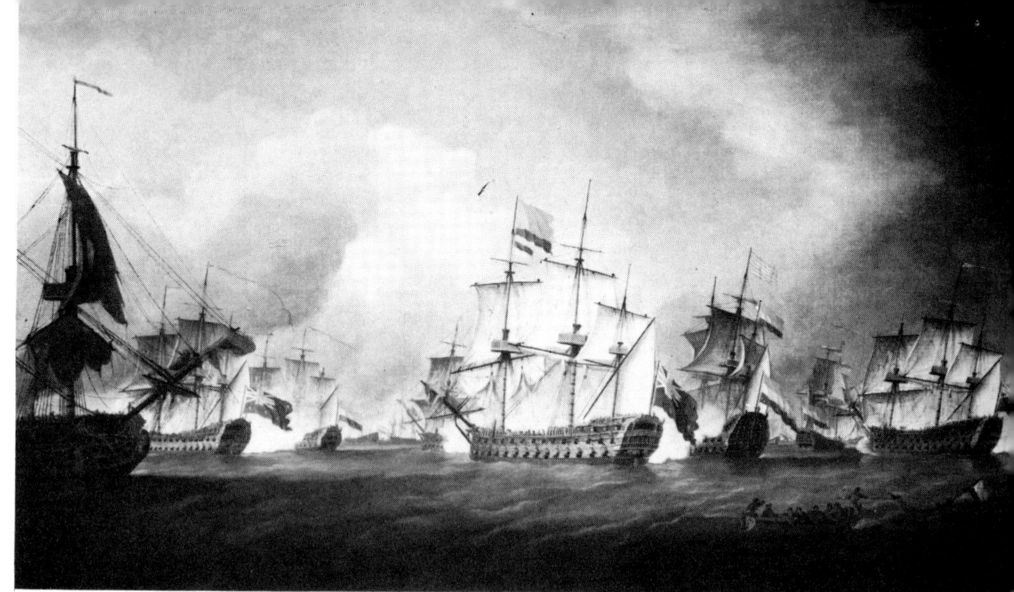

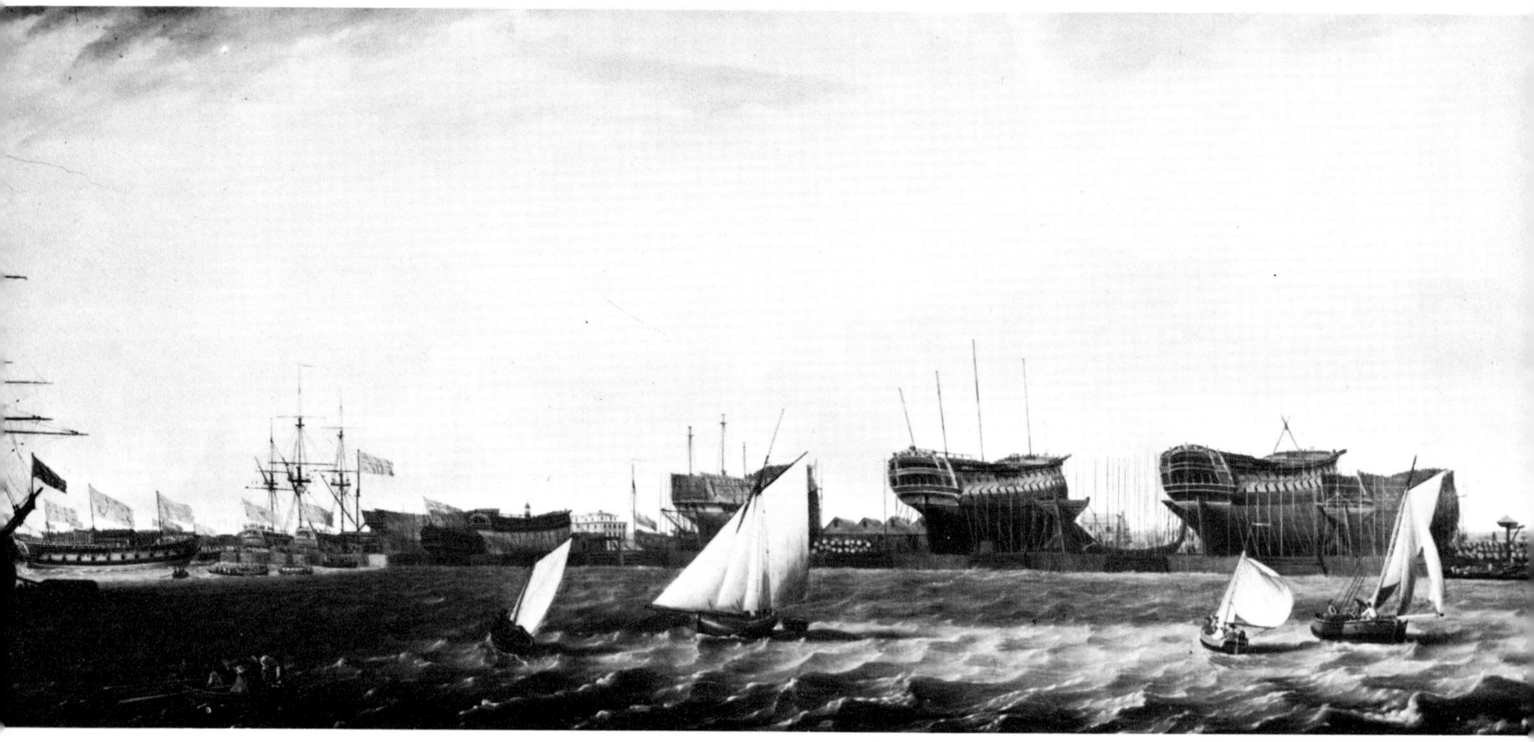

Plate 217. Francis Holman, d.1790. "Blackwall Yard." National Maritime Museum, Greenwich.

Plate 218. Francis Holman, d.1790. "The brig sloop *Roebuck* with her American prizes in 1778." *Note the striped ensigns, see pages 28/29, U.S. flags 2.* National Maritime Museum, Greenwich.

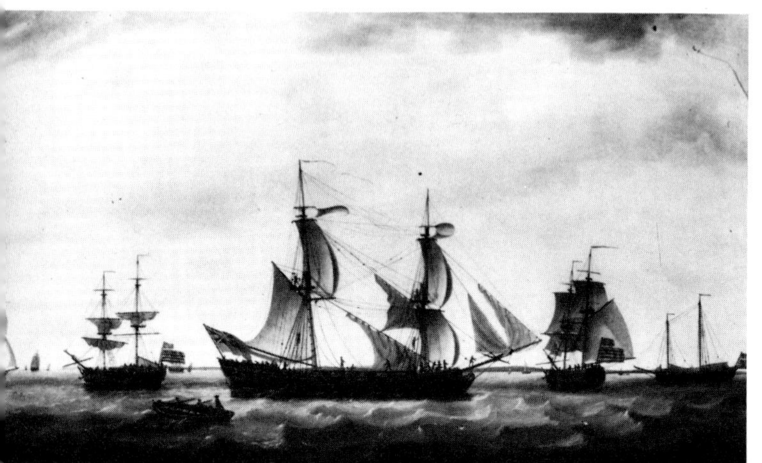

Plate 219. Francis Holman, d.1790. "A small shipyard on the Thames." National Maritime Museum, Greenwich.

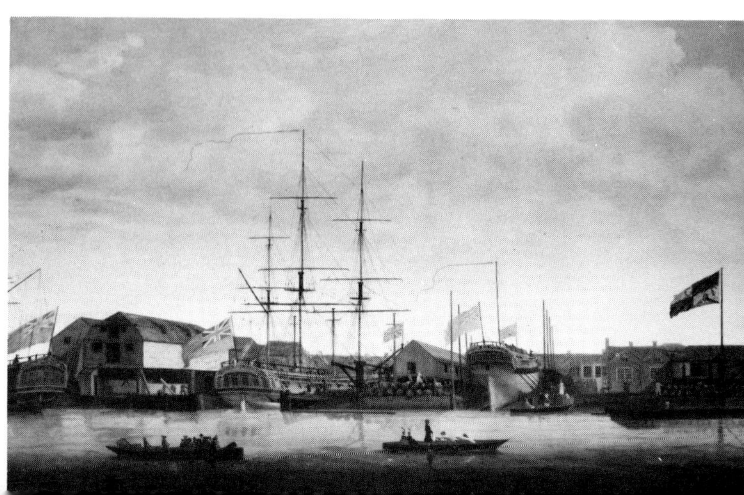

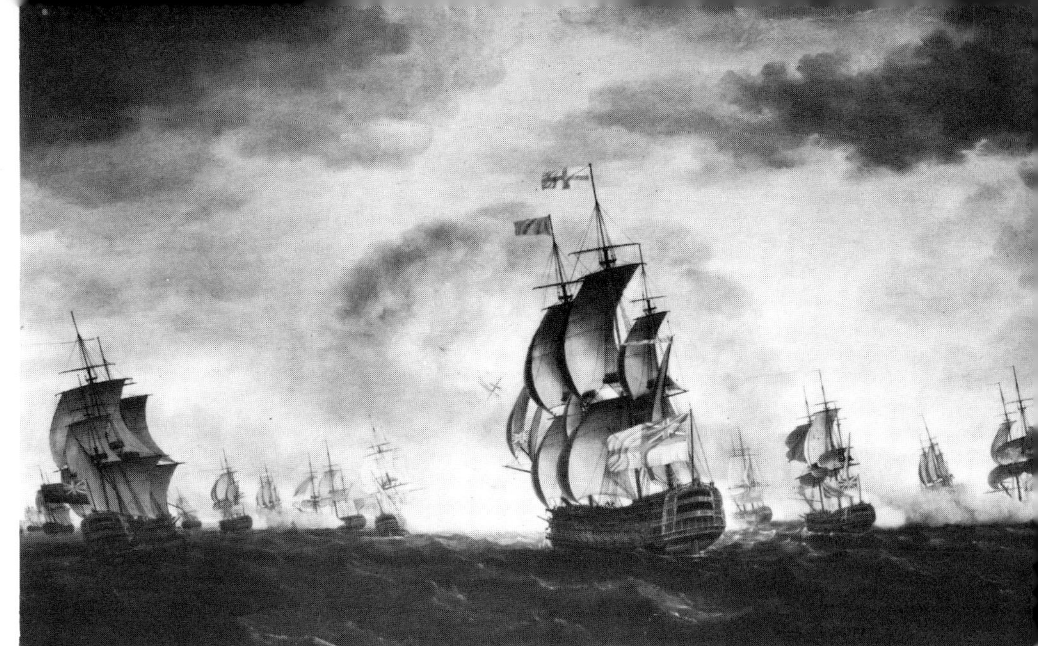

Plate 220. Francis Holman, d.1790. "The Moonlight Battle of St. Vincent in 1780." National Maritime Museum, Greenwich.

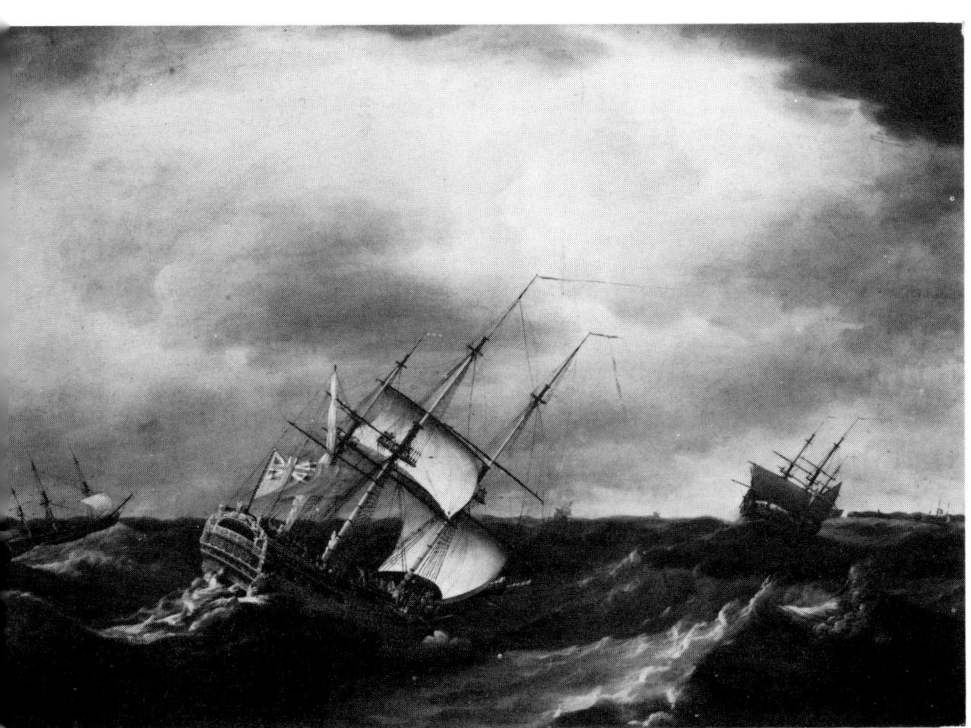

Plate 221. Francis Holman, d.1790. "Men-of-war in a gale, about 1775." Sotheby's.

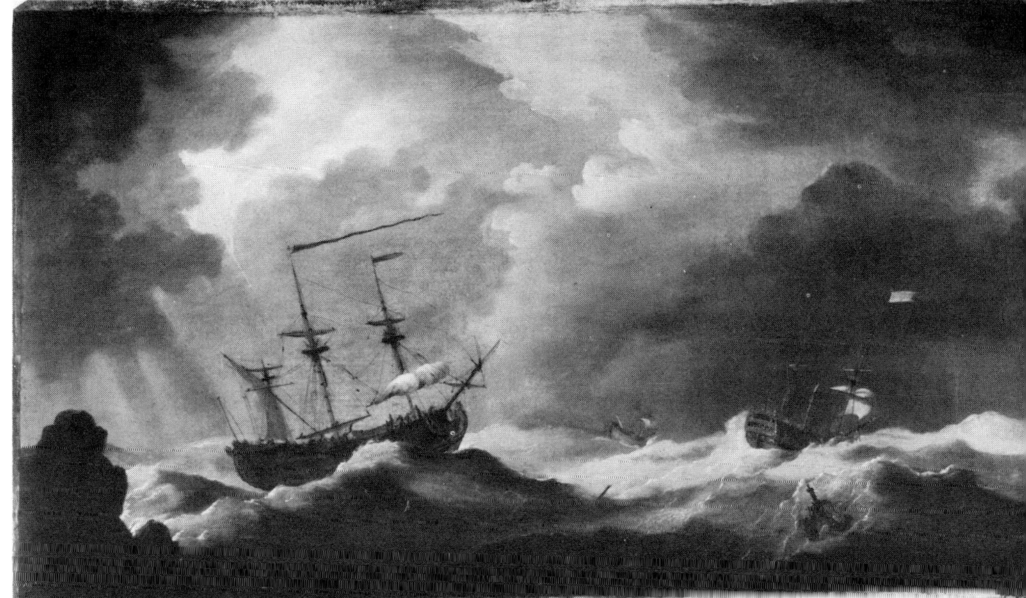

Plate 222. Francis Swaine, c.1720-1782. "English men-of-war in a storm." National Maritime Museum, Greenwich.

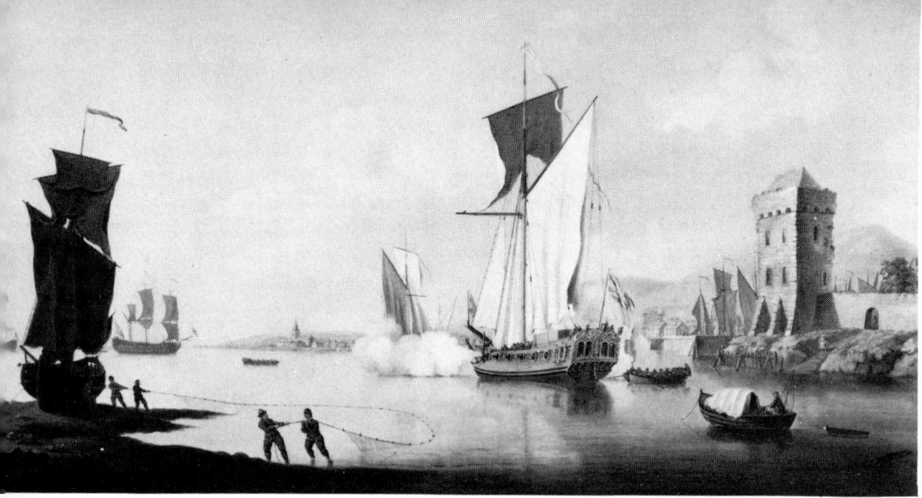

Plate 223. Francis Swaine, c.1720-1782. "A royal yacht becalmed off a castle." National Maritime Museum, Greenwich.

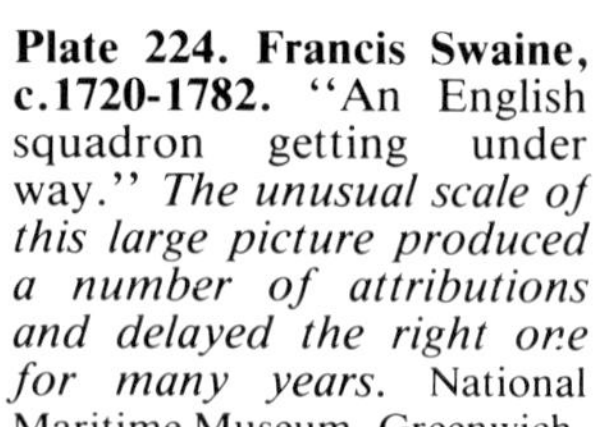

Plate 224. Francis Swaine, c.1720-1782. "An English squadron getting under way." *The unusual scale of this large picture produced a number of attributions and delayed the right one for many years.* National Maritime Museum, Greenwich.

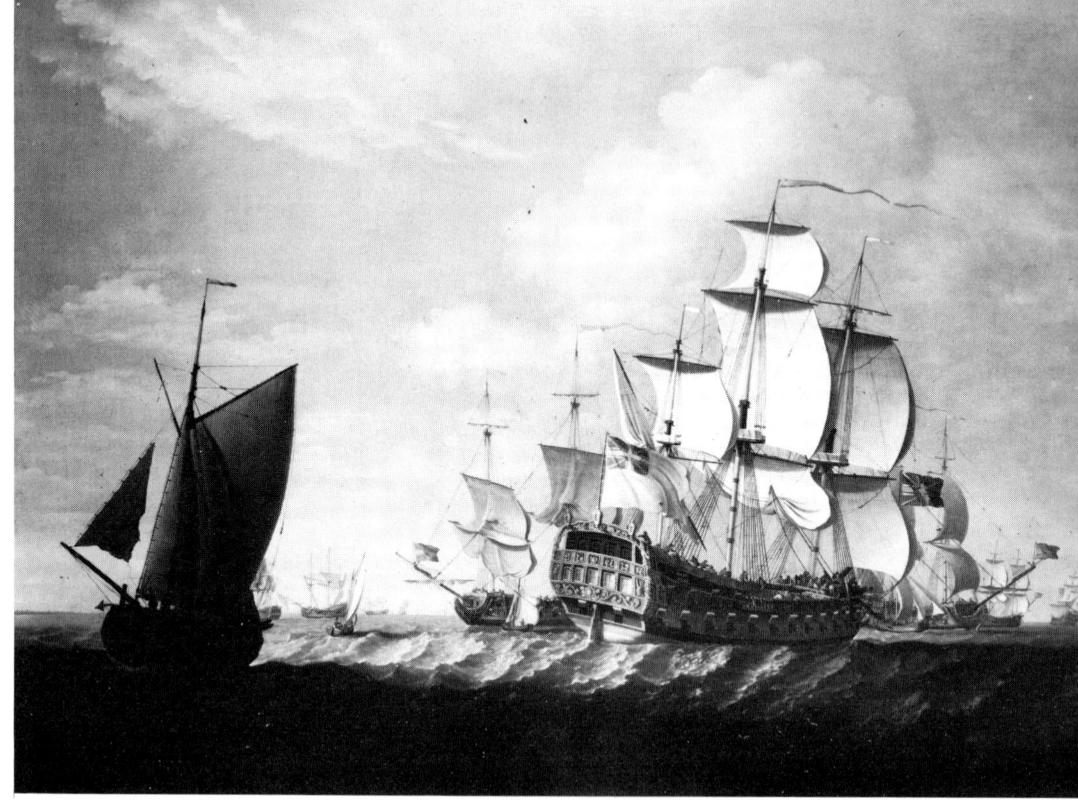

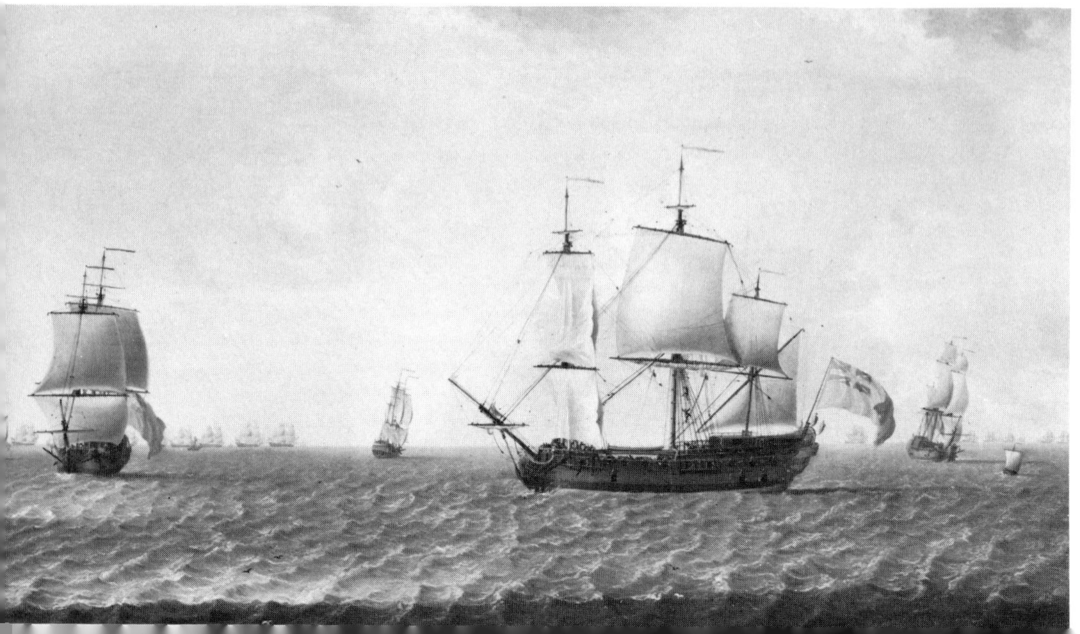

Plate 225. Francis Swaine, c.1720-1782. "An East Indiaman in stays, about 1750." *A fine large Swaine. The East Indiaman has an unusually large coach aft for passenger accommodation.* National Maritime Museum, Greenwich.

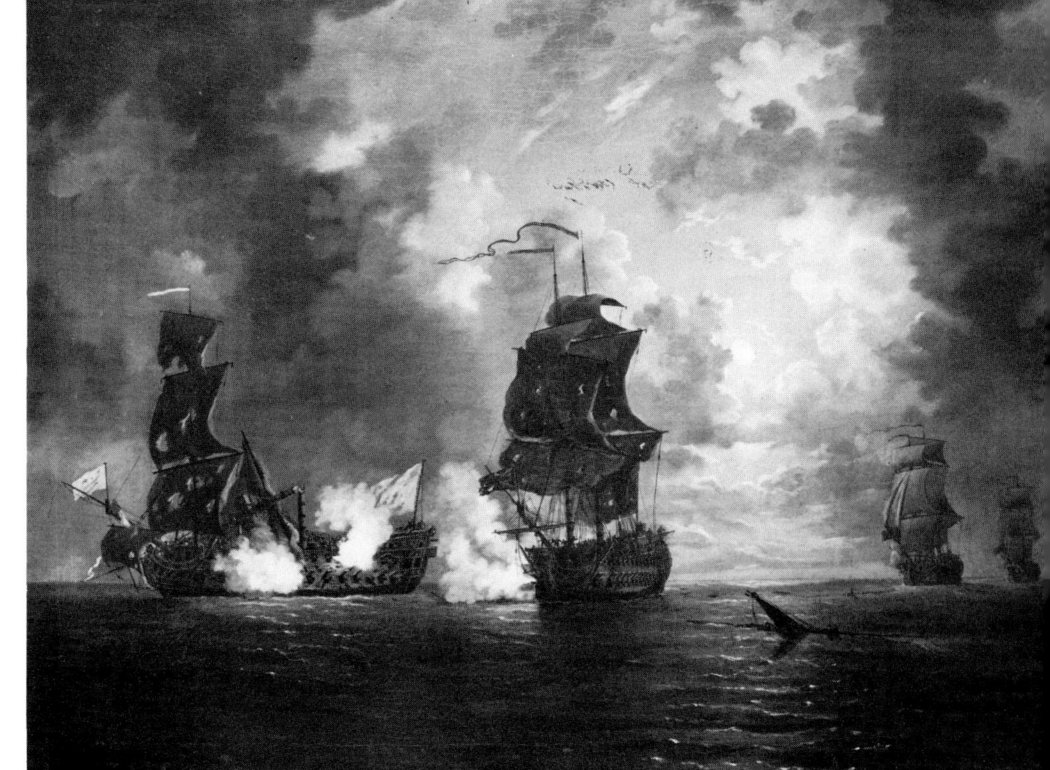

Plate 226. Francis Swaine, c.1720-1782. "The action between the *Monmouth* and *Foudroyant,* 1758." *Swaine often painted moonlight scenes, both on sea and land.* National Maritime Museum, Greenwich.

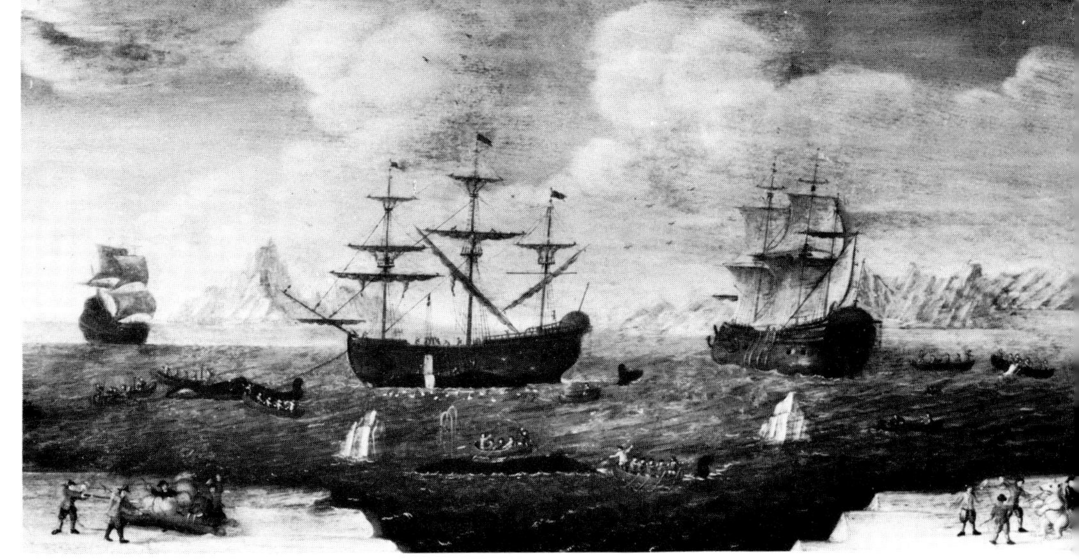

Plate 227. Thomas Schuhmacher, fl. mid-18th century. "Three whalers in the ice, 1755." *A primitive painting by an obscure artist whose work is rarely seen. Note that the boat in the middle of the picture is using her main yard to swing the blubber aboard.* Altonaer Museum, Hamburg.

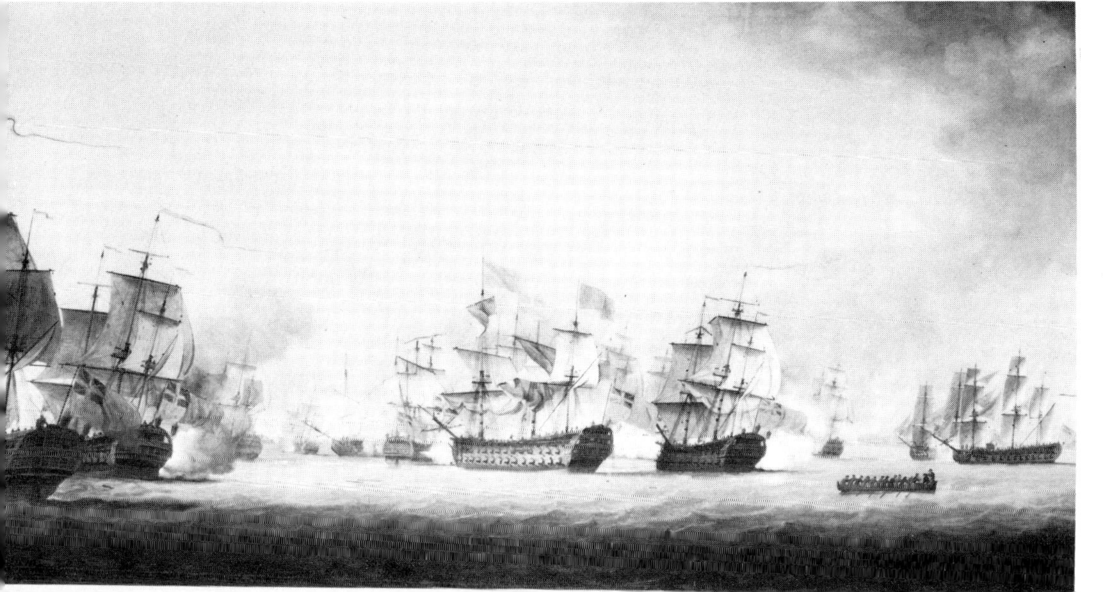

Plate 228. ?Thomas Craskell, fl.1748. "The Battle of Havana in 1748." *Little known artist who may well have painted in Scott's studio but no written evidence exists to suggest this.* National Maritime Museum, Greenwich.

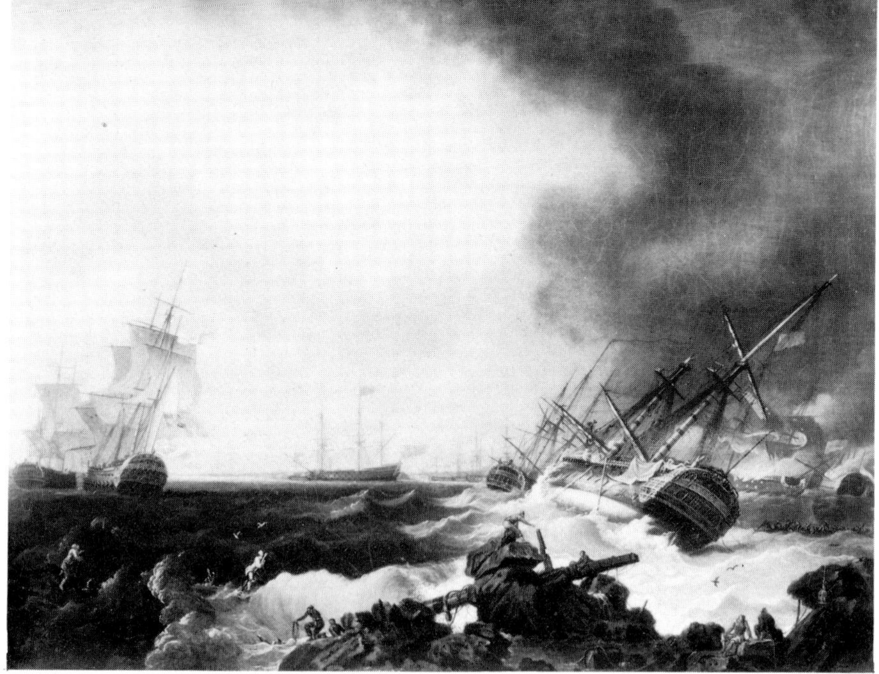

Plate 229. Richard Wright, 1735-1775. "The morning after the Battle of Quiberon Bay in 1759." *The ship wrecked in the foreground shows below the waterline the pease-pudding bottom (creamy white) which was used as a preservative.* National Maritime Museum, Greenwich.

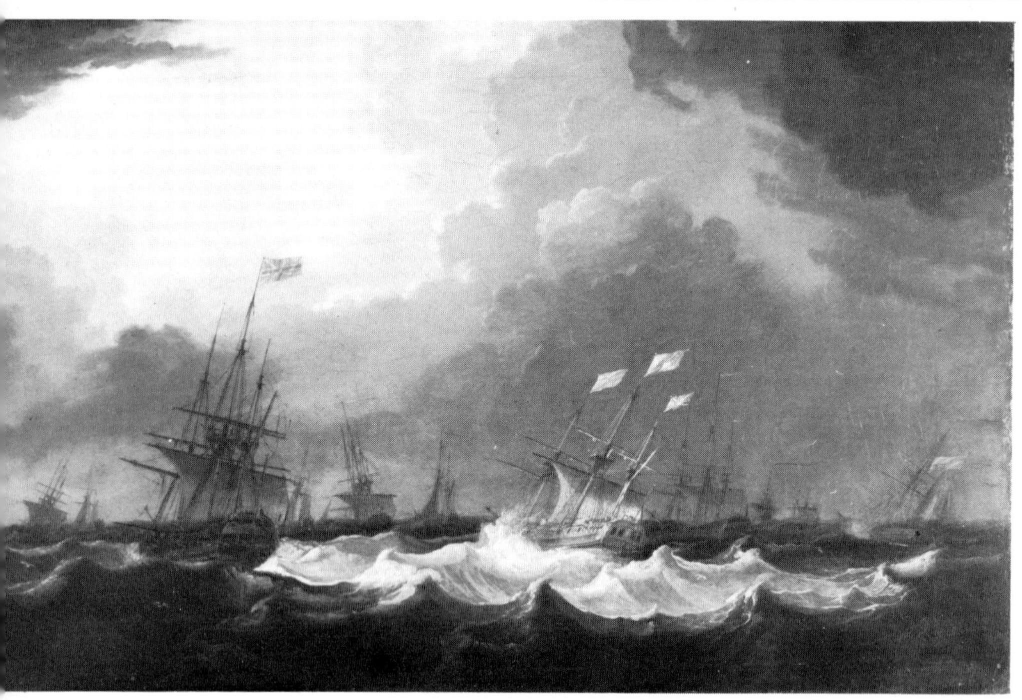

Plate 230. Richard Wright, 1735-1775. "Princess Charlotte on passage to England, 1761." *Three storms blew the squadron over to Norway and the journey from Kiel to Harwich took ten days. The Princess enjoyed it, in the refurbished and renamed yacht the* Royal Charlotte. National Maritime Museum, Greenwich.

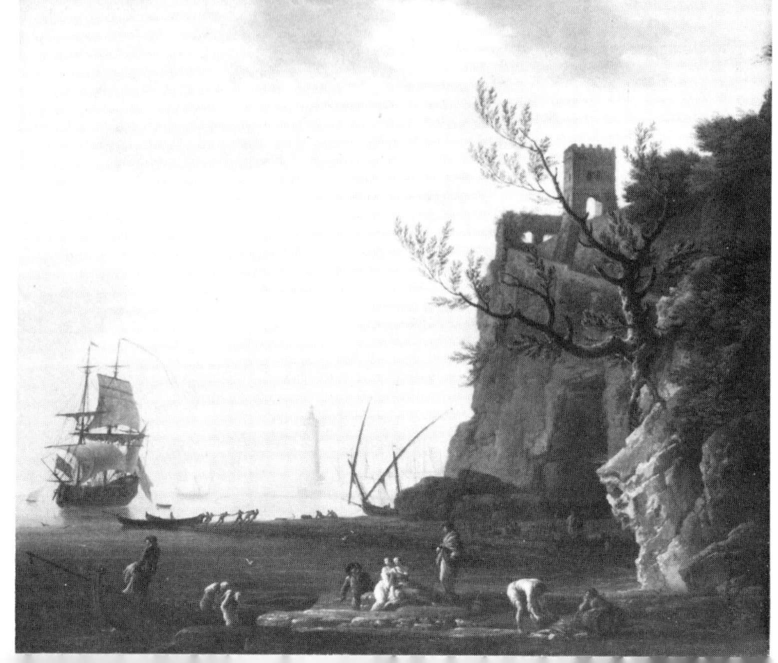

Plate 231. Claude-Joseph Vernet, 1714-1789. "A coast scene at Naples." Dulwich College Picture Gallery.

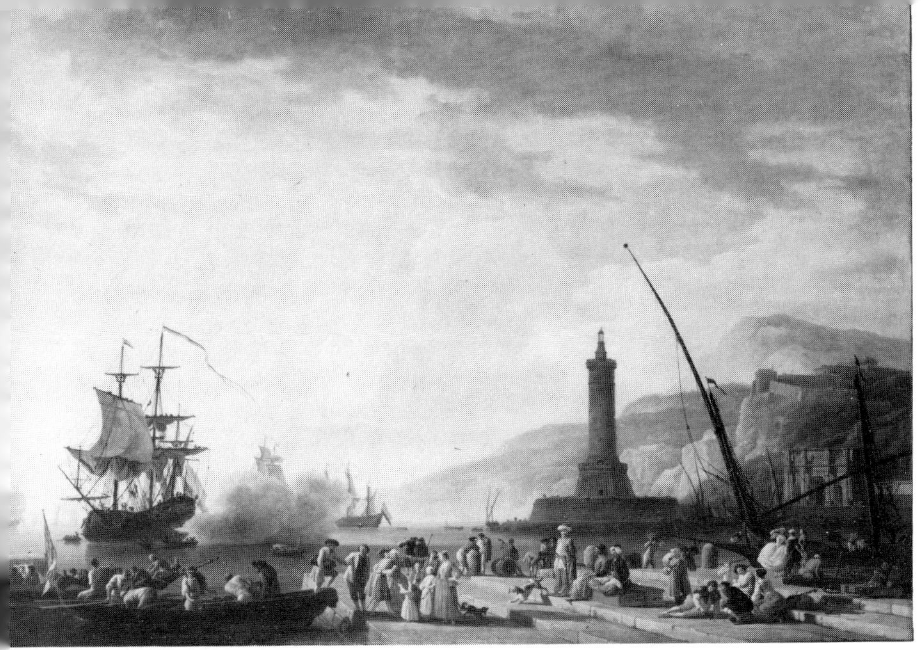

Plate 232. Claude-Joseph Vernet, 1714-1789. "Harbour scene at Naples, dated 1749." Sotheby's.

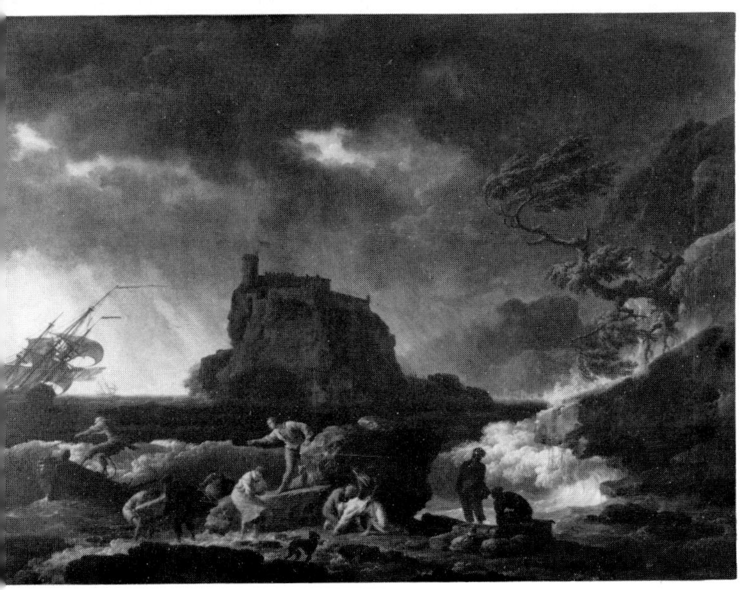

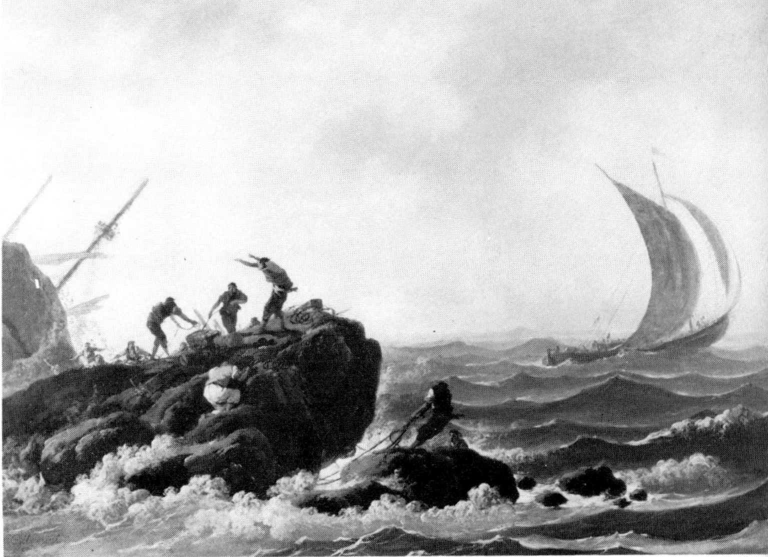

Plate 233 *(above)*. **Claude-Joseph Vernet, 1714-1789.** "Beaching a boat in a gale, 1759." *Although not primarily a ship painter, Vernet can be counted as one of the most attractive marine painters of the 18th century, with a superb command of figures.* Christie's.

Plate 234 *(above right)*. **Jean Baptiste Pillement, 1728-1808.** "Sailors shipwrecked on a rock, dated 1786." *Perhaps the poor man's Vernet, following very much in his style a generation later, though without the same success.* Christie's.

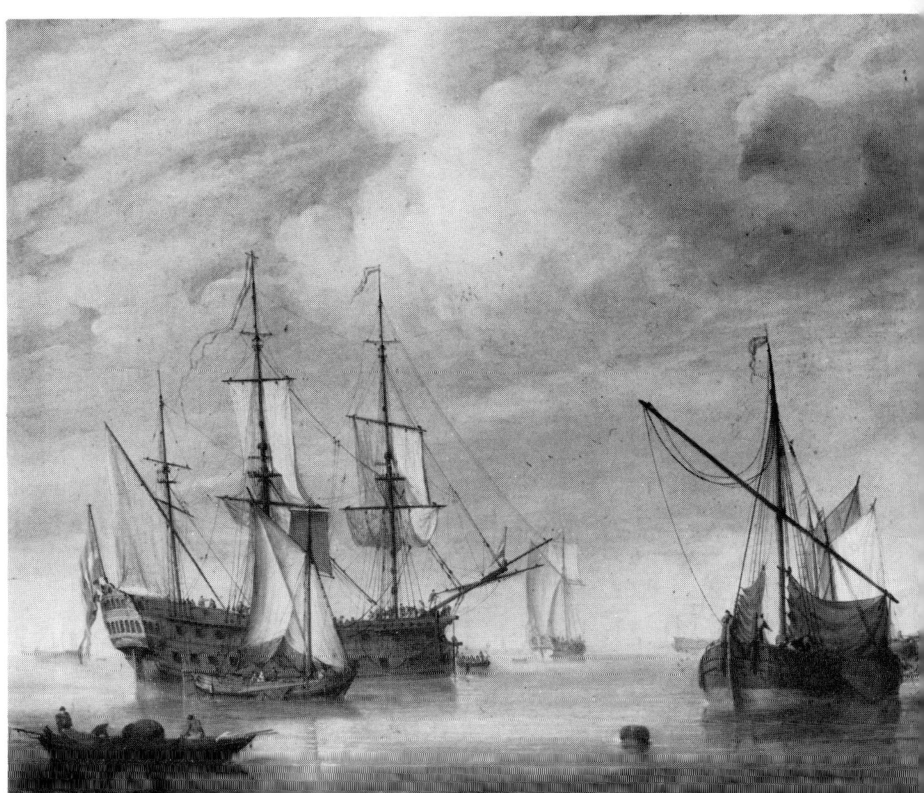

Plate 235. Jan Verbruggen, 1712-1780. "A Dutch ship of the line and shipping in a calm." *A good quality example of a Dutch marine painter of the 18th century. By this period the British school had come to the fore and little is known about the Dutch counterparts who were less in demand.* Private collection.

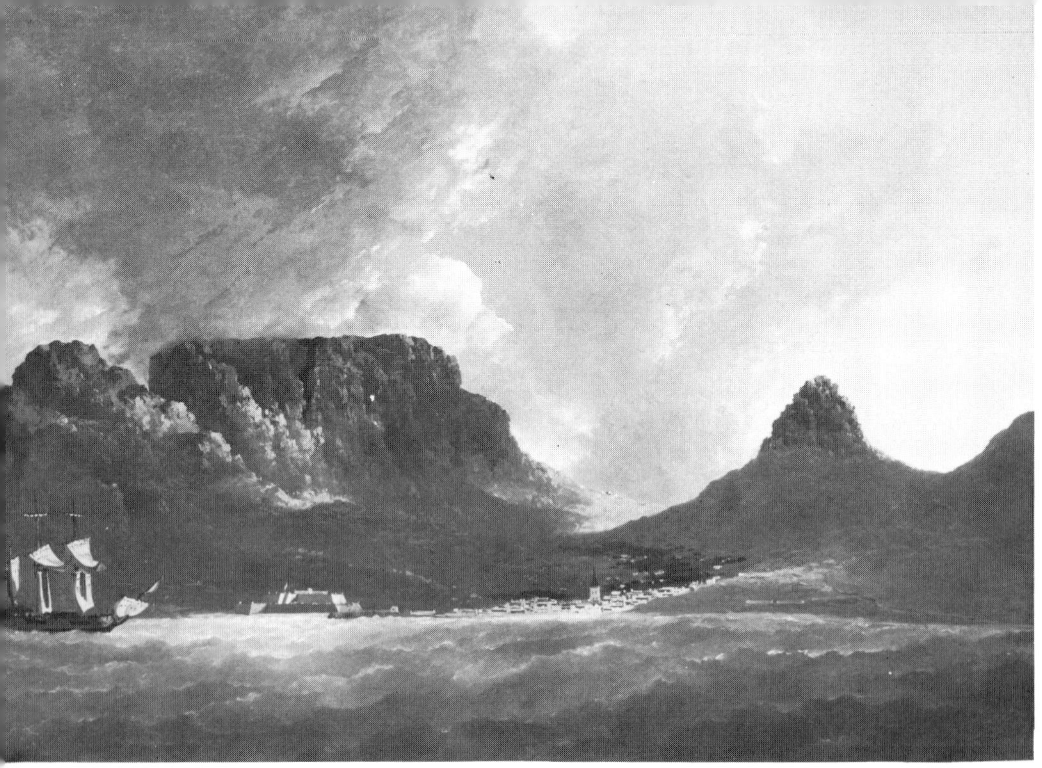

Plate 236. William Hodges, 1744-1797. "Capetown 1773." *Painted from the* Resolution *looking at the* Adventure. *The artist was with Cook on his second voyage. Strongly impressionistic, it did not meet with approval from his contemporaries. One of a series of twenty-five paintings for the Admiralty.* Ministry of Defence (on loan to the National Maritime Museum, Greenwich).

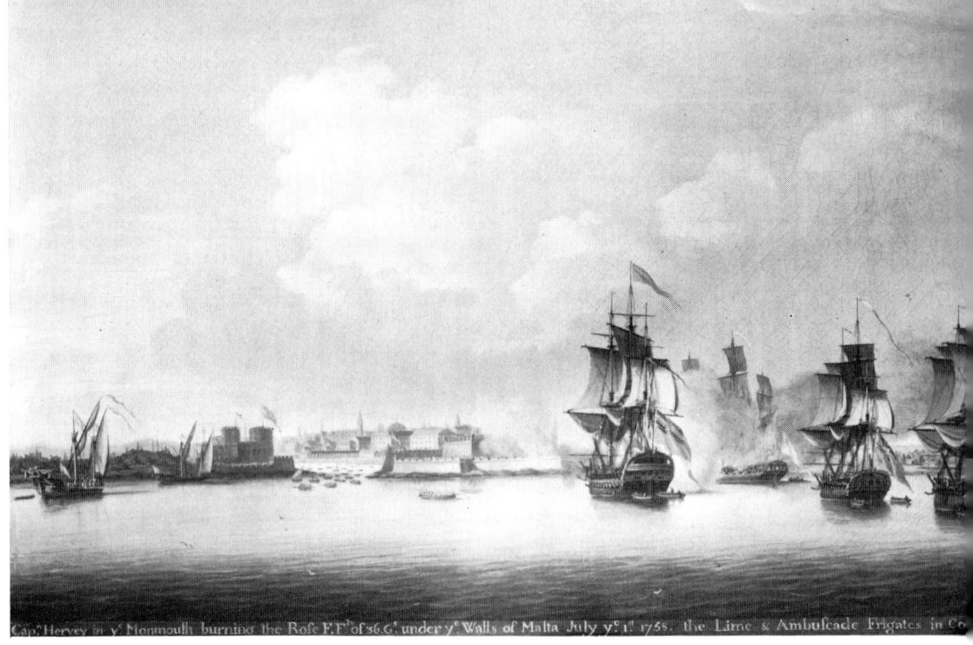

Plate 237. Dominic Serres, the Elder, 1722-1793. "The *Monmouth* burning the French frigate *Rose* at Malta in 1758." National Maritime Museum, Greenwich.

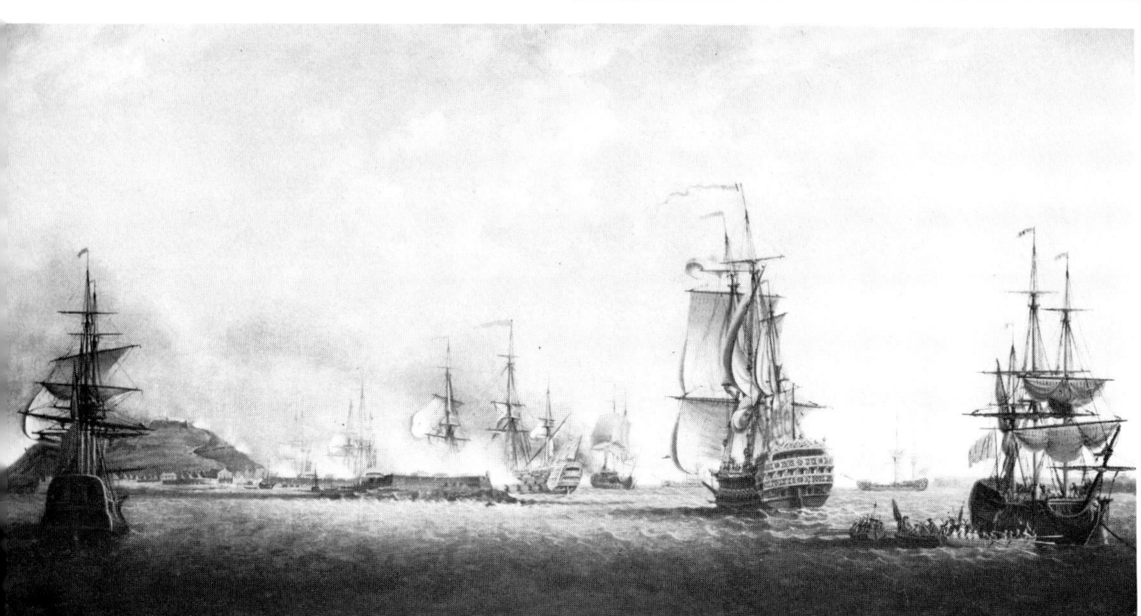

Plate 238. Dominic Serres, the Elder, 1722-1793. "The attack on Goree in 1758." National Maritime Museum, Greenwich.

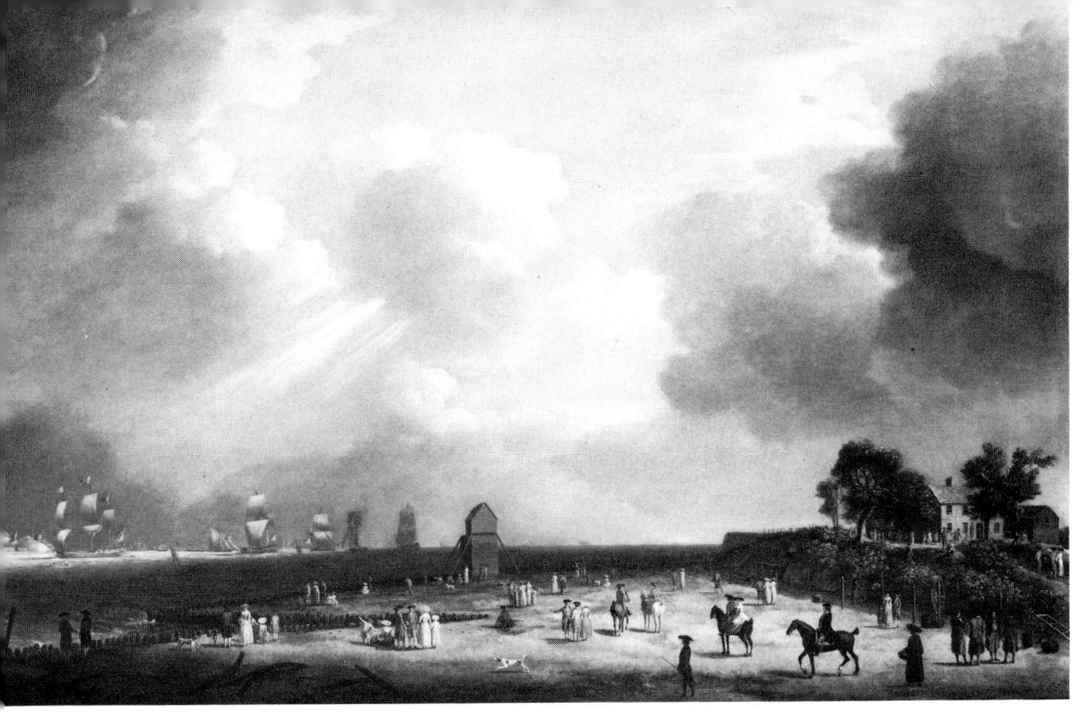

Plate 239. Dominic Serres, the Elder, 1722-1793. "The arrival of Princess Charlotte at Harwich in 1761." National Maritime Museum, Greenwich.

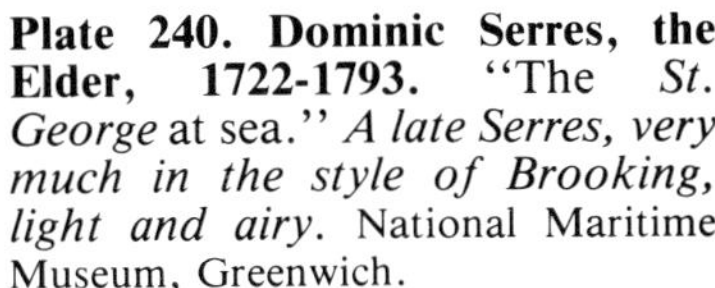

Plate 240. Dominic Serres, the Elder, 1722-1793. "The *St. George* at sea." *A late Serres, very much in the style of Brooking, light and airy.* National Maritime Museum, Greenwich.

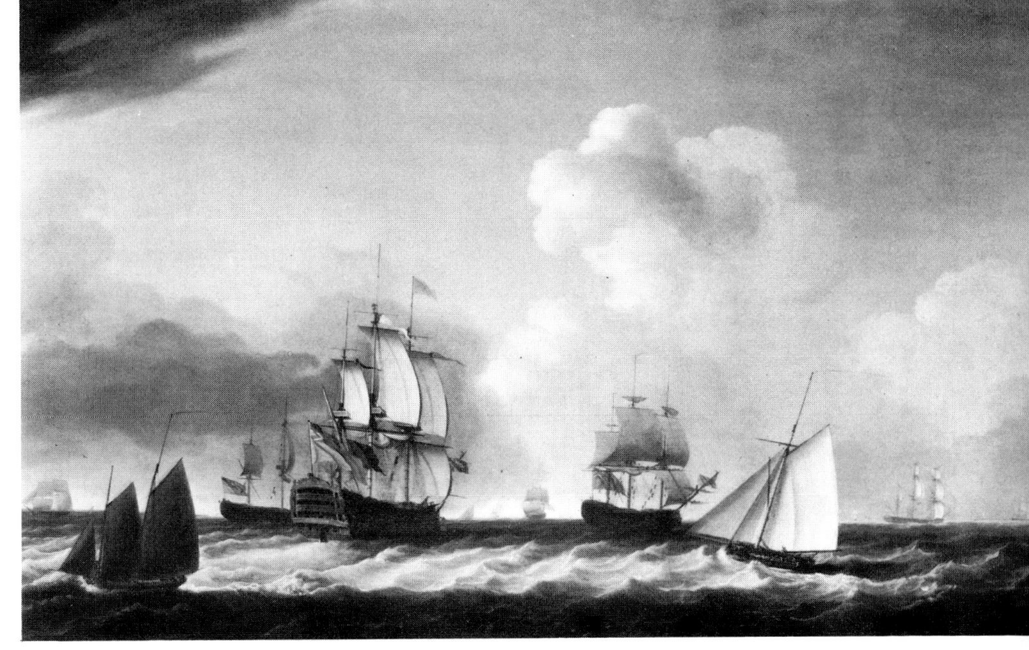

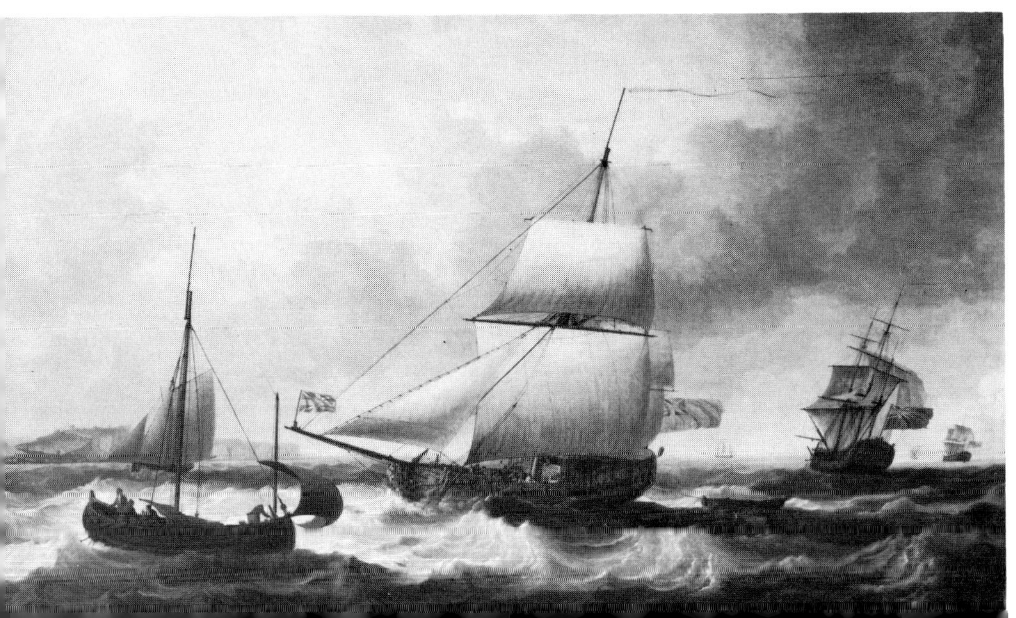

Plate 241. Dominic Serres, the Elder, 1722-1793. "The yacht *Dorset* close hauled off Dover." *A straight copy of a Brooking. The* Dorset *was one of the royal yachts.* National Maritime Museum, Greenwich.

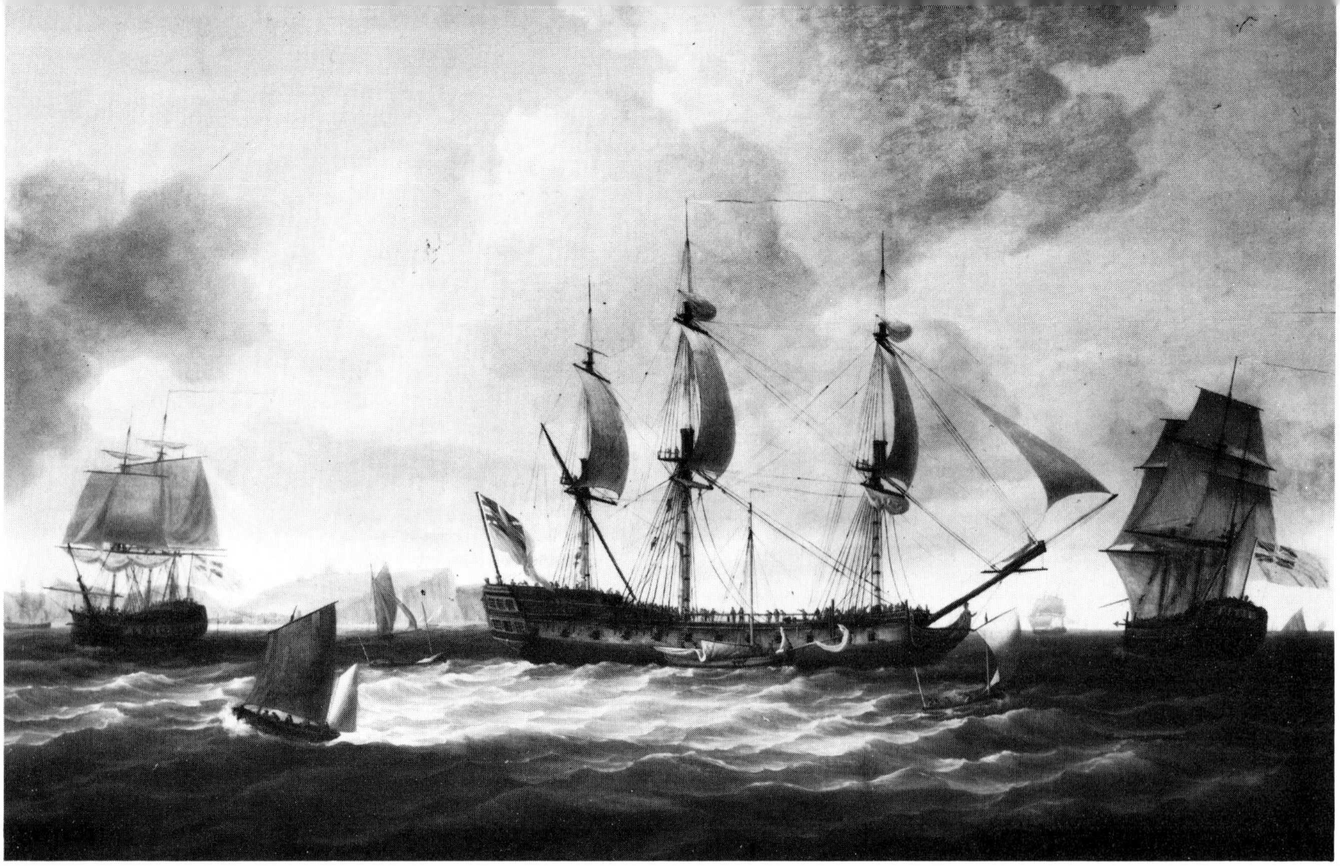

Plate 242. Dominic Serres, the Elder, 1722-1793. "The East Indiaman *Pitt* off Dover, dated 1786." National Maritime Museum, Greenwich.

Plate 243. Dominic Serres, the Elder, 1722-1793. "The arrival of Their Sicilian Majesties at Naples in 1785." *The slight stiffness of the figures in the foreground is typical.* National Maritime Museum, Greenwich.

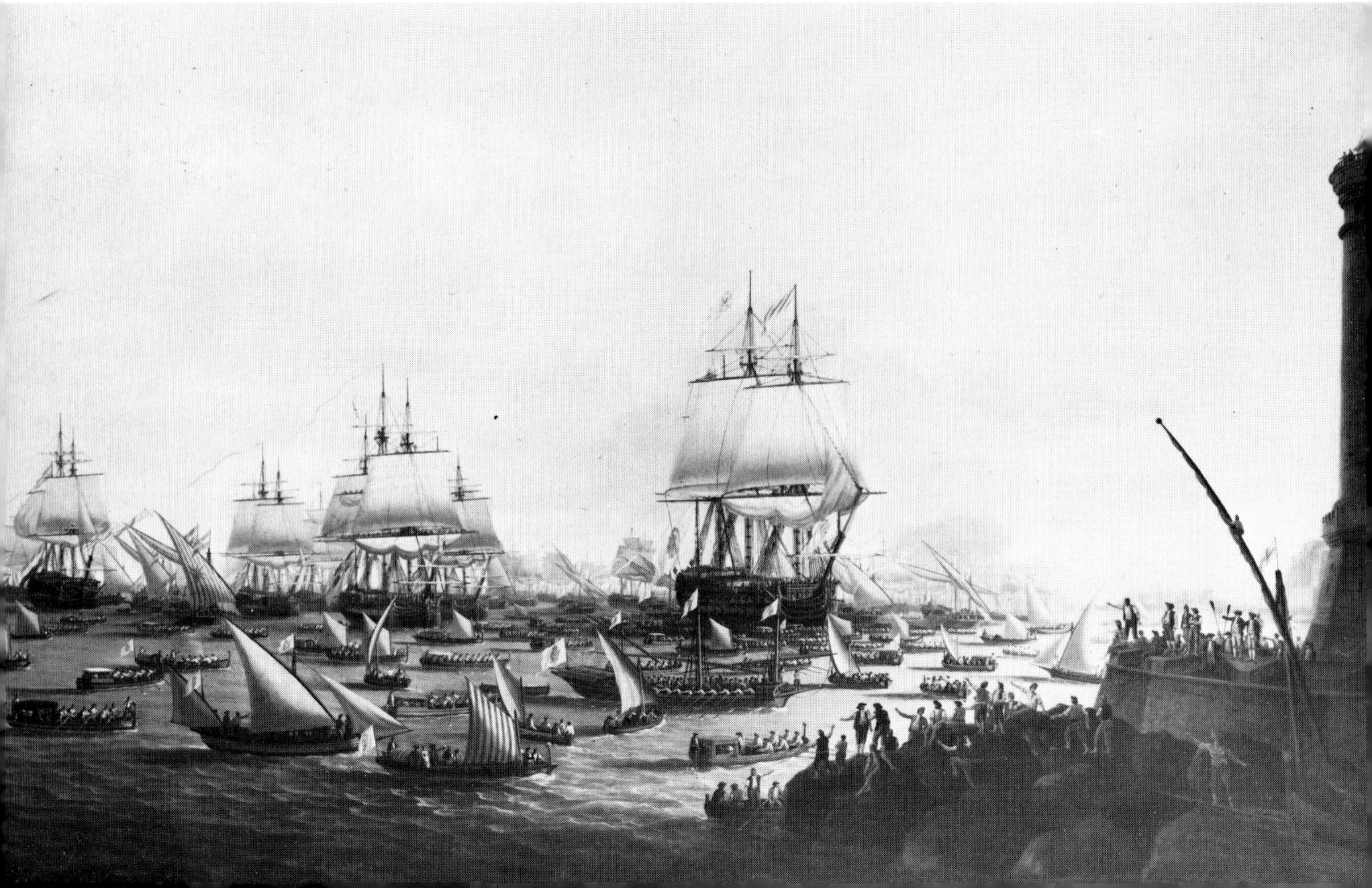

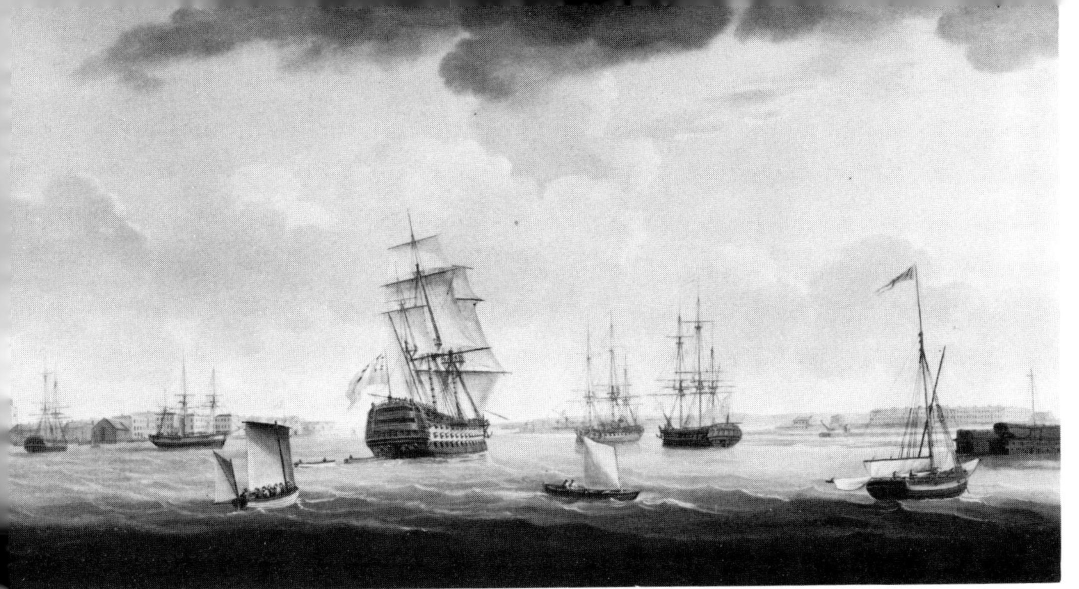

Plate 244. Thomas Elliot, fl.1790-1800. "Portsmouth harbour about 1795." *A composition which Elliot employed consistently with minor variations, painting in the manner of Dominic Serres, but without his sureness of touch.* Sotheby's.

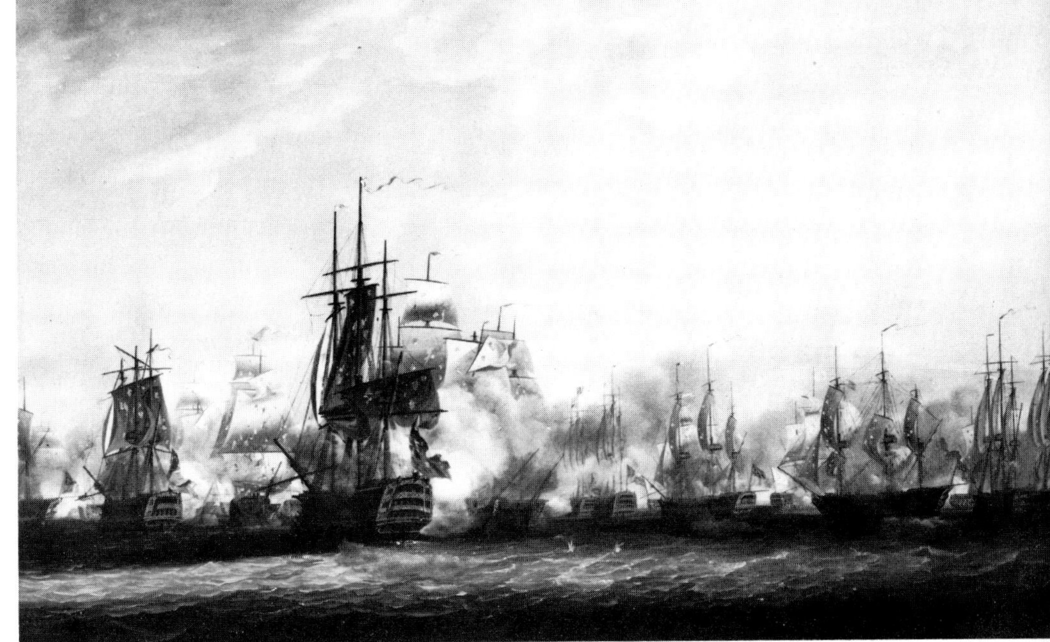

Plate 245. Nicholas Pocock, 1740-1821. "Battle of The Saints in 1782." National Maritime Museum, Greenwich.

Plate 246. Nicholas Pocock, 1740-1821. "Chatham Dockyard, 1790." *One of a number of almost palatial delineations commissioned by the Admiralty of the five dockyards in the early 1790s.* National Maritime Museum, Greenwich (Greenwich Hospital Collection).

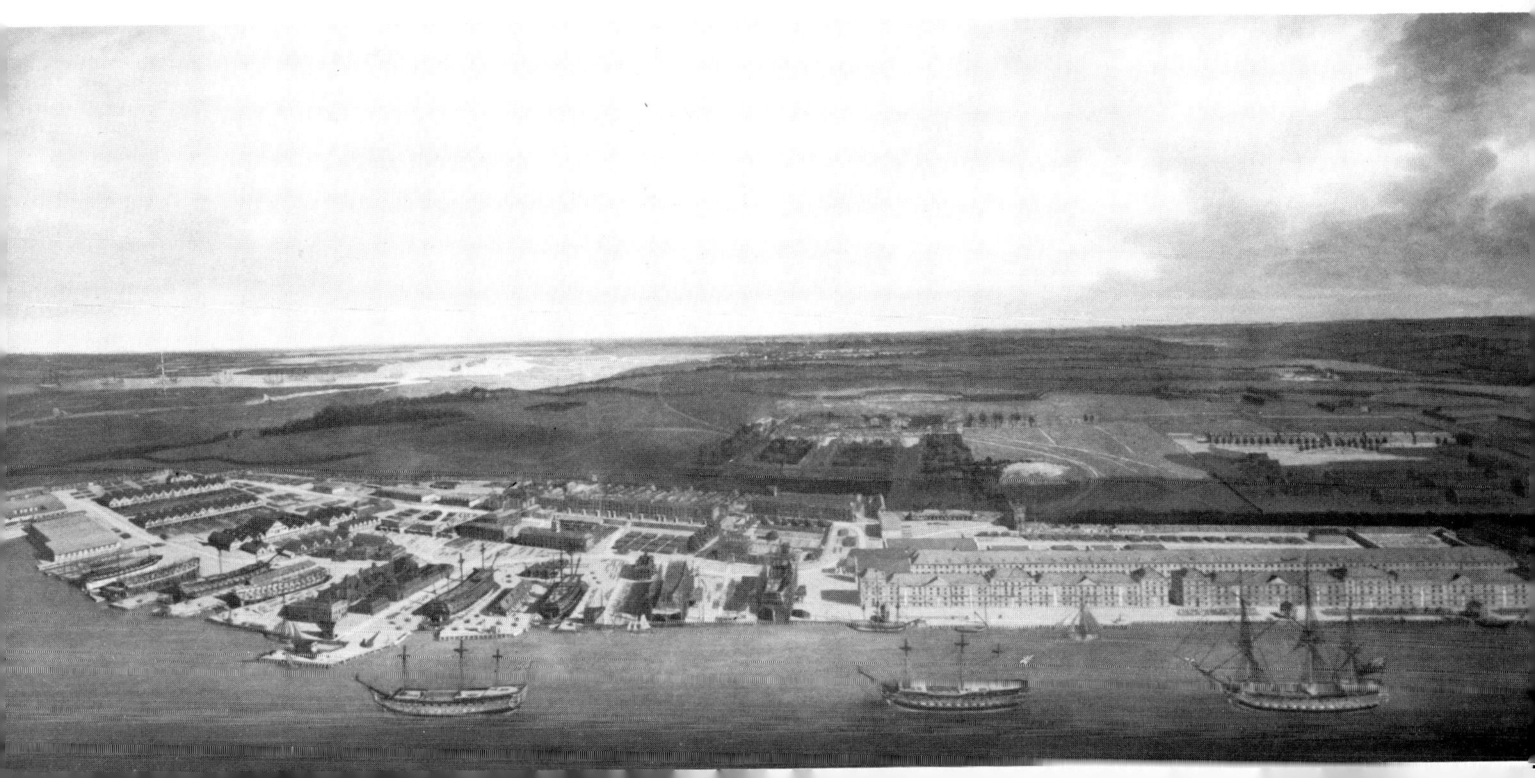

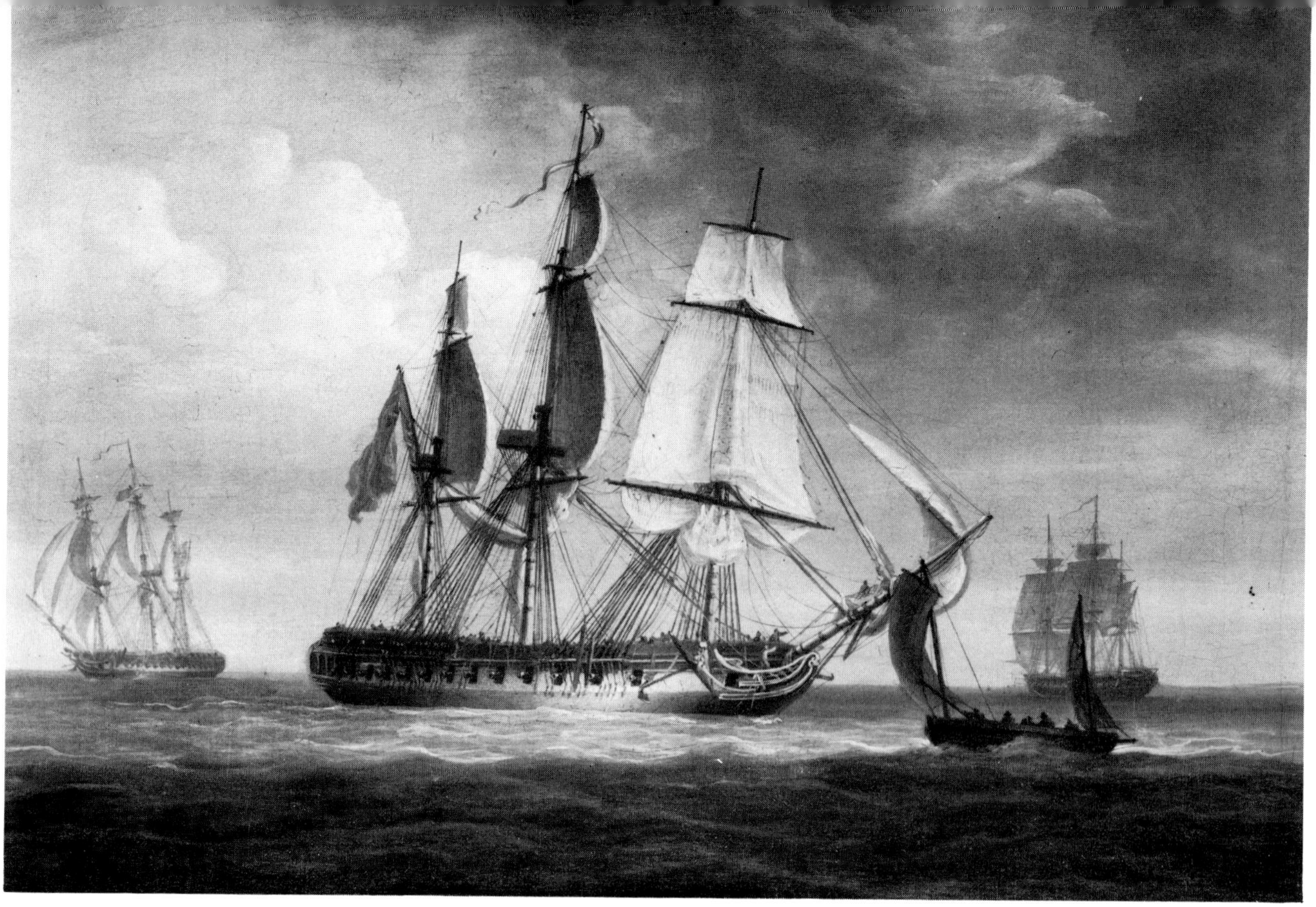

Plate 247. Nicholas Pocock, 1740-1821. "The frigate H.M.S. *Triton,* dated 1797." *A typical example of the carefully drawn work of this artist. There is a small lugger in the right foreground.* National Maritime Museum, Greenwich.

Plate 248. Nicholas Pocock, 1740-1821. "Nelson's commands and flagships." *This and the next example were commissioned for engravings for Clark and McArthur's biography of Lord Nelson.* National Maritime Museum, Greenwich.

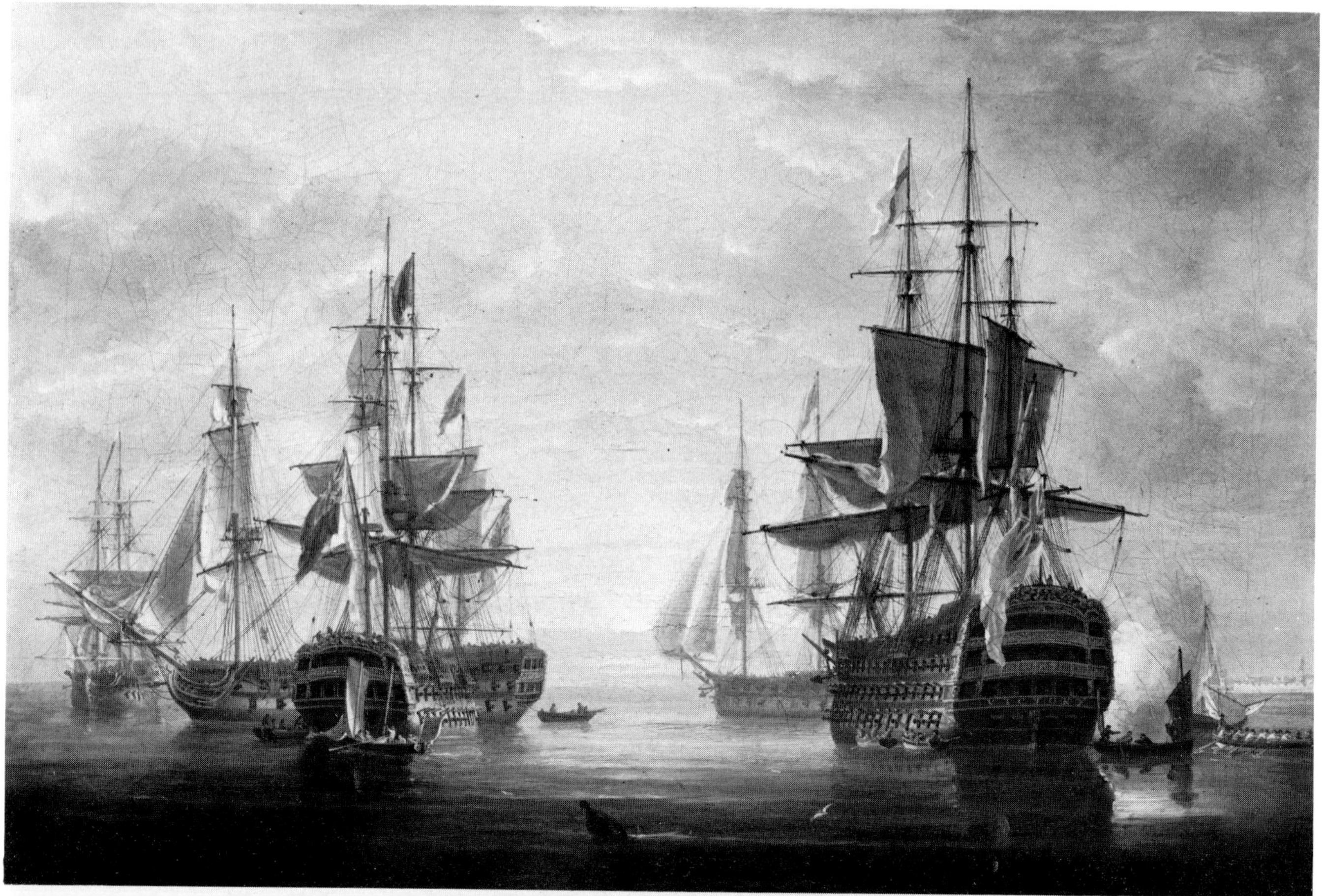

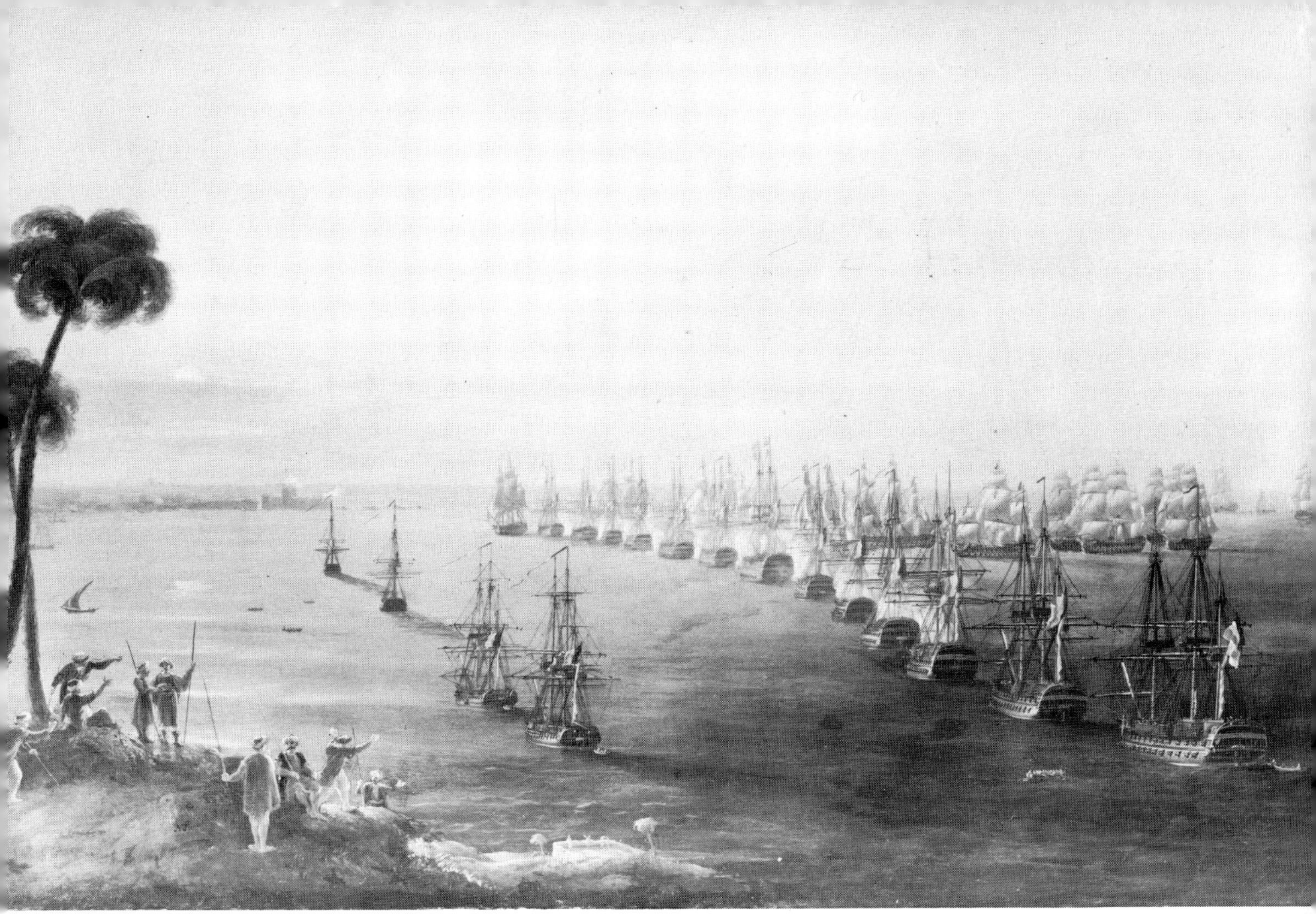

Plate 249. Nicholas Pocock, 1740-1821. "The Battle of the Nile in 1798." National Maritime Museum, Greenwich.

Plate 250. Nicholas Pocock, 1740-1821. "Duckworth's action off San Domingo in 1806." *Pocock made a prodigious coverage of the naval side of the long French Revolutionary Wars.* National Maritime Museum, Greenwich.

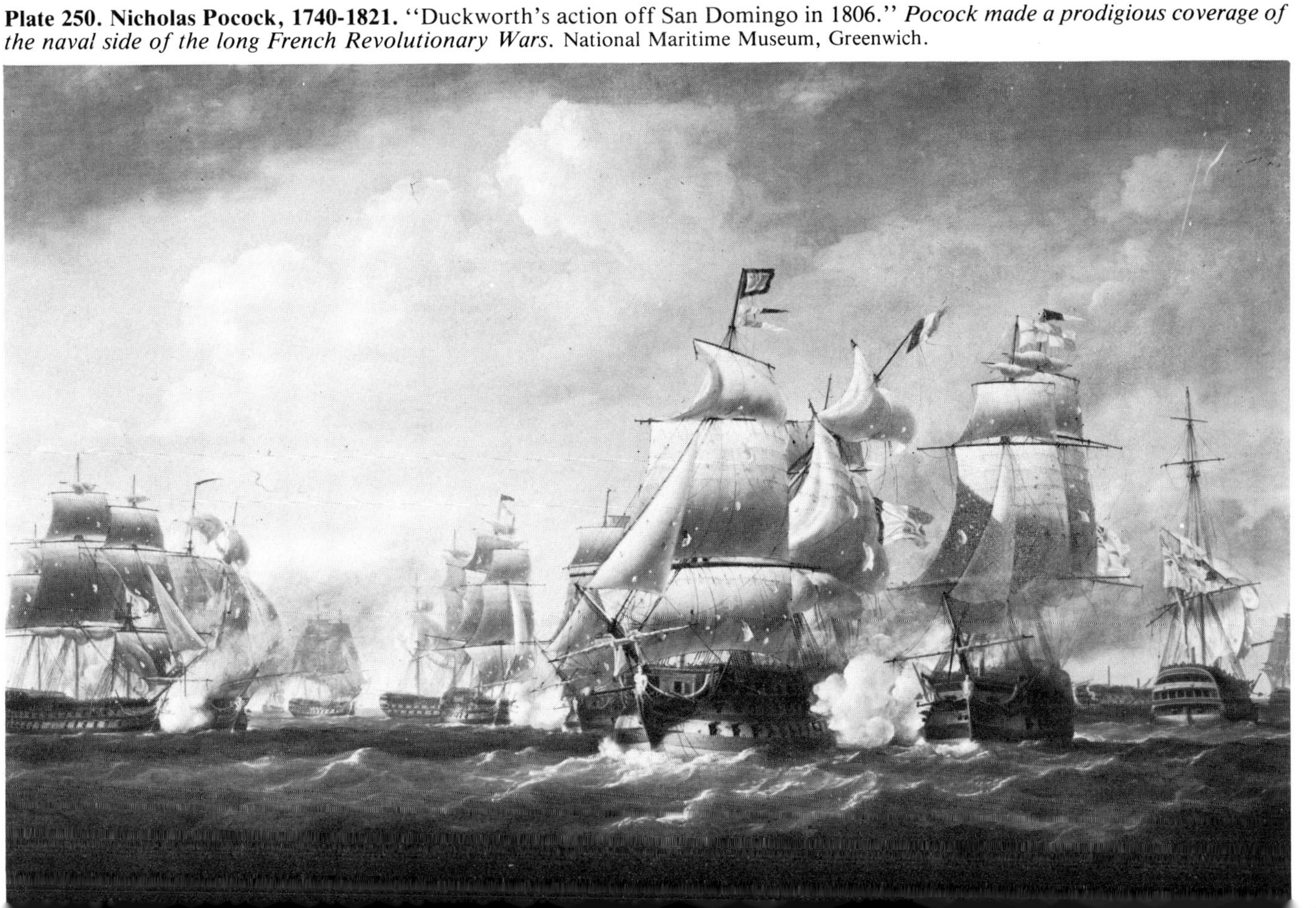

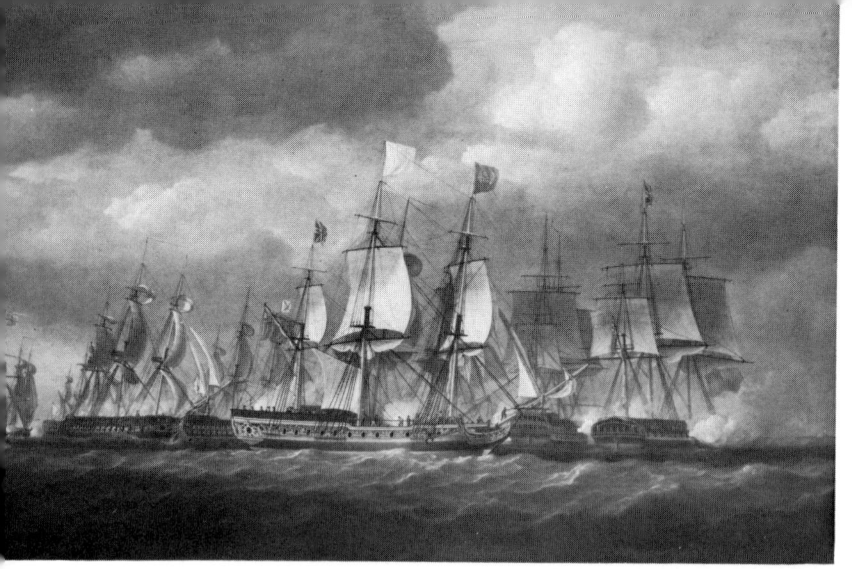

Plate 251. William Innes Pocock, 1783-1836. "The return of Louis XVIII to France in the *Royal Sovereign* in 1814." *A less successful artist painting somewhat in the style of his father, with the same gingery greyish palette. The presence on board of Louis XVIII is the reason for the replacement of the British royal arms by a French flag, the white flag of the House of Bourbon. One would have thought that Louis XVIII's own standard (blue with three fleurs-de-lis) would have been flown.* National Maritime Museum, Greenwich.

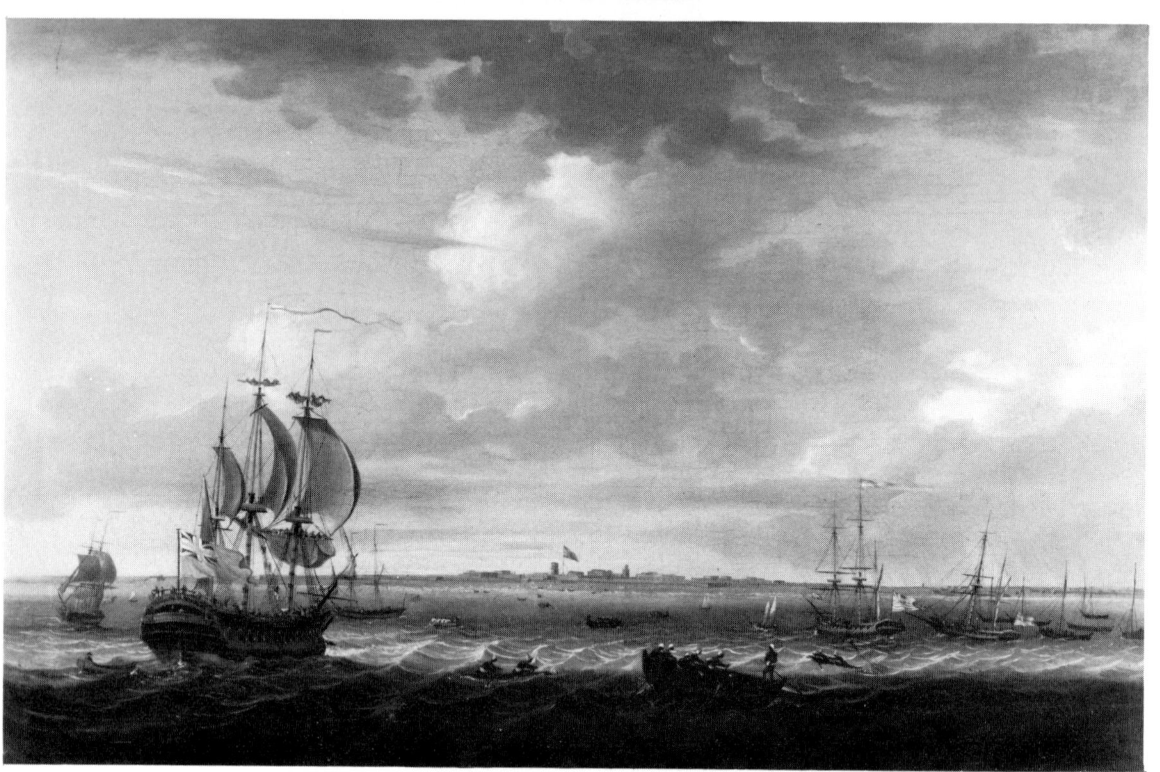

Plate 252. Adam Callander, fl.1780-1811. "Shipping off Madras, c.1780." National Maritime Museum, Greenwich.

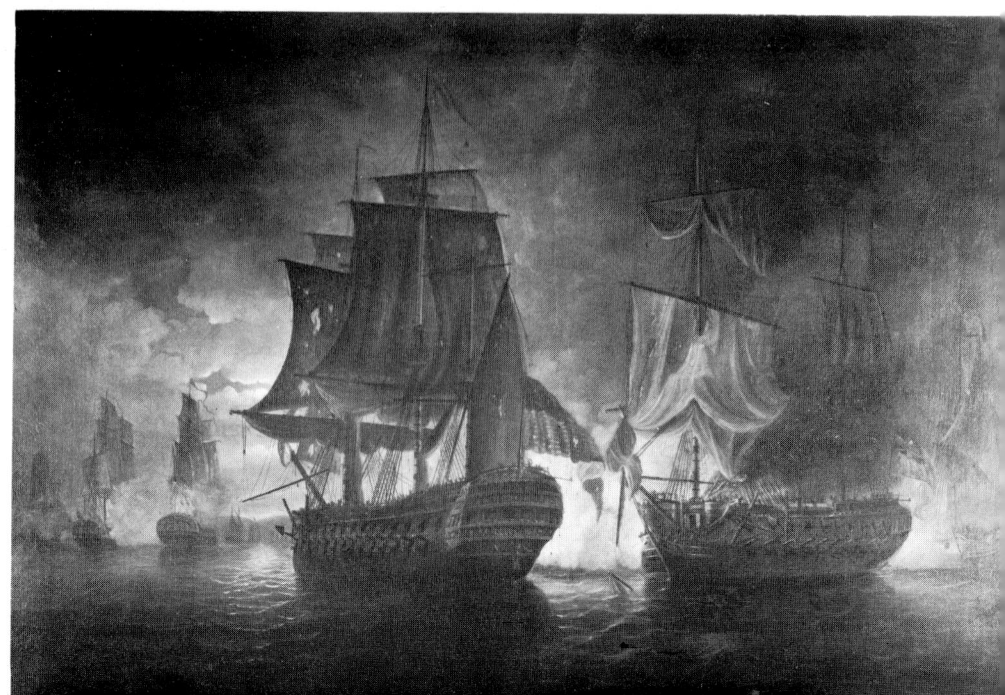

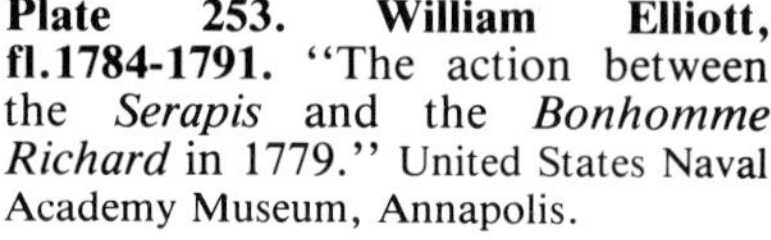

Plate 253. William Elliott, fl.1784-1791. "The action between the *Serapis* and the *Bonhomme Richard* in 1779." United States Naval Academy Museum, Annapolis.

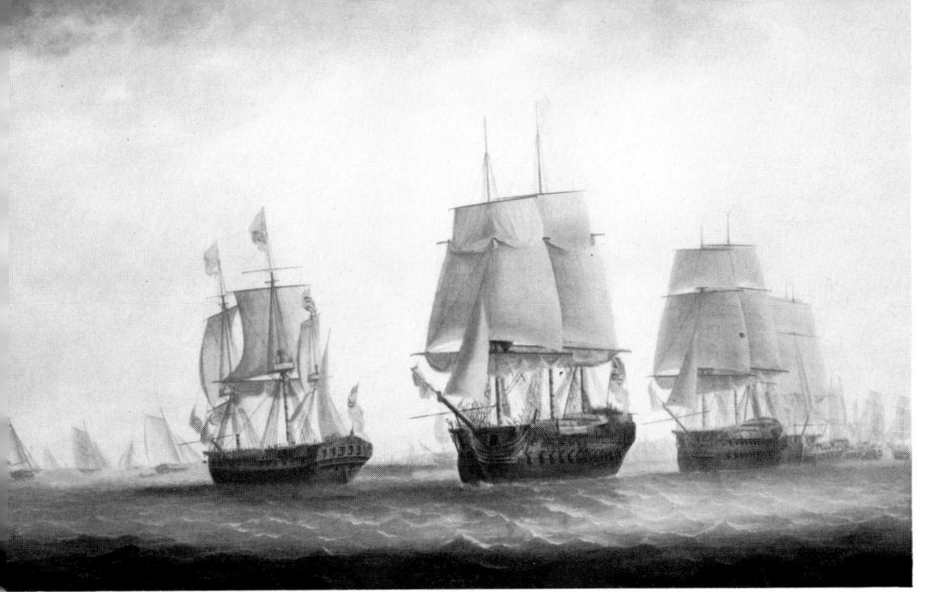

Plate 254. William Elliott, fl.1784-1791. "King George III in the *Southampton* reviewing the fleet at Spithead in 1789." National Maritime Museum, Greenwich.

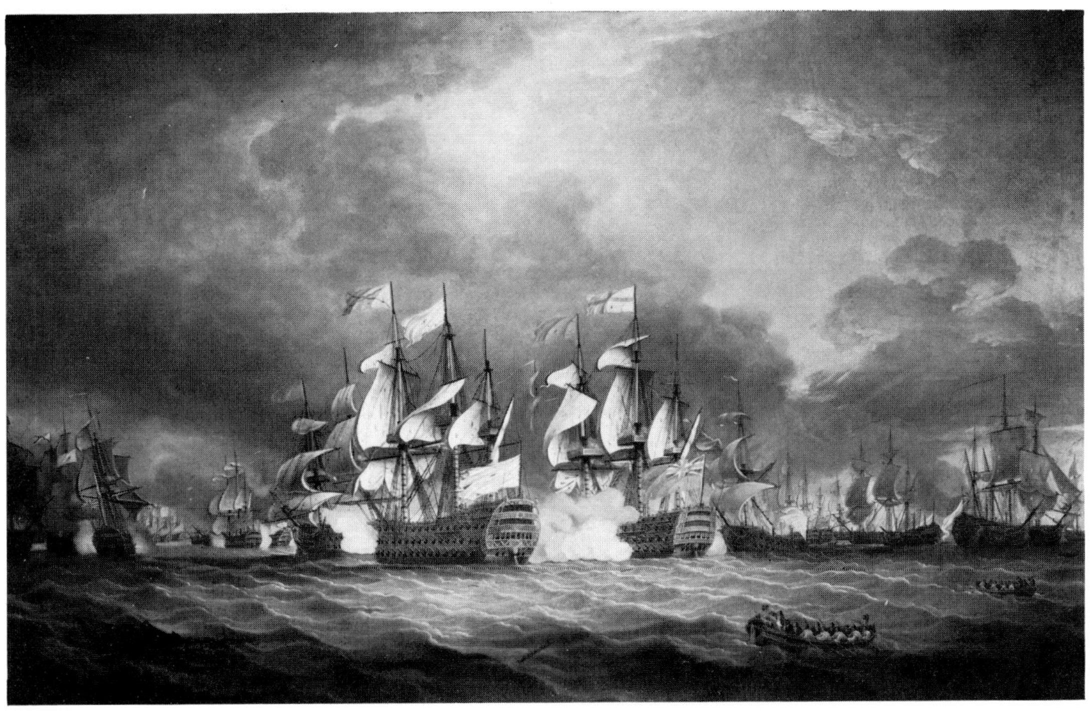

Plate 255. Thomas Mitchell, 1735-1790. "The Battle of the Saints in 1782." *A painter of historical scenes, often large ones. The ship on the left is the* Ville de Paris, *captured in the action, but lost in a hurricane on passage to England.* National Maritime Museum, Greenwich.

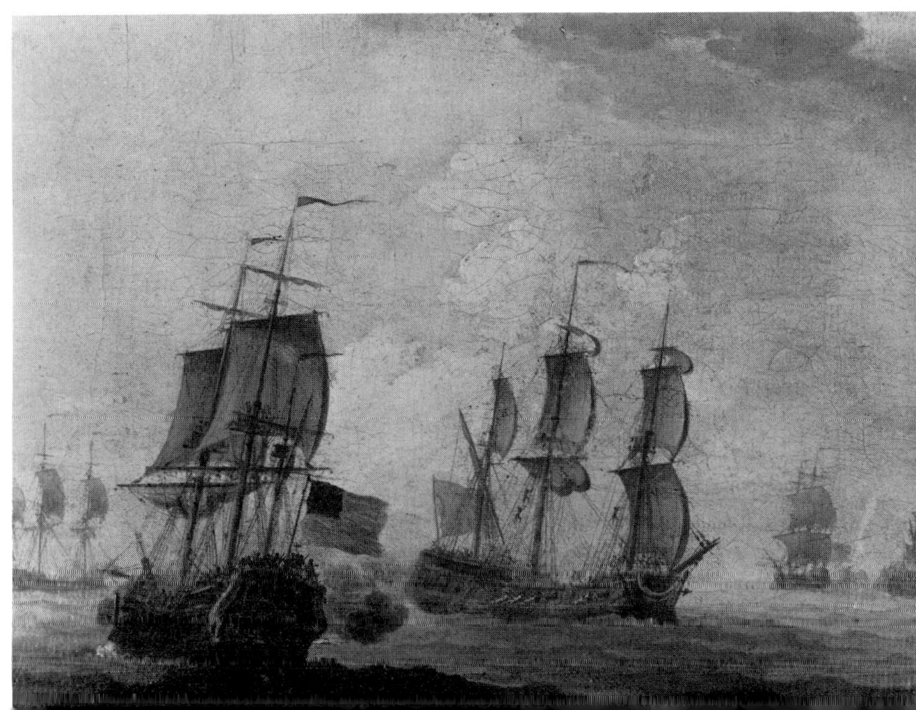

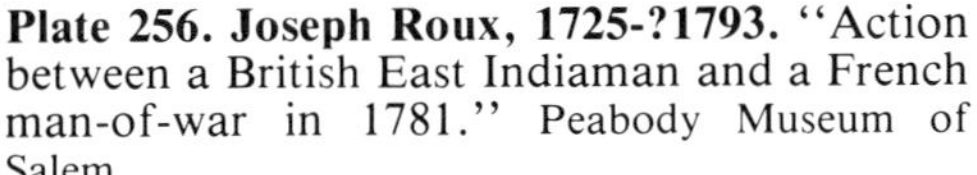

Plate 256. Joseph Roux, 1725-?1793. "Action between a British East Indiaman and a French man-of-war in 1781." Peabody Museum of Salem.

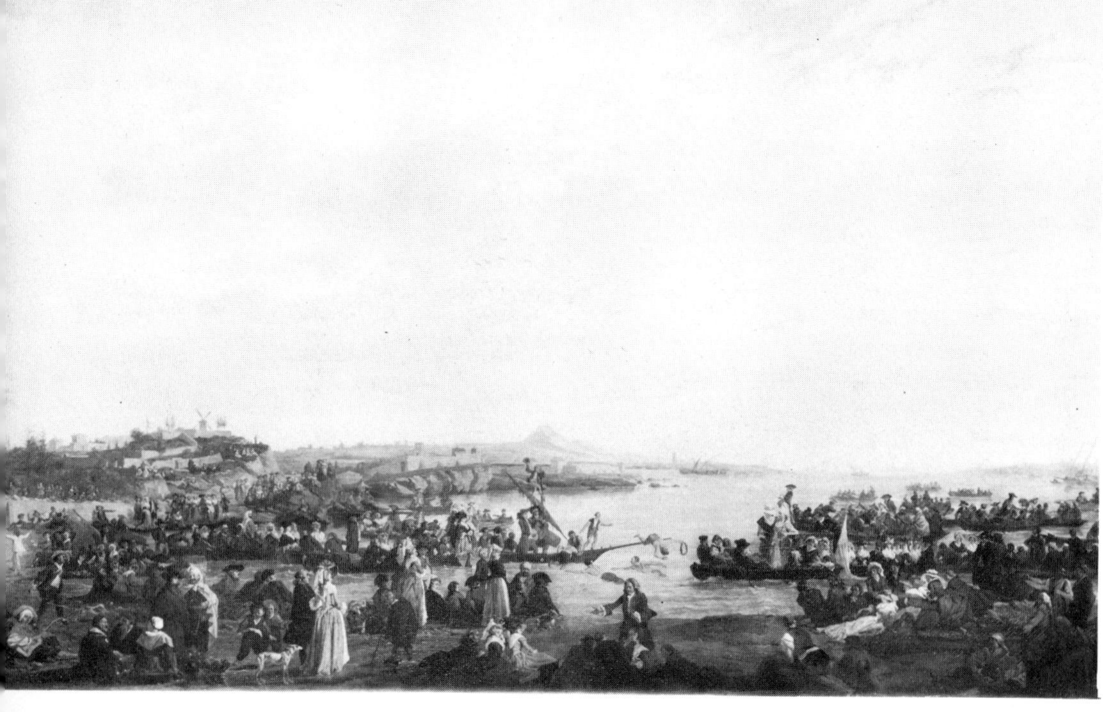

Plate 257. Philippe Jacques de Loutherbourg, 1740-1812. "The Fête of the Tunny Fishers at Marseilles about 1770." *In sharp contrast to the next example by this artist, the carefully delineated figures are controlled and disciplined. His range of work, however, was much wider than sea paintings.* Metropolitan Museum of Art, New York.

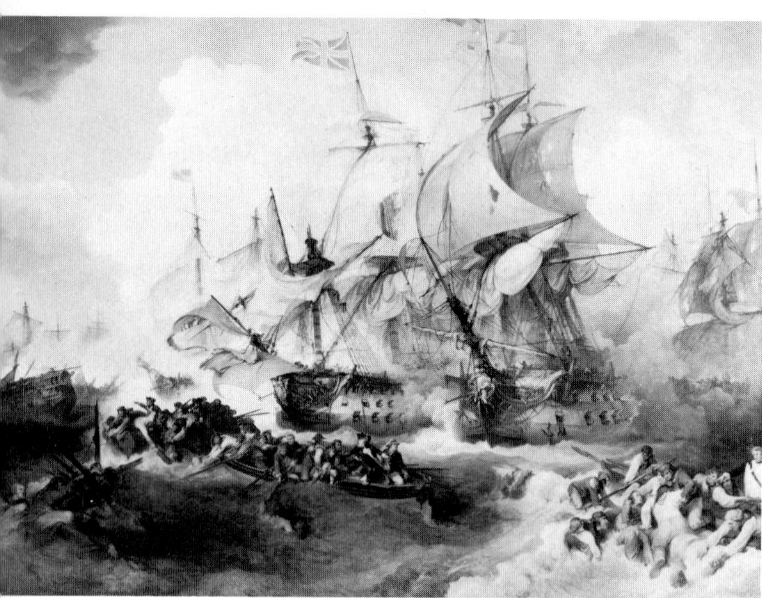

Plate 258. Philippe Jacques de Loutherbourg, 1740-1812. "The Battle of the Glorious First of June, 1794." *It is easy to see from this highly emotional scene the influence this artist must have had on the young Turner. A huge picture.* National Maritime Museum, Greenwich (Greenwich Hospital Collection).

Plate 259. Philippe Jacques de Loutherbourg, 1740-1812. "The Battle of Camperdown in 1797." *This large historical scene and the one that follows clearly demonstrate an ability to handle successfully subject matter on a large canvas, perhaps learnt from his work as a scene painter.* Tate Gallery.

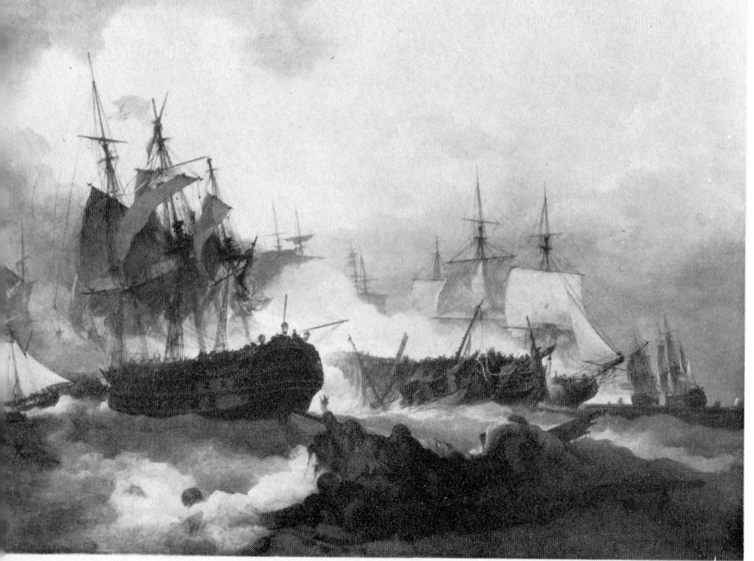

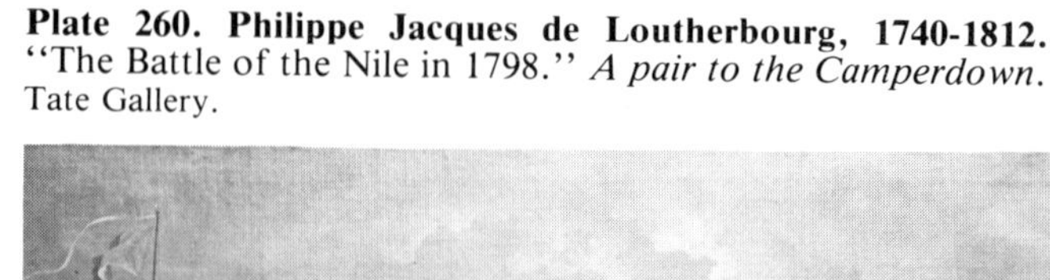

Plate 260. Philippe Jacques de Loutherbourg, 1740-1812. "The Battle of the Nile in 1798." *A pair to the Camperdown.* Tate Gallery.

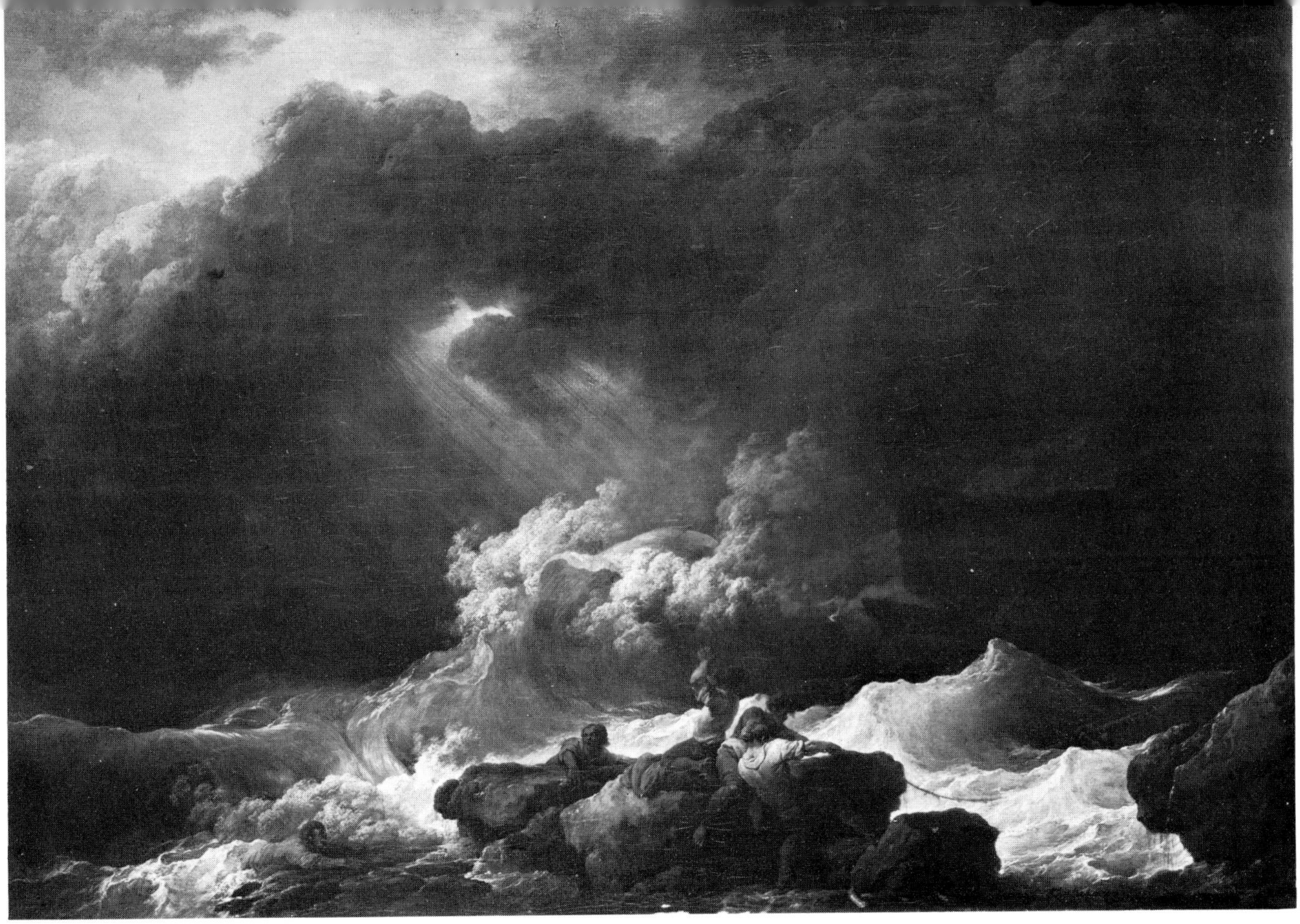

Plate 261. Philippe Jacques de Loutherbourg, 1740-1812. "A storm with rocks and figures." *Yet another contrast. The drama is intensified by the sharply contrasting light and darkness in this horrific scene of a wreck.* Fine Art Academy, Vienna.

Plate 262. John Thomas Serres, 1759-1825. "The royal yacht *Dorset* passing Dublin lighthouse." *An artist strongly influenced by de Loutherbourg, though not really attuned to the Romantic Movement.* Victoria and Albert Museum.

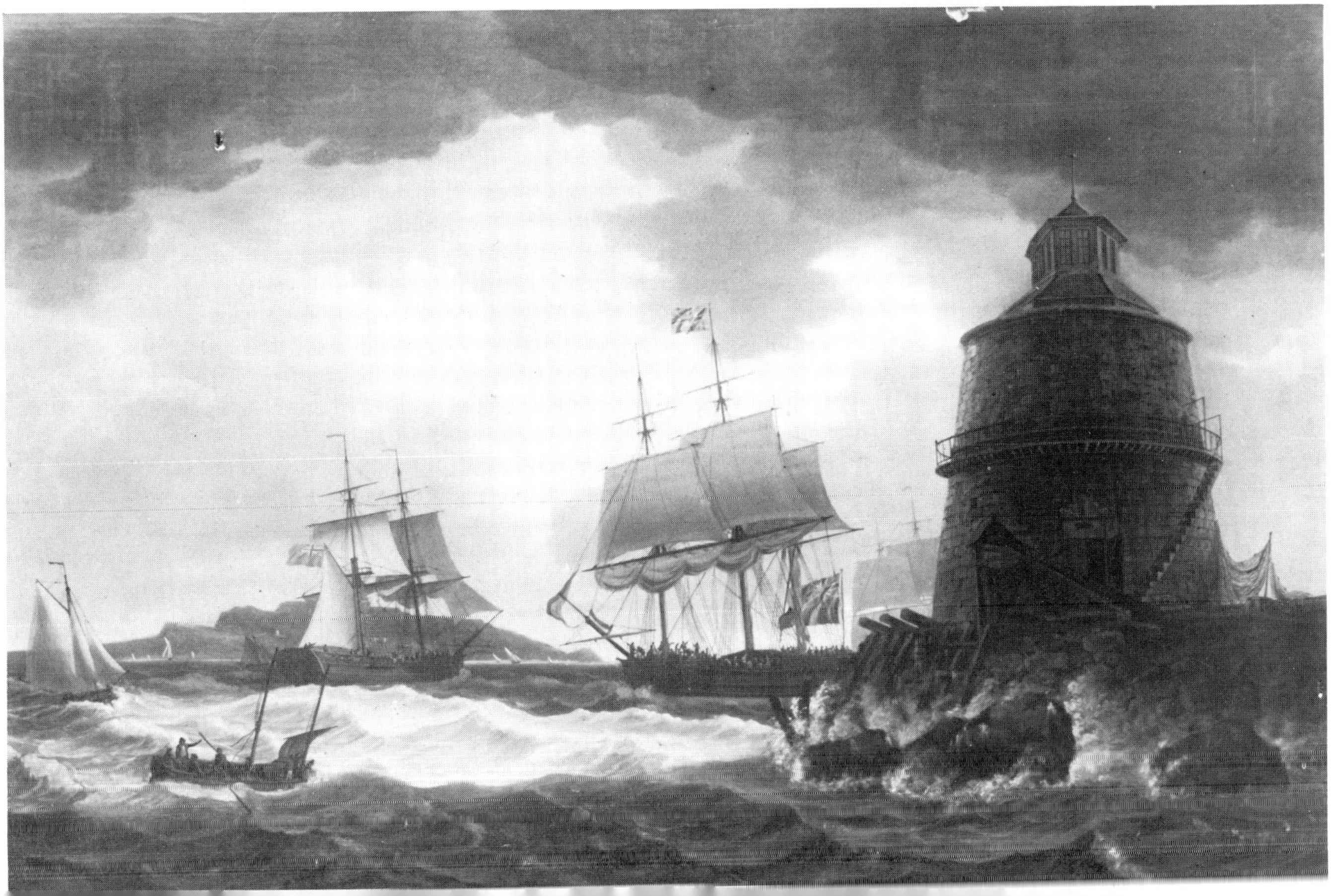

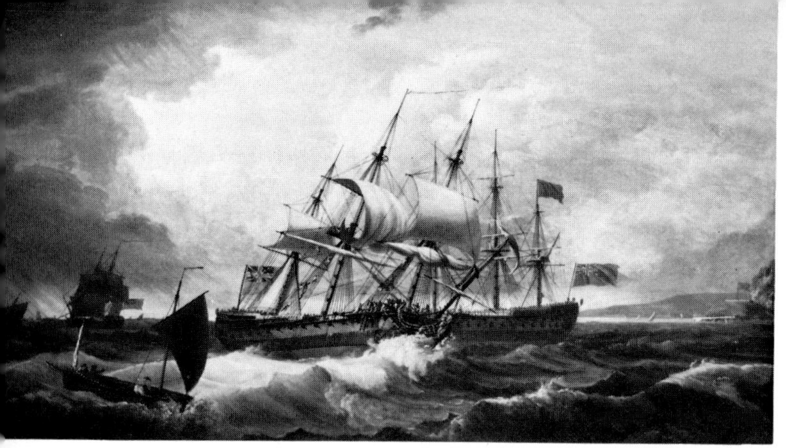

Plate 263. John Thomas Serres, 1759-1825. "British third rates in a squall, 1793." National Maritime Museum, Greenwich.

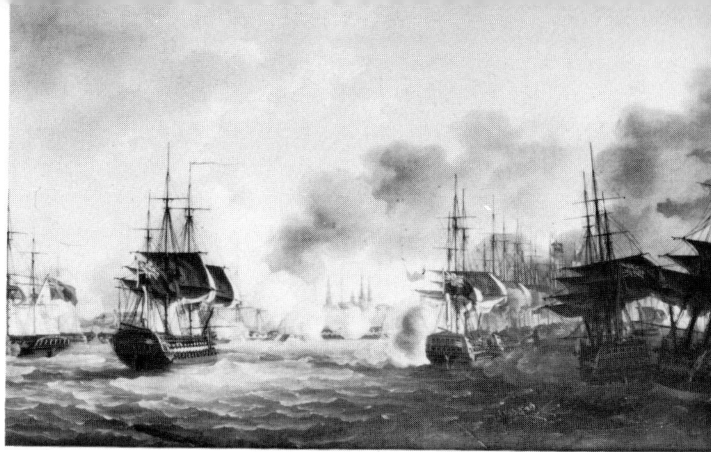

Plate 264. John Thomas Serres, 1759-1825. "The Battle of Copenhagen in 1801." National Maritime Museum, Greenwich.

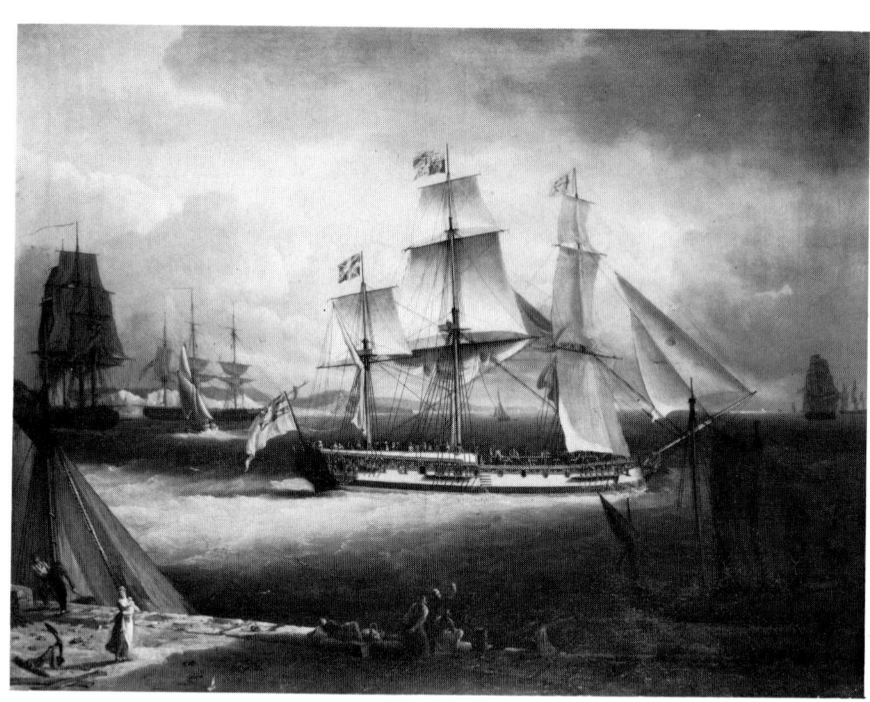

Plate 265. John Thomas Serres, 1759-1825. "King George III aboard the *Royal Sovereign* off Weymouth in 1806." *A large canvas, very successfully executed.* National Maritime Museum, Greenwich.

Plate 266. John Thomas Serres, 1759-1825. "The Thames at Shillingford, 1823." *Painted within two years of his death this peaceful scene is in sharp contrast to previous examples and is very 18th century in flavour. The tranquillity of the scene, the tree and figures in the foreground combine to add to its atmosphere.* National Maritime Museum, Greenwich.

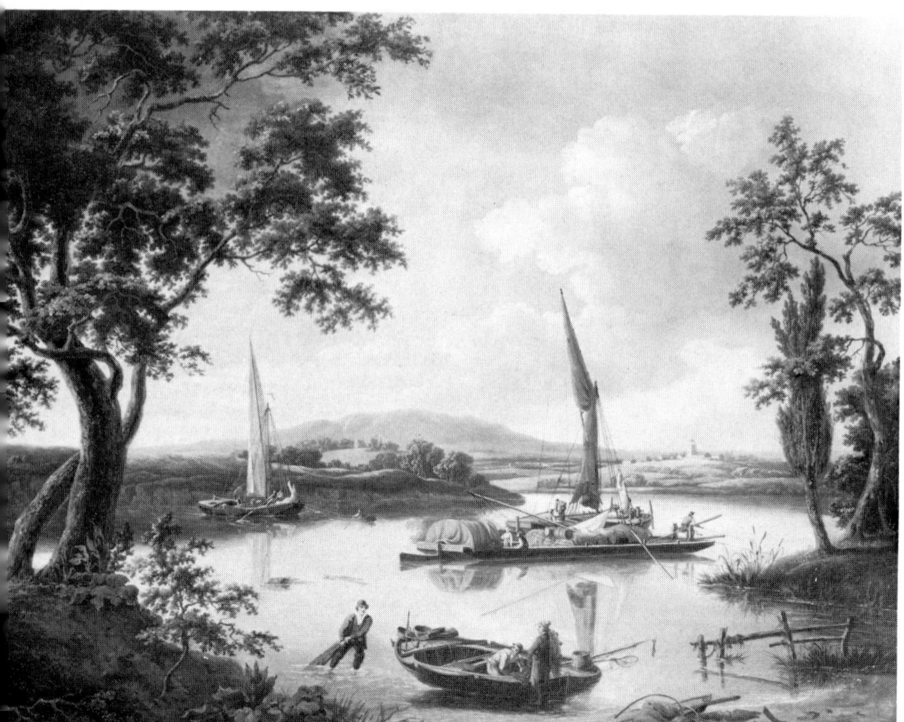

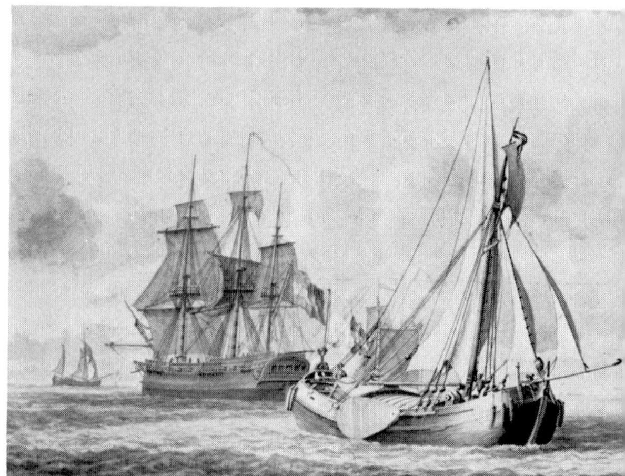

Plate 267. Pieter Aartsze Blaauw, 1744-1808. "A Dutch merchantman and a kaag." Wash drawing. Prins Hendrik Museum, Rotterdam.

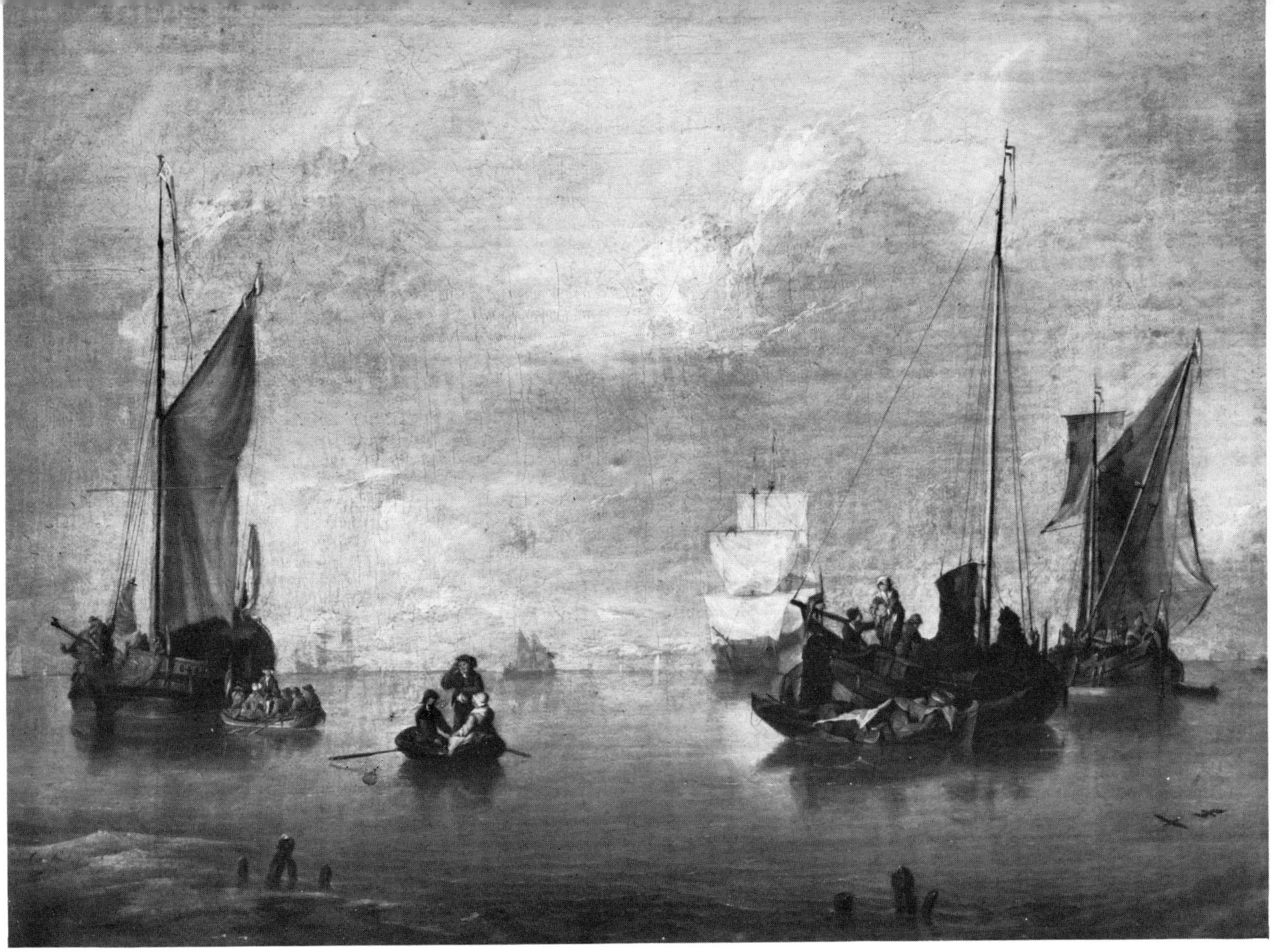

Plate 268. Jan van Os, 1744-1808. "A calm off the Dutch coast." *A picture which harks back to the earlier Dutch school of such painters as Cuyp, but with a freer application of paint.* Christie's.

Plate 269. Robert Cleveley, 1747-1809. "The Battle of Saint Vincent in 1797." *An example typical of the work of Robert Cleveley, painted on similar material (twill canvas) to the very much larger signed examples. The* Salvadore del Mundo, *112 guns, receives a raking broadside from the* Victory. National Maritime Museum, Greenwich.

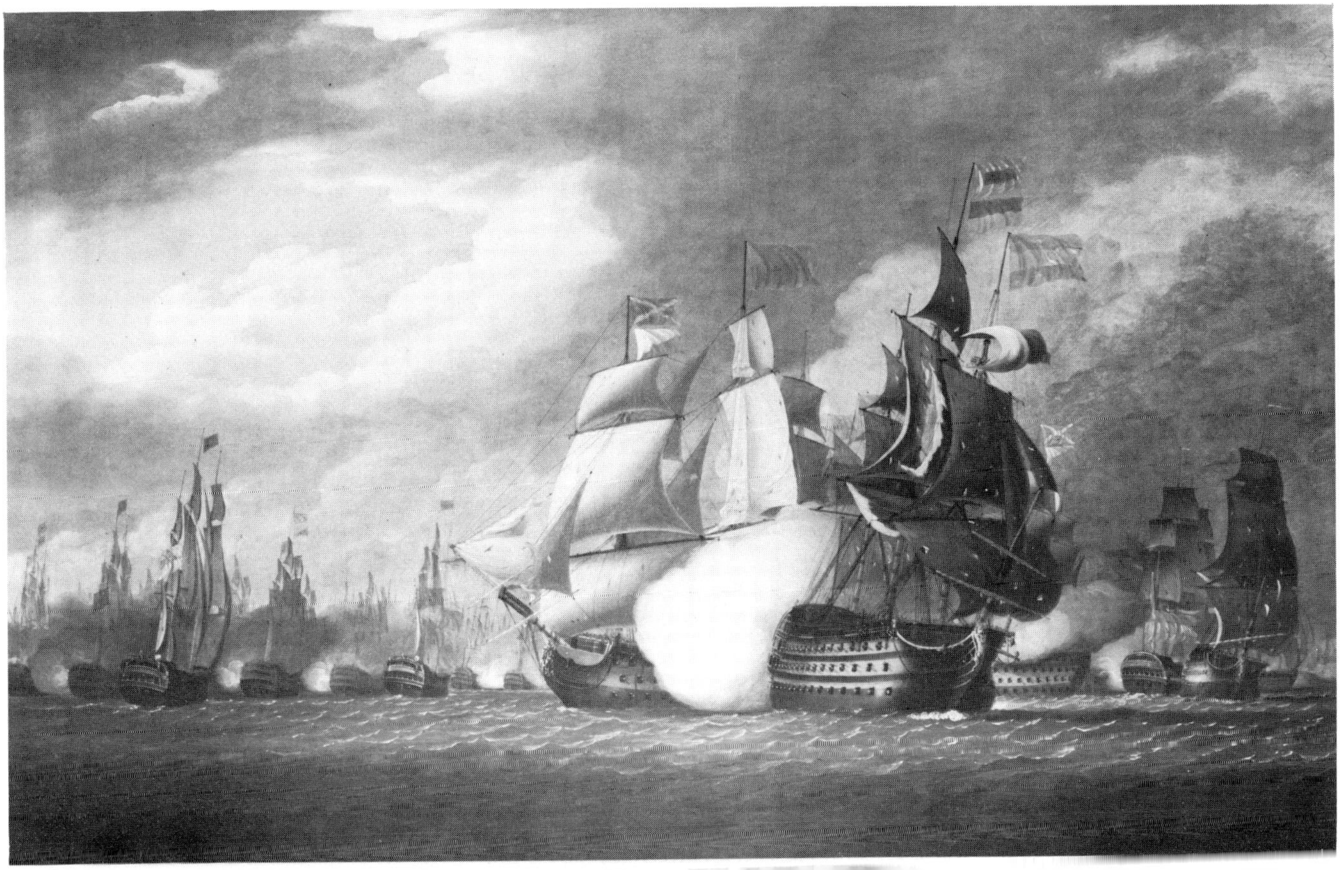

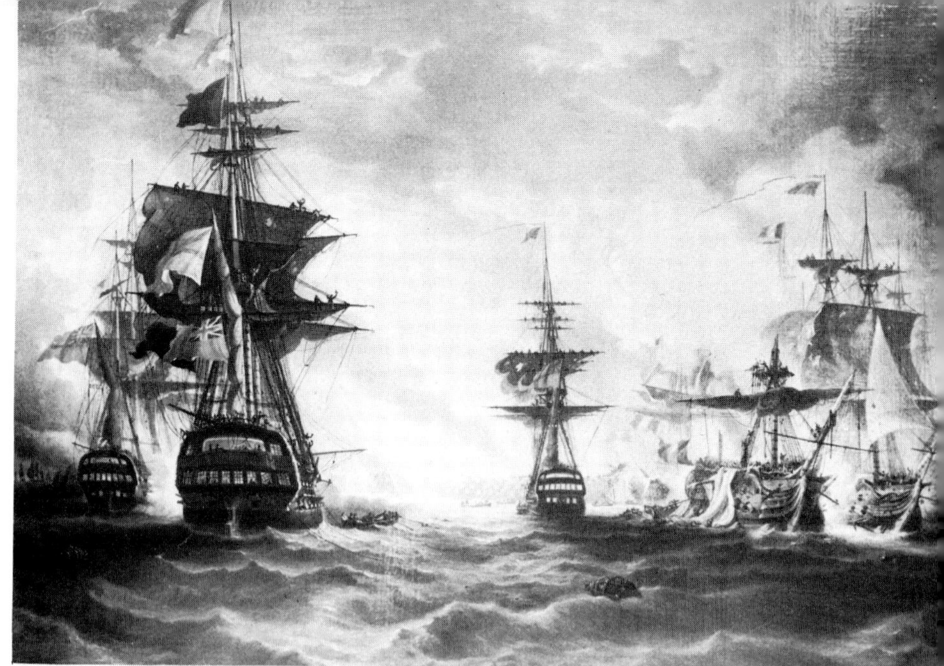

Plate 270. Robert Cleveley, 1747-1809. "Battle of the Nile in 1798." *Comparison with the previous example shows the wide variation of style that is claimed for this artist.* Mariners Museum, Newport News.

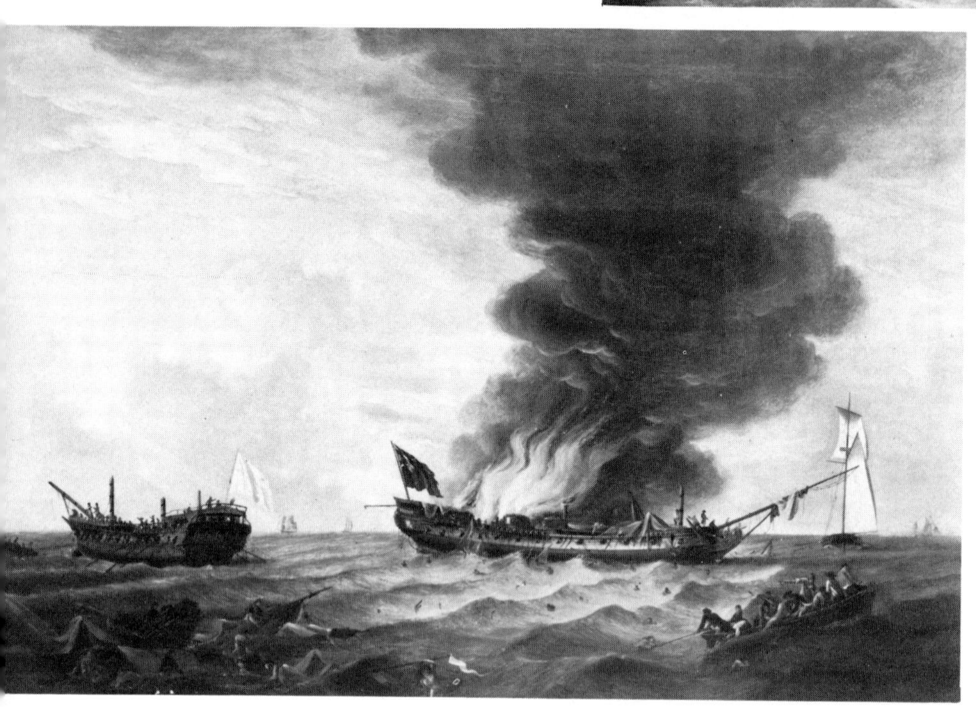

Plate 271. Robert Dodd, 1748-1815. "The *Quebec* on fire after the action with the *Surveillante* in 1779." *A prolific painter and engraver of historical scenes, Dodd's ownership of the means of publishing his work ensured him wide recognition.* National Maritime Museum, Greenwich.

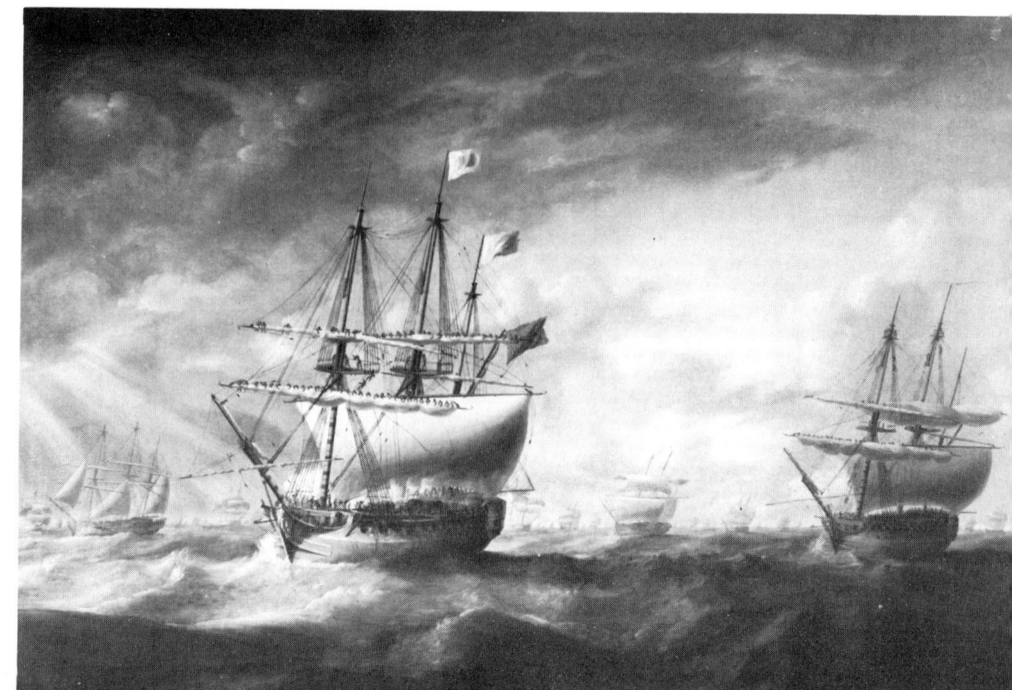

Plate 272. Robert Dodd, 1748-1815. "The shortening sail at the approach of the fatal hurricane, 1782." *The first of a set of five paintings of the loss of the* Ramillies *in a hurricane in 1782. She was the flagship of a squadron escorting the French prizes taken at the Battle of the Saints back to England. The French flagship, the* Ville de Paris, *was also lost.* National Maritime Museum, Greenwich.

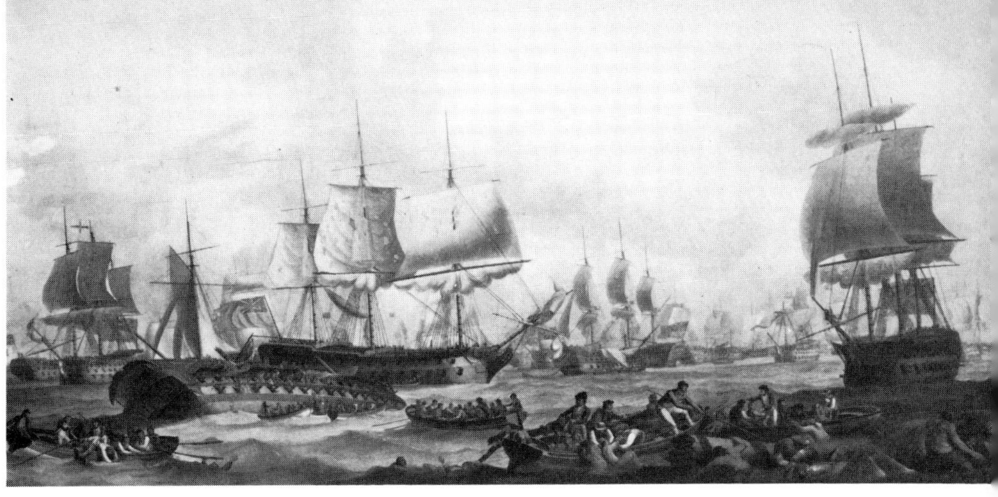

Plate 273. Robert Dodd, 1748-1815. "The sinking of the *Vengeur du Peuple* at the Battle of the Glorious First of June in 1794." *A very large example painted for the dining-room in Dodd's local hostelry.* National Maritime Museum, Greenwich.

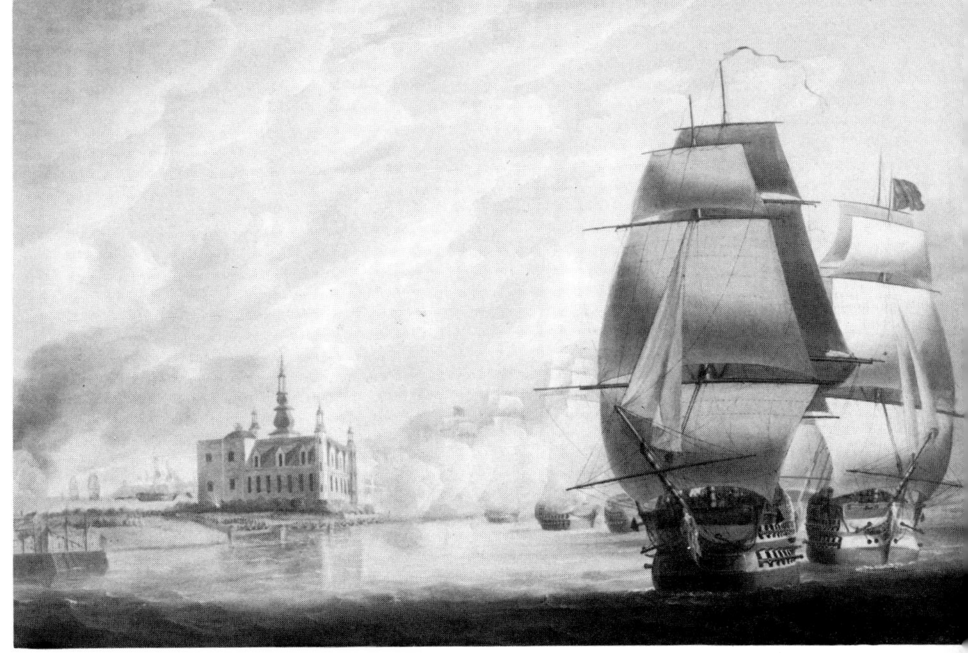

Plate 274. Robert Dodd, 1748-1815. "Sir Hyde Parker forcing a passage through the Sound, off Kronborg Castle in 1801." *The second ship in the line is Nelson's flagship, the* St. George. National Maritime Museum, Greenwich.

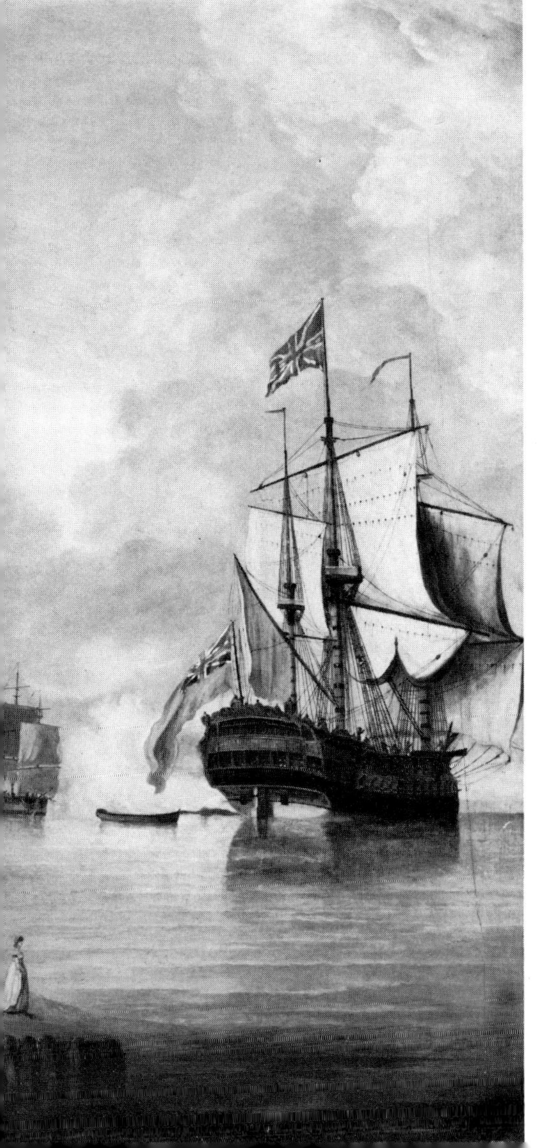

Plate 275. Monamy Swaine, b.c. 1750. "An English flagship saluting, c.1775." *Without the quality of his father's work, Monamy Swaine is fairly often mistaken for Brooking. His facility for figures was not great.* National Maritime Museum, Greenwich.

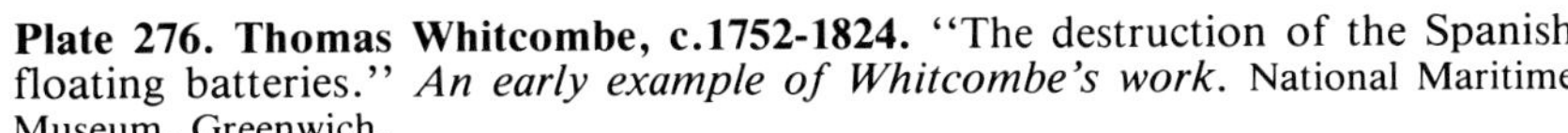

Plate 276. Thomas Whitcombe, c.1752-1824. "The destruction of the Spanish floating batteries." *An early example of Whitcombe's work.* National Maritime Museum, Greenwich.

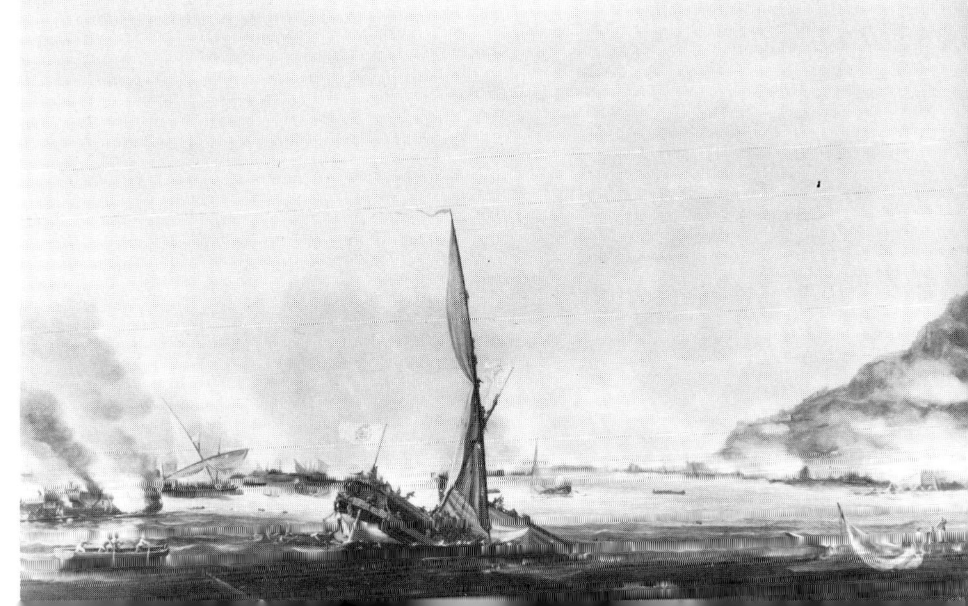

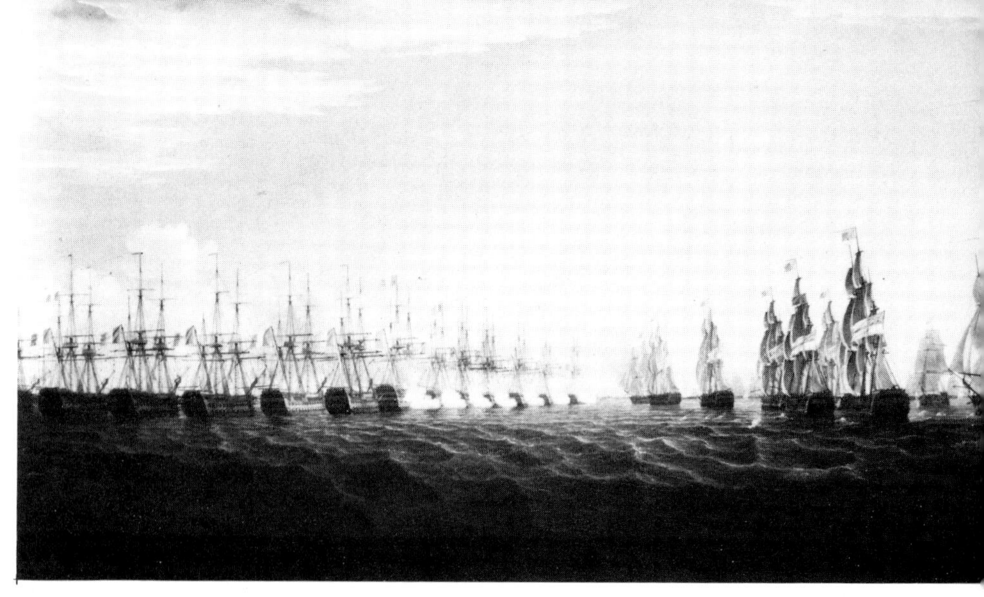

Plate 277. Thomas Whitcombe, c.1752-1824. "The beginning of the Battle of the Nile in 1798." *One of two pictures of the Battle of the Nile. The arrangement of the ships has a slightly awkward appearance.* National Maritime Museum, Greenwich.

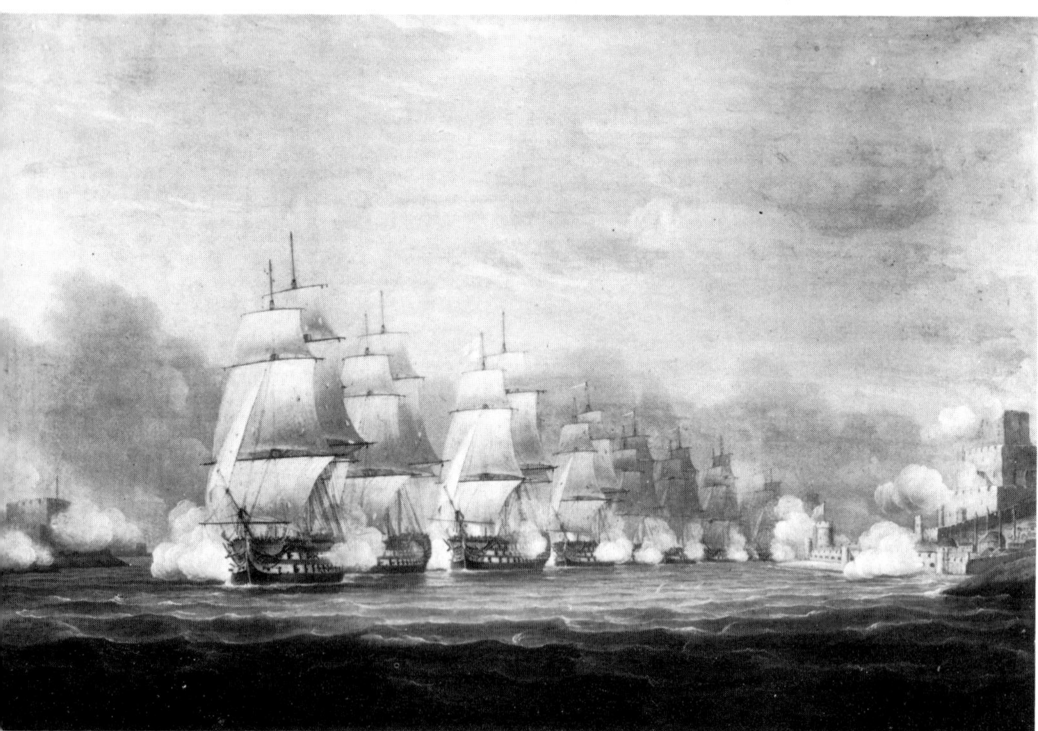

Plate 278. Thomas Whitcombe, c.1752-1824. "Duckworth's fleet forcing a passage through the Dardanelles in 1807." *The fleet is being bombarded from the shore by massive (2ft. 6ins.) stone cannonballs from mediaeval fixed bombards, some of which got into the ships, were subsequently dug out, and are to be seen at the National Maritime Museum.* National Maritime Museum, Greenwich.

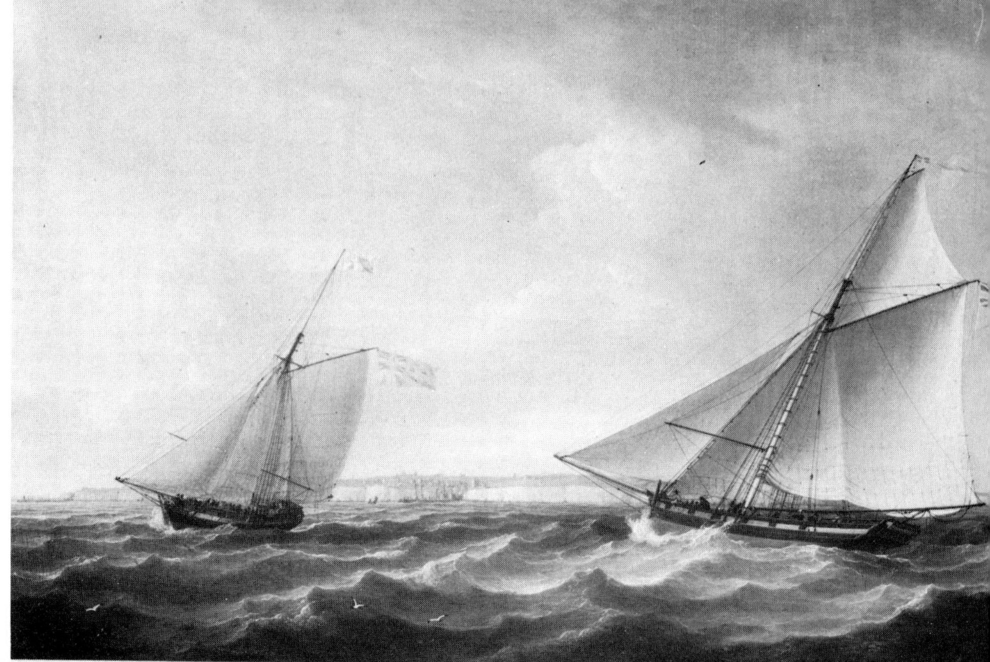

Plate 279. Thomas Whitcombe, c.1752-1824. "A Trinity House cutter and a naval cutter off Ramsgate." *A high quality picture. The yacht on the left flies from the peak the Trinity House flag. The one on the right is a revenue cutter.* National Maritime Museum, Greenwich.

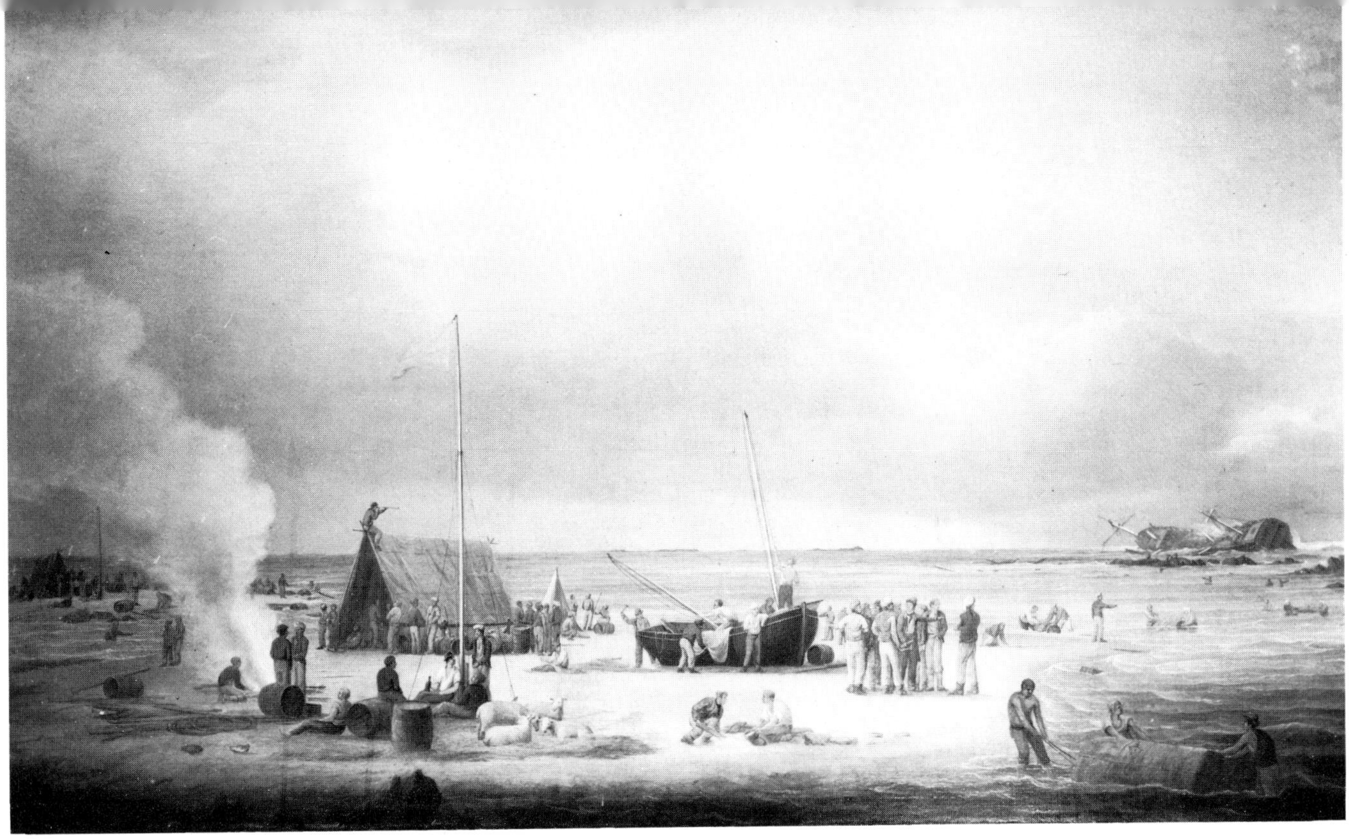

Plate 280. Thomas Whitcombe, c.1752-1824. "The survivors safe ashore from the wrecked East Indiaman *Cabalva,* Mauritius, in 1818." *An unusual subject which nevertheless is very successfully handled.* National Library of Australia (Rex Nan Kivell Collection), Canberra.

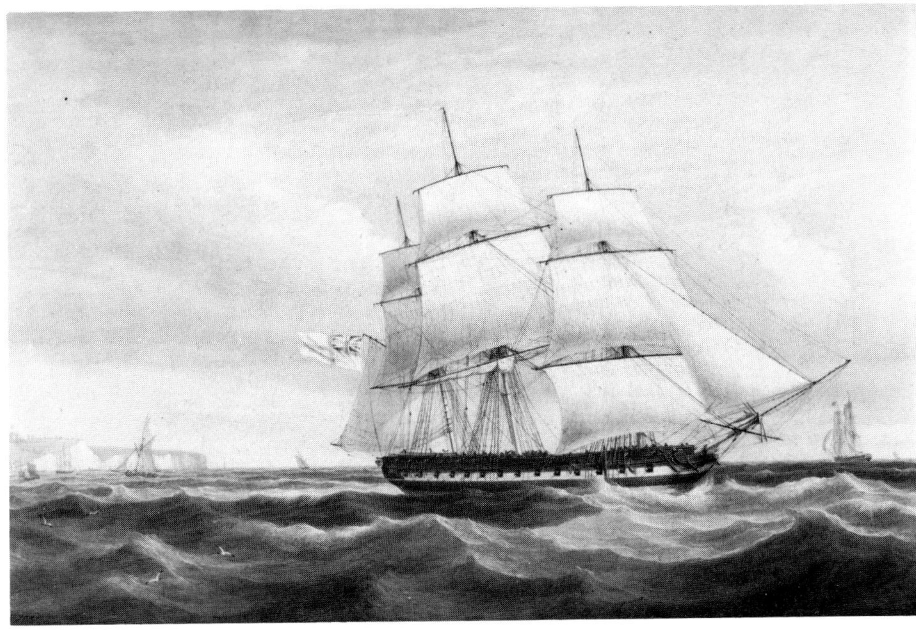

Plate 281. Thomas Whitcombe, c.1752-1824. "The frigate H.M.S. *Undaunted,* off Dover, dated 1820." *46 guns, built 1807, she was the ship that took Napoleon to Elba in May 1814. This is a good example, typical of Whitcombe's work.* National Maritime Museum, Greenwich.

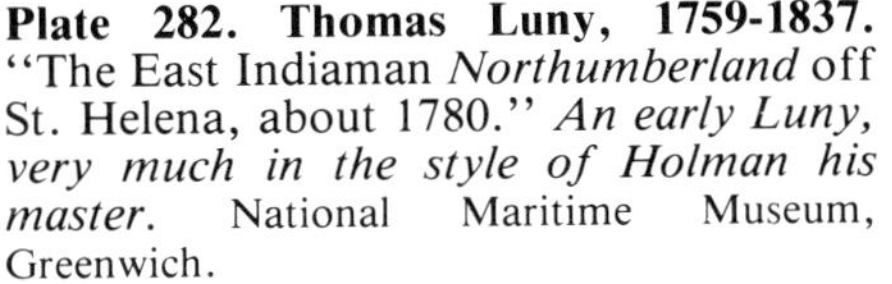

Plate 282. Thomas Luny, 1759-1837. "The East Indiaman *Northumberland* off St. Helena, about 1780." *An early Luny, very much in the style of Holman his master.* National Maritime Museum, Greenwich.

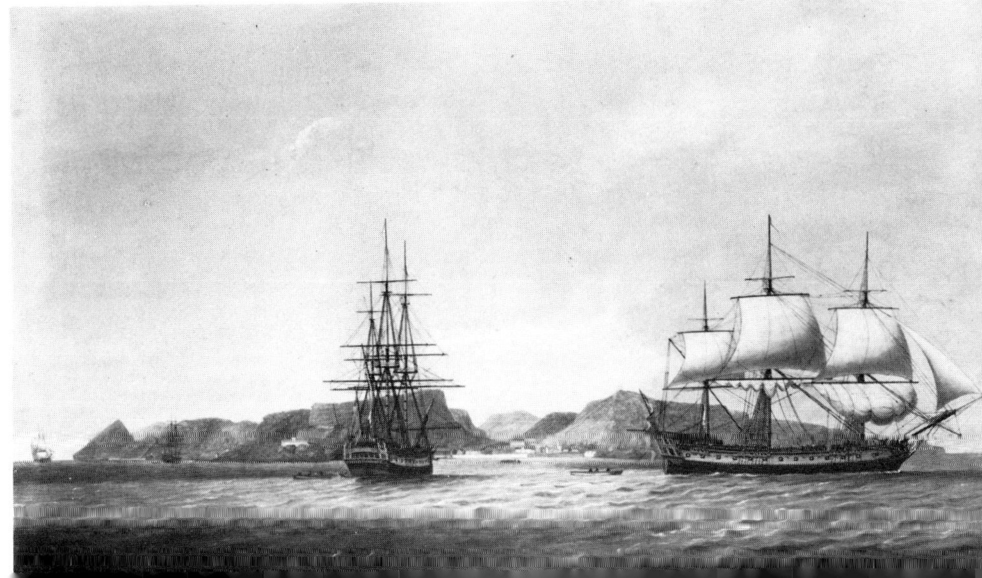

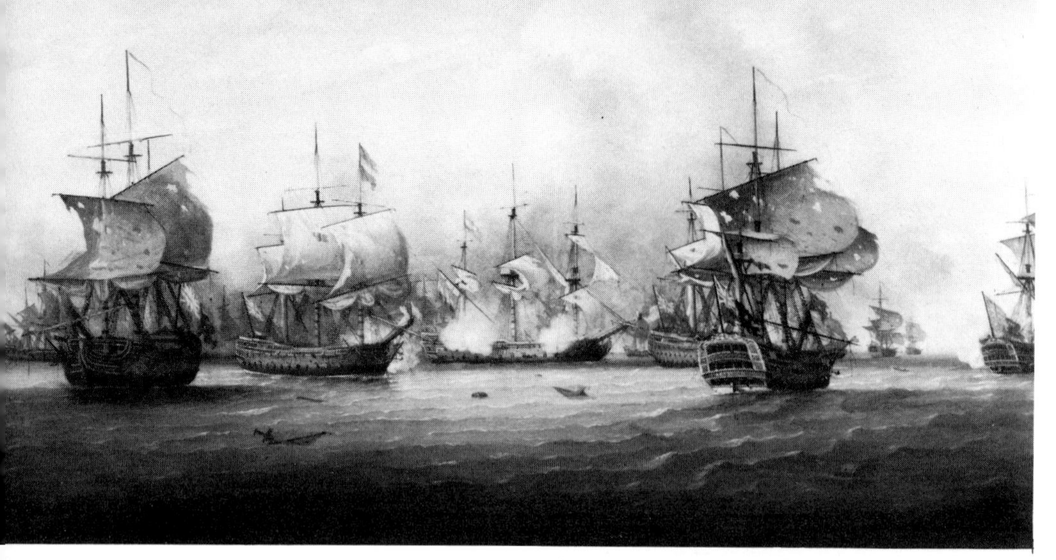

Plate 283. Thomas Luny, 1759-1837. "The Battle of Dogger Bank on August 5th, 1781." *In the centre of the picture the* Fortitude, *flagship of Vice Admiral Hyde Parker, is engaged with the Dutch flagship of Rear Admiral Zoutman.* National Maritime Museum, Greenwich.

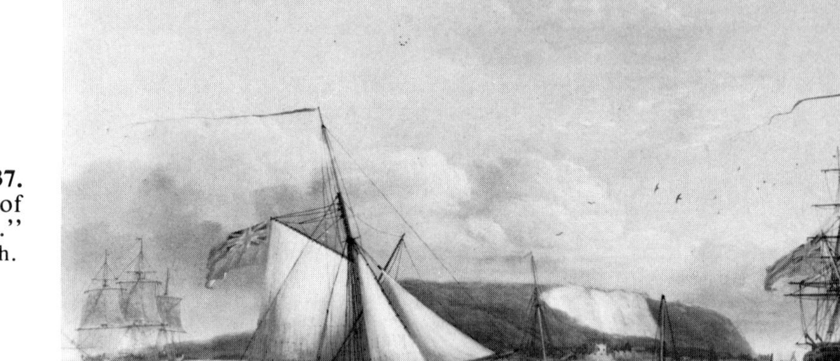

Plate 284. Thomas Luny, 1759-1837. "A cutter passing under the stern of an anchored frigate, about 1803." National Maritime Museum, Greenwich.

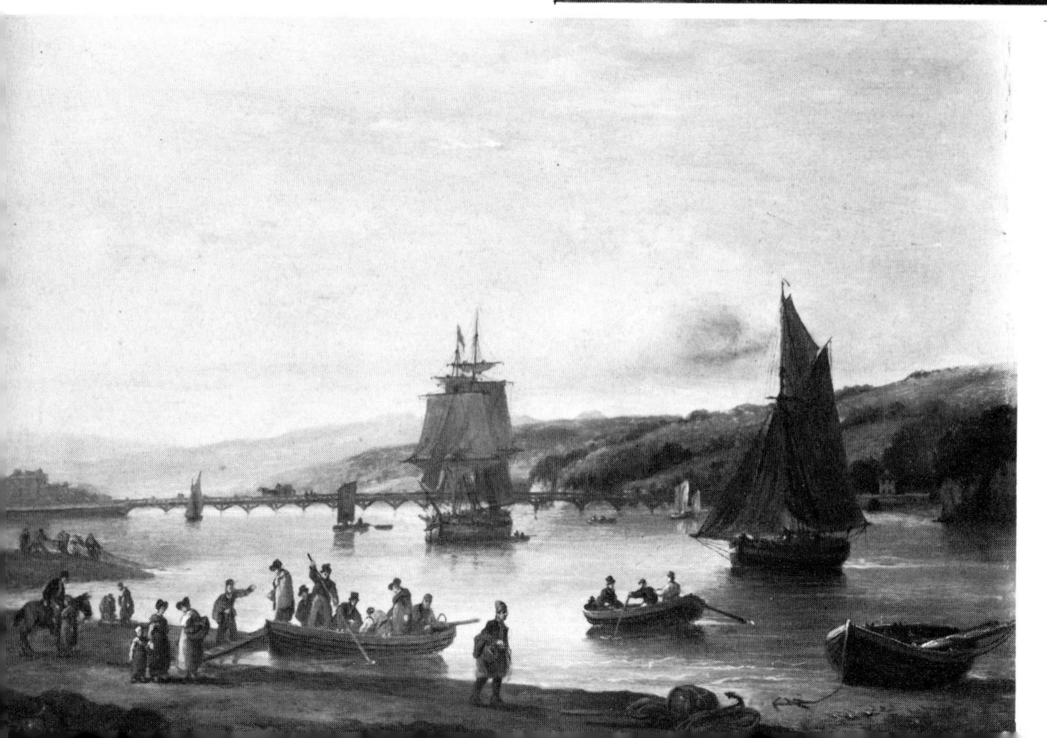

Plate 285. Thomas Luny, 1759-1837. "Landing from the ferry at Teignmouth, Devon, dated 1824." *One from Luny's later period when physical disabilities were taking their toll. Nevertheless, a very well executed work.* National Maritime Museum, Greenwich.

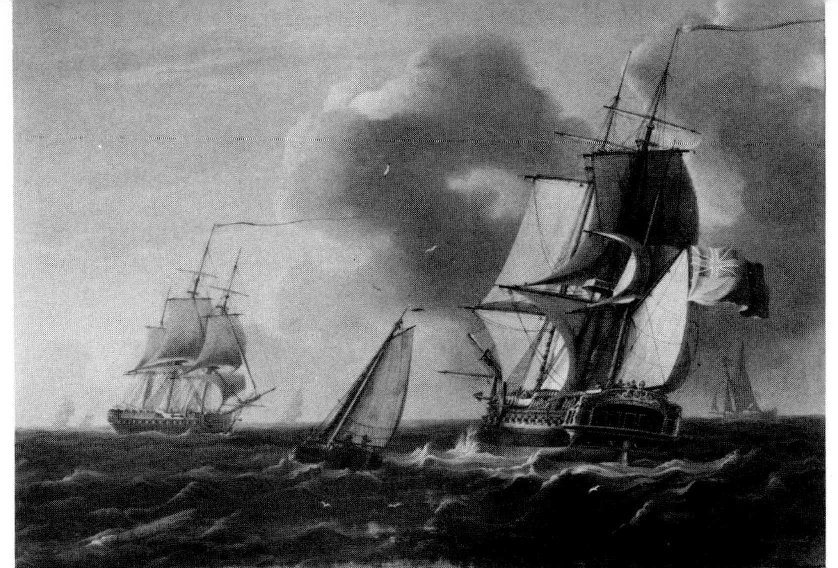

Plate 286. David Kleijne, 1754-1805. "English frigates at sea." *A somewhat stylised picture rather like Buttersworth.* Private collection.

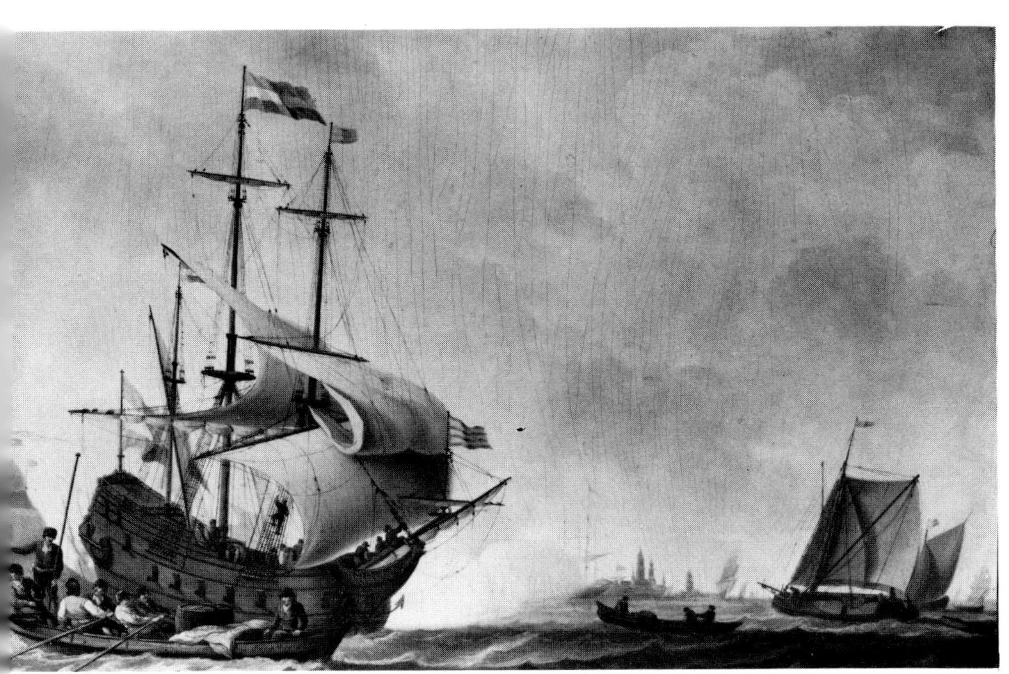

Plate 287. Franz Swagers, 1756-1836. "Shipping off the Dutch coast in the second half of the 17th century, dated 1791." *A painting of an historical scene. The design of the ship is more appropriate to the early 17th century.* Christie's.

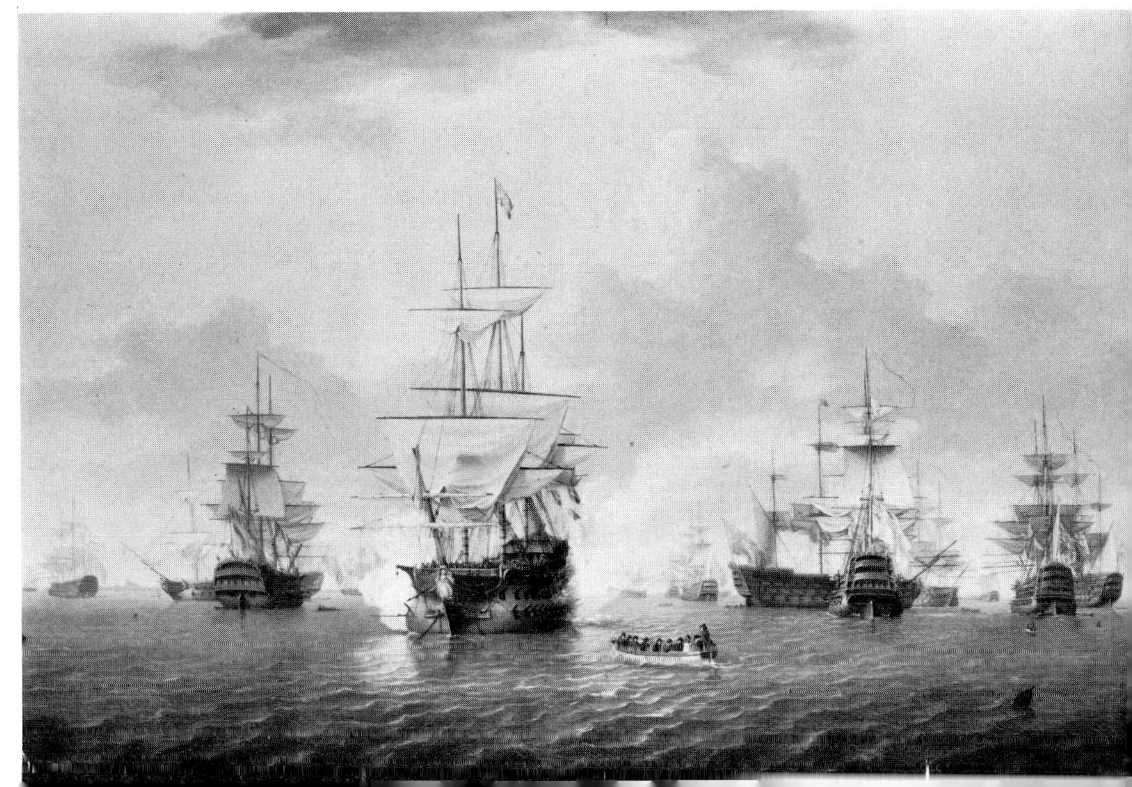

Plate 288. William Anderson, 1757-1837. "The *Queen Charlotte* at Spithead, dated 1791." *A good example of his work showing his ability to handle light successfully in his best work.* Richard Green Gallery.

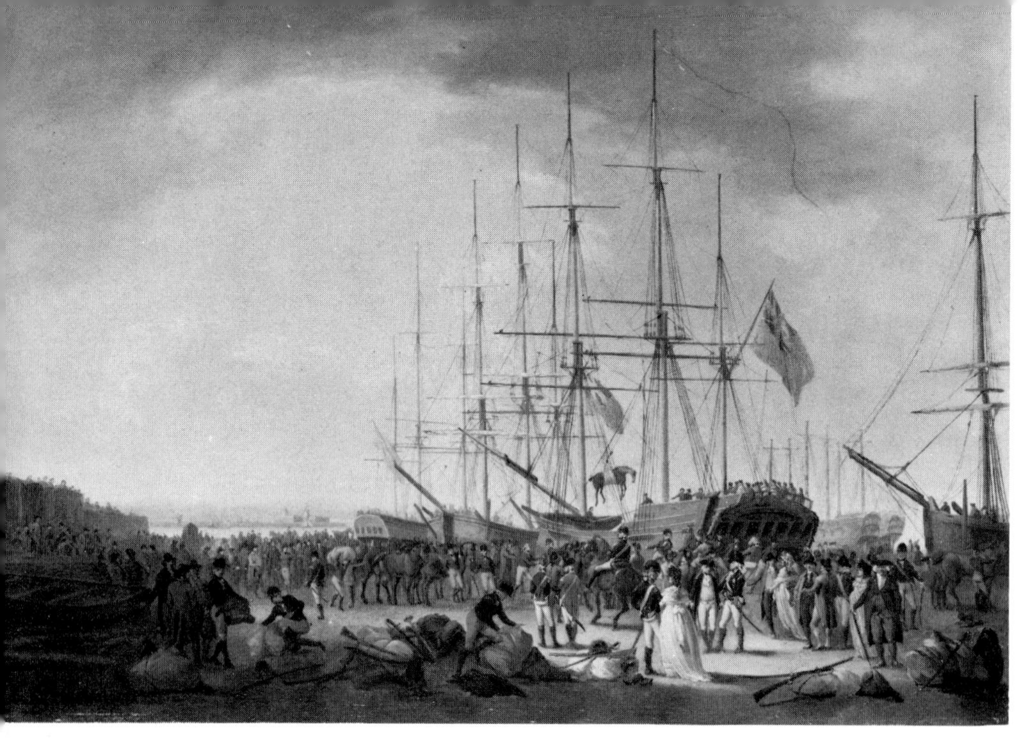

Plate 289. William Anderson, 1757-1837. "Troops embarking near Greenwich, 1798." *Anderson demonstrates here considerable accomplishment, both in his figure painting and in his ability to create the atmosphere of embarkation.* National Maritime Museum, Greenwich.

Plate 290. William Anderson, 1757-1837. "Greenwich Reach". *There is a copy of this painting by John Ward of Hull, recording Anderson's stay there and his influence on the Hull school.* Ferens Art Gallery, Hull.

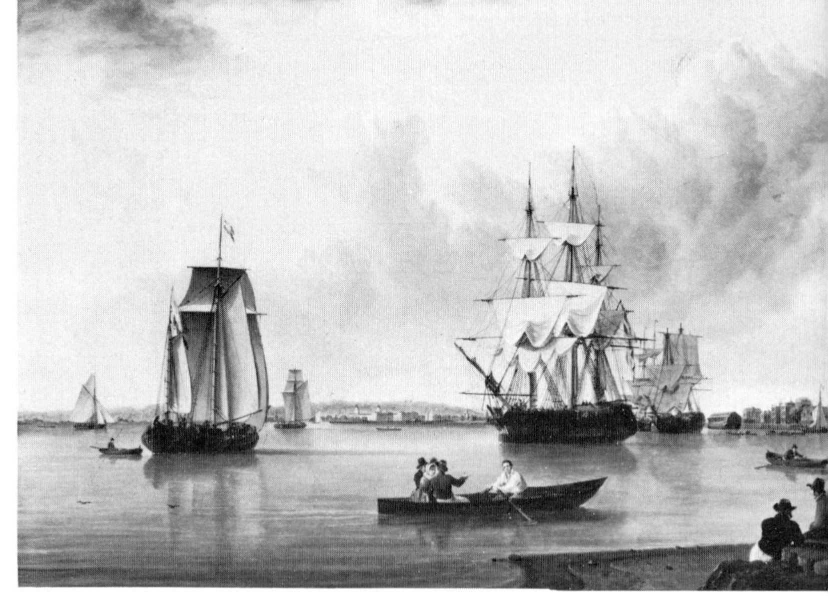

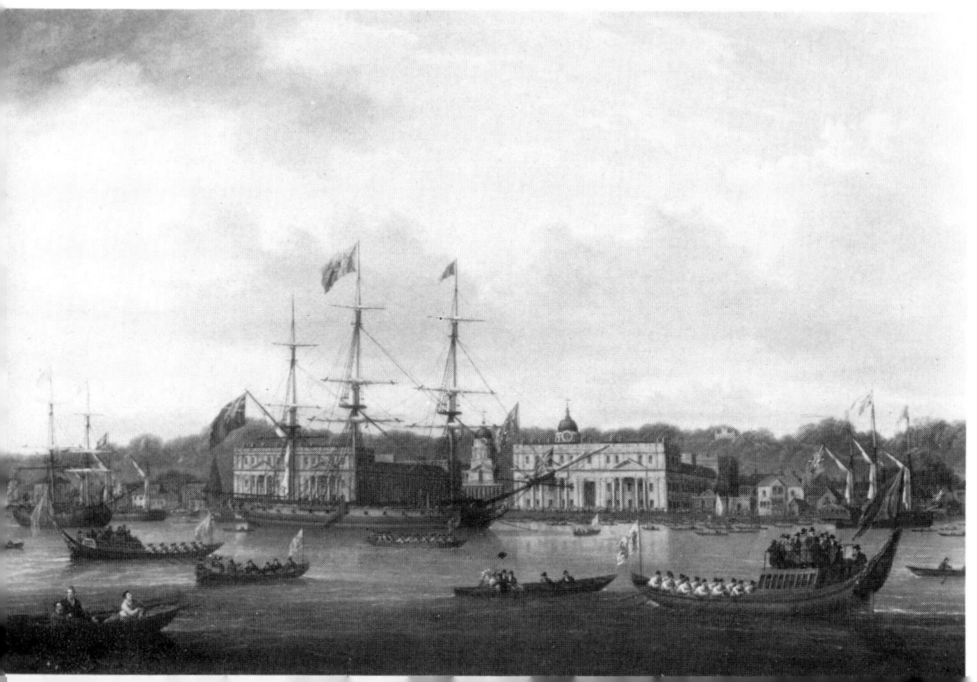

Plate 291. William Anderson, 1757-1837. "The return of King George IV to Greenwich from Edinburgh in 1822." National Maritime Museum, Greenwich.

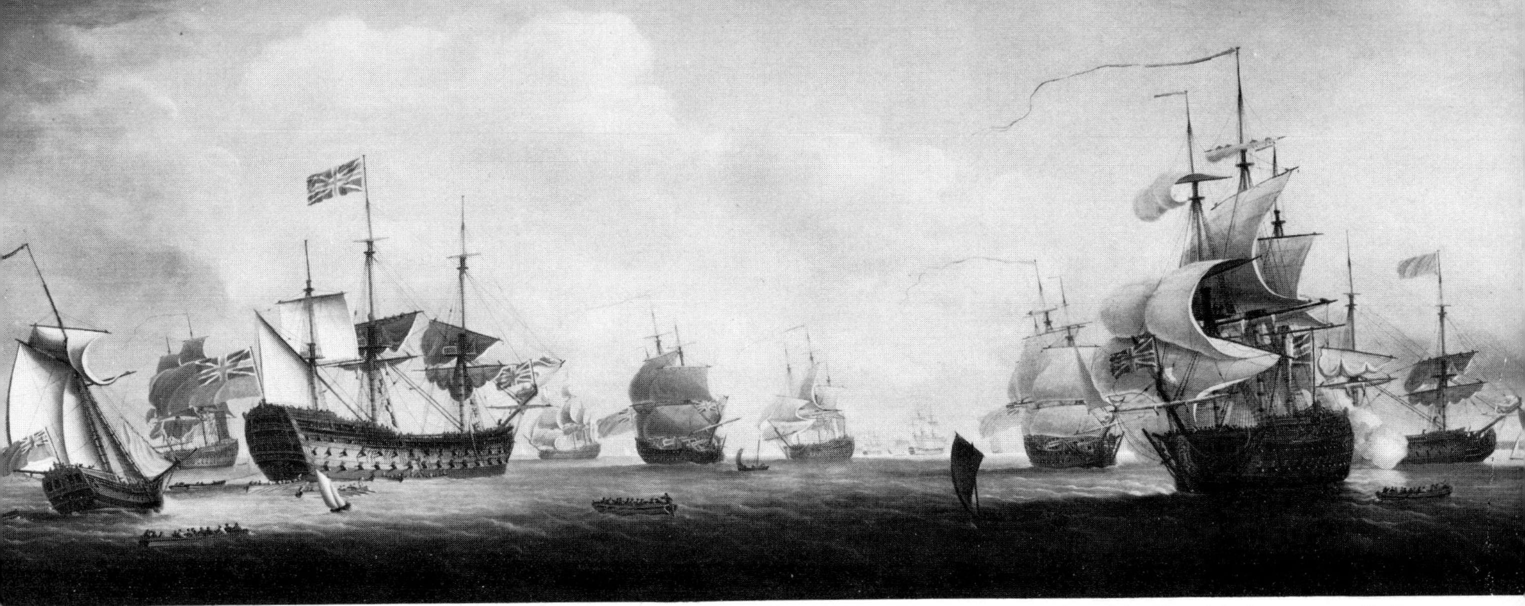

Plate 292. J. Nicholls, fl. late 18th century. "Lord Howe's flagship, the *Queen Charlotte,* and units of the Spanish Armament." *A little known artist of some quality. The scene depicts the mobilisation of the British fleet for a threatened war with Spain. The work is signed and dated 1790.* Ministry of Defence.

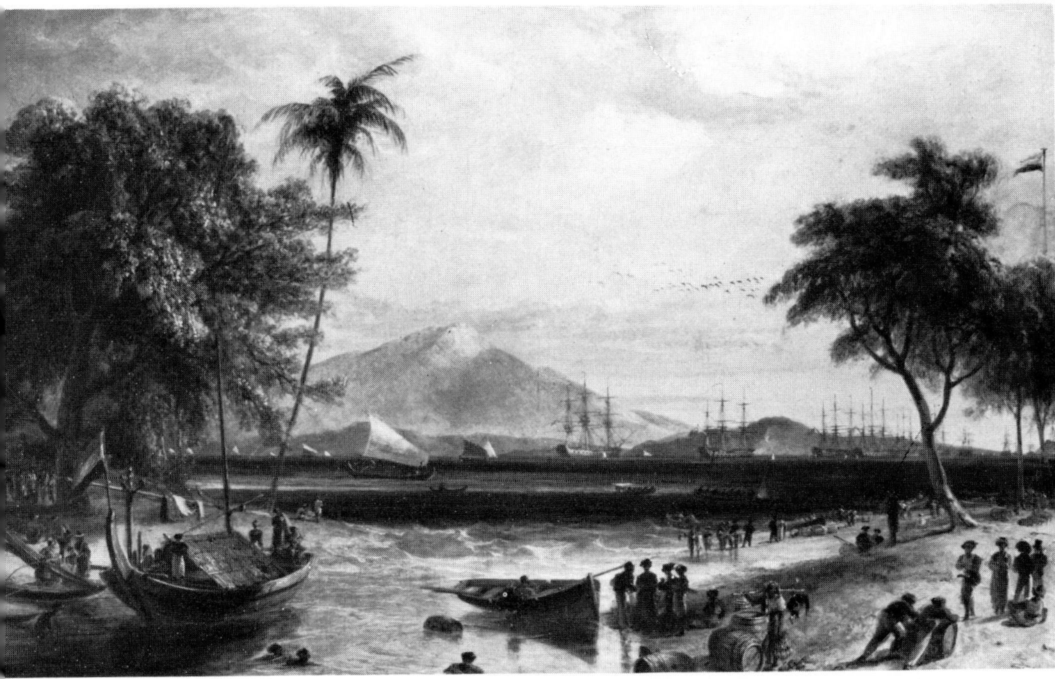

Plate 293. William Daniell, 1769-1837. "The East India fleet anchored off the watering place at Angere Point, Java, 1794." *Daniell produced a large number of topographical aquatints, both of Britain and abroad, to a high professional standard.* National Maritime Museum, Greenwich.

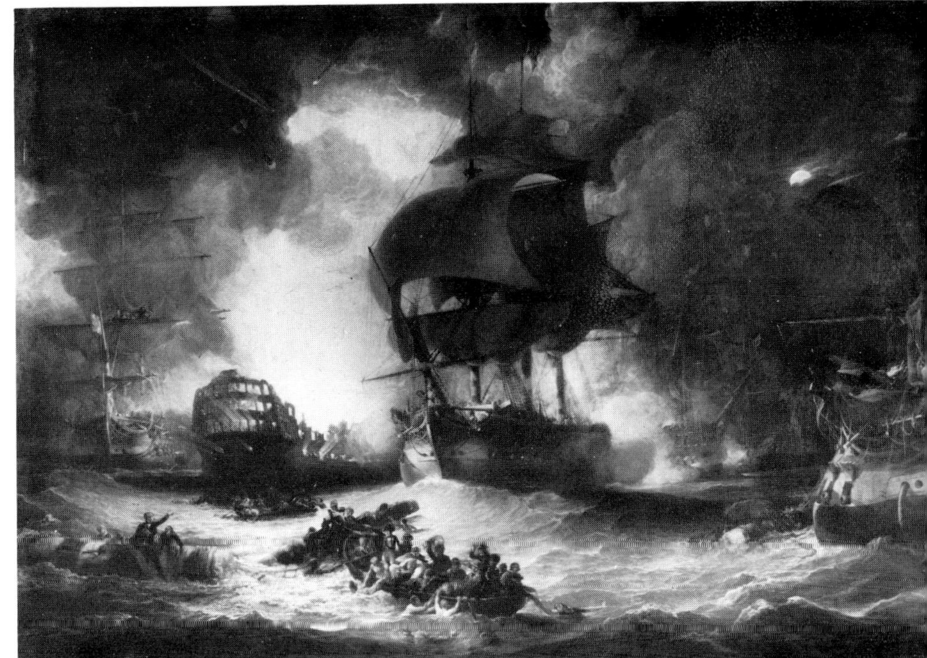

Plate 294. George Arnald, 1763-1841. "The French flagship *L'Orient* blowing up at the Battle of the Nile in 1798." *A pupil of William Pether whose name, in landscape painting, is connected with the effect of darkness, and this example bears witness to the use of dramatic effects, particularly the orange glow of the exploding ship which dominates the whole picture.* National Maritime Museum, Greenwich (Greenwich Hospital Collection).

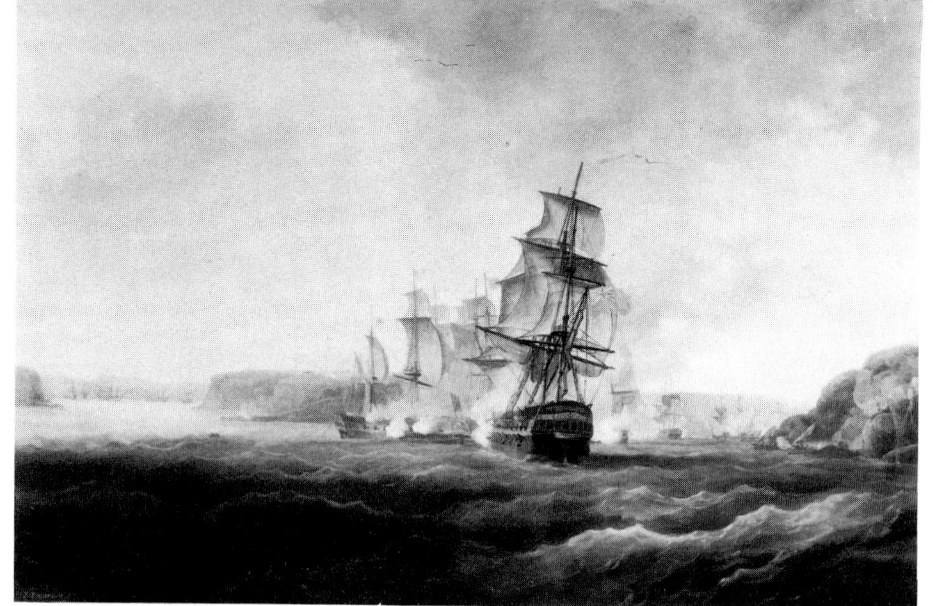

Plate 295. Jeffrey de Raigersfeld, c.1770-1844. "The *Montagu* forcing the French to move from Bertheaume Bay in 1800." *The artist was an English naval officer who painted more in the mid-18th century manner.* National Maritime Museum, Greenwich.

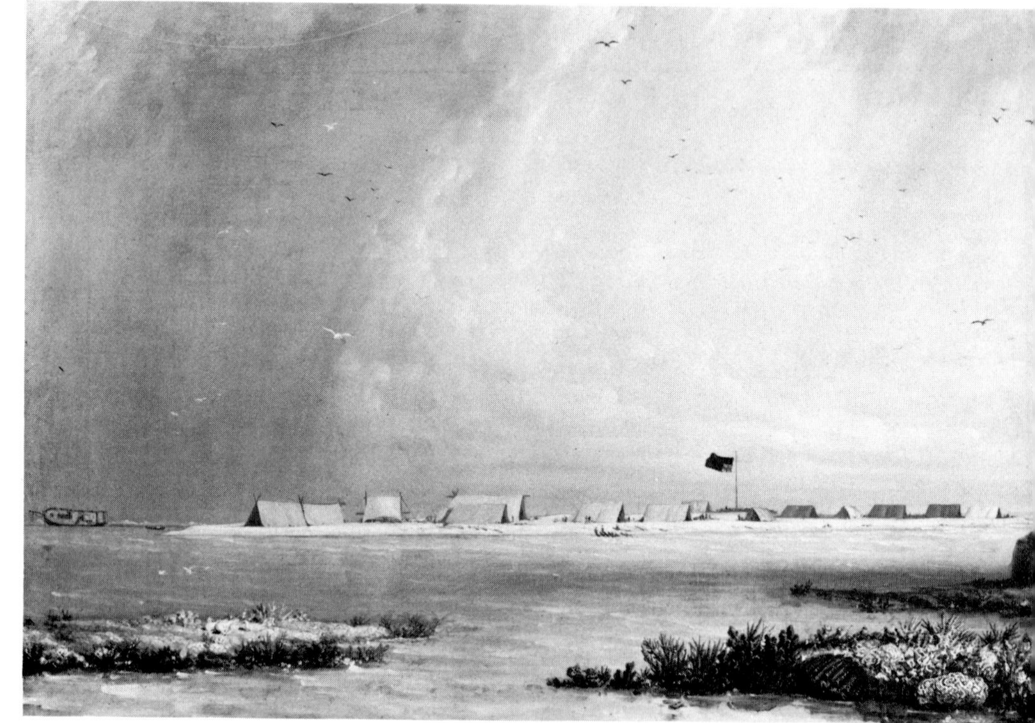

Plate 296. William Westall, 1781-1850. "Wreck Reef: the encampment after the wreck of the *Porpoise* on the Australian Great Barrier Reef, 1803." *Principally a landscape painter, Westall nevertheless successfully conveyed the atmosphere of the encampment. Note the careful delineation of the shells in the foreground. The inverted ensign is a distress signal.* Ministry of Defence (on loan to the National Maritime Museum).

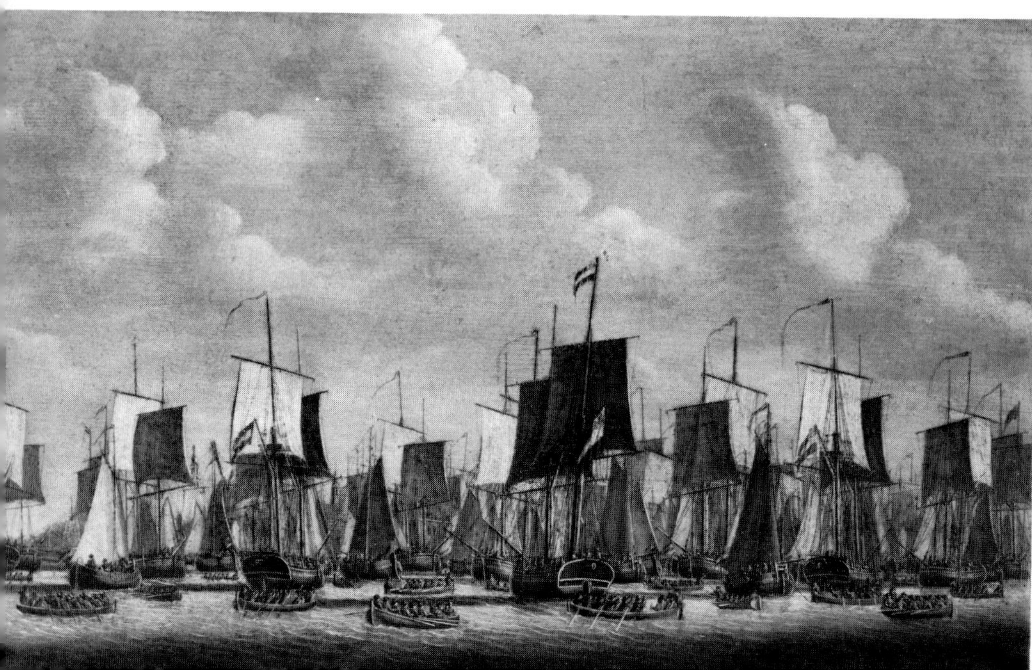

Plate 297. Jacob Schwartzenbach, 1763-1805. "The Dutch fleet at Flushing in 1804." *Painted together with Engel Hoogerheyden.* Rijksmuseum, Amsterdam.

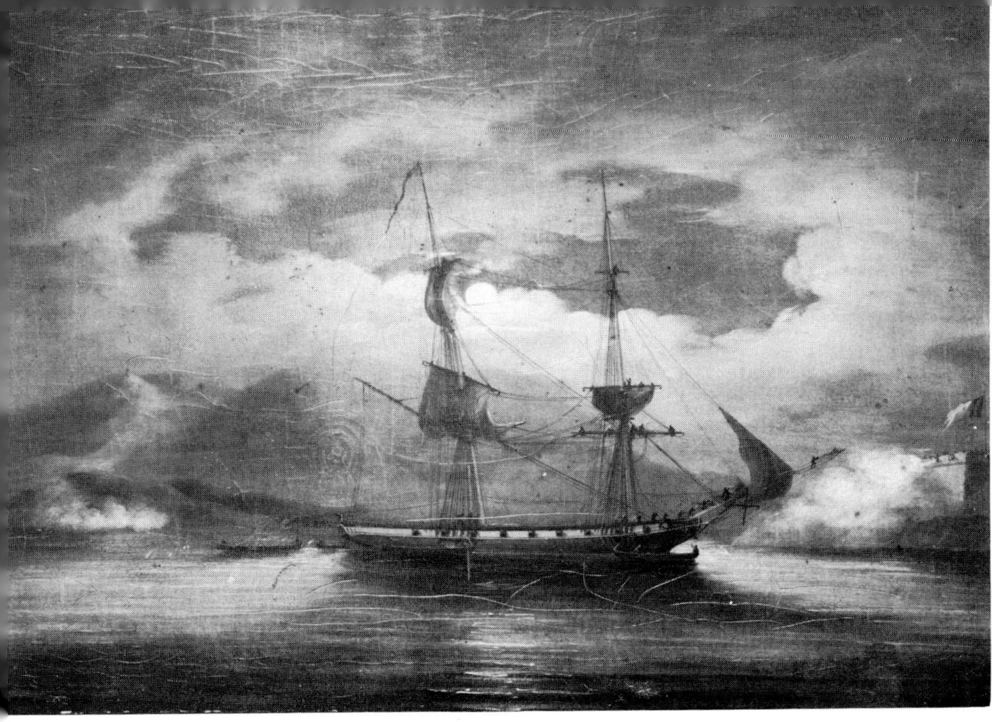

Plate 298. Francis Sartorius, 1782-aft.1808. "The cutting out of the *Curieux* at Martinique in 1804." National Maritime Museum, Greenwich.

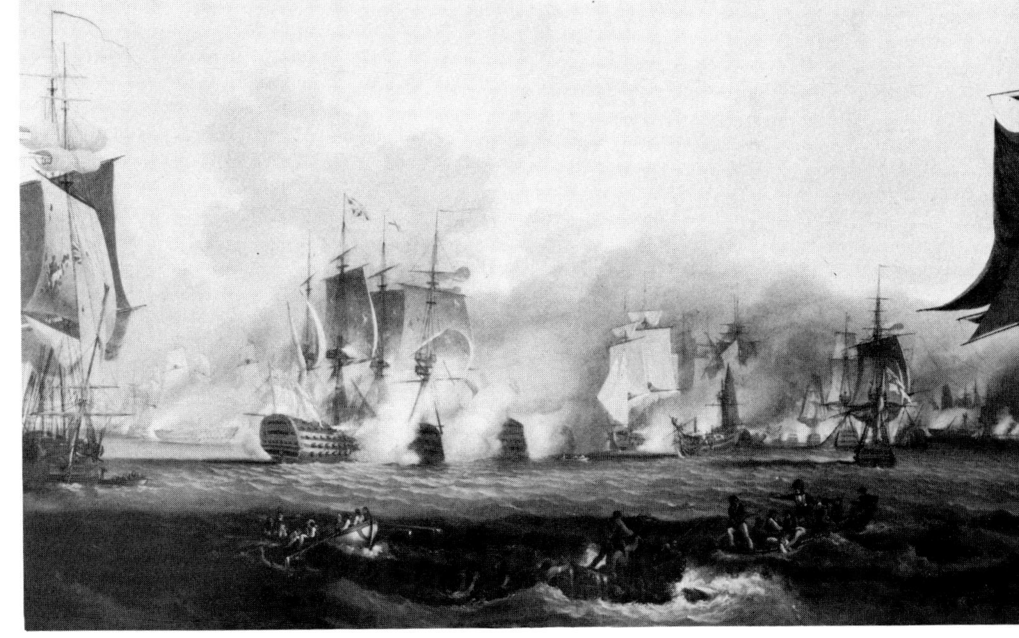

Plate 299. Samuel Drummond, 1765-1844. "The Battle of Trafalgar in 1805." *A large canvas and one of the few marine examples of this artist's work.* National Maritime Museum, Greenwich.

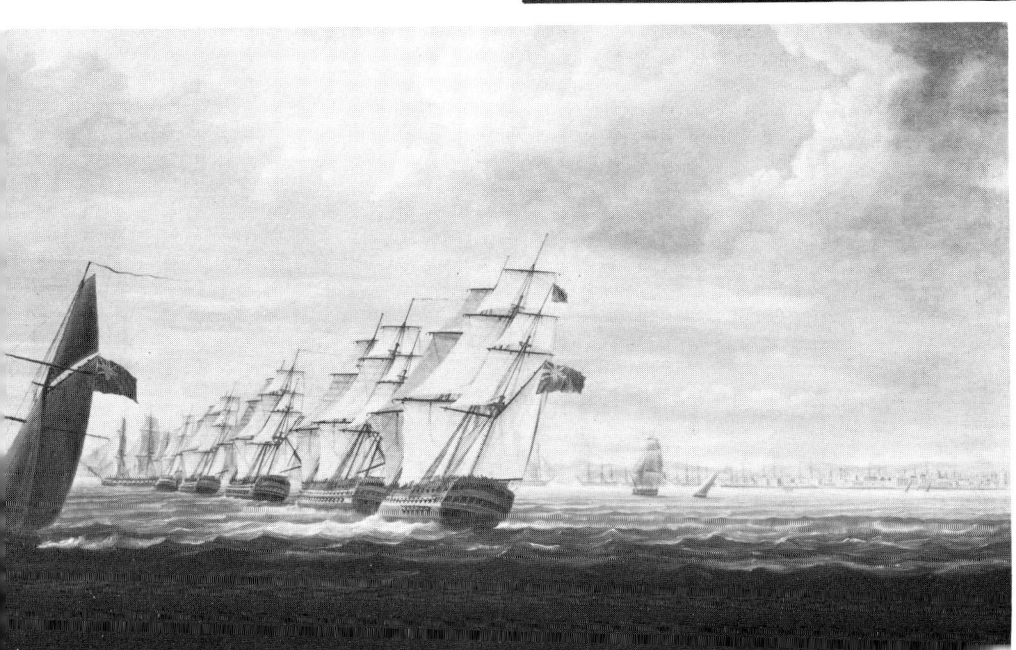

Plate 300. Thomas Buttersworth, 1768-1842. "The inshore blockading squadron off Cadiz in 1797." *Buttersworth also did a series of large watercolours of this squadron, commanded by Sir Horatio Nelson. He was probably still in the Royal Navy and present at this action.* National Maritime Museum, Greenwich.

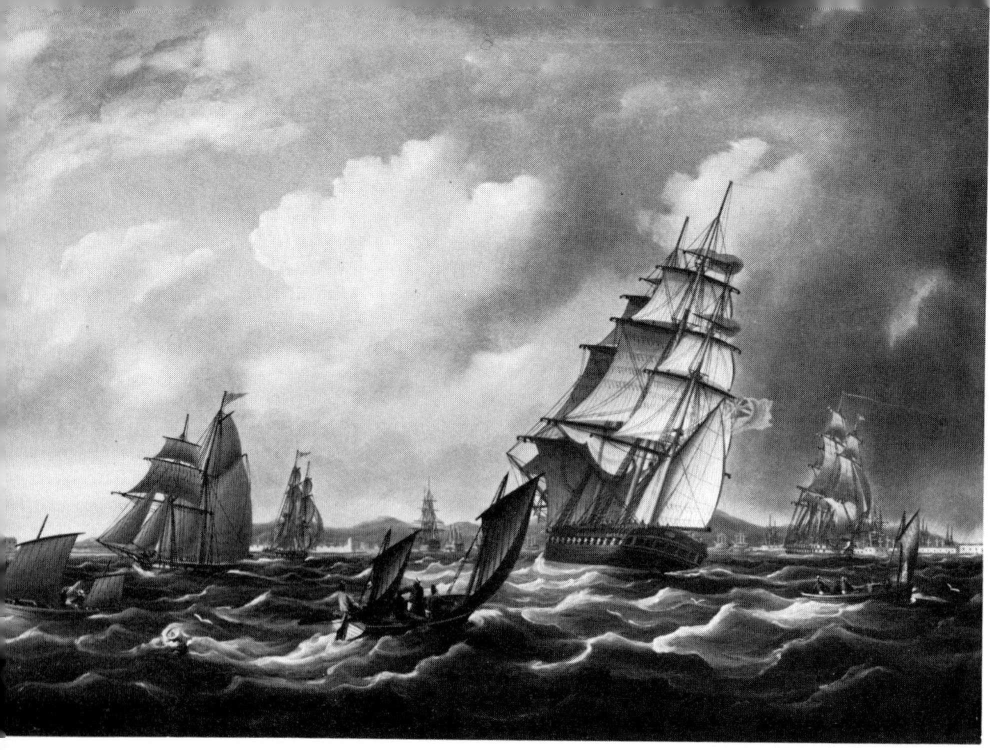

Plate 301. Thomas Buttersworth, 1768-1842. "Shipping off Plymouth." City Museum and Art Gallery, Plymouth.

Plate 302. Thomas Buttersworth, 1768-1842. "The *Ville de Paris* (100 guns), in the Downs in 1803/4." *Wearing the flag of Admiral the Hon. William Cornwallis. In spite of her name, she was not a French prize, but was launched at Chatham in 1795 and was named after the French flagship captured at the Battle of the Saints in 1782.* National Maritime Museum, Greenwich.

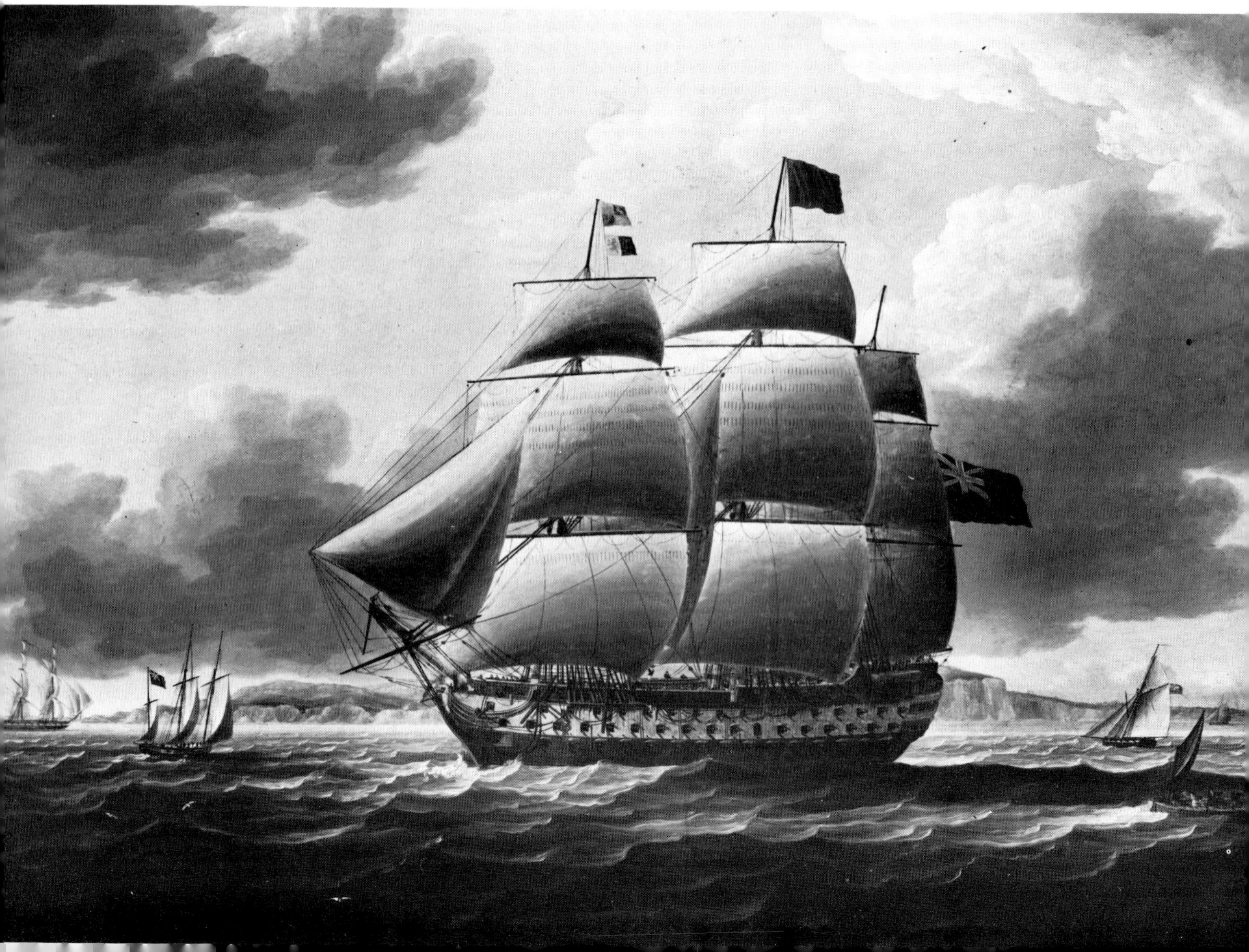

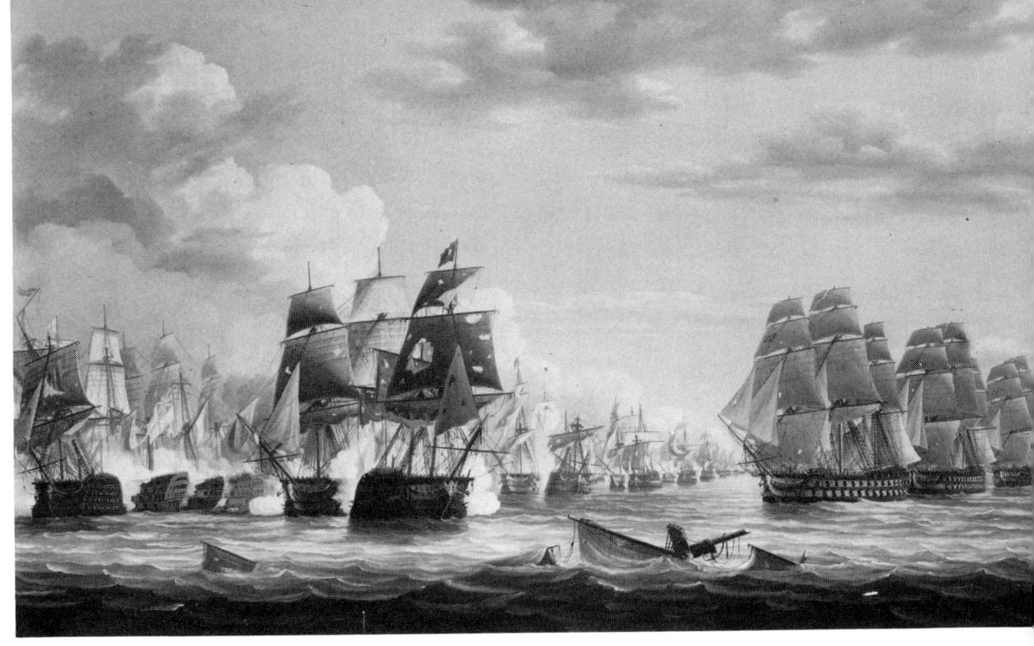

Plate 303. Thomas Buttersworth, 1768-1842. "The Battle of Trafalgar, 21st October, 1805." *On the extreme left of the picture is the great Spanish four-decker* Santisima Trinidad *(136 guns) being raked by the* Victory *(100), which is also in action with the* Redoutable *(74). In the centre is the French flagship the* Bucentaure *(80) being raked by the* Neptune *(98), while on the right the* Leviathan *(74) leads the rest of the line into action.* Richard Green (Fine Paintings).

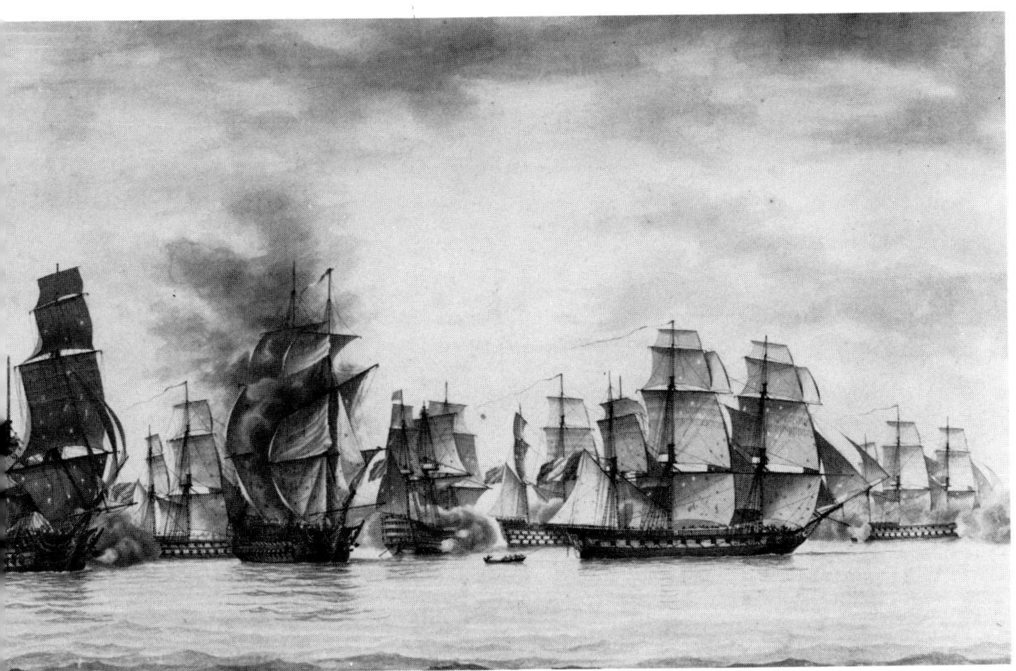

Plate 304. Joseph Ange Antoine Roux, 1765-1835. "Saumarez's action in the Bay of Algeciras in 1801." Watercolour. *The British squadron of four 74-gun and one 80-gun ships of the line, attacked a Franco-Spanish squadron of two 112s, one 94, three 80s and three 74s. Both the Spanish 112s were burnt and sunk and one of the French 74s taken.* Peabody Museum of Salem.

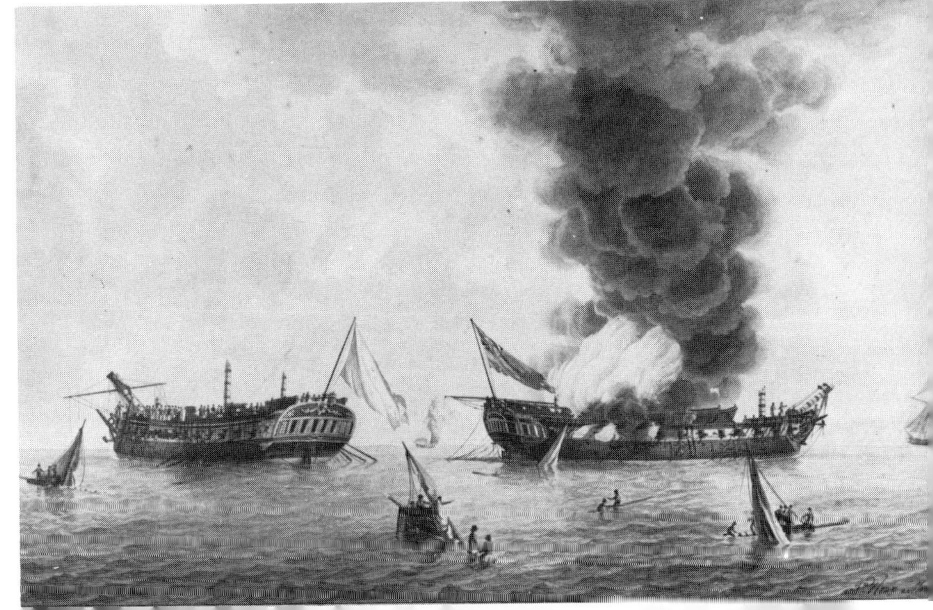

Plate 305. Joseph Ange Antoine Roux, 1765-1835. "The action between the *Quebec* and *Surveillante* in 1779." *Painted in 1811. In this furious action the* Surveillante's *masts and sails fell clear into the sea, but the* Quebec's *fell forwards across the guns which set fire to them, and she eventually blew up killing Captain Farmer. The French captain also died of his wounds.* Mariners Museum, Newport News.

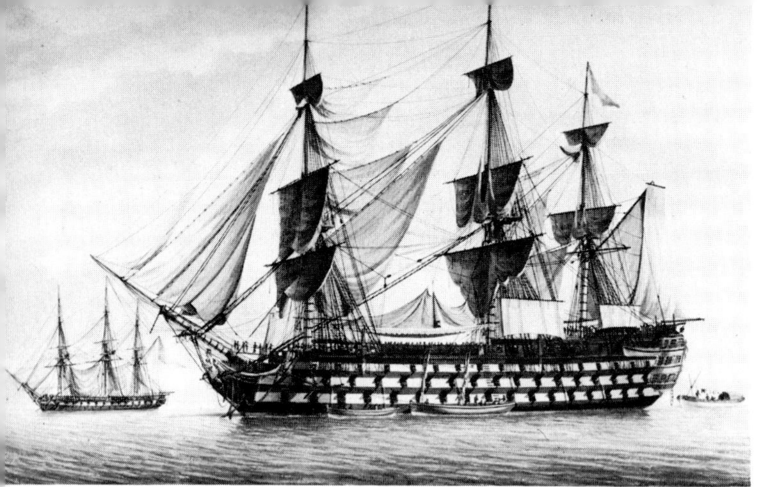

Plate 306. Joseph Ange Antoine Roux, 1765-1835. "The French three-decker *La Wagram,* dated 1811." Watercolour. Peabody Museum of Salem.

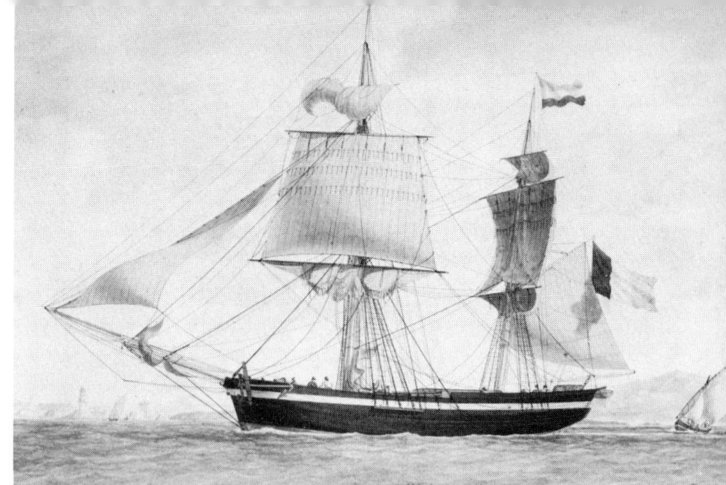

Plate 307. Mathieu Antoine Roux, 1799-1872. "The French merchant brig *Mne & Julie,* dated 1815." Watercolour. Peabody Museum of Salem.

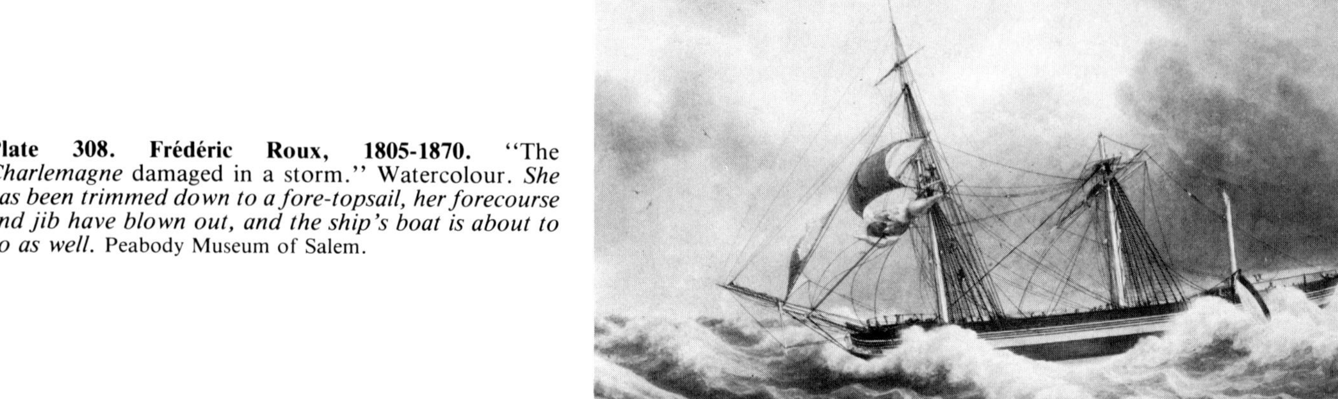

Plate 308. Frédéric Roux, 1805-1870. "The *Charlemagne* damaged in a storm." Watercolour. *She has been trimmed down to a fore-topsail, her forecourse and jib have blown out, and the ship's boat is about to go as well.* Peabody Museum of Salem.

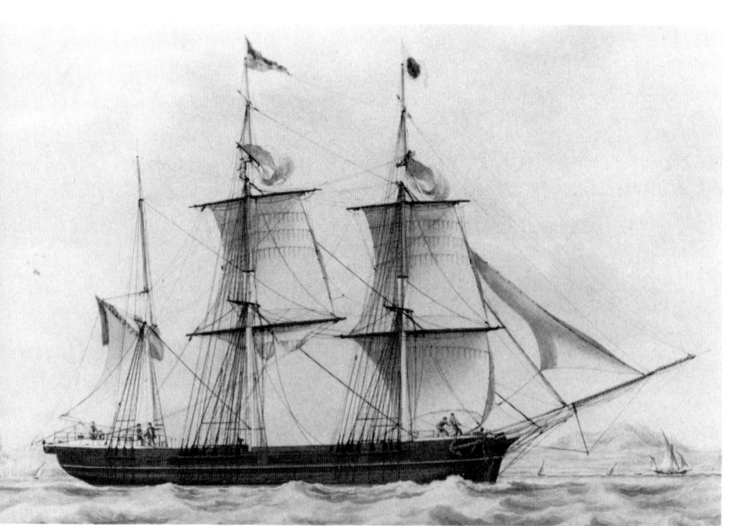

Plate 309. François Geoffroi Roux, 1811-1882. "The French barque *Montaudevert.*" Watercolour. Peabody Museum of Salem.

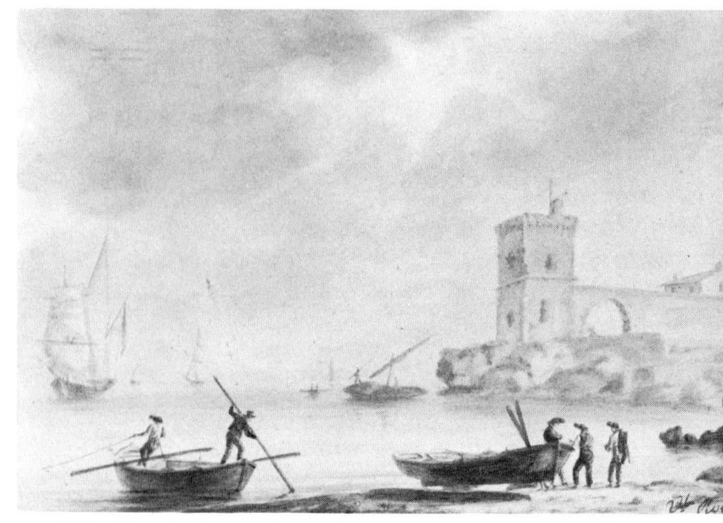

Plate 310. Ursula Roux, fl. early 19th century. "Marseilles Harbour, dated 1827." Watercolour. *A marine painter but not a ship portraitist like the other members of the Roux family.* Peabody Museum of Salem.

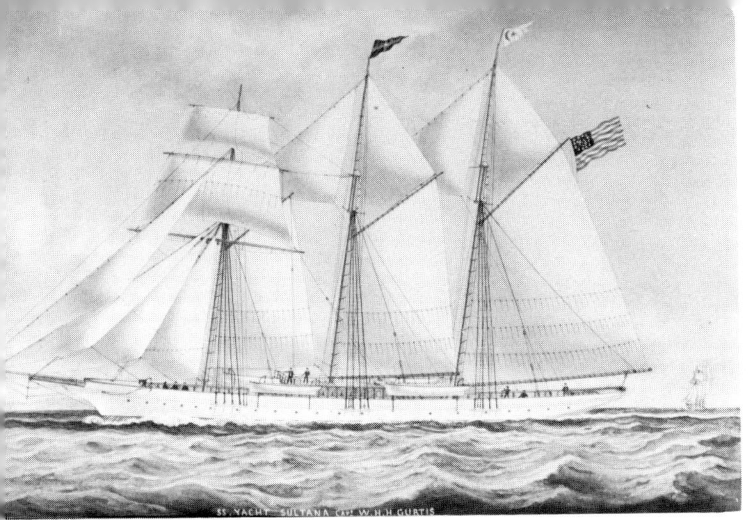

Plate 311. Louis Roux, 1817-1903. ''The American schooner yacht *Sultana.*'' Watercolour. *A rather grand ocean-going yacht by a Roux not thought to have been related to the extensive Roux family of sea painters.* Peabody Museum of Salem.

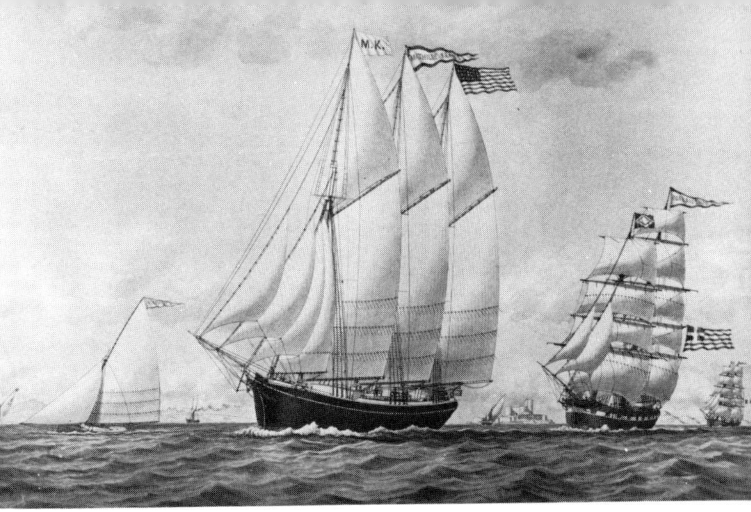

Plate 312. Louis Roux, 1817-1903. ''The American schooner *Mathilde Krans.*'' *Behind the schooner is a Greek brig, with a cutter yacht to the left.* Mariners Museum, Newport News.

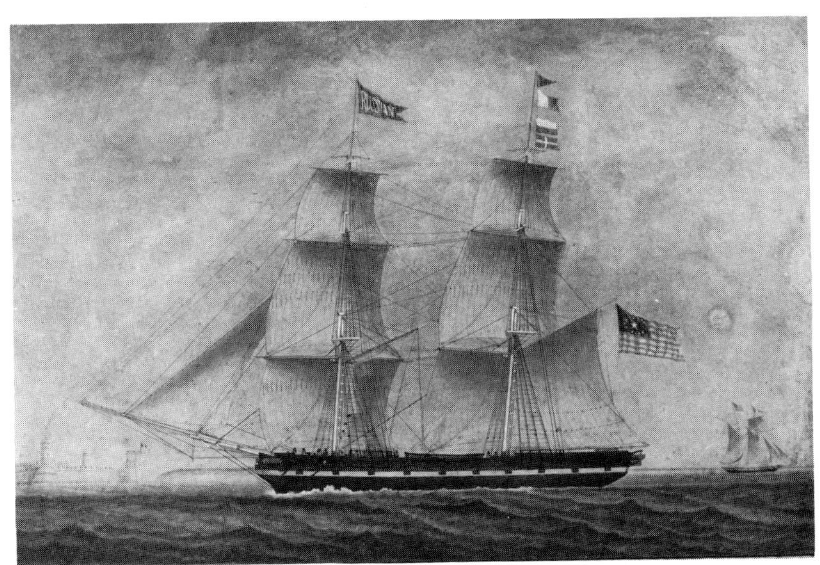

Plate 313. Honoré Pellegrini, 1793-1869. ''The American brig *Russian.*'' Mariners Museum, Newport News.

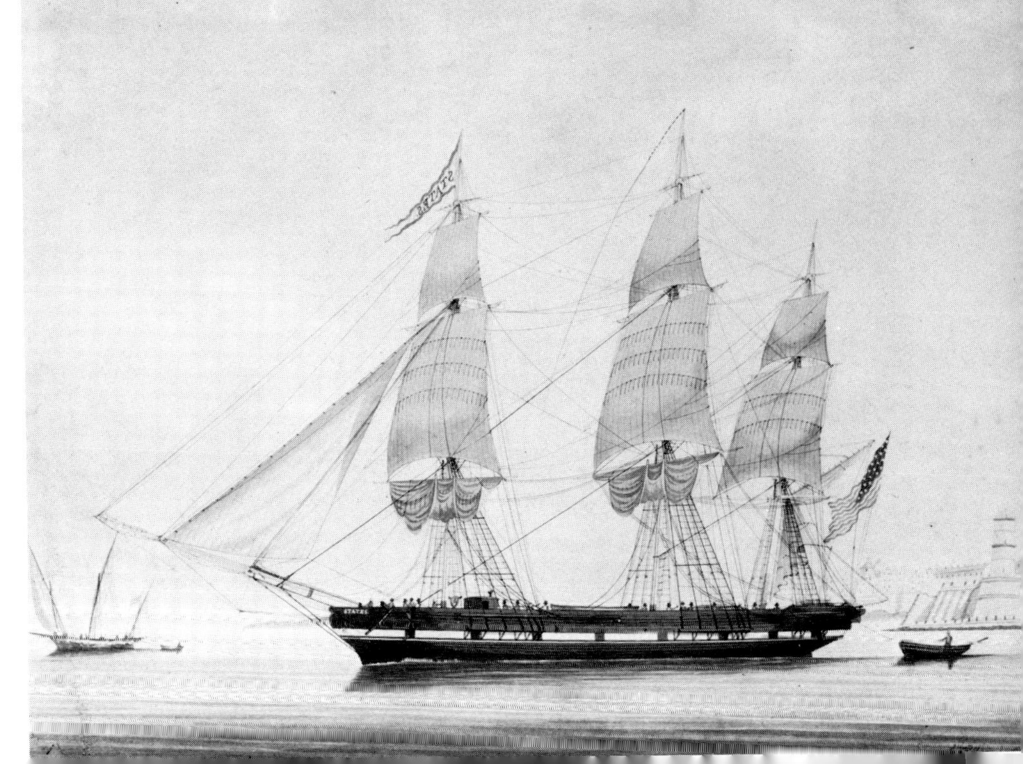

Plate 314. Honoré Pellegrini, 1793-1869. ''The American ship *States* leaving Marseilles in April 1832.'' *From the number of ship portraits by Mediterranean artists that survive in America, it must have been the fashion for the owners and captains to commission them.* Peabody Museum of Salem.

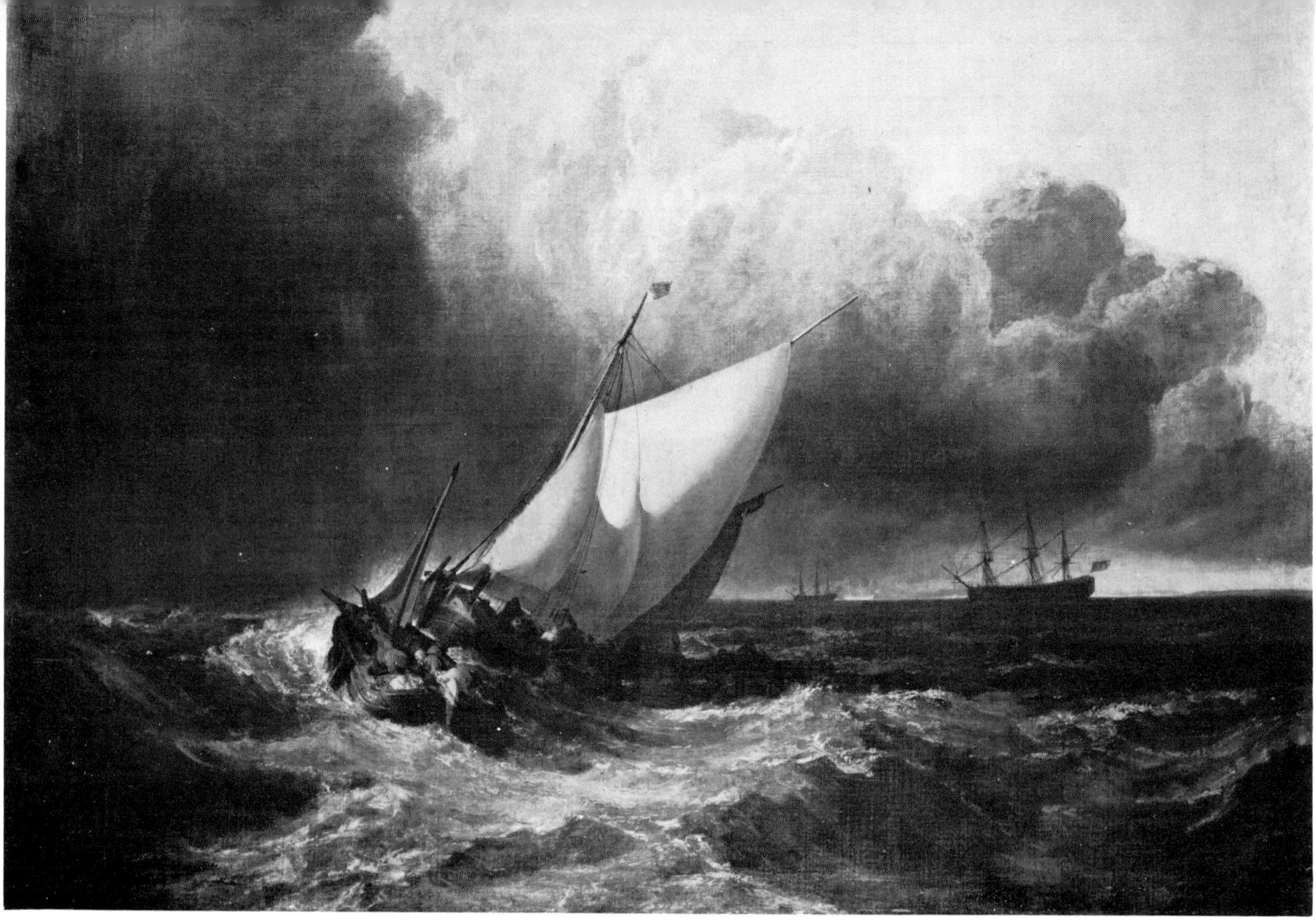

Plate 315. Joseph Mallord William Turner, 1775-1851. "The Bridgewater Sea Piece, 1801." *Turner was commissioned to paint this as a companion to the painting by Willem van de Velde, the Younger, now at the Toledo Museum of Art, Plate 149.* Christie's.

Plate 316. Joseph Mallord William Turner, 1775-1851. "The Battle of Trafalgar in 1805." *Turner saw this subject as emotional rather than historical. Painted in 1824, it didn't help that the sketches by Schetky, from which he painted the* Victory, *were done when most of her guns had been landed, so she was far too high in the water. A fault Turner had to redress after it was pointed out to him.* National Maritime Museum, Greenwich (Greenwich Hospital Collection).

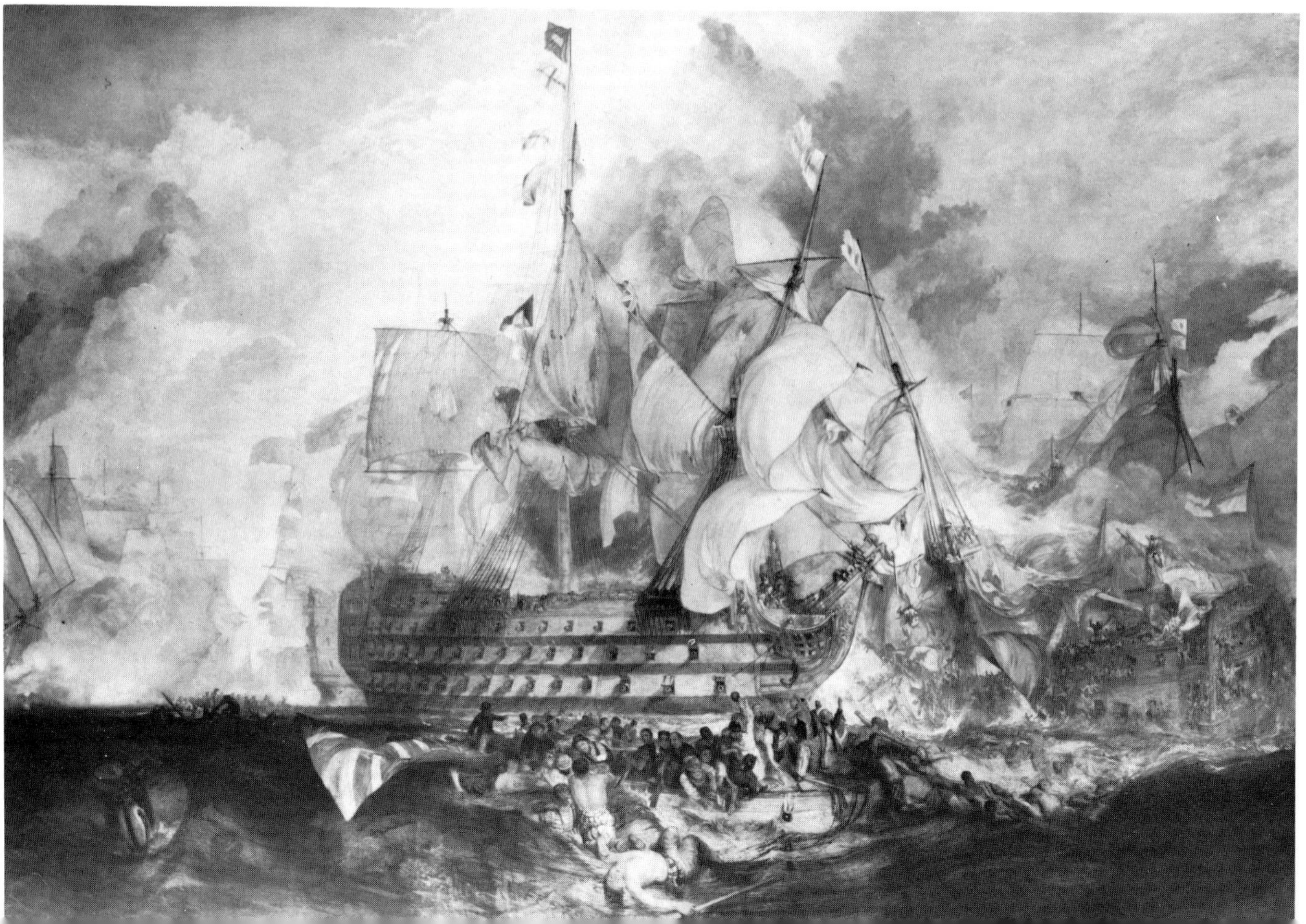

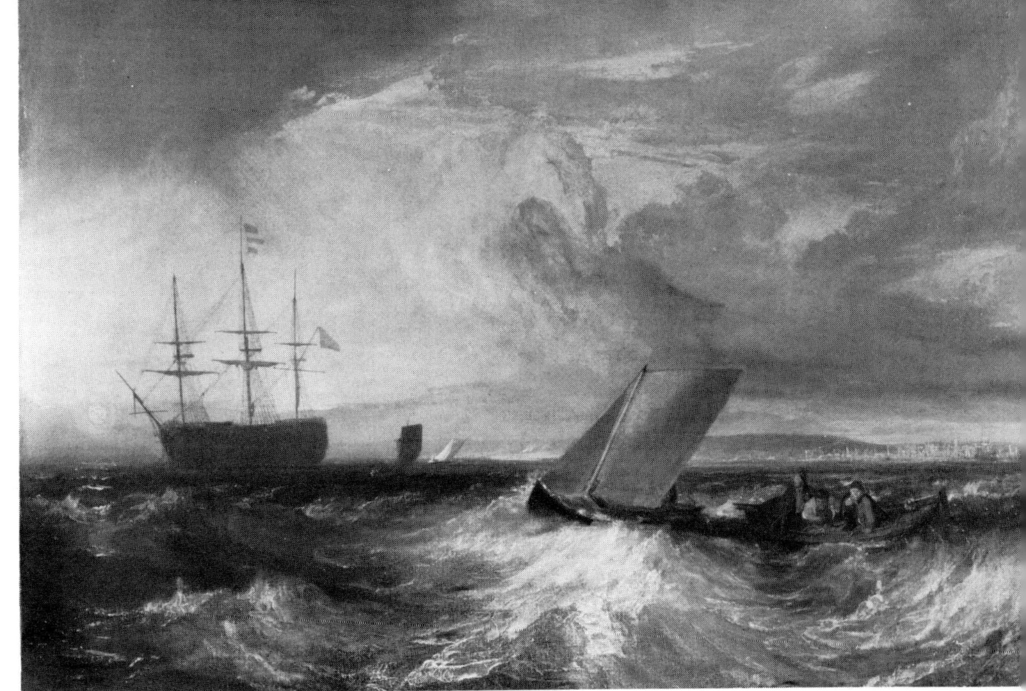

Plate 317. Joseph Mallord William Turner, 1775-1851. "Sheerness seen from the Nore, 1808." Private collection.

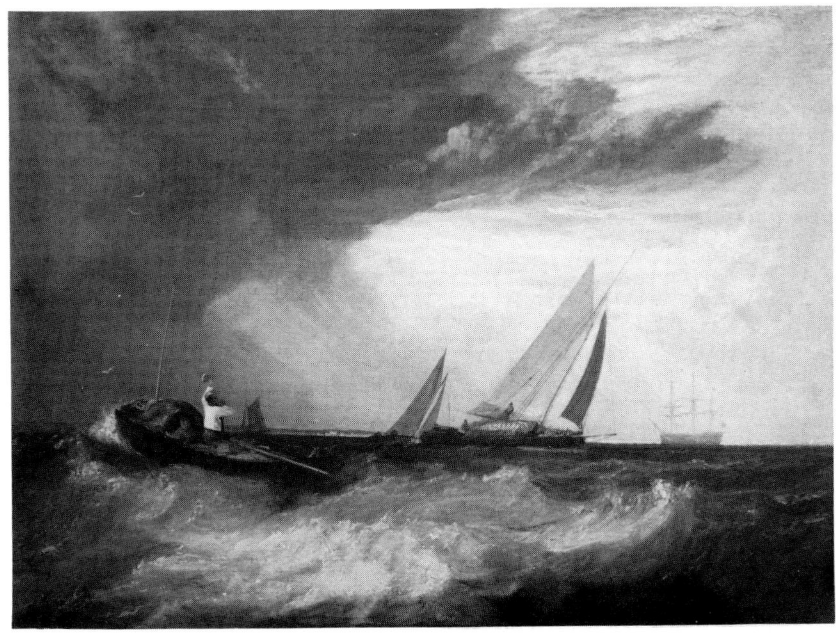

Plate 318. Joseph Mallord William Turner, 1775-1851. "Shoeburyness fishermen hailing a Whitstable hoy, 1809." National Gallery of Canada, Ottawa.

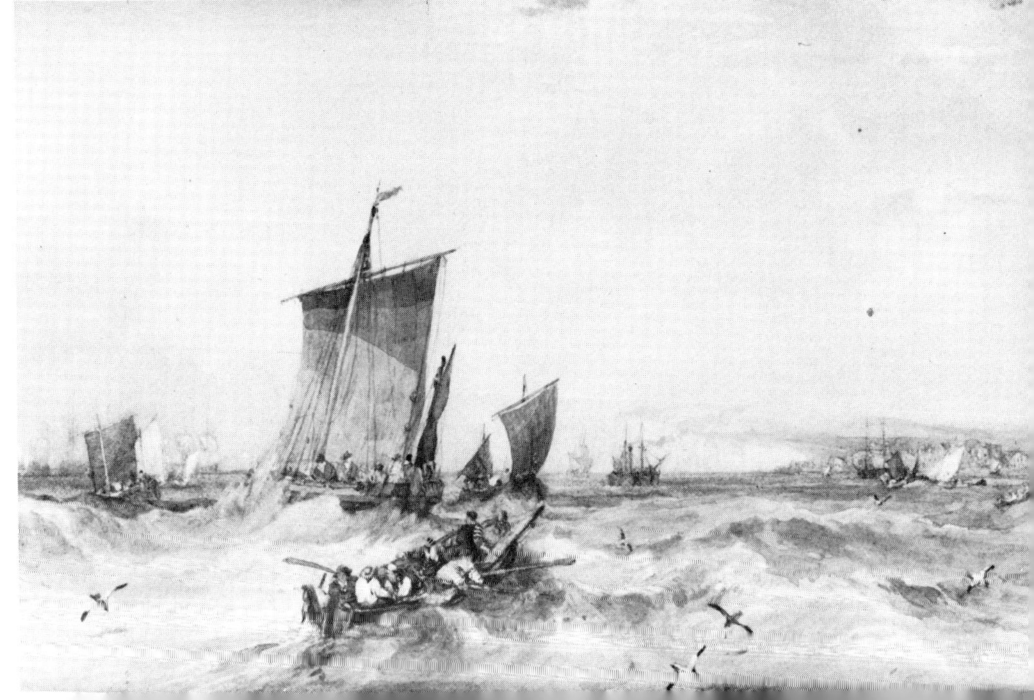

Plate 319. Samuel Owen, 1768/9-1857. "Fishing luggers off Dover." Watercolour. *The style anticipates that of George Chambers — Owen was part of the naturalistic movement of which Chambers was a leading light.* Christie's.

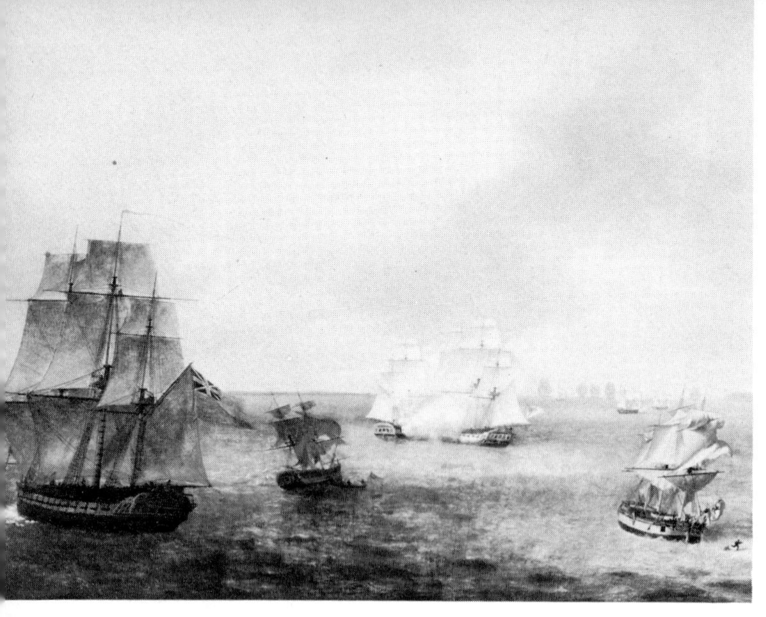

Plate 320. Louis Philipe Crepin, 1772-1851. "The action between the *Hyder Ally* and the *General Monck* in 1782." United States Naval Academy Museum, Annapolis.

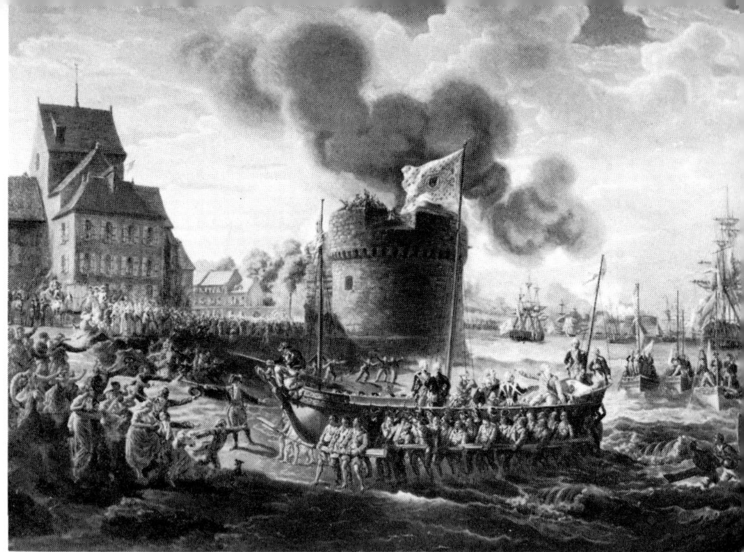

Plate 321. Louis Philippe Crepin, 1772-1851. "The visit of Louis XVI to Cherbourg in 1786." Musée de la Marine, Paris.

Plate 322. Pierre Julien Gilbert, 1783-1860. "Anglo-French action off Mauritius in 1810." Musée de la Marine, Paris.

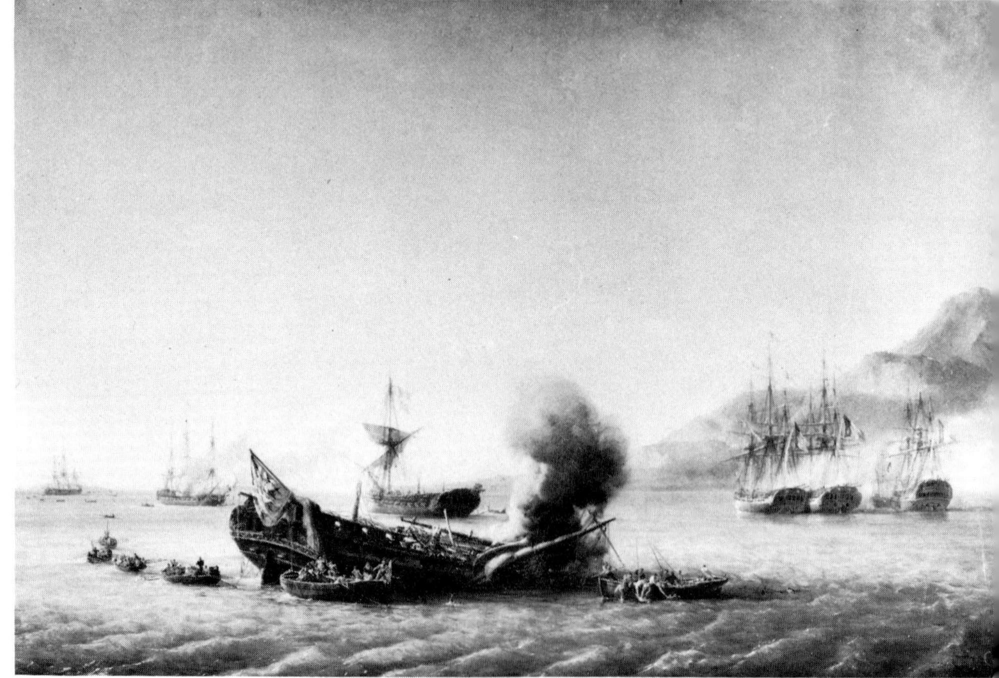

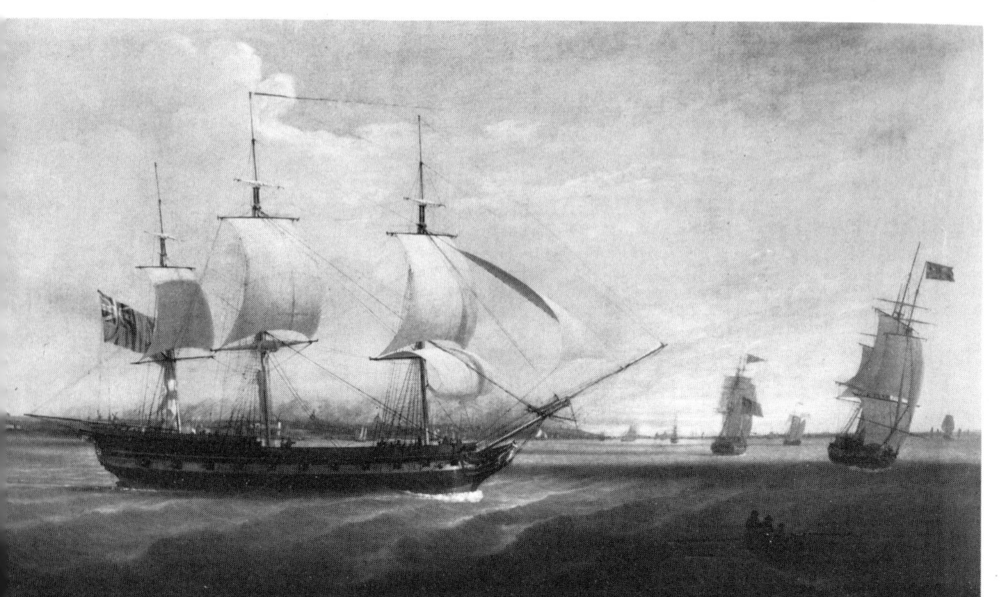

Plate 323. J. Jenkinson, fl. early 19th century. "A packet ship off Liverpool about 1810." *A member of the early 19th century school whose work has been confused with Robert Salmon's.* Christie's.

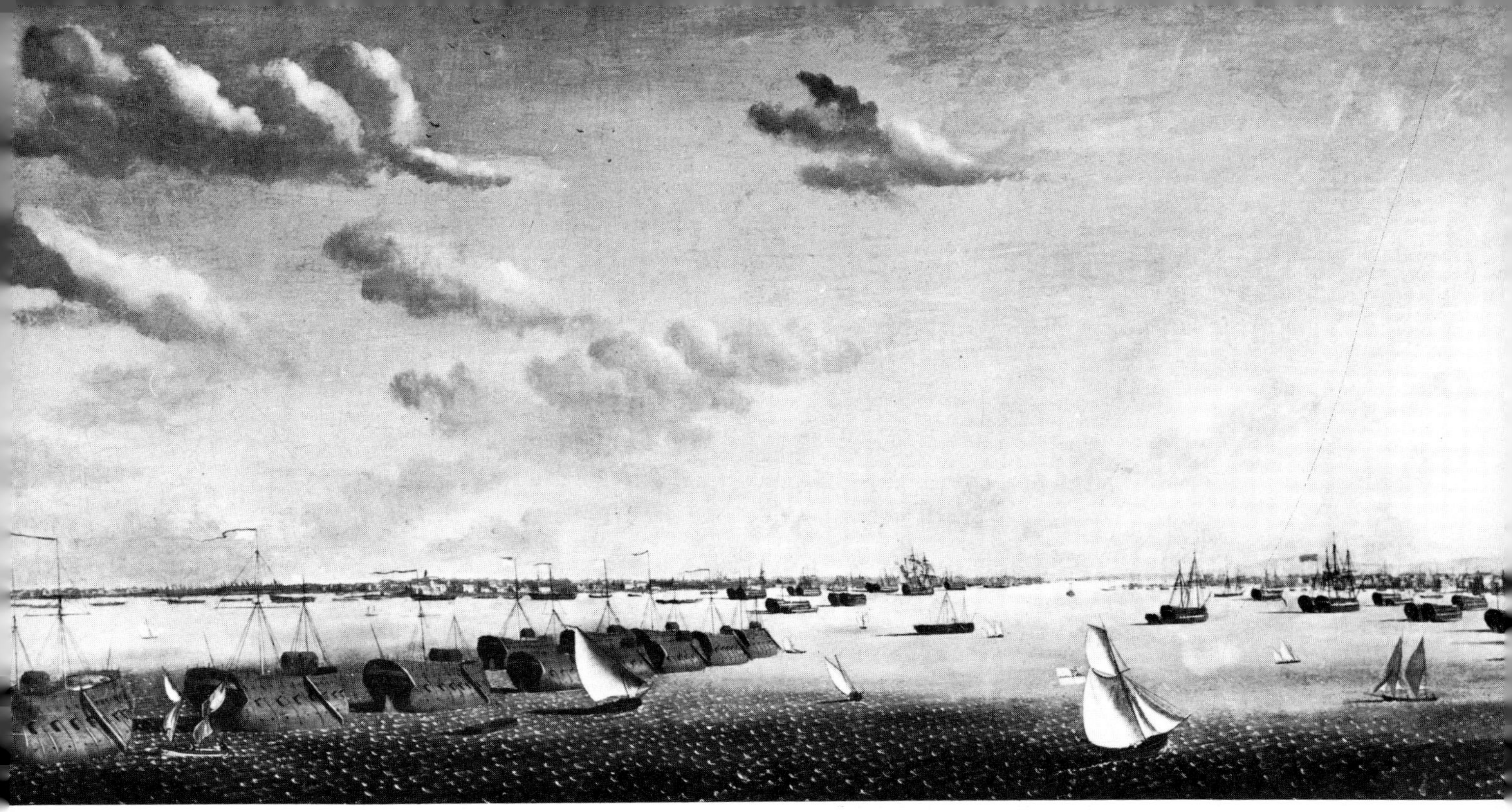

Plate 324. Ambroise Louis Garneray, 1783-1857. "Prison hulks in Portsmouth harbour, about 1810." *One of a series of paintings of this subject by a Frenchman on parole who had been a prisoner in one of them.* National Library of Australia (Rex Nan Kivell Collection), Canberra.

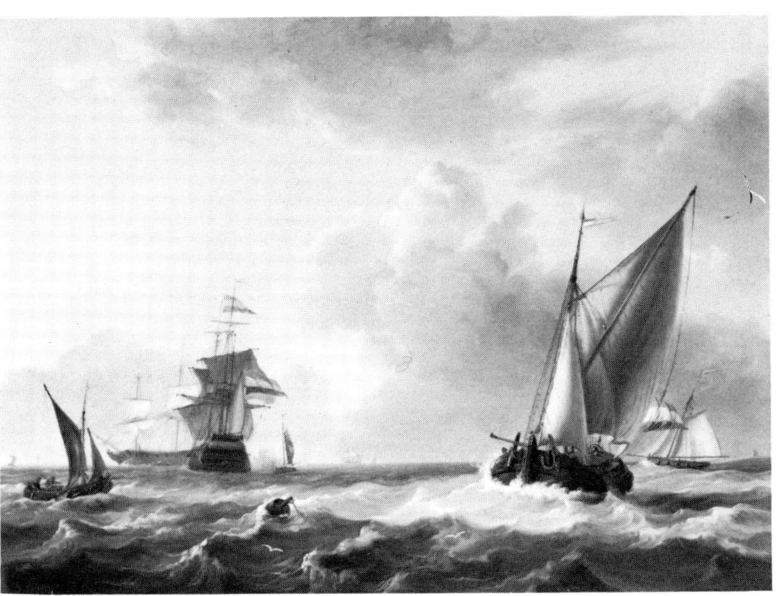

Plate 325. Nicolas Lodewijk Penning, c.1764-1818. "Dutch shipping in a fresh breeze, 1812." *A similar background to those of the Schotels (see Plates 370-372) and indicative of the Dutch revival of fine marine painting in the late 18th and early 19th century.* Phillips.

Plate 326. Michele-Felice Corne, 1762-1832. "The American merchant ship *John,* 1803." Watercolour. *One of his straight ship portraits.* Peabody Museum of Salem.

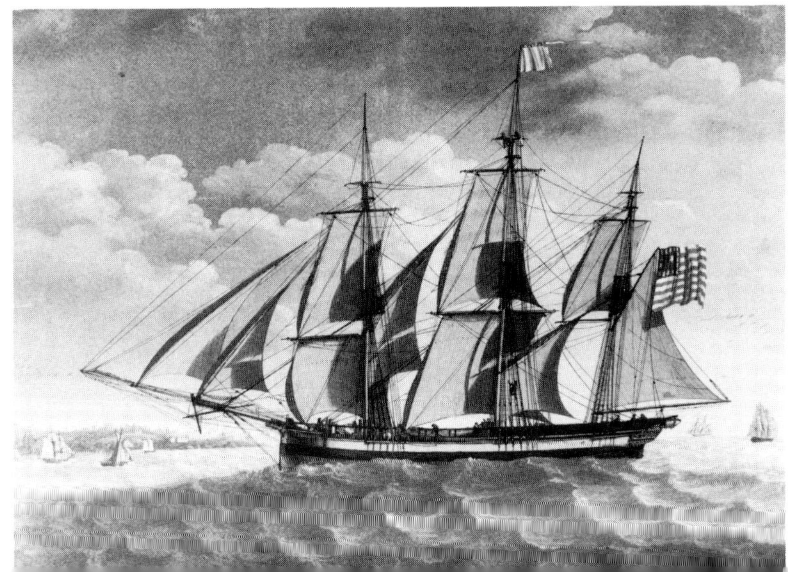

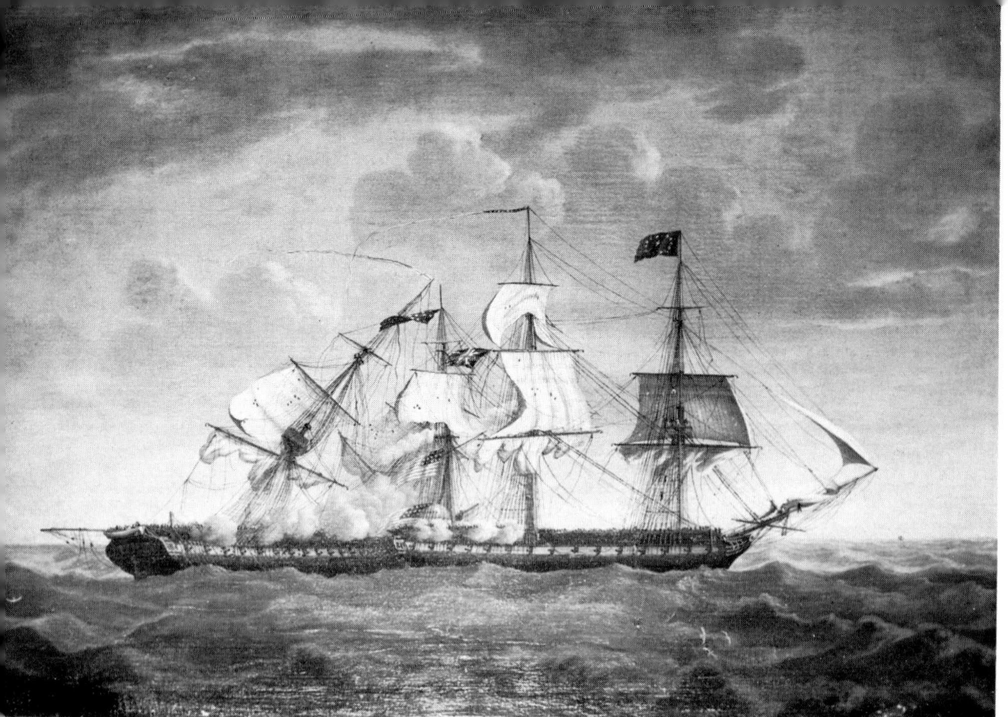

Plate 327. Michele-Felice Corne, 1762-1832. "The action between the U.S.S. *Constitution* and the British frigate *Guerriere* in 1812." United States Naval Academy, Annapolis.

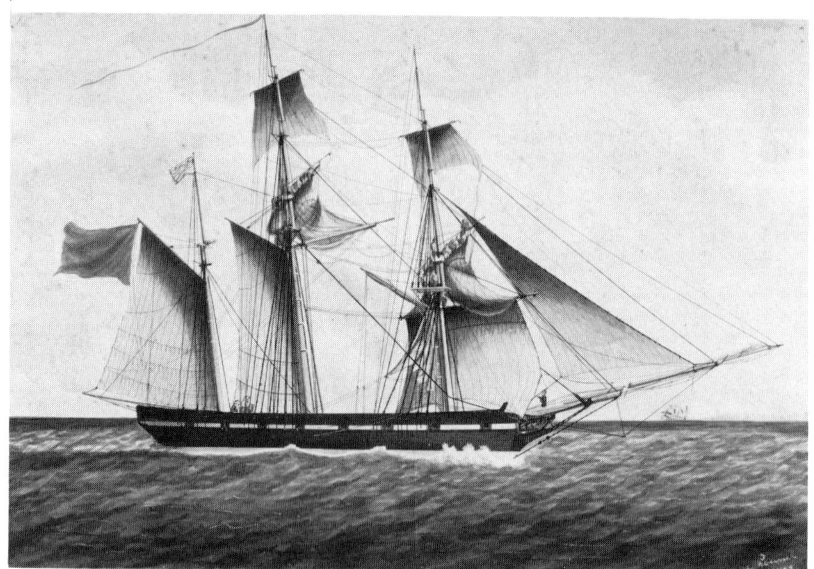

Plate 328. C. Roussel, fl. early 19th century. "The corsair *Alligator,* dated 1813." *Strictly speaking the ship was a pirate.* Private collection.

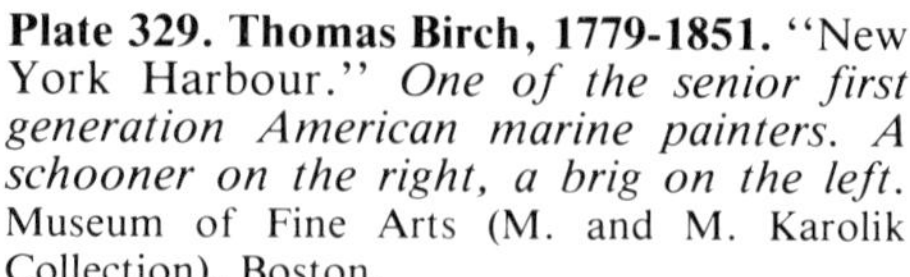

Plate 329. Thomas Birch, 1779-1851. "New York Harbour." *One of the senior first generation American marine painters. A schooner on the right, a brig on the left.* Museum of Fine Arts (M. and M. Karolik Collection), Boston.

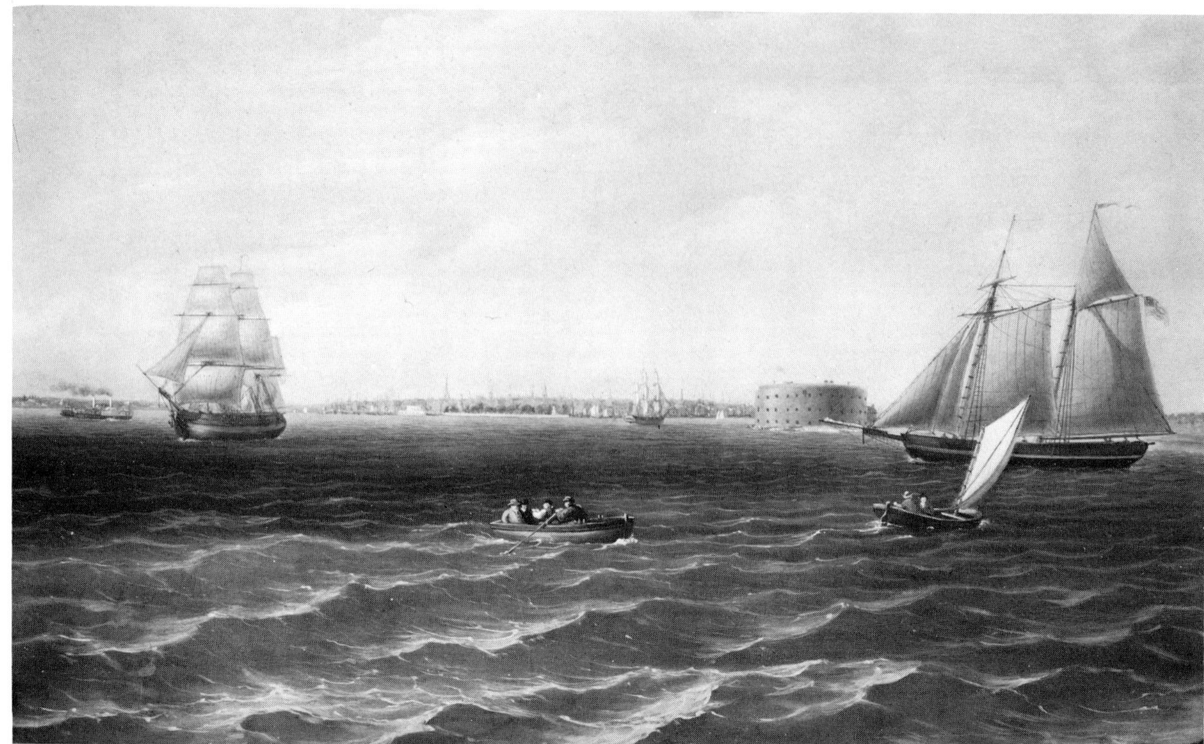

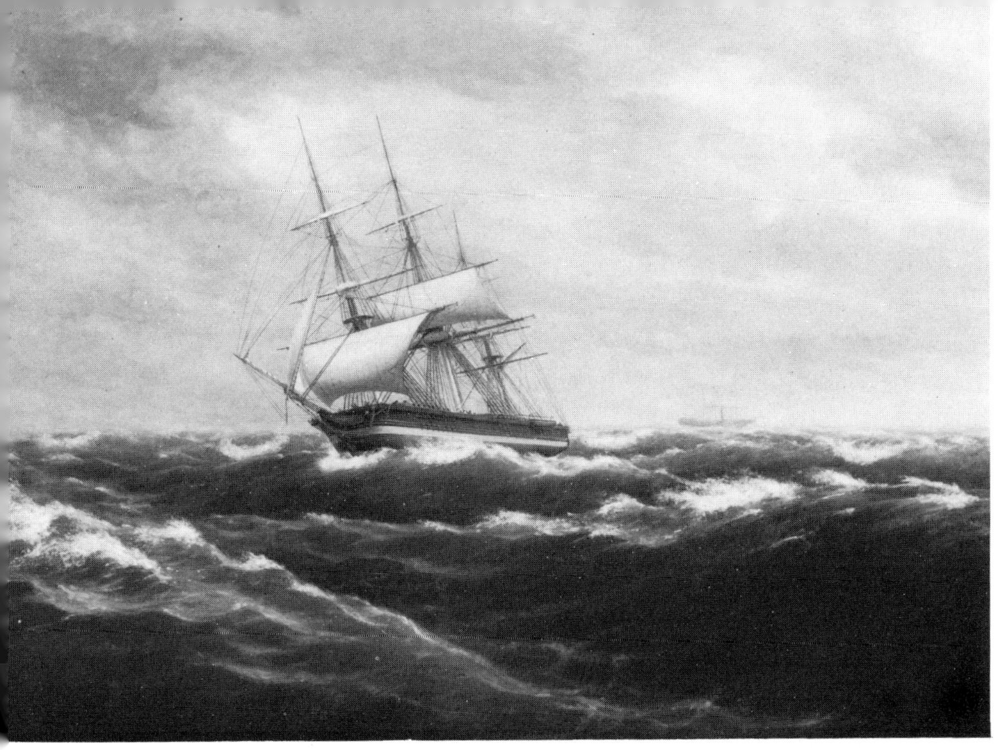

Plate 330. Thomas Birch, 1779-1851. "An American packet ship in a stormy sea." *The ship is running under main topsail and forecourse.* Mariners Museum, Newport News.

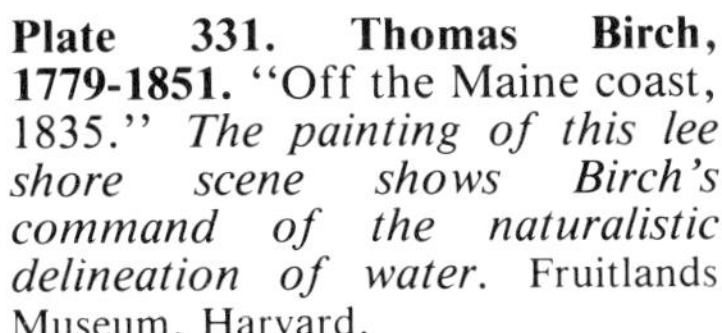

Plate 331. Thomas Birch, 1779-1851. "Off the Maine coast, 1835." *The painting of this lee shore scene shows Birch's command of the naturalistic delineation of water.* Fruitlands Museum, Harvard.

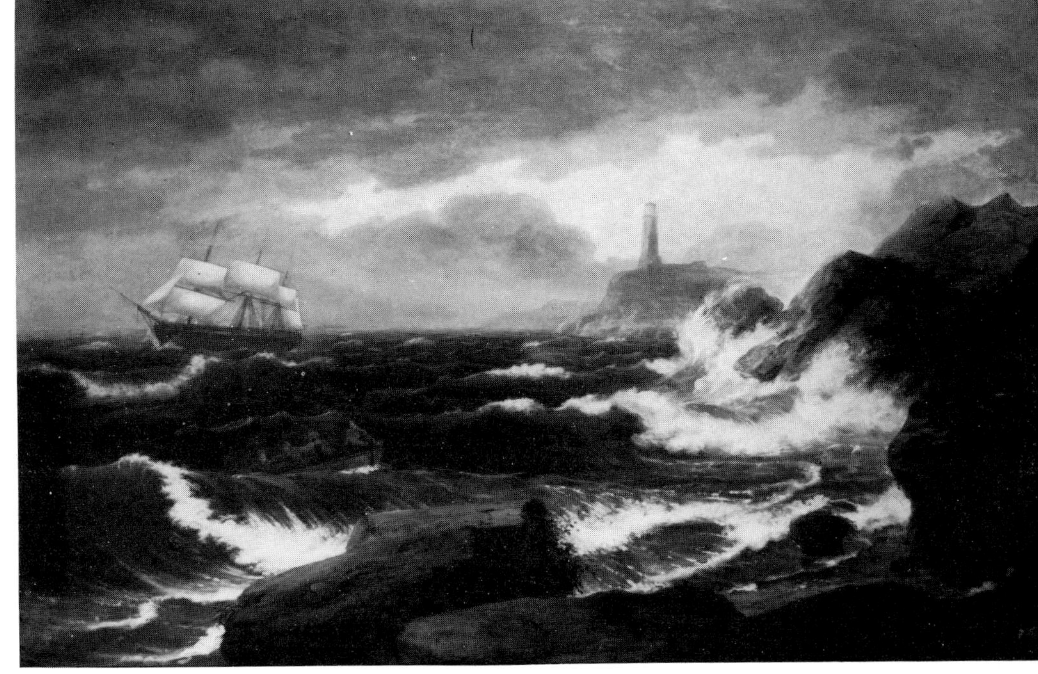

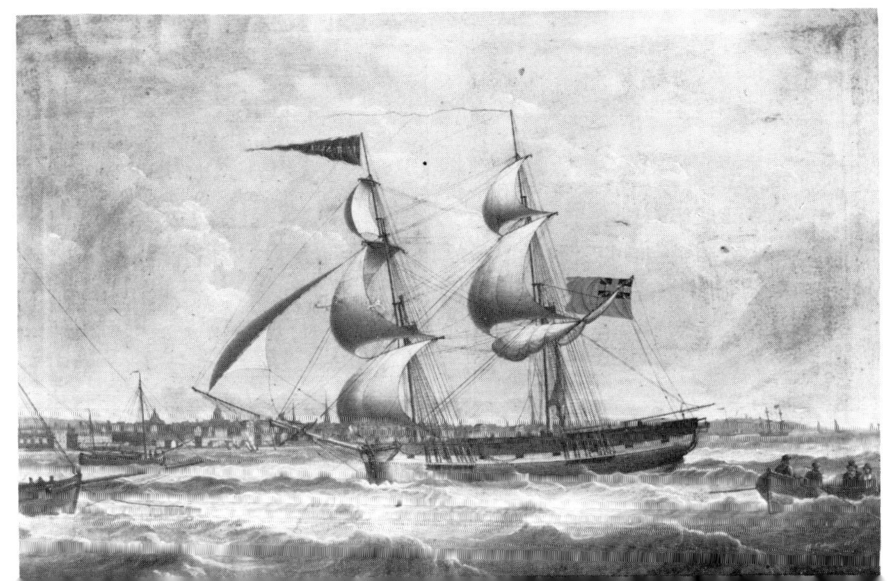

Plate 332. H. Collins, fl. early 19th century. "A snow in a stiff breeze off Liverpool, dated 1813." *A work by one of the earliest Liverpool ship portraitists.* Bonham's.

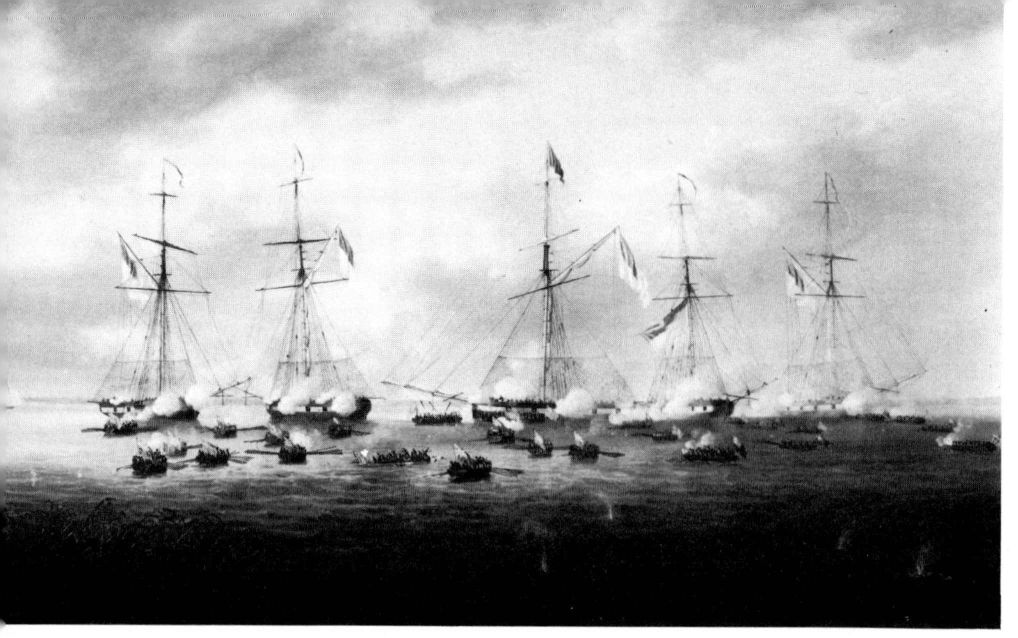

Plate 333. Thomas Lyde Hornbrook, 1780-1850. "The Anglo-American action on Lake Borgne in 1814." *An incident in the American War of 1812. The nets round the lower part of the rigging were designed to make boarding difficult, but in this case not difficult enough, for the British took the American vessels.* National Maritime Museum, Greenwich.

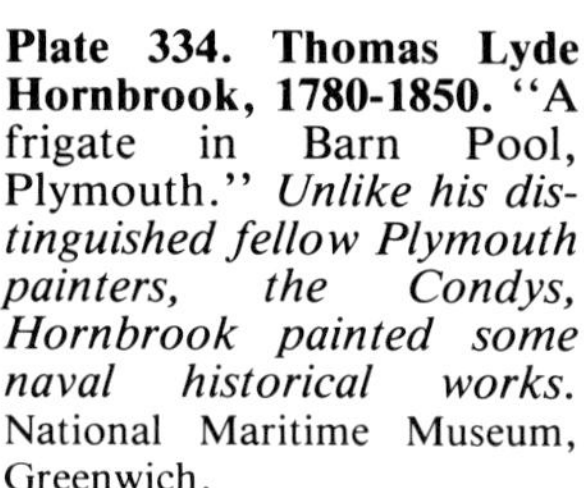

Plate 334. Thomas Lyde Hornbrook, 1780-1850. "A frigate in Barn Pool, Plymouth." *Unlike his distinguished fellow Plymouth painters, the Condys, Hornbrook painted some naval historical works.* National Maritime Museum, Greenwich.

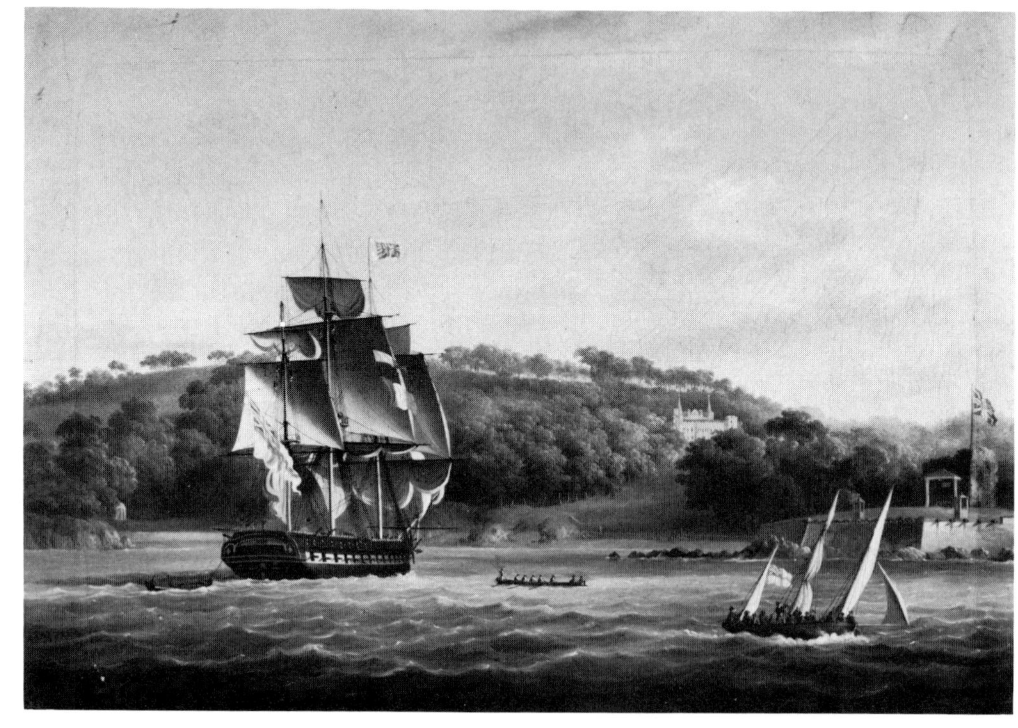

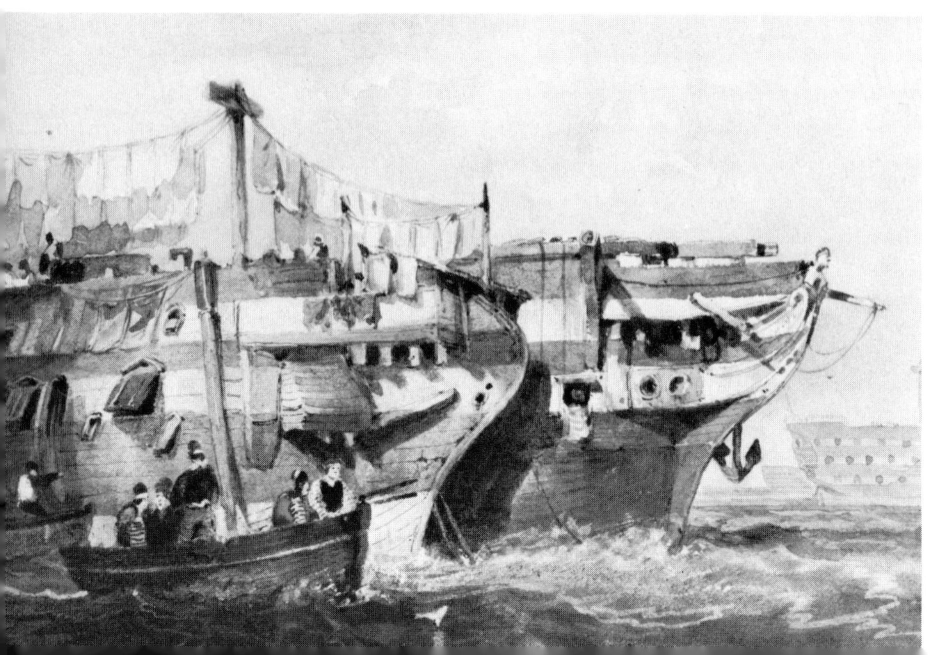

Plate 335. Samuel Prout, 1783-1852. "Royal Naval hulks at Plymouth." Watercolour. *Great immediacy and visual impact, more from the selection of the subject than from any facility for draughtsmanship.* Christie's.

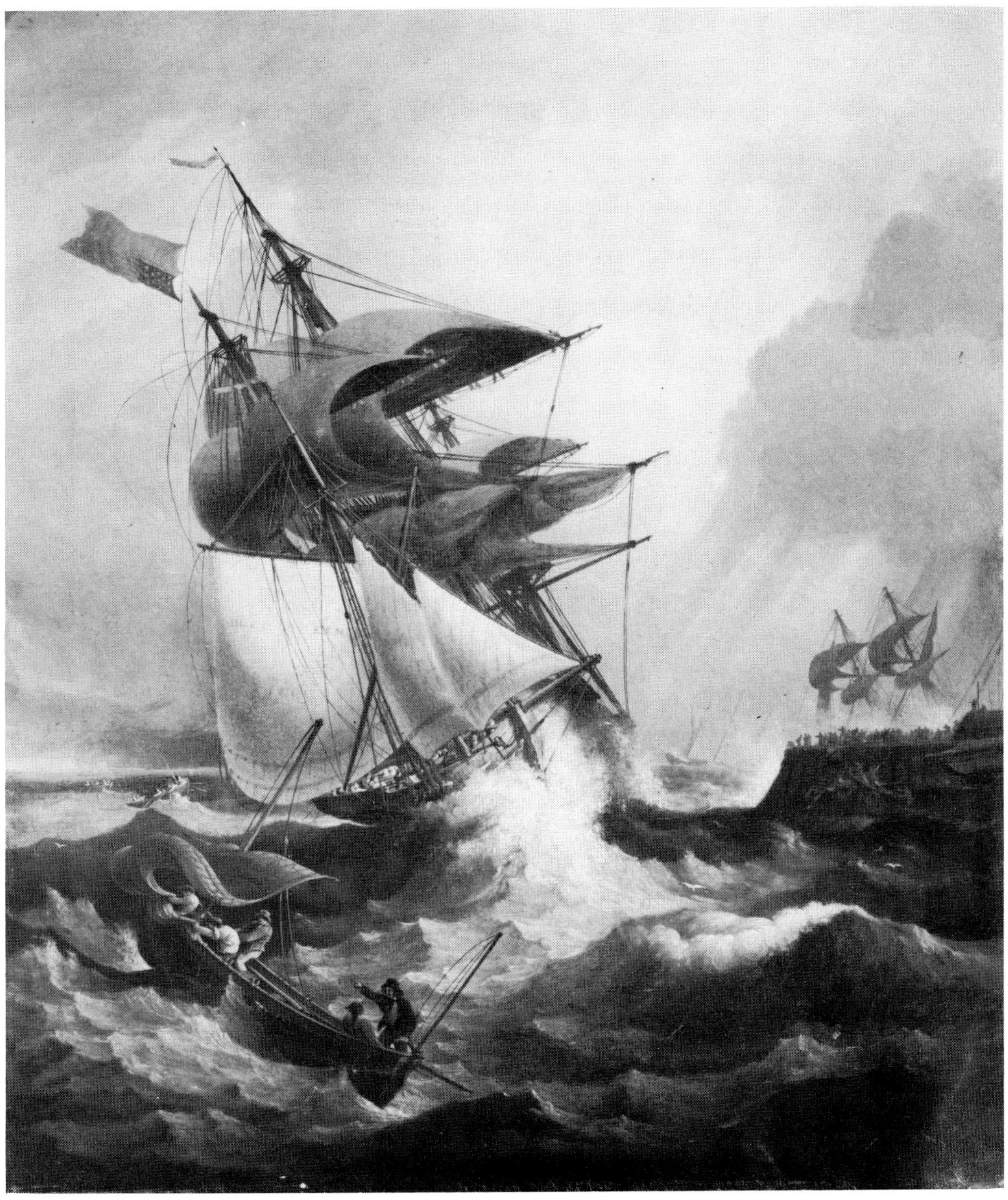

Plate 336. C. John Whichelo, 1784-1865. "A packet and an American ship in distress entering Margate in a storm."
National Maritime Museum, Greenwich.

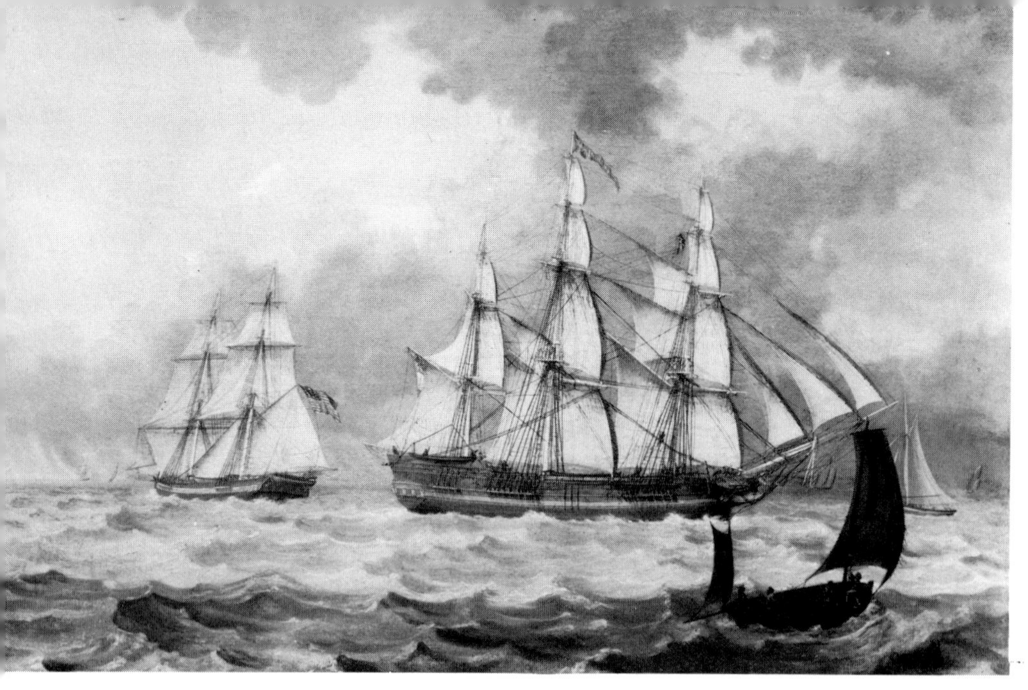

Plate 337. Thomas Binks, 1799-1852. "The ship *East Indian,* 1819." *Binks was a member of the Hull school, and a contemporary of Willoughby.* National Maritime Museum, Greenwich.

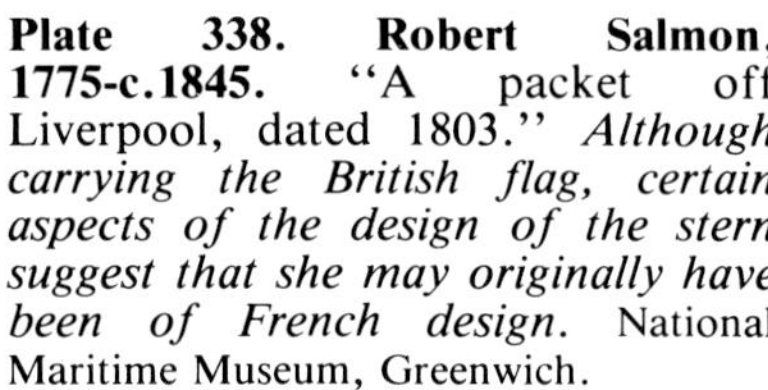

Plate 338. Robert Salmon, 1775-c.1845. "A packet off Liverpool, dated 1803." *Although carrying the British flag, certain aspects of the design of the stern suggest that she may originally have been of French design.* National Maritime Museum, Greenwich.

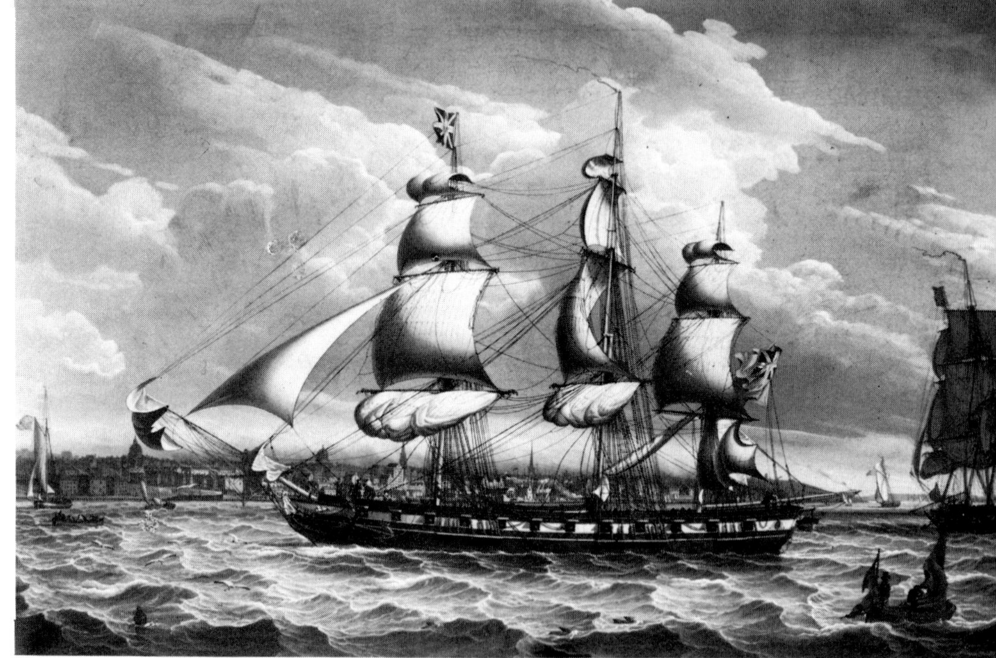

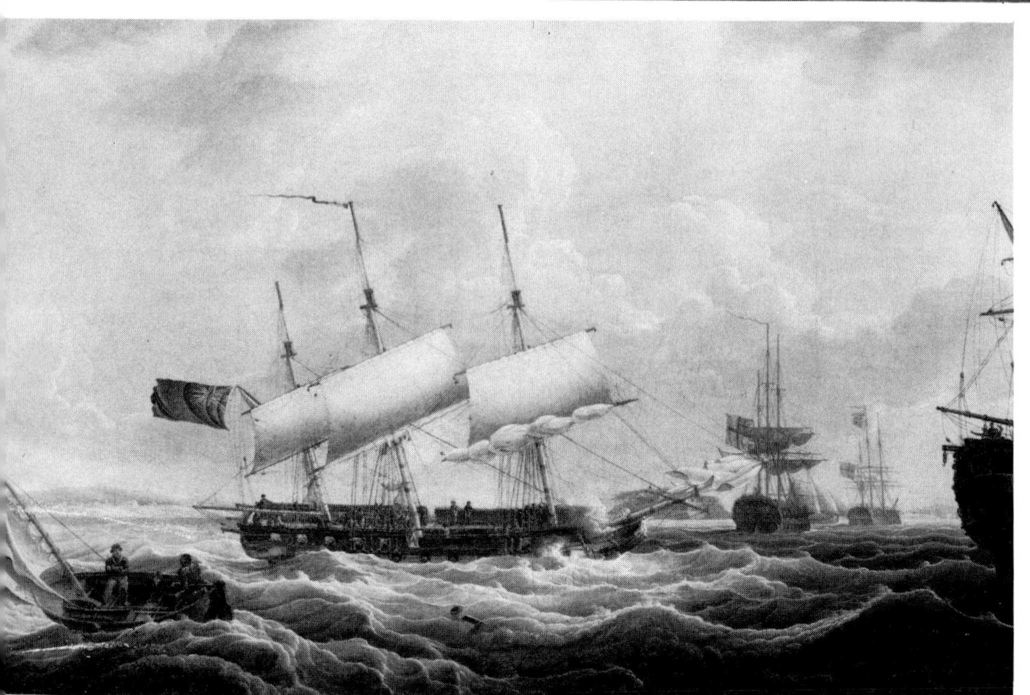

Plate 339. Robert Salmon, 1775-c.1845. "A frigate coming to anchor in the Mersey." *Perch Rock Fort with a frigate close hauled in rough seas.* National Maritime Museum, Greenwich.

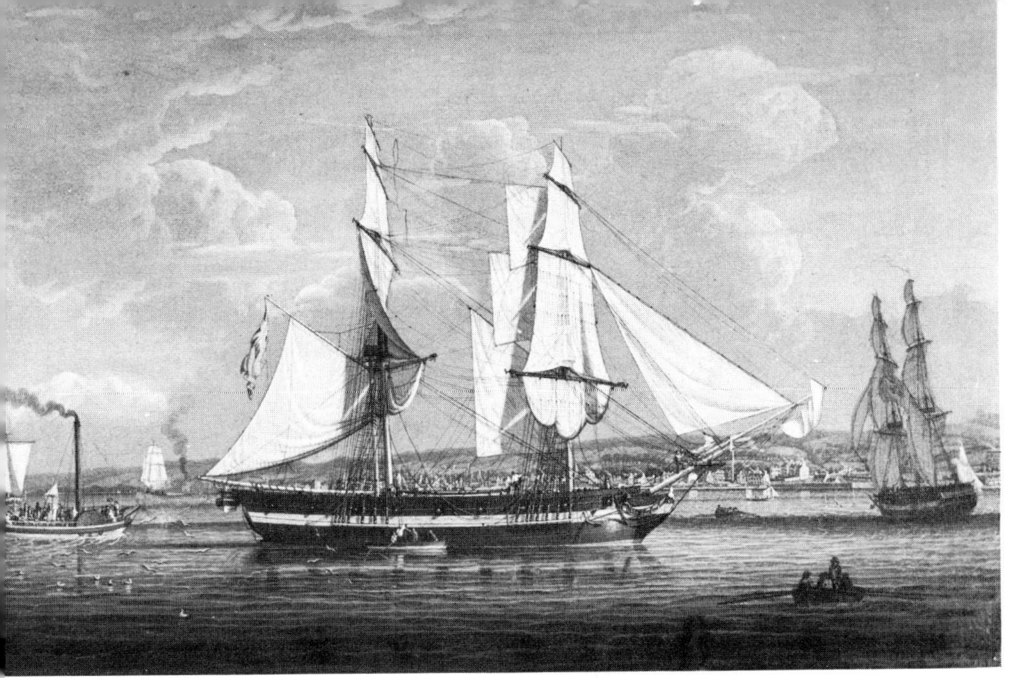

Plate 340. Robert Salmon, 1775-c.1845. "A packet brig off Greenock, with a very early steam ferry, about 1815." *Painted only two years after steam was introduced on the Clyde. Note the stylised sea.* Mariners Museum, Newport News.

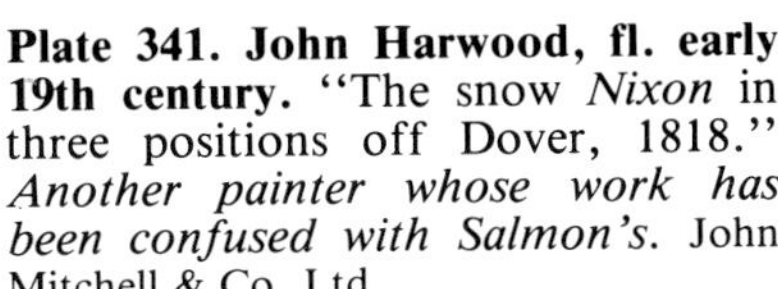

Plate 341. John Harwood, fl. early 19th century. "The snow *Nixon* in three positions off Dover, 1818." *Another painter whose work has been confused with Salmon's.* John Mitchell & Co. Ltd.

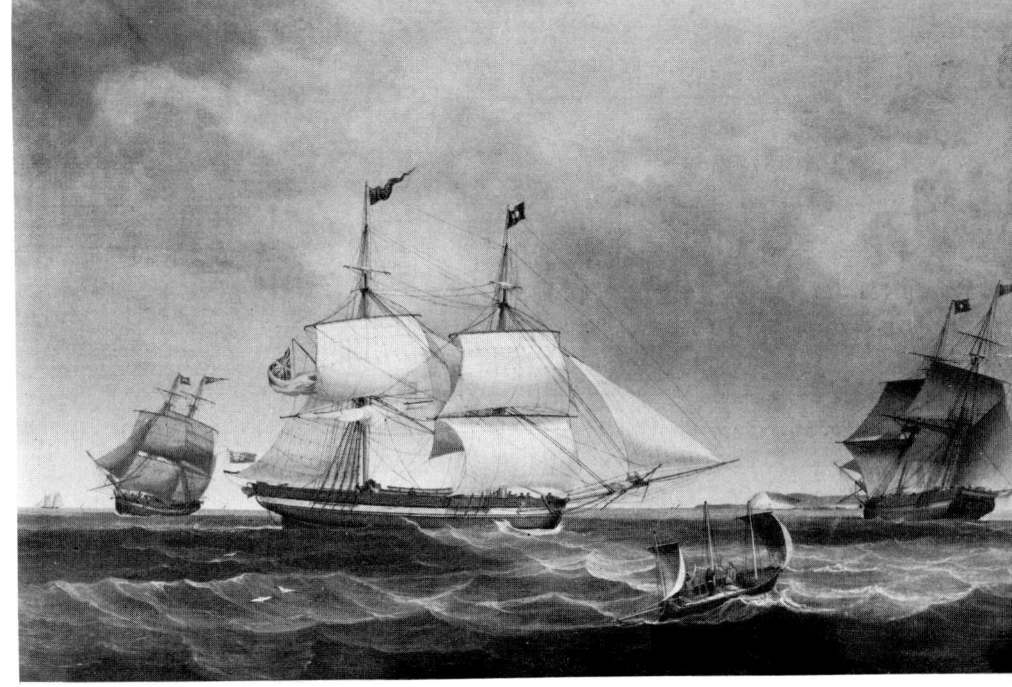

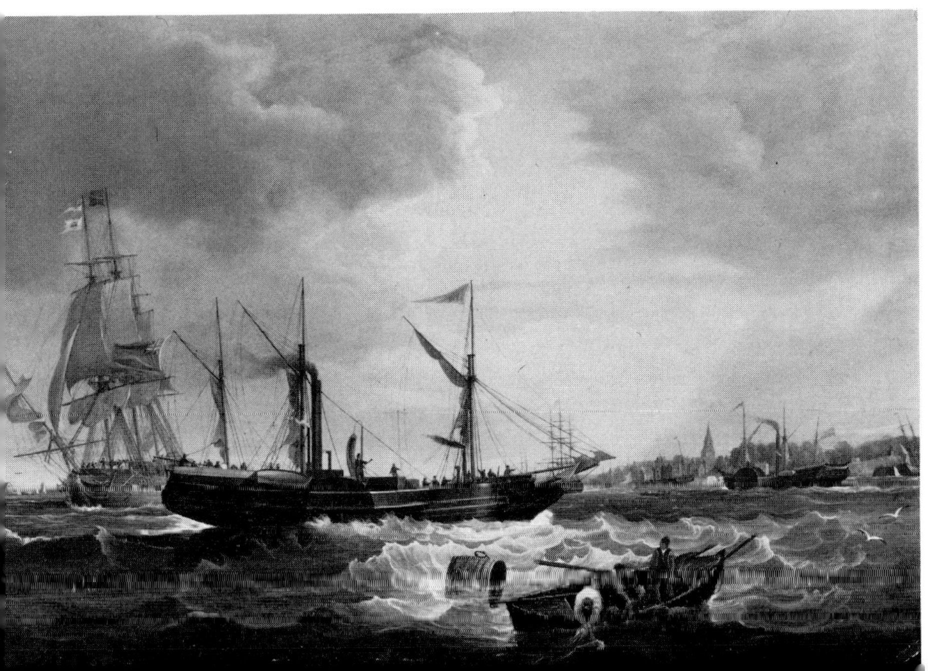

Plate 342. John Harwood, fl. early 19th century. "Shipping off Gravesend, 1821." N.R. Omell.

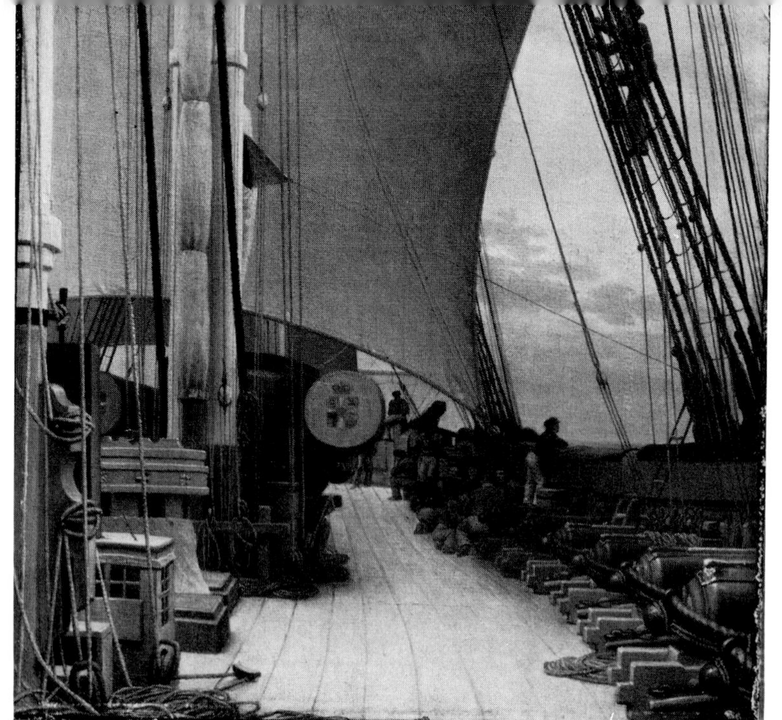

Plate 343. Christoffer Wilhelm Eckersberg, 1783-1853. "The starboard battery of the Danish corvette *Najaden,* 1833." State Museum for Art, Copenhagen.

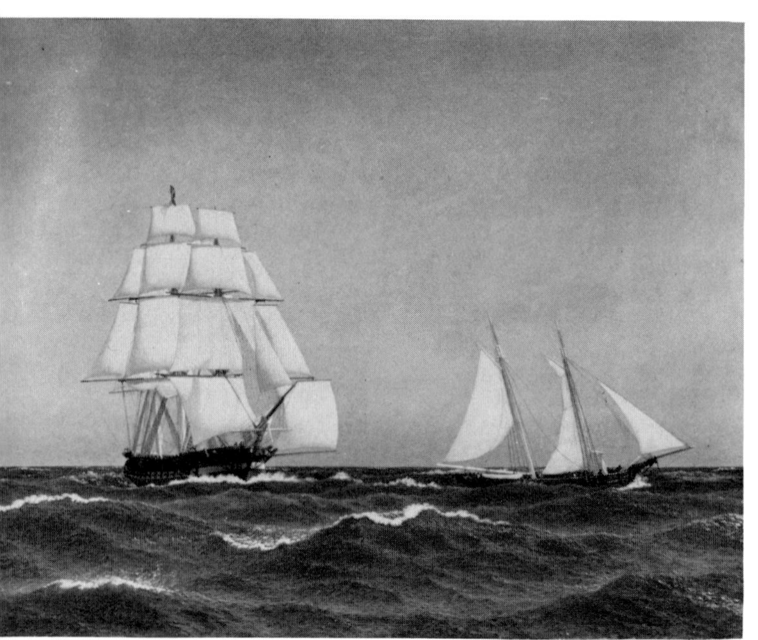

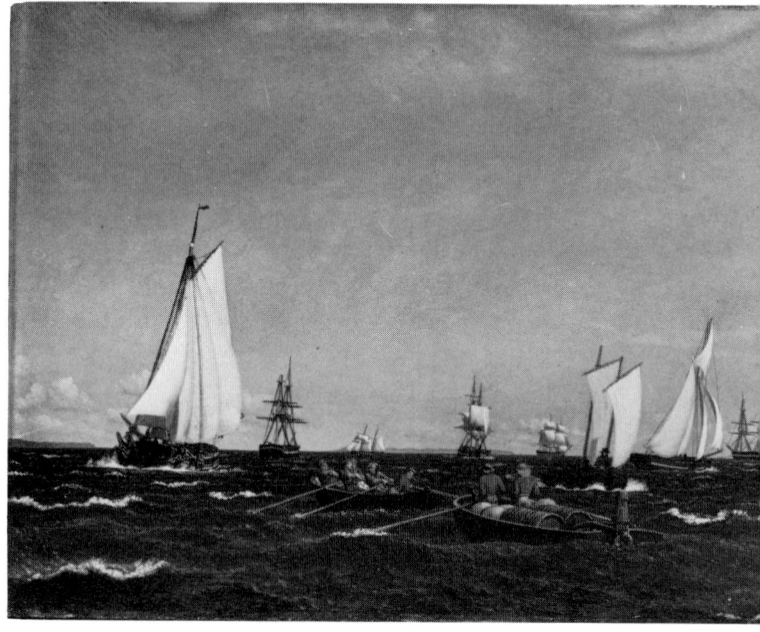

Plate 344 *(above)*. **Christoffer Wilhelm Eckersberg, 1783-1853.** "A privateer outsailing a pursuing frigate, dated 1845." *A good example of the work of Denmark's best marine painter.* State Museum for Art, Copenhagen.

Plate 345 *(above right)*. **Christoffer Wilhelm Eckersberg, 1783-1853.** "Ships in Copenhagen roads, a barge being towed out, 1847." State Museum for Art, Copenhagen.

Plate 346. Johan Christian Clausen Dahl, 1788-1857. "A wreck on the Norwegian coast, 1832." National Gallery, Oslo.

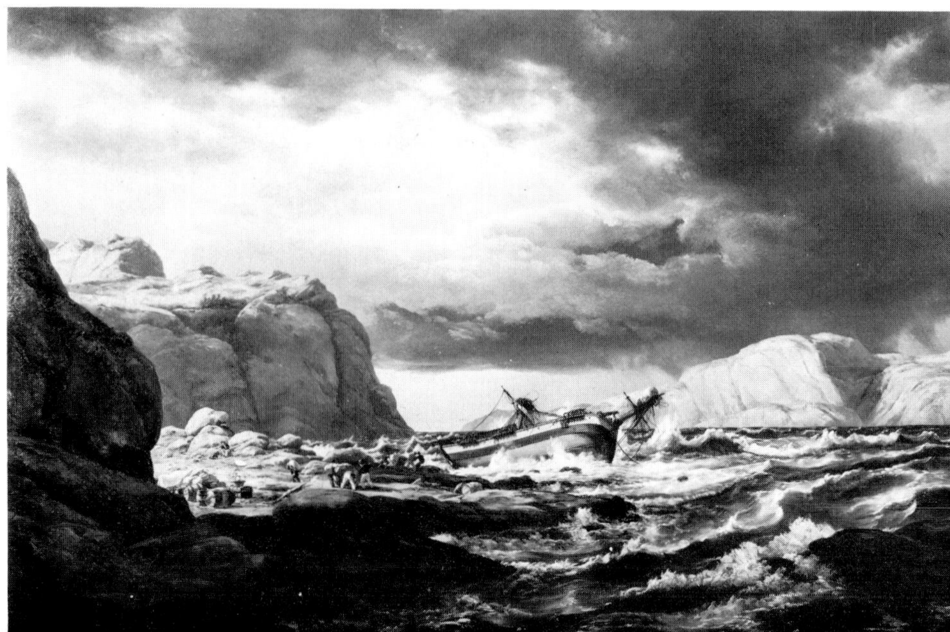

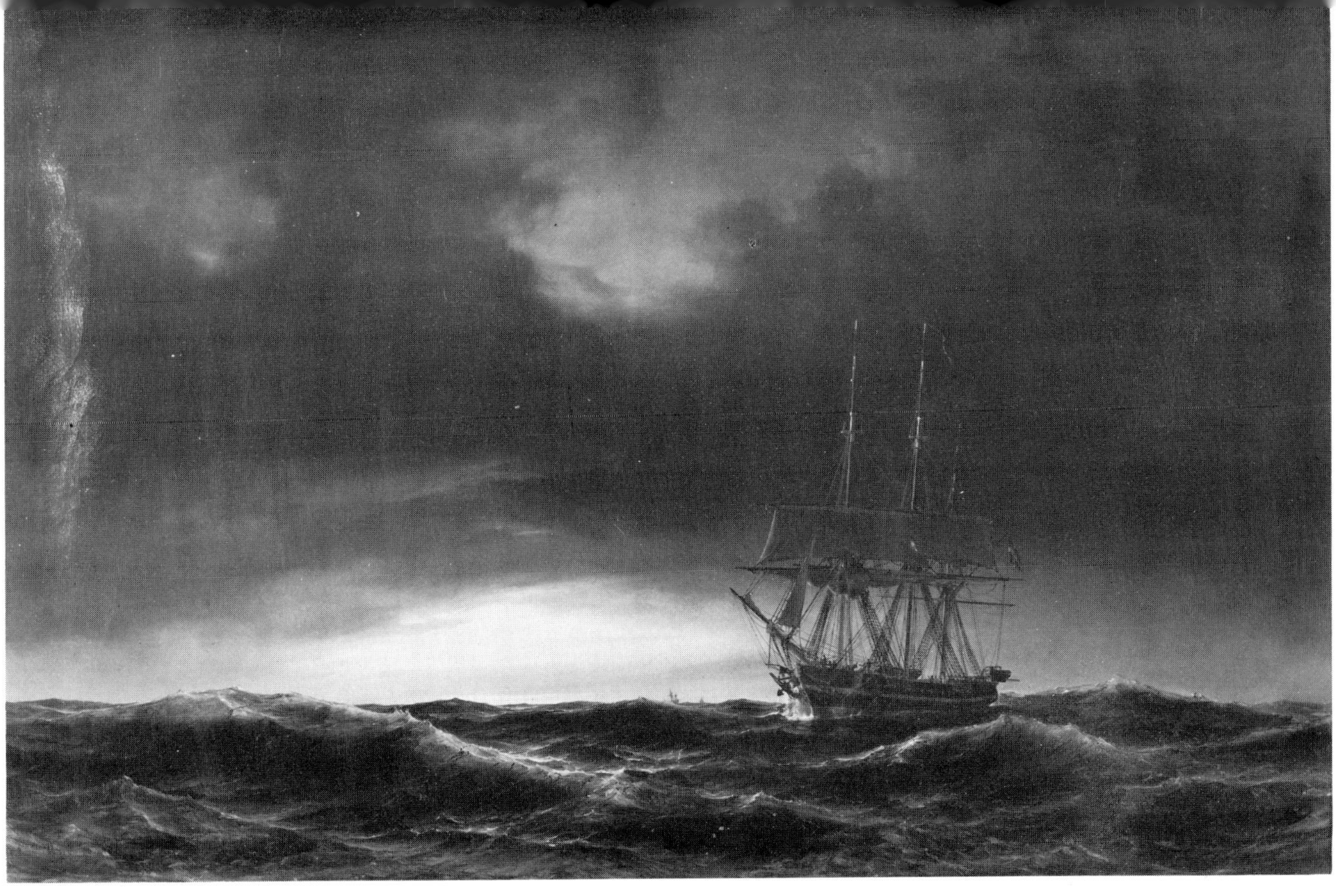

Plate 347. Daniel Hermann Anton Melbye, 1818-1875. "A Danish corvette at sea after a gale, dated 1848." State Museum for Art, Copenhagen.

Plate 348. Daniel Hermann Anton Melbye, 1818-1875. "The Battle of Koge Bay in 1677, dated 1855." State Museum for Art, Copenhagen.

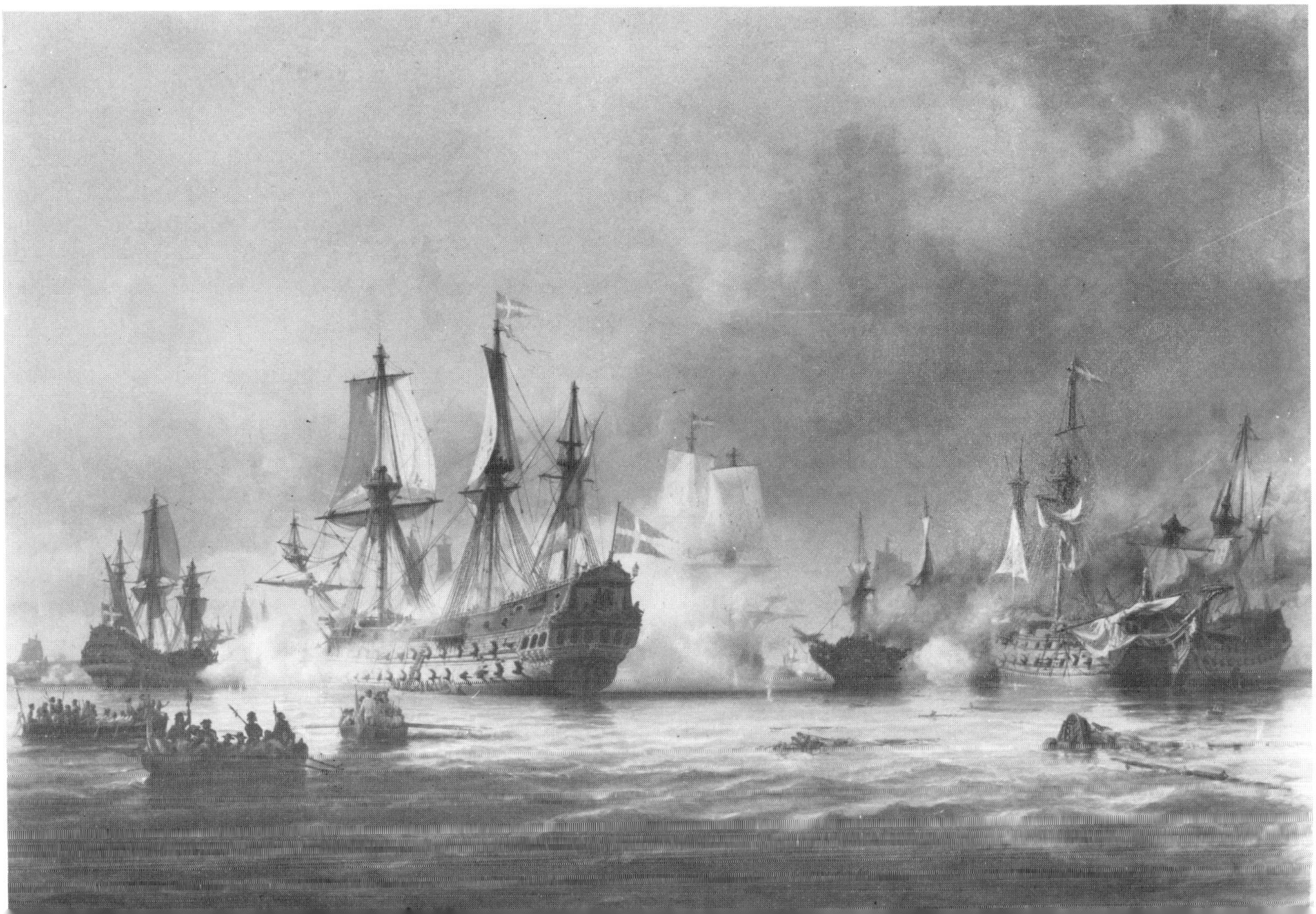

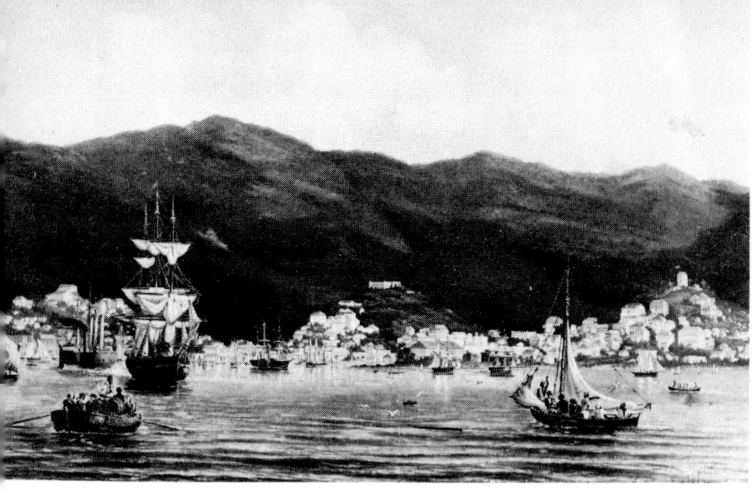

Plate 349. Fritz Sigfried Georg Melbye, 1826-1896. "*Charlotte Amalie,* St. Thomas, West Indies, dated 1861." Maritime Museum, Kronborg Castle.

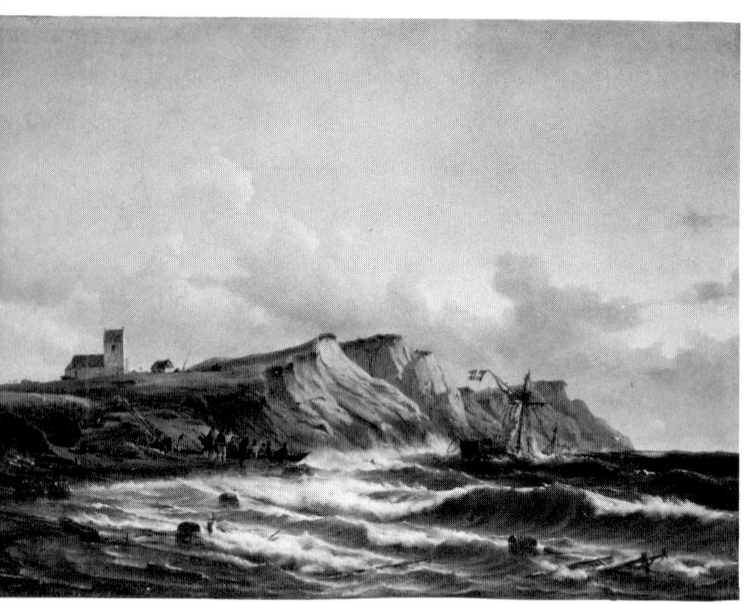

Plate 350. Carl Fredrik Sorensen, 1818-1879. "Shipwreck after a gale on the west coast of Jutland, dated 1848." State Museum for Art, Copenhagen.

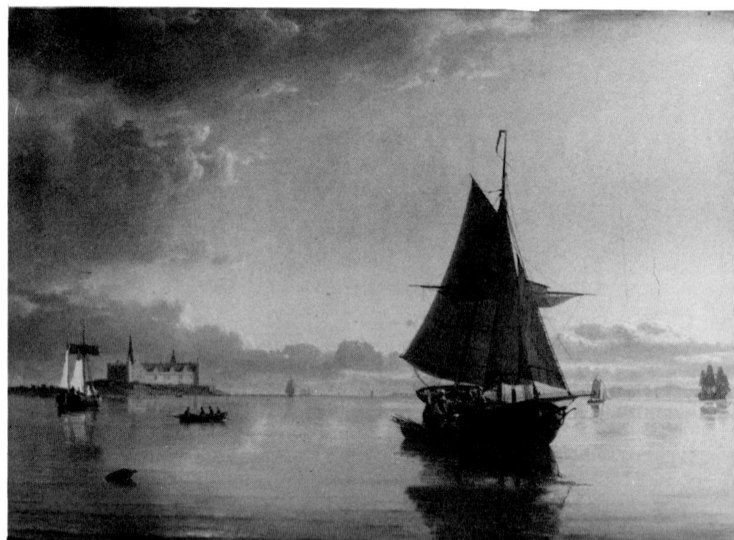

Plate 351. Carl Fredrik Sorensen, 1818-1879. "Early summer morning: the roads of Elsinore, 1860." State Museum for Art, Copenhagen.

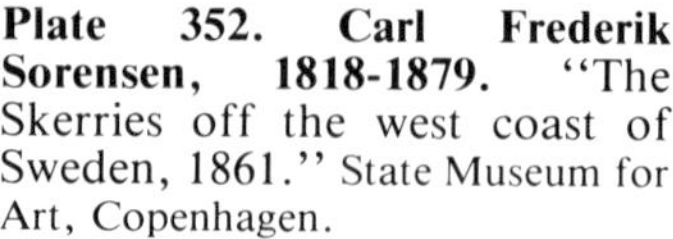

Plate 352. Carl Frederik Sorensen, 1818-1879. "The Skerries off the west coast of Sweden, 1861." State Museum for Art, Copenhagen.

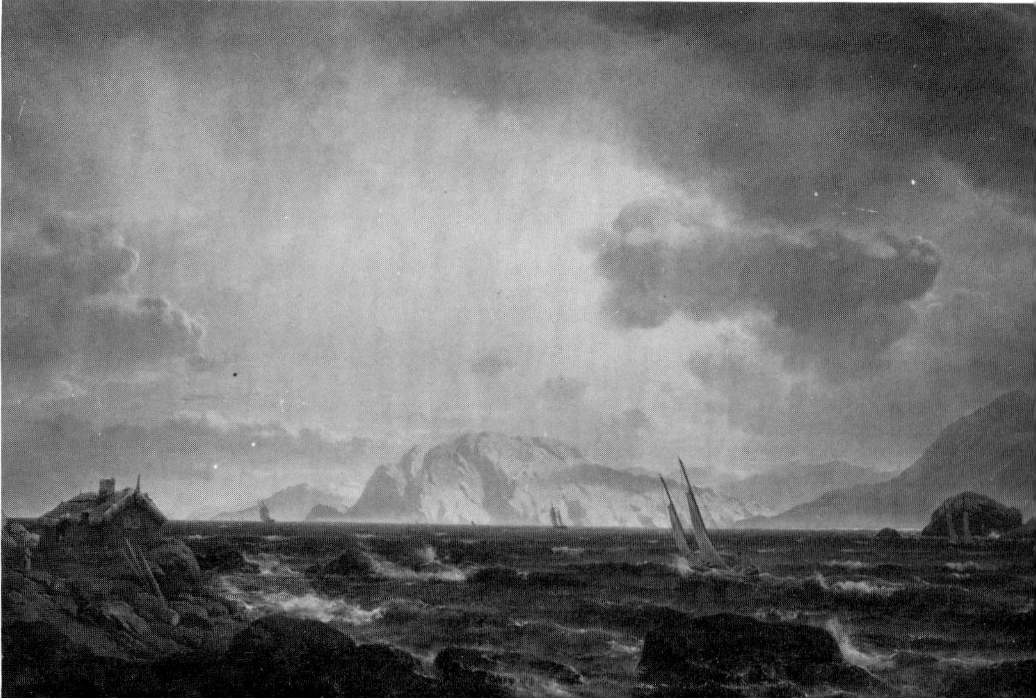

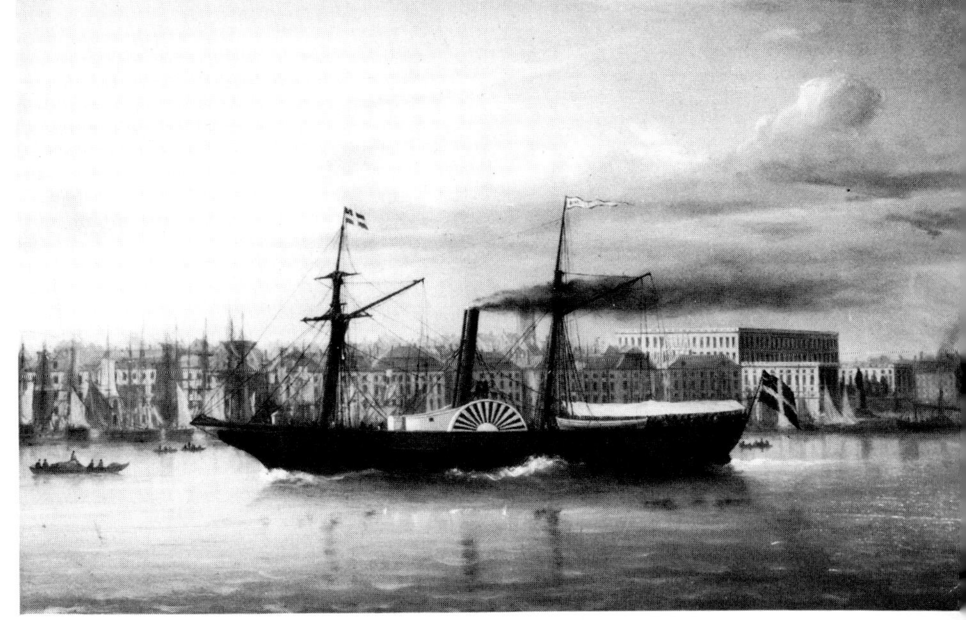

Plate 353. Per Vilhelm Cedergren, 1823-1896. "The paddle steamer *Norrland* in Stockholm harbour." National Maritime Museum, Stockholm.

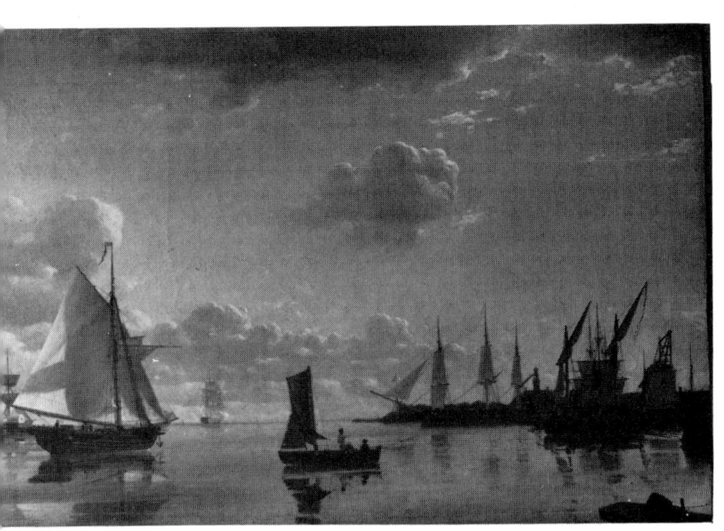

Plate 354. Carl Frederick Emmanuel Larsen, 1823-1859. "The roads of Copenhagen, morning light." State Museum for Art, Copenhagen.

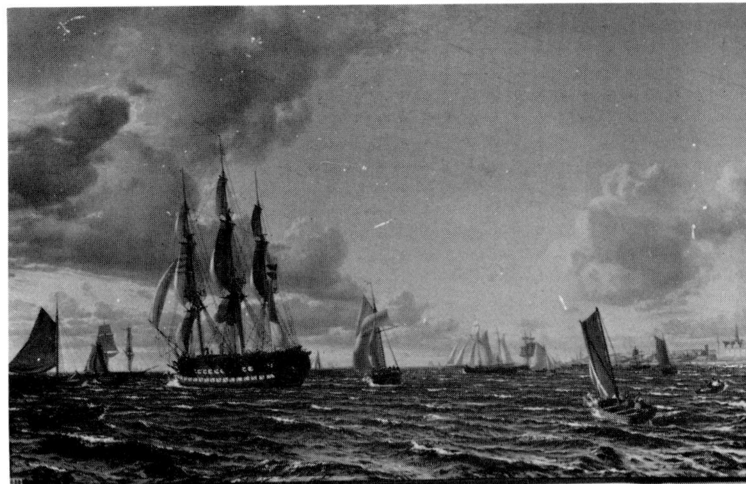

Plate 355. Carl Frederick Emmanuel Larsen, 1823-1859. "The Danish ship of the line *Valdemar* in the Sound, 1856." State Museum for Art, Copenhagen.

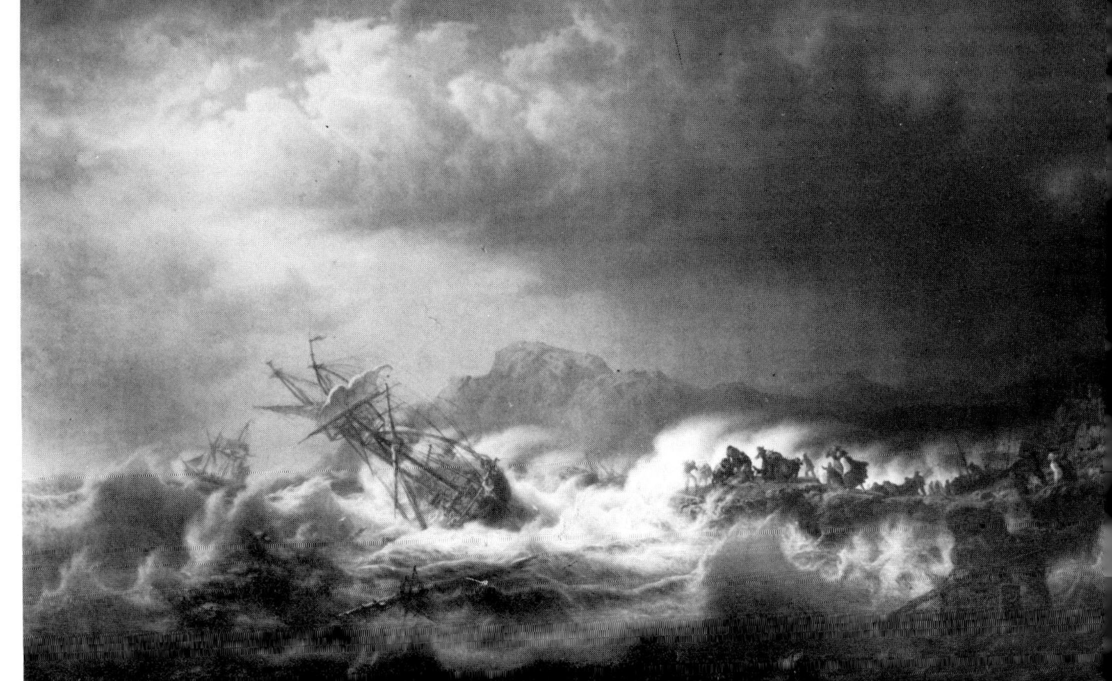

Plate 356. Simeon Markus Larsson, 1825-1864. "Shipwreck." Nationalmuseum, Stockholm.

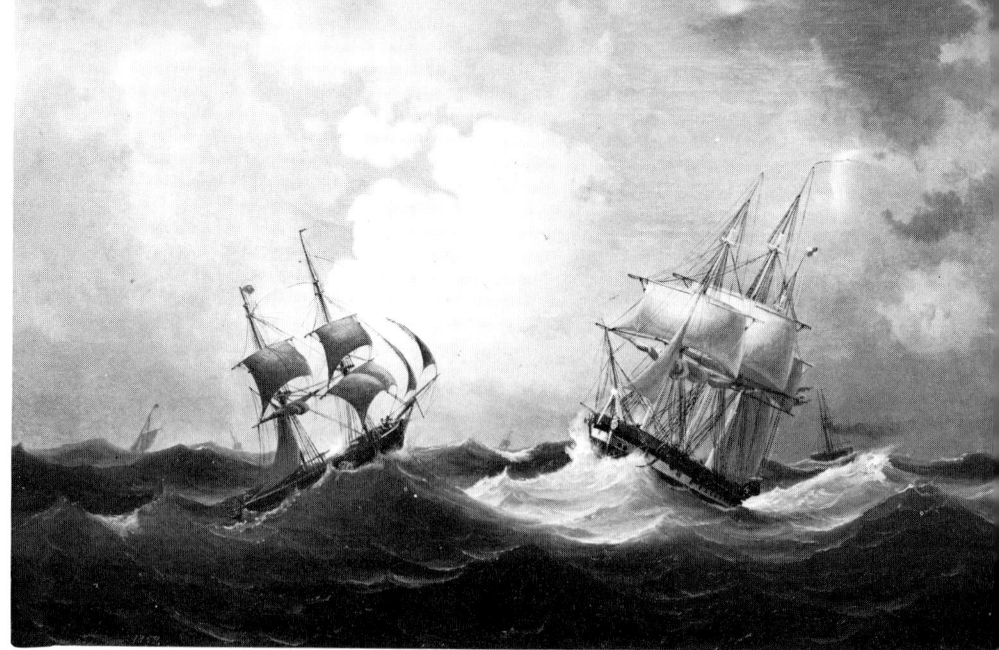

Plate 357. Simeon Markus Larsson, 1825-1864. "A frigate and a brig in a storm, dated 1852." *Another highly competent painting by this artist. His use of exaggerated light and shade is a technique he shared with the early masters.* Lansmuseum, Linkoping, Sweden.

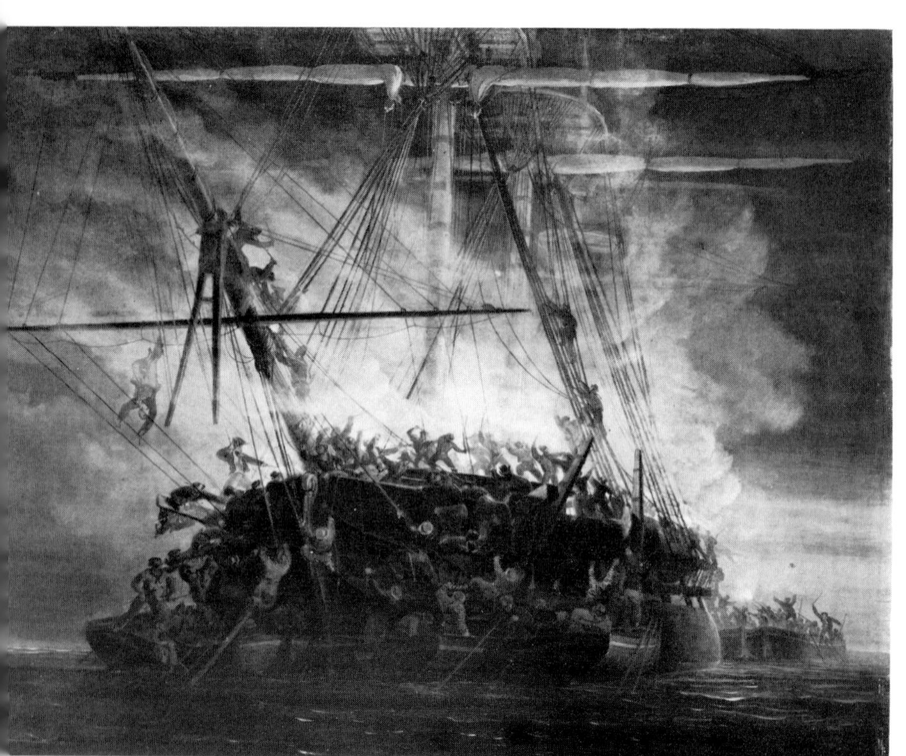

Plate 358. John Christian Schetky, 1778-1874. "The cutting out of the *Chevrette* in 1801." National Maritime Museum, Greenwich.

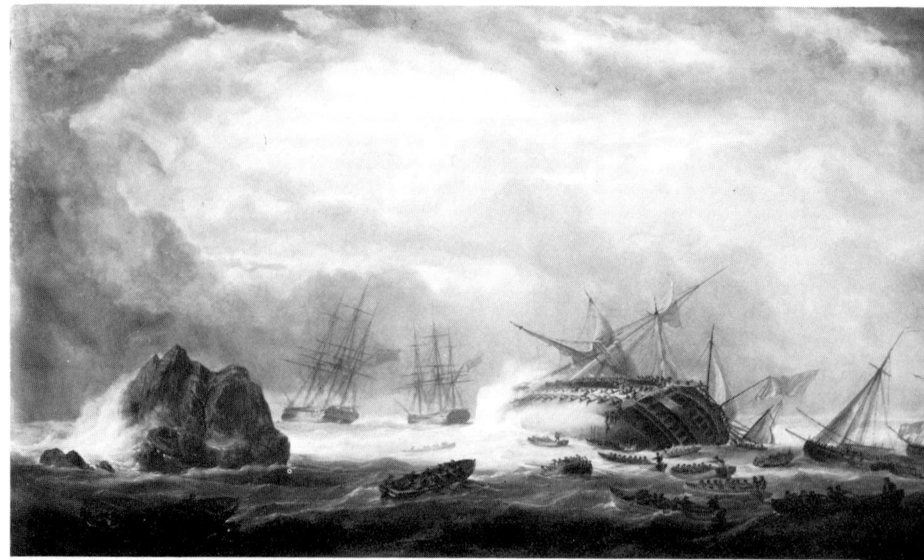

Plate 359. John Christian Schetky, 1778-1874. "The loss of the *Magnificent* on an uncharted rock off Brest in 1804." *The coppering on the underside of the boat has a gingerish quality which is also to be seen in the work of some of his students, R.B. Beechey, for example.* National Maritime Museum, Greenwich.

Plate 360. John Christian Schetky, 1778-1874. "H.M.S. *Columbine* and the Experimental Squadron, 1827." *The brig appears to be barque rigged, but at this time it was common for brigs serving as postal packets, and others on long voyages like Darwin's* Beagle, *to have a light mizzen-mast, stepped well aft. It carried no topsail (see Plate 382).* National Maritime Museum, Greenwich.

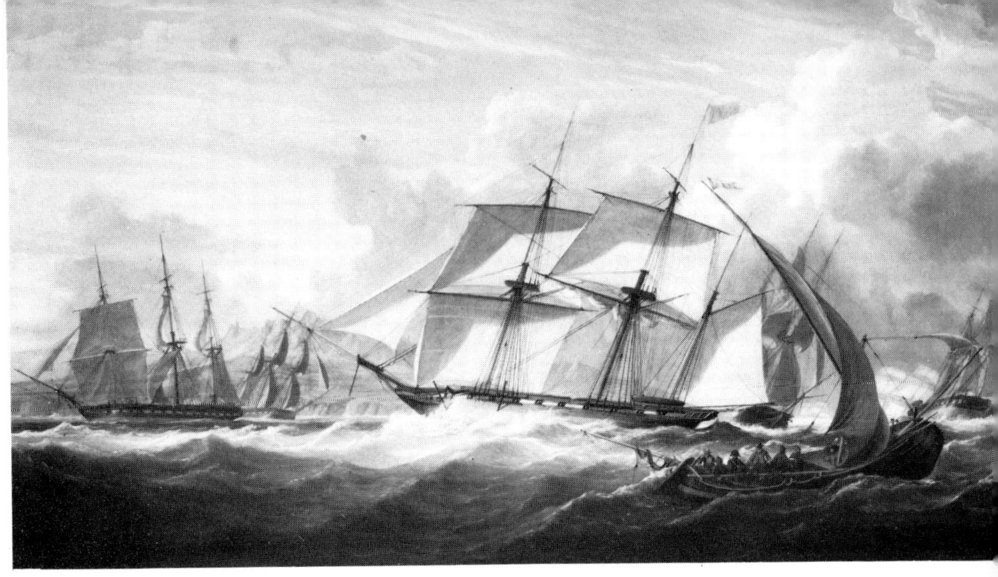

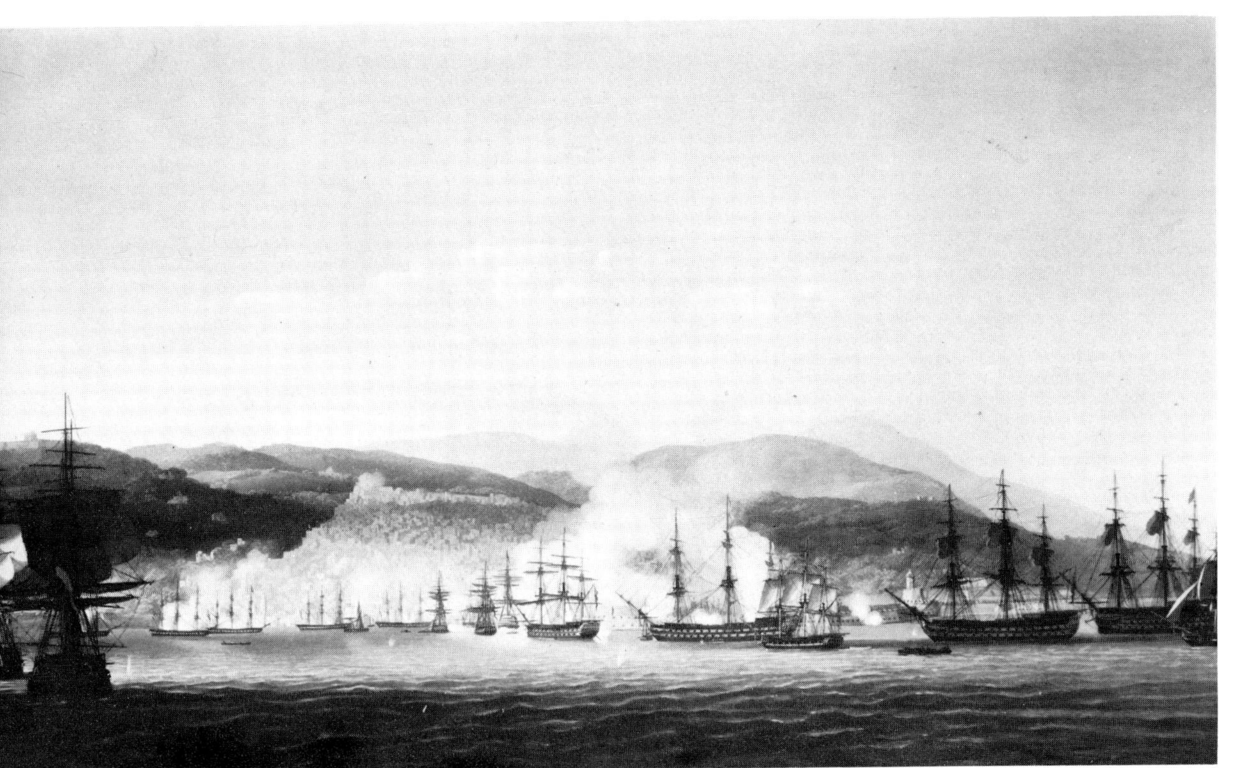

Plate 361. Henry Parke, c.1790-1845. "The bombardment of Algiers in 1816." *Painted more in the 18th century style by an amateur artist with architectural training.* Bonham's.

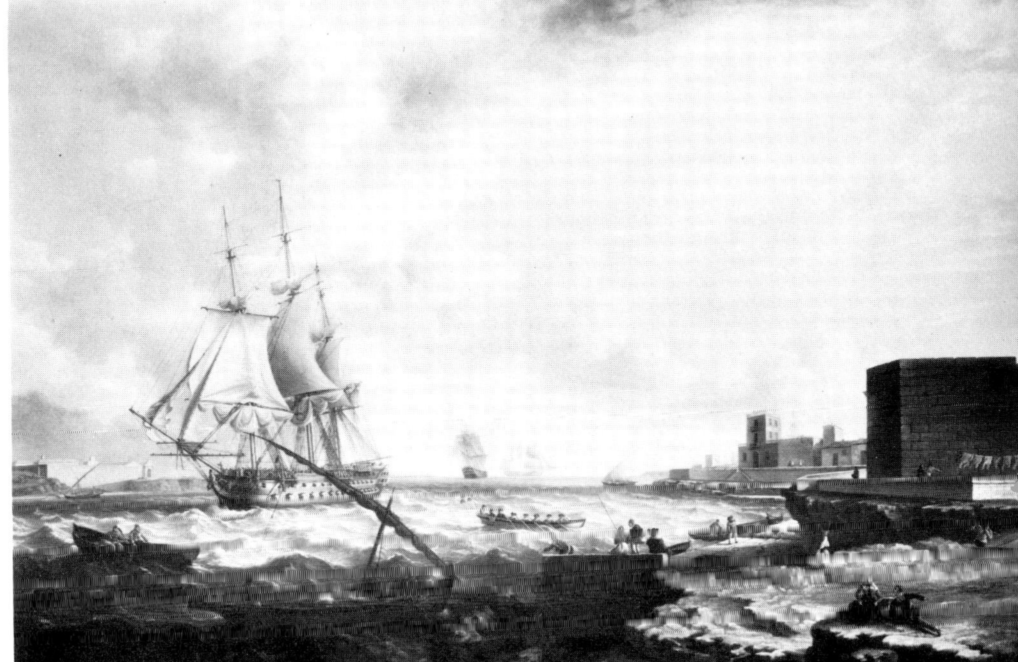

Plate 362. Charles Martin Powell, 1775-1824. "A British two-decker running into Port Mahon, 1820." *An ex-sailor who painted in the Dutch style.* National Maritime Museum, Greenwich.

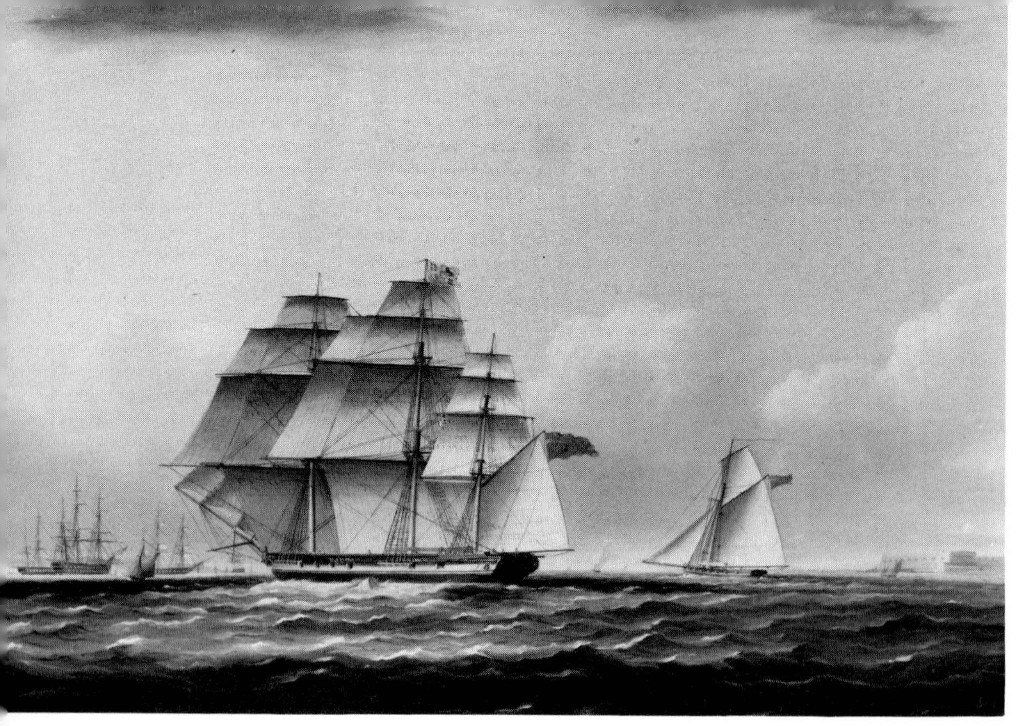

Plate 363. Henry Moses, c.1782-1870. "The royal yacht *Royal Sovereign* with the Duchess of Clarence aboard, sailing out to the Russian squadron at Spithead in 1827." *The* Royal Sovereign *is now painted much more plainly than previously, quite different from the painting of 1806 by J.T. Serres (see Plate 265).* National Maritime Museum, Greenwich.

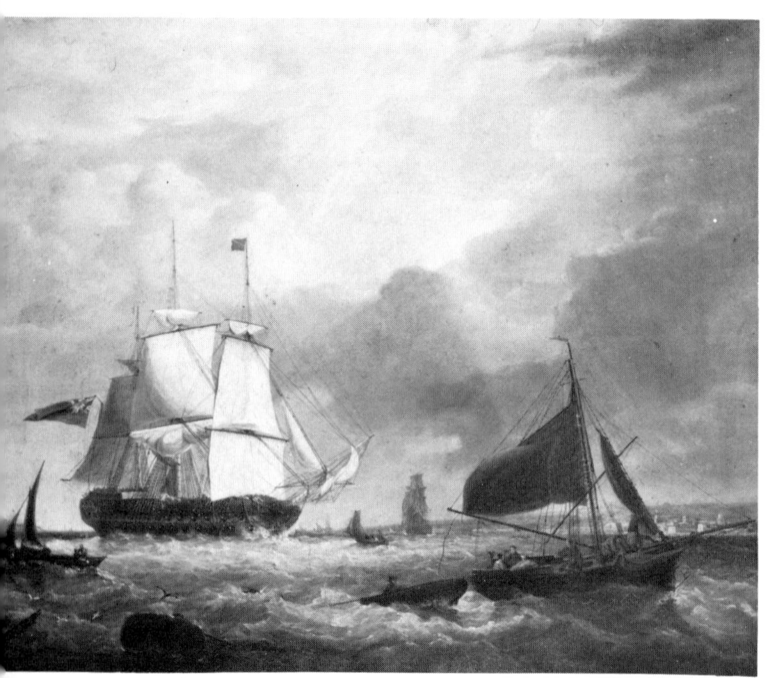

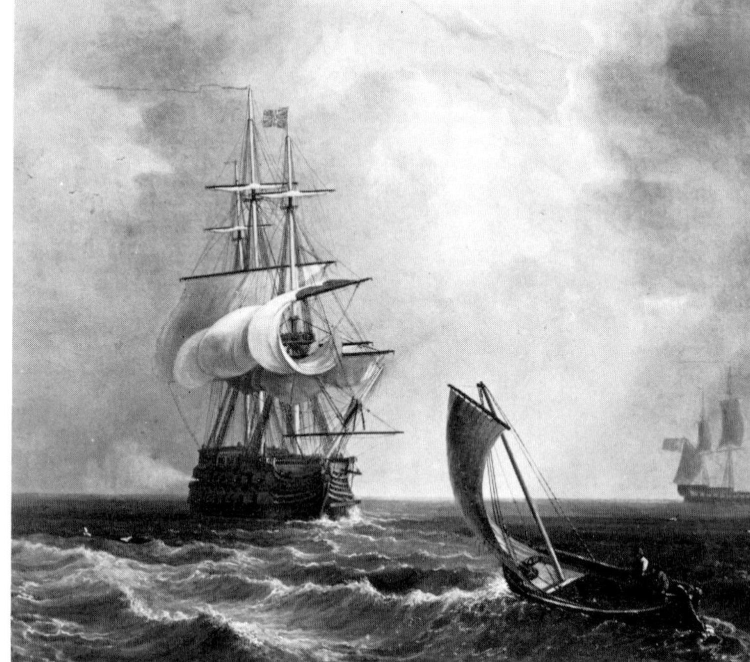

Plate 364 *(above)*. **George Webster, fl.1797-1832.** "A two-decker hove to." *Typical well-filled, action-packed canvas.* Sotheby's.

Plate 365 *(above right)*. **Joseph F. Ellis, c.1783-1848.** "A two-decker dropping anchor and saluting, with a lugger under her bow." *Very much like the work of Sempel, an artist of the mid-19th century.* Sotheby's.

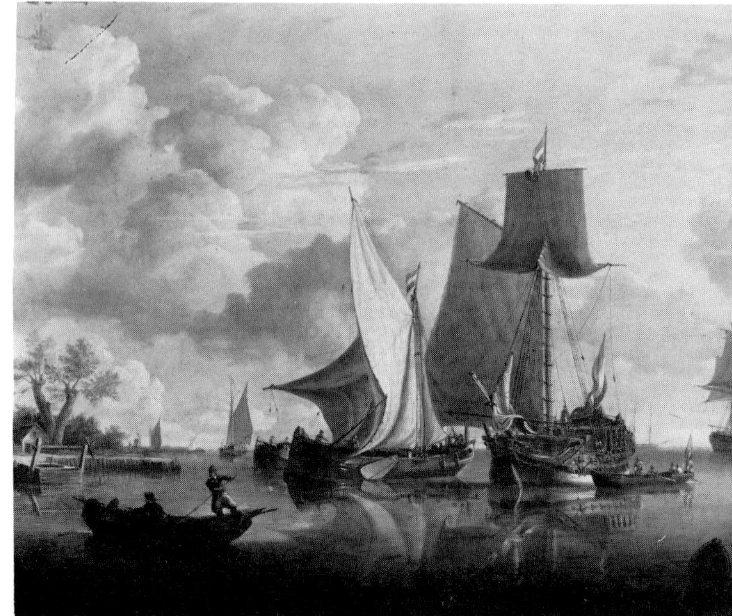

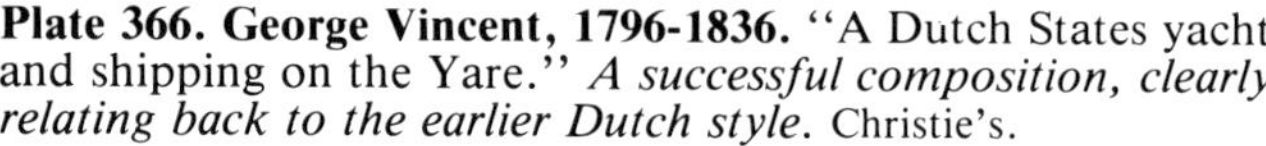

Plate 366. George Vincent, 1796-1836. "A Dutch States yacht and shipping on the Yare." *A successful composition, clearly relating back to the earlier Dutch style.* Christie's.

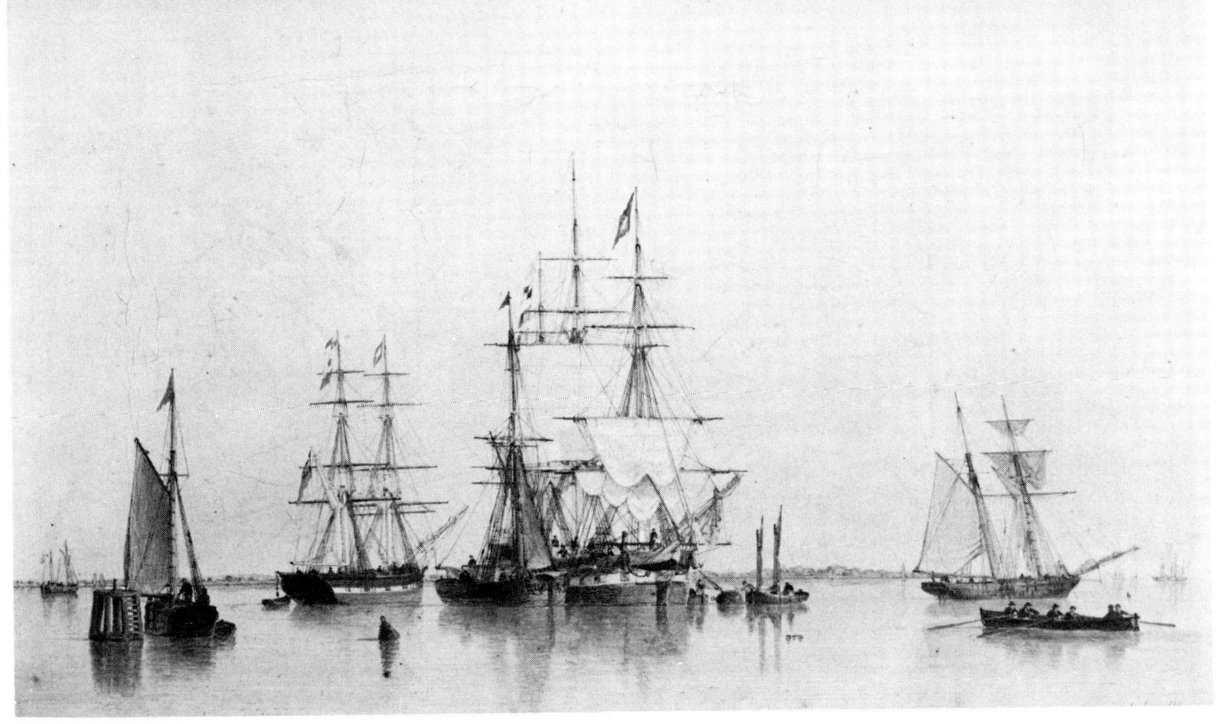

Plate 367. John Ward, 1798-1849. "Ships becalmed in the Humber Estuary." *Ward was the leader of the Hull School and this painting is well drawn and finished.* Christie's.

Plate 368. John Ward, 1798-1849. "The Hull whaler *Isabella* in Baffin Bay." *A good example of a finely composed whaling subject.* Kendall Whaling Museum, Mass.

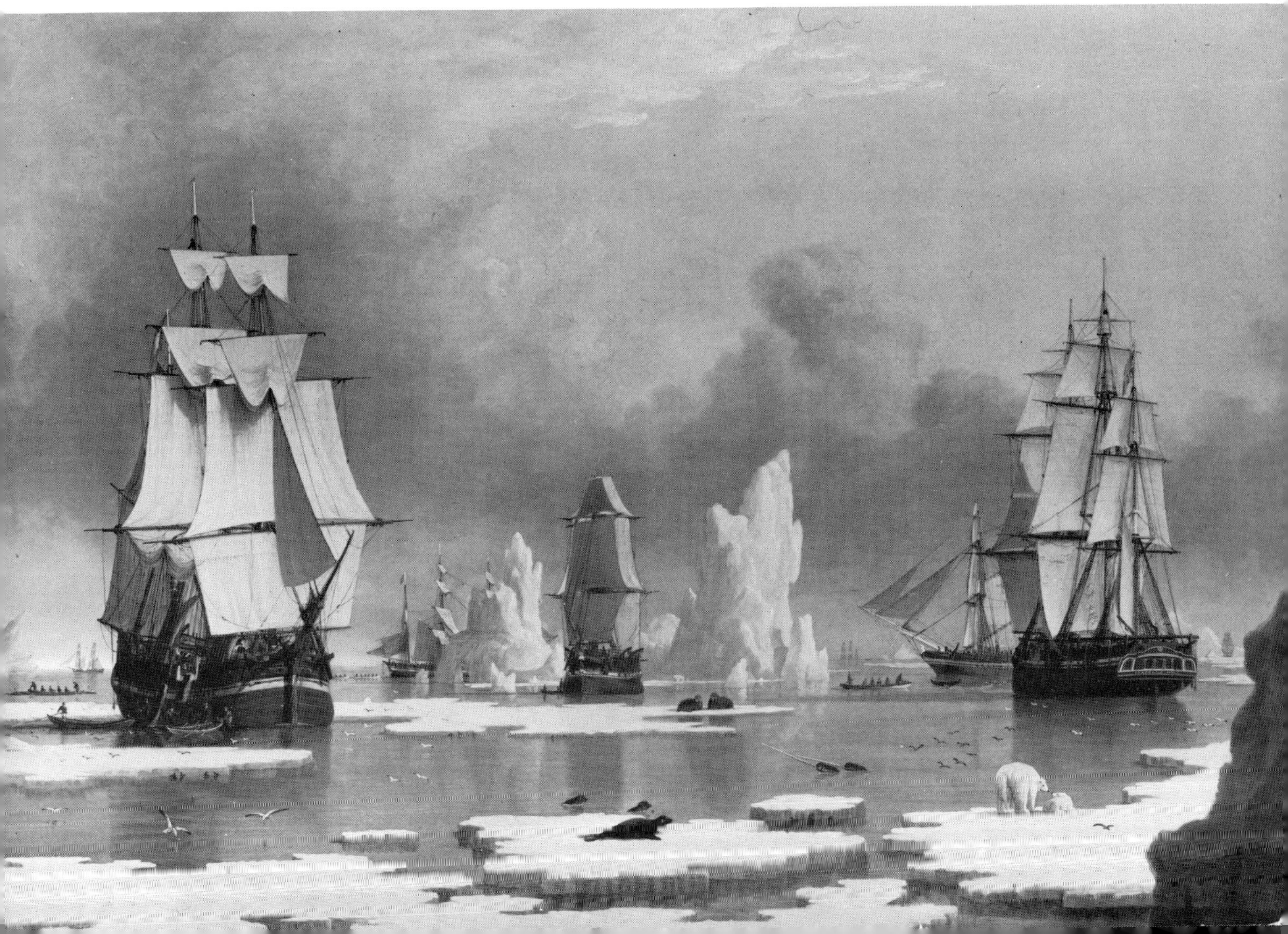

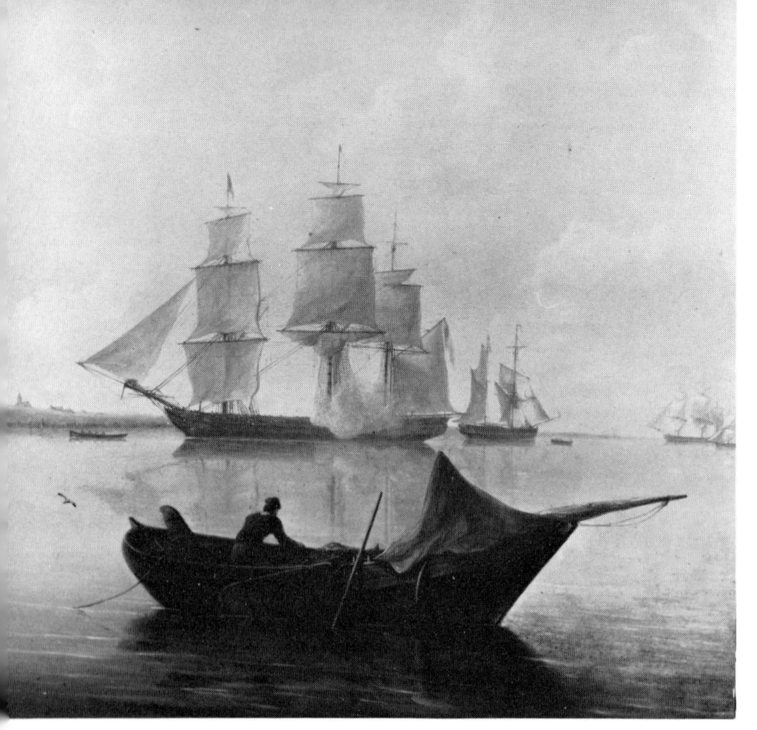

Plate 369. Martinus Schouman, 1770-1838. "A fishing boat and beyond a Dutch naval sloop becalmed close inshore and firing a salute, about 1820." Glasgow Art Gallery.

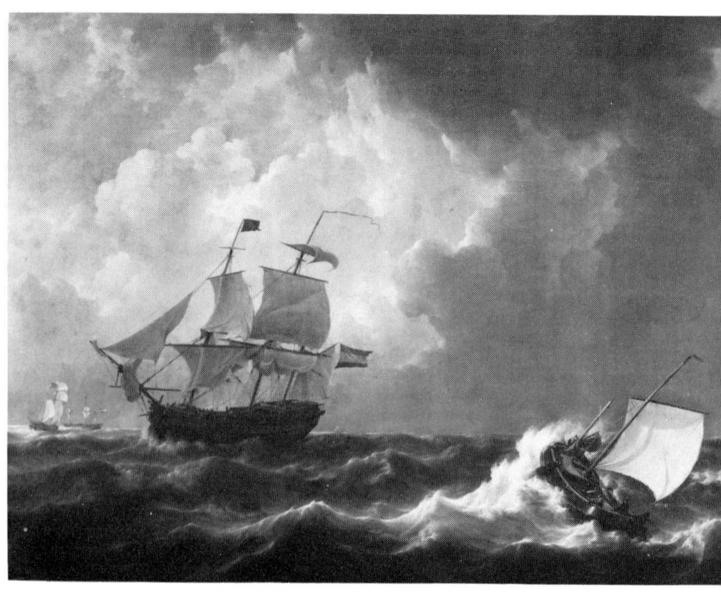

Plate 370. Johannes Christiaan Schotel, 1787-1838. "A Dutch ship of the line and coastal craft in a rough sea." *A return to painting in the great Dutch manner of the 17th century, highly accomplished and with a strong use of light.* Rijksmuseum, Amsterdam.

Plate 371. Johannes Christiaan Schotel, 1787-1838. "Bombardment of Algiers in 1816." Scheepvaart Museum, Amsterdam.

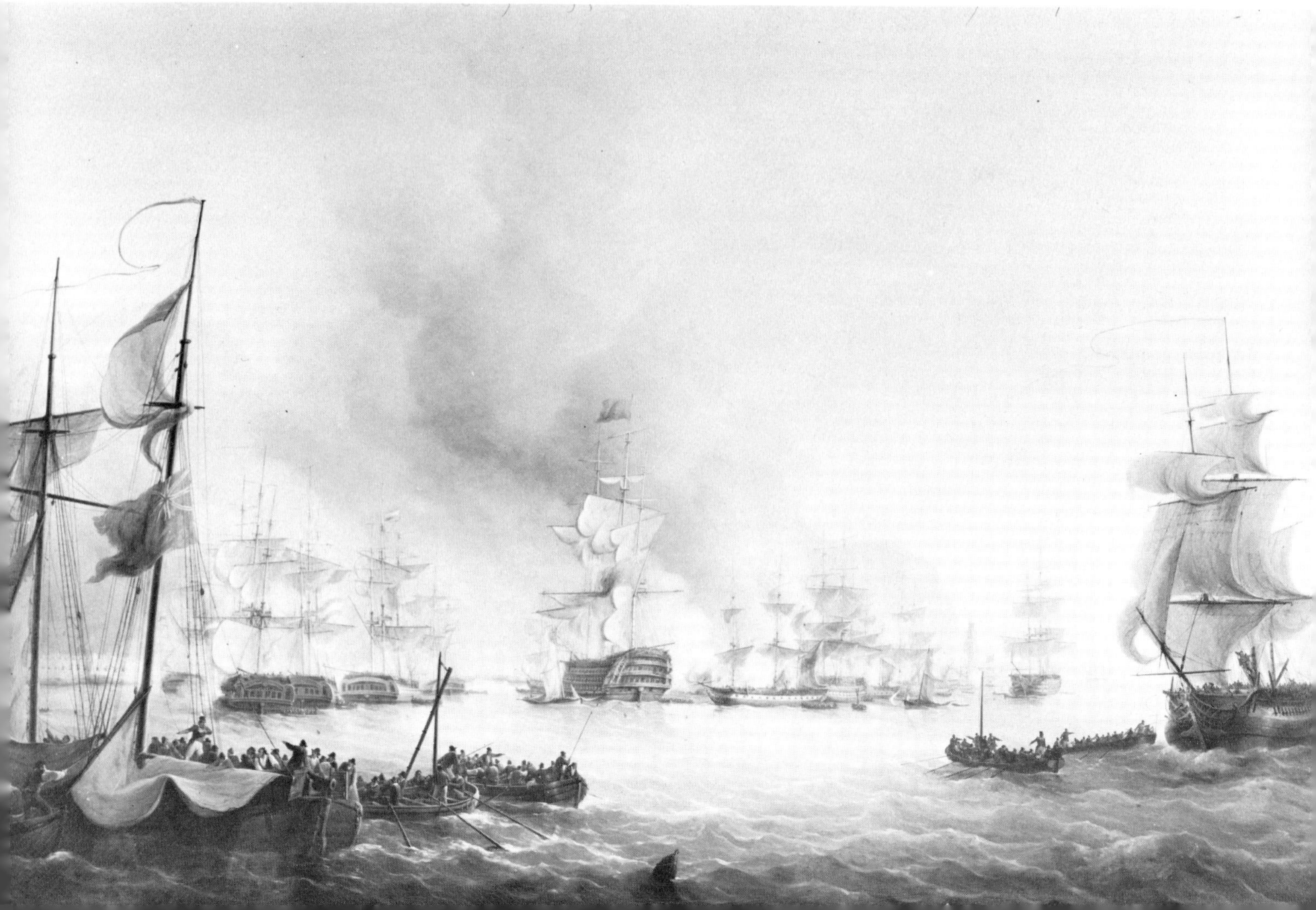

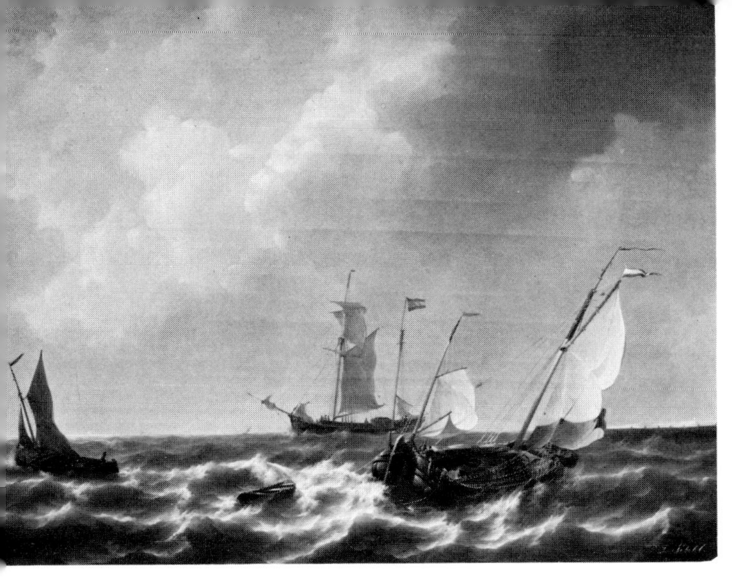

Plate 372. Petrus Johannes Schotel, 1808-1865. "A rough sea off Schouwen Island." *The son followed very much in his father's manner as comparison between this and Plate 370 clearly shows.* Rijksmuseum, Amsterdam.

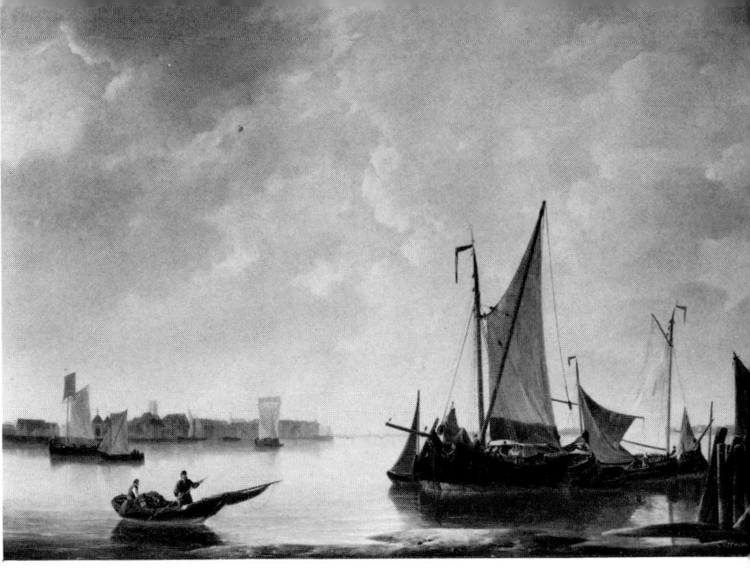

Plate 373. Christiaan Lodewijk Willem Dreibholz, 1799-1874. "A view of Dordrecht seen from Papendrecht." *Not a well-known artist, but clearly in the mainstream of Dutch marine revivals.* Rijksmuseum, Amsterdam.

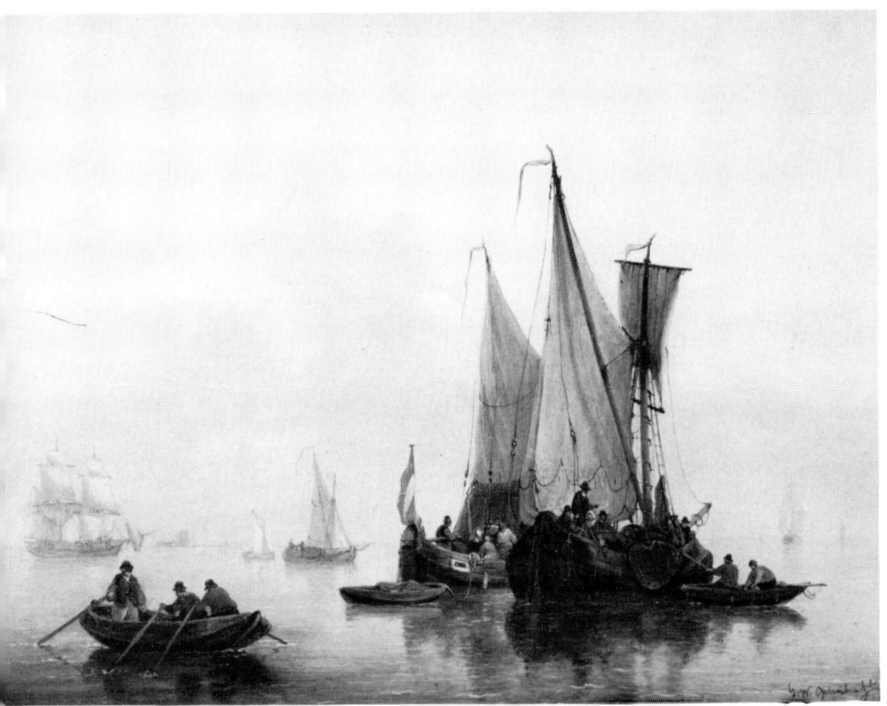

Plate 374. George Willem Opdenhoff, 1807-1873. "Two wijdschips and other Dutch coastal craft." *Looking backward to the successful period of Dutch painting — reminiscent of Capelle. Painters of this late date usually sign their paintings.* Lansmuseum, Linkoping, Sweden.

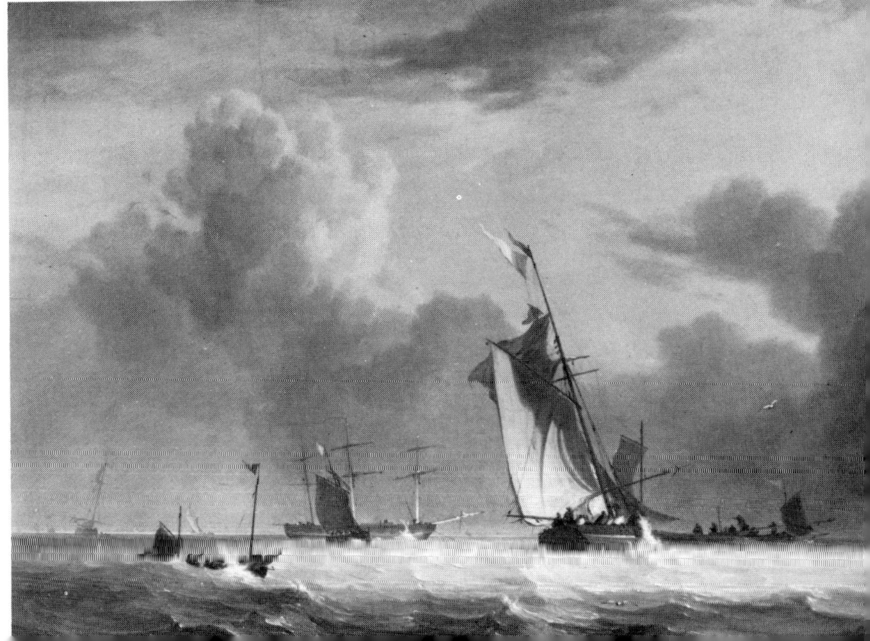

Plate 375. Joseph Stannard, 1797-1830. "Coastal craft in a stiff breeze." *A sea painter of good quality who created an atmosphere of drama in his works.* Sotheby's.

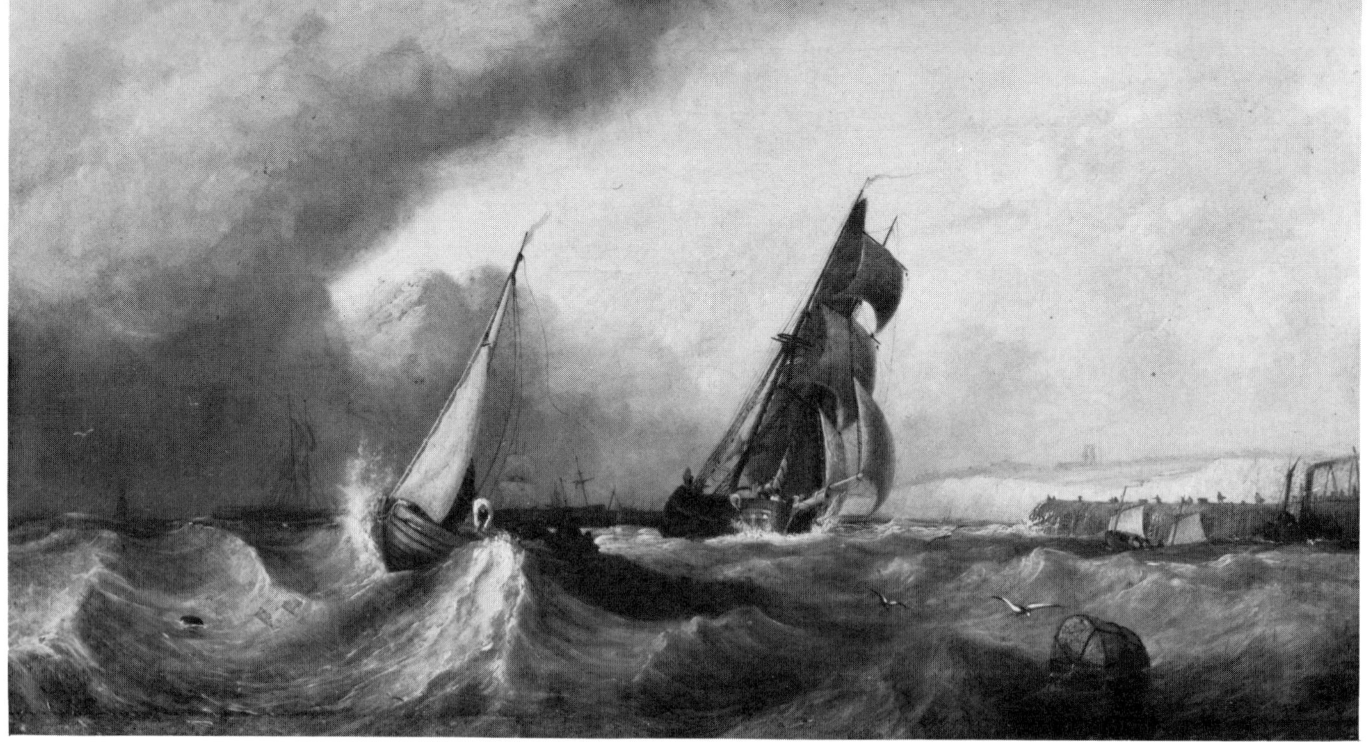

Plate 376. Alfred Stannard, 1806-1889. "Shipping off the coast of Kent." *Another gifted amateur painter, though not quite as talented as his brother (see previous Plate).* Christie's.

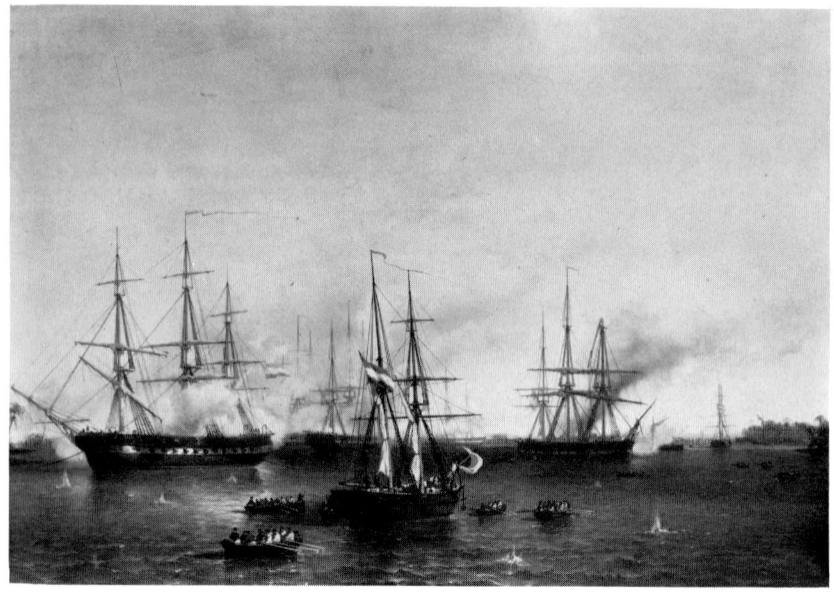

Plate 377. Johan Hendrik Louis Meijer, 1809-1866. "The capture of Palembang." *A very well painted battle scene with effective light on the gun ports in the ship on the left.* Rijksmuseum, Amsterdam.

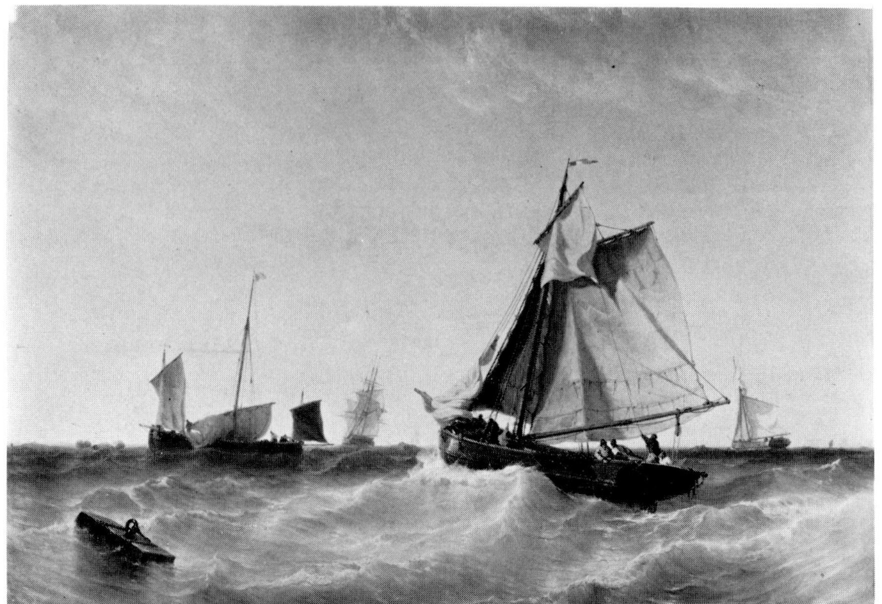

Plate 378. Johan Hendrik Louis Meijer, 1809-1866. "Dutch fishing boats at sea, dated 1829." Rijksmuseum, Amsterdam.

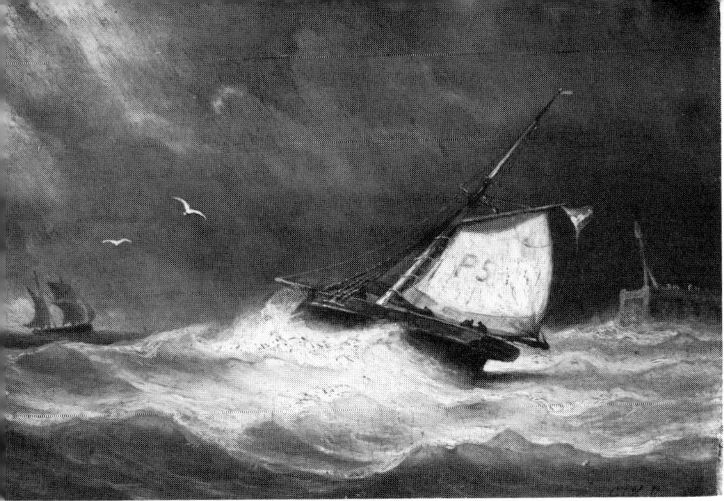

Plate 379. Georges Johannes Hoffman, 1833-1873. "A fishing vessel in a rough sea." *A second flight painter whose work is not always highly finished, using heavy applications of paint.* Rijksmuseum, Amsterdam.

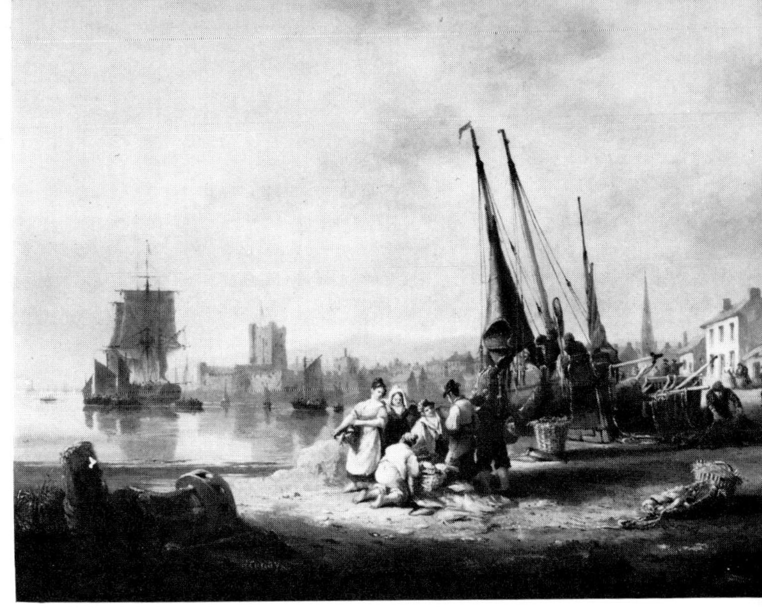

Plate 380. Nicholas Condy, the Elder, 1799-1857. "Carrickfergus about 1830." *This picture is typical of the type of work undertaken by the elder Condy, figures on the seashore, liquid calms, etc.* Christie's.

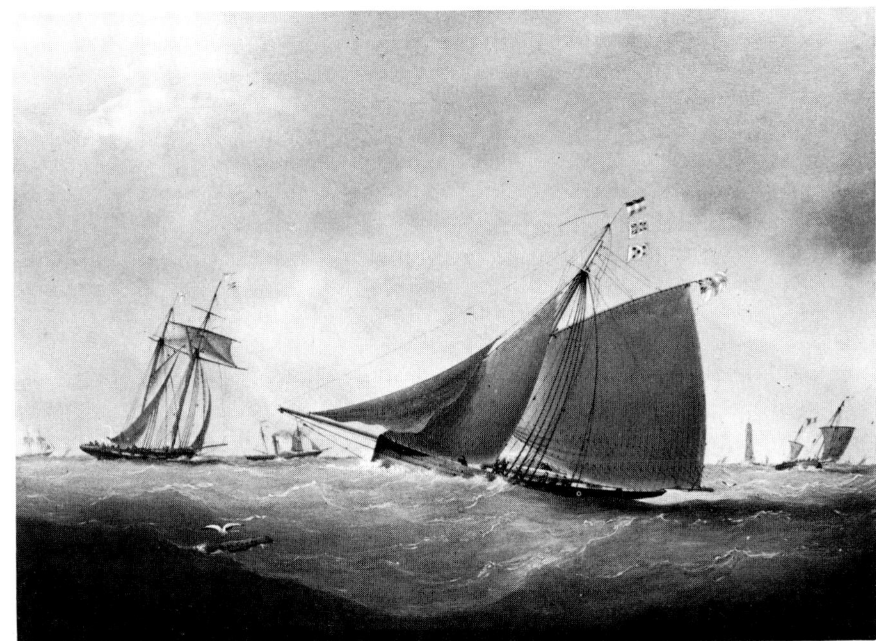

Plate 381. Nicholas Matthew Condy, the Younger, 1818-1851. "A cutter of the Royal Yacht Squadron off Eddystone lighthouse about 1840." *Again, this is typical of the son who paints in a quite distinct style from that of his father and was more interested in shipping as a subject than in figure painting.* Sotheby's.

Plate 382. Nicholas Matthew Condy, the Younger, 1818-1851. "The Post Office packet *Sheldrake* off Falmouth." *Another example of the younger Condy's work showing a typical coastal scene. Although he was working for a shorter time than his father he was more prolific.* National Maritime Museum, Greenwich.

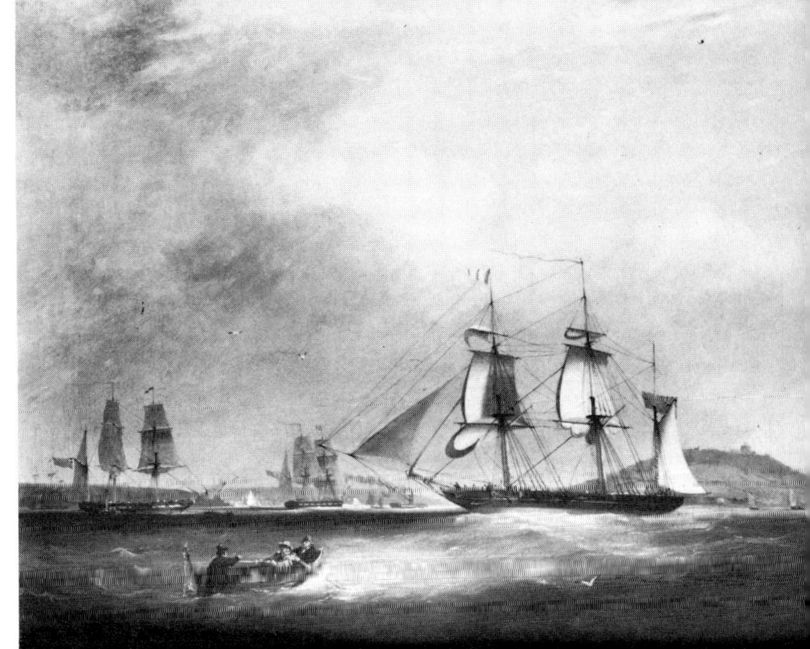

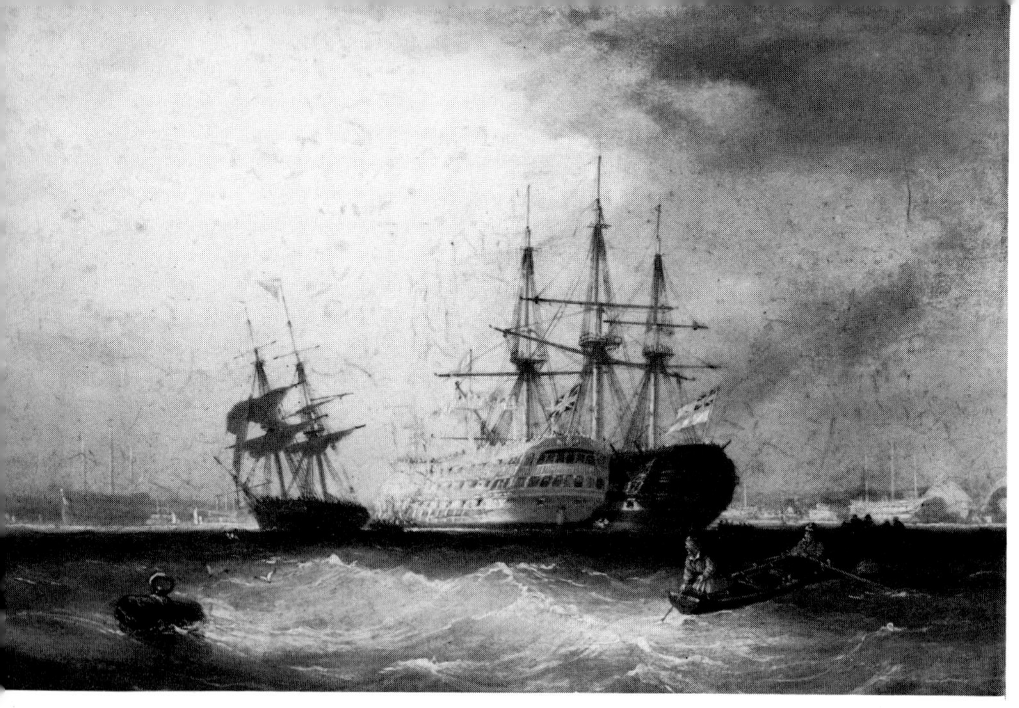

Plate 383. Nicholas Matthew Condy, the Younger, 1818-1851. "Ships off Devonport." *Presumably a fitting out scene, beside a hulk. The imperfections on the picture result from the fact that it is painted on cardboard.* National Maritime Museum, Greenwich.

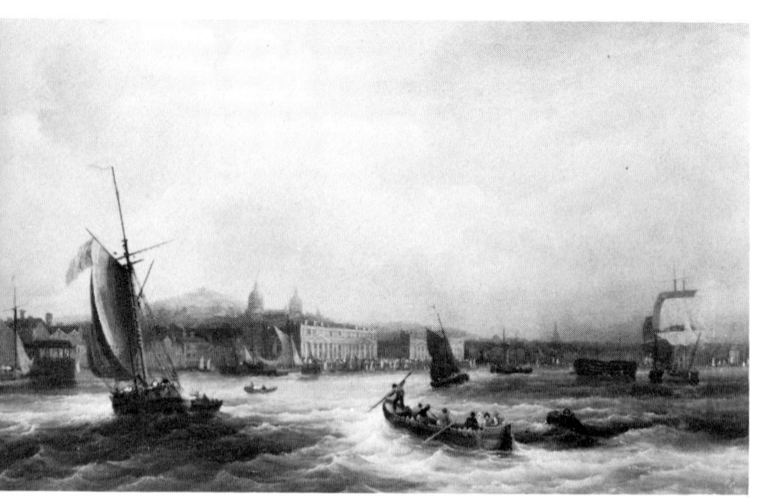

Plate 384. Frederick Calvert, fl.1815-1844. "Greenwich Reach." *A view of Greenwich with Greenwich Hospital in the centre background.* Christie's.

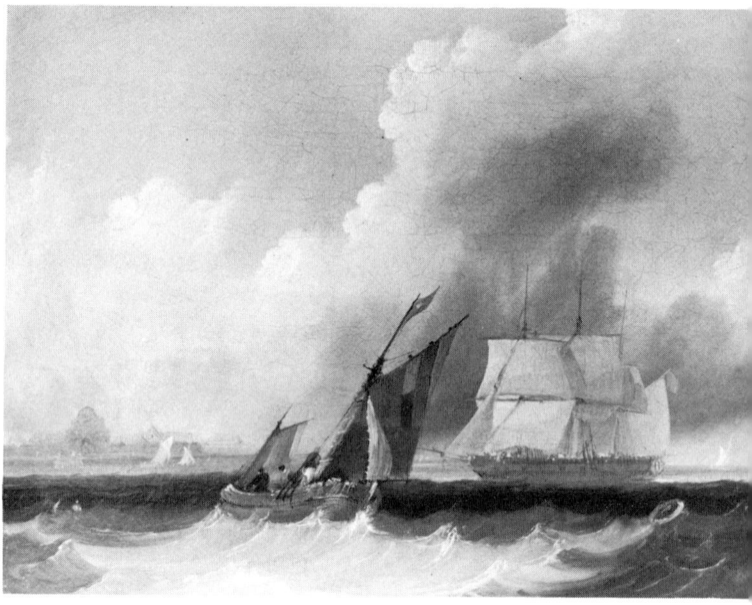

Plate 385. Joseph Molloy, 1798-1877. "Shipping off Tilbury Fort." Ulster Museum, Belfast.

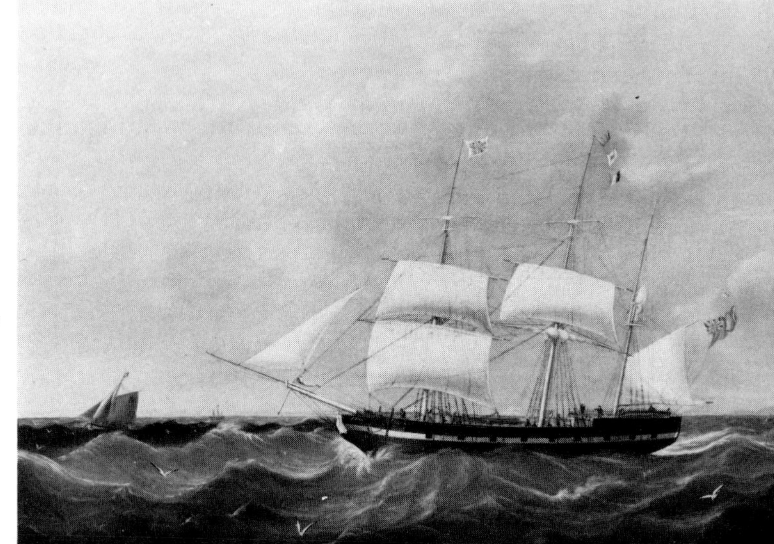

Plate 386. Joseph Heard, 1799-1859. "The barque *Mary.*" National Maritime Museum, Greenwich.

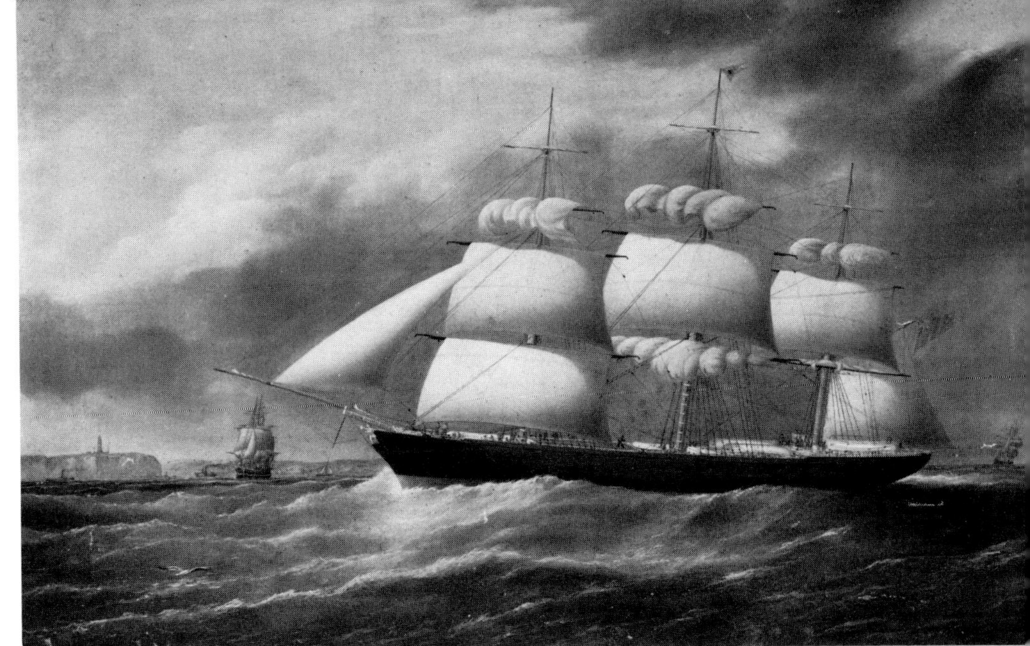

Plate 387. R. Bell, fl.1845. "The ship *Gladiator*." National Maritime Museum, Greenwich.

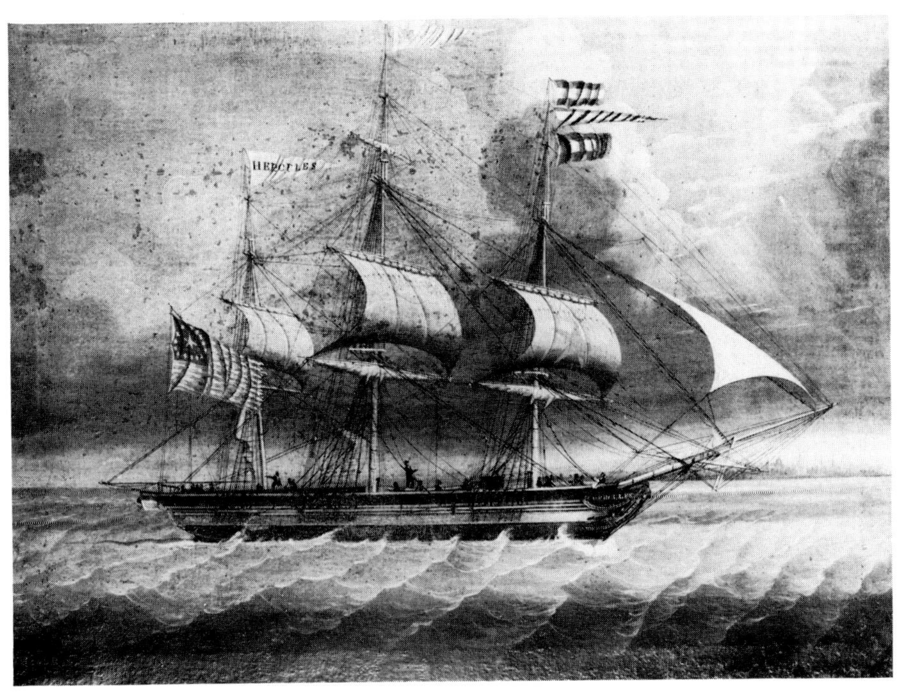

Plate 388. Miles Walters, 1774-1849. "The American ship *Hercules,* built 1816." *This oil painting is attributed.* Peabody Museum of Salem.

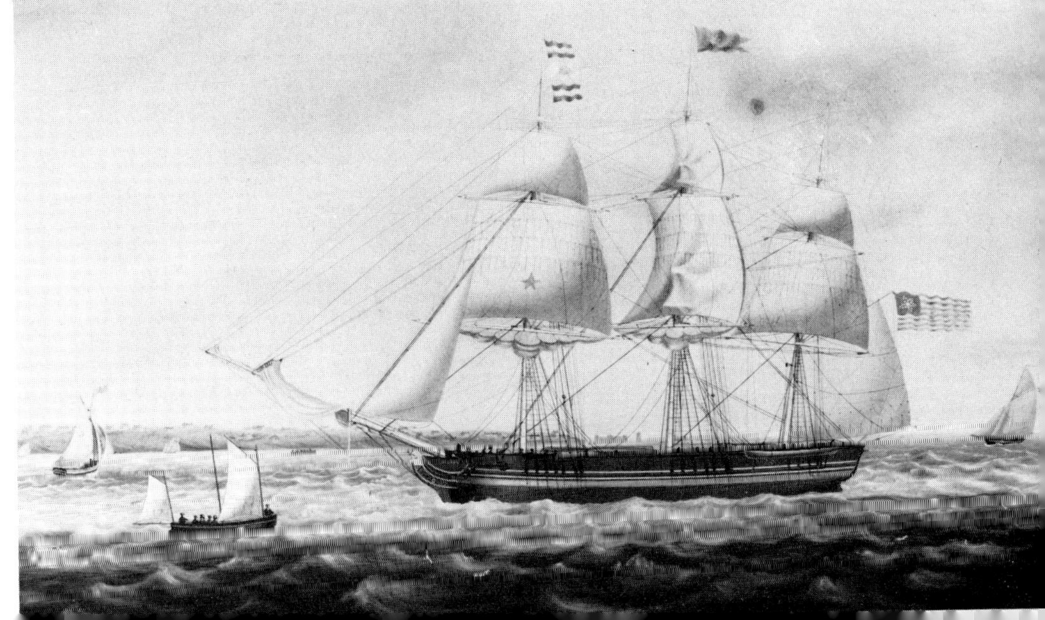

Plate 389. Miles, 1774-1849, and Samuel Walters, 1811-1882. "The Red Star Line packet ship *Birmingham* picking up a pilot at the entrance to the Mersey, 1830." Peabody Museum of Salem.

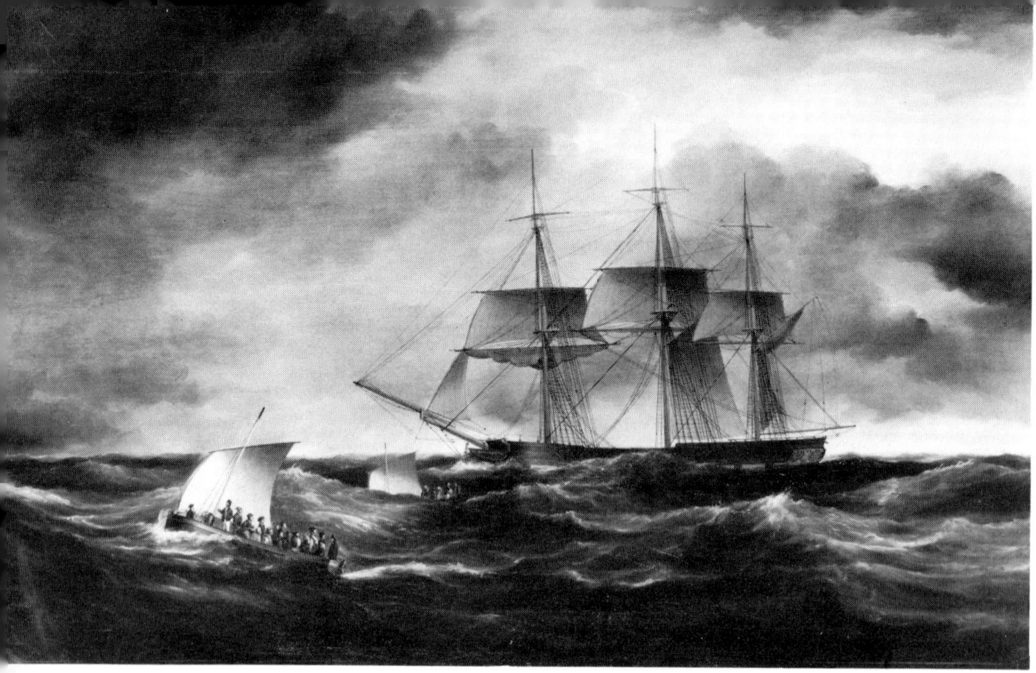

Plate 390. Miles, 1774-1849, and Samuel Walters, 1811-1882. "The loss of the *Dorothy,* dated 1833." Private collection.

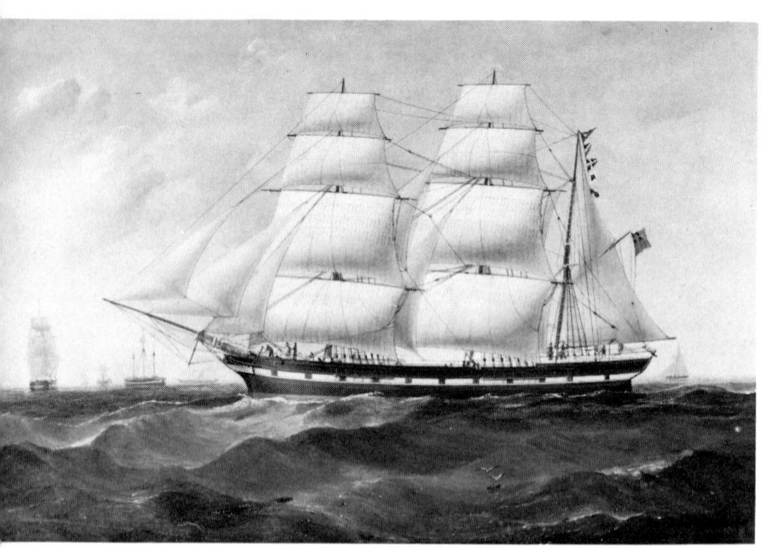

Plate 391. Samuel Walters, 1811-1882. "The barque *British Monarch.*" National Maritime Museum, Greenwich.

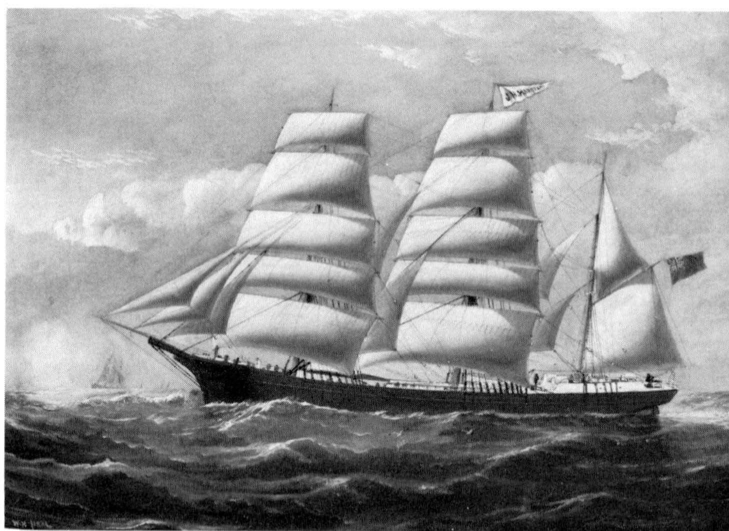

Plate 392. William Howard Yorke, fl.1858-aft.1913. "The barque *J.H. Marsters.*" National Maritime Museum, Greenwich.

Plate 393. Johannes Hermanus Koekkoek, 1778-1851. "A tjalk under sail, dated 1820." *A tjalk is a small, coastal cargo boat, similar to a barge. Of the Koekkoek family of painters, J.H. Koekkoek, the father and grandfather, was the most gifted.* Scheepvaart Museum, Amsterdam.

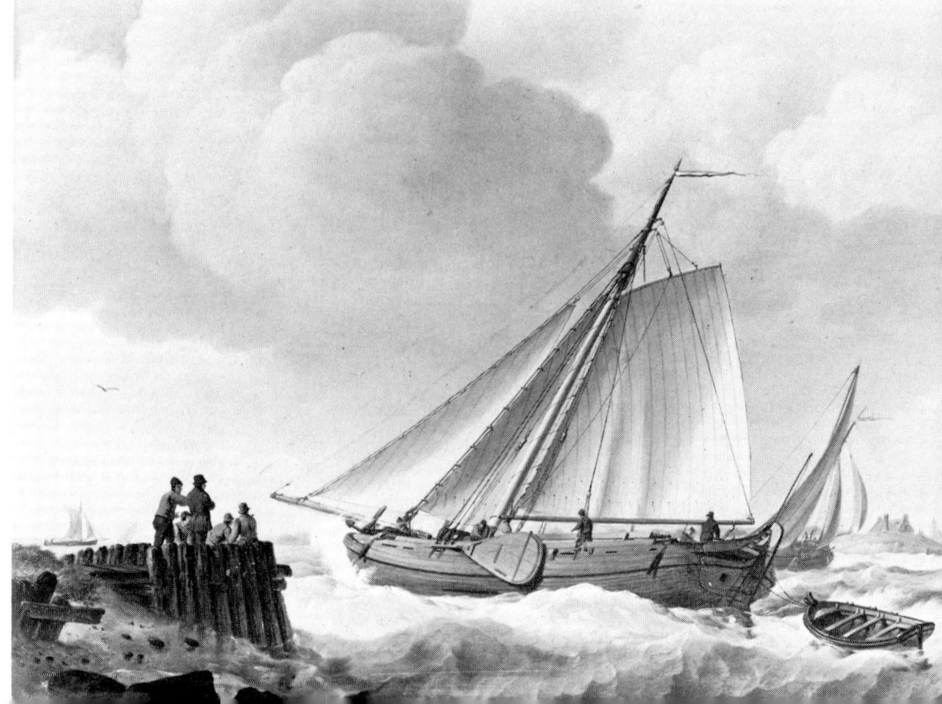

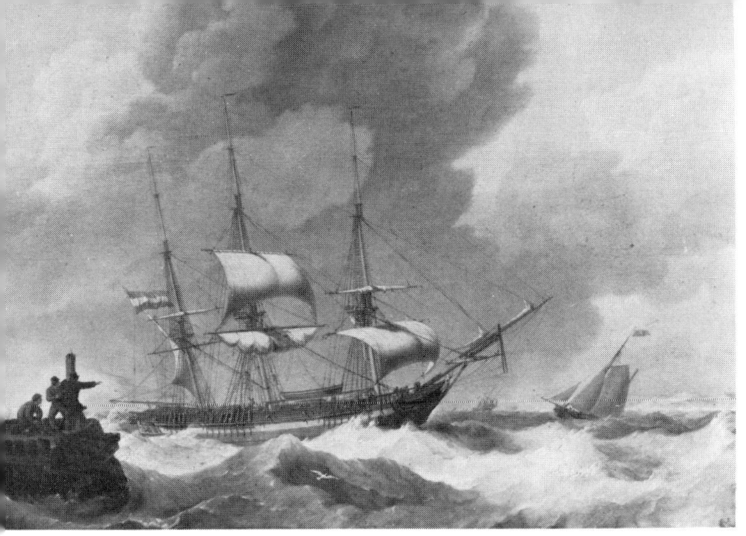

Plate 394. Johannes Hermanus Koekkoek, 1778-1851. "A Dutch ship in a gale off a jetty, dated 1821." Christie's.

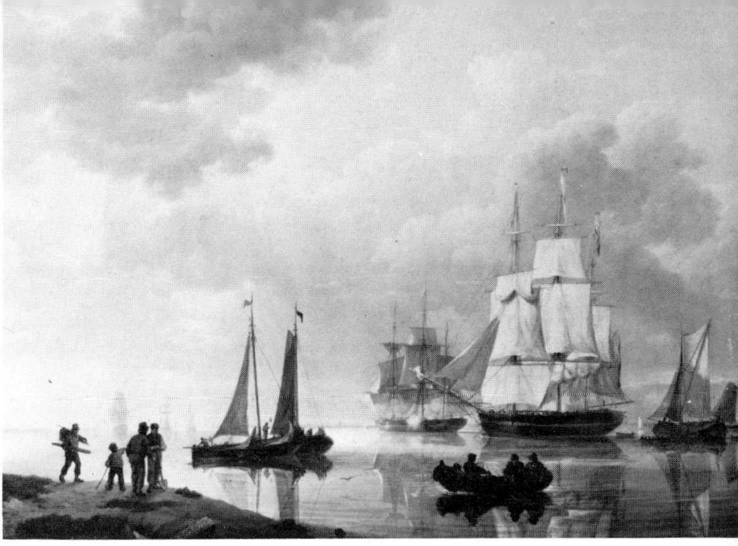

Plate 395. Johannes Hermanus Koekkoek, 1778-1851. "Shipping off shore in a calm, dated 1828." Christie's.

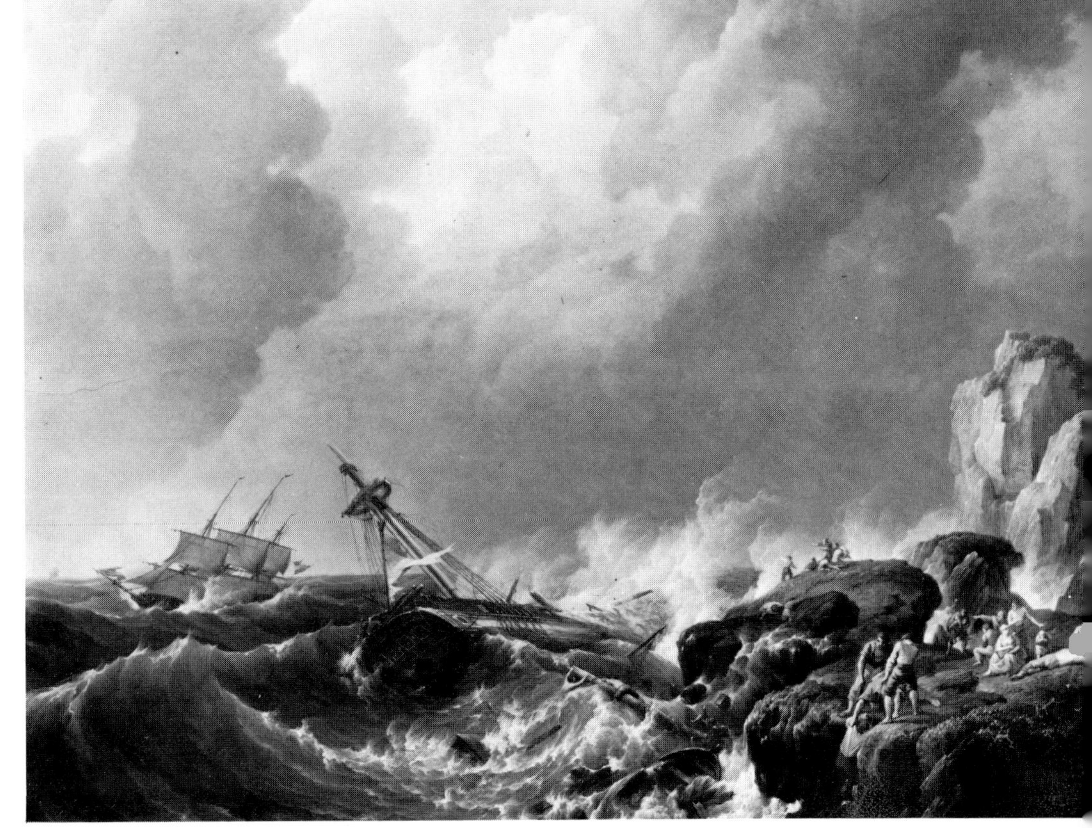

Plate 396. Johannes Hermanus Koekkoek, 1778-1851. "Shipwreck, 1834." Christie's.

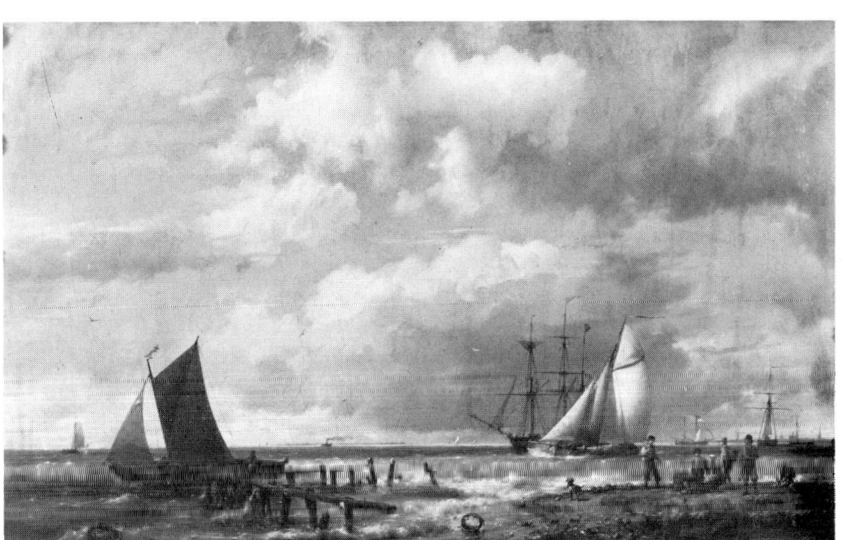

Plate 397. Hermanus Koekkoek, Senior, 1815-1882. "Shipping from the shore, dated 1862." Christie's.

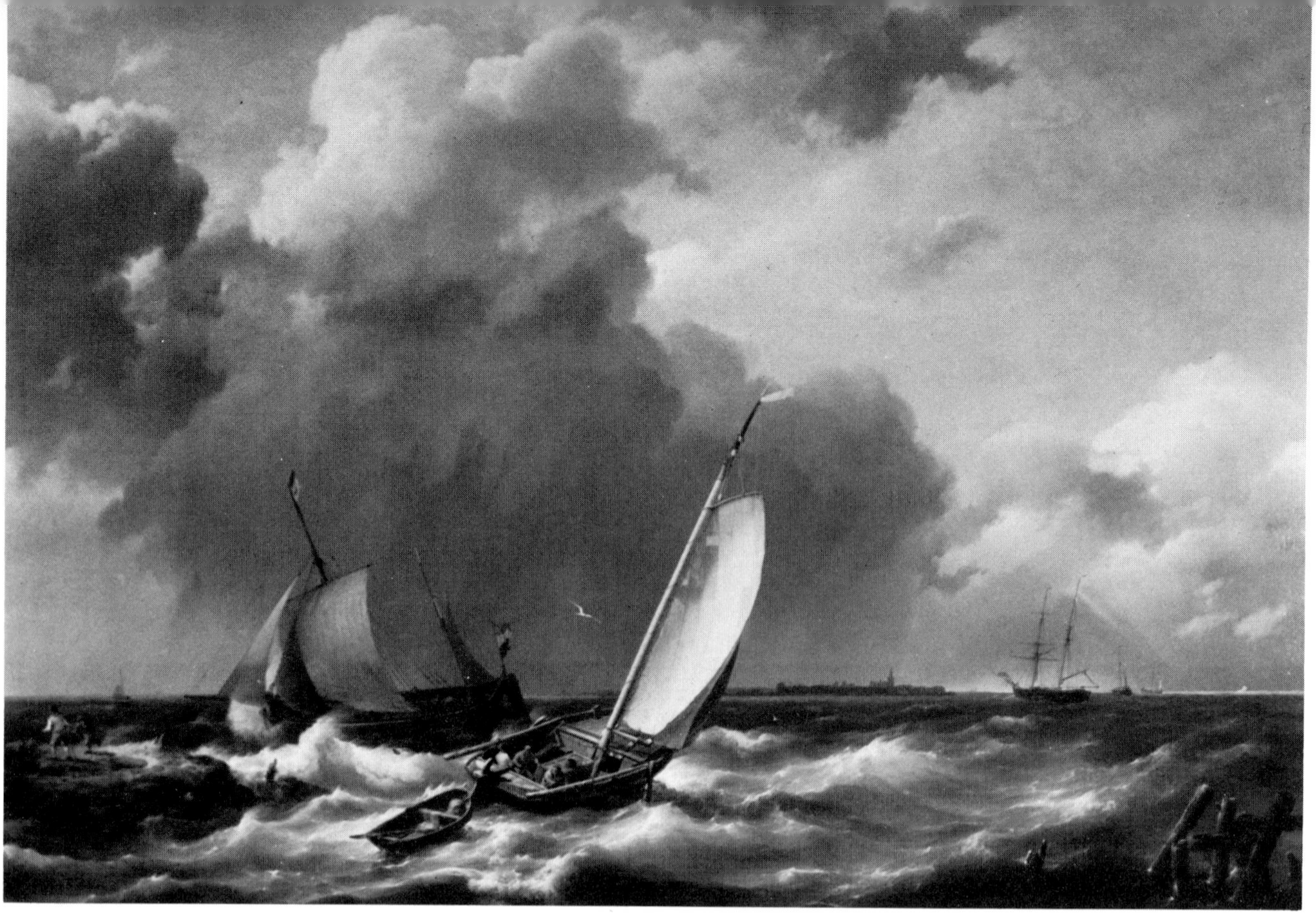

Plate 398. Hermanus Koekkoek, Senior, 1815-1882. "A botter and a hooker in a rough sea off the Dutch coast." *The botter, a high bowed fishing boat that worked in the Zuider Zee, is in the foreground.* Prins Hendrik Museum, Rotterdam (on loan from the Boymans van Beuningen Museum).

Plate 399. William John Huggins, 1781-1845. "King George IV aboard the *Lightning,* the first Post Office steam packet to ply to Dublin, 1821." *In 1821 King George IV made a state visit to Dublin. Strong westerly winds in the Irish Sea held up the sailing yacht* Royal George, *so the King transferred to the steam packet* Lightning *off Holyhead, and arrived in Dublin unannounced early the following morning.* National Maritime Museum, Greenwich.

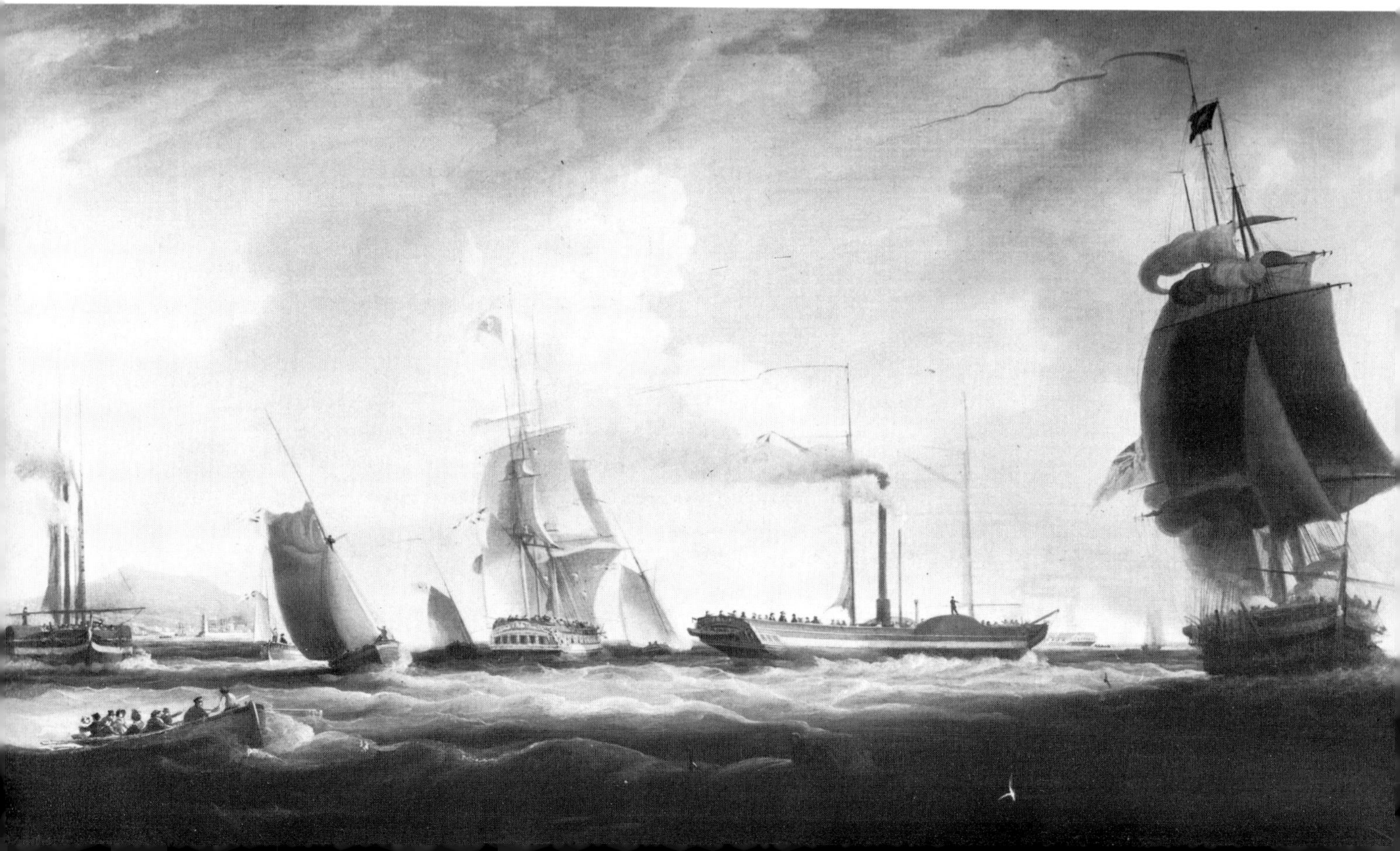

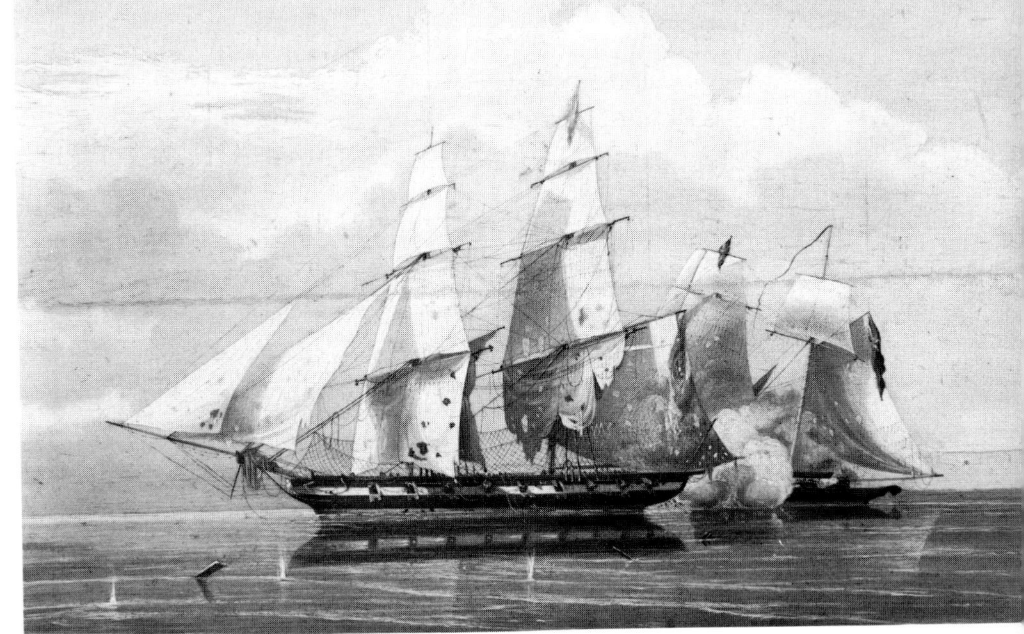

Plate 400. William John Huggins, 1781-1845. "The capture of the slaver *Formidable* by H.M. schooner *Buzzard* in 1834." *Although painted in the 19th century it has a distinct feel of the 18th century.* National Maritime Museum, Greenwich.

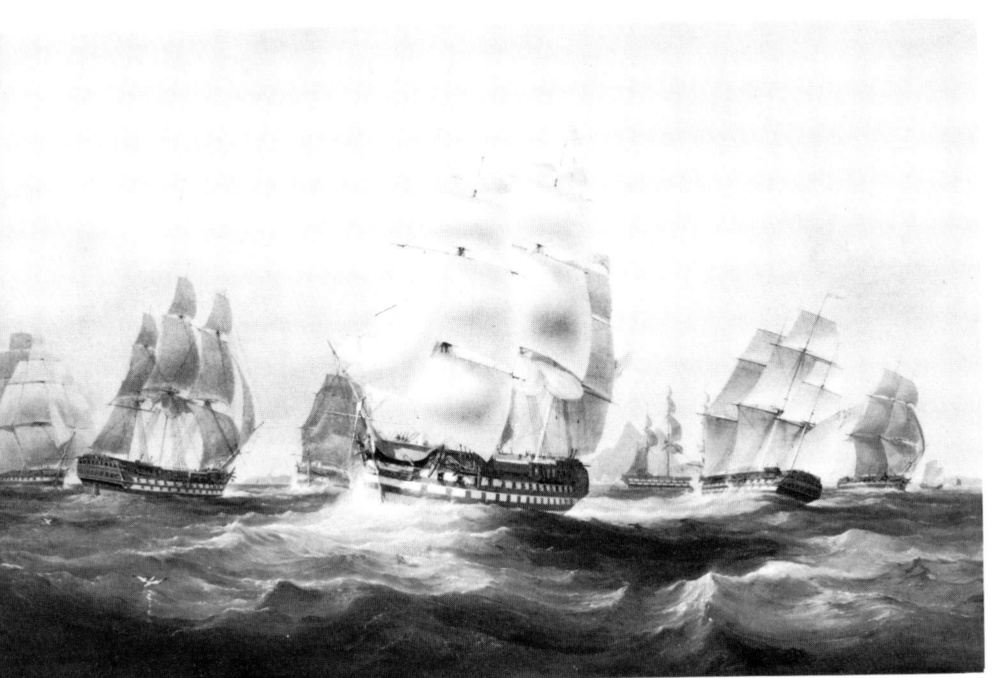

Plate 401. William John Huggins, 1781-1845, and Edward Duncan, 1803-1882. "East Indiamen off the China coast." *An important example of the joint work of these artists, the water probably painted by Duncan. These vessels, the largest merchant craft in the world, technically have a frigate connotation, but with an extra coach (upper layer of stern galleries) attachment to the stern to provide more accommodation. This pertained until 1837 when the new Blackwall frigates were introduced, the coach disappeared and the quarter-deck was extended. The* Seringapatam *was the first of the new craft. The ships' names are recorded on the painting. From left to right:* Ceres, Lowther Castle, Glatton, Winchelsea, Marquis of Ely, Princess Amelia, Castle Huntley. Ministry of Defence (on loan to the National Maritime Museum, Greenwich).

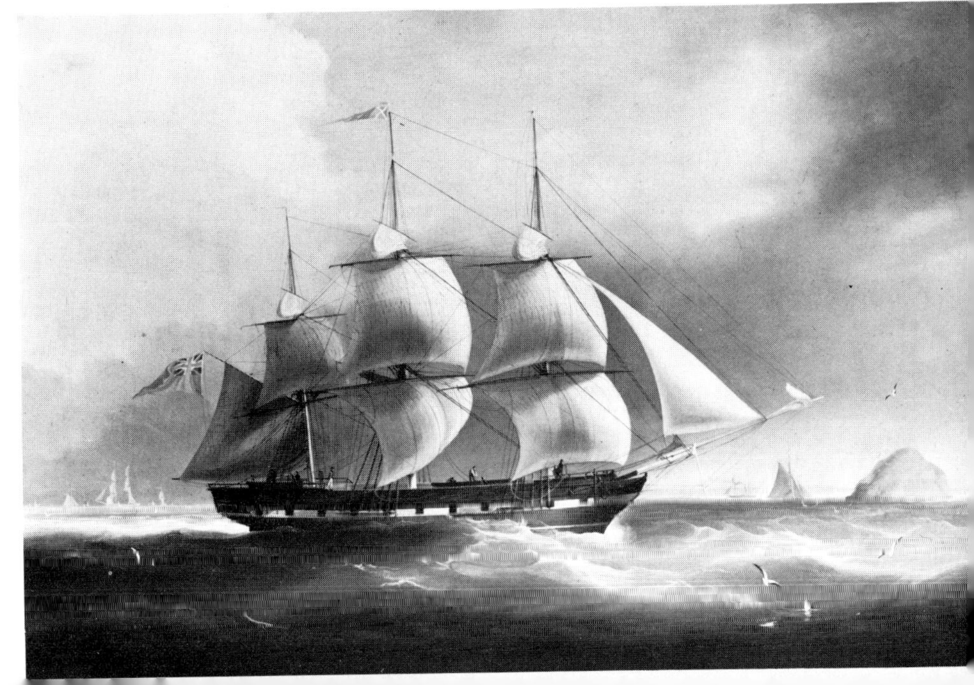

Plate 402. J.M. Huggins, fl.1840. "The East Indiaman *Thomas Coutts* off Ailsa Craig." *Probably the son of W.J. Huggins. A very competently executed ship portrait.* National Maritime Museum, Greenwich.

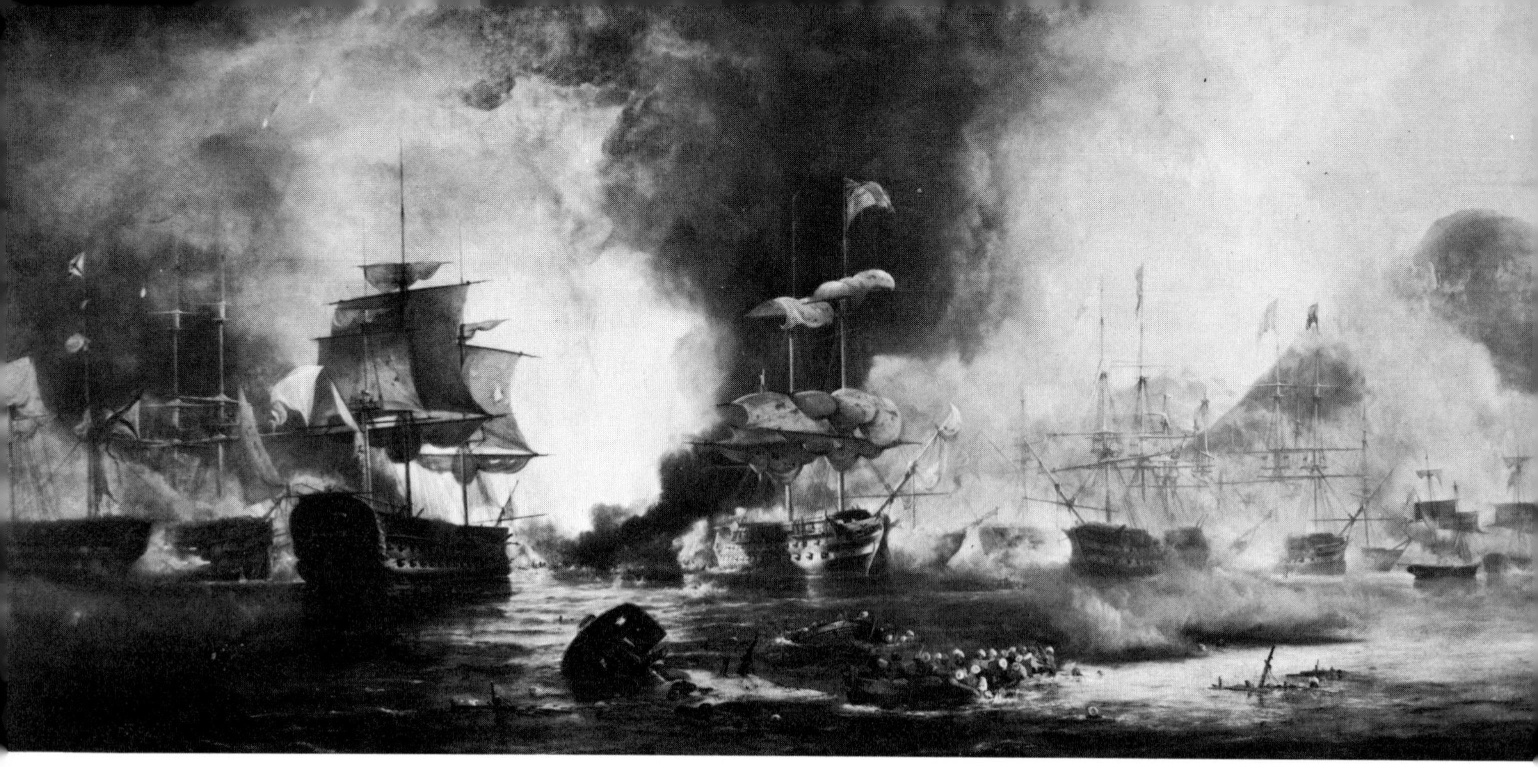

Plate 403. George Philip Reinagle, 1802-1835. "The Battle of Navarino in 1827." *This was the last great action under sail, when an Anglo-Franco-Russian fleet commanded by Sir Edward Codrington, destroyed the Turco-Egyptian one. Reinagle painted many Navarino Campaign scenes from which lithographs were made.* National Maritime Museum, Greenwich.

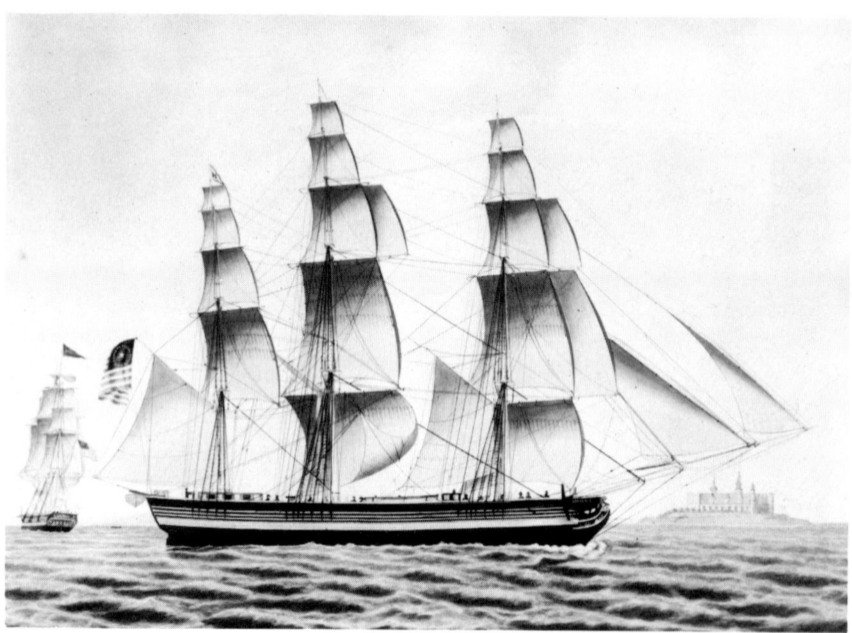

Plate 404. Jacob Petersen, 1774-1854. "The American merchant ship *Arbella* off Kronborg Castle about 1830." Watercolour. Peabody Museum of Salem.

Plate 405. Friederic Theodor Kloss, 1802-1876. "Danish men-of-war in the roads of Copenhagen, 1837." State Museum for Art, Copenhagen.

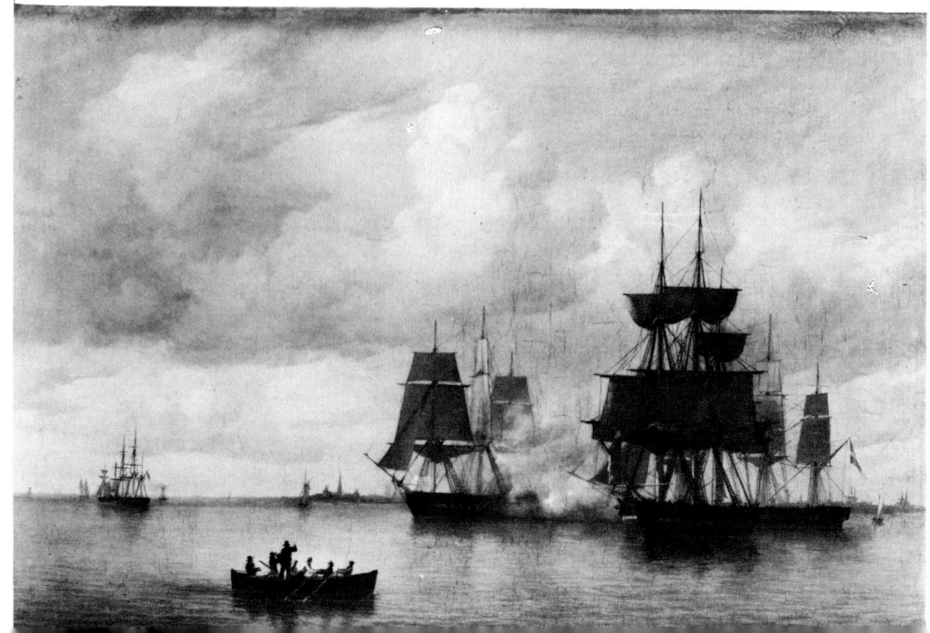

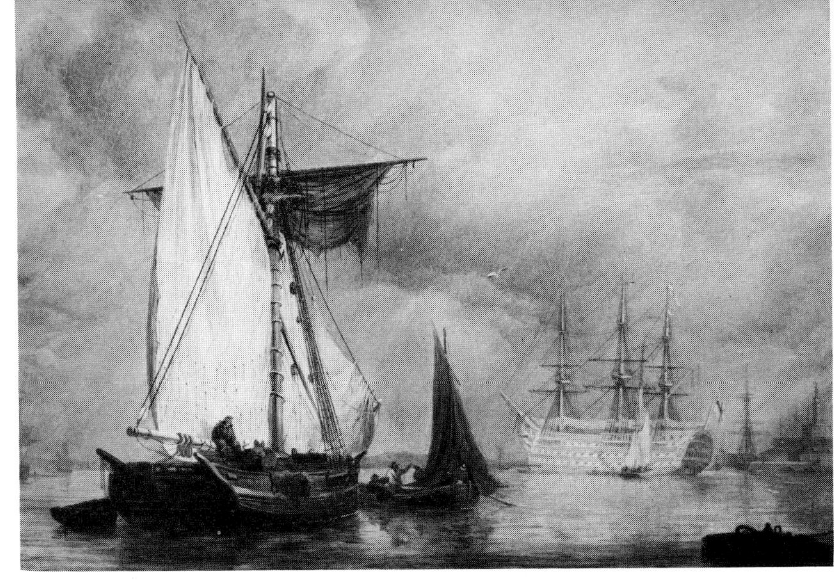

Plate 406. Johann Christian Berger, 1803-1871. "Portsmouth Harbour." Lansmuscum, Linkoping, Sweden.

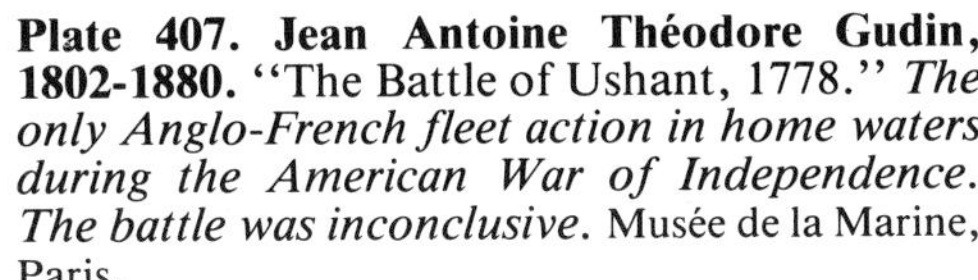

Plate 407. Jean Antoine Théodore Gudin, 1802-1880. "The Battle of Ushant, 1778." *The only Anglo-French fleet action in home waters during the American War of Independence. The battle was inconclusive.* Musée de la Marine, Paris.

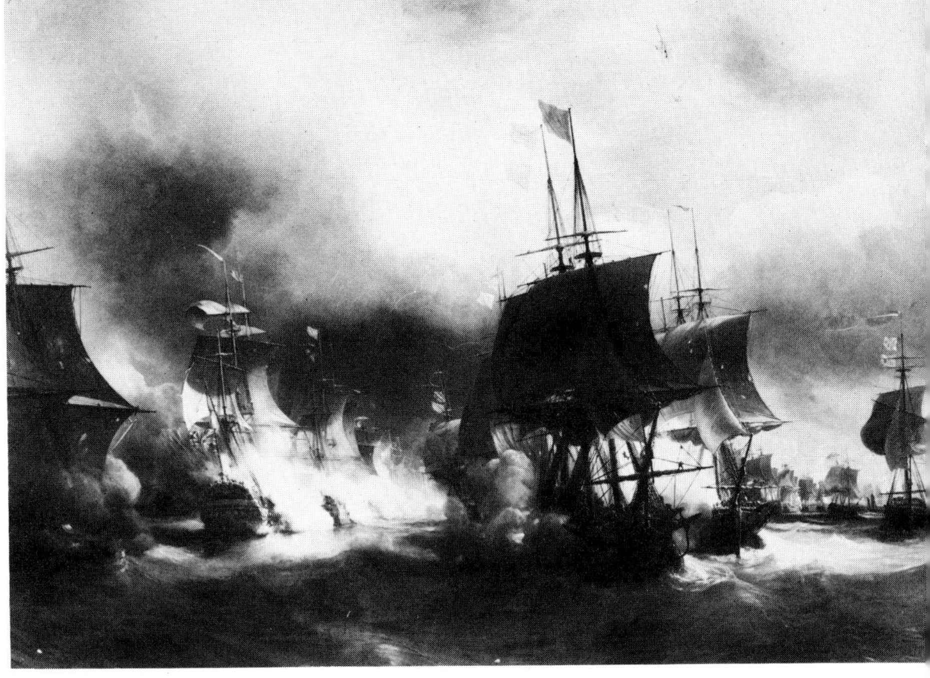

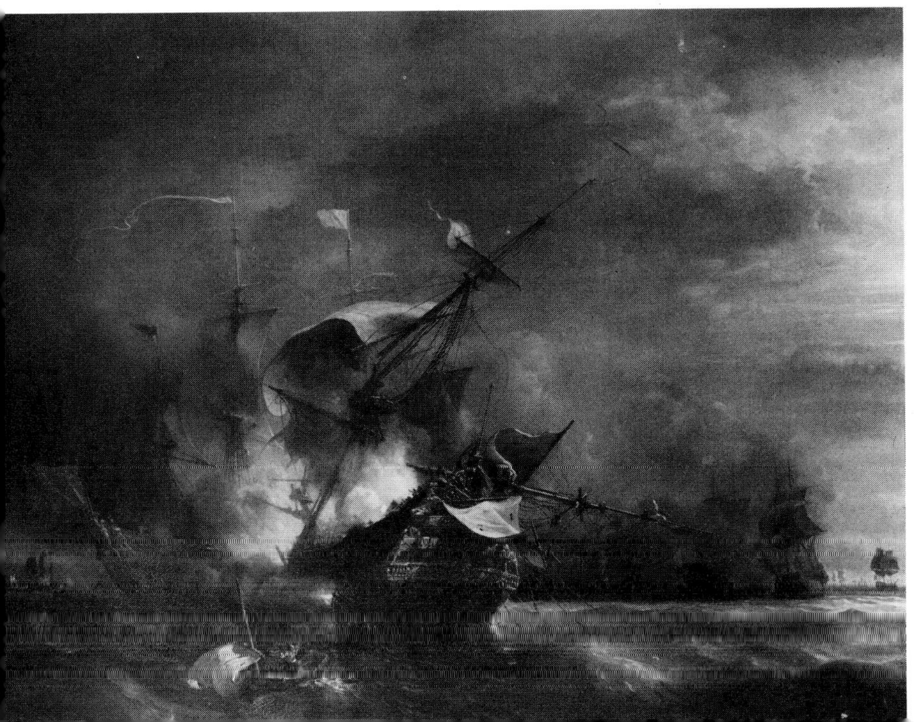

Plate 408. Jean Antoine Théodore Gudin, 1802-1880. "The Battle of Cape Tezard." Musées Nationaux de France, Musée de Versailles.

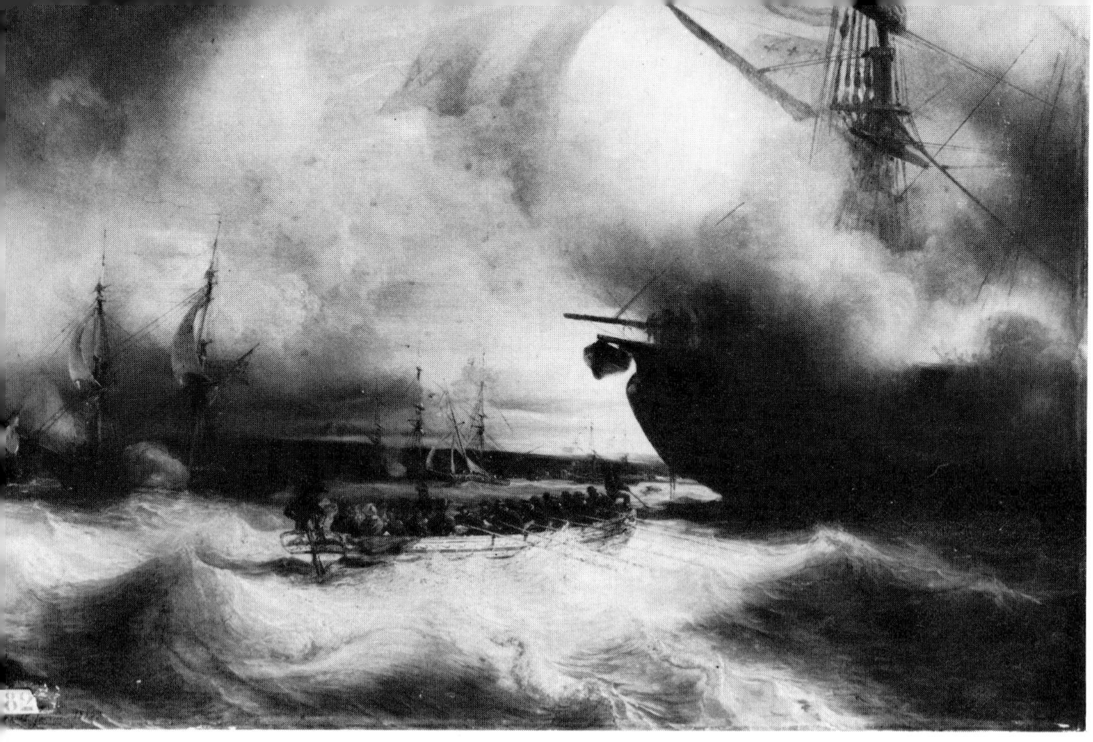

Plate 409. Jean Antoine Théodore Gudin, 1802-1880. "King Louis Philippe and his family going aboard the *Atlantic* at Cherbourg, dated 1834." Musées Nationaux de France, Musée de Versailles.

Plate 410. Jean Antoine Théodore Gudin, 1802-1880. "A Storm at Seaton, dated 1840." Trustees of the Wallace Collection.

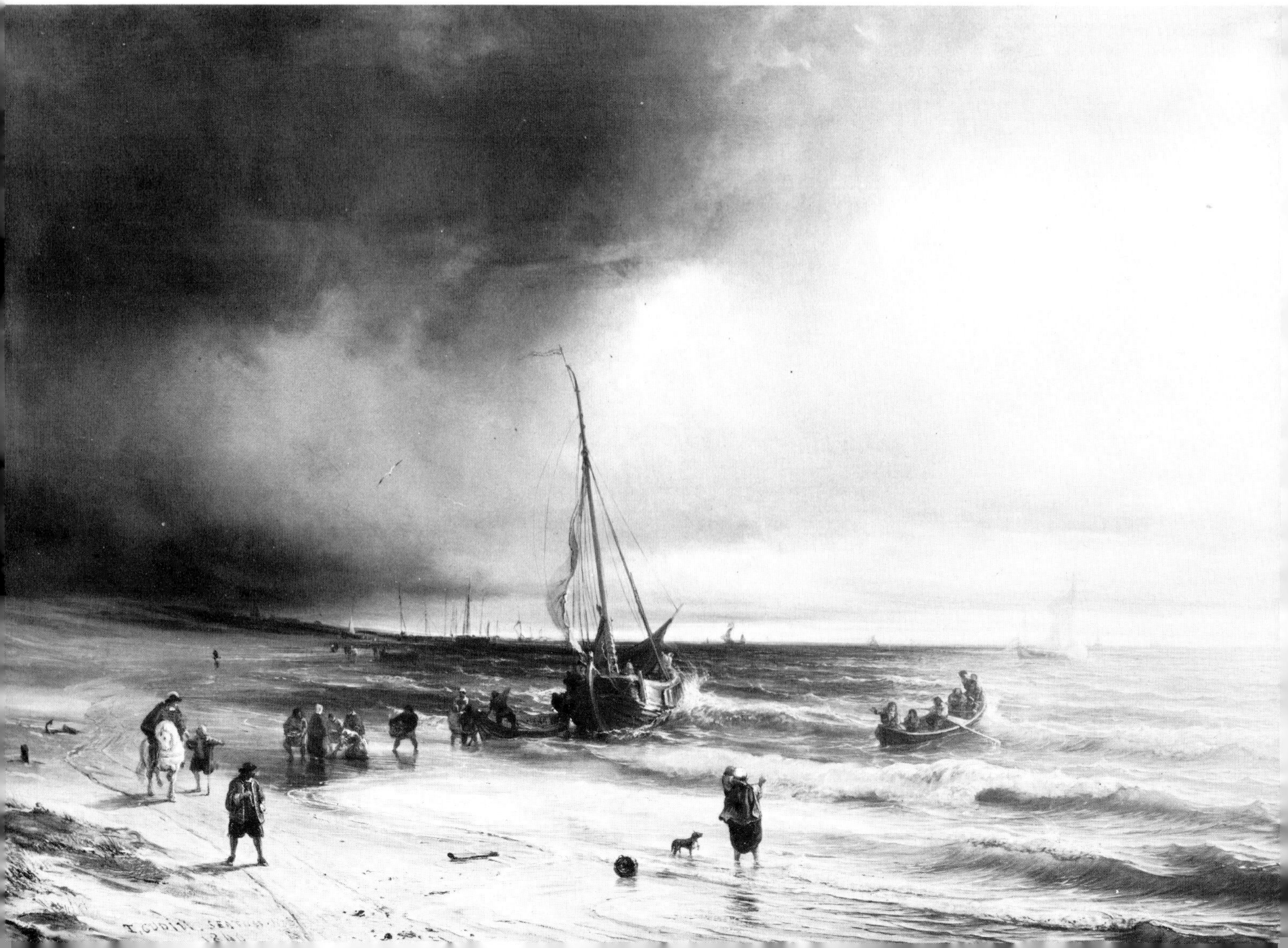

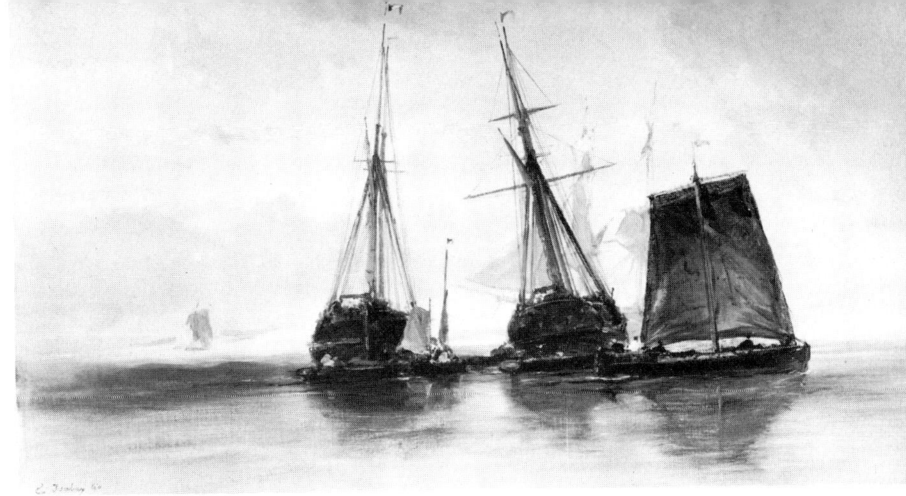

Plate 411. Louis Gabriel Eugène Isabey, 1803-1886. "Ships at anchor." National-museum, Stockholm.

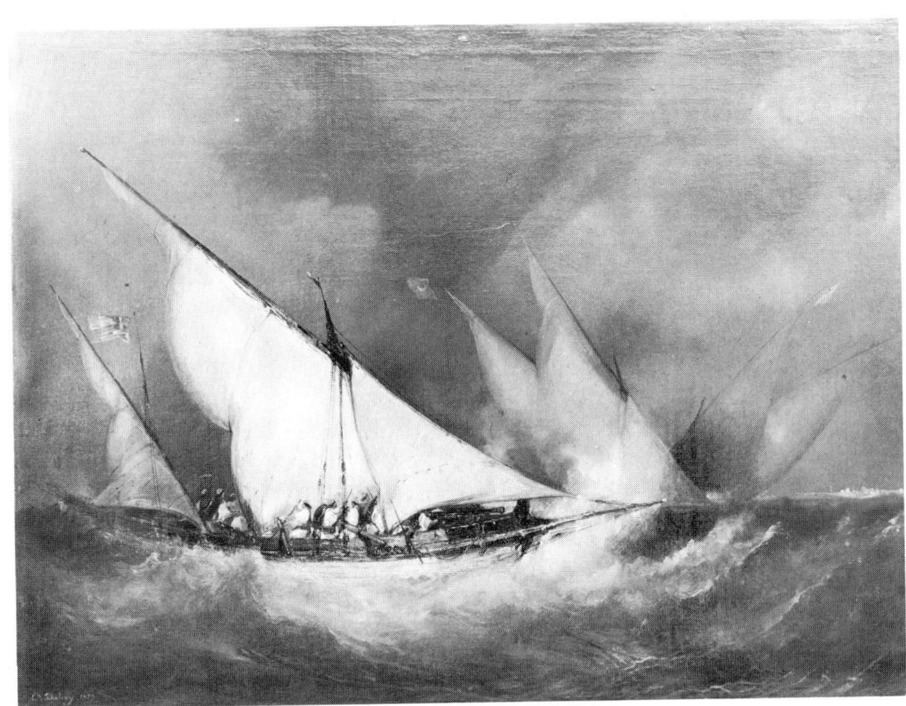

Plate 412. Louis Gabriel Eugène Isabey, 1803-1886. "Greek pirates attacking a Turkish vessel, dated 1827." *Isabey tended towards the school of romantic painters, influenced by Turner.* Cleveland Museum of Art (gift of Mr. and Mrs. J.H. Wade).

Plate 413. Jean Marie Auguste Jugelet, 1805-1875. "The arrival of King Louis-Philippe at Dieppe." *Musée de Dieppe.*

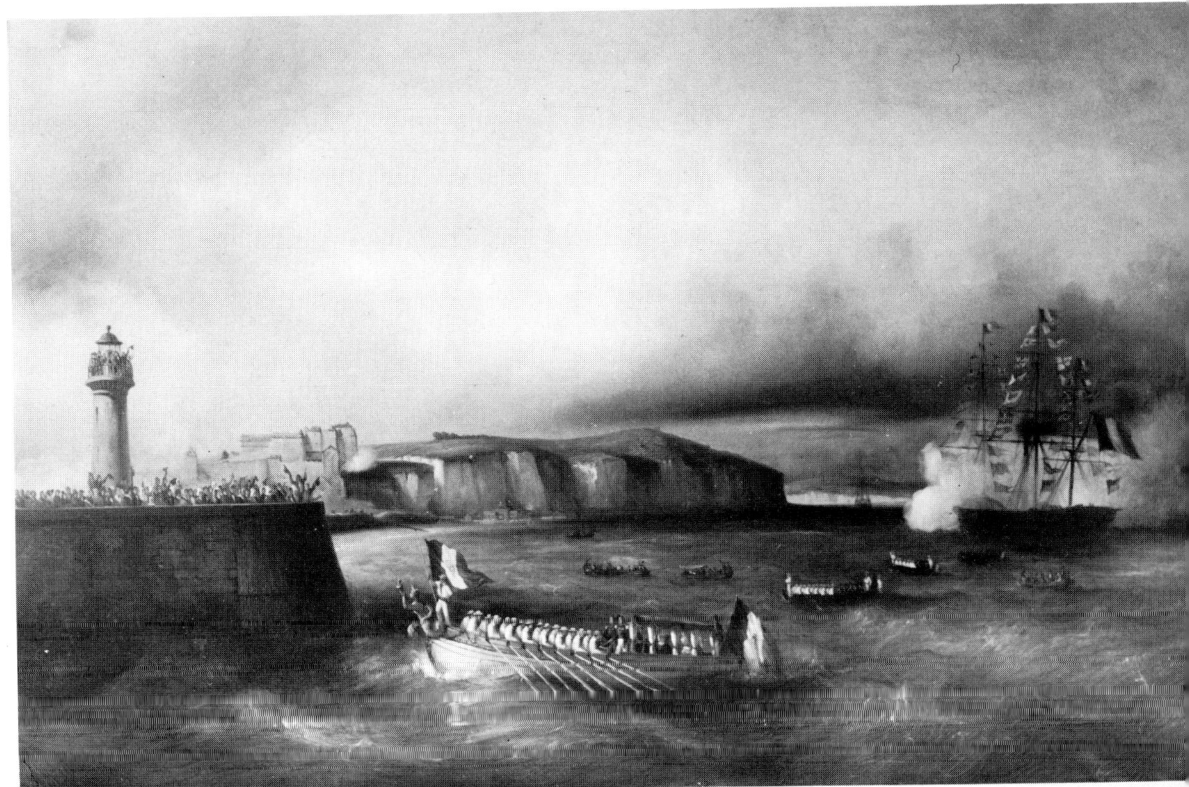

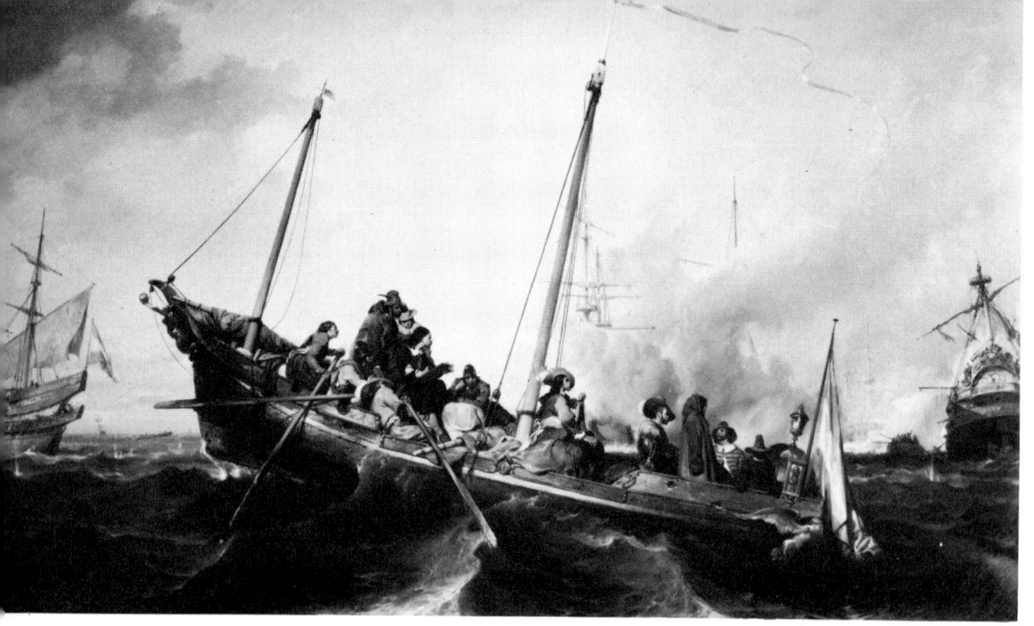

Plate 414. Eugène Modeste Edmond Lepoittevin, 1806-1870. "Willem van de Velde sketching a battle of the Anglo-Dutch Wars." *The great artist is shown in the centre sketching a battle. Lepoittevin, however, portrays on the left a ship's stern of a type which is at least fifty years earlier than any ship that took part in the Dutch War.* Oscar and Peter Johnson Ltd.

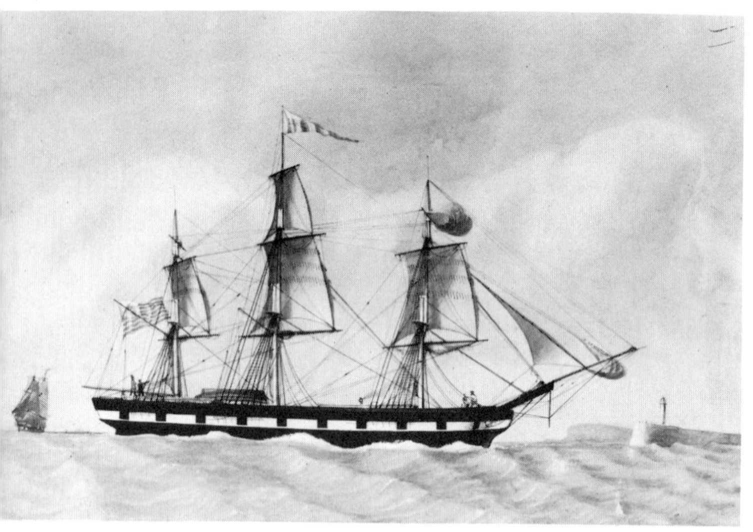

Plate 415. H. Cassinelli, fl. mid-19th century. "The American merchant ship *Lochinvar* entering the port of Le Havre in February 1854." Watercolour. Peabody Museum of Salem.

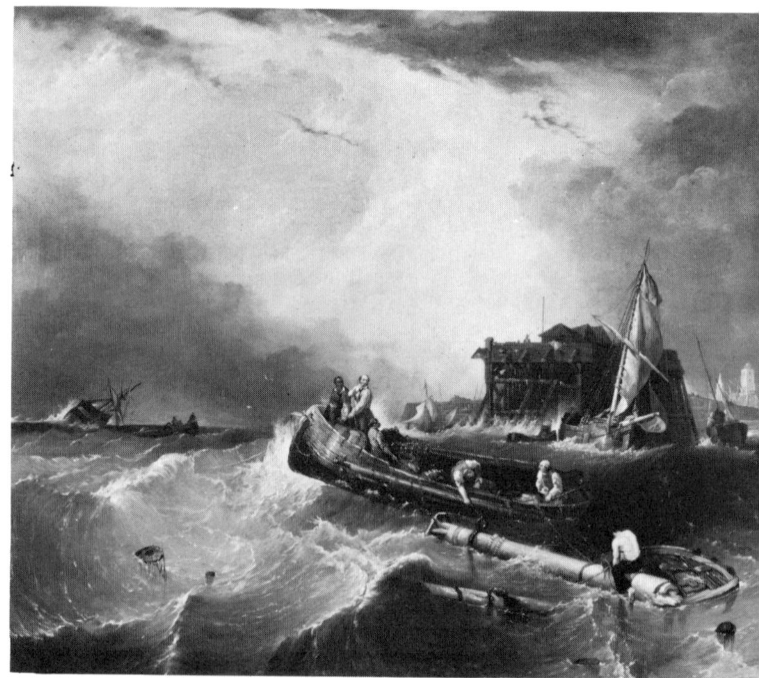

Plate 416. Clarkson Stanfield, 1793-1867. "Wreckers off Fort Rouge, Calais, 1828." Sotheby's.

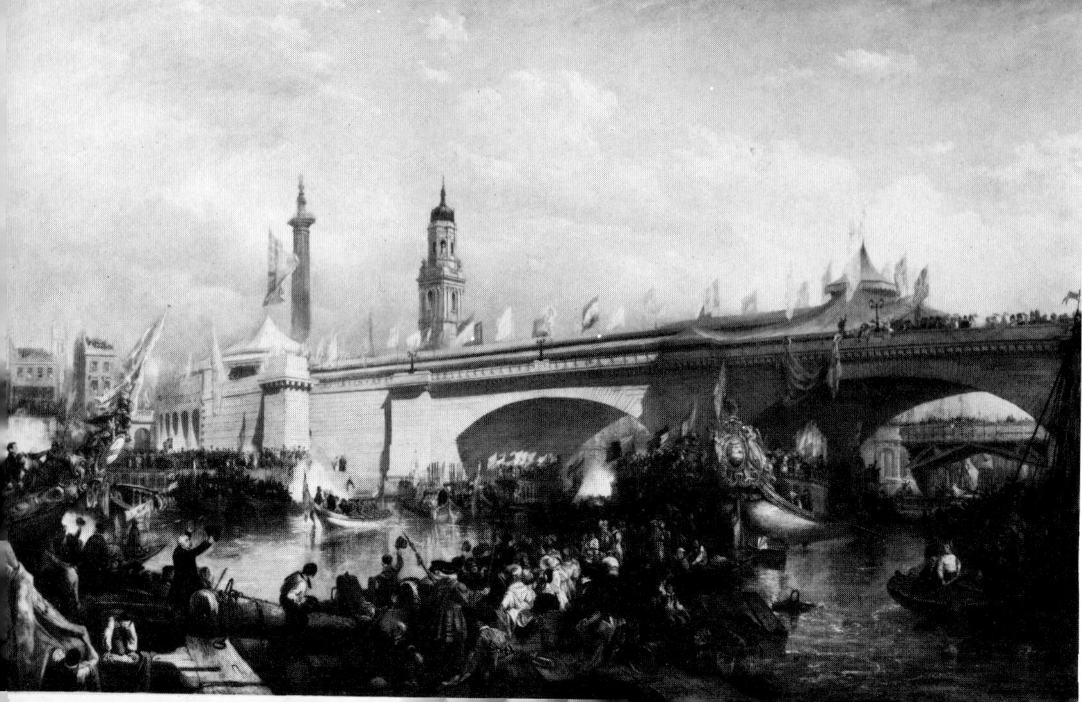

Plate 417. Clarkson Stanfield, 1793-1867. "The opening of the new London Bridge, 1832." *The choice of Stanfield by King William III to record this scene provoked ill feeling among Royal Academicians who thought the commission should have gone to one of them.* Royal collection.

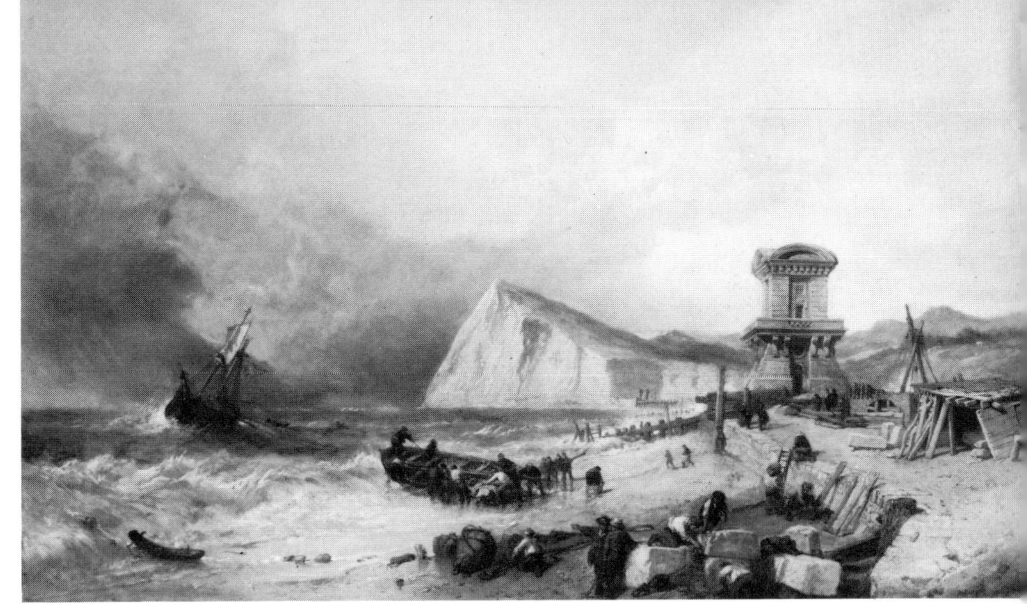

Plate 418. Clarkson Stanfield, 1793-1867. "A brig in distress near Shakespeare Cliffe, Dover, dated 1864." National Maritime Museum, Greenwich.

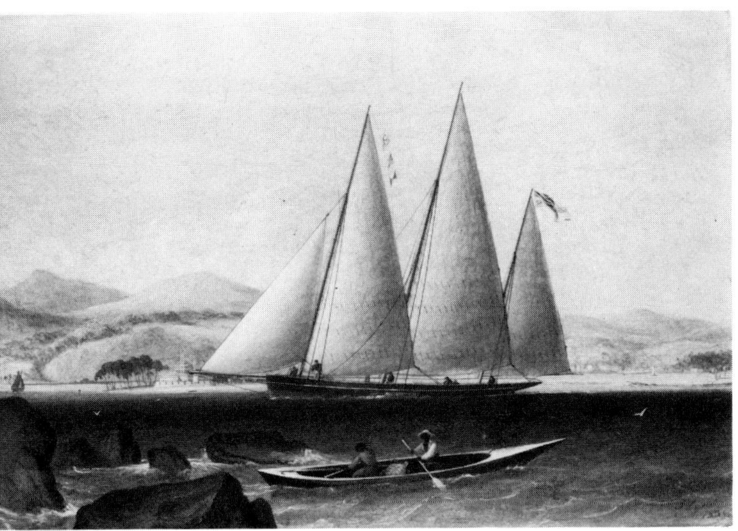

Plate 419. John Lynn, fl.1828-1838. "Bermudan schooner yacht." National Maritime Museum, Greenwich.

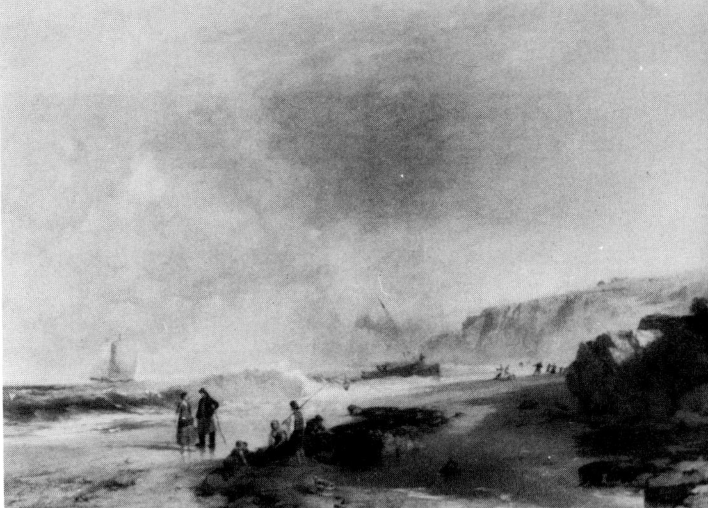

Plate 420. James Baker Pyne, 1800-1870. "The Beach at Whitby." *A coastal painter much impressed by Turner's use of light which he strove to emulate.* Leicester Art Gallery.

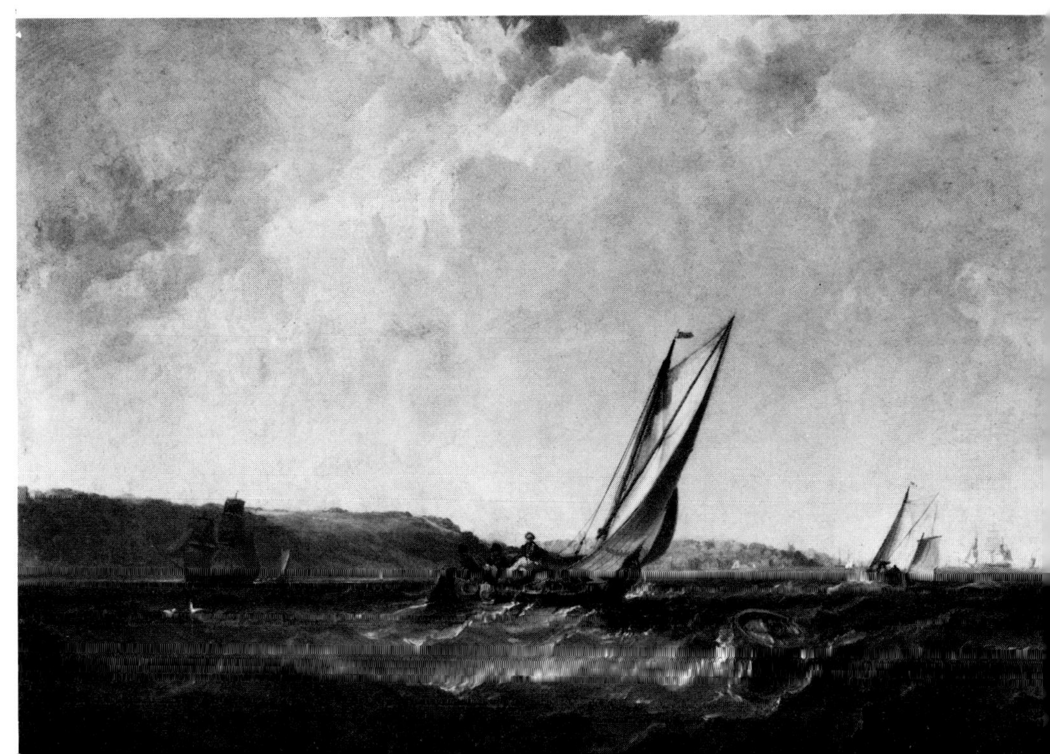

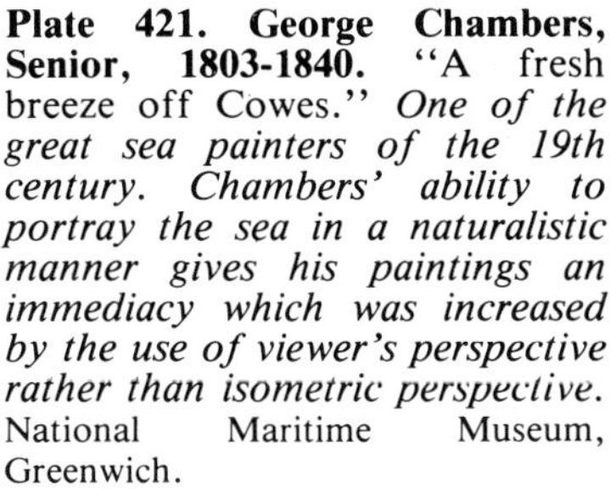

Plate 421. George Chambers, Senior, 1803-1840. "A fresh breeze off Cowes." *One of the great sea painters of the 19th century. Chambers' ability to portray the sea in a naturalistic manner gives his paintings an immediacy which was increased by the use of viewer's perspective rather than isometric perspective.* National Maritime Museum, Greenwich.

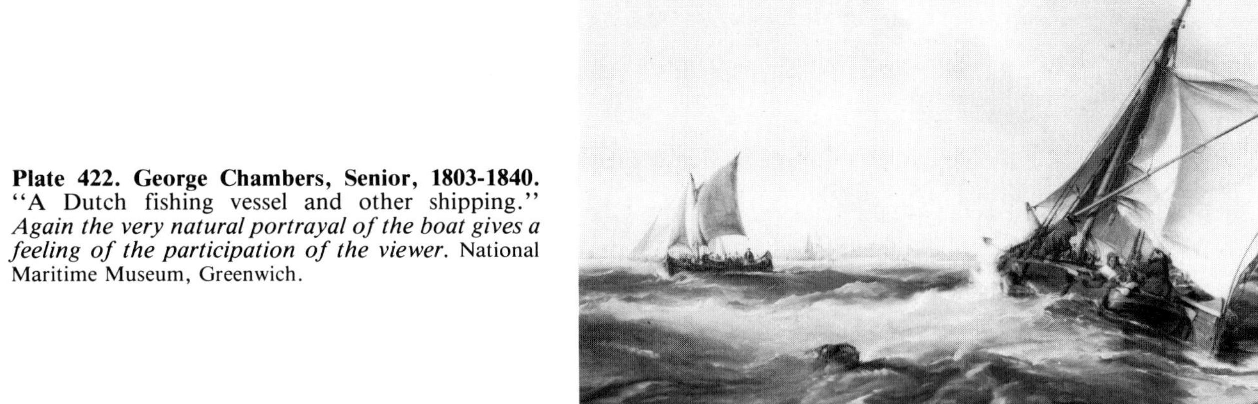

Plate 422. George Chambers, Senior, 1803-1840. "A Dutch fishing vessel and other shipping." *Again the very natural portrayal of the boat gives a feeling of the participation of the viewer.* National Maritime Museum, Greenwich.

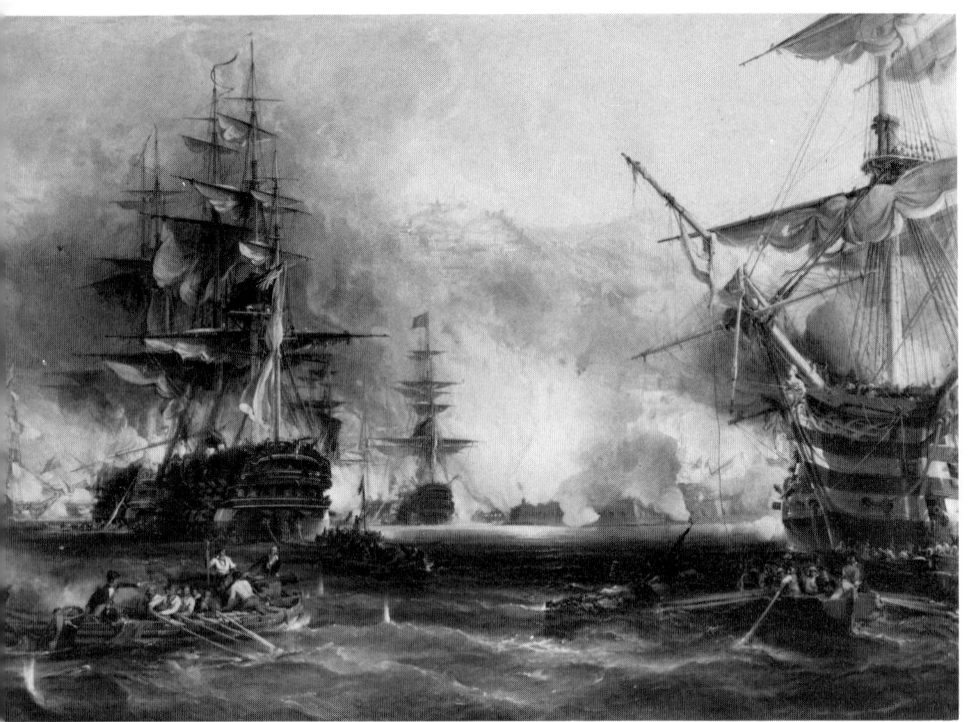

Plate 423. George Chambers, Senior, 1803-1840. "The bombardment of Algiers in 1816." *Admiral Sir Edward Pellew took a squadron out to Algiers to secure the release of 3,000 Christian slaves, in which he was successful. Congreve rockets fired from boats supplemented the ships' guns.* National Maritime Museum, Greenwich.

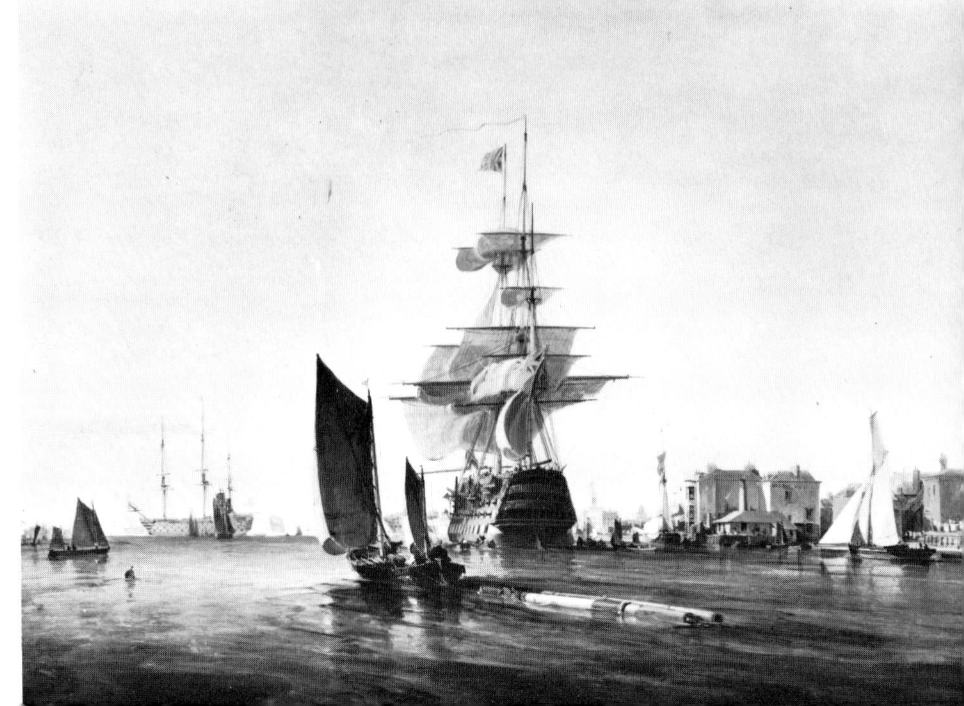

Plate 424. George Chambers, Senior, 1803-1840. "The *Britannia* entering Portsmouth harbour, 1835." National Maritime Museum, Greenwich.

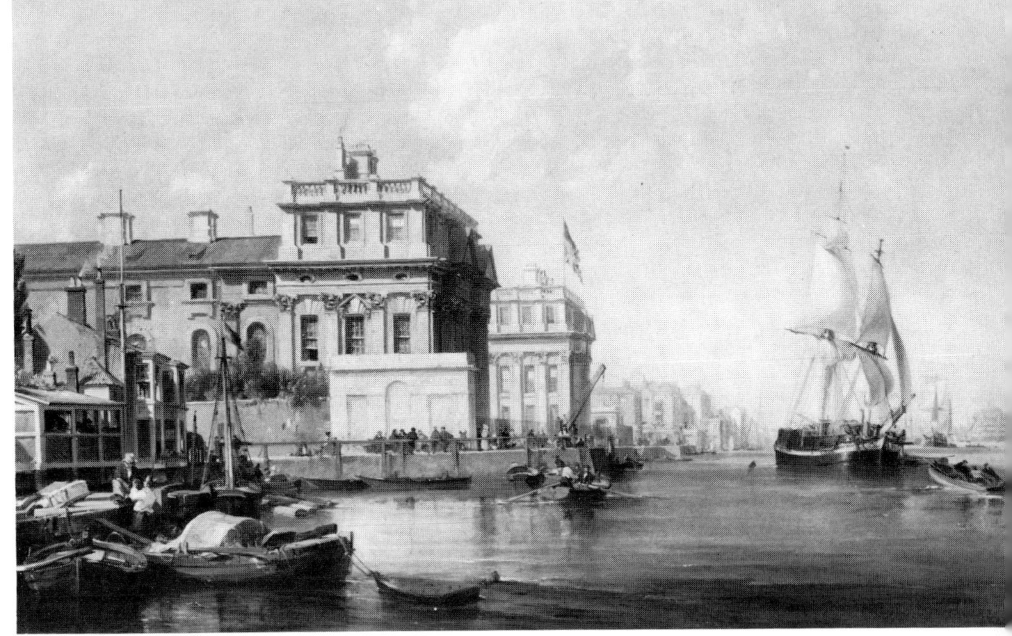

Plate 425. George Chambers, Senior, 1803-1840. "Greenwich Hospital from the east, 1836." *Chambers' early death robbed the world of many potential great works.* National Maritime Museum, Greenwich.

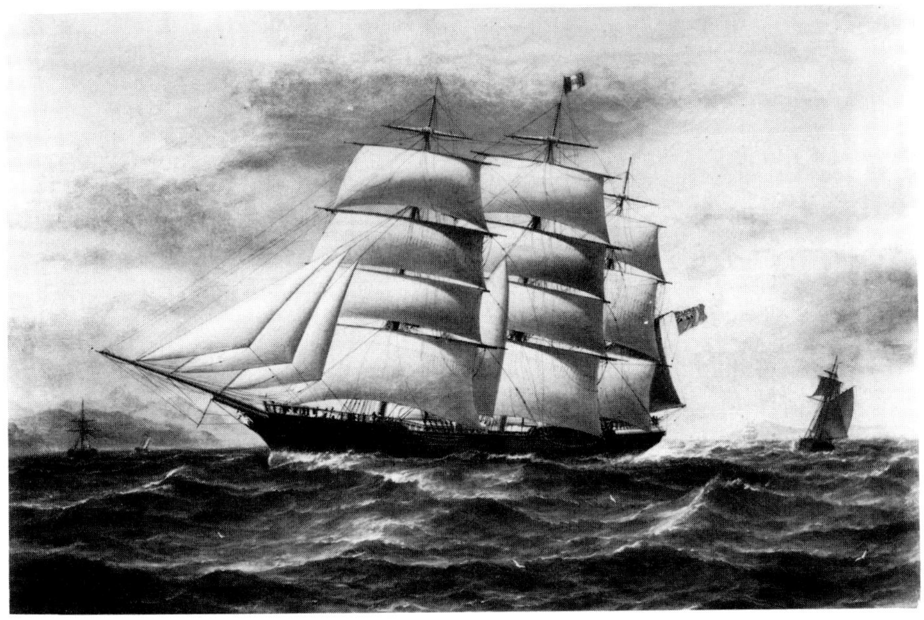

Plate 426. William Clark, 1803-1883. "The ship *Margaret Galbraith.*" *Scotland's best ship portraitist, Clark worked all his life in Greenock.* National Maritime Museum, Greenwich.

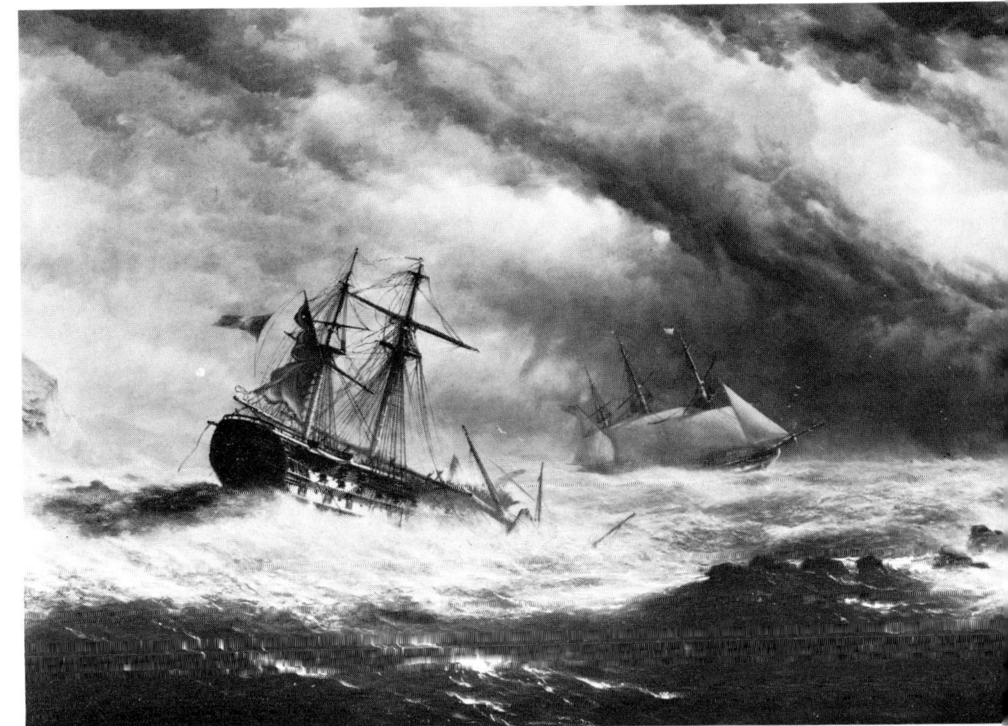

Plate 427. Ebenezer Colls, fl.1850s. "The rescue of an embayed French ship of the line by the British frigate *Endymion* about 1803." *This painting (copied from one by J.C. Schetky) depicts an actual incident, though one would think the chances of rescuing such a boat with the wind directly ashore seem improbable.* National Maritime Museum, Greenwich.

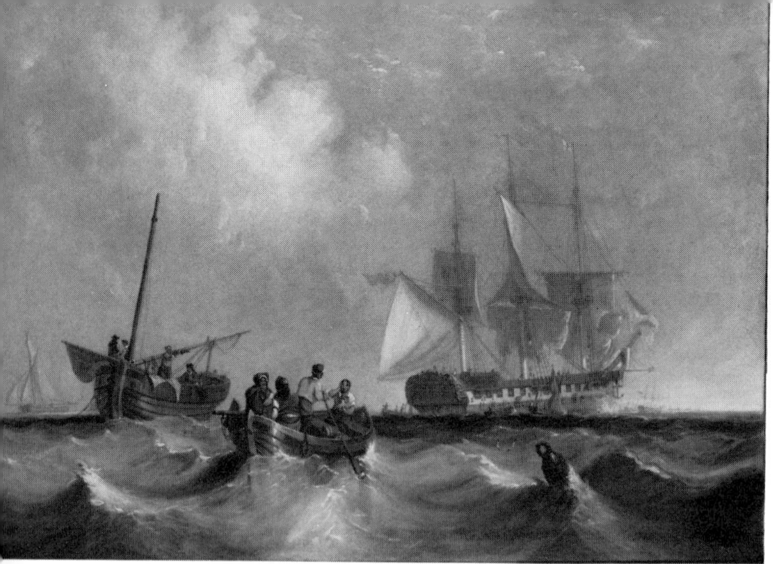

Plate 428. F.W. Ovenden, early 19th century. "A rowing boat going out to a ship of the line hove to." Sotheby's.

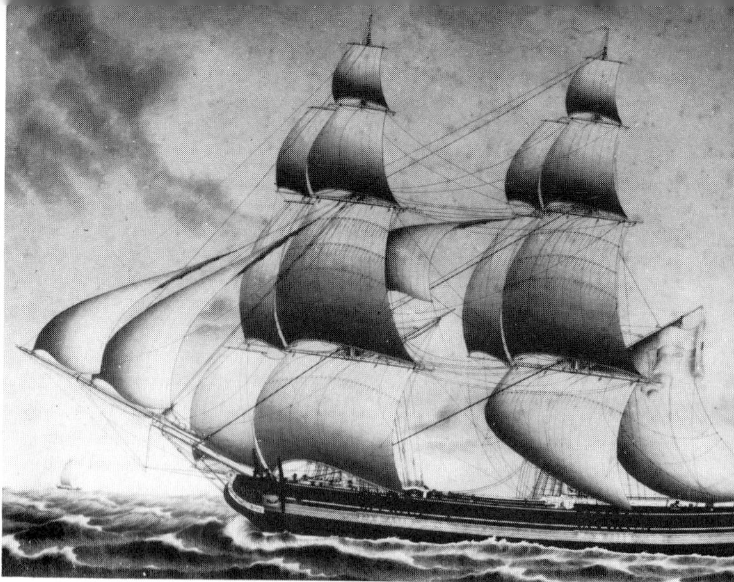

Plate 429. Jacob Ahrend Heinrich Bottger, 1781-1860. "The brig *Triton* out of Flensburg, 1832." Altonaer Museum, Hamburg.

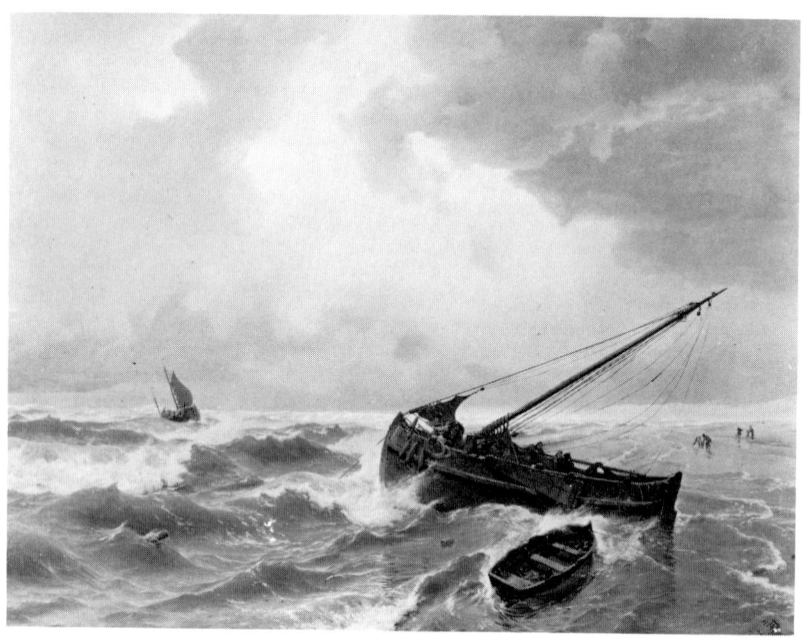

Plate 430. Andreas Achenbach, 1815-1910. "The beach at Scheveningen, dated 1835." *This painter was one of the best of the German school.* Rheinisches Landesmuseum, Bonn.

Plate 431. Andreas Achenbach, 1815-1910. "Departure of a steamer, dated 1870." *A beautifully delineated and drawn work. Painted later than the features of the steamer suggest, since the quarter gallery went out in about the 1850s, and such small steamers date from the 1830s and '40s.* Wallraf-Richartz Museum, Cologne.

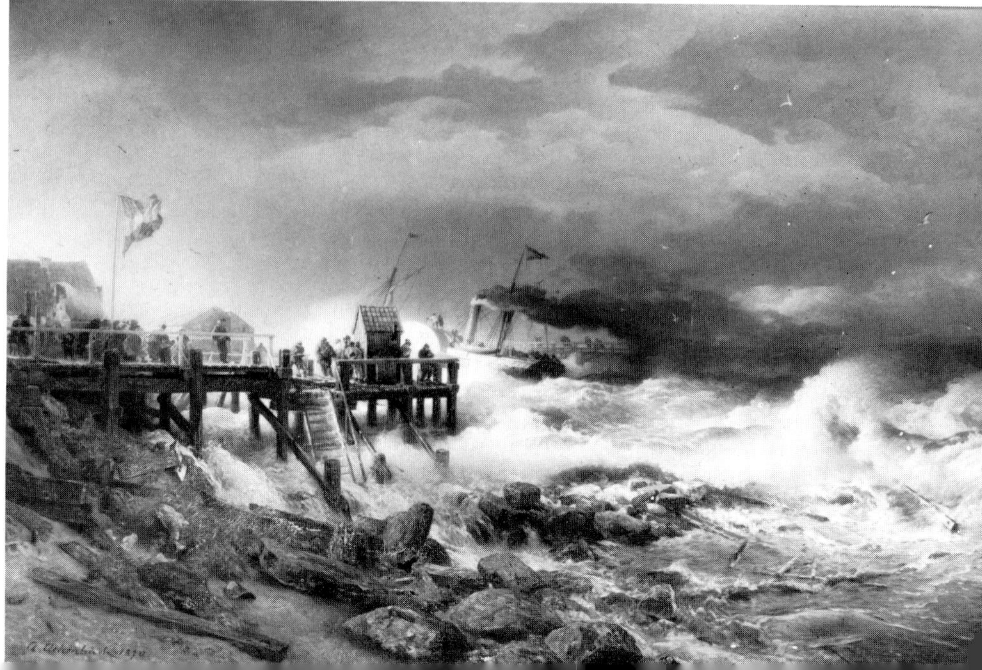

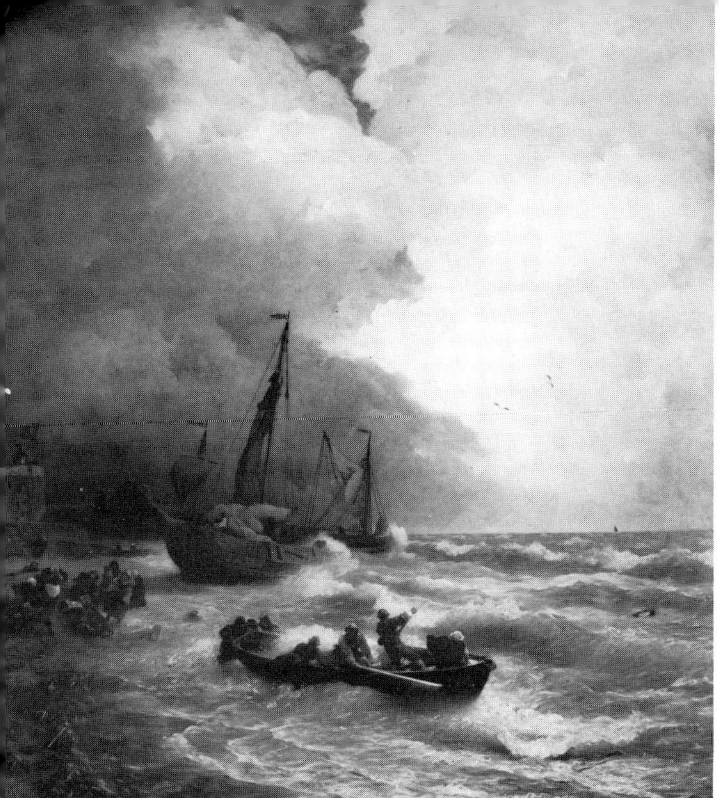

Plate 432. Andreas Achenbach, 1815-1910. ''Approaching storm.'' *Achenbach was adept at creating realistic light, as in this moody and carefully observed painting.* Kunstmuseum, Düsseldorf.

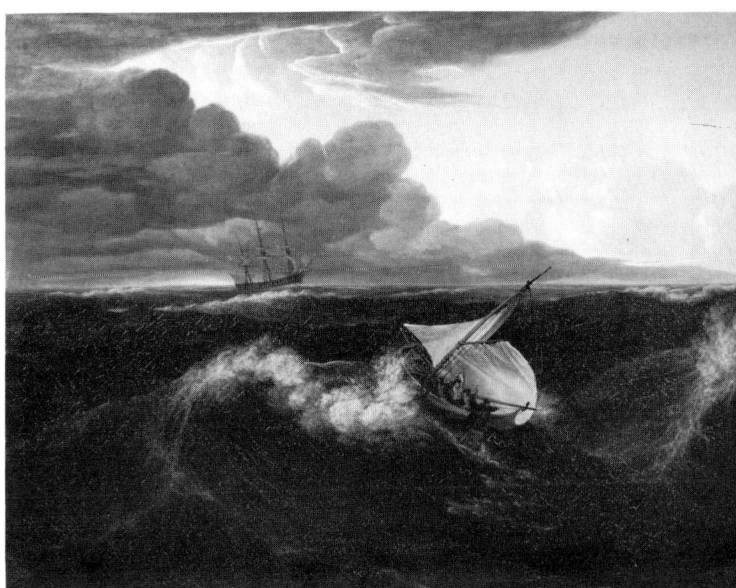

Plate 433. Washington Allston, 1779-1843. ''The Rising of a Thunderstorm at Sea.'' *A heavily dramatic storm scene by an artist who has been called the 'American Titian'.* Museum of Fine Arts, Boston.

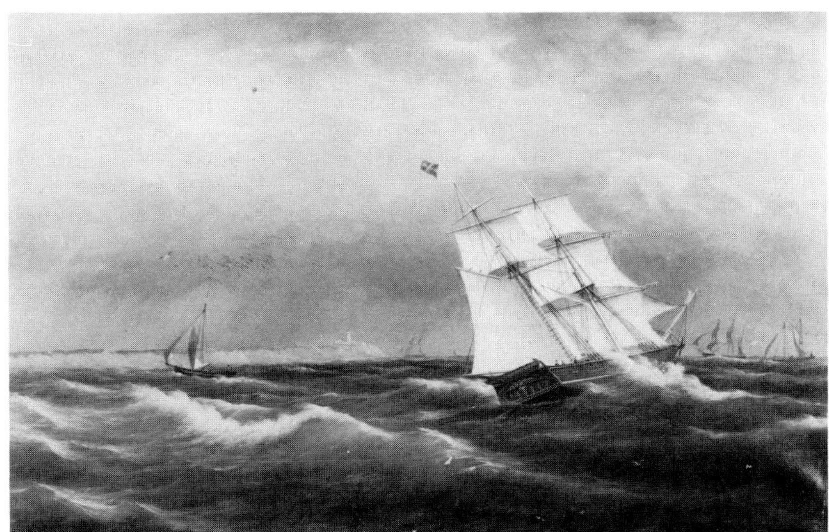

Plate 434. George Robert Bonfield, 1805-1898. ''The American brig *Mail.*'' Mariners Museum, Newport News, Virginia.

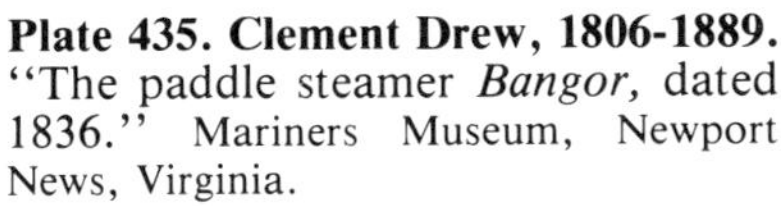

Plate 435. Clement Drew, 1806-1889. ''The paddle steamer *Bangor,* dated 1836.'' Mariners Museum, Newport News, Virginia.

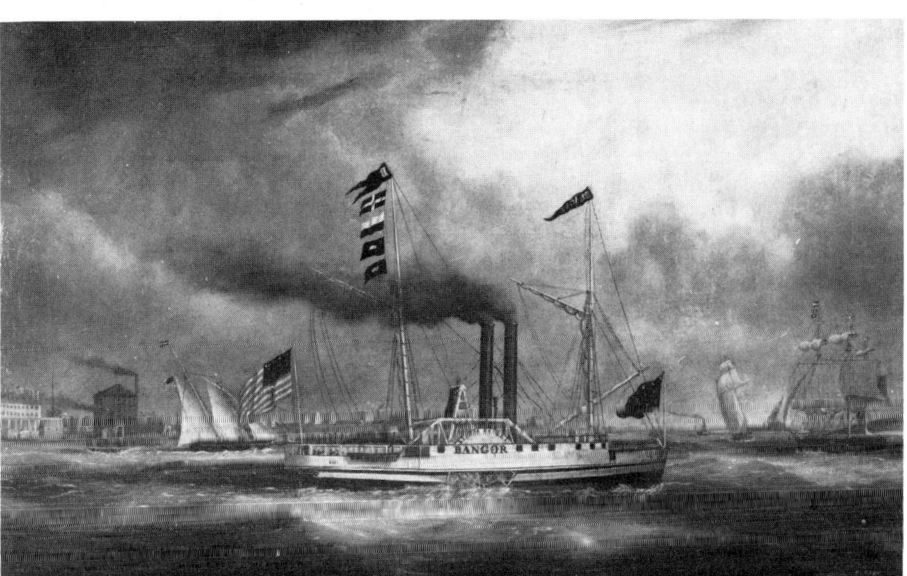

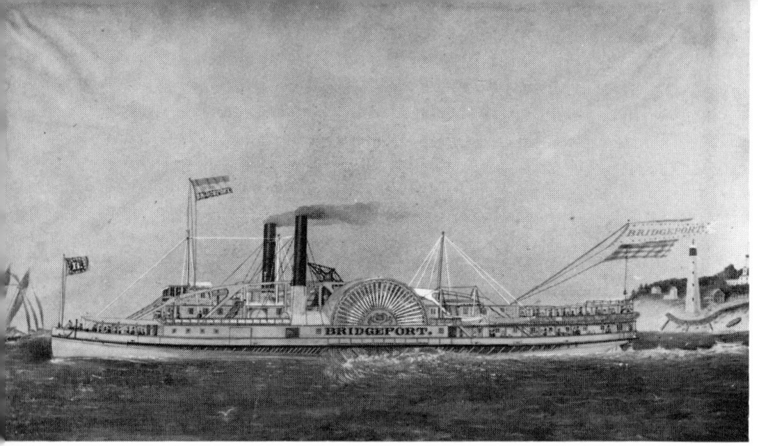

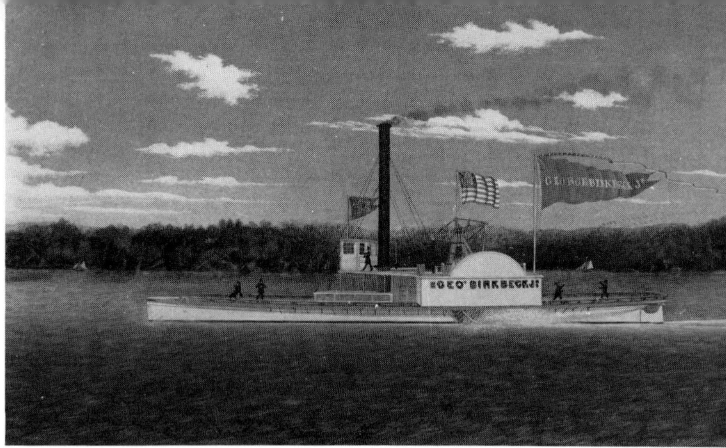

Plate 436. Jurgan Frederick Huge, 1809-1878. "The paddle ferry *Bridgeport.*" *Probably painted in the 1860s or '70s, when a system of ferries similar to this plied the great water inlets of the east coast of America.* Mariners Museum, Newport News.

Plate 437. James Bard, 1815-1897. "The paddle steamer *George Birkbeck Jr.*" *An American paddle steamer of about the 1850s.* Mariners Museum, Newport News.

Plate 438. William Adolphus Knell, c.1808-1875. "The Battle of Camperdown in 1797." *The chef-d'oeuvre of this artist. Despite a certain coarseness, the high sense of drama suggests at least an admiration for the work of Turner.* Private collection (on loan to the National Maritime Museum, Greenwich).

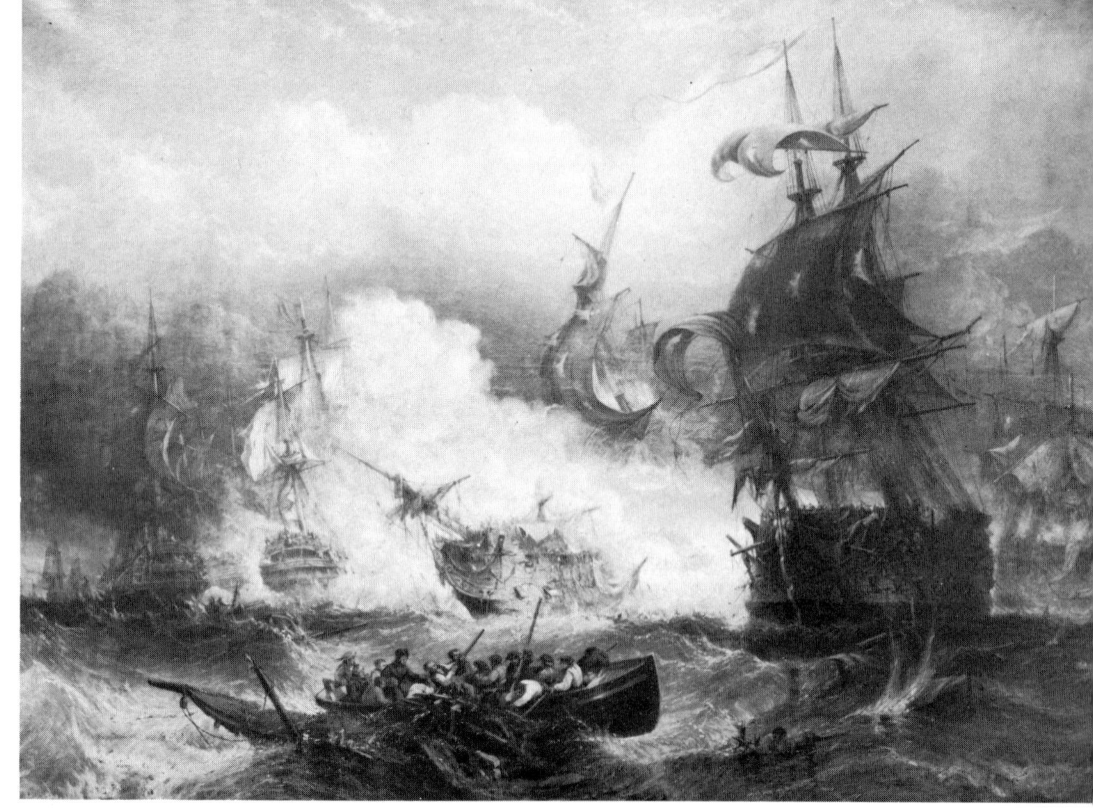

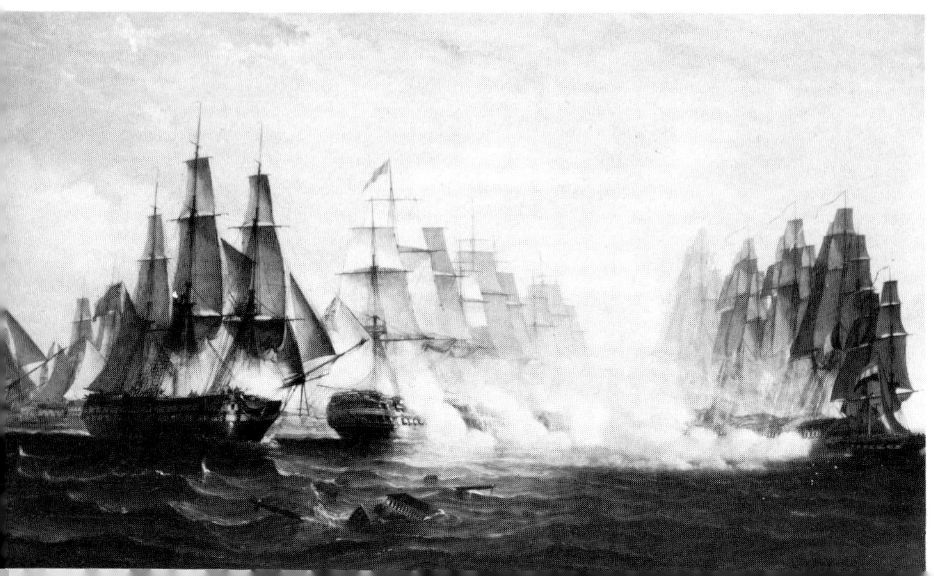

Plate 439. William Adolphus Knell, c.1808-1875. "Commodore Dance's action with Admiral le Comte de La Linois in the Strait of Malocca in 1804." *Linois, in the 80-gun* Marengo, *with his squadron, waited for the China East India Company fleet, with cargoes worth £7,000,000. But when it appeared its commander, Dance, pretending his biggest East Indiamen were ships of the line, attacked him. Linois was fooled and broke and fled.* National Maritime Museum, Greenwich.

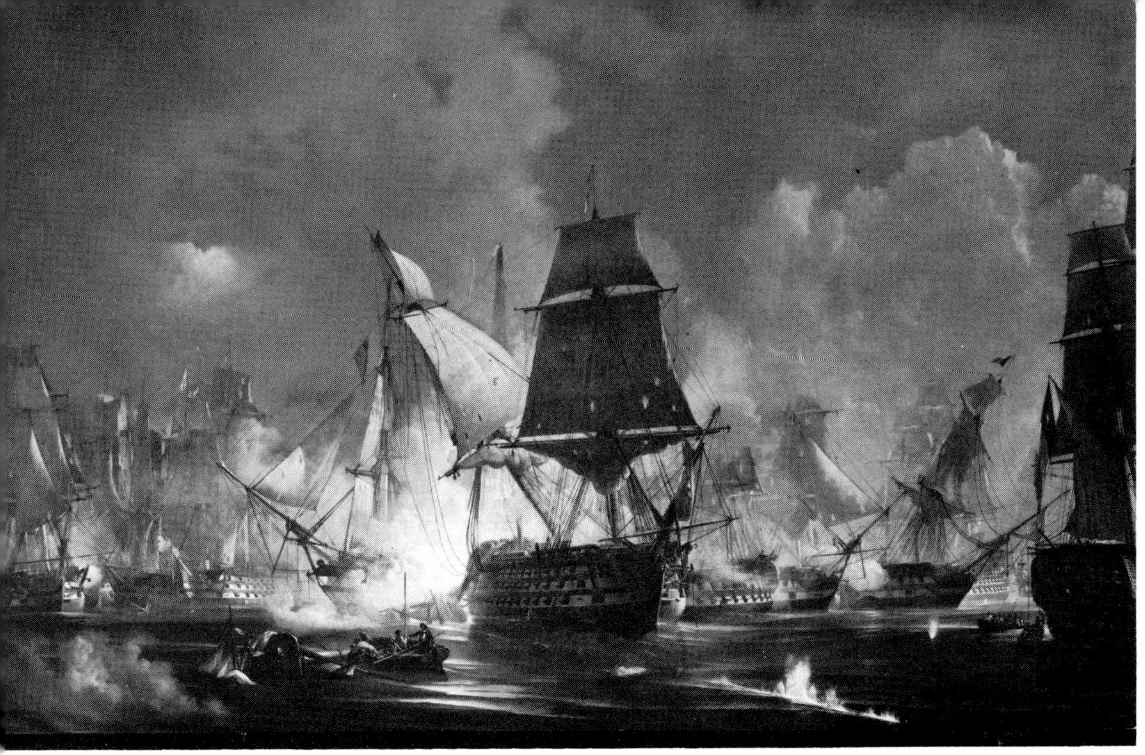

Plate 440. Charles Henry Seaforth, 1801-aft.1853. "The Battle of Trafalgar in 1805." Christie's.

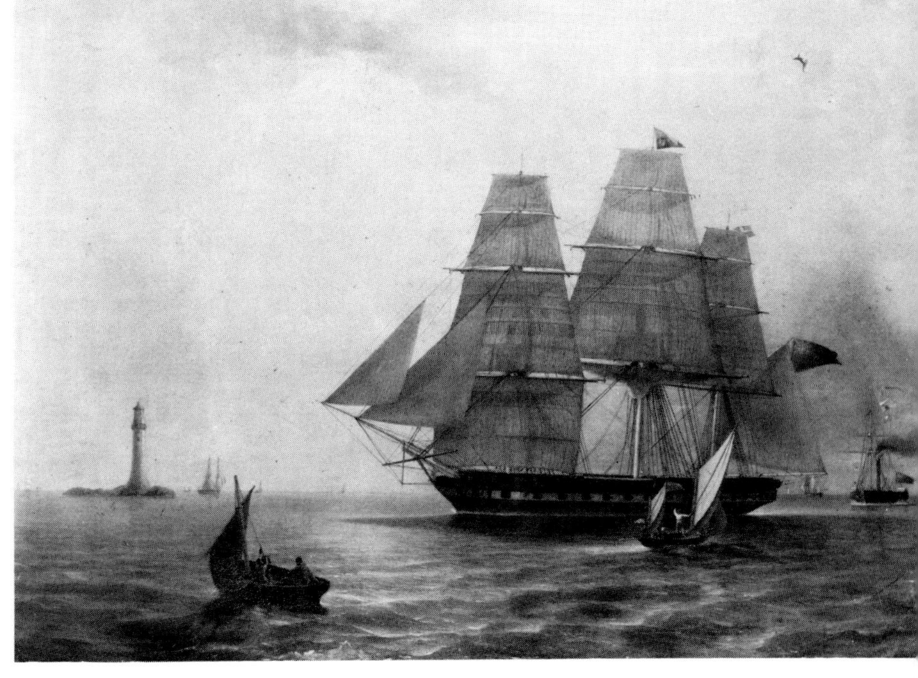

Plate 441. Charles Henry Seaforth, 1801-aft.1853. "H.M. frigate *Forte* off the Eddystone lighthouse with the Duchess of Kent and Princess Victoria aboard, 1833." National Maritime Museum, Greenwich.

Plate 442 *(below)*. **Joseph Walter, 1783-1856.** "The West Indiaman *Britannia,* dated 1838." *Thomas Daniels, the distinguished Bristolian who owned this fine ship, was deeply involved in the slave trade, and was a leading petitioner against the Bill to abolish it. The West Indiamen were second only to the East Indiamen in size and prestige.* National Maritime Museum, Greenwich.

Plate 443 *(below right)*. **Joseph Walter, 1783-1856.** "A brig at the mouth of the Bristol Avon, dated 1838." National Maritime Museum, Greenwich.

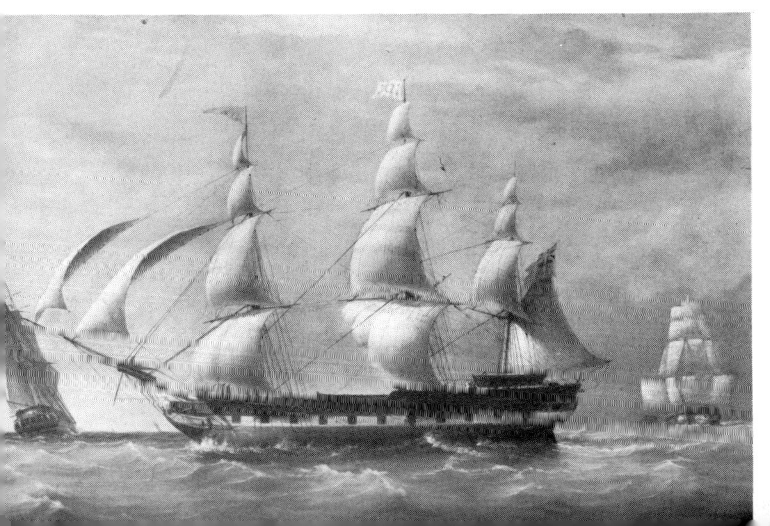

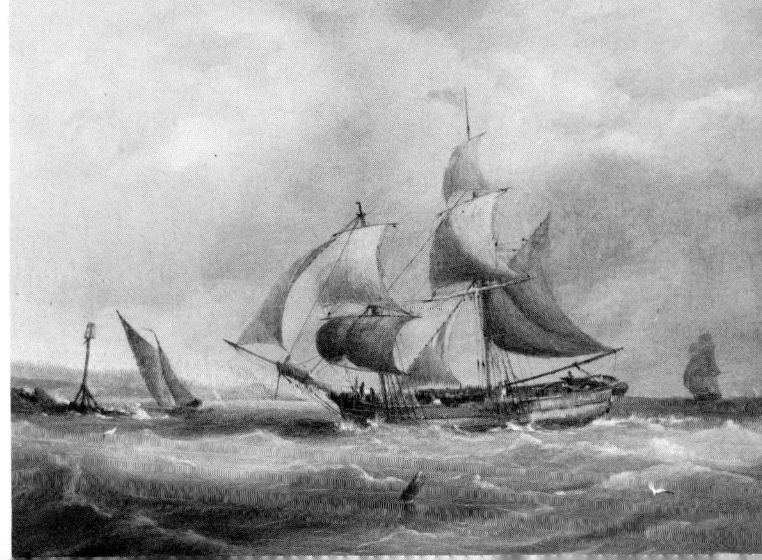

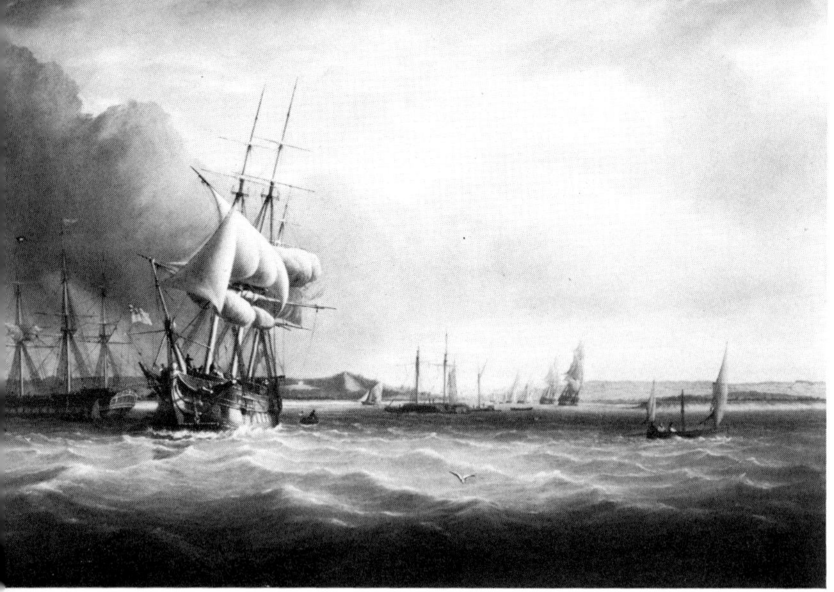

Plate 444. Joseph Walter, 1783-1856. "Shipping in the Bristol Channel." *Walter was unusual among British 19th century marine painters in using a grey palette.* National Maritime Museum, Greenwich.

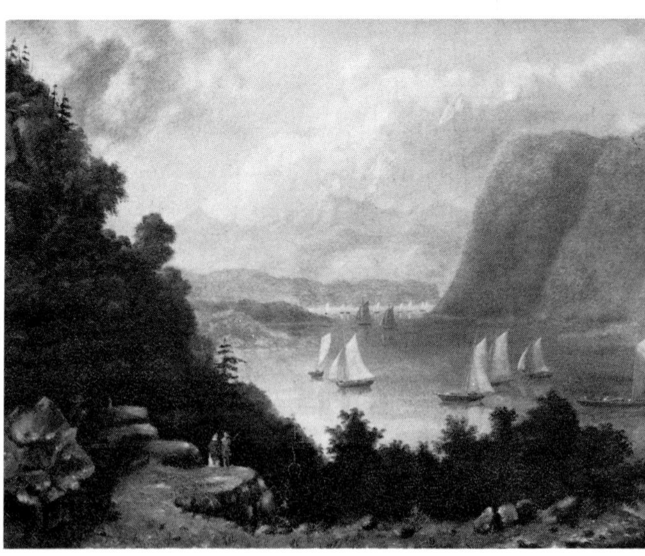

Plate 445. Thomas Cole, 1801-1848. "View of North River." Wadsworth Atheneum (bequest of James B. Hosmer), Conn.

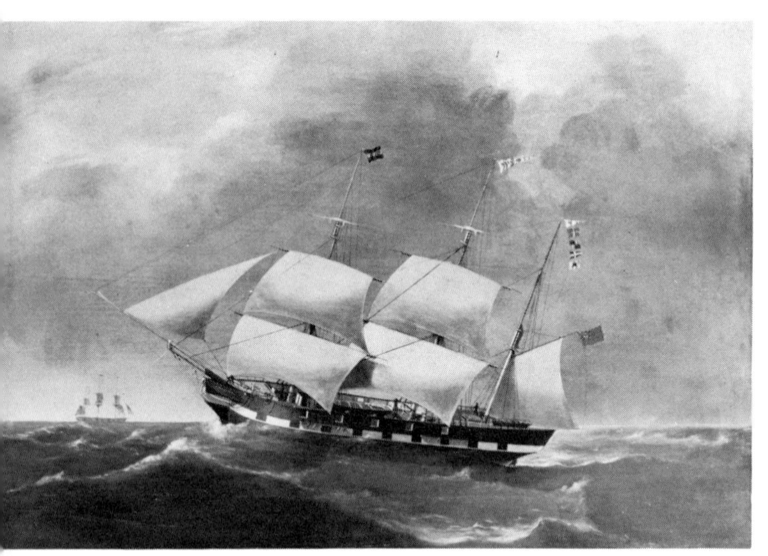

Plate 446. George F. Gregory, 1815-?1885. "The ship Marmion, 1838." *Typical mid-19th century commercial vessel. The aft mast carries a flag hoist in the Marryatt code which indicates the ship's name — "makes her number".* Bonham's.

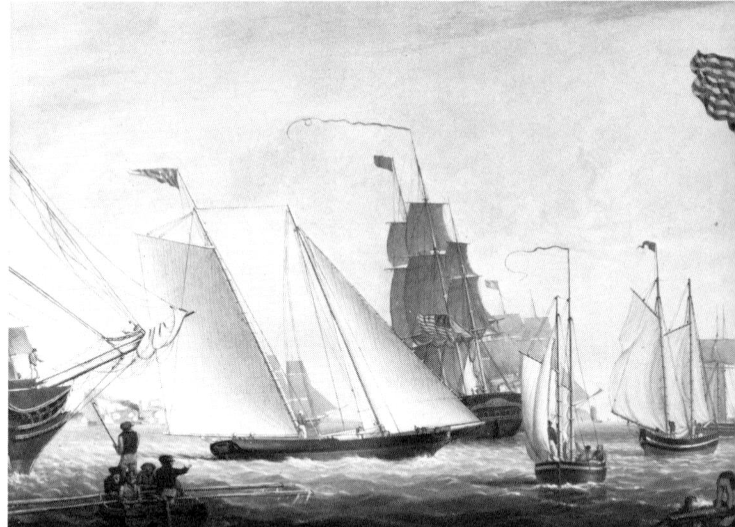

Plate 447. Fitz Hugh Lane, 1804-1865. "The yacht *Northern Light* in Boston Harbour." Shelburne Museum, Vermont.

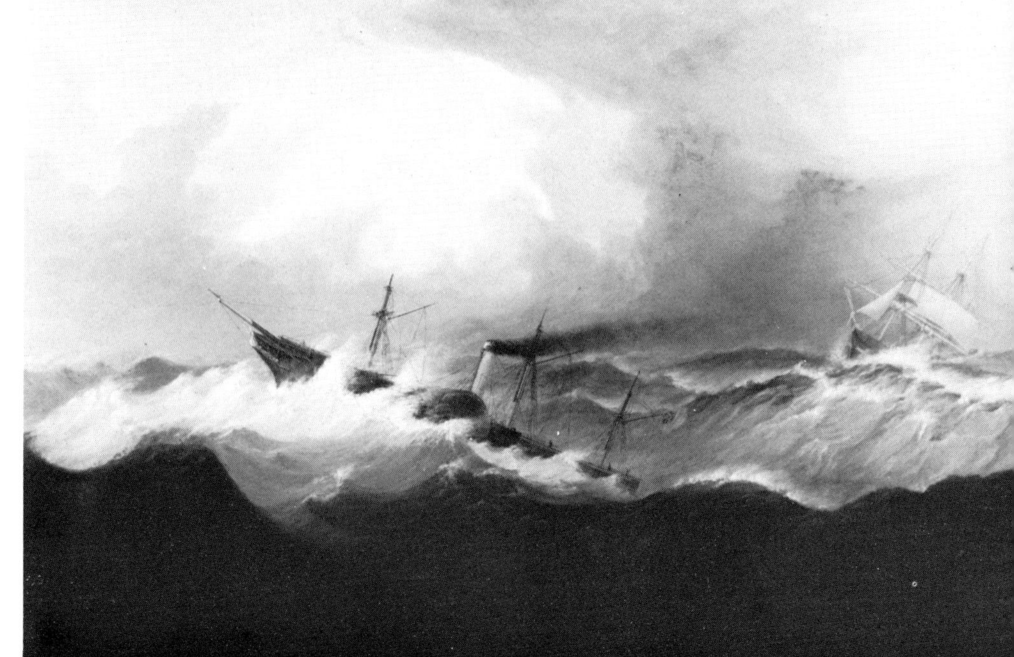

Plate 448. Fitz Hugh Lane, 1804-1865. "The first Cunard transatlantic liner *Britannia* in a storm, 1842." *One of the great problems encountered by paddle steamers, especially in conditions such as these, was that water pulled up into the box caused a loss of power.* Peabody Museum of Salem.

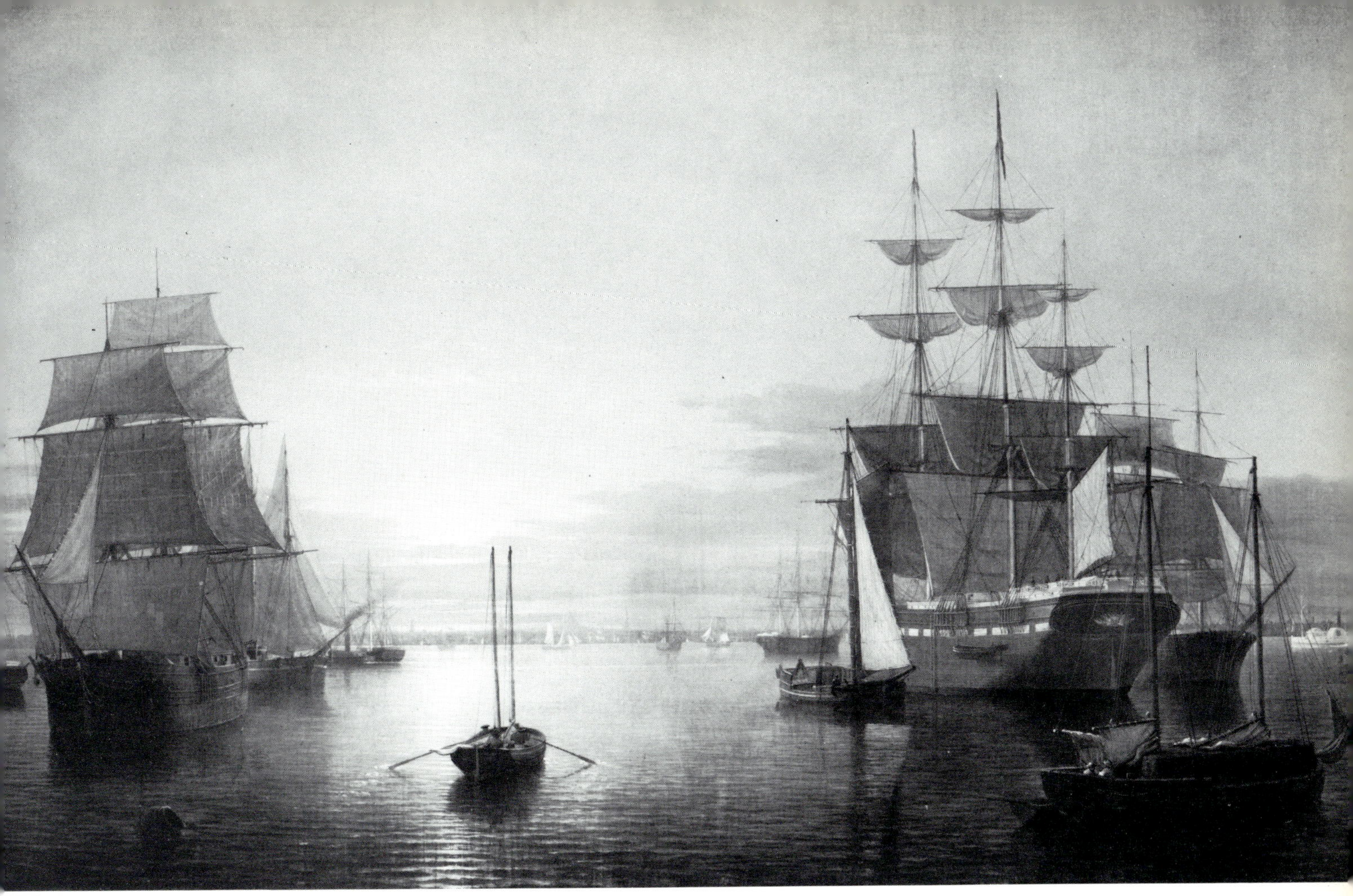

Plate 449. Fitz Hugh Lane, 1804-1865. "View of Boston Harbour, c.1850." *This much admired American artist has created a feeling of serenity and light here. The ship on the right has a sawn off stern, an American convention at this date.* Museum of Fine Arts (M. and M. Karolik Collection), Boston.

Plate 450. Martin Johnson Heade, 1819-1904. "Approaching storm: beach near Newport." *Both this and the next example are dramatic, stylised paintings by another much admired American artist whose influence on his generation was considerable.* Museum of Fine Arts (M. and M. Karolik Collection), Boston.

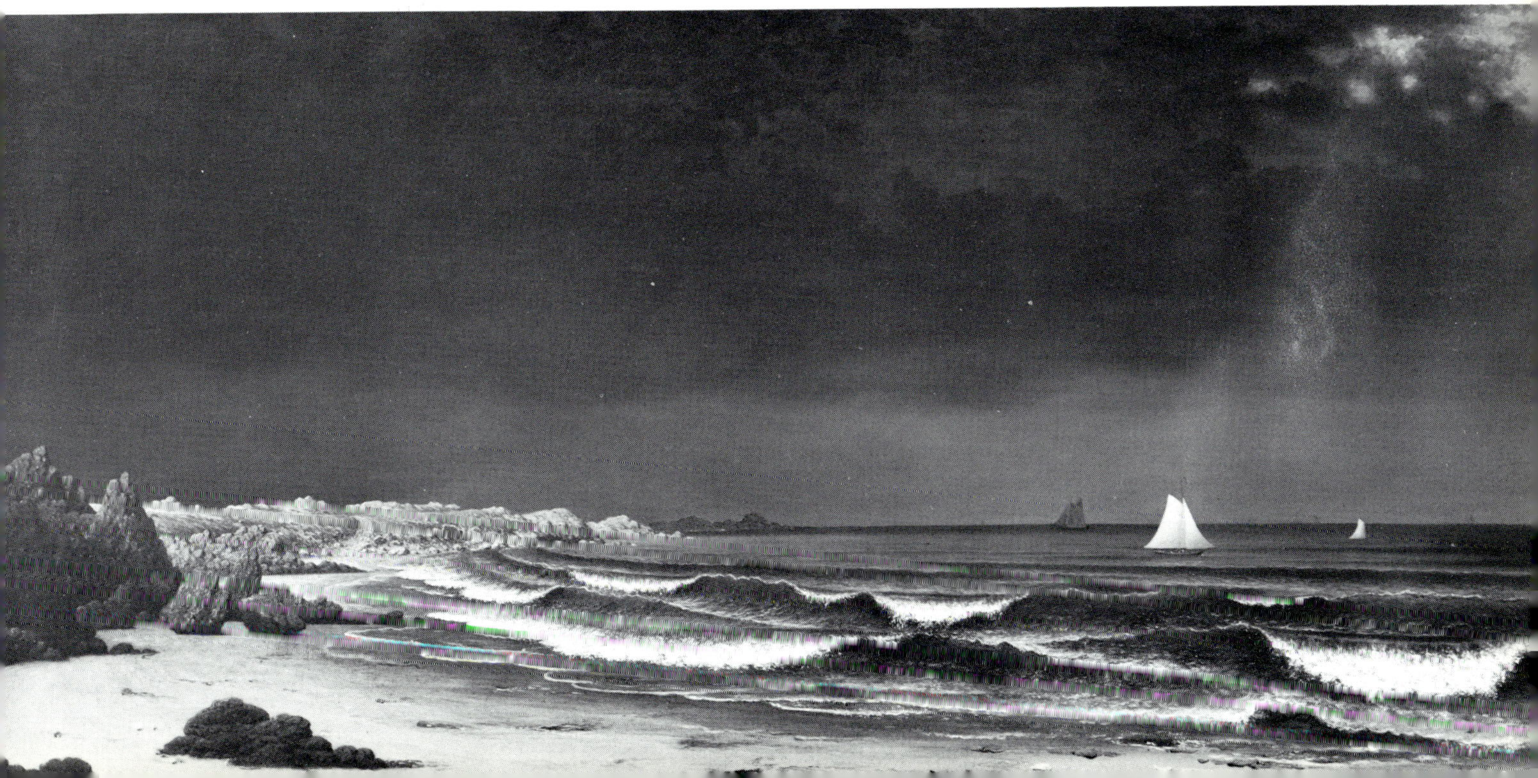

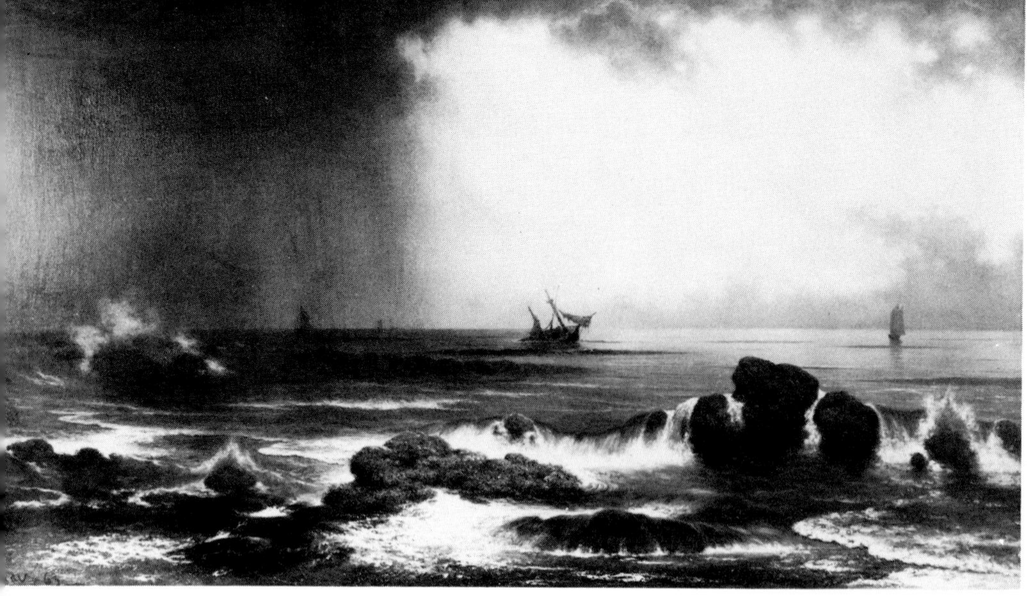

Plate 451. Martin Johnson Heade, 1819-1904. "Coastal scene with a sinking ship." Shelburne Museum, Vermont.

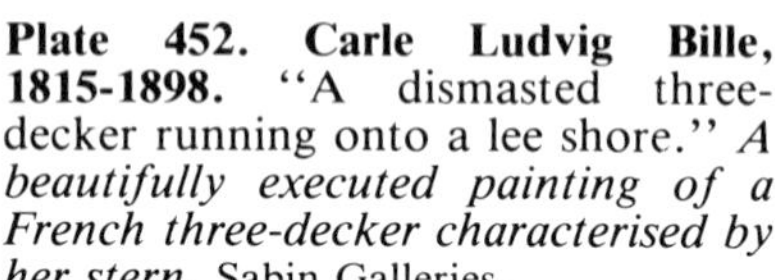

Plate 452. Carle Ludvig Bille, 1815-1898. "A dismasted three-decker running onto a lee shore." *A beautifully executed painting of a French three-decker characterised by her stern.* Sabin Galleries.

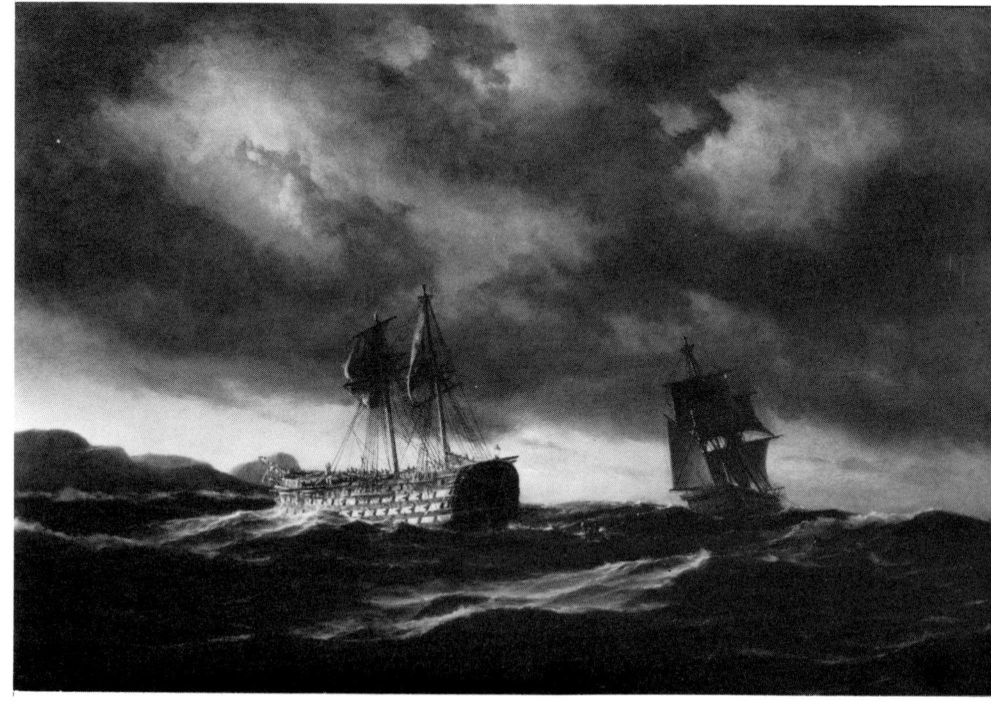

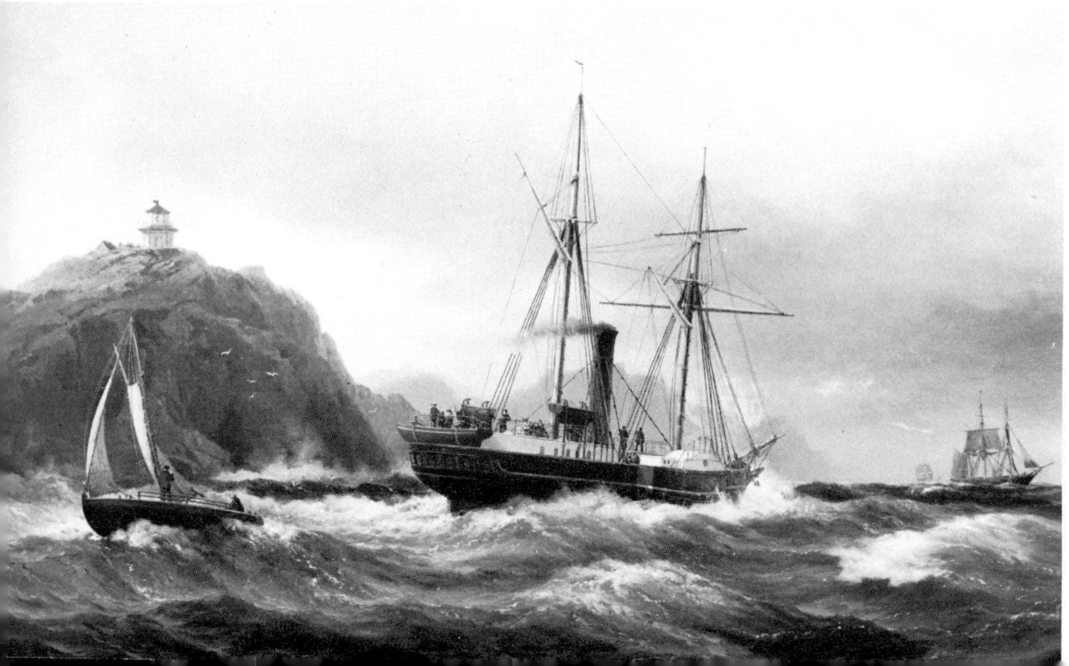

Plate 453. Vilhelm Melbye, 1824-1882. "A paddle-steamer passing a Norwegian lighthouse, dated 1863." *Short haul passenger ships doing a regular run are called packets because they carried mail.* Lansmuseum, Linkoping, Sweden.

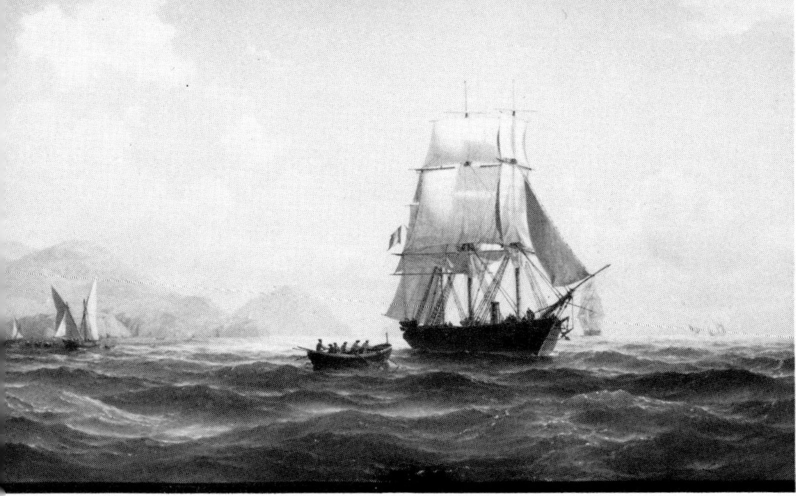

Plate 454. Vilhelm Melbye, 1824-1882. "The Gulf of Naples, dated 1875." *The ship is a French steam-assisted cruiser. The naval ships had such big crews, they never went in for double topsails* . The National Gallery of Canada (gift of Allan Gilmour), Ottawa.

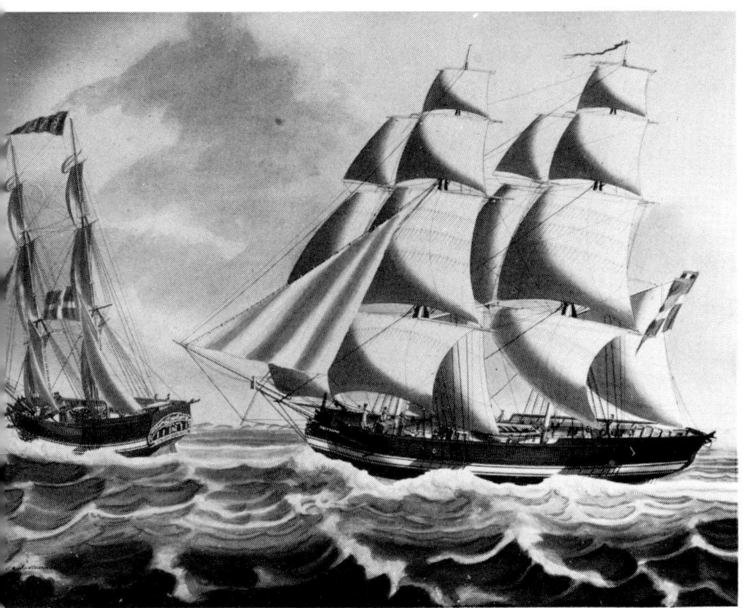

Plate 455. D.A. Teupken, 1801-1845. "The brig *Balticum* out of Altona in two positions, dated 1838." Altonaer Museum, Hamburg.

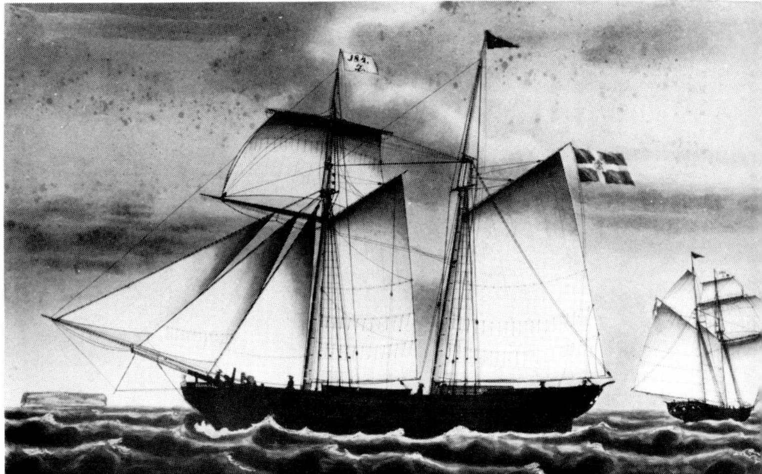

Plate 456. J. Hansen, fl. early 19th century. "The schooner *Regina,* out of Muhlerberg/Blankenese, 1840." Altonaer Museum, Hamburg.

Plate 457. Albertus van Beest, 1820-1860. "New Bedford from Fairhaven." Pen and wash. *Already an established artist, van Beest went to America in 1845 where he worked with William Bradford.* Museum of Fine Arts, Boston.

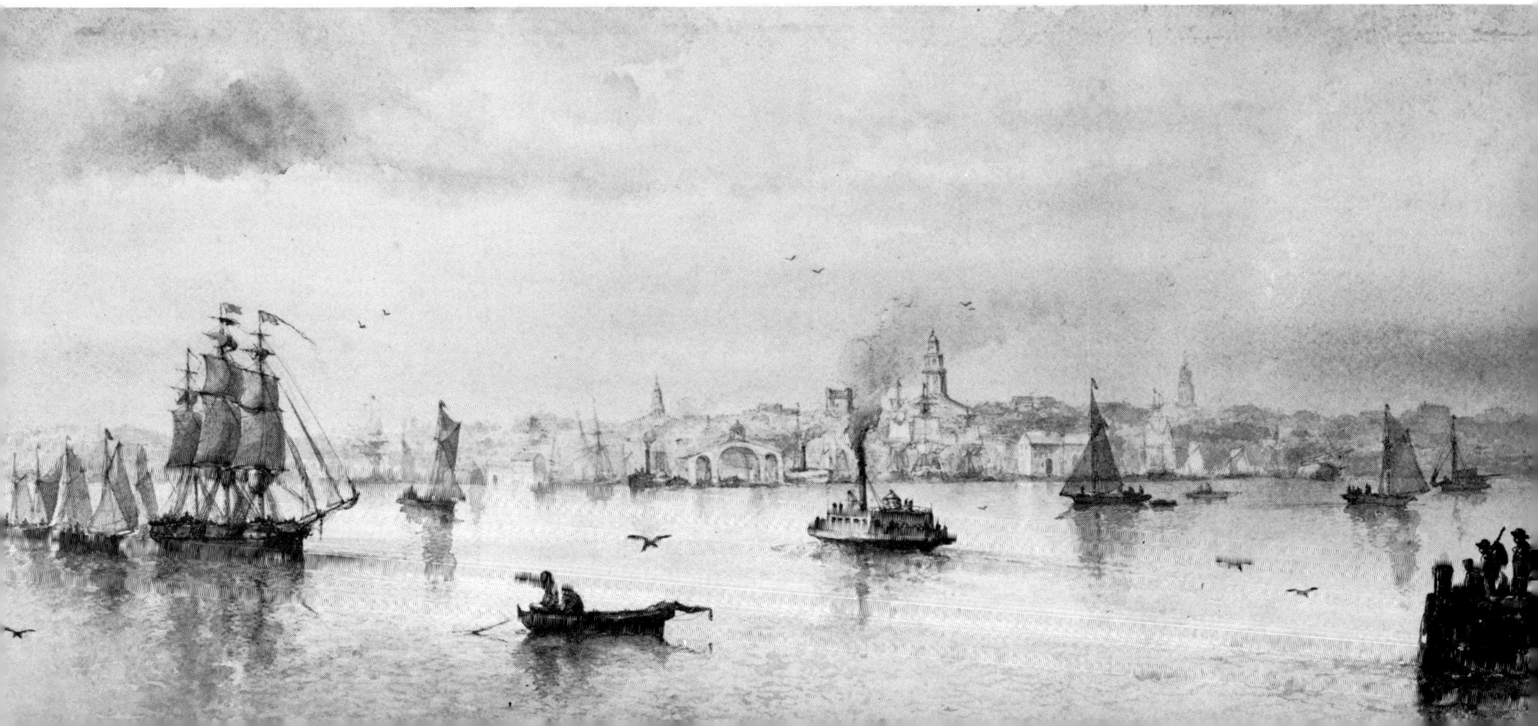

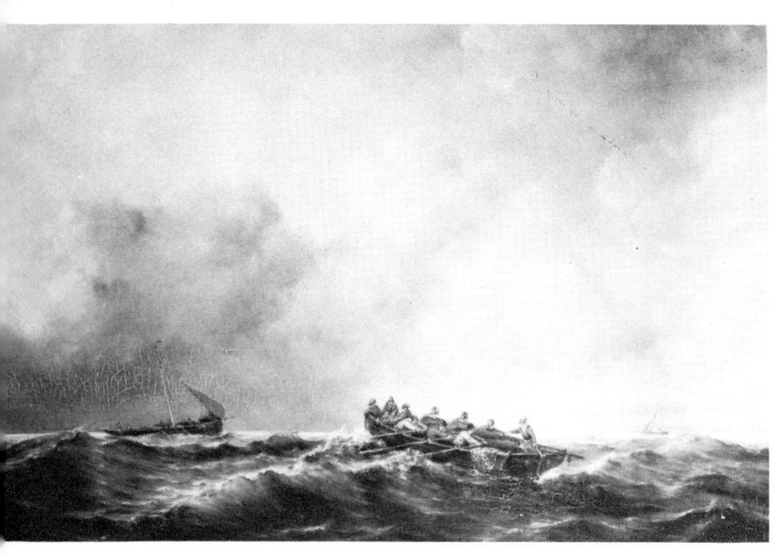

Plate 458. Albertus van Beest, 1820-1860. "Fishermen rowing in a heavy sea." *Van Beest's ability to portray the sea is well shown in this example.* Boymans van Beuningen Museum, Rotterdam.

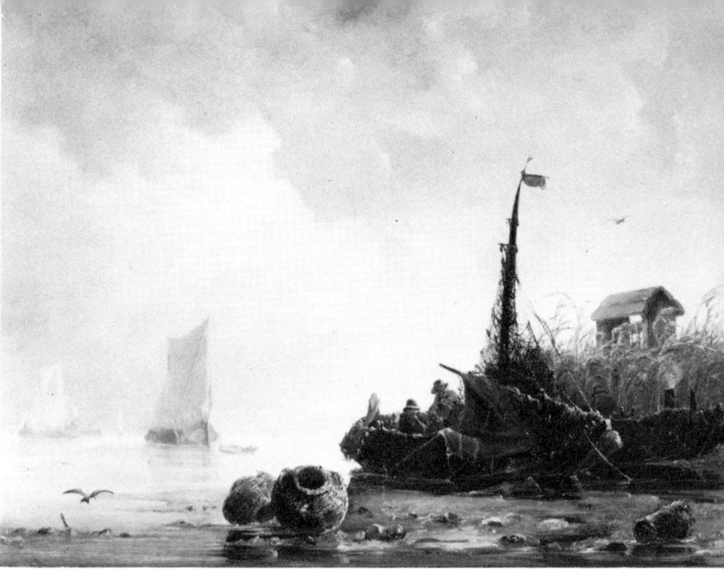

Plate 459. Albertus van Beest, 1820-1860. "Shore scene on the Zeeland coast, dated 1843." *By contrast, a clear return to the traditions of Dutch painting.* Boymans van Beuningen Museum, Rotterdam.

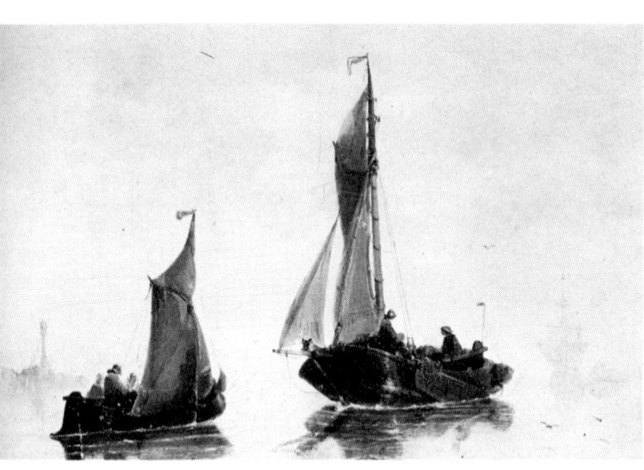

Plate 460. Albertus van Beest, 1820-1860. "Calm with fishing craft, 1848." Boymans van Beuningen Museum, Rotterdam.

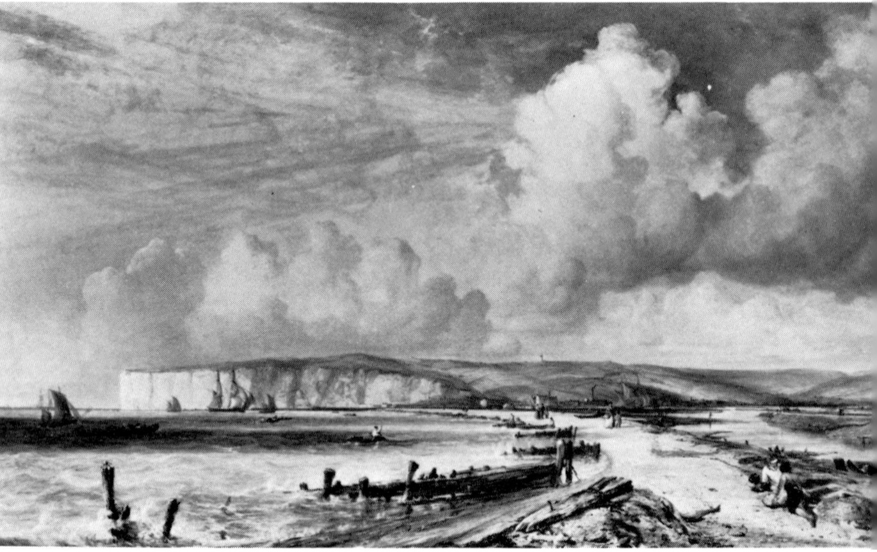

Plate 461. Alfred Clint, 1807-1883. "Scene on the south coast, dated 1845." *Clint was a coastal painter of fine quality.* Sotheby's.

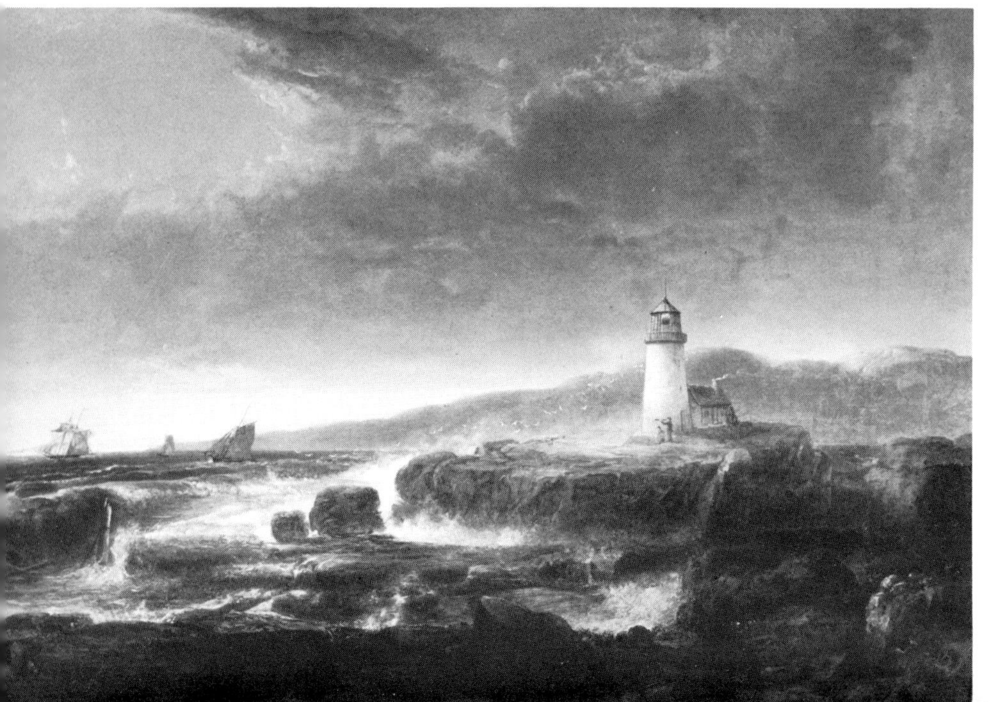

Plate 462. Thomas Doughty, 1793-1856. "Mount Desert Lighthouse, 1847." *An American painter of the Hudson River School, emerging from the primitive.* The Newark Museum Collection, N.J.

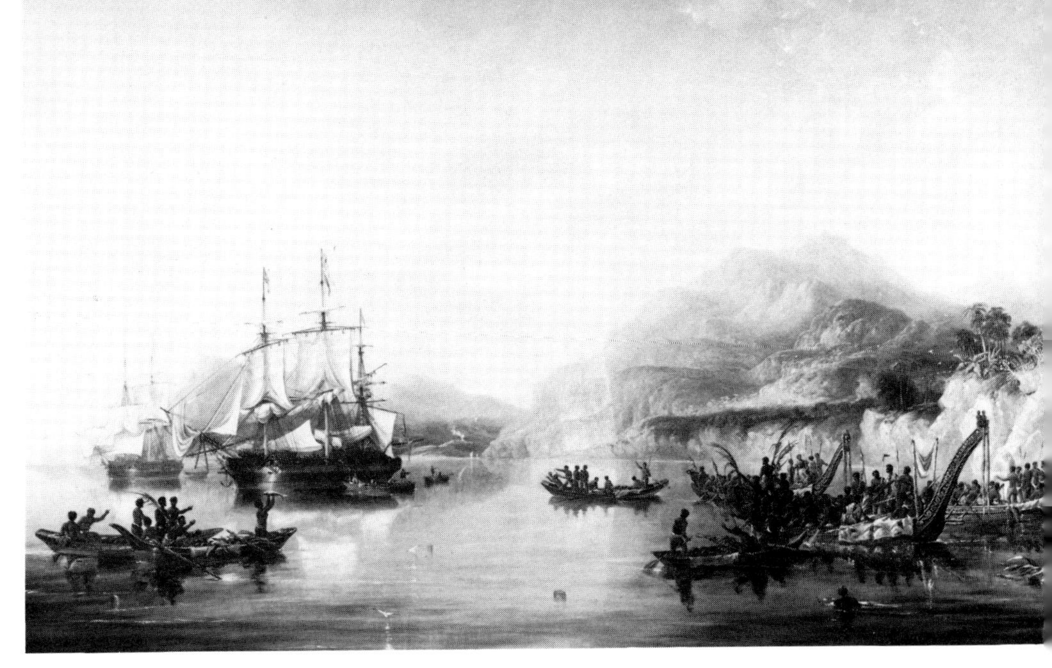

Plate 463. John Wilson Carmichael, 1800-1868. "Survey ships in the South Seas, dated 1847." *Survey ships were usually small cruising vessels, lightly armed.* National Maritime Museum, Greenwich.

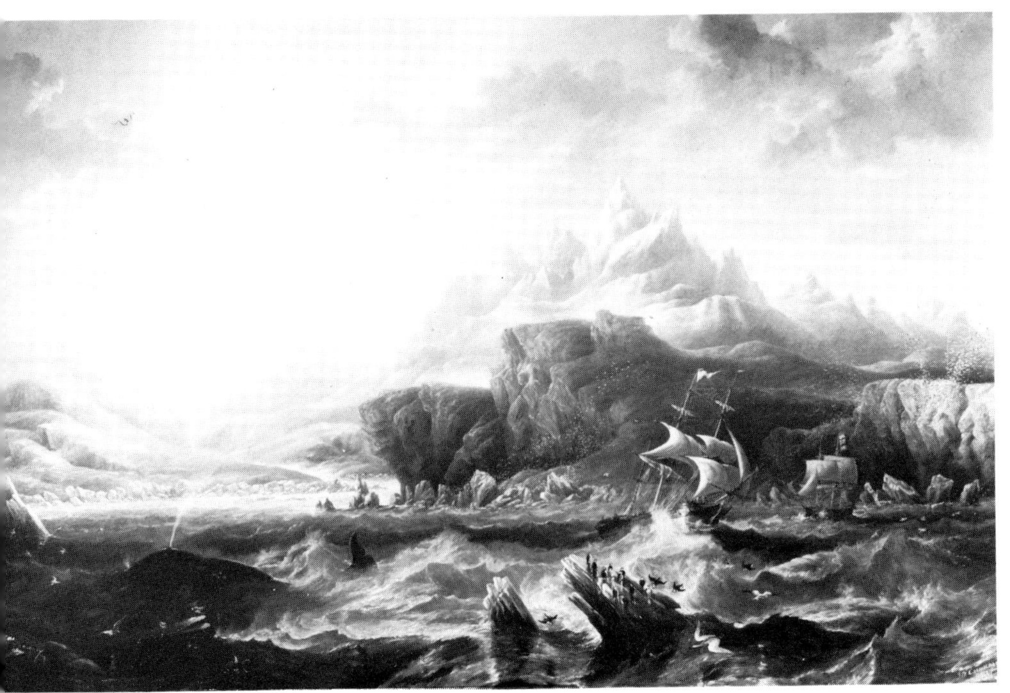

Plate 464. John Wilson Carmichael, 1800-1868. "Survey ships in the Antarctic, dated 1847." *The pair to the preceding illustration.* National Maritime Museum, Greenwich.

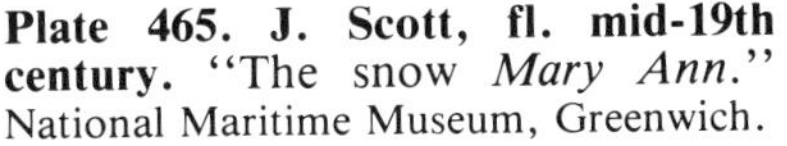

Plate 465. J. Scott, fl. mid-19th century. "The snow *Mary Ann.*" National Maritime Museum, Greenwich.

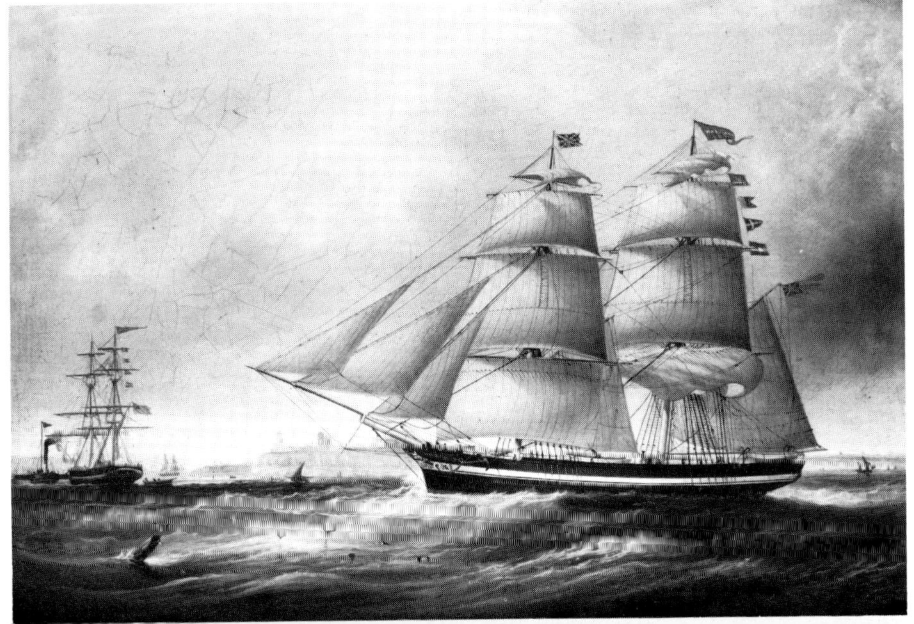

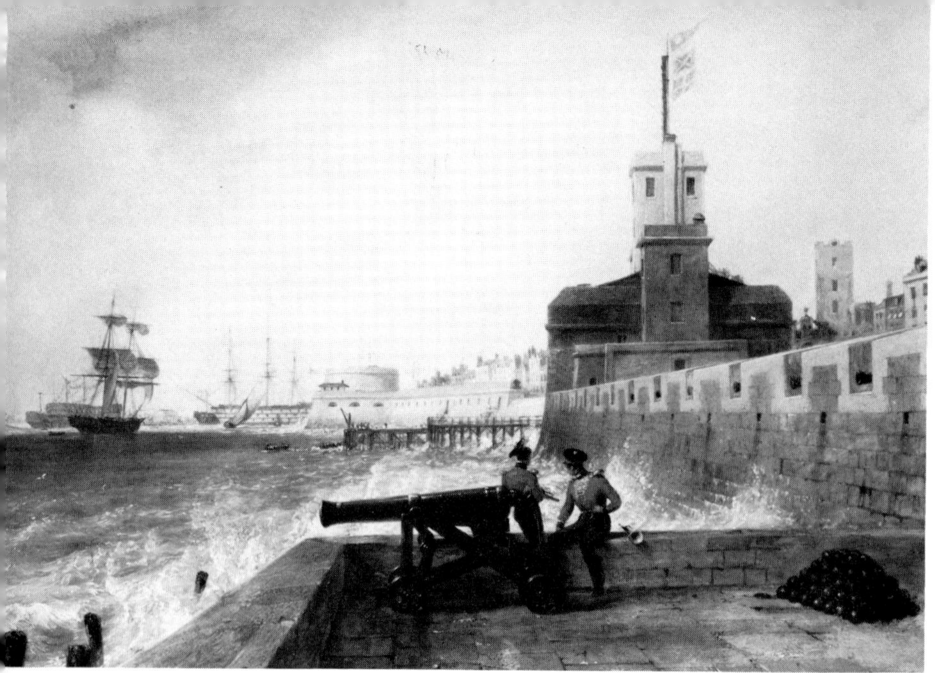

Plate 466. Edward William Cooke, 1811-1880. "The battery, Portsmouth harbour." National Maritime Museum, Greenwich.

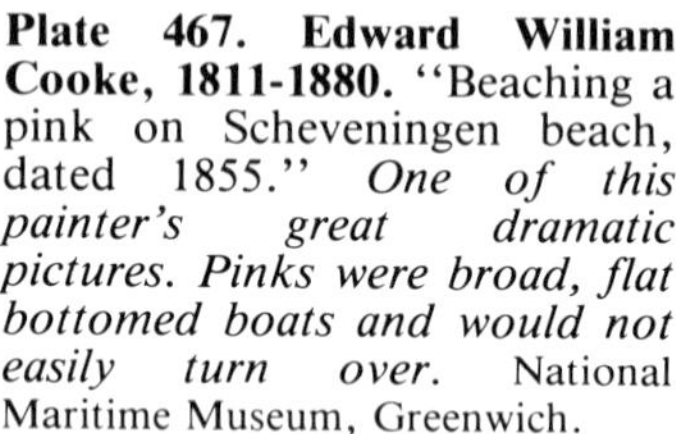

Plate 467. Edward William Cooke, 1811-1880. "Beaching a pink on Scheveningen beach, dated 1855." *One of this painter's great dramatic pictures. Pinks were broad, flat bottomed boats and would not easily turn over.* National Maritime Museum, Greenwich.

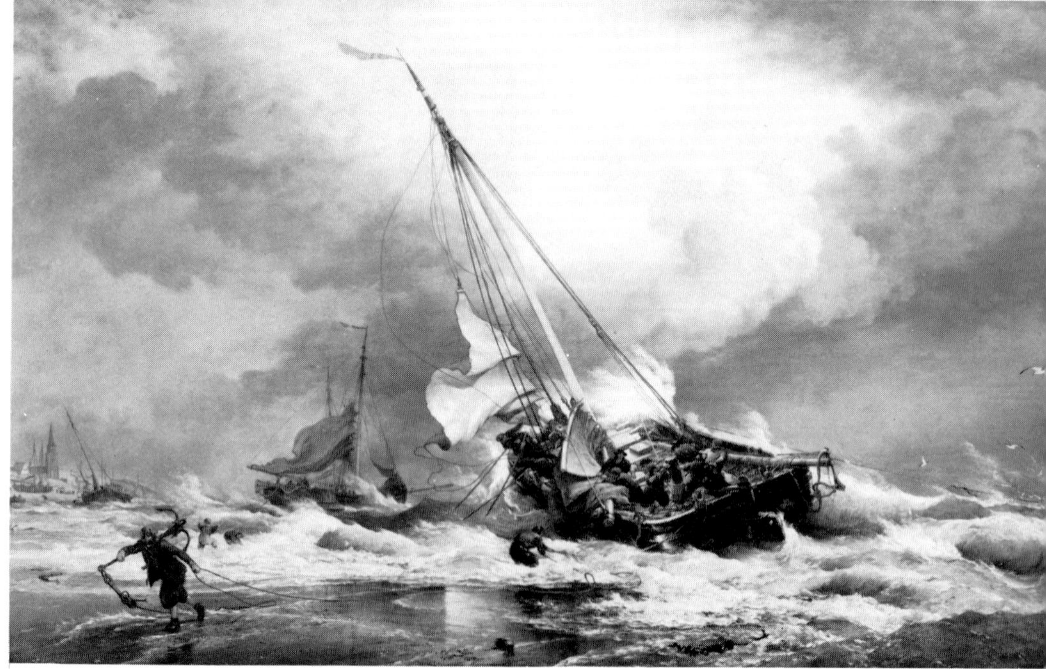

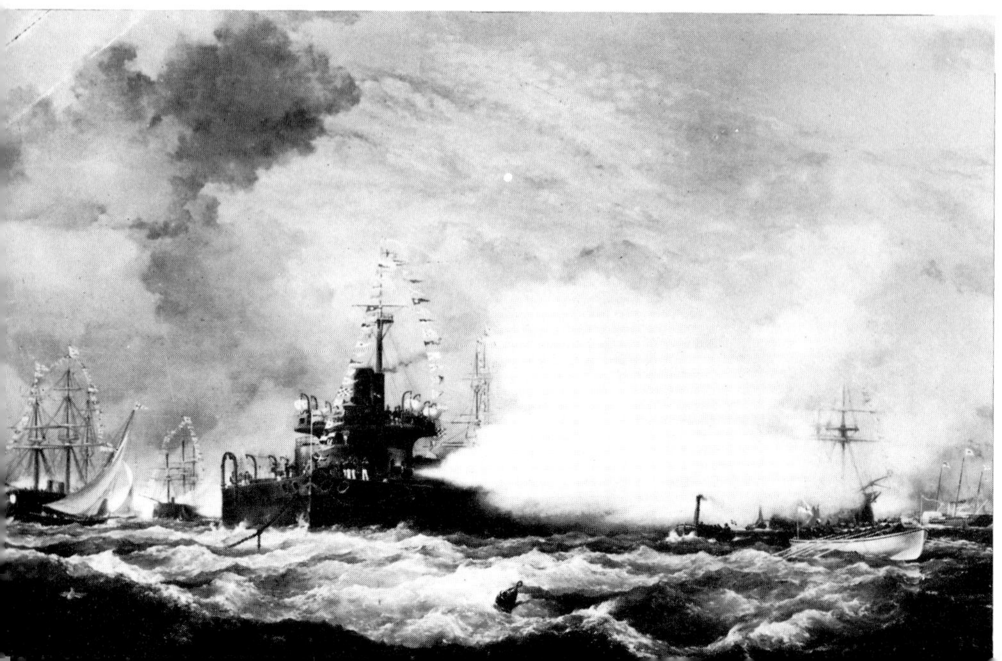

Plate 468. Edward William Cooke, 1811-1880. "H.M.S. *Devastation* at the review at Spithead for the Shah of Persia in 1873." National Maritime Museum, Greenwich (Greenwich Hospital Collection).

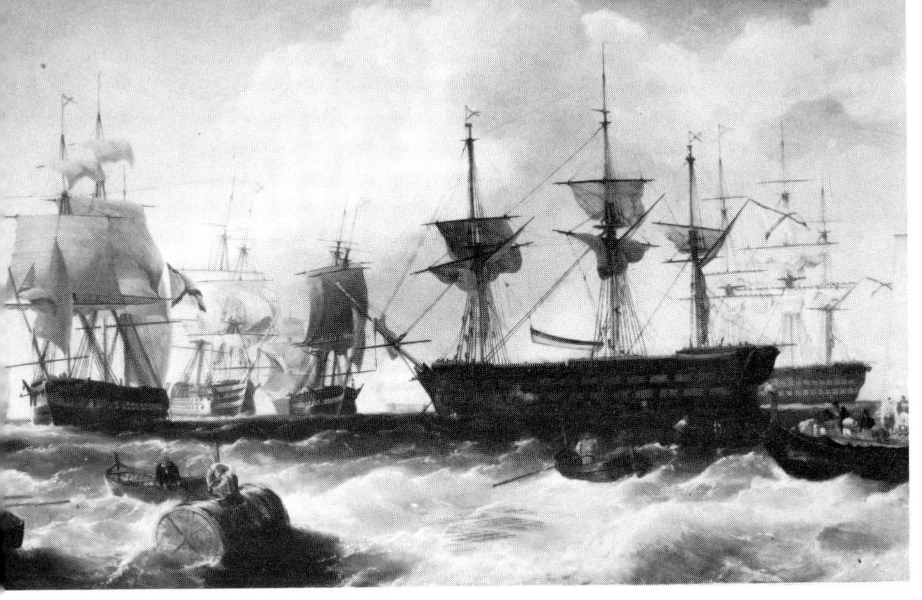

Plate 469. G.W. Butland, fl.1831-1843. "The Russian fleet at Malta in 1827." *A Gravesend artist who has been confused with E.W. Cooke. The ship's boat in the centre is being slung aboard.* National Maritime Museum, Greenwich.

Plate 470 *(right)*. **William E.D. Stuart, fl. mid-19th century.** "Battle of Trafalgar in 1805, exhibited 1848." *A stylised representation of an historical incident.* Christie's.

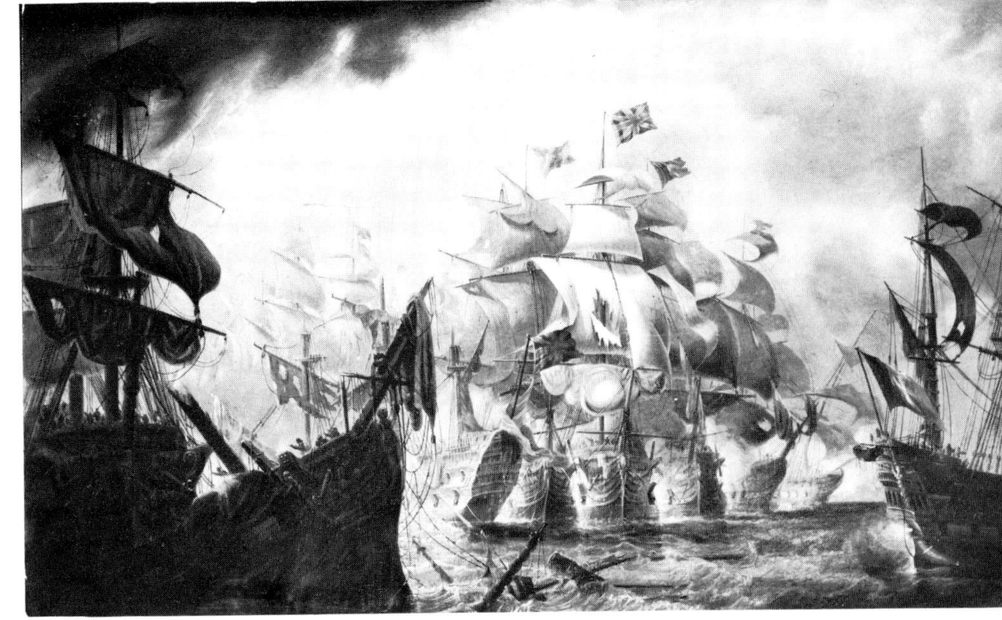

Plate 471 *(below)*. **Miles Edmund Cotman, 1810-1858.** "Dutch boats on the Medway." *The strongly drawn, heavily contrasting shades are typical of the Cotman style. The work is like his father's, but inferior.* Castle Museum, Norwich.

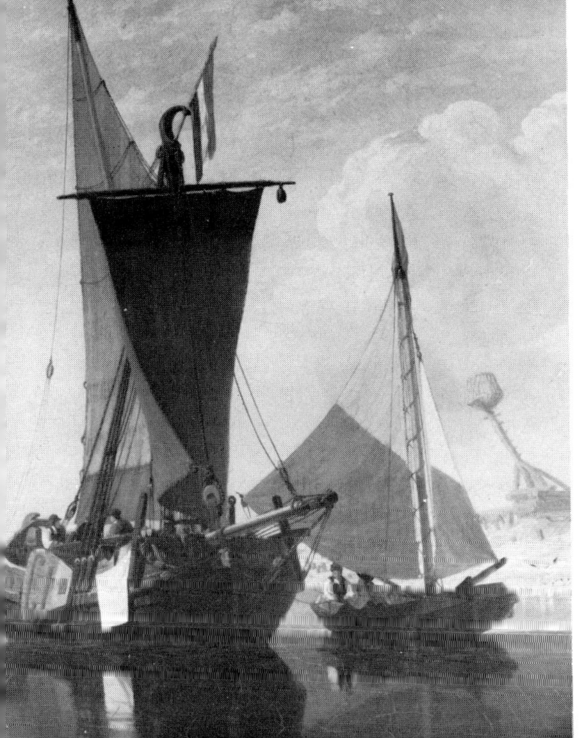

Plate 472. Miles Edmund Cotman, 1810-1858. "Dutch coastal craft becalmed." Sotheby's.

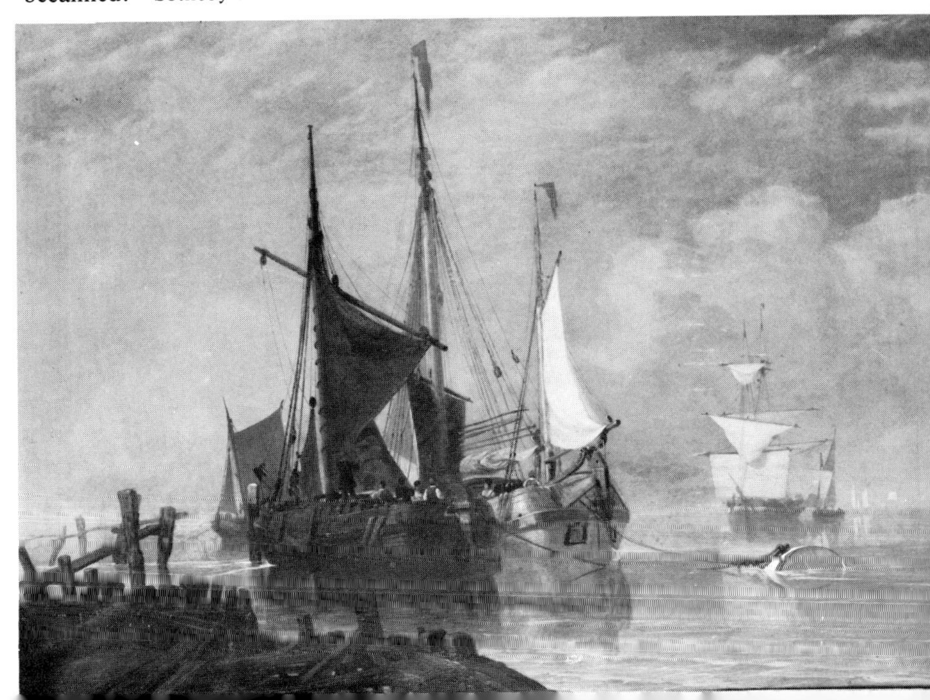

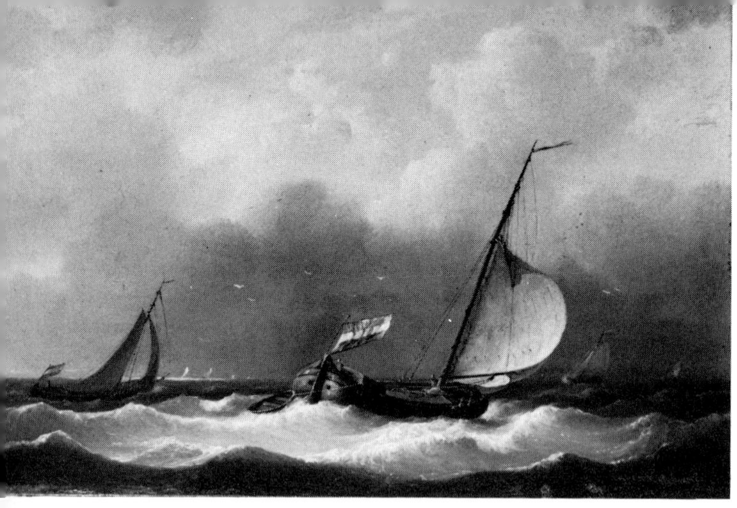

Plate 473. Jacobus Hendricus Johannes Nooteboom, 1811-1878. "Dutch coastal craft in a gale." *In the drawing of the sea and the use of light and colour, he might be considered to be an unsuccessful follower of J.C. Schotel.* Sotheby's.

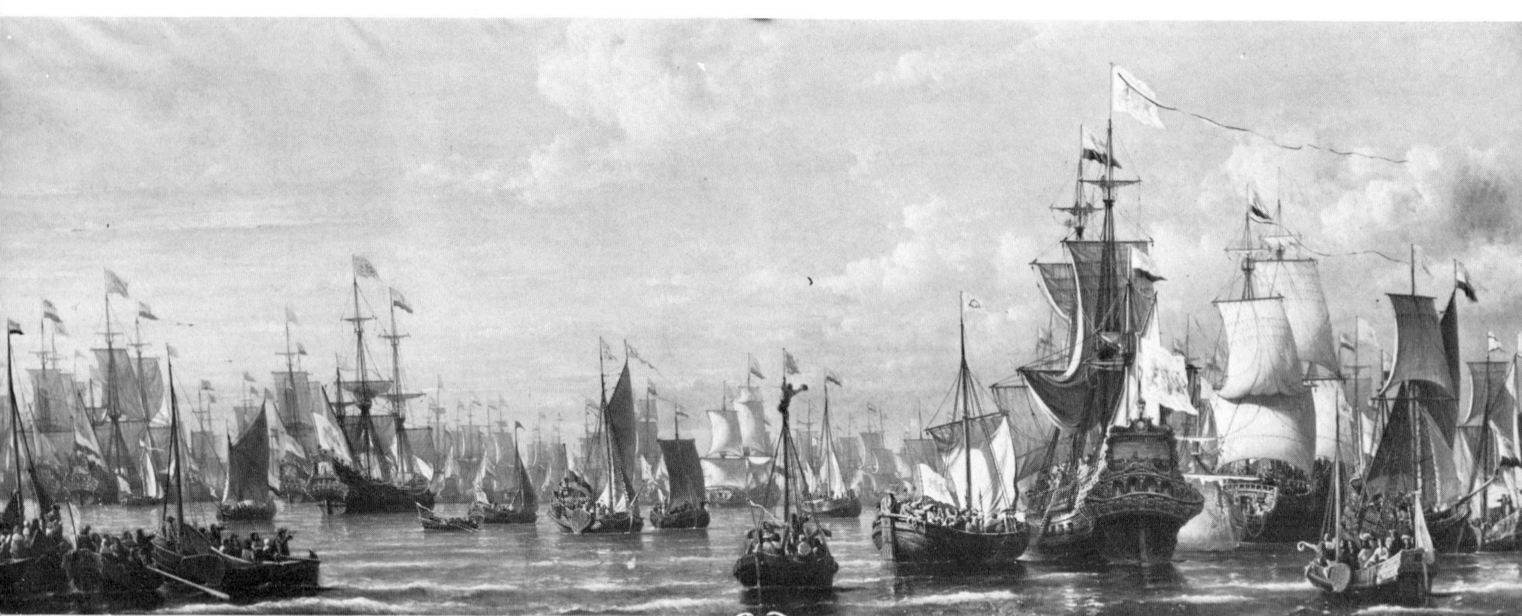

Plate 474. Everhardus Koster, 1817-1892. "King William III inspecting the Dutch fleet in 1691." *One of a pair of very large paintings. Despite the numerous vessels the composition is successful and the sea well executed.* Victoria and Albert Museum.

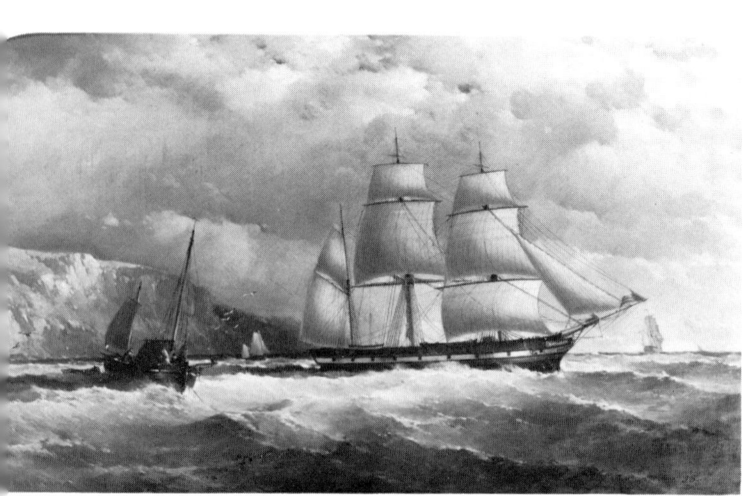

Plate 475. John Syer, 1815-1885. "A barque hove to off the English coast." Christie's.

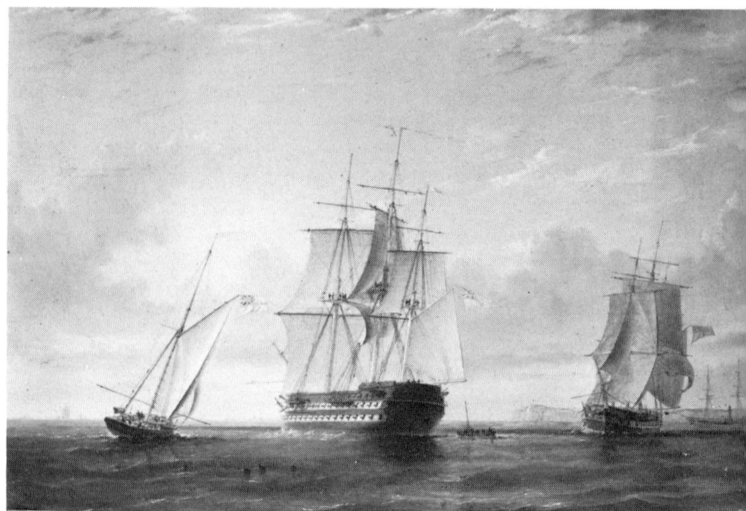

Plate 476. John Warkup Swift, 1815-1869. "A two-decker and a frigate in the Downs." *A little-known but prolific painter producing rather stiff paintings.* Private collection.

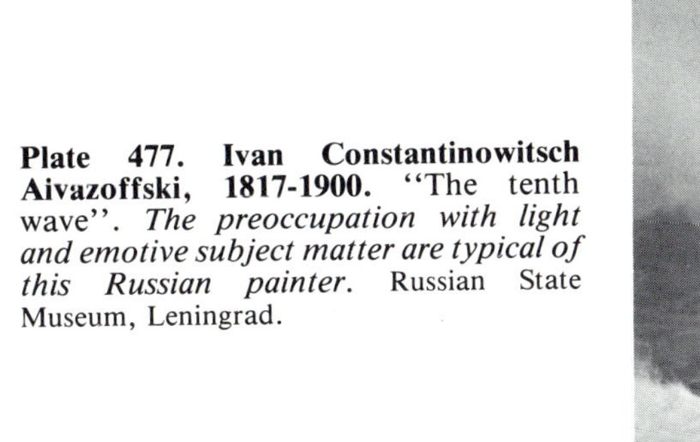

Plate 477. Ivan Constantinowitsch Aivazoffski, 1817-1900. "The tenth wave". *The preoccupation with light and emotive subject matter are typical of this Russian painter.* Russian State Museum, Leningrad.

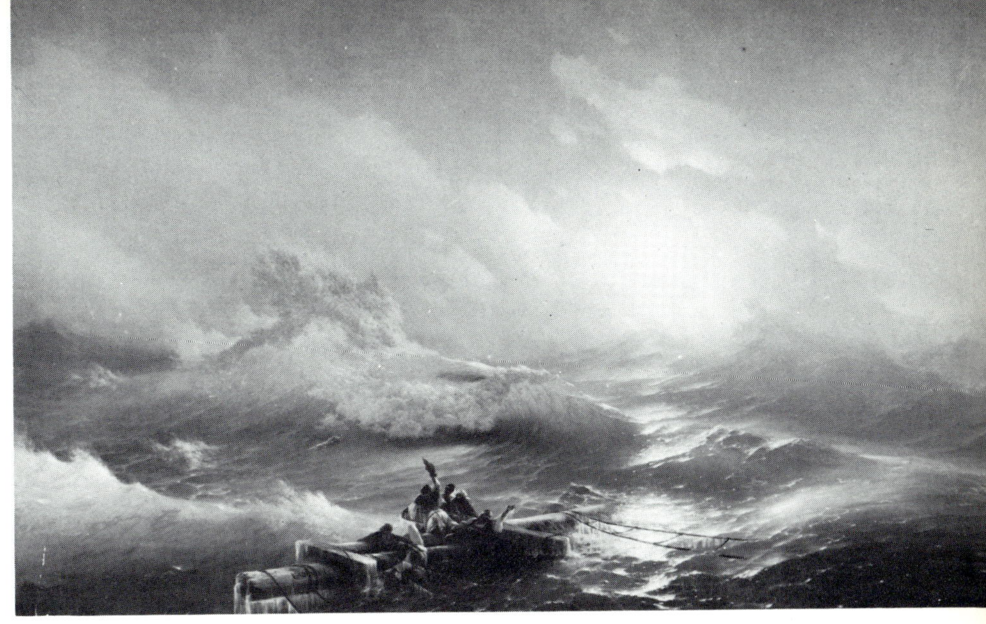

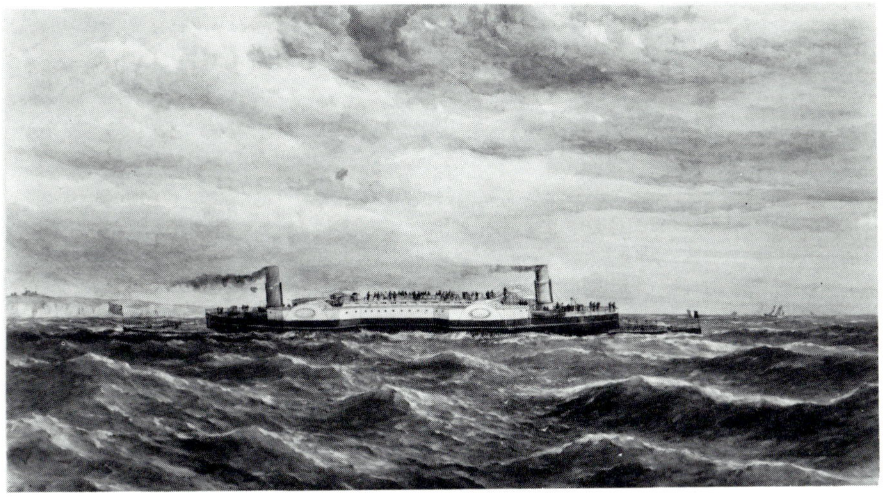

Plate 478. Thomas Goldsworth Dutton, c.1819-1891. "The double ended cross Channel packet *Bessemer*." Watercolour. *The* Bessemer *was a complete failure. With two sets of paddles, two boilers and power assistance (and a central saloon on fully articulated gimbals) it was found too difficult to control, and took chunks out of Calais pier on its first crossing. The cabin was re-erected at a house in Kent, which became a girls' school, and was in use as a summer house until the 1950s.* National Maritime Museum, Greenwich.

Plate 479. Thomas Goldsworth Dutton, c.1819-1891. "The ship *Orient* off Gibraltar." *Dutton was an important and prolific marine painter as well as lithographer. This painting can be dated to around the early 1860s. The* Orient *still has simple topsails and an advanced clipper hull which could also be seen in the 1870s.* National Maritime Museum, Greenwich.

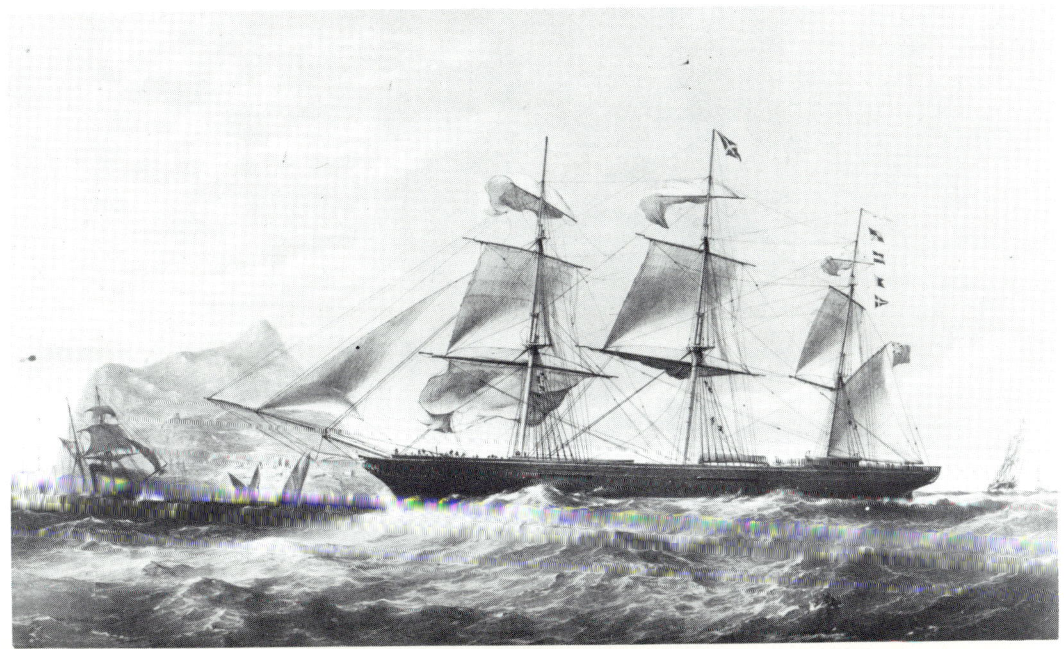

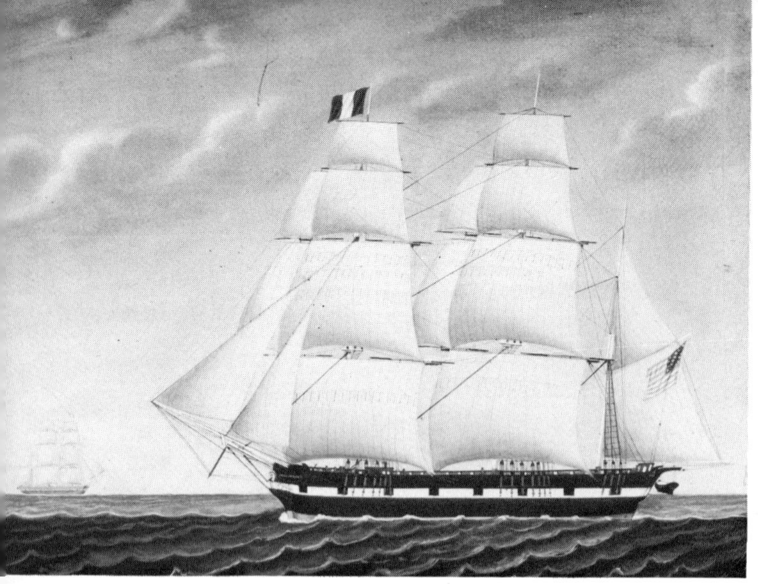

Plate 480. Benjamin Franklin West, 1818-1854. "The barque *Chalcedony* of Salem." *A charming formal American ship portrait.* Peabody Museum of Salem.

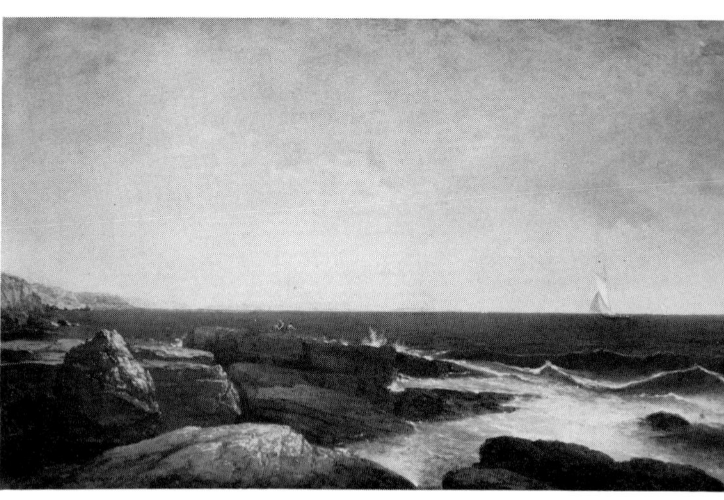

Plate 481. John Frederick Kensett, 1818-1872, and David Huntington. "Seascape, Newport." Museum of Fine Arts (M. and M. Karolik Collection), Boston.

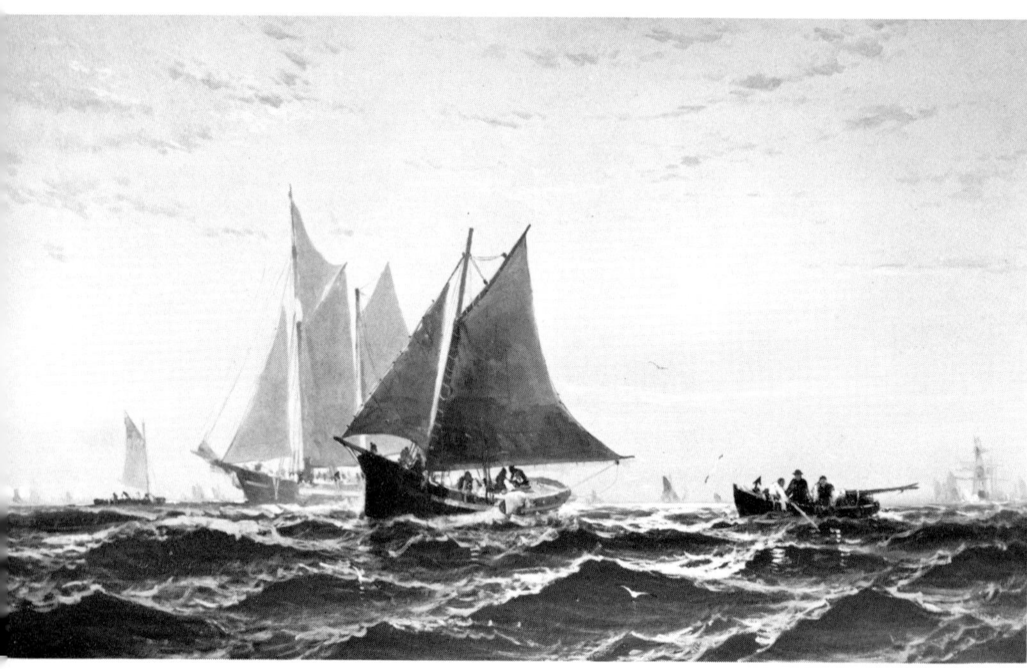

Plate 482. James Hamilton, 1819-1878. "Fishermen at sea." *This work is attributed to Hamilton.* Shelburne Museum, Vermont.

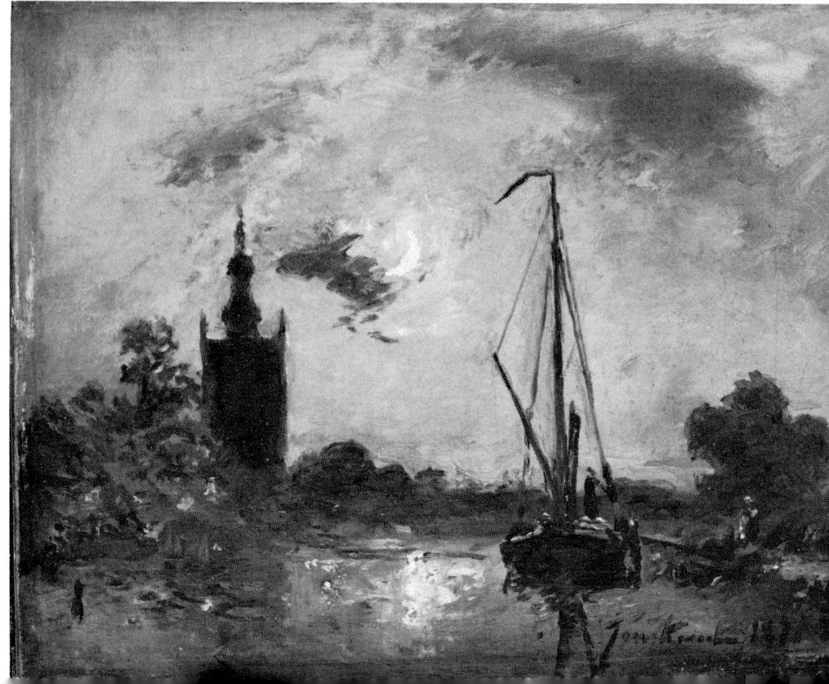

Plate 483. Johan Barthold Jongkind, 1819-1891. "Moonlit river scene." Rijksmuseum, Amsterdam.

Plate 484. **Johan Frederick Schutz, 1817-1888.** "A Dutch steam packet driven ashore in a storm, about 1850." Zeeland Museum, Middelburg.

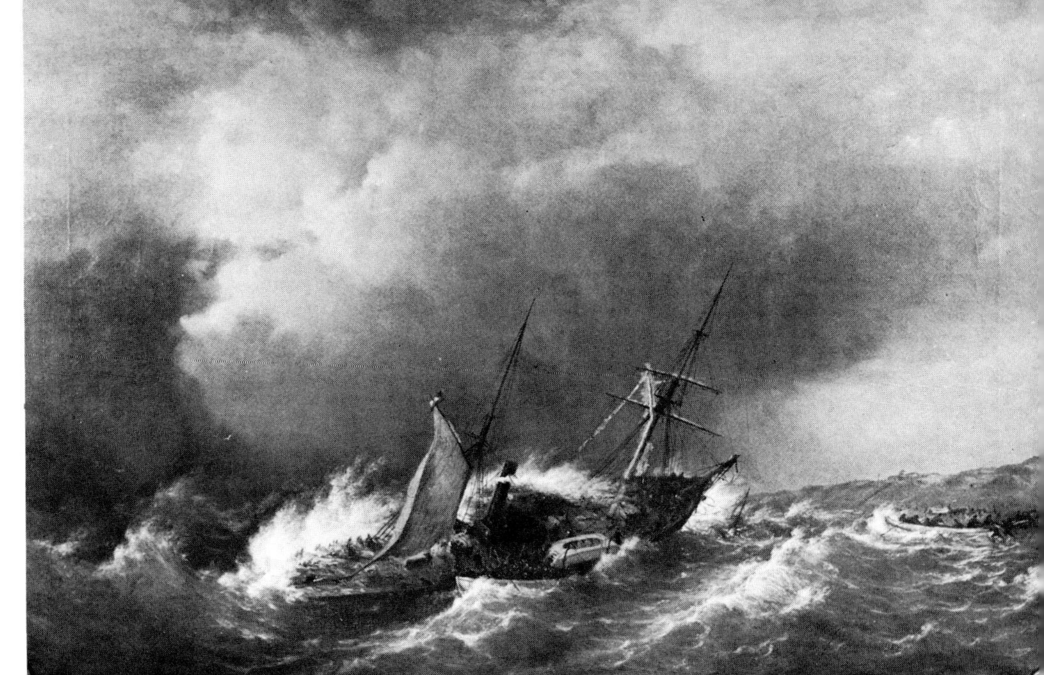

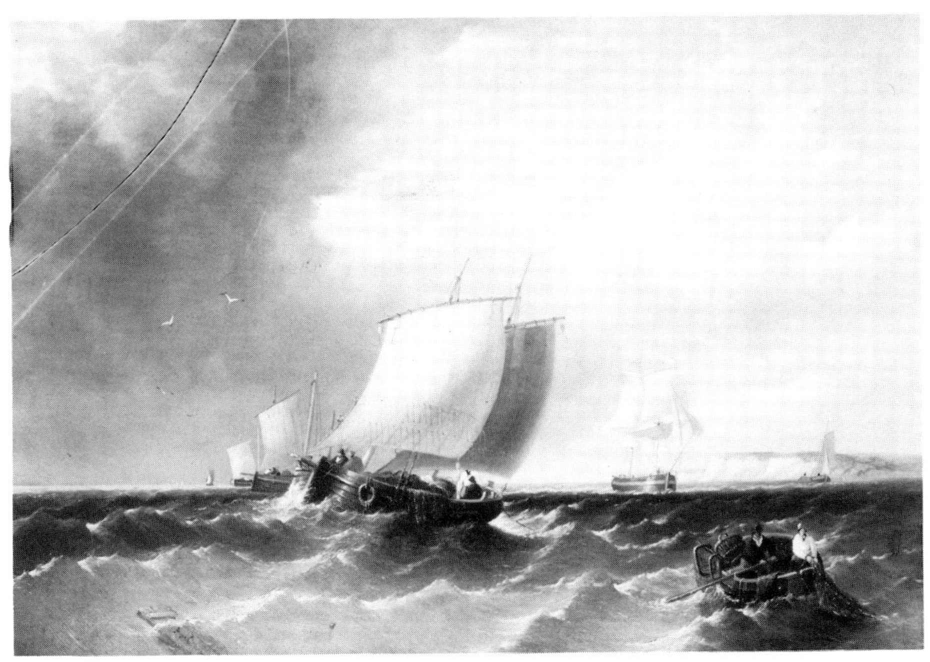

Plate 485. Archibald Webb, c.1800-c.1866. "A fishing lugger off the coast of Kent, about 1850." National Maritime Museum, Greenwich.

Plate 486. Thomas Sewell Robins, 1809-1880. "The *America* yacht racing against yachts of the Royal Yacht Squadron, dated 1851." Royal Yacht Squadron.

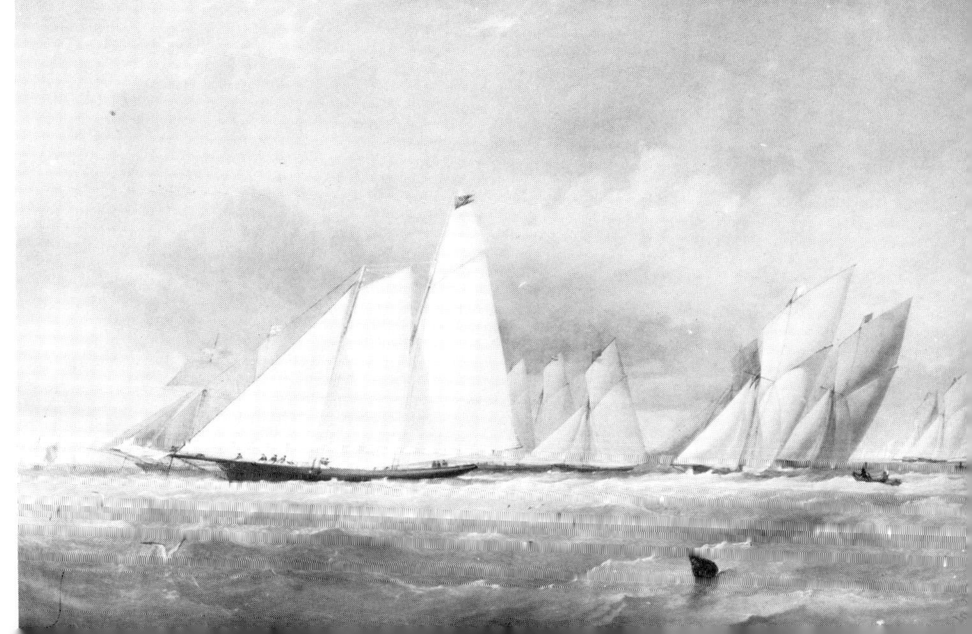

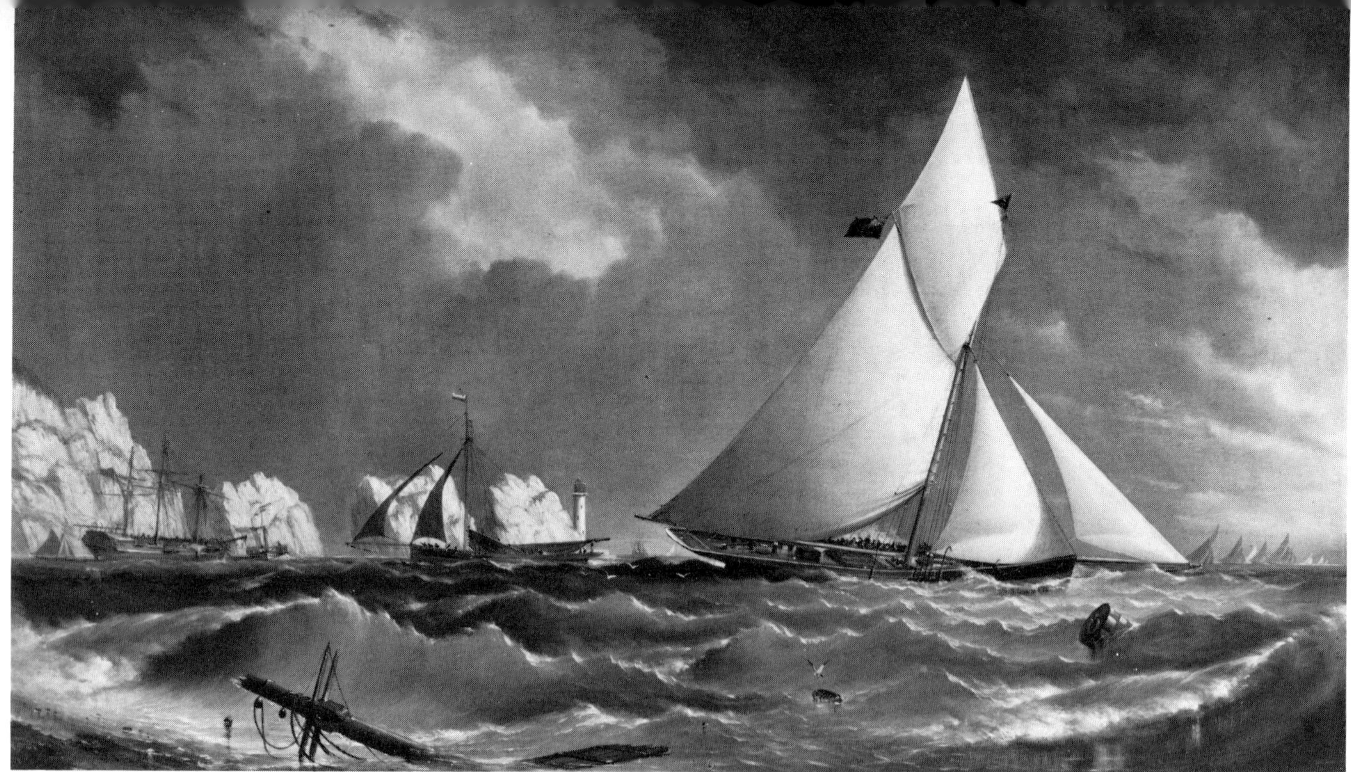

Plate 487. Haughton Forrest, 1825-1924. "The cutter *Julia* off the Needles in the Royal Yacht Squadron Cup Race in 1853." *The American racing yacht of the period was extremely broad in the beam, making her very powerful in strong winds.* John Mitchell & Co.

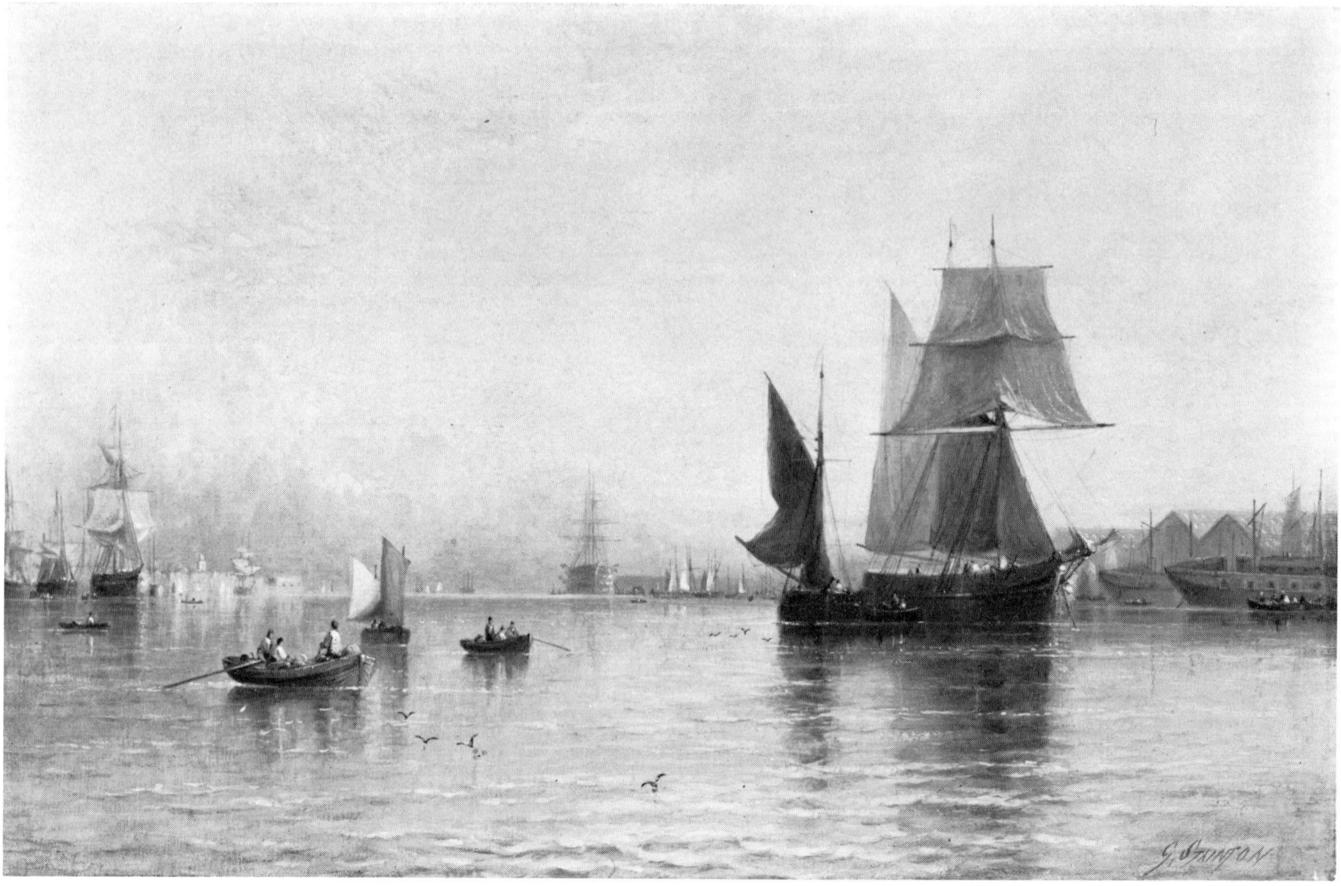

Plate 488. George Stainton, fl. mid-19th century. "Portsmouth Harbour." Malcolm Henderson Esq.

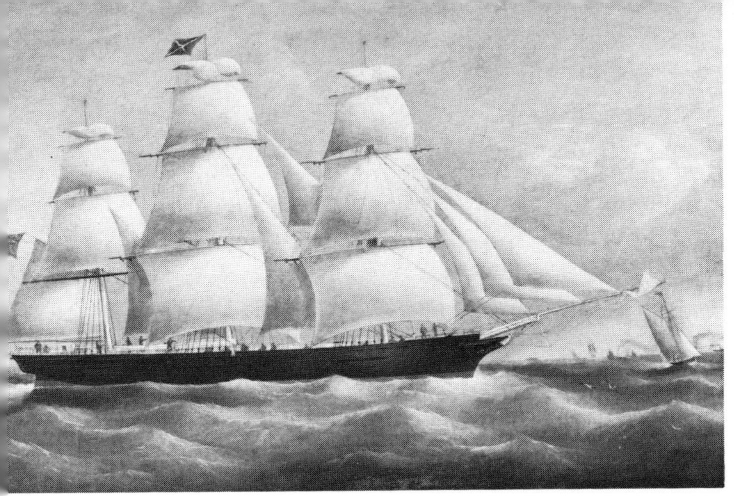

Plate 489. Richard B. Spencer, fl. mid-19th century. "The ship *Eveline.*" National Maritime Museum, Greenwich.

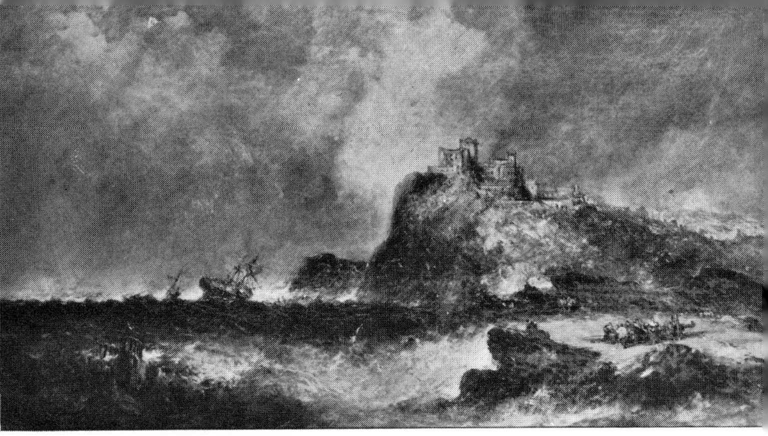

Plate 490. William MacAlpine, fl. mid-19th century. "Coast scene with a wreck." *An artist whose strange, stylised paintings of the aftermath of storms and sea battles often include awkward, ill drawn ships.* Sotheby's.

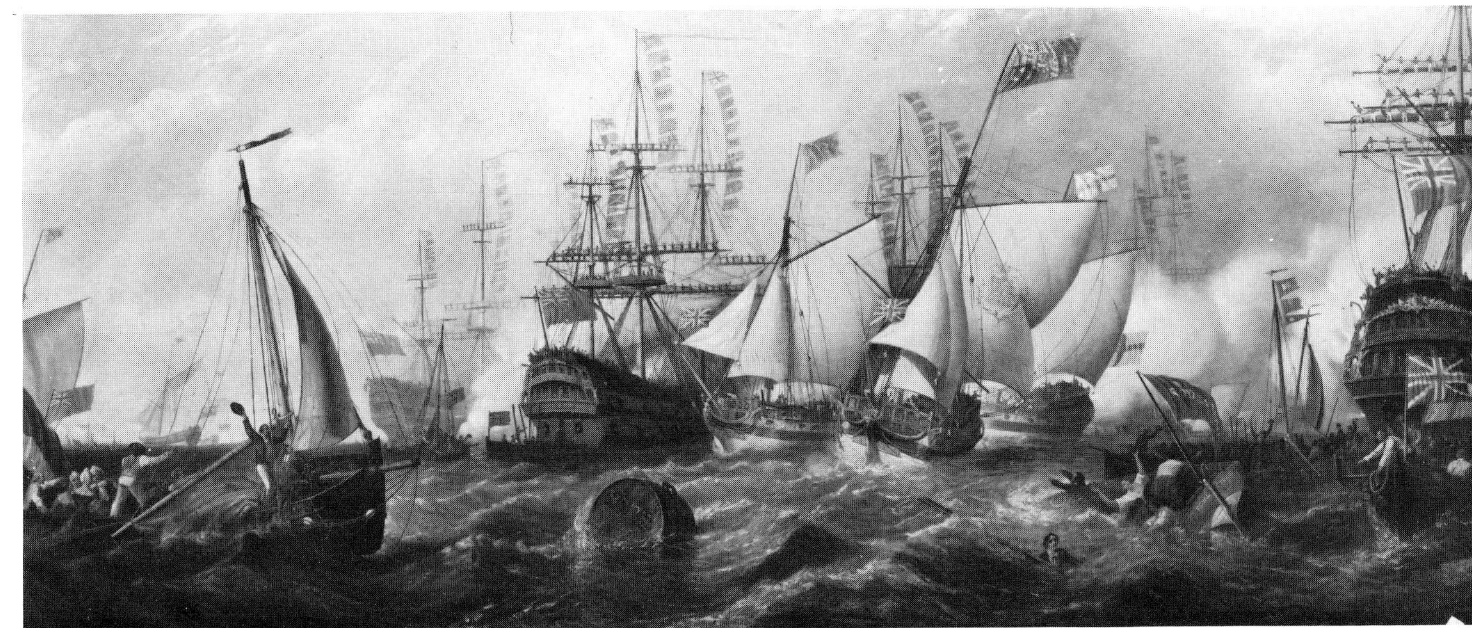

Plate 491. William Stuart, fl. mid-19th century. "The arrival in England of King George I in April 1714." *Typical of the high interest in historical scenes of this period. There is perhaps more spirit than accuracy in the delineation of the shipping though this example is very successful.* Sotheby's.

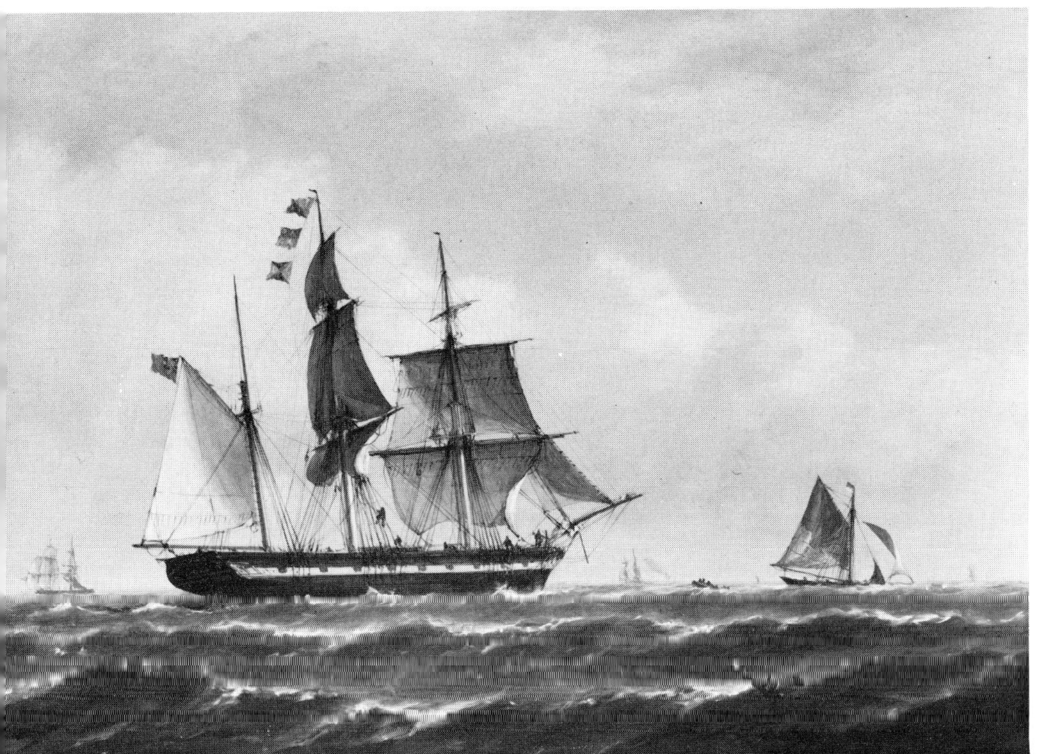

Plate 492. Richard Henry Nibbs, c.1816-1893. "The barque *Peeress* hove to." *The mainsails are backed and the foresails and mizzen are filling, the effect being to stop her completely.* National Maritime Museum, Greenwich.

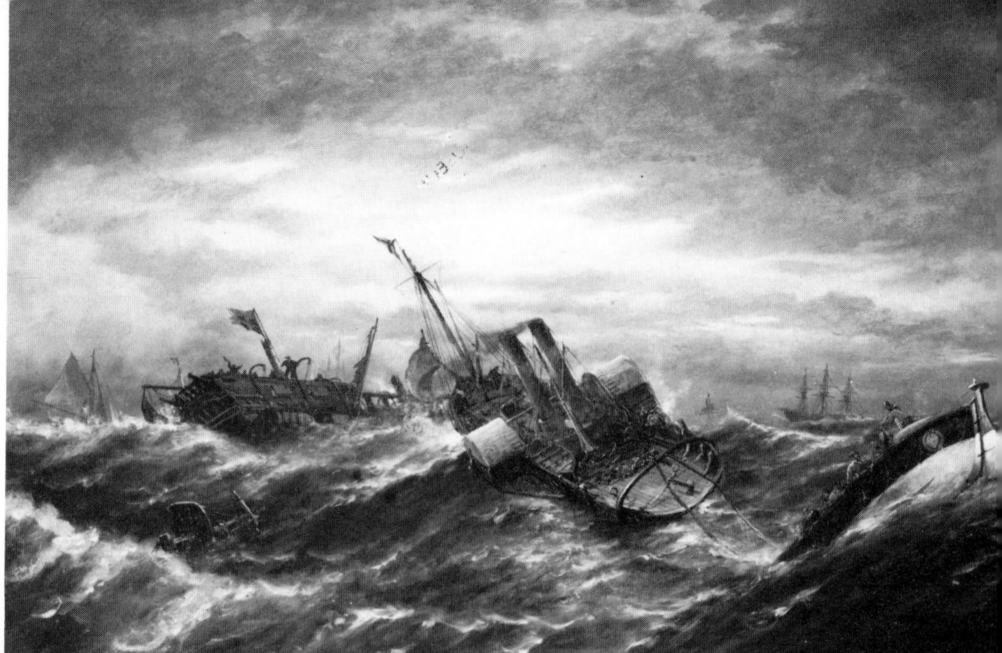

Plate 493. Richard Henry Nibbs, c.1816-1893. "A paddle tug towing a lifeboat to a wreck on the Goodwin Sands." National Maritime Museum, Greenwich.

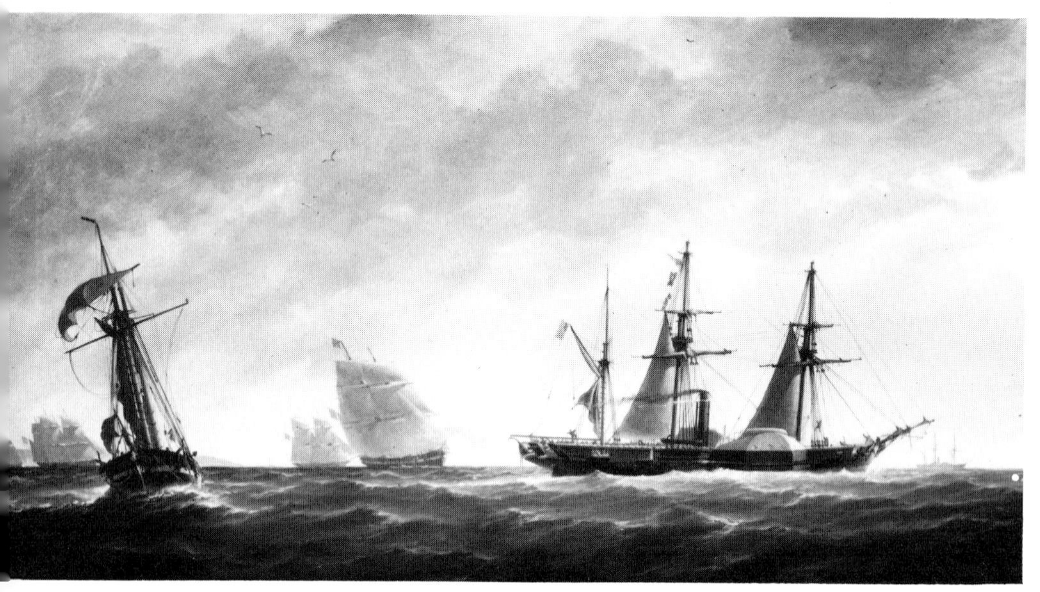

Plate 494. Richard Henry Nibbs, c.1816-1893. " 'The First Shot of the War', H.M.S. *Fury* in action off Odessa in 1854." *The reference is to the Crimean War. The* Fury *had captured the brig in the foreground, but had to abandon her when the Russian squadron drew close enough to fire a shot.* National Maritime Museum, Greenwich.

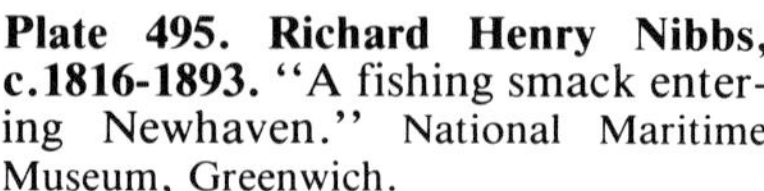

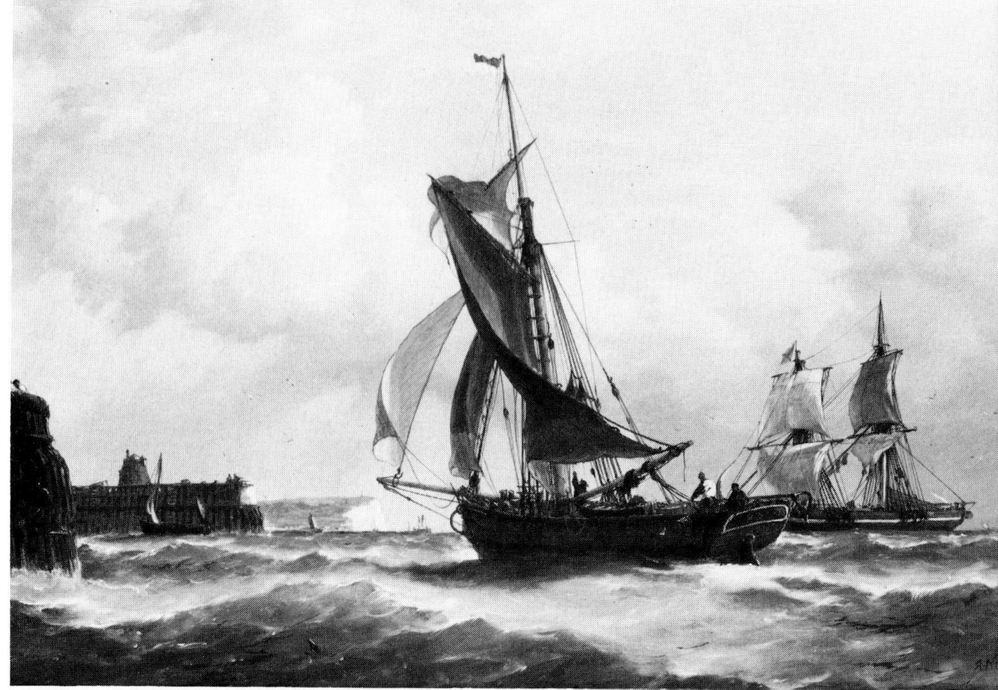

Plate 495. Richard Henry Nibbs, c.1816-1893. "A fishing smack entering Newhaven." National Maritime Museum, Greenwich.

Plate 496. Oswald Walter Brierly, 1817-1894. " 'Man overboard', from H.M.S. *St. Jean d'Acre* in the Baltic in 1854." *A rare oil painting by an artist whose usual medium was watercolour. He went with the Baltic Fleet as the guest of Captain Harry Keppel of the* St. Jean d'Acre *in the first year of the Russian War and many of the resulting paintings were lithographed.* National Maritime Museum, Greenwich.

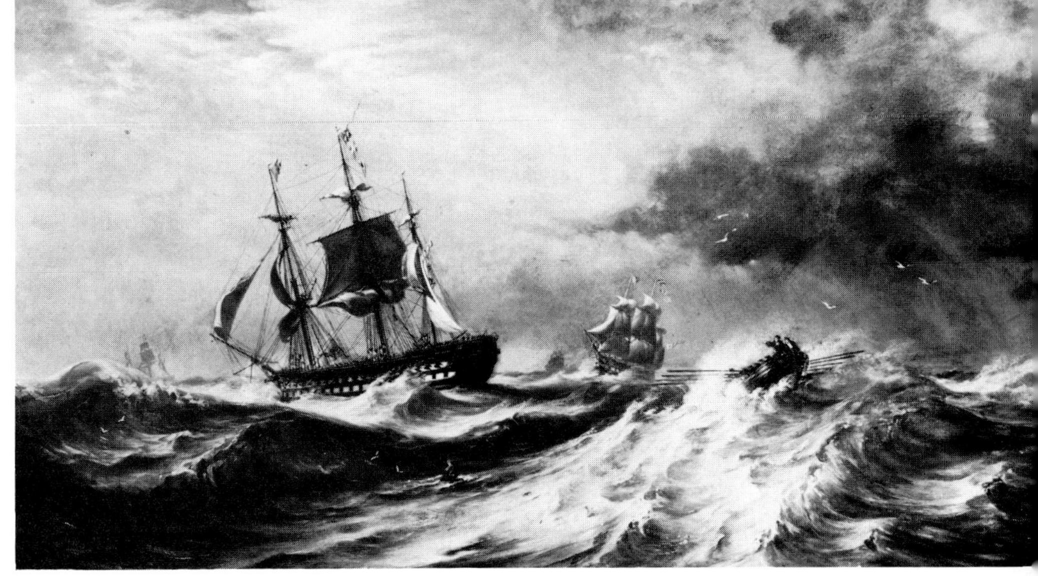

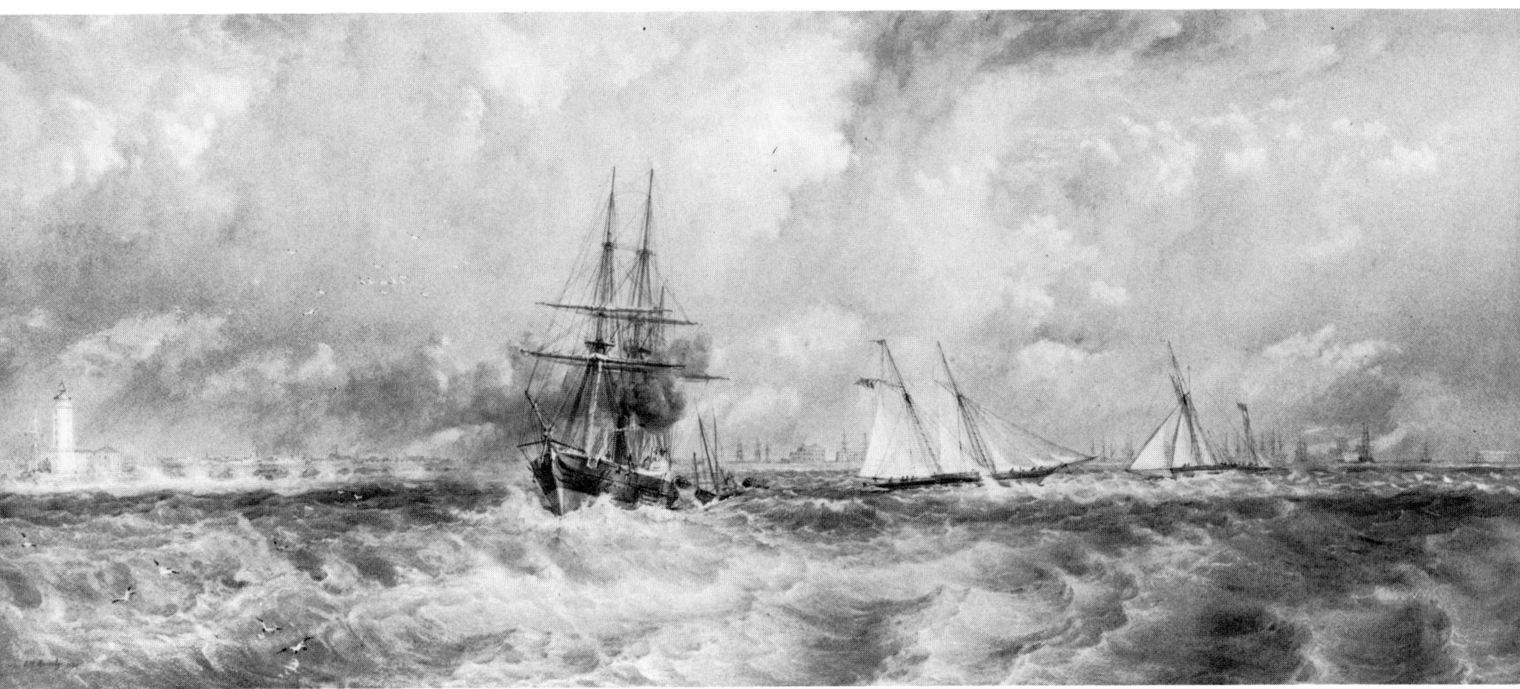

Plate 497. Oswald Walter Brierly, 1817-1894. "H.M.S. *Driver* with the yachts *Gondolier* and *Esmeralda* off Kronstadt in 1854, dated 1858." Watercolour. Sotheby's.

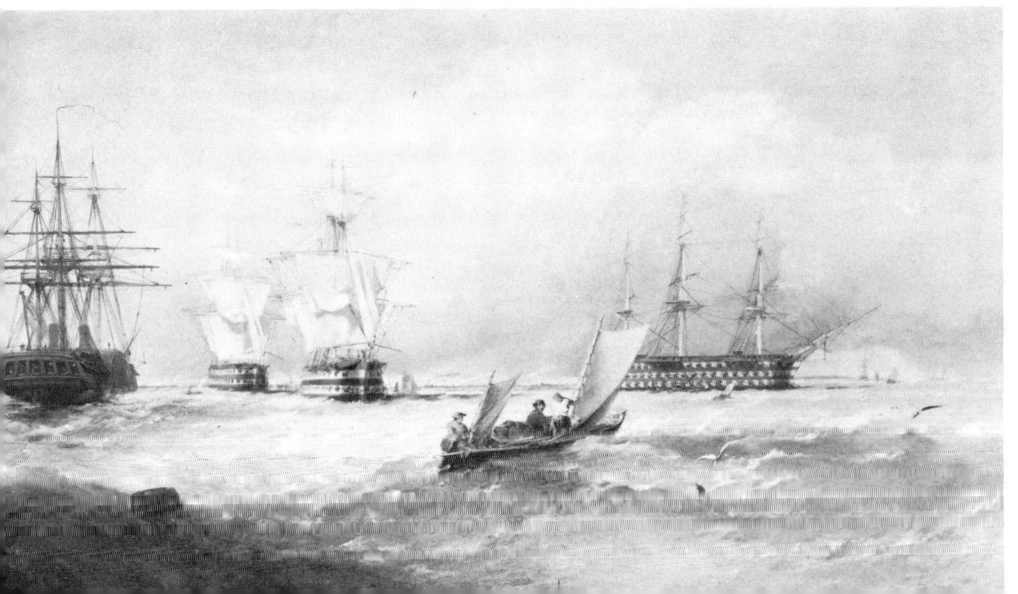

Plate 498. Edmund John Niemann, 1813-1876. "A paddle frigate and ships of the line at Spithead, dated 1855." *Niemann was not previously a sea painter which may explain this rather 'solid' painting.* Christie's.

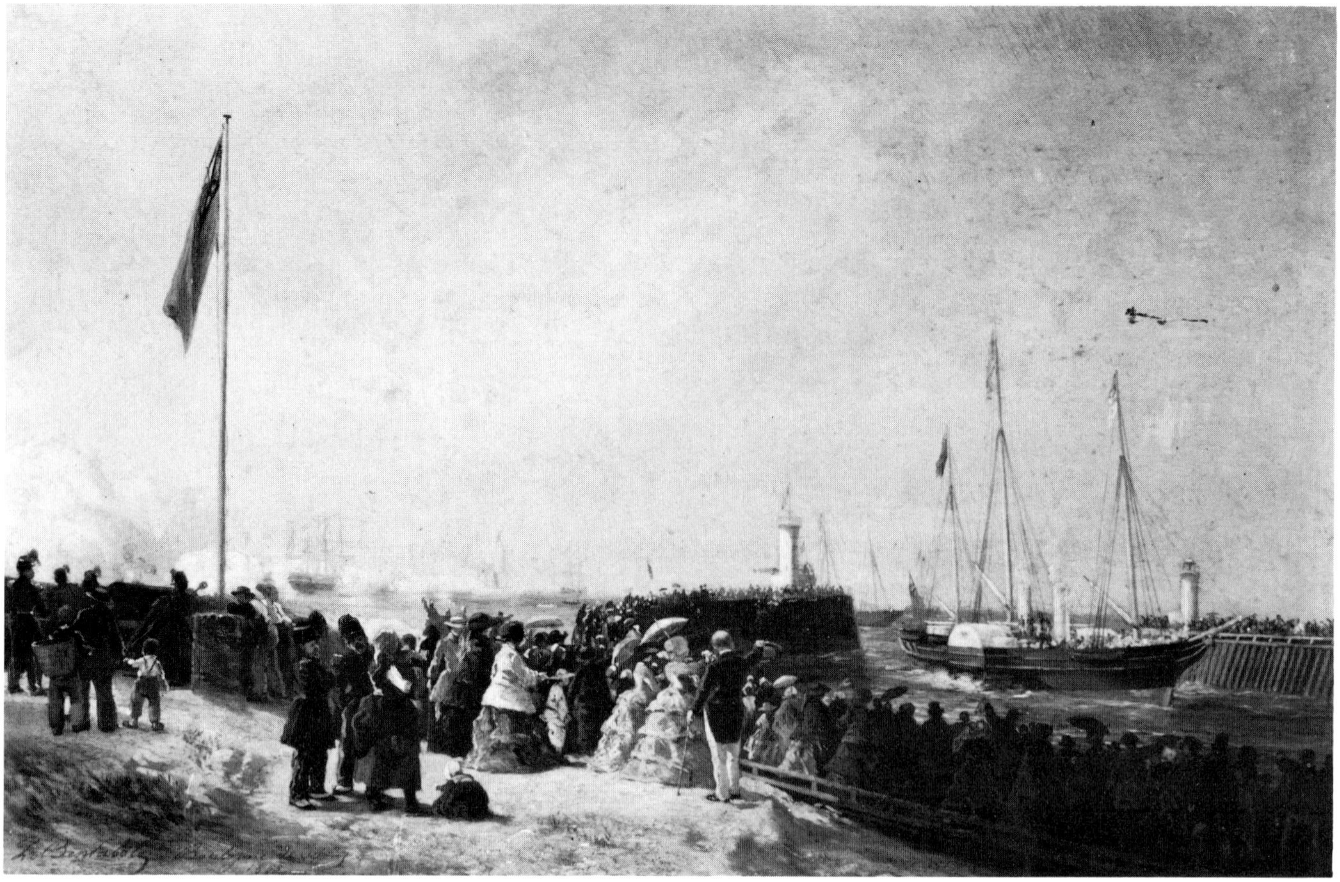

Plate 499. Louis Bentabole, 1827-1880. "Queen Victoria and Prince Albert arriving at Boulogne on a state visit in August 1855." *This was the first occasion on which the royal yacht* Victoria and Albert II *was used.* Trafalgar Galleries.

Plate 500. Louis Lebreton, d.1866. "The French exploration ships *Astrolobe* and *Zelée* stranded on the Detract de Torres, dated 1856." Peabody Museum of Salem.

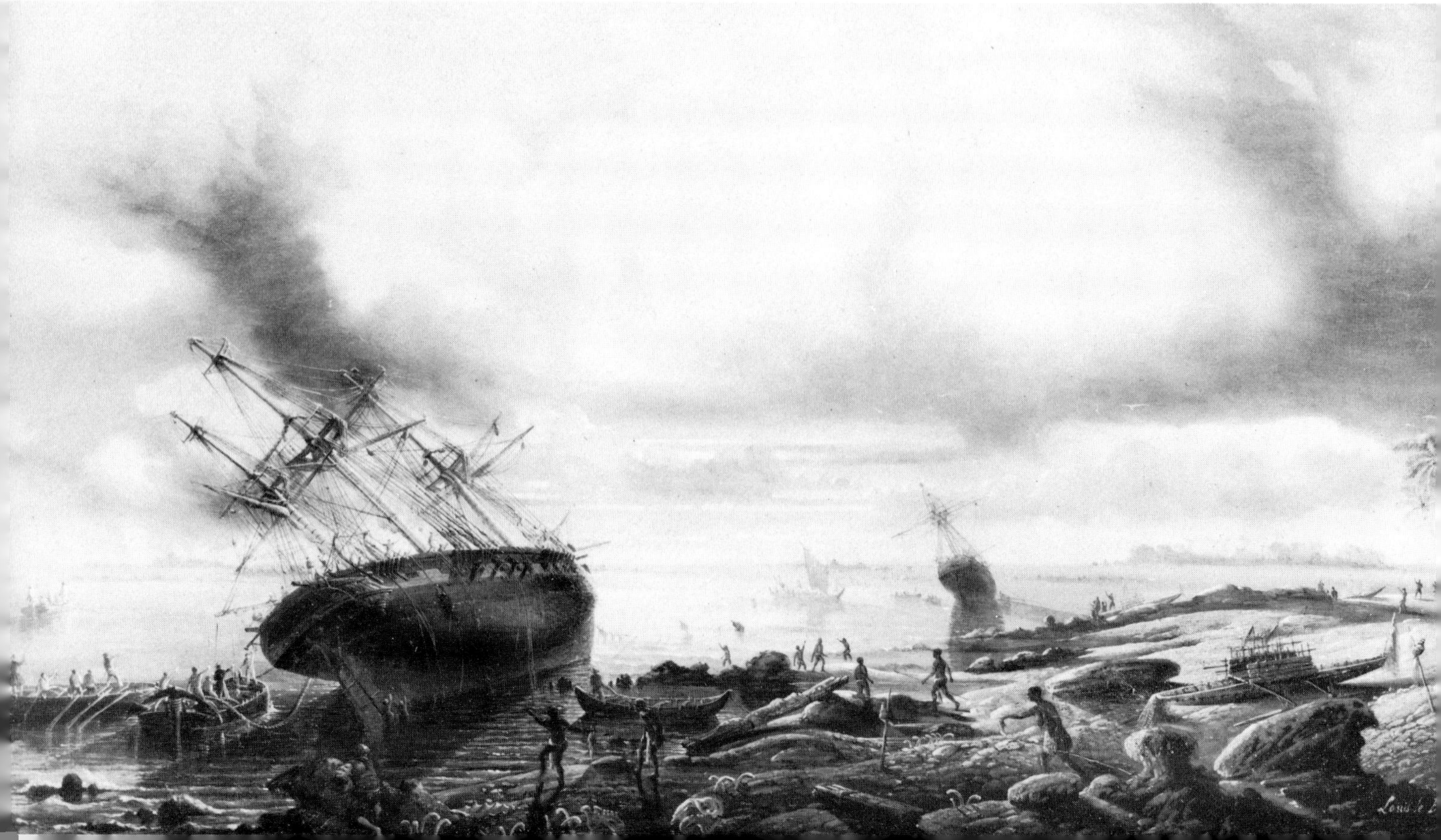

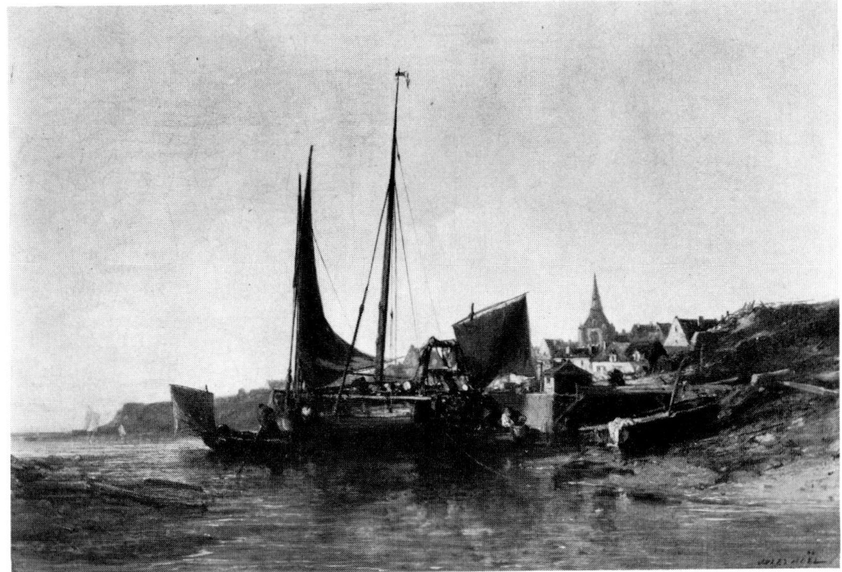

Plate 501. Jules Achille Noël, 1815-1881. "Low tide at a Normandy fishing village, dated 1857." *An excellent work by this French painter.* Christie's.

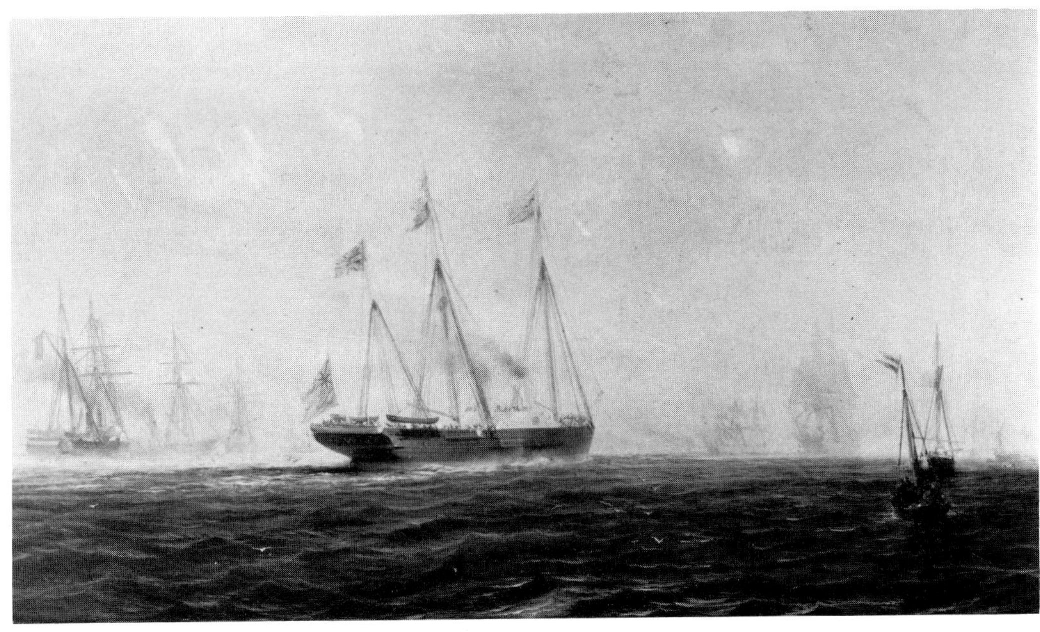

Plate 502. Jean Baptiste Henri Durand-Brager, 1814-1879. "The arrival of Queen Victoria at Cherbourg in August 1858." *The Royal yacht* Victoria and Albert II *was built in 1855.* Sotheby's.

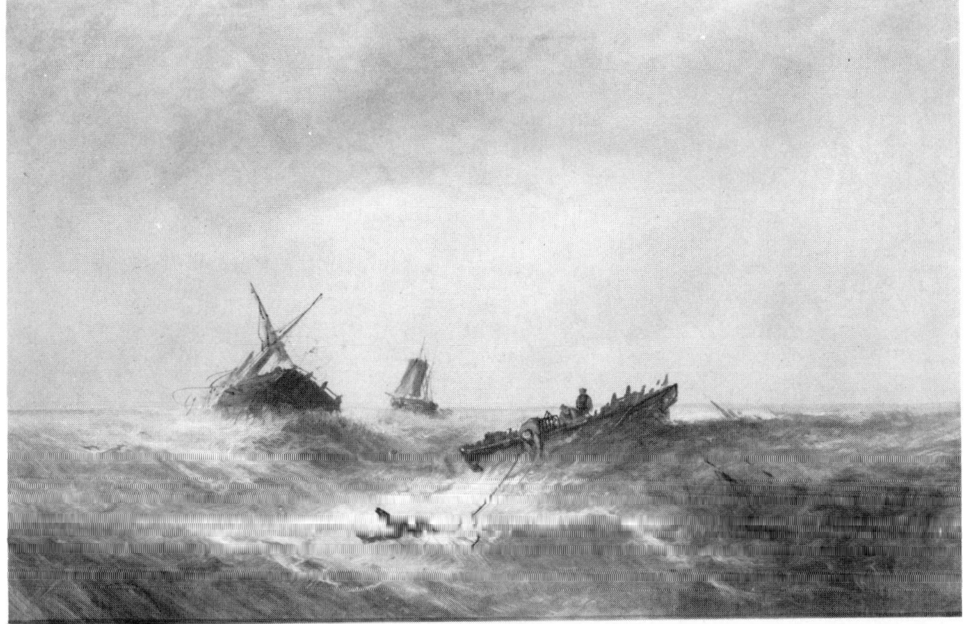

Plate 503. Richard Faxon, fl.1859-1875. "After the storm." Sotheby's.

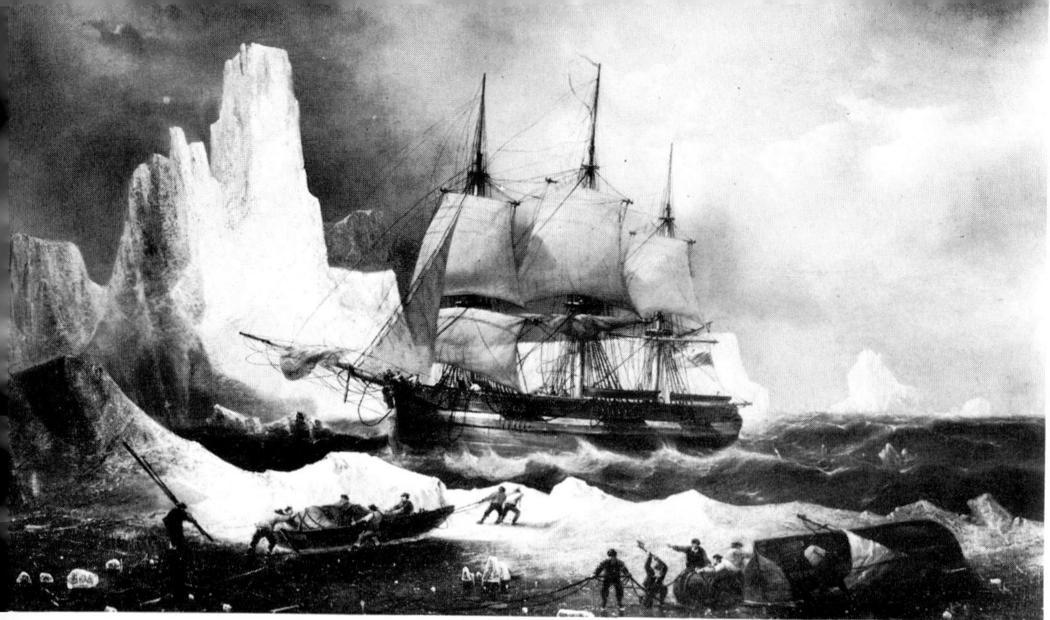

Plate 504. François Etienne Musin, 1826-1888. ''H.M.S. *Erebus* in the ice.'' National Maritime Museum, Greenwich.

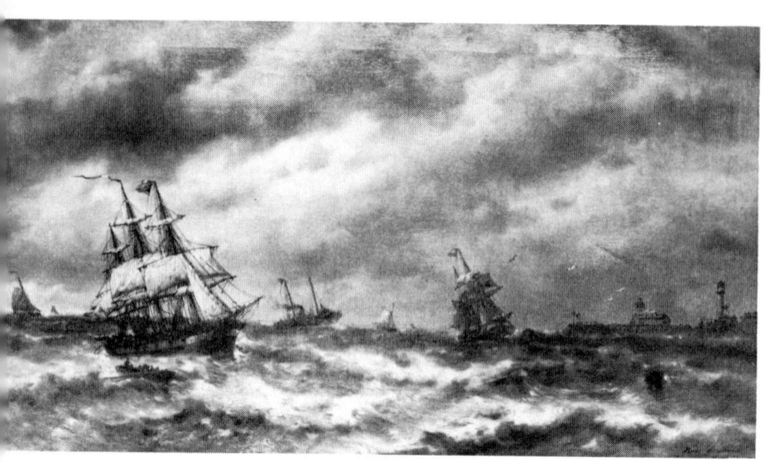

Plate 505. François Etienne Musin, 1826-1888. ''Shipping off Ostend.'' Museum of Fine Art, Ostend.

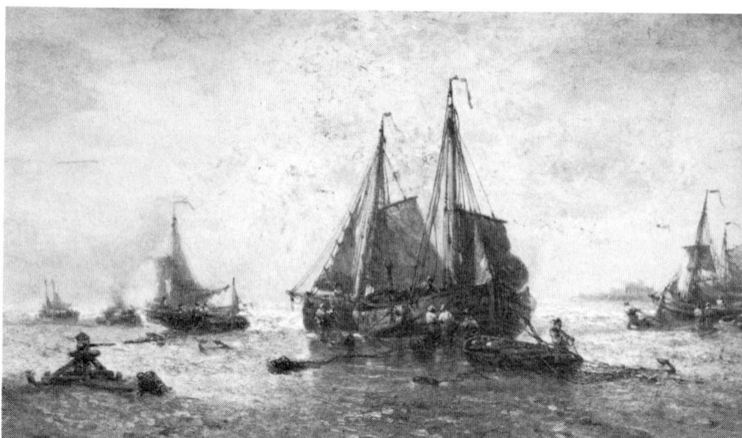

Plate 506. François Etienne Musin, 1826-1888. ''Fishing boats on the beach.'' Museum of Fine Art, Ostend.

Plate 507. Nicolaas Riegen, 1827-1889. ''Dutch coastal craft off a jetty.'' Phillips.

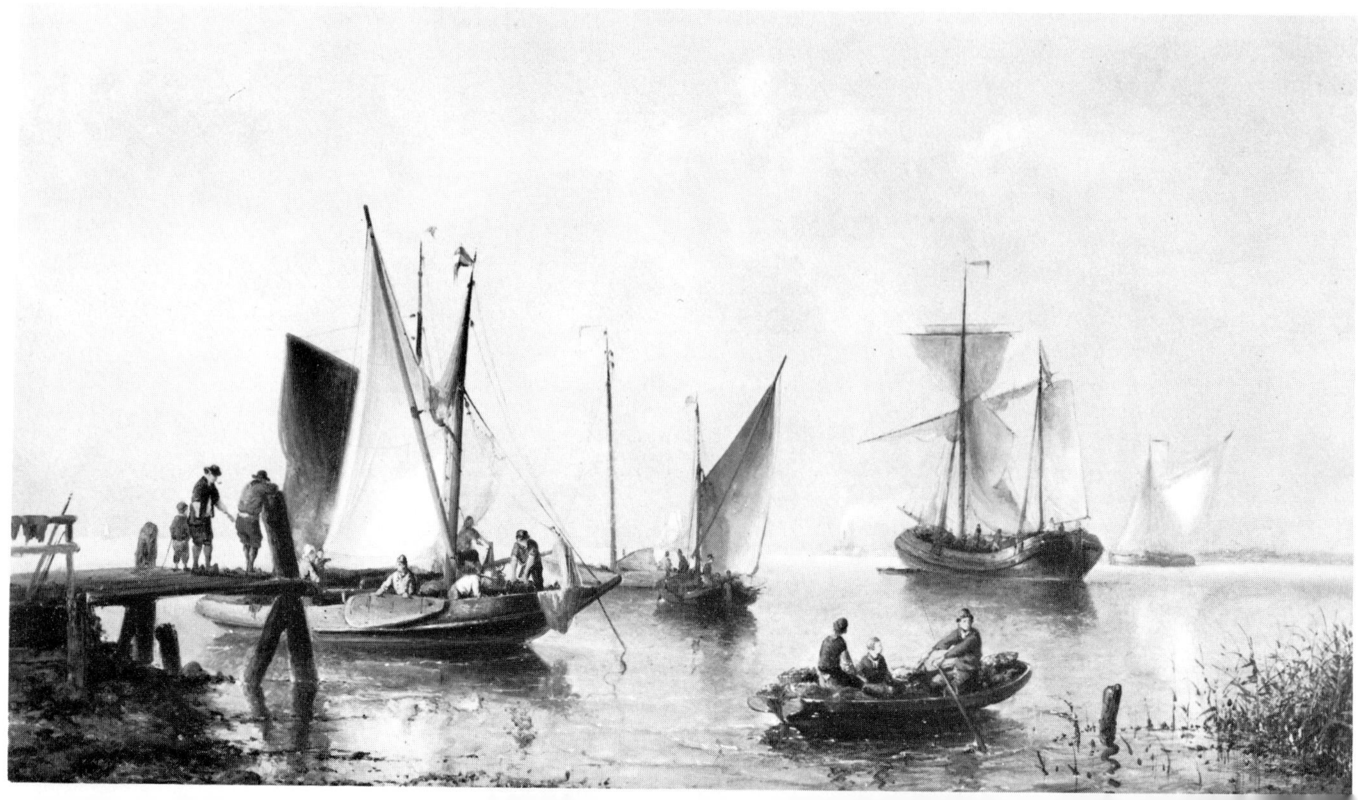

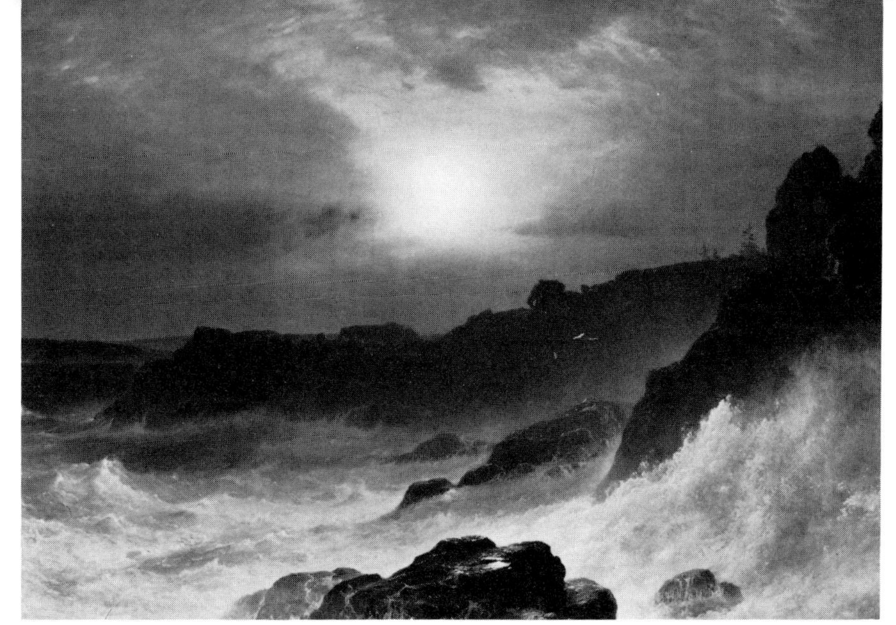

Plate 508. Frederick Edwin Church, 1826-1900. "Sunrise off the Maine coast." Wadsworth Atheneum (bequest of Mrs. Clara Hinton Gould), Hartford.

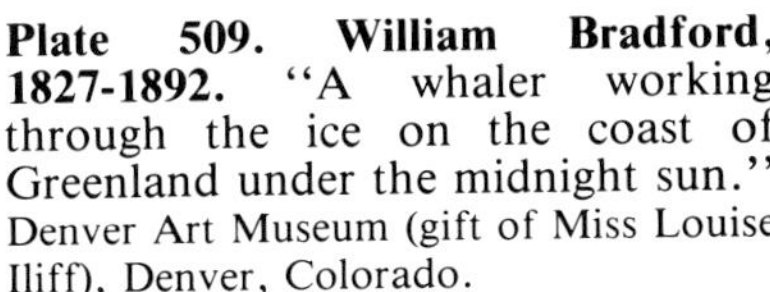

Plate 509. William Bradford, 1827-1892. "A whaler working through the ice on the coast of Greenland under the midnight sun." Denver Art Museum (gift of Miss Louise Iliff), Denver, Colorado.

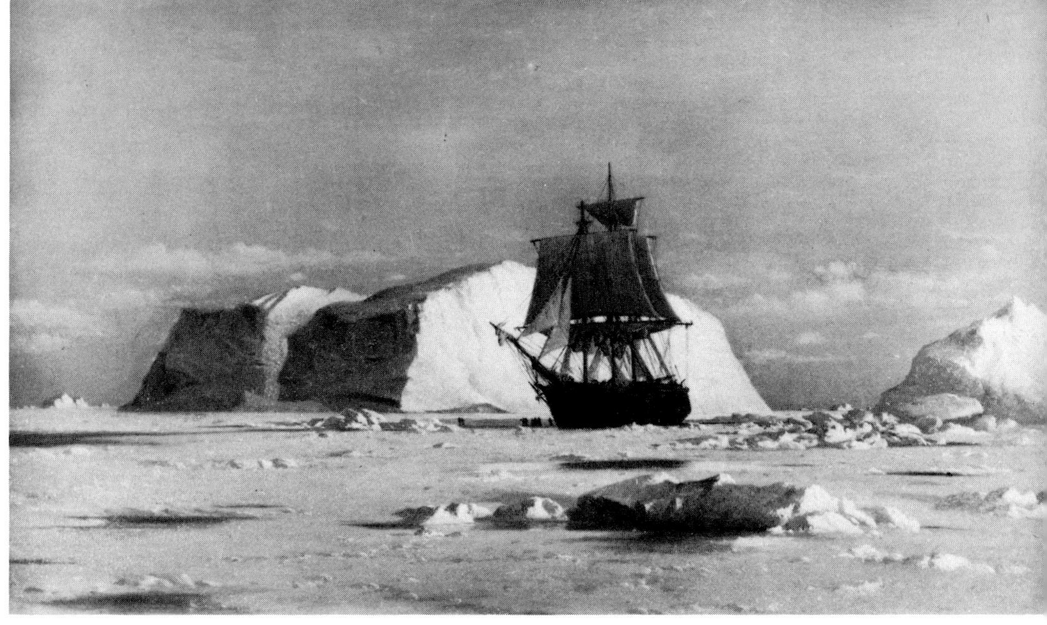

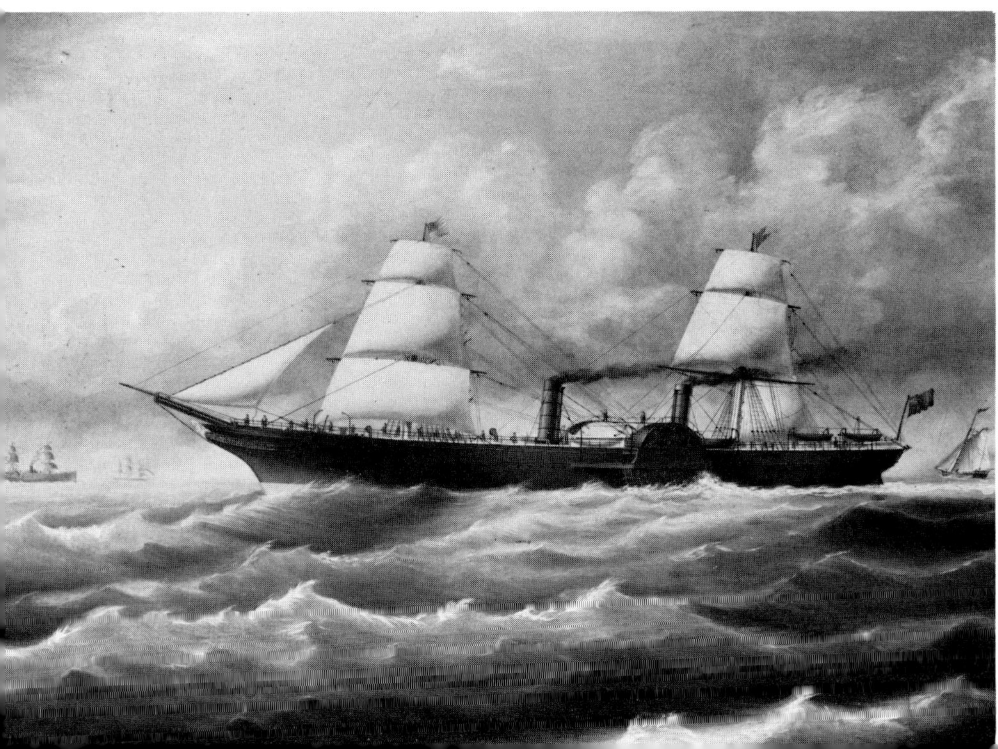

Plate 510. D. Lyle, fl. mid-19th century. "The Cunarder *Persia,* 1856." *The first Cunard iron ship, built in response to the challenge to Cunard by the American Collins Line ships — enormous wooden ships with elaborate interiors, one of which can be seen in the left background.* National Maritime Museum, Greenwich.

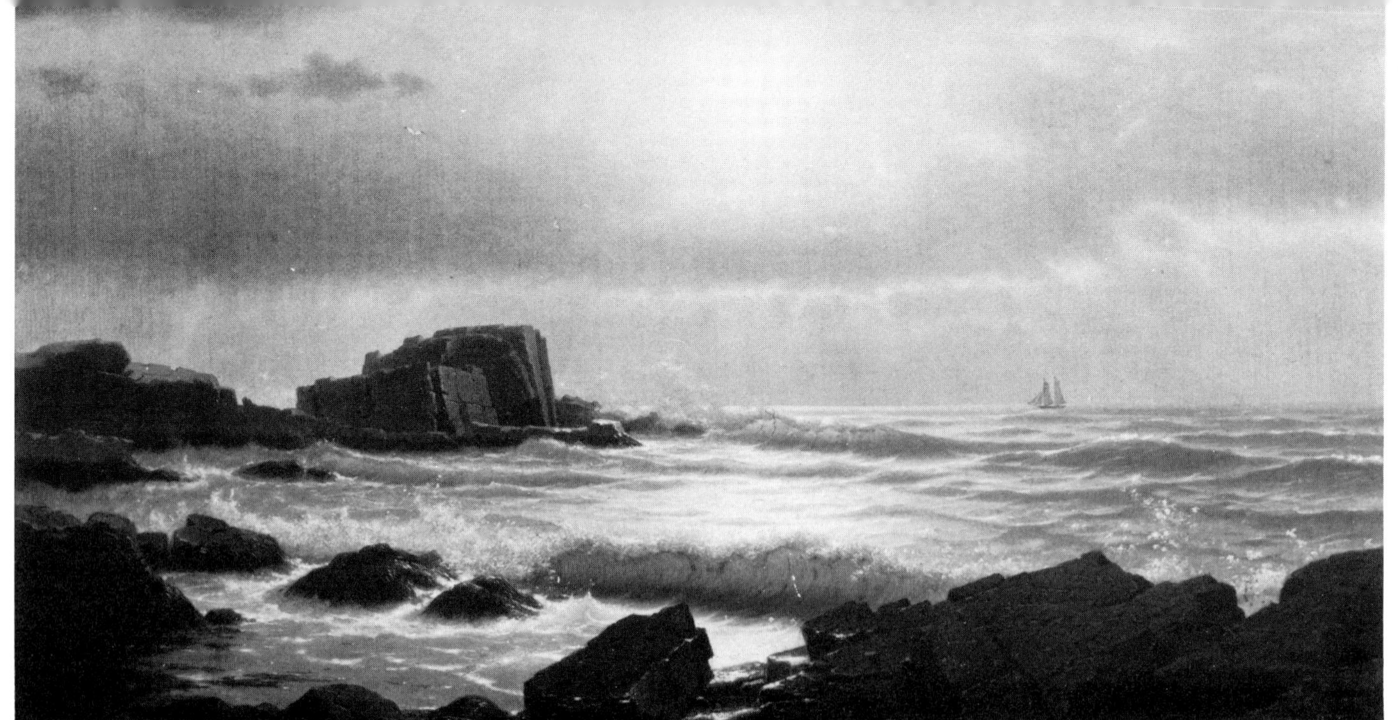

Plate 511. William Stanley Haseltine, 1835-1900. ''Rocks at Nahant.'' Mariners Museum, Newport News.

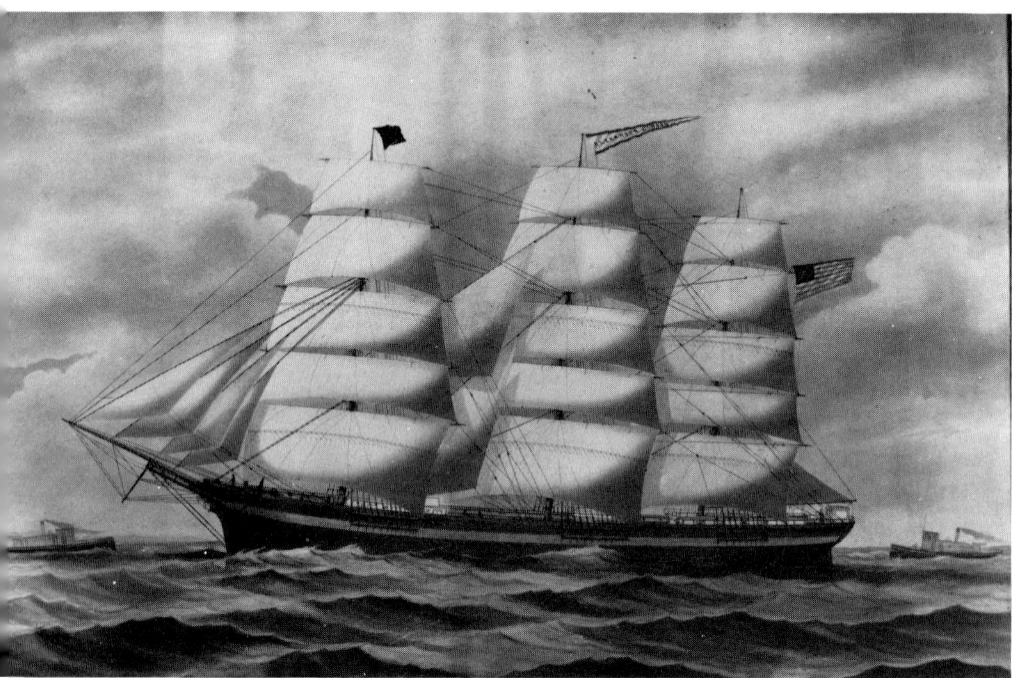

Plate 512. Edward J. Russell, 1835-1906. ''The American ship *Alexander Gibson*.'' Mariners Museum, Newport News.

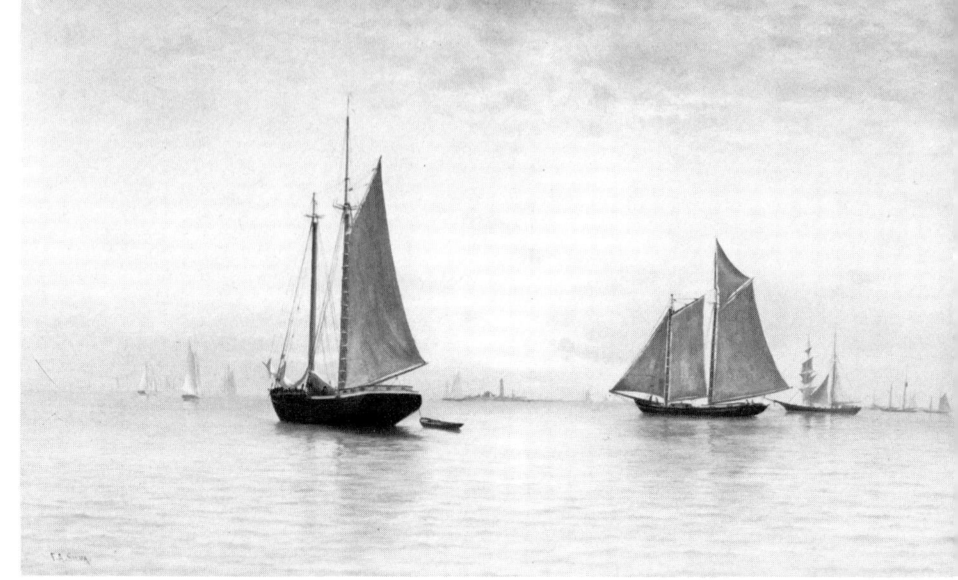

Plate 513. Francis Augustus Silva, 1835-1886. ''Coastal craft in Boston Bay at sunset.'' Peabody Museum of Salem.

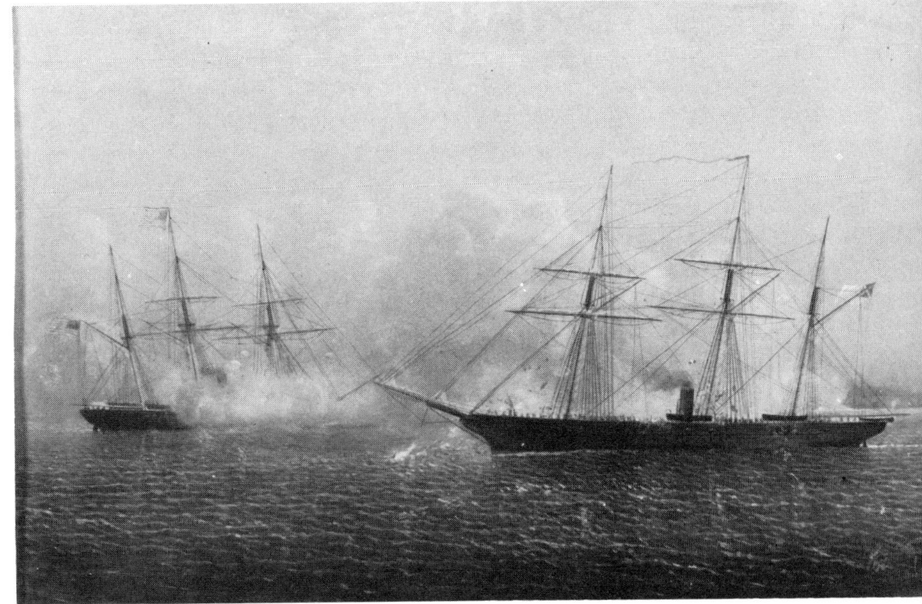

Plate 514. Xanthus R. Smith, 1838-1929. "The action between the *Kearsage* and the *Alabama,* 1864." *A well-known action between the Confederates and Unionists during the American Civil War; the Confederate ship* Kearsage *was sunk.* Mariners Museum, Newport News.

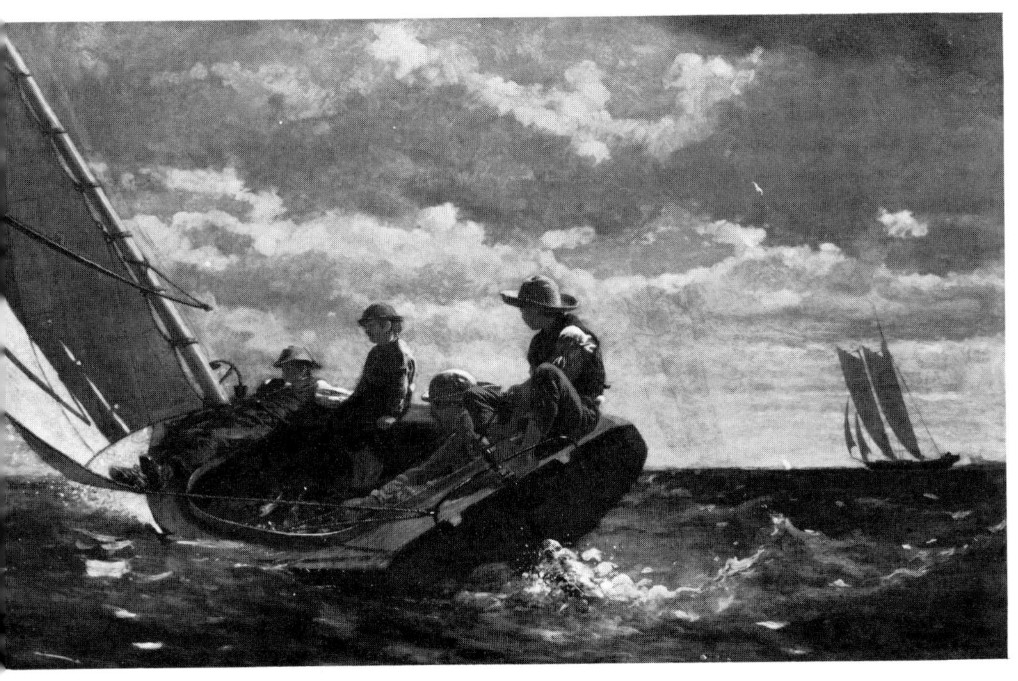

Plate 515. Winslow Homer, 1836-1910. "Breezing up." *A painting with enormous impact by a painter who is very much admired in America.* National Gallery of Art (gift of the W.L. and May T. Mellon Foundation), Washington.

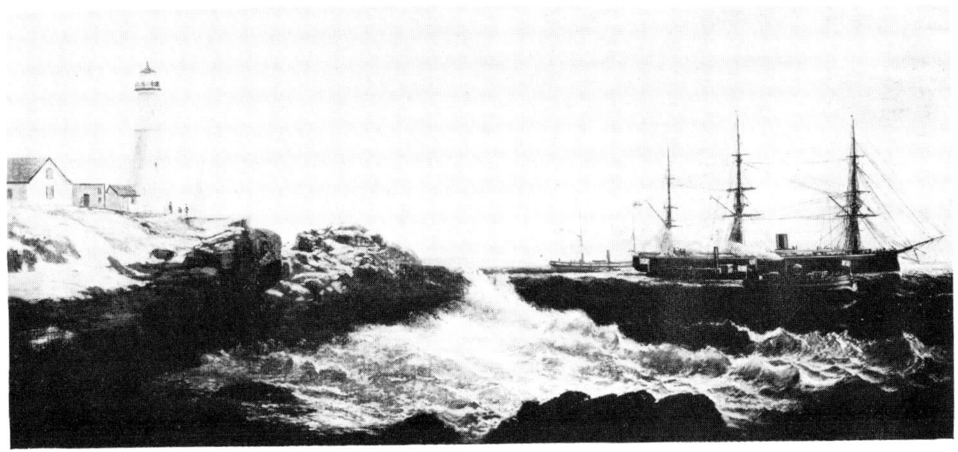

Plate 516. Harrison B. Brown, 1831-1915. "H.M.S. *Monarch* off Portland light taking the body of George Peabody to the United States of America in February 1870." Peabody Museum of Salem.

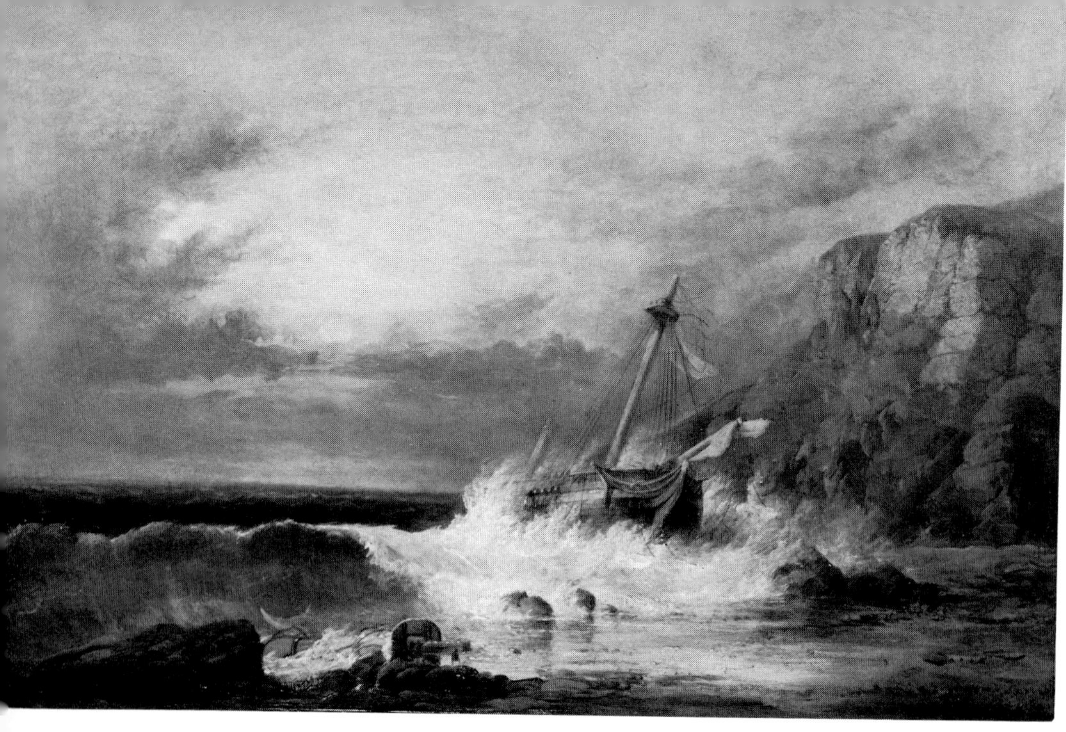

Plate 517. Samuel Bough, 1822-1878. "A wrecked brig on a beach." Private collection.

Plate 518. Samuel Bough, 1822-1878. "Dumbarton 1855." National Maritime Museum, Greenwich.

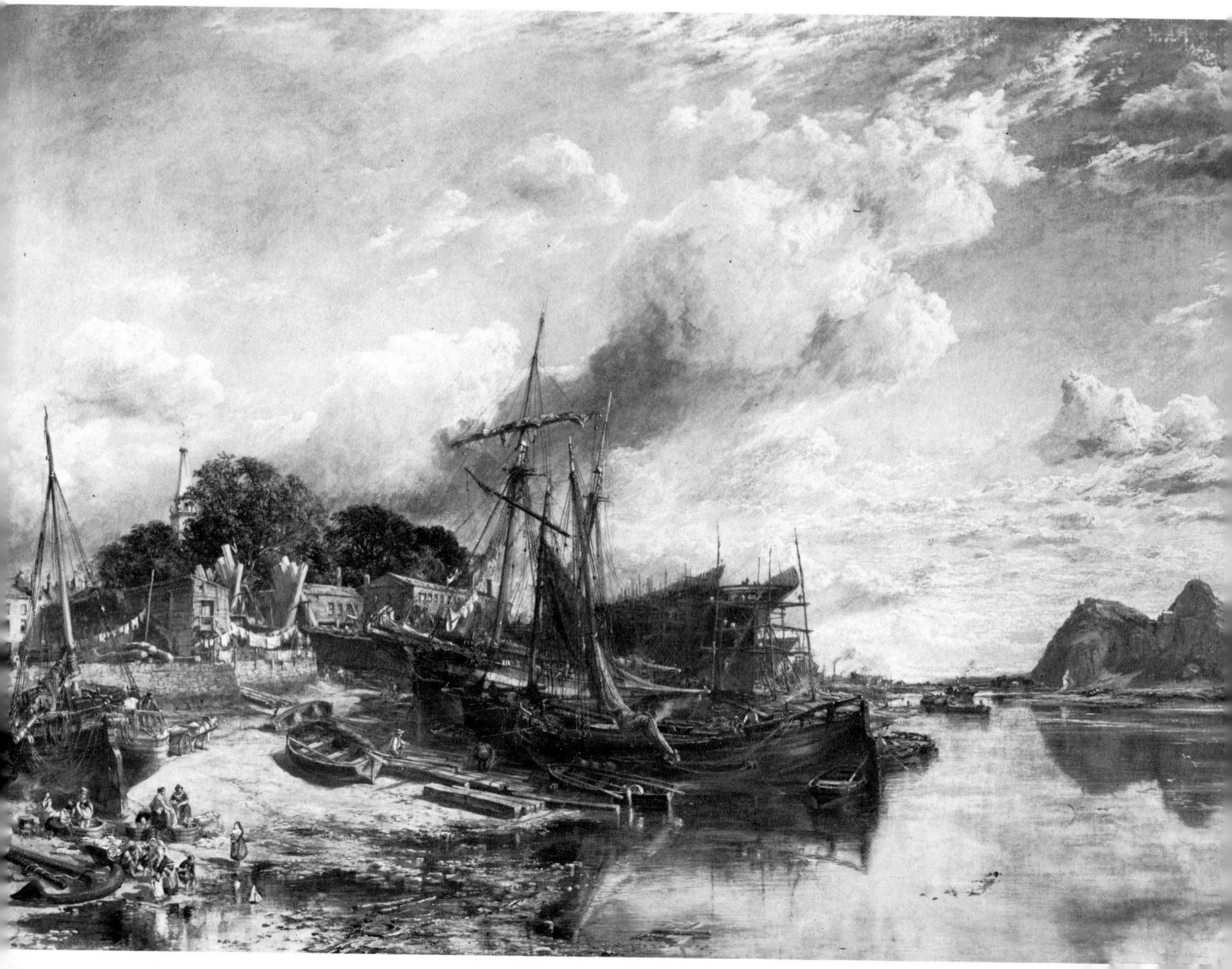

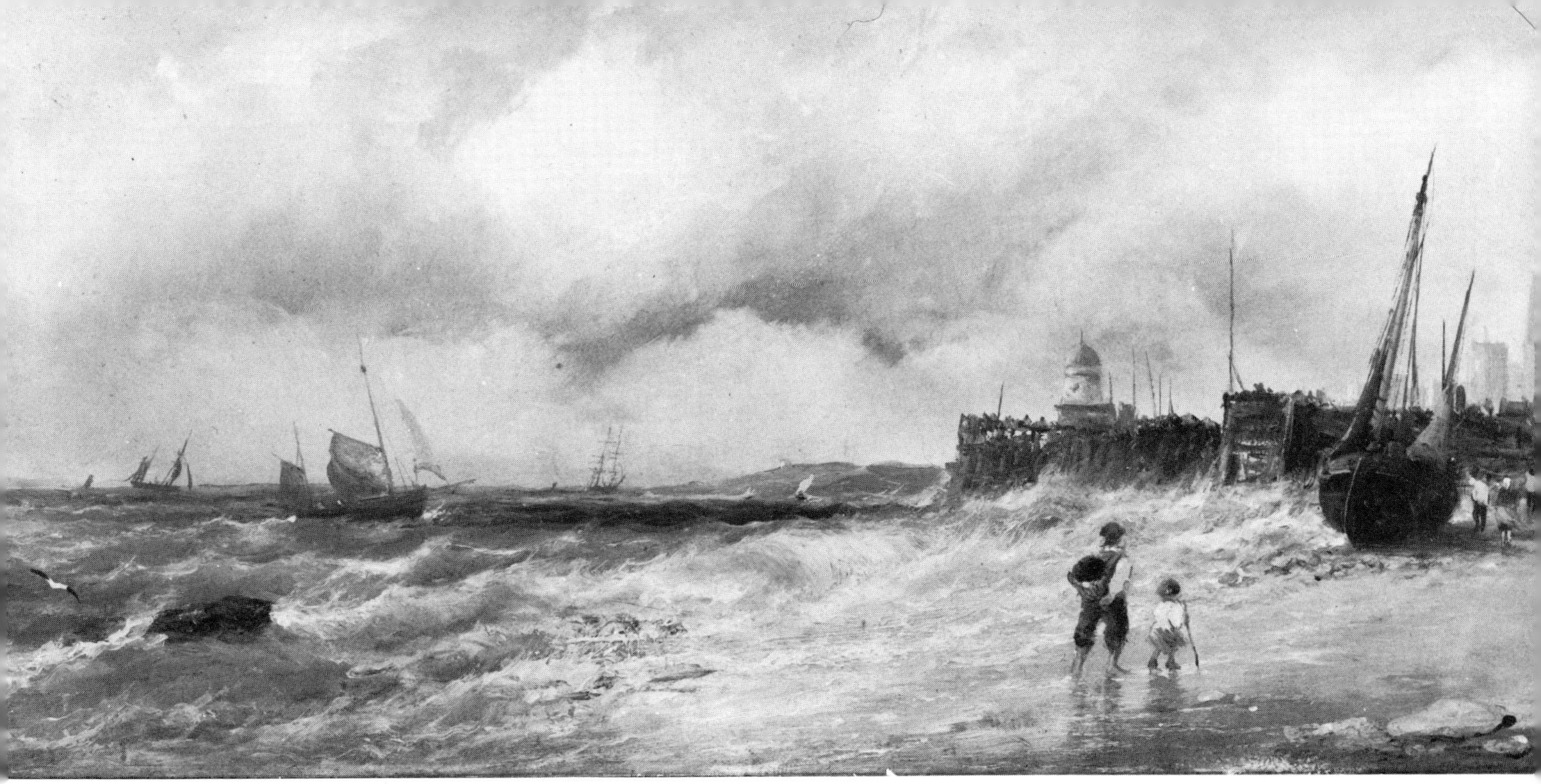

Plate 519. William James Durant Ready, 1823-1873. "Beach scene near Folkestone." Christie's.

Plate 520. George Chambers, Junior, b.1830. "The Bellot Memorial at Greenwich Hospital, dated 1857." *Joseph René Bellot was a French naval lieutenant who was seconded to the Royal Navy and served on Arctic expeditions. He perished after being blown off an ice floe in 1853. George Chambers Junior was not as good an artist as his father. He painted with rather a fluid oil medium and also produced a number of pleasing oil sketches, at best when on a small scale.* National Maritime Museum, Greenwich.

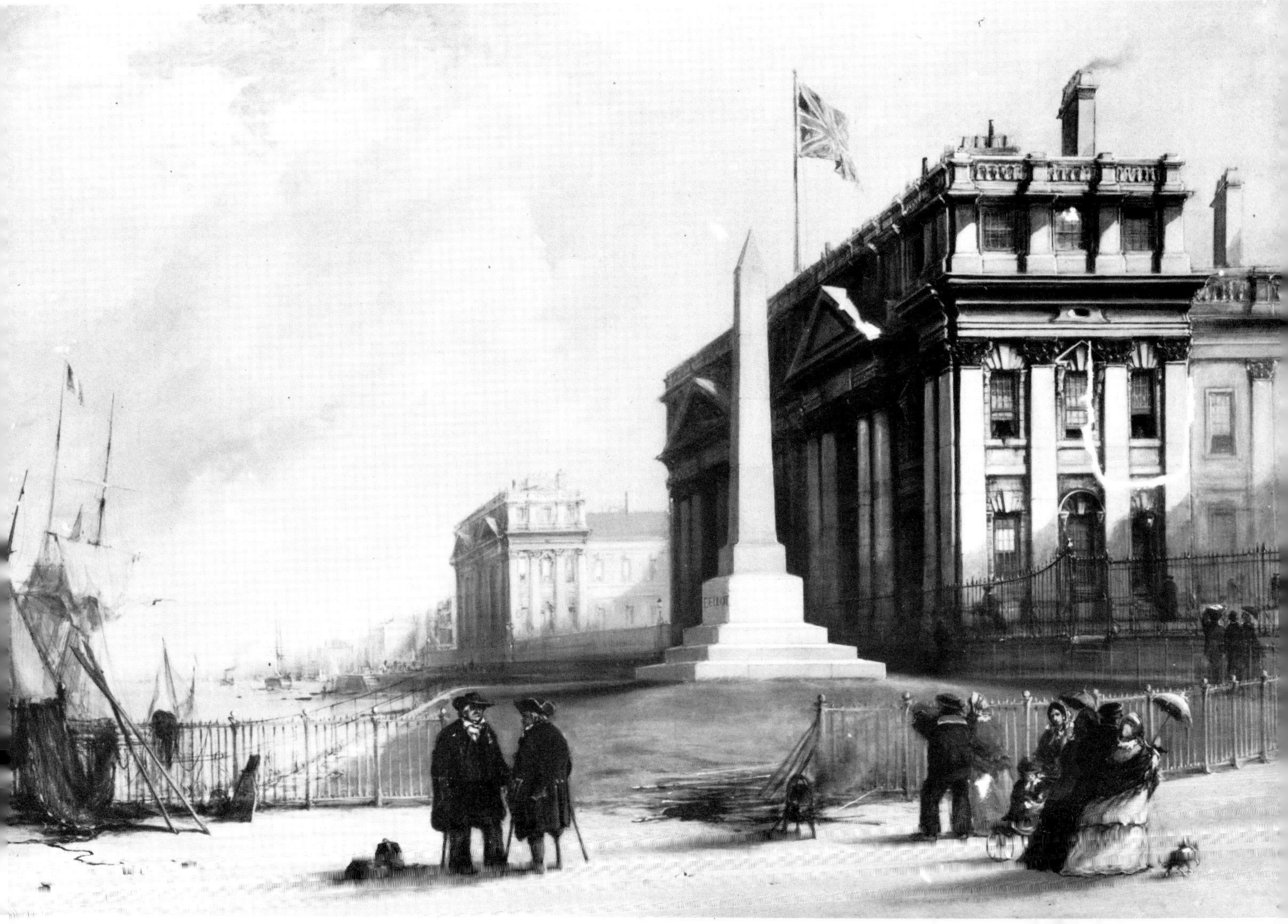

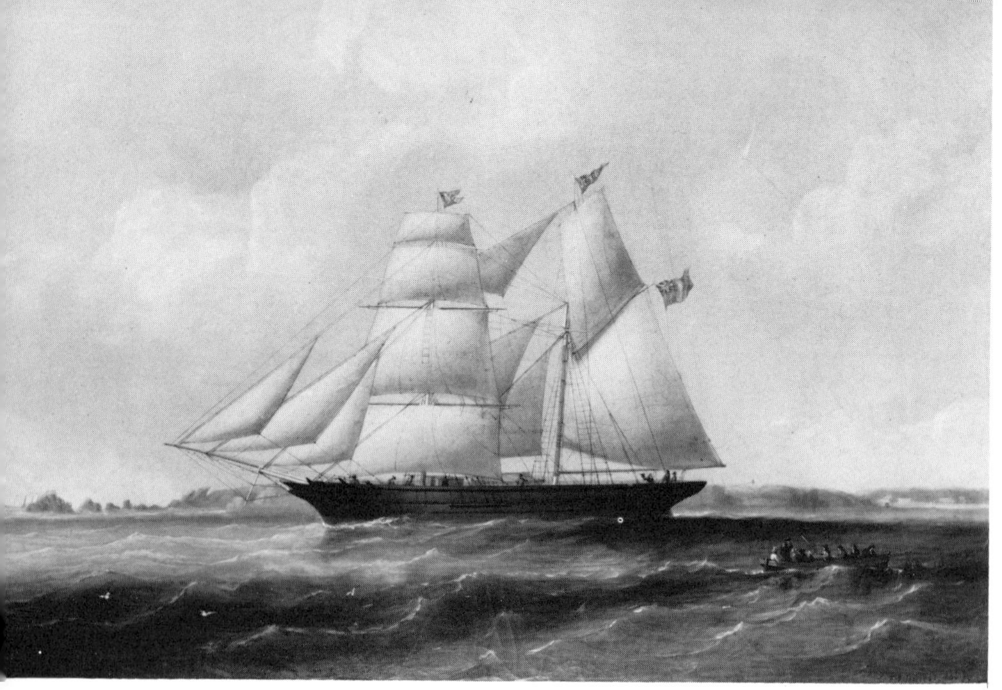

Plate 521. Philip John Ouless, 1817-1885. "The briganteen *Jessie,* dated 1857." National Maritime Museum, Greenwich (on loan from the Société Jersiaise).

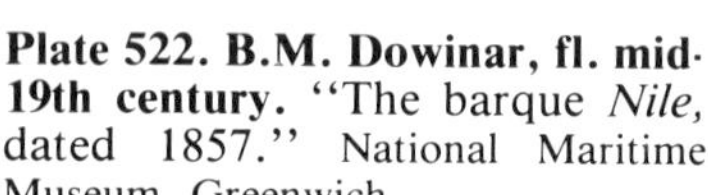

Plate 522. B.M. Dowinar, fl. mid-19th century. "The barque *Nile,* dated 1857." National Maritime Museum, Greenwich.

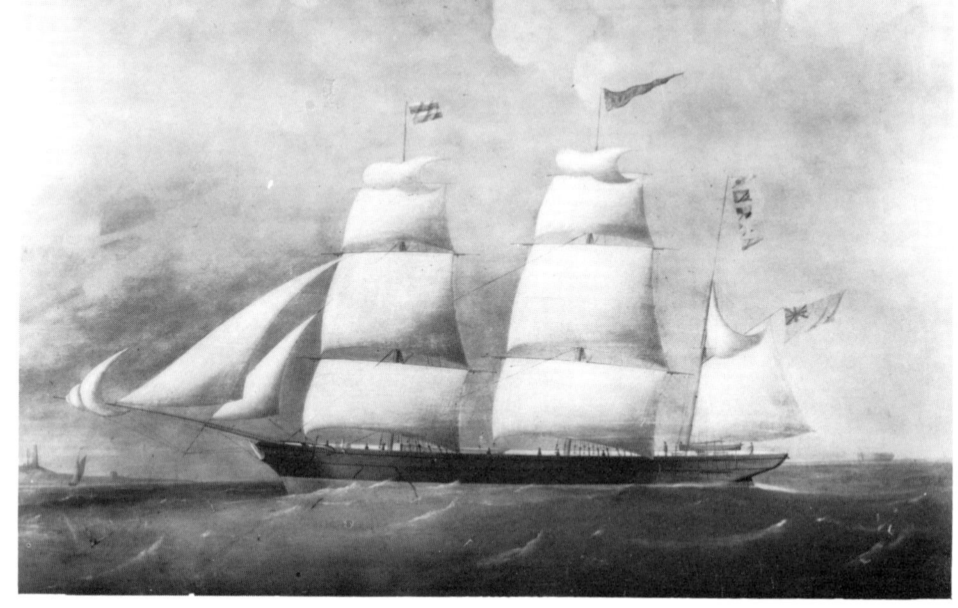

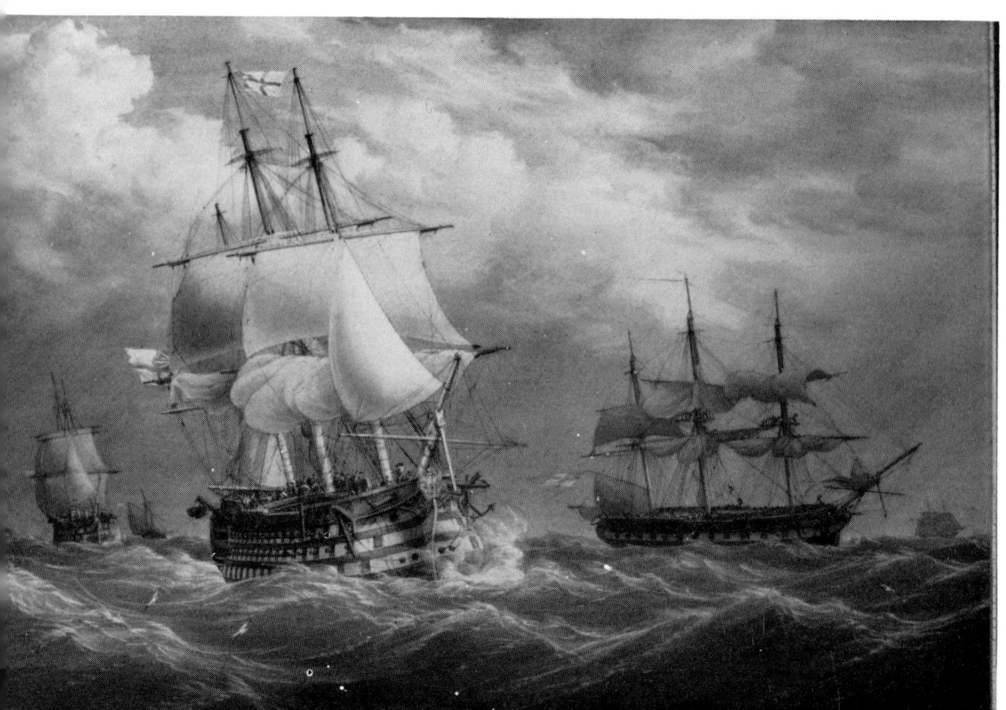

Plate 523. John Cantiloe Joy, 1806-1866, and William Joy, 1803-1867. "H.M.S. *Victory* wearing the flag of Vice Admiral Sir Philip de Saumarez, 1810 to 1812, dated 1858." Watercolour. *The* Victory *towards the end of her sea going service, by then painted black and white.* Sotheby's.

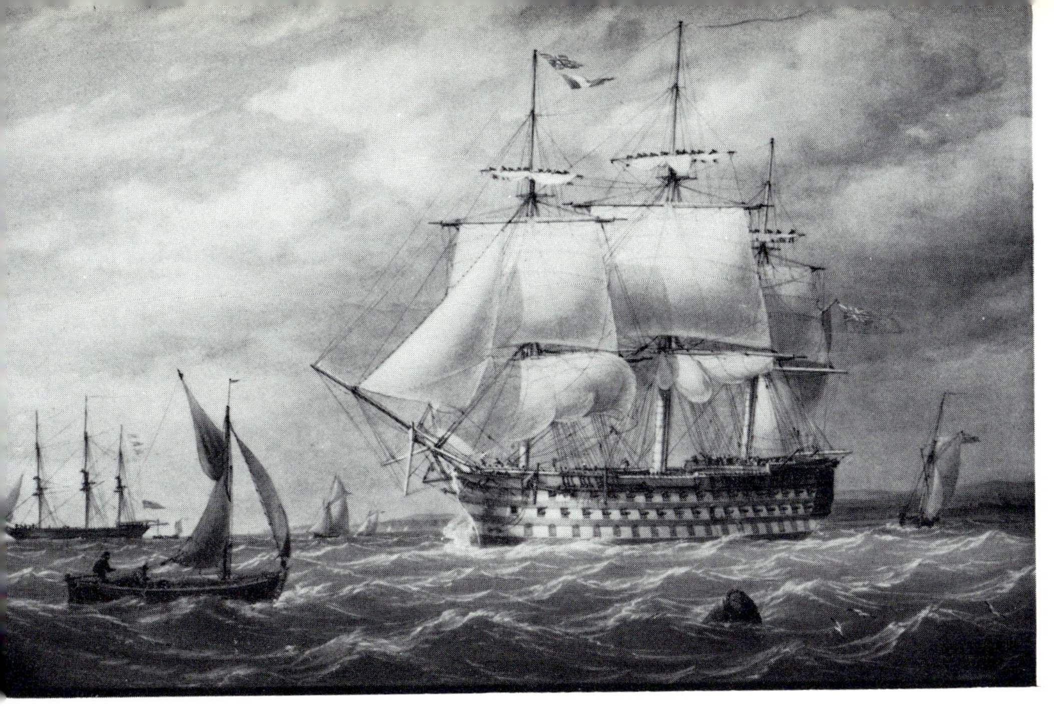

Plate 524. John Cantiloe Joy, 1806-1866, and William Joy, 1803-1867. "H.M.S. *Britannia* at sea about 1830, dated 1858". *Another well painted watercolour by the Joy brothers who frequently collaborated. This shows the* Britannia *as a private ship during a Mediterranean commission, 1830-35.* Sotheby's.

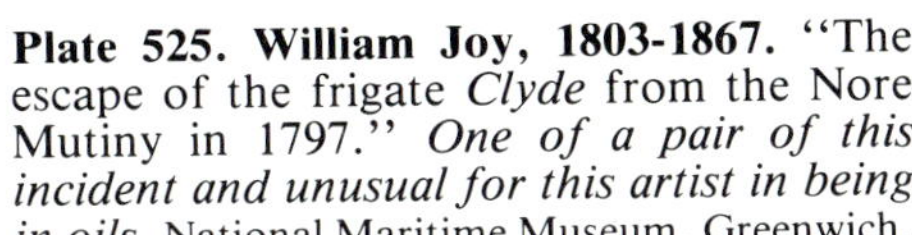

Plate 525. William Joy, 1803-1867. "The escape of the frigate *Clyde* from the Nore Mutiny in 1797." *One of a pair of this incident and unusual for this artist in being in oils.* National Maritime Museum, Greenwich.

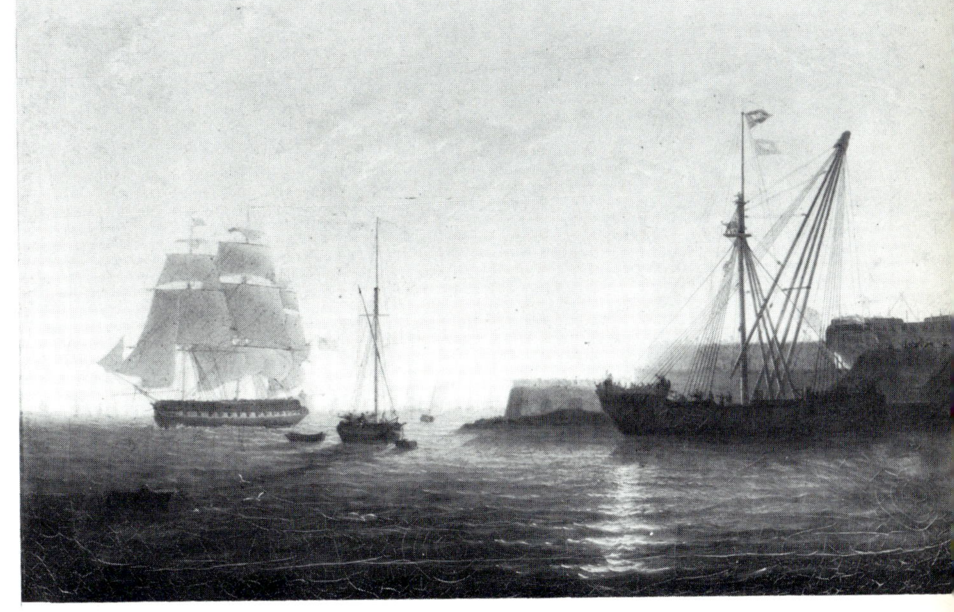

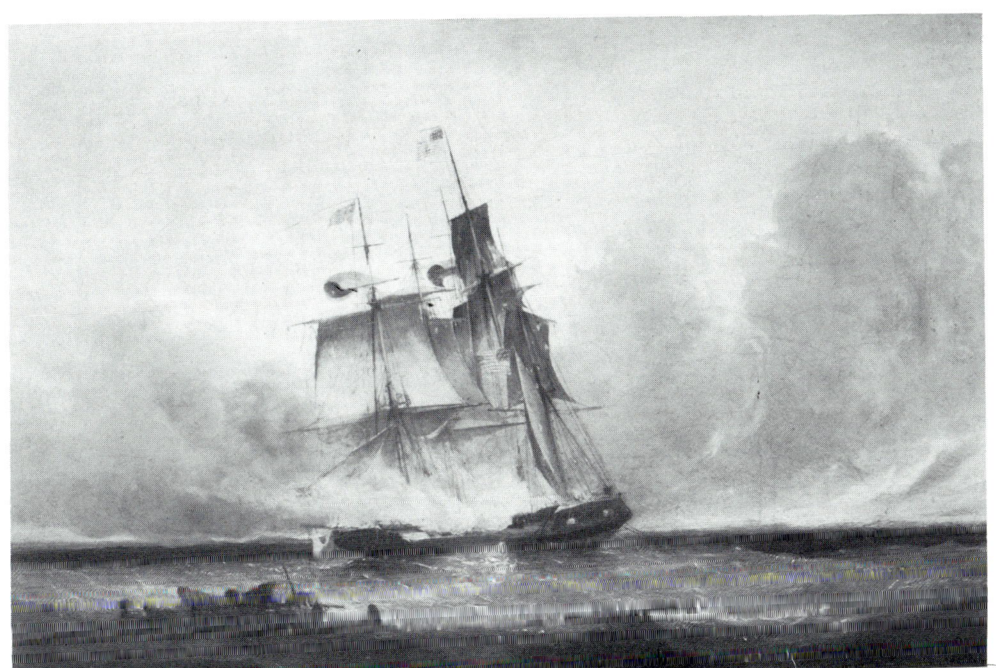

Plate 526. Edwin Hayes, 1819-1904. "The action between the U.S.S. *Wasp* and H.M. brig *Reindeer* in 1814." *One of his rare historical subjects.* National Maritime Museum, Greenwich.

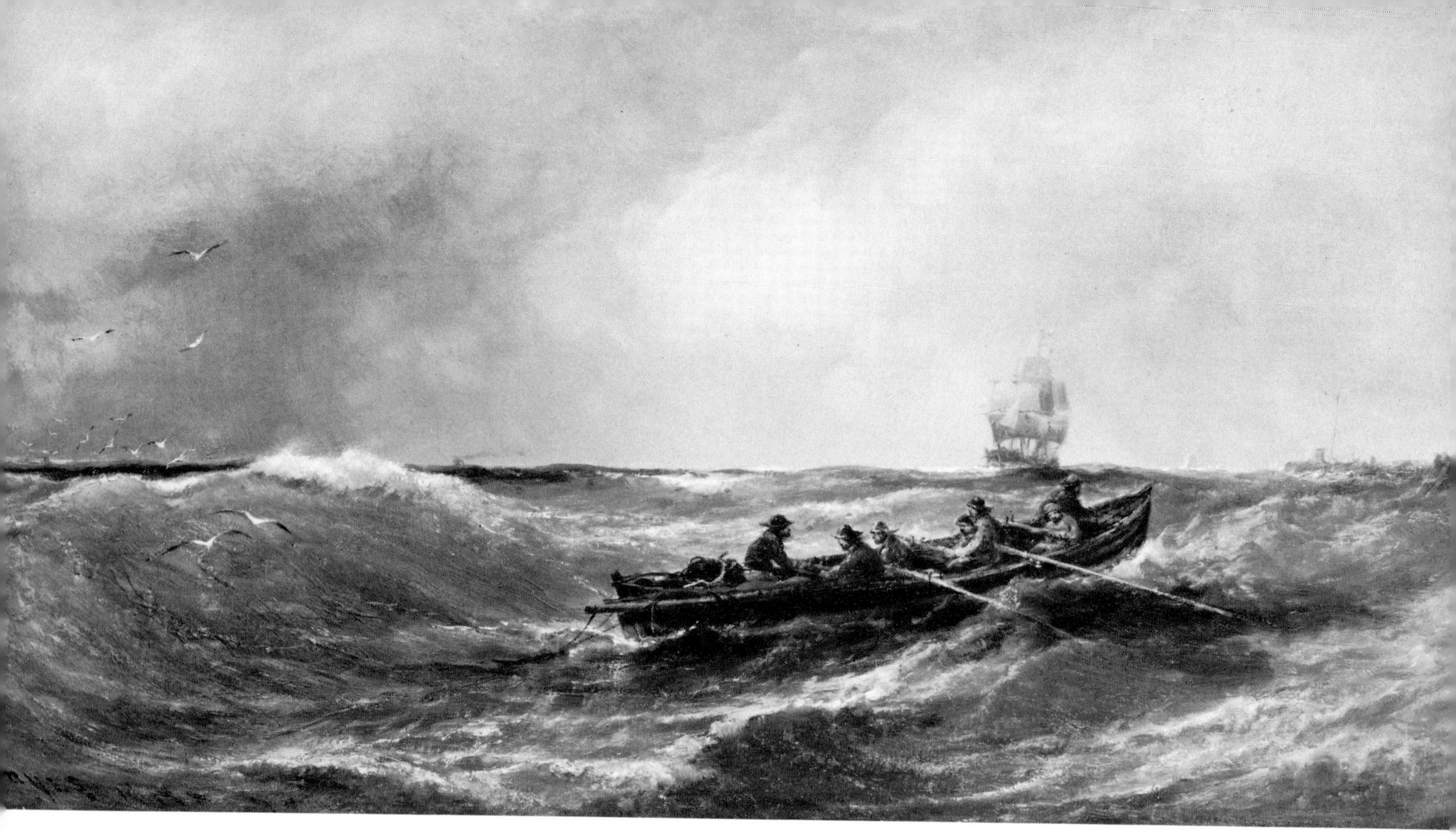

Plate 527. Edwin Hayes, 1819-1904. ''A fishing boat off a coast in a heavy sea, 1874.'' *A fine example of Hayes' work in which he clearly demonstrates his ability to portray the sea, sky and the general atmosphere.* William Barnett Esq.

Plate 528. Edwin Hayes, 1819-1904. ''A kaag and other small craft off the Dutch coast.'' Ulster Museum, Belfast

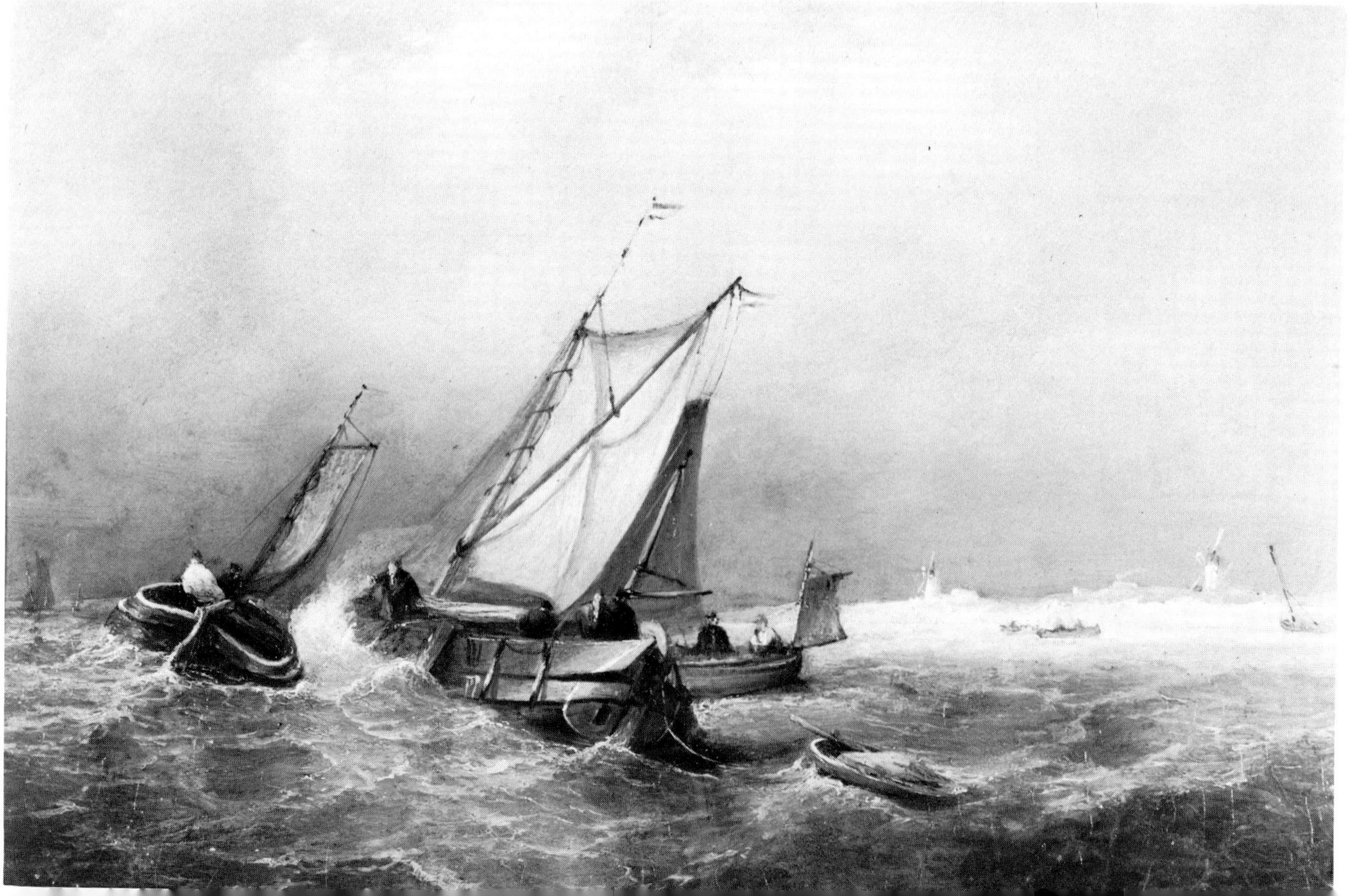

Plate 529. G.R. Barr, fl. mid-19th century. "The ship *Ellen Rodgers,* dated 1858." National Maritime Museum, Greenwich.

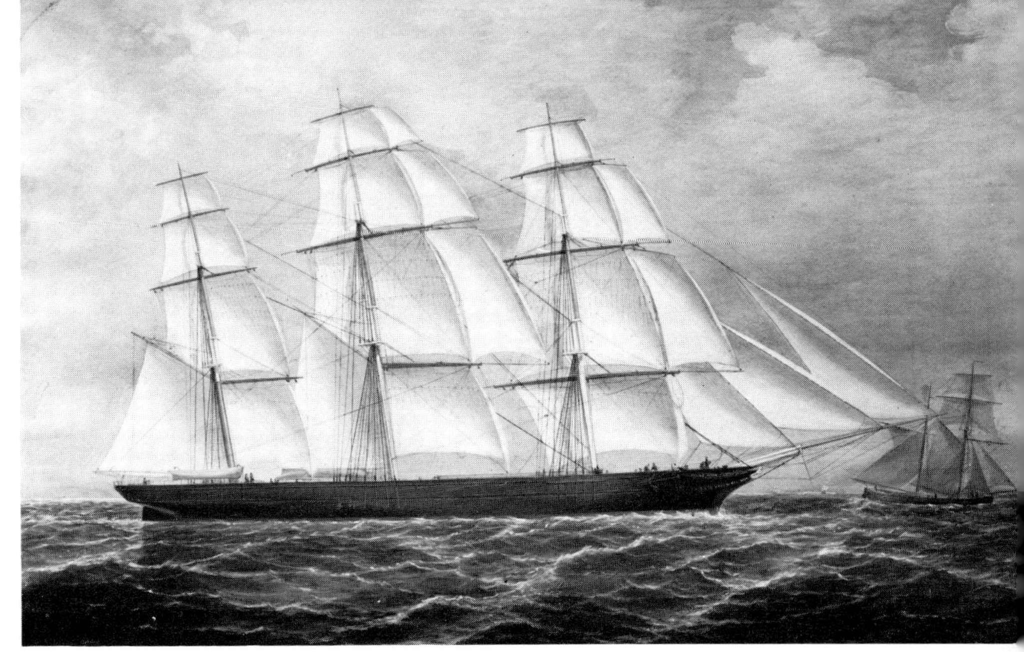

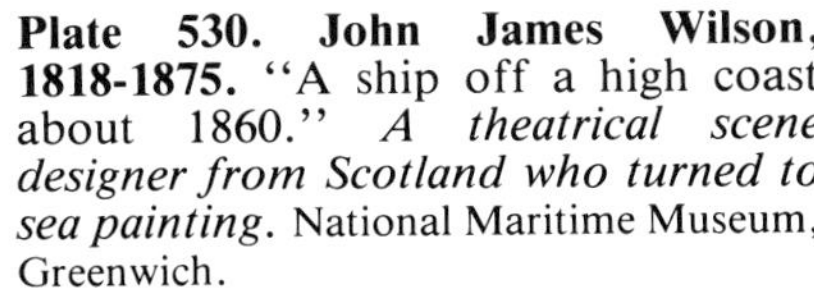

Plate 530. John James Wilson, 1818-1875. "A ship off a high coast about 1860." *A theatrical scene designer from Scotland who turned to sea painting.* National Maritime Museum, Greenwich.

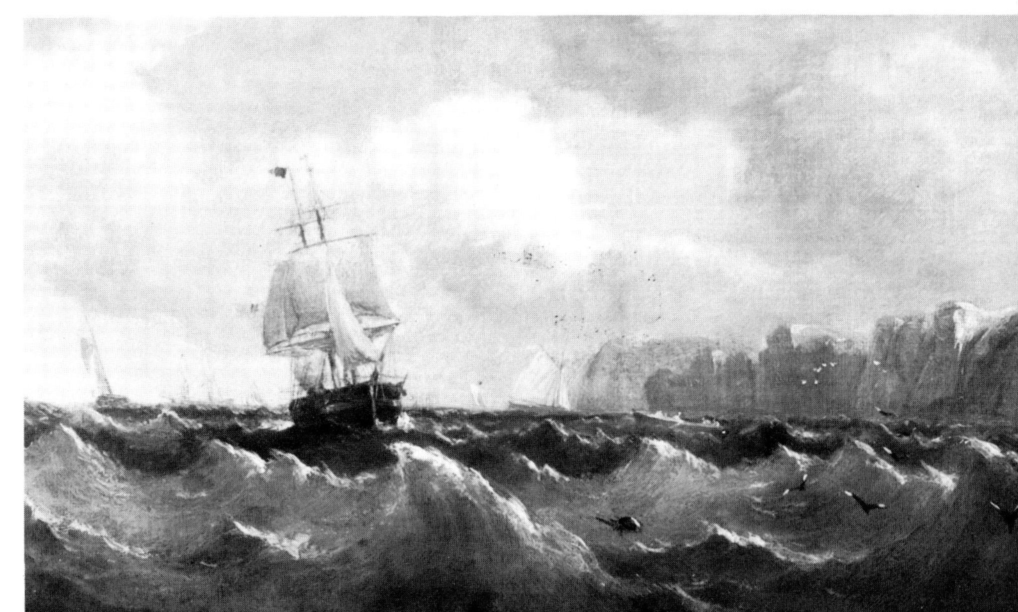

Plate 531. J. Salmon, fl. mid-19th century. "Fishing boats off a beach in a gale, dated 1861." Sotheby's.

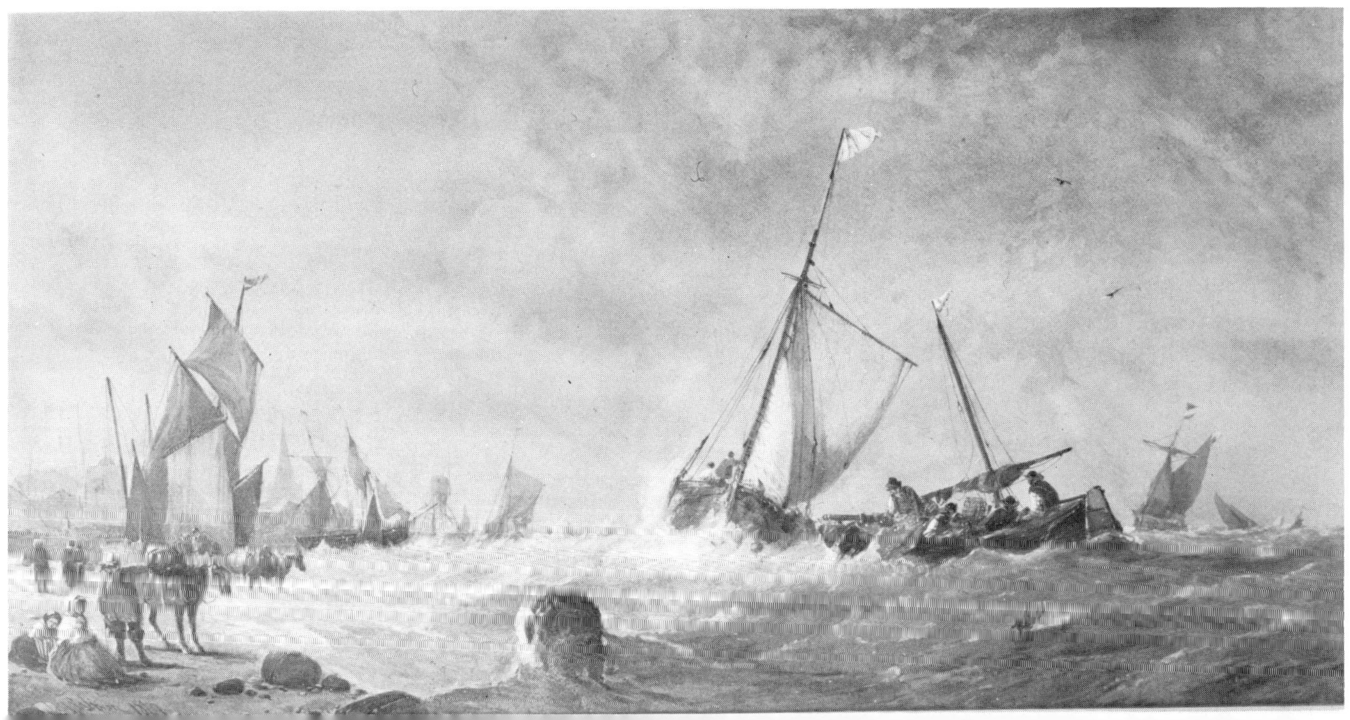

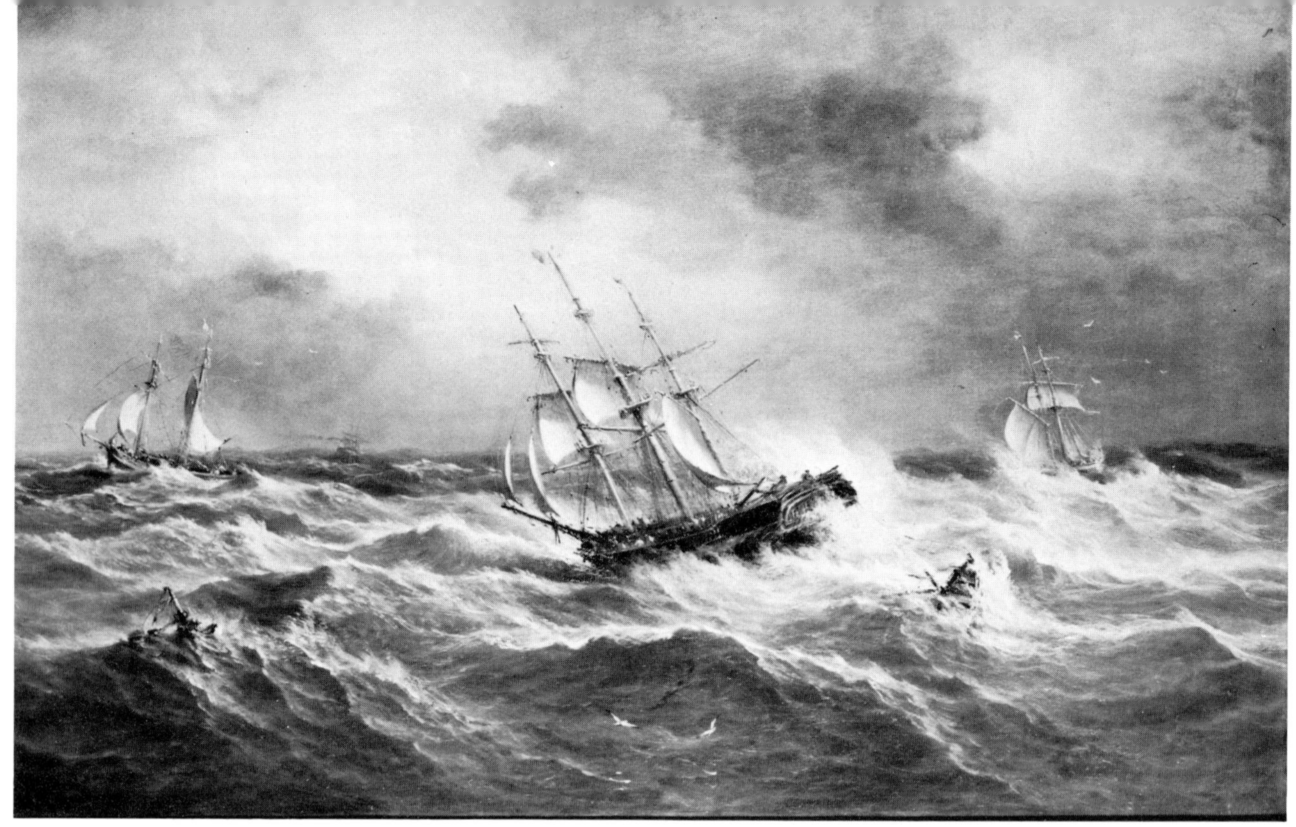

Plate 532. John Moore, 1820-1902. "Shipping in a gale." Sotheby's.

Plate 533. Henry Dawson, 1811-1878. "A hay barge and shipping off Greenwich, dated 1867." *These enormous hay barges with their equally large loads came up river on the incoming tide, while the small 'sweeps' adjusted the positions and kept the barges on course.* M. Newman Ltd.

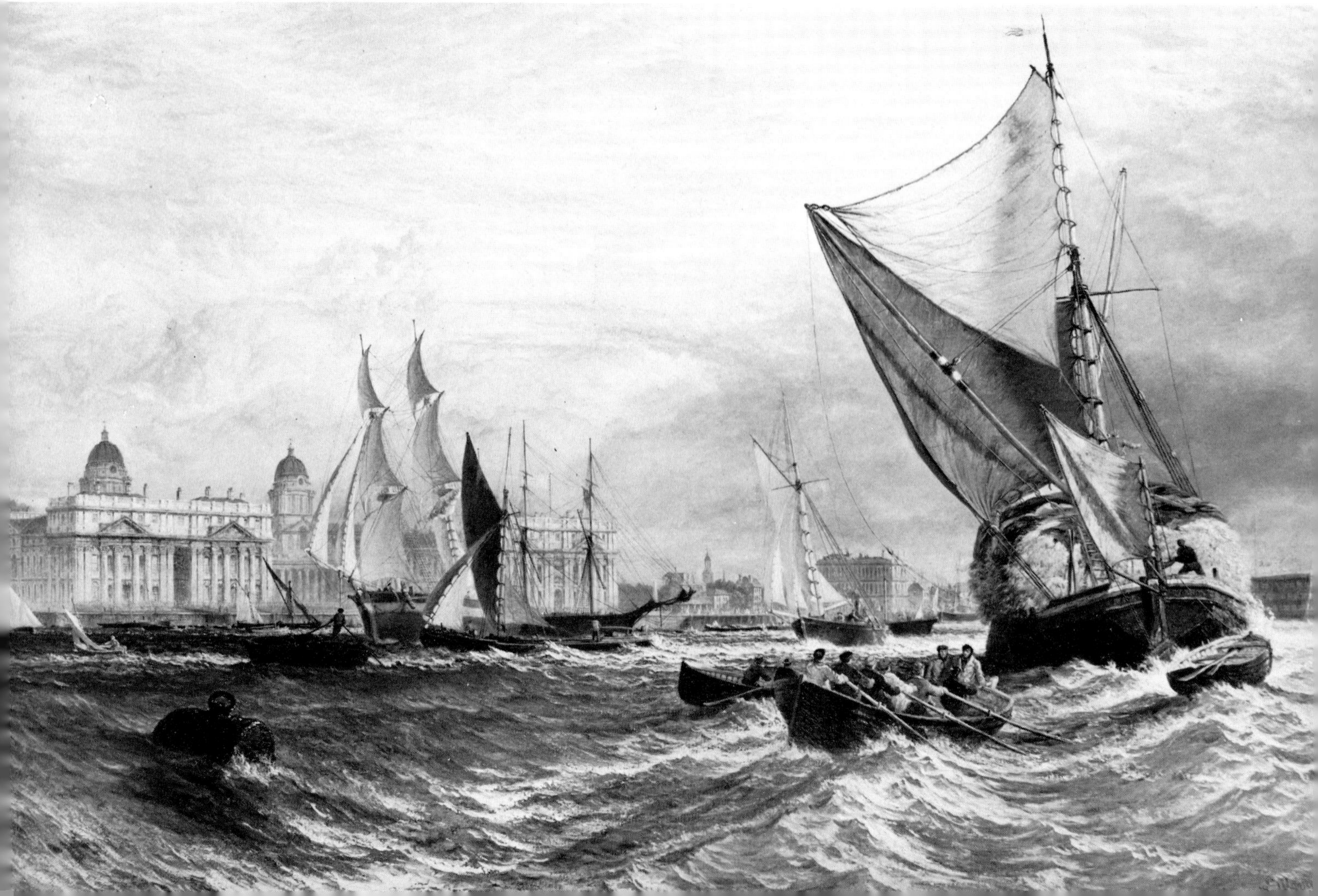

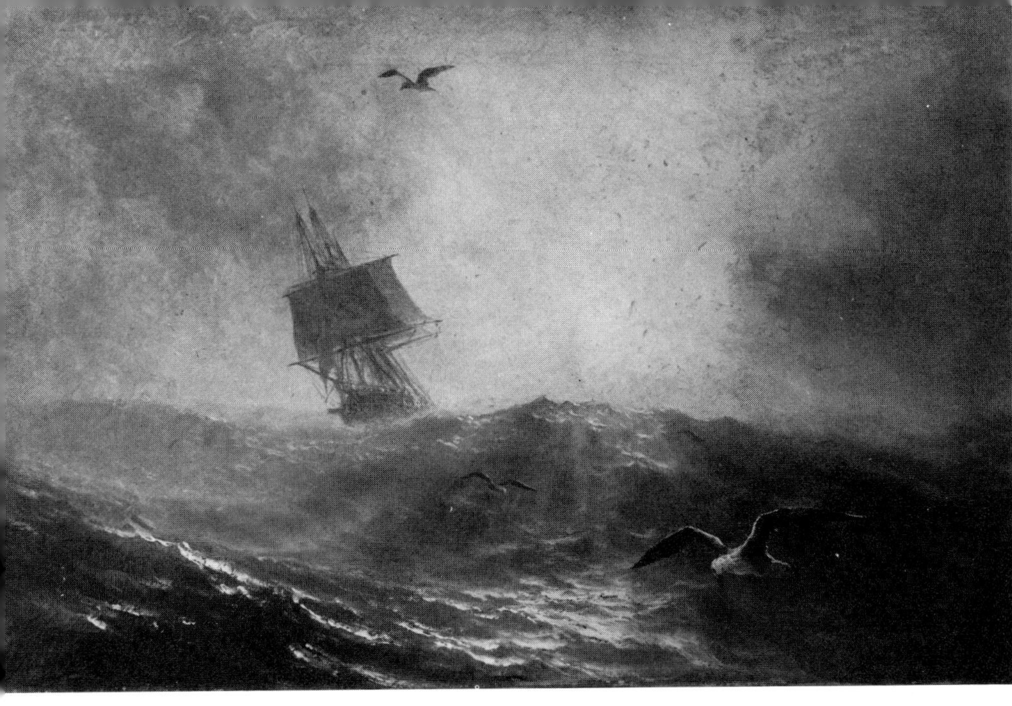

Plate 534. Henry T. Dawson, fl.1860-1873. "A ship running in a heavy sea, after a storm." Bonham's.

Plate 535. William Frederick Settle, 1821-1897. "H.M. frigate *Immortalité* with the royal yacht *Victoria and Albert II,* H.M.S. *Warrior* and a cutter of the Royal Yacht Squadron, in the Solent about 1862." National Maritime Museum, Greenwich.

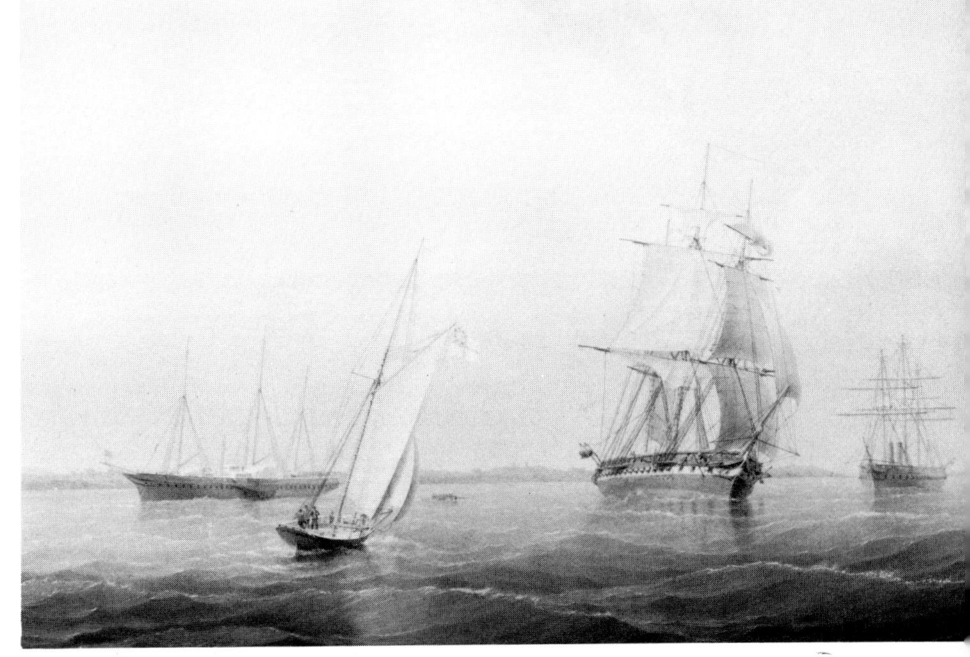

Plate 536. George Clarkson Stanfield, 1828-1878. "Coastal craft off the Dutch coast, dated 1862." King & Chasemore.

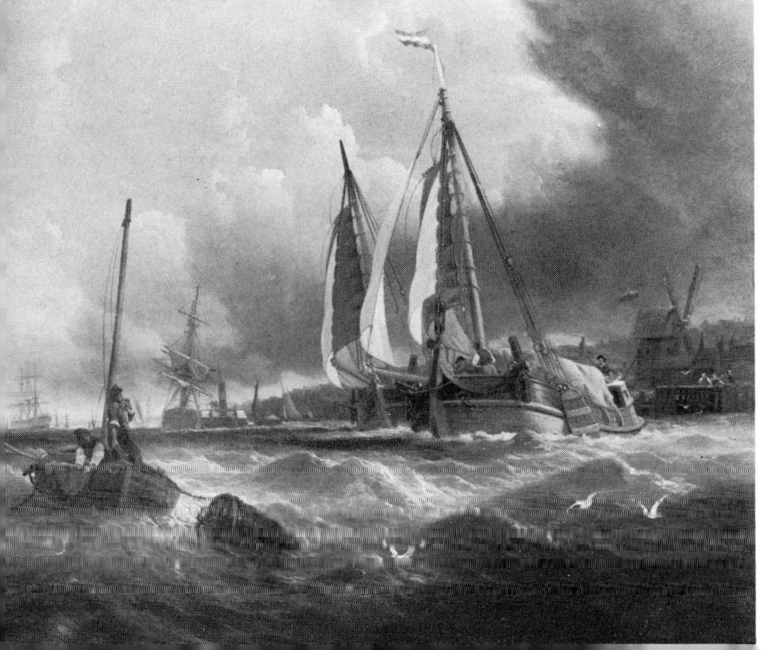

Plate 537. Alfred Montague, fl.1835-1870. "Fishing boats in a gale off a town, dated 1864." Christie's.

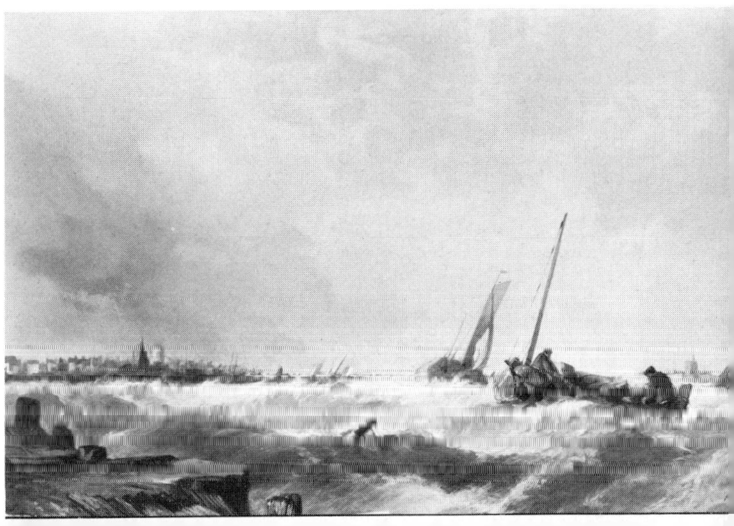

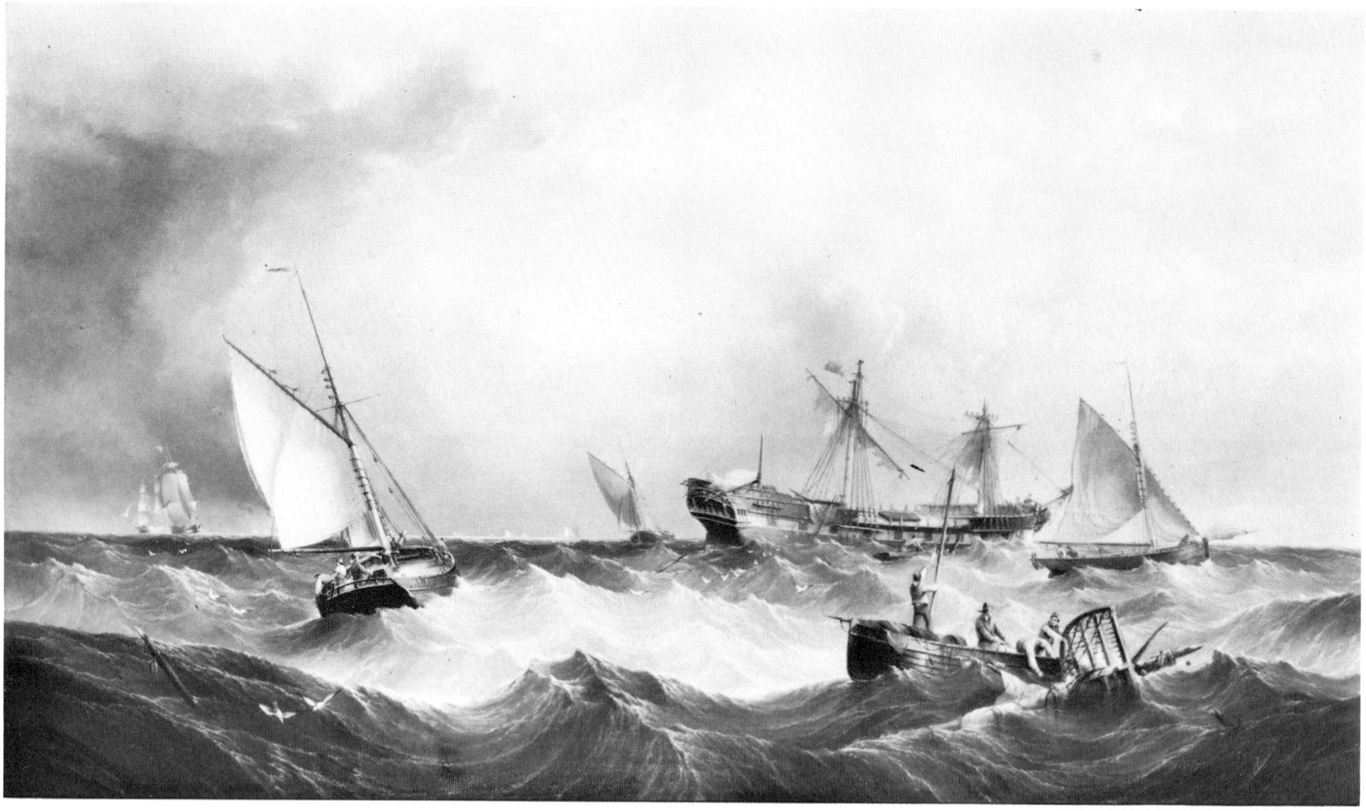

Plate 538. Henry Redmore, 1820-1887. "A merchantman dismasted after a storm." *He painted with a grey palette rather like Joseph Walter.* Bonham's.

Plate 539. Henry Redmore, 1820-1887. "A Dutch merchantman, a British ship of the line and small craft in a stiff breeze, dated 1865." Bonham's.

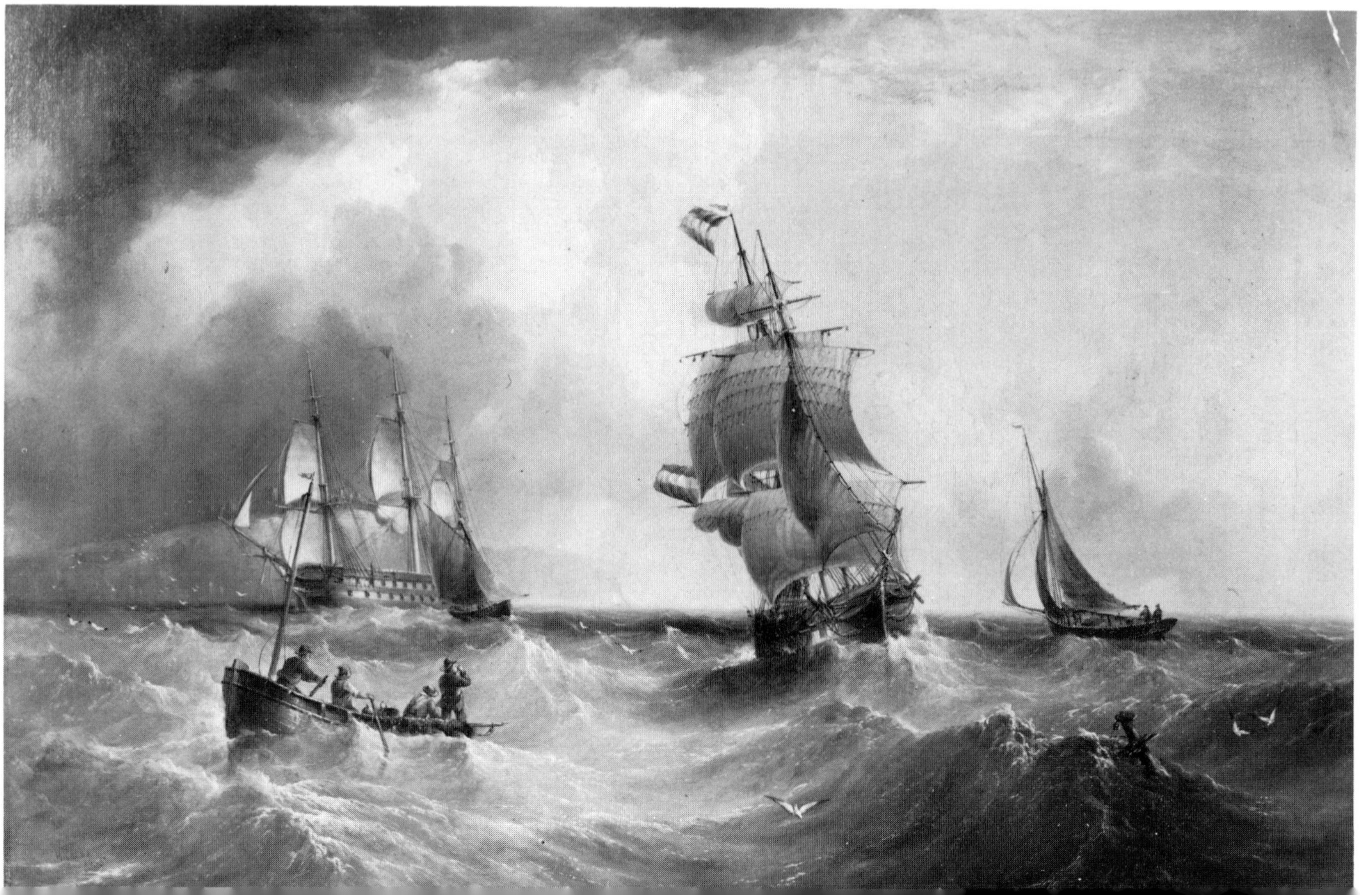

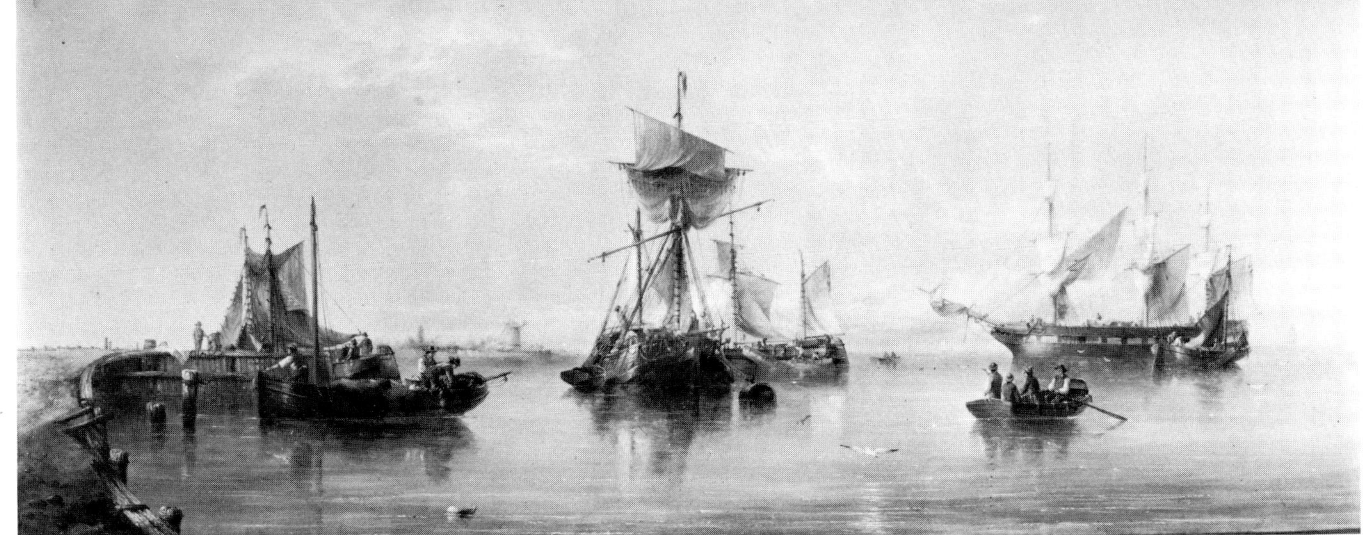

Plate 540. Henry Redmore, 1820-1887. "Shipping off the Dutch coast." *The artist has created a 'Dutch' atmosphere in this scene of shipping off the Dutch coast.* Sotheby's.

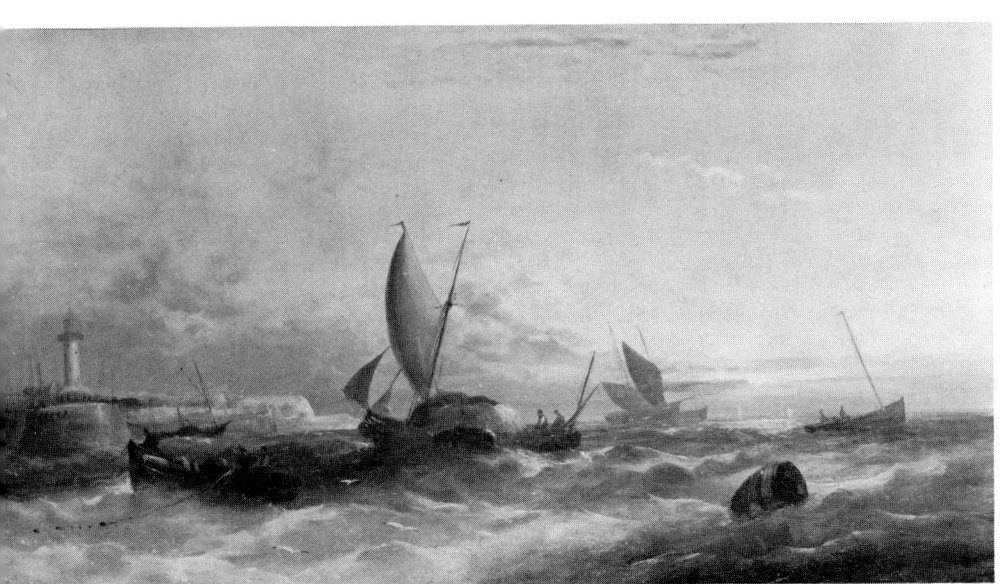

Plate 541. W.H. Williamson, fl. mid- to late 19th century. "Fishing boats off Folkestone, dated 1864." Sotheby's.

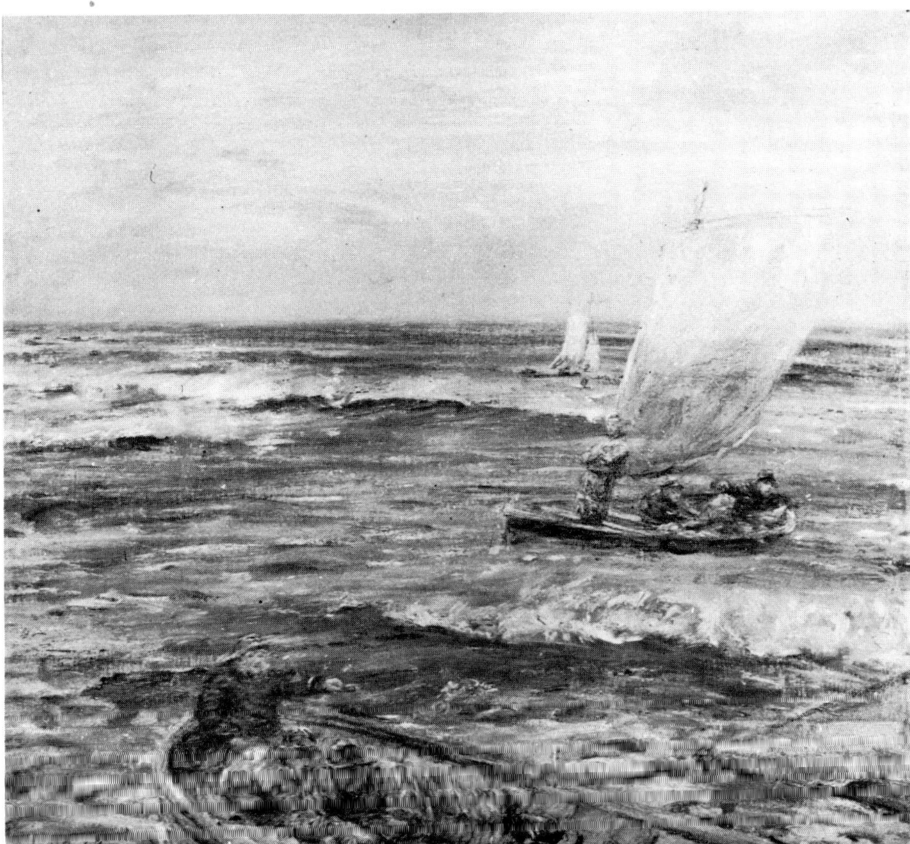

Plate 542. William McTaggart, 1835-1910. "The lobster fishers." *McTaggart's early work was carefully delineated, while his later style became more experimental, to the extent that in many cases the sea and the figures merge.* National Gallery of Victoria, Melbourne.

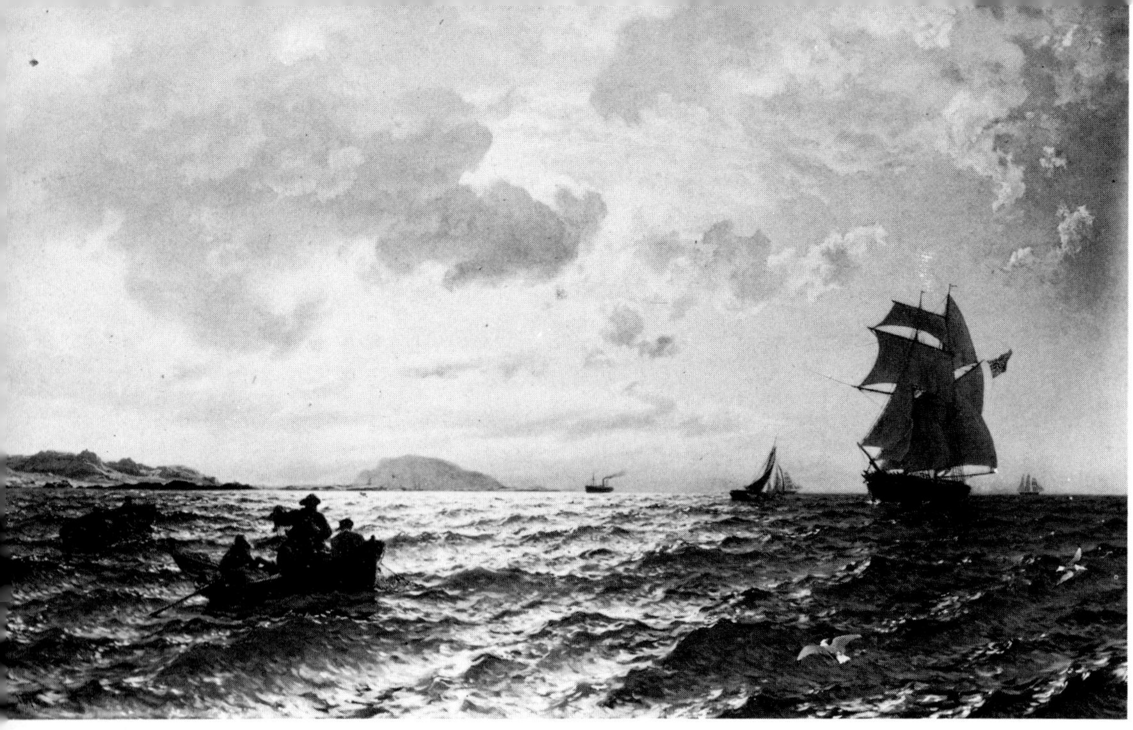

Plate 543. Hans Frederick Gude, 1825-1903. "Fishing boats off-shore with a topsail schooner." *A painting with excellent sky, sea and lighting effects.* National Gallery, Oslo.

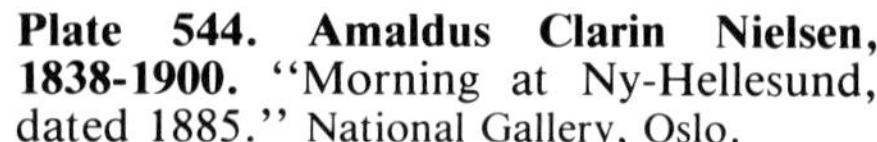

Plate 544. Amaldus Clarin Nielsen, 1838-1900. "Morning at Ny-Hellesund, dated 1885." National Gallery, Oslo.

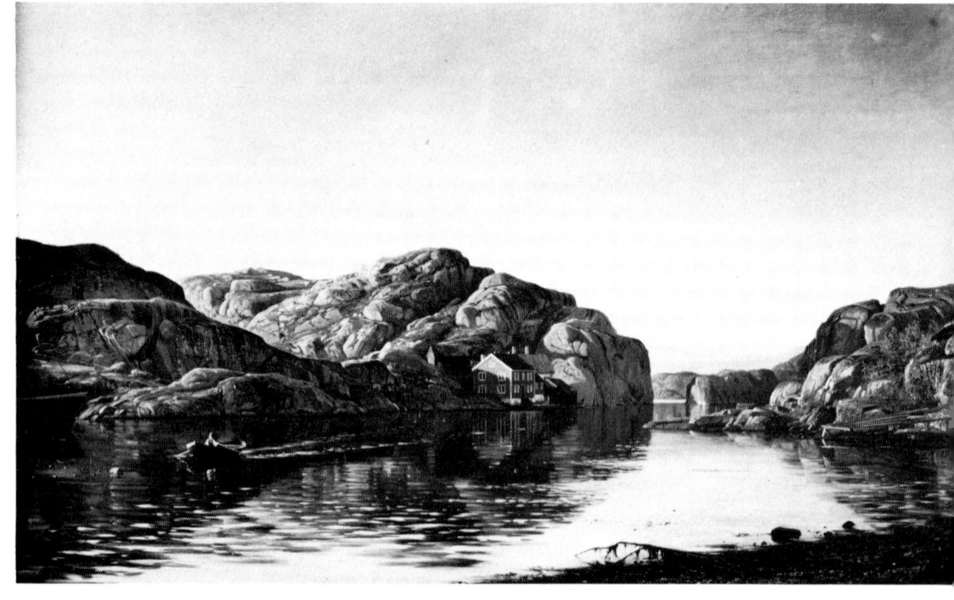

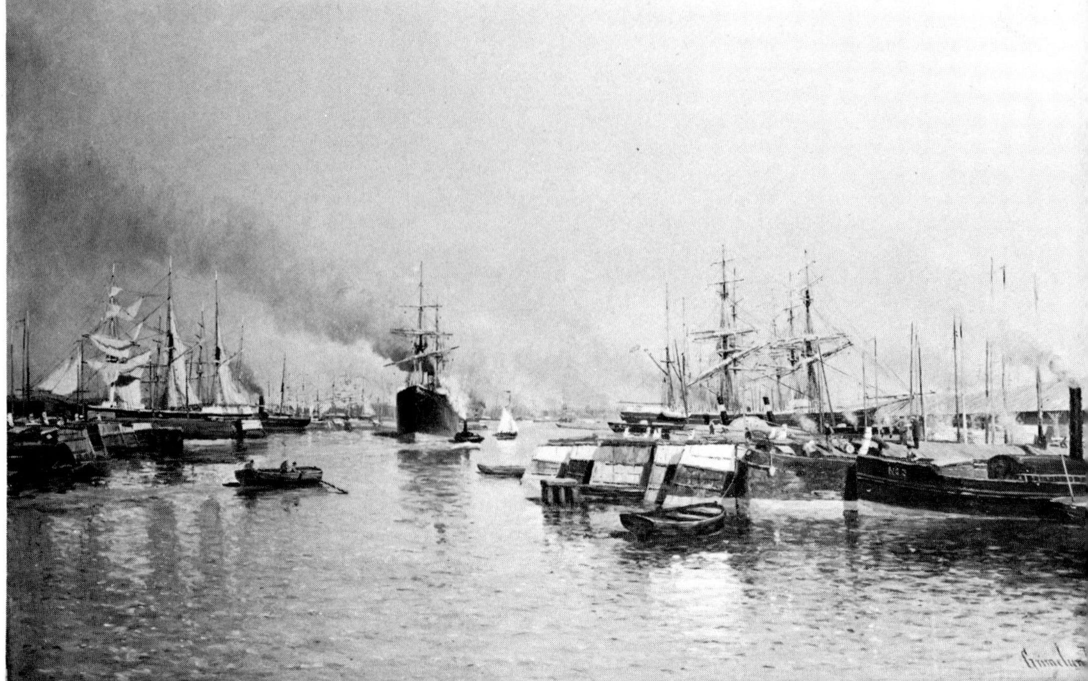

Piate 545. Johannes Martin Grimelund, b.1842. "The port of Antwerp." National Gallery, Oslo.

Plate 546. F. Sorvig. "Norwegian merchant ships, dated 1861." Bergen Maritime Museum.

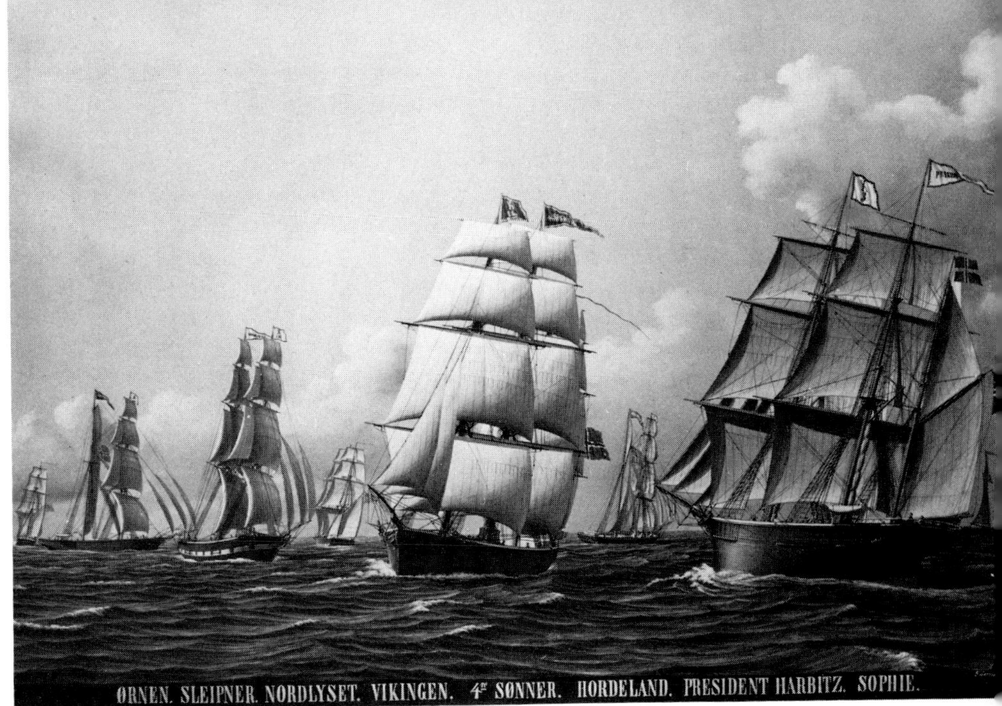

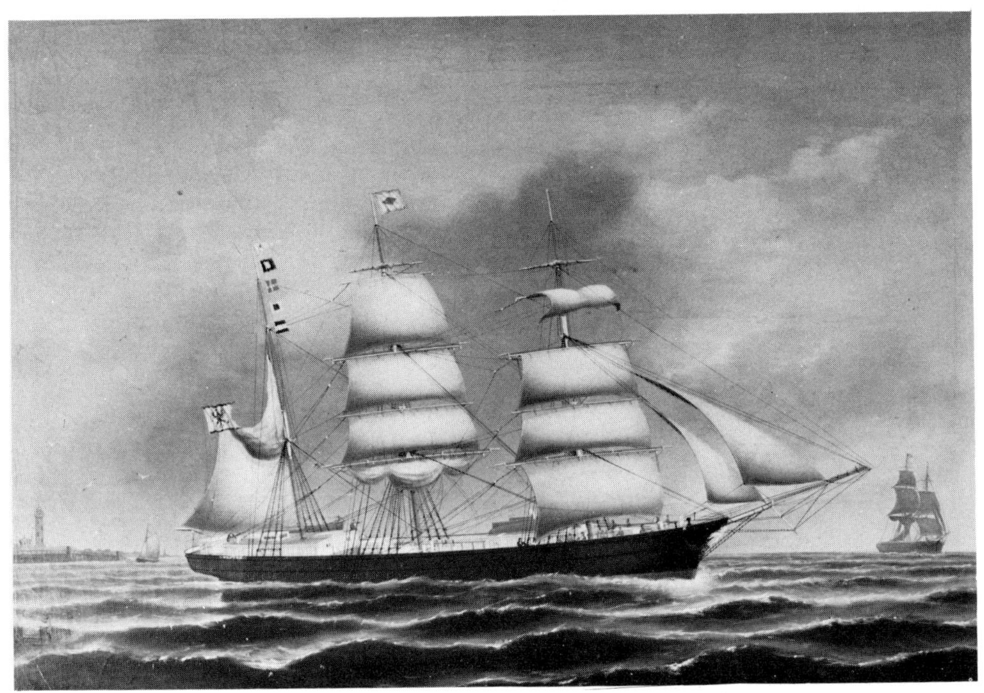

Plate 547. Peter Christian Holm, 1823-1888. "The barque *Neptun,* out of Altona, dated 1866." Altonaer Museum, Hamburg.

Plate 548. Peter Christian Holm, 1823-1888, and Lorenz Petersen, 1803-1870. "The barque *Joachim Christian,* out of Altona, dated 1865." Altonaer Museum, Hamburg.

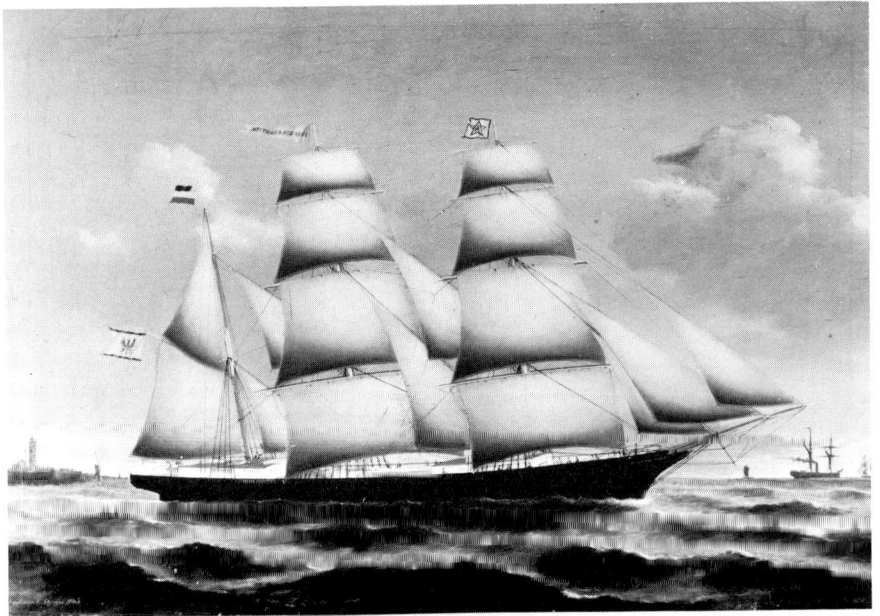

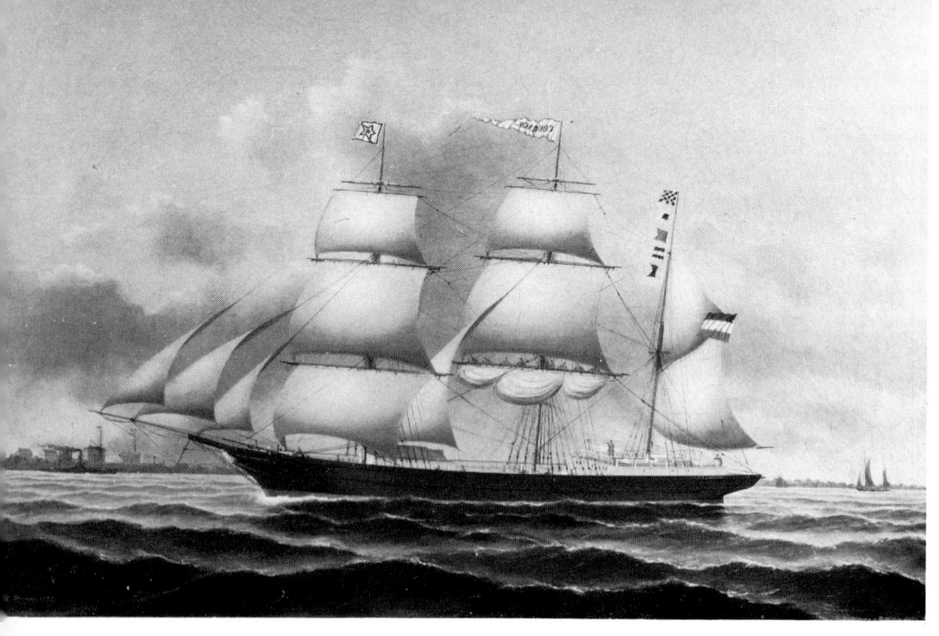

Plate 549. Peter Christian Holm, 1823-1888, and Lorenz Petersen, 1803-1870. "The barque *Courage,* out of Altona, dated 1867." Altonaer Museum, Hamburg.

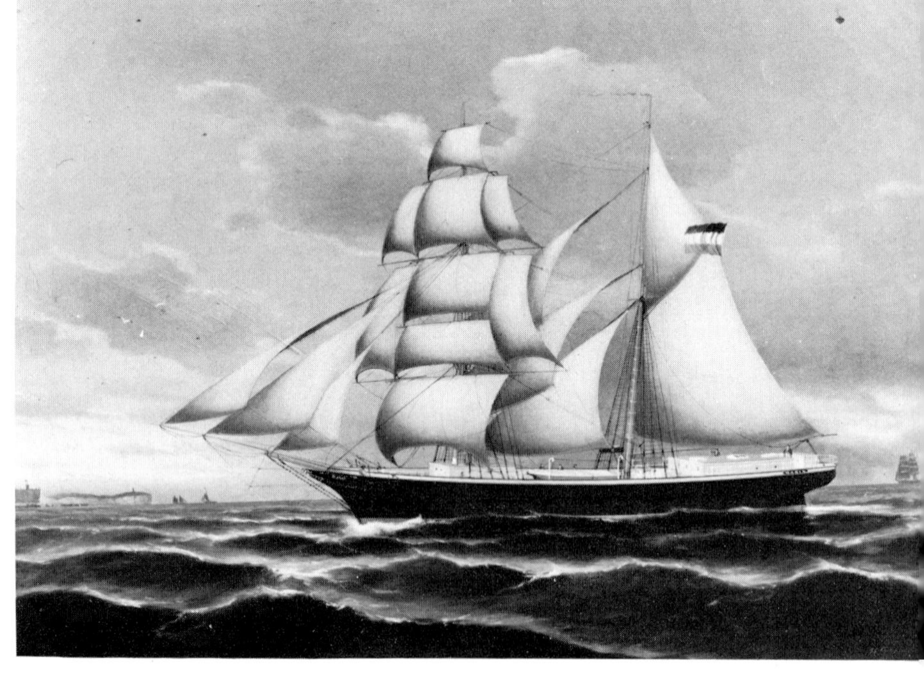

Plate 550. Peter Christian Holm, 1823-1888, and Heinrich Andreas Sophus Petersen, 1834-1916. "The brigantine *Maria,* out of Blankenese, dated 1872." *The brigantine is running with stunsails set.* Altonaer Museum, Hamburg.

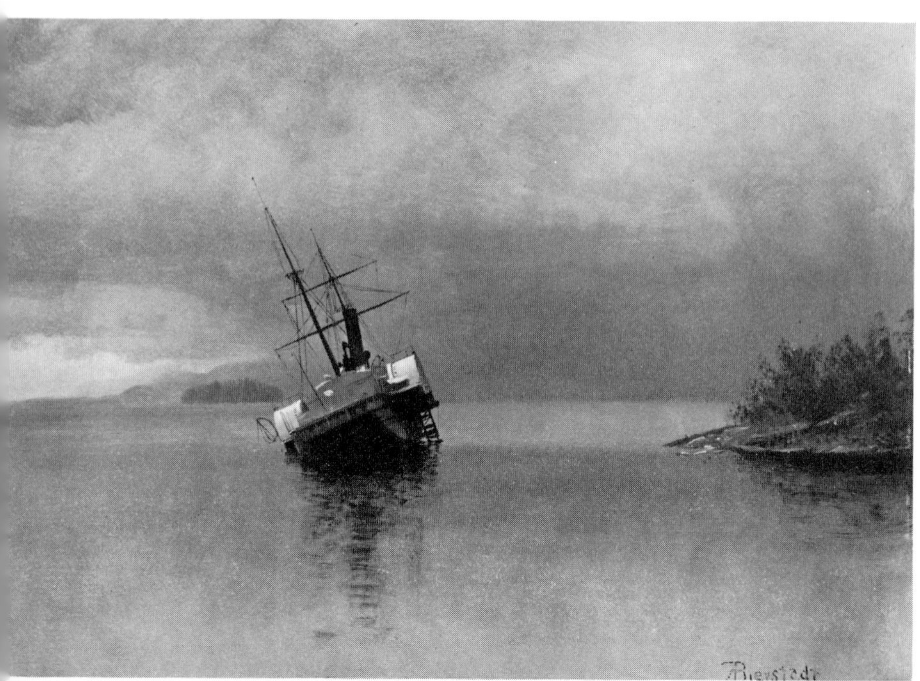

Plate 551. Albert Bierstadt, 1830-1902. "The Wreck of the *Ancon* in Loring Bay, Alaska." Museum of Fine Arts (M. and M. Karolik Collection), Boston.

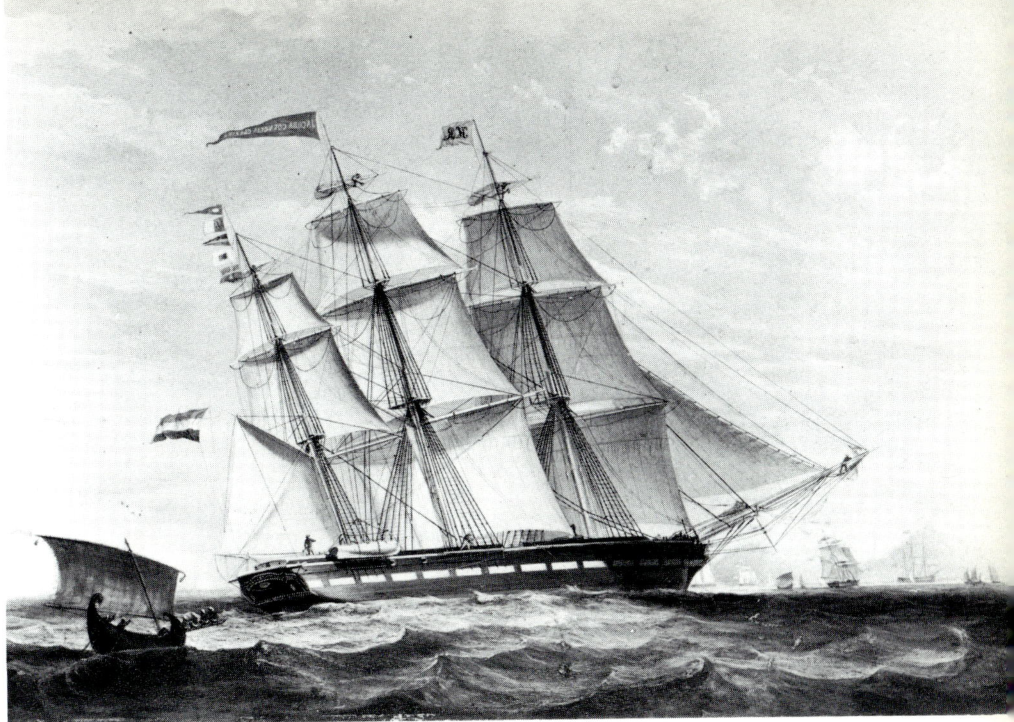

Plate 552. Casparus Johannes Morel, 1798-1861. "The Dutch merchantman *Jacoba Cornelia Clasina,* dated 1857." *The small vessel on the left is an Indonesian caracore which indicates the merchantman is probably in the China Seas. From her mizzen-mast she is wearing her number in the Maryatt code.* Scheepvaart Museum, Amsterdam.

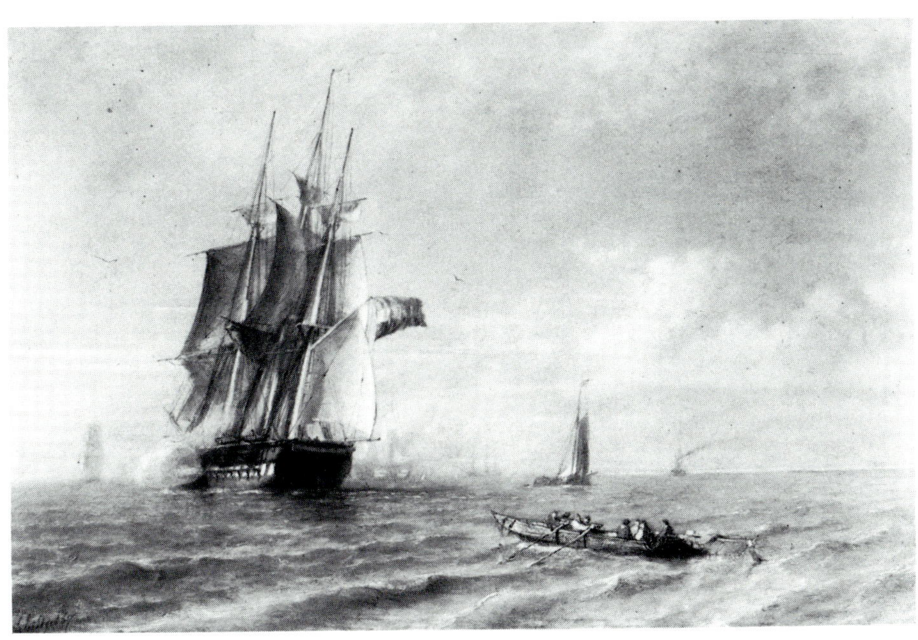

Plate 553. Petrus Paulus Schiedges, 1813-1876. "A Dutch frigate in stays firing a salute, dated 1867." Scheepvaart Museum, Amsterdam.

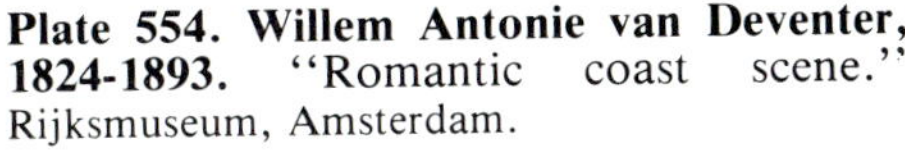

Plate 554. Willem Antonie van Deventer, 1824-1893. "Romantic coast scene." Rijksmuseum, Amsterdam.

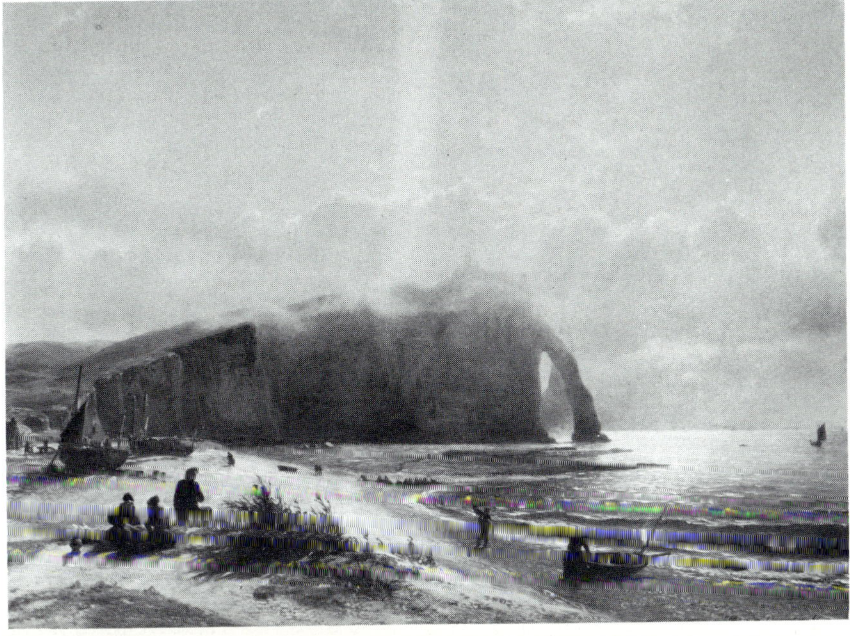

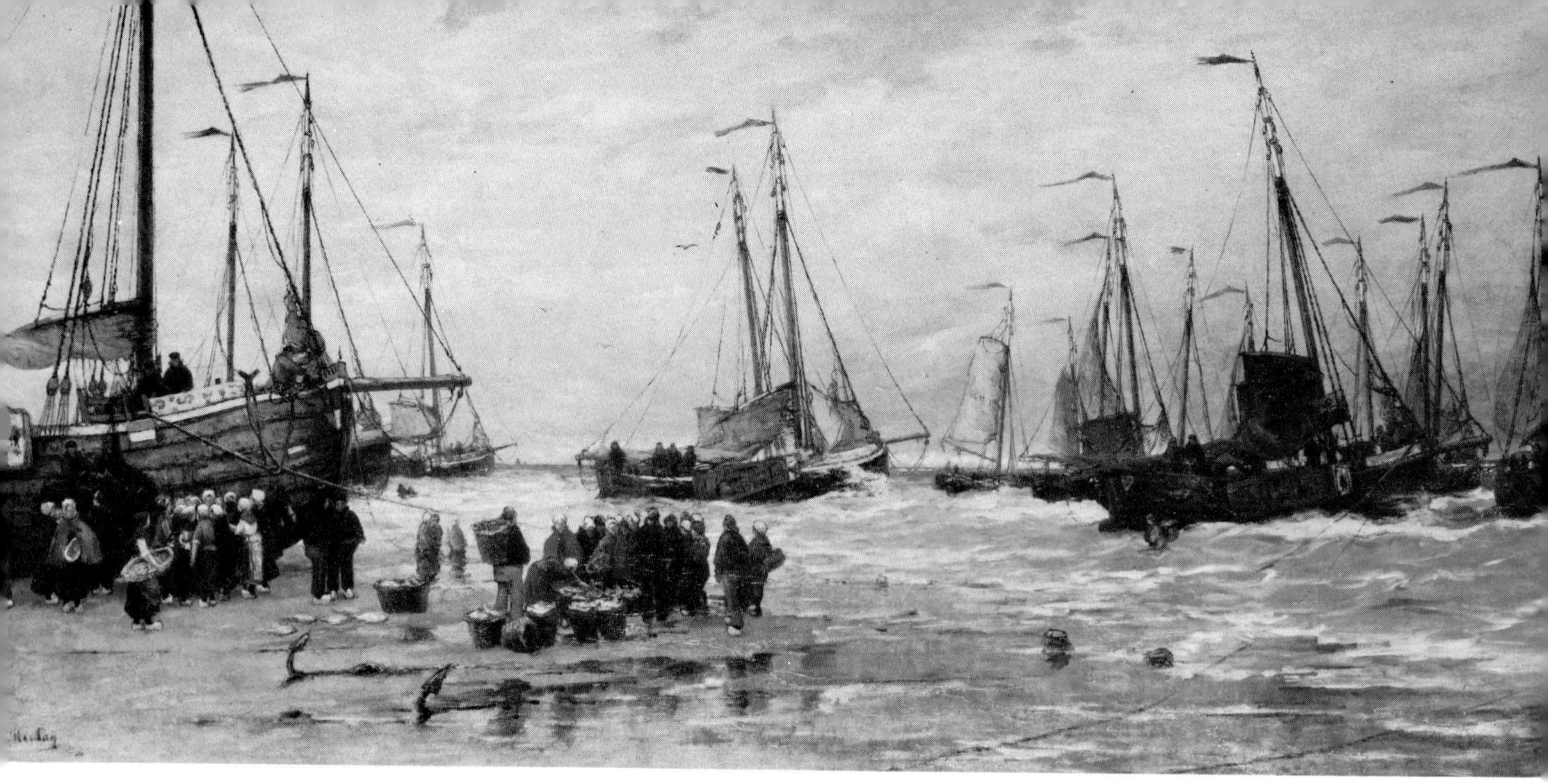

Plate 555. Hendrik Willem Mesdag, 1831-1915. "Fishing pinks in the breakers." *The pinks are unloading their hauls stern on to the beach.* Rijksmuseum, Amsterdam.

Plate 556. Hendrik Willem Mesdag, 1831-1915. "Dutch fishing boats beaching with their catches at sunset." Martin van Mesdag.

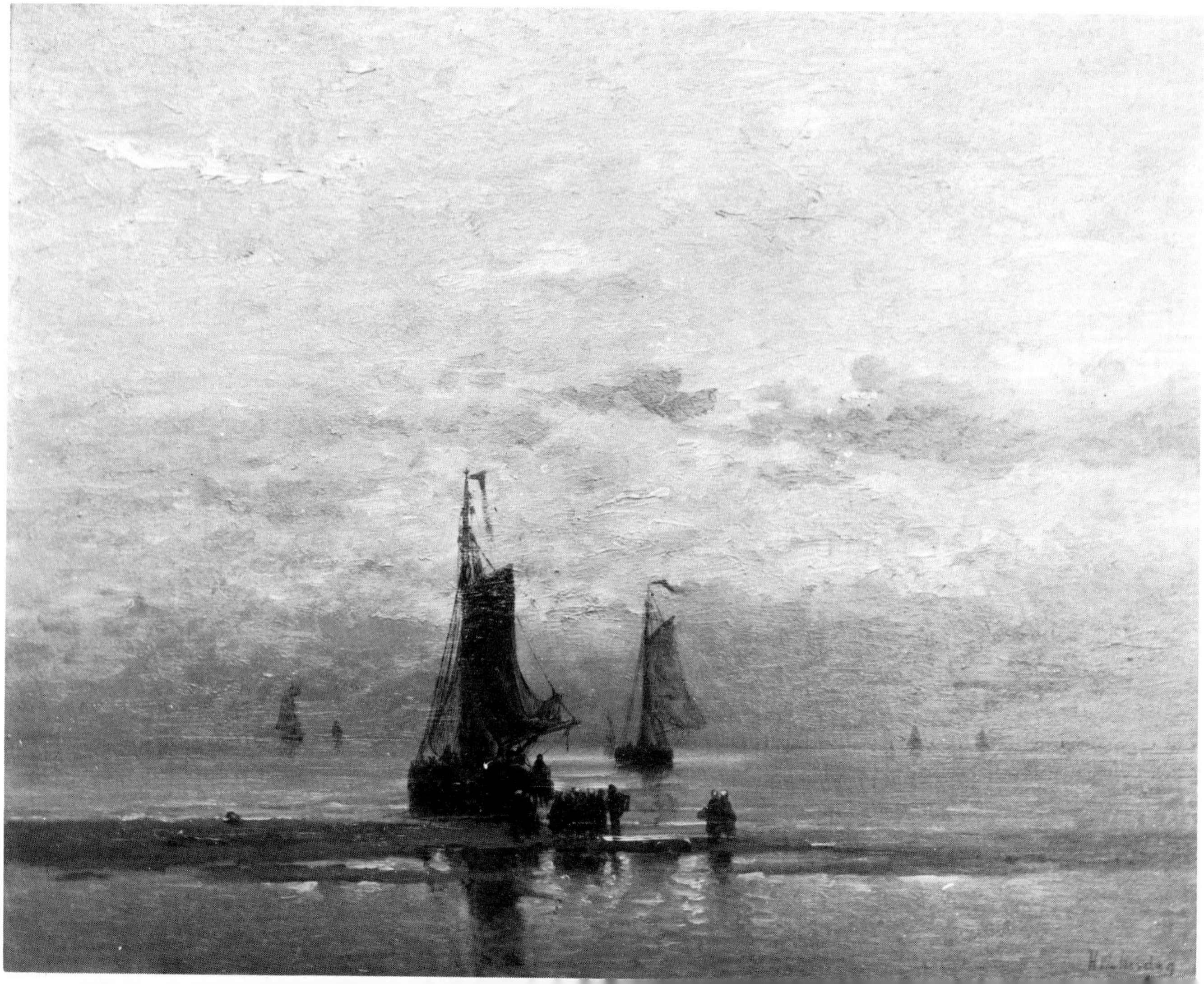

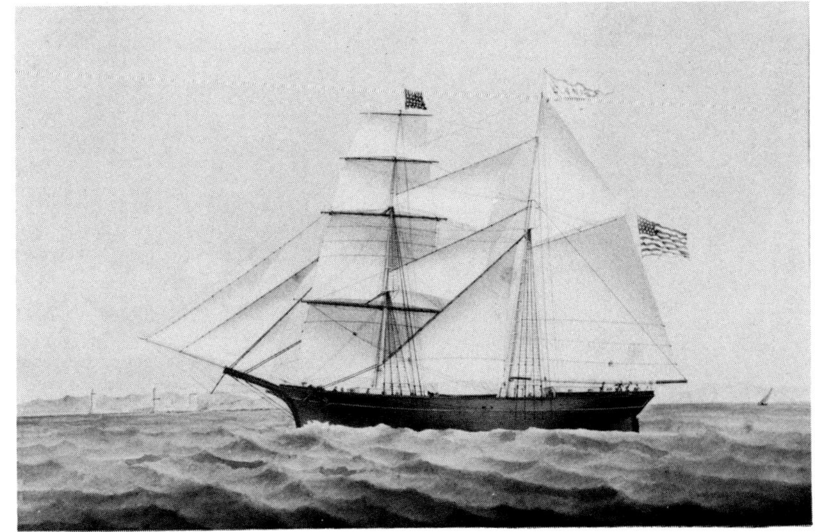

Plate 557. Paul Soulies, fl. mid- to late 19th century. "The American brigantine *Betsy Ames,* dated 1858." *The sails between the masts are staysails.* Mariners Museum, Newport News.

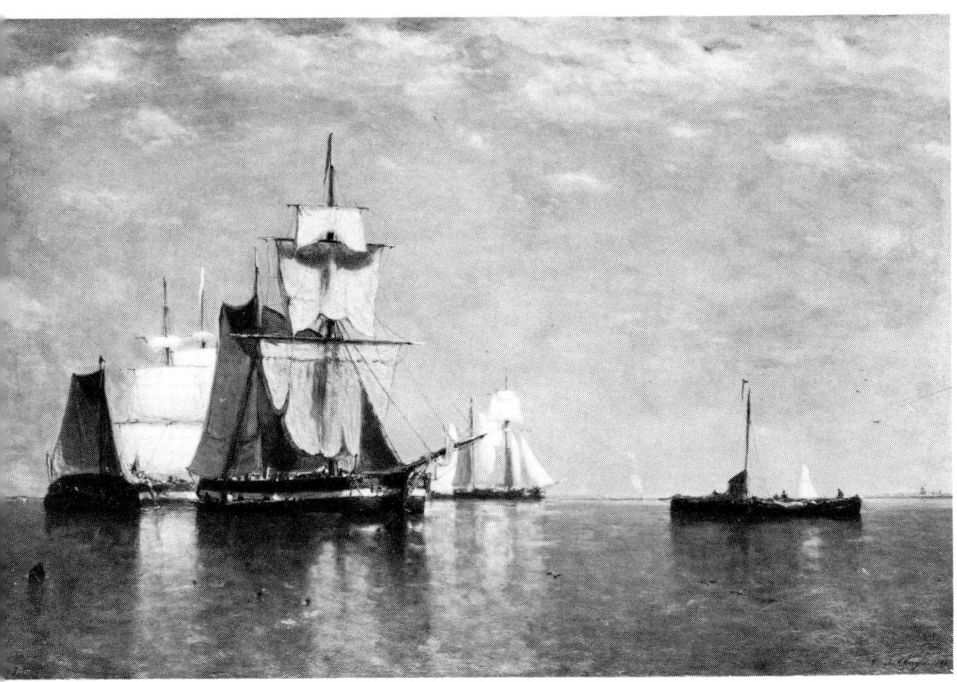

Plate 558. Paul-Jean Clays, 1819-1900. "Dutch coastal craft becalmed, dated 1869." National Gallery, London.

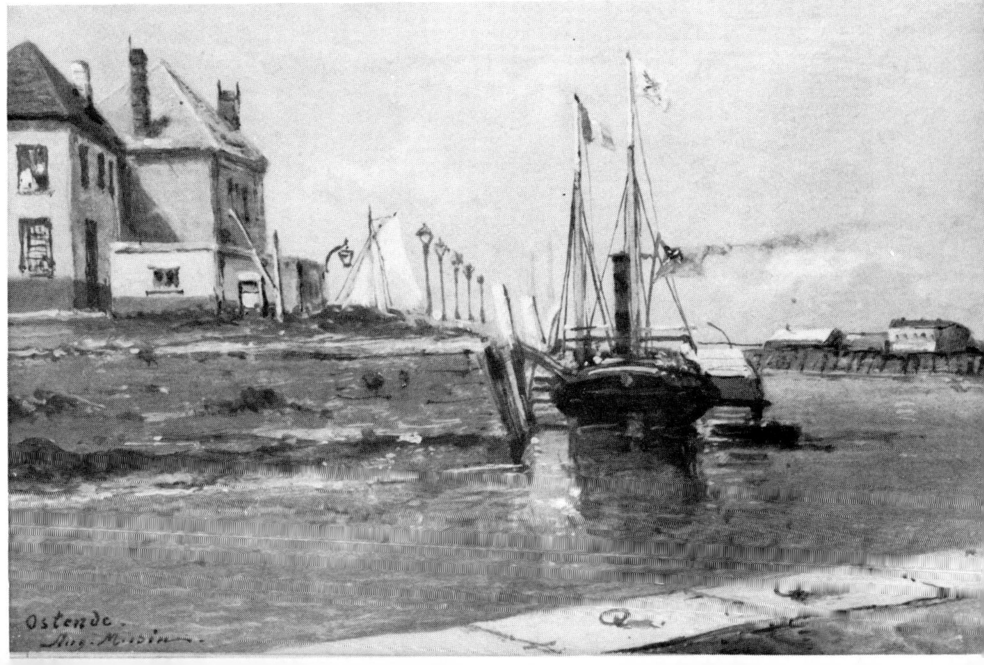

Plate 559. Auguste Henri Musin, b.1852. "The port of Ostend." Museum of Fine Art, Ostend.

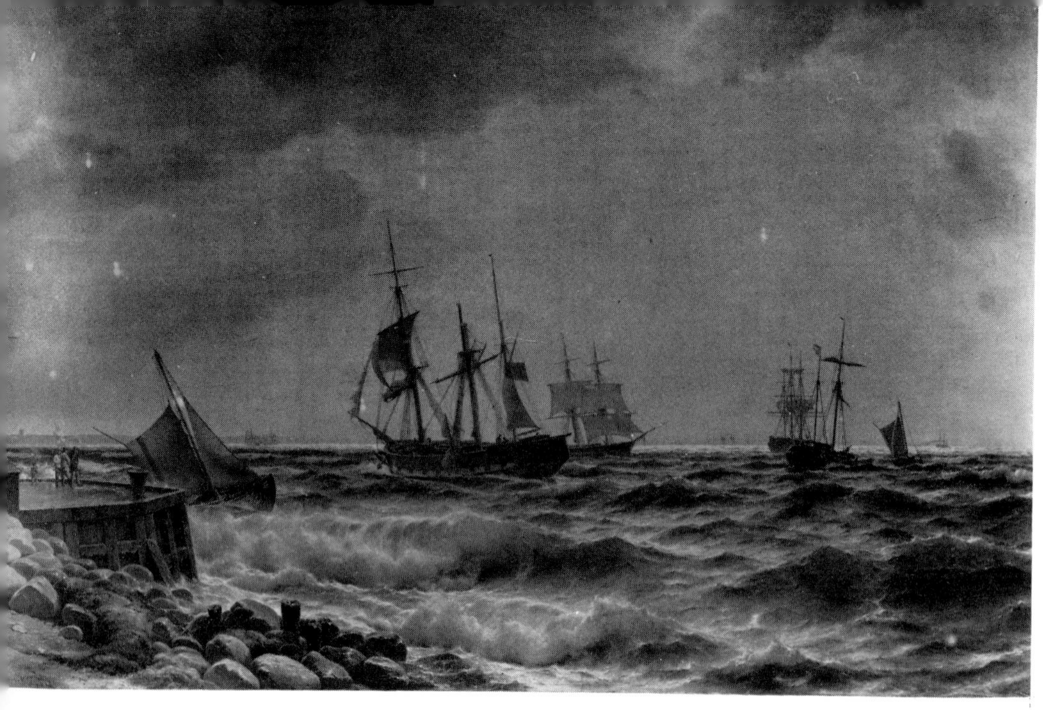

Plate 560. Johan Carl Neumann, 1833-1891. "Ships inshore after a squall, dated 1867." State Museum for Art, Copenhagen.

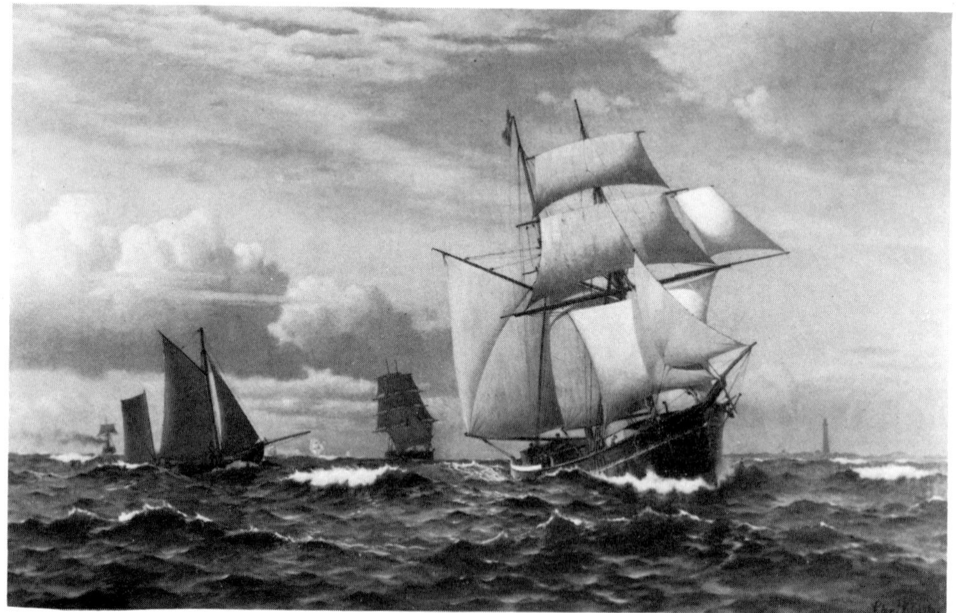

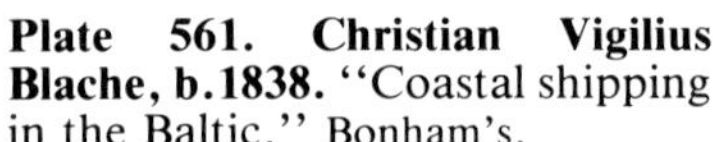

Plate 561. Christian Vigilius Blache, b.1838. "Coastal shipping in the Baltic." Bonham's.

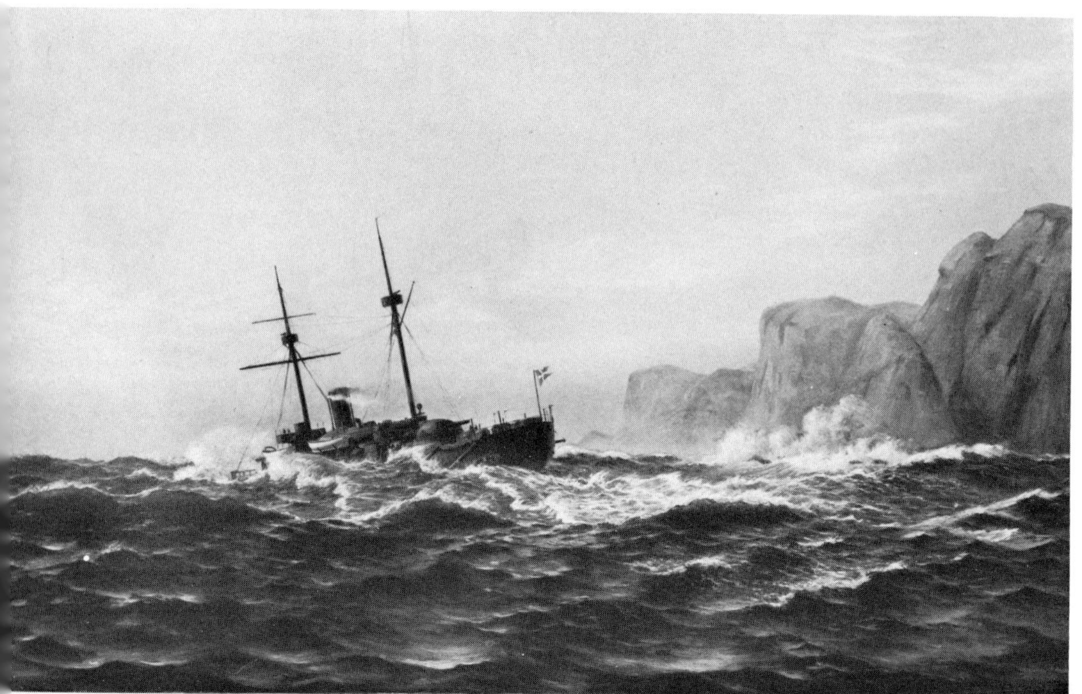

Plate 562. Christian Vigilius Blache, b.1838. "A Danish warship in a heavy sea off rocks." State Museum for Art, Copenhagen.

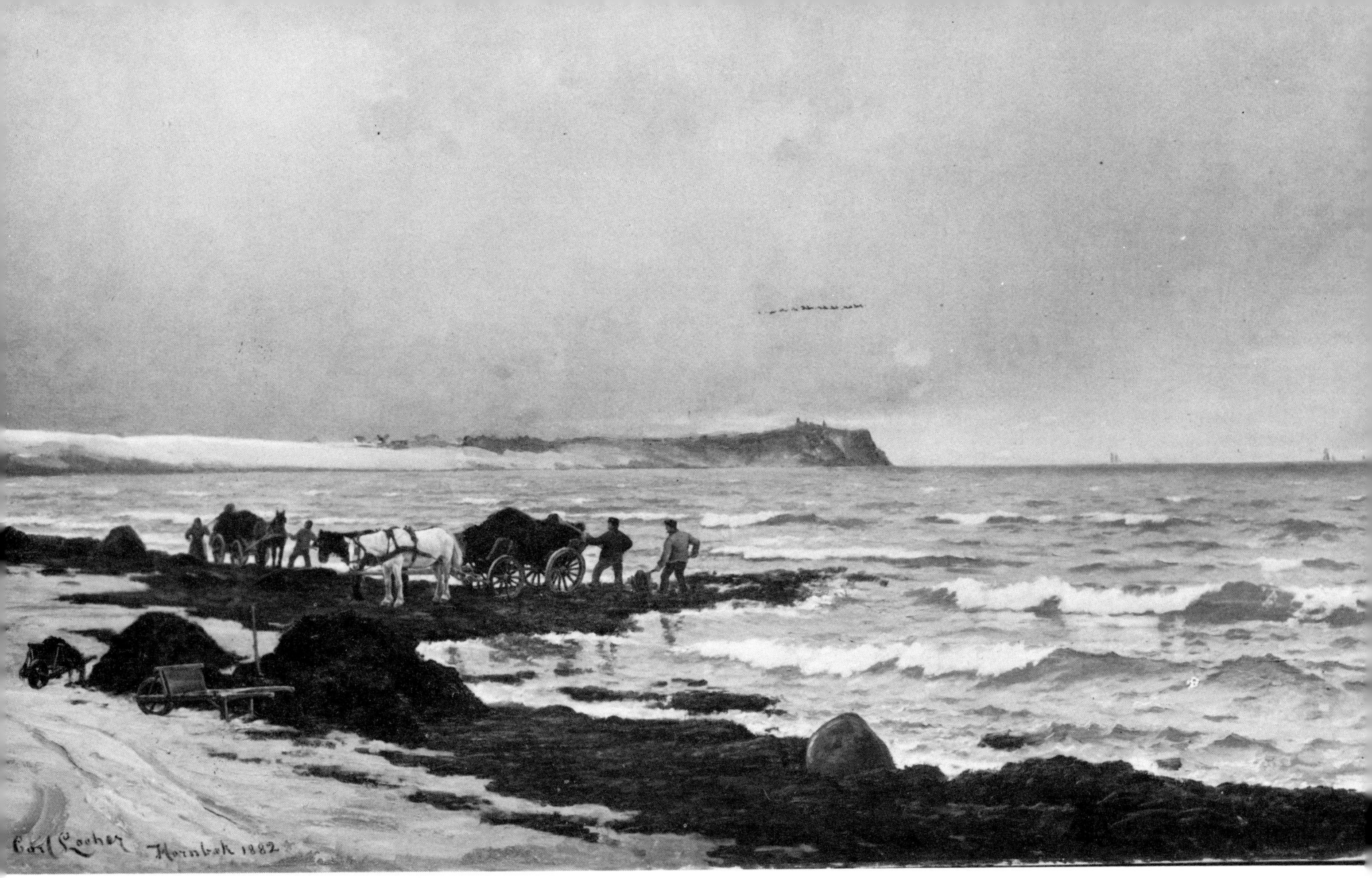

Plate 563. Carl Locher, 1851-1915. "Loading sea weed on Hornbaek beach, Zeeland, dated 1882." Statens Museum for Kunst, Copenhagen.

Plate 564. Giovani Serritelli, fl. mid-19th century. "H.M.S. *Caledonia,* flagship Mediterranean fleet, off Naples, about 1867-9." *Funnels on such ships were retractable — here one is shown up with boilers fired, the other down with fires drawn.* Christie's.

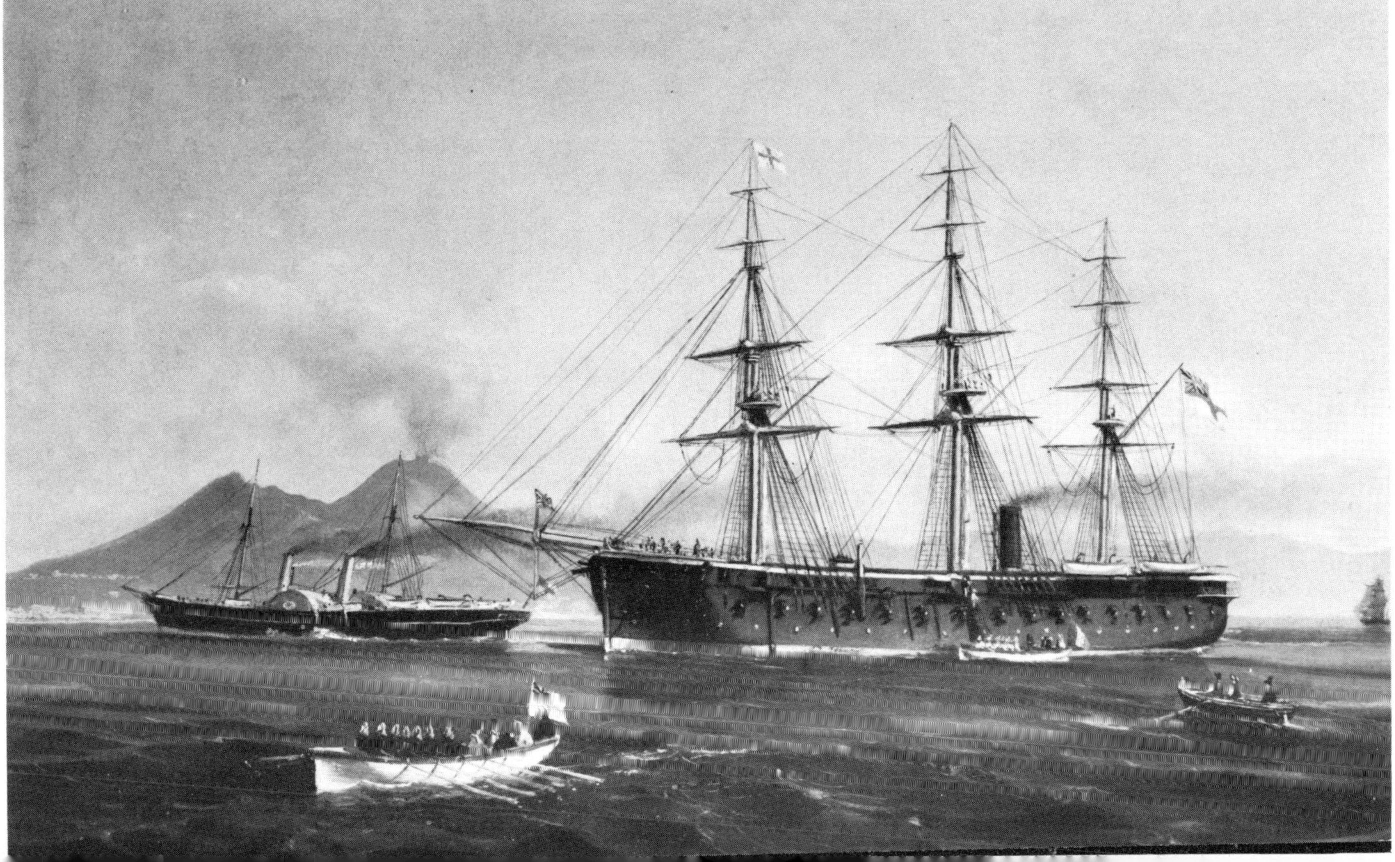

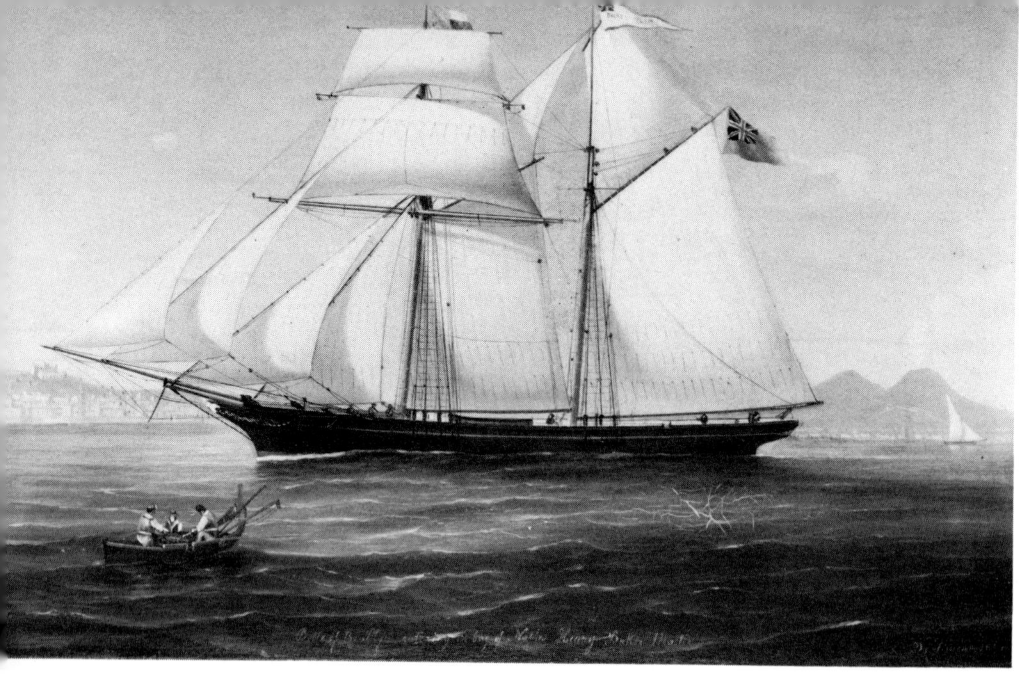

Plate 565. A. de Simone, fl. mid- to late 19th century. "The topsail schooner *Belle of Plym,* dated 1877." National Maritime Museum, Greenwich.

Plate 566. A. de Simone, fl. mid- to late 19th century. "H.M.S. *Inflexible* off Naples about 1883." National Maritime Museum, Greenwich.

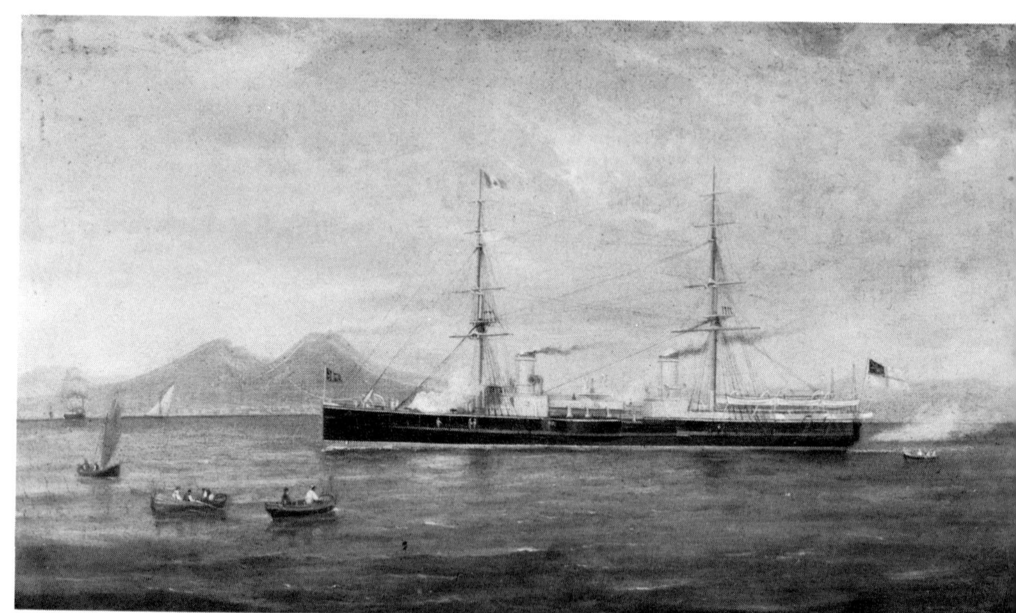

Plate 567. Henry A. Luscombe, 1820-aft.1868. "A Russian squadron at Plymouth in 1868, the ships' yards a-cockbill, in mourning for a dead prince." City Museum and Art Gallery, Plymouth.

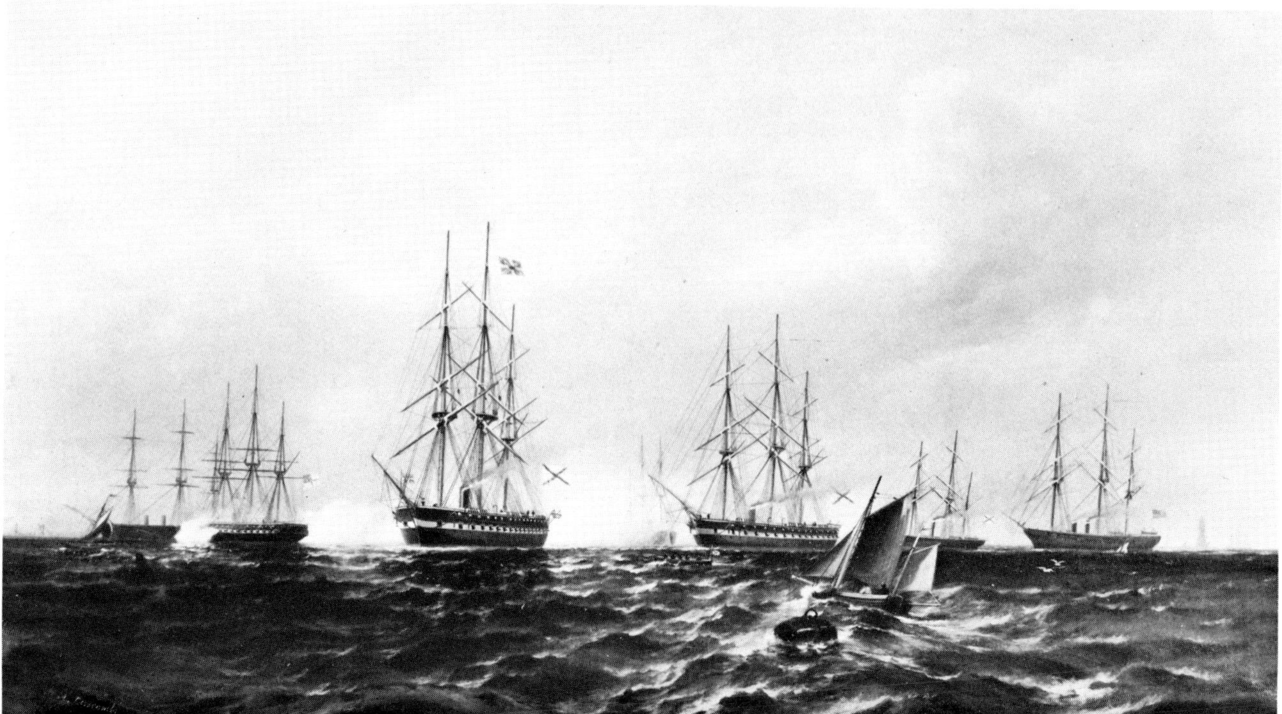

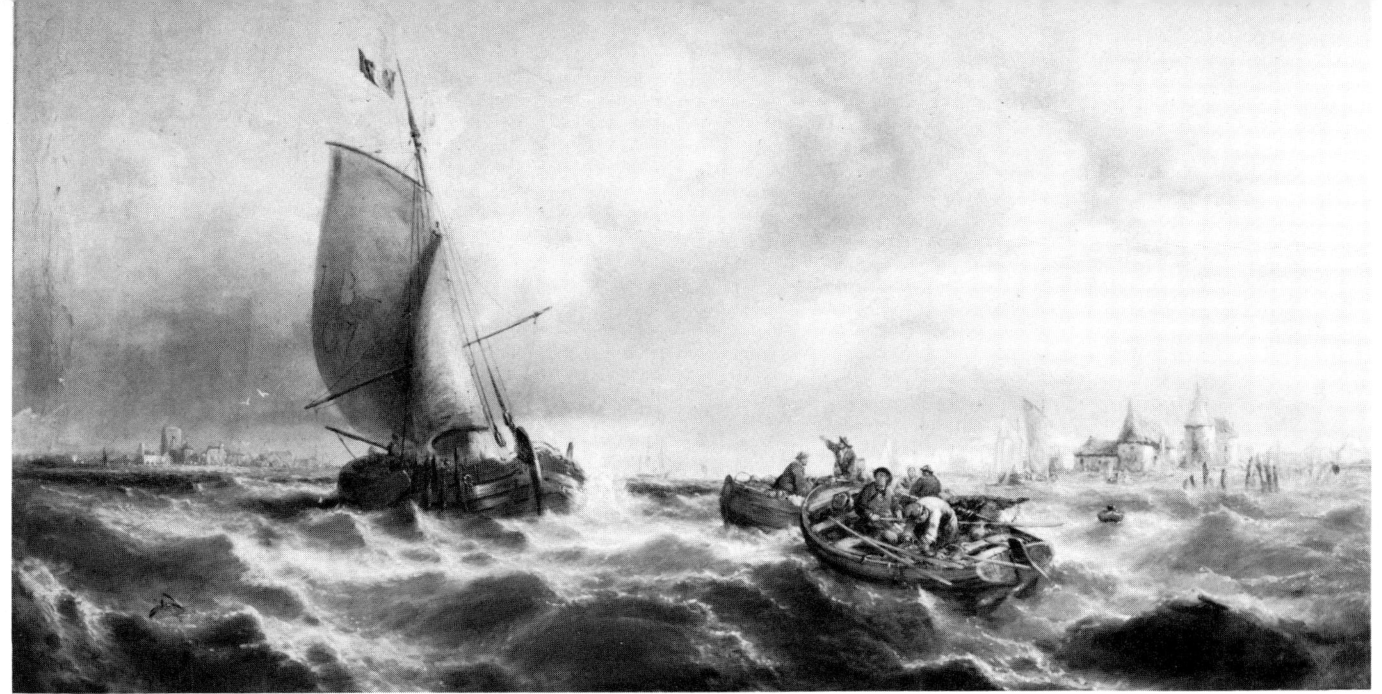

Plate 568. James Burrell, fl. mid- to late 19th century. "Dutch fishing boats in a choppy sea, 1868." Christie's.

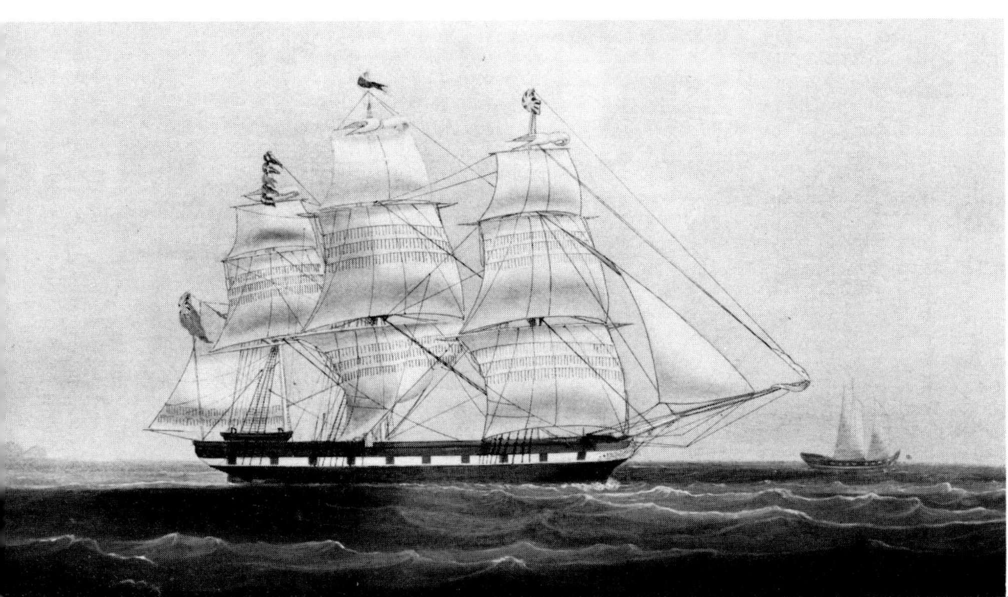

Plate 569. H. Callow, fl. mid- to late 19th century. "The ship *Maidstone* in the China Seas, dated 1869." National Maritime Museum, Greenwich.

Plate 570. George Mears, fl. mid-to late 19th century. "The cross Channel paddle packet *Plymouth Belle,* built 1895." National Maritime Museum, Greenwich.

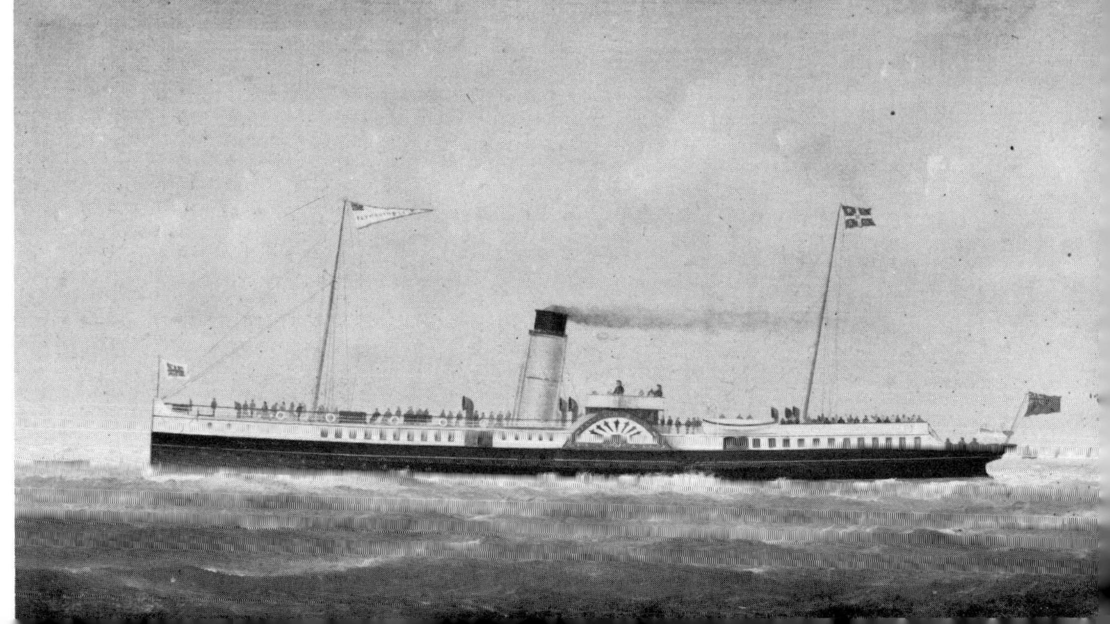

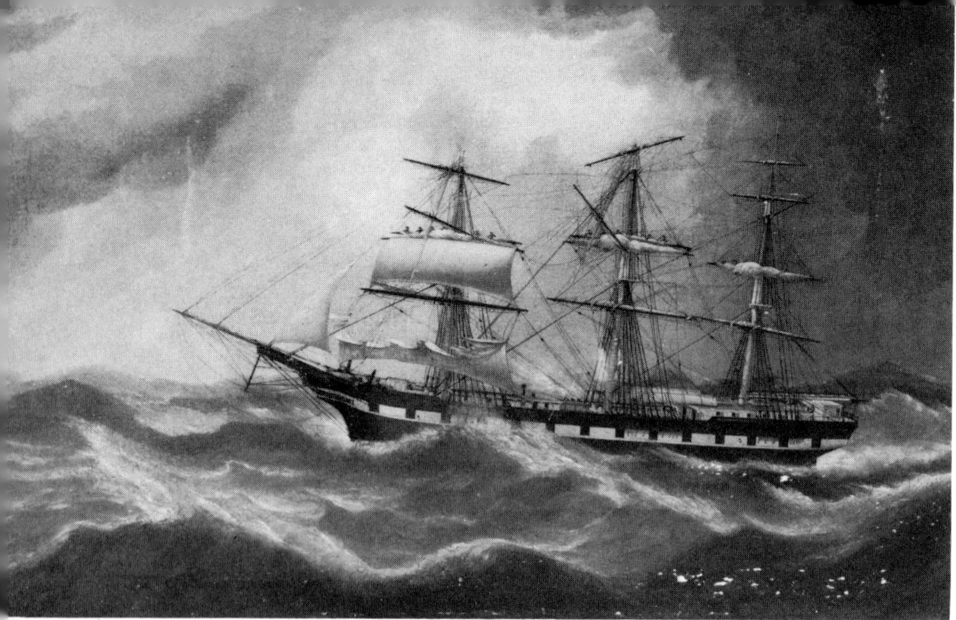

Plate 571. D. Macfarlane, fl. mid- to late 19th century. "The ship *Thomas Harward.*" National Maritime Museum, Greenwich.

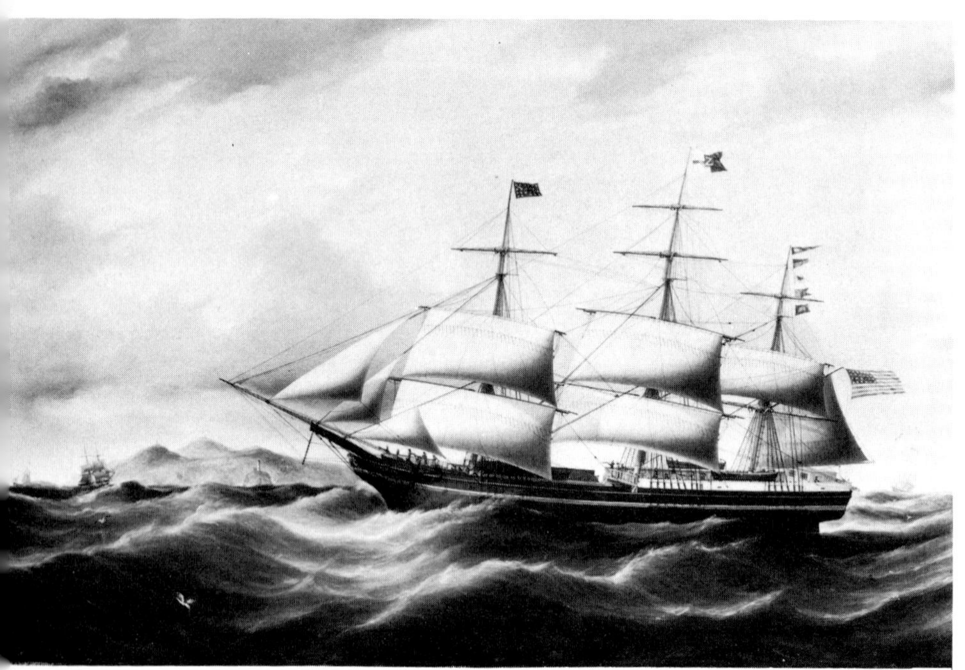

Plate 572. D. Macfarlane, fl. mid-19th century. "The American transantlantic packet *Antarctic.*" *The artist's trade mark — a hovering seagull — can be clearly seen.* National Maritime Museum, Greenwich.

Plate 573. George Stanfield Walters, 1838-1924. "Rye Harbour, Sussex." *A good marine artist, though not as competent as his father Samuel Walters (Plate 391).* Sotheby's.

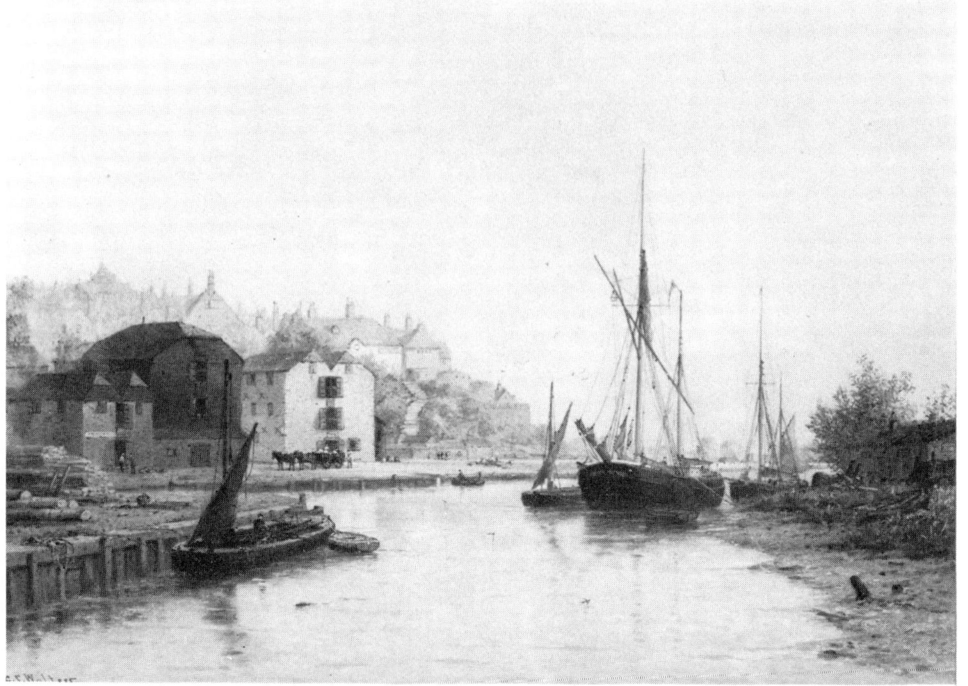

Plate 574. Charles Taylor, the Younger, fl.1843-1866. "A schooner of the Royal Yacht Squadron racing in the Solent, dated 1870." Private collection.

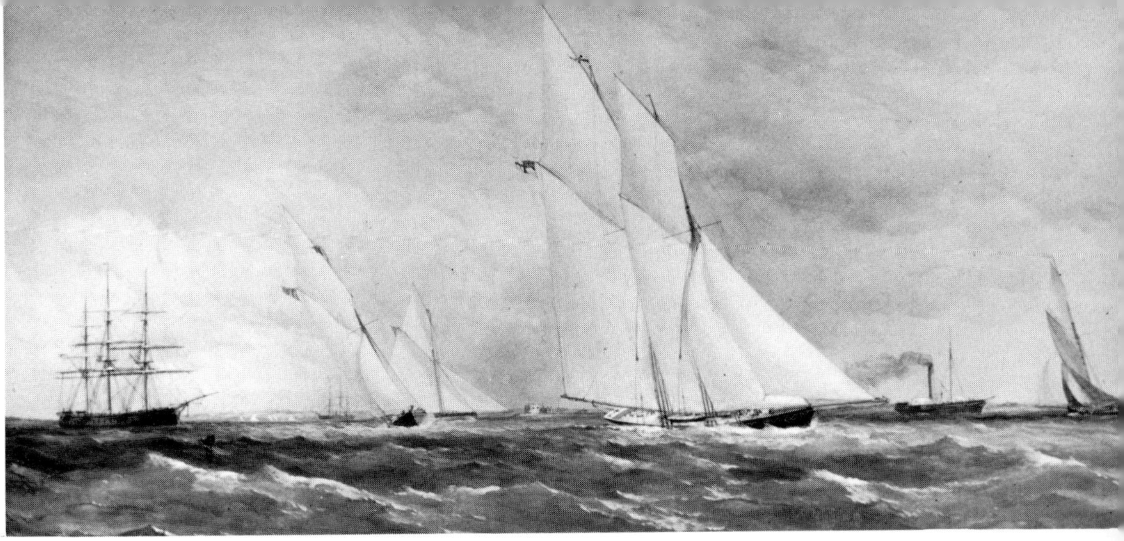

Plate 575. J. Hoskins, fl. mid- to late 19th century. "The screw steamer *Teuton,* launched 1869." *A funnel screw steamer of the early type.* National Maritime Museum, Greenwich.

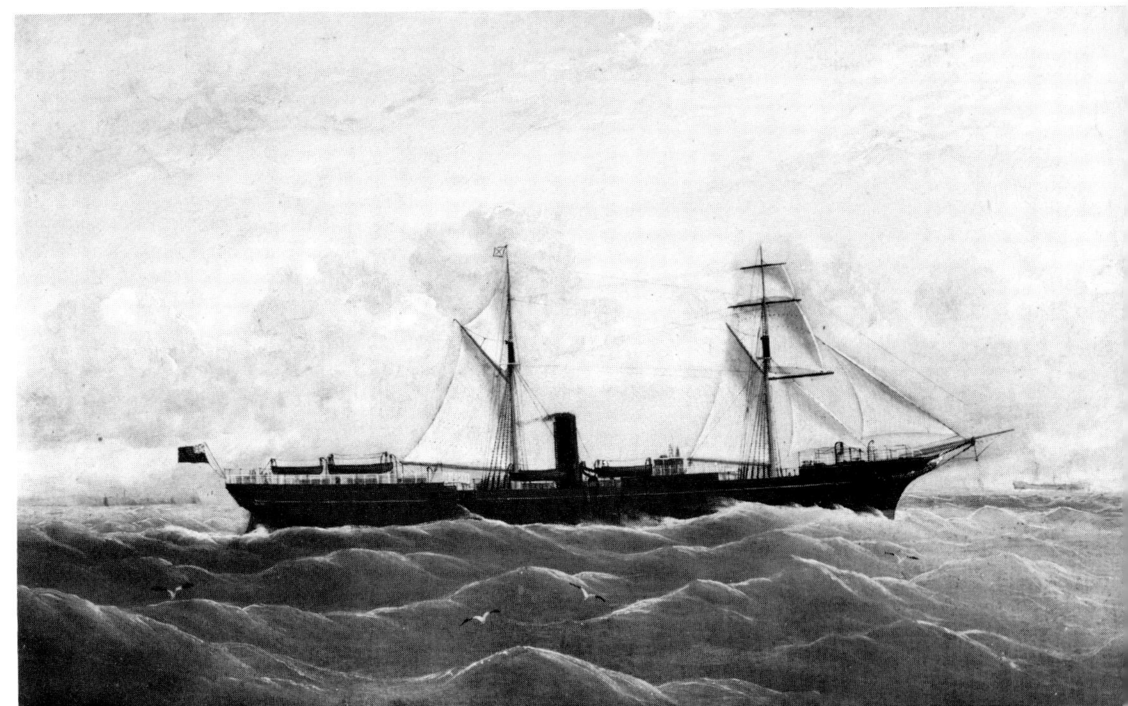

Plate 576. Arthur Joseph Meadows, 1843-1907. "Fishing boats off a jetty about 1870." National Maritime Museum, Greenwich.

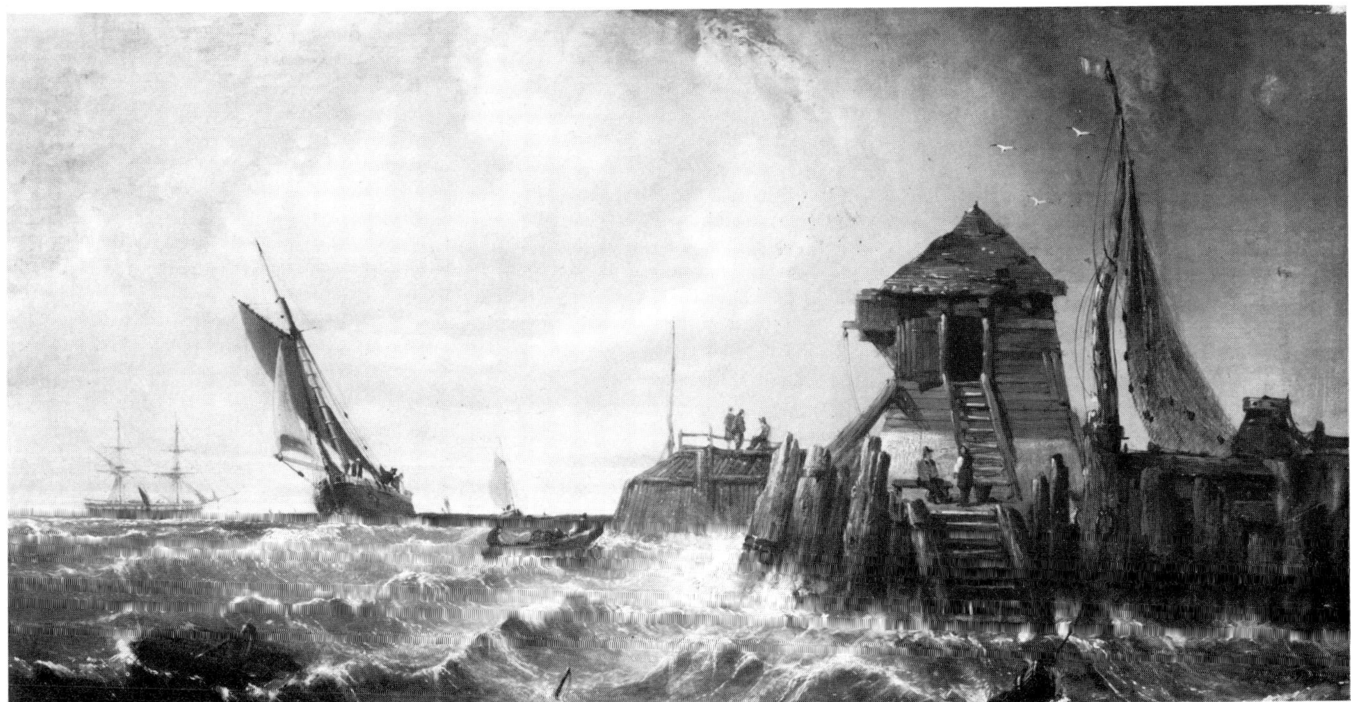

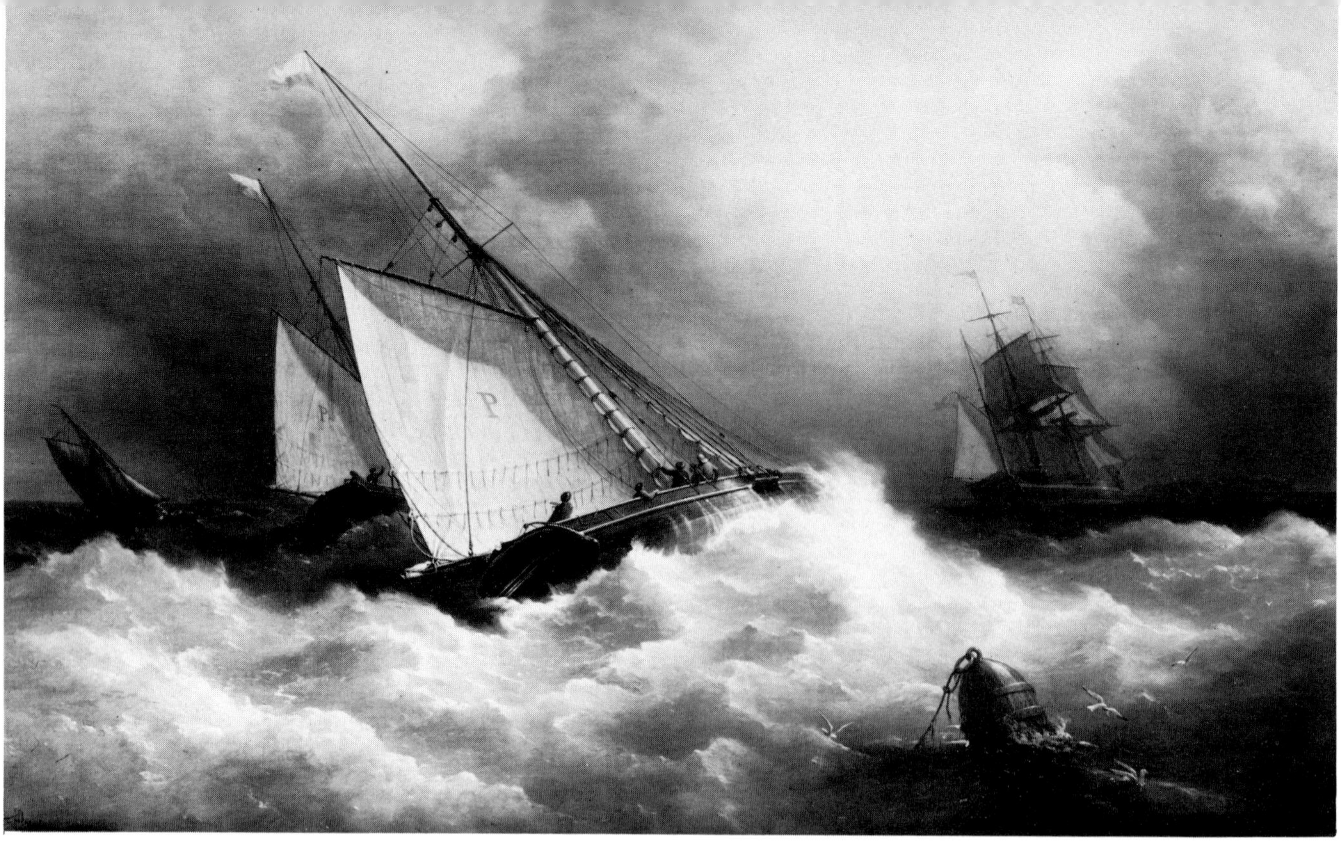

Plate 577. Richard Brydges Beechey, 1808-1895. " 'First Come First Served', pilot cutters racing to a Brocklebank Company ship, dated 1873." *Beechey was an artist of uneven quality, but this painting is well executed.* National Maritime Museum, Greenwich.

Plate 578. Richard Brydges Beechey, 1808-1895. "H.M.S. *Lord Warden* crossing the Brown Ridge shoal, dated 1888." *One of the armoured 'Black Battlefleet', she and her sister, the* Lord Clyde, *had the biggest wooden hulls ever built for the Royal Navy.* Royal Naval College (on loan to the National Maritime Museum, Greenwich).

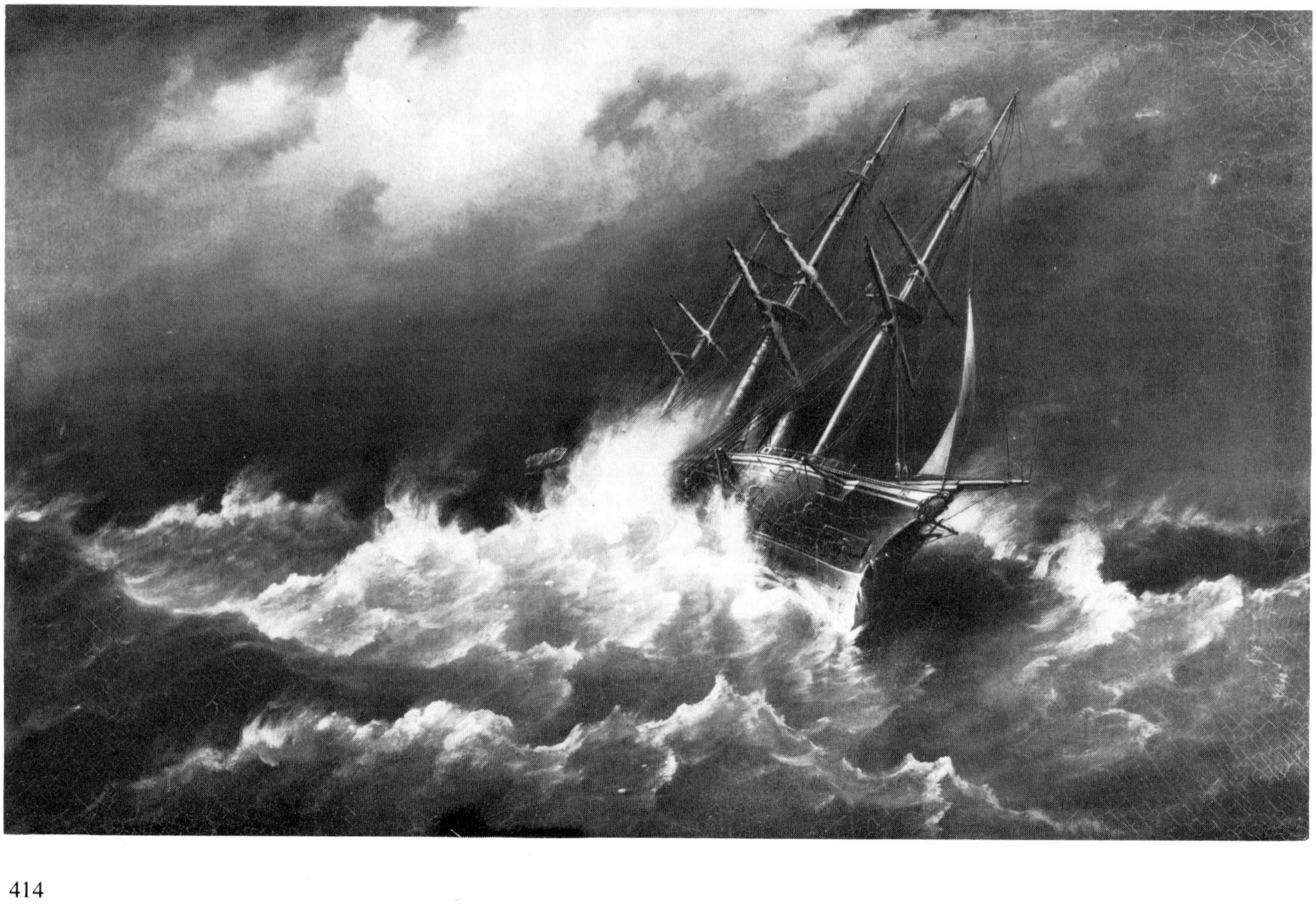

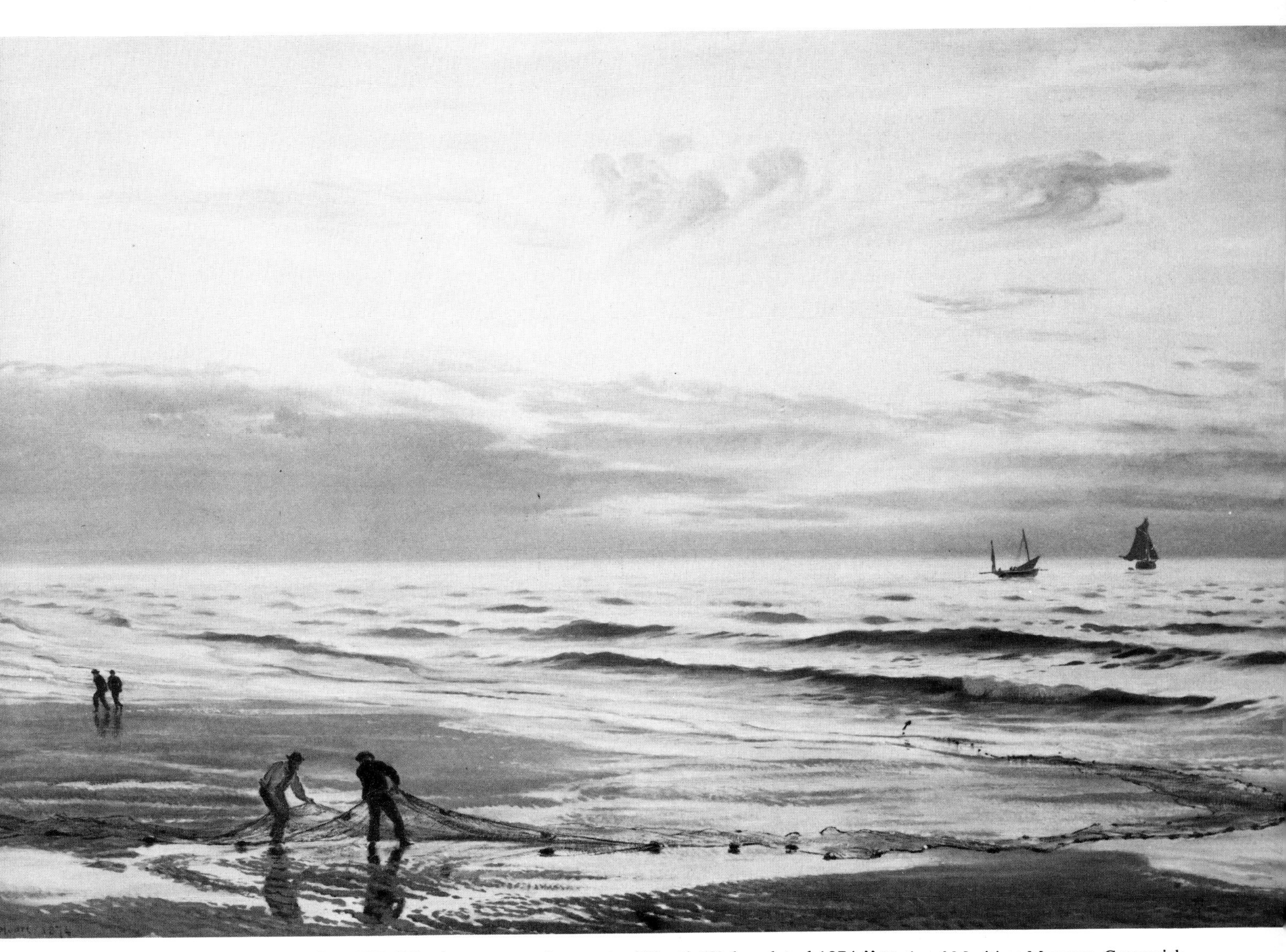

Plate 579. Henry Moore, 1831-1895. "Setting nets on the coast of North Wales, dated 1874." National Maritime Museum, Greenwich.

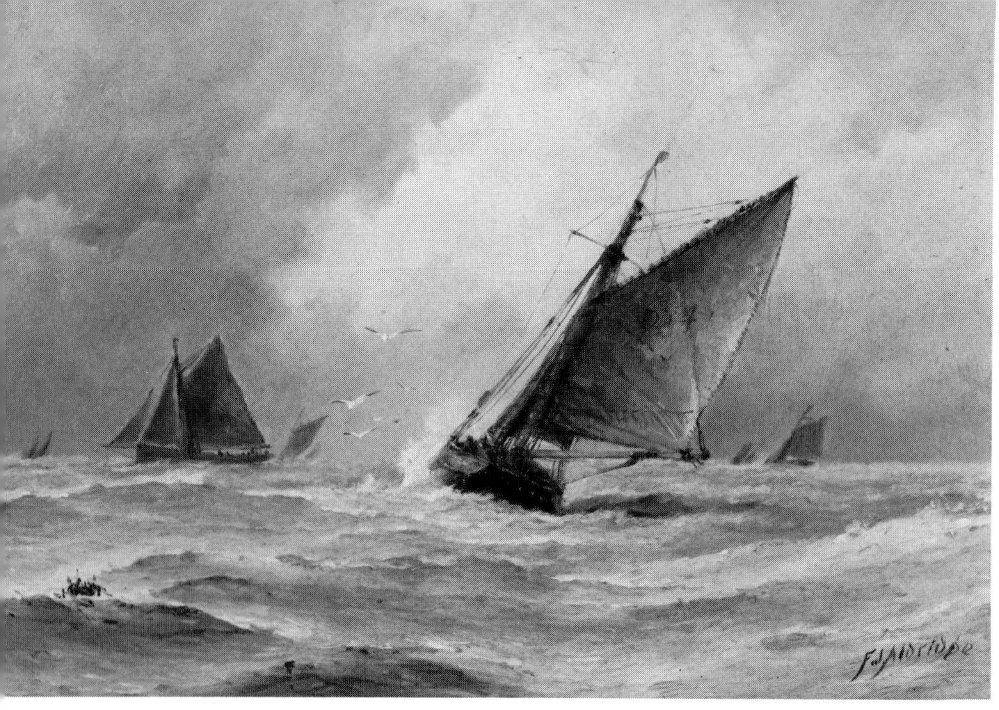

Plate 580. Frederick James Aldridge, 1850-1933. "Fishing smacks in the Channel." Private collection.

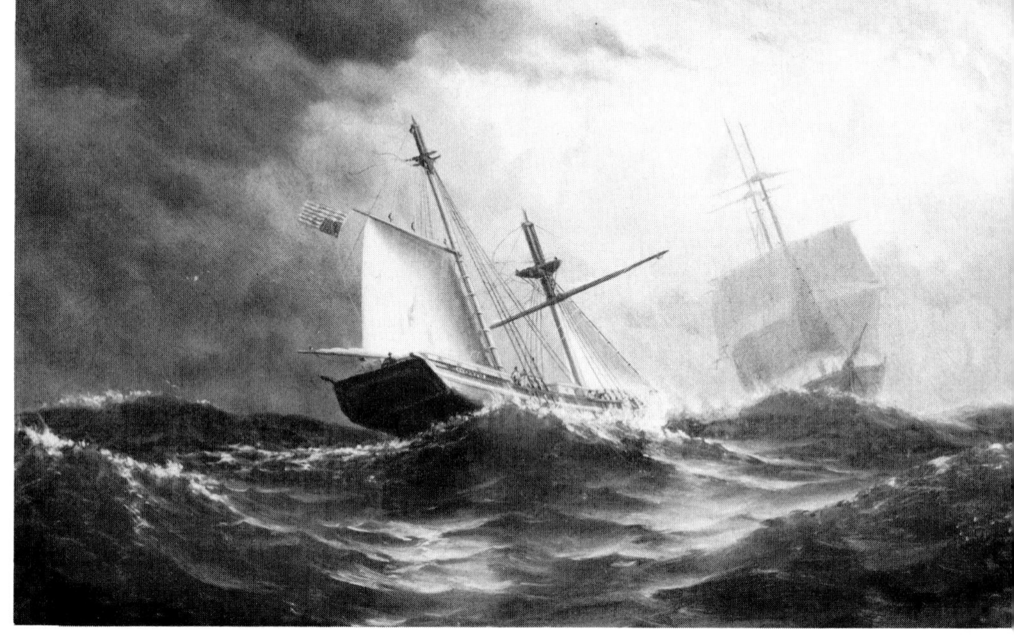

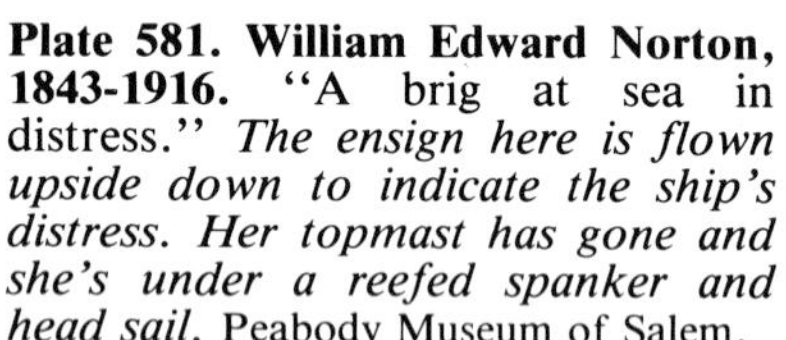

Plate 581. William Edward Norton, 1843-1916. "A brig at sea in distress." *The ensign here is flown upside down to indicate the ship's distress. Her topmast has gone and she's under a reefed spanker and head sail.* Peabody Museum of Salem.

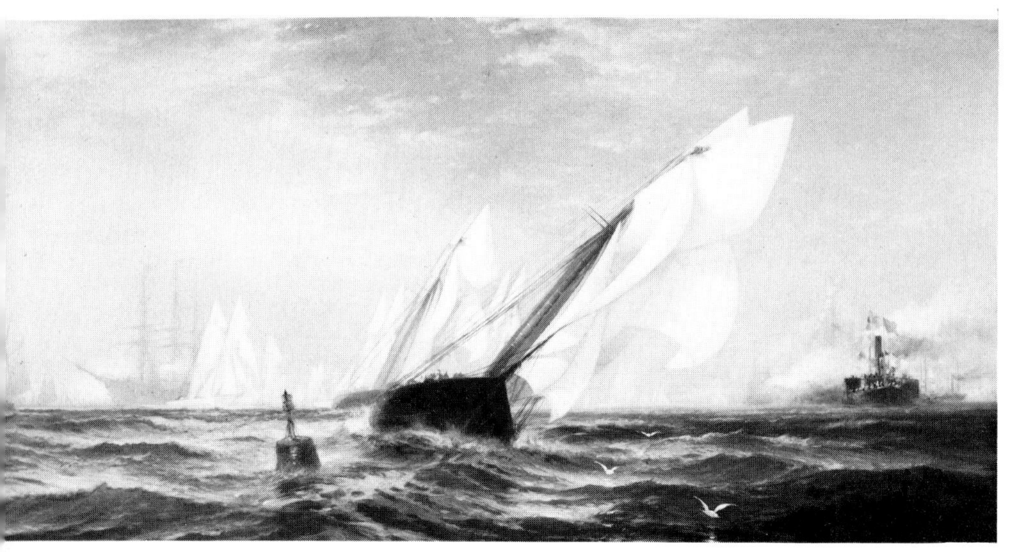

Plate 582. Edward Moran, 1829-1901. "The American schooner yacht *Sappho* beating the English Yacht *Livonia,* 1871." Peabody Museum of Salem.

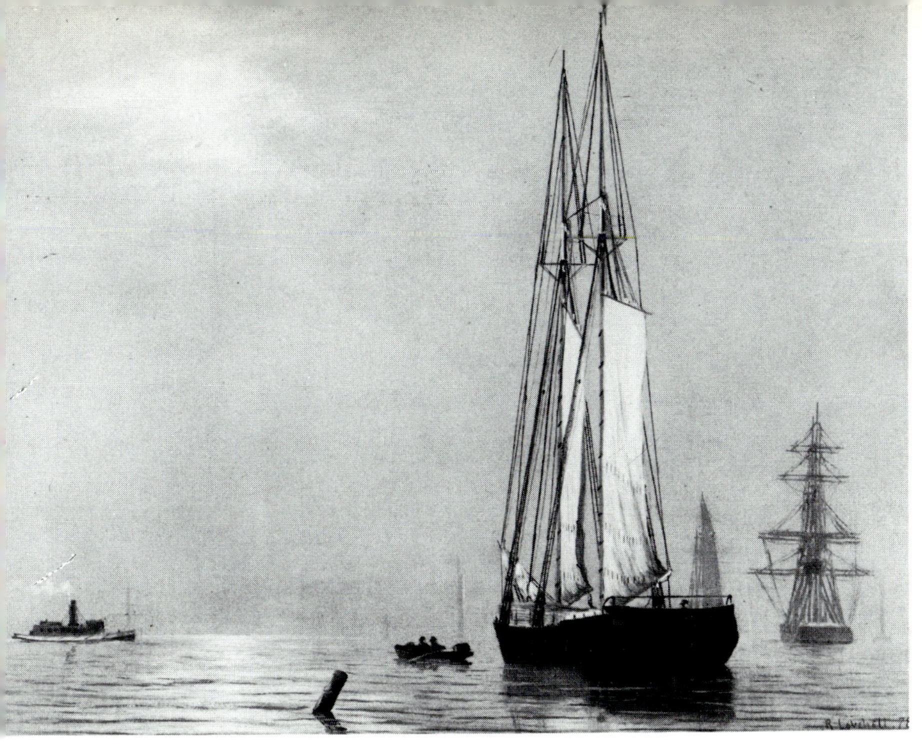

Plate 583. R. Lovewell, fl. late 19th century. "The American lumber schooner *War Eagle,* dated 1878." Peabody Museum of Salem.

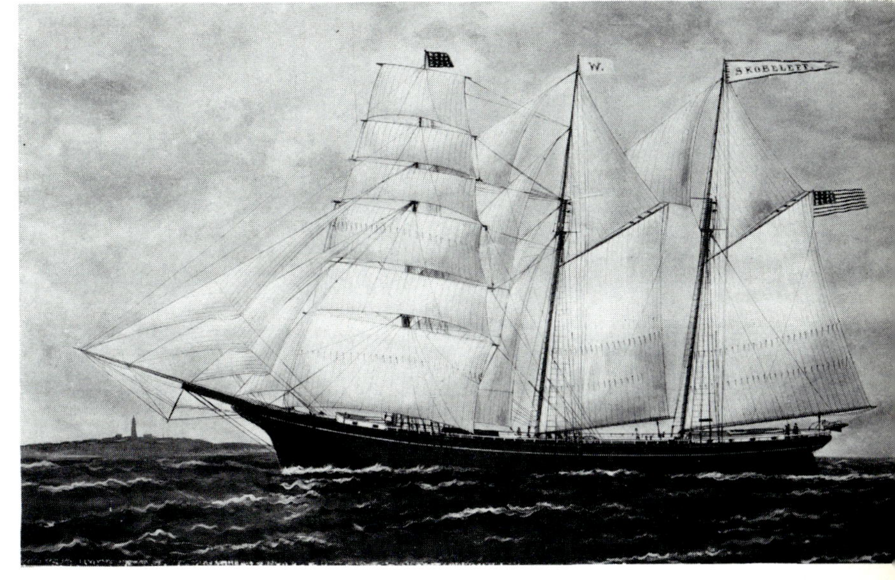

Plate 584. William Pierce Stubbs, 1842-1909. "The barquentine *Skobeleff,* built 1882." Peabody Museum of Salem.

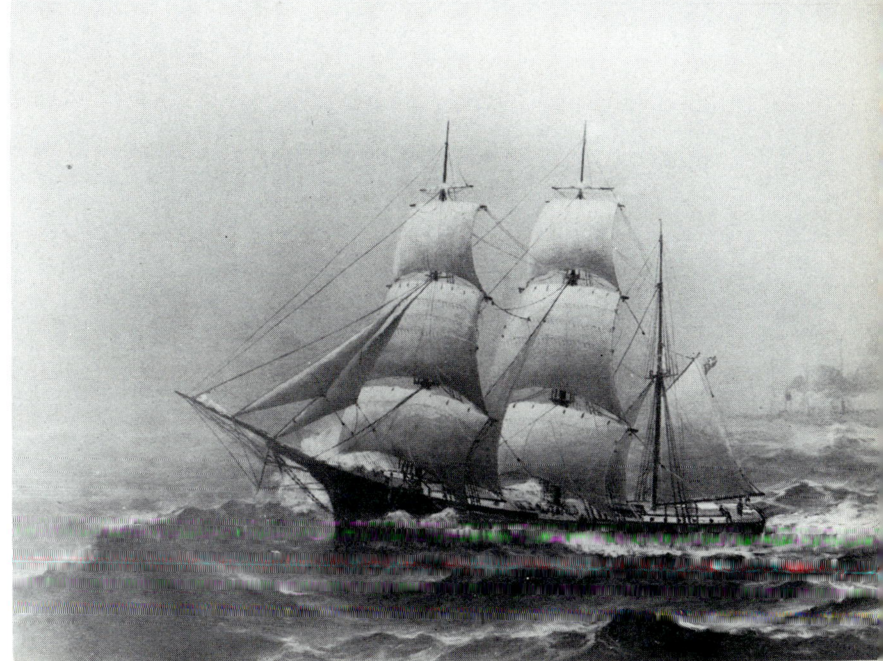

Plate 585. William Formby Halsall, 1841-1919. "The American barque *Roebuck,* 1883." Peabody Musem of Salem.

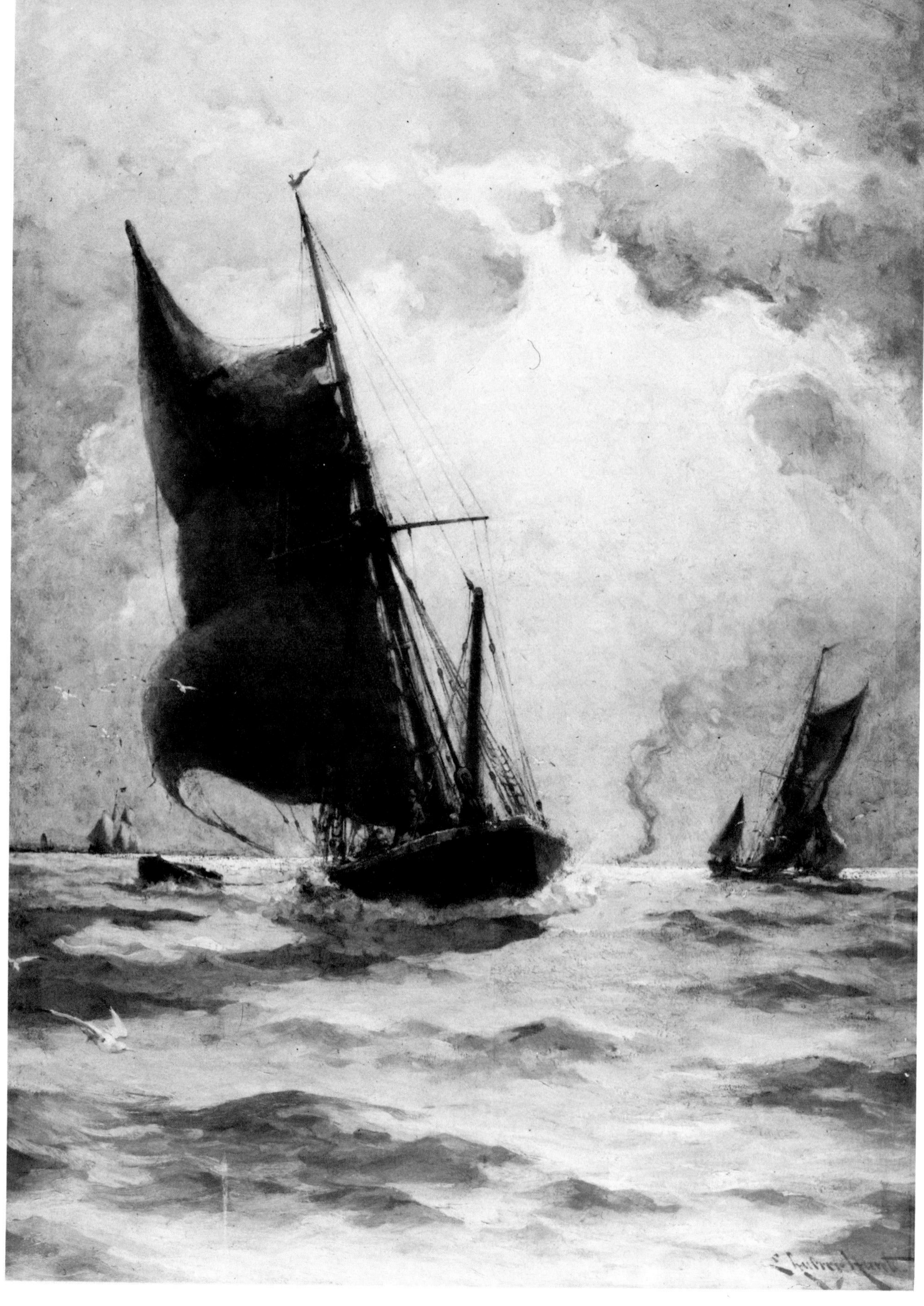

Plate 586. E. Aubrey Hunt, 1855-1922. "A swim headed Thames barge." National Maritime Museum, Greenwich.

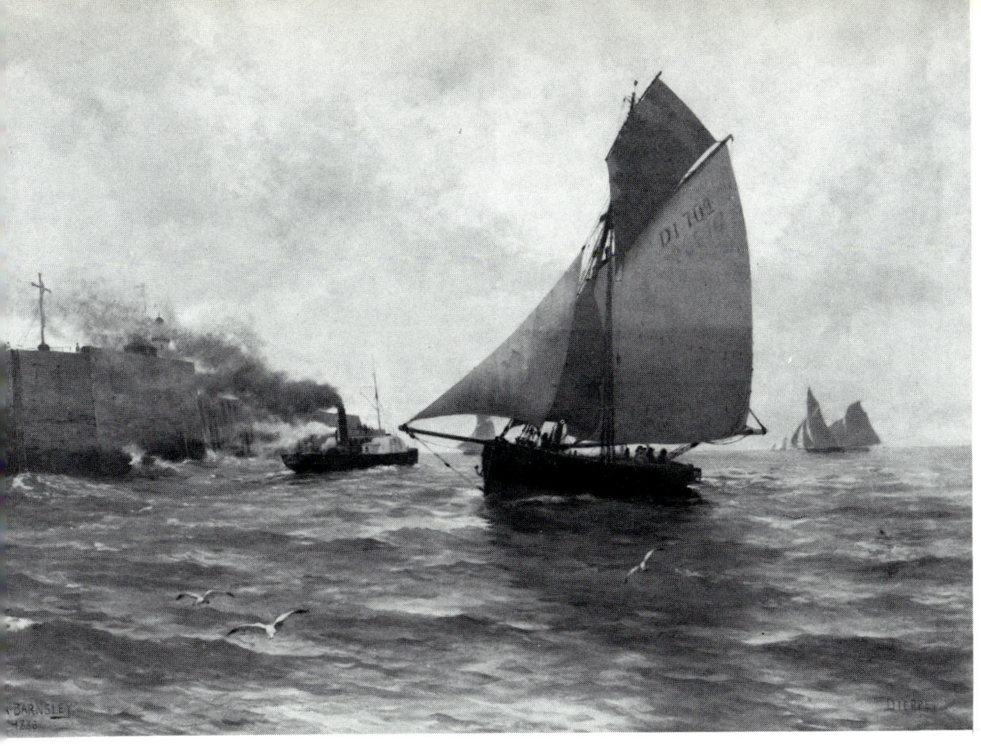

Plate 587. James MacDonald Barnsley, fl. late 19th century. "A fishing boat entering Dieppe harbour, dated 1886." *In the 1870s fishing boats were required to register — hence the numbers seen on the sails.* The Montreal Museum of Fine Arts.

Plate 588. G. Gianni, fl. late 19th century. "H.M.S. *Agincourt* at Malta, about 1882." *The* Agincourt *was one of three five-masted ironclads, the others being* Minotaur *and* Northumberland. National Maritime Museum, Greenwich.

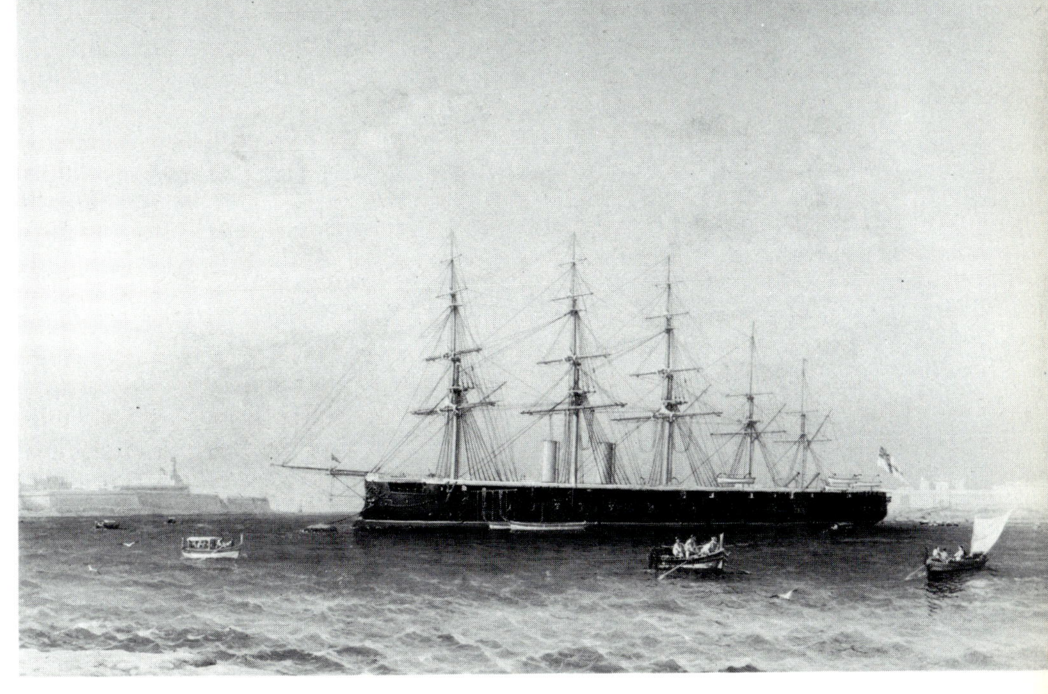

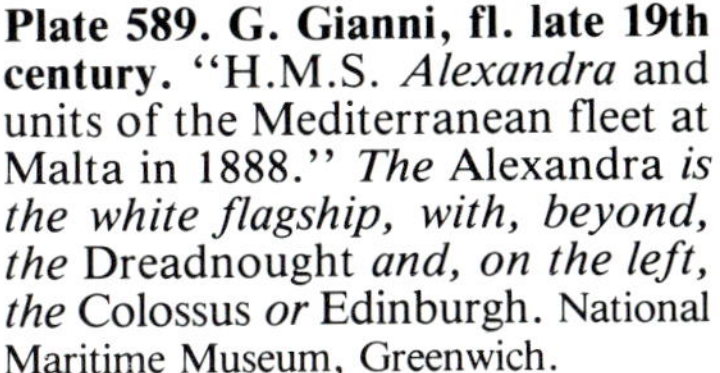

Plate 589. G. Gianni, fl. late 19th century. "H.M.S. *Alexandra* and units of the Mediterranean fleet at Malta in 1888." *The* Alexandra *is the white flagship, with, beyond, the* Dreadnought *and, on the left, the* Colossus *or* Edinburgh. National Maritime Museum, Greenwich.

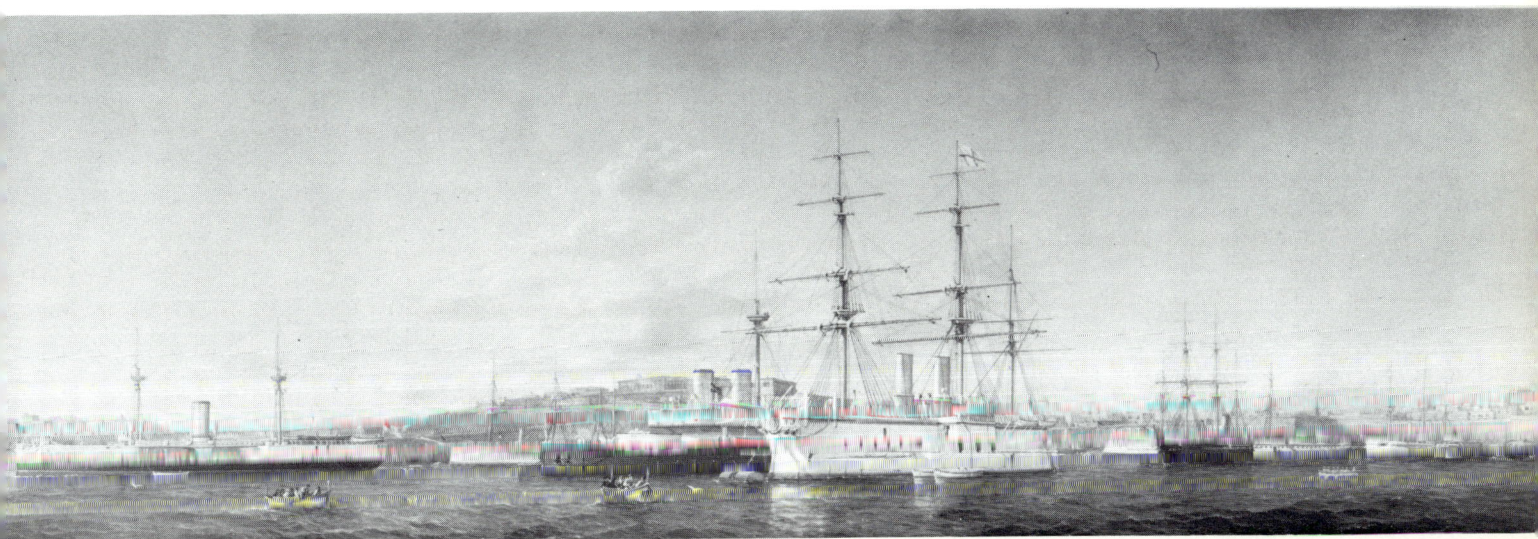

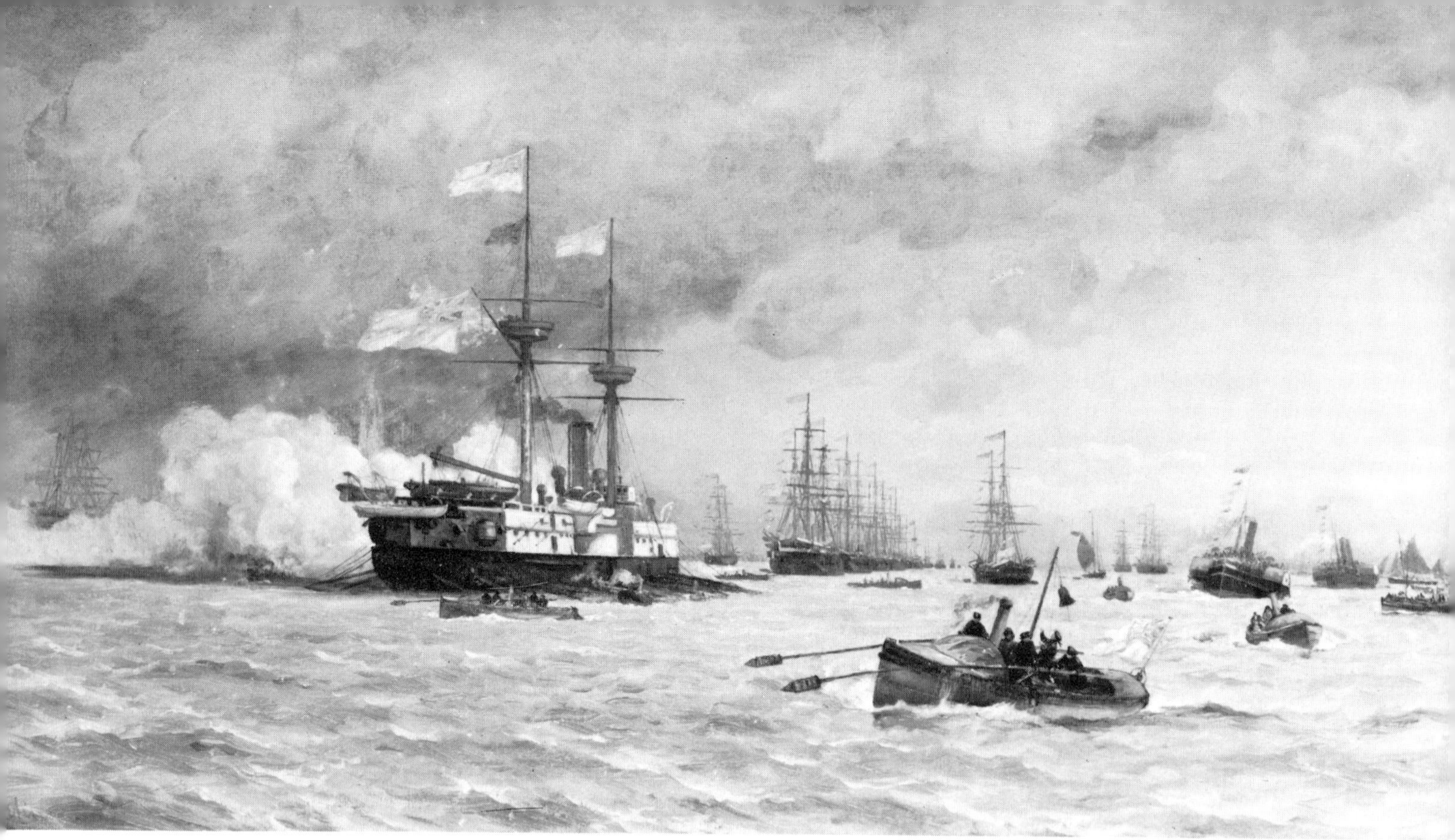

Plate 590. Edoardo de Martino, 1838-1912. "H.M.S. *Edinburgh* with anti-torpedo nets out in a mock exercise against torpedo boats, about 1887." *The torpedo boats carried two pole spars with explosive charges attached to the ends of them and attacked by ramming. The torpedo boat crews were, in effect, on a suicide mission.* National Maritime Museum, Greenwich.

Plate 591. James Webb, 1825-1895. "San Sebastian." *A beautiful painting by an artist who excelled in painting dramatic coastal scenes.* National Maritime Museum, Greenwich.

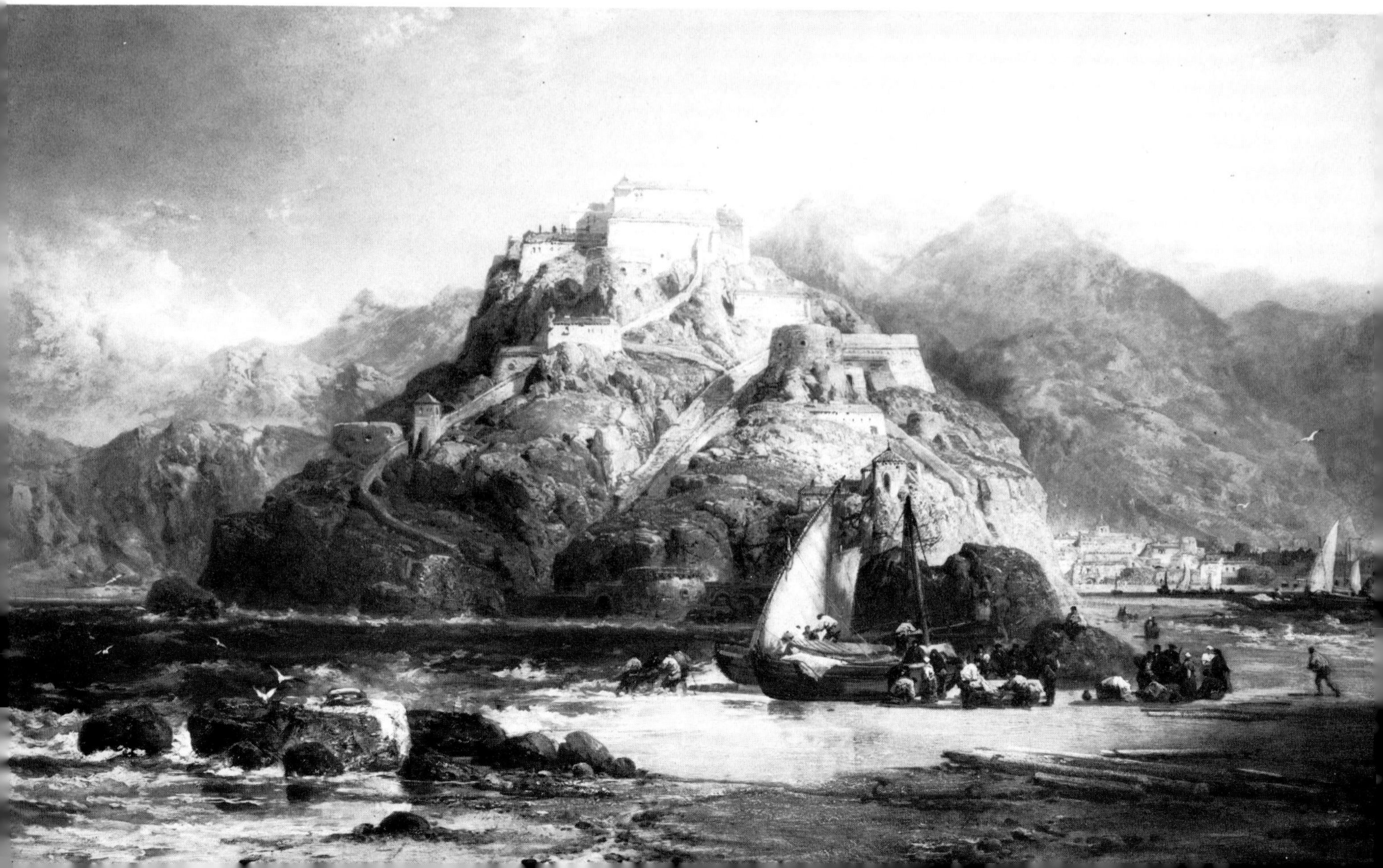

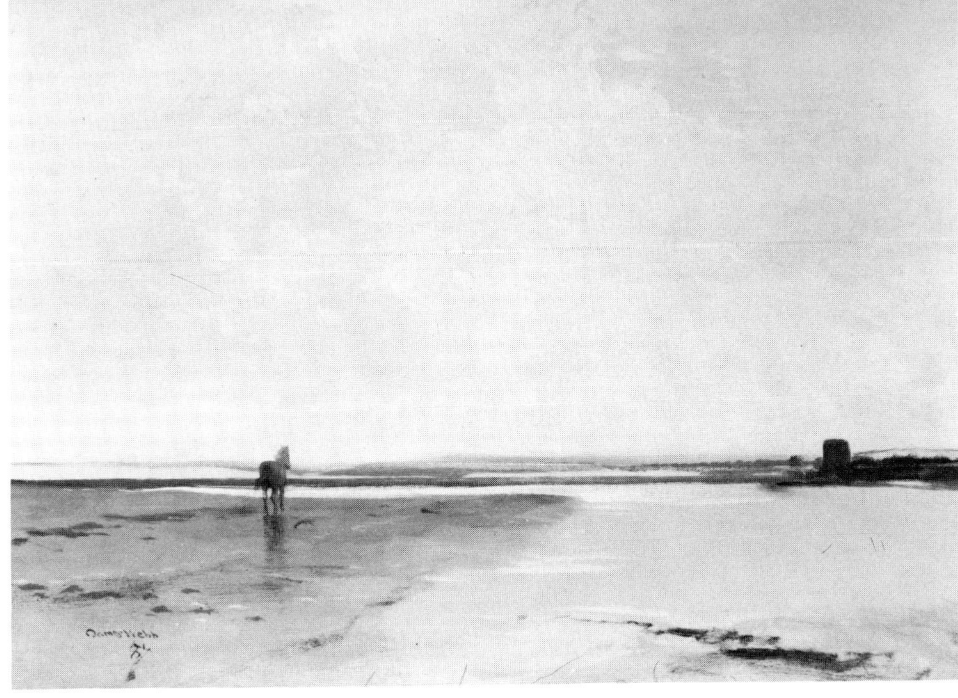

Plate 592. James Webb, 1825-1895. "Beach scene, dated 1887." Christie's.

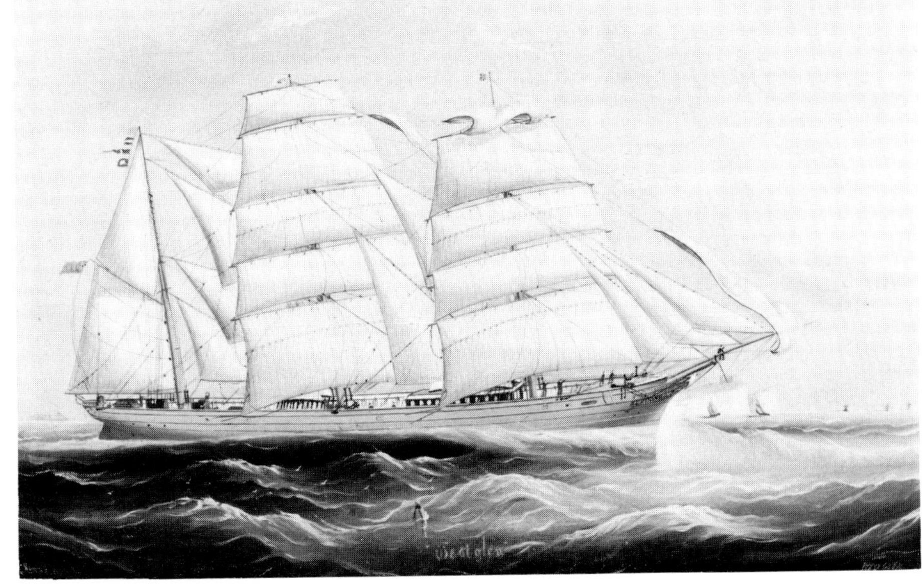

Plate 593. C. Kensington, fl. late 19th and early 20th century. "The barque *Westglen,* dated 1888." National Maritime Museum, Greenwich.

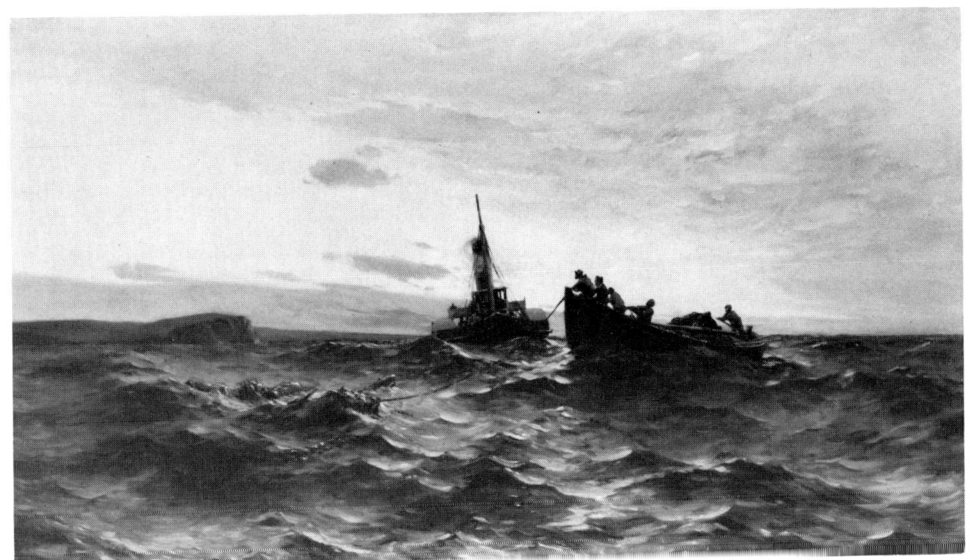

Plate 594. Edmund G. Fuller, fl.1888-1916. "A paddle tug and a boat salving wreckage." Bonham's.

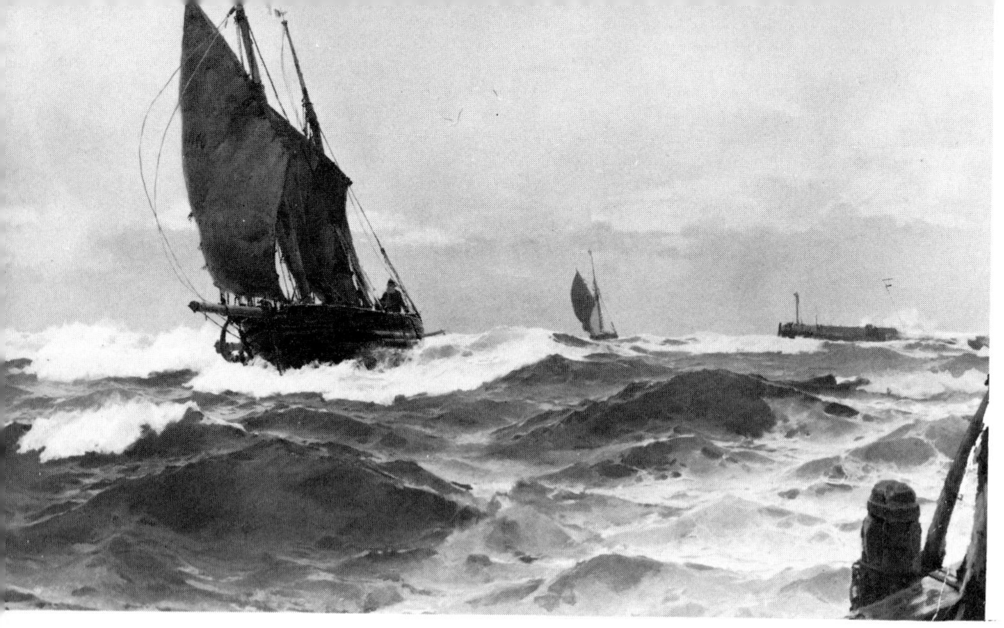

Plate 595. John Fraser, 1858-1927. "Fishing luggers running into Shoreham Harbour, dated 1888." *An artist in the same stream as Somerscales and de Martino. His style changed little, as can be seen in comparing this and the next, later, example.* William Barnett Esq.

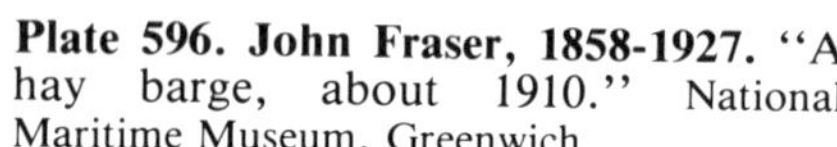

Plate 596. John Fraser, 1858-1927. "A hay barge, about 1910." National Maritime Museum, Greenwich.

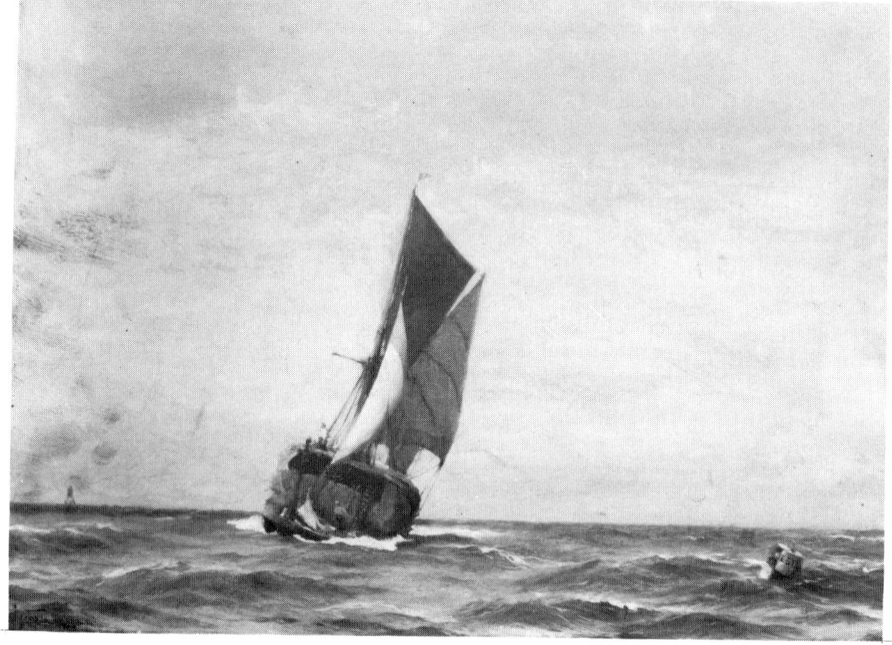

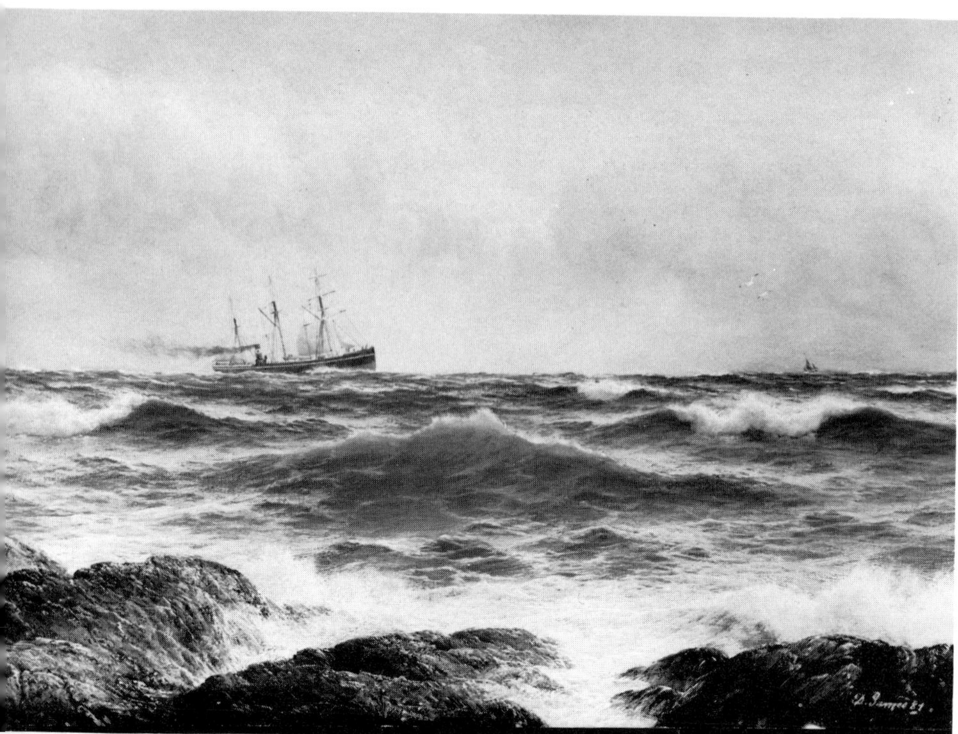

Plate 597. David James, fl. late 19th century. "A passing coaster, dated 1889." *A painter of the sea, who sometimes included shipping in the backgrounds of his paintings, as here.* William Barnett Esq.,

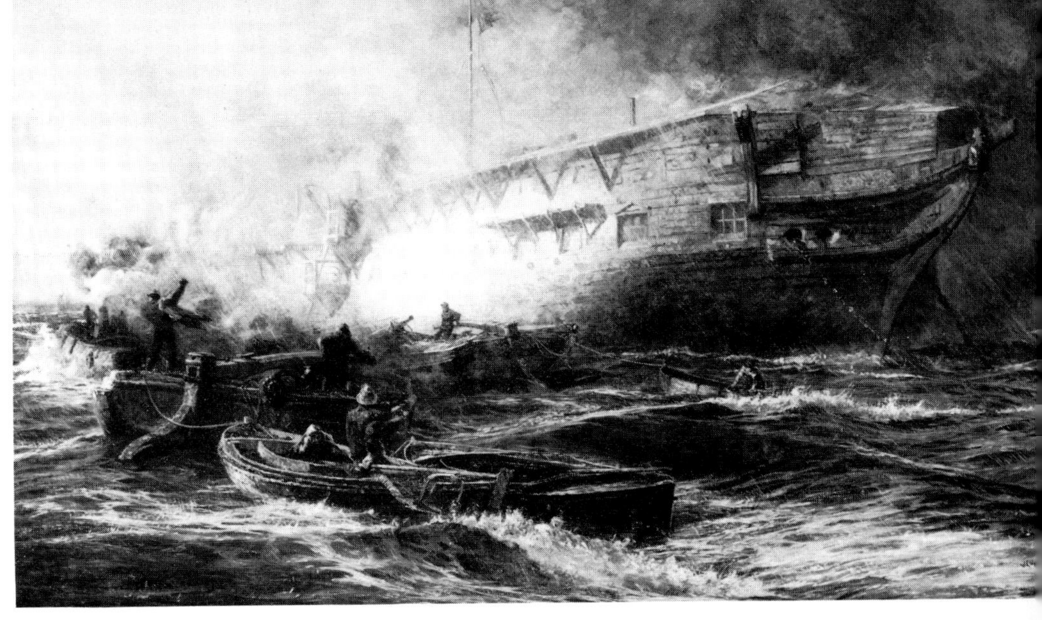

Plate 598. William Lionel Wyllie, 1851-1931. " 'Storm and Sunshine, a battle with the Elements', the powder hulk *Leonidas* in the Medway, dated 1885." *Powder hulks were painted red because of their dangerous loads, and supplied gunpowder to the Navy at Chatham and elsewhere.* National Maritime Museum, Greenwich.

Plate 599. William Lionel Wyllie, 1851-1931. "The White Star liner *Teutonic* leaving Liverpool on her maiden voyage to take her to Spithead for the review for Kaiser Wilhelm II, August 1889." *With the aid of an Admiralty grant, she and her sister, the* Majestic, *were built with gun mountings for four six inch and smaller guns, and extra bunkerage, so that they could serve as merchant cruisers, which the* Teutonic *did in the First World War. These liners were faster than contemporary battleships or cruisers.* National Maritime Museum, Greenwich.

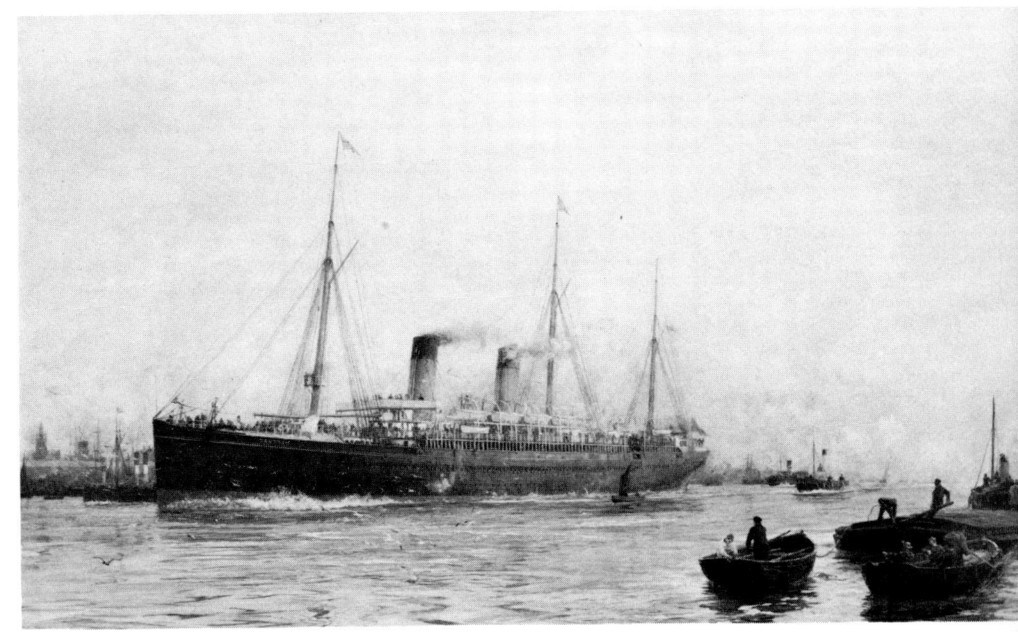

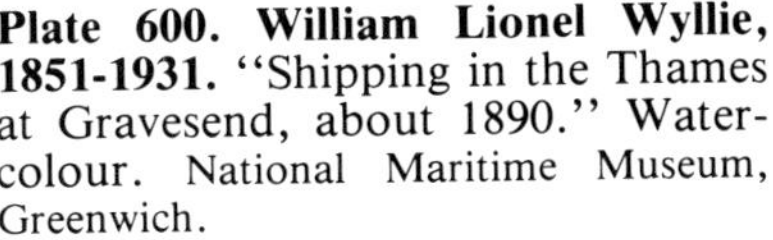

Plate 600. William Lionel Wyllie, 1851-1931. "Shipping in the Thames at Gravesend, about 1890." Watercolour. National Maritime Museum, Greenwich.

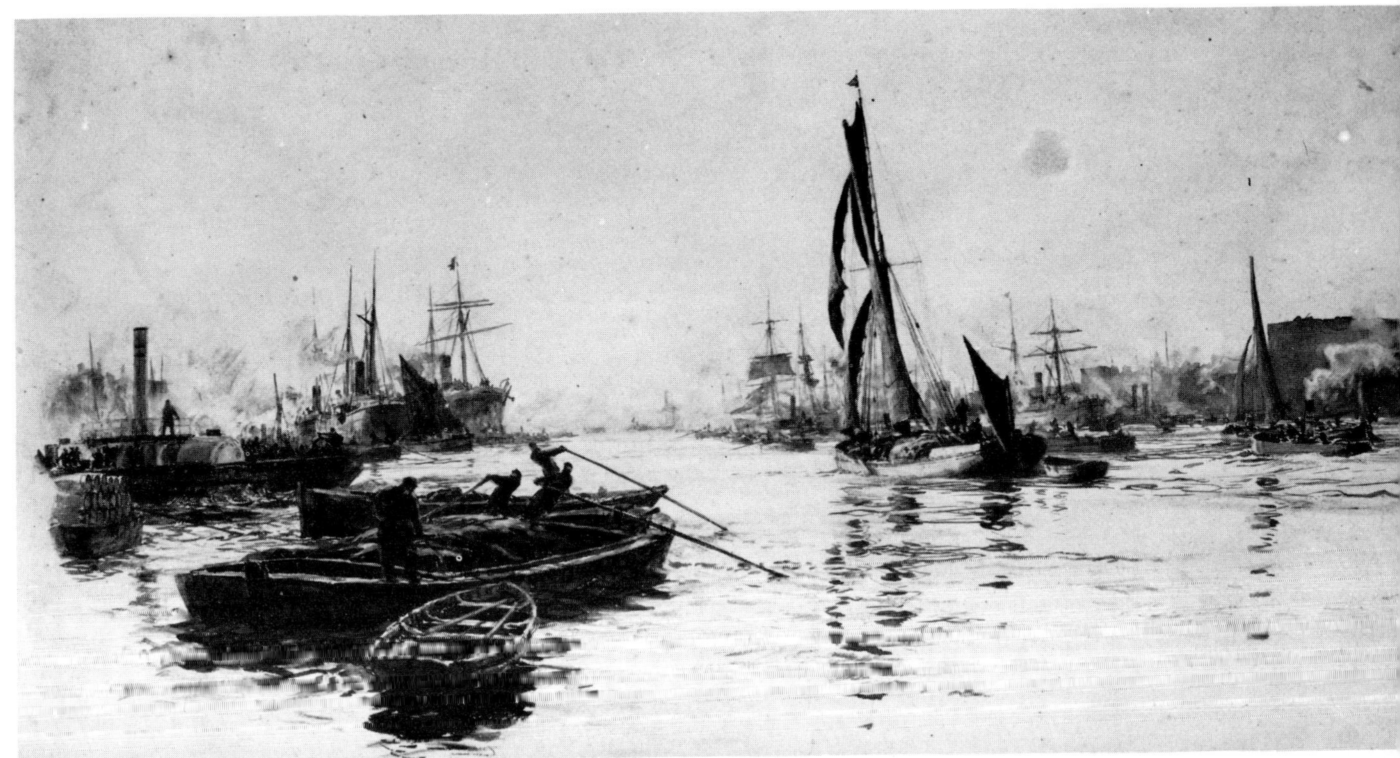

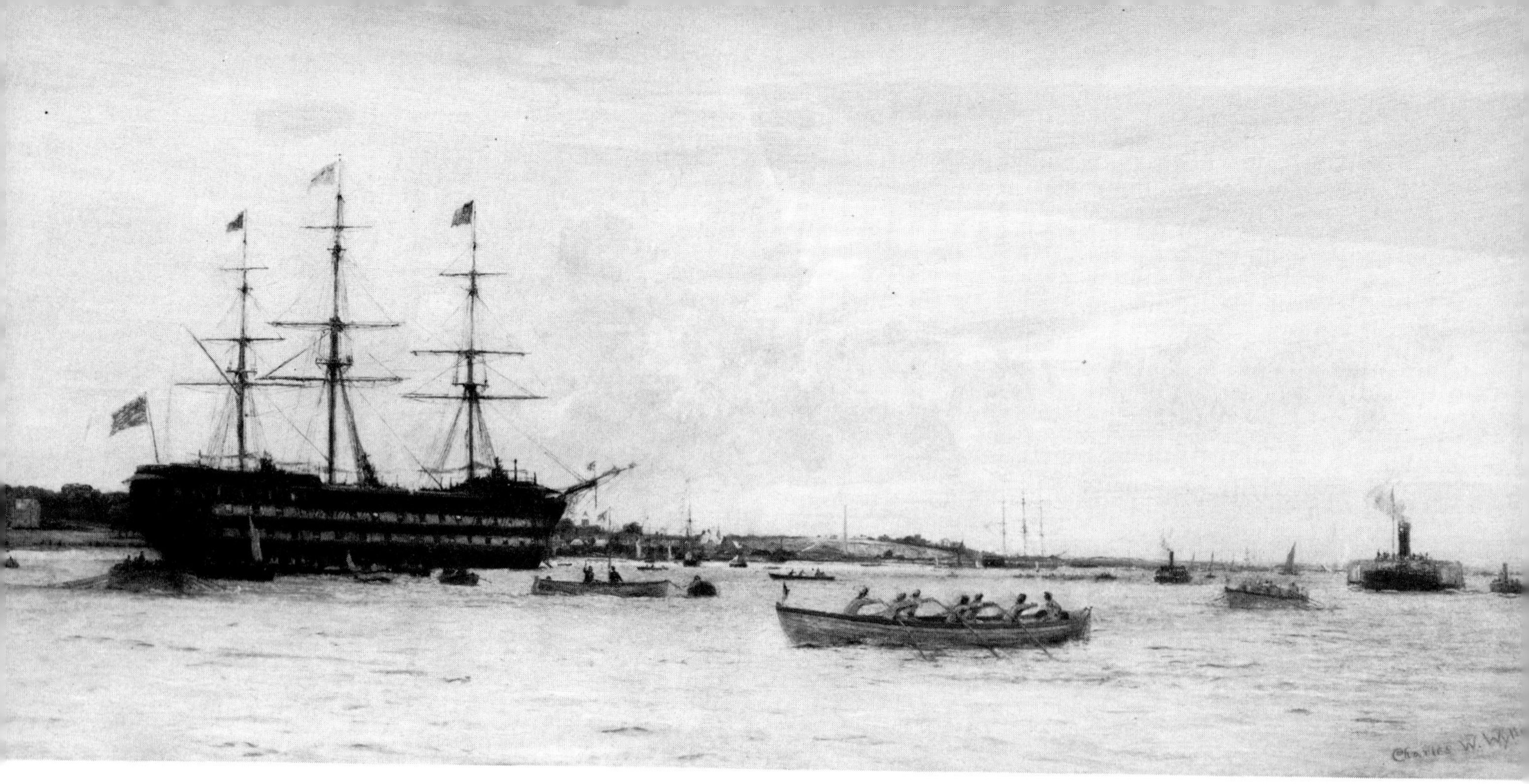

Plate 601. Charles William Wyllie, 1859-1923. "A rowing regatta off the *Worcester,* about 1910." *The* Worcester *was a training ship; in the right distance a paddle steamer.* National Maritime Museum, Greenwich.

Plate 602. Thomas Jacques Somerscales, 1842-1927. "A ship off the coast of Chile, dated 1903." *Somerscales continued to paint Chilean subjects long after he had settled back in England. His work had similarites with that of Fraser and de Martino, though it developed into his individual and realistic style.* Sotheby's.

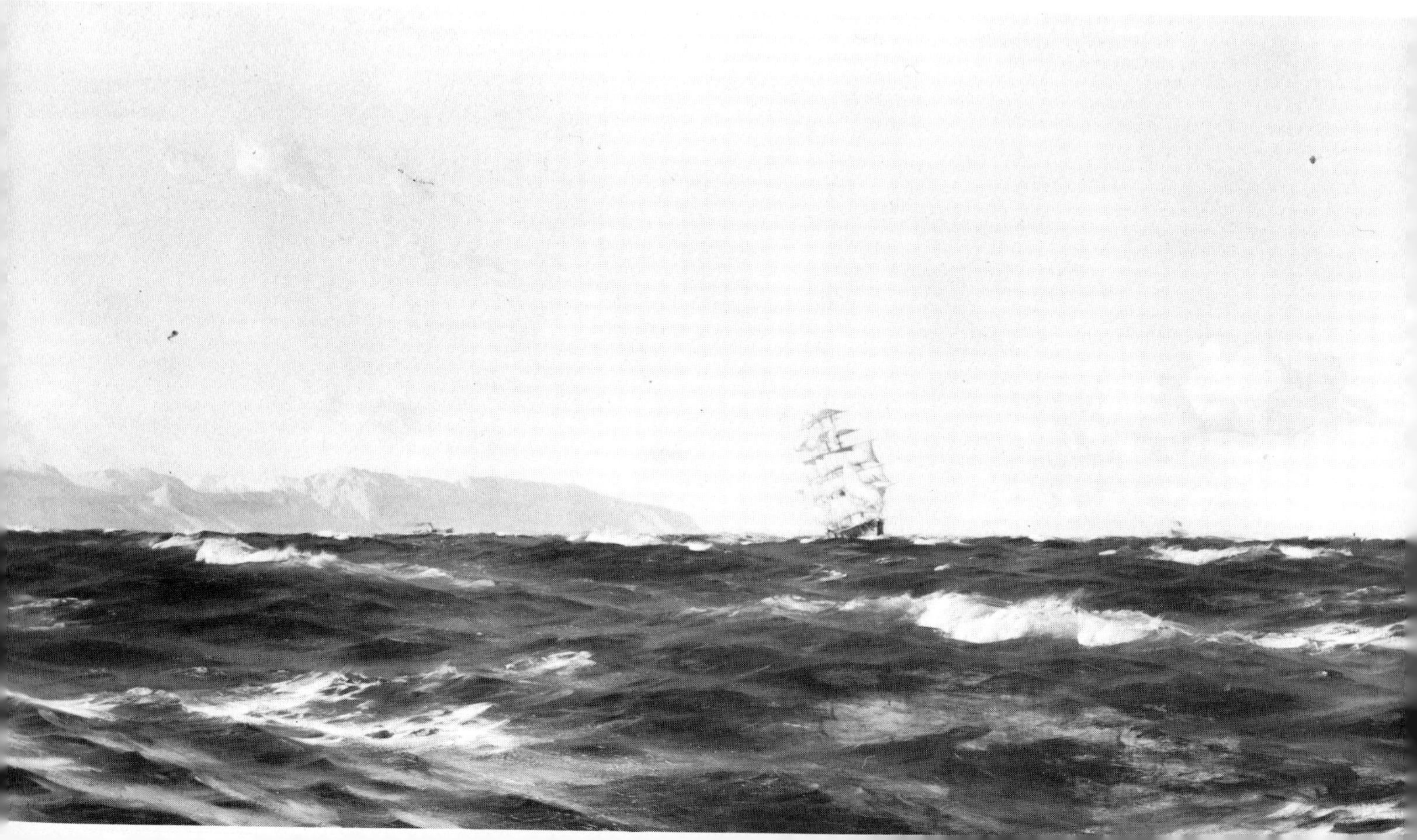

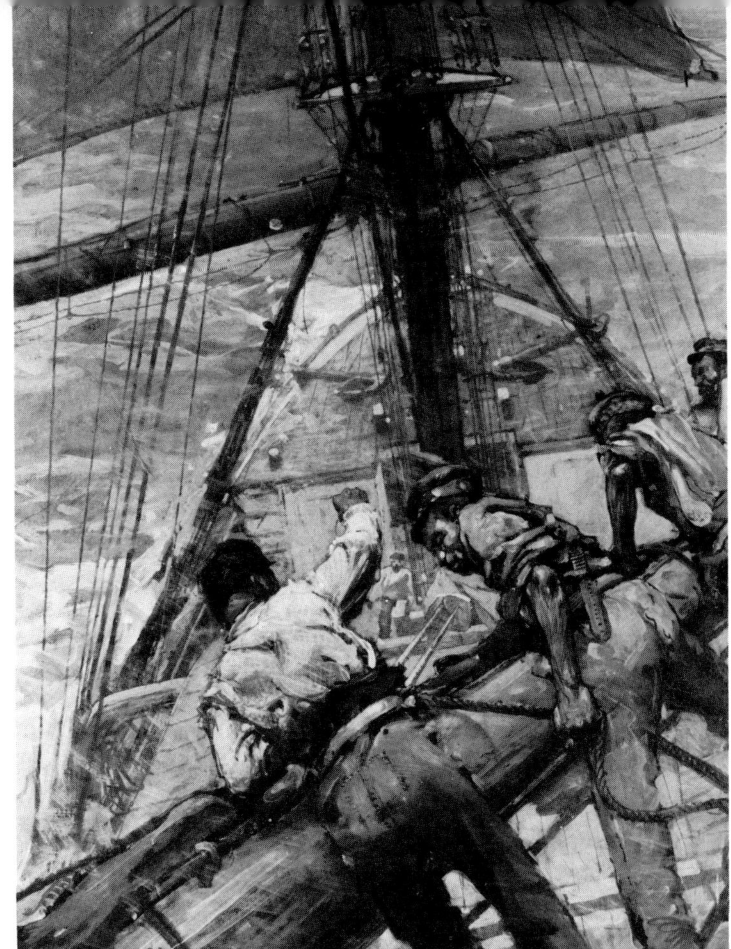

Plate 603. Frank William Brangwyn, 1867-1956. "Heavy weather in the Channel, stowing the mainsail, dated 1894." National Maritime Museum, Greenwich.

Plate 604. Julius Olsson, 1864-1942. "Moonlit shore, near St. Ives, Cornwall." *This picture was exhibited at the RA in 1911 and bought by the Chantrey Bequest.* Tate Gallery, London.

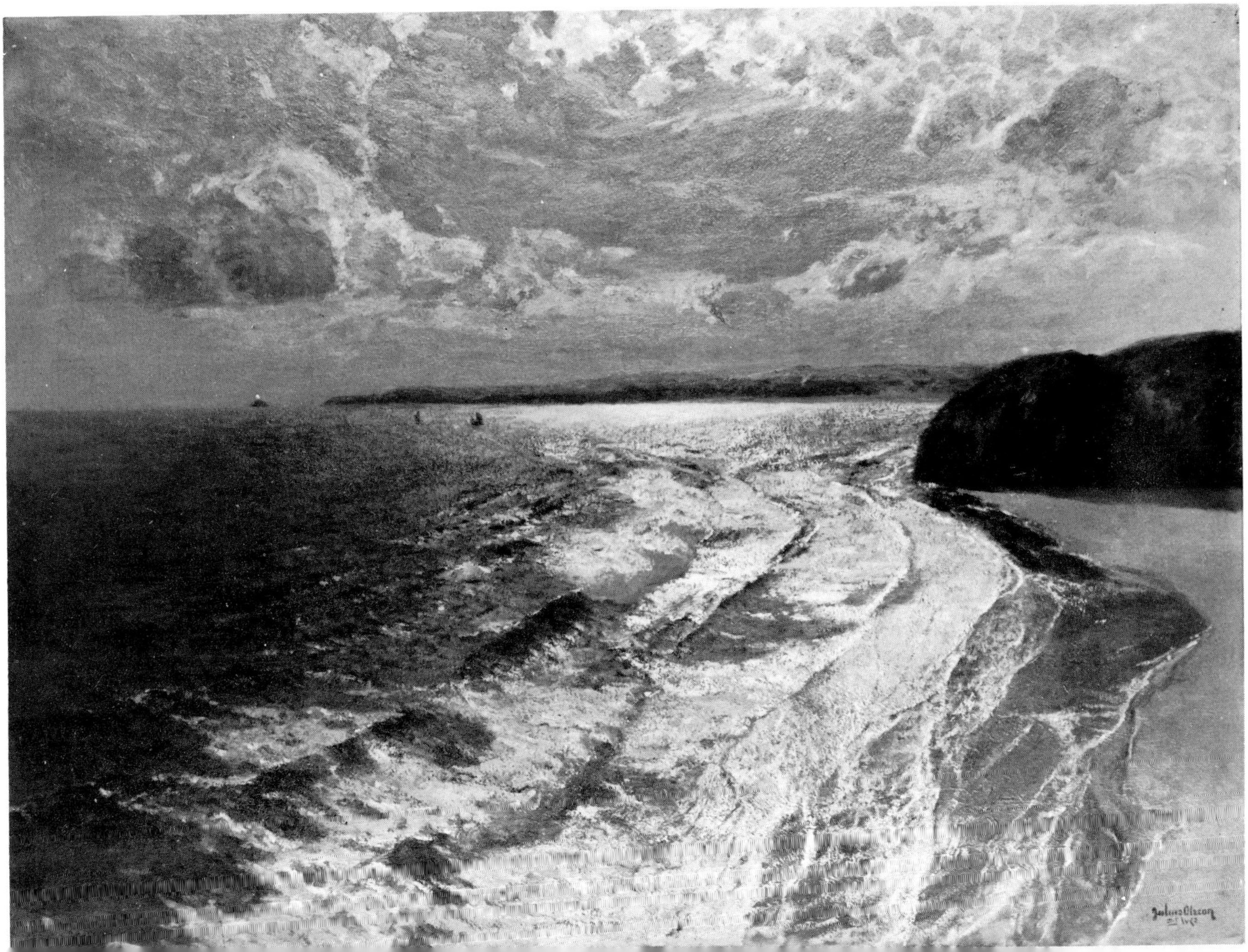

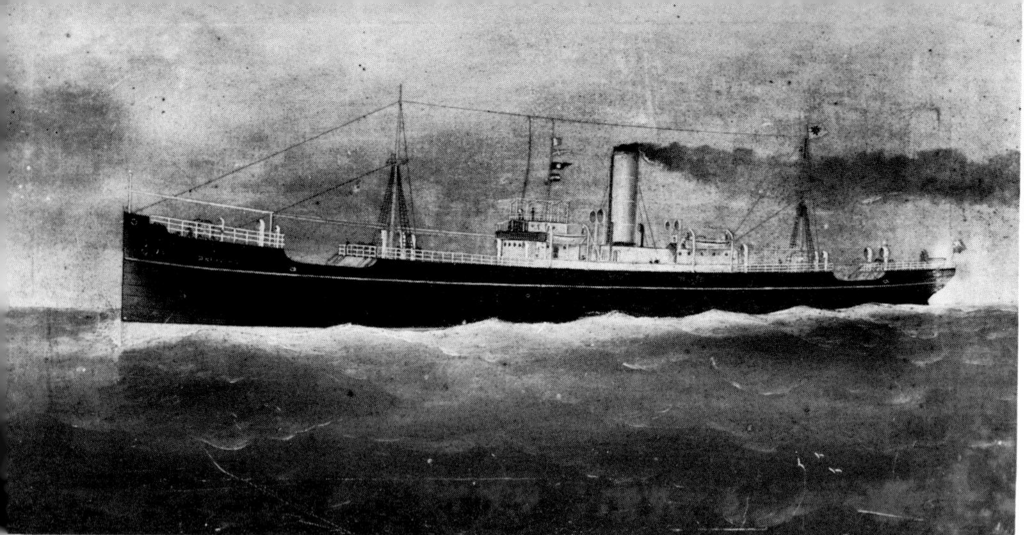

Plate 605. W. Murell, fl. late 19th and early 20th century. "The steamer *Drumcree,* built 1905." *The ship is equipped with a wireless aerial, an innovation dating to around the early 1900s.* National Maritime Museum, Greenwich.

Plate 606. T.G. Purvis, fl. late 19th and early 20th century. "The four masted barque *Colonial Empire.*" National Maritime Museum, Greenwich.

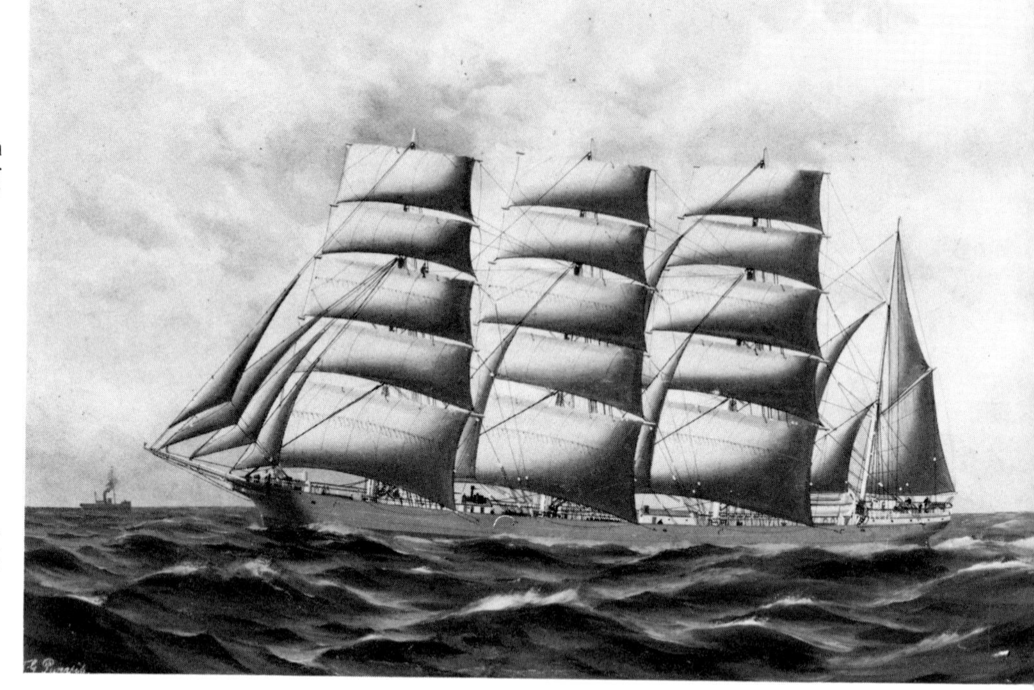

Plate 607. Thomas Rose Miles, fl. late 19th century. "A pilot boat steaming out to a barque hove to." Sotheby's.

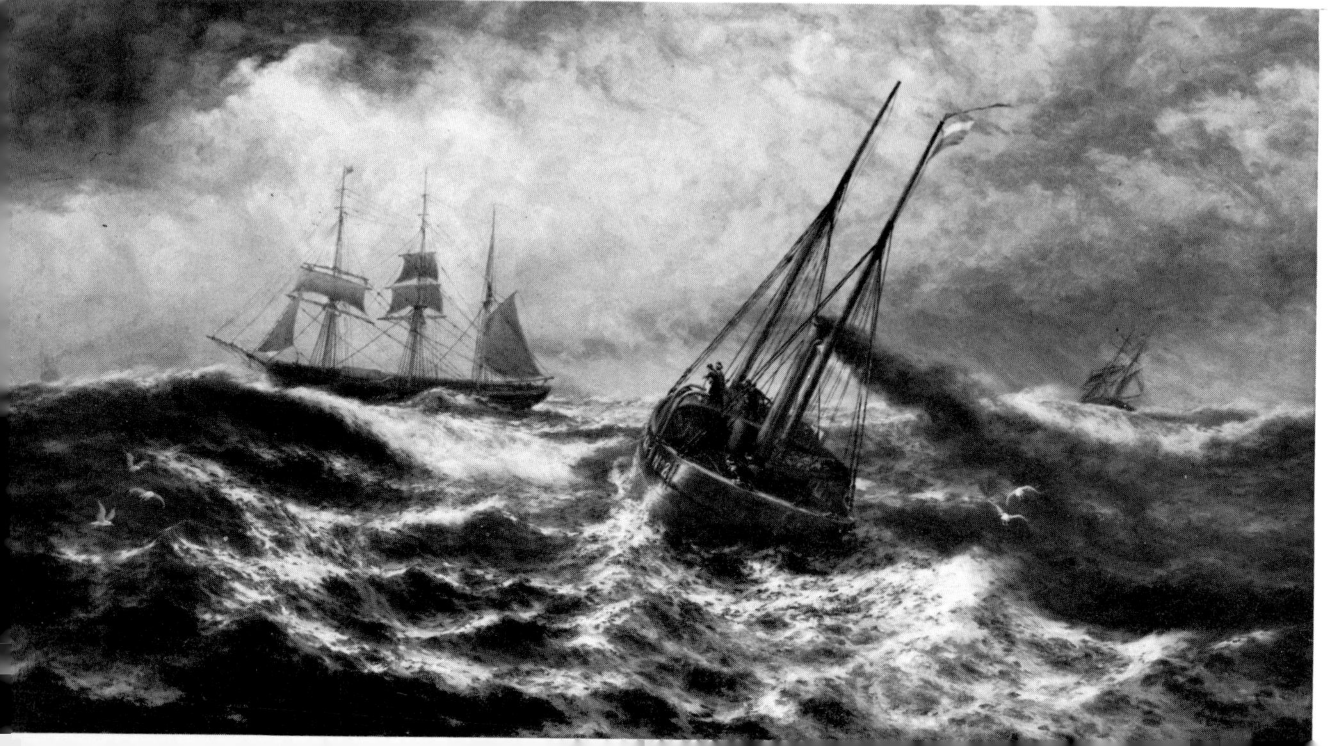

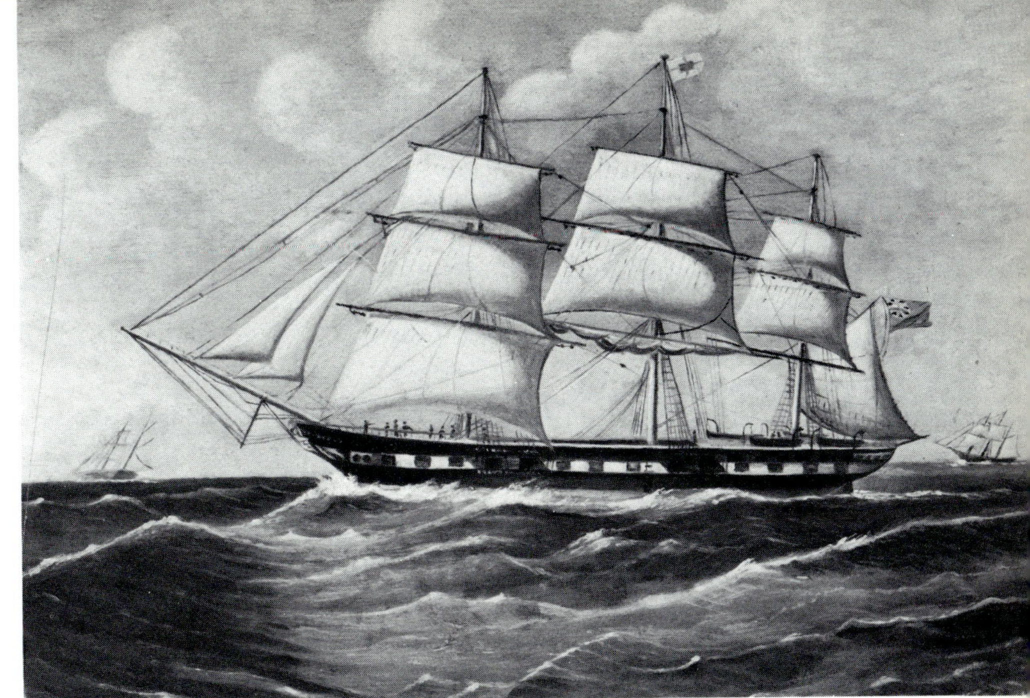

Plate 608. J.W. Corby, fl. mid- to late 19th century. "The ship *St. Lawrence.*" National Maritime Museum, Greenwich.

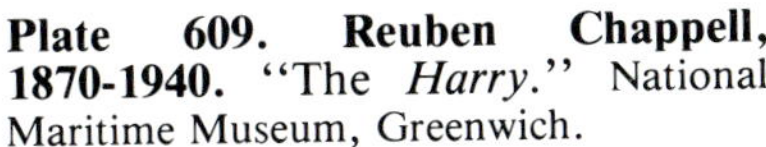

Plate 609. Reuben Chappell, 1870-1940. "The *Harry.*" National Maritime Museum, Greenwich.

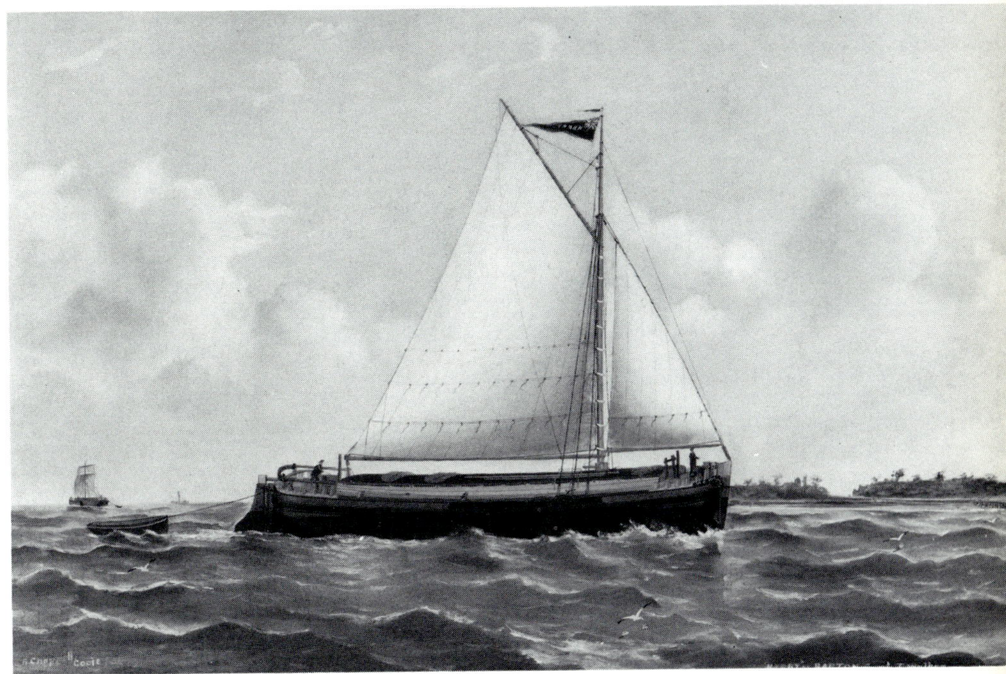

Plate 610. Charles John De Lacy, c.1860-1936. "The departure of the *Kinfauns Castle* for the Boer War in South Africa in 1900." National Maritime Museum, Greenwich.

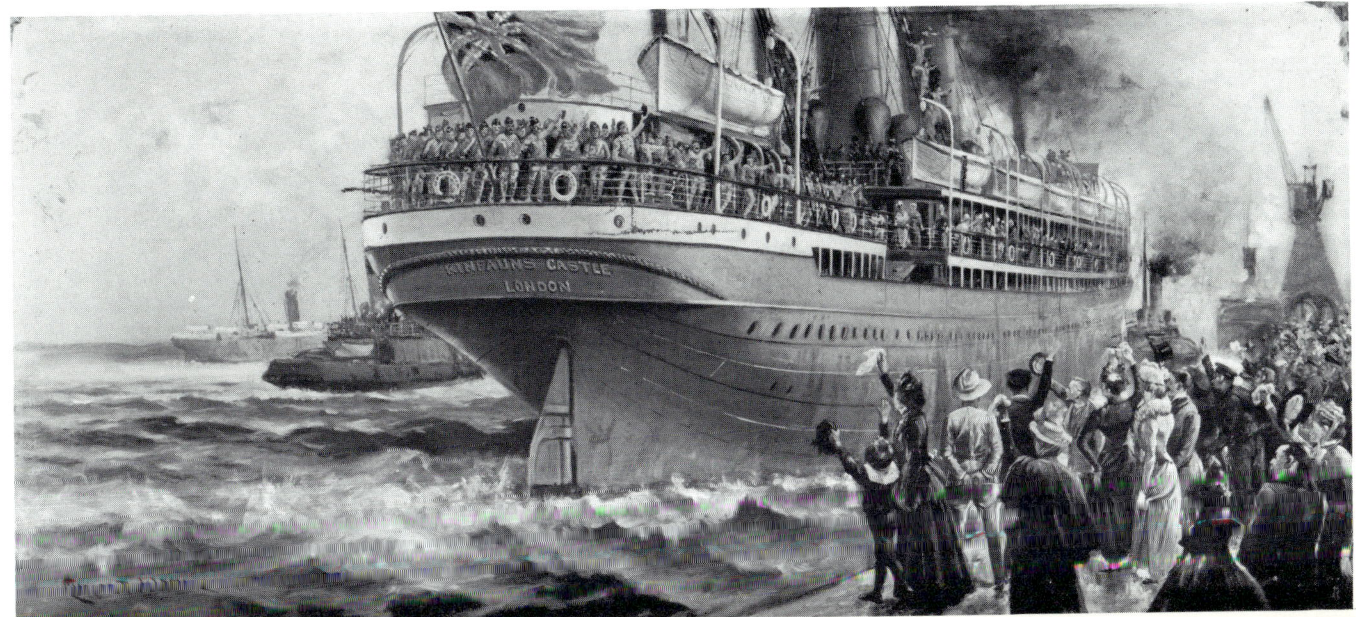

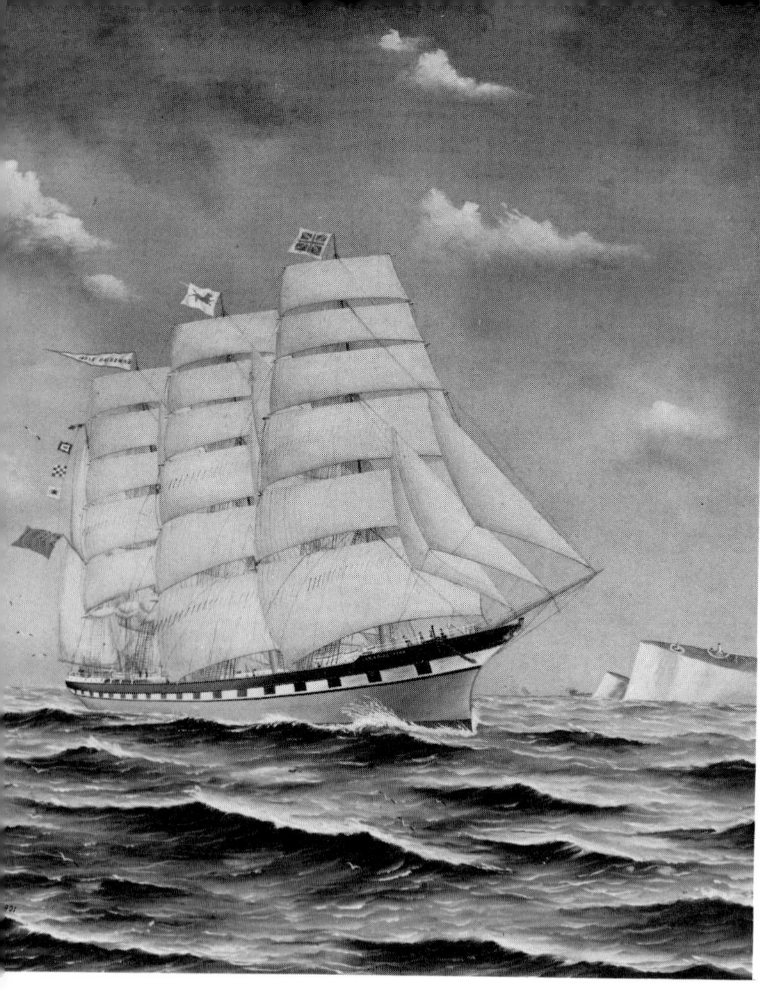

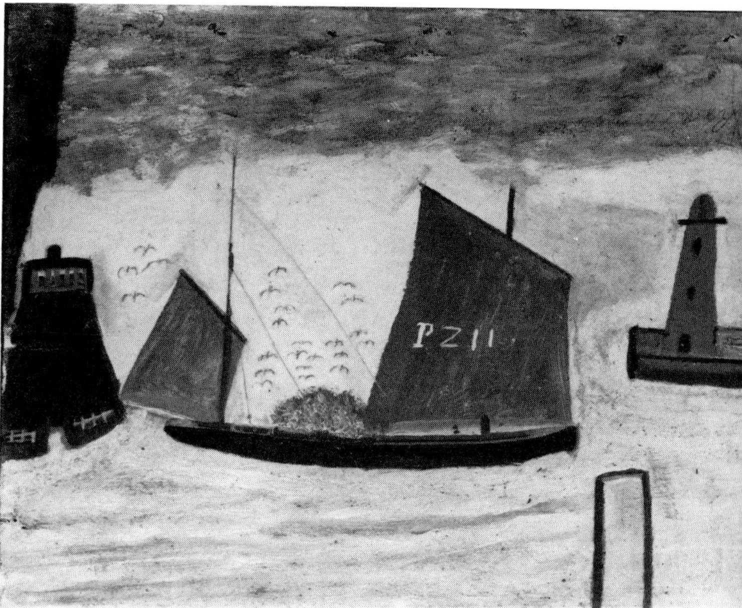

Plate 612. Alfred Wallis, 1855-1942. "A Penzance fishing lugger entering harbour." *A semi-literate fisherman, Wallis painted in a truly primitive style. His work is much sought after today.* Tate Gallery, London.

Plate 611. J. Fannen, fl.1893-1900. "The four-masted barque *Cambrian King,* dated 1901." *The black squares are painted ports which, when on the leeward side, let out water; the ports closed automatically against the sea. This decoration was a fashion which started in the 1880s and finished with sail.* National Maritime Museum, Greenwich.

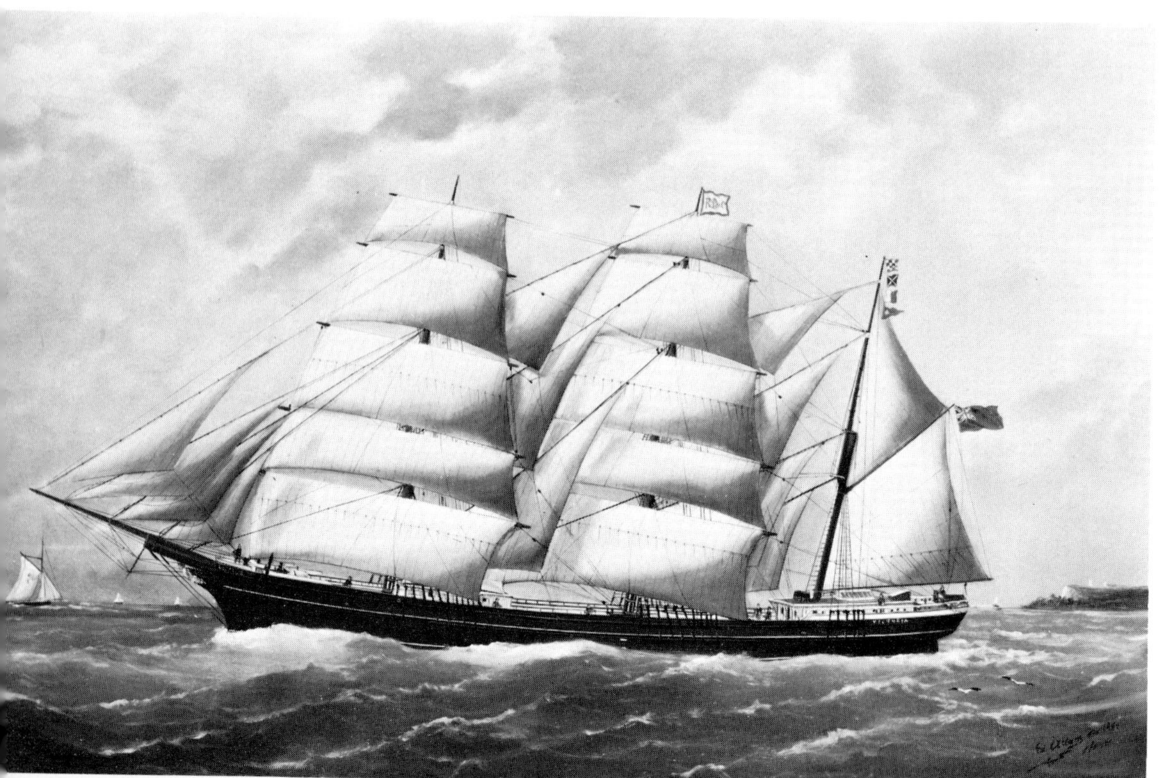

Plate 613. Edmond Adam, fl. late 19th, early 20th century. "The barque *Victoria,* dated 1889." National Maritime Museum, Greenwich.

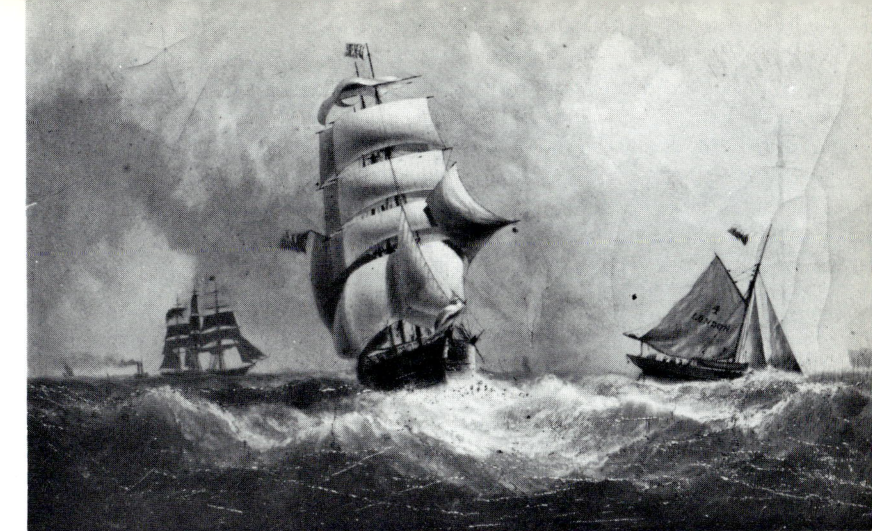

Plate 614. Edouard Adam, d.c.1930. ''Shipping in a stiff breeze.'' Sotheby's.

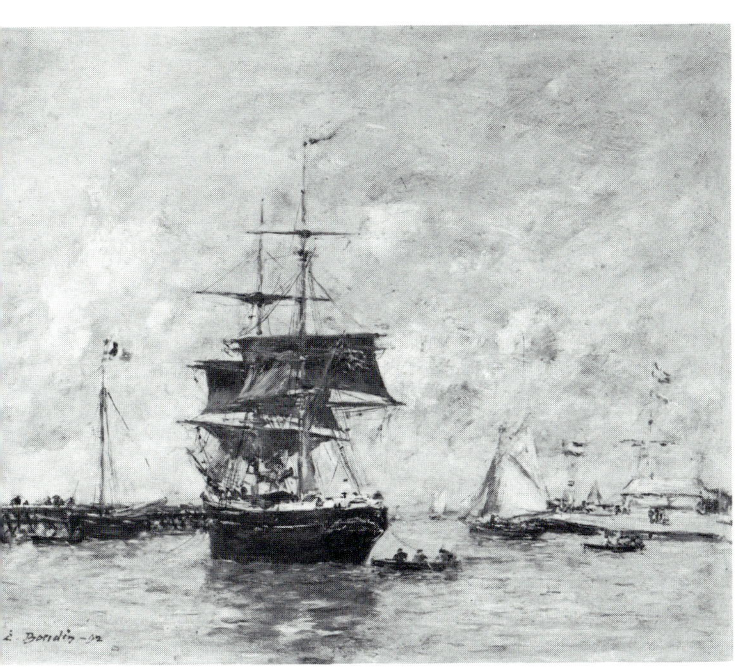

Plate 615. Eugène Louis Boudin, 1825-1908. ''The piers at Trouville, dated 1892.'' *A prolific painter of coast scenes, this is a typically Impressionist work of the French artist.* The Montreal Museum of Fine Arts.

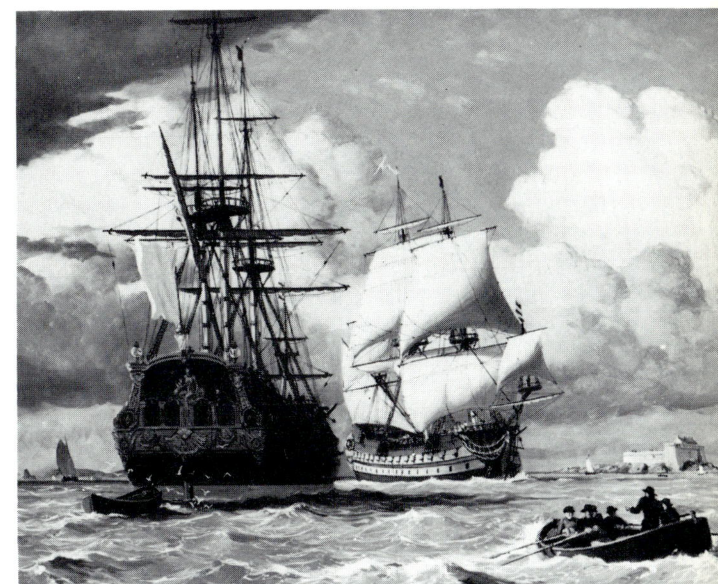

Plate 616. Etienne Blandin, b.1903. ''A French ship of the line passing an anchored ship in St. Malo Roads, about 1690.'' Artist's collection.

Plate 617. Fred Pansing, b.1844. ''The German transatlantic liner *Kaiser Wilhelm der Grosse.*'' *The first of the four stackers, she immediately took the Blue Riband when she went into service in 1898. She was fitted with gun mountings and extra bunkerage so that she could serve as a merchant cruiser. On the outbreak of the First World War she immediately assumed this role and was sunk three weeks later off the coast of West Africa by H.M.S.* Highflyer. Mariners Museum, Newport News, Virginia.

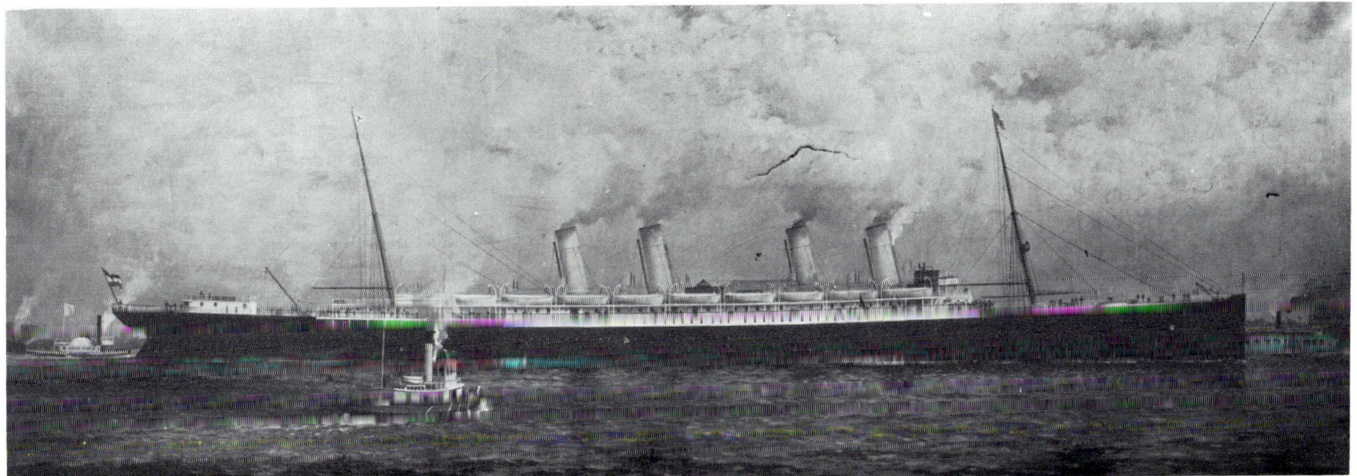

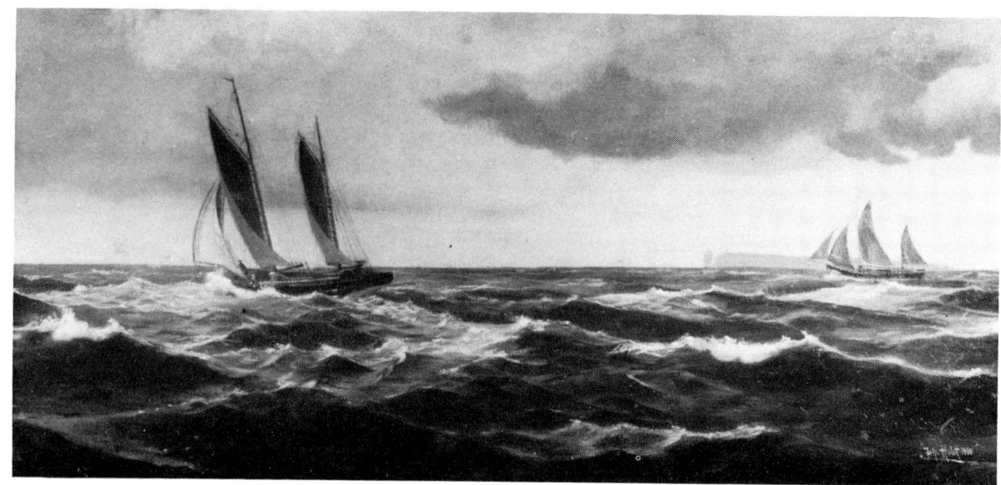

Plate 618. Johannes Holst, 1880-1965. "Fishing boats out of Finkenwerder, dated 1900." Altonaer Museum, Hamburg.

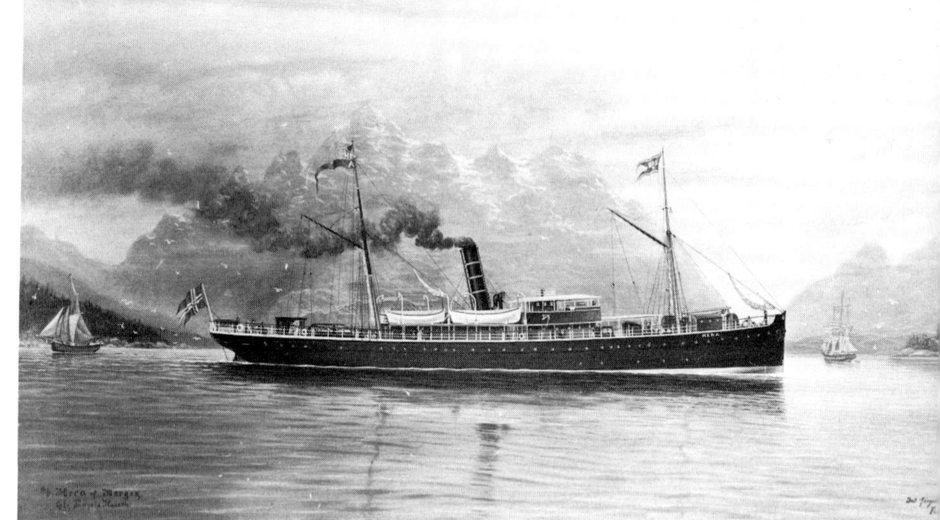

Plate 619. Julius Gregersen, 1860-1935. "The Norwegian steamer *Hera,* dated 1904." Maritime Museum, Bergen.

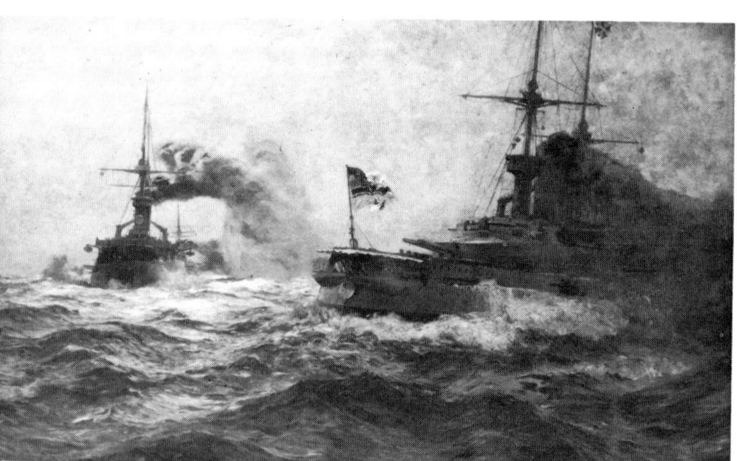

Plate 620. Carl Saltzmann, 1847-1923. "The German High Seas Fleet exercising in 1908." *A big picture by this German marine painter.* National Maritime Museum, Greenwich.

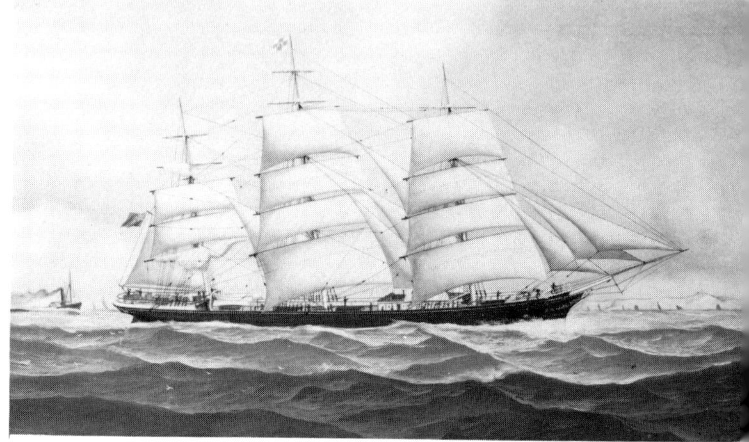

Plate 621. John Henry Mohrmann, 1857-1916. "The ship *British General,* built 1874." *The feature which differentiated iron from wooden built ships in the second half of the 19th century, was the whale back stern in most iron ships, not possible in wooden ones.* National Maritime Museum, Greenwich.

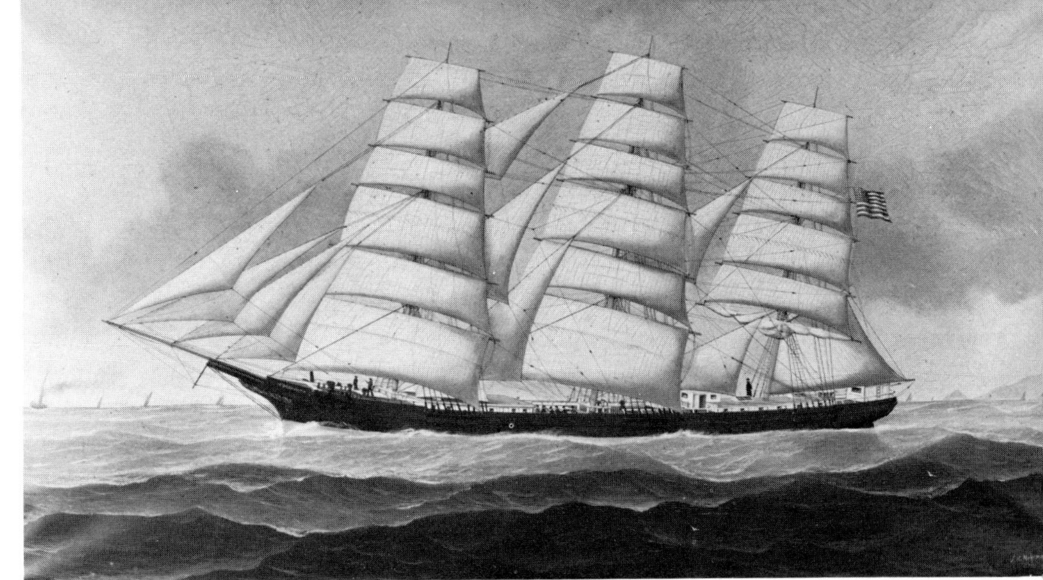

Plate 622. John Henry Mohrmann, 1857-1916. "The ship *Paramita,* dated 1892." *Another Mohrmann given very similar treatment to the preceding plate, especially in the sea.* Peabody Museum of Salem.

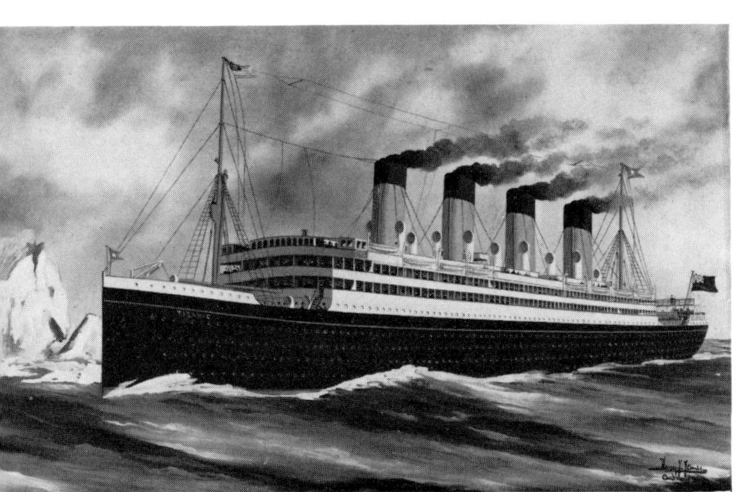

Plate 623. Harry J. Jansen, fl. early 20th century. "The *Titanic* off an iceberg on her maiden and last voyage in 1912." National Maritime Museum, Greenwich.

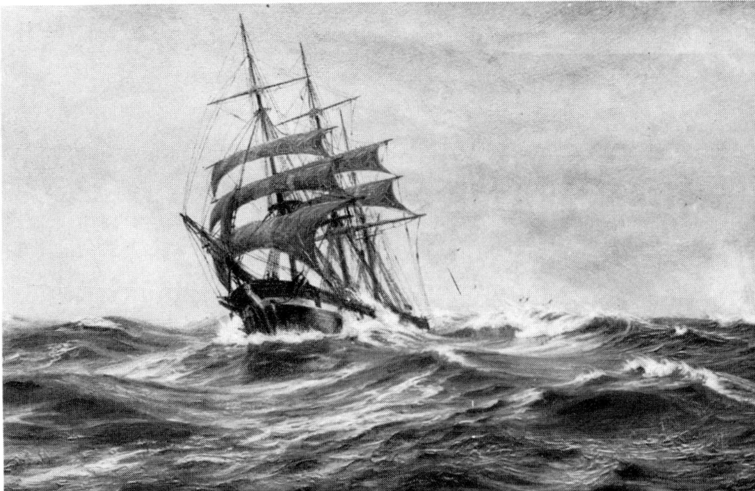

Plate 624. Vilk Arnesen, fl. late 19th century. "A barque running in a heavy sea, dated 1892." National Maritime Museum, Stockholm.

Plate 625. Herman Gustave af Sillen, 1857-1908. "The Swedish armoured turret ships *Gota, Svea* and *Thule* exercising at speed, dated 1897." *Sillen was very much a naval painter, both of commissioned naval events as well as such scenes as illustrated here.* National Maritime Museum, Stockholm.

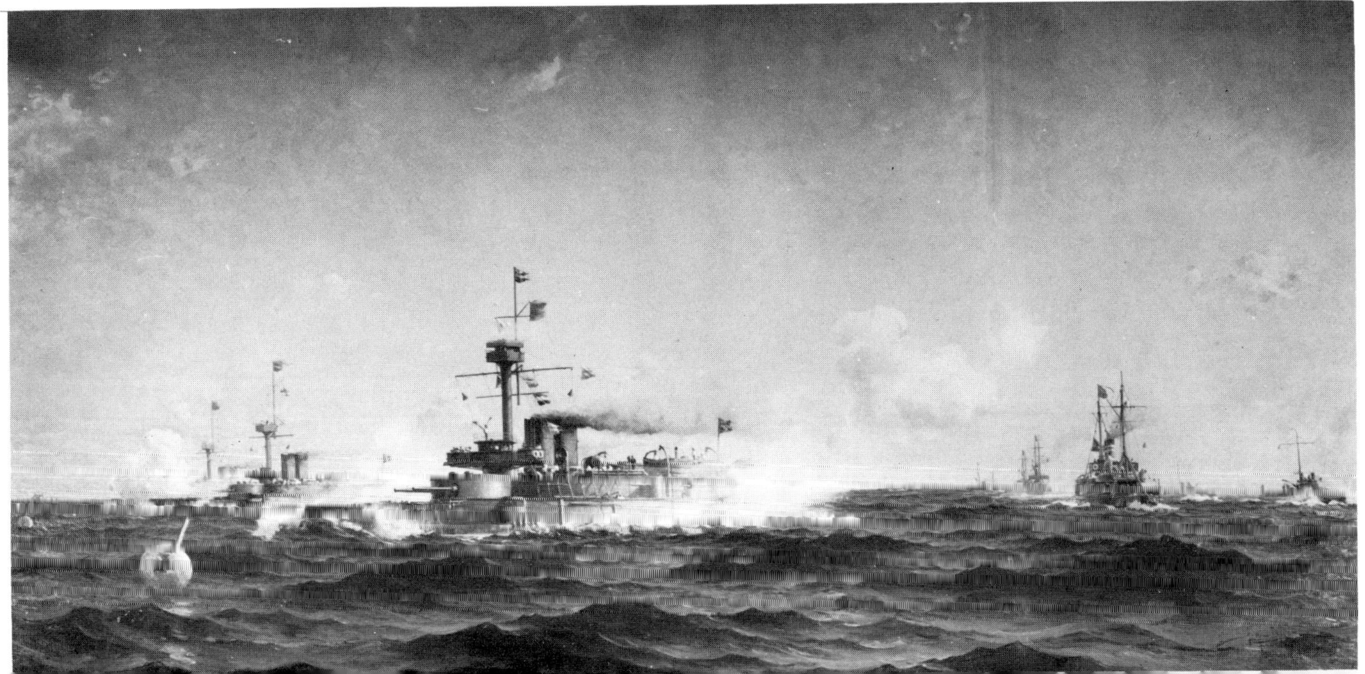

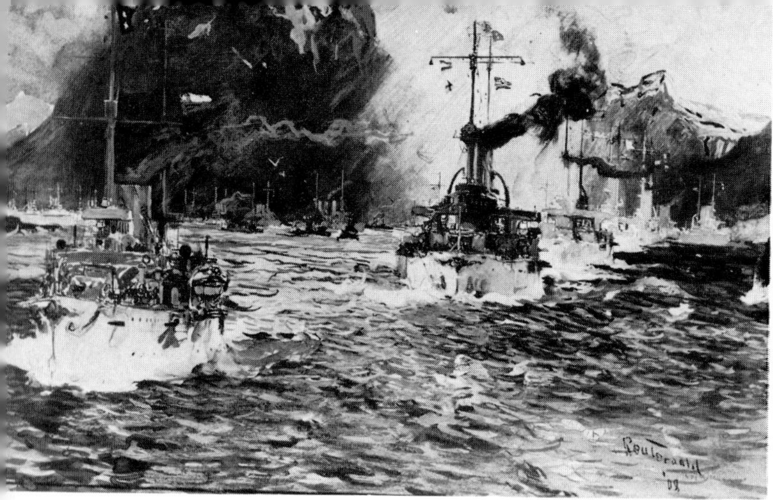

Plate 626. Henry Reuterdahl, 1870-1925. "The Great White Fleet in the Straits of Magellan on its world cruise, February 8th, 1908." *Reuterdahl was the leading naval history painter in America.* United States Naval Academy Museum, Annapolis.

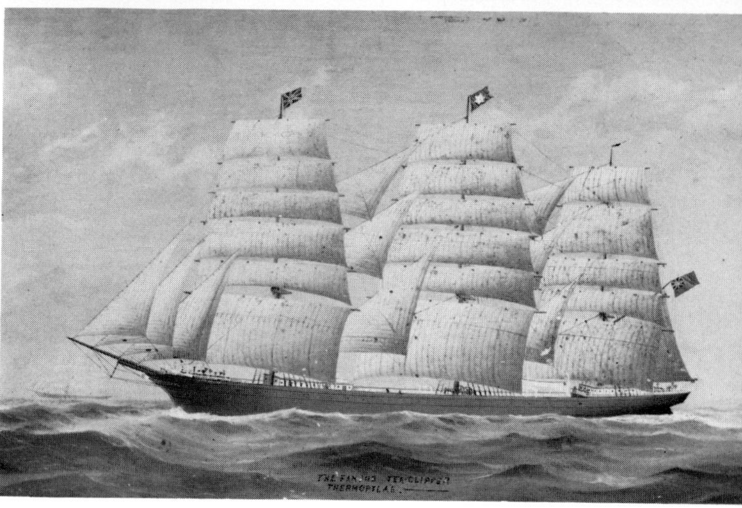

Plate 627. F.I. Sorensen, fl. early 20th century. "The famous tea-clipper *Thermopylae,* built 1868." National Maritime Museum, Greenwich.

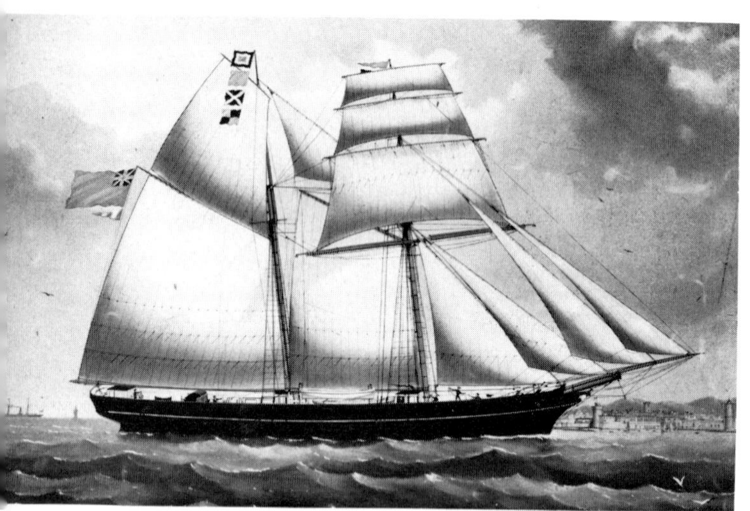

Plate 628. Luigi P. Renault, fl. mid- to late 19th century. "The topsail schooner *Ocean Wave* entering Leghorn." National Maritime Museum, Greenwich.

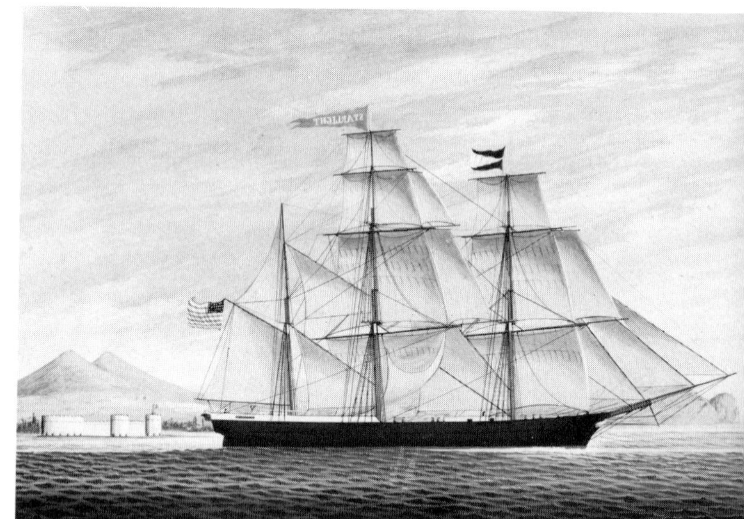

Plate 629. Raffael Corsini, fl. mid- to late 19th century. "The American barque *Starlight,* built 1854." Watercolour. Peabody Museum of Salem.

Plate 630. Antonio Nicolo Gasparo Jacobsen, 1850-1921. "The Inman Line transatlantic liner *City of Paris,* about 1890." *This work is attributed.* Peabody Museum of Salem.

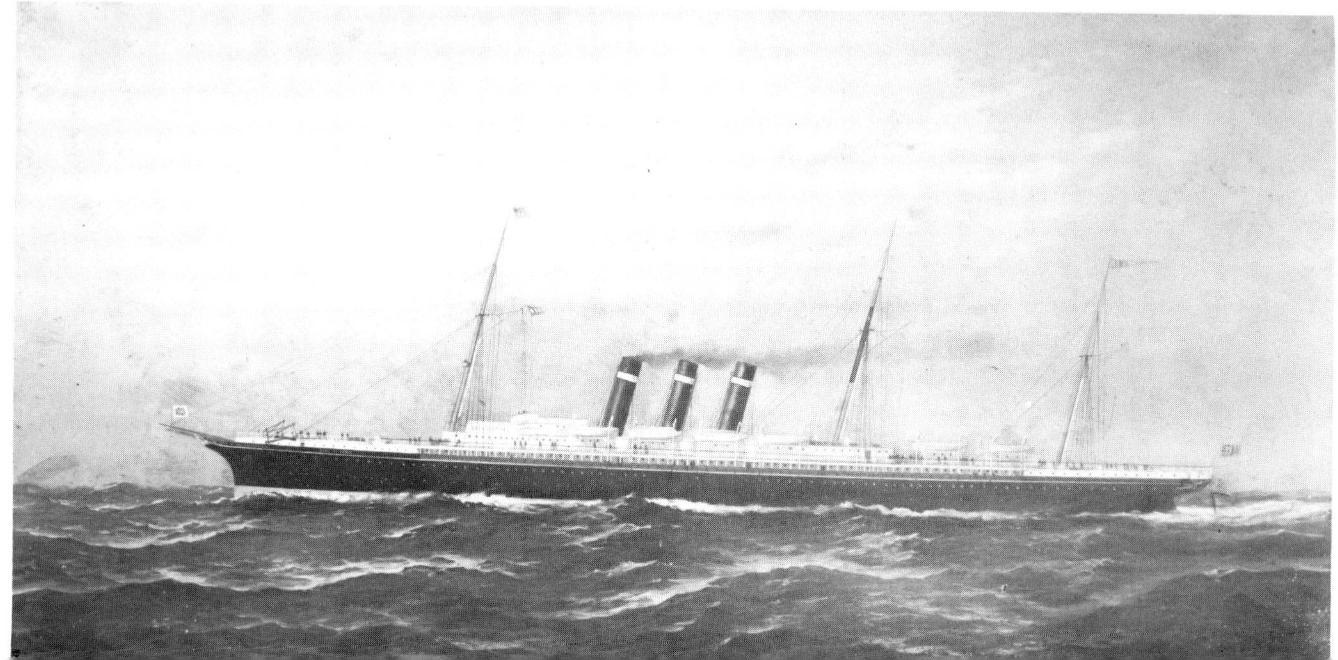

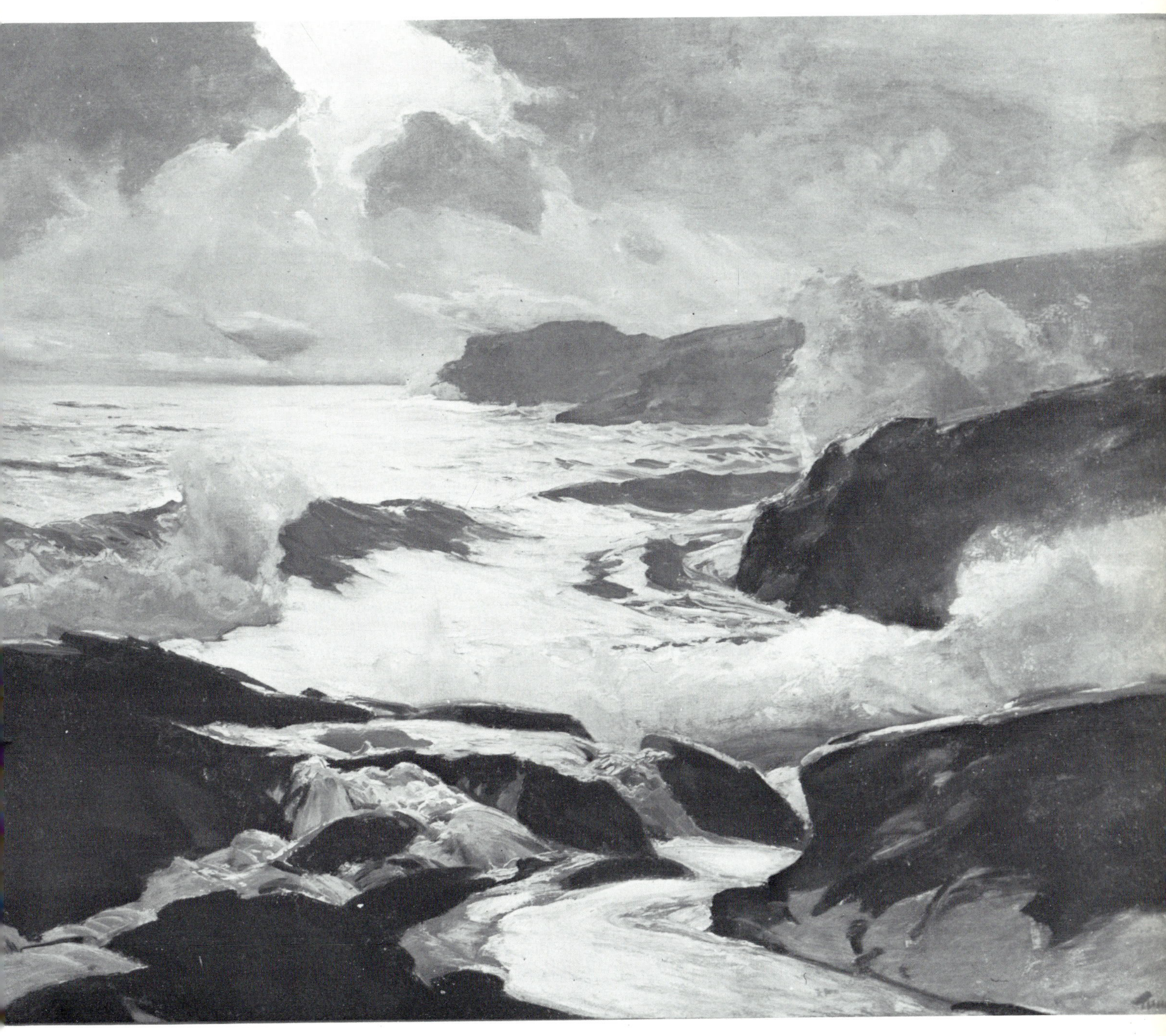

Plate 631. Frederick Judd Waugh, 1861-1940. "Full tide." Mariners Museum, Newport News.

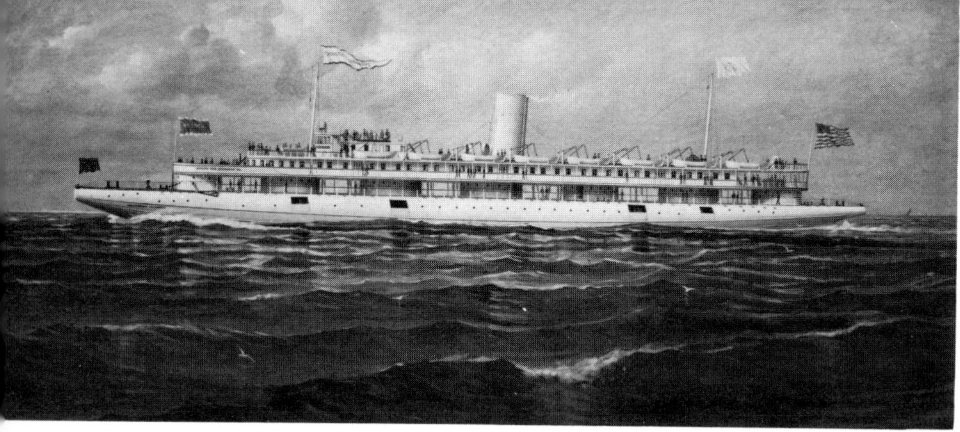

Plate 632. Howard Freeman Sprague, 1871-1899. "The ferry *Christopher Columbus,* built 1893." *A turret ship so called because of her tremendous tumblehome, with the narrow deck construction used to avoid deck tax.* Mariners Museum, Newport News.

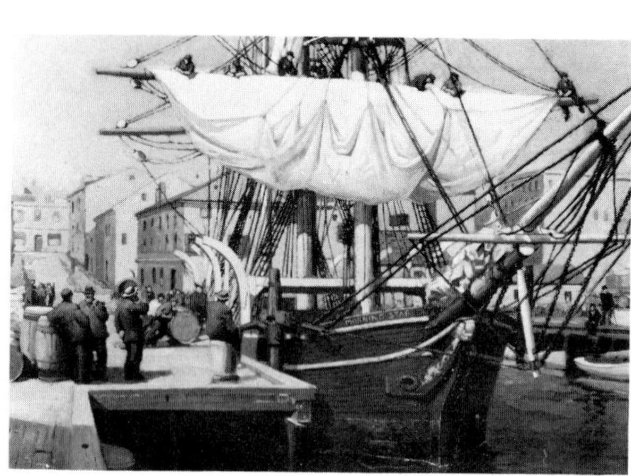

Plate 633. Percy Elton Cowen, 1888-1923. "The *Morning Star* whaling barque." Peabody Museum of Salem.

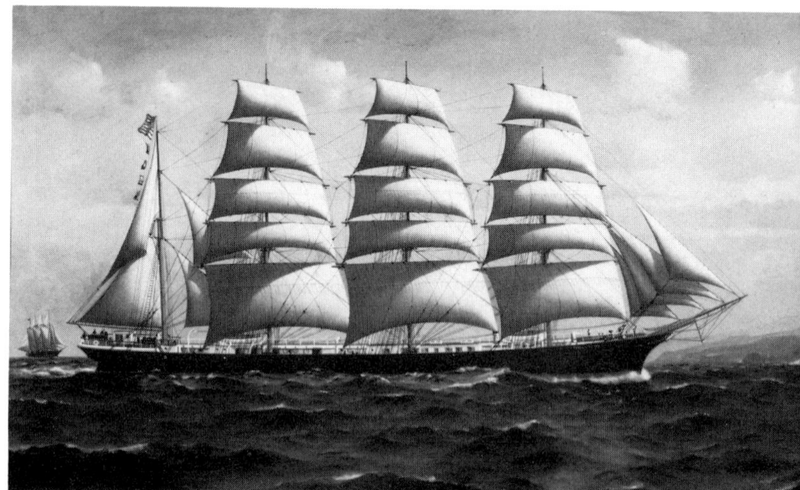

Plate 634. W. Edgar, fl. early 20th century. "The *Falls of Clyde,* dated 1912." *A four-poster barque with, in the background, a large schooner.* San Francisco Maritime Museum (Tidewater-Associated Oil Co. Collection).

Plate 635. J.E. Carville, fl. early 20th century. "The Norwegian steamer *Caloric,* built 1914." Maritime Museum, Bergen.

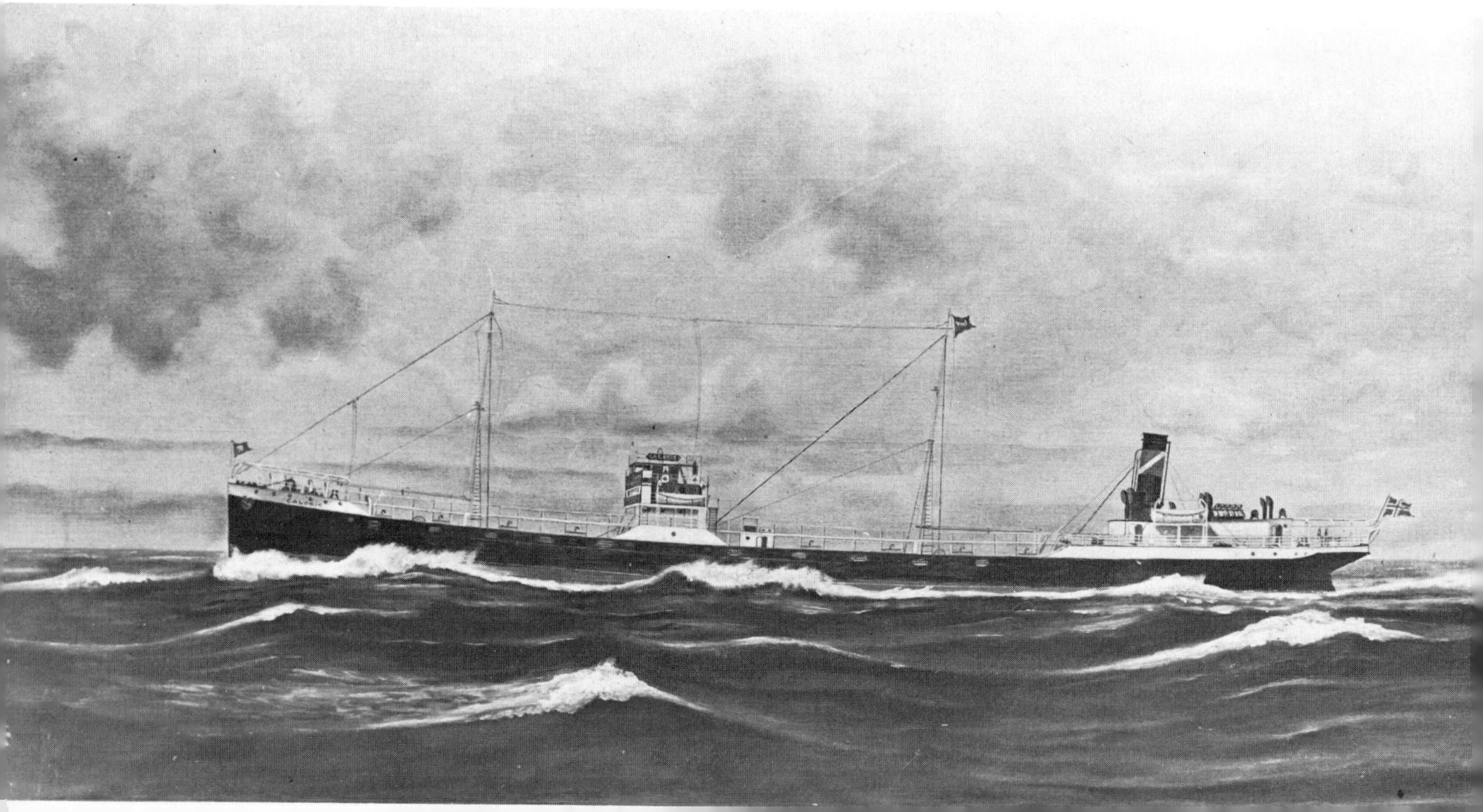

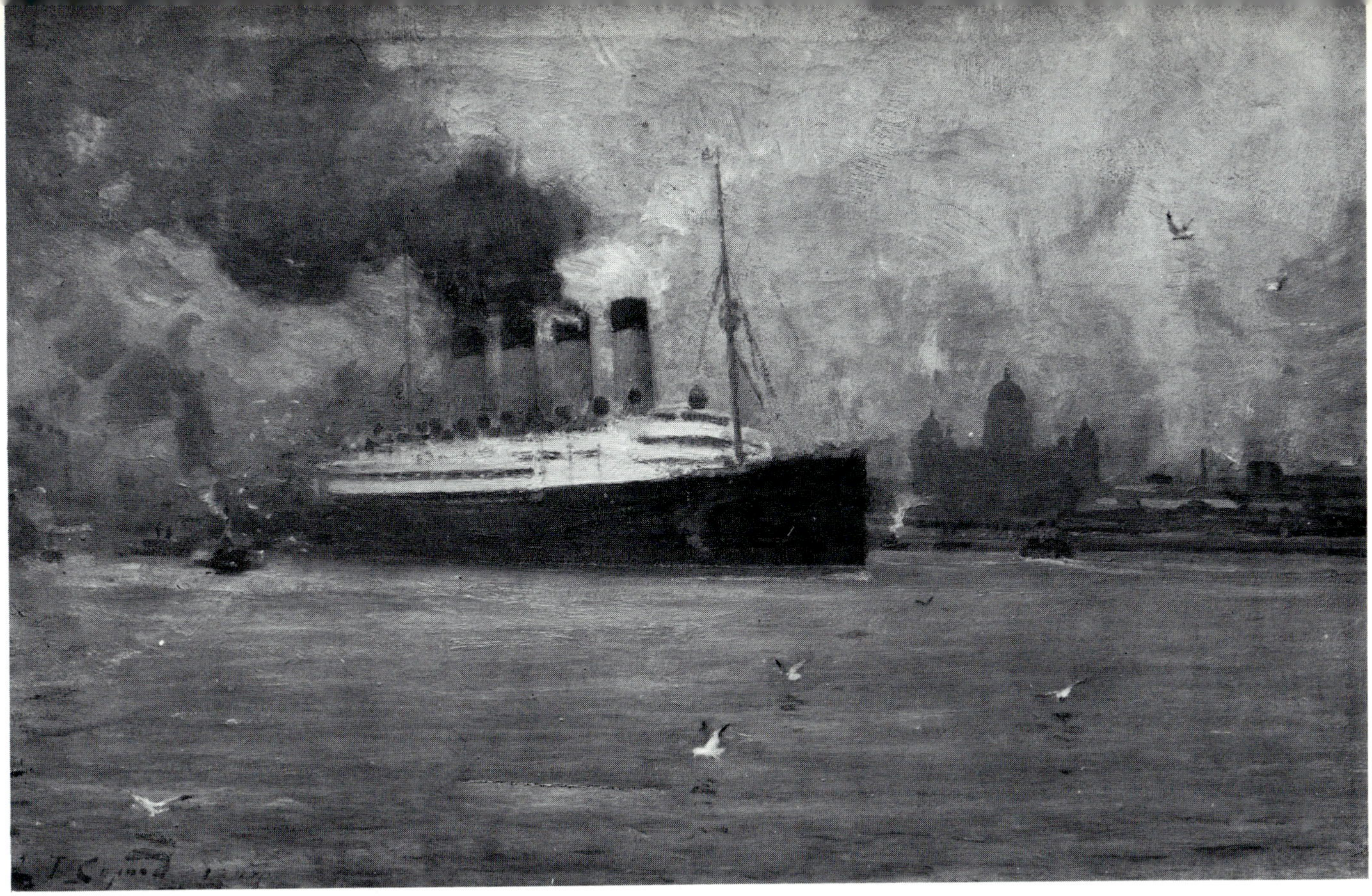

Plate 636. Frank T. Copnall, b.1870. "The Cunarder *Lusitania* at Liverpool in 1907." *The sister ship of the* Mauretania, *the* Lusitania *is seen at the start of her maiden voyage. In the background the Cunard Building.* National Maritime Museum, Greenwich.

Plate 637. Arthur James Wetherall Burgess, 1879-1957. " 'The Brotherhood of Seamen', the *Glengyle* rescuing a boatload of survivors." National Maritime Museum, Greenwich.

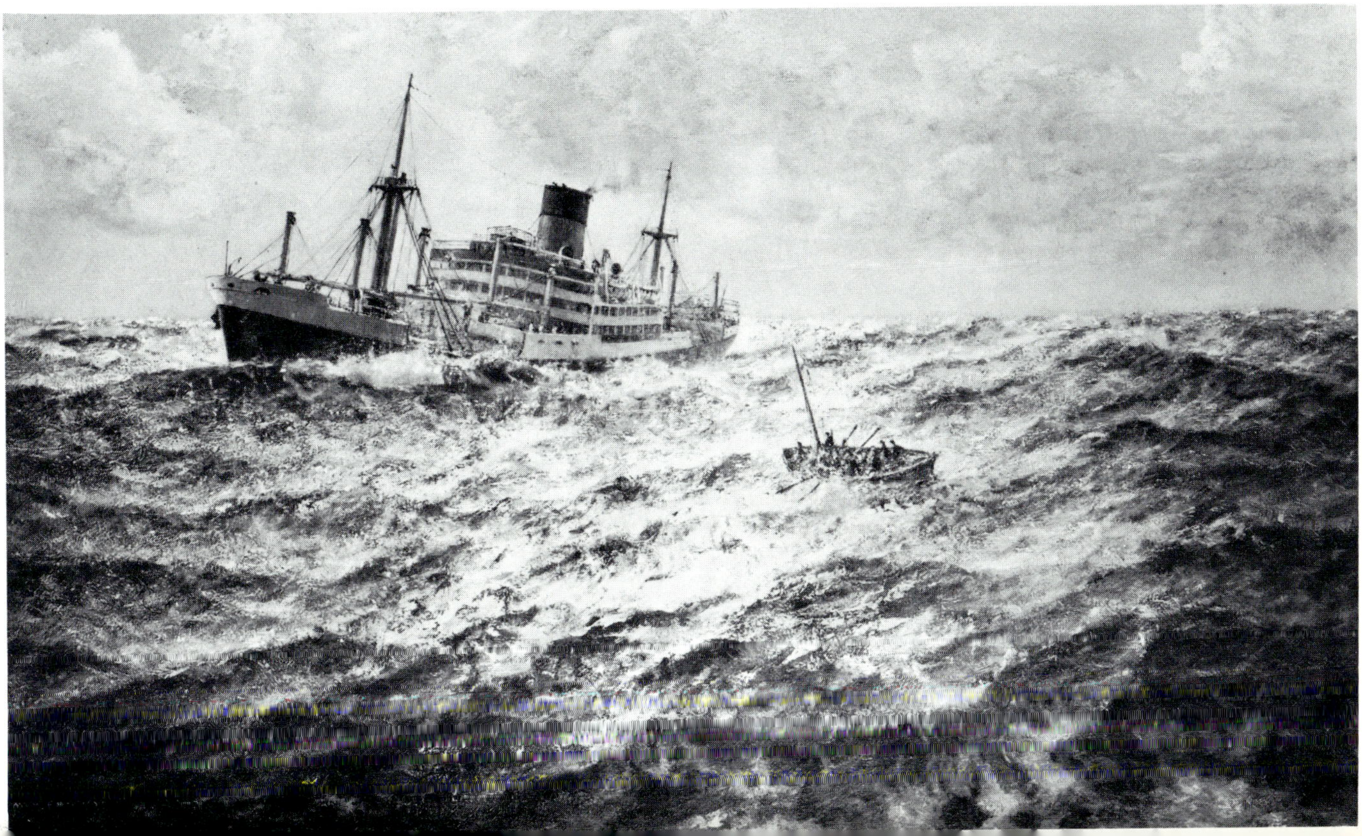

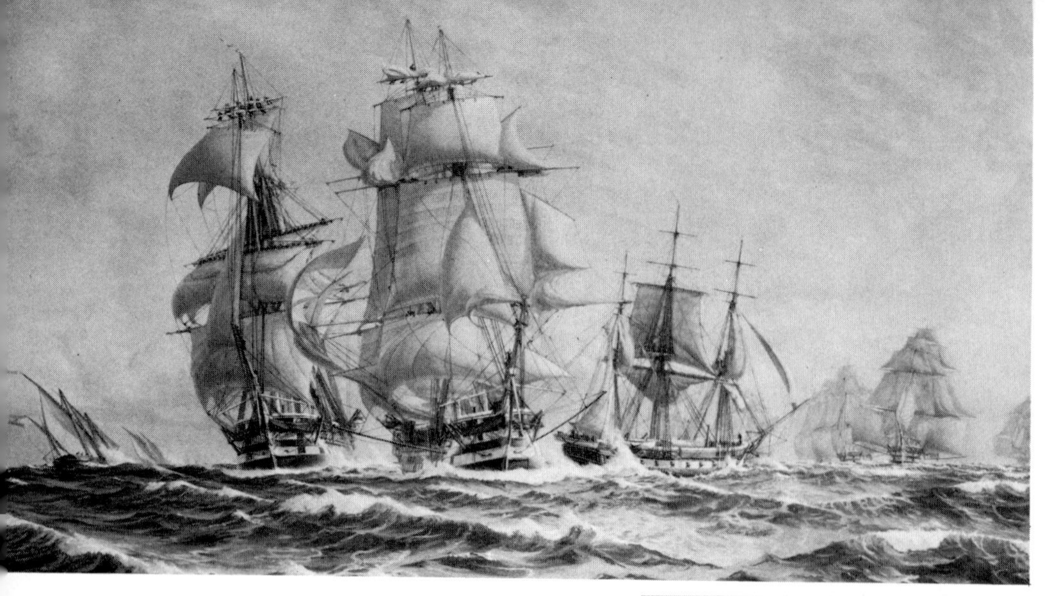

Plate 638. Harold Wyllie, 1880-1973. "The sailing trial of the Channel fleet off Lisbon in 1847." *An exciting moment during the famous race in 1847 when the old ex-French liner* Canopus *beat all Sir William Symonds new liners. The* Canopus *had been captured from the French in 1798, but was still in the Channel fleet in 1847, and because she sailed so well sixteen further ships had been built to her lines. During the race* Canopus' *captain put those crew not needed aloft in hammocks with a 32lb. shot to give moving weight.* Royal Society of Marine Artists (on loan to the National Maritime Museum, Greenwich).

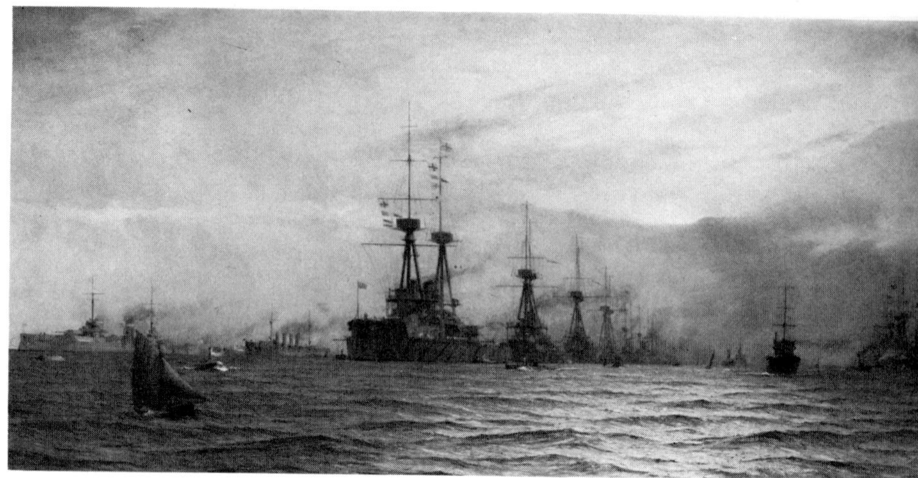

Plate 639. Alma Claude Burlton Cull, 1880-1931. "The eve of King George V's Coronation Review in 1911." *The flagship, the dreadnought* Neptune, *makes the signal to bank fires to a fleet of 125 vessels, including thirty-seven capital ships that packed the Solent.* National Maritime Museum, Greenwich.

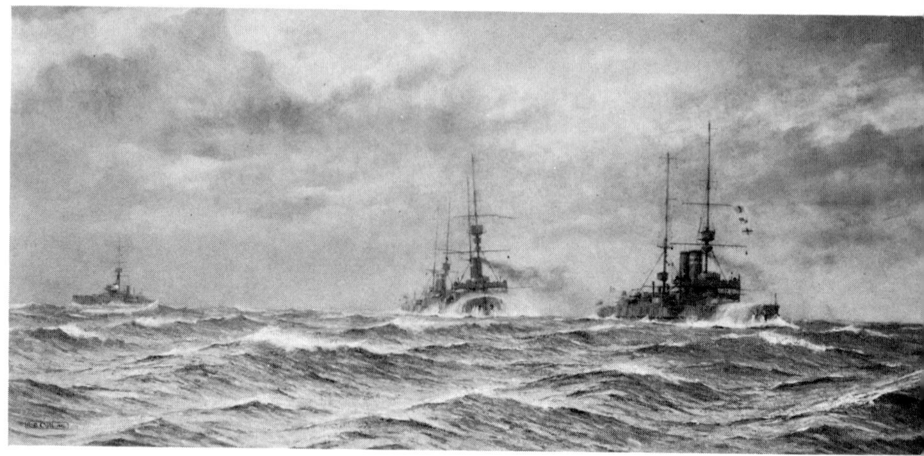

Plate 640. Alma Claude Burlton Cull, 1880-1931. "King Edward VII class battleships at sea, dated 1912." *The last big class of pre-dreadnought battleships, they were affectionately known as the 'Wobbly Eight' because they steered crabwise as the painting shows.* National Maritime Museum, Greenwich.

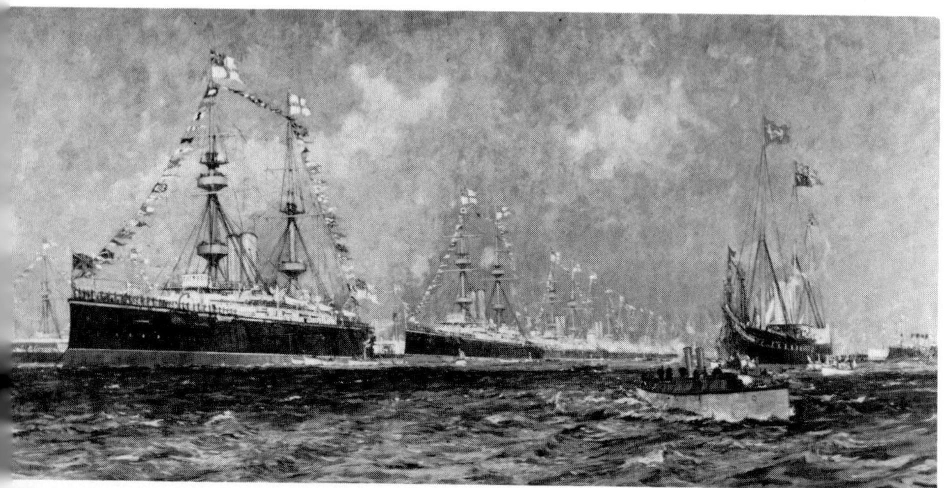

Plate 641. Charles Dixon, 1872-1934. "Queen Victoria's Diamond Jubilee Review in 1897." *The ships of the Royal Navy were not painted grey until 1903. Here H.M.S.* Renown *heads one of the lines of twenty-one battleships and fifty-six cruisers plus other craft, thirty-six miles long, and not one ship recalled from a foreign station. On the right is the royal yacht* Victoria and Albert II. National Maritime Museum, Greenwich.

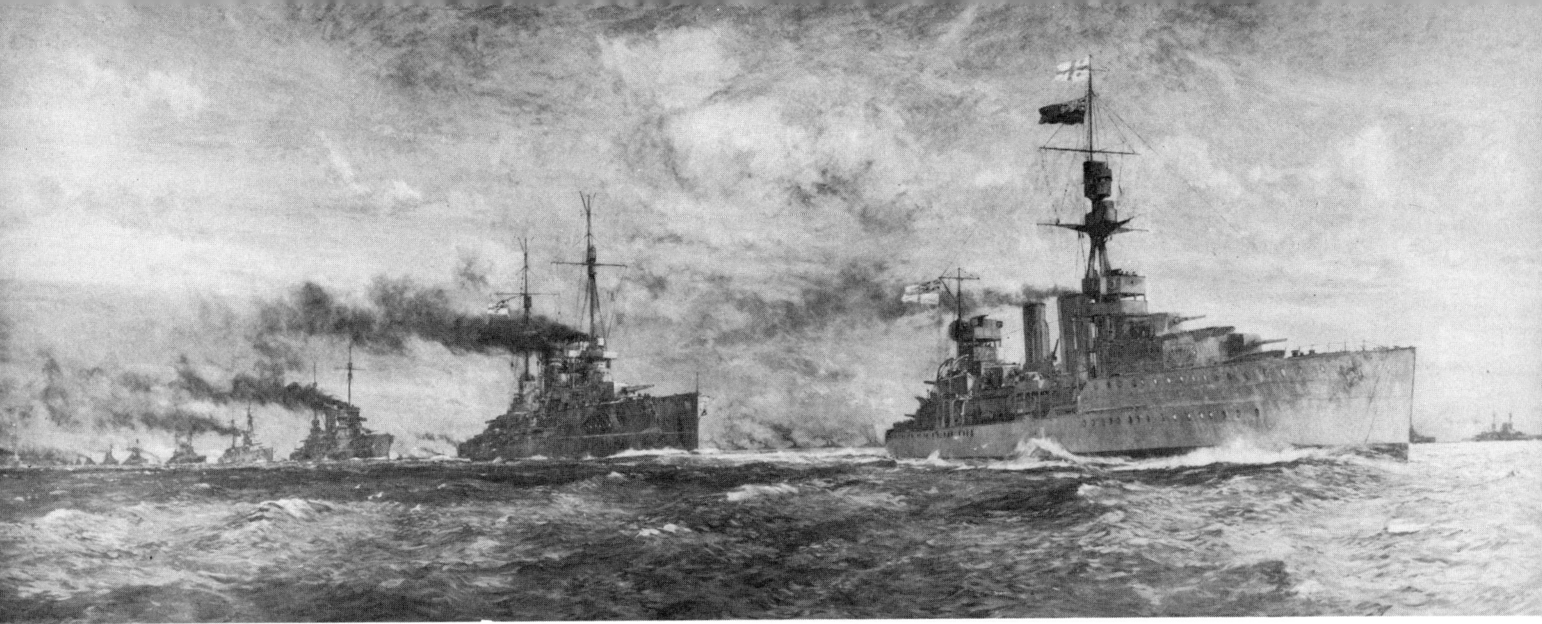

Plate 642. Charles Dixon, 1872-1934. "H.M.S. *Cardiff* leading the surrendered German High Seas Fleet to Rosyth in 1918." National Maritime Museum, Greenwich.

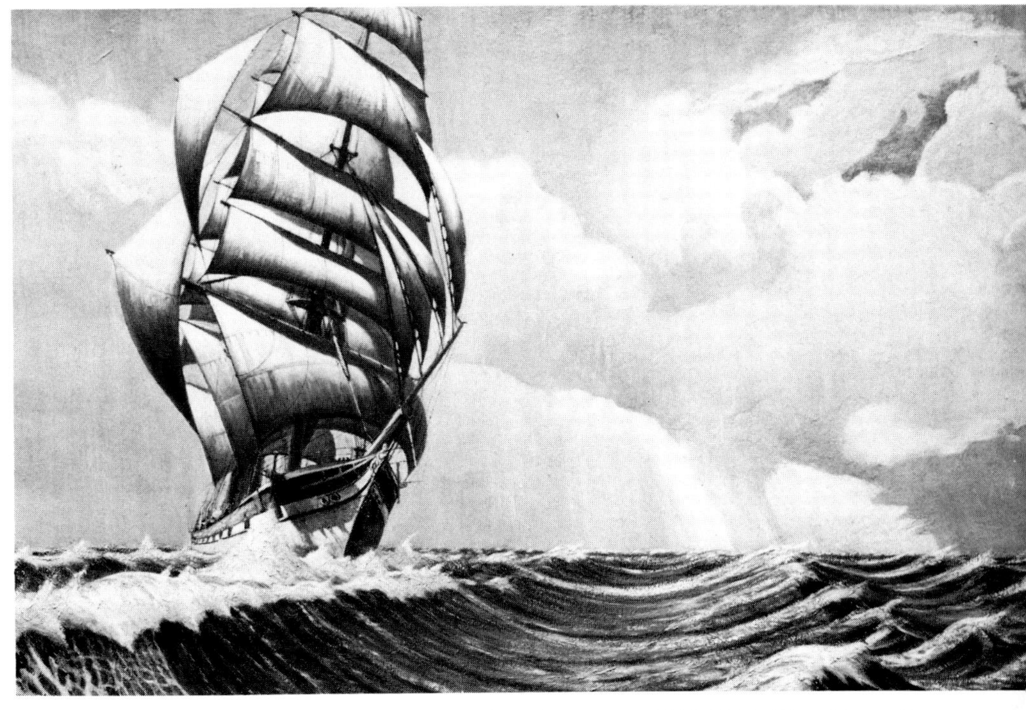

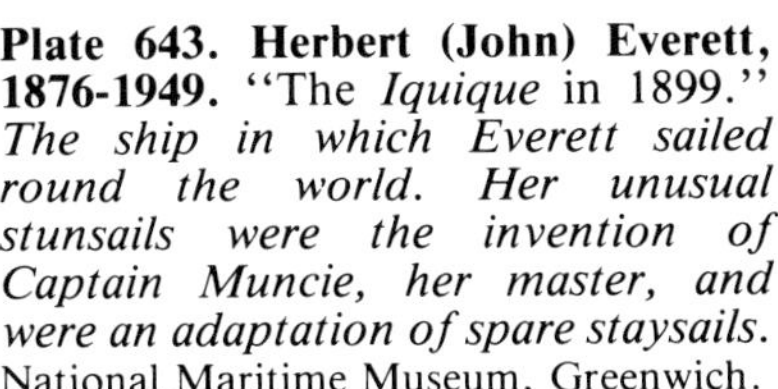

Plate 643. Herbert (John) Everett, 1876-1949. "The *Iquique* in 1899." *The ship in which Everett sailed round the world. Her unusual stunsails were the invention of Captain Muncie, her master, and were an adaptation of spare staysails.* National Maritime Museum, Greenwich.

Plate 644. Herbert (John) Everett, 1876-1949. "A convoy of the First World War." *Painted for the Ministry of Information, the ships are camouflaged with 'dazzle' painting — an idea put forward by Norman Wilkinson and adopted by the Navy and merchant fleets.* National Maritime Museum, Greenwich.

Plate 645. Herbert (John) Everett, 1876-1949. "Looking aft from the fo'c'sle of the *Kylemore*, 1925." *Everett is unique as a marine painter in that much of his output consisted of deck scenes, many, like this one, done on the spot at sea.* National Maritime Museum, Greenwich.

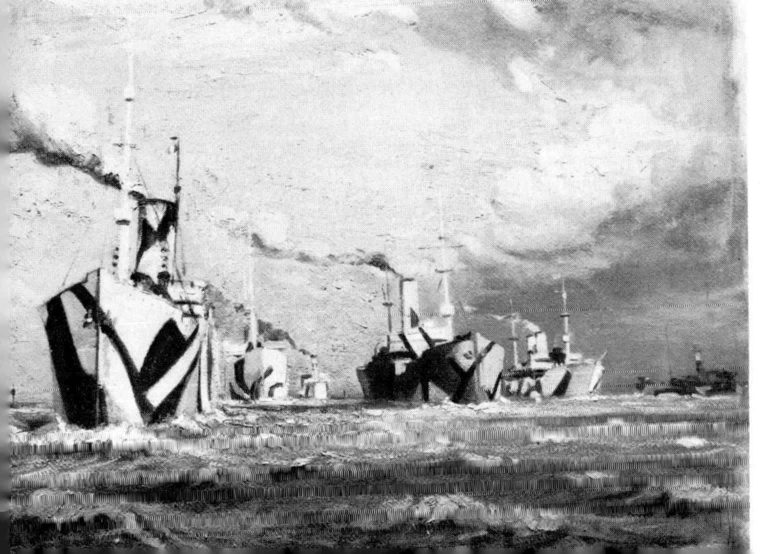

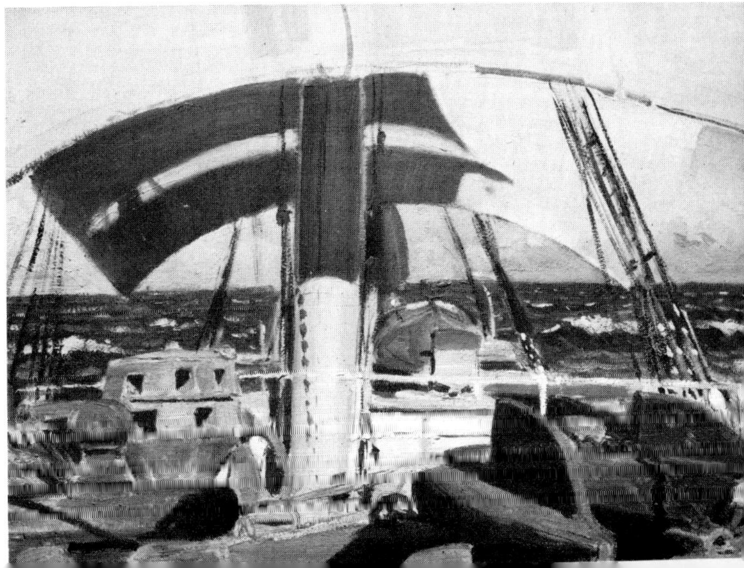

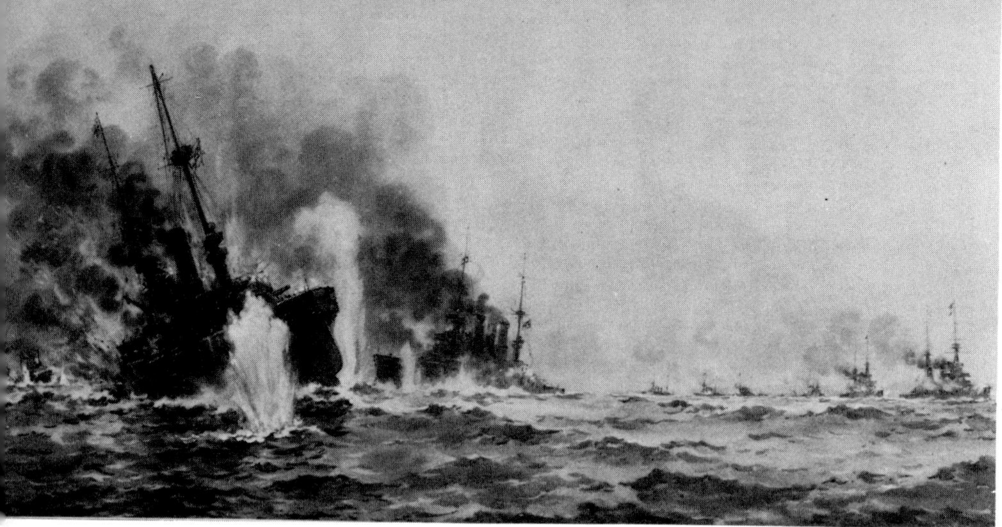

Plate 646. Frank Watson Wood, 1862-1953. "The Battle of the Falkland Islands in 1914." *The* Scharnhorst, *on the left, sunk first, while the* Gneisenau, *centre, survived a little longer. On the extreme right H.M.S.* Invincible. Christie's.

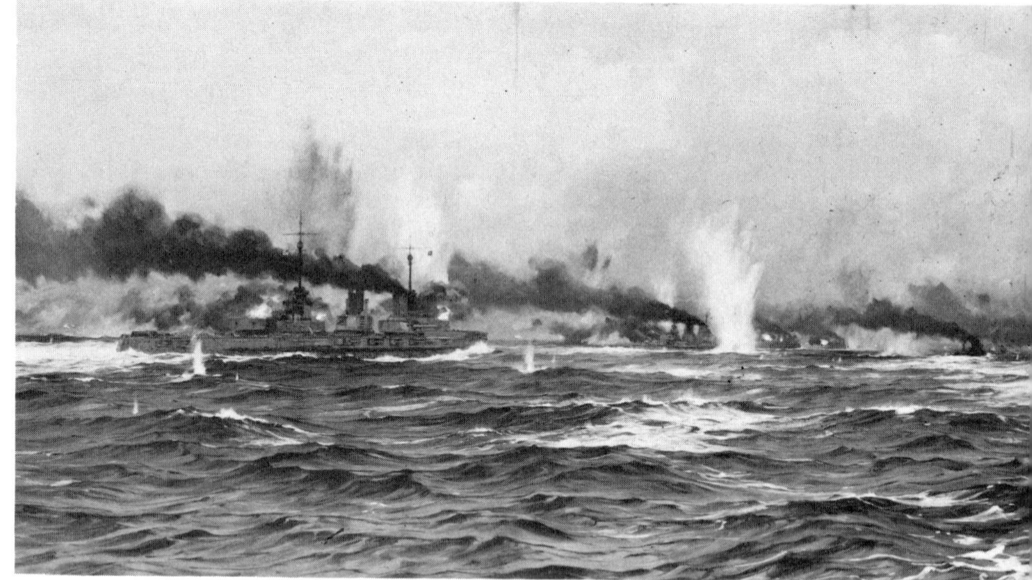

Plate 647. Claus Bergen, 1885-1964. "Hipper's battle-cruisers at the Battle of Jutland in 1916." *German battle-cruisers with flashes from Beatty's battle-cruisers in the background.* National Maritime Museum, Greenwich.

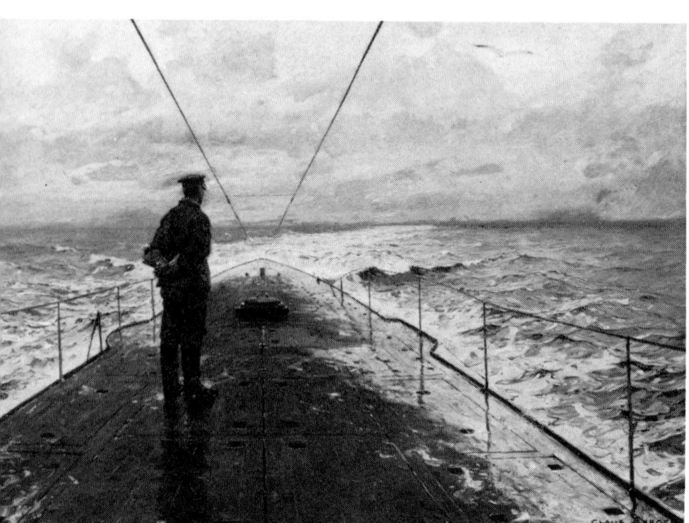

Plate 648. Claus Bergen, 1885-1964. "A German U-boat commander on the fore-deck of his submarine, dated 1918." National Maritime Museum, Greenwich.

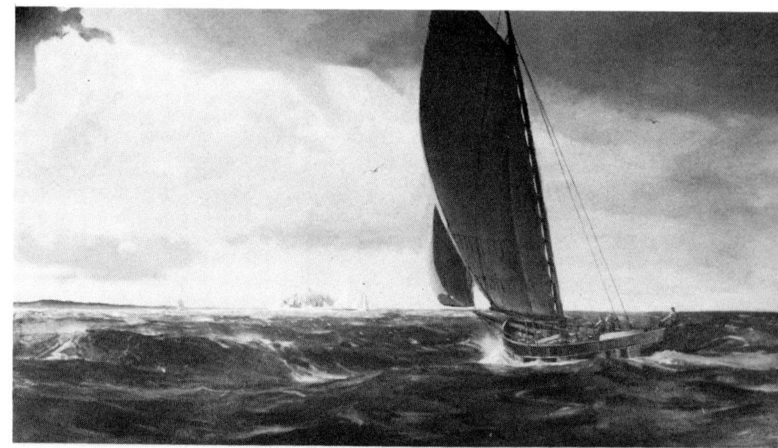

Plate 649. John P. Benson, 1865-1947. "A sloop off Egg Rock, Nahant Bay, 1931." *This work is attributed.* Peabody Museum of Salem

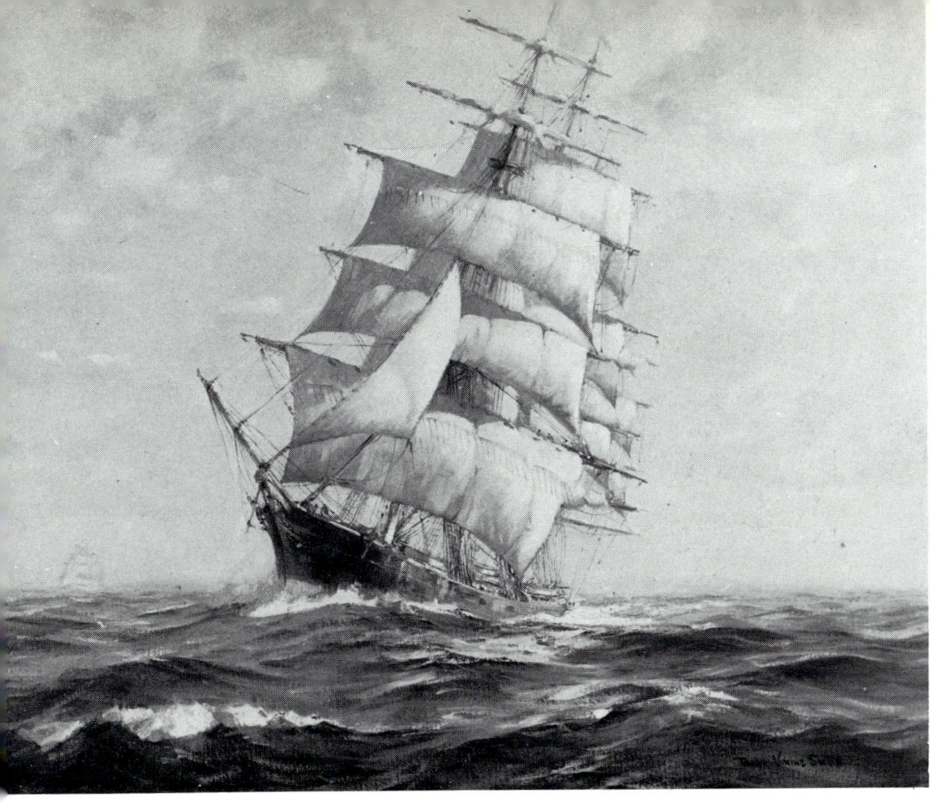

Plate 650. Frank Vining Smith, 1879-1967. "The ship *Tonawanda.*" *Built at Greenock for a Hamburg firm in 1892 as the* Lita. *In 1915, as the* Indra, *bought by the U.S. Ship Board and renamed* Tonawanda. *Finally, sold to the Columbia River Packers' Association in 1924 and renamed* Astoria. Mariners Museum, Newport News, Virginia.

Plate 651. William M. Birchall, b.1884. "The Cunard transatlantic liner *Campania* at anchor in the Mersey, dated 1934." Watercolour. *She was in service from 1893 to 1914, when she was bought by the Admiralty and converted, first to a seaplane carrier and, later, had a flight-deck added from which land planes could take off, but not land. Sunk in collision with H.M.S.* Revenge *just before the armistice in 1918.* Peabody Museum of Salem.

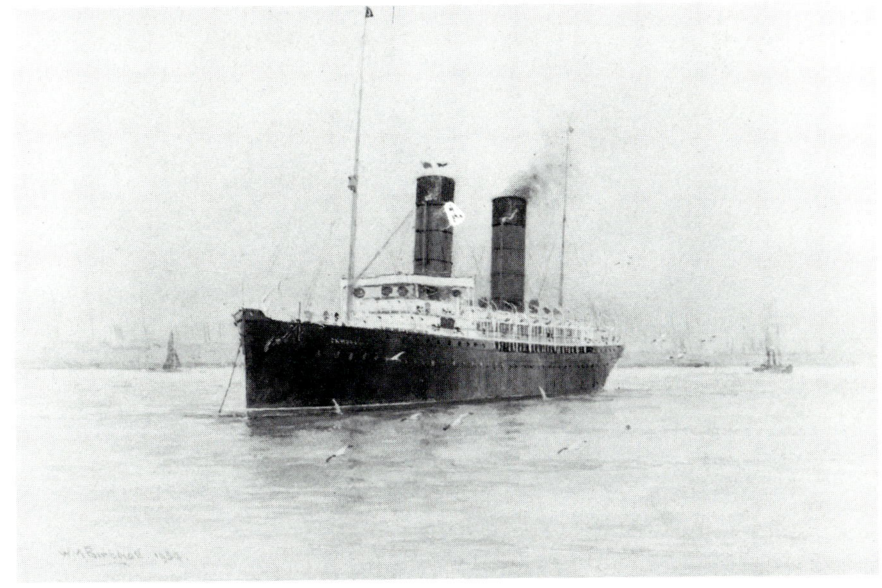

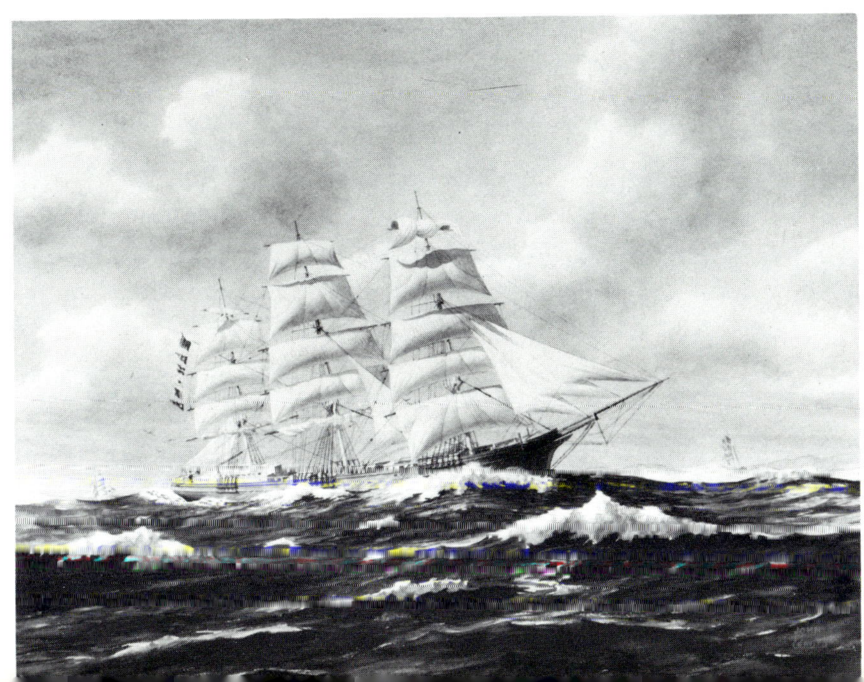

Plate 652. John Faunce Leavitt, b.1905. "The ship *Panay,* built Boston 1877." Watercolour. Peabody Museum of Salem.

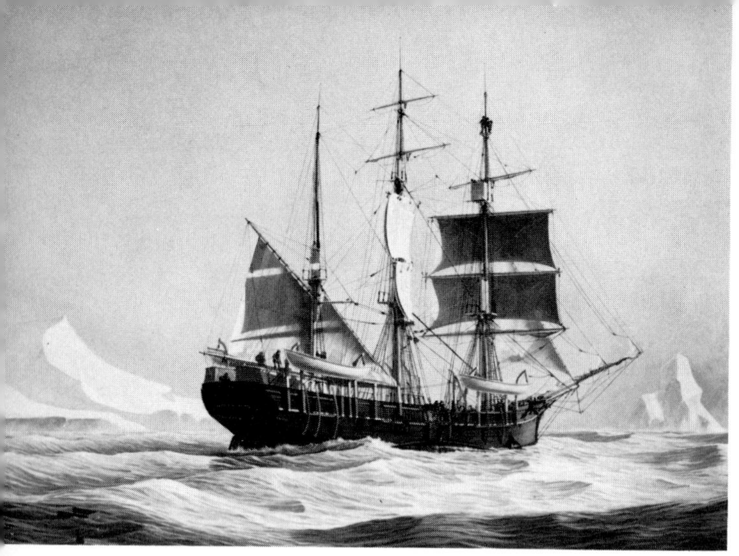

Plate 653. William Gilkerson, b.1936. "The whaling barque *John and Winthrop* in the ice, cutting a bowhead whale, 1913." *Such wooden vessels which sailed in icy waters and carried heavy whales were specially strengthened in order to take the added strains.* The Barkentine Co., Rochester, Mass.

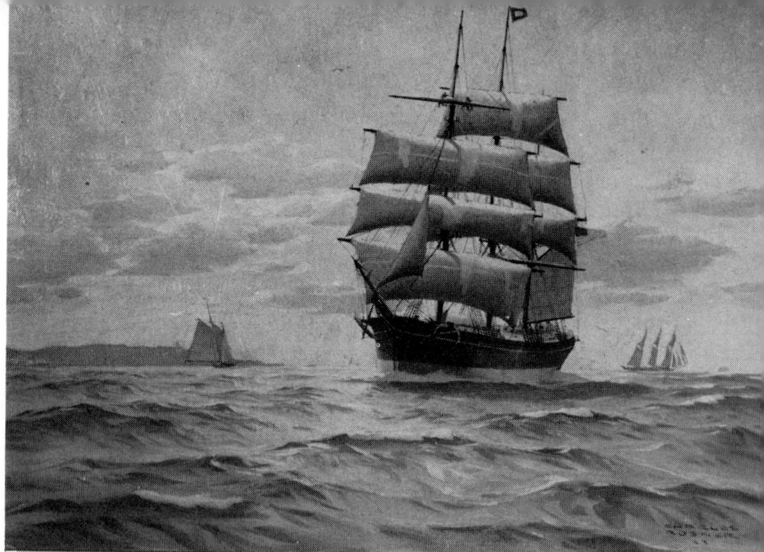

Plate 654. Charles Rosner, 1894-aft.1975. "The American barque *Adam W. Speiss,* dated 1933." Mariners Museum, Newport News.

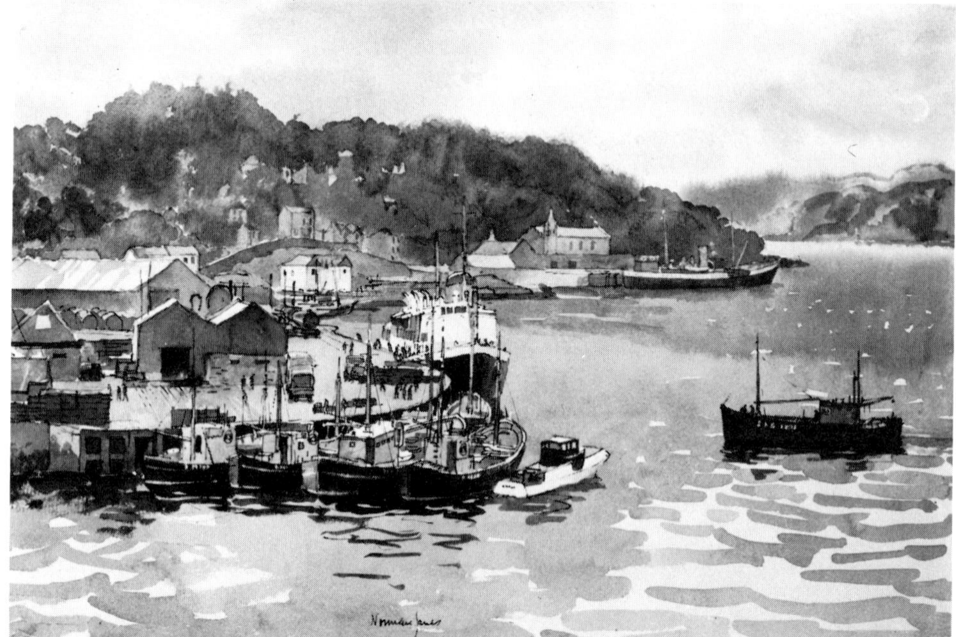

Plate 655. Norman Janes, b.1892. "Oban Quays." Artist's collection.

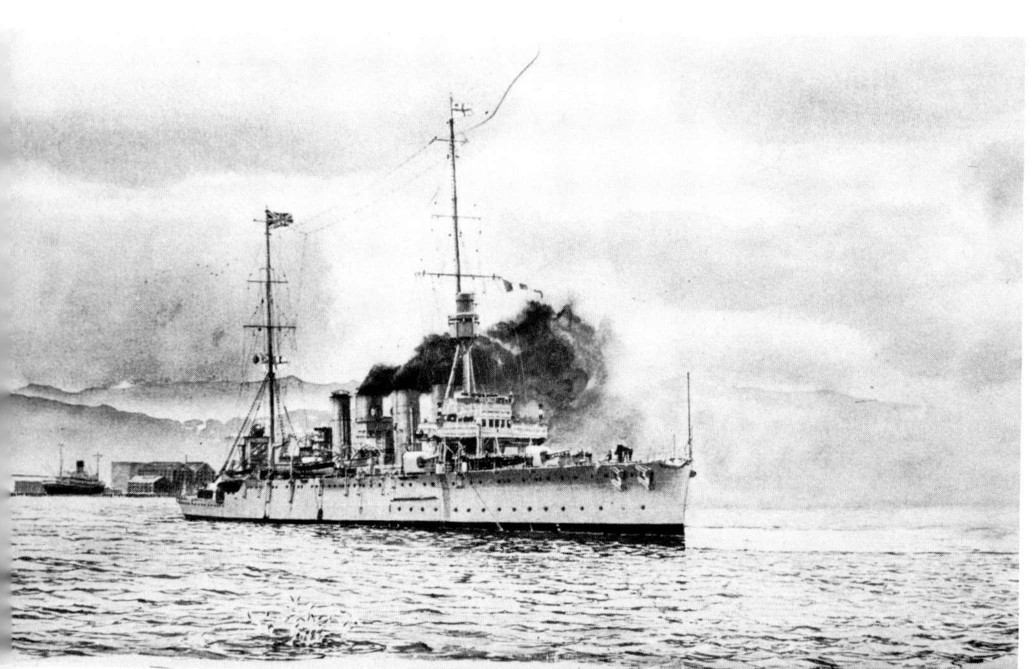

Plate 656. John A. Speer, b.1904. "H.M.N.Z.S. *Chatham.*" *Admiral of the Fleet, Viscount Jellicoe, when he was Governor General of New Zealand, 1920-24, is aboard the* Chatham. Artist's collection.

Plate 657. Vic Ellis, b.1921. "The Lower Thames in the 1930s." *Paddle steamers were seen on the Thames until the Second World War, while the Thames barges are still a regular sight.* Royal Society of Marine Artists (on loan to the National Maritime Museum, Greenwich).

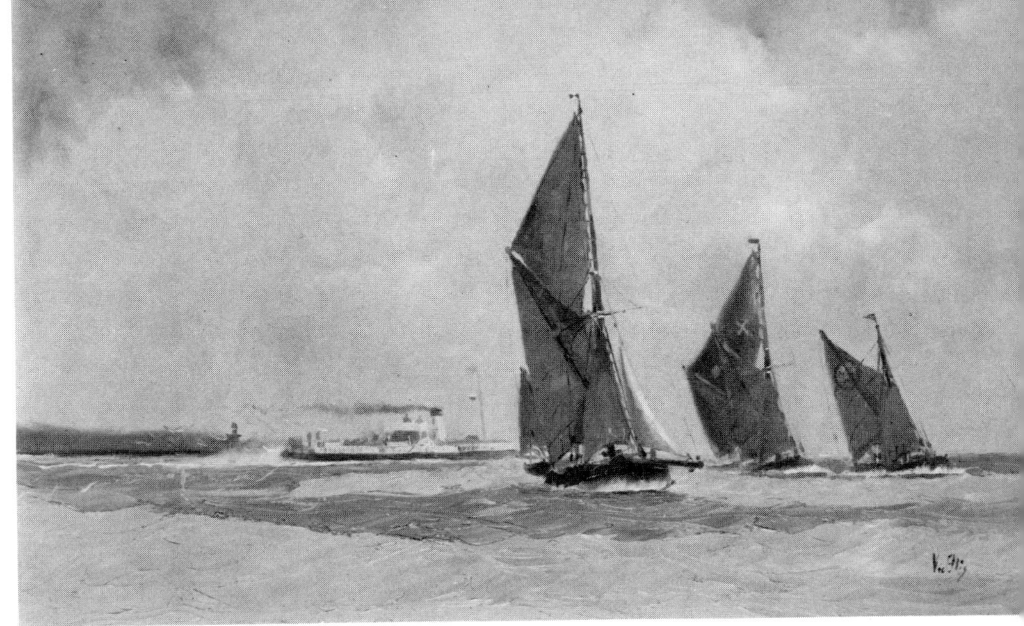

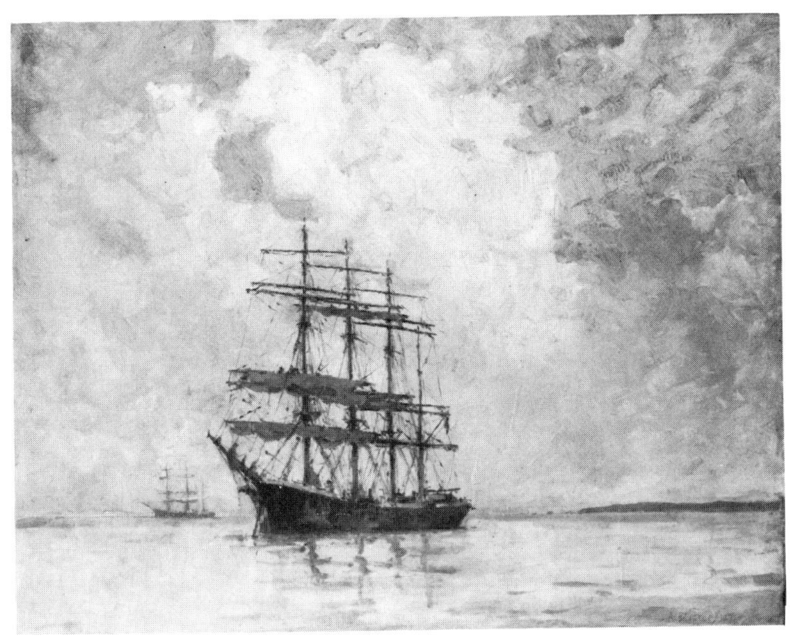

Plate 658. Arthur John Trevor Briscoe, 1873-1943. "The ship *Olivebank,* dated 1937." *Typical of the work of Briscoe who was an engraver as well as a painter.* Sotheby's.

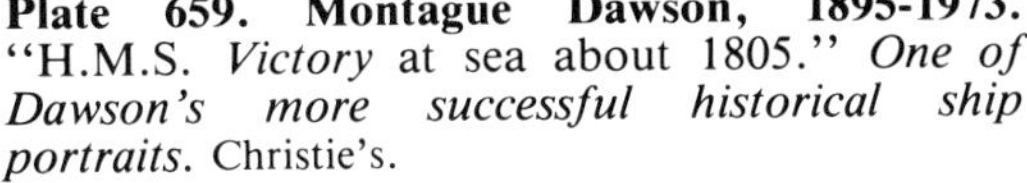

Plate 659. Montague Dawson, 1895-1973. "H.M.S. *Victory* at sea about 1805." *One of Dawson's more successful historical ship portraits.* Christie's.

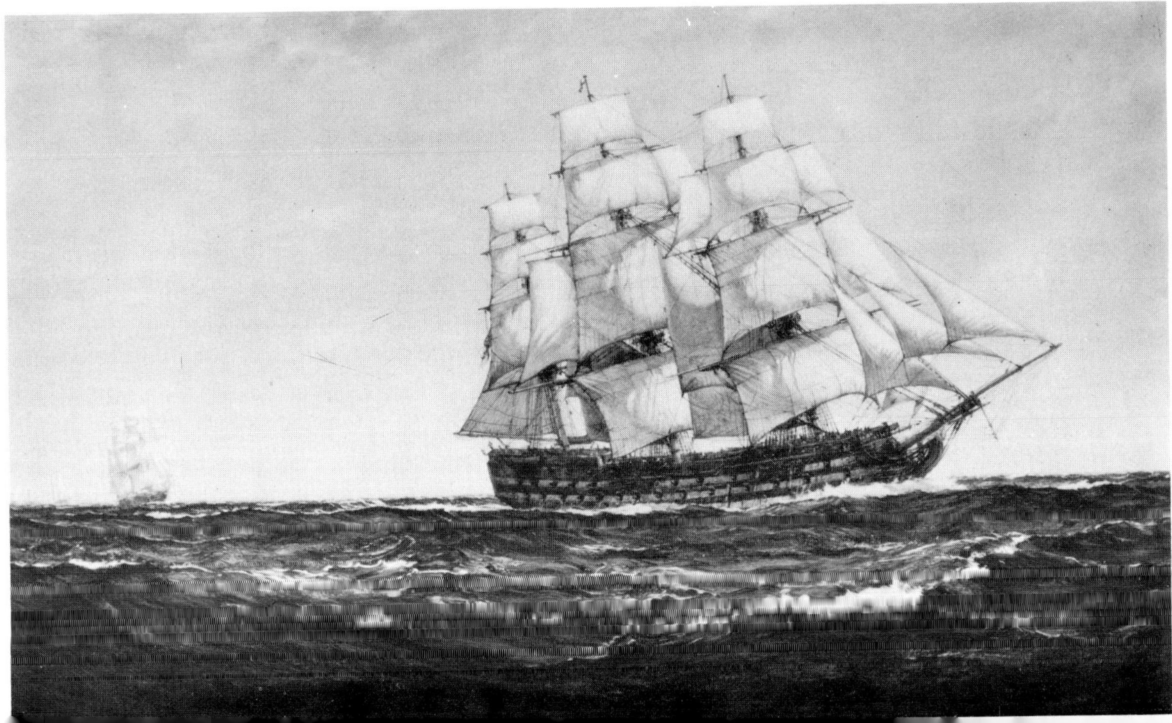

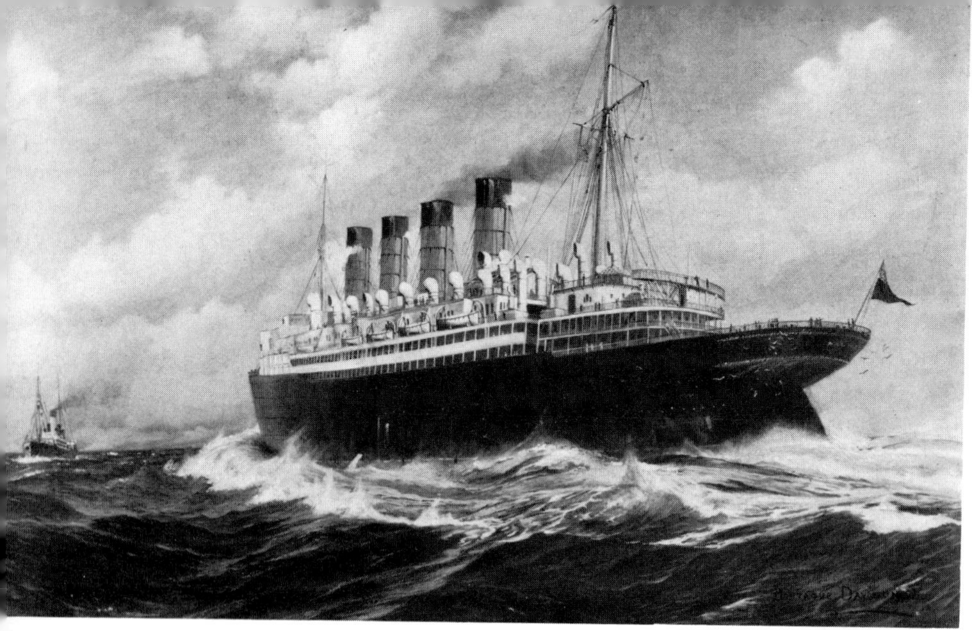

Plate 660. Montague Dawson, 1895-1973. "R.M.S. *Mauretania* about 1910." *An early work of the great Cunarder which held the Blue Riband for the Atlantic run from 1907 to 1929.* National Maritime Museum, Greenwich.

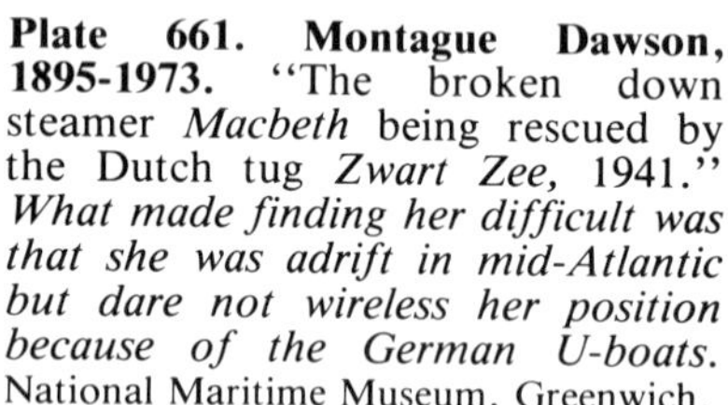

Plate 661. Montague Dawson, 1895-1973. "The broken down steamer *Macbeth* being rescued by the Dutch tug *Zwart Zee,* 1941." *What made finding her difficult was that she was adrift in mid-Atlantic but dare not wireless her position because of the German U-boats.* National Maritime Museum, Greenwich.

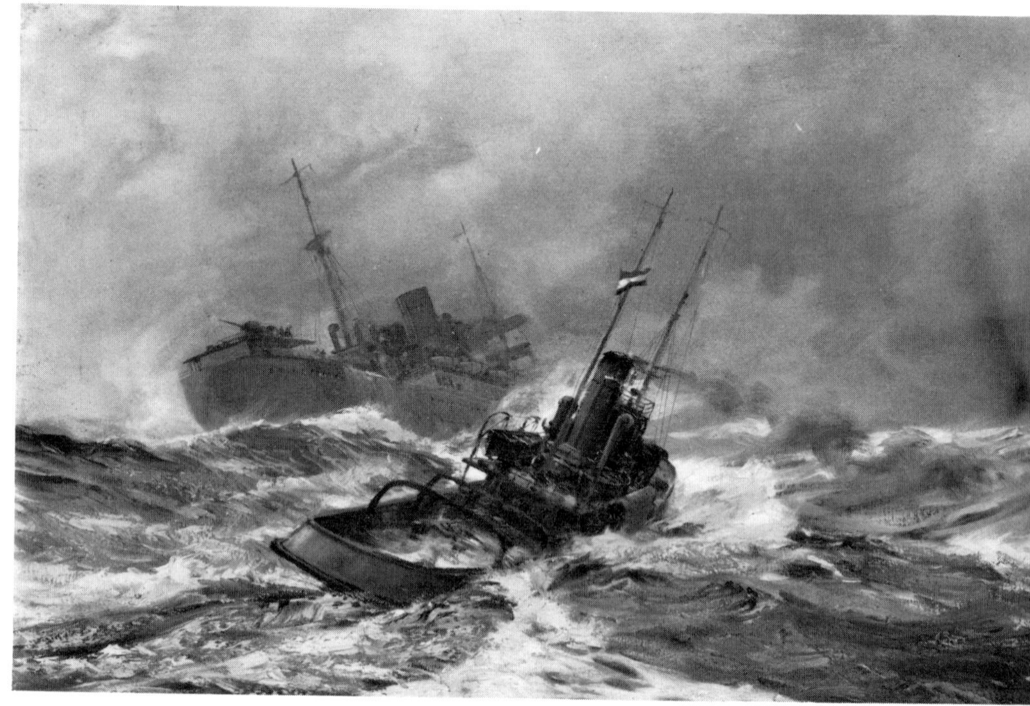

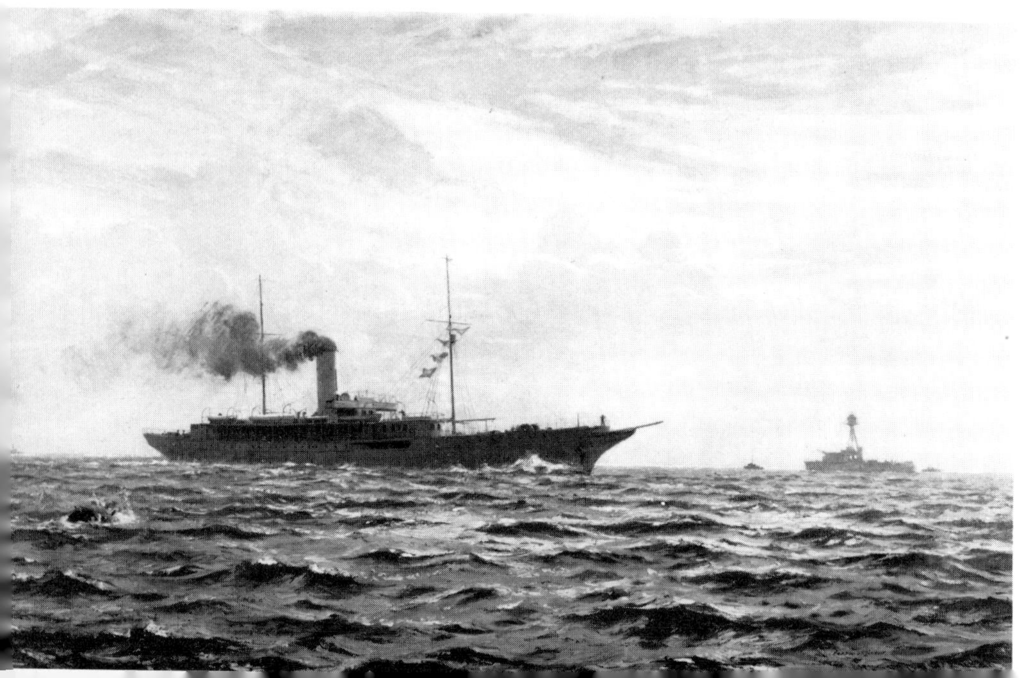

Plate 662. Norman Wilkinson, 1878-1971. "H.M.S. *Liberty* in the First World War." *At her launch at Leith in 1908 she was the seventh largest steam yacht in the world. She was built for the blind American publisher Joly Pulitzer and, after his death in 1911, she came back to Britain, served through the First World War and in the late 1920s and early 1930s was famous as the property of Lady Houston.* National Maritime Museum, Greenwich.

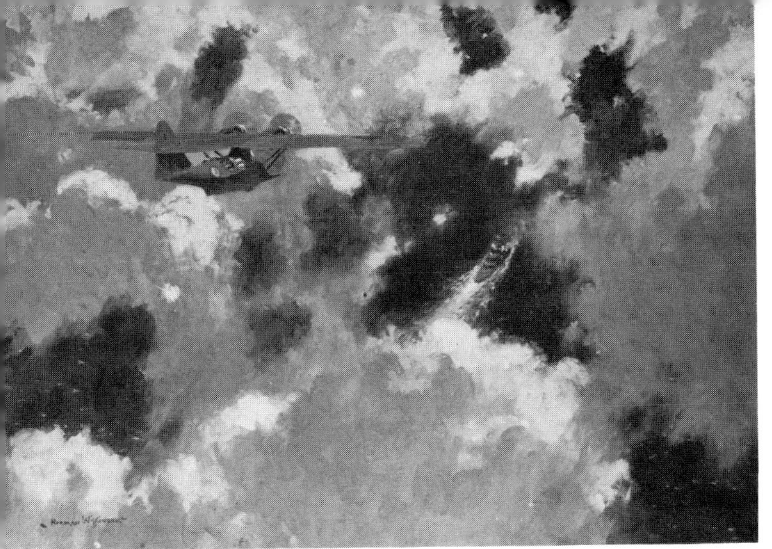

Plate 663. Norman Wilkinson, 1878-1971. A Catalina sighting the *Bismarck* in 1941.'' National Maritime Museum, Greenwich

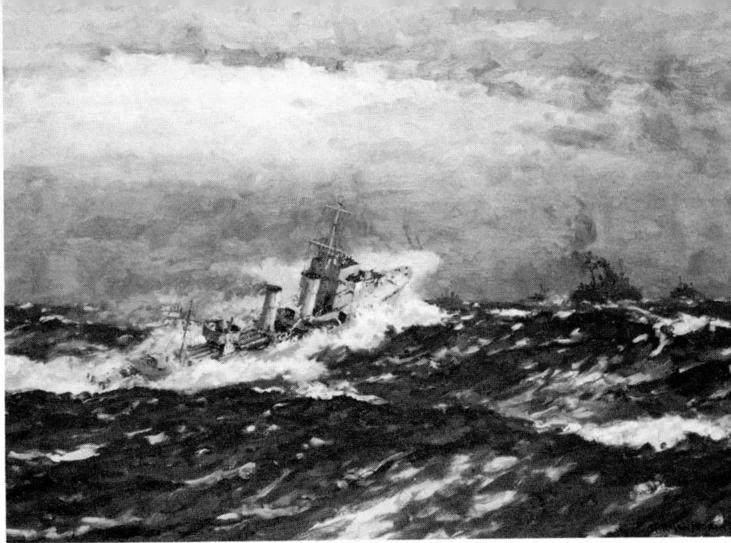

Plate 664. Norman Wilkinson, 1878-1971. ''Atlantic convoy.'' National Maritime Museum, Greenwich.

Plate 665. Norman Wilkinson, 1878-1971. ''The *Ohio* in the Malta convoy in 1942.'' National Maritime Museum, Greenwich.

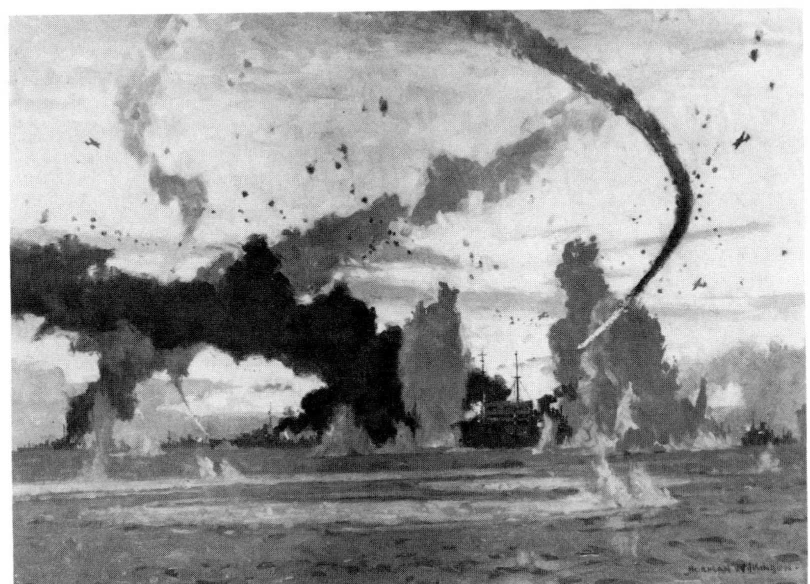

Plate 666. Roland John Robb Langmaid, c.1897-c.1960. ''Force H leaving Gibraltar in 1940.'' *Force H led by the battle cruiser* Renown, *followed by the aircraft carrier* Ark Royal. National Maritime Museum, Greenwich.

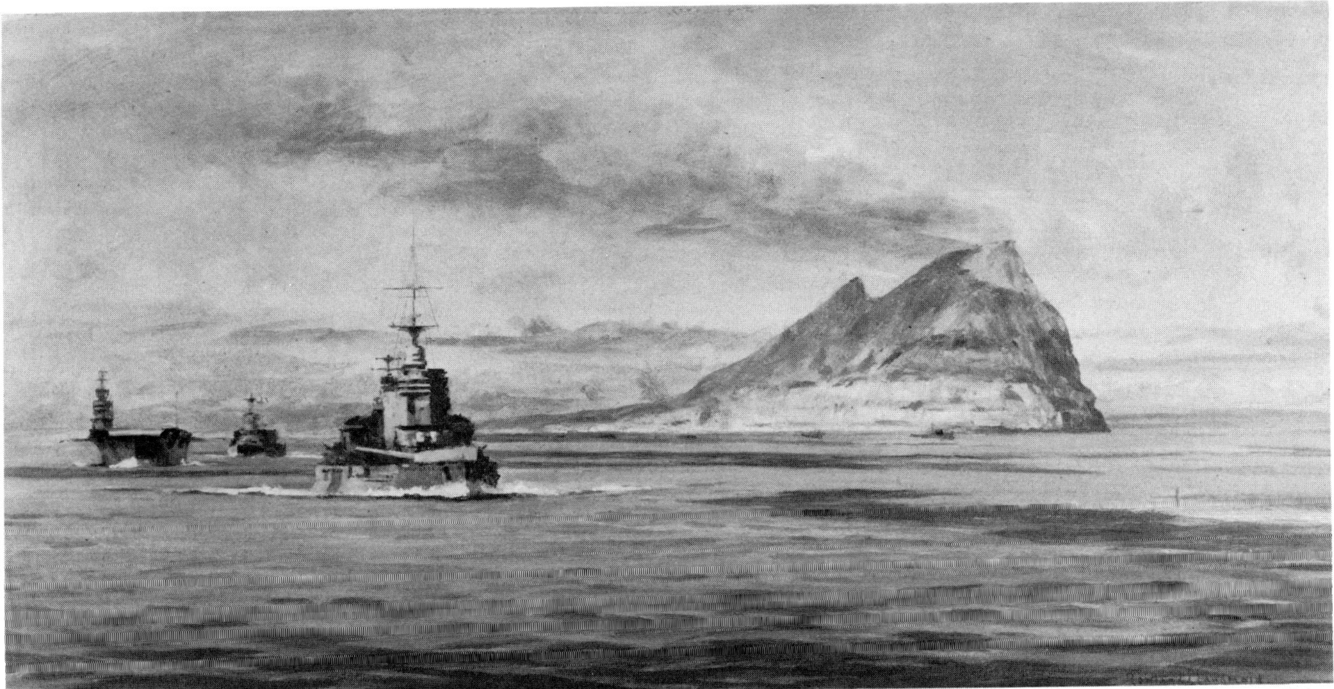

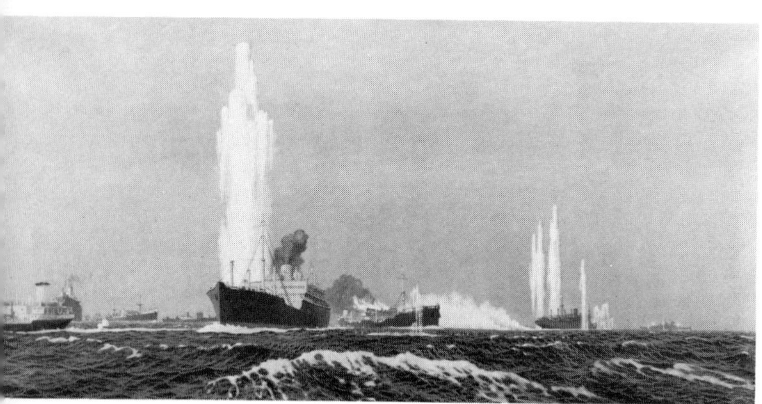

Plate 667. Charles Pears, 1873-1958. "The *Jervis Bay* Action, 1940." National Maritime Museum, Greenwich.

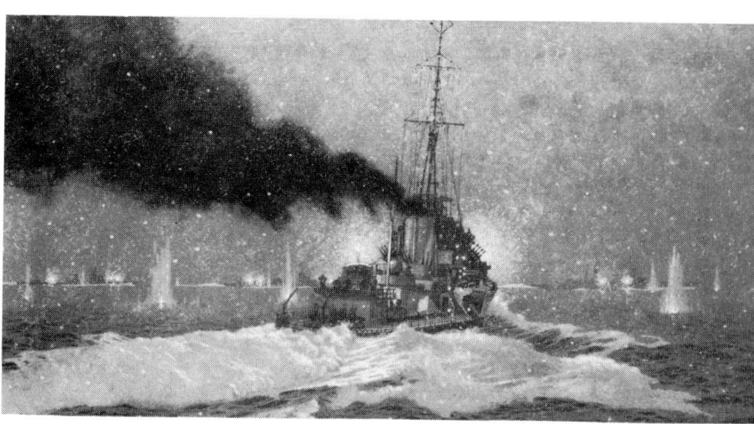

Plate 668. Charles Pears, 1873-1958. "Captain Sherbrooke's Action, 1942." National Maritime Museum, Greenwich.

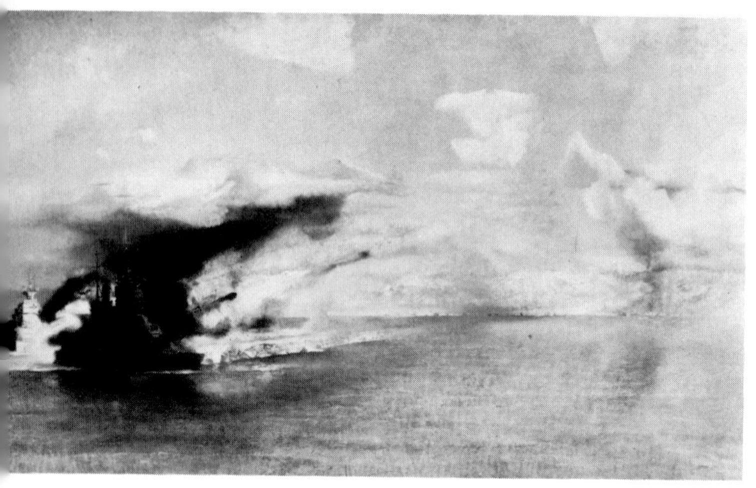

Plate 669. Richard Ernst Eurich, b.1903. "Battleships of the King George V class bombarding a port in the Second World War." *An extraordinarily dramatic and effective painting with an excellent use of colour.* National Maritime Museum, Greenwich.

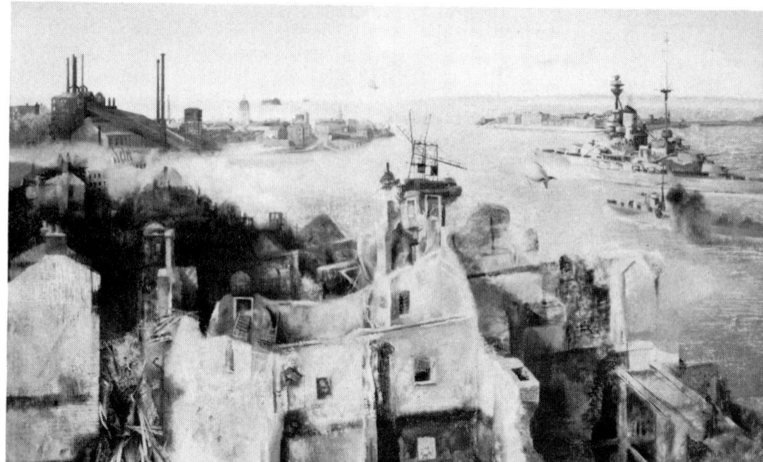

Plate 670. Richard Ernst Eurich, b.1903. "H.M.S. *Revenge* leaving Portsmouth after a raid, dated 1942." *The words 'Good old Bubbles V', under a representation of the famous Pear's picture, can just be seen in the centre foreground. The real 'Bubbles', Admiral Sir William James (Millais' grandson), was then C-in-C Portsmouth.* National Maritime Museum, Greenwich.

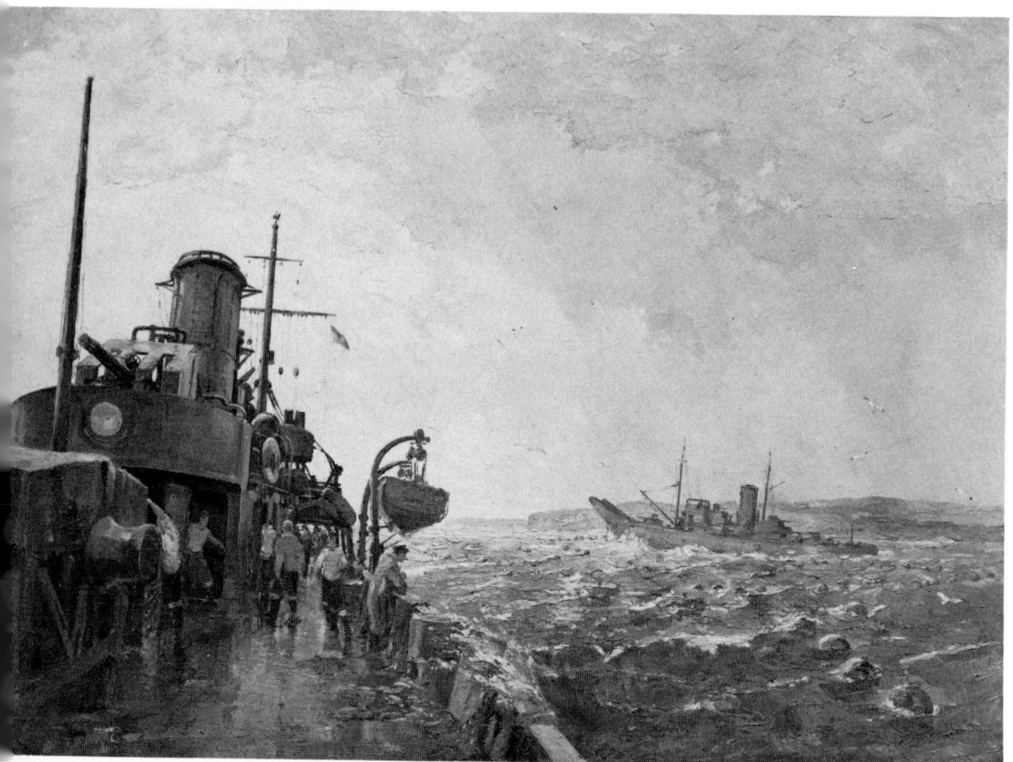

Plate 671. Charles Ernest Cundall, 1890-1971. "Boom defence ships, Second World War." *The booms supported heavy steel nets in order to keep submarines out of the path of shipping.* National Maritime Museum, Greenwich.

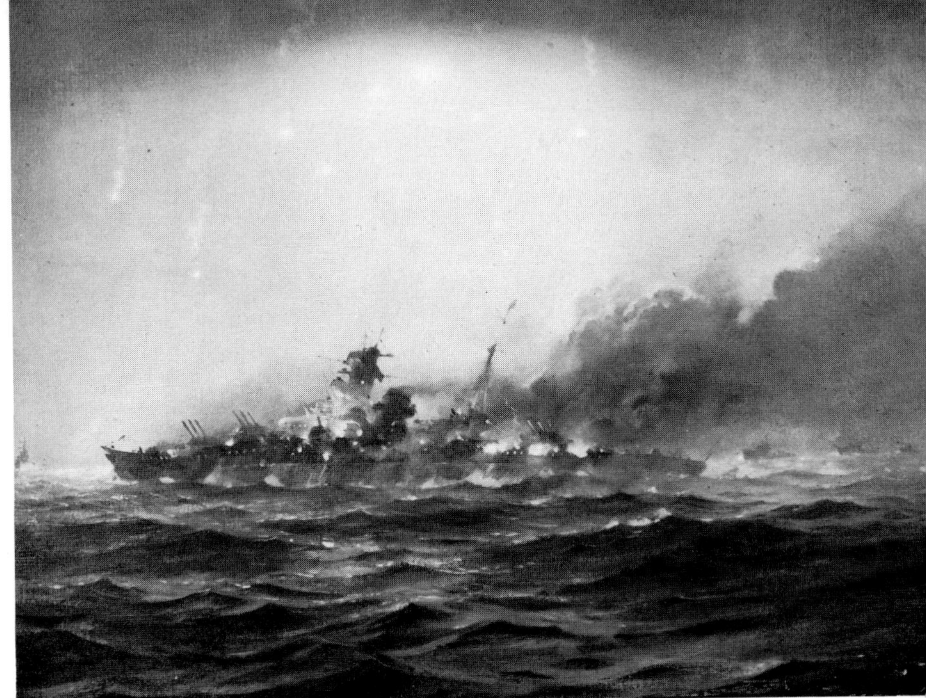

Plate 672. Charles E. Turner, 1883-1965. "The sinking of the *Scharnhorst,* 1943." National Maritime Museum, Greenwich.

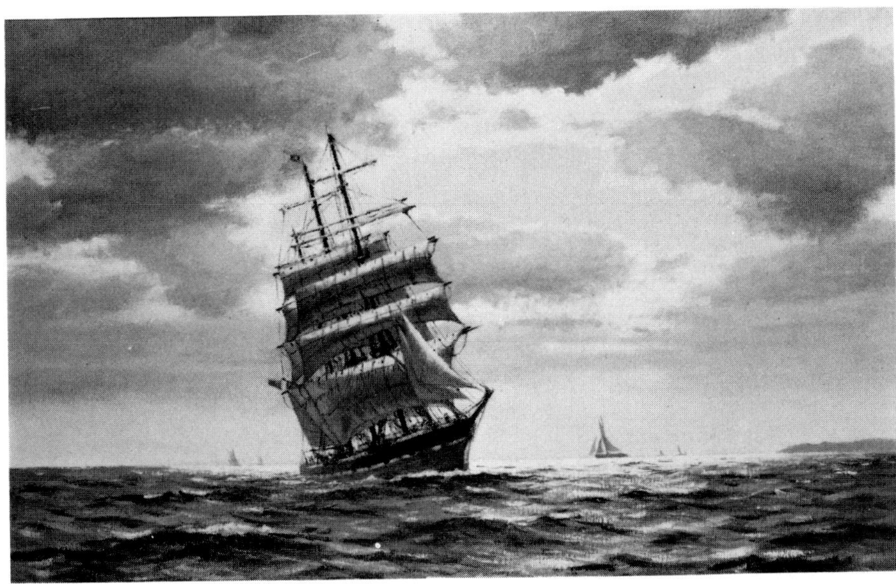

Plate 673. Roger Roland Sutton Fisher, b.1919. "The three-masted barque *Willscott* making a landfall off The Lizard." Artist's collection.

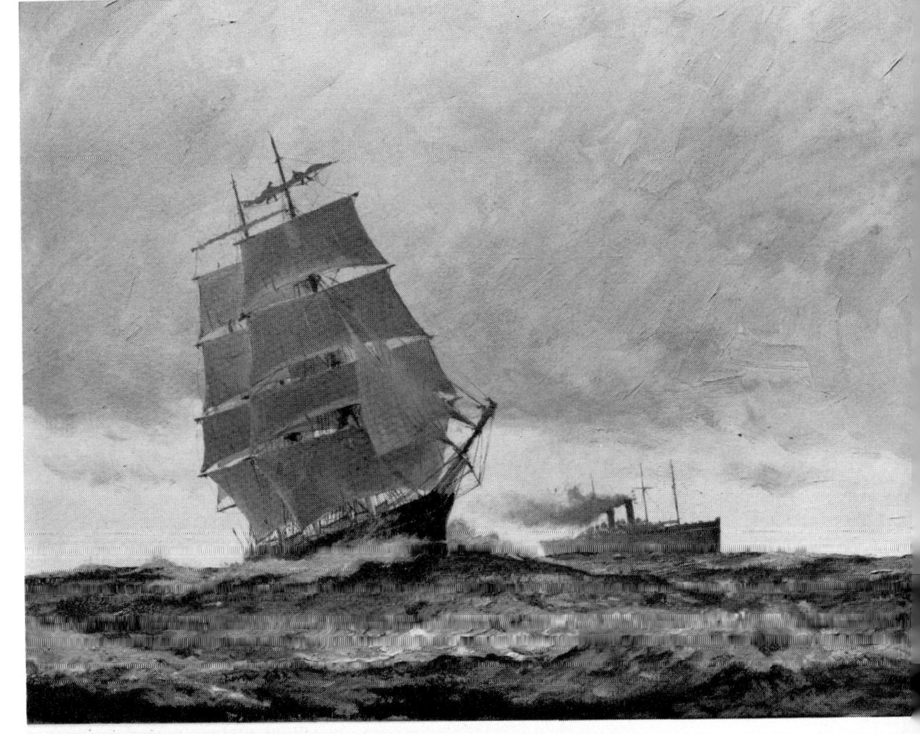

Plate 674. Charles David Cobb, b.1921. "The *Cutty Sark* and the liner *Britannia.*" *In 1889, on passage from Melbourne to Sydney, the wool clipper* Cutty Sark *was overtaken by the new P. & O. liner* Britannia *heading for the same port. That night it blew hard from the south and the watch keeper was surprised to see the lights of a sailing ship overhauling them. On the following morning the* Britannia *passed through Sydney Heads to find the* Cutty Sark *at anchor, sails furled.* Royal Society of Marine Artists (on loan to the National Maritime Museum, Greenwich).

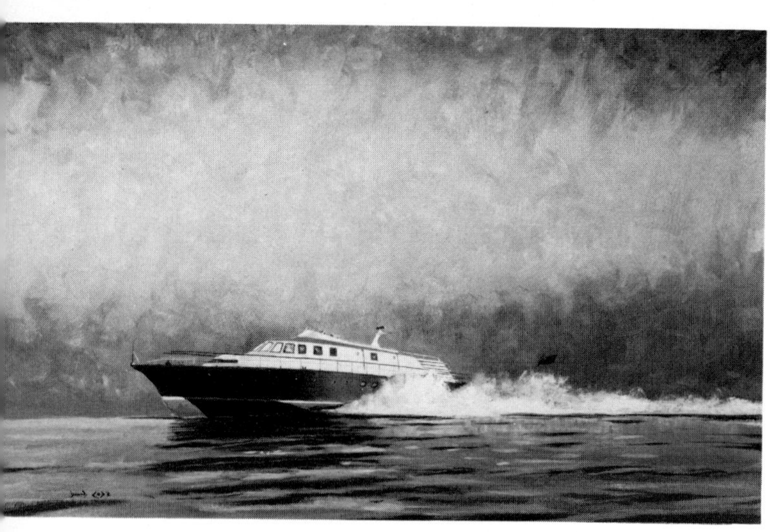

Plate 675. Charles David Cobb, b.1921. "The gas turbined engined yacht *Mercury.*" *Built by Vosper for Mr. Stavros Niarchos in 1960, she was an adaptation of the Brave class torpedo boats, which were capable of 55 knots, and were powered by three Proteus gas turbine engines.* National Maritime Museum, Greenwich.

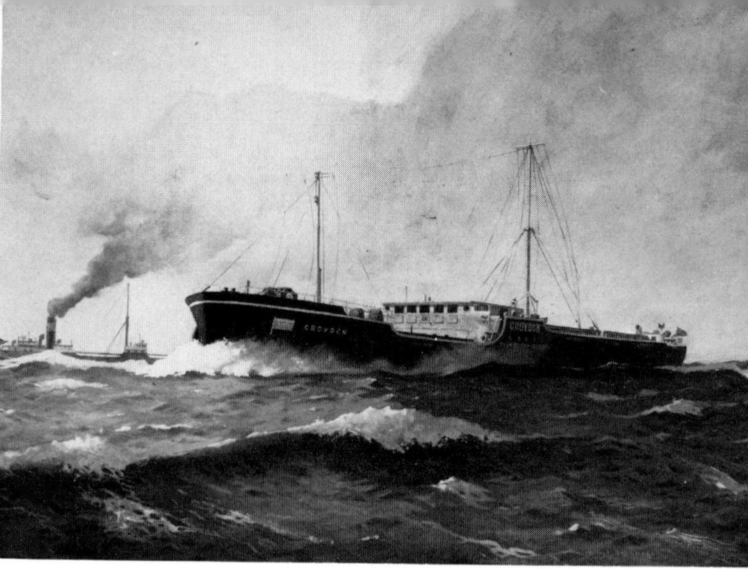

Plate 676. Southby Bramwell, fl. mid-20th century. "The flat iron collier *Croydon,* launched 1951." *The colliers which came up the Thames to London power stations had to have masts which collapsed to enable the ships to pass under the many bridges.* National Maritime Museum, Greenwich.

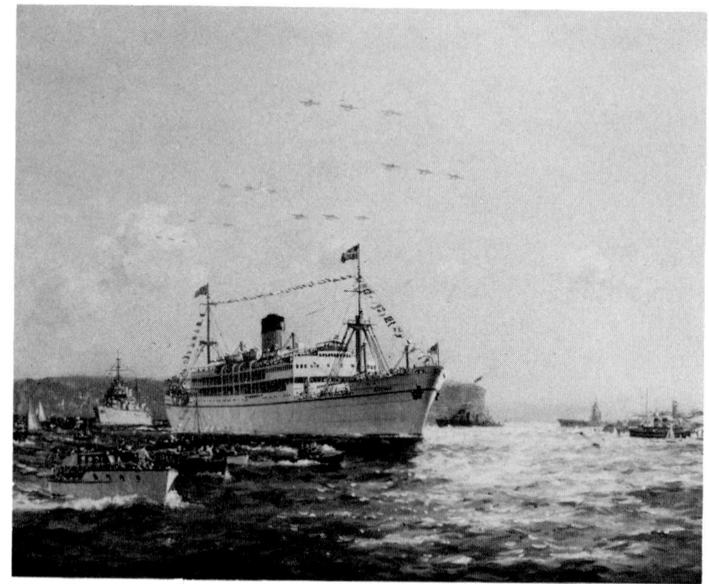

Plate 677. John Allcot, 1888-1973. "H.M. Queen Elizabeth arriving at Sydney in the *Gothic,* February 3rd, 1954." *Photo:* National Maritime Museum, Greenwich.

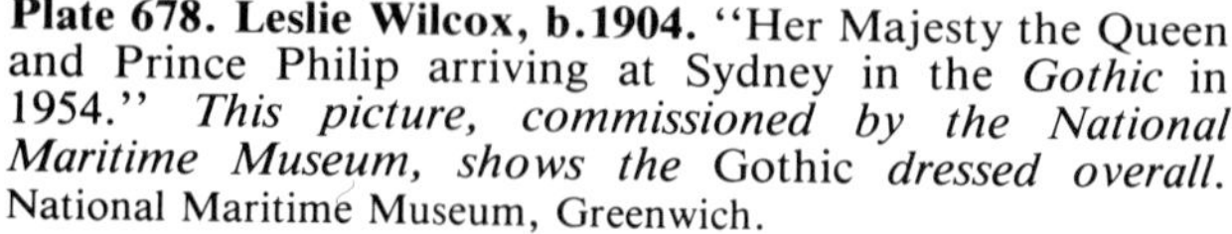

Plate 678. Leslie Wilcox, b.1904. "Her Majesty the Queen and Prince Philip arriving at Sydney in the *Gothic* in 1954." *This picture, commissioned by the National Maritime Museum, shows the* Gothic *dressed overall.* National Maritime Museum, Greenwich.

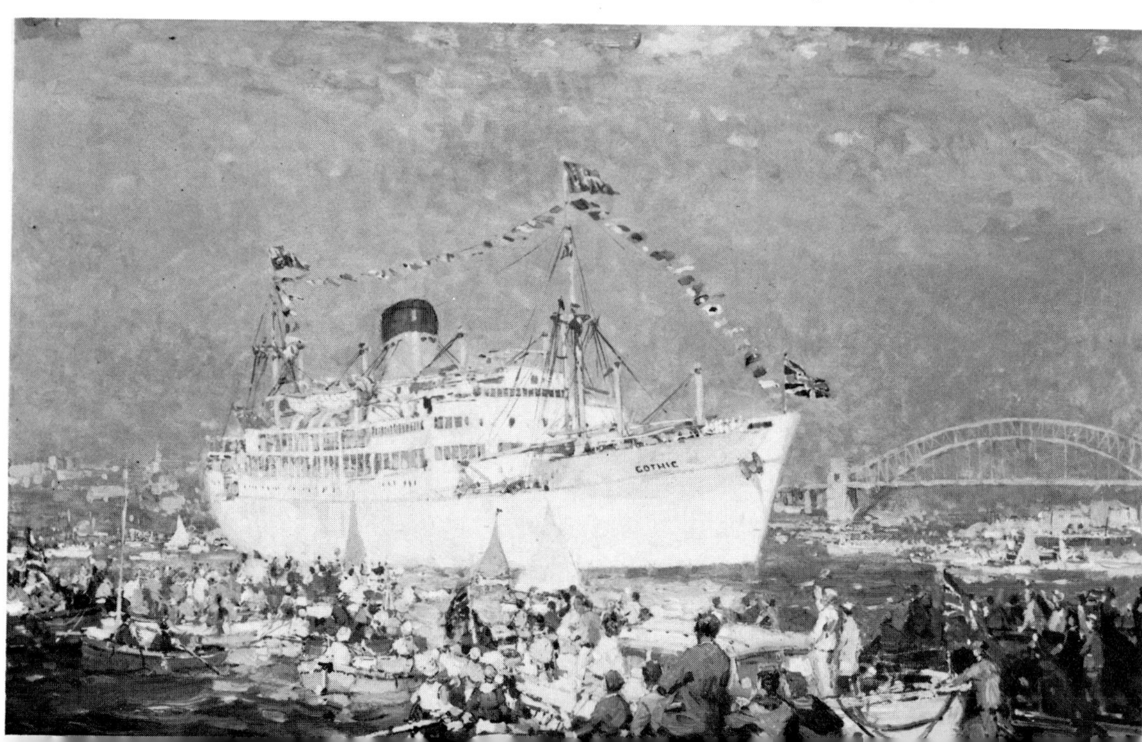

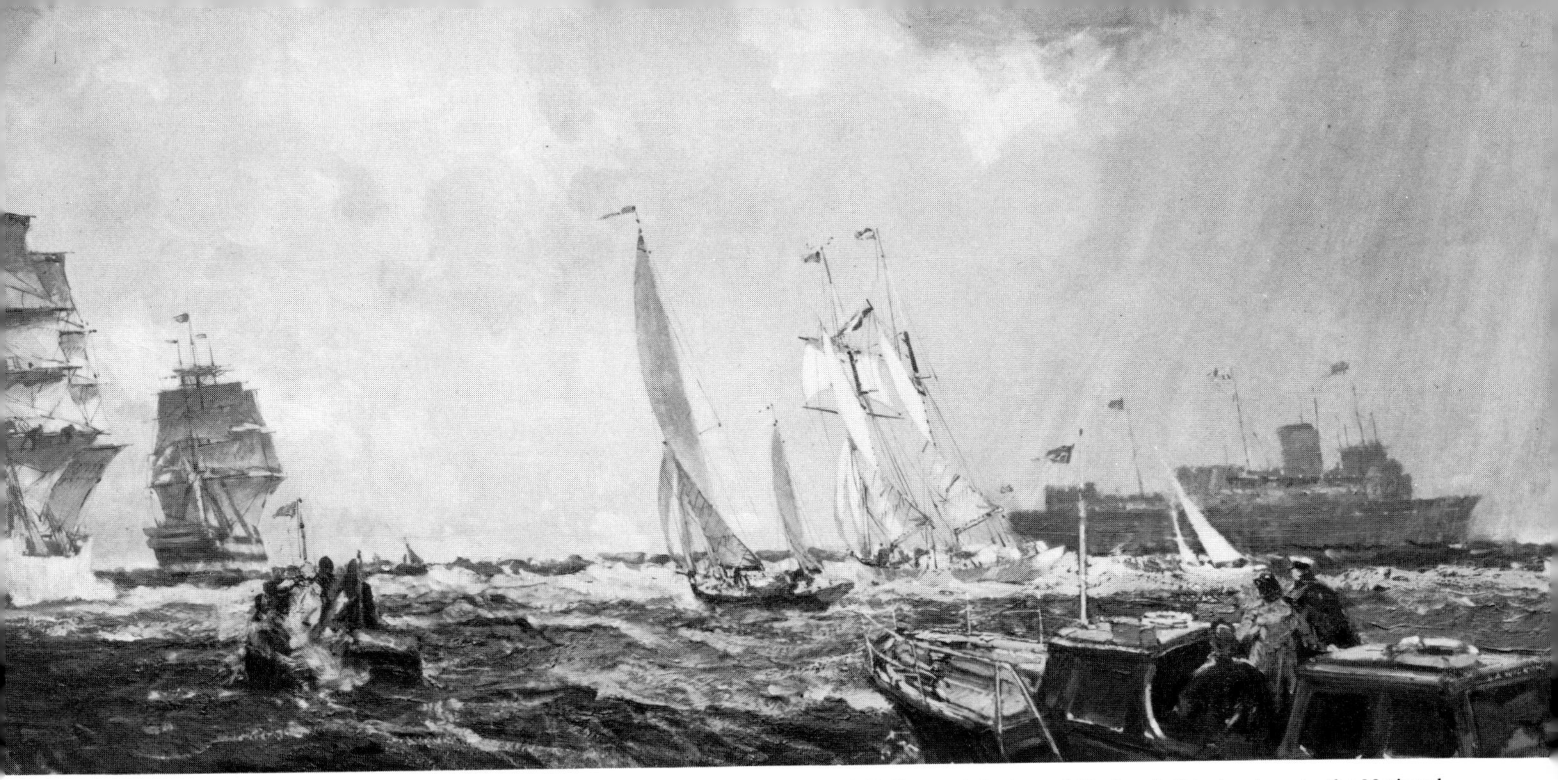

Plate 679. Leslie Wilcox, b.1904. "The start of the Tall Ships Race, 1962." Royal Society of Marine Artists (on loan to the National Maritime Museum, Greenwich).

Plate 680. John Stobart, b.1929. "H.M.Y. *Britannia* at the opening of the St. Lawrence Seaway in 1959." *On her mizzen-mast the Canadian flag, then the Royal and U.S. President's standards fly from the main mast.* National Maritime Museum, Greenwich.

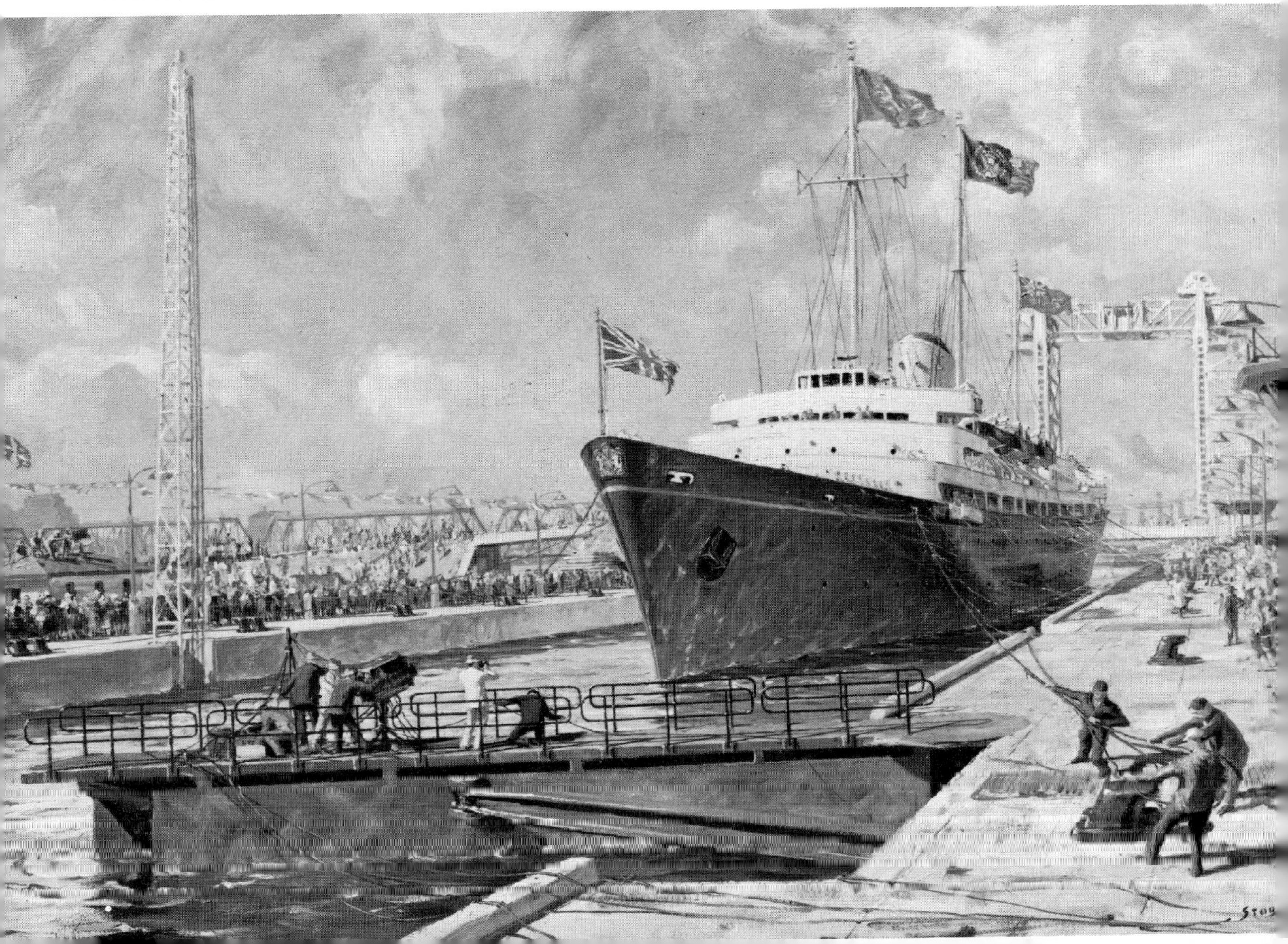

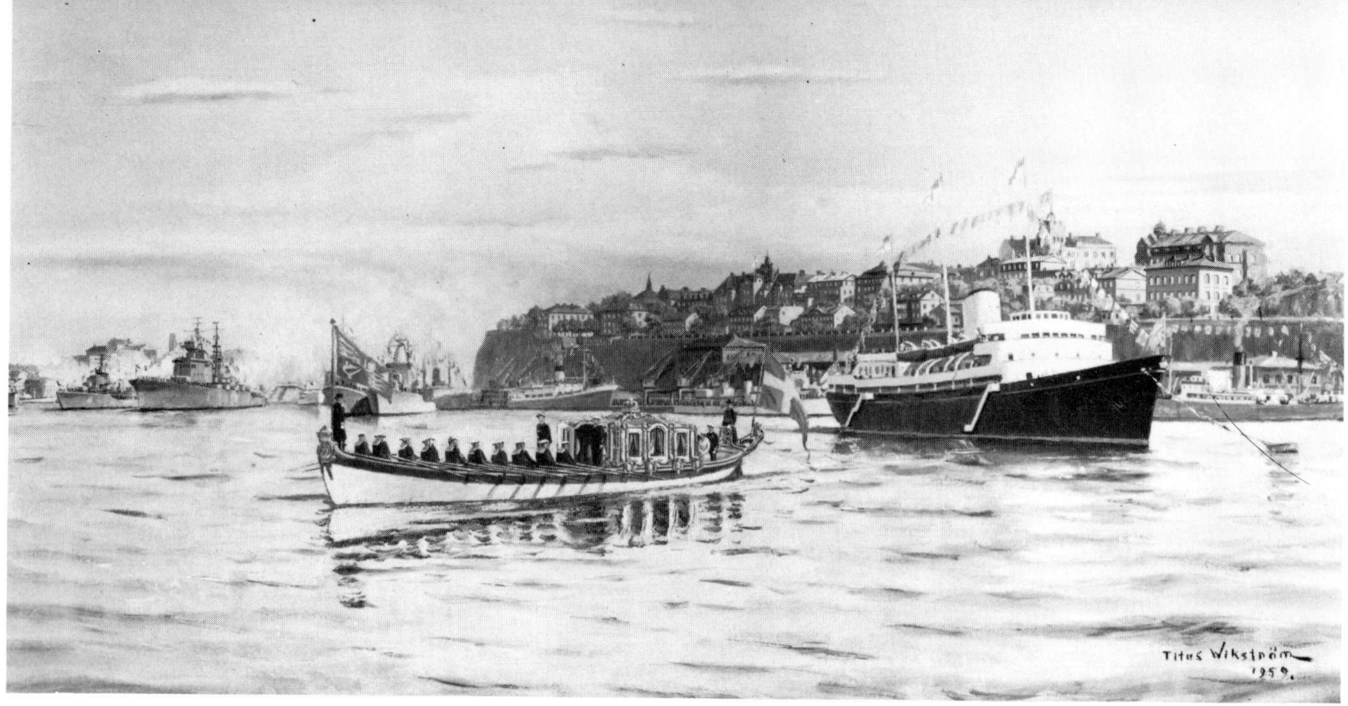

Plate 681. Titus Wikstrom, fl.1950. "Her Majesty the Queen and Prince Philip arriving at Stockholm in 1956." Royal Collection (on loan to the National Maritime Museum, Greenwich).

Plate 682. Derek George Montague Gardner, b.1914. "The ship *Garthpool,* dated 1967." *The artist has conveyed particularly well the poor visibility.* National Maritime Museum, Greenwich.

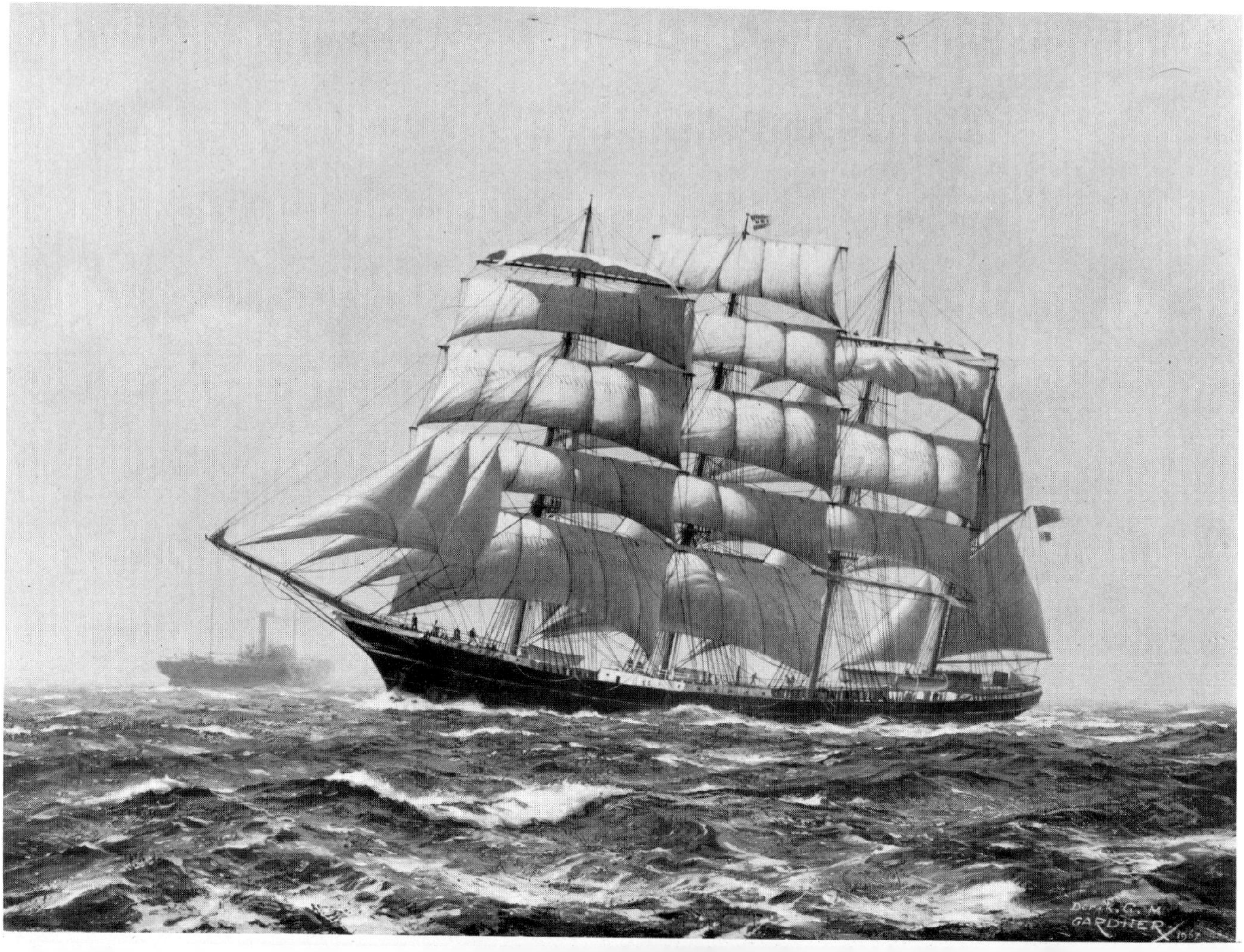

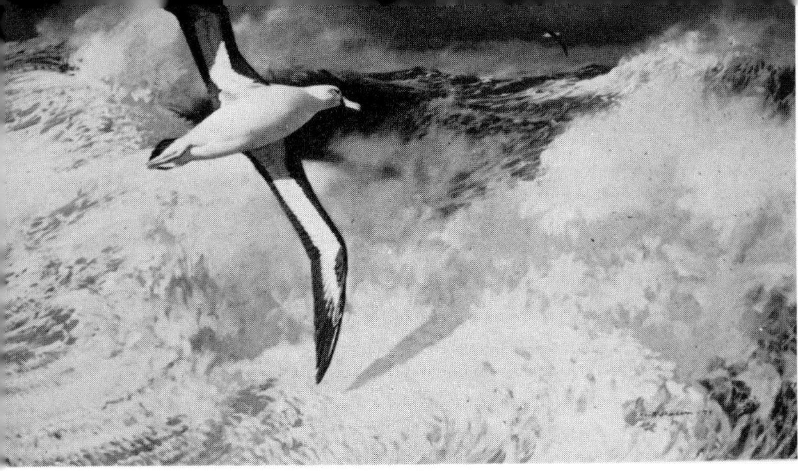

Plate 683. Keith Shackleton, b.1923. "The wandering albatross, dated 1974." Artist's collection.

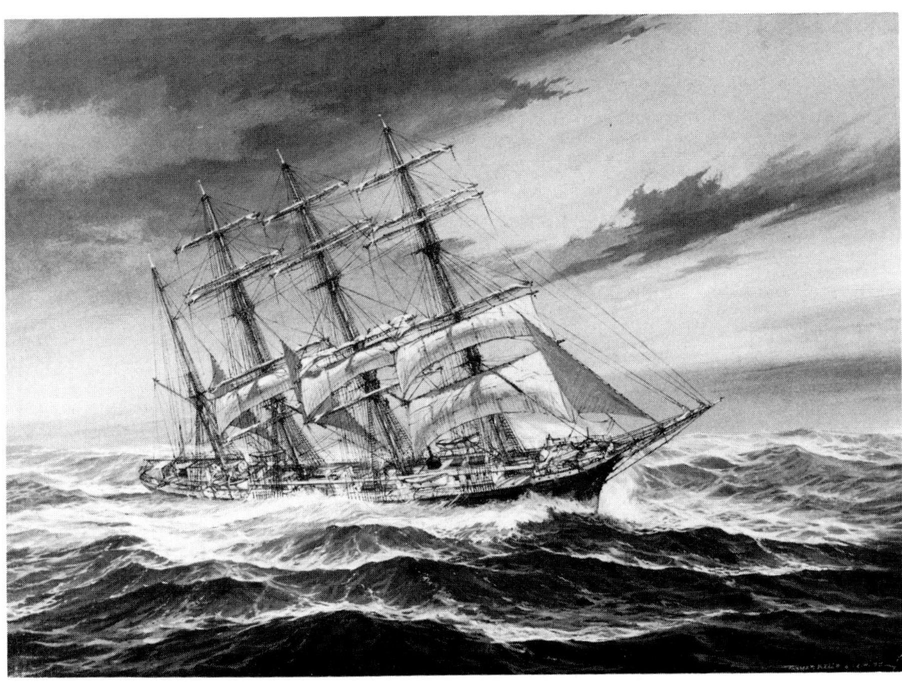

Plate 684. Thomas Winchester Wells, b.1916. " 'Cape Horner Down Under', painted 1975." Artist's collection.

Plate 685. Oswald Longfield Brett, b.1921. "The U.S. frigate *Congress* in New York Harbour in 1853, dated 1966." Seamen's Bank for Savings, New York.

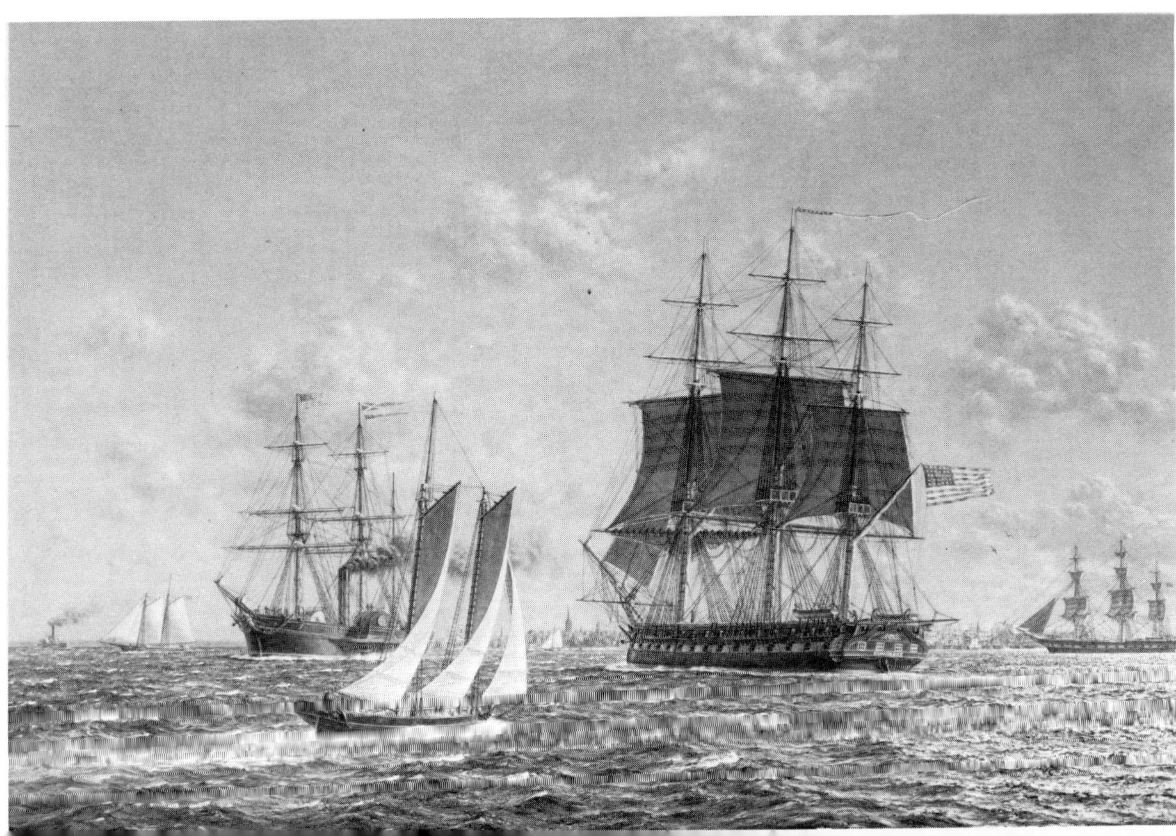

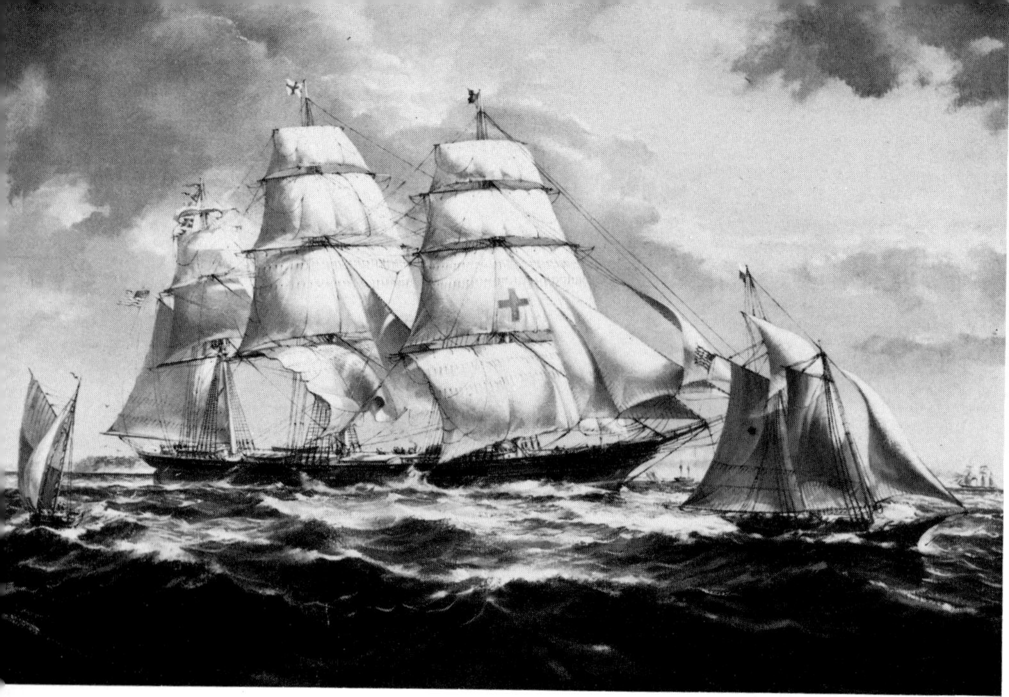

Plate 686. Robert Back, b.1922. "The *Dreadnought* parts with her pilot off Sandy Hook." *The cross on the mainsail is probably a company symbol.* Atlantic Gallery, Washington.

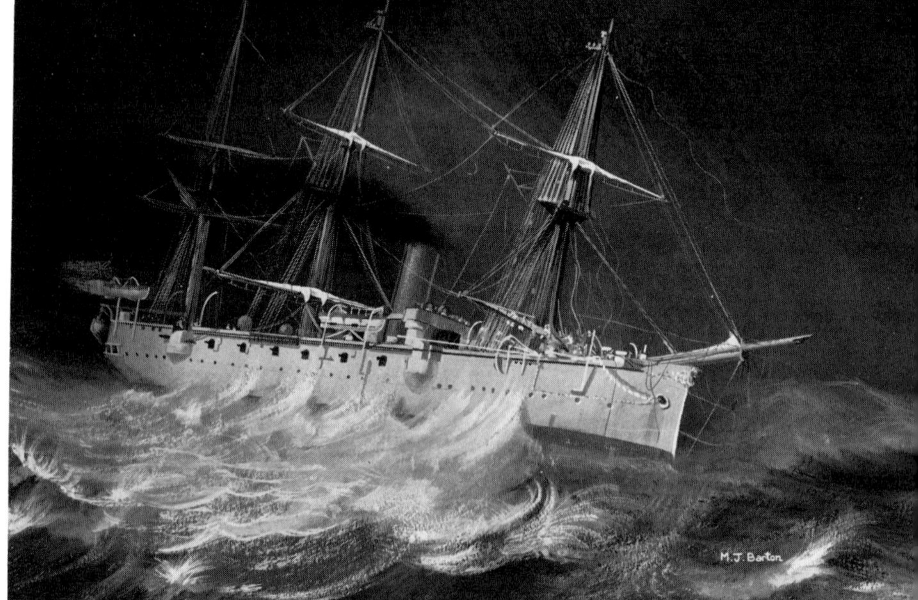

Plate 687. Mike J. Barton, 1933. H.M.S. *Calliope* weathering the hurricane at Apia in 1889." *A sea class cruiser she weathered the famous Pacific storm, but two German gun boats and an American cruiser were not so fortunate.* Artist's collection.

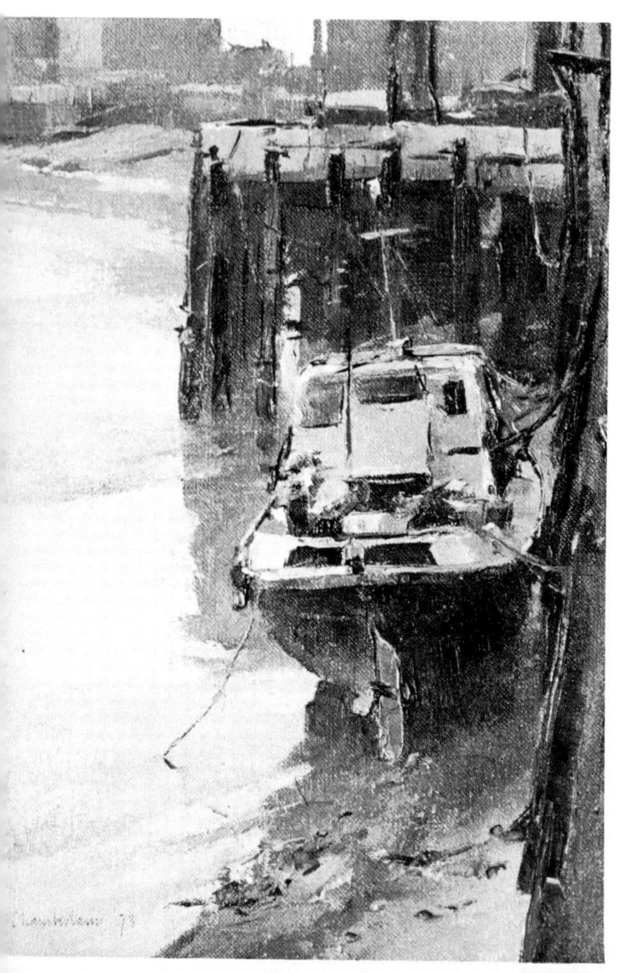

Plate 688. Trevor Chamberlain, b.1933. "Low Water, Rotherhithe." Artist's collection.

Plate 689. Hugh Boycott-Brown, b.1909. "Before the start, Blakeney, Norfolk, 1977." *A typical work both of the artist and the period.* Artist's collection.

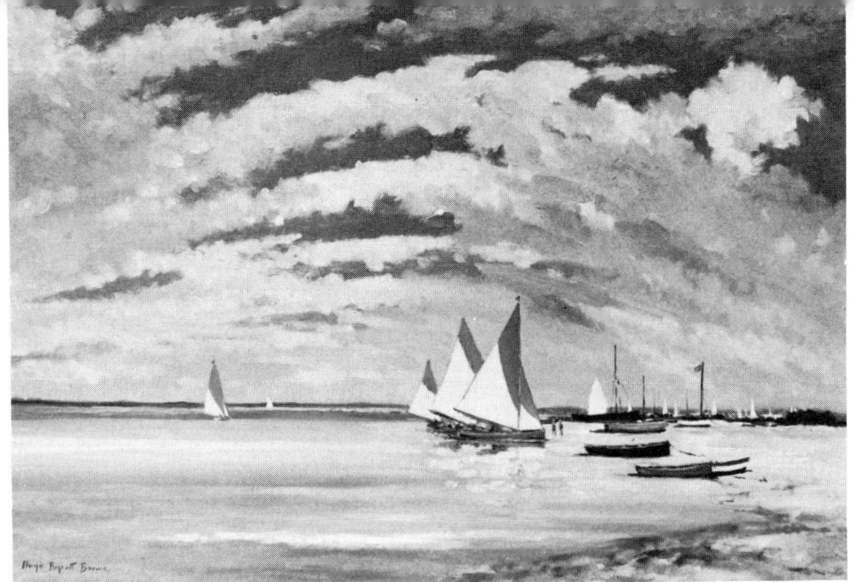

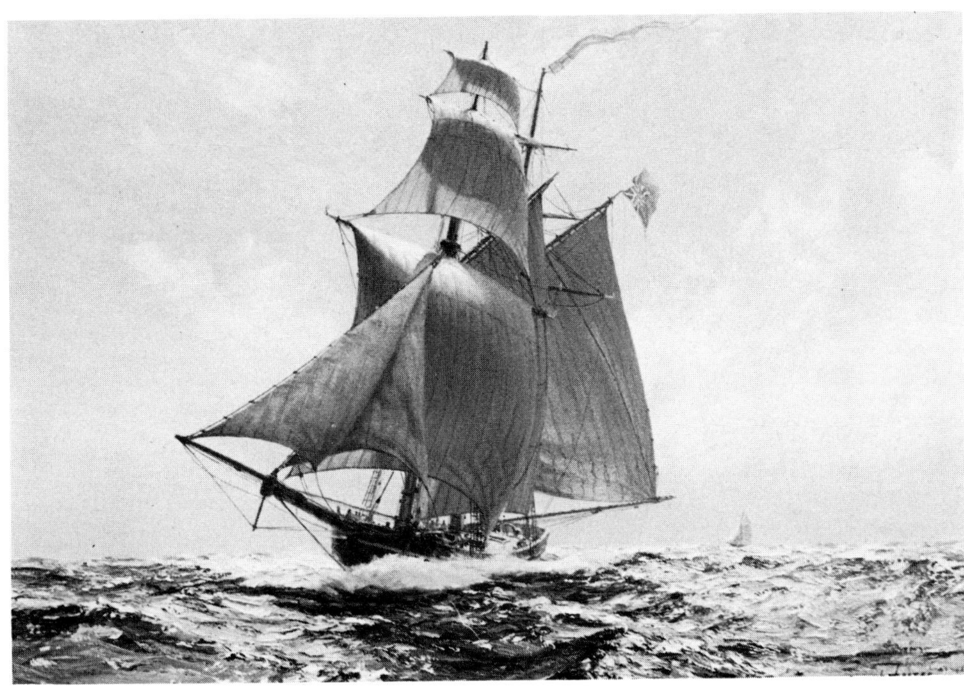

Plate 690. Deryck Foster, b.1924. "*Fast Lady,* a schooner of the Royal Navy about 1794, dated 1977." Artist's collection.

Plate 691. Mark Richard Myers, b.1945. "The barque *Epsilon* of Swansea nearing Cape Horn, dated 1977." Artist's collection.

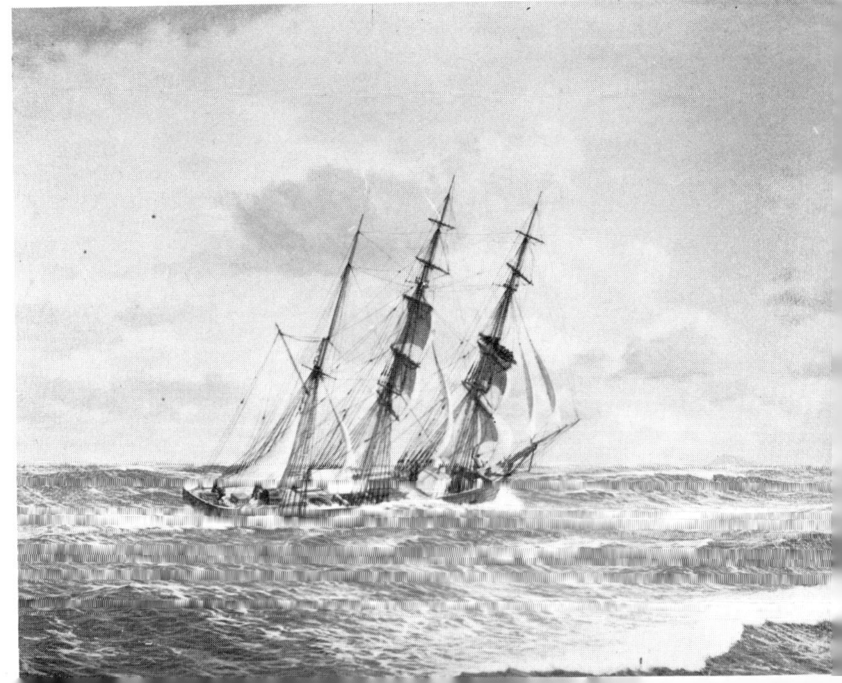

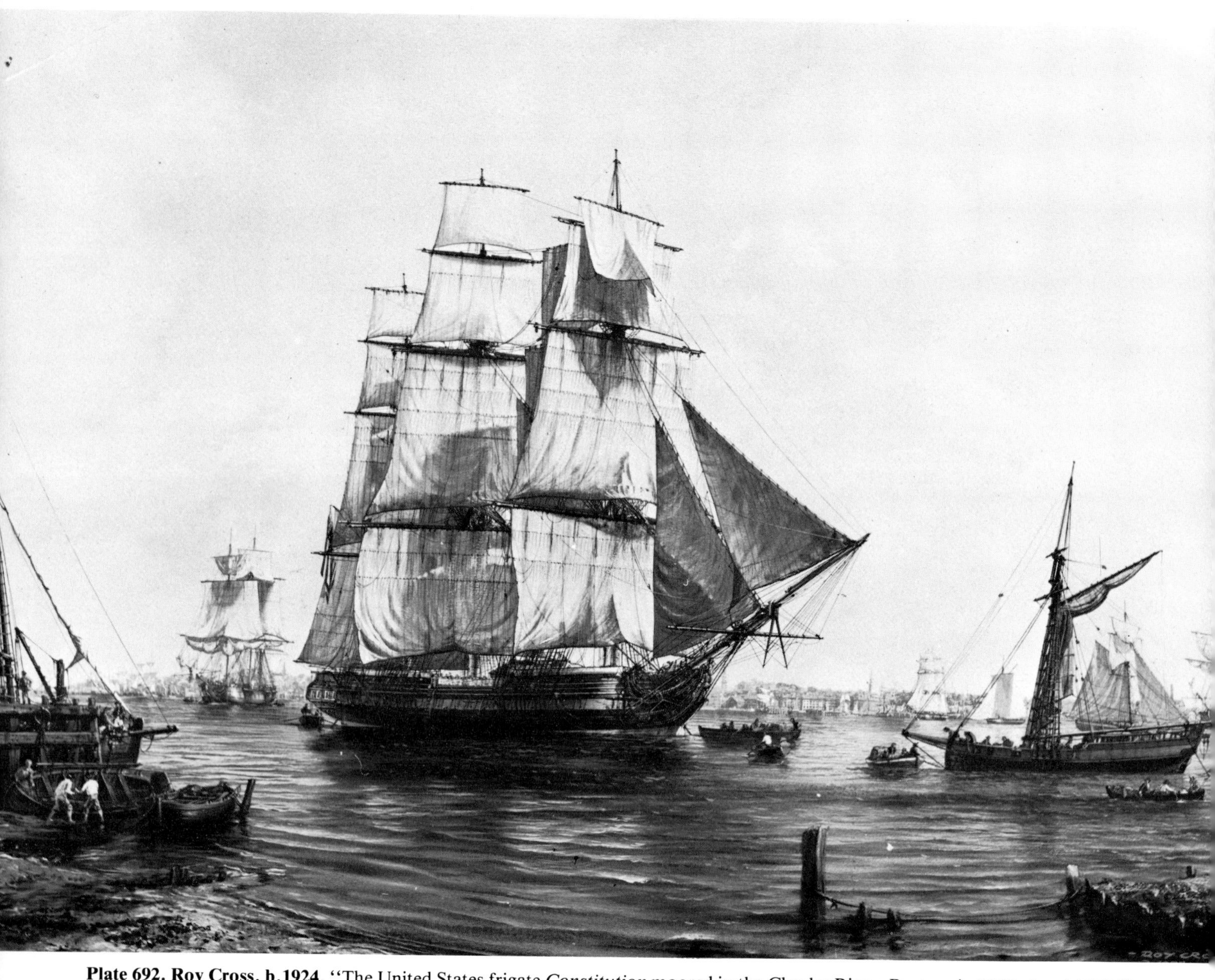

Plate 692. Roy Cross, b.1924. "The United States frigate *Constitution* moored in the Charles River, Boston, in 1803, dated 1978." Artist's collection.

Plate 693. **Kenneth Denton, b.1932.** "Low tide at Pinmill." Artist's collection.

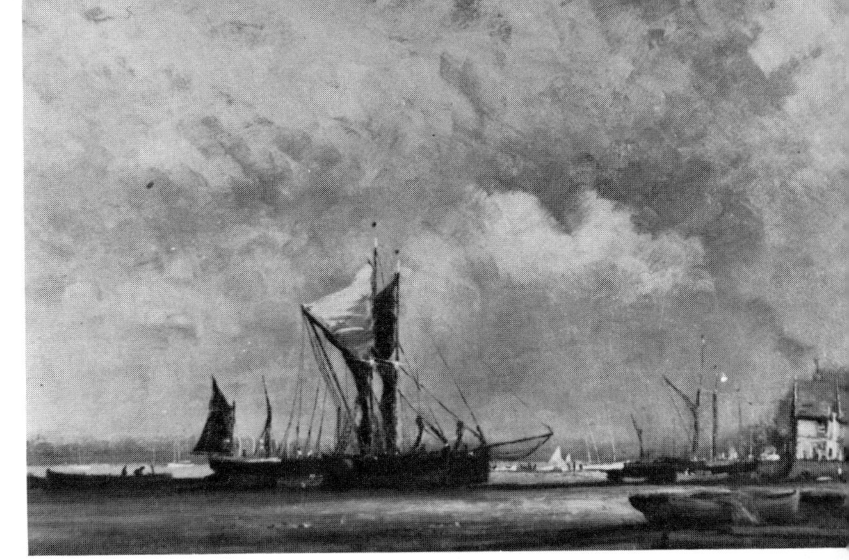

Plate 694. Sybil Mullen Glover, fl. late 20th century. "Off Plymouth Sound." Plymouth Museum and Art Gallery.

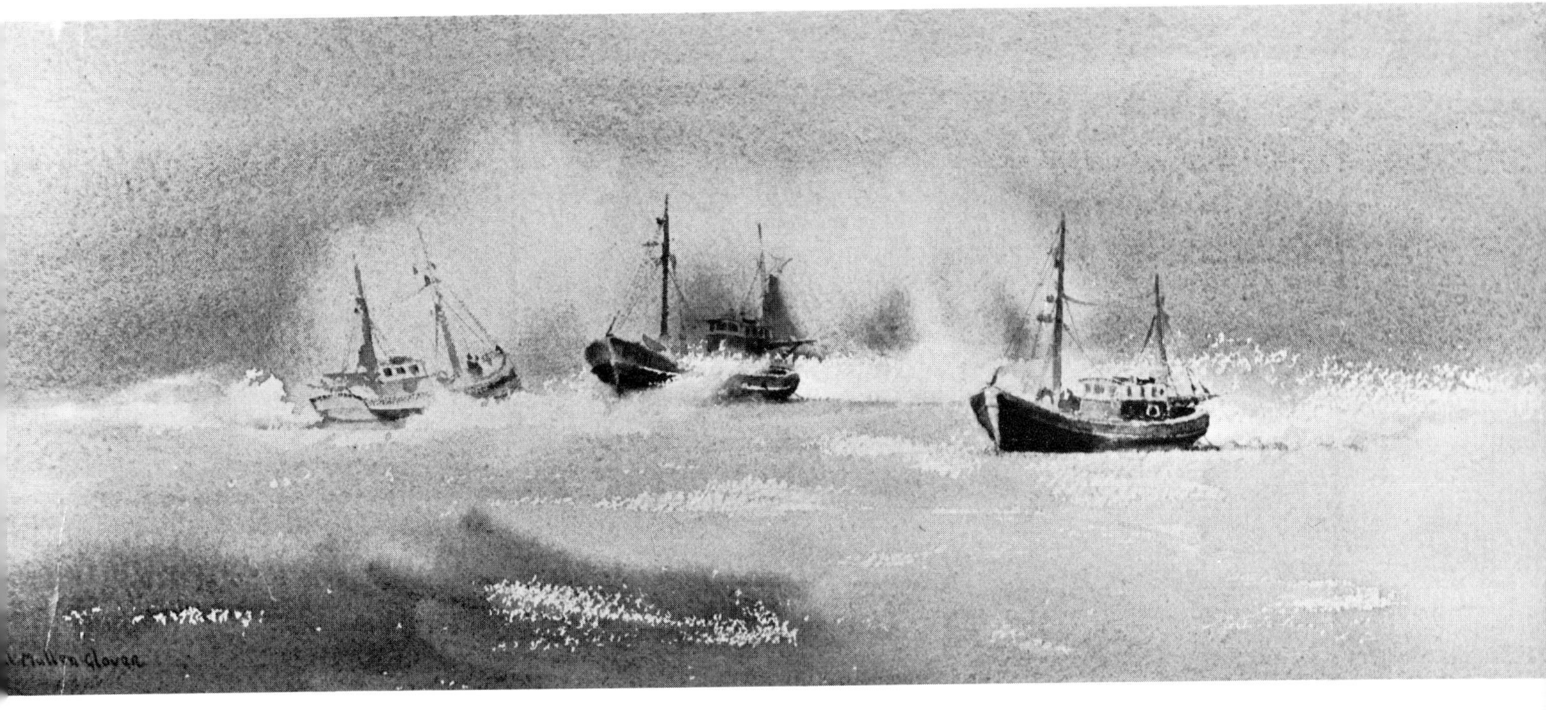

Plate 695. Louis Dodd, fl. late 20th century. "A ketch rigged royal yacht and sixth rate off Greenwich." Sotheby's.

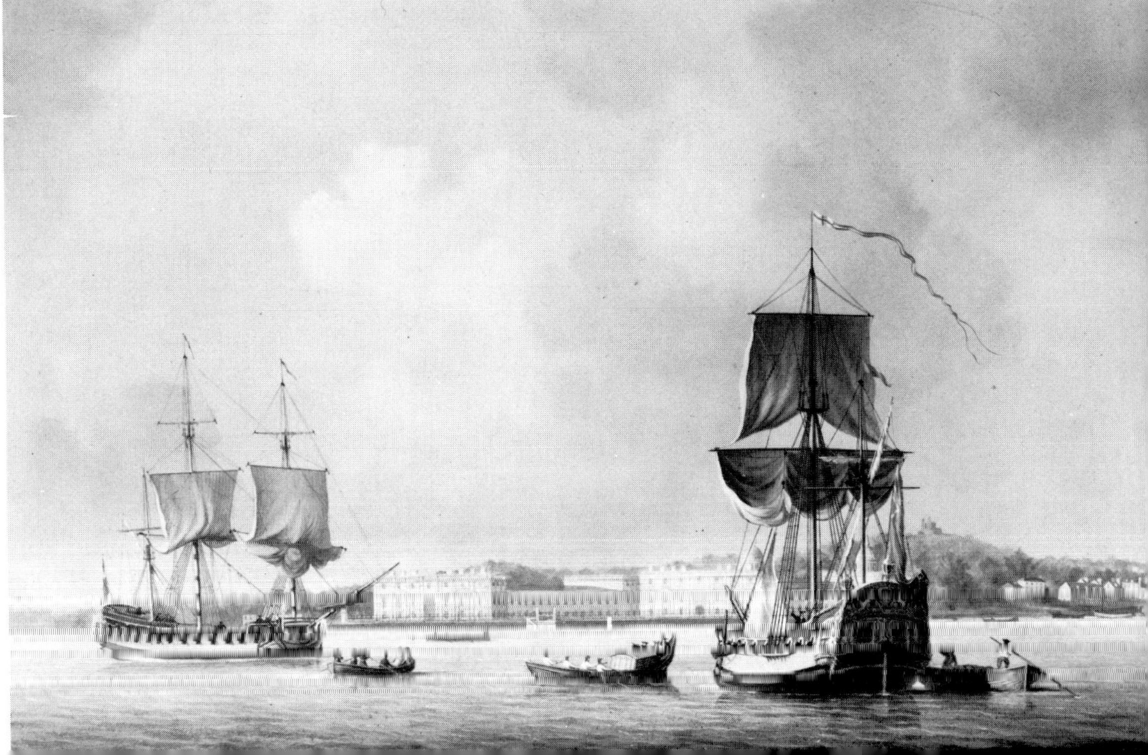

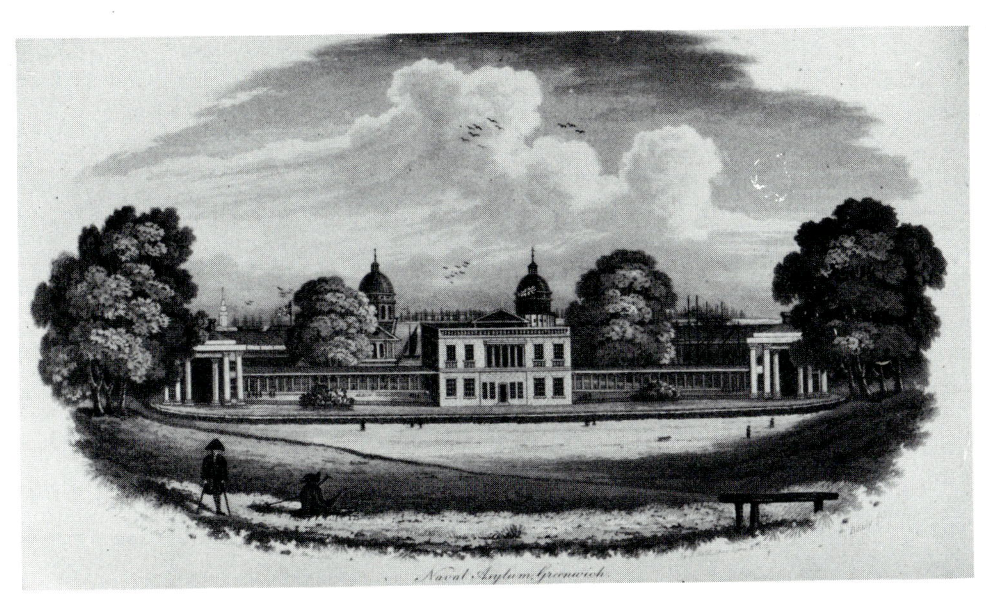
Naval Asylum, Greenwich.

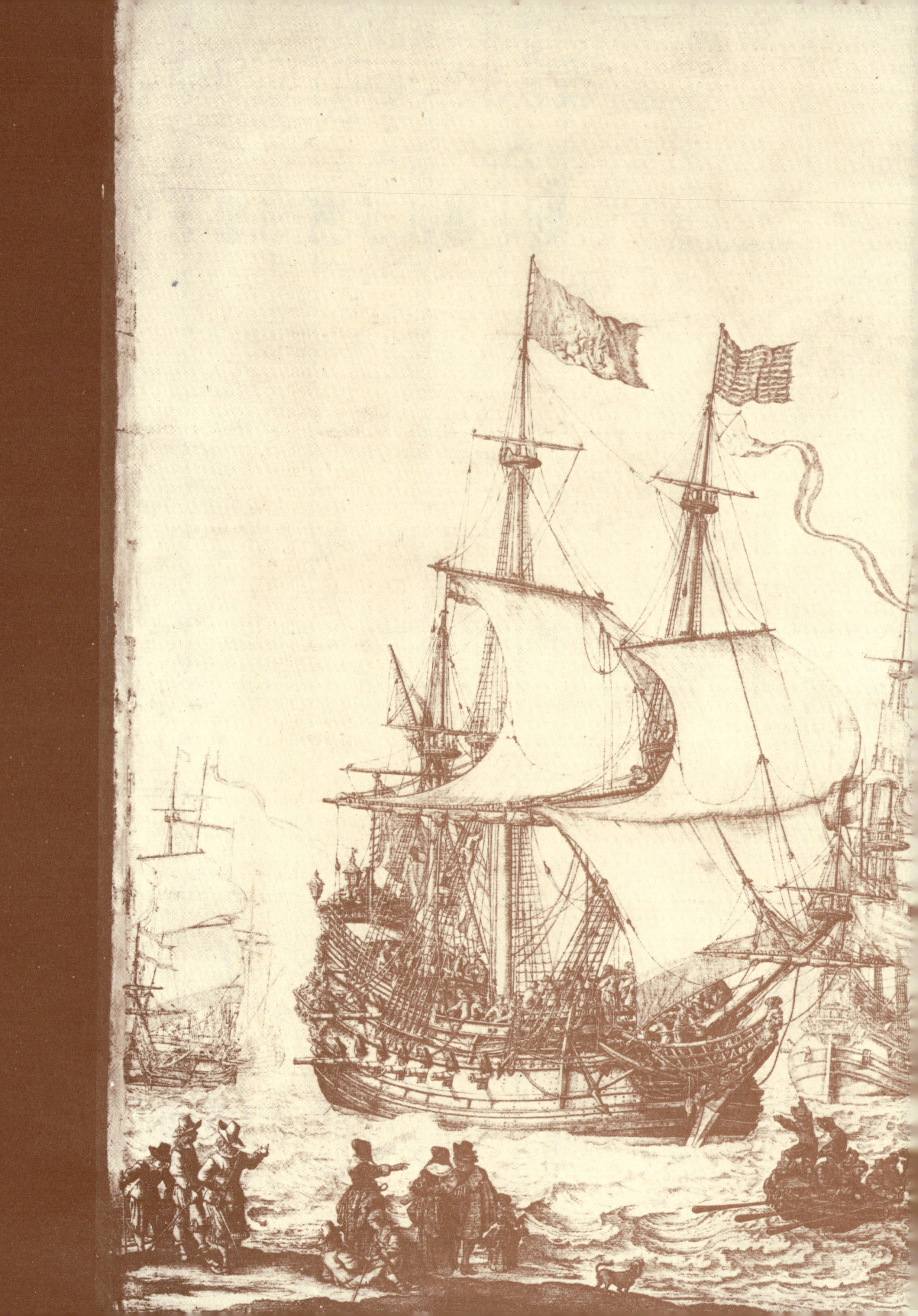